Less managing. More teaching. Greater learning.

INSTRUCTORS...

Would you like your **students** to show up for class more **prepared**? *(Let's face it, class is much more fun if everyone is engaged and prepared...)*

Want ready-made application-level **interactive assignments,** student progress reporting, and auto-assignment grading? *(Less time grading means more time teaching...)*

Want an **instant view of student or class performance** relative to learning objectives? *(No more wondering if students understand...)*

Need to **collect data and generate reports** required for administration or accreditation? *(Say goodbye to manually tracking student learning outcomes...)*

Want to **record and post your lectures** for students to view online?

With **McGraw-Hill's** *Connect*™ **Management,**

INSTRUCTORS GET:

- Interactive Applications – **book-specific interactive assignments** that require students to APPLY concepts and tools of strategic analysis.

- Simple **assignment management,** allowing you to spend more time teaching.

- **Auto-graded** assignments, quizzes, and tests.

- **Detailed Visual Reporting** where student and section results can be viewed and analyzed.

- Sophisticated **online testing** capability.

- A **filtering and reporting** function that allows you to easily assign and report on materials that are correlated to accreditation standards, learning outcomes, and Bloom's taxonomy.

- An easy-to-use **lecture capture** tool.

STUDENTS...

Want to get more **value** from your textbook purchase?

Think learning strategic management should be a bit more **interesting**?

Check out the STUDENT RESOURCES section under the *Connect*™ Library tab.

Here you'll find a wealth of resources designed to help you achieve your goals in the course. You'll find things like **quizzes, PowerPoints, and Guide to Case Analysis** to help you study. Every student has different needs, so explore the STUDENT RESOURCES to find the materials best suited to you.

INSTRUCTORS...

McGraw-Hill Higher Education and Blackboard have teamed up. What does this mean **for you**?

- **Your life, simplified.** Now you and your students can access McGraw-Hill's Connect™ and Create™ right from within your Blackboard course—all with one single sign-on.

- **Deep integration of content and tools.** Whether you're choosing a book for your course or building Connect™ assignments, all the tools you need are right where you want them—inside of Blackboard.

- **Seamless Gradebooks.** Multiple gradebooks? No thanks! When a student completes an integrated Connect™ assignment, the grade for that assignment automatically (and instantly) feeds your Blackboard grade center.

- **A solution for everyone.** Whether your institution is already using Blackboard or you just want to try Blackboard on your own, we have a solution for you. Be sure to ask your local McGraw-Hill representative for details.

Do More

www.domorenow.com

Crafting and Executing Strategy

Concepts and Readings

Crafting and Executing Strategy

Concepts and Readings

EIGHTEENTH EDITION

Arthur A. Thompson
The University of Alabama

Margaret A. Peteraf
Dartmouth College

John E. Gamble
University of South Alabama

A. J. Strickland III
The University of Alabama

CRAFTING AND EXECUTING STRATEGY: CONCEPTS AND READINGS

Published by McGraw-Hill/Irwin, a business unit of The McGraw-Hill Companies, Inc., 1221 Avenue of the Americas, New York, NY, 10020. Copyright © 2012, 2010, 2007, 2005, 2003, 2001, 1999, 1998, 1996, 1995, 1993, 1992, 1990, 1987, 1984, 1981, 1978 by The McGraw-Hill Companies, Inc. All rights reserved. No part of this publication may be reproduced or distributed in any form or by any means, or stored in a database or retrieval system, without the prior written consent of The McGraw-Hill Companies, Inc., including, but not limited to, in any network or other electronic storage or transmission, or broadcast for distance learning.

Some ancillaries, including electronic and print components, may not be available to customers outside the United States.

With respect to Ivey cases, Richard Ivey School of Business Foundation prohibits any form of reproduction, storage or transmission without its written permission. This material is not covered under authorization from any reproduction rights organization. To order copies or request permission to reproduce materials, contact Ivey Publishing, Richard Ivey School of Business Foundation, The University of Western Ontario, London, Ontario, Canada, N6A 3K7; phone (519) 661-3208, fax (519) 661-3882, e-mail cases@ivey.uwo.ca.

One time permission to reproduce Ivey cases granted by Richard Ivey School of Business Foundation on 11-11-10.

This book is printed on acid-free paper.

2 3 4 5 6 7 8 9 0 DOW/DOW 1 0 9 8 7 6 5 4 3 2 1

ISBN 978-0-07-732517-6
MHID 0-07-732517-6

Vice president and editor-in-chief: *Brent Gordon*
Editorial director: *Paul Ducham*
Executive editor: *Michael Ablassmeir*
Executive director of development: *Ann Torbert*
Development editor II: *Laura Griffin*
Editorial assistant: *Andrea Heirendt*
Vice president and director of marketing: *Robin J. Zwettler*
Marketing director: *Amee Mosley*
Executive marketing manager: *Anke Braun Weekes*
Vice president of editing, design, and production: *Sesha Bolisetty*
Manager of editing, design, and production: *Lori Koetters*
Manager of photo, design & publishing tools: *Mary Conzachi*

Lead project manager: *Harvey Yep*
Senior buyer: *Michael R. McCormick*
Cover and interior designer: *Cara Hawthorne, cara david DESIGN*
Senior photo research coordinator: *Keri Johnson*
Photo researcher: *Bill Van Werden*
Executive producer, Media technology: *Mark Christianson*
Senior media project manager: *Susan Lombardi*
Cover image credit: © *MIPAN/Veer*
Typeface: *10.5/12 Times New Roman MT Std*
Compositor: *Laserwords Private Limited*
Printer: *R. R. Donnelley*

Library of Congress Cataloging-in-Publication Data

Crafting and executing strategy : concepts and readings.—18th ed. / Arthur A. Thompson . . . [et al.].
    p. cm.
    Rev. ed. of: Crafting and executing strategy / Arthur A. Thompson. 17th ed. 2010.
    Includes index.
    ISBN-13: 978-0-07-732517-6 (alk. paper)
    ISBN-10: 0-07-732517-6 (alk. paper)
    1. Strategic planning. 2. Business planning. I. Thompson, Arthur A., 1940- II. Thompson, Arthur A., 1940- Crafting and executing strategy.
HD30.28.T525 2012
658.4'012—dc22

                                                                2010050241

www.mhhe.com

To our families and especially our spouses:
Hasseline, Paul, and Kitty.

Arthur A. Thompson, Jr., earned his B.S. and Ph.D. degrees in economics from The University of Tennessee, spent three years on the economics faculty at Virginia Tech, and served on the faculty of The University of Alabama's College of Commerce and Business Administration for 24 years. In 1974 and again in 1982, Dr. Thompson spent semester-long sabbaticals as a visiting scholar at the Harvard Business School.

His areas of specialization are business strategy, competition and market analysis, and the economics of business enterprises. In addition to publishing over 30 articles in some 25 different professional and trade publications, he has authored or co-authored five textbooks and six computer-based simulation exercises. His textbooks and strategy simulations have been used at well over 1,000 college and university campuses worldwide.

Dr. Thompson and his wife of 49 years have two daughters, two grandchildren, and a Yorkshire Terrier.

Margaret Peteraf is the Leon E. Williams Professor of Management at the Tuck School of Business at Dartmouth College. She is an internationally recognized scholar of strategic management, with a long list of publications in top management journals. She has earned myriad honors and prizes for her contributions, including the 1999 Strategic Management Society Best Paper Award recognizing the deep influence of her work on the field of Strategic Management. Professor Peteraf is on the Board of Directors of the Strategic Management Society and has been elected as a Fellow of the Society. She served previously as a member of the Academy of Management's Board of Governors and as Chair of the Business Policy and Strategy Division of the Academy. She has also served in various editorial roles and is presently on 9 editorial boards, including the *Strategic Management Journal,* the *Academy of Management Review,* and *Organization Science.* She has taught in Executive Education programs in various programs around the world and has won teaching awards at the MBA and Executive level.

Professor Peteraf earned her Ph.D., M.A., and M.Phil. at Yale University and held previous faculty appointments at Northwestern University's Kellogg Graduate School of Management and at the University of Minnesota's Carlson School of Management.

John E. Gamble is currently a Professor of Management in the Mitchell College of Business at the University of South Alabama. His teaching specialty at USA is strategic management and he also conducts a course in strategic management in Germany, which is sponsored by the University of Applied Sciences in Worms.

Dr. Gamble's research interests center on strategic issues in entrepreneurial, health care, and manufacturing settings. His work has been published in various scholarly journals and he is the author or co-author of more than 50 case studies published in an assortment of strategic management and strategic marketing texts. He has done consulting on industry and market analysis for clients in a diverse mix of industries.

Professor Gamble received his Ph.D. in management from The University of Alabama in 1995. Dr. Gamble also has a Bachelor of Science degree and a Master of Arts degree from The University of Alabama.

Dr. A. J. (Lonnie) Strickland is the Thomas R. Miller Professor of Strategic Management at the Culverhouse School of Business at The University of Alabama. He is a native of North Georgia, and attended the University of Georgia, where he received a Bachelor of Science degree in math and physics; Georgia Institute of Technology, where he received a Master of Science in industrial management; and Georgia State University, where he received his Ph.D. in business administration.

Lonnie's experience in consulting and executive development is in the strategic management arena, with a concentration in industry and competitive analysis. He has developed strategic planning systems for numerous firms all over the world. He served as Director of Marketing and Strategy at Bell-South, has taken two companies to the New York Stock Exchange, is one of the founders and directors of American Equity Investment Life Holding (AEL), and serves on numerous boards of directors. He is a very popular speaker in the area of Strategic Management.

Lonnie and his wife, Kitty, have been married for 44 years; they have two children, and two grandchildren. Each summer Lonnie and his wife live on their private game reserve in South Africa where they enjoy taking their friends on safaris.

PREFACE

This 18th edition represents one of our most important and thoroughgoing revisions ever. The newest member of the author team, Margie Peteraf, played the lead role in conducting a thorough reexamination of every paragraph on every page of the 17th-edition chapters. The overriding objective was to give all the chapters a major facelift by injecting new perspectives and the best academic thinking, strengthening linkages to the latest research findings, and modifying the coverage and exposition as needed to ensure squarely on-target content. The 18th edition features an attractive new collection of contemporary readings that amplify important topics in managing a company's strategy-making, strategy-executing process and help drive the chapter lessons home.

This edition retains the 12-chapter organization of the prior edition, but topical coverage and discussions have been trimmed in some areas and expanded in others. New material has been added here and there. The presentations of some topics were recast, others fine-tuned, and still others left largely intact. As with past editions, scores of new examples have been added, along with fresh Illustration Capsules, to make the content come alive and to provide students with a ringside view of strategy in action. The result is a major step forward in terms of punch, up-to-date coverage, clarity, and classroom effectiveness. But none of the changes have altered the fundamental character that has driven the text's success over three decades. The chapter content continues to be solidly mainstream and balanced, mirroring *both* the penetrating insight of academic thought and the pragmatism of real-world strategic management. And, as always, painstaking attention has been paid to keeping the chapters very reader-friendly and exceptionally teachable.

Through our experiences as business school faculty members, we fully understand the assessment demands on faculty teaching strategic management and business policy courses. In many institutions, capstone courses have emerged as the logical home for assessing student achievement of program learning objectives. The 18th edition includes a set of Assurance of Learning Exercises at the end of each chapter that link to the specific learning objectives appearing at the beginning of each chapter and highlighted throughout the text. *An important new instructional feature of the 18th edition is the linkage of selected chapter-end Assurance of Learning Exercises to the publisher's Web-based assignment and assessment platform called Connect.* Your students will be able to use the online Connect supplement to complete two or three of the Assurance of Learning Exercises appearing at the end of each of the 12 chapters and also to complete chapter-end self-quizzes, each consisting of 20 multiple-choice questions. All of the Connect exercises are automatically graded, thereby enabling you to easily assess the learning that has occurred.

For some years now, growing numbers of strategy instructors at business schools worldwide have been transitioning to a course structure that includes use of a strategy simulation. Incorporating a competition-based strategy simulation has the strong appeal of providing class members with *an immediate and engaging opportunity to apply the concepts and analytical tools covered in the chapters and to become personally involved in crafting and executing a strategy for a virtual company that they have been assigned to manage and that competes head-to-head with companies run by other class members.* Two widely used and pedagogically effective online strategy simulations, *The Business Strategy Game* and *GLO-BUS,* are optional companions for this text. Both simulations were created by this text's senior author and are closely linked to the content of each chapter in the text. The Exercises for Simulation Participants, found at the end of each chapter, provide clear guidance to class members in applying the concepts and analytical tools covered in the chapters to the issues and decisions that they have to wrestle with in managing their simulation company.

REVITALIZED AND EFFECTIVE CONTENT: THE SIGNATURE OF THE 18TH EDITION

Our objective in undertaking a major revision of this text was to ensure that its content was current, with respect to both scholarship and managerial practice, and was presented in as clear and compelling a fashion as possible. We established four criteria for meeting this objective, namely, that the final product must:

- Explain core concepts in language that students can grasp and provide first-rate examples of their relevance and use by actual companies.
- Thoroughly describe the tools of strategic analysis, how they are used, and where they fit into the managerial process of crafting and executing strategy.
- Incorporate the latest developments in the theory and practice of strategic management in every chapter to keep the content solidly in the mainstream of contemporary strategic thinking.
- Focus squarely on what every student needs to know about crafting, implementing, and executing business strategies in today's market environments.

We believe the 18th edition measures up on all four criteria. Chapter discussions cut straight to the chase about what students really need to know. At the same time, our explanations of core concepts and analytical tools are covered in enough depth to make them understandable and usable, since a shallow explanation carries little punch and almost no instructional value. Chapter content is driven by the imperative of including well-settled strategic management principles, fresh examples that illustrate the principles through the practices of real-world companies, recent research findings and contributions to the literature on strategic management, and the latest thinking of prominent academics and practitioners. There's a logical flow from one chapter to the next, as well as a complementary set of readings with which to spark discussions and drive the lessons home. And we have worked hard to hammer home the whys and hows of successfully crafting and executing strategy in an engaging, cogent, and convincing fashion.

Three standout features strongly differentiate our 12-chapter presentation:

1. *Our coverage of the resource-based theory of the firm in the 18th edition is unsurpassed by any other leading strategy text.* RBV principles and concepts are prominently and comprehensively integrated into our coverage of crafting both single-business and multibusiness strategies. In Chapters 3 through 8 it is repeatedly emphasized that a company's strategy must be matched *not only* to its external market circumstances *but also* to its internal resources and competitive capabilities. Moreover, an RBV perspective is thoroughly integrated into the presentation on strategy execution (Chapters 10, 11, and 12) to make it unequivocally clear how and why the tasks of assembling intellectual capital and building core competencies and competitive capabilities are absolutely critical to successful strategy execution and operating excellence.

2. *Our coverage of the relational view, which focuses on cooperative strategies and the role that interorganizational activity can play in the pursuit of competitive advantage, is similarly unsurpassed by other leading texts.* The topics of alliances, joint ventures, franchising, and other types of cooperative and collaborative relationships are featured prominently in a number of chapters and are integrated into other material throughout the text as well. We show how strategies of this nature can contribute to the success of single business companies as well as multibusiness enterprises. And while we begin with coverage of such topics with respect to firms operating in domestic markets, we extend our discussion of this material to the international realm as well.

3. *In addition, our coverage of business ethics, core values, social responsibility, and environmental sustainability is unsurpassed by any other leading strategy text.* In this new edition, we have embellished the highly important chapter "Ethics, Corporate Social Responsibility, Environmental Sustainability, and Strategy" with fresh content so that it can better fulfill the important functions of (1) alerting students to the role and importance of ethical and socially responsible decision making and (2) addressing the accreditation requirement of the AACSB International that business ethics be visibly and thoroughly embedded in the core curriculum. Moreover, discussions of the roles of values and ethics are integrated into portions of other chapters to further reinforce why and how considerations relating to ethics, values, social responsibility, and sustainability should figure prominently into the managerial task of crafting and executing company strategies.

ORGANIZATION, CONTENT, AND FEATURES OF THE 18TH-EDITION TEXT CHAPTERS

The following rundown summarizes the noteworthy features and topical emphasis in this new edition:

- Although Chapter 1 continues to focus on the central questions of *"What is strategy?"* and *"Why is it important?"* the presentation of this material has been sharpened considerably, with more concise definitions of the key concepts and significant updating to improve the currency of the material. We introduce students to the primary approaches to building competitive advantage and the key elements of business-level strategy. Following Henry Mintzberg's process approach, we explain why a company's strategy is partly planned and partly reactive and why a strategy and its environment tend to co-evolve over time. We discuss the importance of a viable business model that outlines the company's customer value proposition and its profit formula, framing this discussion in terms of key elements of value, price, and cost. We show how the mark of a winning strategy is its ability to pass three tests: (1) the *fit test* (for internal and external fit), (2) the *competitive advantage test,* and (3) the *performance test.* And we explain why good company performance depends upon good strategy execution as well as a sound strategy. In short, this brief chapter is a perfect accompaniment for your opening-day lecture on what the course is all about and why it matters.

- Chapter 2 delves more deeply into the managerial process of actually crafting and executing a strategy—it makes a great assignment for the second day of class and provides a smooth transition into the heart of the course. The focal point of the chapter is the five-step managerial process of crafting and executing strategy: (1) forming a strategic vision of where the company is headed and why, (2) developing strategic as well as financial objectives with which to measure the company's progress, (3) crafting a strategy to achieve these targets and move the company toward its market destination, (4) implementing and executing the strategy, and (5) monitoring progress and making corrective adjustments as needed. Students are introduced to such core concepts as strategic visions, mission statements and core values, the balanced scorecard, strategic intent, and business-level versus corporate-level strategies. There's a robust discussion of why *all managers are on a company's strategy-making, strategy-executing team* and why a company's strategic plan is a collection of strategies devised by different managers at different levels in the organizational hierarchy. The chapter winds up with a section on how to exercise good corporate governance and examines the conditions that led to recent high-profile corporate governance failures.

- Chapter 3 sets forth the now-familiar analytical tools and concepts of industry and competitive analysis and demonstrates the importance of tailoring strategy to fit the circumstances of a company's industry and competitive environment. The standout feature of this chapter is a presentation of Michael Porter's "five-forces model of competition" *that has long been the clearest, most straightforward discussion of any text in the field.* This edition also provides expanded coverage of a company's macro-environment to enable students to conduct what some call *Pestel analysis* of *p*olitical, *e*conomic, *s*ocial, *t*echnological, *e*nvironmental, and *l*egal factors.

- Chapter 4 presents the resource-based view of the firm and convincingly argues why a company's strategy must be built around its most competitively valuable resources and capabilities. We provide students with a simple taxonomy for identifying a company's resources and capabilities and frame our discussion of how a firm's resources and capabilities can provide a sustainable competitive advantage with the *VRIN model.* We introduce the notion of a company's *dynamic capabilities* and cast SWOT analysis as a simple, easy-to-use way to assess a company's overall situation in terms of its ability to seize market opportunities and ward off external threats. There is solid coverage of value chain analysis, benchmarking, and competitive strength assessments—standard tools for appraising a company's relative cost position and customer value proposition vis-à-vis rivals. *An important feature of this chapter is a table showing how key financial and operating ratios are calculated and how to interpret them;* students will find this table handy in doing the number crunching needed to evaluate whether a company's strategy is delivering good financial performance.

- Chapter 5 deals with the basic approaches used to compete successfully and gain a competitive advantage over market rivals. This discussion is framed around the five generic competitive strategies—low-cost leadership, differentiation, best-cost provider, focused differentiation, and focused low cost. We emphasize that regardless of a company's choice, competitive success depends upon a company's capacity to deliver more customer value—one way or another. We provide a fuller treatment of *cost drivers* and *uniqueness drivers* as the keys to bringing down a company's cost and enhancing its differentiation, respectively, in support of this overall goal.

- Chapter 6 continues the theme of competitive strategies for single-business firms with its spotlight on *strategic actions (offensive and defensive) and their timing,* including blue-ocean strategies and first-mover advantages and disadvantages. It also serves to segue into the material covered in the next two chapters (on international and diversification strategies) by introducing the topic of *strategies that alter a company's scope of operations.* The chapter features sections on the strategic benefits and risks of horizontal mergers and acquisitions, vertical integration, and outsourcing of certain value chain activities. The concluding section of this chapter covers the advantages and drawbacks of using strategic alliances and cooperative arrangements to alter a company's scope of operations, with some pointers on how to make strategic alliances work.

- Chapter 7 explores the full range of strategy options for expanding a company's geographic scope and competing in foreign markets: export strategies, licensing, franchising, establishing a wholly owned subsidiary via acquisition or "greenfield" venture, and alliance strategies. In the 18th edition, we've added new coverage of topics such as Porter's *Diamond of National Advantage;* the choice between *multidomestic, global, and transnational strategies; profit sanctuaries* and cross-border strategic moves; and *the quest for competitive advantage via sharing, transferring, or accessing valuable resources and capabilities across national borders.* The chapter concludes with a discussion of the special issues of competing in the markets of developing countries and the strategies that local companies can use to defend against global giants.

- Chapter 8 introduces the topic of corporate-level strategy—a topic of concern for multibusiness companies pursuing diversification. This chapter begins by explaining why successful diversification strategies must create shareholder value and lays out the three essential tests that a strategy must pass to achieve this goal *(the industry attractiveness, cost-of-entry, and better-off tests).* We discuss alternative means of entering new businesses (acquisition, internal start-up, or joint venture) and offer a method for discerning which choice is a firm's best option. Then we turn our attention to a comparison of related versus unrelated diversification strategies, showing that they differ in terms of the nature of their critical resources *(specialized versus general parenting capabilities)* and whether they can exploit cross-business strategic fit for competitive gain. The chapter's analytical spotlight is trained on the techniques and procedures for assessing the strategic attractiveness of a diversified company's business portfolio—the relative attractiveness of the various industries the company has diversified into, the company's competitive strength in each of its lines of business, and the extent to which there is *strategic fit* and *resource fit* among its different businesses. The chapter concludes with a brief survey of a company's four main postdiversification strategy alternatives: (1) sticking closely with the existing business lineup, (2) broadening the diversification base, (3) divesting some businesses and retrenching to a narrower diversification base, and (4) restructuring the makeup of the company's business lineup.

• Chapter 9 reflects the very latest in the literature on (1) a company's duty to operate according to ethical standards, (2) a company's obligation to demonstrate socially responsible behavior and corporate citizenship, and (3) why more companies are limiting strategic initiatives to those that meet the needs of consumers in a manner that protects natural resources and ecological support systems needed by future generations. The discussion includes approaches to ensuring consistent ethical standards for companies with international operations. The contents of this chapter will definitely give students some things to ponder and will help to make them more *ethically aware* and conscious of *why all companies should conduct their business in a socially responsible and sustainable manner.* Chapter 9 has been written as a stand-alone chapter that can be assigned in the early, middle, or late part of the course.

• Chapter 10 begins a three-chapter module on executing strategy (Chapters 10 to 12), anchored around a pragmatic, compelling conceptual framework. Chapter 10 presents an overview of this 10-step framework and then develops the first three pieces of it: (1) *staffing the organization* with capable managers and employees, (2) *marshaling the resources and building the organizational capabilities* required for successful strategy execution, and (3) *creating a strategy-supportive organizational structure* and structuring the work effort. We discuss three approaches to building and strengthening a company's capabilities, ranging from internal development to acquisitions to collaborative arrangements, and consider outsourcing as an option for structuring the work effort. We argue for matching a company's organizational structure to its strategy execution requirements, describe four basic types of organizational structures (simple, functional, multidivisional, and matrix), and discuss centralized versus decentralized decision making. We conclude with some further perspectives on facilitating collaboration with external partners and structuring the company's work effort.

• Chapter 11 covers five important topics concerning strategy execution: (1) *allocating ample resources* to strategy-critical activities, (2) ensuring that *policies and procedures* facilitate rather than impede strategy execution, (3) employing *process management tools* and adopting *best practices* to drive continuous improvement in the performance of value chain activities, (4) installing *information and operating systems* that enable company personnel to better carry out their strategic roles proficiently, and (5) tying *rewards and incentives* directly to good strategy execution and the achievement of performance targets.

• Chapter 12 concludes the text with a discussion of corporate culture and leadership in relation to good strategy execution. The recurring theme throughout the final three chapters is that implementing strategy entails figuring out the specific actions, behaviors, and conditions that are needed for a smooth strategy-supportive operation and then following through to get things done and deliver results. The goal here is to ensure that students understand that the strategy-executing phase is a make-things-happen and make-them-happen-right kind of managerial exercise—one that is critical for achieving operating excellence and reaching the goal of strong company performance.

We have done our best to ensure that the 12 chapters convey the best thinking of academics and practitioners in the field of strategic management and hit the bull's-eye in topical coverage for senior- and MBA-level strategy courses. The ultimate test of the text, of course, is the positive pedagogical impact it has in the classroom. If this edition sets a more effective stage for your lectures and does a better job of helping you persuade students that the discipline of strategy merits their rapt attention, then it will have fulfilled its purpose.

THE COLLECTION OF READINGS

The readings that accompany the chapter presentations were chosen with three criteria in mind: relevance, readability, and recency of publication. The *relevance* criterion led us to seek out articles that connected clearly to the material in the text chapters and either extended the chapter coverage or expanded on a topic of strategic importance. The *readability* criterion helped us identify articles that were clearly written, engaging, practically oriented, and relatively short. The *recency* criterion limited our selections to those that appeared in the 2009–2010 period. We endeavored to be highly selective in our choices, deciding that a manageable number of on-target readings was a better fit with the teaching/learning objectives of most senior and MBA courses in strategy than a more sweeping collection of readings. The 20 readings we chose came from recent issues of *Academy of Management Perspectives, McKinsey Quarterly, MIT Sloan Management Review, Business Strategy Review, Business Horizons, Harvard Business Review, Long Range Planning, Journal of Business Strategy, Ivey Business Journal, Strategy & Leadership, Strategic Change,* and *IESE Insight.*

The first reading, by David Teece, "Business Models, Business Strategy and Innovation," provides an outstanding discussion of the connection between a good business model and a successful strategy—one capable of not only pleasing a company's customers but enabling a company to gain a competitive advantage over its market rivals and earn a good profit. With its rich discussion of today's business models and its many examples drawn from companies that students will recognize, this reading is the perfect accompaniment to our introductory chapter, "What Is Strategy and Why Is It Important?"

Reading 2, "The Power of Vision: Statements That Resonate," is a practically oriented article that ties tightly to the material in Chapter 2. It offers explicit advice on how to develop a powerful vision and shows how effective vision statements can produce results.

The next four articles connect to Chapters 3 and 4, with their presentations of the basic concepts and analytical tools for conducting external (industry environment) and internal (single-business firm) analyses. Pankaj Ghemawat's article, "Finding Your Strategy in the New Landscape," takes a broad view of the industry environment and discusses the challenges companies face in navigating the harsher competitive terrain of a postbubble world. Hugh Courtney and his co-authors argue that because the business world is increasingly interdependent, the success of a company's strategy often depends upon the strategies of its rivals. Therefore those companies that can most accurately predict their competitors' moves have a distinct competitive advantage. Their article provides step-by-step advice on how managers can improve their competitive intelligence skills.

Reading 5, "Operational Capabilities: Hidden in Plain View," adds considerable depth to the coverage of the resource-based view of the firm that dominates the presentation in Chapter 4 (and that is integral to other chapters as well). The extended example from a restaurant's kitchen provides a concrete and easy-to-follow illustration of exactly what we mean by the terms *resources* and *capabilities* and how they apply to everyday business operations. The article by Amy Shuen and Sandra Sieber, "Orchestrating the New Dynamic Capabilities," provides a nice counterpart to this, showing how the advent of Web 2.0 is making the development of dynamic capabilities for orchestrating knowledge and ecosystems across multiple industry and geographic boundaries a top strategic priority.

There are five readings that complement and expand on topics covered in Chapters 5 through 7. The timely article "Low-Cost Strategy through Product Architecture: Lessons from China" will provide students with some insight on how upstart Chinese car makers, such as Chery and BYD, have been able to follow a low-cost strategy while still producing cars that are roughly equivalent to those of their higher-cost foreign rivals. "Innovation Strategies Combined," by Frank Rothaermel and Andrew Hess, concerns the kind of continuous innovation that is a necessity for companies wanting to improve and maintain differentiation strategies or best-cost provider strategies. This article also serves to introduce some of the material on alliances and acquisitions that is covered more fully in the next two readings and that pairs nicely with Chapter 6. Prashant Kale and Harbir Singh identify the primary drivers of alliance success in their article "Managing Strategic Alliances: What Do We Know Now, and Where Do We Go from Here?" They offer advice on how companies can develop the capabilities needed to enhance the success of their strategic alliances, and they suggest that these capabilities can improve the success of acquisitions and other cooperative arrangements as well. In "How Emerging Giants Are Rewriting the Rules of M&A," Nirmalya Kumar describes how companies such as India's Tata and Hindalco have successfully used M&A strategies to access the technology, knowledge, and competencies available in more developed economies. This article provides the perfect segue into the topics covered in Chapter 7 regarding cross-border competition and international strategies. Indeed, Mauro Guillén and Esteban García-Canal expand on Kumar's theme in "The American Model of the Multinational Firm and the 'New' Multinationals from Emerging Economies," showing that the "new MNEs" could not succeed as they have been without having intangible assets and capabilities of their own to provide a foundation for their international expansion.

We included two readings to be assigned in conjunction with Chapter 8, on diversification strategies. The article "Core Competencies for Diversifying: Case Study of a Small Business" provides a practical approach that young or small firms can use to identify their core competencies as they chart a strategy of related diversification. Klaus Meyer's piece, "Globalfocusing: Corporate Strategies under Pressure," treats an issue facing companies that have already diversified: how they should restructure their operations in response to changes taking place in our volatile global economy.

We chose three articles to complement and expand on the topics of ethical business strategies, social responsibility, and environmental sustainability, covered in Chapter 9. "Making the Most of Corporate Social Responsibility" tackles the question of how companies can truly deliver on their lofty ambitions for strengthening their businesses and contributing to society at the same time. Reading 15, "Business as Environmental Steward: The Growth of Greening," shows that risk mitigation through active environmental stewardship by businesses not only can lessen the potential for adverse environmental impact but can open up attractive new business opportunities in the process. In "Recurring Failures in Corporate Governance: A Global Disease?" Nandini Rajagopalan and Anthea Zhang take on the troubling topic of recent ethical failures, ranging from the outsized payouts received by executives of collapsing U.S. financial firms to the melamine-tainted-milk scandal in China. They suggest that effective and sustainable efforts to curb ethical violations in business will require reforms in corporate governance that simultaneously reduce the benefits and increase the costs to the perpetrators.

Four readings were chosen for use with the three chapters on executing strategy (Chapters 10 to 12). "Creative Execution" is a practical guide to executing strategy in a way that helps to differentiate a firm from its competitors; it fits in nicely with the framework we use in Chapters 10 to 12 to introduce students to the managerial tasks of implementing and executing the chosen strategy. "Only the Right People Are Strategic Assets" provides a guide to recruiting, retaining, and developing the kinds of human resources that match a company's core strategy. "Six Sigma at Your Service" is a good fit with the material in Chapter 11, while "The Story Is the Message: Shaping Corporate Culture" brings home the lessons of Chapter 12 and provides a strong and inspirational conclusion for a course on strategic management.

TWO ACCOMPANYING ONLINE, FULLY AUTOMATED SIMULATION EXERCISES: *THE BUSINESS STRATEGY GAME* AND *GLO-BUS*

The Business Strategy Game and *GLO-BUS: Developing Winning Competitive Strategies*—two competition-based strategy simulations that are delivered online and that feature automated processing of decisions and grading of performance—are being marketed by the publisher as companion supplements for use with this book (and other texts in the field).

- *The Business Strategy Game* is the world's most popular strategy simulation, having been used in courses involving over 600,000 students at more than 700 university campuses in over 40 countries.
- *GLO-BUS,* a somewhat simpler strategy simulation introduced in 2004, has been used at more than 400 university campuses worldwide in courses involving over 120,000 students.

How the Strategy Simulations Work

In both *The Business Strategy Game (BSG)* and *GLO-BUS,* class members are divided into teams of one to five persons and assigned to run a company that competes head-to-head against companies run by other class members.

- In *BSG,* team members run an athletic footwear company, producing and marketing both branded and private-label footwear.
- In *GLO-BUS,* team members operate a digital camera company that designs, assembles, and markets entry-level digital cameras and upscale, multifeatured cameras.

In both simulations, companies compete in a global market arena, selling their products in four geographic regions—Europe-Africa, North America, Asia-Pacific, and Latin America. Each management team is called upon to craft a strategy for their company and make decisions relating to plant operations, workforce compensation, pricing and marketing, social responsibility/citizenship, and finance.

Company co-managers are held accountable for their decision making. Each company's performance is scored on the basis of earnings per share, return on equity investment, stock price, credit rating, and image rating. Rankings of company performance, along with a wealth of industry and company statistics, are available to company co-managers after each decision round to use in making strategy adjustments and decisions for the next competitive round. You can be certain that the market environment, strategic issues, and operating challenges that company co-managers must contend with are *very tightly linked* to what your class members will be reading about in the text chapters. The circumstances that co-managers face in running their simulation company embrace the very concepts, analytical tools, and strategy options they encounter in the text chapters (this is something you can quickly confirm by skimming through some of the Exercises for Simulation Participants that appear at the end of each chapter).

We suggest that you schedule 1 or 2 practice rounds and anywhere from 4 to 10 regular (scored) decision rounds (more rounds are better than fewer rounds). Each decision round represents a year of company operations and will entail roughly two hours of time for company co-managers to complete. In traditional 13-week, semester-long courses, there is merit is scheduling one decision round per week. In courses that run 5 to 10 weeks, it is wise to schedule two decision rounds per week for the last several weeks of the term (sample course schedules are provided for courses of varying length and varying numbers of class meetings).

When the instructor-specified deadline for a decision round arrives, the simulation server automatically accesses the saved decision entries of each company, determines the competitiveness and buyer appeal of each company's product offering relative to the other companies being run by students in your class, and then awards sales and market shares to the competing companies, geographic region by geographic region. The unit sales volumes awarded to each company *are totally governed by:*

- How its prices compare against the prices of rival brands.,
- How its product quality compares against the quality of rival brands.,
- How its product line breadth and selection compare.
- How its advertising effort compares.
- And so on, for a total of 11 competitive factors that determine unit sales and market shares.

The competitiveness and overall buyer appeal of each company's product offering *in comparison to the product offerings of rival companies* is all-decisive—this algorithmic feature is what makes *BSG* and *GLO-BUS* "competition-based" strategy simulations. Once each company's sales and market shares are awarded based on the competitiveness of its respective overall product offering, the various company and industry reports detailing the outcomes of the decision round are then generated. Company co-managers can access the results of the decision round 15 to 20 minutes after the decision deadline.

The Compelling Case for Incorporating Use of a Strategy Simulation

There are *three exceptionally important benefits* associated with using a competition-based simulation in strategy courses taken by seniors and MBA students:

- *A three-pronged text-case-simulation course model delivers significantly more teaching-learning power than the traditional text-case model.* Using *both* cases and a strategy simulation to drill students in thinking strategically and applying what they read in the text chapters is a stronger, more effective means of helping them connect theory with practice and develop better business judgment. What cases do that a simulation cannot is give class members broad exposure to a variety of companies and industry situations and insight into the kinds of strategy-related problems managers face. But what a competition-based strategy simulation does far better than case analysis is thrust class members squarely into *an active, hands-on managerial role* where they are totally responsible for assessing market conditions, determining how to respond to the actions of competitors, forging a long-term direction and strategy for their company, and making all kinds of operating decisions. Because they are held fully accountable for their decisions and their company's performance, *co-managers are strongly motivated* to dig deeply into company operations, probe for ways to be more cost-efficient and competitive, and ferret out strategic moves and decisions calculated to boost company performance. *Consequently, incorporating both case assignments and a strategy simulation to develop the skills of class members in thinking strategically and applying the concepts and tools of strategic analysis turns out to be more pedagogically powerful than relying solely on case assignments—there's stronger retention of the lessons learned and better achievement of course learning objectives.*

    To provide you with quantitative evidence of the learning that occurs with using *The Business Strategy Game* or *GLO-BUS,* there is a built-in Learning Assurance Report showing how well each class member performs on nine skills/learning measures versus tens of thousands of students worldwide who have completed the simulation in the past 12 months.

- *The competitive nature of a strategy simulation arouses positive energy and steps up the whole tempo of the course by a notch or two.* Nothing sparks class excitement quicker or better than the concerted efforts on the part of class members at each decision round to achieve a high industry ranking and avoid the perilous consequences of being outcompeted by other class members. Students really enjoy taking on the role of a manager, running their own company, crafting strategies, making all kinds of operating decisions, trying to outcompete rival companies, and getting immediate feedback on the resulting company performance. Lots of back-and-forth chatter occurs when the results of the latest simulation round become available and co-managers renew their quest for strategic moves and actions that will strengthen company performance. Co-managers become *emotionally invested* in running their company and figuring out what strategic moves to make to boost their company's performance. Interest levels climb. All this stimulates learning and causes students to see the practical relevance of the subject matter and the benefits of taking your course.

    As soon as your students start to say "Wow! Not only is this fun but I am learning a lot," *which they will,* you have won the battle of engaging students in the subject matter and moved the value of taking your course to a much higher plateau in the business school curriculum. This translates into *a livelier, richer learning experience from a student perspective and better instructor-course evaluations.*

- *Use of a fully automated online simulation reduces the time instructors spend on course preparation, course administration, and grading.* Since the simulation exercise involves a 20- to 30-hour workload for student teams (roughly 2 hours per decision round times 10 to 12 rounds, plus optional assignments), simulation adopters often compensate by trimming the number of assigned cases from, say, 10 to 12 to perhaps 4 to 6. This significantly reduces the time instructors spend reading cases, studying teaching notes, and otherwise getting ready to lead class discussion of a case or grade oral team presentations. Course preparation time is further cut because you can use several class days to have students meet in the computer lab to work on upcoming decision rounds or a three-year strategic plan (in lieu of lecturing on a chapter or covering an additional assigned case). Not only does use of a simulation permit assigning fewer cases, but it also permits you to eliminate at least one assignment that entails considerable grading on your part. Grading one less written case or essay exam or other written assignment saves enormous time. With *BSG* and *GLO-BUS,* grading is effortless and takes only minutes; once you enter percentage weights for each assignment in your online grade book, a suggested overall grade is calculated for you. You'll be pleasantly surprised—and quite pleased—at how little time it takes to gear up for and to administer *The Business Strategy Game* or *GLO-BUS.*

In sum, incorporating use of a strategy simulation turns out to be *a win-win proposition for both students and instructors.* Moreover, a very convincing argument can be made that a competition-based strategy simulation is *the single most effective teaching/learning tool that instructors can employ to teach the discipline of business and competitive strategy, to make learning more enjoyable, and to promote better achievement of course learning objectives.*

A Bird's-Eye View of *The Business Strategy Game*

The setting for *The Business Strategy Game (BSG)* is the global athletic footwear industry (there can be little doubt in today's world that a globally competitive strategy simulation is *vastly superior* to a simulation with a domestic-only setting). Global market demand for footwear grows at the rate of 7 to 9 percent annually for the first five years and 5 to 7 percent annually for the second five years. However, market growth rates vary by geographic region—North America, Latin America, Europe-Africa, and Asia-Pacific.

Companies begin the simulation producing branded and private-label footwear in two plants, one in North America and one in Asia. They have the option to establish production facilities in Latin America and Europe-Africa, either by constructing new plants or by buying previously constructed plants that have been sold by competing companies. Company co-managers exercise control over production costs on the basis of the styling and quality they opt to manufacture, plant location (wages and incentive compensation vary from region to region), the use of best practices and Six Sigma programs to reduce the production of defective footwear and to boost worker productivity, and compensation practices.

All newly produced footwear is shipped in bulk containers to one of four geographic distribution centers. All sales in a geographic region are made from footwear inventories in that region's distribution center. Costs at the four regional distribution centers are a function of inventory storage costs, packing and shipping fees, import tariffs paid on incoming pairs shipped from foreign plants, and exchange rate impacts. At the start of the simulation, import tariffs average $4 per pair in Europe-Africa, $6 per pair in Latin America, and $8 in the Asia-Pacific region. However, the Free Trade Treaty of the Americas allows tariff-free movement of footwear between North America and Latin America. Instructors have the option to alter tariffs as the game progresses.

Companies market their brand of athletic footwear to footwear retailers worldwide and to individuals buying online at the company's Web site. Each company's sales and market share in the branded footwear segments hinge on its competitiveness on 11 factors: attractive pricing, footwear styling and quality, product line breadth, advertising, use of mail-in rebates, appeal of celebrities endorsing a company's brand, success in convincing footwear retailers to carry its brand, number of weeks it takes to fill retailer orders, effectiveness of a company's online sales effort at its Web site, and customer loyalty. Sales of private-label footwear hinge solely on being the low-price bidder.

All told, company co-managers make as many as 53 types of decisions each period that cut across production operations (up to 10 decisions per plant, with a maximum of four plants), plant capacity additions/sales/upgrades (up to 6 decisions per plant), worker compensation and training (3 decisions per plant), shipping (up to 8 decisions per plant), pricing and marketing (up to 10 decisions in four geographic regions), bids to sign celebrities (2 decision entries per bid), financing of company operations (up to 8 decisions), and corporate social responsibility and environmental sustainability (up to 6 decisions).

Each time company co-managers make a decision entry, an assortment of on-screen calculations instantly shows the projected effects on unit sales, revenues, market shares, unit costs, profit, earnings per share, ROE, and other operating statistics. The on-screen calculations help team members evaluate the relative merits of one decision entry versus another and put together a promising strategy.

Companies can employ any of the five generic competitive strategy options in selling branded footwear—low-cost leadership, differentiation, best-cost provider, focused low cost, and focused differentiation. They can pursue essentially the same strategy worldwide or craft slightly or very different strategies for the Europe-Africa, Asia-Pacific, Latin America, and North America markets. They can strive for competitive advantage based on more advertising, a wider selection of models, more appealing styling/quality, bigger rebates, and so on.

Any well-conceived, well-executed competitive approach is capable of succeeding, provided it is not overpowered by the strategies of competitors or defeated by the presence of too many copycat strategies that dilute its effectiveness. The challenge for each company's management team is to craft and execute a competitive strategy that produces good performance on five measures: earnings per share, return on equity investment, stock price appreciation, credit rating, and brand image.

All activity for *The Business Strategy Game* takes place at www.bsg-online.com.

A Bird's-Eye View of *GLO-BUS*

The industry setting for *GLO-BUS* is the digital camera industry. Global market demand grows at the rate of 8 to 10 percent annually for the first five years and 4 to 6 percent annually for the second five years. Retail sales of digital cameras are seasonal, with about 20 percent of consumer demand coming in each of the first three quarters of each calendar year and 40 percent coming during the big fourth-quarter retailing season.

Companies produce entry-level and upscale, multifeatured cameras of varying designs and quality in a Taiwan assembly facility and ship assembled cameras directly to retailers in North America, Asia-Pacific, Europe-Africa, and Latin America. All cameras are assembled as retail orders come in and are shipped immediately upon completion of the assembly process—companies maintain no finished-goods inventories, and all parts and components are delivered on a just-in-time basis (which eliminates the need to track inventories and simplifies the accounting for plant operations and costs). Company co-managers exercise control over production costs on the basis of the designs and components they specify for their cameras, workforce compensation and training, the length of warranties offered (which affects warranty costs), the amount spent for technical support provided to buyers of the company's cameras, and their management of the assembly process.

Competition in each of the two product market segments (entry-level and multifeatured digital cameras) is based on 10 factors: price, camera performance and quality, number of quarterly sales promotions, length of promotions in weeks, size of the promotional discounts offered, advertising, number of camera models, size of retail dealer network, warranty period, and amount/caliber of technical support provided to camera buyers. Low-cost leadership, differentiation strategies, best-cost provider strategies, and focus strategies are all viable competitive options. Rival companies can strive to be the clear market leader in either entry-level cameras or upscale multifeatured cameras or both. They can focus on one or two geographic regions or strive for geographic balance. They can pursue essentially the same strategy worldwide or craft slightly or very different strategies for the Europe-Africa, Asia-Pacific, Latin America, and North America markets. Just as with *The Business Strategy Game,* almost any well-conceived, well-executed competitive approach is capable of succeeding, *provided it is not overpowered by the strategies of competitors or defeated by the presence of too many copycat strategies that dilute its effectiveness.*

Company co-managers make 49 types of decisions each period, ranging from R&D, camera components, and camera performance (10 decisions) to production operations and worker compensation (15 decisions) to pricing and marketing (15 decisions) to the financing of company operations (4 decisions) to corporate social responsibility (5 decisions). Each time participants make a decision entry, an assortment of on-screen calculations instantly shows the projected effects on unit sales, revenues, market shares, unit costs, profit, earnings per share, ROE, and other operating statistics. These on-screen calculations help team members evaluate the relative merits of one decision entry versus another and stitch the separate decisions into a cohesive and promising strategy. Company performance is judged on five criteria: earnings per share, return on equity investment, stock price, credit rating, and brand image.

All activity for *GLO-BUS* occurs at www.glo-bus.com.

Administration and Operating Features of the Two Simulations

The Internet delivery and user-friendly designs of both *BSG* and *GLO-BUS* make them incredibly easy to administer, even for first-time users. And the menus and controls are so similar that you can readily switch between the two simulations or use one in your undergraduate class and the other in a graduate class. If you have not yet used either of the two simulations, you may find the following of particular interest:

- Setting up the simulation for your course is done online and takes about 10 to 15 minutes. Once setup is completed, no other administrative actions are required beyond those of moving participants to a different team (should the need arise) and monitoring the progress of the simulation (to whatever extent desired).

- Participant's Guides are delivered at the Web site—students can read the guide on their monitors or print out a copy, as they prefer.
- There are 2- to 4-minute Video Tutorials scattered throughout the software (including each decision screen and each page of each report) that provide on-demand guidance to class members who may be uncertain about how to proceed.
- Complementing the Video Tutorials are detailed and clearly written Help sections explaining "all there is to know" about (a) each decision entry and the relevant cause-effect relationships, (b) the information on each page of the Industry Reports, and (c) the numbers presented in the Company Reports. *The Video Tutorials and the Help screens allow company co-managers to figure things out for themselves, thereby curbing the need for students to ask the instructor "how things work."*
- Built-in chat capability on each screen enables company co-managers to collaborate online in the event that a face-to-face meeting to review results and make decision entries is not convenient (or feasible, as is usually the case for class members taking an online course). Company co-managers can also use their cell phones to talk things over while online looking at the screens.
- Both simulations are quite suitable for use in distance-learning or online courses (and are currently being used in such courses on numerous campuses).
- Participants and instructors are notified via e-mail when the results are ready (usually about 15 to 20 minutes after the decision round deadline specified by the instructor/game administrator).
- Following each decision round, participants are provided with a complete set of reports—a six-page Industry Report, a one-page Competitive Intelligence report for each geographic region that includes strategic group maps and bulleted lists of competitive strengths and weaknesses, and a set of Company Reports (income statement, balance sheet, cash flow statement, and assorted production, marketing, and cost statistics).
- Two "open-book" multiple-choice tests of 20 questions are built into each simulation. The quizzes, which you can require or not as you see fit, are taken online and automatically graded, with scores reported instantaneously to participants and automatically recorded in the instructor's electronic grade book. Students are automatically provided with three sample questions for each test.
- Both simulations contain a three-year strategic plan option that you can assign. Scores on the plan are automatically recorded in the instructor's online grade book.
- At the end of the simulation, you can have students complete online peer evaluations (again, the scores are automatically recorded in your online grade book).
- Both simulations have a Company Presentation feature that enables each team of company co-managers to easily prepare PowerPoint slides for use in describing their strategy and summarizing their company's performance in a presentation to either the class, the instructor, or an "outside" board of directors.
- *A Learning Assurance Report provides you with hard data concerning how well your students performed vis-à-vis students playing the simulation worldwide over the past 12 months.* The report is based on nine measures of student proficiency, business know-how, and decision-making skill and can also be used in evaluating the extent to which your school's academic curriculum produces the desired degree of student learning insofar as accreditation standards are concerned.

For more details on either simulation, please consult Section 2 of the Instructor's Manual accompanying this text or register as an instructor at the simulation Web sites (www.bsg-online.com and www.glo-bus.com) to access even more comprehensive information. Using Internet conferencing technology, the simulation authors conduct seminars several times each month (sometimes each week) to demonstrate how the software works, walk you through the various features and menu options, and answer any questions. By all means, please feel free to call the senior author of this text at (205) 722-9145 to arrange a personal demonstration or talk about how one of the simulations might work in one of your courses. We think you'll be quite impressed with the capabilities that have been programmed into *The Business Strategy Game* and *GLO-BUS,* the simplicity with which both simulations can be administered, and their exceptionally tight connection to the text chapters, core concepts, and standard analytical tools.

RESOURCES AND SUPPORT MATERIALS FOR THE 18TH EDITION

For Students

Key Points Summaries   At the end of each chapter is a synopsis of the core concepts, analytical tools, and other key points discussed in the chapter. These chapter-end synopses, along with the core concept definitions and margin notes scattered throughout each chapter, help students focus on basic strategy principles, digest the messages of each chapter, and prepare for tests.

Two Sets of Chapter-End Exercises   Each chapter concludes with two sets of exercises. The *Assurance of Learning Exercises* can be used as the basis for class discussion, oral presentation assignments, short written reports, and substitutes for case assignments. The *Exercises for Simulation Participants* are designed expressly for use by adopters who have incorporated use of a simulation and want to go a step further in tightly and explicitly connecting the chapter content to the simulation company their students are running. The questions in both sets of exercises (along with those Illustration Capsules that qualify as "mini-cases") can be used to round out the rest of a 75-minute class period should your lecture on a chapter last for only 50 minutes.

A Value-Added Web Site   The student section of the Online Learning Center (OLC) at Web site www.mhhe.com/thompson contains a number of helpful aids:

- Ten-question self-scoring chapter tests that students can take to measure their grasp of the material presented in each of the 12 chapters.
- The "Guide to Case Analysis," containing sections on what a case is, why cases are a standard part of courses in strategy, preparing a case for class discussion, doing a written case analysis, doing an oral presentation, and using financial ratio analysis to assess a company's financial condition. We suggest having students read this guide before the first class discussion of a case.
- PowerPoint slides for each chapter.

The *Connect*™ *Management* Web-Based Assignment and Assessment Platform

Beginning with this edition, we have taken advantage of the publisher's innovative *Connect*™ assignment and assessment platform and created several features that simplify the task of assigning and grading three types of exercises for students:

- There are self-scoring chapter tests consisting of 20 to 25 multiple-choice questions that students can take to measure their grasp of the material presented in each of the 12 chapters.
- There are one to two author-developed Interactive Application exercises for each of the 12 chapters that drill students in the use and application of the concepts and tools of strategic analysis.

All of the *Connect*™ exercises are automatically graded (with the exception of a few exercise components that entail student entry of essay answers), thereby simplifying the task of evaluating each class member's performance and monitoring the learning outcomes. The progress-tracking function built into the *Connect*™ *Management* system enables you to:

- View scored work immediately and track individual or group performance with assignment and grade reports.
- Access an instant view of student or class performance relative to learning objectives.
- Collect data and generate reports required by many accreditation organizations, such as AACSB.

For Instructors

Online Learning Center (OLC)

In addition to the student resources, the instructor section of www.mhhe.com/thompson includes an Instructor's Manual and other support materials. Your McGraw-Hill representative can arrange delivery of instructor support materials in a format-ready Standard Cartridge for Blackboard, WebCT, and other Web-based educational platforms.

Instructor's Manual

The accompanying IM contains a section on suggestions for organizing and structuring your course, sample syllabi and course outlines, a set of lecture notes on each chapter and a copy of the test bank.

Test Bank and EZ Test Online

There is a test bank containing over 900 multiple-choice questions and short-answer/essay questions. It has been tagged with AACSB and Bloom's Taxonomy criteria. All of the test bank questions are also accessible within a computerized test bank powered by McGraw-Hill's flexible electronic testing program EZ Test Online (www.eztestonline.com). Using EZ Test Online allows you to create paper and online tests or quizzes. With EZ Test Online, instructors can select questions from multiple McGraw-Hill test banks or author their own and then either print the test for paper distribution or give it online.

PowerPoint Slides

To facilitate delivery preparation of your lectures and to serve as chapter outlines, you'll have access to approximately 500 colorful and professional-looking slides displaying core concepts, analytical procedures, key points, and all the figures in the text chapters.

Instructor's Resource CD-ROM   All of our instructor supplements are available in this one-stop multimedia resource, which includes the complete Instructor's Manual, computerized test bank (EZ Test), accompanying Power-Point slides, and the Digital Image Library with all of the figures from the text. It is a useful aid for compiling a syllabus and daily course schedule, preparing customized lectures, and developing tests on the text chapters.

The Business Strategy Game and GLO-BUS Online Simulations
Using one of the two companion simulations is a powerful and constructive way of emotionally connecting students to the subject matter of the course. We know of no more effective and interesting way to stimulate the competitive energy of students and prepare them for the rigors of real-world business decision making than to have them match strategic wits with classmates in running a company in head-to-head competition for global market leadership.

ACKNOWLEDGMENTS

A great number of colleagues and students at various universities, business acquaintances, and people at McGraw-Hill provided inspiration, encouragement, and counsel during the course of this project. Like all text authors in the strategy field, we are intellectually indebted to the many academics whose research and writing have blazed new trails and advanced the discipline of strategic management. In addition, we'd like to thank the following reviewers who provided seasoned advice and splendid suggestions for improving the chapters in this 18th edition:

Joan H. Bailar, Lake Forest Graduate School of Management
David Blair, University of Nebraska at Omaha
Jane Boyland, Johnson & Wales University
William J. Donoher, Missouri State University
Stephen A. Drew, Florida Gulf Coast University
Jo Ann Duffy, Sam Houston State University
Alan Ellstrand, University of Arkansas
Susan Fox-Wolfgramm, Hawaii Pacific University
Rebecca M. Guidice, University of Nevada–Las Vegas
Mark Hoelscher, Illinois State University
Sean D. Jasso, University of California–Riverside
Xin Liang, University of Minnesota–Duluth
Paul Mallette, Colorado State University
Dan Marlin, University of South Florida–St. Petersburg
Raza Mir, William Paterson University
Mansour Moussavi, Johnson & Wales University
James D. Spina, University of Maryland
Monica A. Zimmerman, West Chester University

We also express our thanks to Dennis R. Balch, Jeffrey R. Bruehl, Edith C. Busija, Donald A. Drost, Randall Harris, Mark Lewis Hoelscher, Phyllis Holland, James W. Kroeger, Sal Kukalis, Brian W. Kulik, Paul Mallette, Anthony U. Martinez, Lee Pickler, Sabine Reddy, Thomas D. Schramko, V. Seshan, Charles Strain, Sabine Turnley, S. Stephen Vitucci, Andrew Ward, Sibin Wu, Lynne

Patten, Nancy E. Landrum, Jim Goes, Jon Kalinowski, Rodney M. Walter, Judith D. Powell, Seyda Deligonul, David Flanagan, Esmerlda Garbi, Mohsin Habib, Kim Hester, Jeffrey E. McGee, Diana J. Wong, F. William Brown, Anthony F. Chelte, Gregory G. Dess, Alan B. Eisner, John George, Carle M. Hunt, Theresa Marron-Grodsky, Sarah Marsh, Joshua D. Martin, William L. Moore, Donald Neubaum, George M. Puia, Amit Shah, Lois M. Shelton, Mark Weber, Steve Barndt, J. Michael Geringer, Ming-Fang Li, Richard Stackman, Stephen Tallman, Gerardo R. Ungson, James Boulgarides, Betty Diener, Daniel F. Jennings, David Kuhn, Kathryn Martell, Wilbur Mouton, Bobby Vaught, Tuck Bounds, Lee Burk, Ralph Catalanello, William Crittenden, Vince Luchsinger, Stan Mendenhall, John Moore, Will Mulvaney, Sandra Richard, Ralph Roberts, Thomas Turk, Gordon Von Stroh, Fred Zimmerman, S. A. Billion, Charles Byles, Gerald L. Geisler, Rose Knotts, Joseph Rosenstein, James B. Thurman, Ivan Able, W. Harvey Hegarty, Roger Evered, Charles B. Saunders, Rhae M. Swisher, Claude I. Shell, R. Thomas Lenz, Michael C. White, Dennis Callahan, R. Duane Ireland, William E. Burr II, C. W. Millard, Richard Mann, Kurt Christensen, Neil W. Jacobs, Louis W. Fry, D. Robley Wood, George J. Gore, and William R. Soukup. These reviewers provided valuable guidance in steering our efforts to improve earlier editions.

We owe a special debt of gratitude to Catherine Maritan, for her detailed comments on a number of chapters, and to Richard S. Shreve and Anant K. Sundaram, who gave us sage advice regarding the material in Chapter 9. We'd like to thank the following students of the Tuck School of Business for their assistance with the chapter revisions: C. David Morgan, Amy E. Florentino, John R. Moran, Mukund Kulashakeran, Jeffrey L. Boyink, Jonathan D. Keith, Anita Natarajan, Alison F. Connolly, and Melissa E. Vess. And we'd like to acknowledge the help of Dartmouth students Catherine Wu, Jack McNeily, and Jenna Pfeffer, as well as Feldberg librarians Karen Sluzenski and Sarah J. Buckingham and Tuck staff members Annette Lyman, Mary Biathrow, Doreen Aher, and Karen H. Summer.

As always, we value your recommendations and thoughts about the book. Your comments regarding coverage and contents will be taken to heart, and we always are grateful for the time you take to call our attention to printing errors, deficiencies, and other shortcomings. Please e-mail us at athompso@cba.ua.edu, mpeteraf@dartmouth.edu, jgamble@usouthal.edu, or astrickl@cba.ua.edu.

Arthur A. Thompson

Margaret A. Peteraf

John E. Gamble

A. J. Strickland

Chapter Structure and Organization

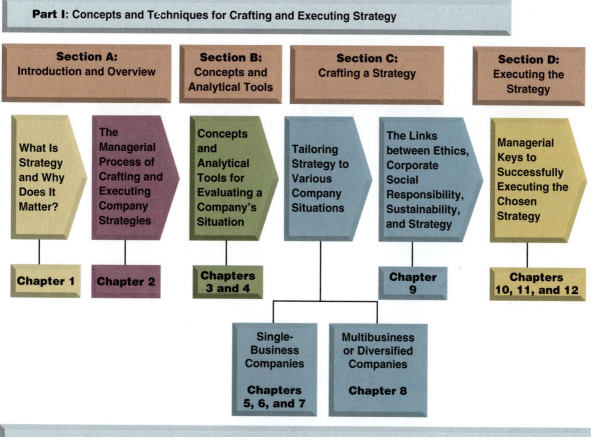

Part I: Concepts and Techniques for Crafting and Executing Strategy

Section A: Introduction and Overview

Section B: Concepts and Analytical Tools

Section C: Crafting a Strategy

Section D: Executing the Strategy

What Is Strategy and Why Does It Matter?

The Managerial Process of Crafting and Executing Company Strategies

Concepts and Analytical Tools for Evaluating a Company's Situation

Tailoring Strategy to Various Company Situations

The Links between Ethics, Corporate Social Responsibility, Sustainability, and Strategy

Managerial Keys to Successfully Executing the Chosen Strategy

Chapter 1

Chapter 2

Chapters 3 and 4

Chapter 9

Chapters 10, 11, and 12

Single-Business Companies

Chapters 5, 6, and 7

Multibusiness or Diversified Companies

Chapter 8

Part II: Readings in Crafting and Executing Strategy
Section A: What Is Strategy and How Is the Process of Crafting and Executing Strategy Managed? (2 readings)
Section B: Crafting Strategy in Single-Business Companies (9 readings)
Section C: Crafting Strategy in Diversified Companies (2 readings)
Section D: Strategy, Ethics, Social Responsibility, and Sustainability (3 readings)
Section E: Executing Strategy (4 readings)

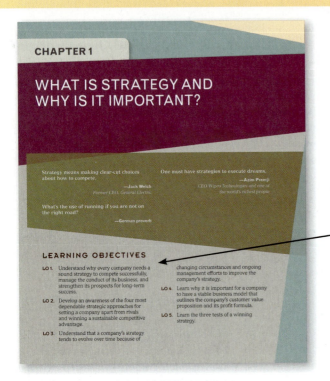

CHAPTER 1

WHAT IS STRATEGY AND WHY IS IT IMPORTANT?

Strategy means making clear-cut choices about how to compete.
—Jack Welch
Former CEO, General Electric

One must have strategies to execute dreams.
—Azim Premji
CEO Wipro Technologies and one of the world's richest people

What's the use of running if you are not on the right road?
—German proverb

LEARNING OBJECTIVES

LO 1. Understand why every company needs a sound strategy to compete successfully, manage the conduct of its business, and strengthen its prospects for long-term success.

LO 2. Develop an awareness of the four most dependable strategic approaches for setting a company apart from rivals and winning a sustainable competitive advantage.

LO 3. Understand that a company's strategy tends to evolve over time because of changing circumstances and ongoing management efforts to improve the company's strategy.

LO 4. Learn why it is important for a company to have a viable business model that outlines the company's customer value proposition and its profit formula.

LO 5. Learn the three tests of a winning strategy.

Learning Objectives are listed at the beginning of each chapter; corresponding numbered indicators in the margins show where learning objectives are covered in the text.

ILLUSTRATION CAPSULE 2.3

Examples of Company Objectives

NORDSTROM

Increase same store sales by 2–4%. Expand credit revenue by $25–$35 million while also reducing associated expenses by $10–$20 million as a result of lower bad debt expenses. Continue moderate store growth by opening three new Nordstrom stores, relocating one store and opening 17 Nordstrom Racks. Find more ways to connect with customers on a multi-channel basis, including plans for an enhanced online experience, improved mobile shopping capabilities and better engagement with customers through social networking. Improve customer focus: "Most important, we continue to do everything in our power to elevate our focus on the customer. Our challenge is to keep building on this momentum. Our number one goal firmly remains improving customer service" (Blake Nordstrom, CEO).

MICROSOFT

On a broad level, deliver end-to-end experiences that connect users to information, communications, entertainment, and people in new and compelling ways across their lives at home, at work, and the broadest-possible range of mobile scenarios. Given the dramatic changes in the way people interact with technology, as touch, gestures, handwriting, and speech recognition become a normal part of how we control devices, focus on making technology more accessible and simpler to use, which will create opportunities to reach new markets and deliver new kinds of computing experiences.

More specifically, grow revenue in the PC Division slightly faster than the overall PC market fueled especially by emerging market trends.

Launch Office 2010 for the business market and promote adoption followed by a 2011 launch of the WindowsPhone 7 in the Entertainment and Devices Division. Grow annuity revenue between 4–6% in the Server and Tools Business segment. Target overall gross margin increases of 1% fueled in part by improved operational efficiency. Operating expenses are targeted at $26.1–$26.3 billion for the year with projected capital spending at $2 billion.

MCDONALD'S

Reinvest $2.4 billion in the business; 50% of this will be spent on opening 1,000 new restaurants around the world, including roughly 500 in Asia Pacific, 250 in Europe, and 150 in the U.S. The other half will be allocated toward "re-imagining" the décor and menu of over 2,000 existing locations. Re-imagining has a direct positive impact on sales as market share increases after re-imagining restaurants in the U.S., France and Australia demonstrate. Continue to expand refranchising; 80% of restaurants have been refranchised and this will be augmented by 200–300 restaurants in the next year. Focus on menu choice with a balance of familiar and popular core products as well as new items to keep products relevant.

Illustration Capsules appear in boxes throughout each chapter to provide in-depth examples, connect the text presentation to real-world companies, and convincingly demonstrate "strategy in action." Some are appropriate for use as mini-cases.

Margin Notes define core concepts and call attention to important ideas and principles.

and changes taking place in the business environment that might affect the company. The answer to the question *"Where do we want to go from here?"* lies within management's vision of the company's future direction—what new customer groups and customer needs to endeavor to satisfy and what new capabilities to build or acquire. The question *"How are we going to get there?"* challenges managers to craft and execute a strategy capable of moving the company in the intended direction.

Developing clear answers to the question *"How are we going to get there?"* is the essence of managing strategically. Rather than relying on the status quo as a road map and dealing with new opportunities or threats as they emerge, managing strategically involves developing a full-blown game plan that spells out the competitive moves and business approaches that will be employed to compete successfully, attract and please customers, conduct operations, achieve targeted levels of performance, and grow the business. Thus, a company's strategy is all about *how:*

- *How* to outcompete rivals.
- *How* to respond to changing economic and market conditions and capitalize on growth opportunities.
- *How* to manage each functional piece of the business (e.g., R&D, supply chain activities, production, sales and marketing, distribution, finance, and human resources).
- *How* to improve the company's financial and market performance.

CORE CONCEPT

A company's **strategy** consists of the competitive moves and business approaches that managers are employing to compete successfully, improve performance, and grow the business.

The specific elements that constitute management's answer to the question *"How are we going to get there?"* define a company's business strategy. Thus, a company's **strategy** is management's *action plan* for competing successfully and operating profitably, based on an integrated array of considered choices.[1] The crafting of a strategy represents a managerial commitment to pursuing a particular set of actions. In choosing a strategy, management is in effect saying, "Among all the many different business approaches and ways of competing we could have chosen, we have decided to employ this particular combination of approaches in moving the company in the intended direction, strengthening its market position and competitiveness, and boosting performance." The strategic choices a company

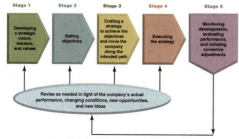

22 **Part 1** Concepts and Techniques for Crafting and Executing Strategy

Figure 2.1 The Strategy-Making, Strategy-Executing Process

Figure 2.1 displays this five-stage process, which we examine next in some detail.

STAGE 1: DEVELOPING A STRATEGIC VISION, A MISSION, AND A SET OF CORE VALUES

Figures scattered throughout the chapters provide conceptual and analytical frameworks.

KEY POINTS

The strategic management process consists of five interrelated and integrated stages:

1. *Developing a strategic vision* of the company's future, a *mission* that defines the company's current purpose, and a set of *core values* to guide the pursuit of the vision and mission. This managerial step provides direction for the company, motivates and inspires company personnel, aligns and guides actions throughout the organization, and communicates to stakeholders management's aspirations for the company's future.
2. *Setting objectives* to convert the vision and mission into performance targets and using the targeted results as yardsticks for measuring the company's performance. Objectives need to spell out *how much* of *what kind* of performance *by when.* Two broad types of objectives are required: *financial objectives* and *strategic objectives.* A *balanced-scorecard* approach provides a popular method for linking financial objectives to specific, measurable strategic objectives.
3. *Crafting a strategy* to achieve the objectives and move the company along the strategic course that management has charted. Crafting deliberate strategy calls for strategic analysis, based on the business model. Crafting emergent strategy is a learning-by-doing process involving experimentation. Who participates in the process of crafting strategy depends on (1) whether the process is emergent or deliberate and (2) the level of strategy concerned. Deliberate strategies are mostly top-down, while emergent strategies are bottom-up, although both cases require two-way interaction between different types of managers. In large, diversified companies, there are four levels of strategy, each of which involves a corresponding level of management: corporate strategy (multibusiness strategy), business strategy (strategy for individual businesses that compete in a single industry), functional-area strategies within each business (e.g., marketing, R&D, logistics), and operating strategies (for key operating units, such as manufacturing plants). Thus, strategy making is an inclusive, collaborative activity involving not only senior company executives but also the heads of major business divisions, functional-area managers, and operating managers on the frontlines. The larger and more diverse the operations of an enterprise, the more points of strategic initiative it has and the more levels of management that play a significant strategy-making role.

Key Points at the end of each chapter provide a handy summary of essential ideas and things to remember.

2. Based on the strategic group map in Illustration Capsule 3.1, who are Nordstrom's closest competitors? Between which two strategic groups is competition the strongest? Why do you think no retail chains are positioned in the upper right corner of the map? Which company/strategic group faces the weakest competition from the members of other strategic groups?

LO 1, LO 4

3. Using your knowledge as a snack-food consumer and your analysis of the five forces in that industry (from question 1), describe the key success factors for the snack-food industry. Your list should contain no more than six industry KSFs. In deciding on your list, it's important to distinguish between factors critical for the success of *any* firm in the industry and factors that pertain only to specific companies.

EXERCISES FOR SIMULATION PARTICIPANTS

LO 1

1. Which of the five competitive forces is creating the strongest competitive pressures for your company?
2. What are the "competitive weapons" that rival companies in your industry can use to gain sales and market share? See Table 3.2 to help you identify possible competitive tactics. (You may be able to think of others.)
3. What are the factors affecting the intensity of rivalry in the industry in which your company is competing. Use Figure 3.4 and the accompanying discussion to help you pinpoint the specific factors most affecting competitive intensity. Would you characterize the rivalry among the companies in your industry as brutal, strong, moderate, or relatively weak? Why?

LO 2

4. Are there any factors driving change in the industry in which your company is competing? What impact will these drivers of change have? How will they change demand or supply? Will they cause competition to become more or less intense? Will they act to boost or squeeze profit margins? List at least two actions your company should consider taking in order to combat any negative impacts of the factors driving change.

LO 3

5. Draw a strategic group map showing the market positions of the companies in your industry. Which companies do you believe are in the most attractive position on the map? Which companies are the most weakly positioned? Which companies do you believe are likely to try to move to a different position on the strategic group map?

LO 4

6. What do you see as the key factors for being a successful competitor in your industry? List at least three.

Exercises at the end of each chapter, linked to learning objectives, provide a basis for class discussion, oral presentations, and written assignments. Several chapters have exercises that qualify as mini-cases.

FOR STUDENTS: An Assortment of Support Materials

Web site: www.mhhe.com/thompson The student portion of the Web site features 10-question self-scoring chapter tests, the "Guide to Case Analysis," and PowerPoint slides for each chapter.

The Business Strategy Game or *GLO-BUS* **Simulation Exercises** Either one of these text supplements involves teams of students managing companies in a head-to-head contest for global market leadership. Company co-managers have to make decisions relating to product quality, production, workforce compensation and training, pricing and marketing, and financing of company operations. The challenge is to craft and execute a strategy that is powerful enough to deliver good financial performance despite the competitive efforts of rival companies. Each company competes in North America, Latin America, Europe-Africa, and Asia-Pacific.

BRIEF CONTENTS

xxxiv

TABLE OF CONTENTS

PART TWO Readings in Crafting and Executing Strategy

PART 1

Concepts and Techniques for Crafting and Executing Strategy

WHAT IS STRATEGY AND WHY IS IT IMPORTANT?

Strategy means making clear-cut choices about how to compete.

—**Jack Welch**
Former CEO, General Electric

What's the use of running if you are not on the right road?

—**German proverb**

One must have strategies to execute dreams.

—**Azim Premji**
CEO Wipro Technologies and one of the world's richest people

LEARNING OBJECTIVES

LO 1. Understand why every company needs a sound strategy to compete successfully, manage the conduct of its business, and strengthen its prospects for long-term success.

LO 2. Develop an awareness of the four most dependable strategic approaches for setting a company apart from rivals and winning a sustainable competitive advantage.

LO 3. Understand that a company's strategy tends to evolve over time because of changing circumstances and ongoing management efforts to improve the company's strategy.

LO 4. Learn why it is important for a company to have a viable business model that outlines the company's customer value proposition and its profit formula.

LO 5. Learn the three tests of a winning strategy.

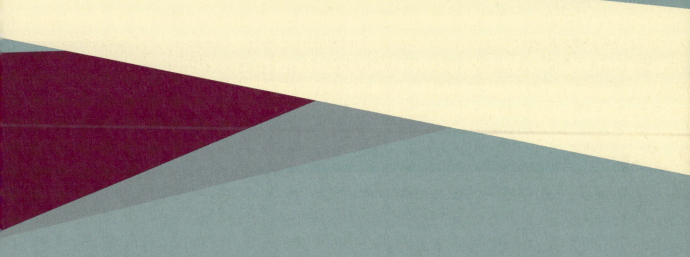

In any given year, a group of companies will stand out as the top performers, in terms of metrics such as profitability, sales growth, or growth in shareholder value. Some of these companies will find that their star status fades quickly, due to little more than a fortuitous constellation of circumstances, such as being in the right business at the right time. But other companies somehow manage to rise to the top and stay there, year after year, pleasing their customers, shareholders, and other stakeholders alike in the process. Companies such as Apple, Google, Coca-Cola, Procter & Gamble, McDonald's, and Microsoft come to mind—but long-lived success is not just the province of U.S. companies. Diverse kinds of companies, both large and small, from many different countries have been able to sustain strong performance records, including Sweden's IKEA (in home furnishings), Australia's BHP Billiton (in mining), Korea's Hyundai Heavy Industries (in shipbuilding and construction), Mexico's America Movil (in telecommunications), and Japan's Nintendo (in video game systems).

What can explain the ability of companies like these to beat the odds and experience prolonged periods of profitability and growth? Why is it that some companies, like Southwest Airlines and Walmart, continue to do well even when others in their industry are faltering? Why can some companies survive and prosper even through economic downturns and industry turbulence?

Many factors enter into a full explanation of a company's performance, of course. Some come from the external environment; others are internal to the firm. But only one thing can account for the kind of long-lived success records that we see in the world's greatest companies—and that is a cleverly crafted and well executed *strategy,* one that facilitates the capture of emerging opportunities, produces enduringly good performance, is adaptable to changing business conditions, and can withstand the competitive challenges from rival firms.

In this opening chapter, we define the concept of strategy and describe its many facets. We will explain what is meant by a competitive advantage, discuss the relationship between a company's strategy and its business model, and introduce you to the kinds of competitive strategies that can give a company an advantage over rivals in attracting customers and earning above-average profits. We will look at what sets a winning strategy apart from others and why the caliber of a company's strategy determines whether it will enjoy a competitive advantage over other firms or be burdened by competitive disadvantage. By the end of this chapter, you will have a clear idea of why the tasks of crafting and executing strategy are core management functions and why excellent execution of an excellent strategy is the most reliable recipe for turning a company into a standout performer over a long-term horizon.

WHAT DO WE MEAN BY *STRATEGY*?

In moving a company forward, managers of all types of organizations—small family-owned businesses, rapidly growing entrepreneurial firms, not-for-profit organizations, and the world's leading multinational corporations—face the same three central questions:

- What is our present situation?
- Where do we want to go from here?
- How are we going to get there?

The first question, *"What is our present situation?"* prompts managers to evaluate industry conditions, the company's current financial performance and market standing, its resources and capabilities, its competitive strengths and weaknesses, and changes taking place in the business environment that might affect the company. The answer to the question *"Where do we want to go from here?"* lies within management's vision of the company's future direction—what new customer groups and customer needs to endeavor to satisfy and what new capabilities to build or acquire. The question *"How are we going to get there?"* challenges managers to craft and execute a strategy capable of moving the company in the intended direction.

Developing clear answers to the question *"How are we going to get there?"* is the essence of managing strategically. Rather than relying on the status quo as a road map and dealing with new opportunities or threats as they emerge, managing strategically involves developing a full-blown game plan that spells out the competitive moves and business approaches that will be employed to compete successfully, attract and please customers, conduct operations, achieve targeted levels of performance, and grow the business. Thus, a company's strategy is all about *how:*

- *How* to outcompete rivals.
- *How* to respond to changing economic and market conditions and capitalize on growth opportunities.
- *How* to manage each functional piece of the business (e.g., R&D, supply chain activities, production, sales and marketing, distribution, finance, and human resources).
- *How* to improve the company's financial and market performance.

CORE CONCEPT

A company's **strategy** consists of the competitive moves and business approaches that managers are employing to compete successfully, improve performance, and grow the business.

The specific elements that constitute management's answer to the question *"How are we going to get there?"* define a company's business strategy. Thus, a company's **strategy** is management's *action plan* for competing successfully and operating profitably, based on an integrated array of considered choices.[1] The crafting of a strategy represents a managerial commitment to pursuing a particular set of actions. In choosing a strategy, management is in effect saying, "Among all the many different business approaches and ways of competing we could have chosen, we have decided to employ this particular combination of approaches in moving the company in the intended direction, strengthening its market position and competitiveness, and boosting performance." The strategic choices a company makes are seldom easy decisions and often involve difficult trade-offs—but that does not excuse failure to pursue a concrete course of action.[2]

In most industries, there are many different avenues for outcompeting rivals and boosting company performance, thus giving managers considerable freedom in choosing the specific elements of their company's strategy.[3] Consequently, some companies strive to improve their performance by employing strategies aimed at achieving lower costs than rivals, while others pursue strategies aimed at achieving product superiority or personalized customer service or quality dimensions that rivals cannot match. Some companies opt for wide product lines, while others concentrate their energies on a narrow product lineup. Some position themselves in only one part of the industry's chain of production/distribution activities (preferring to be just in manufacturing or wholesale distribution or retailing), while others are partially or fully integrated, with operations ranging from components production to manufacturing and assembly to wholesale distribution and retailing. Some competitors deliberately confine their operations to local or regional markets; others opt to compete nationally, internationally (several countries), or globally (all or most of the major country markets worldwide). Some companies decide to operate in only one industry, while others diversify broadly or narrowly into related or unrelated industries.

There is no shortage of opportunity to fashion a strategy that both tightly fits a company's own particular situation and is discernibly different from the strategies of rivals. In fact, competitive success requires a company's managers to make strategic choices about the key building blocks of its strategy that differ from the choices made by competitors—not 100 percent different but at least different in several important respects. A strategy stands a better chance of succeeding when it is predicated on actions, business approaches, and competitive moves aimed at appealing to buyers *in ways that set a company apart from rivals.* Simply trying to mimic the strategies of the industry's successful companies rarely works. Rather, every company's strategy needs to have some distinctive element that draws in customers and produces a competitive edge. Strategy, at its essence, is about competing differently—doing what rival firms *don't* do or what rival firms *can't* do.[4]

> Strategy is about competing differently from rivals—doing what competitors *don't* do or, even better, doing what they *can't* do! Every strategy needs a distinctive element that attracts customers and produces a competitive edge.

A company's strategy provides direction and guidance, in terms of not only what the company *should* do but also what it *should not* do. Knowing what not to do can be as important as knowing what to do, strategically. At best, making the wrong strategic moves will prove a distraction and a waste of company resources. At worst, it can bring about unintended long-term consequences that put the company's very survival at risk.

Figure 1.1 illustrates the broad types of actions and approaches that often characterize a company's strategy in a particular business or industry. For a more concrete example of the specific actions constituting a firm's strategy, see Illustration Capsule 1.1, describing McDonald's strategy in the quick-service restaurant industry.

Strategy and the Quest for Competitive Advantage

The heart and soul of any strategy is the actions and moves in the marketplace that managers are taking to gain a competitive edge over rivals. A creative, distinctive strategy that sets a company apart from rivals and

> **CORE CONCEPT**
>
> A company achieves **sustainable competitive advantage** when it can meet customer needs more effectively or efficiently than rivals and when the basis for this is durable, despite the best efforts of competitors to match or surpass this advantage.

Figure 1.1   Identifying a Company's Strategy—What to Look For

provides a competitive advantage is a company's most reliable ticket for earning above-average profits. Competing in the marketplace on the basis of a competitive advantage tends to be more profitable than competing with no advantage. And a company is almost certain to earn significantly higher profits when it enjoys a competitive advantage as opposed to when it is hamstrung by competitive disadvantage.

Competitive advantage comes from an ability to meet customer needs more *effectively,* with products or services that customers value more highly, or more *efficiently,* at lower cost. Meeting customer needs more effectively can translate into the ability to command a higher price (e.g., Godiva chocolate), which can improve profits by boosting revenues. Meeting customer needs more cost-effectively can translate into being able to charge lower prices and achieve higher sales volumes (e.g., Walmart), thereby improving profits on the revenue side as well as the cost side. Furthermore, if a company's competitive edge holds promise for being sustainable (as opposed to just temporary), then so much the better for both the strategy and the company's future profitability. What makes a competitive advantage **sustainable** (or durable), as opposed to temporary, are elements of the strategy that give buyers *lasting reasons to prefer* a company's products or services over those of competitors—reasons that competitors are unable to nullify or overcome despite their best efforts.

LO 2

Develop an awareness of the four most-dependable strategic approaches for setting a company apart from rivals and winning a sustainable competitive advantage.

McDonald's Strategy in the Quick-Service Restaurant Industry

In 2010, McDonald's was setting new sales records despite a global economic slowdown and declining consumer confidence in the United States. More than 60 million customers visited one of McDonald's 32,000 restaurants in 117 countries each day, which allowed the company to record 2009 revenues and earnings of more than $22.7 billion and $6.8 billion, respectively. McDonald's performance in the marketplace made it one of only two companies listed on the Dow Jones Industrial Average (the other was Walmart Stores, Inc.) that actually increased in share value in spite of the economic meltdown. The company's sales were holding up well amid the ongoing economic uncertainty in early 2010, with global sales as measured in constant currencies increasing by more than 4 percent in the first quarter. Its combined operating margin had risen to nearly 30 percent. The company's success was a result of its well-conceived and executed Plan-to-Win strategy that focused on "being better, not just bigger." Key initiatives of the Plan-to-Win strategy included:

- *Improved restaurant operations.* McDonald's global restaurant operations improvement process involved employee training programs ranging from on-the-job training for new crew members to college-level management courses offered at the company's Hamburger University. The company also sent nearly 200 high-potential employees annually to its McDonald's Leadership Institute to build the leadership skills needed by its next generation of senior managers. McDonald's commitment to employee development earned the company a place on *Fortune*'s list of Top 25 Global Companies for Leaders in 2010. The company also trained its store managers to closely monitor labor, food, and utility costs.

- *Affordable pricing.* In addition to tackling operating costs in each of its restaurants, McDonald's kept its prices low by closely scrutinizing administrative costs and other corporate expenses. McDonald's saw the poor economy in the United States as an opportunity to renegotiate its advertising contracts with newspapers and television networks in early 2009. The company also began to replace its company-owned vehicles with more fuel-efficient models when gasoline prices escalated dramatically in the United States during 2008. However, McDonald's did not choose to sacrifice product quality in order to offer lower prices. The company implemented extensive supplier monitoring programs to ensure that its suppliers did not change product specifications to lower costs. For example, the company's chicken breasts were routinely checked for weight when arriving from suppliers' production facilities. The company's broad approach to minimizing non-value-adding expenses allowed it to offer more items on its Dollar Menu in the United States, its Ein Mal Eins menu in Germany, and its 100 Yen menu in Japan.

- *Wide menu variety and beverage choices.* McDonald's has expanded its menu beyond the popular-selling Big Mac and Quarter Pounder to include such new, healthy quick-service items as grilled chicken salads, chicken snack wraps, and premium chicken sandwiches in the United States, Lemon Shrimp Burgers in Germany, and Ebi shrimp wraps in Japan. The company has also added an extensive line of premium coffees that include espressos,

(continued)

cappuccinos, and lattes sold in its McCafe restaurant locations in the United States, Europe, and the Asia/Pacific region. McDonald's latte was judged "as good [as] or better" than lattes sold by Starbucks or Dunkin' Donuts in a review by the *Chicago Tribune*'s Good Eating and Dining staff in December 2008.

- *Convenience and expansion of dining opportunities.* The addition of McCafes helped McDonald's increase same store sales by extending traditional dining hours. Customers wanting a midmorning coffee or an afternoon snack helped keep store traffic high after McDonald's had sold its last Egg McMuffin, McGriddle, or chicken biscuit and before the lunch crowd arrived to order Big Macs, Quarter Pounders, chicken sandwiches, or salads. The company also extended its drive-thru hours to 24 hours in more than 25,000 locations in cities around the world where consumers tended to eat at all hours of the day and night. At many high-traffic locations in the United States, double drive-thru lanes were added to serve customers more quickly.

- *Ongoing restaurant reinvestment and international expansion.* With more than 14,000 restaurants in the United States, the focus of McDonald's expansion of units was in rapidly growing emerging markets such as Russia and China. The company opened 125 new restaurants in China and 40 new restaurants in Russia in 2008. The company also refurbished about 10,000 of its locations in the United States between 2004 and 2008 as a part of its McCafe rollout and as a way to make its restaurants pleasant places for both customers to dine and employees to work.

Sources: Janet Adamy, "McDonald's Seeks Way to Keep Sizzling," *Wall Street Journal Online,* March 10, 2009; various annual reports; various company press releases.

Four of the most frequently used and dependable strategic approaches to setting a company apart from rivals, building strong customer loyalty, and winning a competitive advantage are:

1. *Striving to be the industry's low-cost provider, thereby aiming for a cost-based competitive advantage over rivals.* Walmart and Southwest Airlines have earned strong market positions because of the low-cost advantages they have achieved over their rivals and their consequent ability to underprice competitors. These advantages in meeting customer needs *efficiently* have translated into volume advantages, with Walmart as the world's largest discount retailer and Southwest as the largest U.S. air carrier, based on the number of domestic passengers.[5]

2. *Outcompeting rivals on the basis of differentiating features, such as higher quality, wider product selection, added performance, value-added services, more attractive styling, and technological superiority.* Successful adopters of differentiation strategies include Apple (innovative products), Johnson & Johnson in baby products (product reliability), Rolex (top-of-the-line prestige), and Mercedes (engineering design). These companies have achieved a competitive advantage because of their ability to meet customer needs more effectively than rivals can, thus driving up their customers' willingness to pay higher prices. One way to sustain this type of competitive advantage is to be sufficiently innovative to thwart the efforts of clever rivals to copy or closely imitate the product offering.

3. *Focusing on a narrow market niche and winning a competitive edge by doing a better job than rivals of serving the special needs and tastes of buyers in the niche.* Firms using a focus strategy can achieve an advantage through either greater efficiency in serving the niche or greater effectiveness in meeting the special needs. Prominent companies that enjoy competitive success in a specialized market niche include eBay in online auctions, Jiffy Lube International

in quick oil changes, McAfee in virus protection software, and The Weather Channel in cable TV.

4. *Aiming to offer the lowest (best) prices for differentiated goods that at least match the features and performance of higher-priced rival brands.* This is known as a *best-cost provider strategy,* and it rests on the ability to be the most cost-effective provider of an upscale product or service. This option is a hybrid strategy that blends elements of the previous approaches. Target is an example of a company that is known for its hip product design (a reputation it built by featuring cheap-chic designers such as Isaac Mizrahi), as well as a more appealing shopping ambience than other "big-box" discounters, such as Walmart and Kmart. It offers the perfect illustration of a best-cost provider strategy.

Winning a *sustainable* competitive edge over rivals with any of the above four strategies generally hinges as much on building competitively valuable expertise and capabilities that rivals cannot readily match as it does on having a distinctive product offering. Clever rivals can nearly always copy the attributes of a popular product or service, but for rivals to match the experience, know-how, and specialized capabilities that a company has developed and perfected over a long period of time is substantially harder to do and takes much longer. FedEx, for example, has superior capabilities in next-day delivery of small packages. Walt Disney has hard-to-beat capabilities in theme park management and family entertainment. In recent years, Apple has demonstrated impressive product innovation capabilities in digital music players, smart phones, and e-readers. Hyundai has become the world's fastest-growing automaker as a result of its advanced manufacturing processes and unparalleled quality control system. Ritz Carlton and Four Seasons have uniquely strong capabilities in providing their hotel guests with an array of personalized services. Each of these capabilities has proved hard for competitors to imitate or best.

The tight connection between competitive advantage and profitability means that the quest for sustainable competitive advantage always ranks center stage in crafting a strategy. The key to successful strategy making is to come up with one or more strategy elements that act as a magnet to draw customers and that produce a lasting competitive edge over rivals. Indeed, what separates a powerful strategy from a run-of-the-mill or ineffective one is management's ability to forge a series of moves, both in the marketplace and internally, that sets the company apart from its rivals, tilts the playing field in the company's favor by giving buyers reason to prefer its products or services, and produces a sustainable competitive advantage over rivals. The bigger and more sustainable the competitive advantage, the better are a company's prospects for winning in the marketplace and earning superior long-term profits relative to its rivals. Without a strategy that leads to competitive advantage, a company risks being outcompeted by stronger rivals and locked into mediocre financial performance.

Why a Company's Strategy Evolves over Time

The appeal of a strategy that yields a sustainable competitive advantage is that it offers the potential for an enduring edge over rivals. However, managers of every company must be willing and ready to modify the strategy in response to changing market conditions, advancing technology, the fresh moves of competitors, shifting buyer needs, emerging market opportunities, and new ideas for improving the strategy. In some industries, conditions change at a fairly slow pace, making it feasible for the major components of a good strategy to remain in place for long

LO 3

Understand that a company's strategy tends to evolve over time because of changing circumstances and ongoing management efforts to improve the company's strategy.

periods. But in industries where industry and competitive conditions change frequently and in sometimes dramatic ways, the life cycle of a given strategy is short. Industry environments characterized by high-velocity change require companies to repeatedly adapt their strategies.[6] For example, companies in industries with rapid-fire advances in technology like medical equipment, electronics, and wireless devices often find it essential to adjust key elements of their strategies several times a year, sometimes even finding it necessary to "reinvent" their approach to providing value to their customers.

Regardless of whether a company's strategy changes gradually or swiftly, the important point is that the task of crafting strategy is not a one-time event but always a work in progress. Adapting to new conditions and constantly evaluating what is working well enough to continue and what needs to be improved are normal parts of the strategy-making process, resulting in an *evolving strategy*.[7]

> Changing circumstances and ongoing management efforts to improve the strategy cause a company's strategy to evolve over time—a condition that makes the task of crafting strategy *a work in progress*, not a one-time event.

A Company's Strategy Is Partly Proactive and Partly Reactive

The evolving nature of a company's strategy means that the typical company strategy is a blend of (1) *proactive* actions to improve the company's financial performance and secure a competitive edge and (2) *adaptive* reactions to unanticipated developments and fresh market conditions. In most cases, much of a company's current strategy flows from previously initiated actions and business approaches that are working well enough to merit continuation and from newly launched initiatives aimed at boosting financial performance and edging out rivals. This part of management's action plan for running the company is its **deliberate strategy,** consisting of strategy elements that are both planned and realized as planned (while other planned strategy elements may not work out).

> A company's strategy is shaped partly by management analysis and choice and partly by the necessity of adapting and learning by doing.

But managers must always be willing to supplement or modify the proactive strategy elements with as-needed reactions to unanticipated conditions. Inevitably, there will be occasions when market and competitive conditions take an unexpected turn that calls for some kind of strategic reaction or adjustment. Hence, *a portion of a company's strategy is always developed on the fly,* coming as a response to fresh strategic maneuvers on the part of rival firms, unexpected shifts in customer requirements, fast-changing technological developments, newly appearing market opportunities, a changing political or economic climate, or other unanticipated happenings in the surrounding environment. Under conditions of high uncertainty, strategy elements are more likely to emerge from experimentation, trial-and-error, and adaptive learning processes than from a proactive plan. These unplanned, reactive, and adaptive strategy adjustments make up the firm's **emergent strategy,** consisting of the new strategy elements that emerge as changing conditions warrant. A company's strategy in toto (its *realized* strategy) thus tends to be a *combination* of proactive and reactive elements, with certain strategy elements being *abandoned* because they have become obsolete or ineffective—see Figure 1.2.[8] A company's realized strategy can be observed in the pattern of its actions over time—a far better indicator than any of its strategic plans on paper or public pronouncements about its strategy.

> ### CORE CONCEPTS
>
> A company's **proactive (or deliberate) strategy** consists of strategy elements that are both planned and realized as planned; its **reactive (or emergent) strategy** consists of new strategy elements that emerge as changing conditions warrant.

Figure 1.2   **A Company's Strategy Is a Blend of Proactive Initiatives and Reactive Adjustments**

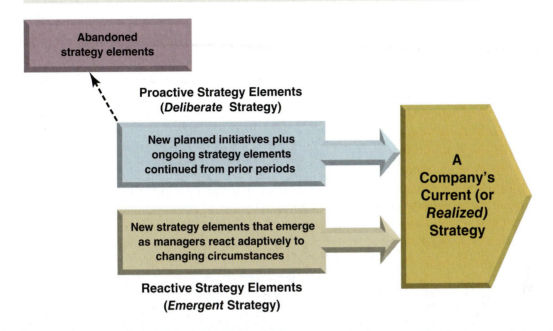

THE RELATIONSHIP BETWEEN A COMPANY'S STRATEGY AND ITS BUSINESS MODEL

LO 4

Learn why it is important for a company to have a viable business model that outlines the company's customer value proposition and its profit formula.

Closely related to the concept of strategy is the company's **business model.** A company's business model is management's blueprint for delivering a valuable product or service to customers in a manner that will generate ample revenues to cover costs and yield an attractive profit.[9] It is management's story line for how the strategy will be a moneymaker. Without the ability to deliver good profitability, the strategy is not viable and the survival of the business is in doubt.

The two crucial elements of a company's business model are (1) its *customer value proposition* and (2) its *profit formula.* The customer value proposition lays out the company's approach to satisfying buyer wants and needs at a price customers will consider a good value. The greater the value provided (V) and the lower the price (P), the more attractive the value proposition is to customers. The profit formula describes the company's approach to determining a cost structure that will allow for acceptable profits, given the pricing tied to its customer value proposition. More specifically, a company's profit formula depends on three basic elements: V—the *value* provided to customers, in terms of how effectively the goods or services of the company meet customers' wants and needs; P—the *price* charged to customers; and C—the company's *costs*. The lower the costs (C), given the customer value proposition ($V - P$), the greater the ability of the business model to be a moneymaker. Thus

CORE CONCEPT

A company's **business model** sets forth the economic logic for making money in a business, given the company's strategy. It describes two critical elements: (1) the customer value proposition and (2) the profit formula.

the profit formula reveals how efficiently a company can meet customer wants and needs and deliver on the value proposition.

Magazines and newspapers employ a business model keyed to delivering information and entertainment they believe readers will find valuable and a profit formula aimed at securing sufficient revenues from subscriptions and advertising to more than cover the costs of producing and delivering their products to readers. Mobile phone providers, satellite radio companies, and broadband providers also employ a subscription-based business model. The business model of network TV and radio broadcasters entails providing free programming to audiences but charging advertising fees based on audience size. Gillette's business model in razor blades involves selling a "master product"—the razor—at an attractively low price and then making money on repeat purchases of razor blades that can be produced very cheaply and sold at high profit margins. Printer manufacturers like Hewlett-Packard, Lexmark, and Epson pursue much the same business model as Gillette—selling printers at a low (virtually break-even) price and making large profit margins on the repeat purchases of printer supplies, especially ink cartridges.

The nitty-gritty issue surrounding a company's business model is whether it can execute its customer value proposition profitably. Just because company managers have crafted a strategy for competing and running the business, this does not automatically mean that the strategy will lead to profitability—it may or it may not. The relevance of a company's business model is to clarify *how the business will (1) provide customers with value and (2) generate revenues sufficient to cover costs and produce attractive profits.*[10] Illustration Capsule 1.2 describes two contrasting business models in radio broadcasting.

WHAT MAKES A STRATEGY A WINNER?

Three tests can be applied to determine whether a strategy is a *winning strategy:*

1. ***The Fit Test:*** *How well does the strategy fit the company's situation?* To qualify as a winner, a strategy has to be well matched to industry and competitive conditions, a company's best market opportunities, and other pertinent aspects of the business environment in which the company operates. No strategy can work well unless it exhibits good *external fit* and is in sync with prevailing market conditions. At the same time, a winning strategy has to be tailored to the company's resources and competitive capabilities and be supported by a complementary set of functional activities (i.e., activities in the realms of supply chain management, operations, sales and marketing, and so on). That is, it must also exhibit *internal fit* and be compatible with a company's ability to execute the strategy in a competent manner. Unless a strategy exhibits good fit with both the external and internal aspects of a company's overall situation, it is likely to be an underperformer and fall short of producing winning results. Winning strategies also exhibit *dynamic fit* in the sense that they evolve over time in a manner that maintains close and effective alignment with the company's situation even as external and internal conditions change.[11]

A **winning strategy** must pass three tests:

1. The Fit Test
2. The Competitive Advantage Test
3. The Performance Test

Sirius XM and Over-the-Air Broadcast Radio: Two Contrasting Business Models

	Sirius XM	Over-the-Air Radio Broadcasters
Customer value proposition	Digital music, news, national and regional weather, traffic reports in limited areas, and talk radio programming provided for a monthly subscription fee. Programming was interrupted only by brief, occasional ads.	Free-of-charge music, national and local news, local traffic reports, national and local weather, and talk radio programming. Listeners could expect frequent programming interruption for ads.
Profit formula	***Revenue generation:*** Monthly subscription fees, sales of satellite radio equipment, and advertising revenues. ***Cost structure:*** Fixed costs associated with operating a satellite-based music delivery service. Fixed and variable costs related to programming and content royalties, marketing, and support activities.	***Revenue generation:*** Advertising sales to national and local businesses. ***Cost structure:*** Fixed costs associated with terrestrial broadcasting operations. Fixed and variable costs related to local news reporting, advertising sales operations, network affiliate fees, programming and content royalties, commercial production activities, and support activities.
	Profit margin: Sirius XM's profitability was dependent on attracting a sufficiently large number of subscribers to cover its costs and provide attractive profits.	***Profit margin:*** The profitability of over-the-air radio stations was dependent on generating sufficient advertising revenues to cover costs and provide attractive profits.

2. ***The Competitive Advantage Test:*** *Can the strategy help the company achieve a sustainable competitive advantage?* Strategies that fail to achieve a durable competitive advantage over rivals are unlikely to produce superior performance for more than a brief period of time. Winning strategies enable a company to

achieve a competitive advantage over key rivals that is long-lasting. The bigger and more durable the competitive advantage, the more powerful it is.

3. ***The Performance Test:*** *Is the strategy producing good company performance?* The mark of a winning strategy is strong company performance. Two kinds of performance indicators tell the most about the caliber of a company's strategy: (1) profitability and financial strength and (2) competitive strength and market standing. Above-average financial performance or gains in market share, competitive position, or profitability are signs of a winning strategy.

Strategies that come up short on one or more of the above tests are plainly less appealing than strategies passing all three tests with flying colors. Managers should use the same questions when evaluating either proposed or existing strategies. New initiatives that don't seem to match the company's internal and external situations should be scrapped before they come to fruition, while existing strategies must be scrutinized on a regular basis to ensure they have good fit, offer a competitive advantage, and are contributing to above-average performance or performance improvements.

WHY CRAFTING AND EXECUTING STRATEGY ARE IMPORTANT TASKS

Crafting and executing strategy are top-priority managerial tasks for a very big reason. A clear and reasoned strategy is management's prescription for doing business, its road map to competitive advantage, its game plan for pleasing customers, and its formula for improving performance. High-achieving enterprises are nearly always the product of astute, creative, proactive strategy making. Companies don't get to the top of the industry rankings or stay there with illogical strategies, copy-cat strategies, or timid attempts to try to do better. Only a handful of companies can boast of hitting home runs in the marketplace due to lucky breaks or the good fortune of having stumbled into the right market at the right time with the right product. And even then, unless they subsequently craft a strategy that capitalizes on their luck, building in what's working and discarding the rest, success of this sort will be fleeting. So there can be little argument that a company's strategy matters—and matters a lot.

The chief executive officer of one successful company put it well when he said:

> In the main, our competitors are acquainted with the same fundamental concepts and techniques and approaches that we follow, and they are as free to pursue them as we are. More often than not, the difference between their level of success and ours lies in the relative thoroughness and self-discipline with which we and they develop and execute our strategies for the future.

Good Strategy + Good Strategy Execution = Good Management

Crafting and executing strategy are thus core management functions. Among all the things managers do, nothing affects a company's ultimate success or failure more fundamentally than how well its management team charts the company's direction, develops competitively effective strategic moves and business approaches, and pursues what needs to be done internally to produce good day-in, day-out strategy execution and operating excellence. Indeed, *good strategy and good strategy execution are the most telling signs of good management.* Managers don't deserve a gold star for designing a potentially brilliant strategy but failing to put the organizational means in place to carry it out in high-caliber fashion. Competent execution of a mediocre strategy scarcely merits enthusiastic applause for management's efforts either. The rationale for using the twin standards of good strategy making and good strategy execution to determine whether a company is well managed is therefore compelling: *The better conceived a company's strategy and the more competently it is executed, the more likely that the company will be a standout performer in the marketplace.* In stark contrast, a company that lacks clear-cut direction, has a flawed strategy, or can't execute its strategy competently is a company whose financial performance is probably suffering, whose business is at long-term risk, and whose management is sorely lacking.

> How well a company performs is directly attributable to the caliber of its strategy and the proficiency with which the strategy is executed.

THE ROAD AHEAD

Throughout the chapters to come and the accompanying case collection, the spotlight is trained on the foremost question in running a business enterprise: *What must managers do, and do well, to make a company a winner in the marketplace?* The answer that emerges, and that becomes the message of this book, is that doing a good job of managing inherently requires good strategic thinking and good management of the strategy-making, strategy-executing process.

The mission of this book is to provide a solid overview of what every business student and aspiring manager needs to know about crafting and executing strategy. We will explore what good strategic thinking entails, describe the core concepts and tools of strategic analysis, and examine the ins and outs of crafting and executing strategy. The accompanying cases will help build your skills both in diagnosing how well the strategy-making, strategy-executing task is being performed and in prescribing actions for how the strategy in question or its execution can be improved. In the process, we hope to convince you that first-rate capabilities in crafting and executing strategy are basic to managing successfully and are skills every manager needs to possess.

As you tackle the following pages, ponder the following observation by the essayist and poet Ralph Waldo Emerson: "Commerce is a game of skill which many people play, but which few play well." If the content of this book helps you become a savvy player and equips you to succeed in business, then your journey through these pages will indeed be time well spent.

KEY POINTS

The tasks of crafting and executing company strategies are the heart and soul of managing a business enterprise and winning in the marketplace. The key points to take away from this chapter include the following:

1. A company's strategy is the *game plan* management is using to stake out a market position, conduct its operations, attract and please customers, compete successfully, and achieve the desired performance targets.

2. The central thrust of a company's strategy is undertaking moves to build and strengthen the company's long-term competitive position and financial performance by *competing differently* from rivals and gaining a sustainable competitive advantage over them.

3. A company achieves a sustainable competitive advantage when it can meet customer needs more effectively or efficiently than rivals and when the basis for this is durable, despite the best efforts of competitors to match or surpass this advantage.

4. A company's strategy typically evolves over time, emerging from a blend of (1) proactive and deliberate actions on the part of company managers to improve the strategy and (2) reactive, as-needed adaptive responses to unanticipated developments and fresh market conditions.

5. A company's business model is management's story line for how the strategy will be a moneymaker. It contains two crucial elements: (1) the *customer value proposition*—a plan for satisfying customer wants and needs at a price customers will consider good value, and (2) the *profit formula*—a plan for a cost structure that will enable the company to deliver the customer value proposition profitably. In effect, a company's business model sets forth the economic logic for making money in a particular business, given the company's current strategy.

6. A winning strategy will pass three tests: (1) *Fit* (external, internal, and dynamic consistency), (2) *Competitive Advantage* (durable competitive advantage), and (3) *Performance* (outstanding financial and market performance).

7. Crafting and executing strategy are core management functions. How well a company performs and the degree of market success it enjoys are directly attributable to the caliber of its strategy and the proficiency with which the strategy is executed.

ASSURANCE OF LEARNING EXERCISES

LO 1, LO 2

1. Go to www.bestbuy.com, click on the investor relations section, and explore Best Buy's latest annual reports and 10-K filings to see if you can identify the key elements of Best Buy's strategy. Use the framework provided in Figure 1.1 to help identify these key elements. What approach toward winning a competitive advantage does Best Buy seem to be pursuing?

LO 1, LO 2, LO 5

2. On the basis of what you know about the quick-service restaurant industry, does McDonald's strategy as described in Illustration Capsule 1.1 seem to be well matched to industry and competitive conditions? Does the strategy seem to be keyed to having a cost-based advantage, offering differentiating features, serving the unique needs of a narrow market niche, or being the best-cost provider? What is there about the action elements of McDonald's strategy that is consistent with its approach to competitive advantage? From the information provided, which tests of a winning strategy does McDonald's strategy pass?

LO 4, LO 3

3. Go to www.nytco.com/investors and check whether the New York Times Company's recent financial reports indicate that its business model is working. Can the company's business model remain sound as more consumers go to the Internet to find general information and stay abreast of current events and news stories? Is its revenue stream from advertisements growing or declining? Are its subscription fees and circulation increasing or declining? Read the company's latest press releases. Is there evidence that the company's business model is evolving? To what degree does its strategic response to changing industry conditions seem proactive and deliberate versus reactive and adaptive (emergent)?

EXERCISE FOR SIMULATION PARTICIPANTS

This chapter discusses three questions that must be answered by managers of organizations of all sizes:

- What is our present situation?
- Where do we want to go from here?
- How are we going to get there?

After you read the Participant's Guide or Player's Manual for the strategy simulation exercise that you will participate in this academic term, you and your co-managers should come up with brief one- or two-paragraph answers to these three questions *before* entering your first set of decisions. While the management team's answer to the first of the three questions can be developed from your reading of the manual, the second and third questions will require a collaborative discussion among the members of your company's management team about how you intend to manage the company you have been assigned to run.

LO 1, LO 2

1. *What is our company's current situation?* A substantive answer to this question should cover the following issues:

   - Is your company in a good, average, or weak competitive position vis-à-vis rival companies?
   - Does your company appear to be in sound financial condition?
   - What problems does your company have that need to be addressed?

LO 3, LO 5

2. *Where do we want to take the company during the time we are in charge?* A complete answer to this question should say something about each of the following:

   - What goals or aspirations do you have for your company?
   - What do you want the company to be known for?
   - What market share would you like your company to have after the first five decision rounds?

- By what amount or percentage would you like to increase total profits of the company by the end of the final decision round?
- What kinds of performance outcomes will signal that you and your co-managers are managing the company in a successful manner?

LO 3, LO 4

3. *How are we going to get there?* Your answer should cover these issues:

- Which of the basic strategic and competitive approaches discussed in this chapter do you think makes the most sense to pursue?
- What kind of competitive advantage over rivals will you try to achieve?
- How would you describe the company's business model?
- What kind of actions will support these objectives?

ENDNOTES

[1] Jan Rivkin, "An Alternative Approach to Making Strategic Choices," Harvard Business School, 9-702-433, 2001.

[2] Costas Markides, "What Is Strategy and How Do You Know If You Have One?" *Business Strategy Review* 15, no. 2 (Summer 2004), pp. 5–6. See also David J. Collis and Michael F. Rukstad, "Can You Say What Your Strategy Is?" *Harvard Business Review* 86, no. 4 (April 2008), pp. 82–90.

[3] For a discussion of the different ways that companies can position themselves in the marketplace, see Michael E. Porter, "What Is Strategy?" *Harvard Business Review* 74, no. 6 (November–December 1996), pp. 65–67.

[4] Ibid.

[5] Walmartstores.com/download/2230.pdf; Southwest Airlines Fact Sheet, July 16, 2009.

[6] For more on the strategic challenges posed by high-velocity changes, see Shona L. Brown and Kathleen M. Eisenhardt, *Competing on the Edge: Strategy as Structured Chaos* (Boston, MA: Harvard Business School Press, 1998), chap. 1.

[7] For an excellent discussion of strategy as a dynamic process involving continuous, unending creation and re-creation of strategy, see Cynthia A. Montgomery, "Putting Leadership Back into Strategy," *Harvard Business Review* 86, no. 1 (January 2008), pp. 54–60.

[8] See Henry Mintzberg and Joseph Lampel, "Reflecting on the Strategy Process," *Sloan Management Review* 40, no. 3 (Spring 1999), pp. 21–30; Henry Mintzberg and J. A. Waters, "Of Strategies, Deliberate and Emergent," *Strategic Management Journal* 6 (1985), pp. 257–72; Costas Markides, "Strategy as Balance: From 'Either-Or' to 'And,'" *Business Strategy Review* 12, no. 3 (September 2001), pp. 1–10.

[9] Mark W. Johnson, Clayton M. Christensen, and Henning Kagermann, "Reinventing Your Business Model," *Harvard Business Review* 86, no. 12 (December 2008), pp. 52–53; Joan Magretta, "Why Business Models Matter," *Harvard Business Review* 80, no. 5 (May 2002), p. 87.

[10] For further discussion of the meaning and role of a company's customer value proposition and profit proposition,see W. Chan Kim and Renée Mauborgne, "How Strategy Shapes Structure," *Harvard Business Review* 87, no. 9 (September 2009), pp. 74–75.

[11] For a discussion of the three types of fit, see Rivkin, "An Alternative Approach to Making Strategic Choices." For an example of managing internal fit dynamically, See M. Peteraf and R. Reed, "Managerial Discretion and Internal Alignment under Regulatory Constraints and Change," *Strategic Management Journal* 28 (2007), pp. 1089–1112.

CHAPTER 2

CHARTING A COMPANY'S DIRECTION: VISION AND MISSION, OBJECTIVES, AND STRATEGY

> The vision we have . . . determines what we do and the opportunities we see or don't see.
>
> **—Charles G. Koch**
> *CEO of Koch Industries, the second-largest privately held company in the U.S.*

> If you don't know where you are going, any road will take you there.
>
> **—Cheshire Cat to Alice**
> *Lewis Carroll, Alice in Wonderland*

> A good goal is like a strenuous exercise—it makes you stretch.
>
> **—Mary Kay Ash**
> *Founder of Mary Kay Cosmetics*

LEARNING OBJECTIVES

LO 1. Grasp why it is critical for company managers to have a clear strategic vision of where a company needs to head and why.

LO 2. Understand the importance of setting both strategic and financial objectives.

LO 3. Understand why the strategic initiatives taken at various organizational levels must be tightly coordinated to achieve companywide performance targets.

LO 4. Become aware of what a company must do to achieve operating excellence and to execute its strategy proficiently.

LO 5. Become aware of the role and responsibility of a company's board of directors in overseeing the strategic management process.

Crafting and executing strategy are the heart and soul of managing a business enterprise. But exactly what is involved in developing a strategy and executing it proficiently? What are the various components of the strategy-making, strategy-executing process and to what extent are company personnel—aside from senior management—involved in the process? In this chapter we present an overview of the ins and outs of crafting and executing company strategies. Special attention will be given to management's direction-setting responsibilities—charting a strategic course, setting performance targets, and choosing a strategy capable of producing the desired outcomes. We will also explain why strategy making is a task for a company's entire management team and discuss which kinds of strategic decisions tend to be made at which levels of management. The chapter concludes with a look at the roles and responsibilities of a company's board of directors in the strategy-making, strategy-executing process and how good corporate governance protects shareholder interests and promotes good management.

WHAT DOES THE STRATEGY-MAKING, STRATEGY-EXECUTING PROCESS ENTAIL?

The process of crafting and executing a company's strategy consists of five interrelated managerial stages:

1. *Developing a strategic vision* of the company's long-term direction, a *mission* that describes the company's purpose, and a set of *values* to guide the pursuit of the vision and mission.
2. *Setting objectives* and using them as yardsticks for measuring the company's performance and progress.
3. *Crafting a strategy* to achieve the objectives and move the company along the strategic course that management has charted.
4. *Executing the chosen strategy* efficiently and effectively.
5. *Monitoring developments, evaluating performance, and initiating corrective adjustments* in the company's vision and mission, objectives, strategy, or execution in light of actual experience, changing conditions, new ideas, and new opportunities.

Figure 2.1   The Strategy-Making, Strategy-Executing Process

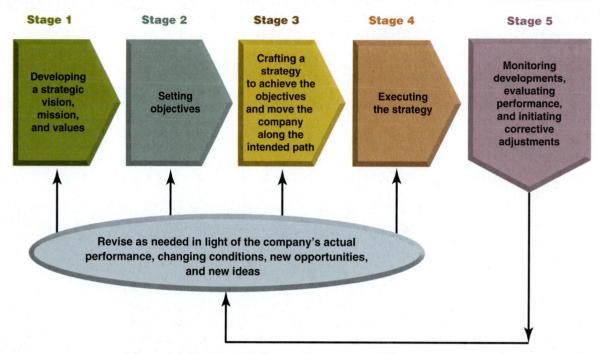

Figure 2.1 displays this five-stage process, which we examine next in some detail.

STAGE 1: DEVELOPING A STRATEGIC VISION, A MISSION, AND A SET OF CORE VALUES

LO 1

Grasp why it is critical for company managers to have a clear strategic vision of where a company needs to head and why.

Very early in the strategy-making process, a company's senior managers must wrestle with the issue of what directional path the company should take. Can the company's prospects be improved by changing its product offerings and/or the markets in which it participates and/or the customers it caters to and/or the technologies it employs? Deciding to commit the company to one path versus another pushes managers to draw some carefully reasoned conclusions about whether the company's present strategic course offers attractive opportunities for growth and profitability or whether changes of one kind or another in the company's strategy and long-term direction are needed.

Developing a Strategic Vision

Top management's views and conclusions about the company's long-term direction and what product-customer-market-technology mix seems optimal for the road ahead constitute a **strategic vision** for the company. A strategic vision delineates management's aspirations for the business, providing a panoramic view of "where we are going" and a convincing rationale for why this makes good business sense for the company. A strategic vision thus points an organization in a particular direction, charts a strategic path for it to follow in preparing for the future, and builds commitment to the future course of action. A clearly articulated strategic vision communicates management's aspirations to stakeholders and helps steer the energies of company personnel in a common direction.

Well-conceived visions are *distinctive* and *specific* to a particular organization; they avoid generic, feel-good statements like "We will become a global leader and the first choice of customers in every market we serve"—which could apply to hundreds of organizations.[1] And they are not the product of a committee charged with coming up with an innocuous but well-meaning one-sentence vision that wins consensus approval from various stakeholders. Nicely worded vision statements with no specifics about the company's product-market-customer-technology focus fall well short of what it takes for a vision to measure up.

A sampling of vision statements currently in use shows a range from strong and clear to overly general and generic. A surprising number of the vision statements found on company Web sites and in annual reports are vague and unrevealing, saying very little about the company's future direction. Some could apply to almost any company in any industry. Many read like a public relations statement—high-sounding words that someone came up with because it is fashionable for companies to have an official vision statement.[2] But the real purpose of a vision statement is to serve as a management tool for giving the organization a sense of direction. Like any tool, it can be used properly or improperly, either clearly conveying a company's future strategic path or not.

For a strategic vision to function as a valuable managerial tool, it must convey what management wants the business to look like and provide managers with a reference point in making strategic decisions and preparing the company for the future. It must say something definitive about how the company's leaders intend to position the company beyond where it is today. Table 2.1 provides some dos and don'ts in composing an effectively worded vision statement. Illustration Capsule 2.1 provides a critique of the strategic visions of several prominent companies.

Communicating the Strategic Vision

Effectively communicating the strategic vision down the line to lower-level managers and employees is as important as the strategic soundness of the long-term direction top management has chosen. Company personnel can't be expected to unite behind managerial efforts to get the organization moving in the intended direction until they understand why the strategic course that management has charted is reasonable and beneficial. It is particularly important for executives to provide a compelling rationale for a dramatically *new* strategic vision and company direction. When company personnel don't understand or accept the need for redirecting organizational efforts, they are prone to resist change. Hence, reiterating the basis for the new direction, addressing employee concerns head-on, calming fears, lifting spirits, and providing updates and progress reports as events unfold all become part of the task in mobilizing support for the vision and winning commitment to needed actions.

Winning the support of organization members for the vision nearly always means putting "where we are going and why" in writing, distributing the statement organizationwide, and having executives personally explain the vision and its

> **CORE CONCEPT**
>
> A **strategic vision** describes management's aspirations for the future and delineates the company's strategic course and long-term direction.

> An effectively communicated vision is a tool for enlisting the commitment of company personnel to actions that move the company forward in the intended direction.

Table 2.1 Wording a Vision Statement—the Dos and Don'ts

The Dos	The Don'ts
Be graphic. Paint a clear picture of where the company is headed and the market position(s) the company is striving to stake out.	**Don't be vague or incomplete.** Never skimp on specifics about where the company is headed or how the company intends to prepare for the future.
Be forward-looking and directional. Describe the strategic course that management has charted and the kinds of product-market-customer-technology changes that will help the company prepare for the future.	**Don't dwell on the present.** A vision is not about what a company once did or does now; it's about "where we are going."
Keep it focused. Be specific enough to provide managers with guidance in making decisions and allocating resources.	**Don't use overly broad language.** All-inclusive language that gives the company license to head in almost any direction, pursue almost any opportunity, or enter almost any business must be avoided.
Have some wiggle room. Language that allows some flexibility is good. The directional course may have to be adjusted as market-customer-technology circumstances change, and coming up with a new vision statement every one to three years signals rudderless management.	**Don't state the vision in bland or uninspiring terms.** The best vision statements have the power to motivate company personnel and inspire shareholder confidence about the company's direction and business outlook.
Be sure the journey is feasible. The path and direction should be within the realm of what the company can pursue and accomplish; over time, a company should be able to demonstrate measurable progress in achieving the vision.	**Don't be generic.** A vision statement that could apply to companies in any of several industries (or to any of several companies in the same industry) is incapable of giving a company its own unique identity.
Indicate why the directional path makes good business sense. The directional path should be in the long-term interests of stakeholders (especially shareowners, employees, and customers).	**Don't rely on superlatives only.** Visions that claim the company's strategic course is one of being the "best" or "the most successful" or "a recognized leader" or the "global leader" usually shortchange the essential and revealing specifics about the path the company is taking to get there.
Make it memorable. To give the organization a sense of direction and purpose, the vision needs to be easily communicated. Ideally, it should be reducible to a few choice lines or a memorable "slogan" (like Henry Ford's famous vision of "a car in every garage").	**Don't run on and on.** Vison statements that are overly long tend to be unfocused and meaningless. A vision statement that is not short and to-the-point will tend to lose its audience.

Sources: John P. Kotter, *Leading Change* (Boston: Harvard Business School Press, 1996), p. 72; Hugh Davidson, *The Committed Enterprise* (Oxford: Butterworth Heinemann, 2002), chap. 2; and Michel Robert, *Strategy Pure and Simple II* (New York: McGraw-Hill, 1992), chaps. 2, 3, and 6.

Strategic visions become real only when the vision statement is imprinted in the minds of organization members and then translated into hard objectives and strategies.

rationale to as many people as feasible. *A strategic vision can usually be stated adequately in one to two paragraphs, and managers should be able to explain it to company personnel and outsiders in 5 to 10 minutes.* Ideally, executives should present their vision for the company in a manner that reaches out and grabs people. An engaging and convincing strategic vision has enormous motivational value—for the same reason that a stonemason is more inspired by building a great cathedral for the ages than simply laying stones to create floors and walls. When managers articulate a vivid and compelling case for where the company is headed, organization members begin to say "This is interesting and has a lot of merit. I want to be involved and do my part to help make it happen." The more that a vision evokes positive support and excitement, the greater its impact in terms of arousing a committed organizational effort and getting company personnel to move in a common direction.[3] Thus executive ability to paint a convincing and inspiring picture of a company's journey and destination is an important element of effective strategic leadership.

ILLUSTRATION CAPSULE 2.1

Examples of Strategic Visions—How Well Do They Measure Up?

Vision Statement	Effective Elements	Shortcomings
Coca-Cola Our vision serves as the framework for our Roadmap and guides every aspect of our business by describing what we need to accomplish in order to continue achieving sustainable, quality growth.	• Graphic • Focused • Flexible • Makes good business sense	• Long • Not forward-looking

- **People:** Be a great place to work where people are inspired to be the best they can be.
- **Portfolio:** Bring to the world a portfolio of quality beverage brands that anticipate and satisfy people's desires and needs.
- **Partners:** Nurture a winning network of customers and suppliers; together we create mutual, enduring value.
- **Planet:** Be a responsible citizen that makes a difference by helping build and support sustainable communities.
- Profit: Maximize long-term return to shareowners while being mindful of our overall responsibilities.
- Productivity: Be a highly effective, lean and fast-moving organization.

Vision Statement	Effective Elements	Shortcomings
UBS We are determined to be the best global financial services company. We focus on wealth and asset management, and on investment banking and securities businesses. We continually earn recognition and trust from clients, shareholders, and staff through our ability to anticipate, learn and shape our future. We share a common ambition to succeed by delivering quality in what we do. Our purpose is to help our clients make financial decisions with confidence. We use our resources to develop effective solutions and services for our clients. We foster a distinctive, meritocratic culture of ambition, performance and learning as this attracts, retains and develops the best talent for our company. By growing both our client and our talent franchises, we add sustainable value for our shareholders.	• Focused • Feasible • Desirable	• Not forward-looking • Bland or uninspiring • Hard to communicate
Walmart Saving People Money So They Can Live Better	• Focused • Memorable • Feasible • Makes good business sense	• Dwells on the present

Sources: Company documents and Web sites (accessed April 23, 2010, and June 6, 2010).

Expressing the Essence of the Vision in a Slogan   The task of effectively conveying the vision to company personnel is assisted when management can capture the vision of where to head in a catchy or easily remembered slogan. A number of organizations have summed up their vision in a brief phrase:

- Levi Strauss & Company: "We will clothe the world by marketing the most appealing and widely worn casual clothing in the world."
- Nike: "To bring innovation and inspiration to every athlete in the world."
- Mayo Clinic: "The best care to every patient every day."
- Scotland Yard: "To make London the safest major city in the world."
- Greenpeace: "To halt environmental abuse and promote environmental solutions."

Creating a short slogan to illuminate an organization's direction and purpose helps rally organization members to hurdle whatever obstacles lie in the company's path and maintain their focus.

The Payoffs of a Clear Vision Statement   A well-conceived, forcefully communicated strategic vision pays off in several respects: (1) It crystallizes senior executives' own views about the firm's long-term direction; (2) it reduces the risk of rudderless decision making; (3) it is a tool for winning the support of organization members for internal changes that will help make the vision a reality; (4) it provides a beacon for lower-level managers in setting departmental objectives and crafting departmental strategies that are in sync with the company's overall strategy; and (5) it helps an organization prepare for the future. When management is able to demonstrate significant progress in achieving these five benefits, the first step in organizational direction setting has been successfully completed.

Crafting a Mission Statement

The defining characteristic of a strategic vision is what it says about the company's *future strategic course*—"the direction we are headed and our aspirations for the future." In contrast, a **mission statement** describes the enterprise's *current business and purpose*—"who we are, what we do, and why we are here." The mission statements that one finds in company annual reports or posted on company Web sites are typically quite brief; some do a better job than others of conveying what the enterprise is all about. Consider, for example, the mission statement of Trader Joe's (a specialty grocery chain):

> The mission of Trader Joe's is to give our customers the best food and beverage values that they can find anywhere and to provide them with the information required for informed buying decisions. We provide these with a dedication to the highest quality of customer satisfaction delivered with a sense of warmth, friendliness, fun, individual pride, and company spirit.

The distinction between a strategic vision and a mission statement is fairly clear-cut: A **strategic vision** portrays a company's aspirations for its *future* ("where we are going"), whereas a company's **mission** describes its *purpose* and its *present* business ("who we are, what we do, and why we are here").

Note that Trader Joe's mission statement does a good job of conveying "who we are, what we do, and why we are here," but it says nothing about the company's long-term direction.

Another example of a well-stated mission statement with ample specifics about what the organization does is that of the Occupational Safety and Health Administration (OSHA): "to assure the safety and health of America's workers by setting and enforcing standards; providing training, outreach, and education; establishing partnerships; and encouraging continual improvement in workplace safety and health." Microsoft's gran-diloquent mission statement—"To help people and businesses throughout the world realize their full potential"—says so little about the customer needs it is satisfying that it could be applied to almost any firm. A well-conceived mission statement should employ language specific enough to give the company its own identity.

Ideally, a company mission statement is sufficiently descriptive to:

- Identify the company's product or services.
- Specify the buyer needs it seeks to satisfy.
- Identify the customer groups or markets it is endeavoring to serve.
- Specify its approach to pleasing customers.
- Give the company its own identity.

Not many company mission statements fully reveal *all* these facets of the business or employ language specific enough to give the company an identity that is distinguishably different from those of other companies in much the same business or industry. A few companies have worded their mission statements so obscurely as to mask what they are all about. Occasionally, companies couch their mission in terms of making a profit. This is misguided. Profit is more correctly an *objective* and a *result* of what a company does. Moreover, earning a profit is the obvious intent of every commercial enterprise. Such companies as BMW, McDonald's, Shell Oil, Procter & Gamble, Nintendo, and Nokia are each striving to earn a profit for shareholders; but plainly the fundamentals of their businesses are substantially different when it comes to "who we are and what we do." It is management's answer to "make a profit doing what and for whom?" that reveals the substance of a company's true mission and business purpose.

Linking the Vision and Mission with Company Values

The **values** of a company (sometimes called *core values*) are the beliefs, traits, and behavioral norms that management has determined should guide the pursuit of its vision and mission. They relate to such things as fair treatment, integrity, ethical behavior, innovativeness, teamwork, top-notch quality, superior customer service, social responsibility, and community citizenship. Many companies have developed a statement of values to emphasize the expectation that the values be reflected in the conduct of company operations and the behavior of company personnel.

Most companies have identified four to eight core values. At FedEx, the six core values concern people (valuing employees and promoting diversity), service (putting customers at the heart of all it does), innovation (inventing services and technologies to improve what it does), integrity (managing with honesty, efficiency, and reliability), and loyalty (earning the respect of the FedEx people, customers, and investors every day, in everything it does). Home Depot embraces eight values—entrepreneurial spirit, excellent customer service, giving back to the community, respect for all people, doing the right thing, taking care of people, building strong relationships, and creating shareholder value—in its quest to be the world's leading home improvement retailer.

Do companies practice what they preach when it comes to their professed values? Sometimes no, sometimes yes—it runs the gamut. At one extreme are

CORE CONCEPT

A well-conceived **mission statement** conveys a company's *purpose* in language specific enough to give the company its own identity.

CORE CONCEPT

A company's **values** are the beliefs, traits, and behavioral norms that company personnel are expected to display in conducting the company's business and pursuing its strategic vision and mission.

companies with window-dressing values; the values are given lip service by top executives but have little discernible impact on either how company personnel behave or how the company operates. Such companies have value statements because they are in vogue and make the company look good. At the other extreme are companies whose executives are committed to infusing the company with the desired character, traits, and behavioral norms so that they are ingrained in the company's corporate culture—the core values thus become an integral part of the company's DNA and what makes it tick. At such value-driven companies, executives "walk the talk" and company personnel are held accountable for displaying the stated values.

At companies where the stated values are real rather than cosmetic, managers connect values to the pursuit of the strategic vision and mission in one of two ways. In companies with long-standing values that are deeply entrenched in the corporate culture, senior managers are careful to craft a vision, mission, and strategy that match established values; they also reiterate how the value-based behavioral norms contribute to the company's business success. If the company changes to a different vision or strategy, executives take care to explain how and why the core values continue to be relevant. In new companies or companies having unspecified values, top management has to consider what values, behaviors, and business conduct should characterize the company and then draft a value statement that is circulated among managers and employees for discussion and possible modification. A final value statement that incorporates the desired behaviors and traits and that connects to the vision and mission is then officially adopted. Some companies combine their vision, mission, and values into a single statement or document, circulate it to all organization members, and in many instances post the vision, mission, and value statement on the company's Web site. Illustration Capsule 2.2 describes how core values drive the company's mission at the Zappos Family of Companies, a widely known and quite successful online shoe and apparel retailer that was acquired recently by Amazon (but will continue to operate separately).

STAGE 2: SETTING OBJECTIVES

LO 2

Understand the importance of setting both strategic and financial objectives.

The managerial purpose of setting **objectives** is to convert the vision and mission into specific performance targets. Well-stated objectives are *specific, quantifiable* or *measurable,* and contain a *deadline for achievement.* As Bill Hewlett, cofounder of Hewlett-Packard, shrewdly observed, "You cannot manage what you cannot measure. . . . And what gets measured gets done."[4] Concrete, measurable objectives are managerially valuable for three reasons: (1) They focus efforts and align actions throughout the organization, (2) they serve as *yardsticks* for tracking a company's performance and progress, and (3) they provide motivation and inspire employees to greater levels of effort. Ideally, managers should develop challenging yet achievable objectives that *stretch* an organization to perform at its full potential.

CORE CONCEPT

Objectives are an organization's performance targets—the specific results management wants to achieve.

What Kinds of Objectives to Set

Two very distinct types of performance targets are required: those relating to financial performance and those relating to strategic performance. **Financial objectives** communicate management's targets for financial

ILLUSTRATION CAPSULE 2.2

Zappos Family Mission and Core Values

We've been asked by a lot of people how we've grown so quickly, and the answer is actually really simple. . . . We've aligned the entire organization around one mission: *to provide the best customer service possible.* Internally, we call this our **WOW** philosophy.

These are the ten core values that we live by:

Deliver Wow through Service. At the Zappos Family of Companies, anything worth doing is worth doing with WOW. WOW is such a short, simple word, but it really encompasses a lot of things. To WOW, you must differentiate yourself, which means doing something a little unconventional and innovative. You must do something that's above and beyond what's expected. And whatever you do must have an emotional impact on the receiver. We are not an average company, our service is not average, and we don't want our people to be average. We expect every employee to deliver WOW.

Embrace and Drive Change. Part of being in a growing company is that change is constant. For some people, especially those who come from bigger companies, the constant change can be somewhat unsettling at first. If you are not prepared to deal with constant change, then you probably are not a good fit for the company.

Create Fun and a Little Weirdness. At Zappos, We're Always Creating Fun and A Little Weirdness! One of the things that makes our company different from a lot of other companies is that we value being fun and being a little weird. We don't want to become one of those big companies that feels corporate and boring. We want to be able to laugh at ourselves. We look for both fun and humor in our daily work.

Be Adventurous, Creative, and Open Minded. We think it's important for people and the company as a whole to be bold and daring (but not reckless). We do not want people to be afraid to take risks and make mistakes. We believe if people aren't making mistakes, then that means they're not taking enough risks. Over time, we want everyone to develop his/her gut about business decisions. We want people to develop and improve their decision-making skills. We encourage people to make mistakes as long as they learn from them.

Pursue Growth and Learning. We think it's important for employees to grow both personally and professionally. It's important to constantly challenge and stretch yourself

and not be stuck in a job where you don't feel like you are growing or learning.

Build Open and Honest Relationships With Communication. Fundamentally, we believe that openness and honesty make for the best relationships because that leads to trust and faith. We value strong relationships in all areas: with managers, direct reports, customers (internal and external), vendors, business partners, team members, and co-workers.

Build a Positive Team and Family Spirit. At our company, we place a lot of emphasis on our culture because we are both a team and a family. We want to create an environment that is friendly, warm, and exciting. We encourage diversity in ideas, opinions, and points of view.

Do More with Less. The Zappos Family of Companies has always been about being able to do more with less. While we may be casual in our interactions with each other, we are focused and serious about the operations of our business. We believe in working hard and putting in the extra effort to get things done.

Be Passionate and Determined. Passion is the fuel that drives us and our company forward. We value passion, determination, perseverance, and the sense of urgency. We are inspired because we believe in what we are doing and where we are going. We don't take "no" or "that'll never work" for an answer because if we had, then our company would have never started in the first place.

Be Humble. While we have grown quickly in the past, we recognize that there are always challenges ahead to tackle. We believe that no matter what happens we should always be respectful of everyone.

performance. **Strategic objectives** are related to a company's marketing standing and competitive vitality. Examples of commonly used financial and strategic objectives include the following:

Financial Objectives	Strategic Objectives
• An *x* percent increase in annual revenues • Annual increases in after-tax profits *of x* percent • Annual increases in earnings per share of *x* percent • Annual dividend increases of *x* percent • Profit margins of *x* percent • An *x* percent return on capital employed (ROCE) or return on shareholders' equity investment (ROE) • Increased shareholder value—in the form of an upward-trending stock price • Bond and credit ratings of *x* • Internal cash flows of *x* dollars to fund new capital investment	• Winning an *x* percent market share • Achieving lower overall costs than rivals • Overtaking key competitors on product performance or quality or customer service • Deriving *x* percent of revenues from the sale of new products introduced within the past five years • Having broader or deeper technological capabilities than rivals • Having a wider product line than rivals • Having a better-known or more powerful brand name than rivals • Having stronger national or global sales and distribution capabilities than rivals • Consistently getting new or improved products to market ahead of rivals

The importance of setting and achieving financial objectives is intuitive. Without adequate profitability and financial strength, a company's long-term health and ultimate survival are jeopardized. Furthermore, subpar earnings and a weak balance sheet alarm shareholders and creditors and put the jobs of senior executives at risk. However, good financial performance, by itself, is not enough.

The Balanced Scorecard: Improved Strategic Performance Fosters Better Financial Performance

A company's financial performance measures are really *lagging indicators* that reflect the results of past decisions and organizational activities.[5] But a company's past or current financial performance is not a reliable indicator of its future prospects—poor financial performers often turn things around and do better, while good financial performers can fall upon hard times. The best and most reliable *leading indicators* of a company's future financial performance and business prospects are strategic outcomes that indicate whether the company's competitiveness and market position are stronger or weaker. The accomplishment of strategic objectives signals that the company is well positioned to sustain or improve its performance. For instance, if a company is achieving ambitious strategic objectives such that its competitive strength and market position are on the rise, then there's reason to expect that its *future* financial performance will be better than its current or past performance. If a company begins to lose competitive strength and fails to achieve important strategic objectives, then its ability to maintain its present profitability is highly suspect.

Consequently, utilizing a performance measurement system that strikes a *balance* between financial objectives and strategic objectives is optimal.[6] Just tracking a company's financial performance overlooks the fact that what ultimately enables a company to deliver better financial results from its operations is the achievement of strategic objectives that improve its competitiveness and market strength. Indeed, *the surest path to boosting company profitability* quarter after quarter and year after year *is to relentlessly pursue strategic outcomes* that strengthen the company's market position and produce a growing competitive advantage over rivals.

The most widely used framework for balancing financial objectives with strategic objectives is known as the **Balanced Scorecard.**[7] This is a method for linking financial performance objectives to specific strategic objectives that derive from a company's business model. It provides a company's employees with clear guidelines about how their jobs are linked to the overall objectives of the organization, so they can contribute most productively and collaboratively to the achievement of these goals. In 2008, nearly 60 percent of global companies used a balanced-scorecard approach to measuring strategic and financial performance.[8] Examples of organizations that have adopted a balanced-scorecard approach to setting objectives and measuring performance include UPS, Ann Taylor Stores, UK Ministry of Defense, Caterpillar, Daimler AG, Hilton Hotels, Duke University Hospital, and Siemens AG.[9] Illustration Capsule 2.3 provides selected strategic and financial objectives of four prominent companies.

The Merits of Setting Stretch Objectives

Ideally, managers ought to use the objective-setting exercise as a tool for *stretching an organization to perform at its full potential and deliver the best possible results.* Challenging company personnel to go all out and deliver "stretch" gains in performance pushes an enterprise to be more inventive, to exhibit more urgency in improving both its financial performance and its business position, and to be more intentional and focused in its actions. Stretch objectives spur exceptional performance and help build a firewall against contentment with modest gains in organizational performance. As Mitchell Leibovitz, former CEO of the auto parts and service retailer Pep Boys, once said, "If you want to have ho-hum results, have ho-hum objectives." *There's no better way to avoid unimpressive results than by setting stretch objectives and using compensation incentives to motivate organization members to achieve the stretch performance targets.*

Why Both Short-Term and Long-Term Objectives Are Needed

A company's set of financial and strategic objectives should include both near-term and longer-term performance targets. Short-term (quarterly or annual) objectives focus attention on delivering performance improvements in the current period and satisfy shareholder expectations for near-term progress. Longer-term targets (three to five years off) force managers to consider what to do *now* to put the company in position to perform better later. Long-term objectives are critical for achieving optimal long-term performance and stand as a barrier to a nearsighted management philosophy and an undue focus on short-term results. When trade-offs have to be made between achieving long-run objectives and achieving short-run objectives, long-run objectives should take precedence (unless the achievement of one or more short-run performance targets has unique importance).

The Need for Objectives at All Organizational Levels

Objective setting should not stop with top management's establishing of company-wide performance targets. Company objectives need to be broken down into

ILLUSTRATION CAPSULE 2.3
Examples of Company Objectives

NORDSTROM

Increase same store sales by 2–4%. Expand credit revenue by $25–$35 million while also reducing associated expenses by $10–$20 million as a result of lower bad debt expenses. Continue moderate store growth by opening three new Nordstrom stores, relocating one store and opening 17 Nordstrom Racks. Find more ways to connect with customers on a multi-channel basis, including plans for an enhanced online experience, improved mobile shopping capabilities and better engagement with customers through social networking. Improve customer focus: "Most important, we continue to do everything in our power to elevate our focus on the customer. Our challenge is to keep building on this momentum. Our number one goal firmly remains improving customer service" (Blake Nordstrom, CEO).

MICROSOFT

On a broad level, deliver end-to-end experiences that connect users to information, communications, entertainment, and people in new and compelling ways across their lives at home, at work, and the broadest-possible range of mobile scenarios. Given the dramatic changes in the way people interact with technology, as touch, gestures, handwriting, and speech recognition become a normal part of how we control devices, focus on making technology more accessible and simpler to use, which will create opportunities to reach new markets and deliver new kinds of computing experiences.

More specifically, grow revenue in the PC Division slightly faster than the overall PC market fueled especially by emerging market trends.

Launch Office 2010 for the business market and promote adoption followed by a 2011 launch of the WindowsPhone 7 in the Entertainment and Devices Division. Grow annuity revenue between 4–6% in the Server and Tools Business segment. Target overall gross margin increases of 1% fueled in part by improved operational efficiency. Operating expenses are targeted at $26.1–$26.3 billion for the year with projected capital spending at $2 billion.

MCDONALD'S

Reinvest $2.4 billion in the business; 50% of this will be spent on opening 1,000 new restaurants around the world, including roughly 500 in Asia Pacific, 250 in Europe, and 150 in the U.S. The other half will be allocated toward "re-imagining" the décor and menu of over 2,000 existing locations. Re-imagining has a direct positive impact on sales as market share increases after re-imagining restaurants in the U.S., France and Australia demonstrate. Continue to expand refranchising; 80% of restaurants have been refranchised and this will be augmented by 200–300 restaurants in the next year. Focus on menu choice with a balance of familiar and popular core products as well as new items to keep products relevant.

Developed with C. David Morgan.

Sources: "Nordstrom 2009 Annual Report," http://phx.corporate-ir.net/phoenix.zhtml?c=93295&p=irol-irhome, https://materials.proxyvote.com/Approved/655664/20100312/AR_57243/images/Nordstrom-AR2009.pdf (accessed April 4, 2010); "Nordstrom Fourth Quarter and Fiscal Year 2009 Earning, February 22, 2010," http://phx.corporate-ir.net/phoenix.zhtml?c=93295&p=irol-newsArticle&ID=1393755&highlight= (accessed April 30, 2010); Nordstrom "4Q 2009 Financial Results," http://investor.nordstrom.com/phoenix.zhtml?c=93295&p=irol-audioArchives (accessed April 30, 2010); Thompson Reuters Street Events, "JWN – Q4 2009 Nordstrom Earnings Conference Call," www.streetevents.com, February 2010 (transcribed version of Webcast accessed April 30, 2010, through InvesText database); "Microsoft Annual Report" www.microsoft.com/msft/reports/default.mspx (accessed April 23, 2010); "Microsoft Third Quarter Earnings Call," www.microsoft.com/msft/earnings/fy10/earn_rel_q3_10.mspx (accessed April 30, 2010); Thompson Reuters Street Events, "MCD – Q4 2009 McDonald's Corporate Earnings Conference Call," www.streetevents.com, January 2010 (transcribed version of Webcast accessed April 30, 2010, through InvesText database).

performance targets for each of the organization's separate businesses, product lines, functional departments, and individual work units. Company performance can't reach full potential unless each organizational unit sets and pursues performance targets that contribute directly to the desired companywide outcomes and results. Objective-setting is thus a *top-down process* that must extend to the lowest organizational levels. And it means that each organizational unit must take care to set performance targets that support—rather than conflict with or negate—the achievement of companywide strategic and financial objectives.

The ideal situation is a team effort in which each organizational unit strives to produce results in its area of responsibility that contribute to the achievement of the company's performance targets and strategic vision. Such consistency signals that organizational units know their strategic role and are on board in helping the company move down the chosen strategic path and produce the desired results.

STAGE 3: CRAFTING A STRATEGY

The task of stitching a strategy together entails addressing a series of hows: *how* to grow the business, *how* to please customers, *how* to outcompete rivals, *how* to respond to changing market conditions, *how* to manage each functional piece of the business, *how* to develop needed capabilities, and *how* to achieve strategic and financial objectives. It also means choosing among the various strategic alternatives—proactively searching for opportunities to do new things or to do existing things in new or better ways.[10] The faster a company's business environment is changing, the more critical it becomes for its managers to be good entrepreneurs in diagnosing the direction and force of the changes under way and in responding with timely adjustments in strategy. Strategy makers have to pay attention to early warnings of future change and be willing to experiment with dare-to-be-different ways to establish a market position in that future. When obstacles appear unexpectedly in a company's path, it is up to management to adapt rapidly and innovatively. *Masterful strategies come from doing things differently from competitors where it counts—out-innovating them, being more efficient, being more imaginative, adapting faster—rather than running with the herd.* Good strategy making is therefore inseparable from good business entrepreneurship. One cannot exist without the other.

Strategy Making Involves Managers at All Organizational Levels

LO 3

Understand why the strategic initiatives taken at various organizational levels must be tightly coordinated to achieve companywide performance targets.

A company's senior executives obviously have important strategy-making roles. The chief executive officer (CEO), as captain of the ship, carries the mantles of chief direction setter, chief objective setter, chief strategy maker, and chief strategy implementer for the total enterprise. Ultimate responsibility for *leading* the strategy-making, strategy-executing process rests with the CEO. In some enterprises the CEO or owner functions as strategic visionary and chief architect of strategy, personally deciding what the key elements of the company's strategy will be, although others may well assist with data gathering and analysis and the CEO may seek the advice of senior executives or board members. A CEO-centered approach to strategy development is characteristic of small owner-managed companies and sometimes large corporations that were founded by the present CEO or that have a CEO with strong strategic leadership skills. Steve Jobs at Apple, Andrea Jung at Avon, and Howard Schultz at Starbucks are prominent examples of corporate CEOs who have wielded a heavy hand in shaping their company's strategy.

Even here, however, it is a mistake to view strategy making as a *top* management function, the exclusive province of owner-entrepreneurs, CEOs, other senior executives, and board members. The more a company's operations cut across different products, industries, and geographic areas, the more that headquarters executives have little option but to delegate considerable strategy-making authority to down-the-line managers in charge of particular subsidiaries, divisions, product lines, geographic sales offices, distribution centers, and plants. On-the-scene managers who oversee specific operating units can be reliably counted on to have more detailed command of the strategic issues and choices for the particular operating unit under their supervision—knowing the prevailing market and competitive conditions, customer requirements and expectations, and all the other relevant aspects affecting the several strategic options available. Managers with day-to-day familiarity of, and authority over, a specific operating unit thus have a big edge over headquarters executives in making wise strategic choices for their operating unit.

Take, for example, a company like General Electric, a $183 billion global corporation with 325,000 employees, operations in some 100 countries, and businesses that include jet engines, lighting, power generation, electric transmission and distribution equipment, housewares and appliances, medical equipment, media and entertainment, locomotives, security devices, water purification, and financial services. While top-level headquarters executives may well be personally involved in shaping GE's *overall* strategy and fashioning *important* strategic moves, it doesn't follow that a few senior executives in GE's headquarters have either the expertise or a sufficiently detailed understanding of all the relevant factors to wisely craft all the strategic initiatives taken for hundreds of subsidiaries and thousands of products. They simply cannot know enough about the situation in every GE organizational unit to decide on every strategy detail and direct every strategic move made in GE's worldwide organization. Rather, it takes involvement on the part of GE's whole management team—top executives, business group heads, the heads of specific business units and product categories, and key managers in plants, sales offices, and distribution centers—to craft the thousands of strategic initiatives that end up constituting the whole of GE's strategy.

The *level* of strategy also has a bearing on who participates in crafting strategy. In diversified companies, where multiple businesses have to be managed, the strategy-making task involves four distinct levels of strategy. Each of these involves different facets of the company's overall strategy and calls for the participation of different types of managers, as shown in Figure 2.2.

1. *Corporate strategy* is strategy at the multibusiness level—how to achieve a competitive edge through a multibusiness, multimarket strategy. It concerns how to boost the combined performance of *the set of businesses* the company has diversified into and the means of capturing cross-business synergies and turning them into competitive advantage. It addresses the questions of what businesses to hold or divest, which new markets to enter, and what mode of

CORE CONCEPT

In most companies, crafting and executing strategy is a *collaborative team effort* in which every manager has a role for the area he or she heads. It is flawed thinking to view crafting and executing strategy as something only high-level managers do.

Figure 2.2 A Company's Strategy-Making Hierarchy

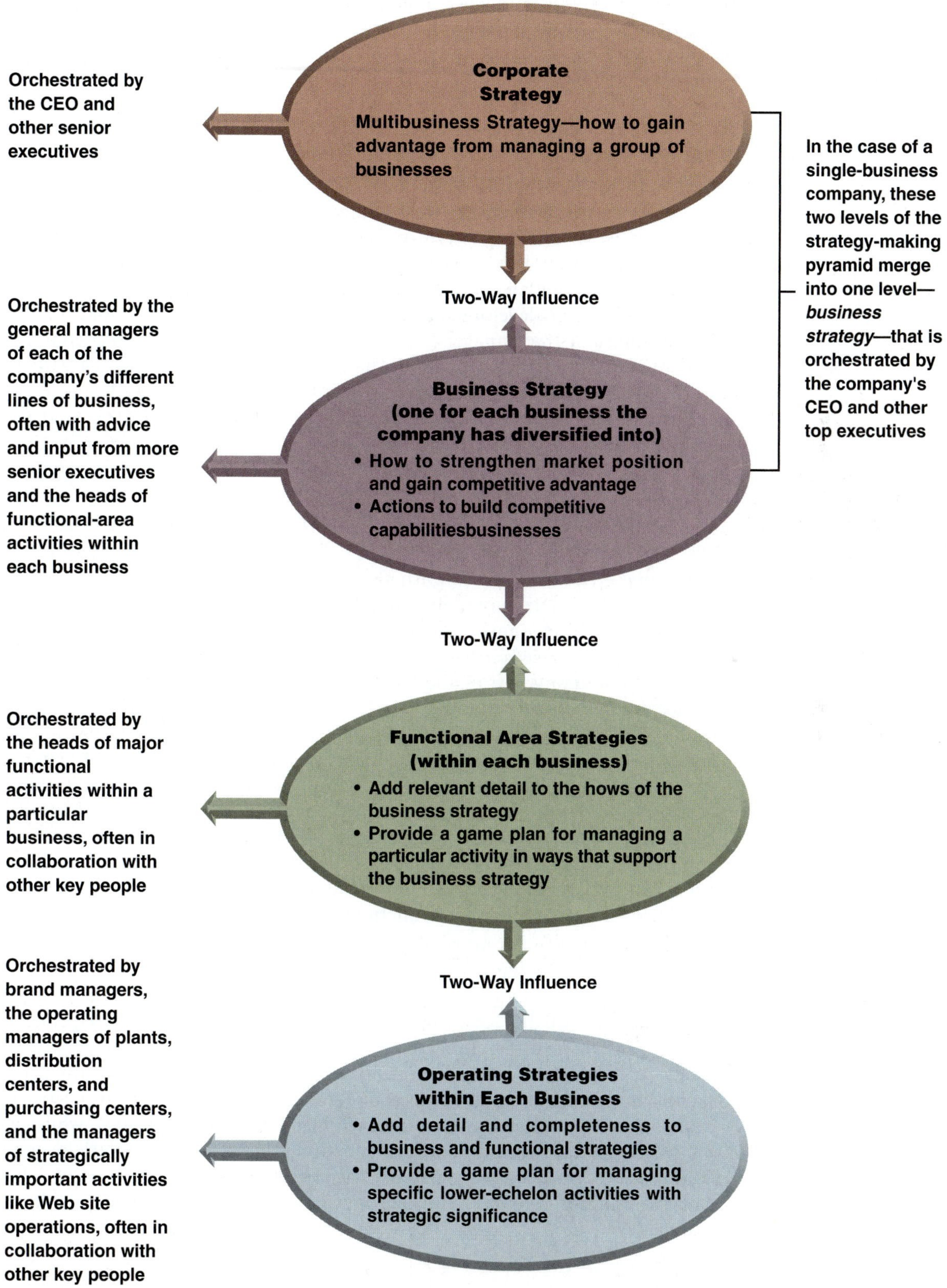

Orchestrated by the CEO and other senior executives

Corporate Strategy

Multibusiness Strategy—how to gain advantage from managing a group of businesses

In the case of a single-business company, these two levels of the strategy-making pyramid merge into one level— *business strategy*—that is orchestrated by the company's CEO and other top executives

Two-Way Influence

Orchestrated by the general managers of each of the company's different lines of business, often with advice and input from more senior executives and the heads of functional-area activities within each business

Business Strategy (one for each business the company has diversified into)
- How to strengthen market position and gain competitive advantage
- Actions to build competitive capabilitiesbusinesses

Two-Way Influence

Orchestrated by the heads of major functional activities within a particular business, often in collaboration with other key people

Functional Area Strategies (within each business)
- Add relevant detail to the hows of the business strategy
- Provide a game plan for managing a particular activity in ways that support the business strategy

Two-Way Influence

Orchestrated by brand managers, the operating managers of plants, distribution centers, and purchasing centers, and the managers of strategically important activities like Web site operations, often in collaboration with other key people

Operating Strategies within Each Business
- Add detail and completeness to business and functional strategies
- Provide a game plan for managing specific lower-echelon activities with strategic significance

entry to employ (e.g., through an acquisition, strategic alliance, or franchising). It concerns the *scope* of the firm and thus includes diversification strategies, vertical integration strategies, and geographic expansion strategies. Senior corporate executives normally have lead responsibility for devising corporate strategy and for choosing among whatever recommended actions bubble up from the organization below. Key business-unit heads may also be influential regarding issues related to the businesses they head. Major strategic decisions are usually reviewed and approved by the company's board of directors. We will look deeper into crafting corporate strategy in Chapter 8.

2. *Business strategy* is strategy at the level of a single line of business—one that competes in a relatively well-defined industry or market domain. The key focus is on crafting responses to changing market circumstances and initiating actions to develop strong competitive capabilities, build competitive advantage, strengthen market position, and enhance performance. Orchestrating the development of business-level strategy is typically the responsibility of the manager in charge of the business, although corporate-level managers may be influential. The business head has at least two other strategy-related roles: (1) seeing that lower-level strategies are well conceived, consistent, and adequately matched to the overall business strategy and (2) getting major business-level strategic moves approved by corporate-level officers and keeping them informed of emerging strategic issues. In diversified companies, business-unit heads have the additional obligation of making sure business-level objectives and strategy conform to corporate-level objectives and strategy themes.

3. *Functional-area strategies* concern the actions and approaches employed in managing particular functions within a business—like R&D, production, sales and marketing, customer service, and finance. A company's marketing strategy, for example, represents the managerial game plan for running the sales and marketing part of the business. A company's product development strategy represents the game plan for keeping the company's product lineup in tune with what buyers are looking for. The primary role of functional strategies is to flesh out the details of a company's business strategy. Lead responsibility for functional strategies within a business is normally delegated to the heads of the respective functions, with the general manager of the business having final approval. Since the different functional-level strategies must be compatible with the overall business strategy and with one another to have beneficial impact, the general business manager may at times exert stronger influence on the content of the functional strategies.

4. *Operating strategies* concern the relatively narrow strategic initiatives and approaches for managing key operating units (e.g., plants, distribution centers, purchasing centers) and specific operating activities with strategic significance (e.g., quality control, materials purchasing, brand management, Internet sales). A distribution center manager of a company promising customers speedy delivery must have a strategy to ensure that finished goods are rapidly turned around and shipped out to customers once they are received from the company's manufacturing facilities. Operating strategies, while of limited scope, add further detail to functional strategies and to the overall business strategy. Lead responsibility for operating strategies is usually delegated to frontline managers, subject to review and approval by higher-ranking managers.

Even though operating strategy is at the bottom of the strategy-making hierarchy, its importance should not be downplayed. A major plant that fails in its strategy to achieve production volume, unit cost, and quality targets can damage the company's reputation for quality products and undercut the achievement of company sales and profit objectives. Frontline managers are thus an important part of an organization's strategy-making team. One cannot reliably judge the strategic importance of a given action simply by the strategy level or location within the managerial hierarchy where it is initiated.

In single-business enterprises, the corporate and business levels of strategy making merge into one level—business strategy—because the strategy for the whole company involves only one distinct line of business. Thus a single-business enterprise has three levels of strategy: business strategy for the company as a whole, functional-area strategies for each main area within the business, and operating strategies undertaken by lower-echelon managers to flesh out strategically significant aspects of the company's business and functional-area strategies. Proprietorships, partnerships, and owner-managed enterprises may have only one or two strategy-making levels since their strategy-making process can be handled by just a few key people. The larger and more diverse the operations of an enterprise, the more points of strategic initiative it has and the more levels of management that have a significant strategy-making role.

The overall point is this: Regardless of the type of enterprise and whether the strategy is primarily deliberate or primarily emergent, crafting strategy involves managers in various positions and at various organizational levels. And while managers farther down in the managerial hierarchy obviously have a narrower, more specific strategy-making role than managers closer to the top, the important understanding is that in most of today's companies *every company manager typically has a strategy-making role—ranging from minor to major—for the area he or she heads.* Hence any notion that an organization's strategists are at the top of the management hierarchy and that midlevel and frontline personnel merely carry out the strategic directives of senior managers needs to be cast aside. In companies with wide-ranging operations, it is far more accurate to view strategy making as a *collaborative team effort* involving managers (and sometimes other key employees) down through the whole organizational hierarchy. A valuable strength of collaborative strategy making is that the team of people charged with crafting the strategy include the very people who will also be charged with implementing and executing it. Giving people an influential stake in crafting the strategy they must later help execute not only builds motivation and commitment but also enhances accountability at multiple levels of management—the excuse of "It wasn't my idea to do this" won't fly.

> In most companies, crafting strategy is a *collaborative team effort* that includes managers in various positions and at various organizational levels. Crafting strategy is rarely something only high-level executives do.

A Strategic Vision + Objectives + Strategy = A Strategic Plan

Developing a strategic vision and mission, setting objectives, and crafting a strategy are basic direction-setting tasks. They map out where a company is headed, its purpose, the targeted strategic and financial outcomes, the basic business model, and the competitive moves and internal action approaches to be used in achieving the desired business results. Together, they constitute a **strategic plan** for coping with industry conditions, outcompeting rivals, meeting objectives,

CORE CONCEPT

A company's **strategic plan** lays out its future direction and business purpose, performance targets, and strategy.

CORE CONCEPT

A company exhibits **strategic intent** when it relentlessly pursues an exceptionally ambitious strategic objective, committing to do whatever it takes to achieve the goals.

and making progress toward the strategic vision.[11] Typically, a strategic plan includes a commitment to allocate resources to the plan and specifies a time period for achieving goals (usually three to five years).

In some companies, the strategic plan is focused around achieving exceptionally bold strategic objectives—stretch goals requiring resources that are well beyond the current means of the company. This type of strategic plan is more the expression of a **strategic intent** to rally the organization through an *unshakable—often obsessive—commitment* to do whatever it takes to acquire the resources and achieve the goals. Nike's strategic intent during the 1960s was to overtake Adidas—an objective far beyond Nike's means at the time. Starbucks strategic intent is to make the Starbucks brand the world's most recognized and respected brand.

In companies that do regular strategy reviews and develop explicit strategic plans, the strategic plan usually ends up as a written document that is circulated to most managers and perhaps selected employees. Near-term performance targets are the part of the strategic plan most often spelled out explicitly and communicated to managers and employees. A number of companies summarize key elements of their strategic plans in the company's annual report to shareholders, in postings on their Web sites, or in statements provided to the business media, whereas others, perhaps for reasons of competitive sensitivity, make only vague, general statements about their strategic plans.[12] In small, privately owned companies, it is rare for strategic plans to exist in written form. Small-company strategic plans tend to reside in the thinking and directives of owners/executives, with aspects of the plan being revealed in meetings and conversations with company personnel, and in the understandings and commitments among managers and key employees about where to head, what to accomplish, and how to proceed.

STAGE 4: EXECUTING THE STRATEGY

LO 4

Become aware of what a company must do to achieve operating excellence and to execute its strategy proficiently.

Managing the implementation of a strategy is an operations-oriented, make-things-happen activity aimed at performing core business activities in a strategy-supportive manner. It is easily the most demanding and time-consuming part of the strategy management process. Converting strategic plans into actions and results tests a manager's ability to direct organizational action, motivate people, build and strengthen company competencies and competitive capabilities, create and nurture a strategy-supportive work climate, and meet or beat performance targets. Initiatives to put the strategy in place and execute it proficiently have to be launched and managed on many organizational fronts.

Management's action agenda for executing the chosen strategy emerges from assessing what the company will have to do to achieve the targeted financial and strategic performance. Each company manager has to think through the answer to "What has to be done in my area to execute my piece of the strategic plan, and what actions should I take to get the process under way?" How much internal change is needed depends on how much of the strategy is new, how far internal practices and competencies deviate from what the strategy requires, and how well the present work climate/culture supports good strategy execution. Depending on the amount of internal change involved, full implementation and proficient execution of company strategy (or important new pieces thereof) can take several months to several years.

In most situations, managing the strategy execution process includes the following principal aspects:

- Staffing the organization with the needed skills and expertise.
- Building and strengthening strategy-supporting resources and competitive capabilities.
- Organizing the work effort along the lines of best practice.
- Allocating ample resources to the activities critical to strategic success.
- Ensuring that policies and procedures facilitate rather than impede effective strategy execution.
- Installing information and operating systems that enable company personnel to carry out their roles effectively and efficiently.
- Motivating people and tying rewards and incentives directly to the achievement of performance objectives.
- Creating a company culture and work climate conducive to successful strategy execution.
- Exerting the internal leadership needed to propel implementation forward and drive continuous improvement of the strategy execution processes.

Good strategy execution requires diligent pursuit of operating excellence. It is a job for a company's whole management team. Success hinges on the skills and cooperation of operating managers who can push for needed changes in their organizational units and consistently deliver good results. Management's handling of the strategy implementation process can be considered successful if things go smoothly enough that the company meets or beats its strategic and financial performance targets and shows good progress in achieving management's strategic vision.

STAGE 5: EVALUATING PERFORMANCE AND INITIATING CORRECTIVE ADJUSTMENTS

The fifth component of the strategy management process—monitoring new external developments, evaluating the company's progress, and making corrective adjustments—is the trigger point for deciding whether to continue or change the company's vision and mission, objectives, strategy, and/or strategy execution methods.[13] As long as the company's strategy continues to pass the three tests of a winning strategy (good fit, competitive advantage, strong performance), company executives may well decide to stay the course. Simply fine-tuning the strategic plan and continuing with efforts to improve strategy execution are sufficient.

However, whenever a company encounters disruptive changes in its environment, questions need to be raised about the appropriateness of its direction and strategy. If a company experiences a downturn in its market position or persistent shortfalls in performance, then company managers are obligated

A company's vision and mission, objectives, strategy, and approach to strategy execution are never final; managing strategy is an ongoing process.

to ferret out the causes—do they relate to poor strategy, poor strategy execution, or both?—and take timely corrective action. A company's direction, objectives, and strategy have to be revisited anytime external or internal conditions warrant. It is to be expected that a company will modify its strategic vision, direction, objectives, and strategy over time.

Likewise, it is not unusual for a company to find that one or more aspects of its strategy execution are not going as well as intended. Proficient strategy execution is always the product of much organizational learning. It is achieved unevenly—coming quickly in some areas and proving nettlesome in others. It is both normal and desirable to periodically assess strategy execution to determine which aspects are working well and which need improving. Successful strategy execution entails vigilantly searching for ways to improve and then making corrective adjustments whenever and wherever it is useful to do so.

CORPORATE GOVERNANCE: THE ROLE OF THE BOARD OF DIRECTORS IN THE STRATEGY-CRAFTING, STRATEGY-EXECUTING PROCESS

LO 5

Become aware of the role and responsibility of a company's board of directors in overseeing the strategic management process.

Although senior managers have *lead responsibility* for crafting and executing a company's strategy, it is the duty of a company's board of directors to exercise strong oversight and see that the five tasks of strategic management are conducted in a manner that is in the best interests of shareholders and other stakeholders.[14] A company's board of directors has four important obligations to fulfill:

1. *Critically appraise the company's direction, strategy, and business approaches.* Board members must ask probing questions and draw on their business acumen to make independent judgments about whether strategy proposals have been adequately analyzed and whether proposed strategic actions appear to have greater promise than alternatives. Asking incisive questions is usually sufficient to test whether the case for management's proposals is compelling and to exercise vigilant oversight. However, when the company's strategy is failing or is plagued with faulty execution, and certainly when there is a precipitous collapse in profitability, board members have a duty to be more proactive, expressing their concerns about the validity of the strategy and/or operating methods, initiating debate about the company's strategic path, having one-on-one discussions with key executives and other board members, and perhaps directly intervening as a group to alter the company's executive leadership and, ultimately, its strategy and business approaches.

2. *Evaluate the caliber of senior executives' strategic leadership skills.* The board is always responsible for determining whether the current CEO is doing a good job of strategic leadership.[15] The board must also evaluate the leadership skills of other senior executives, since the board must elect a successor when the incumbent CEO steps down, either going with an insider

or deciding that an outsider is needed. Evaluation of senior executives' skills is enhanced when outside directors visit company facilities and talk with company personnel to personally evaluate whether the strategy is on track, how well the strategy is being executed, and how well issues and problems are being addressed. Independent board members at GE visit operating executives at each major business unit once a year to assess the company's talent pool and stay abreast of emerging strategic and operating issues affecting the company's divisions.

3. *Institute a compensation plan for top executives that rewards them for actions and results that serve stakeholder interests—especially those of shareholders.* A basic principle of corporate governance is that the owners of a corporation (the shareholders) delegate managerial control to a team of executives who are compensated for their efforts on behalf of the owners. In their role as an *agent* of shareholders, corporate managers have a clear and unequivocal duty to make decisions and operate the company in accord with shareholder interests. (This does not mean disregarding the interests of other stakeholders—employees, suppliers, the communities in which the company operates, and society at large.) Most boards of directors have a compensation committee, composed entirely of directors from *outside* the company, to develop a salary and incentive compensation plan that rewards senior executives for boosting the company's *long-term* performance and growing the economic value of the enterprise on behalf of shareholders; the compensation committee's recommendations are presented to the full board for approval. But during the past 10 to 15 years, many boards of directors have done a poor job of ensuring that executive salary increases, bonuses, and stock option awards are tied tightly to performance measures that are truly in the long-term interests of shareholders. Rather, compensation packages at many companies have increasingly rewarded executives for short-term performance improvements that led to undue risk taking and compensation packages that, in the view of many people, were obscenely large. This has proved damaging to long-term company performance and has worked against shareholder interests—witness the huge loss of shareholder wealth that occurred at many financial institutions in 2008–2009 because of executive risk taking in subprime loans, credit default swaps, and collateralized mortgage securities in 2006–2007. As a consequence, the need to overhaul and reform executive compensation has become a hot topic in both public circles and corporate boardrooms. Illustration Capsule 2.4 discusses how weak governance at the mortgage companies Fannie Mae and Freddie Mac allowed opportunistic senior managers to boost their compensation while making decisions that imperiled the futures of the companies they managed.

4. *Oversee the company's financial accounting and financial reporting practices.* While top executives, particularly the company's CEO and CFO (chief financial officer), are primarily responsible for seeing that the company's financial statements fairly and accurately report the results of the company's operations, board members have a fiduciary duty to protect shareholders by exercising oversight of the company's financial practices. In addition, corporate boards must ensure that generally acceptable accounting principles (GAAP) are properly used in preparing the company's financial statements

ILLUSTRATION CAPSULE 2.4

Corporate Governance Failures at Fannie Mae and Freddie Mac

Executive compensation in the financial services industry during the mid-2000s ranks high among examples of failed corporate governance. Corporate governance at the government-sponsored mortgage giants Fannie Mae and Freddie Mac was particularly weak. The politically appointed boards at both enterprises failed to understand the risks of the subprime loan strategies being employed, did not adequately monitor the decisions of the CEO, did not exercise effective oversight of the accounting principles being employed (which led to inflated earnings), and approved executive compensation systems that allowed management to manipulate earnings to receive lucrative performance bonuses. The audit and compensation committees at Fannie Mae were particularly ineffective in protecting shareholder interests, with the audit committee allowing the company's financial officers to audit reports prepared under their direction and used to determine performance bonuses. Fannie Mae's audit committee also was aware of management's use of questionable accounting practices that reduced losses and recorded one-time gains to achieve financial targets linked to bonuses. In addition, the audit committee failed to investigate formal charges of accounting improprieties filed by a manager in the Office of the Controller.

Fannie Mae's compensation committee was equally ineffective. The committee allowed the company's CEO, Franklin Raines, to select the consultant employed to design the mortgage firm's executive compensation plan and agreed to a tiered bonus plan that would permit Raines and other senior managers to receive maximum bonuses without great difficulty. The compensation plan allowed Raines to earn performance-based bonuses of $52 million and total compensation of $90 million between 1999 and 2004. Raines was forced to resign in December 2004 when the Office of Federal Housing Enterprise Oversight found that Fannie Mae executives had fraudulently inflated earnings to receive bonuses linked to financial performance. Securities and Exchange Commission investigators also found evidence of improper accounting at Fannie Mae and required the company to restate its earnings between 2002 and 2004 by $6.3 billion.

Poor governance at Freddie Mac allowed its CEO and senior management to manipulate financial data to receive performance-based compensation as well. Freddie Mac CEO Richard Syron received 2007 compensation of $19.8 million while the mortgage company's share price declined from a high of $70 in 2005 to $25 at year-end 2007. During Syron's tenure as CEO, the company became embroiled in a multibillion-dollar accounting scandal, and Syron personally disregarded internal reports dating to 2004 that cautioned of an impending financial crisis at the company. Forewarnings within Freddie Mac and by federal regulators and outside industry observers proved to be correct, with loan underwriting policies at Freddie Mac and Fannie Mae leading to combined losses at the two firms in 2008 of more than $100 billion. The price of

(continued)

Freddie Mac's shares had fallen to below $1 by the time of Syron's resignation in September 2008.

Both organizations were placed into a conservatorship under the direction of the U.S. government in September 2008 and were provided bailout funds of nearly $60 billion by April 2009. In May 2009, Fannie Mae requested another $19 billion of the $200 billion committed by the U.S. government to cover the operating losses of the two government-sponsored mortgage firms. By June 2010, the bill for bailing out the two enterprises had risen to $145 billion, with the expectation that still more aid would be required to get them back on sound financial footing.

Sources: "Adding Up the Government's Total Bailout Tab," *New York Times Online,* February 4, 2009; Eric Dash, "Fannie Mae to Restate Results by $6.3 Billion because of Accounting," *New York Times Online,* December 7, 2006; Annys Shin, "Fannie Mae Sets Executive Salaries," *Washington Post,* February 9, 2006, p. D4; Scott DeCarlo, Eric Weiss, Mark Jickling, James R. Cristie, *Fannie Mae and Freddie Mac: Scandal in U.S. Housing* (Nova, 2006), pp. 266–86; "Chaffetz, Conyers, Smith, Issa and Bachus Call for FOIA to Apply to Fannie-Freddie," June 17, 2010 (June 2010 Archives), http://chaffetz.house.gov/2010/06/ (accessed June 24, 2010).

and that proper financial controls are in place to prevent fraud and misuse of funds. Virtually all boards of directors have an audit committee, always composed entirely of *outside directors* (*inside directors* hold management positions in the company and either directly or indirectly report to the CEO). The members of the audit committee have lead responsibility for overseeing the decisions of the company's financial officers and consulting with both internal and external auditors to ensure that financial reports are accurate and that adequate financial controls are in place. Faulty oversight of corporate accounting and financial reporting practices by audit committees and corporate boards during the early 2000s resulted in the federal investigation of more than 20 major corporations between 2000 and 2002. The investigations of such well-known companies as Global Crossing, Enron, Qwest Communications, and WorldCom found that upper management had employed fraudulent or unsound accounting practices to artificially inflate revenues, overstate assets, and reduce expenses. The scandals resulted in the conviction of a number of corporate executives and the passage of the Sarbanes-Oxley Act of 2002, which tightened financial reporting standards and created additional compliance requirements for public boards.

Every corporation should have a strong, independent board of directors that (1) is well informed about the company's performance, (2) guides and judges the CEO and other top executives, (3) has the courage to curb management actions the board believes are inappropriate or unduly risky, (4) certifies to shareholders that the CEO is doing what the board expects, (5) provides insight and advice to management, and (6) is intensely involved in debating the pros and cons of key decisions and actions.[16] Boards of directors that lack the backbone to challenge a strong-willed or "imperial" CEO or that rubber-stamp almost anything the CEO recommends without probing inquiry and debate (perhaps because the board is stacked with the CEO's cronies) abdicate their duty to represent and protect shareholder interests.

> Effective corporate governance requires the board of directors to oversee the company's strategic direction, evaluate its senior executives, handle executive compensation, and oversee financial reporting practices.

KEY POINTS

The strategic management process consists of five interrelated and integrated stages:

1. *Developing a strategic vision* of the company's future, a *mission* that defines the company's current purpose, and a set of *core values* to guide the pursuit of the vision and mission. This managerial step provides direction for the company, motivates and inspires company personnel, aligns and guides actions throughout the organization, and communicates to stakeholders management's aspirations for the company's future.

2. *Setting objectives* to convert the vision and mission into performance targets and using the targeted results as yardsticks for measuring the company's performance. Objectives need to spell out *how much* of *what kind* of performance *by when*. Two broad types of objectives are required: *financial objectives* and *strategic objectives*. A *balanced-scorecard* approach provides a popular method for linking financial objectives to specific, measurable strategic objectives.

3. *Crafting a strategy* to achieve the objectives and move the company along the strategic course that management has charted. Crafting deliberate strategy calls for strategic analysis, based on the business model. Crafting emergent strategy is a learning-by-doing process involving experimentation. Who participates in the process of crafting strategy depends on (1) whether the process is emergent or deliberate and (2) the level of strategy concerned. Deliberate strategies are mostly top-down, while emergent strategies are bottom-up, although both cases require two-way interaction between different types of managers. In large, diversified companies, there are four levels of strategy, each of which involves a corresponding level of management: corporate strategy (multibusiness strategy), business strategy (strategy for individual businesses that compete in a single industry), functional-area strategies within each business (e.g., marketing, R&D, logistics), and operating strategies (for key operating units, such as manufacturing plants). Thus, strategy making is an inclusive, collaborative activity involving not only senior company executives but also the heads of major business divisions, functional-area managers, and operating managers on the frontlines. The larger and more diverse the operations of an enterprise, the more points of strategic initiative it has and the more levels of management that play a significant strategy-making role.

4. *Executing the chosen strategy* and converting the strategic plan into action. Managing the execution of strategy is an operations-oriented, make-things-happen activity aimed at shaping the performance of core business activities in a strategy-supportive manner. Management's handling of the strategy implementation process can be considered successful if things go smoothly enough that the company meets or beats its strategic and financial performance targets and shows good progress in achieving management's strategic vision.

5. *Monitoring developments, evaluating performance, and initiating corrective adjustments* in light of actual experience, changing conditions, new ideas, and new opportunities. This stage of the strategy management process is the trigger point for deciding whether to continue or change the company's vision and mission, objectives, strategy, and/or strategy execution methods.

The sum of a company's strategic vision and mission, objectives, and strategy constitutes a *strategic plan* for coping with industry conditions, outcompeting rivals, meeting objectives, and making progress toward the strategic vision. A company whose strategic plan is based around ambitious *stretch goals* that require an unwavering commitment to do whatever it takes to achieve them is said to have *strategic intent.*

Boards of directors have a duty to shareholders to play a vigilant role in overseeing management's handling of a company's strategy-making, strategy-executing process. This entails four important obligations: (1) Critically appraise the company's direction, strategy, and strategy execution, (2) evaluate the caliber of senior executives' strategic leadership skills, (3) institute a compensation plan for top executives that rewards them for actions and results that serve stakeholder interests—*especially those of shareholders,* and (4) ensure that the company issues accurate financial reports and has adequate financial controls.

ASSURANCE OF LEARNING EXERCISES

LO 1

1. Using the information in Table 2.1, critique the adequacy and merit of the following vision statements, listing effective elements and shortcomings. Rank the vision statements from best to worst once you complete your evaluation.

Vision Statement	Effective Elements	Shortcomings
Wells Fargo We want to satisfy all of our customers' financial needs, help them succeed financially, be the premier provider of financial services in every one of our markets, and be known as one of America's great companies.		
Hilton Hotels Corporation Our vision is to be the first choice of the world's travelers. Hilton intends to build on the rich heritage and strength of our brands by: • Consistently delighting our customers • Investing in our team members • Delivering innovative products and services • Continuously improving performance • Increasing shareholder value • Creating a culture of pride • Strengthening the loyalty of our constituents		
The Dental Products Division of 3M Corporation Become THE supplier of choice to the global dental professional markets, providing world-class quality and innovative products. [*Note:* All employees of the division wear badges bearing these words, and whenever a new product or business procedure is being considered, management asks "Is this representative of THE leading dental company?"]		

(continued)

Vision Statement	Effective Elements	Shortcomings
H. J. Heinz Company Be the world's premier food company, offering nutritious, superior tasting foods to people everywhere. Being the premier food company does not mean being the biggest but it does mean being the best in terms of consumer value, customer service, employee talent, and consistent and predictable growth.		
Chevron To be *the* global energy company most admired for its people, partnership and performance. Our vision means we: • provide energy products vital to sustainable economic progress and human development throughout the world; • are people and an organization with superior capabilities and commitment; • are the partner of choice; • deliver world-class performance; • earn the admiration of all our stakeholders—investors, customers, host governments, local communities and our employees—not only for the goals we achieve but how we achieve them.		

Source: Company Web sites and annual reports.

LO 2

2. Go to the company Web sites for Home Depot (http://corporate.homedepot.com/wps/portal); Avon (www.avoncompany.com/); and Yum Brands, a restaurant company that includes KFC, Pizza Hut, and Taco Bell (www.yum.com), to find some examples of strategic and financial objectives. Make a list of four objectives for each company, and indicate which of these are strategic and which are financial.

LO 5

3. Go to www.dell.com/leadership, and read the sections dedicated to Dell's board of directors and corporate governance. Is there evidence of effective governance at Dell in regard to (1) accurate financial reports and controls, (2) a critical appraisal of strategic action plans, (3) evaluation of the strategic leadership skills of the CEO, and (4) executive compensation?

EXERCISES FOR SIMULATION PARTICIPANTS

LO 1, LO 2, LO 3

1. Meet with your co-managers and prepare a strategic vision statement for your company. It should be at least one sentence long and no longer than a brief paragraph. When you are finished, check to see if your vision statement is in compliance with the dos and don'ts set forth in Table 2.1. If not, revise it accordingly. What would be a good slogan that captures the essence of your strategic vision and that could be used to help communicate the vision to company personnel, shareholders, and other stakeholders?

2.   What is your company's strategic intent? Write a sentence that expresses your company's strategic intent.

3.   What are your company's financial objectives?

4.   What are your company's strategic objectives?

5.   What are the three or four key elements of your company's strategy?

ENDNOTES

[1] For a more in-depth discussion of the challenges of developing a well-conceived vision, as well as some good examples, see Hugh Davidson, *The Committed Enterprise: How to Make Vision and Values Work* (Oxford: Butterworth Heinemann, 2002), chap. 2; W. Chan Kim and Renée Mauborgne, "Charting Your Company's Future," *Harvard Business Review* 80, no. 6 (June 2002), pp. 77–83; James C. Collins and Jerry I. Porras, "Building Your Company's Vision," *Harvard Business Review* 74, no. 5 (September–October 1996), pp. 65–77; Jim Collins and Jerry Porras, *Built to Last: Successful Habits of Visionary Companies* (New York: HarperCollins, 1994), chap. 11; Michel Robert, *Strategy Pure and Simple II: How Winning Companies Dominate Their Competitors* (New York: McGraw-Hill, 1998), chaps. 2, 3 and 6.

[2] Davidson, *The Committed Enterprise,* pp. 20 and 54.

[3] Ibid., pp. 36, 54.

[4] As quoted in Charles H. House and Raymond L. Price, "The Return Map: Tracking Product Teams," *Harvard Business Review* 60, no. 1 (January–February 1991), p. 93.

[5] Robert S. Kaplan and David P. Norton, *The Strategy-Focused Organization* (Boston: Harvard Business School Press, 2001), p. 3. Also see Robert S. Kaplan and David P. Norton, *The Balanced Scorecard: Translating Strategy into Action* (Boston: Harvard Business School Press, 1996), chap. 1.

[6] Kaplan and Norton, p.7. Also see Kevin B. Hendricks, Larry Menor, and Christine Wiedman, "The Balanced Scorecard: To Adopt or Not to Adopt," *Ivey Business Journal* 69, no. 2 (November–December 2004), pp. 1–7; Sandy Richardson, "The Key Elements of Balanced Scorecard Success," *Ivey Business Journal*

69, no. 2 (November–December 2004), pp.7–9.

[7] Kaplan and Norton, *The Balanced Scorecard.*

[8] Information posted on the Web site of Bain and Company, www.bain.com (accessed May 27, 2009).

[9] Information posted on the Web site of Balanced Scorecard Institute, http://www.balancedscorecard.org/ (accessed May 27, 2009).

[10] For a fuller discussion of strategy as an entrepreneurial process, see Henry Mintzberg, Bruce Ahlstrand, and Joseph Lampel, *Strategy Safari: A Guided Tour through the Wilds of Strategic Management* (New York: Free Press, 1998), chap. 5. Also see Bruce Barringer and Allen C. Bluedorn, "The Relationship between Corporate Entrepreneurship and Strategic Management," *Strategic Management Journal* 20 (1999), pp. 421–44; Jeffrey G. Covin and Morgan P. Miles, "Corporate Entrepreneurship and the Pursuit of Competitive Advantage," *Entrepreneurship: Theory and Practice* 23, no. 3 (Spring 1999), pp. 47–63; David A. Garvin and Lynned C. Levesque, "Meeting the Challenge of Corporate Entrepreneurship," *Harvard Business Review* 84, no. 10 (October 2006), pp. 102–12.

[11] For an excellent discussion of why a strategic plan needs to be more than a list of bullet points and should in fact tell an engaging, insightful, stage-setting story that lays out the industry and competitive situation as well as the vision, objectives, and strategy, see Gordon Shaw, Robert Brown, and Philip Bromiley, "Strategic Stories: How 3M Is Rewriting Business Planning," *Harvard Business Review* 76, no. 3 (May–June 1998), pp. 41–50.

[12] In many companies, there is often confusion or ambiguity about exactly what a company's strategy is; see David J. Collis and Michael G. Rukstad, "Can You Say What Your Strategy Is?" *Harvard Business Review* 86, no. 4 (April 2008), pp. 82–90.

[13] For an excellent discussion of why effective strategic leadership on the part of senior executives involves continuous re-creation of a company's strategy, see Cynthia A. Montgomery, "Putting Leadership Back into Strategy," *Harvard Business Review* 86, no. 1 (January 2008), pp. 54–60.

[14] For a timely and insightful discussion of the strategic and leadership functions of a company's board of directors, see Jay W. Lorsch and Robert C. Clark, "Leading from the Boardroom," *Harvard Business Review* 86, no. 4 (April 2008), pp. 105–11.

[15] For a deeper discussion of this function, see Stephen P. Kaufman, "Evaluating the CEO," *Harvard Business Review* 86, no. 10 (October 2008), pp. 53–57.

[16] For a discussion of what it takes for the corporate governance system to function properly, see David A. Nadler, "Building Better Boards," *Harvard Business Review* 82, no. 5 (May 2004), pp. 102–5; Cynthia A. Montgomery and Rhonda Kaufman, "The Board's Missing Link," *Harvard Business Review* 81, no. 3 (March 2003), pp. 86–93; John Carver, "What Continues to Be Wrong with Corporate Governance and How to Fix It," *Ivey Business Journal* 68, no. 1 (September–October 2003), pp. 1–5. See also Gordon Donaldson, "A New Tool for Boards: The Strategic Audit," *Harvard Business Review* 73, no. 4 (July–August 1995), pp. 99–107.

CHAPTER 3

EVALUATING A COMPANY'S EXTERNAL ENVIRONMENT

Analysis is the critical starting point of strategic thinking.

—Kenichi Ohmae
Consultant and Author

Things are always different—the art is figuring out which differences matter.

—Laszlo Birinyi
Investments Manager

In essence, the job of a strategist is to understand and cope with competition.

—Michael Porter
Harvard Business School professor and Cofounder of Monitor Consulting

LEARNING OBJECTIVES

LO 1. Gain command of the basic concepts and analytical tools widely used to diagnose the competitive conditions in a company's industry.

LO 2. Learn how to diagnose the factors shaping industry dynamics and to forecast their effects on future industry profitability.

LO 3. Become adept at mapping the market positions of key groups of industry rivals.

LO 4. Understand why in-depth evaluation of a business's strengths and weaknesses in relation to the specific industry conditions it confronts is an essential prerequisite to crafting a strategy that is well-matched to its external situation.

In Chapter 1, we learned that one of the three central questions that managers must address in evaluating their business prospects is "What's the company's present situation?" Two facets of a company's situation are especially pertinent: (1) competitive conditions in the industry in which the company operates—its external environment; and (2) the company's resources and organizational capabilities—its internal environment.

Insightful diagnosis of a company's external and internal environments is a prerequisite for managers to succeed in crafting a strategy that is an excellent *fit* with the company's situation—the first test of a winning strategy. As depicted in Figure 3.1, the task of crafting a strategy should always begin with an appraisal of the company's external environment and internal environment (as a basis for deciding on a long-term direction and developing a strategic vision), then move toward an evaluation of the most promising alternative strategies and business models, and culminate in choosing a specific strategy.

This chapter presents the concepts and analytical tools for zeroing in on those aspects of a company's external environment that should be considered in making strategic choices about where and how to compete. Attention centers on the competitive arena in which a company operates, the drivers of market change, the market positions of rival companies, and the factors that determine competitive success. In Chapter 4 we explore the methods of evaluating a company's internal circumstances and competitive capabilities.

Figure 3.1   **From Thinking Strategically about the Company's Situation to Choosing a Strategy**

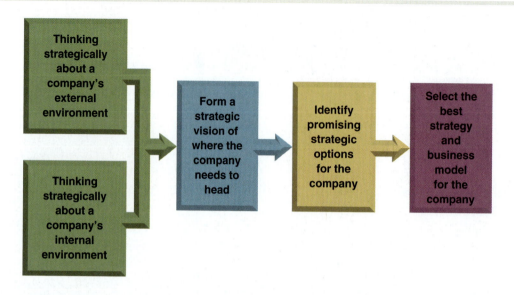

THE STRATEGICALLY RELEVANT COMPONENTS OF A COMPANY'S MACRO-ENVIRONMENT

Every company operates in a larger environment that goes well beyond just the industry in which it operates; this **"macro-environment"** includes seven principal components: population demographics; societal values and lifestyles; political, legal, and regulatory factors; the natural environment and ecological factors; technological factors; general economic conditions; and global forces. Each of these components has the potential to affect the firm's more immediate industry and competitive environment, although some are likely to have a more important effect than others (see Figure 3.2). Since macroeconomic factors affect different industries in different ways and to different degrees, it is important for managers to determine which of these represent the most *strategically relevant factors* outside the firm's industry boundaries. By *strategically relevant,* we mean important enough to have a bearing on the decisions the company ultimately makes about its direction, objectives, strategy, and business model. Strategically relevant influences coming from the outer ring of the external environment can sometimes have a high impact on a company's business situation and have a very significant impact on the company's direction and strategy. For example, the strategic opportunities of cigarette producers to grow their businesses are greatly reduced by antismoking ordinances, the decisions of governments to impose higher cigarette taxes, and the growing cultural stigma attached to smoking. Motor vehicle companies must adapt their strategies to customer concerns about high gasoline prices and to environmental concerns about

Figure 3.2   The Components of a Company's Macro-Environment

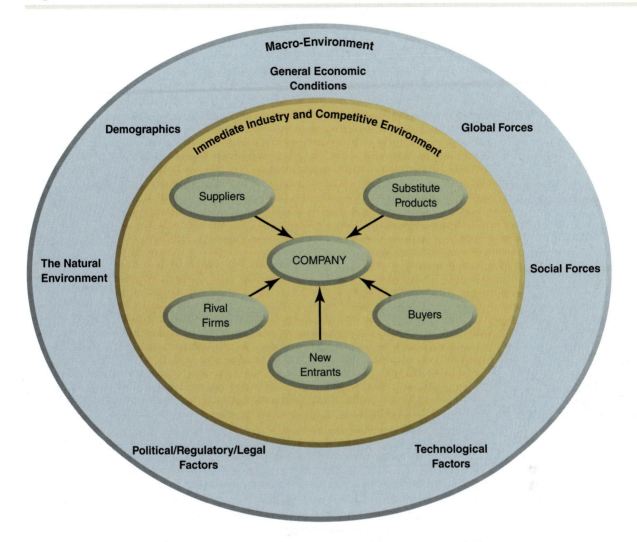

carbon emissions. Companies in the food processing, restaurant, sports, and fitness industries have to pay special attention to changes in lifestyles, eating habits, leisure-time preferences, and attitudes toward nutrition and fitness in fashioning their strategies. Table 3.1 provides a brief description of the components of the macro-environment and some examples of the industries or business situations that they might affect.

Happenings in the outer ring of the environment may occur rapidly or slowly, with or without advance warning. As company managers scan the external environment, they must be alert for potentially important outer-ring developments, assess their impact and influence, and adapt the company's direction and strategy as needed. However, the factors and forces in a company's environment having the *biggest* strategy-shaping impact typically pertain to the company's immediate industry and competitive environment—competitive pressures, the actions of rival firms, buyer behavior, supplier-related considerations, and so on. Consequently, it is on a company's industry and competitive environment that we concentrate the bulk of our attention in this chapter.

Table 3.1   The Seven Components of the Macro-Environment

Component	Description
Demographics	Demographics includes the size, growth rate, and age distribution of different sectors of the population. It includes the geographic distribution of the population, the distribution of income across the population, and trends in these factors. Population demographics can have large implications for industries such as health care, where costs and service needs vary with demographic factors such as age and income distribution.
Social forces	Social forces include the societal values, attitudes, cultural factors, and lifestyles that impact businesses. Social forces vary by locale and change over time. An example includes the attitudes toward gender roles and diversity in the workforce. Another example is the trend toward healthier lifestyles, which can shift spending toward exercise equipment and health clubs and away from alcohol and snack foods.
Political, legal, and regulatory factors	These factors include political policies and processes, as well as the regulations and laws with which companies must comply. Examples include labor laws, antitrust laws, tax policy, regulatory policies, the political climate, and the strength of institutions such as the court system. Some political factors, such as banking deregulation, are industry-specific. Others, such as minimum wage legislation, affect certain types of industries (low-wage, labor-intensive industries) more than others.
Natural environment	This includes ecological and environmental forces such as weather, climate, climate change, and associated factors like water shortages. These factors can directly impact industries such as insurance, farming, energy production, and tourism. They may have an indirect but substantial effect on other industries such as transportation and utilities.
Technological factors	Technological factors include the pace of technological change and technical developments that have the potential for wide-ranging effects on society, such as genetic engineering, the rise of the Internet, and changes in communication technologies. They include activities and institutions involved in creating new knowledge and controlling the use of technology, such as R&D consortia, university-sponsored technology incubators, patent and copyright laws, and government control over the Internet. Technological change can encourage the birth of new industries, such as those based on nanotechnology, and disrupt others, such as the recording industry.
Global forces	Global forces include conditions and changes in global markets, including political events and policies toward international trade. They also include sociocultural practices and the institutional environment in which global markets operate. Global forces influence the degree of international trade and investment through such mechanisms as trade barriers, tariffs, import restrictions, and trade sanctions. Their effects are often industry-specific, such as import restrictions on steel.
General economic conditions	General economic conditions include economic factors at the local, state, national, or international level that affect firms and industries. These include the rate of economic growth, unemployment rates, inflation rates, interest rates, trade deficits or surpluses, savings rates, and per capita domestic product. Economic factors also include conditions in the markets for stocks and bonds, which can affect consumer confidence and discretionary income. Some industries, such as construction, are particularly vulnerable to economic downturns but are positively affected by factors such as low interest rates. Others, such as discount retailing, may benefit when general economic conditions weaken, as consumers become more price-conscious.

THINKING STRATEGICALLY ABOUT A COMPANY'S INDUSTRY AND COMPETITIVE ENVIRONMENT

To gain a deep understanding of a company's industry and competitive environment, managers do not need to gather all the information they can find and spend lots of time digesting it. Rather, they can focus more directly on using some well-defined concepts and analytical tools to get clear answers to seven questions:

1. Does the industry offer attractive opportunities for growth?
2. What kinds of competitive forces are industry members facing, and how strong is each force?
3. What factors are driving changes in the industry, and what impact will these changes have on competitive intensity and industry profitability?
4. What market positions do industry rivals occupy—who is strongly positioned and who is not?
5. What strategic moves are rivals likely to make next?
6. What are the key factors for competitive success in the industry?
7. Does the industry offer good prospects for attractive profits?

Analysis-based answers to these seven questions provide managers with the understanding needed to craft a strategy that fits the company's external situation and positions the company to best meet its competitive challenges. The remainder of this chapter is devoted to describing the methods of obtaining solid answers to the seven questions and explaining how the nature of a company's industry and competitive environment weighs upon the strategic choices of company managers.

QUESTION 1: DOES THE INDUSTRY OFFER ATTRACTIVE OPPORTUNITIES FOR GROWTH?

Answering the question of whether or not an industry will offer the prospect of attractive profits begins with a consideration of whether it offers good opportunities for growth. Growth, of course, cannot guarantee profitability—a lesson that too many firms that have pursued growth for growth's sake have learned the hard way. But it is an indicator of how much customers value the industry's products (or services) and whether the industry demand is strong enough to support profitable sales growth.

Key economic indicators of an industry's growth prospects include market size, in terms of overall unit sales and sales volume, as well as the industry growth rate. Assessing the market size and growth rate will depend, however, on whether the industry is defined broadly or narrowly, in terms of its product or service characteristics. For example, the freight transport industry is far more inclusive than the air freight industry, and market size will vary accordingly. Market size and growth rates will also depend on where the geographic boundary lines are drawn (local, regional, national, or global). In addition, market size and growth rates often vary markedly by region (e.g., Europe versus Asia) and by demographic market segment (e.g., Gen Y versus baby boomers). Looking at the market in a variety of ways can help managers assess the various opportunities for growth and its limits.

One reason for differences among industries in the size of the market and the rate of growth stems from what is known as the "industry life cycle." This is the notion that industries commonly follow a general pattern of development and maturation, consisting of four stages: emergence, rapid growth, maturity, and decline.[1] The size of a market and its growth rate, then, depend on which stage of the life cycle best characterizes the industry in question.

QUESTION 2: WHAT KINDS OF COMPETITIVE FORCES ARE INDUSTRY MEMBERS FACING, AND HOW STRONG ARE THEY?

LO 1

Gain command of the basic concepts and analytical tools widely used to diagnose the competitive conditions in a company's industry.

The character and strength of the competitive forces operating in an industry are never the same from one industry to another. Far and away the most powerful and widely used tool for systematically diagnosing the principal competitive pressures in a market is the *five-forces model of competition.*[2] This model holds that the competitive forces affecting industry profitability go beyond rivalry among competing sellers and include pressures stemming from four coexisting sources. As depicted in Figure 3.3, the five competitive forces include (1) competition from *rival sellers,* (2) competition from *potential new entrants* to the industry, (3) competition from producers of *substitute products,* (4) *supplier* bargaining power, and (5) *customer* bargaining power.

Using the five-forces model to determine the nature and strength of competitive pressures in a given industry involves building the picture of competition in three steps:

- *Step 1:* For each of the five forces, identify the different parties involved, along with the specific factors that bring about competitive pressures.
- *Step 2:* Evaluate how strong the pressures stemming from each of the five forces are (strong, moderate to normal, or weak).
- *Step 3:* Determine whether the strength of the five competitive forces, overall, is conducive to earning attractive profits in the industry.

Competitive Pressures Created by the Rivalry among Competing Sellers

The strongest of the five competitive forces is often the market maneuvering for buyer patronage that goes on among rival sellers of a product or service. In effect, *a market is a competitive battlefield* where the contest among competitors is ongoing and dynamic. Each competing company endeavors to deploy whatever means in its business arsenal it believes will attract and retain buyers, strengthen its market position, and yield good profits. The challenge is to craft a competitive strategy that, at the very least, allows a company to hold its own against rivals and that, ideally, *produces a competitive edge over rivals.* But when one firm deploys a strategy or makes a new strategic move that produces good results, its rivals typically respond with offensive or defensive countermoves of their own. This pattern of action and reaction, move and countermove, produces a continually evolving competitive landscape where the market battle ebbs and flows, sometimes takes unpredictable twists and turns, and produces winners and losers.[3]

Competitive battles among rival sellers can assume many forms that extend well beyond lively price competition. For example, rivalrous firms may resort to such marketing tactics as special sales promotions, heavy advertising, rebates, or low-interest-rate financing to drum up additional sales. Active rivals may race one another to differentiate their products by offering better performance

Figure 3.3   The Five-Forces Model of Competition: A Key Analytical Tool

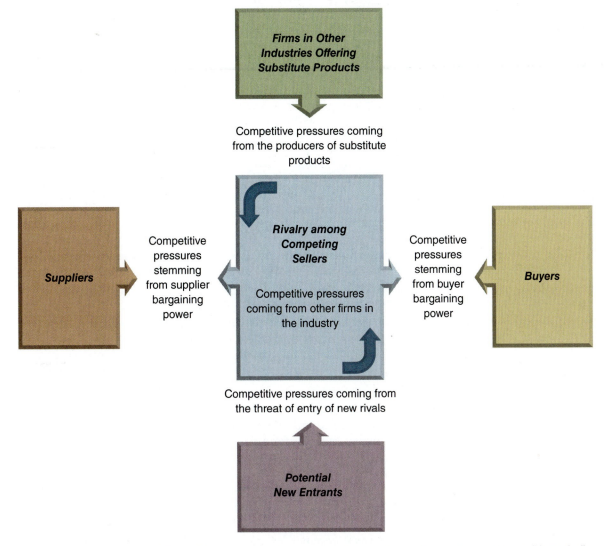

Sources: Adapted from Michael E. Porter, "How Competitive Forces Shape Strategy," *Harvard Business Review* 57, no. 2 (March–April 1979), pp. 137–45, and Michael E. Porter, "The Five Competitive Forces That Shape Strategy," *Harvard Business Review* 86, no. 1 (January 2008), pp. 80–86.

features or higher quality or improved customer service or a wider product selection. Rivals may also compete through the rapid introduction of next-generation products, frequent introduction of new or improved products, and efforts to build stronger dealer networks, establish positions in foreign markets, or otherwise expand distribution capabilities and market presence. Table 3.2 provides a sampling of the types of competitive weapons available to rivals, along with their primary effects.

The intensity of rivalry varies from industry to industry and depends on a number of identifiable factors. Figure 3.4 summarizes these factors, identifying those that intensify or weaken rivalry among direct competitors in an industry. A brief explanation of why these factors affect the degree of rivalry is in order:[4]

Table 3.2   Common "Weapons" for Competing with Rivals

Types of Competitive Weapons	Primary Effects
Price discounting, clearance sales, "blowout" sales	Lowers price (P), acts to boost total sales volume and market share, lowers profit margins per unit sold when price cuts are big and/or increases in sales volume are relatively small
Couponing, advertising items on sale	Acts to increase unit sales volume and total revenues, lowers price (P), increases unit costs (C), may lower profit margins per unit sold ($P - C$)
Advertising product or service characteristics, using ads to enhance a company's image or reputation	Boosts buyer demand, increases product differentiation and perceived value (V), acts to increase total sales volume and market share, may increase unit costs (C) and/or lower profit margins per unit sold
Innovating to improve product performance and quality	Acts to increase product differentiation and value (V), boosts buyer demand, acts to boost total sales volume, likely to increase unit costs (C)
Introducing new or improved features, increasing the number of styles or models to provide greater product selection	Acts to increase product differentiation and value (V), strengthens buyer demand, acts to boost total sales volume and market share, likely to increase unit costs (C)
Increasing customization of product or service	Acts to increase product differentiation and value (V), increases switching costs, acts to boost total sales volume, often increases unit costs (C)
Building a bigger, better dealer network	Broadens access to buyers, acts to boost total sales volume and market share, may increase unit costs (C)
Improving warranties, offering low-interest financing	Acts to increase product differentiation and value (V), increases unit costs (C); increases buyer costs to switch brands, acts to boost total sales volume and market share

- *Rivalry is stronger in markets where buyer demand is growing slowly or declining, and it is weaker in fast-growing markets.* Rapidly expanding buyer demand produces enough new business for all industry members to grow without using volume-boosting sales tactics to draw customers away from rival enterprises. But in markets where buyer demand is growing only 1 to 2 percent or is shrinking, companies anxious (or perhaps desperate) to gain more business typically employ price discounts, sales promotions, and other tactics to boost their sales volumes, sometimes to the point of igniting a fierce battle for market share.

- *Rivalry increases as it becomes less costly for buyers to switch brands.* The less expensive it is for buyers to switch their purchases from the seller of one brand to the seller of another brand, the easier it is for sellers to steal customers away from rivals. But the higher the costs buyers incur to switch brands, the less prone they are to brand switching. Switching costs include not only monetary costs but also the time, inconvenience, and psychological costs involved in switching brands. For example distributors and retailers may not switch to the brands of rival manufacturers because they are hesitant to sever long-standing supplier relationships, incur any technical support costs or retraining expenses in making the switchover, go to the trouble of testing the quality and reliability of the rival brand, or devote resources to marketing the new brand (especially if the brand is not well known).

- *Rivalry increases as the products of rival sellers become more alike, and it diminishes as the products of industry rivals become more strongly differentiated.* When the offerings of rivals are identical or weakly differentiated, buyers have less reason to be brand-loyal—a condition that makes it easier for rivals to convince

Figure 3.4   Factors Affecting the Strength of Rivalry

Substitutes

Rivalry among Competing Sellers:
How strong is seller-related competition?

Rivalry is stronger when:

- Buyer demand is growing slowly
- Buyer demand is falling off and sellers find themselves with excess capacity and/or inventory
- Buyer costs to switch brands are low
- The products of industry members are commodities or else weakly differentiated
- The firms in the industry have high fixed costs or high storage costs
- Competitors are numerous or are of roughly equal size and competitive strength
- Rivals have diverse objectives, strategies, and/or countries of origin
- Rivals have emotional stakes in the business or face high exit barriers

Rivalry is weaker when:

- Buyer demand is growing rapidly
- Buyer costs to switch brands are high
- The products of rival sellers are strongly differentiated and customer loyalty is high
- Fixed and storage costs are low
- Sales are concentrated among a few large sellers
- Industry members are relatively homogeneous in size, strength, objectives, strategy, and country of origin
- Exit barriers are low

Suppliers

Buyers

New Entrants

buyers to switch to their offerings. And since the brands of different sellers have comparable attributes, buyers can shop the market for the best deal and switch brands at will. On the other hand, strongly differentiated product offerings among rivals breed high brand loyalty on the part of buyers—because many buyers view the attributes of certain brands as more appealing or better suited to their needs. Strong brand attachments make it tougher for sellers to draw customers away from rivals. Unless meaningful numbers of buyers are open to considering new or different product attributes being offered by rivals, the high degree of brand loyalty that accompanies strong product differentiation works against fierce rivalry among competing sellers. *The degree of product differentiation also affects switching costs.* When the offerings of rivals are identical or weakly differentiated, it is usually easy and inexpensive for buyers to switch their purchases from one seller to another. But in the case of strongly differentiated brands with quite different features and functionality (like rival brands of cell phones), buyers may be reluctant to go through the brand-switching hassle.

- *Rivalry is more intense when there is unused production capacity, especially if the industry's product has high fixed costs or high storage costs.* Whenever a market is oversupplied (such that sellers have unutilized production capacity and/or too much inventory), the result is a "buyer's market" that intensifies rivalry perhaps even to the point of threatening the survival of competitively weak firms. A similar effect occurs when a product is perishable, seasonal, or costly to hold in inventory, since firms often engage in aggressive price cutting to ensure that they are not left with unwanted or costly inventories. Likewise, whenever fixed costs account for a large fraction of total cost so that unit costs are significantly lower at full capacity, firms come under significant pressure to cut prices to boost sales whenever they are operating below full capacity. Unused capacity imposes a significant cost-increasing penalty because there are fewer units over which to spread fixed costs. The pressure of high fixed or high storage costs can push rival firms into price concessions, special discounts, rebates, and other volume-boosting competitive tactics.

- *Rivalry intensifies as the number of competitors increases and as competitors become more equal in size and competitive strength.* The greater the number of competitors, the higher the probability that one or more companies will be busily engaged in a strategic offensive intended to enhance their market standing, thereby heating up competition and putting new pressures on rivals to respond with offensive or defensive moves of their own. In addition, when rivals are of comparable size and competitive strength, they can usually compete on a fairly equal footing—an evenly matched contest tends to be fiercer than a contest in which one or more industry members have commanding market shares and substantially greater resources and capabilities than their much smaller rivals.

- *Rivalry often becomes more intense—as well as more volatile and unpredictable— as the diversity of competitors increases in terms of long-term directions, objectives, strategies, and countries of origin.* A diverse group of sellers often contains one or more mavericks willing to try novel or rule-breaking market approaches, thus generating a livelier and less predictable competitive environment. Globally competitive markets usually boost the intensity of rivalry, especially when aggressors having lower costs or products with more attractive features are intent on gaining a strong foothold in new country markets.

- *Rivalry is stronger when high exit barriers keep unprofitable firms from leaving the industry.* In industries where the assets cannot easily be sold or transferred to other uses, where workers are entitled to job protection, or where owners are committed to remaining in business for personal reasons, failing firms tend to hold on longer than they might otherwise—even when they are bleeding red ink. This increases rivalry in two ways. Firms that are losing ground or in financial trouble often resort to deep price discounting that can trigger a price war and destabilize an otherwise attractive industry. In addition, high exit barriers result in an industry being more overcrowded than it would otherwise be, and this boosts rivalry and forces the weakest companies to scramble (often pushing them into desperate maneuvers of all kinds) to win sufficient sales and revenues to stay in business.

Rivalry can be characterized as *cutthroat* or *brutal* when competitors engage in protracted price wars or habitually undertake other aggressive strategic moves that prove mutually destructive to profitability. Rivalry can be considered *fierce* to *strong* when the battle for market share is so vigorous that the profit margins of most industry members are squeezed to bare-bones levels. Rivalry can be characterized as *moderate* or *normal* when the maneuvering among industry members, while lively and healthy, still allows most industry members to earn acceptable profits. Rivalry is *weak* when most companies in the industry are relatively well satisfied with their sales growth and market shares, rarely undertake offensives to steal customers away from one another, and—because of weak competitive forces—earn consistently good profits and returns on investment.

Competitive Pressures Associated with the Threat of New Entrants

New entrants to a market bring new production capacity, the desire to establish a secure place in the market, and sometimes substantial resources. Just how serious the competitive threat of entry is in a particular market depends on two classes of factors: *barriers to entry* and the *expected reaction of incumbent firms to new entry.*[5]

Industry incumbents that are willing and able to launch strong defensive maneuvers to maintain their positions can make it hard for a new entrant to gain a sufficient market foothold to survive and eventually become profitable. Entry candidates may have second thoughts if they conclude that existing firms are likely to give newcomers a hard time by offering price discounts (especially to the very customer groups a newcomer is seeking to attract), spending more on advertising, running frequent sales promotions, adding attractive new product features (to match or beat the newcomer's product offering), or providing additional services to customers. Such defensive maneuvers on the part of incumbents raise an entrant's costs and risks and have to be considered likely if one or more incumbents have previously tried to strongly contest the entry of new firms into the marketplace.

A barrier to entry exists whenever it is hard for a newcomer to break into the market and/or the economics of the business put a potential entrant at a disadvantage. The most widely encountered such barriers that entry candidates must hurdle include the following:[6]

- *Sizable economies of scale in production, distribution, advertising, or other areas of operation.* When incumbent companies enjoy cost advantages associated with large-scale operations, outsiders must either enter on a large scale (a costly and perhaps risky move) or accept a cost disadvantage and consequently lower profitability.
- *Significant cost advantages held by existing firms due to experience and learning curve effects.* In many industries, incumbent firms are favored by learning-based cost savings that accrue from experience in performing certain activities such as manufacturing or new product development or inventory management. This gives incumbent firms a first-mover advantage over new entrants that may be difficult to overcome.

- *Other cost advantages enjoyed by industry incumbents.* Existing industry members may also have other types of cost advantages that are hard for a newcomer to replicate. These can stem from (1) preferential access to raw materials, components, or other inputs, (2) cost savings accruing from patents or proprietary technology, (3) favorable locations, and (4) low fixed costs (because they have older facilities that have been mostly depreciated). The bigger the cost advantages of industry incumbents, the more risky it becomes for outsiders to attempt entry (since they will have to accept thinner profit margins or even losses until the cost disadvantages can be overcome).

- *Strong brand preferences and high degrees of customer loyalty.* The stronger the attachment of buyers to established brands, the harder it is for a newcomer to break into the marketplace. In such cases, a new entrant must have the financial resources to spend enough on advertising and sales promotion to overcome customer loyalties and build its own clientele. Establishing brand recognition and building customer loyalty can be a slow and costly process. In addition, if it is difficult or costly for a customer to switch to a new brand, a new entrant may have to offer buyers a discounted price or an extra margin of quality or service. Such barriers discourage new entry because they act to boost financial requirements and lower expected profit margins for new entrants.

- *Strong "network effects" in customer demand.* In industries where buyers are more attracted to a product when there are many other users of the product, there are said to be "network effects," since demand is higher the larger the network of users. Video game systems are an example, since users prefer to have the same systems as their friends so that they can play together on systems they all know and share games. When incumbents have a larger base of users, new entrants with comparable products face a serious disadvantage in attracting buyers.

- *High capital requirements.* The larger the total dollar investment needed to enter the market successfully, the more limited the pool of potential entrants. The most obvious capital requirements for new entrants relate to manufacturing facilities and equipment, introductory advertising and sales promotion campaigns, working capital to finance inventories and customer credit, and sufficient cash to cover start-up costs.

- *The difficulties of building a network of distributors or dealers and securing adequate space on retailers' shelves.* A potential entrant can face numerous distribution channel challenges. Wholesale distributors may be reluctant to take on a product that lacks buyer recognition. Retailers must be recruited and convinced to give a new brand ample display space and an adequate trial period. When existing sellers have strong, well-functioning distributor-dealer networks, a newcomer has an uphill struggle in squeezing its way into existing distribution channels. Potential entrants sometimes have to "buy" their way into wholesale or retail channels by cutting their prices to provide dealers and distributors with higher markups and profit margins or by giving them big advertising and promotional allowances. As a consequence, a potential entrant's own profits may be squeezed unless and until its product gains enough consumer acceptance that distributors and retailers are anxious to carry it.

- *Restrictive government policies.* Regulated industries like cable TV, telecommunications, electric and gas utilities, radio and television broadcasting, liquor retailing, and railroads entail government-controlled entry. Government agencies can also limit or even bar entry by requiring licenses and permits, such as the medallion required to drive a taxicab in New York City. Government-mandated safety regulations and environmental pollution standards also create entry barriers because they raise entry costs. In international markets, host governments commonly limit foreign entry and must approve all foreign investment applications. National governments commonly use tariffs and trade restrictions (antidumping rules, local content requirements, quotas, etc.) to raise entry barriers for foreign firms and protect domestic producers from outside competition.

The threat of entry changes as the industry's prospects grow brighter or dimmer and as entry barriers rise or fall. For example, in the pharmaceutical industry the expiration of a key patent on a widely prescribed drug virtually guarantees that one or more drug makers will enter with generic offerings of their own. Use of the Internet for shopping is making it much easier for e-tailers to enter into competition against some of the best-known retail chains. Moreover, new strategic actions by incumbent firms to increase advertising, strengthen distributor-dealer relations, step up R&D, or improve product quality can erect higher roadblocks to entry.

> High entry barriers and weak entry threats today do not always translate into high entry barriers and weak entry threats tomorrow.

Additional Entry Threat Considerations   There are two additional factors that need to be considered in evaluating whether the threat of entry is strong or weak. The first concerns how attractive the growth and profit prospects are for new entrants. *Rapidly growing market demand and high potential profits act as magnets, motivating potential entrants to commit the resources needed to hurdle entry barriers.*[7] When growth and profit opportunities are sufficiently attractive, certain types of entry barriers are unlikely to provide an effective entry deterrent. At most, they limit the pool of candidate entrants to enterprises with the requisite competencies and resources and with the creativity to fashion a strategy for competing with incumbent firms. Hence, *the best test of whether potential entry is a strong or weak competitive force in the marketplace is to ask if the industry's growth and profit prospects are strongly attractive to potential entry candidates with sufficient expertise and resources to hurdle prevailing entry barriers.* When the answer is no, potential entry is a weak competitive force. When the answer is yes, then potential entry adds significantly to competitive pressures in the marketplace.

A second factor concerns the pool of potential entrants and their capabilities in relation to the particular entry barriers in place. Companies with sizable financial resources, proven competitive capabilities, and a respected brand name may be able to marshal the resources to hurdle certain types of entry barriers rather easily, while small start-up enterprises may find the same entry barriers insurmountable. Thus, how hard it will be for potential entrants to compete on a level playing field is always relative to the financial resources and competitive capabilities of likely entrants. The big take-away is this: *Whether an industry's entry barriers ought to be considered high or low depends on the resources and capabilities possessed by the pool of potential entrants.*[8] As a rule, the bigger the pool of entry candidates that have what it takes, the stronger is the threat of entry.

> The threat of entry is stronger when entry barriers are low, when incumbent firms are unable or unwilling to vigorously contest a newcomer's entry, and when there's a sizable pool of entry candidates with resources and capabilities well suited for competing in the industry.

For example, when Honda opted to enter the U.S. lawn mower market in competition against Toro, Snapper, Craftsman, John Deere, and others, it was easily able to hurdle entry barriers that would have been formidable to other newcomers because it had long-standing expertise in gasoline engines; its well-known reputation for quality and durability in automobiles gave it instant credibility with homeowners. In fact, the strongest competitive pressures associated with potential entry frequently come not from outsiders but from current industry participants with strong capabilities looking for growth opportunities. *Existing industry members are often strong candidates to enter market segments or geographic areas where they currently do not have a market presence.* Companies already well established in certain product categories or geographic areas often possess the resources, competencies, and competitive capabilities to hurdle the barriers of entering a different market segment or new geographic area.

Figure 3.5 summarizes the factors that cause the overall competitive threat from potential new entrants to be strong or weak.

Figure 3.5   Factors Affecting the Threat of Entry

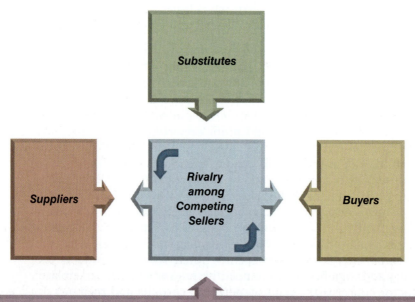

Potential New Entrants

How strong are the competitive pressures coming from the threat of entry of new rivals?

Entry threats are stronger when:
- Entry barriers are low
- Industry members are unwilling or unable to strongly contest the entry of newcomers
- There is a large pool of potential entrants, some of which have the capabilities to overcome high entry barriers
- Existing industry members are looking to expand their market reach by entering product segments or geographic areas where they do not have a presence
- Buyer demand is growing rapidly and newcomers can expect to earn attractive profits without inviting a strong reaction from incumbents

Entry threats are weaker when:
- Entry barriers are high
  - High economies of scale
  - Significant experience-based cost advantages
  - Other cost advantages held by industry members (e.g., access to inputs, technology, favorable location) or low fixed costs
  - Strong product differentiation and brand loyalty
  - Strong network effects
  - High capital requirements
  - Limited new access to distribution channels
  - Restrictive government policies
- Industry members are willing and able to contest new entry
- Industry outlook is risky and uncertain, discouraging entry

Competitive Pressures from the Sellers of Substitute Products

Companies in one industry come under competitive pressure from the actions of companies in a closely adjoining industry whenever buyers view the products of the two industries as good substitutes. For instance, the producers of sugar experience competitive pressures from the sales and marketing efforts of the makers of Equal, Splenda, and Sweet'N Low. Newspapers are struggling to maintain their relevance to subscribers who can watch the news on any of numerous TV channels and use Internet sources to get information about sports results, stock quotes, and job opportunities. The retailers of music CDs are experiencing competitive pressure from downloadable digital music on sites such as iTunes.

As depicted in Figure 3.6, whether the competitive pressures from substitute products are strong, moderate, or weak depends on three factors:

1. *Whether substitutes are readily available.* The presence of readily available substitutes creates competitive pressure by placing a ceiling on the prices industry members can charge without giving customers an incentive to switch to substitutes and risking sales erosion.[9] This price ceiling, at the same time, puts a lid on the profits that industry members can earn unless they find ways to cut costs.

2. *Whether buyers view the substitutes as attractively priced in relation to their quality, performance, and other relevant attributes.* In deciding whether to switch to a substitute product, customers compare its performance, features, ease of use, and other attributes as well as price to see if the substitute offers more value for the money than the industry's product. The users of paper cartons constantly weigh the price/performance trade-offs with plastic containers and metal cans, for example.

3. *Whether the costs that buyers incur in switching to the substitutes are low or high.* Low switching costs make it easier for the sellers of attractive substitutes to lure buyers to their offerings; high switching costs deter buyers from purchasing substitute products.[10] Typical switching costs include the time and inconvenience involved in switching, payments for technical help in making the changeover, the cost of any additional equipment needed, employee retraining costs, the cost of testing the quality and reliability of the substitute, and the psychological costs of severing old supplier relationships and establishing new ones.

Before assessing the competitive pressures coming from substitutes, company managers must identify the substitutes, which is less easy than it sounds since it involves (1) determining where the industry boundaries lie and (2) figuring out which other products or services can address the same basic customer needs as those produced by industry members. Deciding on the industry boundaries is necessary for determining which firms are direct rivals and which produce substitutes. This is a matter of perspective—there are no hard-and-fast rules, other than to say that other brands of the same basic product constitute rival products and not substitutes.

As a rule, *the lower the price of substitutes, the higher their quality and performance; and the lower the user's switching costs, the more intense the competitive pressures posed by substitute products.* Other market indicators of the competitive strength of substitute products include (1) whether the sales of substitutes are growing faster than the sales of the industry being analyzed (a sign that the

Figure 3.6   Factors Affecting Competition from Substitute Products

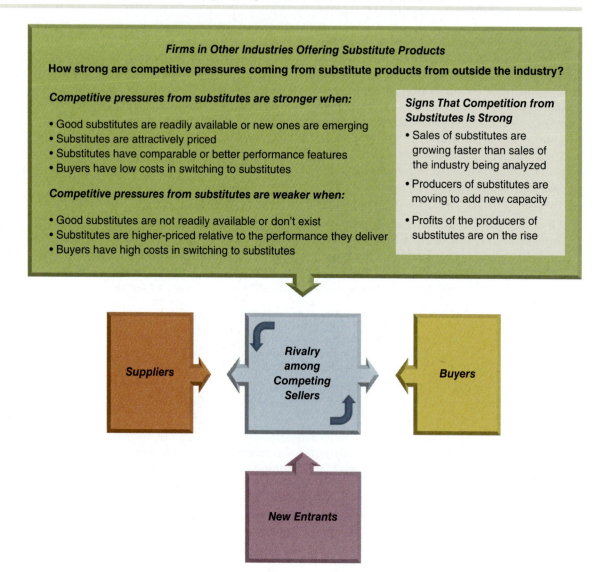

sellers of substitutes may be drawing customers away from the industry in question), (2) whether the producers of substitutes are moving to add new capacity, and (3) whether the profits of the producers of substitutes are on the rise.

Competitive Pressures Stemming from Supplier Bargaining Power

Whether the suppliers of industry members represent a weak or strong competitive force depends on the degree to which suppliers have sufficient *bargaining power* to influence the terms and conditions of supply in their favor. Suppliers with strong bargaining power can erode industry profitability by charging industry members higher prices, passing costs on to them, and limiting their opportunities to find better deals. For instance, Microsoft and Intel, both of whom supply PC makers with essential components, have been known to use their dominant market status not only to charge PC makers premium prices but also to leverage PC makers in other ways. The bargaining power of these two companies over their customers is so great that both companies have faced antitrust charges on numerous occasions. Before a legal agreement ending the practice, Microsoft pressured PC makers to load only Microsoft products on the screens of new computers that come with factory-loaded software. Intel has also defended against antitrust charges but continues to give PC makers who use the biggest percentages of Intel chips in their PC models top priority in filling orders for newly introduced Intel chips. Being on Intel's list of preferred customers helps a PC maker get an allocation of the first production runs of Intel's latest chips and thus get new PC models to market ahead of rivals. Microsoft's and Intel's pressuring of PC makers has helped them maintain their dominant positions in their industries.

Small-scale retailers often must contend with the power of manufacturers whose products enjoy well-known brand names, since consumers expect to find these products on the shelves of the retail stores where they shop. This provides the manufacturer with a degree of pricing power and often the ability to push hard for favorable shelf displays. Similarly, the operators of franchised units of such chains as McDonald's, Dunkin' Donuts, Pizza Hut, Sylvan Learning Centers, and Hampton Inns must frequently agree to source some of their supplies from the franchisor at prices and terms favorable to that franchisor. Supplier bargaining power is also a competitive factor in industries where unions have been able to organize the workforce (which supplies labor). Air pilot unions, for example, have employed their bargaining power to increase pilots' wages and benefits in the air transport industry.

As shown in Figure 3.7, a variety of factors determines the strength of suppliers' bargaining power:[11]

- *Whether suppliers' products are in short supply.* Suppliers of items in short supply have pricing power and bargaining leverage, whereas a surge in the available supply of particular items shifts the bargaining power to the industry members.

- *Whether suppliers provide a differentiated input that enhances the performance or quality of the industry's product.* The more differentiated and valuable a particular input is in terms of enhancing the performance or quality of the products of industry members, the more bargaining leverage and pricing power suppliers have.

- *Whether the item being supplied is a standard item or a commodity that is readily available from a host of suppliers.* The suppliers of commodities (like copper or steel reinforcing rods or shipping cartons) are in a weak position to demand a premium price or insist on other favorable terms because industry members can readily obtain essentially the same item at the same price from many other suppliers eager to win their business.

- *Whether it is difficult or costly for industry members to switch their purchases from one supplier to another.* The higher the switching costs of industry members, the stronger the bargaining power of their suppliers. Low switching costs limit supplier bargaining power by enabling industry members to change suppliers if any one supplier attempts to raise prices by more than the costs of switching.

- *Whether there are good substitutes available for the suppliers' products.* The ready availability of substitute inputs lessens the bargaining power of suppliers by reducing the dependence of industry members on the suppliers. The better

Figure 3.7   Factors Affecting the Bargaining Power of Suppliers

Suppliers

How strong are the competitive pressures stemming from supplier bargaining power?

Supplier bargaining power is stronger when:

- Supplier products/services are in short supply (which gives suppliers leverage in setting prices)
- Supplier products/services are differentiated
- Supplier products/services are critical to industry members' production processes
- Industry members incur high costs in switching their purchases to alternative suppliers
- There are no good substitutes for what the suppliers provide
- Suppliers are not dependent on the industry for a large portion of their revenues
- The supplier industry is more concentrated than the industry it sells to and is dominated by a few large companies

Supplier bargaining power is weaker when:

- There is a surge in the availability of supplies
- The item being supplied is a "commodity" that is readily available from many suppliers at the going market price
- Industry members' switching costs to alternative suppliers are low
- Good substitutes for supplier products/services exist
- Industry members account for a big fraction of suppliers' sales
- The number of suppliers is large relative to the number of industry members and there are no suppliers with large market shares
- Industry members have the potential to integrate backward into the business of suppliers and to self-manufacture their own requirements

Substitutes

Rivalry among Competing Sellers

Buyers

New Entrants

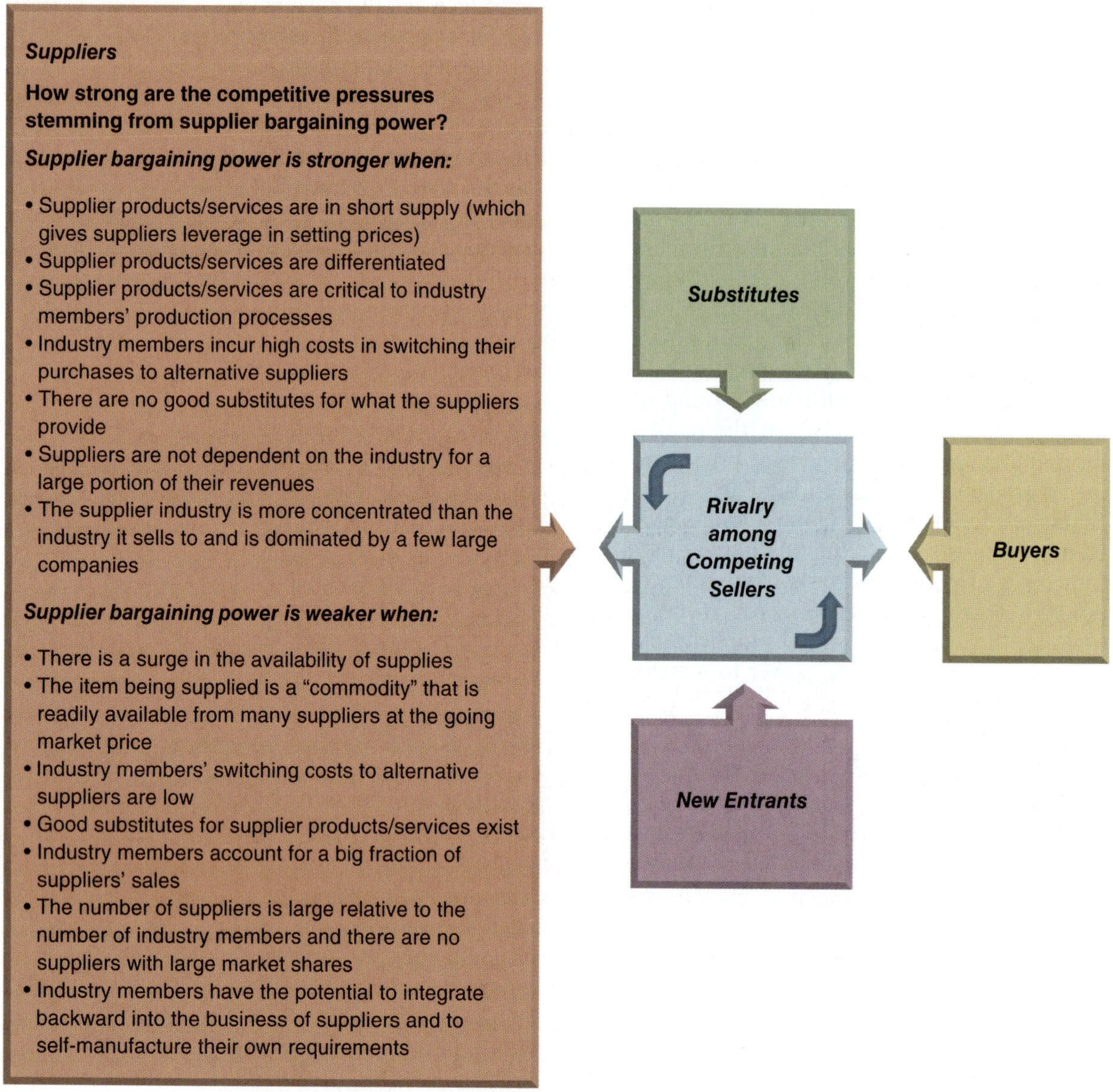

the price and performance characteristics of the substitute inputs, the weaker the bargaining power of suppliers.

- *Whether industry members account for a sizable fraction of suppliers' total sales.* As a rule, suppliers have less bargaining leverage when their sales to members of the industry constitute a big percentage of their total sales. In such cases, the well-being of suppliers is closely tied to the well-being of their major customers. Suppliers have a big incentive to protect and enhance the competitiveness of their major customers via reasonable prices, exceptional quality, and ongoing advances in the technology of the items supplied.
- *Whether the supplier industry is dominated by a few large companies and whether it is more concentrated than the industry it sells to.* Suppliers with sizable market

shares and strong demand for the items they supply generally have sufficient bargaining power to charge high prices and deny requests from industry members for lower prices or other concessions.

- *Whether it makes good economic sense for industry members to integrate backward and self-manufacture items they have been buying from suppliers.* The make-or-buy issue generally boils down to whether suppliers who specialize in the production of particular parts or components and make them in volume for many different customers have the expertise and scale economies to supply as-good or better components at a lower cost than industry members could achieve via self-manufacture. Frequently, it is difficult for industry members to self-manufacture parts and components more economically than they can obtain them from suppliers who specialize in making such items. For instance, most producers of outdoor power equipment (lawn mowers, rotary tillers, leaf blowers, etc.) find it cheaper to source the small engines they need from outside manufacturers that specialize in small-engine manufacture than to make their own engines, because the quantity of engines they need is too small to justify the investment in manufacturing facilities, master the production process, and capture scale economies. Specialists in small-engine manufacture, by supplying many kinds of engines to the whole power equipment industry, can obtain a big-enough sales volume to fully realize scale economies, become proficient in all the manufacturing techniques, and keep costs low. As a rule, suppliers are safe from the threat of self-manufacture by their customers *until* the volume of parts a customer needs becomes large enough for the customer to justify backward integration into self-manufacture of the component.

In identifying the degree of supplier power in an industry, it is important to recognize that different types of suppliers are likely to have different amounts of bargaining power. Thus, the first step is for managers to identify the different types of suppliers, paying particular attention to those that provide the industry with important inputs. The next step is to assess the bargaining power of each type of supplier separately. Figure 3.7 summarizes the conditions that tend to make supplier bargaining power strong or weak.

Competitive Pressures Stemming from Buyer Bargaining Power and Price Sensitivity

Whether buyers are able to exert strong competitive pressures on industry members depends on (1) the degree to which buyers have bargaining power and (2) the extent to which buyers are price-sensitive. Buyers with strong bargaining power can limit industry profitability by demanding price concessions, better payment terms, or additional features and services that increase industry members' costs. Buyer price sensitivity limits the profit potential of industry members by restricting the ability of sellers to raise prices without losing revenue.

The strength of buyers as a competitive force depends on a set of factors that predict the degree of bargaining power and price sensitivity, which may vary according to buyer group (e.g., wholesalers, large retail chains, small retailers, consumers). Retailers tend to have greater bargaining power over industry sellers if they have influence over the purchase decisions of the end user or if they are critical in providing sellers with access to the end user. For example, large retail chains like Walmart, Best Buy, Staples, Home Depot, and Kroger typically have considerable negotiating leverage in purchasing products from manufacturers because of manufacturers' need for broad retail exposure and the most appealing shelf locations. Retailers may stock two or three competing brands of a product but rarely all competing brands, so competition among rival manufacturers for visibility on the shelves of popular multistore retailers gives such retailers significant bargaining strength. Major supermarket chains like Kroger, Safeway, Food Lion, and Publix have sufficient bargaining power to demand promotional allowances and lump-sum payments (called slotting fees) from food products manufacturers in return for stocking certain brands or putting them in the best shelf locations. Motor vehicle manufacturers have strong bargaining power in negotiating to buy original-equipment tires from Goodyear, Michelin, Bridgestone/Firestone, Continental, and Pirelli not only because they buy in large quantities but also because tire makers believe they gain an advantage in supplying replacement tires to vehicle owners if their tire brand is original equipment on the vehicle.

In contrast, individual consumers rarely have any real bargaining power in negotiating price concessions or other favorable terms with sellers. While an individual with other purchase options may refuse to buy a high-priced item, her actions will have no discernible effect on industry profitability. As a buyer group, however, consumers can limit the profit potential of an industry for the same reasons that other buyer groups exert competitive pressure. These reasons are discussed below and summarized in Figure 3.8:[12]

- *Buyers' bargaining power is greater when their costs of switching to competing brands or substitutes are relatively low.* Buyers who can readily switch brands have more leverage than buyers who have high switching costs. Switching costs limit industry profitability, in essence, by putting a cap on how much producers can raise price or reduce quality before they will lose the buyer's business.

- *Buyer power increases when industry goods are standardized or differentiation is weak.* In such circumstances, buyers make their selections on the basis of price, which increases price competition among vendors. When products are differentiated, buyers' options are more limited and they are less focused on obtaining low prices, which may signal poor quality.

- *Buyers have more power when they are large and few in number relative to the number of sellers.* The smaller the number of buyers, the more sellers have to compete for their business and the less easy it is for sellers to find alternative buyers when a customer is lost to a competitor. The prospect of losing a customer not easily replaced often makes a seller more willing to grant concessions of one kind or another. The larger the buyer, the more important their business is to the seller and the more sellers will be willing to grant concessions.

- *Buyer power increases when buyer demand is weak and industry members are scrambling to sell more units.* Weak or declining demand creates a "buyers' market," in which bargain-hunting buyers are able to press for better deals and special treatment; conversely, strong or rapidly growing demand creates a "sellers' market" and shifts bargaining power to sellers.

- *Buyers gain leverage if they are well informed about sellers' products, prices, and costs.* The more information buyers have, the better bargaining position they are in. The mushrooming availability of product information on the Internet is giving added bargaining power to consumers. Buyers can easily use the Internet to compare prices and features of vacation packages, shop for the best interest rates on mortgages and loans, and find the best prices on big-ticket items such as digital cameras. Bargain hunters can shop around for the best deal on the Internet and use that information to negotiate better deals

Figure 3.8 Factors Affecting the Bargaining Power of Buyers

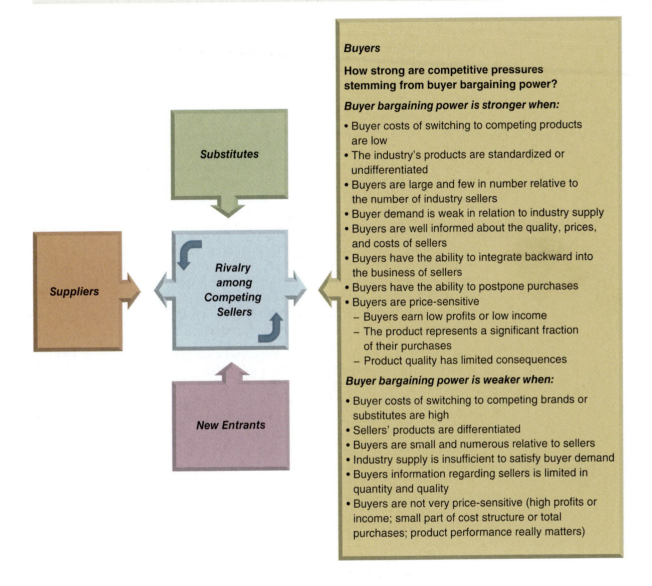

Buyers

How strong are competitive pressures stemming from buyer bargaining power?

Buyer bargaining power is stronger when:

• Buyer costs of switching to competing products are low
• The industry's products are standardized or undifferentiated
• Buyers are large and few in number relative to the number of industry sellers
• Buyer demand is weak in relation to industry supply
• Buyers are well informed about the quality, prices, and costs of sellers
• Buyers have the ability to integrate backward into the business of sellers
• Buyers have the ability to postpone purchases
• Buyers are price-sensitive
  – Buyers earn low profits or low income
  – The product represents a significant fraction of their purchases
  – Product quality has limited consequences

Buyer bargaining power is weaker when:

• Buyer costs of switching to competing brands or substitutes are high
• Sellers' products are differentiated
• Buyers are small and numerous relative to sellers
• Industry supply is insufficient to satisfy buyer demand
• Buyers information regarding sellers is limited in quantity and quality
• Buyers are not very price-sensitive (high profits or income; small part of cost structure or total purchases; product performance really matters)

from local retailers; this method is becoming commonplace in buying new and used motor vehicles.

• *Buyers' bargaining power is greater when they pose a credible threat of integrating backward into the business of sellers.* Companies like Anheuser-Busch, Coors, and Heinz have integrated backward into metal can manufacturing to gain bargaining power in obtaining the balance of their can requirements from otherwise powerful metal can manufacturers. Retailers gain bargaining power by stocking and promoting their own private-label brands alongside manufacturers' name brands.

• *Buyer leverage increases if buyers have discretion to delay their purchases or perhaps even not make a purchase at all.* Consumers often have the option to delay purchases of durable goods, such as major appliances, or discretionary goods, such as hot tubs and home entertainment centers, if they are not happy with the prices offered. Business customers may also be able to defer their purchases of certain items, such as plant equipment or maintenance services. This puts pressure on sellers to provide concessions to buyers so that the sellers can keep their sales numbers from dropping off.

- *Buyer price sensitivity increases when buyers are earning low profits or have low income.* Price is a critical factor in the purchase decisions of low-income consumers and companies that are barely scraping by. In such cases, their high price sensitivity limits the ability of sellers to charge high prices.

- *Buyers are more price-sensitive if the product represents a large fraction of their total purchases.* When a purchase eats up a large portion of a buyer's budget or represents a significant part of his or her cost structure, the buyer cares more about price than might otherwise be the case. When the item is a small fraction of total purchases, buyers are less likely to feel that negotiating or shopping for a better deal is worth the time and trouble.

- *Buyers are more price-sensitive if product performance has limited consequences.* When product performance has limited consequences for the buyer, then purchase decisions are based mostly on price. On the other hand, when product quality is important, such as when it materially affects the quality of an intermediate buyer's goods, then price becomes a less important factor. Price is particularly unimportant to intermediate buyers when a good has the potential to pay for itself by reducing a buyer's other production costs.

The starting point for the analysis of buyers as a competitive force is to identify the different types of buyers along the value chain—then proceed to analyzing the bargaining power and price sensitivity of each type separately. Overall, buyers exert strong competitive pressures and force industry profitability downward if the majority of industry member sales are made to buyer groups that have either strong bargaining power or high price sensitivity. Buyers are able to exert only moderate competitive pressures on sellers when the majority of sellers' revenues come from buyers with intermediate levels of power or price sensitivity. Competitive pressures exerted by buyers are weak when a big portion of sellers' sales revenues comes from buyers with weak bargaining power and price sensitivity.

Is the Collective Strength of the Five Competitive Forces Conducive to Good Profitability?

Assessing whether each of the five competitive forces gives rise to strong, moderate, or weak competitive pressures sets the stage for evaluating whether, overall, the strength of the five forces is conducive to good profitability. Is the state of competition in the industry stronger than "normal"? Can companies in this industry reasonably expect to earn decent profits in light of the prevailing competitive forces? Are some of the competitive forces sufficiently powerful to undermine industry profitability?

The most extreme case of a "competitively unattractive" industry occurs when all five forces are producing strong competitive pressures: Rivalry among sellers is vigorous, low entry barriers allow new rivals to gain a market foothold, competition from substitutes is intense, and both suppliers and buyers are able to exercise considerable leverage. Fierce to strong competitive pressures coming from all five directions drive industry profitability to unacceptably low levels, frequently producing losses for many industry members and forcing some out of business. But an industry can be competitively unattractive without all five competitive forces being strong. In fact, intense competitive pressures *from just one or two* of the five forces may suffice to destroy the conditions for good profitability and prompt some companies to exit the business.

As a rule, *the strongest competitive forces determine the extent of the competitive pressure on industry profitability.*[13] Thus, in evaluating the strength of the five forces overall and their effect on industry profitability, managers should look to the strongest forces. Having more than one strong force will not worsen the effect on industry profitability, but it does mean that the industry has multiple competitive challenges with which to cope. In that sense, an industry with three to five strong forces is even more "unattractive" as a place to compete. Especially intense competitive conditions seem to be the norm in tire manufacturing, apparel, and commercial airlines, three industries where profit margins have historically been thin.

In contrast, when the overall impact of the five competitive forces is moderate to weak, an industry is "attractive" in the sense that the *average* industry member can reasonably expect to earn good profits and a nice return on investment. The ideal competitive environment for earning superior profits is one in which both suppliers and customers are in weak bargaining positions, there are no good substitutes, high barriers block further entry, and rivalry among present sellers generates only limited competitive pressures. Weak competition is the best of all possible worlds for also-ran companies because even they can usually eke out a decent profit—if a company can't make a decent profit when competition is weak, then its business outlook is indeed grim.

In most industries, the collective strength of the five competitive forces is somewhere near the middle of the two extremes of very intense and very weak, typically ranging from slightly stronger than normal to slightly weaker than normal and typically allowing well-managed companies with sound strategies to earn moderately attractive profits.

Matching Company Strategy to Competitive Conditions

Working through the five-forces model step by step not only aids strategy makers in assessing whether the intensity of competition allows good profitability but also promotes sound strategic thinking about how to better match company strategy to the specific competitive character of the marketplace. Effectively matching a company's business strategy to prevailing competitive conditions has three aspects:

1. Pursuing avenues that shield the firm from as many of the different competitive pressures as possible.
2. Initiating actions calculated to shift the competitive forces in the company's favor by altering the underlying factors driving the five forces.
3. Spotting attractive arenas for expansion, where competitive pressures in the industry are somewhat weaker.

But making headway on these three fronts first requires identifying competitive pressures, gauging the relative strength of each of the five competitive forces, and gaining a deep enough understanding of the state of competition in the industry to know which strategy buttons to push.

CORE CONCEPT

The strongest of the five forces determines how strong the forces of competition are overall and the extent of the downward pressure on an industry's level of profitability.

A company's strategy is increasingly effective the more it provides some insulation from competitive pressures, shifts the competitive battle in the company's favor, and positions firms to take advantage of attractive growth opportunities.

QUESTION 3: WHAT FACTORS ARE DRIVING INDUSTRY CHANGE, AND WHAT IMPACTS WILL THEY HAVE?

LO 2

Learn how to diagnose the factors shaping industry dynamics and to forecast their effects on future industry profitability.

While it is critical to understand the nature and intensity of the competitive forces in an industry, it is just as important to understand that the intensity of these forces and the level of an industry's attractiveness are fluid and subject to change. All industries are affected by new developments and ongoing trends that alter industry conditions, some more speedily than others. Many of these changes are important enough to require a strategic response. Since the five competitive forces have such significance for an industry's profit potential, it is critical that managers remain alert to the changes most likely to affect the strength of the five forces. Environmental scanning for changes of this nature will enable managers to forecast changes in the expected profitability of the industry and to adjust their company's strategy accordingly.

Changes that affect the competitive forces in a positive manner may present opportunities for companies to reposition themselves to take advantage of these forces. Changes that affect the five forces negatively may require a defensive strategic response. Regardless of the direction of change, managers will be able to react in a more timely fashion, with lower adjustment costs, if they have advance notice of the coming changes. Moreover, with early notice, managers may be able to influence the direction or scope of environmental change and improve the outlook.

Analyzing Industry Dynamics

CORE CONCEPT

Dynamic industry analysis involves determining how the **drivers of change** are affecting industry and competitive conditions.

Managing under changing conditions begins with a strategic analysis of the industry dynamics. This involves three steps: (1) identifying the **drivers of change,** (2) assessing whether the drivers of change are, individually or collectively, acting to make the industry more or less attractive, and (3) determining what strategy changes are needed to prepare for the impacts of the anticipated change. All three steps merit further discussion.

Identifying an Industry's Drivers of Change

While many types of environmental change can affect industries in one way or another, it is important to focus on the most powerful agents of change—those with the biggest influence in reshaping the industry landscape and altering competitive conditions. Many drivers of change originate in the outer ring of the company's external environment (see Figure 3.2), but others originate in the company's more immediate industry and competitive environment. Although some drivers of change are unique and specific to a particular industry situation, most drivers of industry and competitive change fall into one of the following categories:[14]

- *Changes in an industry's long-term growth rate.* Shifts in industry growth up or down are a key driver of industry change, affecting the balance between industry supply and buyer demand, entry and exit, and the character and strength of competition. Whether demand is growing or declining is one of the key factors influencing the intensity of rivalry in an industry, as explained earlier. But the strength of this effect will depend on how changes in the industry growth rate affect entry and exit in the industry. If entry barriers are low, then growth in demand will attract new entrants, increasing the number of industry rivals. If exit barriers are low, then shrinking demand will induce exit, resulting in fewer remaining rivals. Since the numbers of firms in an industry also affects the strength of rivalry, these secondary effects via entry and exit would counteract the more direct effects of the change in demand on rivalry. Depending on how much entry or exit takes place, the net result might be that the overall force of rivals remains the same. A change in the long-term growth rate may affect industry conditions in other ways as well. For example, if growth prospects induce the entry of a large, established firm with ambitious growth goals, the intensity of rivalry may increase markedly due to the added diversity or changes in the size mix of incumbents. The exact effect of growth rate changes will vary depending on the specific industry situation. In analyzing the effects of any change driver, managers need to keep in mind the various factors that influence the five forces.

- *Increasing globalization.* Globalization can be precipitated by the blossoming of consumer demand in more and more countries and by the actions of government officials in many countries to reduce trade barriers or open up once-closed markets to foreign competitors, as is occurring in many parts of Europe, Latin America, and Asia. Significant differences in labor costs among countries give manufacturers a strong incentive to locate plants for labor-intensive products in low-wage countries and use these plants to supply market demand across the world. Wages in China, India, Singapore, Mexico, and Brazil, for example, are about one-fourth those in the United States, Germany, and Japan. Because globalization is a complex phenomenon that affects different industries in different ways, analyzing its effects on industry dynamics is a challenging task that requires a consideration of how each of the five forces may be affected. For example, globalization increases the diversity and number of competitors, and this in turn increases the force of rivalry in an industry. At the same time, the lowering of trade barriers increases the threat of entry, putting further pressure on industry profitability. On the other hand, globalization is likely to weaken supplier power by increasing the number of suppliers and increasing the possibility of substituting cheap labor for other inputs. The specific effects vary by industry and will impact some industries more than others. Globalization is very much a driver of industry change in such industries as motor vehicles, steel, petroleum, personal computers, video games, public accounting, and textbook publishing.

- *Changes in who buys the product and how they use it.* Shifts in buyer demographics and the ways products are used can greatly alter industry and competitive conditions. Longer life expectancies and growing percentages of relatively well-to-do retirees, for example, are driving demand growth in such industries as health care, prescription drugs, recreational living, and vacation travel. This is the most common effect of changes in buyer demographics, and it affects industry rivalry, as observed above. But other effects are possible as well. Dell's "buy direct" strategy lessened the buyer power of big-box middlemen in the PC industry by cutting out the intermediate buyers and selling directly to end users. Buyer power increased in the pharmaceutical industry when large HMOs created lists of approved drugs, reducing the role of individual (powerless) doctors in the choice process.

- *Technological change.* Advances in technology can cause disruptive change in an industry by introducing substitutes that offer buyers an irresistible price/performance combination. At the least, this increases the power of substitutes; it may change the business landscape in more fundamental ways if it has a devastating effect on demand. Technological change can also impact the manufacturing process in an industry. This might lead to greater economies of scale, for example, which would increase industry entry barriers. Or it could lead to greater product differentiation, as did the introduction of "mass-customization" techniques. Increasing product differentiation tends to lower buyer power, increase entry barriers, and reduce rivalry—all of which have positive implications for industry profitability.

- *Emerging new Internet capabilities and applications.* The emergence of high-speed Internet service and Voice-Over-Internet-Protocol technology, along with an ever-growing series of Internet applications, provides a special case of technological change that has been a major driver of change in industry after industry. It has reshaped many aspects of the business landscape and can affect the five forces in various ways. The ability of companies to reach consumers via the Internet increases the number of rivals a company faces and often escalates rivalry by pitting pure online sellers against combination brick-and-click sellers against pure brick-and-mortar sellers (increasing diversity and size mix). The Internet gives buyers increasing power through unprecedented ability to research the product offerings of competitors and shop the market for the best value (making buyers better informed). Widespread use of e-mail has forever eroded the business of providing fax services and the first-class-mail delivery revenues of government postal services worldwide (substitute power). Videoconferencing via the Internet erodes the demand for business travel (increasing rivalry in the travel market). The Internet of the future will feature faster speeds, dazzling applications, and over a billion connected gadgets performing an array of functions, thus driving further industry and competitive changes. But Internet-related impacts vary from industry to industry. The challenges here are to assess precisely how emerging Internet developments are altering a particular industry's landscape and to factor these impacts into the strategy-making equation.

- *Product and marketing innovation.* An ongoing stream of product innovations tends to alter the pattern of competition in an industry by attracting more first-time buyers, rejuvenating industry growth, and/or increasing product differentiation, with concomitant effects on rivalry, entry threat, and buyer power. Product innovation has been a key driving force in such industries as digital cameras, golf clubs, video games, toys, and prescription drugs. Similarly, when firms are successful in introducing *new ways* to market their products, they can spark a burst of buyer interest, widen industry demand, increase or lower entry barriers, and increase product differentiation—any or all of which can alter the competitiveness of an industry.

- *Entry or exit of major firms.* The entry of one or more foreign companies into a geographic market once dominated by domestic firms nearly always changes the balance between demand and supply and shakes up competitive conditions by adding diversity. Likewise, when an established domestic firm from another industry attempts entry either by acquisition or by launching its own start-up venture, it usually applies its skills and resources in some innovative fashion that pushes competition in new directions. Entry by a major firm thus often produces a new ball game, with greater rivalry as the result. Similarly, exit of a major firm changes the competitive structure by reducing the number of market leaders and increasing the dominance of the leaders who remain. The primary effect is on the degree of rivalry in the industry, through changes in industry concentration.

- *Diffusion of technical know-how across more companies and more countries.* As knowledge about how to perform a particular activity or execute a particular manufacturing technology spreads, products tend to become more commodity-like. This increases the intensity of rivalry, buyer power, and the threat of entry into an industry, as described earlier.

- *Improvements in cost and efficiency in closely adjoining markets.* Big changes in the costs of substitute producers can dramatically alter the state of competition by changing the price/performance trade-off between an industry's products and that of substitute goods. For example, lower production costs and longer-life products have allowed the makers of super-efficient, fluorescent-based spiral lightbulbs to cut deeply into the sales of incandescent lightbulbs. This has occurred because the spiral lightbulbs, despite being priced two to three times higher than incandescent bulbs, are still far cheaper to use because of their energy-saving efficiency (as much as $50 per bulb) and longer lives (up to eight years between replacements).

- *Reductions in uncertainty and business risk.* Many companies are hesitant to enter industries with uncertain futures or high levels of business risk, and firms already in these industries may be cautious about making aggressive capital investments to expand—often because it is unclear how much time and money it will take to overcome various technological hurdles and achieve acceptable production costs (as is the case in the infant solar power industry). Likewise, firms entering foreign markets where demand is just emerging or where political conditions are volatile may be cautious and limit their downside exposure by using less risky strategies. Over time, however, diminishing risk levels and uncertainty tend to stimulate new entry and capital investments on the part of growth-minded companies seeking new opportunities. This can dramatically alter industry and competitive conditions by increasing rivalry, as the numbers of firms in the industry and their diversity increases.

- *Regulatory influences and government policy changes.* Changes in regulations and government policies can affect competitive conditions in industries in a variety of ways. For example, regulatory actions can affect barriers to entry directly, as they have in industries such as airlines, banking, and broadcasting. Regulations regarding product quality, safety, and environmental protection can affect entry barriers more indirectly, by altering capital requirements or economies of scale. Government actions can also affect rivalry through antitrust policies, as they have in soft-drink bottling, where exclusive territorial rights were granted, and in automobile parts, where a loosening of restrictions led to increasing supplier power.[15] In international markets, host governments can affect industry rivalry or supplier and buyer power by opening their domestic markets to foreign participation or closing them to protect domestic companies.

- *Changing societal concerns, attitudes, and lifestyles.* Emerging social issues and changing attitudes and lifestyles can be powerful instigators of industry change. Growing concerns about global warming have emerged as a major driver of change in the energy industry, changing the rate of industry growth in different sectors. The greater attention and care being given to household pets has driven growth across the whole pet industry. Changes in the industry growth rate, as we have seen, can affect the intensity of industry rivalry and entry conditions.

Table 3.3 lists these 12 most common drivers of change. That there are so many different *potential* drivers of change explains why a full understanding of all types of change drivers is a fundamental part of analyzing industry dynamics. However, for each industry no more than three or four of these drivers are likely to be powerful enough to qualify as the *major determinants* of why and how an industry's competitive conditions are changing. The true analytical task is to evaluate the forces of industry and competitive change carefully enough to separate major factors from minor ones.

Assessing the Impact of the Factors Driving Industry Change

Just identifying the factors driving industry change is not sufficient, however. The second, and more important, step in dynamic industry analysis is to determine whether the prevailing change drivers, on the whole, are acting to make the industry environment more or less attractive. Answers to three questions are needed:

1. Overall, are the factors driving change causing demand for the industry's product to increase or decrease?
2. Is the collective impact of the drivers of change making competition more or less intense?
3. Will the combined impacts of the change drivers lead to higher or lower industry profitability?

Getting a handle on the collective impact of the factors driving industry change requires looking at the likely effects of each factor separately, since the drivers of change may not all be pushing change in the same direction. For example, one change driver may be acting to spur demand for the industry's product while

Table 3.3   The Most Common Drivers of Industry Change

1.   Changes in the long-term industry growth rate
2.   Increasing globalization
3.   Changes in who buys the product and how they use it
4.   Technological change
5.   Emerging new Internet capabilities and applications
6.   Product and marketing innovation
7.   Entry or exit of major firms
8.   Diffusion of technical know-how across companies and countries
9.   Improvements in efficiency in adjacent markets
10. Reductions in uncertainty and business risk
11. Regulatory influences and government policy changes
12. Changing societal concerns, attitudes, and lifestyles

another is working to curtail demand. Whether the net effect on industry demand is up or down hinges on which driver of change is the more powerful. Similarly, the effects of the drivers of change on each of the five forces should be looked at individually first, and then collectively, to view the overall effect. In summing up the overall effect of industry change on the five forces, it is important to recall that it is the *strongest* of the five forces that determines the degree of competitive pressure on industry profitability and therefore the industry's profit potential. The key question, then, is whether a new strong force is emerging or whether forces that are strong presently are beginning to weaken.

> The most important part of dynamic industry analysis is to determine whether the collective impact of the change drivers will be to increase or decrease market demand, make competition more or less intense, and lead to higher or lower industry profitability.

Developing a Strategy That Takes the Changes in Industry Conditions into Account

The third step in the strategic analysis of industry dynamics—where the real payoff for strategy making comes—is for managers to draw some conclusions about *what strategy adjustments will be needed to deal with the impacts of the changes in industry conditions.* The value of analyzing industry dynamics is to gain better understanding of what strategy adjustments will be needed to cope with the drivers of industry change and the impacts they are likely to have on competitive intensity and industry profitability. Indeed, without understanding the forces driving industry change and the impacts these forces will have on the character of the industry environment and on the company's business over the next one to three years, managers are ill-prepared to craft a strategy tightly matched to emerging conditions. To the extent that managers are unclear about the drivers of industry change and their impacts, or if their views are off-base, the chances of making astute and timely strategy adjustments are slim. So dynamic industry analysis is not something to take lightly; it has practical value and is basic to the task of thinking strategically about where the industry is headed and how to prepare for the changes ahead.

> Dynamic industry analysis, when done properly, pushes company managers to think about what's around the corner and what the company needs to be doing to get ready for it.

QUESTION 4: HOW ARE INDUSTRY RIVALS POSITIONED—WHO IS STRONGLY POSITIONED AND WHO IS NOT?

Since competing companies commonly sell in different price/quality ranges, emphasize different distribution channels, incorporate product features that appeal to different types of buyers, have different geographic coverage, and so on, it stands to reason that some companies enjoy stronger or more attractive market positions than other companies. Understanding which companies are strongly positioned and which are weakly positioned is an integral part of analyzing an industry's competitive structure. The best technique for revealing the market positions of industry competitors is **strategic group mapping.**[16]

LO 3

Become adept at mapping the market positions of key groups of industry rivals.

Using Strategic Group Maps to Assess the Market Positions of Key Competitors

> **CORE CONCEPT**
>
> A **strategic group** is a cluster of industry rivals that have similar competitive approaches and market positions.

A **strategic group** consists of those industry members with similar competitive approaches and positions in the market.[17] Companies in the same strategic group can resemble one another in any of several ways: They may have comparable product-line breadth, sell in the same price/quality range, emphasize the same distribution channels, use essentially the same product attributes to appeal to similar types of buyers, depend on identical technological approaches, or offer buyers similar services and technical assistance.[18] An industry contains only one strategic group when all sellers pursue essentially identical strategies and have similar market positions. At the other extreme, an industry may contain as many strategic groups as there are competitors when each rival pursues a distinctively different competitive approach and occupies a substantially different market position.

The procedure for constructing a *strategic group map* is straightforward:

- Identify the competitive characteristics that differentiate firms in the industry. Typical variables are price/quality range (high, medium, low), geographic coverage (local, regional, national, global), product-line breadth (wide, narrow), degree of service offered (no frills, limited, full), use of distribution channels (retail, wholesale, Internet, multiple), degree of vertical integration (none, partial, full), and degree of diversification into other industries (none, some, considerable).
- Plot the firms on a two-variable map using pairs of these differentiating characteristics.
- Assign firms occupying about the same map location to the same strategic group.
- Draw circles around each strategic group, making the circles proportional to the size of the group's share of total industry sales revenues.

This produces a two-dimensional diagram like the one for the retail chain store industry in Illustration Capsule 3.1.

Several guidelines need to be observed in creating strategic group maps.[19]

> **CORE CONCEPT**
>
> **Strategic group mapping** is a technique for displaying the different market or competitive positions that rival firms occupy in the industry.

First, the two variables selected as axes for the map should *not* be highly correlated; if they are, the circles on the map will fall along a diagonal and reveal nothing more about the relative positions of competitors than would be revealed by comparing the rivals on just one of the variables. For instance, if companies with broad product lines use multiple distribution channels while companies with narrow lines use a single distribution channel, then looking at broad versus narrow product lines reveals just as much about industry positioning as looking at single versus multiple distribution channels; that is, one of the variables is redundant.

Second, the variables chosen as axes for the map should reflect key approaches to offering value to customers and expose big differences in how rivals position themselves to compete in the marketplace. This, of course, means analysts must identify the characteristics that differentiate rival firms and use these differences as variables for the axes and as the basis for deciding which firm belongs in which strategic group. Third, the variables used as axes don't have to be either quantitative or continuous; rather, they can be discrete variables, defined in terms of distinct classes and combinations. Fourth, drawing the sizes of the circles on the map proportional to the combined sales of the firms in each strategic group allows the map to reflect the relative sizes of each strategic

ILLUSTRATION CAPSULE 3.1

Comparative Market Positions of Selected Retail Chains: A Strategic Group Map Example

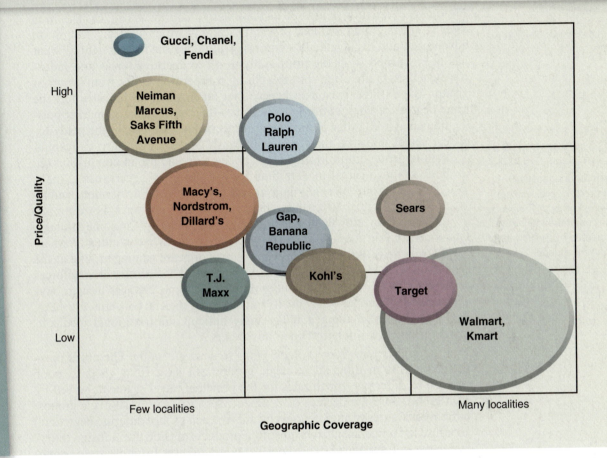

Note: Circles are drawn roughly proportional to the sizes of the chains, based on revenues.

group. Fifth, if more than two good variables can be used as axes for the map, then it is wise to draw several maps to give different views of the relationships among the competitive positions present in the industry's structure—there is not necessarily one best map for portraying how competing firms are positioned.

What Can Be Learned from Strategic Group Maps?

Strategic group maps are revealing in several respects. The most important has to do with identifying which industry members are close rivals and which are distant rivals. Firms in the same strategic group are the closest rivals; the next closest rivals are in the immediately adjacent groups. Often, firms in strategic groups that are far apart on the map hardly compete at all. For instance, Walmart's clientele, merchandise selection, and pricing points are much too different to justify calling Walmart a close

> Strategic group maps reveal which companies are close competitors and which are distant competitors.

79

competitor of Neiman Marcus or Saks Fifth Avenue. For the same reason, Timex is not a meaningful competitive rival of Rolex.

The second thing to be gleaned from strategic group mapping is that *not all positions on the map are equally attractive.*[20] Two reasons account for why some positions can be more attractive than others:[21]

1. *Prevailing competitive pressures in the industry and drivers of change favor some strategic groups and hurt others.* Discerning which strategic groups are advantaged and disadvantaged requires scrutinizing the map in light of what has been learned from the prior analyses of competitive forces and industry dynamics. Quite often the strength of competition varies from group to group—there's little reason to believe that all firms in an industry feel the same degrees of competitive pressure, since their strategies and market positions may well differ in important respects. For instance, in the ready-to-eat cereal industry, there are significantly higher entry barriers (capital requirements, brand loyalty, etc.) for the strategic group comprising the large branded-cereal makers than for the group of generic-cereal makers or the group of small natural-cereal producers. Furthermore, industry dynamics may affect different groups in different ways. For example, the long-term growth in demand may be increasing for some strategic groups and shrinking for others—as is the case in the news industry, where Internet news services and cable news networks are gaining ground at the expense of newspapers and network television. The industry driving forces of emerging Internet capabilities and applications, changes in who buys the product and how they use it, and changing societal concerns, attitudes, and lifestyles are making it increasingly difficult for traditional media to increase audiences and attract new advertisers.

2. *Profit prospects vary from strategic group to strategic group.* The profit prospects of firms in different strategic groups can vary from good to poor because of differing growth rates for the principal buyer segments served by each group, differing degrees of competitive rivalry within strategic groups, differing pressures from potential entrants to each group, differing degrees of exposure to competition from substitute products outside the industry, differing degrees of supplier or customer bargaining power from group to group, and differing impacts from the industry's drivers of change.

Thus, part of strategic group map analysis always entails drawing conclusions about where on the map is the "best" place to be and why. Which companies/strategic groups are destined to prosper because of their positions? Which companies/strategic groups seem destined to struggle because of their positions? What accounts for why some parts of the map are better than others?

> Some strategic groups are more favorably positioned than others because they confront weaker competitive forces and/or because they are more favorably impacted by the drivers of industry change.

QUESTION 5: WHAT STRATEGIC MOVES ARE RIVALS LIKELY TO MAKE NEXT?

Unless a company pays attention to the strategies and situations of competitors and has some inkling of what moves they will be making, it ends up flying blind into competitive battle. As in sports, scouting the opposition is an essential part of game plan development. **Competitive intelligence** about rivals' strategies, their latest actions and announcements, their financial performance, their strengths and weaknesses, and the thinking and leadership styles of their executives is valuable for anticipating the strategic moves competitors are likely to make next. Having good information about the strategic direction and likely moves of key competitors allows a company to prepare defensive countermoves, to craft its own strategic moves with some confidence about what market maneuvers to expect from rivals in response, and to exploit any openings that arise from competitors' missteps.

> Good **competitive intelligence** helps managers avoid the damage to sales and profits that comes from being caught napping by the surprise moves of rivals.

One indicator of the types of moves a rival is likely to make is its financial performance—how much pressure it is under to improve. Rivals with good financial performance are likely to continue their present strategy with only minor fine-tuning. Poorly performing rivals are virtually certain to make fresh strategic moves. Ambitious rivals looking to move up in the industry ranks are strong candidates for launching new strategic offensives to pursue emerging market opportunities and exploit the vulnerabilities of weaker rivals.

Other good clues about what actions a specific company is likely to undertake can often be gleaned from what its management is saying in company press releases, information posted on the company's Web site (especially the presentations management has recently made to securities analysts), and such public documents as annual reports and 10-K filings. (Figure 1.1 in Chapter 1 indicates what to look for in identifying a company's strategy.) Company personnel may be able to pick up useful information from a rival's exhibits at trade shows and from conversations with a rival's customers, suppliers, and former employees. (See Illustration Capsule 3.2 for a discussion of the ethical limits to gathering competitive intelligence.)[22] Many companies have a competitive intelligence unit that sifts through the available information to construct up-to-date strategic profiles of rivals—their current strategies, resources, competitive capabilities, and competitive shortcomings. Such profiles are typically updated regularly and made available to managers and other key personnel.

There are several useful questions that company managers can pose to help predict the likely actions of important rivals:

1. Which competitors have strategies that are producing good results—and thus are likely to make only minor strategic adjustments?

2. Which competitors are losing ground in the marketplace or otherwise struggling to come up with a good strategy—and thus are strong candidates for altering their prices, improving the appeal of their product offerings, moving to a different part of the strategic group map, and otherwise adjusting important elements of their strategy?

3. Which competitors are poised to gain market share, and which ones seem destined to lose ground?

4. Which competitors are likely to rank among the industry leaders five years from now? Do the up-and-coming competitors have strong ambitions and the resources needed to overtake the current industry leader?

5. Which rivals badly need to increase their unit sales and market share? What strategic options are they most likely to pursue: lowering prices, adding new models and styles, expanding their dealer networks, entering additional geographic markets, boosting advertising to build better brand-name awareness, acquiring a weaker competitor, or placing more emphasis on direct sales via their Web sites?

6. Which rivals are likely to enter new geographic markets or make major moves to substantially increase their sales and market share in a particular geographic region?

7. Which rivals are strong candidates to expand their product offerings and enter new product segments where they do not currently have a presence?

8. Which rivals are good candidates to be acquired? Which rivals may be looking to make an acquisition and are financially able to do so?

To succeed in predicting a competitor's next moves, company strategists need to have a good understanding of each rival's situation, its pattern of behavior in the past, how its managers think, and what the rival's best strategic options are. Doing the necessary detective work can be time-consuming, but scouting competitors well enough to anticipate their next moves allows managers to prepare effective countermoves (perhaps even beat a rival to the punch) and to take rivals' probable actions into account in crafting their own best course of action.

QUESTION 6: WHAT ARE THE KEY FACTORS FOR FUTURE COMPETITIVE SUCCESS?

An industry's **key success factors (KSFs)** are those competitive factors that affect industry members' ability to survive and prosper in the marketplace—the particular strategy elements, product attributes, operational approaches, resources, and competitive capabilities that spell the difference between being a strong competitor and a weak competitor—and between profit and loss. KSFs by their very nature are so important to competitive success that *all firms* in the industry must pay close attention to them or risk becoming an industry laggard or failure. To indicate the significance of KSFs another way, how well the elements of a company's strategy measure up against an industry's KSFs determines just how financially and competitively successful that company will be. Identifying KSFs, in light of the prevailing and anticipated industry and competitive conditions, is therefore always a top priority in analytical and strategy-making considerations. Company strategists need to understand the industry landscape well enough to separate the factors most important to competitive success from those that are less important.

Key success factors vary from industry to industry, and even from time to time within the same industry, as drivers of change and competitive conditions change. But regardless of the circumstances, an industry's key success factors can always be deduced by asking the same three questions:

1. On what basis do buyers of the industry's product choose between the competing brands of sellers? That is, what product attributes and service characteristics are crucial?

2. Given the nature of competitive rivalry and the competitive forces prevailing in the marketplace, what resources and competitive capabilities must a company have to be competitively successful?

3. What shortcomings are almost certain to put a company at a significant competitive disadvantage?

Only rarely are there more than five key factors for competitive success. When there appear to be more, usually some are of greater importance than others. Managers should therefore bear in mind the purpose of identifying key success factors—to determine which factors are most important to competitive success—and resist the temptation to label a factor that has only minor importance as a KSF. Compiling a list of every factor that matters even a little bit defeats the purpose of concentrating management attention on the factors truly critical to long-term competitive success.

In the beer industry, for example, although there are many types of buyers (wholesale, retail, end consumer), it is most important to understand the preferences and buying behavior of the beer drinkers. Their purchase decisions are driven by price, taste, convenient access, and marketing. Thus the KSFs include a *strong network of wholesale distributors* (to get the company's brand stocked and favorably displayed in retail outlets, bars, restaurants, and stadiums, where beer is sold) and *clever advertising* (to induce beer drinkers to buy the company's brand and thereby pull beer sales through the established wholesale/retail channels). Because there is a potential for strong buyer power on the part of large distributors and retail chains, competitive success depends on some mechanism to offset that power, of which advertising (to create demand pull) is one. Thus the KSFs also include *superior product differentiation* (as in microbrews) or *superior firm size and branding capabilities* (as in national brands). The KSFs also include *full utilization of brewing capacity* (to keep manufacturing costs low and offset the high advertising, branding, and product differentiation costs).

Correctly diagnosing an industry's KSFs raises a company's chances of crafting a sound strategy. The key success factors of an industry point to those things that every firm in the industry needs to attend to in order to retain customers and weather the competition. If the company's strategy cannot deliver on the key success factors of its industry, it is unlikely to earn enough profits to remain a viable business. The goal of strategists, however, should be to do more than just meet the KSFs, since all firms in the industry need to clear this bar to survive. The goal of company strategists should be to design a strategy that allows it to compare favorably vis-à-vis rivals on each and every one of the

CORE CONCEPT

Key success factors are the strategy elements, product and service attributes, operational approaches, resources, and competitive capabilities with the greatest impact on competitive success in the marketplace.

LO 4

Understand why in-depth evaluation of a business's strengths and weaknesses in relation to the specific industry conditions it confronts is an essential prerequisite to crafting a strategy that is well-matched to its external situation.

industry's KSFs and that aims at being *distinctively better* than rivals on one (or possibly two) of the KSFs.

QUESTION 7: DOES THE INDUSTRY OFFER GOOD PROSPECTS FOR ATTRACTIVE PROFITS?

The final step in evaluating the industry and competitive environment is to use the results of the analyses performed in answering Questions 1 to 6 to determine whether the industry presents the company with strong prospects for attractive profits. The important factors on which to base a conclusion include:

- The industry's growth potential.
- Whether strong competitive forces are squeezing industry profitability to sub-par levels.
- Whether industry profitability will be favorably or unfavorably affected by the prevailing drivers of change in the industry (i.e., whether the industry growth potential and competition appear destined to grow stronger or weaker).
- Whether the company occupies a stronger market position than rivals (one more capable of withstanding negative competitive forces) and whether this is likely to change in the course of competitive interactions.
- How well the company's strategy delivers on the industry key success factors.

As a general proposition, if a company can conclude that its overall profit prospects are above average in the industry, then the industry environment is basically attractive *(for that company)*; if industry profit prospects are below average, conditions are unattractive *(for the company)*. However, it is a mistake to think of a particular industry as being equally attractive or unattractive to all industry participants and all potential entrants.[24] Attractiveness is relative, not absolute, and conclusions one way or the other have to be drawn from the perspective of a particular company. For instance, a favorably positioned competitor may see ample opportunity to capitalize on the vulnerabilities of weaker rivals even though industry conditions are otherwise somewhat dismal. And even if an industry has appealing potential for growth and profitability, a weak competitor (one that may be part of an unfavorably positioned strategic group) may conclude that having to fight a steep uphill battle against much stronger rivals holds little promise of eventual market success or good return on shareholder investment. Similarly, industries attractive to insiders may be unattractive to outsiders because of the difficulty of challenging current market leaders with their particular resources and competencies or because they have more attractive opportunities elsewhere.

> The degree to which an industry is attractive or unattractive is not the same for all industry participants and all potential entrants.

When a company decides an industry is fundamentally attractive and presents good opportunities, a strong case can be made that it should invest aggressively to capture the opportunities it sees and to improve its long-term competitive position in the business. When a strong competitor concludes an industry is becoming less attractive, it may elect to simply protect its present position, investing cautiously if at all and looking for opportunities in other industries. A competitively weak company in an unattractive industry may see its best option as finding a buyer, perhaps a rival, to acquire its business.

KEY POINTS

Thinking strategically about a company's external situation involves probing for answers to the following seven questions:

1. *Does the industry offer attractive opportunities for growth?* Industries differ significantly on such factors as market size and growth rate, geographic scope, life-cycle stage, the number and sizes of sellers, industry capacity, and other conditions that describe the industry's demand-supply balance and opportunities for growth. Identifying the industry's basic economic features and growth potential sets the stage for the analysis to come, since they play an important role in determining an industry's potential for attractive profits.

2. *What kinds of competitive forces are industry members facing, and how strong is each force?* The strength of competition is a composite of five forces: (1) competitive pressures stemming from the competitive jockeying among industry rivals, (2) competitive pressures associated with the market inroads being made by the sellers of substitutes, (3) competitive pressures associated with the threat of new entrants into the market, (4) competitive pressures stemming from supplier bargaining power, and (5) competitive pressures stemming from buyer bargaining. The nature and strength of the competitive pressures have to be examined force by force and their collective strength must be evaluated. The strongest forces, however, are the ultimate determinant of the intensity of the competitive pressure on industry profitability. Working through the five-forces model aids strategy makers in assessing how to insulate the company from the strongest forces, identify attractive arenas for expansion, or alter the competitive conditions so that they offer more favorable prospects for profitability.

3. *What factors are driving changes in the industry, and what impact will these changes have on competitive intensity and industry profitability?* Industry and competitive conditions change because of a variety of forces, some coming from the industry's macro-environment and others originating within the industry. The most common change drivers include changes in the long-term industry growth rate, increasing globalization, changing buyer demographics, technological change, Internet-related developments, product and marketing innovation, entry or exit of major firms, diffusion of know-how, efficiency improvements in adjacent markets, reductions in uncertainty and business risk, government policy changes, and changing societal factors. Once an industry's change drivers have been identified, the analytical task becomes one of determining whether they are acting, individually and collectively, to make the industry environment more or less attractive. Are the change drivers causing demand for the industry's product to increase or decrease? Are they acting to make competition more or less intense? Will they lead to higher or lower industry profitability?

4. *What market positions do industry rivals occupy—who is strongly positioned and who is not?* Strategic group mapping is a valuable tool for understanding the similarities, differences, strengths, and weaknesses inherent in the market positions of rival companies. Rivals in the same or nearby strategic groups

are close competitors, whereas companies in distant strategic groups usually pose little or no immediate threat. The lesson of strategic group mapping is that some positions on the map are more favorable than others. The profit potential of different strategic groups varies due to strengths and weaknesses in each group's market position. Often, industry competitive pressures and change drivers favor some strategic groups and hurt others.

5. *What strategic moves are rivals likely to make next?* Scouting competitors well enough to anticipate their actions can help a company prepare effective countermoves (perhaps even beating a rival to the punch) and allows managers to take rivals' probable actions into account in designing their own company's best course of action. Managers who fail to study competitors risk being caught unprepared by the strategic moves of rivals.

6. *What are the key factors for competitive success?* An industry's key success factors (KSFs) are the particular strategy elements, product attributes, operational approaches, resources, and competitive capabilities that all industry members must have in order to survive and prosper in the industry. KSFs vary by industry and may vary over time as well. For any industry, however, they can be deduced by answering three basic questions: (1) On what basis do buyers of the industry's product choose between the competing brands of sellers, (2) what resources and competitive capabilities must a company have to be competitively successful, and (3) what shortcomings are almost certain to put a company at a significant competitive disadvantage? Correctly diagnosing an industry's KSFs raises a company's chances of crafting a sound strategy.

7. *Does the outlook for the industry present the company with sufficiently attractive prospects for profitability?* The last step in industry analysis is summing up the results from answering questions 1 to 6. If the answers reveal that a company's overall profit prospects in that industry are above average, then the industry environment is basically attractive *for that company;* if industry profit prospects are below average, conditions are unattractive for them. What may look like an attractive environment for one company may appear to be unattractive from the perspective of a different company.

Clear, insightful diagnosis of a company's external situation is an essential first step in crafting strategies that are well matched to industry and competitive conditions. To do cutting-edge strategic thinking about the external environment, managers must know what questions to pose and what analytical tools to use in answering these questions. This is why this chapter has concentrated on suggesting the right questions to ask, explaining concepts and analytical approaches, and indicating the kinds of things to look for.

ASSURANCE OF LEARNING EXERCISES

LO 1, LO 2

1. Prepare a brief analysis of the snack-food industry using the information provided on industry trade association Web sites. On the basis of information provided on these Web sites, draw a five-forces diagram for the snack-food industry and briefly discuss the nature and strength of each of the five competitive forces. What factors are driving change in the industry?

LO 1, LO 3

2. Based on the strategic group map in Illustration Capsule 3.1, who are Nordstrom's closest competitors? Between which two strategic groups is competition the strongest? Why do you think no retail chains are positioned in the upper right corner of the map? Which company/strategic group faces the weakest competition from the members of other strategic groups?

LO 1, LO 4

3. Using your knowledge as a snack-food consumer and your analysis of the five forces in that industry (from question 1), describe the key success factors for the snack-food industry. Your list should contain no more than six industry KSFs. In deciding on your list, it's important to distinguish between factors critical for the success of *any* firm in the industry and factors that pertain only to specific companies.

EXERCISES FOR SIMULATION PARTICIPANTS

LO 1

1. Which of the five competitive forces is creating the strongest competitive pressures for your company?
2. What are the "competitive weapons" that rival companies in your industry can use to gain sales and market share? See Table 3.2 to help you identify possible competitive tactics. (You may be able to think of others.)
3. What are the factors affecting the intensity of rivalry in the industry in which your company is competing. Use Figure 3.4 and the accompanying discussion to help you pinpoint the specific factors most affecting competitive intensity. Would you characterize the rivalry among the companies in your industry as brutal, strong, moderate, or relatively weak? Why?

LO 2

4. Are there any factors driving change in the industry in which your company is competing? What impact will these drivers of change have? How will they change demand or supply? Will they cause competition to become more or less intense? Will they act to boost or squeeze profit margins? List at least two actions your company should consider taking in order to combat any negative impacts of the factors driving change.

LO 3

5. Draw a strategic group map showing the market positions of the companies in your industry. Which companies do you believe are in the most attractive position on the map? Which companies are the most weakly positioned? Which companies do you believe are likely to try to move to a different position on the strategic group map?

LO 4

6. What do you see as the key factors for being a successful competitor in your industry? List at least three.

ENDNOTES

[1] For a more extended discussion of the problems with the life-cycle hypothesis, see Michael E. Porter, *Competitive Strategy: Techniques for Analyzing Industries and Competitors* (New York: Free Press, 1980), pp. 157–62.

[2] The five-forces model of competition is the creation of Professor Michael Porter of the Harvard Business School. See Michael E. Porter, "How Competitive Forces Shape Strategy," *Harvard Business Review* 57, no. 2 (March–April 1979), pp. 137–45; Porter, *Competitive Strategy,* chap. 1; and Porter's most recent discussion of the model, "The Five Competitive Forces That Shape Strategy," *Harvard Business Review* 86, no. 1 (January 2008), pp. 78–93.

[3] For a discussion of how a company's actions to counter the moves of rival firms tend to escalate competitive pressures, see Pamela J. Derfus, Patrick G. Maggitti, Curtis M. Grimm, and Ken G. Smith, "The Red Queen Effect: Competitive Actions and Firm Performance," *Academy of Management Journal* 51, no. 1 (February 2008), pp. 61–80.

[4] Many of these indicators of whether rivalry produces intense competitive pressures are based on Porter, *Competitive Strategy,* pp. 17–21.

[5] Porter, *Competitive Strategy,* p. 7; Porter, "The Five Competitive Forces That Shape Strategy," p. 81.

[6] The role of entry barriers in shaping the strength of competition in a particular market has long been a standard topic in the literature of microeconomics. For a discussion of how entry barriers affect competitive pressures associated with potential entry, see J. S. Bain, *Barriers to New Competition* (Cambridge, MA: Harvard University Press, 1956); F. M. Scherer, *Industrial Market Structure and Economic Performance* (Chicago: Rand McNally, 1971), pp. 216–20, 226–33; Porter, *Competitive Strategy,* pp. 7–17; Porter, "The Five Competitive Forces That Shape Strategy," pp. 80–82.

[7] For a good discussion of this point, see George S. Yip, "Gateways to Entry," *Harvard Business Review* 60, no. 5 (September–October 1982), pp. 85–93.

[8] C. A. Montgomery and S. Hariharan, "Diversified Expansion by Large Established Firms," *Journal of Economic Behavior & Organization* 15, no. 1 (January 1991), pp. 71–89.

[9] Porter, "How Competitive Forces Shape Strategy," p. 142; Porter, *Competitive Strategy,* pp. 23–24.

[10] Porter, *Competitive Strategy,* p. 10.

[11] Ibid., pp. 27–28.

[12] Ibid., pp. 24–27.

[13] Porter, "The Five Competitive Forces That Shape Strategy," p. 80.

[14] Most of the candidate driving forces described here are based on the discussion in Porter, *Competitive Strategy,* pp. 164–83.

[15] D. Yoffie, "Cola Wars Continue: Coke and Pepsi in 2006," Harvard Business School case 9-706-447, rev. April 2, 2007; B. C. Lynn, "How Detroit Went Bottom-Up," *American Prospect,* October 2009, pp. 21–24.

[16] Porter, *Competitive Strategy,* chap. 7.

[17] Ibid., pp. 129–30.

[18] For an excellent discussion of how to identify the factors that define strategic groups, see Mary Ellen Gordon and George R. Milne, "Selecting the Dimensions That Define Strategic Groups: A Novel Market-Driven Approach," *Journal of Managerial Issues* 11, no. 2 (Summer 1999), pp. 213–33.

[19] Porter, *Competitive Strategy,* pp. 152–54.

[20] For other benefits of strategic group analysis, see Avi Fiegenbaum and Howard Thomas, "Strategic Groups as Reference Groups: Theory, Modeling and Empirical Examination of Industry and Competitive Strategy," *Strategic Management Journal* 16 (1995), pp. 461–76; S. Ade Olusoga, Michael P. Mokwa, and Charles H. Noble, "Strategic Groups, Mobility Barriers, and Competitive Advantage," *Journal of Business Research* 33 (1995), pp. 153–64.

[21] Porter, *Competitive Strategy,* pp. 130, 132–38, and 152–55.

[22] For further discussion of legal and ethical ways of gathering competitive intelligence on rival companies, see Larry Kahaner, *Competitive Intelligence* (New York: Simon & Schuster, 1996).

[23] Ibid., pp. 84–85.

[24] B. Wernerfelt and C. Montgomery, "What Is an Attractive Industry?" *Management Science* 32, no. 10 (October 1986), pp. 1223–30.

CHAPTER 4

EVALUATING A COMPANY'S RESOURCES, CAPABILITIES, AND COMPETITIVENESS

> Before executives can chart a new strategy, they must reach common understanding of the company's current position.
>
> **—W. Chan Kim and Renée Mauborgne**
> *Consultants and INSEAD Professors*

> You have to learn to treat people as a resource ... you have to ask not what do they cost, but what is the yield, what can they produce?
>
> **—Peter F. Drucker**
> *Business Thinker and Management Consultant*

> Organizations succeed in a competitive marketplace over the long run because they can do certain things their customers value better than can their competitors.
>
> **—Robert Hayes, Gary Pisano, and David Upton**
> *Harvard Business School Professors*

> Only firms who are able to continually build new strategic assets faster and cheaper than their competitors will earn superior returns over the long term.
>
> **—C. C. Markides and P. J. Williamson**
> *London Business School Professors and Consultants*

LEARNING OBJECTIVES

LO 1. Learn how to take stock of how well a company's strategy is working.

LO 2. Understand why a company's resources and capabilities are central to its strategic approach and how to evaluate their potential for giving the company a competitive edge over rivals.

LO 3. Discover how to assess the company's strengths and weaknesses in light of market opportunities and external threats.

LO 4. Grasp how a company's value chain activities can affect the company's cost structure, degree of differentiation, and competitive advantage.

LO 5. Understand how a comprehensive evaluation of a company's competitive situation can assist managers in making critical decisions about their next strategic moves.

n Chapter 3 we described how to use the tools of industry analysis to assess the profit potential and key success factors of a company's external environment. This laid the groundwork for matching a company's strategy to its external situation. In this chapter we discuss techniques for evaluating a company's internal situation, including its collection of resources and capabilities and the activities it performs along its value chain. Internal analysis enables managers to determine whether their strategy has appealing prospects for giving the company a significant competitive edge over rival firms. Combined with external analysis, it facilitates an understanding of how to reposition a firm to take advantage of new opportunities and to cope with emerging competitive threats. The analytical spotlight will be trained on six questions:

1. How well is the company's present strategy working?

2. What are the company's competitively important resources and capabilities?

3. Is the company able to take advantage of market opportunities and overcome external threats to its external well-being?

4. Are the company's prices and costs competitive with those of key rivals, and does it have an appealing customer value proposition?

5. Is the company competitively stronger or weaker than key rivals?

6. What strategic issues and problems merit front-burner managerial attention?

In probing for answers to these questions, five analytical tools—resource and capability analysis, SWOT analysis, value chain analysis, benchmarking, and competitive strength assessment—will be used. All five are valuable techniques for revealing a company's competitiveness and for helping company managers match their strategy to the company's own particular circumstances.

QUESTION 1: HOW WELL IS THE COMPANY'S PRESENT STRATEGY WORKING?

LO 1

Learn how to take stock of how well a company's strategy is working.

In evaluating how well a company's present strategy is working, the best way to start is with a clear view of what the strategy entails. Figure 4.1 shows the key components of a single-business company's strategy. The first thing to examine is the company's competitive approach. What moves has the company made recently to attract customers and improve its market position—for instance, has it cut prices, improved the design of its product, added new features, stepped up advertising, entered a new geographic market (domestic or foreign), or merged with a competitor? Is it striving for a competitive advantage based on low costs or an appealingly different or better product offering? Is it concentrating on serving a broad spectrum of customers or a narrow market niche? The company's functional strategies in R&D, production, marketing, finance, human resources, information technology, and so on further characterize company strategy, as do any efforts to establish competitively valuable alliances or partnerships with other enterprises.

The two best indicators of how well a company's strategy is working are (1) whether the company is achieving its stated financial and strategic objectives and (2) whether the company is an above-average industry performer. Persistent shortfalls in meeting company performance targets and weak performance relative to rivals are reliable warning signs that the company has a weak strategy or suffers from poor strategy execution or both. Other indicators of how well a company's strategy is working include:

- Whether the firm's sales are growing faster than, slower than, or about the same pace as the market as a whole, thus resulting in a rising, eroding, or stable market share.
- Whether the company is acquiring new customers at an attractive rate as well as retaining existing customers.
- Whether the firm's profit margins are increasing or decreasing and how well its margins compare to rival firms' margins.
- Trends in the firm's net profits and return on investment and how they compare to the same trends for other companies in the industry.
- Whether the company's overall financial strength and credit rating are improving or declining.
- How shareholders view the company on the basis of trends in the company's stock price and shareholder value (relative to the stock price trends at other companies in the industry).
- Whether the firm's image and reputation with its customers are growing stronger or weaker.
- How well the company stacks up against rivals on technology, product innovation, customer service, product quality, delivery time, price, getting newly developed products to market quickly, and other relevant factors on which buyers base their choices.
- Whether key measures of operating performance (such as days of inventory, employee productivity, unit cost, defect rate, scrap rate, order-filling accuracy, delivery times, and warranty costs) are improving, remaining steady, or deteriorating.

Figure 4.1   Identifying the Components of a Single-Business Company's Strategy

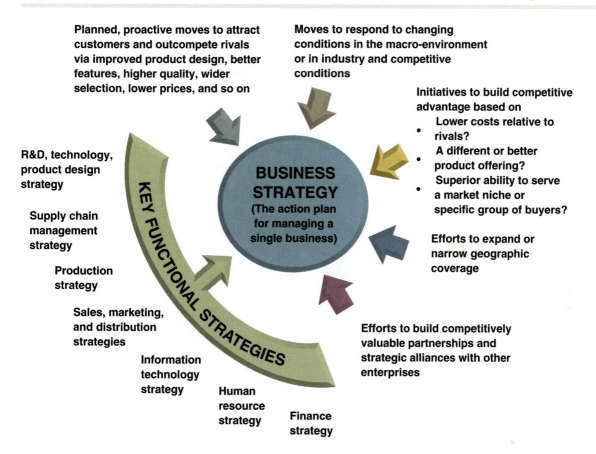

The stronger a company's current overall performance, the less likely the need for radical changes in strategy. The weaker a company's financial performance and market standing, the more its current strategy must be questioned. Weak performance is almost always a sign of weak strategy, weak execution, or both.

Evaluating how well a company's strategy is working should include quantitative as well as qualitative assessments. Table 4.1 provides a compilation of the financial ratios most commonly used to evaluate a company's financial performance and balance sheet strength.

> The stronger a company's financial performance and market position, the more likely it has a well-conceived, well-executed strategy.

QUESTION 2: WHAT ARE THE COMPANY'S COMPETITIVELY IMPORTANT RESOURCES AND CAPABILITIES?

Regardless of how well the strategy is working, it is important for managers to understand the underlying reasons. Clearly, this is critical if strategy changes are needed. But even when the strategy is working well, this can help managers to bolster a

Table 4.1   Key Financial Ratios: How to Calculate Them and What They Mean

Ratio	How Calculated	What It Shows
Profitability Ratios		
1. Gross profit margin	$$\frac{\text{Revenues} - \text{Cost of goods sold}}{\text{Revenues}}$$	Shows the percentage of revenues available to cover operating expenses and yield a profit. Higher is better, and the trend should be upward.
2. Operating profit margin (or return on sales)	$$\frac{\text{Revenues} - \text{Operating expenses}}{\text{Revenues}}$$ *or* $$\frac{\text{Operating income}}{\text{Revenues}}$$	Shows how much profit is earned on each dollar of sales, before paying interest charges and income taxes. Earnings before interest and taxes is known as *EBIT* in financial and business accounting. Higher is better, and the trend should be upward.
3. Net profit margin (or net return on sales)	$$\frac{\text{Profits after taxes}}{\text{Revenues}}$$	Shows after-tax profits per dollar of sales. Higher is better, and the trend should be upward.
4. Return on total assets	$$\frac{\text{Profits after taxes} + \text{Interest}}{\text{Total assets}}$$	A measure of the return on total investment in the enterprise. Interest is added to after-tax profits to form the numerator, since total assets are financed by creditors as well as by stockholders. Higher is better, and the trend should be upward.
5. Return on stockholder's equity	$$\frac{\text{Profits after taxes}}{\text{Total stockholders' equity}}$$	Shows the return stockholders are earning on their investment in the enterprise. A return in the 12% to 15% range is "average," and the trend should be upward.
6. Return on invested capital	$$\frac{\text{Profits after taxes}}{\text{Long-term debt} + \text{total equity}}$$	Shows how effectively a company uses the monetary capital invested in its operations and the returns to those investments. Higher is better, and the trend should be upward.
7. Earnings per share	$$\frac{\text{Profits after taxes}}{\text{Number of shares of common stock outstanding}}$$	Shows the earnings for each share of common stock outstanding. The trend should be upward, and the bigger the annual percentage gains, the better.
Liquidity Ratios		
1. Current ratio	$$\frac{\text{Current assets}}{\text{Current liabilities}}$$	Shows a firm's ability to pay current liabilities using assets that can be converted to cash in the near term. The ratio should definitely be higher than 1.0; a ratio of 2.0 or higher is better still.
2. Working capital	$\text{Current assets} - \text{Current liabilities}$	Shows the cash available for a firm's day-to-day operations. Bigger amounts are better because the company has more internal funds available to (1) pay its current liabilities on a timely basis and (2) finance inventory expansion, additional accounts receivable, and a larger base of operations without resorting to borrowing or raising more equity capital.

(Continued)

Ratio	How Calculated	What It Shows
Leverage Ratios		
1. Debt-to-assets ratio	$$\frac{\text{Total debt}}{\text{Total assets}}$$	Measures the extent to which borrowed funds have been used to finance the firm's operations. A low fraction or ratio is better—a high fraction indicates overuse of debt and greater risk of bankruptcy.
2. Long-term debt-to-capital ratio	$$\frac{\text{Long-term debt}}{\text{Long-term debt} + \text{Total stockholders' equity}}$$	An important measure of creditworthiness and balance sheet strength. It indicates the percentage of capital investment that has been financed by creditors and bondholders. A ratio below 0.25 is usually preferable since monies invested by stockholders account for 75% or more of the company's total capital. The lower the ratio, the greater the capacity to borrow additional funds. A debt-to capital ratio above 0.50 and certainly above 0.75 indicates a heavy and perhaps excessive reliance on debt, lower creditworthiness, and weak balance sheet strength.
3. Debt-to-equity ratio	$$\frac{\text{Total debt}}{\text{Total stockholders' equity}}$$	Should usually be less than 1.0. A high ratio (especially above 1.0) signals excessive debt, lower creditworthiness, and weaker balance sheet strength.
4. Long-term debt-to-equity ratio	$$\frac{\text{Long-term debt}}{\text{Total stockholders' equity}}$$	Shows the balance between debt and equity in the firm's *long-term* capital structure. A low ratio indicates greater capacity to borrow additional funds if needed.
5. Times-interest-earned (or coverage) ratio	$$\frac{\text{Operating income}}{\text{Interest expenses}}$$	Measures the ability to pay annual interest charges. Lenders usually insist on a minimum ratio of 2.0, but ratios above 3.0 signal better creditworthiness.
Activity Ratios		
1. Days of inventory	$$\frac{\text{Inventory}}{\text{Cost of goods sold} \div 365}$$	Measures inventory management efficiency. Fewer days of inventory are usually better.
2. Inventory turnover	$$\frac{\text{Cost of goods sold}}{\text{Inventory}}$$	Measures the number of inventory turns per year. Higher is better.
3. Average collection period	$$\frac{\text{Accounts receivable}}{\text{Total sales} \div 365}$$ *or* $$\frac{\text{Accounts receivable}}{\text{Average daily sales}}$$	Indicates the average length of time the firm must wait after making a sale to receive cash payment. A shorter collection time is better.
Other Important Measures of Financial Performance		
1. Dividend yield on common stock	$$\frac{\text{Annual dividends per share}}{\text{Current market price per share}}$$	A measure of the return to owners received in the form of dividends.

(Continued)

Ratio	How Calculated	What It Shows
2. Price-earnings ratio	$$\frac{\text{Current market price per share}}{\text{Earnings per share}}$$	A P/E ratio above 20 indicates strong investor confidence in a firm's outlook and earnings growth. Firms whose future earnings are at risk or likely to grow slowly typically have ratios below 12.
3. Dividend payout ratio	$$\frac{\text{Annual dividends per share}}{\text{Earnings per share}}$$	Indicates the percentage of after-tax profits paid out as dividends.
4. Internal cash flow	After tax profits + Depreciation	A quick and rough estimate of the cash a company's business is generating after payment of operating expenses, interest, and taxes. Such amounts can be used for dividend payments or funding capital expenditures.
5. Free cash flow	After tax profits + Depreciation − Capital Expenditures − Dividends	A quick and rough estimate of the cash a company's business is generating after payment of operating expenses, interest, taxes, dividends, and desirable reinvestments in the business. The larger a company's free cash flow, the greater is its ability to internally fund new strategic initiatives, repay debt, make new acquisitions, repurchase shares of stock, or increase dividend payments.

CORE CONCEPT

A company's resources and capabilities represent its **competitive assets** and are big determinants of its competitiveness and ability to succeed in the marketplace.

LO 2

Understand why a company's resources and capabilities are central to its strategic approach and how to evaluate their potential for giving the company a competitive edge over rivals.

successful strategy and avoid harmful missteps. How well a strategy works depends a great deal on the relative strengths and weaknesses of a company's resources and capabilities. A company's resources and capabilities are its **competitive assets** and determine whether its competitive power in the marketplace will be impressively strong or disappointingly weak. Companies with minimal or only ordinary competitive assets nearly always are relegated to a trailing position in the industry.

Resource and capability analysis provides managers with a powerful tool for sizing up the company's competitive assets and determining whether they can provide the foundation necessary for competitive success in the marketplace. This is a two step process. The first step is for managers to identify the company's resources and capabilities so that they have a better idea of what they have to work with in crafting the company's competitive strategy. The second step is to examine the company's resources and capabilities more closely to ascertain which of them are the most competitively valuable and to determine whether the best of them can help the firm attain a sustainable competitive advantage over rival firms.[1] This step involves applying the *four tests of a resource's competitive power.*

Identifying the Company's Resources and Capabilities

A firm's resources and capabilities are the fundamental building blocks of its competitive strategy. In crafting strategy, it is essential for managers to be able to recognize a resource or an organizational capability for what it is and to know how to take stock of the company's full complement of resources and capabilities.

To do a good job with this, managers and strategists need to start with a basic understanding of what these terms mean.

In brief, a **resource** is a productive input or competitive asset that is owned or controlled by the firm. Firms have many different types of resources at their disposal that vary not only in kind but in quality as well. Some are higher-quality than others, and some are more competitively valuable, having greater potential to give a firm a competitive advantage over its rivals. For example, a company's brand is a resource, as is an R&D team—yet some brands such as Coca-Cola and Kleenex are well known, with enduring value, while others have little more name recognition than generic products. In similar fashion, some R&D teams are far more innovative and productive than others due to the outstanding talents of the individual team members, the team's composition, and its chemistry.

A **capability** is the capacity of a firm to perform some activity proficiently. Capabilities also vary in form, quality, and competitive importance, with some being more competitively valuable than others. Apple's product innovation capabilities are widely recognized as being far superior to those of its competitors; Nordstrom is known for its superior incentive management capabilities; PepsiCo is admired for its marketing and brand management capabilities.

> Resource and capability analysis is a powerful tool for sizing up a company's competitive assets and determining if they can support a sustainable competitive advantage over market rivals.

> **CORE CONCEPT**
>
> A **resource** is a competitive asset that is owned or controlled by a company; a **capability** is the capacity of a firm to perform some activity proficiently.

Types of Company Resources   A useful way to identify a company's resources is to look for them within categories, as shown in Table 4.2. Broadly speaking, resources can be divided into two main categories:

Table 4.2   Types of Company Resources

Tangible Resources

- *Physical resources:* ownership of or access rights to natural resources (such as mineral deposits); state-of-the-art manufacturing plants, equipment, and/or distribution facilities; land and real estate; the locations of stores, manufacturing plants, or distribution centers, including the overall pattern of their physical locations

- *Financial resources:* cash and cash equivalents; marketable securities; other financial assets such as the borrowing capacity of the firm (as indicated from its balance sheet and credit rating)

- *Technological assets:* patents, copyrights, and trade secrets; production technology, stock of other technologies, technological processes

- *Organizational resources:* IT and communication systems (servers, workstations, etc.); other planning, coordination, and control systems; the company's organizational design and reporting structure

Intangible Resources

- *Human assets and intellectual capital:* the experience, cumulative learning, and tacit knowledge of employees; the education, intellectual capital, and know-how of specialized teams and work groups; the knowledge of key personnel concerning important business functions (e.g., skills in keeping operating costs low, improving product quality, and providing customer service); managerial talent; the creativity and innovativeness of certain personnel

- *Brands, company image, and reputational assets:* brand names, trademarks, product image, buyer loyalty and goodwill; company image, reputation for quality, service, and reliability; reputation with suppliers and partners for fair dealing

- *Relationships:* alliances or joint ventures that provide access to technologies, specialized know-how, or geographic markets; partnerships with suppliers that reduce costs and/or enhance product quality and performance; networks of dealers or distributors; the trust established with various partners

- *Company culture and incentive system:* the norms of behavior, business principles, and ingrained beliefs within the company; the attachment of personnel to the company's ideals; the compensation system and the motivation level of company personnel

tangible and **intangible** resources. Although *human resources* make up one of the most important parts of a company's resource base, we include them in the intangible category to emphasize the role played by the skills, talents, and knowledge of a company's human resources.

Tangible resources are the most easily identified, since tangible resources are those that can be touched or quantified readily. Obviously, they include various types of *physical resources* such as manufacturing facilities and mineral resources, but they also include a company's *financial resources, technological resources,* and *organizational resources* such as the company's communication and control systems.

Intangible resources are harder to discern, but they are often among the most important of a firm's competitive assets. They include various sorts of *human assets and intellectual capital,* as well as a company's *brands, image, and reputational assets.* While intangible resources have no material existence on their own, they are often embodied in something material. Thus the skills and knowledge resources of a firm are embodied in its managers and employees; a company's brand name is embodied in the company logo or product labels. Other important kinds of intangible resources include a company's *relationships* with suppliers, buyers, or partners of various sorts, and the *company's culture and incentive system.* A more detailed listing of the various types of tangible and intangible resources is provided in Table 4.2.

Listing a company's resources category by category can prevent managers from inadvertently overlooking some company resources that might be competitively important. At times, it can be difficult to decide exactly how to categorize certain types of resources. For example, resources such as a work group's specialized expertise in developing innovative products can be considered to be technological assets or human assets or intellectual capital and knowledge assets; the work ethic and drive of a company's workforce could be included under the company's human assets or its culture and incentive system. In this regard, it is important to remember that *it is not exactly how a resource is categorized that matters but, rather, that all of the company's different types of resources are included in the inventory.* The real purpose of using categories in identifying a company's resources is to ensure that none of a company's resources go unnoticed when sizing up the company's competitive assets.

Identifying Capabilities Organizational capabilities are more complex entities than resources; indeed, they are built up through the use of resources and draw on some combination of the firm's resources as they are exercised.[2] Virtually all organizational capabilities are *knowledge-based, residing in people and in a company's intellectual capital or in organizational processes and systems, which embody tacit knowledge.* For example, General Mill's brand management capabilities draw on the knowledge of the company's brand managers, the expertise of its marketing department, and the company's relationships with retailers, since brand building is a cooperative activity requiring retailer support. The capability in video game design for which Electronic Arts is known derives from the creative talents and technological expertise of its highly talented game developers, the company's culture of creativity, and a compensation system that generously rewards talented developers for creating best-selling video games.

Because of their complexity, capabilities are harder to categorize than resources and more challenging to search for as a result. There are, however, two approaches that can make the process of uncovering and identifying a firm's capabilities more systematic. The first method takes the completed listing of a firm's resources as its starting point. Since capabilities are built from resources and utilize resources as they are exercised, a firm's resources can provide a strong set of clues about the types of capabilities the firm is likely to have accumulated. This approach simply involves looking over the firm's resources and considering whether (and to what extent) the firm has built up any related capabilities. So, for example, a fleet of trucks, the latest RFID tracking technology, and a set of large automated distribution centers may be indicative of sophisticated capabilities in logistics and distribution. R&D teams composed of top scientists with expertise in genomics may suggest organizational capabilities in developing new gene therapies or in biotechnology more generally.

The second method of identifying a firm's capabilities takes a functional approach. Many capabilities relate to fairly specific functions; these draw on a limited set of resources and typically involve a single department or organizational unit. Capabilities in injection molding or continuous casting or metal stamping are manufacturing-related; capabilities in direct selling, promotional pricing, or database marketing all connect to the sales and marketing functions; capabilities in basic research, strategic innovation, or new product development link to a company's R&D function. This approach requires managers to survey the various functions a firm performs to find the different capabilities associated with each function.

A problem with this second method is that many of the most important capabilities of firms are inherently *cross-functional*. Cross-functional capabilities draw on a number of different kinds of resources and are generally multidisciplinary in nature—they spring from the effective collaboration among people with different expertise working in different organizational units. An example is the capability for fast-cycle, continuous product innovation that comes from teaming the efforts of groups with expertise in market research, new product R&D, design and engineering, advanced manufacturing, and market testing. Cross-functional capabilities and other complex capabilities involving numerous linked and closely integrated competitive assets are sometimes referred to as **resource bundles.** Although resource bundles are not as easily pigeonholed as other types of resources and capabilities, they can still be identified by looking for company activities that link different types of resources, functions, and departmental units. It is important not to miss identifying a company's resource bundles, since they can be the most competitively important of a firm's competitive assets. Unless it includes a company's cross-functional capabilities and resource bundles, no identification of a company's resources and capabilities can be considered complete.

> **CORE CONCEPT**
>
> A **resource bundle** is a linked and closely integrated set of competitive assets centered around one or more cross-functional capabilities.

Determining Whether a Company's Resources and Capabilities Are Potent Enough to Produce a Sustainable Competitive Advantage

To determine the strategic relevance and competitive power of a firm's resources and capabilities, it is necessary to go beyond merely identifying a company's resources and capabilities. The second step in resource and capability analysis is designed to ascertain which of a company's resources and capabilities are competitively valuable and to what extent they can support a company's quest for a sustainable competitive advantage over market rivals. This involves probing the *caliber* of a firm's competitive assets relative to those of its competitors.[3] When a company has competitive assets that are central to its strategy and superior to those of rival firms, it has a competitive advantage over other firms. If this advantage proves durable despite the best efforts of competitors to overcome it, then the company is said to have a ***sustainable* competitive advantage.** While it may be difficult for a company to achieve a sustainable competitive advantage, it is an important strategic objective because it imparts a potential for attractive and long-lived profitability.

The Four Tests of a Resource's Competitive Power
The competitive power of a resource or capability is measured by how many of the following four tests it can pass.[4] The first two tests determine whether a resource or capability can support a competitive advantage. The last two determine whether the competitive advantage can be sustained in the face of active competition.

1. *Is the resource (or capability) competitively valuable?* To be competitively valuable, a resource or capability must be directly relevant to the company's strategy, making the company a more effective competitor, able to exploit market opportunities and ward off external threats. Unless the resource contributes to the effectiveness of the company's strategy, it cannot pass this first test. An indicator of its effectiveness is whether the resource enables the company to strengthen its business model through a better customer value proposition and/or profit formula. Companies have to guard against contending that something they do well is necessarily competitively valuable. Apple's operating system for its PCs is by most accounts a world beater (compared to Windows Vista and Windows 7), but Apple has failed miserably in converting its strength in operating system design into competitive success in the global PC market—it is an also-ran with a paltry 3 to 5 percent market share worldwide.

2. *Is the resource rare—is it something rivals lack?* Resources and capabilities that are common among firms and widely available cannot be a source of competitive advantage. All makers of branded cereals have valuable marketing capabilities and brands, since the key success factors in the ready-to-eat cereal industry demand this. They are not rare. The brand strength of Cheerios, however, is uncommon and has provided General Mills with greater market share as well as the opportunity to benefit from brand extensions like Honey Nut Cheerios. A resource or capability is considered rare if it is held by only a small number of firms in an industry or specific competitive domain. Thus, while general management capabilities are not rare in an absolute sense, they are relatively rare in some of the less developed regions of the world and in some business domains.

3. *Is the resource hard to copy?* If a resource or capability is both valuable and rare, it will be competitively superior to comparable resources of rival firms. As such, it is a source of competitive advantage for the company. The more difficult and more costly it is for competitors to imitate, the more likely that it can also provide a *sustainable* competitive advantage. Resources tend to be difficult to copy when they are unique (a fantastic real estate location, patent-protected technology, an unusually talented and motivated labor force), when they must be built over time in ways that are difficult to imitate (a well-known brand name, mastery of a complex process technology, a global network of dealers and distributors), and when they entail financial outlays or large-scale operations that few industry members can undertake. Imitation is also difficult for resources that reflect a high level of *social complexity* (company culture, interpersonal

relationships among the managers or R&D teams, trust-based relations with customers or suppliers) and *causal ambiguity,* a term that signifies the hard-to-disentangle nature of the complex resources, such as a web of intricate processes enabling new drug discovery. Hard-to-copy resources and capabilities are important competitive assets, contributing to the longevity of a company's market position and offering the potential for sustained profitability.

4. *Can the resource be trumped by different types of resources and capabilities—are there good substitutes available for the resource?* Even resources and capabilities that are valuable, rare, and hard to copy can lose much of their competitive power if rivals have other types of resources and capabilities that are of equal or greater competitive power. A company may have the most technologically advanced and sophisticated plants in its industry, but any efficiency advantage it enjoys may be nullified if rivals are able to produce equally good products at lower cost by locating their plants in countries where wage rates are relatively low and a labor force with adequate skills is available.

> **CORE CONCEPTS**
>
> **Social complexity** and **causal ambiguity** are two factors that inhibit the ability of rivals to imitate a firm's most valuable resources and capabilities. Causal ambiguity makes it very hard to figure out how a complex resource contributes to competitive advantage and therefore exactly what to imitate.

The vast majority of companies are not well endowed with standout resources or capabilities, capable of passing all four tests with high marks. Most firms have a mixed bag of resources—one or two quite valuable, some good, many satisfactory to mediocre. Resources and capabilities that are valuable pass the first of the four tests. As key contributors to the efficiency and effectiveness of the strategy, they are relevant to the firm's competitiveness but are no guarantee of competitive advantage. They may offer no more than competitive parity with competing firms.

Passing both of the first two tests requires more—it requires resources and capabilities that are not only valuable but also rare. This is a much higher hurdle that can be cleared only by resources and capabilities that are *competitively superior.* Resources and capabilities that are competitively superior are the company's true strategic assets.[5] They provide the company with a competitive advantage over its competitors, if only in the short run.

To pass the last two tests, a resource must be able to maintain its competitive superiority in the face of competition. It must be resistant to imitative attempts and efforts by competitors to find equally valuable substitute resources. Assessing the availability of substitutes is the most difficult of all the tests since substitutes are harder to recognize, but the key is to look for resources or capabilities held by other firms that *can serve the same function* as the company's core resources and capabilities.[6]

Very few firms have resources and capabilities that can pass these tests, but those that do enjoy a sustainable competitive advantage with far greater profit potential. Walmart is a notable example, with capabilities in logistics and supply chain management that have surpassed those of its competitors for over 30 years. Lincoln Electric Company, less well known but no less notable in its achievements, has been the world leader in welding products for over 100 years as a result of its unique piecework incentive system for compensating production workers and the unsurpassed worker productivity and product quality that this system has fostered.

A Company's Resources and Capabilities Must Be Managed Dynamically

Even companies like Walmart and Lincoln Electric cannot afford to rest on their laurels. Rivals that are initially unable to replicate a key resource may develop better and better substitutes over time. Resources and capabilities can depreciate like other assets if they are managed with benign neglect. Disruptive environmental change can also destroy the value of key strategic assets, turning resources and capabilities "from diamonds to rust."[7] Some resources lose their clout quickly when there are rapid changes in technology, customer preferences, distribution channels, or other competitive factors.

> A company requires a dynamically evolving portfolio of resources and capabilities to sustain its competitiveness and help drive improvements in its performance.

For a company's resources and capabilities to have *durable* value, they must be continually refined, updated, and sometimes augmented with altogether new kinds of expertise. Not only are rival companies endeavoring to sharpen and recalibrate their capabilities, but customer needs and expectations are also undergoing constant change. Organizational capabilities grow stale unless they are kept freshly honed and on the cutting edge.[8] A company's resources and capabilities are far more competitively potent when they are (1) in sync with changes in the company's own strategy and its efforts to achieve a resource-based competitive advantage and (2) fully supportive of company efforts to attract customers and combat competitors' newly launched offensives to win bigger sales and market shares. Management's challenge in managing the firm's resources and capabilities dynamically has two elements: attending to ongoing recalibration of existing competitive assets and casting a watchful eye for opportunities to develop totally new kinds of capabilities.

The Role of Dynamic Capabilities   Companies that know the importance of recalibrating and upgrading their most valuable resources and capabilities ensure that these activities are done on a continual basis. By incorporating these activities into their routine managerial functions, they gain the experience necessary to be able to do them consistently well. At that point, their ability to freshen and renew their competitive assets becomes a capability in itself—a **dynamic capability.** A dynamic capability is the ability to modify or augment the company's existing resources and capabilities.[9] This includes the capacity to improve existing resources and capabilities incrementally, in the way that 3M continually upgrades the R&D resources driving its product innovation strategy. It also includes the capacity to add new resources and capabilities to the company's competitive asset portfolio. An example is Pfizer's acquisition capabilities, which have enabled it to replace degraded resources such as expiring patents with newly acquired capabilities in biotechnology.

QUESTION 3: IS THE COMPANY ABLE TO SEIZE MARKET OPPORTUNITIES AND NULLIFY EXTERNAL THREATS?

An essential element in evaluating a company's overall situation entails examining the company's resources and competitive capabilities in terms of the degree to which they enable it to pursue its best market opportunities and defend against the external threats to its future well-being. The simplest and most easily applied tool for conducting this examination is widely known as *SWOT analysis*, so named because it zeros in on a company's internal **S**trengths and **W**eaknesses, market **O**pportunities, and external **T**hreats. Just as important, a first-rate SWOT analysis provides the basis for crafting a strategy that capitalizes on the company's resource strengths, overcomes its resource weaknesses, aims squarely at capturing the company's best opportunities, and defends against the threats to its future well-being.

Identifying a Company's Internal Strengths

A *strength* is something a company is good at doing or an attribute that enhances its competitiveness in the marketplace. A company's strengths depend on the quality of its resources and capabilities. Resource and capability analysis provides a way for managers to assess the quality objectively. While resources and capabilities that pass the four tests of sustainable competitive advantage are among the company's greatest strengths, other types can be counted among the company's strengths as well. A capability that is not potent enough to produce a sustainable advantage over rivals may yet enable a series of temporary advantages if used as a basis for entry into a new market or market segment. A resource bundle that fails to match those of top-tier competitors may still allow a company to compete successfully against the second tier.

Assessing a Company's Competencies—What Activities Does It Perform Well?
One way to appraise the degree of a company's strengths has to do with the company's competence level in performing key pieces of its business—such as supply chain management, R&D, production, distribution, sales and marketing, and customer service. Which activities does it perform especially well? And are there any activities it performs better than rivals? A company's proficiency in conducting different facets of its operations can range from a mere competence in performing an activity to a core competence to a distinctive competence.

A **competence** is an internal activity an organization performs with proficiency—a capability, in other words. A **core competence** is a proficiently performed internal activity that is *central* to a company's strategy and competitiveness. Ben & Jerry's Ice Cream, a subsidiary of Unilever, has a core competence in creating unusual flavors of ice cream and marketing them with catchy names like Chunky Monkey, Chubby Hubby, Cherry Garcia, Karamel Sutra, Imagine Whirled Peace, and Phish Food. A core competence is a more competitively valuable company strength than a competence because of the activity's key role in the company's strategy and the contribution it makes to the company's market success and profitability. Often, core competencies can be leveraged to create new markets or new product demand, as the engine behind a company's growth. 3M Corporation has a core competence in product innovation—its record of introducing new products goes back several decades and new product introduction is central to 3M's strategy of growing its business.

A **distinctive competence** is a competitively valuable activity that a company *performs better than its rivals.* A distinctive competence thus signifies greater proficiency than a core competence. Because a distinctive competence represents a level of proficiency that rivals do not have, it qualifies as a *competitively superior strength* with competitive advantage potential. This is particularly true when the distinctive competence enables

LO 3
Discover how to assess the company's strengths and weaknesses in light of market opportunities and external threats.

SWOT analysis is a simple but powerful tool for sizing up a company's strengths and weaknesses, its market opportunities, and the external threats to its future well-being.

Basing a company's strategy on its most competitively valuable resource and capability strengths gives the company its best chance for market success.

CORE CONCEPT

A **competence** is an activity that a company has learned to perform with proficiency—a capability, in other words.

CORE CONCEPT

A **core competence** is an activity that a company performs proficiently that is also central to its strategy and competitive success.

CORE CONCEPT

A **distinctive competence** is a competitively important activity that a company performs better than its rivals—it thus represents *a competitively superior internal strength.*

CORE CONCEPT

A company's **strengths** represent its competitive assets; its **weaknesses** are shortcomings that constitute competitive liabilities.

a company to deliver standout value to customers (in the form of lower prices, better product performance, or superior service). For instance, Apple has a distinctive competence in product innovation, as exemplified by its iPod, iPhone, and iPad products.

The conceptual differences between a competence, a core competence, and a distinctive competence draw attention to the fact that a company's strengths and competitive assets are not all equal.[10] Some competencies merely enable market survival because most rivals have them—indeed, not having a competence or capability that rivals have can result in competitive disadvantage. If an apparel company does not have the competence to produce its apparel items very cost-efficiently, it is unlikely to survive given the intensely price-competitive nature of the apparel industry. Every Web retailer requires a basic competence in designing an appealing and user-friendly Web site. Core competencies are *competitively* more important strengths than competencies because they are central to the company's strategy. Distinctive competencies are even more competitively important. Because a distinctive competence is a competitively valuable capability that is unmatched by rivals, it can propel the company to greater market success and profitability. A distinctive competence is thus potentially the mainspring of a company's success—unless it is trumped by other, even more powerful types of competencies that rivals hold.

Identifying Company Weaknesses and Competitive Deficiencies

A **weakness,** or *competitive deficiency,* is something a company lacks or does poorly (in comparison to others) or a condition that puts it at a competitive disadvantage in the marketplace. A company's internal weaknesses can relate to (1) inferior or unproven skills, expertise, or intellectual capital in competitively important areas of the business; (2) deficiencies in competitively important physical, organizational, or intangible assets; or (3) missing or competitively inferior capabilities in key areas. *Company weaknesses are thus internal shortcomings that constitute competitive liabilities.* Nearly all companies have competitive liabilities of one kind or another. Whether a company's internal weaknesses make it competitively vulnerable depends on how much they matter in the marketplace and whether they are offset by the company's strengths.

Table 4.3 lists many of the things to consider in compiling a company's strengths and weaknesses. Sizing up a company's complement of strengths and deficiencies is akin to constructing a *strategic balance sheet,* where strengths represent *competitive assets* and weaknesses represent *competitive liabilities.* Obviously, the ideal condition is for the company's competitive assets to outweigh its competitive liabilities by an ample margin—a 50-50 balance is definitely not the desired condition!

Identifying a Company's Market Opportunities

Market opportunity is a big factor in shaping a company's strategy. Indeed, managers can't properly tailor strategy to the company's situation without first identifying its market opportunities and appraising the growth and profit potential each one holds. Depending on the prevailing circumstances, a company's opportunities can be plentiful or scarce, fleeting or lasting, and can range from wildly attractive (an absolute "must" to pursue) to marginally interesting (because of the high risks or questionable profit potentials) to unsuitable (because the company's strengths are ill-suited to successfully capitalizing on the opportunities). A sampling of potential market opportunities is shown in Table 4.3.

Newly emerging and fast-changing markets sometimes present stunningly big or "golden" opportunities, but it is typically hard for managers at one company to peer into "the fog of the future" and spot them much ahead of managers at other companies.[11] But as the fog begins to clear, golden opportunities are nearly always seized rapidly— and the companies that seize them are usually those that have been actively waiting, staying alert with diligent market reconnaissance, and preparing themselves to capitalize on shifting market conditions by patiently assembling an arsenal of competitively valuable resources— talented personnel, technical know-how, strategic partnerships, and a war chest of cash to finance aggressive action when the time comes.[12] In mature markets, unusually attractive market opportunities emerge sporadically, often after long periods of relative calm—but future market conditions may be more predictable, making emerging opportunities easier for industry members to detect.

> A company is well advised to pass on a particular market opportunity unless it has or can acquire the competencies needed to capture it.

In evaluating a company's market opportunities and ranking their attractiveness, managers have to guard against viewing every *industry* opportunity as a *company* opportunity. Not every company is equipped with the competencies to successfully pursue each opportunity that exists in its industry. Some companies are more capable of going after particular opportunities than others, and a few companies may be hopelessly outclassed. *The market opportunities most relevant to a company are those that match up well with the company's competitive assets, offer the best growth and profitability, and present the most potential for competitive advantage.*

Identifying the Threats to a Company's Future Profitability

Often, certain factors in a company's external environment pose *threats* to its profitability and competitive well-being. Threats can stem from the emergence of cheaper or better technologies, rivals' introduction of new or improved products, the entry of lower-cost foreign competitors into a company's market stronghold, new regulations that are more burdensome to a company than to its competitors, vulnerability to a rise in interest rates or tight credit conditions, the potential of a hostile takeover, unfavorable demographic shifts, adverse changes in foreign exchange rates, political upheaval in a foreign country where the company has facilities, and the like. A list of potential threats to a company's future profitability and market position is shown in Table 4.3.

External threats may pose no more than a moderate degree of adversity (all companies confront some threatening elements in the course of doing business), or they may be so imposing as to make a company's situation and outlook quite tenuous. On rare occasions, market shocks can give birth to a *sudden-death* threat that throws a company into an immediate crisis and a battle to survive. Many of the world's major airlines were plunged into an unprecedented financial crisis by the perfect storm of 9/11, rising prices for jet fuel, mounting competition

Table 4.3 **What to Look For in Identifying a Company's Strengths, Weaknesses, Opportunities, and Threats**

Potential Strengths and Competitive Assets	Potential Weaknesses and Competitive Deficiencies
• Competencies that are well matched to industry key success factors • Strong financial condition; ample financial resources to grow the business • Strong brand-name image/company reputation • Attractive customer base • Proprietary technology/superior technological skills/ important patents • Superior intellectual capital • Skills in advertising and promotion • Strong bargaining power over suppliers or buyers • Product innovation capabilities • Proven capabilities in improving production processes • Good supply chain management capabilities • Good customer service capabilities • Superior product quality • Wide geographic coverage and/or strong global distribution capability • Alliances/joint ventures that provide access to valuable technology, competencies, and/or attractive geographic markets • A product that is strongly differentiated from those of rivals • Cost advantages over rivals • Core competencies in _____ • A distinctive competence in _____ • Resources that are hard to copy and for which there are no good substitutes	• Competencies that are not well-matched to industry key success factors • In the wrong strategic group • Losing market share because _____ • Lack of attention to customer needs • Weak balance sheet, short on financial resources to grow the firm, too much debt; • Higher overall unit costs relative to those of key competitors • Weak or unproven product innovation capabilities • A product/service with ho-hum attributes or features inferior to the offerings of rivals • Too narrow a product line relative to rivals • Weak brand image or reputation • Weaker dealer network than key rivals and/or lack of adequate global distribution capability • Behind on product quality, R&D, and/or technological know-how • Lack of management depth • Inferior intellectual capital relative to rivals • Plagued with internal operating problems or obsolete facilities • Too much underutilized plant capacity • No well-developed or proven core competencies • No distinctive competencies or competitively superior resources • Resources that are readily copied or for which there are good substitutes • No clear strategic direction

Potential Market Opportunities	Potential External Threats to a Company's Future Profitability
• Openings to win market share from rivals • Sharply rising buyer demand for the industry's product • Serving additional customer groups or market segments • Expanding into new geographic markets • Expanding the company's product line to meet a broader range of customer needs • Utilizing existing company skills or technological know-how to enter new product lines or new businesses • Online sales via the Internet • Integrating forward or backward • Falling trade barriers in attractive foreign markets • Acquiring rival firms or companies with attractive technological expertise or capabilities • Entering into alliances or joint ventures to expand the firm's market coverage or boost its competitive capability • Openings to exploit emerging new technologies	• Increasing intensity of competition among industry rivals—may squeeze profit margins • Slowdowns in market growth • Likely entry of potent new competitors • Loss of sales to substitute products • Growing bargaining power of customers or suppliers • Vulnerability to industry driving forces • Shift in buyer needs and tastes away from the industry's product • Adverse demographic changes that threaten to curtail demand for the industry's product • Adverse economic conditions that threaten critical suppliers or distributers • Changes in technology—particularly disruptive technology that can undermine the company's distinctive competencies • Restrictive foreign trade policies • Costly new regulatory requirements • Tight credit conditions • Rising prices on energy or other key inputs

from low-fare carriers, shifting traveler preferences for low fares as opposed to lots of in-flight amenities, and higher labor costs. Similarly, the global economic crisis that began with the mortgage lenders, banks, and insurance companies has produced shock waves from which few industries have been insulated, causing even strong performers like General Electric to falter. While not all crises can be anticipated, it is management's job to identify the threats to the company's future prospects and to evaluate what strategic actions can be taken to neutralize or lessen their impact.

What Do the SWOT Listings Reveal?

SWOT analysis involves more than making four lists. The two most important parts of SWOT analysis are *drawing conclusions* from the SWOT listings about the company's overall situation and *translating these conclusions into strategic actions* to better match the company's strategy to its internal strengths and market opportunities, to correct important weaknesses, and to defend against external threats. Figure 4.2 shows the steps involved in gleaning insights from SWOT analysis.

> Simply making lists of a company's strengths, weaknesses, opportunities, and threats is not enough; the payoff from SWOT analysis comes from the conclusions about a company's situation and the implications for strategy improvement that flow from the four lists.

Figure 4.2   **The Steps Involved in SWOT Analysis: Identify the Four Components of SWOT, Draw Conclusions, Translate Implications into Strategic Actions**

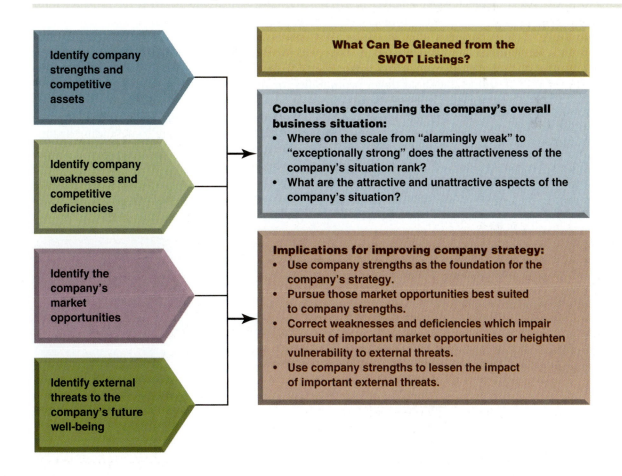

Just what story the SWOT listings tell about the company's overall situation is often revealed in the answers to the following set of questions:

- What aspects of the company's situation are particularly attractive?
- What aspects are of the most concern?
- All things considered, where on a scale of 1 to 10 (where 1 is alarmingly weak and 10 is exceptionally strong) do the company's overall situation and future prospects rank?
- Are the company's internal strengths and competitive assets powerful enough to enable it to compete successfully?
- Are the company's weaknesses and competitive deficiencies mostly inconsequential and readily correctable, or could one or more prove fatal if not remedied soon?
- Do the company's strengths and competitive assets outweigh its weaknesses and competitive liabilities by an attractive margin?
- Does the company have attractive market opportunities that are well suited to its internal strengths? Does the company lack the competitive assets to pursue any of the most attractive opportunities?
- Are the threats alarming, or are they something the company appears able to deal with and defend against?

The final piece of SWOT analysis is to translate the diagnosis of the company's situation into actions for improving the company's strategy and business prospects. *A company's internal strengths should always serve as the basis of its strategy— placing heavy reliance on a company's best competitive assets is the soundest route to attracting customers and competing successfully against rivals.*[13] As a rule, strategies that place heavy demands on areas where the company is weakest or has unproven competencies are suspect and should be avoided. Plainly, managers have to look toward correcting competitive weaknesses that make the company vulnerable, hold down profitability, or disqualify it from pursuing an attractive opportunity. Furthermore, strategy has to be aimed squarely at capturing those market opportunities that are most attractive and suited to the company's collection of competencies. How much attention to devote to defending against external threats to the company's market position and future performance hinges on how vulnerable the company is, whether there are attractive defensive moves that can be taken to lessen their impact, and whether the costs of undertaking such moves represent the best use of company competitive assets.

QUESTION 4: ARE THE COMPANY'S PRICES AND COSTS COMPETITIVE WITH THOSE OF KEY RIVALS, AND DOES IT HAVE AN APPEALING CUSTOMER VALUE PROPOSITION?

Company managers are often stunned when a competitor cuts its price to "unbelievably low" levels or when a new market entrant comes on strong with a very low price. The competitor may not, however, be "dumping" (an economic term for selling at prices that are below cost), buying its way into the market with a super-low price, or waging a desperate move to gain sales—it may simply have substantially lower costs. One of the most telling signs of whether a company's business position is strong or precarious is whether its prices and costs can remain competitive with industry rivals. For a company to retain its market share, its costs must be *in line* with those of close rivals selling similar quality products.

While less common, new entrants can also storm the market with a product that ratchets the quality level up so high that customers will abandon competing sellers even if they have to pay more for the new product. With its vastly greater storage capacity and lightweight, cool design, Apple's iPod left other makers of portable digital music players in the dust when it was first introduced. By introducing new models with even more attractive features, Apple has continued its worldwide dominance of this market. Apple's new iPad appears to be doing the same in the market for e-readers and tablet PCs.

Regardless of where on the quality spectrum a company competes, it must also remain competitive in terms of its customer value proposition in order to stay in the game. Tiffany's value proposition, for example, remains attractive to customers who want customer service, the assurance of quality, and a high-status brand despite the availability of cut-rate diamond jewelry online. Target's customer value proposition has withstood the Walmart low-price juggernaut by attention to product design, image, and attractive store layouts in addition to efficiency.

The value provided to the customer depends on how well a customer's needs are met for the price paid. How well customer needs are met depends on the perceived quality of a product or service as well as other, more tangible attributes. The greater the amount of customer value that the company can offer profitably compared to its rivals, the less vulnerable it will be to competitive attack. For managers, the key is to keep close track of how *cost effectively* the company can deliver value to customers relative to its competitors. If they can deliver the same amount of value with lower expenditures (or more value at the same cost), they will maintain a competitive edge.

Two analytical tools are particularly useful in determining whether a company's prices, costs, and customer value proposition are competitive: value chain analysis and benchmarking.

The Concept of a Company Value Chain

Every company's business consists of a collection of activities undertaken in the course of designing, producing, marketing, delivering, and supporting its product or service. All the various activities that a company performs internally combine to form a **value chain**—so called because the underlying intent of a company's activities is to do things that ultimately *create value for buyers.*

As shown in Figure 4.3, a company's value chain consists of two broad categories of activities: the *primary activities* that are foremost in creating value for customers and the requisite *support activities* that facilitate and enhance the performance of the primary activities.[14] The exact nature of the primary and secondary activities that make up a company's value chain

LO 4

Grasp how a company's value chain activities can affect the company's cost structure, degree of differentiation, and competitive advantage.

The higher a company's costs are above those of close rivals, the more competitively vulnerable it becomes.

The greater the amount of customer value that a company can offer profitably relative to close rivals, the less competitively vulnerable it becomes.

CORE CONCEPT

A company's **value chain** identifies the primary activities that create customer value and the related support activities.

vary according to the specifics of a company's business; hence, the listing of the primary and support activities in Figure 4.3 is illustrative rather than definitive. For example, the primary value-creating activities for a manufacturer of bakery goods, such as Pepperidge Farm, include supply chain management, baking and packaging operations, distribution, and sales and marketing but are unlikely to include service. Its support activities include quality control as well as product R&D, human resource management, and administration. For a department store retailer, such as Macy's, customer service is included among its primary activities, along with merchandise selection and buying, store layout and product display, and advertising; its support activities include site selection, hiring and training, and store maintenance, plus the usual assortment of administrative activities. For a hotel chain like Marriot, the primary activities and costs are in site selection and construction, reservations, operation of its hotel properties, and marketing; principal support activities include accounting, hiring and training hotel staff, supply chain management, and general administration.

With its focus on value-creating activities, the value chain is an ideal tool for examining how a company delivers on its customer value proposition. It permits a deep look at the company's cost structure and ability to offer low prices. It reveals the emphasis that a company places on activities that enhance differentiation and support higher prices, such as service and marketing. Note that there is also a profit margin component to the value chain; this is because profits are necessary to compensate the company's owners/shareholders and investors, who bear risks and provide capital. Tracking the profit margin along with the value-creating activities is critical because unless an enterprise succeeds in delivering customer value profitably (with a sufficient return on invested capital), it can't survive for long. This is the essence of a sound business model.

Illustration Capsule 4.1 shows representative costs for various activities performed by Just Coffee, a cooperative producer and roaster of fair-trade organic coffee.

Comparing the Value Chains of Rival Companies The primary purpose of value chain analysis is to facilitate a comparison, activity-by-activity, of how effectively and efficiently a company delivers value to its customers, relative to its competitors. Segregating the company's operations into different types of primary and secondary activities is the first step in this comparison. The next is to do the same for the company's most significant competitors.

Even rivals in the same industry may differ significantly in terms of the activities they perform. For instance, the "operations" component of the value chain for a manufacturer that makes all of its own parts and components and assembles them into a finished product differs from the "operations" of a rival producer that buys the needed parts and components from outside suppliers and only performs assembly operations. How each activity is performed may affect a company's relative cost position as well as its capacity for differentiation. Thus, even a simple comparison of how the activities of rivals' value chains differ can be revealing of competitive differences.

A Company's Primary and Secondary Activities Identify the Major Components of Its Internal Cost Structure Each activity in the value chain gives rise to costs and ties up assets. For a company to remain competitive, it is critical for it to perform its activities cost-effectively,

Figure 4.3   A Representative Company Value Chain

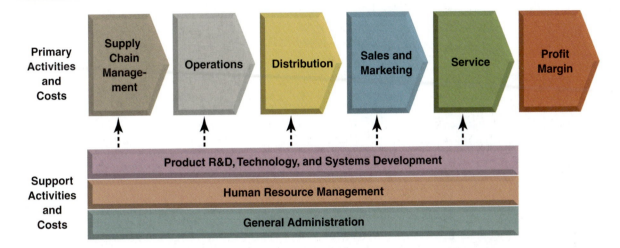

PRIMARY ACTIVITIES

- **Supply Chain Management**—Activities, costs, and assets associated with purchasing fuel, energy, raw materials, parts and components, merchandise, and consumable items from vendors; receiving, storing, and disseminating inputs from suppliers; inspection; and inventory management.

- **Operations**—Activities, costs, and assets associated with converting inputs into final product form (production, assembly, packaging, equipment maintenance, facilities, operations, quality assurance, environmental protection).

- **Distribution**—Activities, costs, and assets dealing with physically distributing the product to buyers (finished goods warehousing, order processing, order picking and packing, shipping, delivery vehicle operations, establishing and maintaining a network of dealers and distributors).

- **Sales and Marketing**—Activities, costs, and assets related to sales force efforts, advertising and promotion, market research and planning, and dealer/distributor support.

- **Service**—Activities, costs, and assets associated with providing assistance to buyers, such as installation, spare parts delivery, maintenance and repair, technical assistance, buyer inquiries, and complaints.

SUPPORT ACTIVITIES

- **Product R&D, Technology, and Systems Development**—Activities, costs, and assets relating to product R&D, process R&D, process design improvement, equipment design, computer software development, telecommunications systems, computer-assisted design and engineering, database capabilities, and development of computerized support systems.

- **Human Resources Management**—Activities, costs, and assets associated with the recruitment, hiring, training, development, and compensation of all types of personnel; labor relations activities; and development of knowledge-based skills and core competencies.

- **General Administration**—Activities, costs, and assets relating to general management, accounting and finance, legal and regulatory affairs, safety and security, management information systems, forming strategic alliances and collaborating with strategic partners, and other "overhead" functions.

Source: Based on the discussion in Michael E. Porter, *Competitive Advantage* (New York: Free Press, 1985), pp. 37–43.

The Value Chain for Just Coffee, a Producer of Fair-Trade Organic Coffee

Value Chain Activities and Costs in Producing, Roasting, and Selling a Pound of Fair-Trade Organic Coffee	
1. Average cost of procuring the coffee from coffee-grower cooperatives	$2.30
2. Import fees, storage costs, and freight charges	.73
3. Labor cost of roasting and bagging	.89
4. Cost of labels and bag	.45
5. Average overhead costs	3.03
6. Total company costs	$7.40
7. Average retail markup over company costs (company operating profit)	2.59
8. Average price to consumer at retail	$9.99

Source: Developed by the authors with help from Jonathan D. Keith from information on Just Coffee's Web site, www.justcoffee.coop/the_coffee_dollar_breakdown (accessed June 16, 2010).

regardless of which it chooses to emphasize. Once the major value chain activities are identified, the next step is to evaluate the company's cost competitiveness using what accountants call *activity-based costing* to determine the costs of performing each value chain activity (and assets required, including working capital).[15] The degree to which a company's costs should be disaggregated into specific activities depends on how valuable it is to develop cost data for narrowly defined activities as opposed to broadly defined activities. Generally speaking, cost estimates are needed at least for each broad category of primary and secondary activities, but finer classifications may be needed if a company discovers that it has a cost disadvantage vis-à-vis rivals and wants to pin down the exact source or activity causing the disadvantage. Quite often, there are links between activities such that the manner in which one activity is done can affect the costs of performing other activities. For instance, how an automobile is designed has a huge impact on the number of different parts and components, their respective manufacturing costs, and the expense of assembling the various parts and components into a finished product.

The combined costs of all the various activities in a company's value chain define the company's internal cost structure. Further, the cost of each activity contributes to whether the company's overall cost position relative to rivals is favorable or unfavorable. But a company's own internal costs are insufficient to assess whether its costs are competitive with those of rivals. Cost and price differences among competing companies can have their origins in activities performed by suppliers or by distribution allies involved in getting the product to the final customer or end user of the product, in which case the company's entire value chain system becomes relevant.

The Value Chain System for an Entire Industry

A company's value chain is embedded in a larger system of activities that includes the value chains of its suppliers and the value chains of whatever wholesale distributors and retailers it utilizes in getting its product or service to end users. This *value chain system* has implications that extend far beyond the company's costs. It can affect attributes like product quality that enhance differentiation and have importance for the company's customer value proposition as well as its profitability.[16] Suppliers' value chains are relevant because suppliers perform activities and incur costs in creating and delivering the purchased inputs utilized in a company's own value-creating activities. The costs, performance features, and quality of these inputs influence a company's own costs and product differentiation capabilities. Anything a company can do to help its suppliers' drive down the costs of their value chain activities or improve the quality and performance of the items being supplied can enhance its own competitiveness—a powerful reason for working collaboratively with suppliers in managing supply chain activities.[17]

> A company's cost competitiveness depends not only on the costs of internally performed activities (its own value chain) but also on costs in the value chains of its suppliers and distribution channel allies.

Similarly, the value chains of a company's distribution channel partners are relevant because (1) the costs and margins of a company's distributors and retail dealers are part of the price the ultimate consumer pays and (2) the activities that distribution allies perform affect sales volumes and customer satisfaction. For these reasons, companies normally work closely with their distribution allies (who are their direct customers) to perform value chain activities in mutually beneficial ways. For instance, motor vehicle manufacturers have a competitive interest in working closely with their automobile dealers to promote higher sales volumes and better customer satisfaction with dealers' repair and maintenance services. Producers of bathroom fixtures are heavily dependent on the sales and promotional activities of their distributors and building supply retailers and on whether distributors/retailers operate cost-effectively enough to be able to sell at prices that lead to attractive sales volumes.

As a consequence, *accurately assessing a company's competitiveness entails scrutinizing the nature and costs of value chain activities throughout the entire value chain system for delivering its products or services to end-use customers.* A typical industry value chain system that incorporates the value chains of suppliers and forward channel allies (if any) is shown in Figure 4.4. As was the case with company value chains, the specific activities constituting industry value chains also vary significantly. The primary value chain system activities in the pulp and paper industry (timber farming, logging, pulp mills, and papermaking) differ from the primary value chain system activities in the home appliance industry (parts and components manufacture, assembly, wholesale distribution, retail sales). The value chain system in the soft-drink industry (syrup manufacture, bottling and can filling, wholesale distribution, advertising, and retail merchandising) differs from that in the computer software industry (programming, disk loading, marketing, distribution).

Figure 4.4 Representative Value Chain System for an Entire Industry

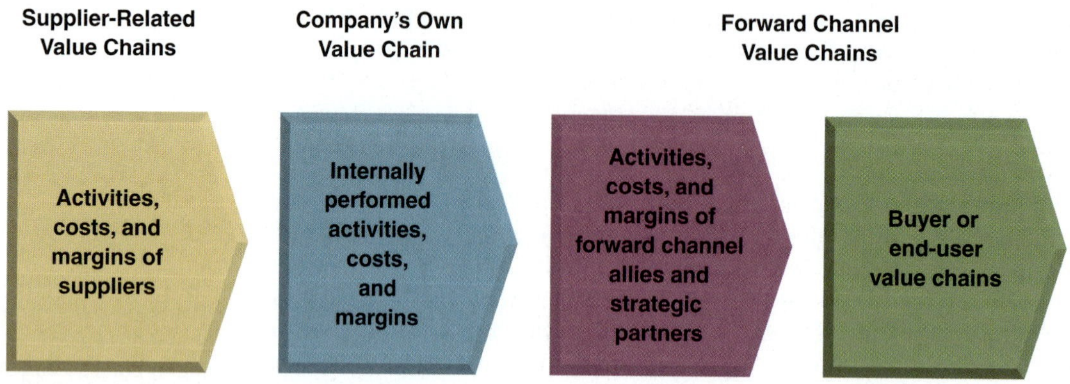

**Supplier-Related
Value Chains**

**Company's Own
Value Chain**

**Forward Channel
Value Chains**

Activities,
costs, and
margins of
suppliers

Internally
performed
activities,
costs,
and
margins

Activities,
costs, and
margins of
forward channel
allies and
strategic
partners

Buyer or
end-user
value chains

Source: Based in part on the single-industry value chain displayed in Michael E. Porter, *Competitive Advantage* (New York: Free Press, 1985), p. 35.

Benchmarking: A Tool for Assessing Whether the Costs and Effectiveness of a Company's Value Chain Activities Are in Line

Once a company has developed good estimates for the costs and effectiveness of each of the major activities in its own value chain and has sufficient data relating to the value chain activities of suppliers and distribution allies, then it is ready to explore how it compares on these dimensions with key rivals. This is where benchmarking comes in. **Benchmarking** entails comparing how different companies perform various value chain activities—how inventories are managed, how products are assembled, how fast the company can get new products to market, how customer orders are filled and shipped—and then making cross-company comparisons of the costs and effectiveness of these activities.[18] The objectives of benchmarking are to identify the best practices in performing an activity, to learn how other companies have actually achieved lower costs or better results in performing benchmarked activities, and to take action to improve a company's competitiveness whenever benchmarking reveals that its costs and results of performing an activity are not on a par with what other companies have achieved.

Xerox became one of the first companies to use benchmarking in 1979 when Japanese manufacturers began selling midsize copiers in the United States for $9,600 each—less than Xerox's production costs.[19] Xerox management suspected its Japanese competitors were dumping, but it sent a team of line managers to Japan, including the head of manufacturing, to study competitors' business processes and costs. With the aid of Xerox's joint venture partner in Japan, Fuji-Xerox, which knew the competitors well, the team found that Xerox's costs were excessive due to gross inefficiencies in the company's manufacturing processes and business practices. The findings triggered a major internal effort at Xerox to become cost-competitive and prompted Xerox to begin benchmarking 67 of its key work processes against companies identified as employing the best practices. Xerox quickly decided not to restrict its benchmarking efforts to its office equipment rivals but to extend them to any company regarded as "world class" in performing *any activity* relevant to Xerox's business. Other companies quickly picked up on Xerox's approach. Toyota managers got their idea for just-in-time inventory deliveries by studying how U.S. supermarkets replenished their shelves. Southwest Airlines reduced the turnaround time of its aircraft at each scheduled stop by studying pit crews on the auto racing circuit. Over 80 percent of Fortune 500 companies reportedly use benchmarking for comparing themselves against rivals on cost and other competitively important measures.

The tough part of benchmarking is not whether to do it but rather how to gain access to information about other companies' practices and costs. Sometimes benchmarking can be accomplished by collecting information from published reports, trade groups, and industry research firms or by talking to knowledgeable industry analysts, customers, and suppliers. Sometimes field trips to the facilities of competing or noncompeting companies can be arranged to observe how things are done, ask questions, compare practices and processes, and perhaps exchange data on productivity, staffing levels, time requirements, and other cost components—but the problem here is that such companies, even if they agree to host facilities tours and answer questions, are unlikely to share competitively sensitive cost information. Furthermore, comparing one company's costs to another's costs may not involve comparing apples to apples if the two companies employ different cost accounting principles to calculate the costs of particular activities.

> Benchmarking the costs of company activities against rivals provides hard evidence of whether a company is cost-competitive.

However, a third and fairly reliable source of benchmarking information has emerged. The explosive interest of companies in benchmarking costs and best practices has prompted numerous consulting firms and business organizations (e.g., Accenture, A.T. Kearney, Benchnet—The Benchmarking Exchange, Best Practices LLC, and the Strategic Planning Institute's Council on Benchmarking and Best Practices, LLC) to gather benchmarking data, distribute information about best practices, and provide comparative cost data without identifying the names of particular companies. Having an independent group gather the information and report it in a manner that disguises the names of individual companies protects competitively sensitive data and lessens the potential for unethical behavior on the part of company personnel in gathering their own data about competitors. Illustration Capsule 4.2 presents a widely recommended code of conduct for engaging in benchmarking.

Strategic Options for Remedying a Disadvantage in Costs or Effectiveness

Examining the costs of a company's own value chain activities and comparing them to rivals' indicates who has how much of a cost advantage or disadvantage and which cost components are responsible. Similarly, much can be learned by comparisons at the activity level of how effectively a company delivers on its value proposition relative to its competitors and which elements in its value chain system are responsible. Such information is vital in strategic actions to eliminate a cost disadvantage, deliver more customer value, enhance differentiation, and improve profitability. Such information can also help a company to recognize and reinforce activities in which it has a comparative advantage and to find

ILLUSTRATION CAPSULE 4.2

Benchmarking and Ethical Conduct

Because discussions between benchmarking partners can involve competitively sensitive data, conceivably raising questions about possible restraint of trade or improper business conduct, many benchmarking organizations urge all individuals and organizations involved in benchmarking to abide by a code of conduct grounded in ethical business behavior. One of the most widely used codes of conduct is the one developed by APQC (formerly the American Productivity and Quality Center) and advocated by the Qualserve Benchmarking Clearinghouse; it is based on the following principles and guidelines:

- Avoid discussions or actions that could lead to or imply an interest in restraint of trade, market and/or customer allocation schemes, price fixing, dealing arrangements, bid rigging, or bribery. Don't discuss costs with competitors if costs are an element of pricing.

- Refrain from the acquisition of trade secrets from another by any means that could be interpreted as improper, including the breach of any duty to maintain secrecy. Do not disclose or use any trade secret that may have been obtained through improper means or that was disclosed by another in violation of duty to maintain its secrecy or limit its use.

- Be willing to provide to your benchmarking partner the same type and level of information that you request from that partner.

- Communicate fully and early in the relationship to clarify expectations, avoid misunderstanding, and establish mutual interest in the benchmarking exchange.

- Be honest and complete with the information submitted.

- The use or communication of a benchmarking partner's name with the data obtained or practices observed requires the prior permission of the benchmarking partner.

- Honor the wishes of benchmarking partners regarding how the information that is provided will be handled and used.

- In benchmarking with competitors, establish specific ground rules up front. For example, "We don't want to talk about things that will give either of us a competitive advantage, but rather we want to see where we both can mutually improve or gain benefit."

- Check with legal counsel if any information-gathering procedure is in doubt. If uncomfortable, do not proceed. Alternatively, negotiate and sign a specific nondisclosure agreement that will satisfy the attorneys representing each partner.

- Do not ask competitors for sensitive data or cause benchmarking partners to feel they must provide data to continue the process.

- Use an ethical third party to assemble and "blind" competitive data, with inputs from legal counsel in direct competitor sharing. (Note: When cost is closely linked to price, sharing cost data can be considered to be the same as sharing price data.)

- Any information obtained from a benchmarking partner should be treated as internal, privileged communications. If "confidential" or proprietary material is to be exchanged, then a specific agreement should be executed to specify the content of the material that needs to be protected, the duration of the period of protection, the conditions for permitting access to the material, and the specific handling requirements necessary for that material.

Sources: APQC, www.apqc.org; Qualserve Benchmarking Clearinghouse, www.awwa.org (accessed October 8, 2010).

new avenues for enhancing its competitiveness through lower costs, greater differentiation, or a more attractive customer value proposition. There are three main areas in a company's total value chain system where company managers can try to improve its efficiency and effectiveness: (1) a company's own activity segments, (2) suppliers' part of the overall value chain, and (3) the distribution channel portion of the chain.

Improving the Efficiency and Effectiveness of Internally Performed Value Chain Activities   Managers can pursue any of several strategic approaches to reduce the costs of internally performed value chain activities and improve a company's cost competitiveness:[20]

1. Implement the use of best practices throughout the company, particularly for high-cost activities.
2. Redesign the product and/or some of its components to eliminate high-cost components or facilitate speedier and more economical manufacture or assembly—computer chip makers regularly design around the patents held by others to avoid paying royalties; automakers have substituted lower-cost plastic and rubber for metal at many exterior body locations.
3. Relocate high-cost activities (such as manufacturing) to geographic areas like Southeast Asia or Latin America or eastern Europe where they can be performed more cheaply.
4. See if certain internally performed activities can be outsourced from vendors or performed by contractors more cheaply than they can be done in-house.
5. Shift to lower-cost technologies and/or invest in productivity-enhancing, cost-saving technological improvements (robotics, flexible manufacturing techniques, state-of-the-art information systems).
6. Stop performing activities that add little or no customer value. Examples include seldom-used customer services, employee training programs that are of marginal value, and maintaining large raw-material or finished-goods inventories.

How successfully a company competes depends on more than low costs. It also depends on how effectively it delivers value to the customer and on its ability to differentiate itself from rivals. To improve the effectiveness of its customer value proposition and enhance differentiation, there are several approaches a manager can take:[21]

1. Implement the use of best practices for quality throughout the company, particularly for high-value activities (those that are important for creating value for the customer).
2. Adopt best practices and technologies that spur innovation, improve design, and enhance creativity.
3. Implement the use of best practices in providing customer service.
4. Reallocate resources to devote more to activities that will have the biggest impact on the value delivered to the customer and that address buyers' most important purchase criteria.
5. For intermediate buyers (distributors or retailers, for example), gain an understanding of how the activities the company performs impact the buyer's value chain. Improve the effectiveness of company activities that have the greatest impact on the efficiency or effectiveness of the buyer's value chain.
6. Adopt best practices for signaling the value of the product and for enhancing customer perceptions.

Improving the Efficiency and Effectiveness of Supplier-Related Value Chain Activities   Improving the efficiency and effectiveness of the value chain activities of suppliers can also address a company's competitive weaknesses with respect to costs and differentiation. On the cost side, a company can gain savings in suppliers' part of the overall value chain by pressuring suppliers for lower prices, switching to lower-priced substitute inputs, and collaborating closely with suppliers to identify mutual cost-saving opportunities.[22] For example, just-in-time deliveries from suppliers can lower a company's inventory and internal logistics costs and may also allow suppliers to economize on their warehousing, shipping, and production scheduling costs—a win-win outcome for both. In a few instances, companies may find that it is cheaper to integrate backward into the business of high-cost suppliers and make the item in-house instead of buying it from outsiders.

Similarly, a company can enhance its differentiation by working with or through its suppliers to do so. Some methods include selecting and retaining suppliers who meet higher-quality standards, coordinating with suppliers to enhance design or other features desired by customers, providing incentives to encourage suppliers to meet higher-quality standards, and assisting suppliers in their efforts to improve. Fewer defects in parts from suppliers not only improve quality and enhance differentiation throughout the value chain system but can lower costs as well since there is less waste and disruption to the production processes.

Improving the Efficiency and Effectiveness of Distribution-Related Value Chain Activities

Taking actions aimed at improvements with respect to the forward or downstream portion of the value chain system can also help to remedy a company's competitive disadvantage with respect to either costs or differentiation. Any of three means can be used to achieve better cost competitiveness in the forward portion of the industry value chain: (1) Pressure distributors, dealers, and other forward channel allies to reduce their costs and markups so as to make the final price to buyers more competitive with the prices of rivals; (2) collaborate with forward channel allies to identify win-win opportunities to reduce costs—a chocolate manufacturer, for example, learned that by shipping its bulk chocolate in liquid form in tank cars instead of as 10-pound molded bars, it could not only save its candy-bar manufacturing customers the costs associated with unpacking and melting but also eliminate its own costs of molding bars and packing them; and (3) change to a more economical distribution strategy, including switching to cheaper distribution channels (perhaps direct sales via the Internet) or perhaps integrating forward into company-owned retail outlets.

The means to enhance differentiation through activities at the forward end of the value chain system include (1) engaging in cooperative advertising and promotions with forward allies (dealers, distributors, retailers, etc.), (2) creating exclusive arrangements with downstream sellers or other mechanisms that increase their incentives to enhance delivered customer value, and (3) creating and enforcing standards for downstream activities and assisting in training channel partners in business practices. Harley-Davidson, for example, enhances the shopping experience and perceptions of buyers by selling through retailers that sell Harley-Davidson motorcycles exclusively and meet Harley-Davidson standards.

Translating Proficient Performance of Value Chain Activities into Competitive Advantage

Value chain analysis and benchmarking are not only useful for identifying and remedying competitive disadvantages; they can also be used to uncover and strengthen competitive advantages. A company's value-creating activities can offer a competitive advantage in one of two ways: (1) They can contribute to greater efficiency and lower costs relative to competitors, or (2) they can provide a basis for differentiation, so customers are willing to pay relatively more for the company's goods and services. A company that does a *first-rate job* of managing its value chain activities *relative to competitors* stands a good chance of profiting from its competitive advantage.

Achieving a cost-based competitive advantage requires determined management efforts to be cost-efficient in performing value chain activities. Such efforts have to be ongoing and persistent, and they have to involve each and every value chain activity. The goal must be continuous cost reduction, not a one-time or on-again–off-again effort. Companies whose managers are truly committed to low-cost performance of value chain activities and succeed in engaging company personnel to discover innovative ways to drive costs out of the business have a real chance of gaining a durable low-cost edge over rivals. It is not as easy as it seems to imitate a company's low-cost practices. Companies like Dollar General, Nucor Steel, Irish airline Ryanair, Greyhound Lines, and French discount retailer Carrefour have been highly successful in managing their values chains in a low-cost manner.

Ongoing and persistent efforts are also required for a competitive advantage based on differentiation. Superior reputations and brands are built up slowly over time, through continuous investment and activities that deliver consistent, reinforcing messages. Differentiation based on quality requires vigilant management of activities for quality assurance throughout the value chain. While the basis for differentiation (e.g., status, design, innovation, customer service, reliability, image) may vary widely among companies pursuing a differentiation advantage, companies that succeed do so on the basis of a commitment to coordinated value chain activities aimed purposefully at this objective. Examples include Grey Goose Vodka (status), IKEA (design), FedEx (reliability), 3M (innovation), Body Shop (image), and Nordstrom (customer service).

How Activities Relate to Resources and Capabilities There is a close relationship between the value-creating activities that a company performs and its resources and capabilities. An organizational capability or competence implies a *capacity* for action; in contrast, a value-creating activity *is* the action. With respect to resources and capabilities, activities are "where the rubber hits the road." When companies engage in a value-creating activity, they do so by drawing on specific company resources and capabilities that underlie and enable the activity. For example, brand-building activities depend on human resources, such as experienced brand managers (including their knowledge and expertise in this arena), as well as organizational capabilities in advertising and marketing. Cost-cutting activities may derive from organizational capabilities in inventory management, for example, and resources such as inventory tracking systems.

Because of this correspondence between activities and supporting resources and capabilities, value chain analysis can complement resource and capability analysis as tools for assessing a company's competitive advantage. Resources and capabilities that are *both valuable and rare* provide a company with *what it takes* for competitive advantage. For a company with competitive assets of this sort, the potential is there. When these assets are deployed in the form of a value-creating activity, that potential is realized due to their competitive superiority. Resource analysis is one tool for identifying competitively superior resources and capabilities. But their value and the competitive superiority of that value can only be assessed objectively *after* they are deployed. Value chain analysis and benchmarking provide the type of data needed to make that objective assessment.

There is also a dynamic relationship between a company's activities and its resources and capabilities. Value-creating activities are more than just the embodiment of a resource's or capability's potential. They also contribute to the formation and development of capabilities. The road to competitive advantage begins with management efforts to build organizational expertise in performing certain competitively important value chain activities. With consistent practice and continuous investment of company resources, these activities rise to the level of a reliable organizational capability or a competence. To the extent that top management makes the growing capability a cornerstone of the company's strategy, this capability becomes a core competence for the company. Later, with further organizational learning and gains in proficiency, the core competence may evolve into a distinctive competence, giving the company superiority over rivals in performing an important value chain activity. Such superiority, if it gives the company significant competitive clout in the marketplace, can produce an attractive competitive edge over rivals. Whether the resulting competitive advantage is on the cost side or on the differentiation side (or both) will depend on the company's choice of which types of competence-building activities to engage in over this time period, as shown in Figure 4.5.

> Performing value chain activities in ways that give a company the capabilities to either outmatch rivals on differentiation or beat them on costs will help the company to secure a competitive advantage.

QUESTION 5: IS THE COMPANY COMPETITIVELY STRONGER OR WEAKER THAN KEY RIVALS?

LO 5

Understand how a comprehensive evaluation of a company's competitive situation can assist managers in making critical decisions about their next strategic moves.

Resource and capability analysis together with value chain analysis and benchmarking will reveal whether a company has a competitive advantage over rivals on the basis of *individual* resources, capabilities, and activities. These tools can also be used to assess the competitive advantage attributable to a *bundle* of resources and capabilities. Resource bundles can sometimes pass the four tests of a resource's competitive power even when the individual components of the resource bundle cannot. For example, although Callaway Golf Company's engineering capabilities and market research capabilities are matched relatively well by rivals Cobra Golf and Ping Golf, the company's bundling of resources used in its product development process (including cross-functional development systems, technological capabilities, knowledge of consumer preferences, and a collaborative organizational culture) gives it a competitive advantage that has allowed it to remain the largest seller of golf equipment for more than a decade.

Resource analysis and value chain/benchmarking analysis of the company's resources, capabilities, and activities (both as individual entities and as bundles) are necessary for determining whether the company is competitively stronger or weaker than key rivals. But they are not sufficient for gaining a complete picture

Figure 4.5 **Translating Company Performance of Value Chain Activities into Competitive Advantage**

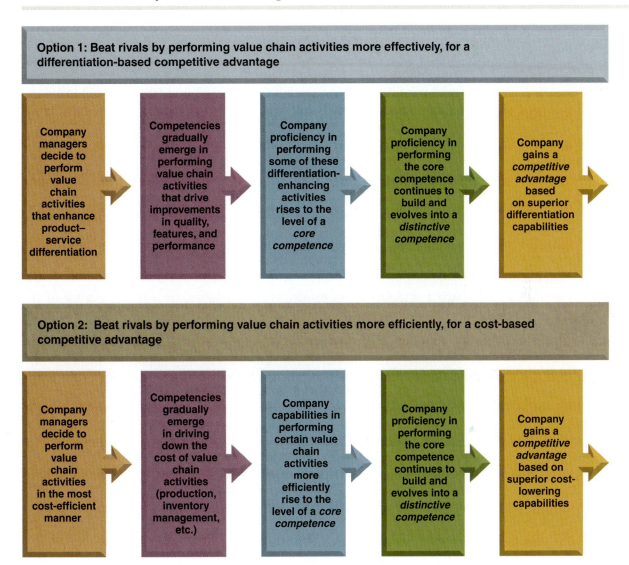

of a company's competitive situation. A more comprehensive assessment needs to be made of the company's *overall* competitive strengths and weaknesses since a competitive advantage along one part of its value chain can be overwhelmed by competitive disadvantages along other parts of the chain. In making an overall assessment of a company's competitiveness, the answers to two questions are of particular interest: First, how does the company rank relative to competitors on each of the important factors that determine market success? Second, all things considered, does the company have a *net* competitive advantage or disadvantage versus major competitors?

An easy-to-use method for answering these two questions involves developing quantitative strength ratings for the company and its key competitors on each industry key success factor and each competitively pivotal resource and capability. Much of the information needed for doing a competitive strength assessment comes from previous analyses. Industry and five-forces analyses reveal the key success factors and competitive forces that separate industry winners from losers. Analyzing benchmarking data and scouting key competitors provide a basis for judging the competitive strength of rivals on such factors as cost, key product attributes, customer service, image and reputation, financial strength, technological skills, distribution capability, and other resources and capabilities. Resource and capability analysis reveals which factors are competitively important, given the external situation. Together with value chain analysis, it also shines a light on the competitive strengths of the company. That is, it reveals whether the company or its rivals have the advantage with respect to competitively important resources, capabilities, and activities. The four tests of a resource's competitive power indicate, further, whether any of these advantages are sustainable. SWOT analysis provides a more comprehensive and forward-looking picture of the company's overall situation by surveying the entire set of its strengths and weaknesses in relation to rivals and the external environment.

Step 1 in doing a competitive strength assessment is to make a list of the industry's key success factors and most telling measures of competitive strength or weakness (6 to 10 measures usually suffice). Step 2 is to assign weights to each of the measures of competitive strength based on their perceived importance—it is highly unlikely that the different measures are equally important. In an industry where the products/services of rivals are virtually identical, for instance, having low unit costs relative to rivals is nearly always the most important determinant of competitive strength. In an industry with strong product differentiation, the most significant measures of competitive strength may be brand awareness, brand image and reputation, product attractiveness, and distribution capability. A weight could be as high as 0.75 (maybe even higher) in situations where one particular competitive variable is overwhelmingly decisive, or a weight could be as low as 0.20 when two or three strength measures are more important than the rest. Lesser competitive strength indicators can carry weights of 0.05 or 0.10. Whether the differences between the importance weights are big or little, *the sum of the weights must add up to 1.*

Step 3 is to rate the firm and its rivals on each competitive strength measure. Numerical rating scales (e.g., from 1 to 10) are best to use, although ratings of stronger (+), weaker (−), and about equal (=) may be appropriate when information is scanty and assigning numerical scores conveys false precision. Step 4 is to multiply each strength rating by its importance weight to obtain weighted strength scores (a strength rating of 4 times a weight of 0.20 gives a weighted strength score of 0.80). Step 5 is to sum the weighted scores on each measure to get overall weighted competitive strength ratings for each company. Step 6 is to use the overall strength ratings to draw conclusions about the size and extent of the company's net competitive advantage or disadvantage and to take specific note of areas of strength and weakness.

Table 4.4 provides an example of competitive strength assessment in which a hypothetical company (ABC Company) competes against two rivals. In the

Table 4.4   A Representative Weighted Competitive Strength Assessment

Key Success Factor/Strength Measure	Importance Weight	Competitive Strength Assessment (Rating scale: 1 = very weak; 10 = very strong)					
		ABC Co.		Rival 1		Rival 2	
		Strength Rating	Weighted Score	Strength Rating	Weighted Score	Strength Rating	Weighted Score
Quality/product performance	0.10	8	0.80	5	0.50	1	0.10
Reputation/image	0.10	8	0.80	7	0.70	1	0.10
Manufacturing capability	0.10	2	0.20	10	1.00	5	0.50
Technological skills	0.05	10	0.50	1	0.05	3	0.15
Dealer network/distribution capability	0.05	9	0.45	4	0.20	5	0.25
New product innovation capability	0.05	9	0.45	4	0.20	5	0.25
Financial resources	0.10	5	0.50	10	1.00	3	0.30
Relative cost position	0.30	5	1.50	10	3.00	1	0.30
Customer service capabilities	0.15	5	0.75	7	1.05	1	0.15
Sum of importance weights	**1.00**						
Overall weighted competitive strength rating			**5.95**		**7.70**		**2.10**

example, relative cost is the most telling measure of competitive strength, and the other strength measures are of lesser importance. The company with the highest rating on a given measure has an implied competitive edge on that measure, with the size of its edge reflected in the difference between its weighted rating and rivals' weighted ratings. For instance, Rival 1's 3.00 weighted strength rating on relative cost signals a considerable cost advantage versus ABC Company (with a 1.50 weighted score on relative cost) and an even bigger cost advantage against Rival 2 (with a weighted score of 0.30). The measure-by-measure ratings reveal the competitive areas where a company is strongest and weakest, and against whom.

The overall competitive strength scores indicate how all the different strength measures add up—whether the company is at a net overall competitive advantage or disadvantage against each rival. The higher a company's *overall weighted strength rating,* the stronger its *overall competitiveness* versus rivals. The bigger the difference between a company's overall weighted rating and the scores of *lower-rated* rivals, the greater is its implied *net competitive advantage.* Thus, Rival 1's overall weighted score of 7.70 indicates a greater net competitive advantage over Rival 2 (with a score of 2.10) than over ABC Company (with a score of 5.95). Conversely, the bigger the difference between a company's overall rating and the scores of *higher-rated* rivals, the greater its implied *net competitive disadvantage.* Rival 2's score of 2.10 gives it a smaller net competitive disadvantage against ABC Company (with an overall score of 5.95) than against Rival 1 (with an overall score of 7.70).

High weighted competitive strength ratings signal a strong competitive position and possession of competitive advantage; low ratings signal a weak position and competitive disadvantage.

Strategic Implications of Competitive Strength Assessments

Competitive strength assessments provide useful conclusions about a company's competitive situation. The ratings show how a company compares against rivals, factor by factor (or capability by capability), thus revealing where it is strongest and weakest, and against whom. Moreover, the overall competitive strength score indicates how all the different factors add up—whether the company is at a net competitive advantage or disadvantage against each rival. The firm with the largest overall competitive strength rating enjoys the strongest competitive position, with the size of its net competitive advantage reflected by how much its score exceeds the scores of rivals.

In addition, the strength ratings provide guidelines for designing wise offensive and defensive strategies. For example, if ABC Co. wants to go on the offensive to win additional sales and market share, such an offensive probably needs to be aimed directly at winning customers away from Rival 2 (which has a lower overall strength score) rather than Rival 1 (which has a higher overall strength score). Moreover, while ABC has high ratings for technological skills (a 10 rating), dealer network/distribution capability (a 9 rating), new product innovation capability (a 9 rating), quality/product performance (an 8 rating), and reputation/image (an 8 rating), these strength measures have low importance weights—meaning that ABC has strengths in areas that don't translate into much competitive clout in the marketplace. Even so, it outclasses Rival 2 in all five areas, plus it enjoys substantially lower costs than Rival 2 (ABC has a 5 rating on relative cost position versus a 1 rating for Rival 2)—and relative cost position carries the highest importance weight of all the strength measures. ABC also has greater competitive strength than Rival 3 as concerns customer service capabilities (which carries the second-highest importance weight). Hence, because ABC's strengths are in the very areas where Rival 2 is weak, ABC is in a good position to attack Rival 2—it may well be able to persuade a number of Rival 2's customers to switch their purchases over to ABC's product.

> A company's competitive strength scores pinpoint its strengths and weaknesses against rivals and point directly to the kinds of offensive/defensive actions it can use to exploit its competitive strengths and reduce its competitive vulnerabilities.

But ABC should be cautious about cutting price aggressively to win customers away from Rival 2, because Rival 1 could interpret that as an attack by ABC to win away Rival 1's customers as well. And Rival 1 is in far and away the best position to compete on the basis of low price, given its high rating on relative cost in an industry where low costs are competitively important (relative cost carries an importance weight of 0.30). Rival 1's very strong relative cost position vis-à-vis both ABC and Rival 2 arms it with the ability to use its lower-cost advantage to thwart any price cutting on ABC's part; clearly ABC is vulnerable to any retaliatory price cuts by Rival 1—Rival 1 can easily defeat both ABC and Rival 2 in a price-based battle for sales and market share. If ABC wants to defend against its vulnerability to potential price cutting by Rival 1, then it needs to aim a portion of its strategy at lowering its costs.

The point here is that a competitively astute company should utilize the strength scores in deciding what strategic moves to make—what strengths to exploit in winning business away from rivals, which rivals to attack, and which competitive weaknesses to try to correct. When a company has important competitive strengths in areas where one or more rivals are weak, it makes sense to consider offensive moves to exploit rivals' competitive weaknesses. When a company has important competitive weaknesses in areas where one or more rivals are strong, it makes sense to consider defensive moves to curtail its vulnerability.

QUESTION 6: WHAT STRATEGIC ISSUES AND PROBLEMS MERIT FRONT-BURNER MANAGERIAL ATTENTION?

The final and most important analytical step is to zero in on exactly what strategic issues company managers need to address—and resolve—for the company to be more financially and competitively successful in the years ahead. This step involves drawing on the results of both industry analysis and the evaluations of the company's own competitiveness. The task here is to get a clear fix on exactly what strategic and competitive challenges confront the company, which of the company's competitive shortcomings need fixing, what obstacles stand in the way of improving the company's competitive position in the marketplace, and what specific problems merit front-burner attention by company managers.

> Zeroing in on the strategic issues a company faces and compiling a "worry list" of problems and roadblocks creates a strategic agenda of problems that merit prompt managerial attention.

The "worry list" of issues and problems that have to be wrestled with can include such things as:

- *How* to stave off market challenges from new foreign competitors.
- *How* to combat the price discounting of rivals.
- *How* to reduce the company's high costs and pave the way for price reductions.
- *How* to sustain the company's present rate of growth in light of slowing buyer demand.
- *Whether* to expand the company's product line.
- *Whether* to correct the company's competitive deficiencies by acquiring a rival company with the missing strengths.
- *Whether* to expand into foreign markets rapidly or cautiously.
- *Whether* to reposition the company and move to a different strategic group.
- *What to do* about growing buyer interest in substitute products.
- *What to do* to combat the aging demographics of the company's customer base.

> Actually deciding on a strategy and what specific actions to take is what comes *after* developing the list of strategic issues and problems that merit front-burner management attention.

The worry list thus always centers on such concerns as "how to … ," "what to do about … ," and "whether to… ." The purpose of the worry list is to identify the specific issues/problems that management needs to address, not to figure out what specific actions to take. Deciding what to do—which strategic actions to take and which strategic moves to take—comes later (when it is time to craft the strategy and choose among the various strategic alternatives).

If the items on the worry list are relatively minor—which suggests that the company's strategy is mostly on track and reasonably well matched to the company's overall situation, company managers seldom need to go much beyond fine-tuning the present strategy. If, however, the issues and problems confronting the company are serious and indicate the present strategy is not well suited for the road ahead, the task of crafting a better strategy has got to go to the top of management's action agenda.

> A good strategy must contain ways to deal with all the strategic issues and obstacles that stand in the way of the company's financial and competitive success in the years ahead.

KEY POINTS

There are six key questions to consider in evaluating a company's ability to compete successfully against market rivals:

1. *How well is the present strategy working?* This involves evaluating the strategy from a qualitative standpoint (completeness, internal consistency, rationale, and suitability to the situation) and also from a quantitative standpoint (the strategic and financial results the strategy is producing). The stronger a company's current overall performance, the less likely the need for radical strategy changes. The weaker a company's performance and/or the faster the changes in its external situation (which can be gleaned from industry and competitive forces analysis), the more its current strategy must be questioned.

2. *Do the company's resources and capabilities have sufficient competitive power to give it a sustainable advantage over competitors?* The answer to this question comes from conducting the four tests of a resource's competitive power. If a company has resources and capabilities that are competitively valuable and rare, the firm will have a competitive advantage over market rivals. If its resources and capabilities are also hard to copy, with no good substitutes, then the firm may be able to sustain this advantage even in the face of active efforts by rivals to overcome it.

3. *Is the company able to seize market opportunities and overcome external threats to its future well-being?* The answer to this question comes from performing a SWOT analysis. The two most important parts of SWOT analysis are (1) drawing conclusions about what story the compilation of strengths, weaknesses, opportunities, and threats tells about the company's overall situation and (2) acting on the conclusions to better match the company's strategy to its internal strengths and market opportunities, to correct the important internal weaknesses, and to defend against external threats. A company's strengths and competitive assets are strategically relevant because they are the most logical and appealing building blocks for strategy; internal weaknesses are important because they may represent vulnerabilities that need correction. External opportunities and threats come into play because a good strategy necessarily aims at capturing a company's most attractive opportunities and at defending against threats to its well-being.

4. *Are the company's prices, costs, and value proposition competitive?* One telling sign of whether a company's situation is strong or precarious is whether its prices and costs are competitive with those of industry rivals. Another sign is how it compares with rivals in terms of differentiation—how effectively it delivers on its customer value proposition. Value chain analysis and benchmarking are essential tools in determining whether the company is performing particular functions and activities efficiently and effectively, learning whether its costs are in line with competitors, whether it is differentiating in ways that really enhance customer value, and deciding which internal activities and business processes need to be scrutinized for improvement. They complement resource and capability analysis by providing data at the level of individual activities that provides more objective evidence of whether individual resources and capabilities, or bundles of resources and linked activity sets, are competitively superior.

5. *On an overall basis, is the company competitively stronger or weaker than key rivals?* The key appraisals here involve how the company matches up against key rivals on industry key success factors and other chief determinants of competitive success and whether and why the company has a *net* competitive advantage or disadvantage. Quantitative competitive strength assessments, using the method presented in Table 4.4, indicate where a company is competitively strong and weak and provide insight into the company's ability to defend or enhance its market position. As a rule, a company's competitive strategy should be built around its competitive strengths and should aim at shoring up areas where it is competitively vulnerable. When a company has important competitive strengths in areas where one or more rivals are weak, it makes sense to consider offensive moves to exploit rivals' competitive weaknesses. When a company has important competitive weaknesses in areas where one or more rivals are strong, it makes sense to consider defensive moves to curtail its vulnerability.

6. *What strategic issues and problems merit front-burner managerial attention?* This analytical step zeros in on the strategic issues and problems that stand in the way of the company's success. It involves using the results of industry analysis as well as resource and value chain analysis of the company's competitive situation to identify a "worry list" of issues to be resolved for the company to be financially and competitively successful in the years ahead. The worry list always centers on such concerns as "how to … ," "what to do about … ," and "whether to … "—the purpose of the worry list is to identify the specific issues/problems that management needs to address. Actually deciding on a strategy and what specific actions to take is what comes after the list of strategic issues and problems that merit front-burner management attention is developed.

Solid analysis of the company's competitive situation vis-à-vis its key rivals, like good industry analysis, is a valuable precondition for good strategy making. A competently done evaluation of a company's resources, capabilities, and competitive strengths exposes strong and weak points in the present strategy and how attractive or unattractive the company's competitive position is and why. Managers need such understanding to craft a strategy that is well suited to the company's competitive circumstances.

ASSURANCE OF LEARNING EXERCISES

LO 2, LO 3, LO 4

1. Review the information in Illustration Capsule 4.1 concerning the average costs of producing and selling fair-trade coffee. Then answer the following questions:

   a. Companies that do not sell fair-trade coffee can buy coffee direct from small farmers for as little as $0.75 per pound. By paying substandard wages, they can also reduce their labor costs of roasting and bagging coffee to $0.70 per pound and reduce their overhead by 20 percent. If they sell their coffee at the same average price as Just Coffee, what would their profit margin be and how would this compare to Just Coffee's?

b. How can Just Coffee respond to this type of competitive threat? Does it have any valuable competitive assets that can help it respond, or will it need to acquire new ones. Would your answer change the company's value chain in any way?

LO 1

2. Using the information in Table 4.1 and the financial statement information for Avon Products below, calculate the following ratios for Avon for both 2008 and 2009:

a. Gross profit margin

b. Operating profit margin

c. Net profit margin.

d. Times interest earned coverage

e. Return on shareholders' equity

f. Return on assets

g. Debt-to-equity ratio

h. Days of inventory

i. Inventory turnover ratio

j. Average collection period

Based on these ratios, did Avon's financial performance improve, weaken, or remain about the same from 2008 to 2009?

Consolidated Statements of Income for Avon Products, Inc., 2008–2009 (in millions, except per-share data)

	Years ended December 31	
	2009	2008
Net sales	$10,284.7	$10,588.9
Other revenue	98.1	101.2
Total revenue	10,382.8	10,690.1
Costs, expenses, and other:		
Cost of sales	3,888.3	3,949.1
Selling, general and administrative expenses	5,476.3	5,401.7
Operating profit	1,018.2	1,339.3
Interest expense	104.8	100.4
Interest income	(20.2)	(37.1)
Other expense, net	7.1	37.7
Total other expenses	91.7	101.0
Income before taxes	926.5	1,238.3
Income taxes	298.3	362.7
Net income	628.2	875.6

(Continued)

	Years ended December 31	
	2009	2008
Net income attributable to noncontrolling interests	(2.4)	(.3)
Net income attributable to Avon	$ 625.8	$ 875.3
Earnings per share:		
Basic	$ 1.45	$ 2.04
Diluted	$ 1.45	$ 2.03

Consolidated Balance Sheets for Avon Products, Inc., 2008–2009 (in millions, except per-share data)

	As of Dec. 31, 2009	As of Dec. 31, 2008
Assets		
Cash and cash equivalents	$ 1,311.6	$ 1,104.7
Accounts receivable (less allowances of $165.5 and $127.9)	779.7	687.8
Inventories	1,067.5	1,007.9
Prepaid expenses and other	1,030.5	756.5
Total current assets	4,189.3	3,556.9
Property, plant, and equipment, at cost		
Land	144.3	85.3
Buildings and improvements	1,048.1	1,008.1
Equipment	1,506.9	1,346.5
Total property, plant, and equipment, at cost	2,699.3	2,439.9
Less accumulated depreciation	(1,169.7)	(1,096.0)
Net property, plant, and equipment	1,529.6	1,343.9
Other assets	1,113.8	1,173.2
Total assets	$ 6,832.7	$ 6,074.0
Liabilities and Shareholders' Equity		
Debt maturing within 1 year	$ 138.1	$1,031.4
Accounts payable	754.7	724.3
Accrued compensation	291.0	234.4
Other accrued liabilities	697.1	581.9
Sales and taxes other than income	259.2	212.2
Income taxes	134.7	128.0
Total current liabilities	2,274.8	2,912.2
Long-term debt	2,307.8	1,456.2
Employee benefit plans	588.9	665.4
Long-term income taxes	173.8	168.9
Other liabilities	174.8	159.0
Total liabilities	$ 5,520.1	$ 5,361.7

Commitments and contingencies

(Continued)

Shareholders' equity

Common stock, par value $.25—authorized 1,500 shares; issued 740.9 and 739.4 shares	$ 186.1	$ 185.6
Additional paid-in capital	1,941.0	1,874.1
Retained earnings	4,383.9	4,118.9
Accumulated other comprehensive loss	(692.6)	(965.9)
Treasury stock, at cost (313.4 and 313.1 shares)	(4,545.8)	(4,537.8)
Total Avon shareholders' equity	1,272.6	674.9
Noncontrolling interest	40.0	37.4
Total shareholders' equity	**$ 1,312.6**	**$ 712.3**
Total liabilities and shareholders' equity	**$ 6,832.7**	**$ 6,074.0**

Source: Avon Products, Inc., 2009 10-K.

EXERCISES FOR SIMULATION PARTICIPANTS

LO 1

1. Using the formulas in Table 4.1 and the data in your company's latest financial statements, calculate the following measures of financial performance for your company:

    a. Operating profit margin

    b. Return on total assets

    c. Current ratio

    d. Working capital

    e. Long-term debt-to-capital ratio

    f. Price-earnings ratio

LO 1

2. On the basis of your company's latest financial statements and all the other available data regarding your company's performance that appear in the Industry Report, list the three measures of financial performance on which your company did "best" and the three measures on which your company's financial performance was "worst."

LO 1, LO 2, LO 3, LO 4, LO 5

3. What hard evidence can you cite that indicates your company's strategy is working fairly well (or perhaps not working so well, if your company's performance is lagging that of rival companies)?

LO 3

4. What internal strengths and weaknesses does your company have? What external market opportunities for growth and increased profitability exist for

your company? What external threats to your company's future well-being and profitability do you and your co-managers see? What does the preceding SWOT analysis indicate about your company's present situation and future prospects—where on the scale from "exceptionally strong" to "alarmingly weak" does the attractiveness of your company's situation rank?

LO 2, LO 3

5. Does your company have any core competencies? If so, what are they?

LO 4

6. What are the key elements of your company's value chain? Refer to Figure 4.3 in developing your answer.

LO 5

7. Using the methodology presented in Table 4.4, do a weighted competitive strength assessment for your company and two other companies that you and your co-managers consider to be very close competitors.

ENDNOTES

[1] In recent years, considerable research has been devoted to the role a company's resources and competitive capabilities play in determining its competitiveness, shaping its strategy, and impacting its profitability. Following the trailblazing article by Birger Wernerfelt, "A Resource-Based View of the Firm," *Strategic Management Journal* 5, no. 5 (September–October 1984), pp. 171–80, the findings and conclusions have merged into what is now referred to as the resource-based view of the firm. Other very important contributions include Jay Barney, "Firm Resources and Sustained Competitive Advantage," *Journal of Management* 17, no. 1 (1991), pp. 99–120; Margaret A. Peteraf, "The Cornerstones of Competitive Advantage: A Resource-Based View," *Strategic Management Journal* 14, no. 3 (March 1993), pp. 179–91; Birger Wernerfelt, "The Resource-Based View of the Firm: Ten Years After," *Strategic Management Journal* 16, no. 3 (March 1995), pp. 171–74. A full-blown overview of the resource-based view of the firm, in its most current form, is presented in Jay B. Barney and Delwyn N. Clark, *Resource-Based Theory: Creating and Sustaining Competitive Advantage* (New York: Oxford University Press, 2007).
[2] A more detailed explanation of the relationship between resources and capabilities can be found in R. Amit and P. Schoemaker, "Strategic Assets and Organizational Rent," *Strategic Management Journal* 14 (1993), pp. 33–46.
[3] See, for example, Jay B. Barney, "Looking Inside for Competitive Advantage," *Academy of Management Executive* 9, no. 4 (November 1995), pp. 49–61; Christopher A. Bartlett and Sumantra Ghoshal, "Building Competitive

Advantage through People," *MIT Sloan Management Review* 43, no. 2 (Winter 2002), pp. 34–41; Danny Miller, Russell Eisenstat,and Nathaniel Foote, "Strategy from the Inside Out: Building Capability-Creating Organizations," *California Management Review* 44, no. 3 (Spring 2002), pp. 37–54.
[4] See Barney , "Firm Resources and Sustained Competitive Advantage," pp. 105–9; M. Peteraf and J. Barney, "Unraveling the Resource-Based Tangle," *Managerial and Decision Economics* 24, no. 4 (June–July 2003), pp. 309–23.
[5] See Amit and Schoemaker, Strategic Assets and Organizational Rent, for more on the power of strategic assets to improve a company's profitability.
[6] For a discussion of how to recognize powerful substitute resources, see Margaret A. Peteraf and Mark E. Bergen, "Scanning Dynamic Competitive Landscapes: A Market-Based and Resource-Based Framework," *Strategic Management Journal* 24 (2003), pp. 1027–42.
[7] See C. Montgomery, "Of Diamonds and Rust: A New Look at Resources," in C. Montgomery (ed.), *Resource-Based and Evolutionary Theories of the Firm* (Boston: Kluwer Academic, 1995), pp. 251–68.
[8] For a good discussion of what happens when a company's capabilities grow stale and obsolete, see D. Leonard-Barton, "Core Capabilities and Core Rigidities: A Paradox in Managing New Product Development," *Strategic Management Journal* 13 (Summer 1992), pp. 111–25; Montgomery, "Of Diamonds and Rust."
[9] The concept of dynamic capabilities was introduced by D. Teece, G. Pisano, and A. Shuen, "Dynamic Capabilities and Strategic Management," *Strategic Management*

Journal 18, no. 7 (1997), pp. 509–33. Other important contributors to the concept include K. Eisenhardt and J. Martin, "Dynamic Capabilities: What Are They?" *Strategic Management Journal* 21, nos. 10–11 (2000), pp. 1105–21; M. Zollo and S. Winter, "Deliberate Learning and the Evolution of Dynamic Capabilities," *Organization Science* 13 (2002), pp. 339–51; C. Helfat et al., *Dynamic Capabilities: Understanding Strategic Change in Organizations* (Malden, MA: Blackwell, 2007).
[10] For a more extensive discussion of how to identify and evaluate the competitive power of a company's capabilities, see David W. Birchall and George Tovstiga, "The Strategic Potential of a Firm's Knowledge Portfolio," *Journal of General Management* 25, no. 1 (Autumn 1999), pp. 1–16; Nick Bontis, Nicola C. Dragonetti, Kristine Jacobsen, and Goran Roos, "The Knowledge Toolbox: A Review of the Tools Available to Measure and Manage Intangible Resources," *European Management Journal* 17, no. 4 (August 1999), pp. 391–401. Also see David Teece, "Capturing Value from Knowledge Assets: The New Economy, Markets for Know-How, and Intangible Assets," *California Management Review* 40, no. 3 (Spring 1998), pp. 55–79.
[11] Donald Sull, "Strategy as Active Waiting," *Harvard Business Review* 83, no. 9 (September 2005), pp. 121–22.
[12] Ibid., pp. 124–26.
[13] See M. Peteraf, "The Cornerstones of Competitive Advantage: A Resource-Based View," *Strategic Management Journal,* March 1993, pp. 179–91.
[14] The value chain concept was developed and articulated by Michael Porter in his 1985

best-seller, *Competitive Advantage* (New York: Free Press).

[15] For discussions of the accounting challenges in calculating the costs of value chain activities, see John K. Shank and Vijay Govindarajan, *Strategic Cost Management* (New York: Free Press, 1993), especially chaps. 2–6, 10, and 11; Robin Cooper and Robert S. Kaplan, "Measure Costs Right: Make the Right Decisions," *Harvard Business Review* 66, no. 5 (September–October 1988), pp. 96–103; Joseph A. Ness and Thomas G. Cucuzza, "Tapping the Full Potential of ABC," *Harvard Business Review* 73, no. 4 (July–August 1995), pp. 130–38.

[16] Porter, *Competitive Advantage,* p. 34.

[17] The strategic importance of effective supply chain management is discussed in Hau L. Lee, "The Triple-A Supply Chain," *Harvard Business Review* 82, no. 10 (October 2004), pp. 102–12.

[18] For more details, see Gregory H. Watson, *Strategic Benchmarking: How to Rate Your Company's Performance Against the World's Best* (New York: Wiley, 1993); Robert C. Camp, *Benchmarking: The Search for Industry Best Practices That Lead to Superior Performance* (Milwaukee: ASQC Quality Press, 1989); Dawn Iacobucci and Christie Nordhielm, "Creative Benchmarking," *Harvard Business Review* 78 no. 6 (November–December 2000), pp. 24–25.

[19] Jeremy Main, "How to Steal the Best Ideas Around," *Fortune,* October 19, 1992, pp. 102–3.

[20] Some of these options are discussed in more detail in Porter, *Competitive Advantage,* chap. 3.

[21] Porter discusses options such as these in *Competitive Advantage,* chap. 4.

[22] An example of how Whirlpool Corporation transformed its supply chain from a competitive liability to a competitive asset is discussed in Reuben E. Stone, "Leading a Supply Chain Turnaround," *Harvard Business Review* 82, no. 10 (October 2004), pp. 114–21.

CHAPTER 5

THE FIVE GENERIC COMPETITIVE STRATEGIES

Which One to Employ?

> I'm spending my time trying to understand our competitive position and how we're serving customers.
>
> **—Lou Gerstner**
> *Former CEO credited with IBM's turnaround*

> Competitive strategy is about being different. It means deliberately choosing to perform activities differently or to perform different activities than rivals to deliver a unique mix of value.
>
> **—Michael E. Porter**
> *Harvard Business School professor and Cofounder of Monitor Consulting*

> The essence of strategy lies in creating tomorrow's competitive advantages faster than competitors mimic the ones you possess today.
>
> **—Gary Hamel and C. K. Prahalad**
> *Professors, authors, and consultants*

LEARNING OBJECTIVES

LO 1. Understand what distinguishes each of the five generic strategies and why some of these strategies work better in certain kinds of industry and competitive conditions than in others.

LO 2. Gain command of the major avenues for achieving a competitive advantage based on lower costs.

LO 3. Learn the major avenues to a competitive advantage based on differentiating a company's product or service offering from the offerings of rivals.

LO 4. Recognize the attributes of a best-cost provider strategy and the way in which some firms use a hybrid strategy to go about building a competitive advantage and delivering superior value to customers.

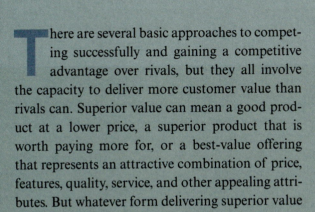

There are several basic approaches to competing successfully and gaining a competitive advantage over rivals, but they all involve the capacity to deliver more customer value than rivals can. Superior value can mean a good product at a lower price, a superior product that is worth paying more for, or a best-value offering that represents an attractive combination of price, features, quality, service, and other appealing attributes. But whatever form delivering superior value takes, it nearly always requires performing value chain activities differently than rivals and building competitively valuable resources and capabilities that rivals cannot readily match or trump.

This chapter describes the five *generic competitive strategy options*. Which of the five to employ is a company's first and foremost choice in crafting an overall strategy and beginning its quest for competitive advantage.

THE FIVE GENERIC COMPETITIVE STRATEGIES

A company's competitive strategy *deals exclusively with the specifics of management's game plan for competing successfully*—its specific efforts to please customers, its offensive and defensive moves to counter the maneuvers of rivals, its responses to shifting market conditions, its initiatives to strengthen its market position, and the specific kind of competitive advantage it is trying to achieve. The chances are remote that any two companies—even companies in the same industry—will employ competitive strategies that are exactly alike in every detail. Why? Because managers at different companies always have a slightly different spin on how best to deal with competitive pressures and industry driving forces, what future market conditions will be like, and what strategy specifics make the most sense for their particular company in light of the company's strengths and weaknesses, its most promising market opportunities, and the external threats to its future well-being.

LO 1

Understand what distinguishes each of the five generic strategies and why some of these strategies work better in certain kinds of industry and competitive conditions than in others.

However, when one strips away the details to get at the real substance, the two factors that most distinguish one competitive strategy from another boil down to (1) whether a company's market target is broad or narrow and (2) whether the company is pursuing a competitive advantage linked to low costs or product differentiation. As shown in Figure 5.1, these two factors give rise to five competitive strategy options for staking out a market position, operating the business, and delivering value to customers:[1]

1. *A low-cost provider strategy:* striving to achieve lower overall costs than rivals on products that attract a broad spectrum of buyers.
2. *A broad differentiation strategy:* seeking to differentiate the company's product offering from rivals' with attributes that will appeal to a broad spectrum of buyers.
3. *A focused (or market niche) low-cost strategy:* concentrating on a narrow buyer segment and outcompeting rivals on costs, thus being in position to win buyer favor by means of a lower-priced product offering.
4. *A focused (or market niche) differentiation strategy:* concentrating on a narrow buyer segment and outcompeting rivals with a product offering that meets the specific tastes and requirements of niche members better than the product offerings of rivals.
5. *A best-cost provider strategy:* giving customers *more value for the money* by offering upscale product attributes at a lower cost than rivals. Being the "best-cost" producer of an upscale product allows a company to underprice rivals whose products have similar upscale attributes. This option is a *hybrid* strategy that *blends elements of differentiation and low-cost strategies* in a unique way.

The remainder of this chapter explores the ins and outs of these five generic competitive strategies and how they differ.

Figure 5.1   The Five Generic Competitive Strategies: Each Stakes Out a Different Market Position

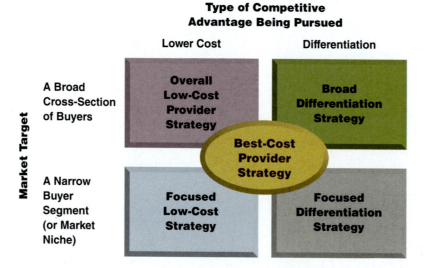

Source: This is an author-expanded version of a three-strategy classification discussed in Michael E. Porter, *Competitive Strategy* (New York: Free Press, 1980), pp. 35–40.

LOW-COST PROVIDER STRATEGIES

LO 2

Gain command of the major avenues for achieving a competitive advantage based on lower costs.

Striving to be the industry's overall low-cost provider is a powerful competitive approach in markets with many price-sensitive buyers. A company achieves **low-cost leadership** when it becomes the industry's lowest-cost provider rather than just being one of perhaps several competitors with comparatively low costs. A low-cost provider's strategic target is to have lower costs than rivals on products of comparable quality. In striving for a cost advantage over rivals, company managers must take care to incorporate features and services that buyers consider essential—*a product offering that is too frills-free sabotages the attractiveness of the company's product and can turn buyers off even if it is cheaper than competing products.* For maximum effectiveness, a low-cost provider needs to pursue cost-saving approaches that are difficult for rivals to copy. When it is relatively easy or inexpensive for rivals to imitate the low-cost firm's methods, then any resulting cost advantage evaporates too quickly to gain a very valuable edge in the marketplace.

> **CORE CONCEPT**
>
> A **low-cost leader**'s basis for competitive advantage is lower overall costs than competitors. Successful low-cost leaders are exceptionally good at finding ways to drive costs out of their businesses and still provide a product or service that buyers find acceptable.

A low-cost advantage over rivals has enormous competitive power, sometimes enabling a company to achieve faster rates of growth (by using price cuts to draw customers away from rivals) and frequently helping to boost a company's profitability. A company can translate a low-cost advantage over rivals into attractive profit performance in either of two ways:

1. By using its lower-cost edge to underprice competitors and attract price-sensitive buyers in great enough numbers to increase total profits.
2. By refraining from using price cuts to steal sales away from rivals (which runs the risk of starting a price war) and, instead, charging a price roughly equal to those of other low-priced rivals. While this strategy will not increase the company's market share, it will enable the company to earn a bigger profit margin per unit sold (because the company's costs per unit are below the unit costs of rivals) and thereby propel it to higher total profits and return on investment than rivals are able to earn.

> A low-cost advantage over rivals can translate into better profitability than rivals attain.

While many companies are inclined to exploit a low-cost advantage by attacking rivals with lower prices (in hopes that the expected gains in sales and market share will lead to higher total profits), this strategy can backfire if rivals respond with retaliatory price cuts of their own (in order to protect their customer base) and the aggressor's price cuts fail to produce sales gains that are big enough to offset the profit erosion associated with charging a lower price. The bigger the risk that rivals will respond with matching price cuts, the more appealing it becomes to employ the second option for using a low-cost advantage to achieve higher profitability.

The Two Major Avenues for Achieving a Cost Advantage

To achieve a low-cost edge over rivals, a firm's cumulative costs across its overall value chain must be lower than competitors' cumulative costs. There are two ways to accomplish this:[2]

1. Do a better job than rivals of performing value chain activities more cost-effectively.

2. Revamp the firm's overall value chain to eliminate or bypass some cost-producing activities.

Let's look at each of the two approaches to securing a cost advantage.

Cost-Efficient Management of Value Chain Activities

For a company to do a more cost-efficient job of managing its value chain than rivals, managers must launch a concerted, ongoing effort to ferret out cost-saving opportunities in every part of the value chain. No activity can escape cost-saving scrutiny, and all company personnel must be expected to use their talents and ingenuity to come up with innovative and effective ways to keep costs down. All avenues for performing value chain activities at a lower cost than rivals have to be explored. Particular attention, however, needs to be paid to a set of factors known as **cost drivers,** which have an especially strong effect on a company's costs and which managers can use as levers to push costs down. (Figure 5.2 provides a list of important cost drivers.) Cost-cutting methods that demonstrate an effective use of the cost drivers include:

1. *Striving to capture all available economies of scale.* Economies of scale stem from an ability to lower unit costs by increasing the scale of operation, and they can affect the unit costs of many activities along the value chain, including manufacturing, R&D, advertising, distribution, and general administration. For example, PepsiCo and Anheuser-Busch have the ability to afford the $3 million cost of a 30-second Super Bowl ad because the cost of such an ad can be spread out over the hundreds of millions of units they sell. In contrast, a small company with a sales volume of only 1 million units would find the $3 million cost of a Super Bowl ad prohibitive—just one ad would raise costs over $2 per unit even if the ad was unusually effective and caused sales volume to jump 25 percent, to 1.25 million units. Similarly, a large manufacturing plant can be more economical to operate than a smaller one. In global industries, making separate products for each country market instead of selling a mostly standard product worldwide tends to boost unit costs because of lost time in model changeover, shorter production runs, and inability to reach the most economic scale of production for each country model.

2. *Taking full advantage of experience and learning-curve effects.* The cost of performing an activity can decline over time as the learning and experience of company personnel build. Learning/experience economies can stem from debugging and mastering newly introduced technologies, using the experiences and suggestions of workers to install more efficient plant layouts and assembly procedures, and the added speed and effectiveness that accrues from repeatedly picking sites for and building new plants, retail outlets, or distribution centers. Aggressively managed low-cost providers pay diligent attention to capturing the benefits of learning and experience and to keeping these benefits proprietary to whatever extent possible.

3. *Trying to operate facilities at full capacity.* Whether a company is able to operate at or near full capacity has a big impact on units costs when

Figure 5.2   Cost Drivers: The Keys to Driving Down Company Costs

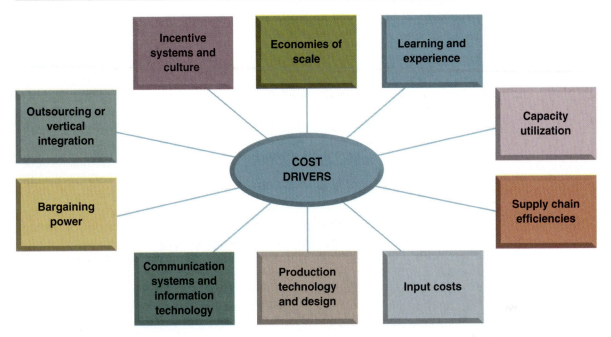

Sources: Adapted by the authors from M. Porter, *Competitive Advantage: Creating and Sustaining Competitive Advantage* (New York: Free Press, 1985).

its value chain contains activities associated with substantial fixed costs. Higher rates of capacity utilization allow depreciation and other fixed costs to be spread over a larger unit volume, thereby lowering fixed costs per unit. The more capital-intensive the business and the higher the fixed costs relative to total costs, the greater the unit-cost penalty for underutilizing existing capacity.

4. *Improving supply chain efficiency.* Partnering with suppliers to streamline the ordering and purchasing process, to reduce inventory carrying costs via just-in-time inventory practices, to economize on shipping and materials handling, and to ferret out other cost-saving opportunities is a much-used approach to cost reduction. A company with a distinctive competence in cost-efficient supply chain management can sometimes achieve a sizable cost advantage over less adept rivals.

5. *Using lower cost inputs wherever doing so will not entail too great a sacrifice in quality.* Some examples include lower-cost raw materials or component parts, nonunion labor "inputs," and lower rental fees due to differences in location. If the costs of certain factors are "too high," a company may even design the high-cost inputs out of the product altogether.

6. *Using the company's bargaining power vis-à-vis suppliers or others in the value chain system to gain concessions.* Home Depot, for example, has sufficient bargaining clout with suppliers to win price discounts on large-volume purchases. PepsiCo similarly uses its bargaining power to win concessions from supermarkets, mass merchandisers, and other forward channel allies.

7. *Using communication systems and information technology to achieve operating efficiencies.* For example, data sharing, starting with customer orders and going all the way back to components production, coupled with the use of enterprise resource planning (ERP) and manufacturing execution system (MES) software, can greatly reduce production times and labor costs. Numerous companies now have online systems and software that turn formerly time-consuming and labor-intensive tasks like purchasing, inventory management, invoicing, and bill payment into speedily performed mouse clicks.

8. *Employing advanced production technology and process design to improve overall efficiency.* Examples range from highly automated robotic production technology to computer-assisted design (CAD) techniques to design for manufacture (DFM) procedures that enable more integrated and efficient production. Dell's highly automated PC assembly plant in Austin, Texas, is a prime example of the use of advanced product and process technologies. Other manufacturers have pioneered the use of production or processing technology that eliminates the need for costly investments in facilities or equipment and that requires fewer employees. Companies can also achieve substantial efficiency gains through process innovation or through approaches such as business process management, business process reengineering, and total quality management that aim to coordinate production activities and drive continuous improvement in productivity and quality.[3] Procter & Gamble is an example of a company known for its successful application of business process reengineering techniques.

9. *Being alert to the cost advantages of outsourcing or vertical integration.* Outsourcing the performance of certain value chain activities can be more economical than performing them in-house if outside specialists, by virtue of their expertise and volume, can perform the activities at lower cost. Indeed, outsourcing has, in recent years, become a widely used cost reduction approach. On the other hand, there can be times when integrating into the activities of either suppliers or distribution channel allies can lower costs through greater production efficiencies, reduced transaction costs, or a better bargaining position.

10. *Motivating employees through incentives and company culture.* A company's incentive system can encourage not only greater worker productivity but also cost-saving innovations that come from worker suggestions. The culture of a company can also spur worker pride in productivity and continuous improvement. Companies that are well known for their cost-reducing incentive systems and culture include Nucor Steel, which characterizes itself as a company of "11,900 teammates," Southwest Airlines, and Walmart.

In addition to the above means of performing value chain activities more efficiently than rivals, managers can also achieve important cost savings by deliberately opting for an inherently economical strategy. For instance, a company can often open up a significant cost advantage over rivals by:

• Having lower specifications for purchased materials, parts, and components than do rivals. Thus, a maker of personal computers can use the cheapest hard drives, microprocessors, monitors, and other components so as to end up with lower production costs than rival PC makers.

• Stripping frills and features from its product offering that are not highly valued by price-sensitive or bargain-hunting buyers. Deliberately restricting the company's product offering to "the essentials" can help a company cut costs associated with snazzy attributes and a full lineup of options and extras. Activities and costs can also be eliminated by offering buyers fewer services.

- Offering a limited product line as opposed to a full product line. Pruning slow-selling items from the product lineup and being content to meet the needs of most buyers rather than all buyers can eliminate activities and costs associated with numerous product versions and wide selection.

- Distributing the company's product only through low-cost distribution channels and avoiding high-cost distribution channels.

- Choosing to use the most economical method for delivering customer orders (even if it results in longer delivery times).

The point here is that a low-cost provider strategy entails not only performing value chain activities cost-effectively but also judiciously choosing cost-saving strategic approaches.

Revamping the Value Chain System to Lower Costs   Dramatic cost advantages can often emerge from redesigning the company's value chain system in ways that eliminate costly work steps and entirely bypass certain cost-producing value chain activities. While using communication technologies and information systems or business process reengineering to drive down costs often involves activities that span the value chain system, other approaches to revamping the value chain system can include:

- *Selling direct to consumers and bypassing the activities and costs of distributors and dealers.* To circumvent the need for distributors-dealers, a company can (1) create its own direct sales force (which adds the costs of maintaining and supporting a sales force but which may well be cheaper than utilizing independent distributors and dealers to access buyers) and/or (2) conduct sales operations at the company's Web site (incurring costs for Web site operations and shipping may be a substantially cheaper way to make sales to customers than going through distributor-dealer channels). Costs in the wholesale/retail portions of the value chain frequently represent 35 to 50 percent of the price final consumers pay, so establishing a direct sales force or selling online may offer big cost savings.

- *Coordinating with suppliers to bypass the need to perform certain value chain activities, speed up their performance, or otherwise increase overall efficiency.* Examples include having suppliers combine particular parts and components into preassembled modules, thus permitting a manufacturer to assemble its own product in fewer work steps and with a smaller workforce, and sharing real-time sales information to lower costs through improved inventory management. At Walmart, some items supplied by manufacturers are delivered directly to retail stores rather than being routed through Walmart's distribution centers and delivered by Walmart trucks; in other instances, Walmart unloads incoming shipments from manufacturers' trucks arriving at its distribution centers directly onto outgoing Walmart trucks headed to particular stores without ever moving the goods into the distribution center. Many supermarket chains have greatly reduced in-store meat butchering and cutting activities by shifting to meats that are cut and packaged at the meatpacking plant and then delivered to their stores in ready-to-sell form.

- *Reducing materials handling and shipping costs by having suppliers locate their plants or warehouses close to the company's own facilities.* Having suppliers locate their plants or warehouses very close to a company's own plant facilitates just-in-time deliveries of parts and components to the exact work station where they will be utilized in assembling the company's product. This not only lowers incoming shipping costs but also curbs or eliminates the need for a company to build and operate storerooms for incoming parts and components and have plant personnel move the inventories to the work stations as needed for assembly.

Illustration Capsule 5.1 describes how Walmart has managed its value chain in the retail grocery portion of its business to achieve a dramatic cost advantage over rival supermarket chains and become the world's biggest grocery retailer.

Examples of Companies That Revamped Their Value Chains to Reduce Costs   Nucor Corporation, the most profitable steel producer in the United States and one of the largest steel producers worldwide, drastically revamped the value chain process for manufacturing steel products by using relatively inexpensive electric arc furnaces where scrap steel and directly reduced iron ore are melted and then sent to a continuous caster and rolling mill to be shaped into steel bars, steel beams, steel plate, and sheet steel. Using electric arc furnaces to make new steel products by recycling scrap steel eliminated many of the steps used by traditional steel mills that made their steel products from iron ore, coke, limestone, and other ingredients using costly coke ovens, basic oxygen blast furnaces, ingot casters, and multiple types of finishing facilities—plus Nucor's value chain system required far few employees. As a consequence, Nucor was able to make steel with a far lower capital investment, a far smaller workforce, and far lower operating costs than traditional steel mills. Nucor's strategy to replace the traditional steelmaking value chain with its simpler, quicker value chain approach has made it one of the lowest-cost producers of steel in the world and enabled Nucor to take huge volumes of sales and market share away from traditional steel companies and earn attractive profits. (Nucor has reported profits for every quarter in every year during the 1966–2008 period—a remarkable accomplishment in a mature and cyclical industry notorious for poor profitability.) While the recession-plagued year of 2009 was not a good one for Nucor, it returned to profits quickly in 2010.

Southwest Airlines has achieved considerable cost savings by reconfiguring the traditional value chain of commercial airlines, thereby allowing it to offer travelers dramatically lower fares. Its mastery of fast turnarounds at the gates (about 25 minutes versus 45 minutes for rivals) allows its planes to fly more hours per day. This translates into being able to schedule more flights per day with fewer aircraft, allowing Southwest to generate more revenue per plane on average than rivals. Southwest does not offer assigned seating, baggage transfer to connecting airlines, or first-class seating and service, thereby eliminating all the cost-producing activities associated with these features. The company's fast and user-friendly online reservation system facilitates e-ticketing and reduces staffing requirements at telephone reservation centers and airport counters. Its use of automated check-in equipment reduces staffing requirements for terminal check-in.

The Keys to Being a Successful Low-Cost Provider

To succeed with a low-cost provider strategy, company managers have to scrutinize each cost-creating activity and determine what factors cause costs to be high or low. Then they have to use this knowledge to streamline or reengineer how activities are performed, exhaustively pursuing cost efficiencies throughout the value chain. Normally, low-cost producers try to engage all company personnel in continuous cost improvement efforts, and they strive to operate with exceptionally small corporate staffs to keep administrative costs to a minimum. Many successful low-cost

ILLUSTRATION CAPSULE 5.1

How Walmart Managed Its Value Chain to Achieve a Huge Low-Cost Advantage over Rival Supermarket Chains

Walmart has achieved a very substantial cost and pricing advantage over rival supermarket chains both by revamping portions of the grocery retailing value chain and by outmanaging its rivals in efficiently performing various value chain activities. Its cost advantage stems from a series of initiatives and practices:

- Instituting extensive information sharing with vendors via online systems that relay sales at its checkout counters directly to suppliers of the items, thereby providing suppliers with real-time information on customer demand and preferences (creating an estimated 6 percent cost advantage). It is standard practice at Walmart to collaborate extensively with vendors on all aspects of the purchasing and store delivery process to squeeze out mutually beneficial cost savings. Procter & Gamble, Walmart's biggest supplier, went so far as to integrate its enterprise resource planning (ERP) system with Walmart's.

- Pursuing global procurement of some items and centralizing most purchasing activities so as to leverage the company's buying power (creating an estimated 2.5 percent cost advantage).

- Investing in state-of-the-art automation at its distribution centers, efficiently operating a truck fleet that makes daily deliveries to Walmart's stores, and putting other assorted cost-saving practices into place at its headquarters, distribution centers, and stores (resulting in an estimated 4 percent cost advantage).

- Striving to optimize the product mix and achieve greater sales turnover (resulting in about a 2 percent cost advantage).

- Installing security systems and store operating procedures that lower shrinkage rates (producing a cost advantage of about 0.5 percent).

- Negotiating preferred real estate rental and leasing rates with real estate developers and owners of its store sites (yielding a cost advantage of 2 percent).

- Managing and compensating its workforce in a manner that produces lower labor costs (yielding an estimated 5 percent cost advantage).

Altogether, these value chain initiatives give Walmart an approximately 22 percent cost advantage over Kroger, Safeway, and other leading supermarket chains. With such a sizable cost advantage, Walmart has been able to underprice its rivals and rapidly become the world's leading supermarket retailer.

Sources: Developed by the authors from information at www.walmart.com and in Marco Iansiti and Roy Levien, "Strategy as Ecology," *Harvard Business Review* 82, no. 3 (March 2004), p. 70.

leaders also use benchmarking to keep close tabs on how their costs compare with those of rivals and firms performing comparable activities in other industries.

But while low-cost providers are champions of frugality, they seldom hesitate to spend aggressively on resources and capabilities *that promise to drive costs out of the business.* Indeed, having resources or capabilities of this type and ensuring that they remain competitively superior is essential for achieving competitive advantage as a low-cost provider. Walmart, one of the world's foremost

> Success in achieving a low-cost edge over rivals comes from out-managing rivals in finding ways to perform value chain activities faster, more accurately, and more cost-effectively.

low-cost providers, has been an early adopter of state-of-the-art technology throughout its operations—its distribution facilities are an automated showcase, it has developed sophisticated online systems to order goods from suppliers and manage inventories, it equips its stores with cutting-edge sales-tracking and checkout systems, and it sends daily point-of-sale data to 4,000 vendors, *but Walmart carefully estimates the cost savings of new technologies before it rushes to invest in them.* By continuously investing in complex technologies that are hard for rivals to match, Walmart has sustained its competitive advantage for over 30 years.

Other companies noted for their successful use of low-cost provider strategies include Vizio in big-screen TVs, Briggs & Stratton in small gasoline engines, Bic in ballpoint pens, Stride Rite in footwear, Poulan in chain saws, and General Electric and Whirlpool in major home appliances.

When a Low-Cost Provider Strategy Works Best

A low-cost provider strategy becomes increasingly appealing and competitively powerful when:

1. *Price competition among rival sellers is vigorous.* Low-cost providers are in the best position to compete offensively on the basis of price, to use the appeal of lower price to grab sales (and market share) from rivals, to win the business of price-sensitive buyers, to remain profitable despite strong price competition, and to survive price wars.

2. *The products of rival sellers are essentially identical and readily available from many eager sellers.* Look-alike products and/or overabundant product supply set the stage for lively price competition; in such markets, it is the less efficient, higher-cost companies whose profits get squeezed the most.

3. *There are few ways to achieve product differentiation that have value to buyers.* When the differences between product attributes or brands do not matter much to buyers, buyers are nearly always very sensitive to price differences and market share winners will tend to be those with the lowest-priced brands.

4. *Most buyers use the product in the same ways.* With common user requirements, a standardized product can satisfy the needs of buyers, in which case low selling price, not features or quality, becomes the dominant factor in causing buyers to choose one seller's product over another's.

5. *Buyers incur low costs in switching their purchases from one seller to another.* Low switching costs give buyers the flexibility to shift purchases to lower-priced sellers having equally good products or to attractively priced substitute products. A low-cost leader is well positioned to use low price to induce its customers not to switch to rival brands or substitutes.

6. *Buyers are large and have significant power to bargain down prices.* Low-cost providers have partial profit-margin protection in bargaining with high-volume buyers, since powerful buyers are rarely able to bargain price down past the survival level of the next most cost-efficient seller.

7. *Industry newcomers use introductory low prices to attract buyers and build a customer base.* A low-cost provider can use price cuts of its own to make it harder for a new rival to win customers. Moreover, the pricing power of a low-cost provider acts as a barrier for new entrants.

As a rule, the more price-sensitive buyers are, the more appealing a low-cost strategy becomes. A low-cost company's ability to set the industry's price floor and still earn a profit erects protective barriers around its market position.

Pitfalls to Avoid in Pursuing a Low-Cost Provider Strategy

Perhaps the biggest mistake a low-cost provider can make to spoil the profitability of its low-cost advantage is getting carried away with overly aggressive price cutting to win sales and market share away from rivals. *Higher unit sales and market shares do not automatically translate into higher total profits.* A low-cost/low-price advantage results in superior profitability only if (1) prices are cut by less than the size of the unit cost advantage or (2) the added gains in unit sales are large enough to bring in a bigger total profit despite lower margins per unit sold. A company with a 5 percent per-unit cost advantage cannot cut prices 20 percent, end up with a volume gain of only 10 percent, and still expect to earn higher profits!

A lower price improves total profitability only if the price cuts lead to total revenues that are big enough to *more than cover* all the added costs associated with selling more units. When the incremental gains in total revenues flowing from a lower price exceed the incremental increases in total costs associated with a higher sales volume, then cutting price is a profitable move. But if a lower selling price results in revenue gains that are smaller than the increases in total costs, company profits end up lower than before and the price cut ends up reducing profits rather than raising them.

A second pitfall of a low-cost provider strategy is failing to emphasize avenues of cost advantage that can be kept proprietary or that relegate rivals to playing catch-up. The real value of a cost advantage depends on its sustainability. Sustainability, in turn, hinges on whether the company achieves its cost advantage in ways difficult for rivals to copy or otherwise overcome.

A third pitfall is becoming too fixated on cost reduction. Low cost cannot be pursued so zealously that a firm's offering ends up being too features-poor to generate buyer appeal. Furthermore, a company driving hard to push its costs down has to guard against misreading or ignoring increased buyer interest in added features or service, declining buyer sensitivity to price, or new developments that start to alter how buyers use the product. Otherwise, it risks losing market ground if buyers start opting for more upscale or feature-rich products.

Even if these mistakes are avoided, a low-cost provider strategy still entails risk. An innovative rival may discover an even lower-cost value chain approach. Important cost-saving technological breakthroughs may suddenly emerge. And if a low-cost provider has heavy investments in its present means of operating, then it can prove very costly to quickly shift to the new value chain approach or a new technology.

> A low-cost provider is in the best position to win the business of price-sensitive buyers, set the floor on market price, and still earn a profit.

> Reducing price does not lead to higher total profits unless the incremental gain in total revenues exceeds the incremental increase in total costs.

> A low-cost provider's product offering must always contain enough attributes to be attractive to prospective buyers—low price, by itself, is not always appealing to buyers.

BROAD DIFFERENTIATION STRATEGIES

Differentiation strategies are attractive whenever buyers' needs and preferences are too diverse to be fully satisfied by a standardized product offering. Successful product differentiation requires careful study of buyers' needs and behaviors to learn what buyers consider important, what they think has value, and what they are

Learn the major
avenues to a
competitive
advantage based
on differentiating a
company's product
or service offering
from the offerings
of rivals.

willing to pay for.[4] Then the trick is for a company to incorporate certain buyer-desired attributes into its product offering such that its offering will not only appeal to a broad range of buyers but also be different enough to stand apart from the product offerings of rivals—in regard to the latter, a strongly differentiated product offering is always preferable to a weakly differentiated one. A differentiation strategy calls for a customer value proposition that is *unique*. The strategy achieves its aim when an attractively large number of buyers find the customer value proposition appealing and become strongly attached to a company's differentiated attributes.

Successful differentiation allows a firm to do one or more of the following:

- Command a premium price for its product.
- Increase unit sales (because additional buyers are won over by the differentiating features).
- Gain buyer loyalty to its brand (because some buyers are strongly bonded to the differentiating features of the company's product offering).

Differentiation enhances profitability whenever a company's product can command a sufficiently higher price or produce sufficiently bigger unit sales *to more than cover the added costs of achieving the differentiation.* Company differentiation strategies fail when buyers don't value the brand's uniqueness and/or when a company's approach to differentiation is easily copied or matched by its rivals.

Companies can pursue differentiation from many angles: a unique taste (Dr Pepper, Listerine); multiple features (Microsoft Office, the iPhone); wide selection and one-stop shopping (Home Depot, Amazon.com); superior service (FedEx); engineering design and performance (Mercedes, BMW); prestige and distinctiveness (Rolex); product reliability (Johnson & Johnson in baby products); quality manufacture (Karastan in carpets, Michelin in tires, Honda in automobiles); technological leadership (3M Corporation in bonding and coating products); a full range of services (Charles Schwab in stock brokerage); wide product selection (Campbell's soups); and high fashion design (Gucci and Chanel).

CORE CONCEPT

The essence of a **broad differentiation strategy** is to offer unique product attributes that a wide range of buyers find appealing and worth paying for.

Managing the Value Chain to Create the Differentiating Attributes

Differentiation is not something hatched in marketing and advertising departments, nor is it limited to the catchalls of quality and service. Differentiation opportunities can exist in activities all along an industry's value chain. The most systematic approach that managers can take, however, involves focusing on the **uniqueness drivers,** a set of factors—analogous to cost drivers—that are particularly effective in creating differentiation. Figure 5.3 contains a list of important uniqueness drivers. Ways that managers can enhance differentiation based on these drivers include the following:

CORE CONCEPT

A **uniqueness driver** is a factor that can have a strong differentiating effect.

1. *Striving to create superior product features, design, and performance.* This applies to the physical and well as functional attributes of a product, including features such as expanded end uses and applications, added user safety, greater recycling capability, or enhanced environmental protection. Design features can be important in enhancing the aesthetic appeal of a product. Ducati's motorcycles, for example, are prized for their designs and have been exhibited in the Guggenheim art museum in New York City.[5]

Figure 5.3   Uniqueness Drivers: The Keys to Creating a Differentiation Advantage

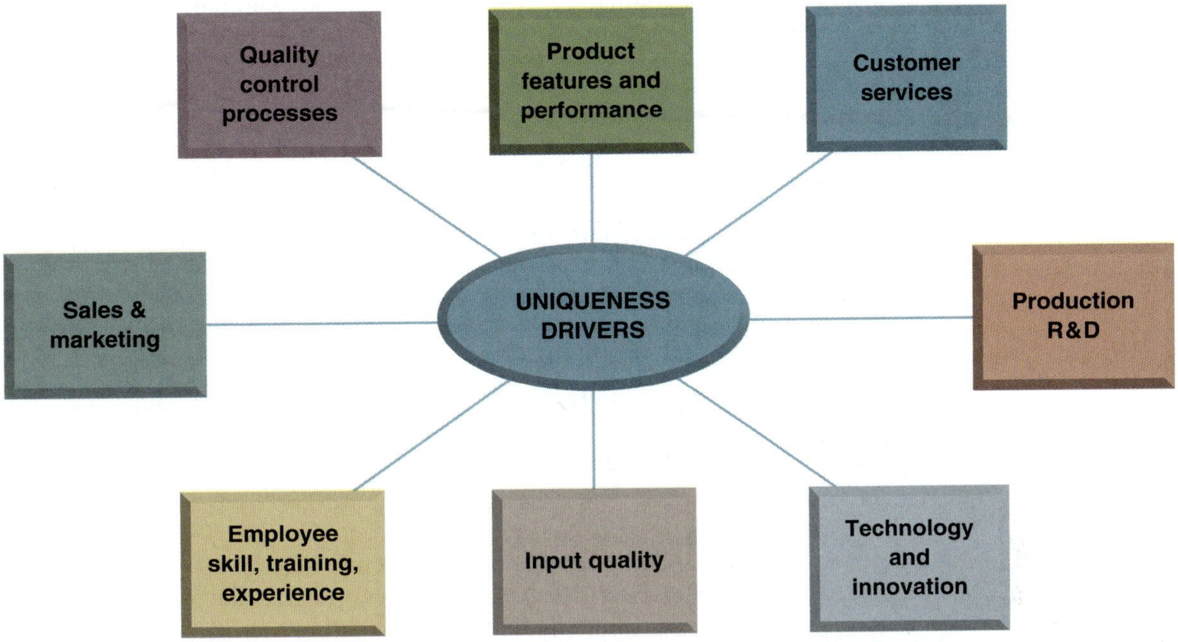

Source: Adapted from M. Porter, *Competitive Advantage: Creating and Sustaining Competitive Advantage* (New York: Free Press, 1985).

2. *Improving customer service or adding additional services.* Better customer services, in areas such as delivery, returns, and repair, can be as important in creating differentiation as superior product features. Examples include superior technical assistance to buyers, higher-quality maintenance services, more and better product information provided to customers, more and better training materials for end users, better credit terms, quicker order processing, or greater customer convenience.

3. *Pursuing production R&D activities.* Engaging in production R&D may permit custom-order manufacture at an efficient cost, provide wider product variety and selection through product "versioning," improve product quality, or make production methods safer for the environment. Many manufacturers have developed flexible manufacturing systems that allow different models and product versions to be made on the same assembly line. Being able to provide buyers with made-to-order products can be a potent differentiating capability.

4. *Striving for innovation and technological advances.* Successful innovation is the route to more frequent first-on-the-market victories and is a powerful differentiator. If the innovation proves hard to replicate, through patent protection or other means, it can provide a company with a first mover advantage that is sustainable.

5. *Pursuing continuous quality improvement.* Perceived quality differences can be an important differentiator in the eyes of customers. Quality control processes can be applied throughout the value chain, including postsale customer service activities. They can reduce product defects, prevent premature product failure, extend product life, make it economical to offer longer warranty

coverage, improve economy of use, result in more end-user convenience, or enhance product appearance. Companies whose quality management systems meet certification standards, such as the ISO 9001 standards, can enhance their reputation for quality with customers.

6. *Increasing the intensity of marketing and sales activities.* Marketing and advertising can have a tremendous effect on the value perceived by buyers and therefore their willingness to pay more for the company's offerings. They can create differentiation even when little tangible differentiation exists otherwise. For example, blind taste tests show that even the most loyal Pepsi or Coke drinkers have trouble telling one cola drink from another.[6] Brands create customer loyalty, which increases the perceived "cost" of switching to another product. Brand management activities are therefore also important in supporting differentiation.

7. *Seeking out high-quality inputs.* Input quality can ultimately spill over to affect the performance or quality of the company's end product. Starbucks, for example, gets high ratings on its coffees partly because it has very strict specifications on the coffee beans purchased from suppliers.

8. *Improving employee skill, knowledge, and experience through human resource management activities.* Hiring, training, and retaining highly skilled and experienced employees is important since such employees are often the source of creative, innovative ideas that are behind new product development. Moreover, they are essential to performing differentiating activities such as design, engineering, marketing, and R&D. Company culture and reward systems can help unleash the potential contribution of high-value employees to a differentiation strategy.

Managers need keen understanding of the sources of differentiation and the activities that drive uniqueness to evaluate various differentiation approaches and design durable ways to set their product offering apart from rival brands.

Revamping the Value Chain System to Increase Differentiation
Just as pursuing a cost advantage can involve the entire value chain system, the same is true for a differentiation advantage. Activities performed upstream by suppliers or downstream by distributors and retailers can have a meaningful effect on customers' perceptions of a company's offerings and its value proposition. Approaches to enhancing differentiation through changes in the value chain system include:[7]

- *Coordinating with channel allies to enhance customer perceptions of value.* Coordinating with downstream partners such as distributors, dealers, brokers, and retailers can contribute to differentiation in a variety of ways. Methods that companies use to influence the value chain activities of their channel allies include setting standards for downstream partners to follow, providing them with templates to standardize the selling environment or practices, training channel personnel, or cosponsoring promotions and advertising campaigns. Coordinating with retailers is important for enhancing the buying experience and building a company's image. Coordinating with distributors or shippers can mean quicker delivery to customers, more accurate order filling, and/or lower shipping costs. The Coca-Cola Company considers coordination with its bottler/distributors so important that it has at times taken over a troubled bottler for the purpose of improving its management and upgrading its plant and equipment before releasing the product to the market.[8]

- *Coordinating with suppliers to better address customer needs.* Collaborating with suppliers can also be a powerful route to a more effective differentiation strategy. Coordinating and collaborating with suppliers can improve many dimensions affecting product features and quality. This is particularly true for companies that only engage in assembly operations, such as Dell in PCs and Ducati in motorcycles. Close coordination with suppliers can also enhance differentiation by speeding up new product development cycles or speeding delivery to end customers. Strong relationships with suppliers can also mean that the company's supply requirements are prioritized when industry supply is insufficient to meet overall demand.

Delivering Superior Value via a Broad Differentiation Strategy

Differentiation strategies depend on meeting customer needs in unique ways or creating new needs, through activities such as innovation or persuasive advertising. The objective is to offer customers something that rivals can't—at least in terms of the level of satisfaction. There are four basic routes to achieving this aim.

The first route is to incorporate product attributes and user features that *lower the buyer's overall costs* of using the company's product. This is the least obvious and most overlooked route to a differentiation advantage. It is a differentiating factor since it can help business buyers be more competitive in their markets and more profitable. Producers of materials and components often win orders for their products by reducing a buyer's raw-material waste (providing cut-to-size components), reducing a buyer's inventory requirements (providing just-in-time deliveries), using online systems to reduce a buyer's procurement and order processing costs, and providing free technical support. This route to differentiation can also appeal to individual consumers who are looking to economize on their overall costs of consumption. Making a company's product more economical for a buyer to use can be done by incorporating energy-efficient features (energy-saving appliances and lightbulbs help cut buyers' utility bills; fuel-efficient vehicles cut buyer costs for gasoline) and/or by increasing maintenance intervals and product reliability so as to lower buyer costs for maintenance and repairs.

A second route is to incorporate *tangible* features that increase customer satisfaction with the product, such as product specifications, functions, and styling. This can be accomplished by including attributes that add functionality, enhance the design, expand the range of uses, save time for the user, are more reliable, or make the product cleaner, safer, quieter, simpler to use, portable, more convenient, or longer-lasting than rival brands. Cell phone manufacturers are in a race to introduce next-generation devices capable of being used for more purposes and having simpler menu functionality.

A third route to a differentiation-based competitive advantage is to incorporate *intangible* features that enhance buyer satisfaction in noneconomic ways. Toyota's Prius appeals to environmentally conscious motorists not only because these drivers want to help reduce global carbon dioxide emissions but also because they identify with the image conveyed. Rolls-Royce, Ralph Lauren, Tiffany, Rolex, and Prada have differentiation-based competitive advantages linked to buyer desires for status, image, prestige, upscale fashion, superior craftsmanship, and the finer things in life.

> Differentiation can be based on *tangible* or *intangible* attributes.

Intangibles that contribute to differentiation can extend beyond product attributes to the reputation of the company and to customer relations or trust.

The fourth route is to *signal the value* of the company's product offering to buyers. Typical signals of value include a high price (in instances where high price implies high quality and performance), more appealing or fancier packaging than competing products, ad content that emphasizes a product's standout attributes, the quality of brochures and sales presentations, the luxuriousness and ambience of a seller's facilities (important for high-end retailers and for offices or other facilities frequented by customers). They make potential buyers aware of the professionalism, appearance, and personalities of the seller's employees and/or make potential buyers realize that a company has prestigious customers. Signaling value is particularly important (1) when the nature of differentiation is based on intangible features and is therefore subjective or hard to quantify, (2) when buyers are making a first-time purchase and are unsure what their experience with the product will be, and (3) when repurchase is infrequent and buyers need to be reminded of a product's value.

Regardless of the approach taken, achieving a successful differentiation strategy requires, first, that the company have strengths in capabilities, such as customer service, marketing, brand management, and technology, that can create and support differentiation. That is, the resources, competencies, and value chain activities of the company must be well matched to the requirements of the strategy. For the strategy to result in competitive advantage, the company's competencies must also be sufficiently unique in delivering value to buyers that they help set its product offering apart from those of rivals. They must be competitively superior. There are numerous examples of companies that have differentiated themselves on the basis of distinctive competencies and capabilities. Apple has set itself apart from rivals on the basis of its capabilities to develop innovative new products and speed next-generation products to market ahead of competitors. When a major new event occurs, many people turn to Fox News and CNN because they have the capability to devote more airtime to breaking news stories and get reporters on the scene very quickly. Avon and Mary Kay Cosmetics have differentiated themselves from other cosmetics and personal care companies by assembling a sales force numbering in the hundreds of thousands that gives them a direct sales capability—their sales associates personally demonstrate products to interested buyers, take their orders on the spot, and deliver the items to buyers' homes.

The most successful approaches to differentiation are those that are hard or expensive for rivals to duplicate. Indeed, this is the route to a sustainable differentiation advantage. While resourceful competitors can, in time, clone almost any tangible product attribute, socially complex intangible attributes, such as company reputation, long-standing relationships with buyers, and image are much harder to imitate. Differentiation that creates switching costs that lock in buyers also provides a route to sustainable advantage. For example, if a buyer makes a substantial investment in learning to use one type of system, that buyer is less likely to switch to a competitor's system. (This has kept many users from switching away from Microsoft Office products, despite the fact that there are other applications with superior features.) As

> Easy-to-copy differentiating features cannot produce sustainable competitive advantage.

a rule, differentiation yields a longer-lasting and more profitable competitive edge when it is based on a well-established brand image, patent-protected product innovation, complex technical superiority, a reputation for superior product quality and reliability, relationship-based customer service, and unique competitive capabilities. Such differentiating attributes are generally tougher and take longer for rivals to match, and buyers widely perceive them as offering superior value.

When a Differentiation Strategy Works Best

Differentiation strategies tend to work best in market circumstances where:

- *Buyer needs and uses of the product are diverse.* Diverse buyer preferences present competitors with a bigger window of opportunity to do things differently and set themselves apart with product attributes that appeal to particular buyers. For instance, the diversity of consumer preferences for menu selection, ambience, pricing, and customer service gives restaurants exceptionally wide latitude in creating a differentiated product offering. Similar opportunities exist for the publishers of magazines, the makers of motor vehicles, and the manufacturers of cabinetry and countertops.

- *There are many ways to differentiate the product or service that have value to buyers.* There's plenty of room for retail apparel competitors to stock different styles and quality of apparel merchandise but very little room for the makers of paper clips or copier paper or sugar to set their products apart. Likewise, the sellers of different brands of gasoline or orange juice have little differentiation opportunity compared to the sellers of high-definition TVs or patio furniture or breakfast cereal. Basic commodities, such as chemicals, mineral deposits, and agricultural products, provide few opportunities for differentiation.

- *Few rival firms are following a similar differentiation approach.* The best differentiation approaches involve trying to appeal to buyers on the basis of attributes that rivals are not emphasizing. A differentiator encounters less head-to-head rivalry when it goes its own separate way in creating uniqueness and does not try to outdifferentiate rivals on the very same attributes. When many rivals are all claiming "ours tastes better than theirs" or "ours gets your clothes cleaner than theirs," the most likely result is weak brand differentiation and "strategy overcrowding"— competitors end up chasing much the same buyers with much the same product offerings.

- *Technological change is fast-paced and competition revolves around rapidly evolving product features.* Rapid product innovation and frequent introductions of next-version products not only provide space for companies to pursue separate differentiating paths but also heighten buyer interest. In video game hardware and video games, golf equipment, PCs, cell phones, and MP3 players, competitors are locked into an ongoing battle to set themselves apart by introducing the best next-generation products; companies that fail to come up with new and improved products and distinctive performance features quickly lose out in the marketplace. In U.S. network TV broadcasting, NBC, ABC, CBS, Fox, and several others are always scrambling to develop a lineup of TV shows that will win higher audience ratings and pave the way for charging higher advertising rates and boosting ad revenues.

Pitfalls to Avoid in Pursuing a Differentiation Strategy

Differentiation strategies can fail for any of several reasons. *A differentiation strategy is always doomed when competitors are able to quickly copy most or all of the appealing product attributes a company comes up with.* Rapid imitation means that no rival achieves differentiation, since whenever one firm introduces some aspect of uniqueness that strikes the fancy of buyers, fast-following copycats quickly reestablish similarity. This is

Any differentiating feature that works well is a magnet for imitators, although imitation attempts are not always successful.

why a firm must seek out sources of uniqueness that are time-consuming or burdensome for rivals to match if it hopes to use differentiation to win a lasting competitive edge over rivals.

A second pitfall is that *the company's attempt at differentiation produces an unenthusiastic response on the part of buyers.* Thus even if a company succeeds in setting its product apart from those of rivals, its strategy can result in disappointing sales and profits if buyers find other brands more appealing. Any time many potential buyers look at a company's differentiated product offering and conclude "so what," the company's differentiation strategy is in deep trouble.

The third big pitfall of a differentiation strategy is *overspending on efforts to differentiate the company's product offering, thus eroding profitability.* Company efforts to achieve differentiation nearly always raise costs, often substantially since marketing and R&D are expensive undertakings. The trick to profitable differentiation is either to keep the unit cost of achieving differentiation below the price premium that the differentiating attributes can command in the marketplace (thus increasing the profit margin per unit sold) or to offset thinner profit margins per unit by selling enough additional units to increase total profits. If a company goes overboard in pursuing costly differentiation efforts and then unexpectedly discovers that buyers are unwilling to pay a sufficient price premium to cover the added costs of differentiation, it ends up saddled with unacceptably thin profit margins or even losses. The need to contain differentiation costs is why many companies add little touches of differentiation that add to buyer satisfaction but are inexpensive to institute. Upscale restaurants often provide valet parking. Laundry detergent and soap manufacturers add pleasing scents to their products. Ski resorts provide skiers with complimentary coffee or hot apple cider at the base of the lifts in the morning and late afternoon.

Other common mistakes in crafting a differentiation strategy include:[9]

- *Being timid and not striving to open up meaningful gaps in quality, service, or performance features vis-à-vis the products of rivals.* Tiny differences between rivals' product offerings may not be visible or important to buyers. If a company wants to generate the fiercely loyal customer following needed to earn superior profits and open up a differentiation-based competitive advantage over rivals, then its strategy must result in *strong rather than weak product differentiation.* In markets where differentiators do no better than achieve weak product differentiation (because the attributes of rival brands are fairly similar in the minds of many buyers), customer loyalty to any one brand is weak, the costs of brand switching are fairly low, and no one company has enough of a market edge that it can get by with charging a price premium over rival brands.
- *Adding so many frills and extra features that the product exceeds the needs and use patterns of most buyers.* A dazzling array of features and options not only drives up costs (and therefore product price) but also runs the risk that many buyers will conclude that a less deluxe and lower-priced brand is a better value since they have little occasion or reason to use some of the deluxe attributes.
- *Charging too high a price premium.* While buyers may be intrigued by a product's deluxe features, they may nonetheless see it as being overpriced relative to the value delivered by the differentiating attributes. A company must guard against turning off would-be buyers with what is perceived as "price gouging." Normally, the bigger the price premium for the differentiating extras, the harder it is to keep buyers from switching to the lower-priced offerings of competitors.

Overdifferentiating and overcharging can be fatal strategy mistakes.

A low-cost provider strategy can defeat a differentiation strategy when buyers are satisfied with a basic product and don't think "extra" attributes are worth a higher price.

FOCUSED (OR MARKET NICHE) STRATEGIES

What sets focused strategies apart from low-cost provider and broad differentiation strategies is concentrated attention on a narrow piece of the total market. The target segment, or niche, can be defined by geographic uniqueness, by specialized requirements in using the product, or by special product attributes that appeal only to niche members. Community Coffee, the largest family-owned specialty coffee retailer in the United States, has a geographic focus on the state of Louisiana and communities across the Gulf of Mexico. Community holds only a 1.1 percent share of the national coffee market but has recorded sales in excess of $100 million and has won a 50 percent share of the coffee business in the 11-state region where it is distributed. Examples of other firms that concentrate on a well-defined market niche keyed to a particular product or buyer segment include Animal Planet and the History Channel (in cable TV); Cannondale (in top-of-the-line mountain bikes); Enterprise Rent-a-Car (a specialist in providing rental cars to repair garage customers); Bandag (a specialist in truck tire recapping that promotes its recaps aggressively at over 1,000 truck stops); CGA, Inc. (a specialist in providing insurance to cover the cost of lucrative hole-in-one prizes at golf tournaments); and Match.com (the world's largest online dating service). Microbreweries, bed-and-breakfast inns, and local owner-managed retail boutiques have also scaled their operations to serve narrow or local customer segments.

A Focused Low-Cost Strategy

A focused strategy based on low cost aims at securing a competitive advantage by serving buyers in the target market niche at a lower cost and lower price than those of rival competitors. This strategy has considerable attraction when a firm can lower costs significantly by limiting its customer base to a well-defined buyer segment. The avenues to achieving a cost advantage over rivals also serving the target market niche are the same as those for low-cost leadership: outmanage rivals in keeping the costs of value chain activities contained to a bare minimum and search for innovative ways to bypass certain value chain activities. The only real difference between a low-cost provider strategy and a focused low-cost strategy is the size of the buyer group that a company is trying to appeal to—the former involves a product offering that appeals broadly to almost all buyer groups and market segments, whereas the latter aims at just meeting the needs of buyers in a narrow market segment.

Focused low-cost strategies are fairly common. Producers of private-label goods are able to achieve low costs in product development, marketing, distribution, and advertising by concentrating on making generic items imitative of name-brand merchandise and selling directly to retail chains wanting a low-priced store brand. The Perrigo Company has become a leading manufacturer of over-the-counter health care products, with 2010 sales of more than $2.2 billion, by focusing on producing private-label brands for retailers such as Walmart, CVS, Walgreens, Rite-Aid, and Safeway. Budget motel chains, like Motel 6, cater to price-conscious travelers who just want to pay for a clean, no-frills place to spend the night. Redbox has established a low-cost network of more than 15,000 vending machines in high-traffic shopping locations that enable it to rent movie DVDs for $1 and sell used movie DVDs for $7. Illustration Capsule 5.2 describes how Vizio's low costs and focus on big-box retailers has allowed it to become the largest seller of flat-panel HDTVs in the United States in less than six years from its startup.

A Focused Differentiation Strategy

A focused strategy keyed to differentiation aims at securing a competitive advantage with a product offering carefully designed to appeal to the unique preferences and needs of a narrow, well-defined group of buyers (as opposed to a broad differentiation strategy aimed at many buyer groups and market segments). Successful use of a focused differentiation strategy depends on the existence of a buyer segment that is looking for special product attributes or seller capabilities and on a firm's ability to stand apart from rivals competing in the same target market niche.

Companies like Godiva Chocolates, Rolls-Royce, Haägen-Dazs, and W. L. Gore (the maker of Gore-Tex) employ successful differentiation-based focused strategies targeted at upscale buyers wanting products and services with world-class attributes. Indeed, most markets contain a buyer segment willing to pay a big price premium for the very finest items available, thus opening the strategic window for some competitors to pursue differentiation-based focused strategies aimed at the very top of the market pyramid. Ferrari markets its 1,500 cars sold in North America each year to a list of just 20,000 highly affluent car enthusiasts. Only the highest echelon of this exclusive group were contacted by Ferrari for a chance to put their names on the waiting list for one of the 29 $1.9 million FXX models planned for sale in North America.

Another successful focused differentiator is "fashion food retailer" Trader Joe's, a 300-store, 25-state chain that is a combination gourmet deli and food warehouse. Customers shop Trader Joe's as much for entertainment as for conventional grocery items—the store stocks out-of-the-ordinary culinary treats like raspberry salsa, salmon burgers, and jasmine fried rice, as well as the standard goods normally found in supermarkets. What sets Trader Joe's apart is not just its unique combination of food novelties and competitively priced grocery items but also its capability to turn an otherwise mundane grocery excursion into a whimsical treasure hunt that is just plain fun. Illustration Capsule 5.3 describes Progressive Insurance's focused differentiation strategy.

When a Focused Low-Cost or Focused Differentiation Strategy Is Attractive

A focused strategy aimed at securing a competitive edge based either on low cost or differentiation becomes increasingly attractive as more of the following conditions are met:

- The target market niche is big enough to be profitable and offers good growth potential.
- Industry leaders do not see that having a presence in the niche is crucial to their own success—in which case focusers can often escape battling head to head against some of the industry's biggest and strongest competitors.

ILLUSTRATION CAPSULE 5.2

Vizio's Focused Low-Cost Strategy

California-based Vizio, Inc., designs flat-panel LCD and plasma TVs that range in size from 20 to 55 inches and are sold only by big-box discount retailers such as Walmart, Sam's Club, Costco Wholesale, and Best Buy. If you've shopped for a flat-panel TV recently, you've probably noticed that Vizio is among the lowest-priced brands and that its picture quality is surprisingly good considering the price. The company is able to keep its cost low by only designing TVs and then sourcing its production to a limited number of contract manufacturers in Taiwan. In fact, 80 percent of its production is handled by a company called AmTran Technology. Such a dependence on a supplier can place a buyer in a precarious situation by making it vulnerable to price increases or product shortages, but Vizio has countered this possible threat by making AmTran a major stockholder. AmTran Technology owns a 23 percent stake in Vizio and earns about 80 percent of its revenues from its sales of televisions to Vizio. Vizio's close relationship with its major supplier and its focus on a single product category sold through limited distribution channels allows it to offer its customers deep price discounts.

Vizio's first major account was landed in 2003 when it approached buyers for Costco with a 46-inch plasma TV whose wholesale price was half that of the next lowest-price competitor. Within two months, Costco was carrying Vizio flat-panel TVs in 320 of its warehouse stores in the United States. In October 2007, Vizio approached buyers for Sam's Club with a 20-inch LCD TV that could be sold at retail for under $350. The price and quality of the 20-inch TV led Sam's Club buyers to place an order for 20,000 TVs for March 2008 delivery. By 2009, Vizio had become the largest seller of flat-panel HDTVs in the United States, with a market share of 21.6 percent.

Sources: "Picture Shift: U.S. Upstart Takes On TV Giants in Price War," *Wall Street Journal,* April 15, 2008, p. A1; Vizio, Inc., "Vizio Achieves #1 LCD HDTV Ranking in North America and #1 Ranking in U.S. Flat Panel HDTV Shipments," press release, May 11, 2009.

- It is costly or difficult for multisegment competitors to put capabilities in place to meet the specialized needs of buyers constituting the target market niche and at the same time satisfy the expectations of their mainstream customers.
- The industry has many different niches and segments, thereby allowing a focuser to pick a competitively attractive niche suited to its most valuable resources and capabilities. Also, with more niches there is more room for focusers to avoid each other in competing for the same customers.
- Few, if any, other rivals are attempting to specialize in the same target segment—a condition that reduces the risk of segment overcrowding.
- The focuser has a reservoir of customer goodwill and loyalty (accumulated from having catered to the specialized needs and preferences of niche members over many years) that it can draw on to help stave off ambitious challengers looking to horn in on its business.

The advantages of focusing a company's entire competitive effort on a single market niche are considerable, especially for smaller and medium-size companies that may lack the breadth and depth of resources to tackle going after a broad customer base with a "something for everyone" lineup of models, styles,

Progressive Insurance's Focused Differentiation Strategy in Auto Insurance

Progressive Insurance has fashioned a strategy in auto insurance focused on people with a record of traffic violations who drive high-performance cars, drivers with accident histories, motorcyclists, teenagers, and other so-called high-risk categories of drivers that most auto insurance companies steer away from. Progressive discovered that some of these high-risk drivers are affluent and pressed for time, making them less sensitive to paying premium rates for their car insurance. Management learned that it could charge such drivers premiums high enough to cover the level of risk they presented, plus the company differentiated itself from other car insurers by expediting the process of obtaining insurance and decreasing the annoyance that high-risk drivers faced in obtaining insurance coverage. In addition, Progressive pioneered the low-cost direct sales model of allowing customers to purchase insurance online and over the phone.

Progressive also studied the market segments for insurance carefully enough to discover that some motorcycle owners were not especially risky (middle-aged suburbanites who sometimes commuted to work or used their motorcycles mainly for recreational trips with their friends). Progressive's strategy allowed it to become a leader in providing car insurance to the owners of high-value vehicles who appreciated Progressive's streamlined approach to doing business.

In further differentiating and promoting Progressive's policies, management created teams of roving claims adjusters who would arrive at accident scenes to assess claims and issue checks for repairs on the spot. Progressive introduced 24-hour claims reporting, now an industry standard. In addition, it developed a sophisticated pricing system so that it could quickly and accurately assess each customer's risk and weed out unprofitable customers.

By being creative and excelling at the nuts and bolts of its business, Progressive has won a 7.6 percent share of the $150 billion market for auto insurance and has the highest underwriting margins in the auto insurance industry.

Sources: www.progressiveinsurance.com; I. McMillan, A. van Putten, and R. McGrath, "Global Gamesmanship," *Harvard Business Review* 81, no. 5 (May 2003), p. 68; *Fortune,* May 16, 2005, p. 34; "Motorcyclists Age, Affluence Trending Upward," *BestWire,* July 24, 2007.

and product selection. YouTube has become a household name by concentrating on short video clips posted online. Papa John's and Domino's Pizza have created impressive businesses by focusing on the home delivery segment. Porsche and Ferrari have done well catering to wealthy sports car enthusiasts.

The Risks of a Focused Low-Cost or Focused Differentiation Strategy

Focusing carries several risks. One is the chance that competitors will find effective ways to match the focused firm's capabilities in serving the target niche—perhaps by coming up with products or brands specifically designed to appeal to buyers in the target niche or by developing expertise and capabilities that offset the focuser's strengths. In the lodging business, large chains like Marriott have launched multibrand strategies that allow them to compete effectively in several lodging segments simultaneously. Marriott has flagship J.W. Marriot and Ritz-Carlton hotels with deluxe accommodations for business travelers and resort vacationers; its Courtyard by Marriott and SpringHill Suites brands cater to business travelers looking for moderately priced lodging; Marriott Residence Inns and TownePlace Suites are designed as a "home away from home" for travelers staying five or more nights; and the 535 Fairfield Inn locations are intended to appeal to travelers looking for quality lodging at an "affordable" price. Multibrand strategies are attractive to large companies like Marriott precisely because they enable a company to enter a market niche and siphon business away from companies that employ a focused strategy.

A second risk of employing a focused strategy is the potential for the preferences and needs of niche members to shift over time toward the product attributes desired by the majority of buyers. An erosion of the differences across buyer segments lowers entry barriers into a focuser's market niche and provides an open invitation for rivals in adjacent segments to begin competing for the focuser's customers. A third risk is that the segment may become so attractive that it is soon inundated with competitors, intensifying rivalry and splintering segment profits.

BEST-COST PROVIDER STRATEGIES

Best-cost provider strategies stake out a middle ground between pursuing a low-cost advantage and a differentiation advantage and between appealing to the broad market as a whole and a narrow market niche—see Figure 5.1. Such a middle ground allows a company to aim squarely at the sometimes great mass of value-conscious buyers looking for a good to very good product or service at an economical price. Value-conscious buyers frequently shy away from both cheap low-end products and expensive high-end products, but they are quite willing to pay a "fair" price for extra features and functionality they find appealing and useful. The essence of a best-cost provider strategy is giving customers more *value for the money* by satisfying buyer desires for appealing features/performance/quality/service and charging a lower price for these attributes compared to rivals with similar caliber product offerings.[10] From a competitive-positioning standpoint, best-cost strategies are thus a *hybrid,* balancing a strategic emphasis on low cost against a strategic emphasis on differentiation (desirable features delivered at a relatively low price).

To profitably employ a best-cost provider strategy, a company *must have the resources and capabilities to incorporate attractive or upscale attributes into its product offering at a lower cost than rivals.* When a company can incorporate appealing features, good to excellent product performance or quality, or more satisfying customer service into its product offering *at a lower cost than rivals,* then it enjoys "best-cost" status—it is the low-cost provider of a product or service with *desirable attributes.* A best-cost provider can use its low-cost advantage to underprice

> **CORE CONCEPT**
>
> **Best-cost provider strategies** are a *hybrid* of low-cost provider and differentiation strategies that aim at providing desired quality/features/performance/service attributes while beating rivals on price.

LO 4

Recognize the attributes of a best-cost provider strategy and the way in which some firms use a hybrid strategy to go about building a competitive advantage and delivering superior value to customers.

rivals whose products or services have similarly desirable attributes and still earn attractive profits. It is usually not difficult to entice buyers away from rivals with an equally good product at a more economical price.

Being a best-cost provider is different from being a low-cost provider because the additional attractive attributes entail additional costs (which a low-cost provider can avoid by offering buyers a basic product with few frills). Moreover, the two strategies aim at a distinguishably different market target. *The target market for a best-cost provider is value-conscious buyers*—buyers who are looking for appealing extras and functionality at an appealingly low price. Value-hunting buyers (as distinct from *price-conscious buyers* looking for a basic product at a bargain-basement price) often constitute a very sizable part of the overall market. Normally, value-conscious buyers are willing to pay a "fair" price for extra features, but they shy away from paying top dollar for items having all the bells and whistles. It is the desire to cater to *value-conscious buyers* as opposed to *budget-conscious buyers* that sets a best-cost provider apart from a low-cost provider—the two strategies aim at distinguishably different market targets.

When a Best-Cost Provider Strategy Works Best

A best-cost provider strategy works best in markets where product differentiation is the norm and there is an attractively large number of value-conscious buyers who prefer midrange products to cheap, basic products or expensive top-of-the-line products. A best-cost provider needs to position itself near the middle of the market with either a medium-quality product at a below-average price or a high-quality product at an average or slightly higher price. The objective is to provide the *best value* for better-quality, differentiated products. Best-cost provider strategies also work well in recessionary times when great masses of buyers become value-conscious and are attracted to economically priced products and services with appealing attributes. *But unless a company has the resources, know-how, and capabilities to incorporate upscale product or service attributes at a lower cost than rivals, adopting a best-cost strategy is ill-advised*—a winning strategy must always be matched to a company's most valuable resources and capabilities.

Illustration Capsule 5.4 describes how Toyota has applied the principles of the best-cost provider strategy in producing and marketing its Lexus brand.

The Big Risk of a Best-Cost Provider Strategy

A company's biggest vulnerability in employing a best-cost provider strategy is getting squeezed between the strategies of firms using low-cost and high-end differentiation strategies. Low-cost providers may be able to siphon customers away with the appeal of a lower price (despite less appealing product attributes). High-end differentiators may be able to steal customers away with the appeal of better product attributes (even though their products carry a higher price tag). Thus, to be successful, a best-cost provider must offer buyers *significantly* better product attributes in order to justify a price above what low-cost leaders are charging. Likewise, it has to achieve significantly lower costs in providing upscale features so that it can outcompete high-end differentiators on the basis of a *significantly* lower price.

ILLUSTRATION CAPSULE 5.4

Toyota's Best-Cost Provider Strategy for Its Lexus Line

Toyota Motor Company is widely regarded as a low-cost producer among the world's motor vehicle manufacturers. Despite its emphasis on product quality, Toyota has achieved low-cost leadership because it has developed considerable skills in efficient supply chain management and low-cost assembly capabilities and because its models are positioned in the low-to-medium end of the price spectrum, where high production volumes are conducive to low unit costs. But when Toyota decided to introduce its new Lexus models to compete in the luxury-car market segment, it employed a classic best-cost provider strategy. Toyota took the following four steps in crafting and implementing its Lexus strategy:

- Designing an array of high-performance characteristics and upscale features into the Lexus models to make them comparable in performance and luxury to other high-end models and attractive to Mercedes, BMW, Audi, Jaguar, Cadillac, and Lincoln buyers.

- Transferring its capabilities in making high-quality Toyota models at low cost to making premium-quality Lexus models at costs below other luxury-car makers. Toyota's supply chain capabilities and low-cost assembly know-how allowed it to incorporate high-tech performance features and upscale quality into Lexus models at substantially less cost than Mercedes, BMW, and other luxury-vehicle makers have been able to achieve in producing their models.

- Using its relatively lower manufacturing costs to underprice comparable Mercedes, BMW, Audi, and Jaguar models. Toyota believed that with its cost advantage it could price

attractively equipped Lexus cars low enough to draw price-conscious buyers away from comparable high-end brands. Toyota's pricing policy also allowed it to induce Toyota, Honda, Ford, or GM owners desiring more luxury to switch to a Lexus. Lexus's pricing advantage has typically been quite significant. For example, in 2009 the Lexus RX 350, a midsize SUV, carried a sticker price in the $38,000 to $48,000 range (depending on how it was equipped), whereas comparable Mercedes M-class SUVs had price tags in the $45,000 to $63,000 range and a comparable BMW X5 SUV could range anywhere from $47,000 to $65,000.

- Establishing a new network of Lexus dealers, separate from Toyota dealers, dedicated to providing a level of personalized, attentive customer service unmatched in the industry.

Toyota's best-cost strategy has resulted in growing sales of Lexus models (now over 400,000 vehicles annually). Lexus has consistently ranked first in the widely watched J. D. Power & Associates quality survey, and Lexus owners enjoy both top-notch dealer service and product quality.

THE CONTRASTING FEATURES OF THE FIVE GENERIC COMPETITIVE STRATEGIES: A SUMMARY

Deciding which generic competitive strategy should serve as the framework on which to hang the rest of the company's strategy is not a trivial matter. Each of the five generic competitive strategies *positions* the company differently in its market and competitive environment. Each establishes a central theme for how the company will endeavor to outcompete rivals. Each creates some boundaries or guidelines for maneuvering as market circumstances unfold and as ideas for improving the strategy are debated. Each points to different ways of experimenting and tinkering with the basic strategy—for example, employing a low-cost leadership strategy means experimenting with ways that costs can be cut and value chain activities can be streamlined, whereas a broad differentiation strategy means exploring ways to add new differentiating features or to perform value chain activities differently if the result is to add value for customers in ways they are willing to pay for. Each entails differences in terms of product line, production emphasis, marketing emphasis, and means of maintaining the strategy, as shown in Table 5.1.

Thus a choice of which generic strategy to employ spills over to affect many aspects of how the business will be operated and the manner in which value chain activities must be managed. Deciding which generic strategy to employ is perhaps the most important strategic commitment a company makes—it tends to drive the rest of the strategic actions a company decides to undertake.

Table 5.1   Distinguishing Features of the Five Generic Competitive Strategies

	Low-Cost Provider	Broad Differentiation	Focused Low-Cost Provider	Focused Differentiation	Best-Cost Provider
Strategic target	• A broad cross-section of the market.	• A broad cross-section of the market.	• A narrow market niche where buyer needs and preferences are distinctively different.	• A narrow market niche where buyer needs and preferences are distinctively different.	• Value-conscious buyers. • A middle market range.
Basis of competitive strategy	• Lower overall costs than competitors.	• Ability to offer buyers something attractively different from competitors' offerings.	• Lower overall cost than rivals in serving niche members.	• Attributes that appeal specifically to niche members.	• Ability to offer better goods at attractive prices.
Product line	• A good basic product with few frills (acceptable quality and limited selection).	• Many product variations, wide selection; emphasis on differentiating features.	• Features and attributes tailored to the tastes and requirements of niche members.	• Features and attributes tailored to the tastes and requirements of niche members.	• Items with appealing attributes; assorted features; better quality, not best.
Production emphasis	• A continuous search for cost reduction without sacrificing acceptable quality and essential features.	• Build in whatever differentiating features buyers are willing to pay for; strive for product superiority.	• A continuous search for cost reduction for products that meet basic needs of niche members.	• Small-scale production or custom-made products that match the tastes and requirements of niche members.	• Build in appealing features and better quality at lower cost than rivals.

	Low-Cost Provider	Broad Differentiation	Focused Low-Cost Provider	Focused Differentiation	Best-Cost Provider
Marketing emphasis	• Low prices, good value. • Try to make a virtue out of product features that lead to low cost.	• Tout differentiating features. • Charge a premium price to cover the extra costs of differentiating features.	• Communicate attractive features of a budget-priced product offering that fits niche buyers' expectations.	• Communicate how product offering does the best job of meeting niche buyers' expectations.	• Tout delivery of *best* value. • Either deliver comparable features at a lower price than rivals or else match rivals on prices and provide better features.
Keys to maintaining the strategy	• Economical prices, good value. • Strive to manage costs down, year after year, in every area of the business.	• Stress constant innovation to stay ahead of imitative competitors. • Concentrate on a few key differentiating features.	• Stay committed to serving the niche at the lowest overall cost; don't blur the firm's image by entering other market segments or adding other products to widen market appeal.	• Stay committed to serving the niche better than rivals; don't blur the firm's image by entering other market segments or adding other products to widen market appeal.	• Unique expertise in simultaneously managing costs down while incorporating upscale features and attributes.
Resources and capabilities required	• Capabilities for driving costs out of the value chain system. • *Examples:* large-scale automated plants, an efficiency-oriented culture, bargaining power.	• Capabilities concerning quality, design, intangibles, and innovation. • *Examples:* marketing capabilities, R&D teams, technology.	• Capabilities to lower costs on niche goods. • *Examples:* lower input costs for the specific product desired by the niche, batch production capabilities.	• Capabilities to meet the highly specific needs of niche members. • *Examples:* custom production, close customer relations.	• Capabilities to simultaneously deliver lower cost and higher-quality/differentiated features. • *Examples:* TQM practices, mass customization.

Successful Competitive Strategies Are Resource-Based

For a company's competitive strategy to succeed in delivering good performance and the intended competitive edge over rivals, it has to be underpinned by an appropriate set of resources, know-how, and competitive capabilities. To succeed in employing a low-cost provider strategy, a company has to have the resources and capabilities needed to keep its costs below those of its competitors; this means having the expertise to cost-effectively manage value chain activities better than rivals and/or having the innovative capability to bypass certain value chain activities being performed by rivals. Successful focused strategies require the capability to do an outstanding job of satisfying the needs and expectations of niche

A company's competitive strategy is unlikely to succeed unless it is predicated on leveraging a competitively valuable collection of resources and capabilities that match the strategy.

buyers. Success in employing a best-cost strategy requires the resources and capabilities to simultaneously incorporate desirable product or service attributes and deliver them at a lower cost than rivals. To succeed in strongly differentiating its product in ways that are appealing to buyers, a company must have the resources and capabilities to incorporate unique attributes into its product offering that a broad range of buyers will find appealing and worth paying for, This is easier said than done because, given sufficient time, competitors can clone almost any product feature buyers find quite appealing. Hence, long-term differentiation success is usually dependent on having a hard-to-imitate portfolio of resource capabilities (like patented technology; strong, socially complex skills in product innovation; expertise in relationship-based customer service) that allow a company to sustain its differentiation-based competitive advantage. Likewise, sustaining the competitive edge inherent in any generic strategy depends on resources, capabilities, and competences that rivals have a hard time duplicating and for which there are no good substitutes.

KEY POINTS

The key points to take away from this chapter include the following:

1. Deciding which of the five generic competitive strategies to employ—overall low-cost, broad differentiation, focused low-cost, focused differentiation, or best-cost—is perhaps the most important strategic commitment a company makes. It tends to drive the remaining strategic actions a company undertakes and sets the whole tone for pursuing a competitive advantage over rivals.

2. In employing a low-cost provider strategy and trying to achieve a low-cost advantage over rivals, a company must do a better job than rivals of cost-effectively managing value chain activities and/or it must find innovative ways to eliminate cost-producing activities. Low-cost provider strategies work particularly well when the products of rival sellers are virtually identical or very weakly differentiated and supplies are readily available from eager sellers, when there are not many ways to differentiate that have value to buyers, when many buyers are price-sensitive and shop the market for the lowest price, and when buyer switching costs are low.

3. Broad differentiation strategies seek to produce a competitive edge by incorporating tangible and intangible attributes that set a company's product/service offering apart from rivals in ways that buyers consider valuable and worth paying for. Successful differentiation allows a firm to (1) command a premium price for its product, (2) increase unit sales (because additional buyers are won over by the differentiating features), and/or (3) gain buyer loyalty to its brand (because some buyers are strongly attracted to the differentiating features and bond with the company and its products). Differentiation strategies work best when diverse buyer preferences open up windows of opportunity to strongly differentiate a company's product offering from those of rival brands, in situations where few other rivals are pursuing a similar differentiation approach, and in circumstances where companies are racing to bring out the most appealing next-generation product. A differentiation strategy is doomed when competitors are able to quickly copy most or all of the appealing product attributes a company comes up with, when a company's differentiation efforts fail to interest many buyers, and when a company overspends

on efforts to differentiate its product offering or tries to overcharge for its differentiating extras.

4. A focused strategy delivers competitive advantage either by achieving lower costs than rivals in serving buyers constituting the target market niche or by developing a specialized ability to offer niche buyers an appealingly differentiated offering that meets their needs better than rival brands do. A focused strategy based on either low cost or differentiation becomes increasingly attractive when the target market niche is big enough to be profitable and offers good growth potential, when it is costly or difficult for multisegment competitors to put capabilities in place to meet the specialized needs of the target market niche and at the same time satisfy the expectations of their mainstream customers, and when few other rivals are attempting to specialize in the same target segment.

5. Best-cost provider strategies combine a strategic emphasis on low cost with a strategic emphasis on more than minimal quality, service, features, or performance. The aim is to create competitive advantage by giving buyers *more value for the money for midrange products*—an approach that entails (1) matching close rivals on key quality/service/features/performance attributes, (2) beating them on the costs of incorporating such attributes into the product or service, and (3) charging a more economical price. A best-cost provider strategy works best in markets with large numbers of value-conscious buyers desirous of purchasing appealingly good products and services for less money.

6. In all cases, competitive advantage depends on having competitively superior resources and capabilities that are a good match for the chosen generic strategy. A sustainable advantage depends on maintaining that competitive superiority with resources, capabilities, and value chain activities that rivals have trouble matching and for which there are no good substitutes.

ASSURANCE OF LEARNING EXERCISES

LO 1, LO 2, LO 3, LO 4

1. Best Buy is the largest consumer electronics retailer in the United States, with 2009 sales of nearly $45 billion. The company competes aggressively on price with such rivals as Costco Wholesale, Sam's Club, Walmart, and Target, but it is also known by consumers for its first-rate customer service. Best Buy customers have commented that the retailer's sales staff is exceptionally knowledgeable about the company's products and can direct them to the exact location of difficult-to-find items. Best Buy customers also appreciate that demonstration models of PC monitors, MP3 players, and other electronics are fully powered and ready for in-store use. Best Buy's Geek Squad tech support and installation services are additional customer service features that are valued by many customers. How would you characterize Best Buy's competitive strategy? Should it be classified as a low-cost provider strategy? A differentiation strategy? A best-cost strategy? Explain your answer.

LO 3

2. Stihl is the world's leading manufacturer and marketer of chain saws, with annual sales exceeding $2 billion. With innovations dating to its 1929

STRENGTHENING A COMPANY'S COMPETITIVE POSITION

Strategic Moves, Timing, and Scope of Operations

> Competing in the marketplace is like war. You have injuries and casualties, and the best strategy wins.
>
> **—John Collins**
> *NHL executive*

> It was our duty to expand.
>
> **—Ingvar Kamprad**
> *Founder of IKEA*

> In the virtual economy, collaboration is a new competitive imperative.
>
> **—Michael Dell**
> *CEO of Dell Inc.*

> In this new wave of technology, you can't do it all yourself, you have to form alliances.
>
> **—Carlos Slim**
> *CEO of Telmex, Telcel and América Móvil and the wealthiest person in the world*

LEARNING OBJECTIVES

LO 1. Learn whether and when to pursue offensive or defensive strategic moves to improve a company's market position.

LO 2. Recognize when being a first mover or a fast follower or a late mover is most advantageous.

LO 3. Become aware of the strategic benefits and risks of expanding a company's horizontal scope through mergers and acquisitions.

LO 4. Learn the advantages and disadvantages of extending the company's scope of operations via vertical integration.

LO 5. Become aware of the conditions that favor farming out certain value chain activities to outside parties.

LO 6. Understand when and how strategic alliances can substitute for horizontal mergers and acquisitions or vertical integration and how they can facilitate outsourcing.

[5] G. Gavetti, "Ducati," Harvard Business School case 9-701-132, rev. March 8, 2002.

[6] http://jrscience.wcp.muohio.edu/nsfall01/FinalArticles/Final-IsitWorthitBrandsan.html.

[7] This section expands on the section on value chain linkages found in Porter, *Competitive Advantage*, p. 125.

[8] D. Yoffie, "Cola Wars Continue: Coke and Pepsi in 2006," Harvard Business School case 9-706-447.

[9] Porter, *Competitive Advantage*, pp. 160–62.

[10] For an excellent discussion of best-cost provider strategies, see Peter J. Williamson and Ming Zeng, "Value-for-Money Strategies for Recessionary Times," *Harvard Business Review* 87, no. 3 (March 2009), pp. 66–74.

CHAPTER 6

STRENGTHENING A COMPANY'S COMPETITIVE POSITION

Strategic Moves, Timing, and Scope of Operations

> Competing in the marketplace is like war. You have injuries and casualties, and the best strategy wins.
>
> **—John Collins**
> *NHL executive*

> It was our duty to expand.
>
> **—Ingvar Kamprad**
> *Founder of IKEA*

> In the virtual economy, collaboration is a new competitive imperative.
>
> **—Michael Dell**
> *CEO of Dell Inc.*

> In this new wave of technology, you can't do it all yourself, you have to form alliances.
>
> **—Carlos Slim**
> *CEO of Telmex, Telcel and América Móvil and the wealthiest person in the world*

LEARNING OBJECTIVES

LO 1. Learn whether and when to pursue offensive or defensive strategic moves to improve a company's market position.

LO 2. Recognize when being a first mover or a fast follower or a late mover is most advantageous.

LO 3. Become aware of the strategic benefits and risks of expanding a company's horizontal scope through mergers and acquisitions.

LO 4. Learn the advantages and disadvantages of extending the company's scope of operations via vertical integration.

LO 5. Become aware of the conditions that favor farming out certain value chain activities to outside parties.

LO 6. Understand when and how strategic alliances can substitute for horizontal mergers and acquisitions or vertical integration and how they can facilitate outsourcing.

on efforts to differentiate its product offering or tries to overcharge for its differentiating extras.

4. A focused strategy delivers competitive advantage either by achieving lower costs than rivals in serving buyers constituting the target market niche or by developing a specialized ability to offer niche buyers an appealingly differentiated offering that meets their needs better than rival brands do. A focused strategy based on either low cost or differentiation becomes increasingly attractive when the target market niche is big enough to be profitable and offers good growth potential, when it is costly or difficult for multisegment competitors to put capabilities in place to meet the specialized needs of the target market niche and at the same time satisfy the expectations of their mainstream customers, and when few other rivals are attempting to specialize in the same target segment.

5. Best-cost provider strategies combine a strategic emphasis on low cost with a strategic emphasis on more than minimal quality, service, features, or performance. The aim is to create competitive advantage by giving buyers *more value for the money for midrange products*—an approach that entails (1) matching close rivals on key quality/service/features/performance attributes, (2) beating them on the costs of incorporating such attributes into the product or service, and (3) charging a more economical price. A best-cost provider strategy works best in markets with large numbers of value-conscious buyers desirous of purchasing appealingly good products and services for less money.

6. In all cases, competitive advantage depends on having competitively superior resources and capabilities that are a good match for the chosen generic strategy. A sustainable advantage depends on maintaining that competitive superiority with resources, capabilities, and value chain activities that rivals have trouble matching and for which there are no good substitutes.

ASSURANCE OF LEARNING EXERCISES

LO 1, LO 2, LO 3, LO 4

1. Best Buy is the largest consumer electronics retailer in the United States, with 2009 sales of nearly $45 billion. The company competes aggressively on price with such rivals as Costco Wholesale, Sam's Club, Walmart, and Target, but it is also known by consumers for its first-rate customer service. Best Buy customers have commented that the retailer's sales staff is exceptionally knowledgeable about the company's products and can direct them to the exact location of difficult-to-find items. Best Buy customers also appreciate that demonstration models of PC monitors, MP3 players, and other electronics are fully powered and ready for in-store use. Best Buy's Geek Squad tech support and installation services are additional customer service features that are valued by many customers. How would you characterize Best Buy's competitive strategy? Should it be classified as a low-cost provider strategy? A differentiation strategy? A best-cost strategy? Explain your answer.

LO 3

2. Stihl is the world's leading manufacturer and marketer of chain saws, with annual sales exceeding $2 billion. With innovations dating to its 1929

invention of the gasoline-powered chain saw, the company holds over 1,000 patents related to chain saws and outdoor power tools. The company's chain saws, leaf blowers, and hedge trimmers sell at price points well above competing brands and are sold only by its network of over 8,000 independent dealers. The company boasts in its advertisements that its products are rated number one by consumer magazines and are *not* sold at Lowe's or Home Depot. How does Stihl's choice of distribution channels and advertisements contribute to its differentiation strategy?

LO 3

3. Explore BMW's Web site (www.bmw.com), and then click on the link for www.bmwgroup.com. The site you find provides an overview of the company's key functional areas, including research and development and production activities (see the page headings). Under Research and Development, click on Innovation & Technology and explore the links at the sidebar to better understand the types of resources and capabilities that underlie BMW's approach to innovation. Also review the statements under Production focusing on automobile production worldwide and sustainable production. How do the resources, capabilities, and activities of BMW contribute to its differentiation strategy and the unique position in the industry that it has achieved?

EXERCISES FOR SIMULATION PARTICIPANTS

LO 1, LO 2, LO 3, LO 4

1. Which one of the five generic competitive strategies best characterizes your company's strategic approach to competing successfully?
2. Which rival companies appear to be employing a low-cost provider strategy?
3. Which rival companies appear to be employing a broad differentiation strategy?
4. Which rival companies appear to be employing some type of focused strategy?
5. Which rival companies appear to be employing a best-cost provider strategy?
6. What is your company's action plan to achieve a sustainable competitive advantage over rival companies? List at least three (preferably more) specific kinds of decision entries on specific decision screens that your company has made or intends to make to win this kind of competitive edge over rivals.

ENDNOTES

[1] This classification scheme is an adaptation of a narrower three-strategy classification presented in Michael E. Porter, *Competitive Strategy: Techniques for Analyzing Industries and Competitors* (New York: Free Press, 1980). For a discussion of the different ways that companies can position themselves in the marketplace, see Michael E. Porter, "What Is Strategy?" *Harvard Business Review* 74, no. 6 (November–December 1996), pp. 65–67.
[2] M. Porter, *Competitive Advantage: Creating and Sustaining Superior Performance* (New York: Free Press, 1985), p. 97.
[3] Michael Hammer and James Champy were the main proponents of business process reengineering. See M. Hammer and J. Champy, *Reengineering the Corporation: A Manifesto for Business Revolution,* rev. and updated (New York: HarperBusiness, 2003).
[4] For a discussion of how unique industry positioning and resource combinations are linked to consumers' perspectives of value and their willingness to pay more for differentiated products or services, see Richard L. Priem, "A Consumer Perspective on Value Creation," *Academy of Management Review* 32, no. 1 (2007), pp. 219–35.

Once a company has settled on which of the five generic competitive strategies to employ, attention turns to how strategic choices along several other dimensions can complement its competitive approach and maximize the power of its overall strategy. The first dimension concerns competitive actions—both offensive and defensive; the second concerns competitive dynamics and the timing of strategic moves; and the third concerns the breadth of a company's activities (or its *scope* of operations along an industry's entire value chain). All in all, the following measures to strengthen a company's competitive position and create a full-blown business strategy have to be considered:

- Whether and when to go on the offensive and initiate aggressive strategic moves to improve the company's market position.
- Whether and when to employ defensive strategies to protect the company's market position.

- When to undertake strategic moves—whether advantage or disadvantage lies in being a first mover, a fast follower, or a late mover.
- Whether to bolster the company's market position by merging with or acquiring another firm in the same industry.
- Whether to integrate backward or forward into more stages of the vertical chain of activities that (typically) begins with raw-material production and ends with sales to the end consumer.
- Whether to outsource certain value chain activities or perform them in-house.
- Whether to enter into strategic alliances or partnership arrangements with other enterprises.

This chapter presents the pros and cons of each of these strategy-enhancing measures.

GOING ON THE OFFENSIVE—STRATEGIC OPTIONS TO IMPROVE A COMPANY'S MARKET POSITION

No matter which one of the five generic competitive strategies a firm employs, there are times when it makes sense for the company to *go on the offensive* to strengthen its market position and improve its overall business performance. Strategic offensives are called for when a company spots opportunities to gain profitable market share at the expense of rivals or when a company has no choice but to try to whittle away at a strong rival's competitive advantage. Companies like Walmart, Apple, and Google play hardball, aggressively pursuing competitive advantage and trying to reap the benefits of a leading market share, superior profit margins, and more rapid growth, as well as the reputational rewards of being known as a winning company on the move.[1] The best offensives tend to incorporate several principles: (1) focusing relentlessly on building competitive advantage and then striving to convert it into sustainable advantage (as described in Chapter 4), (2) creating and deploying company resources in ways that cause rivals to struggle to defend themselves, (3) employing the element of surprise as opposed to doing what rivals expect and are prepared for, and (4) displaying a strong bias for swift, decisive, and overwhelming actions to overpower rivals.[2]

Choosing the Basis for Competitive Attack

As a rule, challenging rivals on competitive grounds where they are strong is an uphill struggle.[3] Offensive initiatives that exploit competitor weaknesses stand a far better chance of succeeding than do those that challenge competitor strengths, especially if the weaknesses represent important vulnerabilities and if weak rivals can be caught by surprise with no ready defense.[4]

Strategic offensives should, as a general rule, be based on exploiting a company's strongest strategic assets—its most valuable resources and capabilities, such as a better-known brand name, a more efficient production or distribution system, greater technological capability, or a superior reputation for quality. But a consideration of the company's strengths should not be made without also considering the rival's strengths and weaknesses. A strategic offensive should be based on those areas of strength where the company has its greatest competitive advantage over the targeted rivals. If a company has especially good customer service capabilities, it can make special sales pitches to the customers of those rivals that provide subpar customer service. Aggressors with a recognized brand name and strong marketing skills can launch efforts to win customers away from rivals with weak brand recognition. There is considerable appeal in emphasizing sales to buyers in geographic regions where a rival has a weak market share or is exerting less competitive effort. Likewise, it may be attractive to pay special attention to buyer segments that a rival is neglecting or is weakly equipped to serve.

Ignoring the need to tie a strategic offensive to a company's resources where they are competitively stronger than rivals' is like going to war with a popgun—the prospects for success are dim. For instance, it is foolish for a company with relatively high costs to employ a price-cutting offensive—price-cutting offensives are best left to financially strong companies whose costs are relatively low in comparison to those of the companies being attacked. Likewise, it is ill-advised to pursue a product innovation offensive without having competitively superior expertise in R&D, new product development, and speeding new products to market.

The principal offensive strategy options include the following:

1. *Using a cost-based advantage to attack competitors on the basis of price or value.* A price-cutting offensive can involve offering customers an equally good or better product at a lower price or offering a low-priced, lower-quality product that gives customers more value for the money. This is the classic offensive for improving a company's market position vis-à-vis rivals, but it works well only

under certain circumstances. Lower prices can produce market share gains if competitors don't respond with price cuts of their own and if the challenger convinces buyers that its product offers them a better value proposition. However, such a strategy increases total profits only if the gains in additional unit sales are enough to offset the impact of lower prices and thinner margins per unit sold. Price-cutting offensives are generally successful only when a company *first achieves a cost advantage and then hits competitors with a lower price.*[5] Walmart's rise to dominance in discount retailing and supermarkets was based on just this type of strategic offensive. Ryanair also used this strategy successfully against rivals such as British Air and Aer Lingus, by first cutting costs to the bone and then targeting leisure passengers who care more about low price than in-flight amenities and service.[6] While some companies have used price-cutting offensives as a means of obtaining the cost advantages associated with greater market share (economies of scale or experience), this has proved to be a highly risky strategy. More often than not, such price-cutting offensives are met with retaliatory attacks that can mire the entire industry in a costly price war.

2. *Leapfrogging competitors by being the first adopter of next-generation technologies or being first to market with next-generation products.* In technology-based industries, the opportune time to overtake an entrenched competitor is when there is a shift to the next generation of the technology. Microsoft got its next-generation Xbox 360 to market a full 12 months ahead of Sony's PlayStation 3 and Nintendo's Wii, helping it convince video gamers to buy an Xbox rather than wait for the new PlayStation 3 and Wii to hit the market. This type of offensive strategy is high-risk, however, since it requires costly investment at a time when consumer reactions to the new technology are yet unknown.

3. *Pursuing continuous product innovation to draw sales and market share away from less innovative rivals.* Ongoing introductions of new and improved products can put rivals under tremendous competitive pressure, especially when rivals' new product development capabilities are weak. But such offensives can be sustained only if a company has sufficient product innovation skills to keep its pipeline full and maintain buyer enthusiasm for its new and better product offerings.

4. *Adopting and improving on the good ideas of other companies (rivals or otherwise).*[7] The idea of warehouse-type home improvement centers did not originate with Home Depot cofounders Arthur Blank and Bernie Marcus; they got the "big-box" concept from their former employer Handy Dan Home Improvement. But they were quick to improve on Handy Dan's business model and take Home Depot to the next plateau in terms of product line breadth and customer service. Casket maker Hillenbrand greatly improved its market position by adapting Toyota's production methods to casket making. Offense-minded companies are often quick to take any good idea (not nailed down by a patent or other legal protection), make it their own, and then aggressively apply it to create competitive advantage for themselves.

5. *Using hit-and-run or guerrilla warfare tactics to grab sales and market share from complacent or distracted rivals.* Options for "guerrilla offensives" include occasional lowballing on price (to win a big order or steal a key account from a rival), surprising key rivals with sporadic but intense bursts of promotional activity (offering a special trial offer for new customers to draw them away

from rival brands), or undertaking special campaigns to attract buyers away from rivals plagued with a strike or problems in meeting buyer demand.[8] Guerrilla offensives are particularly well suited to small challengers that have neither the resources nor the market visibility to mount a full-fledged attack on industry leaders and that may not merit a full retaliatory response from larger rivals.[9]

6. *Launching a preemptive strike to secure an advantageous position that rivals are prevented or discouraged from duplicating.*[10] What makes a move preemptive is its one-of-a-kind nature—whoever strikes first stands to acquire competitive assets that rivals can't readily match. Examples of preemptive moves include (1) securing the best distributors in a particular geographic region or country; (2) obtaining the most favorable sites in terms of customer demographics, cost characteristics, or access to transportation, raw-material supplies, or low-cost inputs; (3) tying up the most reliable, high-quality suppliers via exclusive partnerships, long-term contracts, or acquisition; and (4) moving swiftly to acquire the assets of distressed rivals at bargain prices. To be successful, a preemptive move doesn't have to totally block rivals from following; it merely needs to give a firm a prime position that is not easily replicated or circumvented.

How long it takes for an offensive to yield good results varies with the competitive circumstances.[11] It can be short if buyers respond immediately (as can occur with a dramatic cost-based price cut, an imaginative ad campaign, or an especially appealing new product). Securing a competitive edge can take much longer if winning consumer acceptance of an innovative product will take some time or if the firm may need several years to debug a new technology, put new production capacity in place, or develop and perfect new competitive capabilities. But how long it takes for an offensive move to improve a company's market standing (and whether it can do so) also depends on whether market rivals recognize the threat and begin a counterresponse. And whether rivals will respond depends on whether they are capable of making an effective response and if they believe that a counterattack is worth the expense and the distraction.[12]

Choosing Which Rivals to Attack

Offensive-minded firms need to analyze which of their rivals to challenge as well as how to mount the challenge. The following are the best targets for offensive attacks:[13]

*   *Market leaders that are vulnerable.* Offensive attacks make good sense when a company that leads in terms of size and market share is not a true leader in terms of serving the market well. Signs of leader vulnerability include unhappy buyers, an inferior product line, a weak competitive strategy with regard to low-cost leadership or differentiation, strong emotional commitment to an aging technology the leader has pioneered, outdated plants and equipment, a preoccupation with diversification into other industries, and mediocre or declining profitability. Toyota's massive product recalls in 2009 and 2010 due to safety concerns presented other car companies with a prime opportunity to attack a vulnerable and distracted market leader. GM and Ford used incentives and low-financing offers aimed at winning over Toyota buyers to increase their market share during this period. Offensives to erode the positions of vulnerable market leaders have real promise when the challenger is also able to revamp

its value chain or innovate to gain a fresh cost-based or differentiation-based competitive advantage.[14] To be judged successful, attacks on leaders don't have to result in making the aggressor the new leader; a challenger may "win" by simply becoming a stronger runner-up. Caution is well advised in challenging strong market leaders—there's a significant risk of squandering valuable resources in a futile effort or precipitating a fierce and profitless industrywide battle for market share.

- *Runner-up firms with weaknesses in areas where the challenger is strong.* Runner-up firms are an especially attractive target when a challenger's resources and capabilities are well suited to exploiting their weaknesses.

- *Struggling enterprises that are on the verge of going under.* Challenging a hard-pressed rival in ways that further sap its financial strength and competitive position can weaken its resolve and hasten its exit from the market. In this type of situation, it makes sense to attack the rival in the market segments where it makes the most profits, since this will threaten its survival the most.

- *Small local and regional firms with limited capabilities.* Because small firms typically have limited expertise and resources, a challenger with broader and/or deeper capabilities is well positioned to raid their biggest and best customers—particularly those that are growing rapidly, have increasingly sophisticated requirements, and may already be thinking about switching to a supplier with more full-service capability.

Blue-Ocean Strategy—A Special Kind of Offensive

A **blue-ocean strategy** seeks to gain a dramatic and durable competitive advantage by abandoning efforts to beat out competitors in existing markets and, instead, inventing a new industry or distinctive market segment that renders existing competitors largely irrelevant and allows a company to create and capture altogether new demand.[15] This strategy views the business universe as consisting of two distinct types of market space. One is where industry boundaries are defined and accepted, the competitive rules of the game are well understood by all industry members, and companies try to outperform rivals by capturing a bigger share of existing demand; in such markets, lively competition constrains a company's prospects for rapid growth and superior profitability since rivals move quickly to either imitate or counter the successes of competitors. The second type of market space is a "blue ocean" where the industry does not really exist yet, is untainted by competition, and offers wide-open opportunity for profitable and rapid growth if a company can come up with a product offering and strategy that allows it to create new demand.

> **CORE CONCEPT**
>
> A **blue-ocean strategy** is based on discovering or inventing new industry segments that create altogether new demand, thereby positioning the firm in uncontested market space offering superior opportunities for profitability and growth.

A terrific example of such wide-open or blue-ocean market space is the online auction industry that eBay created and now dominates. Other examples of companies that have achieved competitive advantages by creating blue-ocean market spaces include Starbucks in the coffee shop industry, Dollar General in extreme discount retailing, FedEx in overnight package delivery, and Cirque du Soleil in live entertainment. Cirque du Soleil "reinvented the circus" by creating a distinctively different market space for its performances (Las Vegas nightclubs and theater-type settings) and pulling in a whole new group of customers—adults and corporate clients—who were willing to pay several times more than the price of a conventional circus ticket to have more than the price of a conventional circus ticket to have an "entertainment experience" featuring sophisticated clowns and star-quality acrobatic acts in a comfortable atmosphere. Companies that create blue-ocean market spaces can usually sustain their initial competitive advantage without encountering a major competitive challenge for 10 to 15 years because of high barriers to imitation and the strong brand-name awareness that a blue-ocean strategy can produce.

Zipcar Inc. is presently using a blue-ocean strategy to compete against entrenched rivals in the rental-car industry. It rents cars by the hour or day (rather than by the week) to members who pay a yearly fee for access to cars parked in designated spaces located conveniently throughout large cities. By allowing drivers under 25 years of age to rent cars and by targeting city dwellers who need to supplement their use of public transportation with short-term car rentals, Zipcar entered uncharted waters in the rental-car industry, growing rapidly in the process. Founded in 2000, Zipcar filed to go public in mid-2010.

DEFENSIVE STRATEGIES—PROTECTING MARKET POSITION AND COMPETITIVE ADVANTAGE

Good defensive strategies can help protect a competitive advantage but rarely are the basis for creating one.

In a competitive market, all firms are subject to offensive challenges from rivals. The purposes of defensive strategies are to (1) lower the risk of being attacked, (2) weaken the impact of any attack that occurs, and (3) influence challengers to aim their efforts at other rivals. While defensive strategies usually don't enhance a firm's competitive advantage, they can definitely help fortify the firm's competitive position, protect its most valuable resources and capabilities from imitation, and defend whatever competitive advantage it might have. Defensive strategies can take either of two forms: actions to block challengers and actions to signal the likelihood of strong retaliation.

Blocking the Avenues Open to Challengers

The most frequently employed approach to defending a company's present position involves actions that restrict a challenger's options for initiating a competitive attack. There are any number of obstacles that can be put in the path of would-be challengers.[16] A defender can participate in alternative technologies as a hedge against rivals attacking with a new or better technology. A defender can introduce new features, add new models, or broaden its product line to close off gaps and vacant niches to opportunity-seeking challengers. It can thwart the efforts of rivals to attack with a lower price by maintaining economy-priced options of its own. It can try to discourage buyers from trying competitors' brands by lengthening warranties, offering free training and support services, developing the capability to deliver spare parts to users faster than rivals can, providing coupons and sample giveaways to buyers most prone to experiment, and making early announcements about impending new products or price changes to induce potential buyers to postpone switching. It can challenge the quality or safety of rivals' products. Finally, a defender can grant volume discounts or better financing terms to dealers

There are many ways to throw obstacles in the path of would-be challengers.

and distributors to discourage them from experimenting with other suppliers, or it can convince them to handle its product line *exclusively* and force competitors to use other distribution outlets.

Signaling Challengers That Retaliation Is Likely

The goal of signaling challengers that strong retaliation is likely in the event of an attack is either to dissuade challengers from attacking at all or to divert them to less threatening options. Either goal can be achieved by letting challengers know the battle will cost more than it is worth. Signals to would-be challengers can be given by:[17]

- Publicly announcing management's commitment to maintaining the firm's present market share.
- Publicly committing the company to a policy of matching competitors' terms or prices.
- Maintaining a war chest of cash and marketable securities.
- Making an occasional strong counterresponse to the moves of weak competitors to enhance the firm's image as a tough defender.

Signaling is most likely to be an effective defensive strategy if the signal is accompanied by a credible commitment to follow through.

TIMING A COMPANY'S OFFENSIVE AND DEFENSIVE STRATEGIC MOVES

When to make a strategic move is often as crucial as *what* move to make. Timing is especially important when **first-mover advantages** or **disadvantages** exist.[18] Under certain conditions, being first to initiate a strategic move can have a high payoff in the form of a competitive advantage that later movers can't dislodge. Moving first is no guarantee of success, however, since first movers also face some significant disadvantages. Indeed, there are circumstances in which it is more advantageous to be a fast follower or even a late mover. Because the timing of strategic moves can be consequential, it is important for company strategists to be aware of the nature of first-mover advantages and disadvantages and the conditions favoring each type.[19]

> **CORE CONCEPT**
>
> Because of **first-mover advantages** and **disadvantages,** competitive advantage can spring from *when* a move is made as well as from *what* move is made.

The Potential for First-Mover Advantages

Market pioneers and other types of first movers typically bear greater risks and greater development costs than firms that move later. If the market responds well to its initial move, the pioneer will benefit from a monopoly position (by virtue of being first to market) that enables it to recover its investment costs and make an attractive profit. If the firm's pioneering move gives it a competitive advantage that can be sustained even after other firms enter the market space, its first-mover advantage will be greater still. The extent of this type of advantage, however, will

> **LO 2**
>
> Recognize when being a first mover or a fast follower or a late mover is most advantageous.

depend on whether and how fast follower firms can piggyback on the pioneer's success and either imitate or improve on its move.

The conditions that favor first-mover advantages, then, are those that slow the moves of follower firms or prevent them from imitating the success of the first mover. There are six such conditions in which first-mover advantages are most likely to arise:

1. *When pioneering helps build a firm's reputation with buyers and creates brand loyalty.* A firm's reputation can insulate it from competition when buyer uncertainty about product quality keeps the firm's customers from trying competitors' offerings and when new buyers minimize their risk by choosing on the basis of reputation. Similarly, customer loyalty to an early mover's brand can create a tie that binds, limiting the success of later entrants' attempts to poach from the early mover's customer base and steal market share.

2. *When a first mover's customers will thereafter face significant switching costs.* Switching costs limit the ability of late movers to lure away the customers of early movers by making it expensive for a customer to switch to another company's product or service. Switching costs can arise for a number of reasons. They may be due to the time a consumer invests in learning how to use a specific company's product. They may arise from an investment in complementary products that are also brand-specific. They can also arise from certain types of loyalty programs or long-term contracts that give customers greater incentives to remain with an initial provider.

3. *When property rights protections thwart rapid imitation of the initial move.* In certain types of industries, property rights protections in the form of patents, copyrights, and trademarks prevent the ready imitation of an early mover's initial moves. First-mover advantages in pharmaceuticals, for example, are heavily dependent on patent protections, and patent races in this industry are common. In other industries, however, patents provide limited protection and can frequently be circumvented. Property rights protections also vary among nations, since they are dependent on a country's legal institutions and enforcement mechanisms.

4. *When an early lead enables the first mover to move down the learning curve ahead of rivals.* When there is a steep learning curve and when learning can be kept proprietary, a first mover can benefit from volume-based cost advantages that grow ever larger as its experience accumulates and its scale of operations increases. This type of first-mover advantage is self-reinforcing and, as such, can preserve a first mover's competitive advantage over long periods of time. Honda's advantage in small multiuse motorcycles has been attributed to such an effect, as has the long-lived advantage of Lincoln Electric Company in arc welders, which are used in industries such as construction and shipbuilding.

5. *When a first mover can set the technical standard for the industry.* In many technology-based industries, the market will converge around a single technical standard. By establishing the industry standard, a first mover can gain a powerful advantage that, like experienced-based advantages, builds over time. The greater the importance of technical standards in an industry, the greater the advantage of being the one to set the standard and the more firmly the first mover will be entrenched. The lure of such an advantage, however, can result in standard wars among early movers, as each strives to set the industry standard. The key to winning such wars is to enter early on the

basis of strong fast-cycle product development capabilities, gain the support of key customers and suppliers, employ penetration pricing, and make allies of the producers of complementary products.

To sustain any advantage that may initially accrue to a pioneer, a first mover needs to be a fast learner and continue to move aggressively to capitalize on any initial pioneering advantage. It helps immensely if the first mover has deep financial pockets, important competitive capabilities, and astute managers. What makes being a first mover strategically important is not being the first company to do something but, rather, being the first competitor to put together the precise combination of features, customer value, and sound revenue/cost/profit economics that gives it an edge over rivals in the battle for market leadership.[20] If the marketplace quickly takes to a first mover's innovative product offering, the first mover must have large-scale production, marketing, and distribution capabilities if it is to take full advantage of its market lead. If technology is advancing at a torrid pace, a first mover cannot hope to sustain its lead without having strong capabilities in R&D, design, and new product development, along with the financial strength to fund these activities.

Illustration Capsule 6.1 describes how Amazon.com achieved a first-mover advantage in online retailing.

The Potential for First-Mover Disadvantages or Late-Mover Advantages

There are circumstances when first movers face significant disadvantages and when it is actually better to be an adept follower than a first mover. First-mover disadvantages *(or late-mover advantages)* arise in the following four instances:

1. *When pioneering is more costly than imitating, and only negligible experience or learning-curve benefits accrue to the leader.* Such conditions allow a follower to end up with lower costs than the first mover and either win customers away with lower prices or benefit from more profitable production.

2. *When the products of an innovator are somewhat primitive and do not live up to buyer expectations.* In this situation, a clever follower can study customers' reactions to the pioneer's products and win disenchanted buyers away from the leader with better-performing products. Moreover, the first mover may find itself saddled with a negative reputation that retards its ability to recover from its early missteps.

3. *When rapid market evolution gives fast followers the opening to leapfrog a first mover's products with more attractive next-version products.* Industries characterized by fast-paced changes in either technology or buyer needs and expectations may present opportunities for second movers to improve on the pioneer's products and offer customers a more attractive value proposition as a result.

4. *When market uncertainties make it difficult to ascertain what will eventually succeed.* Under these conditions, first movers are likely to make numerous mistakes that later movers can avoid and learn from. Even if the pioneer manages to please early adopters, it may turn out that the needs of early adopters are very different from mass-market needs. Late movers may find it far more advantageous to wait until these needs are clarified and then focus on satisfying the mass market's demand.

ILLUSTRATION CAPSULE 6.1

Amazon.com's First-Mover Advantage in Online Retailing

Amazon.com's path to becoming the world's largest online retailer began in 1994 when Jeff Bezos, a Manhattan hedge fund analyst at the time, noticed that the number of Internet users was increasing by 2,300 percent annually. Bezos saw the tremendous growth as an opportunity to sell products online that would be demanded by a large number of Internet users and could be easily shipped. Bezos launched the online bookseller Amazon.com in 1995. The start-up's revenues soared to $148 million in 1997, $610 million in 1998, and $1.6 billion in 1999. Bezos' business plan—hatched while on a cross-country trip with his wife in 1994—made him *Time* magazine's Person of the Year in 1999.

The volume-based and reputational benefits of Amazon.com's early entry into online retailing had delivered a first-mover advantage, but between 2000 and 2009 Bezos undertook a series of additional strategic initiatives to solidify the company's number-one ranking in the industry. Bezos undertook a massive building program in the late-1990s that added five new warehouses and fulfillment centers totaling $300 million. The additional warehouse capacity was added years before it was needed, but Bezos wanted to move preemptively against potential rivals and ensure that, as demand continued to grow, the company could continue to offer its customers the best selection, the lowest prices, and the cheapest and most convenient delivery. The company also expanded its product line to include sporting goods, tools, toys, grocery items, electronics, and digital music downloads, giving it another means of maintaining its experience

and scale-based advantages. Amazon.com's 2008 revenues of $19.2 billion made it the world's largest Internet retailer; Jeff Bezos' shares in Amazon.com made him the 110th-wealthiest person in the world in 2009, with an estimated net worth of $8.2 billion.

Moving down the learning curve in Internet retailing was not an entirely straightforward process for Amazon.com. Bezos commented in a *Fortune* article profiling the company, "We were investors in every bankrupt, 1999-vintage e-commerce startup. Pets.com, living.com, kozmo.com. We invested in a lot of high-profile flameouts." He went on to specify that although the ventures were a "waste of money," they "didn't take us off our own mission." Bezos also suggested that gaining advantage as a first mover is "taking a million tiny steps—and learning quickly from your missteps."

Sources: Mark Brohan, "The Top 500 Guide," *Internet Retailer,* June 2009 (accessed at www.internetretailer.com on June 17, 2009); Josh Quittner, "How Jeff Bezos Rules the Retail Space," *Fortune,* May 5, 2008, pp. 126–34.

To Be a First Mover or Not

In weighing the pros and cons of being a first mover versus a fast follower versus a late mover, it matters whether the race to market leadership in a particular industry is a marathon or a sprint. In marathons, a slow mover is not unduly penalized—first-mover advantages can be fleeting, and there's ample time for fast followers and sometimes even late movers to play catch-up.[21] Thus the speed at which the pioneering innovation is likely to catch on matters considerably as companies struggle with whether to pursue a particular emerging market opportunity aggressively (as a first mover or fast follower) or cautiously (as a late mover). For instance, it took 18 months for 10 million users to sign up for Hotmail, 5.5 years for worldwide mobile phone use to grow from 10 million to 100 million, and close to 10 years for the number of at-home broadband subscribers to reach 100 million worldwide. The lesson here is that there is a market penetration curve for every emerging opportunity; typically, the curve has an inflection point at which all the pieces of the business model fall into place, buyer demand explodes, and the market takes off. The inflection point can come early on a fast-rising curve (as with use of e-mail) or farther on up a slow-rising curve (as with the use of broadband). Any company that seeks competitive advantage by being a first mover thus needs to ask some hard questions:

- Does market takeoff depend on the development of complementary products or services that currently are not available?
- Is new infrastructure required before buyer demand can surge?
- Will buyers need to learn new skills or adopt new behaviors? Will buyers encounter high switching costs in moving to the newly introduced product or service?
- Are there influential competitors in a position to delay or derail the efforts of a first mover?

When the answers to any of these questions are yes, then a company must be careful not to pour too many resources into getting ahead of the market opportunity—the race is likely going to be more of a 10-year marathon than a 2-year sprint.[22] On the other hand, if the market is a winner-take-all type of market, where powerful first-mover advantages insulate early entrants from competition and prevent later movers from making any headway, then it may be best to move quickly despite the risks.

STRENGTHENING A COMPANY'S MARKET POSITION VIA ITS SCOPE OF OPERATIONS

Apart from considerations of competitive moves and their timing, there is another set of managerial decisions that can affect the strength of a company's market position. These decisions concern the scope of a company's operations—the breadth of its activities and the extent of its market reach. Decisions regarding the **scope of the firm** focus on which activities a firm will perform internally and which it will not. For example, should Panera Bread Company produce the fresh dough that its company-owned and franchised bakery-cafés use in making baguettes, pastries, bagels, and other types of bread, or should it obtain its dough from outside suppliers? Scope decisions also concern which segments of the market to serve—decisions that can include geographic market segments as well as product and service segments. Should Panera expand its menu to include light dinner entrees? Should it offer delivery or drive-through service? Should it expand into all 50 states or concentrate on strengthening its market presence regionally?

   Decisions such as these, in essence, determine where the boundaries of a firm lie and the degree to which the operations within those boundaries cohere. They also have much to do with the direction and extent of a business's growth. In this chapter, we introduce the topic of company scope and discuss different types of

> **CORE CONCEPT**
>
> The **scope of the firm** refers to the range of activities which the firm performs internally, the breadth of its product and service offerings, the extent of its geographic market presence, and its mix of businesses.

scope decisions in relation to a company's business-level strategy. In the next two chapters, we develop two additional dimensions of a firm's scope. Chapter 7 focuses on international expansion—a matter of extending the company's geographic scope into foreign markets. Chapter 8 takes up the topic of corporate strategy, which concerns diversifying into a mix of different businesses. Scope issues are at the very heart of corporate-level strategy.

Several dimensions of firm scope have relevance for business-level strategy in terms of their capacity to strengthen a company's position in a given market. These include the firm's **horizontal scope,** which is the range of product and service segments that the firm serves within its market. Mergers and acquisitions involving other market participants provide a means for a company to expand its horizontal scope. Expanding the firm's vertical scope by means of vertical integration can also affect the success of its market strategy. **Vertical scope** is the extent to which the firm engages in the various activities that make up the industry's entire value chain system, from initial activities such as raw-material production all the way to retailing and after-sales service activities. Outsourcing decisions concern another dimension of scope since they involve narrowing the firm's boundaries with respect to its participation in value chain activities. We discuss the pros and cons of each of these options in the sections that follow. Since strategic alliances and partnerships provide an alternative to vertical integration and acquisition strategies and are sometimes used to facilitate outsourcing, we conclude this chapter with a discussion of the benefits and challenges associated with cooperative arrangements of this sort.

HORIZONTAL MERGER AND ACQUISITION STRATEGIES

LO 3

Become aware of the strategic benefits and risks of expanding a company's horizontal scope through mergers and acquisitions.

Mergers and acquisitions are much-used strategic options; for example, the total worldwide value of mergers and acquisitions completed in 2008 and 2009 was approximately $5 trillion.[23] A *merger* is the combining of two or more companies into a single corporate entity, with the newly created company often taking on a new name. An *acquisition* is a combination in which one company, the acquirer, purchases and absorbs the operations of another, the acquired. The difference between a merger and an acquisition relates more to the details of ownership, management control, and financial arrangements than to strategy and competitive advantage. The resources and competitive capabilities of the newly created enterprise end up much the same whether the combination is the result of acquisition or merger.

Horizontal mergers and acquisitions, which involve combining the operations of firms within the same general industry, provide an effective means for firms to rapidly increase the scale and horizontal scope of their core business. For example, Microsoft has used an aggressive acquisition strategy to extend its software business into new segments and strengthen its technological capabilities in this domain. Mergers between airlines, such as the 2010 United-Continental merger, have increased their scale of operations and extended their reach geographically. Companies from developing economies are increasingly expanding their businesses through cross-border acquisitions, as we discuss in the following chapter on international strategy.

Combining the operations of two companies, via merger or acquisition, is an attractive strategic option for strengthening the resulting company's competitiveness and opening up avenues of new market opportunity. Increasing a company's horizontal scope can strengthen its business and increase its profitability in five ways: (1) by improving the efficiency of its operations, (2) by heightening its product differentiation, (3) by reducing market rivalry, (3) by increasing the company's bargaining power over suppliers and buyers, and (5) by enhancing its flexibility and dynamic capabilities (discussed in Chapter 4).

To achieve these benefits, horizontal merger and acquisition strategies typically are aimed at any of five outcomes:[24]

1. *Increasing the company's scale of operations and market share.* Many mergers and acquisitions are undertaken with the objective of transforming two or more high-cost companies into one lean competitor with significantly lower costs. When a company acquires another company in the same industry, there's usually enough overlap in operations that less efficient plants can be closed or distribution and sales activities partly combined and downsized. Likewise, it is usually feasible to squeeze out cost savings in administrative activities, again by combining and downsizing such administrative activities as finance and accounting, information technology, human resources, and so on. The combined companies may also be able to reduce supply chain costs because of greater bargaining power over common suppliers and closer collaboration with supply chain partners. By helping to consolidate the industry and remove excess capacity, such combinations can also reduce industry rivalry and improve industry profitability.

2. *Expanding a company's geographic coverage.* One of the best and quickest ways to expand a company's geographic coverage is to acquire rivals with operations in the desired locations. If there is some geographic overlap, then one benefit is being able to reduce costs by eliminating duplicate facilities in those geographic areas where undesirable overlap exists. Since a company's size increases with its geographic scope, another benefit is increased bargaining power with the company's suppliers or buyers. For companies whose business customers require national or international coverage, a broader geographic scope can provide differentiation benefits while also enhancing the company's bargaining power. Food products companies like Nestlé, Kraft, Unilever, and Procter & Gamble have made acquisitions an integral part of their strategies to expand internationally in order to serve key customers such as Walmart on a global basis. Greater geographic coverage can also contribute to product differentiation by enhancing a company's name recognition and brand awareness. Banks like Wells Fargo and Bank of America have used acquisition strategies to establish a market presence and gain name recognition in an ever-growing number of states and localities.

3. *Extending the company's business into new product categories.* Many times a company has gaps in its product line that need to be filled in order to offer customers a more effective product bundle or the benefits of one-stop-shopping.[25] For example, customers might prefer to acquire a suite of software applications from a single vendor that can offer more integrated solutions to the company's problems. Acquisition can be a quicker and more potent way to broaden a company's product line than going through the exercise of introducing a company's own new product to fill the gap. Expanding

into additional market segments or product categories can offer companies benefits similar to those gained by expanding geographically: greater product differentiation, bargaining power, and efficiencies. It can also reduce rivalry by helping to consolidate an industry. Coca-Cola has increased the effectiveness of the product bundle it provides to retailers by acquiring Minute Maid (juices and juice drinks), Odwalla (juices), Hi-C (ready-to-drink fruit beverages), and Glaceau, the maker of VitaminWater. By entering the low-cost segment of the rental-car industry with its 2010 acquisition of Dollar Thrifty (whose brands include Dollar Rent a Car and Thrifty Rent a Car), Hertz can benefit from greater scale and stronger bargaining power over its suppliers.

4. *Gaining quick access to new technologies or complementary resources and capabilities.* By making acquisitions to bolster a company's technological know-how or to expand its skills and capabilities, a company can bypass a time-consuming and expensive internal effort to build desirable new resources and organizational capabilities. From 2000 through April 2009, Cisco Systems purchased 85 companies to give it more technological reach and product breadth, thereby enhancing its standing as the world's biggest provider of hardware, software, and services for building and operating Internet networks. By acquiring technologies and other resources and capabilities that complement its own set, a company can gain many of the types of benefits available from extending its horizontal scope. Among them is the greater flexibility and dynamic capabilities that spring from greater innovativeness and the ability to compete on the basis of a more effective bundle of resources.

5. *Leading the convergence of industries whose boundaries are being blurred by changing technologies and new market opportunities.* In fast-cycle industries or industries whose boundaries are changing, companies can use acquisition strategies to hedge their bets about the direction that an industry will take, increase their capacity to meet changing demands, and respond flexibly to changing buyer needs and technological demands. Such acquisitions add to a company's dynamic capabilities by bringing together the resources and products of several different companies and enabling the company to establish a strong position in the consolidating markets. Microsoft has made a series of acquisitions that have enabled it to launch Microsoft TV Internet Protocol Television (IPTV). Microsoft TV allows broadband users to use their home computers or Xbox game consoles to watch live programming, see video on demand, view pictures, and listen to music. News Corporation has also prepared for the convergence of media services with the purchase of satellite TV companies to complement its media holdings in TV broadcasting (the Fox network and TV stations in various countries), cable TV (Fox News, Fox Sports, and FX), filmed entertainment (Twentieth Century Fox and Fox studios), newspapers, magazines, and book publishing.

Numerous companies have employed a horizontal acquisition strategy to catapult themselves from the ranks of the unknown into positions of market leadership. In 1998, Wells Fargo & Company became the 10th-largest bank in the United States as a result of the merger between Wells Fargo and Norwest Corporation. Although it was still only a network of small midwestern banks at that time, it continued to grow via acquisition over the next decade, pursuing a business model based on selling a full range of financial services to an ever-larger base of customers. New opportunity presented itself, however, in the wake of the 2008 financial crisis. By acquiring troubled Wachovia Bank (which operated primarily in the Southeast and parts of the Atlantic Coast), Wells Fargo & Company was able to double its size and transform itself into a nationwide bank with global presence. By 2010, it was the fourth-largest bank in the United States, with $1.2 trillion in assets and over 10,000 branch banks. Moreover, its reputation had grown along with it; it was listed by *Fortune* magazine as the world's 14th "Most Admired Company in 2009," was among *Barron's* "World's 25 Most Respected Companies," and was on *Forbes*'s list of the "Top 100 Best Companies in the World."

Illustration Capsule 6.2 describes how Clear Channel Worldwide has used acquisitions to build a leading global position in radio broadcasting.

Why Mergers and Acquisitions Sometimes Fail to Produce Anticipated Results

All too frequently, mergers and acquisitions do not produce the hoped-for outcomes.[26] Cost savings may prove smaller than expected. Gains in competitive capabilities may take substantially longer to realize or, worse, may never materialize at all. Efforts to mesh the corporate cultures can stall due to formidable resistance from organization members. Managers and employees at the acquired company may argue forcefully for continuing to do things the way they were done before the acquisition. Key employees at the acquired company can quickly become disenchanted and leave; the morale of company personnel who remain can drop to disturbingly low levels because they disagree with newly instituted changes. Differences in management styles and operating procedures can prove hard to resolve. The managers appointed to oversee the integration of a newly acquired company can make mistakes in deciding which activities to leave alone and which activities to meld into their own operations and systems.

A number of mergers/acquisitions have been notably unsuccessful. Ford's $2.5 billion acquisition of Jaguar was a failure, as was its $2.5 billion acquisition of Land Rover (both were sold to India's Tata Motors in 2008 for $2.3 billion). Daimler AG, the maker of Mercedes-Benz and Smart cars, entered into a high-profile merger with Chrysler only to dissolve it in 2007, taking a loss of $30 billion. A number of recent mergers and acquisitions have yet to live up to expectations—prominent examples include Oracle's acquisition of Sun Microsystems, the Fiat-Chrysler deal, Bank of America's acquisition of Merrill Lynch, and the merger of Sprint and Nextel in the mobile phone industry. Antitrust concerns on the part of regulatory authorities have prevented the successful conclusion of other mergers and acquisitions. Coca-Cola, for example, failed to win approval in 2009 for its proposed $2.4 billion acquisition of Huiyuan Juice Group under China's new antimonopoly law.

VERTICAL INTEGRATION STRATEGIES

Expanding the firm's vertical scope by means of a vertical integration strategy provides another way to strengthen the company's position in its core market. A **vertically integrated firm** is one that participates in multiple segments or stages of an industry's overall value chain. A good example of a vertically integrated

ILLUSTRATION CAPSULE 6.2

Clear Channel Communications: Using Mergers and Acquisitions to Become a Global Market Leader in Radio Broadcasting

In 2009, Clear Channel Communications was among the worldwide leaders in radio broadcasting. Clear Channel owned and operated more than 1,000 radio stations in the United States and operated an additional 240 radio stations in Australia, New Zealand, and Mexico. The company, which was founded in 1972 by Lowry Mays and Billy Joe McCombs, got its start by acquiring an unprofitable country-music radio station in San Antonio, Texas. Over the next 10 years, Mays learned the radio business and slowly bought other radio stations in a variety of states. Going public in 1984 helped the company raise the equity capital needed to continue acquiring radio stations in additional geographic markets.

By 1998, Clear Channel had used acquisitions to build a leading position in radio stations. Domestically, it owned, programmed, or sold airtime for 69 AM radio stations and 135 FM stations in 48 local markets in 24 states. Clear Channel's big move was to begin expanding internationally by acquiring interests in radio station properties in a variety of countries. In October 1999, Clear Channel made a major acquisition that expanded its horizontal scope significantly: It acquired AM-FM, Inc., and changed its name to Clear Channel Communications. The AM-FM, Inc., acquisition gave Clear Channel operations in 32 countries, including 830 radio stations.

Additional acquisitions were completed during the 2000–2003 period. The emphasis was on buying radio broadcasting properties with operations in many of the same local markets, which made it feasible to (1) cut costs by sharing facilities and staffs, (2) improve programming, and (3) sell advertising to customers in packages that not only helped Clear Channel's advertising clients distribute their messages more effectively but also allowed the company to combine its sales activities, achieving significant cost savings and boosting profit margins. In 2008, Clear Channel sought a buyer for 288 of its 1,005 radio stations that operated in small markets. Its remaining 717 radio stations all operated in the top-100 markets in the United States.

Sources: www.clearchannel.com (accessed May 2008); *BusinessWeek,* October 19, 1999, p. 56.

LO 4

Learn the advantages and disadvantages of extending the company's scope of operations via vertical integration.

firm is Maple Leaf Foods, a major Canadian producer of fresh and processed meats whose best-selling brands include Maple Leaf and Schneiders. Maple Leaf Foods participates in hog and poultry production, with company-owned hog and poultry farms; it has its own meat-processing and -rendering facilities; it packages its products and distributes them from company-owned distribution centers; and it conducts marketing, sales, and customer service activities for its wholesale and retail buyers but does not otherwise participate in the final stage of the meat processing vertical chain—the retailing stage.

A vertical integration strategy can expand the firm's range of activities *backward* into sources of supply and/or *forward* toward end users. When Tiffany & Co, a manufacturer and retailer of fine jewelry, began sourcing, cutting, and polishing its own diamonds, it integrated backward along the diamond supply chain. Mining giant De Beers Group and Canadian miner Aber Diamond integrated forward when they entered the diamond retailing business.

A firm can pursue vertical integration by starting its own operations in other stages of the vertical activity chain, by acquiring a company already performing the activities it wants to bring in-house, or by entering into a strategic alliance or joint venture. Vertical integration strategies can aim at *full integration* (participating in all stages of the vertical chain) or *partial integration* (building positions in selected stages of the vertical chain). Firms can also engage in *tapered integration* strategies, which involve a mix of in-house and outsourced activity in any given stage of the vertical chain. Oil companies, for instance, supply their refineries with oil from their own wells as well as with oil that they purchase from other producers—they engage in tapered backward integration. Since Boston Beer Company, the maker of Samuel Adams, sells most of its beer through distributors but also operates brew-pubs, it practices tapered forward integration.

The Advantages of a Vertical Integration Strategy

Under the right conditions, a vertical integration strategy can add materially to a company's technological capabilities, strengthen the firm's competitive position, and boost its profitability.[27] But it is important to keep in mind that vertical integration has no real payoff strategywise or profitwise unless it produces cost savings and/or differentiation benefits sufficient to justify the extra investment.

Integrating Backward to Achieve Greater Competitiveness   It is harder than one might think to generate cost savings or improve profitability by integrating backward into activities such as parts and components manufacture (which could otherwise be purchased from suppliers with specialized expertise in making these parts and components). For backward integration to be a cost-saving and profitable strategy, a company must be able to (1) achieve the same scale economies as outside suppliers and (2) match or beat suppliers' production efficiency with no drop-off in quality. Neither outcome is a slam dunk. To begin with, a company's in-house requirements are often too small to reach the optimum size for low-cost operation—for instance, if it takes a minimum production volume of 1 million units to achieve mass-production economies and a company's in-house requirements are just 250,000 units, then it falls far short of being able to capture the scale economies of outside suppliers (which may readily find buyers for 1 million or more units). Furthermore, matching the production efficiency of suppliers is fraught with problems when suppliers have considerable production experience of their own, when the technology they employ has elements that are hard to master, and/or when substantial R&D expertise is required to develop next-version parts and components or keep pace with advancing technology in parts/components production.

But that said, there are still occasions when a company can improve its cost position and competitiveness by performing a broader range of vertical chain activities in-house rather than having certain of these activities performed by outside suppliers. When the item being supplied is a major cost component, when there is a sole supplier, or when suppliers have outsized profit margins, vertical integration can lower costs by limiting supplier power. Vertical integration can also lower costs by facilitating the coordination of production flows and avoiding bottleneck problems. Furthermore, when a company has proprietary know-how that it wants to keep from rivals, then in-house performance of value-adding activities related to this know-how is beneficial even if such activities could be performed by outsiders. Apple recently decided to integrate backward into producing its own chips for iPhones, chiefly because chips are a major cost component, they have big profit margins, and in-house production would help coordinate design tasks and protect Apple's proprietary iPhone technology. International Paper Company backward integrates into pulp mills that it sets up nearby its paper mills (outside suppliers are generally unwilling to make a site-specific investment for a buyer) and reaps the benefits of coordinated production flows, energy savings, and transportation economies.

Backward vertical integration can produce a differentiation-based competitive advantage when performing activities internally contributes to a better-quality product/service offering, improves the caliber of customer service, or in other ways enhances the performance of the final product. On occasion, integrating into more stages along the vertical added-value chain can add to a company's differentiation capabilities by allowing it to build or strengthen its core competencies, better master key skills or strategy-critical technologies, or add features that deliver greater customer value. Spanish clothing maker Inditex has backward integrated into fabric making, as well as garment design and manufacture, for its successful Zara brand. By tightly controlling the process and postponing dyeing until later stages, Zara can respond quickly to changes in fashion trends and supply its customers with the hottest items. NewsCorp backward integrated into film studios (Twentieth Century Fox) and TV program production to ensure access to high-quality content for its TV stations (and to limit supplier power).

Integrating Forward to Enhance Competitiveness Like backward integration, forward integration can lower costs by increasing efficiency and bargaining power. In addition, it can allow manufacturers to gain better access to end users, strengthen brand awareness, and increase product differentiation. Automakers, for example, have forward integrated into the lending business in order to exercise more control and make auto loans a more attractive part of the car-buying process. Forward integration can also enable companies to make the end users' purchasing experience a differentiating feature. For example, Ducati and Harley motorcycles both have company-owned retail stores that are essentially little museums, filled with iconography, that provide an environment conducive to selling not only motorcycles and gear but memorabilia, clothing, and other items featuring the brand. Insurance companies and brokerages have the ability to make consumers' interactions with local agents and office personnel a differentiating feature by focusing on building relationships.

In many industries, independent sales agents, wholesalers, and retailers handle competing brands of the same product; having no allegiance to any one company's brand, they tend to push whatever earns them the biggest profits. An independent insurance agency, for example, represents a number of different insurance companies and tries to find the best match between a customer's insurance requirements and the policies of alternative insurance companies. Under this arrangement, it's possible for an agent to develop a preference for one company's policies or underwriting practices and neglect other represented insurance companies. An insurance company may conclude, therefore, that it is better off integrating forward and setting up its own local offices, as State Farm and Allstate have done. Likewise, some tire manufacturers (such as Goodyear) have integrated forward into tire retailing to exert better control over sales force/customer interactions. A number of consumer-goods manufacturers, like Coach, Pepperidge Farm, and Samsonite, have integrated forward into retailing so as to move seconds, overstocked items, and slow-selling merchandise through their own branded factory outlet stores.

Some producers have opted to integrate forward by selling directly to customers at the company's Web site. Bypassing regular wholesale/retail channels in favor of direct sales and Internet retailing can have appeal if it reinforces the brand and enhances consumer satisfaction or if it lowers distribution costs, produces a relative cost advantage over certain rivals, and results in lower selling prices to end users. In addition, sellers are compelled to include the Internet as a retail channel when a sufficiently large number of buyers in an industry prefer to make purchases online. However, a company that is vigorously pursuing online sales to consumers at the same time that it is also heavily promoting sales to consumers through its network of wholesalers and retailers is competing directly against its distribution allies. Such actions constitute *channel conflict* and create a tricky route to negotiate. A company that is actively trying to expand online sales to consumers is signaling *a weak strategic commitment to its dealers* and *a willingness to cannibalize dealers' sales and growth potential.* The likely result is angry dealers and loss of dealer goodwill. Quite possibly, a company may stand to lose more sales by offending its dealers than it gains from its own online sales effort. Consequently, in industries where the strong support and goodwill of dealer networks is essential, companies may conclude that it is important to avoid channel conflict and that their Web sites should be designed to partner with dealers rather than compete against them.

The Disadvantages of a Vertical Integration Strategy

Vertical integration has some substantial drawbacks beyond the potential for channel conflict.[28] The most serious drawbacks to vertical integration include the following concerns:

- Vertical integration raises a firm's capital investment in the industry, *increasing business risk.* What if industry growth and profitability go sour?

- Vertically integrated companies are often *slow to embrace technological advances* or more efficient production methods when they are saddled with older technology or facilities. A company that obtains parts and components from outside suppliers can always shop the market for the latest and best parts and components, whereas a vertically integrated firm that is saddled with older technology or facilities that make items it no longer needs is looking at the high costs of premature abandonment.

- Integrating backward into parts and components manufacture *can impair a company's operating flexibility* when it comes to changing out the use of certain parts and components. It is one thing to design out a component made by a supplier and another to design out a component being made in-house (which can mean laying off employees and writing off the associated investment in equipment and facilities). Most of the world's automakers, despite their expertise in automotive technology and manufacturing, have concluded that purchasing many of their key parts and components from manufacturing specialists results in higher quality, lower costs, and greater design flexibility than does the vertical integration option.

- Vertical integration potentially results in *less flexibility in accommodating shifting buyer preferences* when a new product design doesn't include parts and components that the company makes in-house. Integrating forward or backward locks a firm into relying on its own in-house activities and sources of supply.

- Vertical integration *may not enable a company to realize economies of scale* if its production levels are below the minimum efficient scale. Small companies in particular are likely to suffer a cost disadvantage by producing in-house when suppliers of many small companies can realize scale economies that a small company cannot attain on its own.

- Vertical integration poses all kinds of *capacity matching problems.* In motor vehicle manufacturing, for example, the most efficient scale of operation for making axles is different from the most economic volume for radiators and different yet again for both engines and transmissions. Building the capacity to produce just the right number of axles, radiators, engines, and transmissions in-house—and doing so at the lowest unit costs for each—is much easier said than done. If internal capacity for making transmissions is deficient, the difference has to be bought externally. If internal capacity for radiators proves excessive, customers need to be found for the surplus. And if by-products are generated—as occurs in the processing of many chemical products—they require arrangements for disposal. Consequently, integrating across several production stages in ways that achieve the lowest feasible costs can be a monumental challenge.

- Integration forward or backward often calls for *radical new skills and business capabilities.* Parts and components manufacturing, assembly operations, wholesale distribution and retailing, and direct sales via the Internet represent different kinds of businesses, operating in different types of industries, with different key success factors. Managers of a manufacturing company should consider carefully whether it makes good business sense to invest time and money in developing the expertise and merchandising skills to integrate forward into wholesaling or retailing. Many manufacturers learn the hard way that company-owned wholesale/retail networks present many headaches, fit poorly with what they do best, and don't always add the kind of value to their core business they thought they would.

In today's world of close working relationships with suppliers and efficient supply chain management systems, *very few businesses can make a case for integrating backward into the business of suppliers* to ensure a reliable supply of materials and components or to reduce production costs. The best materials and components suppliers stay abreast of advancing technology and are adept in improving their efficiency and keeping their costs and prices as low as possible. A company that pursues a vertical integration strategy and tries to produce many parts and components in-house is likely to find itself very hard-pressed to keep up with technological advances and cutting-edge production practices for each part and component used in making its product

Weighing the Pros and Cons of Vertical Integration

All in all, therefore, a strategy of vertical integration can have both important strengths and weaknesses. The tip of the scales depends on (1) whether vertical integration can enhance the performance of strategy-critical activities in ways that lower cost, build expertise, protect proprietary know-how, or increase differentiation; (2) the impact of vertical integration on investment costs, flexibility and response times, and the administrative costs of coordinating operations across more vertical chain activities; and (3) how difficult it will be for the company to acquire the set of skills and capabilities needed to operate in another stage of the vertical chain. *Vertical integration strategies have merit according to which capabilities and value-adding activities truly need to be performed in-house and which can be performed better or cheaper by outsiders.* Without solid benefits, integrating forward or backward is not likely to be an attractive strategy option.

American Apparel, the largest U.S. clothing manufacturer, has made vertical integration a central part of its strategy, as described in Illustration Capsule 6.3.

OUTSOURCING STRATEGIES: NARROWING THE SCOPE OF OPERATIONS

In contrast to vertical integration strategies, outsourcing strategies narrow the scope of a business's operations (and the firm's boundaries, in terms of what activities are performed internally). **Outsourcing** involves a conscious decision to forgo attempts to perform certain value chain activities internally and instead to farm them out to outside specialists.[29] Many PC makers, for example, have shifted from assembling units in-house to outsourcing the entire assembly process to manufacturing specialists because enterprises that assemble many brands of PCs are better able to bargain down the prices of PC components (by buying in very large volumes) and because they have greater expertise in performing assembly tasks more cost-effectively. Nike has outsourced most of its manufacturing-related value chain activities so that it can concentrate on marketing and managing its brand.

> **CORE CONCEPT**
>
> **Outsourcing** involves farming out certain value chain activities to outside vendors.

Outsourcing certain value chain activities can be advantageous whenever:

- *An activity can be performed better or more cheaply by outside specialists.* A company should generally *not* perform any value chain activity internally that can be performed more efficiently or effectively by outsiders—the chief exception occurs when a particular activity is strategically crucial and internal control over that activity is deemed essential.

- *The activity is not crucial to the firm's ability to achieve sustainable competitive advantage and won't hollow out its core competencies.* Outsourcing of support activities such as maintenance services, data processing and data storage, fringe-benefit management, and Web site operations has become commonplace. Colgate-Palmolive, for instance, has been able to reduce its information technology operational costs by more than 10 percent per year through an outsourcing agreement with IBM. A number of companies have outsourced their call center operations to foreign-based contractors that have access to lower-cost labor supplies and can employ lower-paid call center personnel to respond to customer inquiries or requests for technical support.

- *It streamlines company operations in ways that improve organizational flexibility and speed time to market.* Outsourcing gives a company the flexibility to switch suppliers in the event that its present supplier falls behind competing suppliers. To the extent that its suppliers can speedily get next-generation parts and components into production, then a company can get its own next-generation product offerings into the marketplace quicker. Moreover, seeking out new suppliers with the needed capabilities already in place is frequently quicker,

> **LO 5**
>
> Become aware of the conditions that favor farming out certain value chain activities to outside parties.

ILLUSTRATION CAPSULE 6.3

American Apparel's Vertical Integration Strategy

American Apparel, known for its hip line of basic garments and its provocative advertisements, is no stranger to the concept of "doing it all." The Los Angeles–based casual wear company has made both forward and backward vertical integration a central part of its strategy, making American Apparel a rarity in the U.S. fashion industry. Not only does it do all its own fabric cutting and sewing, but it also owns several knitting and dyeing facilities in southern California, as well as a distribution warehouse, a wholesale operation, and over 270 retail stores in 20 countries. American Apparel even does its own clothing design, marketing, and advertising, often using its employees as photographers and clothing models.

Founder and CEO Dov Charney claims that the company's vertical integration strategy lets American Apparel respond more quickly to rapid market changes, allowing the company to bring an item from design to its stores worldwide in the span of a week. End-to-end coordination also improves inventory control, helping prevent common problems in the fashion business such as stockouts and steep markdowns. The company capitalizes on its California-based vertically integrated operations by using taglines such as "Sweatshop Free. Made in the USA" to bolster its "authentic" image.

However, this strategy is not without risks and costs. In an industry where 97 percent of goods are imported, American Apparel pays its workers wages and benefits above the relatively high mandated American minimum. Furthermore, operating in so many key vertical chain activities makes it impossible to be expert in all of them and creates optimal scale and capacity mismatches—problems with which the firm has partly dealt by tapering its backward integration into knitting and dyeing. Lastly, while the company can respond quickly to new fashion trends, its vertical integration strategy may make it more difficult for the company to scale back in an economic downturn or respond to radical change in the industry environment. Ultimately, only time will tell whether American Apparel will dilute or capitalize on its vertical integration strategy in its pursuit of profitable growth.

Developed with John R. Moran.

Sources: American Apparel Web site, www.americanapparel.net (accessed June 16, 2010); American Apparel investor presentation, June 2009, http://files.shareholder.com/downloads/APP/938846703x0x300331/3dd0b7ca-e458-45b8-8516-e25ca272016d/NYC%20JUNE%202009.pdf; Dov Charney. "American Apparel—Dov Charney Interview," *YouTube,* 2007, http://youtube.com/watch?v=hYqR8UII8A4; Christopher Palmeri, "Living on the Edge at American Apparel," *BusinessWeek,* June 27, 2005.

easier, less risky, and cheaper than hurriedly retooling internal operations to replace obsolete capabilities or trying to install and master new technologies.

- *It reduces the company's risk exposure to changing technology and/or buyer preferences.* When a company outsources certain parts, components, and services, its suppliers must bear the burden of incorporating state-of-the-art technologies and/or undertaking redesigns and upgrades to accommodate a company's plans to introduce next-generation products. If what a supplier provides falls out of favor with buyers, or is designed out of next-generation products, or rendered unnecessary by technological change, it is the supplier's business that suffers rather than a company's own internal operations.

- *It allows a company to assemble diverse kinds of expertise speedily and efficiently.* A company can nearly always gain quicker access to first-rate capabilities and expertise by employing suppliers who already have them in place than it can by trying to build them from scratch with its own company personnel.

- *It allows a company to concentrate on its core business, leverage its key resources, and do even better what it already does best.* A company is better able to heighten its own competitively valuable capabilities when it concentrates its full resources and energies on performing those activities internally that it can perform better than outsiders and/or that it needs to have under its direct control. Coach, for example, devotes its energy to designing new styles of ladies handbags and leather accessories, opting to outsource handbag production to 40 contract manufacturers in 15 countries. Hewlett-Packard, IBM, and others have sold manufacturing plants to suppliers and then contracted to purchase the output.

The Big Risk of Outsourcing Value Chain Activities

The biggest danger of outsourcing is that a company will farm out too many or the wrong types of activities and thereby hollow out its own capabilities.[30] For example, in recent years, companies anxious to reduce operating costs have opted to outsource such strategically important activities as product development, engineering design, and sophisticated manufacturing tasks—the very capabilities that underpin a company's ability to lead sustained product innovation. While these companies may have been able to lower their operating costs by outsourcing these functions to outsiders that can perform them more cheaply, *their ability to lead the development of innovative new products has been weakened in the process.* For example, nearly every U.S. brand of laptop and cell phone (with the notable exception of Apple) is not only manufactured but designed in Asia.[31] It is strategically dangerous for a company to be dependent on outsiders for competitive capabilities that over the long run determine its market success. Companies like IBM, Dell, American Express, and Bank of America are alert to the danger of farming out the performance of strategy-critical value chain activities and generally only outsource relatively mundane functions: IBM outsources customer support operations, Dell outsources manufacturing, American Express outsources IT functions, and BoA outsources human resource management.

> A company must guard against outsourcing activities that hollow out the resources and capabilities that it needs to be a master of its own destiny.

Another risk of outsourcing comes from the lack of direct control. It may be difficult to monitor, control, and coordinate the activities of outside parties by mean of contracts and arm's-length transactions alone; unanticipated problems may arise that cause delays or cost overruns and become hard to resolve amicably. Moreover, contract-based outsourcing can be problematic because outside parties lack incentives to make investments specific to the needs of the outsourcing company's value chain.

STRATEGIC ALLIANCES AND PARTNERSHIPS

Strategic alliances and cooperative partnerships provide one way to gain some of the benefits offered by vertical integration, outsourcing, and horizontal mergers and acquisitions while minimizing the associated problems. Companies

LO 6

Understand
when and how
strategic alliances
can substitute for
horizontal mergers
and acquisitions or
vertical integration
and how they
can facilitate
outsourcing.

frequently engage in cooperative strategies as an alternative to vertical integration or horizontal mergers and acquisitions. Increasingly, companies are also employing strategic alliances and partnerships to extend their scope of operations via international expansion and diversification strategies, as we describe in Chapters 7 and 8. Strategic alliances and cooperative arrangements are now a common means of narrowing a company's scope of operations as well, serving as a useful way to manage outsourcing (in lieu of traditional, purely price-oriented contracts).

For example, oil and gas companies engage in considerable vertical integration—but Shell Oil Company and Pemex (Mexico's state-owned petroleum company) have found that joint ownership of their Deer Park Refinery in Texas lowers their investment costs and risks in comparison to going it alone. The colossal failure of the Daimler-Chrysler merger formed an expensive lesson for Daimler AG about what can go wrong with horizontal mergers and acquisitions; its 2010 strategic alliance with Renault-Nissan may allow the two companies to achieve jointly the global scale required for cost competitiveness in cars and trucks while avoiding the type of problems that so plagued Daimler-Chrysler. Many companies employ strategic alliances to manage the problems that might otherwise occur with outsourcing—Cisco's system of alliances guards against loss of control, protects its proprietary manufacturing expertise, and enables the company to monitor closely the assembly operations of its partners while devoting its energy to designing new generations of the switches, routers, and other Internet-related equipment for which it is known.

Companies in all types of industries and in all parts of the world have elected to form strategic alliances and partnerships to complement their own strategic initiatives and strengthen their competitiveness in domestic and international markets—the very same goals that motivate vertical integration, horizontal mergers and acquisitions, and outsourcing initiatives. This is an about-face from times past, when the vast majority of companies were content to go it alone, confident that they already had or could independently develop whatever resources and know-how were needed to be successful in their markets. But in today's world, large corporations—even those that are successful and financially strong—have concluded that it doesn't always make good strategic and economic sense to be *totally independent* and *self-sufficient* with regard to each and every skill, resource, and capability they may need. When a company needs to strengthen its competitive position, whether through greater differentiation, efficiency improvements, or a stronger bargaining position, the fastest and most effective route may be to partner with other enterprises having similar goals and complementary capabilities; moreover, partnering offers greater flexibility should a company's resource requirements or goals later change.

A **strategic alliance** is a formal agreement between two or more separate companies in which there is strategically relevant collaboration of some sort, joint contribution of resources, shared risk, shared control, and mutual dependence. Often, alliances involve cooperative marketing, sales or distribution, joint production, design collaboration, or projects to jointly develop new technologies or products. They can vary in terms of their duration and the extent of the collaboration; some are intended as long-term arrangements, involving an extensive set of cooperative activities, while others are designed to accomplish more limited, short-term objectives.

CORE CONCEPT

A **strategic alliance** is a formal agreement between two or more separate companies in which they agree to work cooperatively toward some common objective.

Collaborative arrangements may entail a contractual agreement, but they commonly stop short of formal ownership ties between the partners (although sometimes an alliance member will secure minority ownership of another member). A special type of strategic alliance involving ownership ties is the **joint venture.** A joint venture entails forming a new corporate entity that is jointly owned by two or more companies that agree to share in the revenues, expenses, and control of the newly formed entity. Since joint ventures involve setting up a mutually owned business, they tend to be more durable but also riskier than other arrangements. In other types of strategic alliances, the collaboration between the partners involves a much less rigid structure in which the partners retain their independence from one another. If a strategic alliance is not working out, a partner can choose to simply walk away or reduce its commitment to collaborating at any time.

> **CORE CONCEPT**
>
> A **joint venture** is a type of strategic alliance in which the partners set up an independent corporate entity that they own and control jointly, sharing in its revenues and expenses.

Five factors make an alliance "strategic," as opposed to just a convenient business arrangement:[32]

1. It helps build, sustain, or enhance a core competence or competitive advantage.
2. It helps block a competitive threat.
3. It increases the bargaining power of alliance members over suppliers or buyers.
4. It helps open up important new market opportunities.
5. It mitigates a significant risk to a company's business.

Strategic cooperation is a much-favored approach in industries where new technological developments are occurring at a furious pace along many different paths and where advances in one technology spill over to affect others (often blurring industry boundaries). Whenever industries are experiencing high-velocity technological advances in many areas simultaneously, firms find it virtually essential to have cooperative relationships with other enterprises to stay on the leading edge of technology and product performance even in their own area of specialization.

It took a $3.2 billion joint venture involving the likes of Sprint-Nextel, Clearwire, Intel, Time Warner Cable, Google, Comcast, and Bright House Networks to roll out next-generation 4G wireless services based on Sprint's and Clearwire's WiMax mobile networks, with the objective of reaching 100 metropolitan areas and 120 million people by the end of 2010. WiMax was an advanced Wi-Fi technology that allowed people to browse the Internet at speeds as great as 10 times faster than other cellular Wi-Fi technologies. The venture was a necessity for Sprint-Nextel and Clearwire since they lacked the financial resources to handle the rollout on their own. The appeal of the partnership for Time Warner, Comcast, and Bright House was the ability to bundle the sale of wireless services to their cable customers, while Intel had the chip sets for WiMax and hoped that WiMax would become the dominant wireless Internet format. Google's interest in the alliance was to strengthen its lead in desktop search on wireless devices.

Clear Channel Communications has entered into a series of partnerships to provide a multiplatform launchpad for artists like Taylor Swift, Phoenix, and Sara Bareilles. In 2008, they launched iHeartRadio on the iPhone, leveraging their relationships with record labels, artists, TV music channels, and media companies to rake in $175 million in digital revenue as compared to $50 million earned by Pandora in the same period. In 2010, they partnered with MySpace, Hulu, and the artist management company 19 Entertainment for "If I Can Dream," an original reality series where unsigned musicians and actors share a "Real World"-style house in Los Angeles and document their attempts at stardom. Clear Channel has helped promote the show by conducting exclusive radio interviews and performances with the talent, which in turn has helped the show become a top-30 weekly program on Hulu.[33]

Since 2003, Samsung Electronics, a global electronics company headquartered in South Korea, has entered into more than 30 major strategic alliances involving such companies as Sony, Nokia, Intel, Microsoft, Dell, Toshiba, Lowe's, IBM, Hewlett-Packard, and Disney Automation; the alliances involved joint investments, technology transfer arrangements, joint R&D projects, and agreements to supply parts and components—all of which facilitated Samsung's strategic efforts to globalize its business and secure its position as a leader in the worldwide electronics industry. Microsoft collaborates very closely with independent software developers to ensure that their programs will run on the next-generation versions of Windows. Genentech, a leader in biotechnology and human genetics, has formed R&D alliances with over 30 companies to boost its prospects for developing new cures for various diseases and ailments. United Airlines, American Airlines, Continental, Delta, and Northwest created an alliance to form Orbitz, an Internet travel site that enabled them to compete head to head against Expedia and Travelocity and, further, gave them more economical access to travelers and vacationers shopping online for airfares, rental cars, lodging, cruises, and vacation packages.

Toyota has forged long-term strategic partnerships with many of its suppliers of automotive parts and components, both to achieve lower costs and to improve the quality and reliability of its vehicles. In 2008, when Chrysler found itself unable to build hybrid SUVs and trucks using its Two Mode technological innovation (because it lacked the economies of scale necessary to produce proprietary components at a reasonable cost), it entered into a strategic alliance with Nissan whereby Nissan would build Chrysler vehicles with the hybrid technology and Chrysler would take over the production of certain Nissan truck models. Daimler AG has been entering a variety of alliances to lower its risks and improve its prospects in electric cars, where it lacks key capabilities. Its equity-based strategic partnership with Tesla Motors, for example, will allow Daimler to use proven technology to bring its electric vehicles to market quickly, while helping Tesla learn how to mass produce its electric cars. Daimler's 2010 joint venture with Chinese car maker BYD is intended to help Daimler make and sell electric cars for the Chinese market.

Studies indicate that large corporations are commonly involved in 30 to 50 alliances and that a number have hundreds of alliances. One study estimated that corporate revenues coming from activities involving strategic alliances have more than doubled since 1995.[34] Another study reported that the typical large corporation relied on alliances for 15 to 20 percent of its revenues, assets, or income.[35] Companies that have formed a host of alliances have a need to manage their alliances like a portfolio—terminating those that no longer serve a useful purpose or that have produced meager results, forming promising new alliances, and restructuring certain existing alliances to correct performance problems and/or redirect the collaborative effort.[36]

> Company use of alliances is quite widespread.

Why and How Strategic Alliances Are Advantageous

The most common reasons companies enter into strategic alliances are to expedite the development of promising new technologies or products, to overcome deficits in their own technical and manufacturing expertise, to bring together the personnel and expertise needed to create desirable new skill sets and capabilities, to improve supply chain efficiency, to share the risks of high-stake, risky ventures, to gain economies of scale in production and/or marketing, and to acquire or improve market access through joint marketing agreements.[37] Manufacturers frequently pursue alliances with parts and components suppliers to gain the efficiencies of better supply chain management and to speed new products to market. By joining forces in components production and/or final assembly, companies may be able to realize cost savings not achievable with their own small volumes. Allies can learn much from one another in performing joint research, sharing technological know-how, and collaborating on complementary new technologies and products—sometimes enough to enable them to pursue other new opportunities on their own.[38] In industries where technology is advancing rapidly, alliances are all about fast cycles of learning, staying abreast of the latest developments, gaining quick access to the latest round of technological know-how, and developing dynamic capabilities. In bringing together firms with different skills and knowledge bases, alliances open up learning opportunities that help partner firms better leverage their own resources and capabilities.[39]

> The best alliances are highly selective, focusing on particular value-creating activities, whether within or across industry boundaries, and on obtaining a specific competitive benefit. They enable a firm to build on its strengths and to learn.

There are several other instances in which companies find strategic alliances particularly valuable. As we explain in the next chapter, a company that is racing for *global market leadership* needs alliances to:[40]

- *Get into critical country markets quickly* and accelerate the process of building a potent global market presence.

- *Gain inside knowledge about unfamiliar markets and cultures through alliances with local partners.* For example, U.S., European, and Japanese companies wanting to build market footholds in the fast-growing Chinese market have pursued partnership arrangements with Chinese companies to help get products through the customs process, to help guide them through the maze of government regulations, to supply knowledge of local markets, to provide guidance on adapting their products to better match the buying preferences of Chinese consumers, to set up local manufacturing capabilities, and to assist in distribution, marketing, and promotional activities.

- *Access valuable skills and competencies* that are concentrated in particular geographic locations (such as software design competencies in the United States, fashion design skills in Italy, and efficient manufacturing skills in Japan and China).

A company that is racing to *stake out a strong position in an industry of the future* needs alliances to:[41]

- *Establish a stronger beachhead* for participating in the target industry.

- *Master new technologies and build new expertise and competencies* faster than would be possible through internal efforts.

- *Open up broader opportunities* in the target industry by melding the firm's own capabilities with the expertise and resources of partners.

Capturing the Benefits of Strategic Alliances

The extent to which companies benefit from entering into alliances and partnerships seems to be a function of six factors:[42]

1. *Picking a good partner.* A good partner must bring complementary strengths to the relationship. To the extent that alliance members have nonoverlapping strengths, there is greater potential for synergy and less potential for coordination problems and conflict. In addition, a good partner needs to share the company's vision about the overall purpose of the alliance and to have specific goals that either match or complement those of the company. Strong partnerships also depend on good chemistry among key personnel and compatible views about how the alliance should be structured and managed.

2. *Being sensitive to cultural differences.* Cultural differences among companies can make it difficult for their personnel to work together effectively. Cultural differences can be problematic among companies from the same country, but when the partners have different national origins, the problems are often magnified. Unless there is respect among all the parties for company cultural differences, including those stemming from different local cultures and local business practices, productive working relationships are unlikely to emerge.

3. *Recognizing that the alliance must benefit both sides.* Information must be shared as well as gained, and the relationship must remain forthright and trustful. Many alliances fail because one or both partners grow unhappy with what they are learning. Also, if either partner plays games with information or tries to take advantage of the other, the resulting friction can quickly erode the value of further collaboration. Open, trustworthy behavior on both sides is essential for fruitful collaboration.

4. *Ensuring that both parties live up to their commitments.* Both parties have to deliver on their commitments for the alliance to produce the intended benefits. The division of work has to be perceived as fairly apportioned, and the caliber of the benefits received on both sides has to be perceived as adequate. Such actions are critical for the establishment of trust between the parties; research has shown that trust is an important factor in fostering effective strategic alliances.[43]

5. *Structuring the decision-making process so that actions can be taken swiftly when needed.* In many instances, the fast pace of technological and competitive changes dictates an equally fast decision-making process. If the parties get bogged down in discussions or in gaining internal approval from higher-ups, the alliance can turn into an anchor of delay and inaction.

6. *Managing the learning process and then adjusting the alliance agreement over time to fit new circumstances.* One of the keys to long-lasting success is adapting the nature and structure of the alliance to be responsive to shifting market conditions, emerging technologies, and changing customer requirements. Wise allies are quick to recognize the merit of an evolving collaborative arrangement, where adjustments are made to accommodate changing market conditions and to overcome whatever problems arise in establishing an effective working relationship. Most alliances encounter troubles of some kind within a couple of years—those that are flexible enough to evolve are better able to recover.[44]

Most alliances that aim at sharing technology or providing market access turn out to be temporary, lasting only a few years. This is not necessarily an indicator of failure, however. Strategic alliances can be terminated after a few years simply because they have fulfilled their purpose; indeed, many alliances are intended to be of limited duration, set up to accomplish specific short-term objectives. Longer-lasting collaborative arrangements, however, may provide even greater strategic benefits. Alliances are more likely to be long-lasting when (1) they involve collaboration with partners that do not compete directly, (2) a trusting relationship has been established, and (3) both parties conclude that continued collaboration is in their mutual interest, perhaps because new opportunities for learning are emerging.

The Drawbacks of Strategic Alliances and Partnerships

While strategic alliances provide a way of obtaining the benefits of vertical integration, mergers and acquisitions, and outsourcing, they also suffer from some of the same drawbacks. Culture clash and integration problems due to different management styles and business practices can interfere with the success of an alliance, just as they can with vertical integration or horizontal mergers and acquisitions. Anticipated gains may fail to materialize due to an overly optimistic view of the synergies or a poor fit in terms of the combination of resources and capabilities. When outsourcing is conducted via alliances, there is no less risk of becoming dependent on other companies for essential expertise and capabilities— indeed, this may be the Achilles' heel of such alliances.

Moreover, there are additional pitfalls to collaborative arrangements. The greatest danger is that a partner will gain access to a company's proprietary knowledge base, technologies, or trade secrets, enabling the partner to match the company's core strengths and costing the company its hard-won competitive advantage. This risk is greatest when the alliance is among industry rivals or when the alliance is for the purpose of collaborative R&D, since this type of partnership requires an extensive exchange of closely held information.

The question for managers is when to engage in a strategic alliance and when to choose an alternative means of meeting their objectives. The answer to this question depends on the relative advantages of each method and the circumstances under which each type of organizational arrangement is favored.

The principle advantages of strategic alliances over vertical integration or horizontal mergers/acquisitons are threefold:

1. They lower investment costs and risks for each partner by facilitating resource pooling and risk sharing. This can be particularly important when investment needs and uncertainty are high, such as when a dominant technology standard has not yet emerged.

2. They are more flexible organizational forms and allow for a more adaptive response to changing conditions. Flexibility is key when environmental conditions or technologies are changing rapidly. Moreover, strategic alliances under such circumstances may enable the development of each partner's dynamic capabilities.

3. They are more rapidly deployed—a critical factor when speed is of the essence. Speed is of the essence when there is a winner-take-all type of competitive situation, such as the race for a dominant technological design or a race down a steep experience curve, where there is a large first-mover advantage.

The key advantages of using strategic alliances rather than arm's-length transactions to manage outsourcing are (1) the increased ability to exercise control over the partners' activities and (2) a greater willingness for the partners to make relationship-specific investments. Arm's-length transactions discourage such investments since they imply less commitment and do not build trust.

On the other hand, there are circumstances when other organizational mechanisms are preferable to partnering. Mergers and acquisitions are especially suited for situations in which strategic alliances or partnerships do not go far enough in providing a company with access to needed resources and capabilities.[45] Ownership ties are more permanent than partnership ties, allowing the operations of the merger/acquisition participants to be tightly integrated and creating more in-house control and autonomy. Other organizational mechanisms are also preferable to alliances when there is limited property rights protection for valuable know-how and when companies fear being taken advantage of by opportunistic partners.

While it is important for managers to understand when strategic alliances and partnerships are most likely (and least likely) to prove useful, it is also important to know how to manage them.

How to Make Strategic Alliances Work

A surprisingly large number of alliances never live up to expectations. A recent article reported that even though the number of strategic alliances increases by about 25 percent annually, about 60 to 70 percent of alliances continue to fail each year.[46] The success of an alliance depends on how well the partners work together, their capacity to respond and adapt to changing internal and external conditions, and their willingness to renegotiate the bargain if circumstances so warrant. A successful alliance requires real in-the-trenches collaboration, not merely an arm's-length exchange of ideas. Unless partners place a high value on the skills, resources, and contributions each brings to the alliance and the cooperative arrangement results in valuable win-win outcomes, it is doomed.

While the track record for strategic alliances is poor on average, many companies have learned how to manage strategic alliances successfully and routinely defy these averages. Samsung Group, which includes Samsung Electronics and had worldwide sales of $117.8 billion in 2009, successfully manages an ecosystem of over 1,300 partnerships that enable productive activities from global procurement to local marketing to collaborative R&D. Samsung Group takes a systematic approach to managing its partnerships and devotes considerable resources to this enterprise. In 2008, for example, it established a Partner Collaboration and Enhancement Office under the direct control of its CEO. Samsung Group supports its partners with financial help as well as training and development resources to ensure that its alliance partners' technical, manufacturing, and management capabilities remain globally competitive. As a result, some of its equipment providers have emerged as the leading firms in their industries while contributing to Samsung's competitive advantage in the global TV market.

Companies that have greater success in managing their strategic alliances and partnerships often credit the following factors:

- *They create a system for managing their alliances.* Companies need to manage their alliances in a systematic fashion, just as they manage other functions.

This means setting up a process for managing the different aspects of alliance management from partner selection to alliance termination procedures. To ensure that the system is followed on a routine basis by all company managers, many companies create a set of explicit procedures, process templates, manuals, or the like.

- *They build relationships with their partners and establish trust.* Establishing strong interpersonal relationships is a critical factor in making strategic alliances work since they facilitate opening up channels of communication, coordinating activity, aligning interests, and building trust. Cultural sensitivity is a key part of this, particularly for cross-border alliances. Accordingly, many companies include cultural sensitivity training for their managers as a part of their alliance management program.

- *They protect themselves from the threat of opportunism by setting up safeguards.* There are a number of means for preventing a company from being taken advantage of by an untrustworthy partner or unwittingly losing control over key assets. Contractual safeguards, including noncompete clauses, can provide some protection. But if the company's core assets are vulnerable to being appropriated by partners, it may be possible to control their use and strictly limit outside access. Cisco Systems, for example, does not divulge the source code for its designs to its alliance partners, thereby controlling the initiation of all improvements and safeguarding its innovations from imitation.

- *They make commitments to their partners and see that their partners do the same.* When partners make credible commitments to a joint enterprise, they have stronger incentives for making it work and are less likely to "free-ride" on the efforts of other partners. Because of this, equity-based alliances tend to be more successful than nonequity alliances.[47]

- *They make learning a routine part of the management process.* There are always opportunities for learning from a partner, but organizational learning does not take place automatically. Moreover, whatever learning takes place cannot add to a company's knowledge base unless the learning is incorporated into the company's routines and practices. Particularly when the purpose of an alliance is to improve a company's knowledge assets and capabilities, it is important for the company to learn thoroughly and rapidly about its partners' technologies, business practices, and organizational capabilities and then transfer valuable ideas and practices into its own operations promptly.

Finally, managers should realize that alliance management is an organizational capability, much like any other. It develops over time, out of effort, experience, and learning. For this reason, it is wise to begin slowly, with simple alliances, designed to meet limited, short-term objectives. Short-term partnerships that are successful often become the basis for much more extensive collaborative arrangements. Even when strategic alliances are set up with the hope that they will become long-term engagements, they have a better chance of succeeding if they are phased in so that the partners can learn how they can work together most fruitfully.

KEY POINTS

1. Once a company has settled on which of the five generic competitive strategies to employ, attention turns to how strategic choices regarding (1) competitive actions, (2) timing, and (3) scope of operations can complement its competitive approach and maximize the power of its overall strategy.

2. Strategic offensives should, as a general rule, be grounded in a company's strategic assets. The best offensives use a company's resource and capability strengths to attack rivals in the competitive areas where they are comparatively weakest.

3. Companies have a number of offensive strategy options for improving their market positions: using a cost-based advantage to attack competitors on the basis of price or value, leapfrogging competitors with next-generation technologies, pursuing continuous product innovation, adopting and improving the best ideas of others, using hit-and-run tactics to steal sales away from unsuspecting rivals, and launching preemptive strikes. A blue-ocean type of offensive strategy seeks to gain a dramatic and durable competitive advantage by abandoning efforts to beat out competitors in existing markets and, instead, inventing a new industry or distinctive market segment that renders existing competitors largely irrelevant and allows a company to create and capture altogether new demand.

4. The purposes of defensive strategies are to lower the risk of being attacked, weaken the impact of any attack that occurs, and influence challengers to aim their efforts at other rivals. Defensive strategies to protect a company's position usually take one of two forms: (1) actions to block challengers and (2) actions to signal the likelihood of strong retaliation.

5. The timing of strategic moves also has competitive relevance and is especially important when first-mover advantages or disadvantages exist. Company managers are obligated to carefully consider the advantages or disadvantages that attach to being a first mover versus a fast follower versus a wait-and-see late mover.

6. Decisions concerning the scope of a company's operations—which activities a firm will perform internally and which it will not—can also affect the strength of a company's market position. The *scope of the firm* refers to the range of its activities, the breadth of its product and service offerings, the extent of its geographic market presence, and its mix of businesses. Companies can expand their scope horizontally (more broadly within their focal market) or vertically (up or down the chain of value-adding activities that start with raw-material production and end with sales and service to the end consumer). Horizontal mergers and acquisitions (combinations of market rivals) provide a means for a company to expand its horizontal scope. Vertical integration expands a firm's vertical scope.

7. Horizontal mergers and acquisitions can strengthen a firm's competitiveness in five ways: (1) by improving the efficiency of its operations, (2) by heightening its product differentiation, (3) by reducing market rivalry, (3) by increasing the company's bargaining power over suppliers and buyers, and (5) by enhancing its flexibility and dynamic capabilities.

8. Vertical integration, forward or backward, makes strategic sense only if it strengthens a company's position via either cost reduction or creation of a differentiation-based advantage. Otherwise, the drawbacks of vertical integration (increased investment, greater business risk, increased vulnerability to technological changes, less flexibility in making product changes, and the potential for channel conflict) are likely to outweigh any advantages.

9. Outsourcing involves farming out pieces of the value chain formerly performed in-house to outside vendors, thereby narrowing the scope of the firm. Outsourcing can enhance a company's competitiveness whenever (1) an activity can be performed better or more cheaply by outside specialists; (2) having the activity performed by others won't hollow out the outsourcing company's core competencies; (3) it streamlines company operations in ways that improve organizational flexibility, speed decision making, and cut cycle time; (4) it reduces the company's risk exposure; (5) it allows a company to access capabilities more quickly and improves its ability to innovate; and (6) it permits a company to concentrate on its core business and focus on what it does best.

10. Strategic alliances and cooperative partnerships provide one way to gain some of the benefits offered by vertical integration, outsourcing, and horizontal mergers and acquisitions while minimizing the associated problems. They serve as an alternative to vertical integration and mergers and acquisitions; they serve as a supplement to outsourcing, allowing more control relative to outsourcing via arm's-length transactions.

11. Companies that manage their alliances well generally (1) create a system for managing their alliances, (2) build relationships with their partners and establish trust, (3) protect themselves from the threat of opportunism by setting up safeguards, (4) make commitments to their partners and see that their partners do the same, and (5) make learning a routine part of the management process.

ASSURANCE OF LEARNING EXERCISES

LO 3

1. Using your university library's subscription to Lexis-Nexis, EBSCO, or a similar database, perform a search on "acquisition strategy." Identify at least two companies in different industries that are using acquisitions to strengthen their market positions. How have these acquisitions enhanced the acquiring companies' competitive capabilities?

LO 4

2. Go to www.bridgestone.co.jp/english/ir, and review information about Bridgestone Corporation's tire and raw-material operations under the About Bridgestone and IR Library links. To what extent is the company vertically integrated? What segments of the vertical chain has the company chosen to enter? What are the benefits and liabilities of Bridgestone's vertical integration strategy?

LO 5, LO 6

3. Go to **www.google.com**, and do a search on "outsourcing." Identify at least two companies in different industries that have entered into outsourcing agreements with firms with specialized services. In addition, describe what value chain activities the companies have chosen to outsource. Do any of these outsourcing agreements seem likely to threaten any of the companies' competitive capabilities? Are the companies using strategic alliances to manage their outsourcing?

EXERCISES FOR SIMULATION PARTICIPANTS

LO 1

1. What offensive strategy options does your company have? Identify at least two offensive moves that your company should seriously consider to improve the company's market standing and financial performance.

LO 2

2. What options for being a first mover does your company have? Do any of these first-mover options hold competitive advantage potential?

LO 1

3. What defensive strategy moves should your company consider in the upcoming decision round? Identify at least two defensive actions that your company has taken in a past decision round.

LO 3

4. Does your company have the option to merge with or acquire other companies? If so, which rival companies would you like to acquire or merge with?

LO 4

5. Is your company vertically integrated? Explain.

LO 5, LO 6

6. Is your company able to engage in outsourcing? If so, what do you see as the pros and cons of outsourcing? Are strategic alliances involved? Explain.

ENDNOTES

[1] An insightful discussion of aggressive offensive strategies is presented in George Stalk, Jr., and Rob Lachenauer, "Hardball: Five Killer Strategies for Trouncing the Competition," *Harvard Business Review* 82, no. 4 (April 2004), pp. 62–71. For a discussion of offensive strategies to enter attractive markets where existing firms are making above-average profits, see David J. Bryce and Jeffrey H. Dyer, "Strategies to Crack Well-Guarded Markets," *Harvard Business Review* 85, no. 5 (May 2007), pp. 84–92. A discussion of offensive strategies particularly suitable for industry leaders is presented in Richard D'Aveni, "The Empire Strikes Back: Counterrevolutionary Strategies for Industry Leaders," *Harvard Business Review* 80, no. 11 (November 2002), pp. 66–74.

[2] George Stalk, "Playing Hardball: Why Strategy Still Matters," *Ivey Business Journal* 69, no.2 (November–December 2004), pp. 1–2. See K. G. Smith, W. J. Ferrier, and C. M. Grimm, "King of the Hill: Dethroning the Industry Leader," *Academy of Management Executive* 15, no. 2 (May 2001), pp. 59–70; also see W. J. Ferrier, K. G. Smith, and C. M. Grimm, "The Role of Competitive Action

in Market Share Erosion and Industry Dethronement: A Study of Industry Leaders and Challengers," *Academy of Management Journal* 42, no. 4 (August 1999), pp. 372–88.
[3] For a discussion of how to wage offensives against strong rivals, see David B. Yoffie and Mary Kwak, "Mastering Balance: How to Meet and Beat a Stronger Opponent," *California Management Review* 44, no. 2 (Winter 2002), pp. 8–24.
[4] Stalk, "Playing Hardball," pp. 1–2.
[5] Ian C. MacMillan, Alexander B. van Putten, and Rita Gunther McGrath, "Global Gamesmanship," *Harvard Business Review* 81, no. 5 (May 2003), pp. 66–67; also see Ashkay R. Rao, Mark E. Bergen, and Scott Davis, "How to Fight a Price War," *Harvard Business Review* 78, no. 2 (March–April 2000), pp. 107–16.
[6] D. B. Yoffie and M. A. Cusumano, "Judo Strategy—The Competitive Dynamics of Internet Time," *Harvard Business* Review 77, no. 1 (January–February 1999), pp. 70–81.
[7] Stalk and Lachenauer, "Hardball: Five Killer Strategies," p. 64.
[8] For an interesting study of how small firms can successfully employ guerrilla-style tactics, see Ming-Jer Chen and Donald C. Hambrick, "Speed, Stealth, and Selective Attack: How Small Firms Differ from Large Firms in Competitive Behavior," *Academy of Management Journal* 38, no. 2 (April 1995), pp. 453–82. Other discussions of guerrilla offensives can be found in Ian MacMillan, "How Business Strategists Can Use Guerrilla Warfare Tactics," *Journal of Business Strategy* 1, no. 2 (Fall 1980), pp. 63–65; William E. Rothschild, "Surprise and the Competitive Advantage," *Journal of Business Strategy* 4, no. 3 (Winter 1984), pp. 10–18; Kathryn R. Harrigan, *Strategic Flexibility* (Lexington, MA: Lexington Books, 1985), pp. 30–45; Liam Fahey, "Guerrilla Strategy: The Hit-and-Run Attack," in Liam Fahey (ed.), *The Strategic Management Planning Reader* (Englewood Cliffs, NJ: Prentice Hall, 1989), pp. 194–97.
[9] Yoffie and Cusumano, "Judo Strategy." See also D. B. Yoffie and M. Kwak, "Mastering Balance: How to Meet and Beat a Stronger Opponent," *California Management Review* 44, no. 2 (Winter 2002), pp. 8–24.
[10] The use of preemptive strike offensives is treated comprehensively in Ian MacMillan, "Preemptive Strategies," *Journal of Business Strategy* 14, no. 2 (Fall 1983), pp. 16–26.
[11] Ian C. MacMillan, "How Long Can You Sustain a Competitive Advantage?" in Liam Fahey (ed.), *The Strategic Planning Management Reader* (Englewood Cliffs, NJ: Prentice Hall, 1989), pp. 23–24.
[12] For a discussion of competitors' reactions, see Kevin P. Coyne and John Horn, "Predicting Your Competitor's Reactions," *Harvard Business Review* 87 no. 4 (April 2009), pp. 90–97.
[13] Philip Kotler, *Marketing Management,* 5th ed. (Englewood Cliffs, NJ: Prentice Hall, 1984), p. 400.

[14] Michael E. Porter, *Competitive Advantage* (New York: Free Press, 1985), p. 518.
[15] W. Chan Kim and Renée Mauborgne, "Blue Ocean Strategy," *Harvard Business Review* 82, no. 10 (October 2004), pp. 76–84.
[16] Porter, *Competitive Advantage,* pp. 489–94.
[17] Ibid., pp. 495–97. The list here is selective; Porter offers a greater number of options.
[18] Ibid., pp. 232–33.
[19] For research evidence on the effects of pioneering versus following, see Jeffrey G. Covin, Dennis P. Slevin, and Michael B. Heeley, "Pioneers and Followers: Competitive Tactics, Environment, and Growth," *Journal of Business Venturing* 15, no. 2 (March 1999), pp. 175–210; Christopher A. Bartlett and Sumantra Ghoshal, "Going Global: Lessons from Late-Movers," *Harvard Business Review* 78, no. 2 (March–April 2000), pp. 132–45.
[20] Gary Hamel, "Smart Mover, Dumb Mover," *Fortune,* September 3, 2001, p. 195.
[21] Ibid., p.192; Costas Markides and Paul A. Geroski, Racing to be 2nd: Conquering Industries of the Future," *Business Strategy Review* 15, no. 4 (Winter 2004), pp. 25–31.
[22] For a more extensive discussion, see Fernando Suarez and Gianvito Lanzolla, "The Half-Truth of First-Mover Advantage," *Harvard Business Review* 83, no. 4 (April 2005), pp. 121–27.
[23] Henry Gibbon, "Worldwide M&A Declines 28% to US$2trn," *Acquisitions Monthly,* January 2010 (issue 303), pp. 4–11.
[24] For an excellent review of the strategic objectives of various types of mergers and acquisitions and the managerial challenges that different kinds of mergers and acquisitions present, see Joseph L. Bower, "Not All M&As Are Alike—and That Matters," *Harvard Business Review* 79, no. 3 (March 2001), pp. 93–101.
[25] O. Chatain and P. Zemsky, "The Horizontal Scope of the Firm: Organizational Tradeoffs vs. Buyer-Supplier Relationships," *Management Science* 53, no. 4 (April 2007), pp. 550–65.
[26] For a more expansive discussion, see Jeffrey H. Dyer, Prashant Kale, and Harbir Singh, "When to Ally and When to Acquire," *Harvard Business Review* 82, no. 4 (July–August 2004), pp. 109–10.
[27] See Kathryn R. Harrigan, "Matching Vertical Integration Strategies to Competitive Conditions," *Strategic Management Journal* 7, no. 6 (November–December 1986), pp. 535–56; for a more extensive discussion of the advantages and disadvantages of vertical integration, see John Stuckey and David White, "When and When Not to Vertically Integrate," *Sloan Management Review* (Spring 1993), pp. 71–83.
[28] The resilience of vertical integration strategies despite the disadvantages is discussed in Thomas Osegowitsch and Anoop Madhok, "Vertical Integration Is Dead, or Is It?" *Business Horizons* 46, no. 2 (March–April 2003), pp. 25–35.
[29] For a good overview of outsourcing strategies, see Ronan McIvor, "What Is the

Right Outsourcing Strategy for Your Process?" *European Management Journal* 26, no. 1 (February 2008), pp. 24–34.
[30] For a good discussion of the problems that can arise from outsourcing, see Gary P. Pisano and Willy C. Shih, "Restoring American Competitiveness," *Harvard Business Review* 87, no. 7–8 (July–August 2009), pp. 114–25; Jérôme Barthélemy, "The Seven Deadly Sins of Outsourcing," *Academy of Management Executive* 17, no. 2 (May 2003), pp. 87–100.
[31] Pisano and Shih, "Restoring American Competitivness," pp. 116–17.
[32] Jason Wakeam, "The Five Factors of a Strategic Alliance," *Ivey Business Journal* 68, no 3 (May–June 2003), pp. 1–4.
[33] *Advertising Age,* May 24, 2010, p. 14.
[34] Salvatore Parise and Lisa Sasson, "Leveraging Knowledge Management across Strategic Alliances," *Ivey Business Journal* 66, no. 4 (March–April 2002), p. 42.
[35] David Ernst and James Bamford, "Your Alliances Are Too Stable," *Harvard Business Review* 83, no. 6 (June 2005), p.133.
[36] An excellent discussion of the portfolio approach to managing multiple alliances and how to restructure a faltering alliance is presented in Ernst and Bamford, "Your Alliances Are Too Stable," pp. 133–41.
[37] Michael E. Porter, *The Competitive Advantage of Nations* (New York: Free Press, 1990), p. 66. For a discussion of how to realize the advantages of strategic partnerships, see Nancy J. Kaplan and Jonathan Hurd, "Realizing the Promise of Partnerships," *Journal of Business Strategy* 23, no. 3 (May–June 2002), pp. 38–42; Parise and Sasson, "Leveraging Knowledge Management across Strategic Alliances," pp. 41-47; Ernst and Bamford, "Your Alliances Are Too Stable," pp. 133–41; and Jonathan Hughes and Jeff Weiss, "Simple Rules for Making Alliances Work," *Harvard Business Review* 85, no. 11 (November 2007), pp. 122–31.
[38] For a discussion of how to raise the chances that a strategic alliance will produce strategically important outcomes, see M. Koza and A. Lewin, "Managing Partnerships and Strategic Alliances: Raising the Odds of Success," *European Management Journal* 18, no. 2 (April 2000), pp. 146–51.
[39] A. Inkpen, "Learning, Knowledge Acquisition, and Strategic Alliances," *European Management Journal* 16, no. 2 (April 1998), pp. 223–29.
[40] Yves L. Doz and Gary Hamel, *Alliance Advantage: The Art of Creating Value through Partnering* (Boston: Harvard Business School Press), chap. 1.
[41] Ibid.
[42] Ibid., chaps. 4–8; Patricia Anslinger and Justin Jenk, "Creating Successful Alliances," *Journal of Business Strategy* 25, no. 2 (2004), pp. 18–23; Rosabeth Moss Kanter, "Collaborative Advantage: The Art of the Alliance," *Harvard Business Review* 72, no. 4 (July–August 1994), pp. 96–108; Joel Bleeke and David Ernst, "The Way to Win in

Cross-Border Alliances," *Harvard Business Review* 69, no. 6 (November–December 1991), pp. 127–35; Gary Hamel, Yves L. Doz, and C. K. Prahalad, "Collaborate with Your Competitors—and Win," *Harvard Business Review* 67, no. 1 (January–February 1989), pp. 133–39; Hughes and Weiss, "Simple Rules for Making Alliances Work."

[43] J. B. Cullen, J. L. Johnson, and T. Sakano, "Success through Commitment and Trust: The Soft Side of Strategic Alliance Management," *Journal of World Business* 35, no. 3 (Fall 2000), pp. 223–40; T. K. Das and B. S. Teng, "Between Trust and Control: Developing Confidence in Partner Cooperation in Alliances," *Academy of Management Review* 23, no. 3 (July 1998), pp. 491–512.

[44] K. M. Eisenhardt and C. B. Schoonhoven, "Resource-Based View of Strategic Alliance Formation: Strategic and Social Effects in Entrepreneurial Firms," *Organization Science* 7, no. 2 (March–April 1996), pp. 136–50; M. Zollo, J. J. Reuer, and H. Singh, "Interorganizational Routines and Performance in Strategic Alliances," *Organization Science* 13, no. 6 (November–December 2002), pp. 701–13.

[45] The pros and cons of mergers/acquisitions versus strategic alliances are described in Dyer, Kale, and Singh, "When to Ally and When to Acquire," pp. 109–15.

[46] Hughes and Weiss, "Simple Rules for Making Alliances Work," p. 122.

[47] Y. G. Pan and D. K. Tse, "The Hierarchical Model of Market Entry Modes," *Journal of International Business Studies* 31, no. 4 (2000), pp. 535–54.

CHAPTER 7

STRATEGIES FOR COMPETING IN INTERNATIONAL MARKETS

We're not going global because we want to or because of any megalomania, but because it's really necessary. . . . The costs are so enormous today that you really need to have worldwide revenues to cover them.

—Rupert Murdoch
CEO of the media conglomerate News Corporation

Globalization [provides] a long-lasting competitive advantage. If we build a new gas turbine, in 18 months our

competitors also have one. But building a global company is not so easy to copy.

—Percy Barnevik
Former CEO of the Swiss-Swedish industrial corporation ABB

Capital, technology, and ideas flow these days like quicksilver across national boundaries.

—Robert H. Waterman, Jr.
Internationally recognized expert on management practices

LEARNING OBJECTIVES

LO 1. Develop an understanding of the primary reasons companies choose to compete in international markets.

LO 2. Learn how and why differing market conditions across countries and industries make crafting international strategy a complex undertaking.

LO 3. Learn about the major strategic options for entering and competing in foreign markets.

LO 4. Gain familiarity with the three main strategic approaches for competing internationally.

LO 5. Understand how international companies go about building competitive advantage in foreign markets.

Any company that aspires to industry leadership in the 21st century must think in terms of global, not domestic, market leadership. The world economy is globalizing at an accelerating pace as ambitious growth-minded companies race to build stronger competitive positions in the markets of more and more countries, as countries previously closed to foreign companies open up their markets, as companies in developing countries gain competitive strength, and as advances in information technology and communication shrink the importance of geographic distance. The forces of globalization are changing the competitive landscape in many industries, offering companies attractive new opportunities but at the same time introducing new competitive threats. Companies in industries where these forces are greatest are therefore under considerable pressure to come up with a strategy for competing successfully in foreign markets.

This chapter focuses on strategy options for expanding beyond domestic boundaries and competing in the markets of either a few or a great many countries. In the process of exploring these issues, we will introduce such concepts as multidomestic, global, and transnational strategies; the Porter diamond of national advantage; and cross-country differences in cultural, demographic, and market conditions. The chapter also includes sections on strategy options for entering and competing in foreign markets; the importance of locating value chain operations in the most advantageous countries; and the special circumstances of competing in such developing markets as China, India, Brazil, Russia, and eastern Europe.

WHY COMPANIES DECIDE TO ENTER FOREIGN MARKETS

LO 1

Develop an understanding of the primary reasons companies choose to compete in international markets.

A company may opt to expand outside its domestic market for any of five major reasons:

1. *To gain access to new customers.* Expanding into foreign markets offers potential for increased revenues, profits, and long-term growth and becomes an especially attractive option when a company's home markets are mature and nearing saturation levels. Companies often expand internationally to extend the life cycle of their products, as Honda has done with its classic 50-cc motorcycle, the Honda cub (which is still selling well in developing markets, more than 50 years after it was first introduced in Japan). A larger target market also offers companies the opportunity to earn a return on large investments more rapidly. This can be particularly important in R&D-intensive industries, where development is fast-paced or competitors imitate innovations rapidly.

2. *To achieve lower costs through economies of scale, experience, and increased purchasing power.* Many companies are driven to sell in more than one country because domestic sales volume alone is not large enough to fully capture economies of scale in product development, manufacturing, or marketing. Similarly, firms expand internationally to increase the rate at which they accumulate experience and move down the learning curve. International expansion can also lower a company's input costs through greater pooled purchasing power. The relatively small size of country markets in Europe and limited domestic volume explains why companies like Michelin, BMW, and Nestlé long ago began selling their products all across Europe and then moved into markets in North America and Latin America.

3. *To further exploit its core competencies.* A company with competitively valuable resources and capabilities can often extend a market-leading position in its home market into a position of regional or global market leadership by leveraging these resources further. Nokia's competencies and capabilities in mobile phones have propelled it to global market leadership in the wireless telecommunications business. Walmart is capitalizing on its considerable expertise in discount retailing to expand into China, Latin America, Japan, South Korea, and the United Kingdom; Walmart executives believe the company has tremendous growth opportunities in China. Companies can often leverage their resources internationally by replicating a successful business model, using it as a basic blueprint for international operations, as Starbucks and McDonald's have done.[1]

4. *To gain access to resources and capabilities located in foreign markets.* An increasingly important motive for entering foreign markets is to acquire resources and capabilities that cannot be accessed as readily in a company's home market. Companies often enter into cross-border alliances or joint ventures, for example, to gain access to resources and capabilities that complement their own or to learn from their partners.[2] Cross-border acquisitions are commonly made for similar reasons.[3] In other cases, companies choose to establish operations in other countries to utilize local distribution networks, employ low-cost human resources, or acquire technical knowledge. In a few

cases, companies in industries based on natural resources (e.g., oil and gas, minerals, rubber, and lumber) find it necessary to operate in the international arena because attractive raw-material supplies are located in many different parts of the world.

5. *To spread its business risk across a wider market base.* A company spreads business risk by operating in many different countries rather than depending entirely on operations in a few countries. Thus, when a company with operations across much of the world encounters economic downturns in certain countries, its performance may be bolstered by buoyant sales elsewhere.

In addition, companies that are the suppliers of other companies often expand internationally when their major customers do so, to meet their needs abroad and retain their position as a key supply chain partner. Automotive parts suppliers, for example, have followed automobile manufacturers abroad, and retail goods suppliers have followed large retailers into foreign markets.

WHY COMPETING ACROSS NATIONAL BORDERS MAKES STRATEGY MAKING MORE COMPLEX

Crafting a strategy to compete in one or more countries of the world is inherently more complex because of (1) factors that affect industry competitiveness that vary from country to country, (2) the potential for location-based advantages in certain countries, (3) different government policies and economic conditions that make the business climate more favorable in some countries than in others, (4) the risks of adverse shifts in currency exchange rates, and (5) cross-country differences in cultural, demographic, and market conditions.

LO 2

Learn how and why differing market conditions across countries and industries make crafting international strategy a complex undertaking.

Cross-Country Variation in Factors That Affect Industry Competitiveness

Certain countries are known for their strengths in particular industries. For example, Chile has competitive strengths in industries such as copper, fruit, fish products, paper and pulp, chemicals, and wine. Japan is known for competitive strength in consumer electronics, automobiles, semiconductors, steel products, and specialty steel. Where industries are more likely to develop competitive strength depends on a set of factors that describe the nature of each country's business environment and vary across countries. Because strong industries are made up of strong firms, the strategies of firms that expand internationally are usually grounded in one or more of these factors. The four major factors are summarized in a framework known as the *Diamond of National Advantage* (see Figure 7.1).[4]

Demand Conditions
The demand conditions in an industry's home market include the relative size of the market and the nature of domestic buyers' needs and wants. Industry sectors that are larger and more important in their home market tend to attract more resources and grow faster than others. Demanding domestic buyers for an industry's products spur greater innovativeness and improvements in quality. Such conditions foster the development of stronger

Figure 7.1   The Diamond of National Advantage

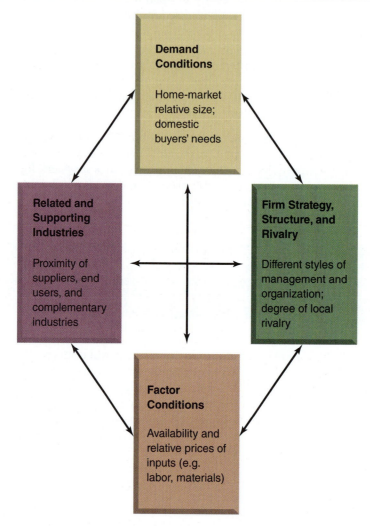

Source: Adapted from M. Porter, "The Competitive Advantage of Nations," *Harvard Business Review,* March–April 1990, pp. 73–93.

industries, with firms that are capable of translating a home-market advantage into a competitive advantage in the international arena.

Factor Conditions   Factor conditions describe the availability, quality, and cost of raw materials and other inputs (called *factors*) that firms in an industry require to produce their products and services. The relevant factors vary from industry to industry but can include different types of labor, technical or managerial knowledge, land, financial capital, and natural resources. Elements of a country's infrastructure may be included as well, such as its transportation, communication, and banking system. For instance, in India there are efficient, well-developed national channels for distributing trucks, scooters, farm equipment, groceries, personal care items, and other packaged products to the country's 3 million retailers, whereas in China distribution is primarily local and there is a limited national network for distributing most products. Competitively strong industries and firms develop where relevant factor conditions are favorable.

Related and Supporting Industries   Robust industries often develop as part of a cluster of related industries, including suppliers of components and capital equipment, end users, and the makers of complementary products, including those that are technologically related. The sports car makers Ferrari and Maserati, for example, are located in an area of Italy known as the "engine technological district" that includes other firms involved in racing, such as Ducati Motorcycles, along with hundreds of small suppliers. The advantage to firms that develop as part of a related-industry cluster comes from the close collaboration with key suppliers and the greater knowledge sharing throughout the cluster, resulting in greater efficiency and innovativeness.

Firm Strategy, Structure, and Rivalry   Different country environments foster the development of different styles of management, organization, and strategy. For example, strategic alliances are a more common strategy for firms from Asian or Latin American countries, which emphasize trust and cooperation in their organizations, than for firms from North American, where individualism is more influential. In addition, countries vary in terms of the competitiveness of their industries. Fierce competitive conditions in home markets tend to hone domestic firms' competitive capabilities and ready them for competing internationally.

For an industry in a particular country to become competitively strong, all four factors must be favorable for that industry. When they are, the industry is likely to contain firms that are capable of competing successfully in the international arena. Thus the diamond framework can be used to reveal the answers to several questions that are important for competing on an international basis. First, it can help predict where foreign entrants into an industry are most likely to come from. This can help managers prepare to cope with new foreign competitors, since the framework also reveals something about the basis of the new rivals' strengths. Second, it can reveal the countries in which foreign rivals are likely to be weakest and thus help managers decide which foreign markets to enter first. And third, because it focuses on the attributes of a country's business environment that allow firms to flourish, it reveals something about the advantages of conducting particular business activities in that country. Thus the diamond framework is an aid to deciding where to locate different value chain activities most beneficially—a topic that we address next.

Locating Value Chain Activities for Competitive Advantage

Increasingly, companies are locating different value chain activities in different parts of the world to exploit location-based advantages that vary from country to country. This is particularly evident with respect to the location of manufacturing activities. Differences in wage rates, worker productivity, energy costs, environmental regulations, tax rates, inflation rates, and the like, create sizable variations in manufacturing costs from country to country. By locating its plants in certain countries, firms in some industries can reap major manufacturing cost advantages because of lower input costs (especially labor), relaxed government regulations, the proximity of suppliers and technologically related industries, or unique natural resources. In such cases, the low-cost countries become principal production sites, with most of the output being exported to markets in other parts of the world. Companies that build production facilities in low-cost countries (or that source their products from contract manufacturers in these countries) gain a competitive advantage over rivals with plants in countries where costs are higher. The competitive role of low manufacturing costs is most evident in low-wage countries like China, India, Pakistan, Cambodia, Vietnam, Mexico, Brazil, Guatemala, the Philippines, and several countries in Africa and eastern Europe that have become production havens for manufactured goods with high labor content (especially textiles and apparel). Hourly compensation for production workers in 2007 averaged about $0.81 in China versus about $1.10 in the Philippines, $2.92 in Mexico, $5.96 in Brazil, $6.58 in Taiwan, $7.91 in Hungary, $8.27 in Portugal, $19.75 in Japan, $24.59 in the United States, $28.91 in Canada, $37.66 in Germany, and $48.56 in Norway.[5] China is fast becoming the manufacturing capital of the world—virtually all of the world's major manufacturing companies now have facilities in China.

For other types of value chain activities, input quality or availability are more important considerations. Tiffany entered the mining industry in Canada to access diamonds that could be certified as "conflict free" and not associated with either the funding of African wars or unethical mining conditions. Many U.S. companies locate call centers in countries such as India and Ireland, where English is spoken and the workforce is well educated. Other companies locate R&D activities in countries where there are prestigious research institutions and well-trained scientists and engineers. Likewise, concerns about short delivery times and low shipping costs make some countries better locations than others for establishing distribution centers.

The Impact of Government Policies and Economic Conditions in Host Countries

Cross-country variations in government policies and economic conditions affect both the opportunities available to a foreign entrant and the risks of operating within that country. The governments of some countries are anxious to attract foreign investments and go all out to create a business climate that outsiders will view as favorable. A good example is Ireland, which has one of the world's most pro-business environments. Ireland offers companies very low corporate tax rates, has a government that is responsive to the needs of industry, and aggressively recruits high-tech manufacturing facilities and international companies. Ireland's policies were a major factor in Intel's decision to locate a $2.5 billion chip manufacturing plant in Ireland that employs over 4,000 people. Governments anxious to spur economic growth, create more jobs, and raise living standards for their citizens usually enact policies aimed at stimulating business innovation and capital investment. They may provide incentives such as reduced taxes, low-cost loans, site location and site development assistance, and government-sponsored training for workers to encourage companies to construct production and distribution facilities. When new business-related issues or developments arise, pro-business governments make a practice of seeking advice and counsel from business leaders. When tougher business-related regulations are deemed appropriate, they endeavor to make the transition to more costly and stringent regulations somewhat business-friendly rather than adversarial.

On the other hand, governments sometimes enact policies that, from a business perspective, make locating facilities within a country's borders less attractive. For example, the nature of a company's operations may make it particularly costly to achieve compliance with a country's environmental regulations. Some governments, desirous of discouraging foreign imports, provide subsidies and low-interest loans to domestic companies (to enable them to better compete against foreign companies), enact deliberately burdensome procedures and requirements for imported goods to pass customs inspection (to make it harder for imported goods to compete against the products of local businesses), and impose tariffs or quotas on the imports of certain goods (also to help protect local businesses from foreign competition). They may also specify that a certain percentage of the parts and components used in manufacturing a product be obtained from local suppliers, require prior approval of capital spending projects, limit withdrawal of funds from the country, and require minority (sometimes majority) ownership of foreign company operations by local companies or investors. Sometimes foreign companies wanting only to sell their products in a country face a web of regulations regarding technical standards and product certification. Political leaders in some countries may be openly hostile to or suspicious of companies from certain foreign countries operating within their borders. Moreover, there are times when a government may place restrictions on exports to ensure adequate local supplies and regulate the prices of imported and locally produced goods. Such government actions make a country's business climate less attractive and in some cases may be sufficiently onerous as to discourage a company from locating production or distribution facilities in that country or maybe even selling its products in that country.

The decision about whether to enter a particular country must take into account the degree of political and economic risk. **Political risks** stem from government hostility to foreign business, weak governments, and political instability. In industries that a government deems critical to the national welfare, there is sometimes a risk that the government will nationalize the industry and expropriate the assets of foreign companies. In 2010, for example, Ecuador threatened to expropriate the holdings of all foreign oil companies that refused to sign new contracts giving the state control of all production. Other political risks include the loss of investments due to war or political unrest, regulatory changes that create operating uncertainties, security risks due to terrorism, and corruption. **Economic risks** are intertwined with political risks but also stem from factors such as inflation rates and the stability of a country's monetary system. The threat of piracy and lack of protection for intellectual property are important sources of economic risk. Another is fluctuations in the value of different currencies—a factor that we discuss in more detail next.

The Risks of Adverse Exchange Rate Shifts

When companies produce and market their products and services in many different countries, they are subject to the impacts of sometimes favorable and sometimes unfavorable changes in currency exchange rates. The rates of exchange between different currencies can vary by as much as 20 to 40 percent annually, with the changes occurring sometimes gradually and sometimes swiftly. Sizable shifts in exchange rates, which tend to be hard to predict because of the variety of factors involved and the uncertainties surrounding when and by how much these factors will change, shuffle the global cards of which countries represent the low-cost manufacturing locations and which rivals have the upper hand in the marketplace.

To understand the economic risks associated with fluctuating exchange rates, consider the case of a U.S. company that has located manufacturing facilities in Brazil (where the currency is reals—pronounced "ray-alls") and that exports most of the Brazilian-made goods to markets in the European Union (where the currency is euros). To keep the numbers simple, assume that the exchange rate is 4 Brazilian reals for 1 euro and that the product being made in Brazil has a manufacturing cost of 4 Brazilian reals (or 1 euro). Now suppose that for some reason the exchange rate shifts from 4 reals per euro to 5 reals per euro (meaning that the real has declined in value and that the euro is stronger). Making the product in Brazil is now more cost-competitive because a Brazilian good costing 4 reals to produce has fallen to only 0.8 euro at the new exchange rate (4 reals divided by 5 reals per euro = 0.8 euro) and this clearly puts the producer of the Brazilian-made good *in a better position to compete* against the European makers of the same good. On the other hand, should the value of the Brazilian real grow stronger in relation to the euro—resulting in an exchange rate of 3 reals to 1 euro—the same Brazilian-made good formerly costing 4 reals (or 1 euro) to produce now has a cost of 1.33 euros (4 reals divided by 3 reals per euro = 1.33 euros) and this puts the producer of the Brazilian-made good in a weaker competitive position vis-à-vis European producers of the same good. Clearly, the attraction of manufacturing a good in Brazil and selling it in Europe is far greater when the euro is strong (an exchange rate of 1 euro for 5 Brazilian reals) than when the euro is weak and exchanges for only 3 Brazilian reals.

But there is one more piece to the story. When the exchange rate changes from 4 reals per euro to 5 reals per euro, not only is the cost competitiveness of the Brazilian manufacturer stronger relative to European manufacturers of the same item but the Brazilian-made good that formerly cost 1 euro and now costs only 0.8 euro can also be sold to consumers in the European Union for a lower euro price than before. In other words, the combination of a stronger euro and a weaker real acts to *lower the price of Brazilian-made goods* in all the countries that are members of the European Union, and this is likely to *spur sales of the Brazilian-made good in Europe and boost Brazilian exports to Europe.* Conversely, should the exchange rate shift from 4 reals per euro to 3 reals per euro—which makes the Brazilian manufacturer less cost competitive with European manufacturers of the same item—the Brazilian-made good that formerly cost 1 euro and now costs 1.33 euros will sell for a higher price in euros than before, thus weakening the demand of European consumers for Brazilian-made goods and acting to reduce Brazilian exports to Europe. Thus *Brazilian exporters are likely to experience (1) rising demand for their goods in Europe whenever the Brazilian real grows weaker relative to the euro and (2) falling demand for their goods in Europe whenever the real grows stronger relative to the euro.*

Insofar as U.S.-based manufacturers are concerned, declines in the value of the U.S. dollar against foreign currencies act to reduce or eliminate whatever cost advantage foreign manufacturers might have over U.S. manufacturers and can even prompt foreign companies to establish production plants in the United States. Likewise, a weak euro versus other currencies enhances the cost competitiveness of companies manufacturing goods in Europe for export to foreign markets; a strong euro versus other currencies weakens the cost competitiveness of

Fluctuating exchange rates pose significant economic risks to a company's competitiveness in foreign markets. Exporters are disadvantaged when the currency of the country where goods are being manufactured grows stronger relative to the currency of the importing country.

European plants that manufacture goods for export. The growing strength of the euro relative to the U.S. dollar has encouraged a number of European manufacturers such as Volkswagen, Fiat, and Airbus to shift production from European factories to new facilities in the United States. Also, the weakening dollar caused Chrysler to discontinue its contract manufacturing agreement with an Austrian firm for assembly of minivans and Jeeps sold in Europe. Beginning in 2008, Chrysler's vehicles sold in Europe were exported from its factories in Illinois and Missouri. The weak dollar was also a factor in Ford's and GM's recent decisions to begin exporting U.S.-made vehicles to China and Latin America.

> Domestic companies facing competitive pressure from lower-cost imports are benefited when their government's currency grows *weaker* in relation to the currencies of the countries where the lower-cost goods are being made.

It is important to note that *currency exchange rates are rather unpredictable,* swinging first one way and then another way, so the competitiveness of any company's facilities in any country is partly dependent on whether exchange rate changes over time have a favorable or unfavorable cost impact. Companies producing goods in one country for export abroad always improve their cost competitiveness when the country's currency grows weaker relative to currencies of the countries where the goods are being exported to, and they find their cost competitiveness eroded when the local currency grow stronger. On the other hand, domestic companies that are under pressure from lower-cost imported goods become more cost competitive when their currency grows weaker in relation to the currencies of the countries where the imported goods are made—in other words, a U.S. manufacturer views a weaker U.S. dollar as a *favorable exchange rate shift* because such shifts help make its costs more competitive than those of foreign rivals.

Cross-Country Differences in Demographic, Cultural, and Market Conditions

Differing population sizes, income levels, and other demographic factors give rise to considerable differences in market size and growth rates from country to country. Less than 20 percent of the populations of Brazil, India, and China have annual purchasing power equivalent to $25,000. Middle-class consumers represent a much smaller portion of the population in these and other developing countries than in North America, Japan, and much of western Europe—China's middle class numbers about 300 million out of a population of 1.35 billion.[6] At the same time, in developing markets like India, China, Brazil, and Malaysia, market growth potential is far higher than it is in the more mature economies of Britain, Denmark, Canada, and Japan. The potential for market growth in automobiles is explosive in China, where 2009 sales of new vehicles amounted to 13.6 million, surpassing U.S. sales of 10 million and making China the world's largest market.[7] Owing to widely differing population demographics and income levels, there is a far bigger market for luxury automobiles in the United States and Germany than in Argentina, India, Mexico, China, and Thailand.

Buyer tastes for a particular product or service sometimes differ substantially from country to country. In France consumers prefer top-loading washing machines, while in most other European countries consumers prefer front-loading machines. Soups that appeal to Swedish consumers are not popular in Malaysia. Italian coffee drinkers prefer espressos, but in North America the preference is for mild-roasted coffees. Sometimes, product designs suitable in one country are inappropriate in another because of differing local standards—for example, in the United States electrical devices run on 110-volt electric systems, but in some

European countries the standard is a 240-volt electric system, necessitating the use of different electrical designs and components. Cultural influences can also affect consumer demand for a product. For instance, in South Korea, many parents are reluctant to purchase PCs even when they can afford them because of concerns that their children will be distracted from their schoolwork by surfing the Web, playing PC-based video games, and becoming Internet "addicts."[8]

Consequently, companies operating in an international marketplace have to wrestle with *whether and how much to customize their offerings in each different country market to match the tastes and preferences of local buyers or whether to pursue a strategy of offering a mostly standardized product worldwide.* While making products that are closely matched to local tastes makes them more appealing to local buyers, customizing a company's products country by country may have the effect of raising production and distribution costs due to the greater variety of designs and components, shorter production runs, and the complications of added inventory handling and distribution logistics. Greater standardization of a multinational company's product offering, on the other hand, can lead to scale economies and learning curve effects, thus contributing to the achievement of a low-cost advantage. *The tension between the market pressures to localize a company's product offerings country by country and the competitive pressures to lower costs is one of the big strategic issues that participants in foreign markets have to resolve.*

THE CONCEPTS OF MULTIDOMESTIC COMPETITION AND GLOBAL COMPETITION

In crafting a strategy to compete on an international basis, it is essential for managers to recognize that the pattern of international competition varies in important ways from industry to industry.[9] At one extreme is **multidomestic competition,** in which there's so much cross-country variation in market conditions and in the companies contending for leadership that the market contest among rivals in one country is localized and not closely connected to the market contests in other countries. The standout features of multidomestic competition are that (1) buyers in different countries are attracted to different product attributes, (2) sellers vary from country to country, and (3) industry conditions and competitive forces in each national market differ in important respects. Take the banking industry in Poland, Mexico, and Australia as an example—the requirements and expectations of banking customers vary among the three countries, the lead banking competitors in Poland differ from those in Mexico or Australia, and the competitive battle going on among the leading banks in Poland is unrelated to the rivalry taking place in Mexico or Australia. Thus, with multidomestic competition, rival firms battle for national championships and winning in one country does not necessarily signal the ability to fare well in other countries. In multidomestic competition, the power of a company's strategy and capabilities in one country has little impact on its competitiveness in other countries where it operates. Moreover, any competitive advantage a company secures in one country is largely confined to that country; the spillover effects to other countries are minimal to nonexistent.

> **CORE CONCEPT**
>
> **Multidomestic competition** exists when the competition among rivals in each country market is localized and not closely connected to the competition in other country markets—there is no world market, just a collection of self-contained local markets.

Industries characterized by multidomestic competition include radio and TV broadcasting, consumer banking, life insurance, apparel, metals fabrication, many types of food products (coffee, cereals, breads, canned goods, frozen foods), and retailing.

At the other extreme is **global competition,** in which prices and competitive conditions across country markets are strongly linked and the term *global* has true meaning. In a globally competitive industry, much the same group of rival companies competes in many different countries but especially in countries where sales volumes are large and where having a competitive presence is strategically important to building a strong global position in the industry. Thus, a company's competitive position in one country both affects and is affected by its position in other countries. In global competition, a firm's overall competitive advantage grows out of its entire worldwide operations; the competitive advantage it creates at its home base is supplemented by advantages growing out of its operations in other countries (having plants in low-wage countries, being able to transfer expertise from country to country, having the capability to serve customers that also have multinational operations, and having brand-name recognition in many parts of the world). Rival firms in globally competitive industries vie for worldwide leadership. Global competition exists in motor vehicles, television sets, tires, cell phones, personal computers, copiers, watches, digital cameras, bicycles, and commercial aircraft.

> **CORE CONCEPT**
>
> **Global competition** exists when competitive conditions across national markets are linked strongly enough to form a true world market and when leading competitors compete head to head in many different countries.

An industry can have segments that are globally competitive and segments in which competition is country by country.[10] In the hotel/motel industry, for example, the low- and medium-priced segments are characterized by multidomestic competition—competitors mainly serve travelers within the same country. In the business and luxury segments, however, competition is more globalized. Companies like Nikki (owned by Japan Airlines), Marriott, Sheraton, and Hilton have hotels at many international locations, use worldwide reservation systems, and establish common quality and service standards to gain marketing advantages in serving businesspeople and other travelers who make frequent international trips. In lubricants, the marine engine segment is globally competitive—ships move from port to port and require the same oil everywhere they stop. Brand reputations in marine lubricants have a global scope, and successful marine engine lubricant producers (ExxonMobil, BP Amoco, and Shell) operate globally. In automotive motor oil, however, multidomestic competition dominates—countries have different weather conditions and driving patterns, production of motor oil is subject to limited scale economies, shipping costs are high, and retail distribution channels differ markedly from country to country. Thus, domestic firms—like Quaker State and Pennzoil in the United States and Castrol in Great Britain—can be leaders in their home markets without competing globally.

It is also important to recognize that an industry can be in transition from multidomestic competition to global competition. In a number of today's industries—beer and major home appliances are prime examples—leading domestic competitors have begun expanding into more and more foreign markets, often acquiring local companies or brands and integrating them into their operations. As some industry members start to build global brands and a global presence, other industry members find themselves pressured to follow the same strategic path—especially if establishing multinational operations results in important scale economies and a powerhouse brand name. As the industry consolidates to fewer players, such that many of the same companies find themselves in head-to-head competition in more and more country markets, global competition begins to replace multidomestic competition.

At the same time, consumer tastes in a number of important product categories are converging across the world. Less diversity of tastes and preferences opens the way for companies to create global brands and sell essentially the same products in almost all countries of the world. Even in industries where consumer tastes remain fairly diverse, companies are learning to use "custom mass production" to economically create different versions of a product and thereby satisfy the tastes of people in different countries.

In addition to taking the obvious cultural and political differences between countries into account, a company must shape its strategic approach to competing in foreign markets according to whether its industry is characterized by multidomestic competition, global competition, or some combination, depending on differences among industry sectors and on how the industry is evolving.

STRATEGIC OPTIONS FOR ENTERING AND COMPETING IN INTERNATIONAL MARKETS

LO 3

Learn about the major strategic options for entering and competing in foreign markets.

Once a company decides to expand beyond its domestic borders it must consider the question of how to enter foreign markets. There are six primary strategic options for doing so:

1. Maintain a national (one-country) production base and export goods to foreign markets.
2. License foreign firms to produce and distribute the company's products abroad.
3. Employ a franchising strategy.
4. Establish a wholly owned subsidiary in the foreign market by acquiring a foreign company.
5. Create a wholly owned foreign subsidiary from the ground up via a "greenfield" venture.
6. Rely on strategic alliances or joint ventures to partner with foreign companies.

Which option to employ depends on a variety of factors, including the nature of the firm's strategic objectives, whether the firm has the full range of resources and capabilities needed to operate abroad, country-specific factors such as trade barriers, and the transaction costs involved (the costs of contracting with a partner and monitoring its compliance with the terms of the contract, for example). The options vary considerably regarding the level of investment required and the associated risks, but higher levels of investment and risk generally provide the firm with the benefits of greater ownership and control.

Export Strategies

Using domestic plants as a production base for exporting goods to foreign markets is an excellent initial strategy for pursuing international sales. It is a conservative way to test the international waters. The amount of capital needed to begin exporting is often quite minimal; existing production capacity may well be sufficient to make goods for export. With an export strategy, a manufacturer can limit its involvement in foreign markets by contracting with foreign wholesalers experienced in importing to handle the entire distribution and marketing function in their countries or regions of the world. If it is more advantageous to maintain control over these functions, however, a manufacturer can establish its own distribution and sales organizations in some or all of the target foreign markets. Either way, a home-based production and export strategy helps the firm minimize its direct investments in foreign countries. Such strategies have been favored traditionally by Chinese, Korean, and Italian companies—products are designed and manufactured at home and then distributed through local channels in the importing countries; the primary functions performed abroad relate chiefly to establishing a network of distributors and perhaps conducting sales promotion and brand awareness activities.

Whether an export strategy can be pursued successfully over the long run hinges on whether its advantages for the company continue to outweigh its disadvantages. This depends in part on the relative cost competitiveness of the home-country production base. In some industries, firms gain additional scale economies and learning curve benefits from centralizing production in one or several giant plants whose output capability exceeds demand in any one country market; exporting is one obvious way to capture such economies. However, an export strategy is vulnerable when (1) manufacturing costs in the home country are substantially higher than in foreign countries where rivals have plants, (2) the costs of shipping the product to distant foreign markets are relatively high, or (3) adverse shifts occur in currency exchange rates. The disadvantages of export strategies can also swell due to high tariffs and other trade barriers, inadequate control over marketing or distribution, and an inability to tap into location advantages available elsewhere, such as skilled low-cost labor.

Licensing Strategies

Licensing makes sense when a firm with valuable technical know-how, an appealing brand, or a unique patented product has neither the internal organizational capability nor the resources to enter foreign markets. Licensing also has the advantage of avoiding the risks of committing resources to country markets that are unfamiliar, politically volatile, economically unstable, or otherwise risky. By licensing the technology, trademark, or production rights to foreign-based firms, the firm does not have to bear the costs and risks of entering foreign markets on its own, yet it is able to generate income from royalties. The big disadvantage of licensing is the risk of providing valuable technological know-how to foreign companies and thereby losing some degree of control over its use; monitoring licensees and safeguarding the company's proprietary know-how can prove quite difficult in some circumstances. But if the royalty potential is considerable and the companies to whom the licenses are being granted are trustworthy and reputable, then licensing can be a very attractive option. Many software and pharmaceutical companies use licensing strategies.

Franchising Strategies

While licensing works well for manufacturers and owners of proprietary technology, franchising is often better suited to the international expansion efforts of service and retailing enterprises. McDonald's, Yum! Brands (the parent of Pizza Hut,

KFC, and Taco Bell), the UPS Store, Jani-King International (the world's largest commercial cleaning franchisor), Roto-Rooter, 7-Eleven, and Hilton Hotels have all used franchising to build a presence in foreign markets. Franchising has much the same advantages as licensing. The franchisee bears most of the costs and risks of establishing foreign locations; a franchisor has to expend only the resources to recruit, train, support, and monitor franchisees. The big problem a franchisor faces is maintaining quality control; foreign franchisees do not always exhibit strong commitment to consistency and standardization, especially when the local culture does not stress the same kinds of quality concerns. Another problem that can arise is whether to allow foreign franchisees to make modifications in the franchisor's product offering so as to better satisfy the tastes and expectations of local buyers. Should McDonald's allow its franchised units in Japan to modify Big Macs slightly to suit Japanese tastes? Should the franchised Pizza Hut units in China be permitted to substitute spices that appeal to Chinese consumers? Or should the same menu offerings be rigorously and unvaryingly required of all franchisees worldwide?

Acquisition Strategies

Acquisition strategies have the advantages of a high level of control as well as speed, which can be a significant factor when a firm wants to enter a foreign market at a relatively large scale. When a strong presence in the market or local economies of scale are a significant competitive factor in the market, these advantages may make acquiring a large local firm preferable to most other entry modes. Similarly, when entry barriers are high—whether in the form of trade barriers, access to a local distribution network, or building key relationships with local constituents and officials—an acquisition may be the only route to overcoming such hurdles. Acquisition may also be the preferred entry strategy if the strategic objective is to gain access to the core capabilities or well-guarded technologies of a foreign firm.

At the same time, acquisition strategies have their downside as a foreign entry strategy. Acquisition strategies are always costly, since it is necessary to pay a premium over the share-price value of a company in order to acquire control. This can saddle the acquiring company with a good deal of debt, increasing its risk of bankruptcy and limiting its other investment options. Acquiring a foreign firm can be particularly tricky due to the challenge of international negotiations, the burden of foreign legal and regulatory requirements, and the added complexity of postacquisition integration efforts when companies are separated by distance, culture, and language.[11] While the potential benefits of a cross-border acquisition can be high, the risk of failure is high as well.

Greenfield Venture Strategies

A **greenfield venture** strategy is one in which the company creates a subsidiary business in the foreign market by setting up the entire operation (plants, distribution system, etc.) from the ground up. Like acquisition strategies, greenfield ventures have the advantage of high control, but to an even greater degree since starting from scratch allows the company to set up every aspect of the operation to its specifications. Since organizational change is notoriously difficult and hampered by a variety of inertial factors, it is much harder to fine-tune the operations of an acquired firm to this degree—particularly a foreign firm. Entering a foreign market from the ground up provides a firm with another potential advantage: It enables the company to *learn by doing* how to operate in the foreign market and how to best serve local needs, navigate the local politics, and compete most effectively against local rivals. This is not to say, however, that the company needs to acquire all the knowledge and experience needed from the ground up; in building its operation, the company can avail itself of local managerial talent and know-how by simply hiring experienced local managers who understand the local market conditions, local buying habits, local competitors, and local ways of doing business. By assembling a management team that also includes senior managers from the parent company (preferably with considerable international experience), the parent company can transfer technology, business practices, and the corporate culture into the new foreign subsidiary and ensure that there is a conduit for the flow of information between the corporate office and local operations.

Greenfield ventures in foreign markets also pose a number of problems, just as other entry strategies do. They represent a costly capital investment, subject to a high level of risk. They require numerous other company resources as well, diverting them from other uses. They do not work well in countries without strong, well-functioning markets and institutions that protect the rights of foreign investors and provide other legal protections.[12] Moreover, an important disadvantage of greenfield ventures relative to other means of international expansion is that they are the slowest entry route—particularly if the objective is to achieve a sizable market share. On the other hand, successful greenfield ventures may offer higher returns to compensate for their high risk and slower path.

Alliance and Joint Venture Strategies

Collaborative agreements with foreign companies in the form of strategic alliances or joint ventures are widely used as a means of entering foreign markets.[13] Often they are used in conjunction with another entry strategy, such as exporting, franchising, or establishing a greenfield venture. Historically, firms in industrialized nations that wanted to export their products and market them in less developed countries sought alliances with local companies in order to do so—such arrangements were often necessary to win approval for entry from the host country's government. Companies wanting to set up a manufacturing operation abroad often had to do so via a joint venture with a foreign firm. Over the last 20 years, those types of restrictions have been lifted in countries such as India and China, and companies have been able to enter these markets via more direct means.[14]

Today, a more important reason for using strategic alliances and joint ventures as a vehicle for international expansion is that they facilitate resource and risk sharing. When firms need access to complementary resources to succeed abroad, when the venture requires substantial investment, and when the risks are high, the attraction of such strategies grows. A company can benefit immensely from a foreign partner's familiarity with local government regulations, its knowledge of the buying habits and product preferences of consumers, its distribution channel relationships, and so on. Both Japanese and American companies are actively forming alliances with European companies to better compete in the 27-nation European Union and to capitalize on emerging but risky opportunities in the countries of eastern Europe. Similarly, many U.S. and European companies

> Collaborative strategies involving alliances or joint ventures with foreign partners are a popular way for companies to edge their way into the markets of foreign countries.

are allying with Asian companies in their efforts to enter markets in China, India, Thailand, Indonesia, and other Asian countries where they lack local knowledge and uncertainties abound. Many foreign companies, of course, are particularly interested in strategic partnerships that will strengthen their ability to gain a foothold in the U.S. market.

Another potential benefit of a collaborative strategy is the learning and added expertise that come from performing joint research, sharing technological know-how, studying one another's manufacturing methods, and understanding how to tailor sales and marketing approaches to fit local cultures and traditions. Indeed, by learning from the skills, technological know-how, and capabilities of alliance partners and implanting the knowledge and know-how of these partners in its own personnel and organization, a company can upgrade its capabilities and become a stronger competitor in its home market. DaimlerChrysler's strategic alliance with Mitsubishi, for example, was motivated by a desire to learn from Mitsubishi's technological strengths in small-size vehicles in order to improve the performance of its loss-making "smart car" division.[15]

> Cross-border alliances enable a growth-minded company to widen its geographic coverage and strengthen its competitiveness in foreign markets; at the same time, they offer flexibility and allow a company to retain some degree of autonomy and operating control.

Many companies believe that cross-border alliances and partnerships are a better strategic means of gaining the above benefits (as compared to acquiring or merging with foreign-based companies to gain much the same benefits) because they allow a company to preserve its independence (which is not the case with a merger), retain veto power over how the alliance operates, and avoid using scarce financial resources to fund acquisitions. Furthermore, an alliance offers the flexibility to readily disengage once its purpose has been served or if the benefits prove elusive, whereas an acquisition is a more permanent sort of arrangement (although the acquired company can, of course, be divested).[16]

Illustration Capsule 7.1 provides four examples of cross-border strategic alliances.

The Risks of Strategic Alliances with Foreign Partners   Alliances and joint ventures with foreign partners have their pitfalls, however. Cross-border allies typically have to overcome language and cultural barriers and figure out how to deal with diverse operating practices. The transaction costs of working out a mutually agreeable arrangement and monitoring partner compliance with the terms of the arrangement can be high. The communication, trust building, and coordination costs are not trivial in terms of management time.[17] Often, partners soon discover they have conflicting objectives and strategies, deep differences of opinion about how to proceed, and/or important differences in corporate values and ethical standards. Tensions build up, working relationships cool, and the hoped-for benefits never materialize.[18] It is not unusual for there to be little personal chemistry among some of the key people on whom success or failure of the alliance depends—the rapport such personnel need to work well together may never emerge. And even if allies are able to develop productive personal relationships, they can still have trouble reaching mutually agreeable ways to deal with key issues or resolve differences. Occasionally, the egos of corporate executives can clash. An alliance between Northwest Airlines and KLM Royal Dutch Airlines resulted in a bitter feud among both companies' top officials (who, according to some reports, refused to speak to each other).[19] Plus there is the thorny problem of getting alliance partners to sort through issues and reach decisions fast enough to stay abreast of rapid advances in technology or fast-changing market conditions.

1. The engine of General Motors' growth strategy in Asia is its three-way joint venture with Wulung, a Chinese producer of mini-commercial vehicles, and SAIC (Shanghai Automotive Industrial Corporation), China's largest automaker. The success of the SAIC-GM-Wulung Automotive Company is also GM's best hope for financial recovery since it emerged from bankruptcy on July 10, 2009. While GM lost $4.8 billion overall before interest and taxes during the last six months of 2009, its international operations (everything except North America and Europe) earned $1.2 billion. Its Chinese joint ventures accounted for approximately one-third of that profit, due in part to the roaring success of the no-frills Wulung Sunshine, a lightweight minivan that has become China's best-selling vehicle. In 2010, General Motors' sales in China topped its U.S. sales—the first time that sales in a foreign market have done so in the 102-year history of the company. GM is now positioning its Chinese joint venture to serve as a springboard for the company's expansion in India, with the possibility of launching a product to rival the Tata Nano there. When GM's president of international operations, Timothy E. Lee, was asked about GM's ability to compete in India, he replied, "When you harvest from your partnerships the collective wisdom of other cultures, it's incredible what you can do."

2. The European Aeronautic Defense and Space Company (EADS) was formed by an alliance of aerospace companies from Britain, Spain, Germany, and France that included British Aerospace, Daimler-Benz Aerospace, and Aerospatiale. The objective of the alliance was to create a European aircraft company capable of competing with U.S.-based Boeing Corp. The alliance has proved highly successful, infusing its commercial airline division, Airbus, with the know-how and resources needed to compete head to head with Boeing for world leadership in large commercial aircraft (those designed for over 100 passengers). The company also established an alliance with U.S. military aircraft manufacturer Northrop Grumman to develop a highly sophisticated refueling tanker based on the A330 airliner for the U.S. Air Force.

3. Cisco, the worldwide leader in networking components, entered into a strategic alliance with Finnish telecommunications firm Nokia Siemens Networks to develop communications networks capable of transmitting data either across the Internet or by mobile technologies. Nokia Siemens Networks itself was created through a 2006 international joint venture between German-based Siemens AG and the Finnish communications giant Nokia. The Cisco–Nokia Siemens alliance was created to better position both companies for convergence among Internet technologies and wireless communication devices that was expected to dramatically change how both computer networks and wireless telephones would be used.

4. Verio, a subsidiary of Japan-based NTT Communications and one of the leading global providers of Web hosting services and IP data transport, operates with the philosophy that in today's highly competitive and challenging technology market, companies must gain and share skills, information, and technology with technology leaders across the world. Believing that no company can be all things to all customers in the Web hosting industry, Verio executives have developed an alliance-oriented business model that combines the company's core competencies with the skills and products of best-of-breed technology partners. Verio's strategic partners include Accenture, Cisco Systems, Microsoft, Sun Microsystems, Oracle, Arsenal Digital Solutions (a provider of worry-free tape backup, data restore, and data storage services), Internet Security Systems (a provider of firewall and intrusion detection systems), and Mercantec (which develops storefront and shopping cart software). Verio's management believes that its portfolio of strategic alliances allows it to use innovative, best-of-class technologies in providing its

(Continued)

221

customers with fast, efficient, accurate data transport and a complete set of Web hosting services. An independent panel of 12 judges recently selected Verio as the winner of the Best Technology Foresight Award for its efforts in pioneering new technologies.

Developed with Mukund Kulashekaran.

Sources: Company Web sites and press releases; Yves L. Doz and Gary Hamel, *Alliance Advantage: The Art of Creating Value through Partnering* (Boston: Harvard Business School Press, 1998); Joanne Muller, "Can China Save GM?" *Forbes.com,* May 10, 2010, www.forbes.com/forbes/2010/0510/global-2000-10-automobiles-china-detroit-whitacre-save-gm.html; "GM's First-Half China Sales Surge Past the U.S.," *Bloomberg Businessweek,* July 2, 2010, www.businessweek.com/news/2010-07-02/gm-s-first-half-china-sales-surge-past-the-u-s-.html; Nandini Sen Gupta, "General Motors May Drive in Nano Rival with Chinese Help," *Economic Times,* May 31, 2010, http://economictimes.indiatimes.com/articleshow/5992589.cms.

One worrisome problem with alliances or joint ventures is that a firm may risk losing some of its competitive advantage if an alliance partner is given full access to its proprietary technological expertise or other unique and competitively valuable capabilities. There is a natural tendency for allies to struggle to collaborate effectively in competitively sensitive areas, thus spawning suspicions on both sides about forthright exchanges of information and expertise. It requires many meetings of many people working in good faith over a period of time to iron out what is to be shared, what is to remain proprietary, and how the cooperative arrangements will work.

Even if a collaborative arrangement proves to be a win-win proposition for both parties, a company has to guard against becoming overly dependent on foreign partners for essential expertise and competitive capabilities. If a company is aiming for global market leadership and needs to develop capabilities of its own, then at some juncture a cross-border merger or acquisition may have to be substituted for cross-border alliances and joint ventures. One of the lessons about cross-border alliances is that they are more effective in helping a company establish a beachhead of new opportunity in world markets than they are in enabling a company to achieve and sustain global market leadership.

When a Cross-Border Alliance May Be Unnecessary   Experienced multinational companies that market in 50 to 100 or more countries across the world find less need for entering into cross-border alliances than do companies in the early stages of globalizing their operations.[20] Multinational companies make it a point to develop senior managers who understand how "the system" works in different countries, plus they can avail themselves of local managerial talent and know-how by simply hiring experienced local managers and thereby detouring the hazards of collaborative alliances with local companies. If a multinational enterprise with considerable experience in entering the markets of different countries wants to detour the hazards of allying with local businesses, it can simply assemble a capable management team consisting of both senior managers with considerable international experience and local managers. The role of its own in-house managers with international business savvy is to transfer technology, business practices, and the corporate culture into the company's operations in the new country market and to serve as conduits for the flow of information between the corporate office and local operations. The role of local managers is to contribute needed understanding of the local market conditions, local buying habits, and local ways of doing business and, often, to head up local operations.

Hence, one cannot automatically presume that a company needs the wisdom and resources of a local partner to guide it through the process of successfully entering the markets of foreign countries. Indeed, experienced multinationals often discover that local partners do not always have adequate local market knowledge—much of the so-called experience of local partners can predate the emergence of current market trends and conditions and sometimes their operating practices can be archaic.[21]

COMPETING INTERNATIONALLY: THE THREE MAIN STRATEGIC APPROACHES

Broadly speaking, a firm's **international strategy** is simply its strategy for competing in two or more countries simultaneously. Typically, a company will start to compete internationally by entering just one or perhaps a select few foreign markets, selling its products or services in countries where there is a ready market for them. But as it expands further internationally, it will have to confront head-on the conflicting pressures of local responsiveness versus efficiency gains from standardizing and integrating operations globally. Moreover, it will have to consider whether the markets abroad are characterized by multidomestic competition, global competition, or some mix. The issue of whether and how to vary the company's competitive approach to fit specific market conditions and buyer preferences in each host country or whether to employ essentially the same strategy in all countries is perhaps the foremost strategic issue that companies must address when they operate in two or more foreign markets.[22] Figure 7.2 shows a company's three options for resolving this issue: a *multidomestic, global,* or *transnational* strategy.

Multidomestic Strategy—Think Local, Act Local

A **multidomestic strategy** is one based on differentiating products and services on a country-by-country or regional basis to meet differing buyer needs and to address divergent local market conditions. It is a good choice for companies that compete primarily in industries characterized by multidomestic competition. This type of strategy involves having plants produce different product versions for different local markets and adapting marketing and distribution to fit local customs, cultures, regulations, and market requirements. Castrol, a specialist in oil lubricants, produces over 3,000 different formulas of lubricants to meet the requirements of different climates, vehicle types and uses, and equipment applications that characterize different country markets. In the food products industry, it is common for companies to vary the ingredients in their products and sell the localized versions under local brand names to cater to country-specific tastes and eating preferences.

In essence, a multidomestic strategy represents a **think-local, act-local** approach to international strategy. A think-local, act-local approach is possible only when decision making is decentralized, giving local managers considerable latitude for crafting and executing strategies for the country markets they are responsible for. Giving local managers

LO 4

Gain familiarity with the three main strategic approaches for competing internationally.

CORE CONCEPT

An **international strategy** is a strategy for competing in two or more countries simultaneously.

CORE CONCEPT

A **multidomestic strategy** is one in which a company varies its product offering and competitive approach from country to country in an effort to be responsive to differing buyer preferences and market conditions. It is a **think-local, act-local** type of international strategy, facilitated by decision making decentralized to the local level.

Figure 7.2   **Three Approaches for Competing Internationally**

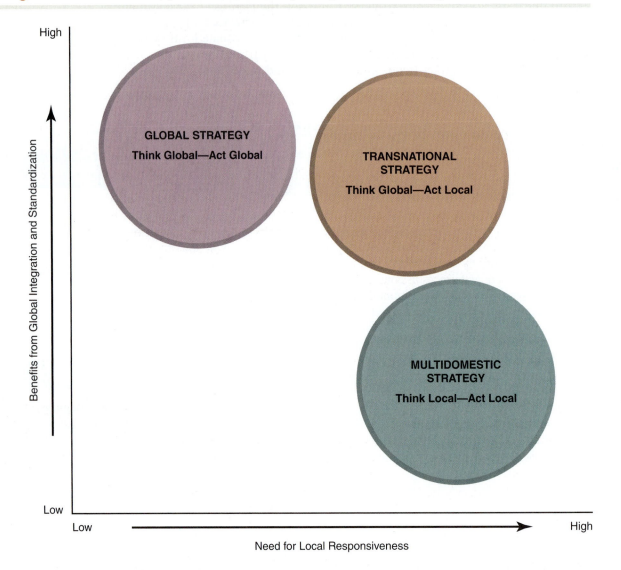

decision-making authority allows them to address specific market needs and respond swiftly to local changes in demand. It also enables them to focus their competitive efforts, stake out attractive market positions vis-à-vis local competitors, react to rivals' moves in a timely fashion, and target new opportunities as they emerge.

A think-local, act-local approach to strategy making is most appropriate when the need for local responsiveness is high due to significant cross-country differences in demographic, cultural, and market conditions and when the potential for efficiency gains from standardization is limited, as depicted in Figure 7.2. Consider, for example, the wide variation in refrigerator usage and preference around the world. Northern Europeans want large refrigerators because they tend to shop once a week in supermarkets; southern Europeans prefer small refrigerators because they shop daily. In parts of Asia refrigerators are a status symbol and may be placed in the living room, leading to preferences for stylish designs and colors—in India bright blue and red are popular colors. In other Asian countries household space is constrained, and many refrigerators are only 4 feet high so that the top can be used for storage. If the minimum efficient scale for producing refrigerators is relatively low, there would be little reason to forgo the benefits of meeting these varying needs precisely in favor of a standardized, one-size-fits-all approach to production.

Despite their obvious benefits, think-local, act-local strategies have three big drawbacks:

1. They hinder transfer of a company's capabilities, knowledge, and other resources across country boundaries, since the company's efforts are not integrated or coordinated across country boundaries. This can make the company less innovative overall.

2. They raise production and distribution costs due to the greater variety of designs and components, shorter production runs for each product version, and complications of added inventory handling and distribution logistics.

3. They are not conducive to building a single, worldwide competitive advantage. When a company's competitive approach and product offering vary from country to country, the nature and size of any resulting competitive edge also tends to vary. At the most, multidomestic strategies are capable of producing a group of local competitive advantages of varying types and degrees of strength.

Global Strategy—Think Global, Act Global

A **global strategy** contrasts sharply with a multidomestic strategy in that it takes a standardized, globally integrated approach to producing, packaging, selling, and delivering the company's products and services worldwide. Companies employing a global strategy sell the same products under the same brand names everywhere, utilize much the same distribution channels in all countries, and compete on the basis of the same capabilities and marketing approaches worldwide. Although the company's strategy or product offering may be adapted in very minor ways to accommodate specific situations in a few host countries, the company's fundamental competitive approach (low cost, differentiation, best cost, or focused) remains very much intact worldwide and local managers stick close to the global strategy.

A **think-global, act-global** strategic theme prompts company managers to integrate and coordinate the company's strategic moves worldwide and to expand into most, if not all, nations where there is significant buyer demand. It puts considerable strategic emphasis on building a *global* brand name and aggressively pursuing opportunities to transfer ideas, new products, and capabilities from one country to another.[23] Global strategies are characterized by relatively centralized value chain activities, such as production and distribution. While there may be more than one manufacturing plant and distribution center to minimize transportation costs, for example, they tend to be few in number. Achieving the efficiency potential of a global strategy requires that resources and best practices be shared, value chain activities be integrated, and capabilities be transferred from one location to another as they are developed. These objectives are best facilitated through centralized decision making and strong headquarters control.

Because a global strategy cannot accommodate varying local needs, it is an appropriate strategic choice when there are pronounced efficiency benefits from standardization and when buyer needs are relatively homogeneous across countries and regions. A globally standardized and integrated approach is

> ### CORE CONCEPT
>
> A **global strategy** is one in which a company employs the same basic competitive approach in all countries where it operates, sells much the same products everywhere, strives to build global brands, and coordinates its actions worldwide with strong headquarters control. It represents a **think-global, act-global** approach.

especially beneficial when high volumes significantly lower costs due to econo-mies of scale or added experience (moving the company further down a learning curve). It can also be advantageous if it allows the firm to replicate a successful business model on a global basis efficiently or engage in higher levels of R&D by spreading the fixed costs and risks over a higher-volume output. It is a fitting response to industry conditions marked by global competition.

The drawbacks of global strategies are several: (1) They do not enable firms to address local needs as precisely as locally based rivals can, (2) they are less responsive to changes in local market conditions, either in the form of new oppor-tunities or competitive threats, (3) they raise transportation costs and may involve higher tariffs, and (4) they involve higher coordination costs due to the more com-plex task of managing a globally integrated enterprise.

Transnational Strategy—Think Global, Act Local

A **transnational strategy** (sometimes called *glocalization*) incorporates elements of both a globalized and a localized approach to strategy making. This type of middle-ground strategy is called for when there are relatively high needs for local responsiveness as well as appreciable benefits to be realized from standardization, as Figure 7.2 suggests. A transnational strategy encourages a company to **think global, act local** to balance these competing objectives.

Often, companies implement a transnational strategy with mass-customization techniques that enable them to address local preferences in an efficient, semistan-dardized manner. Both McDonald's and KFC have discovered ways to custom-ize their menu offerings in various countries without compromising costs, product quality, and operating effectiveness. When it first opened Disneyland Paris, Disney learned the hard way that a global approach to its international theme parks would not work; it has since adapted elements of its strat-egy to accommodate local preferences even though much of its strategy still derives from a globally applied formula. Otis Elevator found that a transnational strategy delivers better results than a global strategy when competing in countries like China where local needs are highly differenti-ated. In 2000, it switched from its customary single-brand approach to a multibrand strategy aimed at serving different segments of the market. By 2009, it had doubled its market share in China and increased its revenues sixfold.[24]

> **CORE CONCEPT**
>
> A **transnational strategy** is a **think-global, act-local** approach that incor-porates elements of both multidomestic and global strategies.

A transnational strategy is far more conducive than other strategies to transferring and leveraging subsidiary skills and capabilities. But, like other approaches to competing internationally, transnational strategies also have sig-nificant drawbacks:

1. They are the most difficult of all international strategies to implement due to the added complexity of varying the elements of the strategy to situational conditions.
2. They place large demands on the organization due to the need to pursue con-flicting objectives simultaneously.
3. Implementing the strategy is likely to be a costly and time-consuming enter-prise, with an uncertain outcome.

Table 7.1 provides a summary of the pluses and minuses of the three approaches to competing internationally.

Table 7.1 **Advantages and Disadvantages of Multidomestic, Global, and Transnational Approaches**

	Advantages	Disadvantages
Multidomestic (think local, act local)	• Can meet the specific needs of each market more precisely • Can respond more swiftly to localized changes in demand • Can target reactions to the moves of local rivals • Can respond more quickly to local opportunities and threats	• Hinders resource and capability sharing or cross-market transfers • Higher production and distribution costs • Not conducive to a worldwide competitive advantage
Transnational (think global, act local)	• Offers the benefits of both local responsiveness and global integration • Enables the transfer and sharing of resources and capabilities across borders • Provides the benefits of flexible coordination	• More complex and harder to implement • Conflicting goals may be difficult to reconcile and require trade-offs • Implementation more costly and time-consuming
Global (think global, act global)	• Lower costs due to scale and scope economies • Greater efficiencies due to the ability to transfer best practices across markets • More innovation from knowledge sharing and capability transfer • The benefit of a global brand and reputation	• Unable to address local needs precisely • Less responsive to changes in local market conditions • Higher transportation costs and tariffs • Higher coordination and integration costs

THE QUEST FOR COMPETITIVE ADVANTAGE IN THE INTERNATIONAL ARENA

There are three important ways in which a firm can gain competitive advantage (or offset domestic disadvantages) by expanding outside its domestic market.[25] First, it can use location to lower costs or achieve greater product differentiation. Second, it can transfer competitively valuable resources, competencies, and capabilities from one country to another or share them across international borders to extend and deepen its competitive advantages. And third, it can benefit from cross-border coordination in ways that a domestic-only competitor cannot.

LO 5

Understand how international companies go about building competitive advantage in foreign markets.

Using Location to Build Competitive Advantage

To use location to build competitive advantage, a company must consider two issues: (1) whether to concentrate each activity it performs in a few select countries or to disperse performance of the activity to many nations, and (2) in which countries to locate particular activities.[26]

When to Concentrate Activities in a Few Locations

It is advantageous for a company to concentrate its activities in a limited number of locations when:

- *The costs of manufacturing or other activities are significantly lower in some geographic locations than in others.* For example, much of the world's athletic footwear is manufactured in Asia (China and Korea) because of low labor costs; much of the production of circuit boards for PCs is located in Taiwan because of both low costs and the high-caliber technical skills of the Taiwanese labor force.

- *There are significant scale economies in production or distribution.* The presence of significant economies of scale in components production or final assembly means that a company can gain major cost savings from operating a few ultra-efficient plants as opposed to a host of small plants scattered across the world. Achieving low-cost provider status often requires a company to have the largest worldwide manufacturing share (as distinct from brand share or market share), with production centralized in one or a few world-scale plants. Some companies even use such plants to manufacture units sold under the brand names of rivals to further boost production-related scale economies. Makers of digital cameras and LCD TVs located in Japan, South Korea, and Taiwan have used their scale economies to establish a low-cost advantage. Likewise, a company may be able to reduce its distribution costs by capturing scale economies associated with establishing large-scale distribution centers to serve major geographic regions of the world market (for example, North America, Latin America, Europe–Middle East, and Asia-Pacific).

- *There are sizable learning and experience benefits associated with performing an activity in a single location.* In some industries, a manufacturer can lower unit costs, boost quality, or master a new technology more quickly by concentrating production in a few locations. The greater the cumulative volume of production at a plant, the faster the buildup of learning and experience of the plant's workforce, thereby enabling quicker capture of the learning/experience benefits.

- *Certain locations have superior resources, allow better coordination of related activities, or offer other valuable advantages.* A research unit or a sophisticated production facility may be situated in a particular nation because of its pool of technically trained personnel. Samsung became a leader in memory chip technology by establishing a major R&D facility in Silicon Valley and transferring the know-how it gained back to its operations in South Korea. Companies also locate activities to benefit from proximity to a cluster of related and supporting industries, as discussed earlier. Cisco Systems, an international firm that sells networking and communications technology, such as routers, restricts its acquisitions to companies located in one of three well-known clusters of high-tech activity.[27] Where just-in-time inventory practices yield big cost savings and/or where an assembly firm has long-term partnering arrangements with its key suppliers, parts manufacturing plants may be located close to final assembly plants. A customer service center or sales office may be opened in a particular country to help cultivate strong relationships with pivotal customers located nearby.

> Companies that compete internationally can pursue competitive advantage in world markets by locating their value chain activities in whatever nations prove most advantageous.

When to Disperse Activities across Many Locations

There are several instances when dispersing activities is more advantageous than concentrating them. Buyer-related activities—such as distribution to dealers, sales and advertising, and after-sale service—usually must take place close to buyers. This means physically locating the capability to perform such activities in every country market where a firm has major customers (unless buyers in several adjoining countries can be served quickly from a nearby central location). For example, firms that make mining and oil-drilling equipment maintain operations in many locations around the world to support customers' needs for speedy equipment repair and technical assistance. The four biggest public accounting firms have offices in numerous countries to serve the foreign operations of their international corporate clients. Dispersing activities to many locations is also competitively advantageous when high transportation costs, diseconomies of large size, and trade barriers make it too expensive to operate from a central location. Many companies distribute their products from multiple locations to shorten delivery times to customers. In addition, it is strategically advantageous to disperse activities to hedge against the risks of fluctuating exchange rates, supply interruptions (due to strikes, mechanical failures, and transportation delays), and adverse political developments. Such risks are usually greater when activities are concentrated in a single location.

As discussed earlier, there are a variety of reasons for locating different value chain activities in different countries—all having to do with location-based advantages that vary from country to country. While the classic reason for locating an activity in a particular country is low cost, input quality and availability are also important considerations.[28] Such activities as materials procurement, parts manufacture, finished-goods assembly, technology research, and new product development can frequently be decoupled from buyer locations and performed wherever advantage lies. Components can be made in Mexico; technology research done in Frankfurt; new products developed and tested in Phoenix; and assembly plants located in Spain, Brazil, Taiwan, or South Carolina. Capital can be raised in whatever country it is available on the best terms.

Sharing and Transferring Resources and Capabilities across Borders to Build Competitive Advantage

When a company has competitively valuable resources and capabilities, it may be able to mount a resource-based strategic offensive to enter additional country markets. If a company's resources retain their value in foreign contexts, then entering new markets can extend the company's resource-based competitive advantage over a broader domain. For example, companies have used powerful brand names such as Rolex, Chanel, and Tiffany to extend their differentiation-based competitive advantages into markets far beyond their home-country origins. In each of these cases, the luxury brand name represents a valuable resource that is *shared among all of the company's international operations* and allows the company to command a higher willingness to pay from its customers in each country.

Transferring resources and capabilities across borders provides another means to extend a company's competitive advantage internationally. For example, if a firm learns how to assemble its product more efficiently at its Brazilian plant, the accumulated expertise can be quickly communicated to assembly plants in other world locations. Whirlpool, the leading global manufacturer of home appliances, with 69 manufacturing and technology research centers around the world and sales in nearly every country, uses an online global information technology platform to quickly and effectively transfer key product innovations and improved production techniques both across national borders and across its various appliance brands.

Sharing or transferring resources and capabilities across borders provides a way for a company to leverage its core competencies more fully and extend its competitive advantages into a wider array of geographic markets. Thus a technology-based competitive advantage in one country market may provide a similar basis for advantage in other country markets (depending on local market conditions). But since sharing or transferring valuable resources across borders is a very cost-effective means of extending a company's competitive advantage, these activities can also contribute to a company's competitive advantage on the costs side, giving multinational companies a powerful edge over domestic-only rivals. Since valuable resources and capabilities (such as brands, technologies, and production capabilities) are often developed at very high cost, deploying them abroad spreads the fixed development cost over greater output, thus lowering the company's unit costs. The cost of transferring already developed resources and capabilities is low by comparison. And even if the resources and capabilities need to be fully replicated in the foreign market or adapted to local conditions, this can usually be done at low additional cost relative to the initial investment in capability building.

Consider the case of Walt Disney's theme parks as an example. The success of the theme parks in the United States derives in part from core resources such as the Disney brand name and characters like Mickey Mouse that have universal appeal and worldwide recognition. These resources can be freely shared with new theme parks as Disney expands internationally. Disney can replicate its theme parks in new countries cost-effectively since it has already borne the costs of developing its core resources, park attractions, basic park design, and operating capabilities. The cost of replicating its theme parks abroad should be relatively low, even if they need to be adapted to a variety of local country conditions. By expanding internationally, Disney is able to enhance its competitive advantage over local theme park rivals. It does so by leveraging the differentiation advantage conferred by resources such as the Disney name and the park attractions. And by moving into new foreign markets, it augments its competitive advantage worldwide through the efficiency gains that come from cross border resource sharing and low-cost capability transfer and business model replication.

Sharing and transferring resources and capabilities across country borders may also contribute to the development of broader or deeper competencies and capabilities—ideally helping a company achieve *dominating depth* in some competitively valuable area. For example, an international company that consistently incorporates the same differentiating attributes in its products worldwide has enhanced potential to build a global brand name with significant power in the marketplace. The reputation for quality that Honda established worldwide began in motorcycles but enabled the company to command a position in both automobiles and outdoor power equipment in multiple-country markets. A one-country customer base is often too small to support the resource buildup needed to achieve such depth; this is particularly true when the market is developing or protected and sophisticated resources have not been required. By deploying capabilities across a larger international domain, a company can gain the experience needed to upgrade them to a higher performance standard. And by facing a more challenging set of international competitors, a company may be spurred to develop a stronger set of competitive capabilities. Moreover, by entering international markets, firms may be able to augment their capability set by learning from international rivals, cooperative partners, or acquisition targets.

However, sharing and transferring resources and capabilities across borders cannot provide a guaranteed recipe for competitive success. Because lifestyles and buying habits differ internationally, resources that are valuable in one country may not have value in another. For example, brands that are popular in one country may not transfer well or may lack recognition in the new context and thus offer no advantage against an established local brand. In addition, whether a resource or capability can confer a competitive advantage abroad depends on the conditions of rivalry in each particular market. If the rivals in a foreign country market have superior resources and capabilities, then an entering firm may find itself at a competitive disadvantage even if it has a resource-based advantage domestically and can transfer the resources at low cost.

Using Cross-Border Coordination for Competitive Advantage

Companies that compete on an international basis have another source of competitive advantage relative to their purely domestic rivals: They are able to benefit from coordinating activities across different countries' domains.[29] For example, an international manufacturer can shift production from a plant in one country to a plant in another to take advantage of exchange rate fluctuations, to cope with components shortages, or to profit from changing wage rates or energy costs. Production schedules can be coordinated worldwide; shipments can be diverted from one distribution center to another if sales rise unexpectedly in one place and fall in another. By coordinating their activities, multinational companies may also be able to enhance their leverage with host-country governments or respond adaptively to changes in tariffs and quotas.

Efficiencies can also be achieved by shifting workloads from where they are unusually heavy to locations where personnel are underutilized. Whirlpool's efforts to link its product R&D and manufacturing operations in North America, Latin America, Europe, and Asia allowed it to accelerate the discovery of innovative appliance features, coordinate the introduction of these features in the appliance products marketed in different countries, and create a cost-efficient worldwide supply chain. Whirlpool's conscious efforts to integrate and coordinate its various operations around the world have helped it become a low-cost producer and also speed product innovations to market, thereby giving Whirlpool an edge over rivals worldwide.

PROFIT SANCTUARIES AND CROSS-BORDER STRATEGIC MOVES

Profit sanctuaries are country markets (or geographic regions) in which a company derives substantial profits because of its protected market position or unassailable competitive advantage. Japan, for example, is the chief profit sanctuary for most Japanese companies because trade barriers erected by the Japanese government effectively block foreign companies from competing for a large share of Japanese sales. Protected from the threat of foreign competition in their home market, Japanese companies can safely charge somewhat higher prices to their Japanese customers and thus earn attractively large profits on sales made in Japan. Other profit sanctuaries may be protected because a company has an unassailable market position due to unrivaled and inimitable capabilities. In most cases, a company's biggest and most strategically crucial profit sanctuary is its home market, but multinational companies may also enjoy profit sanctuary status in other nations where they have a strong position based on some type of competitive advantage. Companies that compete worldwide are likely to have more profit sanctuaries than companies that compete in just a few country markets; a domestic-only competitor, of course, can have only one profit sanctuary at most (see Figure 7.3).

Figure 7.3   **Profit Sanctuary Potential of Domestic-only, International, and Global Competitors**

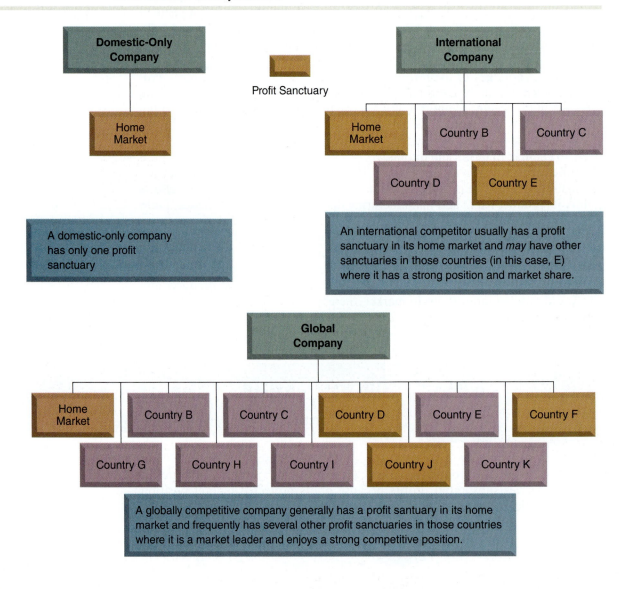

Using Cross-Market Subsidization to Wage a Strategic Offensive

Profit sanctuaries are valuable competitive assets, providing the financial strength to support strategic offensives in selected country markets and fuel a company's race for world-market leadership. The added financial capability afforded by multiple profit sanctuaries gives an international competitor the financial strength to wage a market offensive against a domestic competitor whose only profit sanctuary is its home market. The international company has the flexibility of lowballing its prices or launching high-cost marketing campaigns in the domestic company's home market and grabbing market share at the domestic company's expense. Razor-thin margins or even losses in these markets can be subsidized with the healthy profits earned in its profit sanctuaries—a practice called **cross-market subsidization.** The international company can adjust the depth of its price cutting to move in and capture market share quickly, or it can shave prices slightly to make gradual market inroads (perhaps over a decade or more) so as not to threaten domestic firms precipitously and trigger protectionist government actions. If the domestic company retaliates with matching price cuts or increased marketing expenses, it exposes its entire revenue stream and profit base to erosion; its profits can be squeezed substantially and its competitive strength sapped, even if it is the domestic market leader.

> ### CORE CONCEPT
>
> **Cross-market subsidization**—supporting competitive offensives in one market with resources and profits diverted from operations in another market—can be a powerful competitive weapon.

When taken to the extreme, cut-rate pricing attacks by international competitors may draw charges of unfair dumping. A company is said to be dumping when it sells its goods in foreign markets at prices that are (1) well below the prices at which it normally sells in its home market or (2) well below its full costs per unit. Companies that engage in dumping usually keep their selling prices high enough to cover variable costs per unit, thereby limiting their losses on each unit to some percentage of fixed costs per unit.

Dumping can be a tempting strategy in either of two instances: (1) when selling goods abroad at below-market prices can allow a firm to avoid the high costs of idling plants, and (2) when temporary below-cost pricing can allow a company to make lasting market share gains by driving weak firms from the market. The first may be justified as a legitimate competitive practice, while the latter is usually viewed to be predatory in nature. A charge of unfair dumping is more easily defended when a company with unused production capacity discovers that it is cheaper to keep producing (as long as the selling prices cover average variable costs per unit) than it is to incur the costs associated with idle plant capacity. By keeping its plants operating at or near capacity, not only may a company be able to cover variable costs and earn a contribution to fixed costs, but it also may be able to use its below-market prices to draw price-sensitive customers away from foreign rivals. It is wise for companies pursuing such an approach to court these new customers and retain their business when prices later begin a gradual rise back to normal market levels.

Alternatively, a company may use below-market pricing to drive down the price so far in the targeted country that domestic firms are quickly put in dire financial straits or in danger of being driven out of business. However, using below-market pricing in this way *runs a high risk of host-government retaliation on behalf of the adversely affected domestic companies.* Almost all governments can be expected to retaliate against perceived dumping practices by imposing special tariffs on goods being imported from the countries of the guilty companies.

Indeed, as the trade among nations has mushroomed over the past 10 years, most governments have joined the World Trade Organization (WTO), which promotes fair-trade practices among nations and actively polices dumping. Companies based in France and China were recently found guilty of dumping laminate flooring at unreasonably low prices in Canada to the detriment of Canadian producers.[30] Companies deemed guilty of dumping frequently come under pressure from their government to cease and desist, especially if the tariffs adversely affect innocent companies based in the same country or if the advent of special tariffs raises the specter of an international trade war.

Using Cross-Border Tactics to Defend against International Rivals

Cross-border tactics can also be used as a means of defending against the strategic moves of strong international rivals with multiple profit sanctuaries of their own. If a company finds itself under competitive attack by an international rival in one country market, one way to respond is with a counterattack against one of the rival's key markets in a different country—preferably where the rival is least protected and has the most to lose. This is a possible option when rivals compete against one another in much the same markets around the world.

For companies with at least one profit sanctuary, having a presence in a rival's key markets can be enough to deter the rival from making aggressive attacks. The reason for this is that the combination of some market presence (even at small scale) and a profit sanctuary elsewhere can send a signal to the rival that the company could quickly ramp up production (funded by the profit sanctuary) to mount a competitive attack in that market if the rival attacks one of the company's key markets in another country.

When international rivals compete against one another in multiple-country markets, this type of deterrence effect can restrain them from taking aggressive action against one another due to the fear of a retaliatory response that might escalate the battle into a cross-border competitive war. **Mutual restraint** of this sort tends to stabilize the competitive position of multimarket rivals against one another. And while it may prevent each firm from making any major market share gains at the expense of its rival, it also prevents costly competitive battles that would be likely to erode the profitability of both companies without any compensating gain.

CORE CONCEPT

When the same companies compete against one another in multiple geographic markets, the threat of cross-border counterattacks may be enough to deter aggressive competitive moves and encourage **mutual restraint** among international rivals.

STRATEGIES FOR COMPETING IN THE MARKETS OF DEVELOPING COUNTRIES

Companies racing for global leadership have to consider competing in developing-economy markets like China, India, Brazil, Indonesia, Thailand, Poland, Russia, and Mexico—countries where the business risks are considerable but where the opportunities for growth are huge, especially as their economies develop and living standards climb toward levels in the industrialized world.[31]

With the world now comprising nearly 7 billion people—fully 40 percent of whom live in India and China, and hundreds of millions more live in other, less developed countries in Asia and Latin America—a company that aspires to world market leadership (or to sustained rapid growth) cannot ignore the market opportunities or the base of technical and managerial talent such countries offer. For example, in 2010 China was the world's second-largest economy (behind the United States), as measured by purchasing power. Its population of 1.4 billion people now consumes a quarter of the world's luxury products, due to the rapid growth of a wealthy class.[32] China is also the world's largest consumer of many commodities. China's growth in demand for consumer goods had made it the world's largest market for vehicles by 2009 and put it on track to become the world's largest market for luxury goods by 2014.[33] Thus, no company that aspires to global market leadership can afford to ignore the strategic importance of establishing competitive market positions in China, India, other parts of the Asia-Pacific region, Latin America, and eastern Europe. Illustration Capsule 7.2 describes Yum! Brands' strategy to increase its sales and market share in China.

Tailoring products to fit market conditions in a developing country like China, however, often involves more than making minor product changes and becoming more familiar with local cultures.[34] Ford's attempt to sell a Ford Escort in India at a price of $21,000—a luxury-car price, given that India's best-selling Maruti-Suzuki model sold at the time for $10,000 or less and that fewer than 10 percent of Indian households had an annual purchasing power greater than $20,000—met with a less-than-enthusiastic market response. McDonald's has had to offer vegetable burgers in parts of Asia and to rethink its prices, which are often high by local standards and affordable only by the well-to-do. Kellogg has struggled to introduce its cereals successfully because consumers in many less developed countries do not eat cereal for breakfast and changing habits is difficult and expensive. Single-serving packages of detergents, shampoos, pickles, cough syrup, and cooking oils are very popular in India because they allow buyers to conserve cash by purchasing only what they need immediately. Thus, many companies find that trying to employ a strategy akin to that used in the markets of developed countries is hazardous.[35] Experimenting with some, perhaps many, local twists is usually necessary to find a strategy combination that works.

Strategy Options for Competing in Developing-Country Markets

There are several options for tailoring a company's strategy to fit the sometimes unusual or challenging circumstances presented in developing-country markets:

- *Prepare to compete on the basis of low price.* Consumers in developing markets are often highly focused on price, which can give low-cost local competitors the edge unless a company can find ways to attract buyers with bargain prices as well as better products.[36] For example, when Unilever entered the market for laundry detergents in India, it realized that 80 percent of the population could not afford the brands it was selling to affluent consumers there. To compete against a very low-priced detergent made by a local company, Unilever developed a low-cost detergent (named Wheel), constructed new low-cost production facilities, packaged the detergent in single-use amounts so that it could be sold at a very low unit price, distributed the product to local merchants by handcarts, and crafted an economical marketing campaign that

In 2010, Yum! Brands operated more than 37,000 restaurants in more than 110 countries. Its best-known brands were KFC, Taco Bell, Pizza Hut, A&W, and Long John Silver's. In 2009, its fastest growth in revenues came from its 3,369 restaurants in China, which recorded operating profits of $602 million during the year. KFC was the largest quick-service chain in China, with 2,870 units in 2009, while Pizza Hut was the largest casual-dining chain, with 450 units. Yum! Brands planned to open at least 500 new restaurant locations annually in China, including new Pizza Hut Home delivery units and East Dawning units, which had a menu offering traditional Chinese food. All of Yum! Brands' menu items for China were developed in its R&D facility in Shanghai.

In addition to adapting its menu to local tastes and adding new units at a rapid pace, Yum! Brands also adapted the restaurant ambience and decor to appeal to local consumer preferences and behavior. The company changed its KFC store formats to provide educational displays that supported parents' priorities for their children and to make KFC a fun place for children to visit. The typical KFC outlet in China averaged two birthday parties per day.

In 2009, Yum! Brands operated 60 KFC, Taco Bell, Pizza Hut, A&W, and Long John Silver's restaurants for every 1 million Americans. The company's more than 3,300 units in China represented only 2 restaurants per 1 million Chinese. Yum! Brands management believed that its strategy keyed to continued expansion in the number of units in China and additional menu refinements would allow its operating profits from restaurants located in China to account for 40 percent of systemwide operating profits by 2017.

Sources: Yum! Brands 2009 10-K and other information posted at www.yum.com.

included painted signs on buildings and demonstrations near stores. The new brand quickly captured $100 million in sales and was the number-one detergent brand in India in 2008 based on dollar sales. Unilever later replicated the strategy in India with low-priced packets of shampoos and deodorants and in South America with a detergent brand named Ala.

- *Be prepared to modify aspects of the company's business model or strategy to accommodate local circumstances (but not to such an extent that the company loses the advantage of global scale and branding).*[37] For instance, when Dell entered China, it discovered that individuals and businesses were not accustomed to placing orders through the Internet (whereas over 50 percent of Dell's sales in North America were online). To adapt, Dell modified its direct sales model to rely more heavily on phone and fax orders and decided to be patient in getting Chinese customers to place Internet orders. Further, because numerous Chinese government departments and state-owned enterprises insisted that hardware vendors make their bids through distributors and systems integrators (as opposed to dealing directly with Dell salespeople, as did large enterprises in other countries), Dell opted to use third parties in marketing its products to this buyer segment (although it did sell through its own sales force where it could). But Dell was careful not to abandon the parts of its business model that gave it a competitive edge over rivals. Similarly, when McDonald's moved into Russia in the 1990s, it was forced to alter its practice of obtaining needed supplies from outside vendors because capable local suppliers were not available; to supply its Russian outlets and stay true to its core principle of serving consistent-quality fast food, McDonald's set up its own vertically integrated supply chain—cattle were imported from Holland and russet potatoes were imported from the United States. McDonald's management also worked with a select number of Russian bakers for its bread, brought in agricultural specialists from Canada and Europe to improve the management practices of Russian farmers, built its own 100,000-square-foot McComplex to produce hamburgers, French fries, ketchup, mustard, and Big Mac sauce, and set up a trucking fleet to move supplies to restaurants.

- *Try to change the local market to better match the way the company does business elsewhere.*[38] An international company often has enough market clout to drive major changes in the way a local country market operates. When Hong Kong–based STAR launched its first satellite TV channel in 1991, it generated profound impacts on the TV marketplace in India. The Indian government lost its monopoly on TV broadcasts, several other satellite TV channels aimed at Indian audiences quickly emerged, and the excitement of additional TV channels in India triggered a boom in TV manufacturing in India. When Japan's Suzuki entered India, it triggered a quality revolution among Indian auto parts manufacturers. Local component suppliers teamed up with Suzuki's vendors in Japan and worked with Japanese experts to produce higher-quality products. Over the next two decades, Indian companies became proficient in making top-notch components for vehicles, won more prizes for quality than companies in any country other than Japan, and broke into the global market as suppliers to many automakers in Asia and other parts of the world. Mahindra and Mahindra, one of India's premier automobile manufacturers, has been recognized by a number of organizations for its product quality. Among its most noteworthy awards was its number-one ranking by J.D. Power Asia Pacific in 2007 for new vehicle overall quality.

- *Stay away from developing markets where it is impractical or uneconomic to modify the company's business model to accommodate local circumstances.*[39] Home Depot expanded into Mexico in 2001 and China in 2006, but it has avoided entry into other developing countries because its value proposition of good quality, low prices, and attentive customer service relies on (1) good highways and logistical systems to minimize store inventory costs, (2) employee stock ownership to help motivate store personnel to provide good customer service, and (3) high labor costs for housing construction and home repairs that encourage homeowners to engage in do-it-yourself projects. Relying on these factors in the U.S. and Canadian markets has worked spectacularly for

Home Depot, but the company has found that it cannot count on these factors in nearby Latin America.

Company experiences in entering developing markets like China, India, Russia, and Brazil indicate that profitability seldom comes quickly or easily. Building a market for the company's products can often turn into a long-term process that involves re-education of consumers, sizable investments in advertising and promotion to alter tastes and buying habits, and upgrades of the local infrastructure (transportation systems, distribution channels, etc.). In such cases, a company must be patient, work within the system to improve the infrastructure, and lay the foundation for generating sizable revenues and profits once conditions are ripe for market takeoff.

> Profitability in developing markets rarely comes quickly or easily—new entrants have to adapt their business models and strategies to local conditions and be patient in earning a profit.

DEFENDING AGAINST GLOBAL GIANTS: STRATEGIES FOR LOCAL COMPANIES IN DEVELOPING COUNTRIES

If opportunity-seeking, resource-rich multinational companies are looking to enter developing-country markets, what strategy options can local companies use to survive? As it turns out, the prospects for local companies facing global giants are by no means grim. Studies of local companies in developing markets have disclosed five strategies that have proved themselves in defending against globally competitive companies.[40] Illustration Capsule 7.3 discusses how a travel agency in China used a combination of these strategies to become that country's largest travel consolidator and online travel agent.

1. *Develop business models that exploit shortcomings in local distribution networks or infrastructure.* In many instances, the extensive collection of resources possessed by the global giants is of little help in building a presence in developing markets. The lack of well-established wholesaler and distributor networks, telecommunication systems, consumer banking, or media necessary for advertising makes it difficult for large internationals to migrate business models proved in developed markets to developing countries. Such markets sometimes favor local companies whose managers are familiar with the local language and culture and are skilled in selecting large numbers of conscientious employees to carry out labor-intensive tasks. Shanda, a Chinese producer of massively multiplayer online role-playing games (MMORPG), has overcome China's lack of an established credit card network by selling prepaid access cards through local merchants. The company's focus on online games also addresses shortcomings in China's software piracy laws. Emerge Logistics has used its understanding of China's extensive government bureaucracy and fragmented network of delivery services to deliver goods for international companies doing business in China. Many foreign firms have found it difficult to get their goods to market since the average Chinese trucking company owns only one or two trucks. An India-based electronics company has been able to carve out a market niche for itself by developing an all-in-one business machine designed especially for India's 1.2 million small shopkeepers that tolerates the frequent power outages in that country.[41]

2. *Utilize keen understanding of local customer needs and preferences to create customized products or services.* When developing-country markets are largely made up of customers with strong local needs, a good strategy option is to concentrate on customers who prefer a local touch and to accept the loss of the customers attracted to global brands.[42] A local company may be able to astutely exploit its local orientation—its familiarity with local preferences, its expertise in traditional products, its long-standing customer relationships. A small Middle Eastern cell phone manufacturer competes successfully against industry giants Nokia, Samsung, and Motorola by selling a model designed especially for Muslims—it is loaded with the Koran, alerts people at prayer times, and is equipped with a compass that points them toward Mecca. Shenzhen-based Tencent has become the leader in instant messaging in China through its unique understanding of Chinese behavior and culture.

3. *Take advantage of aspects of the local workforce with which large multinational companies may be unfamiliar.* Local companies that lack the technological capabilities of foreign entrants may be able to rely on their better

understanding of the local labor force to offset any disadvantage. Focus Media is China's largest outdoor advertising firm and has relied on low-cost labor to update its 130,000 LCD displays and billboards in 90 cities in a low-tech manner, while multinational companies operating in China use electronically networked screens that allow messages to be changed remotely. Focus uses an army of employees who ride to each display by bicycle to change advertisements with programming contained on a USB flash drive or DVD. Indian information technology firms such as Infosys Technologies and Satyam Computer Services have been able to keep their personnel costs lower than those of international competitors EDS and Accenture because of their familiarity with local labor markets. While the large internationals have focused recruiting efforts in urban centers like Bangalore and Delhi, driving up engineering and computer science salaries in such cities, local companies have shifted recruiting efforts to second-tier cities that are unfamiliar to foreign firms.

4. *Use acquisition and rapid-growth strategies to better defend against expansion-minded internationals.* With the growth potential of developing markets such as China, Indonesia, and Brazil obvious to the world, local companies must attempt to develop scale and upgrade their competitive capabilities as quickly as possible to defend against the stronger international's arsenal of resources. Most successful companies in developing markets have pursued mergers and acquisitions at a rapid-fire pace to build first a nationwide and then an international presence. Hindalco, India's largest aluminum producer, has followed just such a path to achieve its ambitions for global dominance. By acquiring companies in India first, it gained enough experience and confidence to eventually acquire much larger foreign companies with world-class capabilities.[43] When China began to liberalize its foreign trade policies, Lenovo (the Chinese PC maker) realized that its long-held position of market dominance in China could not withstand the onslaught of new international entrants such as Dell and HP. Its acquisition of IBM's PC business allowed Lenovo to gain rapid access to IBM's globally recognized PC brand, its R&D capability, and its existing distribution in developed countries. This has allowed Lenovo not only to hold its own against the incursion of global giants into its home market but to expand into new markets around the world.[44]

5. *Transfer company expertise to cross-border markets and initiate actions to contend on an international level.* When a company from a developing country has resources and capabilities suitable for competing in other country markets, launching initiatives to transfer its expertise to foreign markets becomes a viable strategic option.[45] Televisa, Mexico's largest media company, used its expertise in Spanish culture and linguistics to become the world's most prolific producer of Spanish-language soap operas. Jollibee Foods, a family-owned company with 56 percent of the fast-food business in the Philippines, combated McDonald's entry first by upgrading service and delivery standards and then by using its expertise in seasoning hamburgers with garlic and soy sauce and making noodle and rice meals with fish to open outlets catering to Asian residents in Hong Kong, the Middle East, and California. By continuing to upgrade its capabilities and learn from its experience in foreign markets, a company can sometimes transform itself into one capable of competing on a worldwide basis, as an emerging global giant.[46] Sundaram Fasteners of India began its foray into foreign markets as a supplier of radiator caps to

GM—an opportunity it pursued when GM first decided to outsource the production of this part. As a participant in GM's supplier network, the company learned about emerging technical standards, built its capabilities, and became one of the first Indian companies to achieve QS 9000 quality certification. With the expertise it gained and its recognition for meeting quality standards, Sundaram was then able to pursue opportunities to supply automotive parts in Japan and Europe.

KEY POINTS

1. Competing in international markets allows companies to (1) gain access to new customers, (2) achieve lower costs through greater scale economies, learning curve effects, or purchasing power, (3) leverage core competencies developed domestically in additional country markets, (4) gain access to resources and capabilities located outside a company's domestic market, and (5) spread business risk across a wider market base.

2. Companies electing to expand into international markets must consider five factors when evaluating strategy options: (1) cross-country variation in factors that affect industry competitiveness, (2) location-based drivers regarding where to conduct different value chain activities, (3) varying political and economic risks, (4) potential shifts in exchange rates, and (5) differences in cultural, demographic, and market conditions.

3. The strategies of firms that expand internationally are usually grounded in home-country advantages concerning demand conditions, factor conditions, related and supporting industries, and firm strategy, structure, and rivalry, as described by the Diamond of National Advantage framework.

4. The pattern of international competition varies in important ways from industry to industry. At one extreme is *multidomestic competition,* in which the market contest among rivals in one country is not closely connected to the market contests in other countries—there is no world market, just a collection of self-contained country (or maybe regional) markets. At the other extreme is *global competition,* in which competitive conditions across national markets are linked strongly enough to form a true world market, wherein leading competitors compete head to head in many different countries.

5. There are six strategic options for entering foreign markets. These include (1) maintaining a national (one-country) production base and exporting goods to foreign markets, (2) licensing foreign firms to produce and distribute the company's products abroad, (3) employing a franchising strategy, (4) establishing a wholly owned subsidiary by acquiring a foreign company, (5) creating a wholly owned foreign subsidiary from the ground up via a greenfield venture, and (6) using strategic alliances or other collaborative partnerships to enter a foreign market.

6. A company must choose among three alternative approaches for competing internationally: (1) a *multidomestic strategy,* which is a *think-local, act-local* approach to crafting international strategy; (2) a *global strategy*—a *think-global, act-global* approach; and (3) a combination *think-global, act-local* approach, known as a *transnational strategy.* A think-local, act-local, or multidomestic, strategy is appropriate for industries or companies that must vary

their product offerings and competitive approaches from country to country in order to accommodate different buyer preferences and market conditions. The think-global, act-global approach that characterizes a global strategy works best when there are substantial cost benefits to be gained from taking a standardized and globally integrated approach and little need for local responsiveness. A transnational approach (think global, act local) is called for when there is a high need for local responsiveness as well as substantial benefits from taking a globally integrated approach. While this is the most challenging international strategy to implement, it can be used when it is feasible for a company to employ essentially the same basic competitive strategy in all markets but still customize its product offering and some aspect of its operations to fit local market circumstances.

7. There are three general ways in which a firm can gain competitive advantage (or offset domestic disadvantages) in international markets. One way involves locating various value chain activities among nations in a manner that lowers costs or achieves greater product differentiation. A second way draws on an international competitor's ability to extend or deepen its competitive advantage by cost-effectively sharing, replicating, or transferring its most valuable resources and capabilities across borders. A third concerns benefiting from cross-border coordination in ways that are unavailable to domestic-only competitors.

8. Profit sanctuaries are country markets in which a company derives substantial profits because of its protected market position. They are valuable competitive assets, providing companies with the financial strength to mount strategic offensives in selected country markets or to support defensive moves that can ward off mutually destructive competitive battles. They may be used to wage strategic offenses in international markets through *cross-subsidization*—a practice of supporting competitive offensives in one market with resources and profits diverted from operations in another market. They may be used defensively to encourage *mutual restraint* among competitors when there is international *multimarket competition* by signaling that each company has the financial capability for mounting a strong counterattack if threatened. For companies with at least one profit sanctuary, having a presence in a rival's key markets can be enough to deter the rival from making aggressive attacks.

9. Companies racing for global leadership have to consider competing in developing markets like China, India, Brazil, Indonesia, and Mexico—countries where the business risks are considerable but the opportunities for growth are huge. To succeed in these markets, companies often have to (1) compete on the basis of low price, (2) be prepared to modify aspects of the company's business model or strategy to accommodate local circumstances (but not so much that the company loses the advantage of global scale and global branding), and/or (3) try to change the local market to better match the way the company does business elsewhere. Profitability is unlikely to come quickly or easily in developing markets, typically because of the investments needed to alter buying habits and tastes, the increased political and economic risk, and/or the need for infrastructure upgrades. And there may be times when a company should simply stay away from certain developing markets until conditions for entry are better suited to its business model and strategy.

10. Local companies in developing-country markets can seek to compete against large multinational companies by (1) developing business models that exploit shortcomings in local distribution networks or infrastructure, (2) utilizing superior understanding of local customer needs and preferences or local relationships, (3) taking advantage of competitively important qualities of the local workforce with which large multinational companies may be unfamiliar, (4) using acquisition strategies and rapid-growth strategies to better defend against expansion-minded multinational companies, or (5) transferring company expertise to cross-border markets and initiating actions to compete on a global level.

ASSURANCE OF LEARNING EXERCISES

LO 2, LO 3, LO 4

1. Harley-Davidson has chosen to compete in various country markets in Europe and Asia using an export strategy. Go to the Investor Relations section at www.harley-davidson.com and read the sections of its latest annual report related to its international operations. Why does it seem that the company has avoided developing production facilities outside the United States?

LO 3, LO 5

2. The Hero Group is among the 10 largest corporations in India, with 20 business segments and annual revenues of $3.2 billion in fiscal 2006. Many of the corporation's business units have utilized strategic alliances with foreign partners to compete in new product and geographic markets. Review the company's statements concerning its alliances and international business operations at www.herogroup.com/alliance.htm, and prepare a two-page report that outlines the group's successful use of international strategic alliances.

LO 2, LO 4, LO 5

3. Assume you are in charge of developing the strategy for an international company selling products in 50 different countries around the world. One of the issues you face is whether to employ a multidomestic strategy, a global strategy, or a transnational strategy.

    a. If your company's product is mobile phones, do you think it would make better strategic sense to employ a multidomestic strategy, a global strategy, or a transnational strategy? Why?

    b. If your company's product is dry soup mixes and canned soups, would a multidomestic strategy seem to be more advisable than a global strategy? Why?

    c. If your company's product is large home appliances such as washing machines, ranges, ovens, and refrigerators, would it seem to make more sense to pursue a multidomestic strategy, a global strategy, or a transnational strategy? Why?

    d. If your company's product is apparel and footwear, would a multidomestic strategy, a global strategy, or a transnational strategy seem to have more appeal? Why?

EXERCISES FOR SIMULATION PARTICIPANTS

The questions below are for simulation participants whose companies operate in an international market arena. If your company competes only in a single country, then skip the questions in this section.

LO 2

1. Does your company compete in a world-market arena characterized by multi-domestic competition or global competition? Explain why.

LO 3, LO 4, LO 5

2. Which one of the following best describes the strategic approach your company is taking in trying to compete successfully on an international basis?

    *   Think local, act local
    *   Think global, act local
    *   Think global, act global

    Explain your answer, and indicate two or three chief elements of your company's strategic approach to competing in two or more different geographic regions.

LO 2

3. To what extent, if any, have you and your co-managers adapted your company's strategy to take shifting exchange rates into account? In other words, have you undertaken any actions to try to minimize the impact of adverse shifts in exchange rates?

LO 2

4. To what extent, if any, have you and your co-managers adapted your company's strategy to take geographic differences in import tariffs or import duties into account?

ENDNOTES

[1] Sidney G. Winter and Gabriel Szulanski, "Replication as Strategy," *Organization Science* 12, no. 6 (November–December 2001), pp. 730–43; Sidney G. Winter and Gabriel Szulanski, "Getting It Right the Second Time," *Harvard Business Review* 80, no. 1 (January 2002), pp. 62–69.

[2] A. C. Inkpen and A. Dinur, "Knowledge Management Processes and International Joint Ventures," *Organization Science* 9, no. 4 (July–August 1998), pp. 454–68; P. Dussauge, B. Garrette, and W. Mitchell, "Learning from Competing Partners: Outcomes and Durations of Scale and Link Alliances in Europe, North America and Asia," *Strategic Management Journal* 21, no. 2 (February 2000), pp. 99–126; C. Dhanaraj, M. A. Lyles, H. K. Steensma et al., "Managing Tacit and Explicit Knowledge Transfer in IJVs: The Role of Relational Embeddedness and the Impact on

Performance," *Journal of International Business Studies* 35, no. 5 (September 2004), pp. 428–42; K. W. Glaister and P. J. Buckley, "Strategic Motives for International Alliance Formation," *Journal of Management Studies* 33, no. 3 (May 1996), pp. 301–32.

[3] J. Anand and B. Kogut, "Technological Capabilities of Countries, Firm Rivalry and Foreign Direct Investment," *Journal of International Business Studies* 28, no. 3 (1997), pp. 445–65; J. Anand and A. Delios, "Absolute and Relative Resources as Determinants of International Acquisitions," *Strategic Management Journal* 23, no. 2 (February 2002), pp. 119–35; A. Seth, K. Song, and A. Pettit, "Value Creation and Destruction in Cross-Border Acquisitions: An Empirical Analysis of Foreign Acquisitions of U.S. Firms," *Strategic Management Journal* 23, no. 10 (October 2002), pp. 921–40; J. Anand, L. Capron, and W. Mitchell, "Using

Acquisitions to Access Multinational Diversity: Thinking beyond the Domestic versus Cross-Border M&A Comparison," *Industrial & Corporate Change* 14, no. 2 (April 2005), pp. 191–224.

[4] M. Porter, "The Competitive Advantage of Nations," *Harvard Business Review,* March–April 1990, pp. 73–93.

[5] U.S. Department of Labor, "International Comparisons of Hourly Compensation Costs in Manufacturing in 2007," *Bureau of Labor Statistics Newsletter,* March 26, 2009, p. 8.

[6] "China's Middle Class Found Wanting for Happiness," *The Independent,* March 19, 2010, www.independent.co.uk/life-style/house-and-home/chinas-middle-class-found-wanting-for-happiness-1924180.html.

[7] "China Car Sales 'Overtook the US' in 2009," *BBC News,* January 11, 2010, http://news.bbc.co.uk/2/hi/8451887.stm.

[8] Sangwon Yoon, "South Korea Targets Internet Addicts; 2 Million Hooked," *Valley News,* April 25, 2010, p. C2.

[9] Michael E. Porter, *The Competitive Advantage of Nations* (New York: Free Press, 1990), pp. 53–54.

[10] Ibid., p. 61.

[11] K.E. Meyer, M. Wright, and S. Pruthi, "Institutions, Resources, and Entry Strategies in Emerging Economies," *Strategic Management Journal* 30, no. 5 (2009), pp. 61–80; E. Pablo, "Determinants of Cross-Border M&As in Latin America," *Journal of Business Research* 62, no. 9 (2009), pp. 861–67; R. Olie, "Shades of Culture and Institutions in International Mergers," *Organization Studies* 15, no. 3 (1994), pp. 381–406.

[12] Meyer et al., "Institutions, Resources, and Entry Strategies in Emerging Economies."

[13] See Yves L. Doz and Gary Hamel, *Alliance Advantage* (Boston: Harvard Business School Press, 1998), especially chaps. 2–4; Joel Bleeke and David Ernst, "The Way to Win in Cross-Border Alliances," *Harvard Business Review* 69, no. 6 (November –December 1991), pp. 127–33; Gary Hamel, Yves L. Doz, and C. K. Prahalad, "Collaborate with Your Competitors—and Win," *Harvard Business Review* 67, no. 1 (January–February 1989), pp. 134–35; Porter, *The Competitive Advantage of Nations,* p. 66.

[14] N. Kumar and A. Chadha, "India's Outward Foreign Direct Investments in Steel Industry in a Chinese Comparative Perspective," *Industrial and Corporate Change* 18, no. 2 (2009), pp. 249–67; R. Chittoor, S. Ray, P. Aulakh, and M. B. Sarkar, "Strategic Responses to Institutional Changes: 'Indigenous Growth' Model of the Indian Pharmaceutical Industry," *Journal of International Management* 14 (2008), pp. 252–69.

[15] F. Froese and L. Goeritz, "Integration Management of Western Acquisitions in Japan," *Asian Business and Management* 6 (2007) pp. 95–114.

[16] For a discussion of the pros and cons of alliances versus acquisitions, see Jeffrey H. Dyer, Prashant Kale, and Harbir Singh, "When to Ally and When to Acquire," *Harvard Business Review* 82, no. 7–8 (July–August 2004), pp. 109–15.

[17] For additional discussion of company experiences with alliances and partnerships, see Doz and Hamel, *Alliance Advantage,* chaps. 2–7; and Rosabeth Moss Kanter, "Collaborative Advantage: The Art of the Alliance," *Harvard Business Review* 72, no. 4 (July–August 1994), pp. 96–108.

[18] Jeremy Main, "Making Global Alliances Work," *Fortune,* December 19, 1990, p. 125.

[19] Details are reported in Shawn Tully, "The Alliance from Hell," *Fortune,* June 24, 1996, pp. 64–72.

[20] C. K. Prahalad and K. Lieberthal, "The End of Corporate Imperialism," *Harvard Business Review,* 81, no. 8 (August 2003), pp.109–117.

[21] Ibid.

[22] For an in-depth discussion of the challenges of crafting strategies suitable for a world in which both production and markets are globalizing, see Pankaj Ghemawat, "Managing Differences: The Central Challenge of Global Strategy," *Harvard Business Review* 85, no. 3 (March 2007), pp. 59–68.

[23] For more details on the merits of and opportunities for cross-border transfer of successful strategy experiments, see C. A. Bartlett and S. Ghoshal, *Managing across Borders: The Transnational Solution,* 2nd ed. (Boston: Harvard Business School Press, 1998), pp. 79–80 and chap. 9. Also see Pankaj Ghemawat, "Managing Differences: The Central Challenge of Global Strategy," *Harvard Business Review* 85, no. 3 (March 2007), pp. 58–68.

[24] Lynn S. Paine, "The China Rules," *Harvard Business Review* 88, no. 6 (June 2010) pp. 103–8.

[25] Porter, *The Competitive Advantage of Nations,* pp. 53–55.

[26] Ibid., pp. 55–58.

[27] A. Inkpen, A. Sundaram, and K. Rockwood, "Cross-Border Acquisitions of U.S. Technology Assets," *California Management Review* 42, no. 3 (Spring 2000), pp. 50–71.

[28] Porter, *The Competitive Advantage of Nations,* p. 57.

[29] C. K. Prahalad and Yves L. Doz, *The Multinational Mission* (New York: Free Press, 1987), pp. 58–60; Ghemawat, "Managing Differences," pp. 58–68.

[30] Canadian International Trade Tribunal, findings issued June 16, 2005, and posted at www.citt-tcce.gc.ca (accessed September 28, 2005).

[31] This point is discussed at greater length in Prahalad and Lieberthal, "The End of Corporate Imperialism," pp. 68–79; also see David J. Arnold and John A. Quelch, "New Strategies in Emerging Markets," *Sloan Management Review* 40, no. 1 (Fall 1998), pp. 7–20. For a more extensive discussion of strategy in emerging markets, see C. K. Prahalad, *The Fortune at the Bottom of the Pyramid: Eradicating Poverty through Profits* (Upper Saddle River, NJ: Wharton, 2005), especially chaps. 1–3.

[32] "Is a Luxury Good Consumption Tax Useful?" *Beijing Review.com.cn,* June 18, 2010, www.bjreview.com.cn/print/txt/2010-06/18/content_280191.htm; "GM's First-Half China Sales Surge Past the U.S.," *Bloomberg Businessweek,* July 2, 2010, http://businessweek.com/news/2010-07-02/gm-s-first-half-china-sales-surge-past-the-u-s-.html.

[33] Joanne Muller, "Can China Save GM?" *Forbes.com,* May 10, 2010, www.forbes.com/forbes/2010/0510/global-2000-10-automobiles-china-detroit-whitacre-save-gm.html; "Is a Luxury Good Consumption Tax Useful?"

[34] Prahalad and Lieberthal, "The End of Corporate Imperialism," pp. 72–73.

[35] Tarun Khanna, Krishna G. Palepu, and Jayant Sinha, "Strategies That Fit Emerging Markets," *Harvard Business Review* 83, no. 6 (June 2005), p. 63; Arindam K. Bhattacharya and David C. Michael, "How Local Companies Keep Multinationals at Bay," *Harvard Business Review* 86, no. 3 (March 2008), pp. 94–95.

[36] Prahalad and Lieberthal, "The End of Corporate Imperialism," p. 72.

[37] Khanna, Palepu, and Sinha, "Strategies That Fit Emerging Markets," pp. 73–74.

[38] Ibid., p. 74.

[39] Ibid., p. 76.

[40] The results and conclusions from a study of 134 local companies in 10 emerging markets are presented in Tarun Khanna and Krishna G. Palepu, "Emerging Giants: Building World-Class Companies in Developing Countries," *Harvard Business Review* 84, no. 10 (October 2006), pp. 60–69; also, an examination of strategies used by 50 local companies in emerging markets is discussed in Arindam K. Bhattacharya and David C. Michael, "How Local Companies Keep Multinationals at Bay," pp. 85–95.

[41] Steve Hamm, "Tech's Future," *BusinessWeek,* September 27, 2004, p. 88.

[42] Niroj Dawar and Tony Frost, "Competing with Giants: Survival Strategies for Local Companies in Emerging Markets," *Harvard Business Review* 77, no. 1 (January–February 1999), p. 122; see also Guitz Ger, "Localizing in the Global Village: Local Firms Competing in Global Markets," *California Management Review* 41, no. 4 (Summer 1999), pp. 64–84; Khanna and Palepu, "Emerging Giants," pp. 63–66.

[43] N. Kumar, "How Emerging Giants Are Rewriting the Rules of M&A," *Harvard Business Review,* May 2009, pp. 115–21.

[44] H. Rui and G. Yip, "Foreign Acquisitions by Chinese Firms: A Strategic Intent Perspective," *Journal of World Business* 43 (2008), pp. 213–26.

[45] Dawar and Frost, "Competing with Giants," p. 124.

[46] Ibid., p. 126; Khanna and Palepu, "Emerging Giants," pp. 60–69.

CHAPTER 8

CORPORATE STRATEGY
Diversification and the Multibusiness Company

Fit between a parent and its businesses is a two-edged sword: A good fit can create value; a bad one can destroy it.

—Andrew Campbell,
Michael Gould, and Marcus Alexander

We are quite pragmatic. If a business does not contribute to our overall vision, it has to go.

—Richard Wambold
CEO, Pactiv

Make winners out of every business in your company. Don't carry losers.

—Jack Welch
Former CEO, General Electric

I think our biggest achievement to date has been bringing back to life an inherent Disney synergy that enables each part of our business to draw from, build upon, and bolster the others.

—Michael Eisner
Former CEO, Walt Disney Company

LEARNING OBJECTIVES

LO 1. Understand when and how business diversification can enhance shareholder value.

LO 2. Gain an understanding of how related diversification strategies can produce cross-business strategic fit capable of delivering competitive advantage.

LO 3. Become aware of the merits and risks of corporate strategies keyed to unrelated diversification.

LO 4. Gain command of the analytical tools for evaluating a company's diversification strategy.

LO 5. Understand a diversified company's four main corporate strategy options for solidifying its diversification strategy and improving company performance.

In this chapter, we move up one level in the strategy-making hierarchy, from strategy making in a single-business enterprise to strategy making in a diversified enterprise. Because a diversified company is a collection of individual businesses, the strategy-making task is more complicated. In a one-business company, managers have to come up with a plan for competing successfully in only a single industry environment—the result is what we labeled in Chapter 2 as *business strategy* (or *business-level strategy*). But in a diversified company, the strategy-making challenge involves assessing multiple industry environments and developing a *set* of business strategies, one for each industry arena in which the diversified company operates. And top executives at a diversified company must still go one step further and devise a companywide or *corporate strategy* for improving the attractiveness and performance of the company's overall business lineup and for making a rational whole out of its diversified collection of individual businesses.

In most diversified companies, corporate-level executives delegate considerable strategy-making authority to the heads of each business, usually giving them the latitude to craft a business strategy suited to their particular industry and competitive circumstances and holding them accountable for producing good results. But the task of crafting a diversified company's overall or corporate strategy falls squarely in the lap of top-level executives and involves four distinct facets:

1. *Picking new industries to enter and deciding on the mode of entry.* The first concerns in diversifying are what new industries to get into and whether to enter by starting a new business from the ground up, acquiring a company already in the target industry, or forming a joint venture or strategic alliance with another company.

2. *Pursuing opportunities to leverage cross-business value chain relationships and strategic fit into competitive advantage.* A company that diversifies into businesses with competitively important value chain matchups (pertaining to common technology, supply chain logistics, production, distribution channels, and/or customers) gains competitive advantage potential not open to a company that diversifies into businesses whose value chains are totally unrelated and that require totally different resources and capabilities. Capturing this competitive advantage potential requires capitalizing on such cross-business opportunities as transferring skills or technology from one business to another, reducing costs via sharing common facilities and resources, utilizing the company's well-known brand names and distribution muscle to increase the sales of newly acquired products, and encouraging knowledge-sharing and collaborative activity among the businesses.

3. *Establishing investment priorities and steering corporate resources into the most attractive*

business units. A diversified company's different businesses are usually not equally attractive from the standpoint of investing additional funds. It is incumbent on corporate management to (a) decide on the priorities for investing capital in the company's different businesses, (b) channel resources into areas where earnings potentials are higher and away from areas where they are lower, and (c) divest business units that are chronically poor performers or are in an increasingly unattractive industry. Divesting poor performers and businesses in unattractive industries frees up unproductive investments either for redeployment to promising business units or for financing attractive new acquisitions.

4. *Initiating actions to boost the combined performance of the corporation's collection of businesses.* Corporate strategists must craft moves to improve the overall performance of the corporation's business lineup and sustain increases in shareholder value. Strategic options for diversified corporations include (a) sticking closely with the existing business lineup and pursuing opportunities presented by these businesses, (b) broadening the scope of diversification by entering additional industries, (c) divesting some businesses and retrenching to a narrower collection of diversified businesses with better overall performance prospects, and (d) restructuring the entire company by divesting some businesses and acquiring others so as to put a whole new face on the company's business lineup.

The demanding and time-consuming nature of these four tasks explains why corporate executives generally refrain from becoming immersed in the details of crafting and executing business-level strategies, preferring instead to delegate lead responsibility for business strategy and business-level operations to the heads of each business unit.

In the first portion of this chapter we describe the various means a company can use to become diversified, and we explore the pros and cons of related versus unrelated diversification strategies. The second part of the chapter looks at how to evaluate the attractiveness of a diversified company's business lineup, decide whether the company has a good diversification strategy, and identify ways to improve its future performance. In the chapter's concluding section, we survey the strategic options open to already diversified companies.

WHEN TO DIVERSIFY

As long as a company has its hands full trying to capitalize on profitable growth opportunities in its present industry, there is no urgency to pursue diversification. But the opportunities for profitable growth are often limited in mature industries and declining markets. A company may also encounter diminishing market opportunities and stagnating sales if its industry becomes competitively unattractive and unprofitable. A company's growth prospects may dim quickly if demand for the industry's product is eroded by the appearance of alternative technologies, substitute products, or fast-shifting buyer preferences. Consider, for example, how digital cameras have virtually destroyed the business of companies dependent on making camera film and doing film processing, how iPods and other brands of digital music players (as well as online music stores) have affected the revenues

of retailers of music CDs, and how the mushrooming use of cell phones and Internet-based voice communication have diminished demand for landline-based telecommunication services and eroded the revenues of such once-dominant long-distance providers as AT&T, British Telecommunications, and NTT in Japan. Under conditions such as these, diversification into new industries always merits strong consideration—particularly if the resources and capabilities of a company can be employed more fruitfully in other industries.[1]

A company becomes a prime candidate for diversifying under the following four circumstances:[2]

1. When it spots opportunities for expanding into industries whose technologies and products complement its present business.

2. When it can leverage its collection of resources and capabilities by expanding into businesses where these resources and capabilities are valuable competitive assets.

3. When diversifying into additional businesses opens new avenues for reducing costs via cross-business sharing or transfer of competitively valuable resources and capabilities.

4. When it has a powerful and well-known brand name that can be transferred to the products of other businesses and thereby used as a lever for driving up the sales and profits of such businesses.

BUILDING SHAREHOLDER VALUE: THE ULTIMATE JUSTIFICATION FOR DIVERSIFYING

Diversification must do more for a company than simply spread its business risk across various industries. In principle, diversification cannot be considered a success unless it results in *added long-term economic value for shareholders*—value that shareholders cannot capture on their own by purchasing stock in companies in different industries or investing in mutual funds so as to spread their investments across several industries.

> **LO 1**
>
> Understand when and how business diversification can enhance shareholder value.

For there to be reasonable expectations of producing added long-term shareholder value, a move to diversify into a new business must pass three tests:[3]

1. *The industry attractiveness test.* The industry to be entered must be attractive enough to yield consistently good returns on investment. Whether an industry is attractive depends chiefly on the presence of industry and competitive conditions that are conducive to earning as-good or better profits and return on investment than the company is earning in its present business(es). It is hard to justify diversifying into an industry where profit expectations are *lower* than those in the company's present businesses.

2. *The cost-of-entry test.* The cost of entering the target industry must not be so high as to erode the potential for good profitability. Industry attractiveness is not a sufficient reason for a firm to diversify into an industry. In fact, the more attractive an industry's prospects are for growth and long-term profitability, the more expensive the industry can be to get into. Entry barriers for start-up companies are likely to be high in attractive industries; were barriers

low, a rush of new entrants would soon erode the potential for high profitability. And buying a well-positioned company in an appealing industry often entails a high acquisition cost that makes passing the cost-of-entry test less likely. Since the owners of a successful and growing company usually demand a price that reflects their business's profit prospects, it's easy for such an acquisition to fail the cost-of-entry test.

3. *The better-off test.* Diversifying into a new business must offer potential for the company's existing businesses and the new business to perform better together under a single corporate umbrella than they would perform operating as independent, stand-alone businesses—an effect known as **synergy.** For example, let's say that company A diversifies by purchasing company B in another industry. If A and B's consolidated profits in the years to come prove no greater than what each could have earned on its own, then A's diversification won't provide its shareholders with added value. Company A's shareholders could have achieved the same $1 + 1 = 2$ result by merely purchasing stock in company B. Diversification does not result in added long-term value for shareholders unless it produces a $1 + 1 = 3$ effect where the businesses *perform better together* as part of the same firm than they could have performed as independent companies.

Diversification moves must satisfy all three tests to grow shareholder value over the long term. Diversification moves that can pass only one or two tests are suspect.

STRATEGIES FOR ENTERING NEW BUSINESSES

The means of entering new businesses can take any of three forms: acquisition, internal start-up, or joint ventures with other companies.

Acquisition of an Existing Business

Acquisition is a popular means of diversifying into another industry. Not only is it quicker than trying to launch a brand-new operation, but it also offers an effective way to hurdle such entry barriers as acquiring technological know-how, establishing supplier relationships, becoming big enough to match rivals' unit costs, having to spend large sums on introductory advertising and promotions, and securing adequate distribution. Acquisitions are also commonly employed to access resources and capabilities that are complementary to those of the acquiring firm and that cannot be developed readily internally. Buying an ongoing operation allows the acquirer to move directly to the task of building a strong market position in the target industry, rather than getting bogged down in trying to develop the knowledge, experience, scale of operation, and market reputation necessary for a start-up entrant to become an effective competitor.

However, acquiring an existing business can prove quite expensive. The costs of acquiring another business include not only the acquisition price but also the costs of negotiating and completing the purchase transaction and the costs of integrating the business into the diversified company's portfolio. If the company to be acquired is a successful company, the acquisition price will include a hefty *premium* over the preacquisition value of the company. For example, the $5.8 billion that Xerox paid to acquire Affiliated Computer Services in 2010 included a 38 percent premium over the service company's market value.[4] Premiums are paid in order to convince the shareholders and managers of the target company that it is in their financial interests to approve the deal. The average premium in deals between U.S. companies rose to 56 percent in 2009, but it is more often in the 30 to 40 percent range.[5]

The big dilemma an acquisition-minded firm faces is whether to pay a premium price for a successful company or to buy a struggling company at a bargain price.[6] If the buying firm has little knowledge of the industry but ample capital, it is often better off purchasing a capable, strongly positioned firm—even if its current owners demand a premium price. However, when the acquirer sees promising ways to transform a weak firm into a strong one and has the resources, the know-how, and the patience to do it, a struggling company can be the better long-term investment.

While acquisitions offer an enticing means for entering a new business, many fail to deliver on their promise.[7] Realizing the potential gains from an acquisition requires a successful integration of the acquired company into the culture, systems, and structure of the acquiring firm. This can be a costly and time-consuming operation. Acquisitions can also fail to deliver long-term shareholder value if the acquirer overestimates the potential gains and pays a premium in excess of the realized gains. High integration costs and excessive price premiums are two reasons that an acquisition might fail the cost-of-entry test. Firms with significant experience in making acquisitions are better able to avoid these types of problems.[8]

> **CORE CONCEPT**
>
> An **acquisition premium** is the amount by which the price offered exceeds the preacquisition market value of the target company.

Internal Development

Internal development of new businesses has become an increasingly important means for companies to diversify and is often referred to as **corporate venturing** or *new venture development*. It involves building a new business from scratch. Although building a new business from the ground up is generally a time-consuming and uncertain process, it avoids the pitfalls associated with entry via acquisition and may allow the firm to realize greater profits in the end. It may offer a viable means of entering a new or emerging industry where there are no good acquisition candidates.

Entering a new business via internal development also poses some significant hurdles. An internal new venture not only has to overcome industry entry barriers but also has to invest in new production capacity, develop sources of supply, hire and train employees, build channels of distribution, grow a customer base, and so on. The risks associated with internal start-ups are substantial, and the likelihood of failure is often high. Moreover, the culture, structures, and organizational systems of some companies may impede innovation and make it difficult for corporate entrepreneurship to flourish.

Generally, internal development of a new business has appeal only when (1) the parent company already has in-house most or all of the skills and resources it needs to piece together a new business and compete effectively; (2) there is ample time to launch the business; (3) the internal cost of entry is lower than the cost of entry via acquisition; (4) the targeted industry is populated with many relatively

> **CORE CONCEPT**
>
> **Corporate venturing** (or *new venture development*) is the process of developing new businesses as an outgrowth of a company's established business operations. It is also referred to as *corporate entrepreneurship* or *intrapreneurship* since it requires entrepreneurial-like qualities within a larger enterprise.

small firms such that the new start-up does not have to compete head to head against larger, more powerful rivals; (5) adding new production capacity will not adversely impact the supply-demand balance in the industry; and (6) incumbent firms are likely to be slow or ineffective in responding to a new entrant's efforts to crack the market.[9]

Joint Ventures

Joint ventures entail forming a new business that is owned jointly by two or more companies. Entering a new business via joint venture can be useful in at least three types of situations.[10] First, a joint venture is a good vehicle for pursuing an opportunity that is too complex, uneconomical, or risky for one company to pursue alone. Second, joint ventures make sense when the opportunities in a new industry require a broader range of competencies and know-how than a company can marshal. Many of the opportunities in satellite-based telecommunications, biotechnology, and network-based systems that blend hardware, software, and services call for the coordinated development of complementary innovations and the tackling of an intricate web of financial, technical, political, and regulatory factors simultaneously. In such cases, pooling the resources and competencies of two or more companies is a wiser and less risky way to proceed. Third, companies sometimes use joint ventures to diversify into a new industry when the diversification move entails having operations in a foreign country—several governments require foreign companies operating within their borders to have a local partner that has minority, if not majority, ownership in the local operations. Aside from fulfilling host-government ownership requirements, companies usually seek out a local partner with expertise and other resources that will aid the success of the newly established local operation.

However, as discussed in Chapters 6 and 7, partnering with another company—in the form of either a joint venture or a collaborative alliance—has significant drawbacks due to the potential for conflicting objectives, disagreements over how to best operate the venture, culture clashes, and so on. Joint ventures are generally the least durable of the entry options, usually lasting only until the partners decide to go their own ways.

Choosing a Mode of Entry

The choice of how best to enter a new business—whether through internal development, acquisition, or joint venture—depends on the answers to four important questions:

- Does the company have all of the resources and capabilities it requires to enter the business through internal development or is it lacking some critical resources?
- Are there entry barriers to overcome?
- Is speed an important factor in the firm's chances for successful entry?
- Which is the least costly mode of entry, given the company's objectives?

The Question of Critical Resources and Capabilities   If a firm has all the resources it needs to start up a new business or will be able to easily purchase or lease any missing resources, it may choose to enter the business via internal development. However, if missing critical resources cannot be easily purchased or leased, a firm wishing to enter a new business must obtain these missing resources through either acquisition or joint venture. Bank of America acquired Merrill Lynch in 2008 to obtain critical investment banking resources and capabilities that it lacked. The acquisition of these additional capabilities complemented Bank of America's strengths in corporate banking and opened up new business opportunities for Bank of America. Firms often acquire other companies as a way to enter foreign markets where they lack local marketing knowledge, distribution capabilities, and relationships with local suppliers or customers. McDonald's acquisition of Burghy, Italy's only national hamburger chain, offers an example.[11] If there are no good acquisition opportunities or if the firm wants to avoid the high cost of acquiring and integrating another firm, it may choose to enter via joint venture. This type of entry mode has the added advantage of spreading the risk of entering a new business, which is particularly attractive when uncertainty is high. DeBeers's joint venture with the luxury goods company LVMH provided DeBeers with the complementary marketing capabilities it needed to enter the diamond retailing business, as well as partner to share the risk.

The Question of Entry Barriers The second question to ask is whether entry barriers would prevent a new entrant from gaining a foothold and succeeding in the industry. If entry barriers are low and the industry is populated by small firms, internal development may be the preferred mode of entry. If entry barriers are high, the company may still be able to enter with ease if it has the requisite resources and capabilities for overcoming high barriers. For example, entry barriers due to reputational advantages may be surmounted by a diversified company with a widely known and trusted corporate name. But if the entry barriers cannot be overcome readily, then the only feasible entry route may be through acquisition of a well-established company. While entry barriers may also be overcome with a strong complementary joint venture, this mode is the more uncertain choice due to the lack of industry experience.

The Question of Speed Speed is another determining factor in deciding how to go about entering a new business. Acquisition is a favored mode of entry when speed is of the essence, as is the case in rapidly changing industries where fast movers can secure long-term positioning advantages. Speed is important in industries where early movers gain experience-based advantages that grow ever larger over time as they move down the learning curve and in technology-based industries where there is a race to establish an industry standard or leading technological platform. But in other cases it can be better to enter a market after the uncertainties about technology or consumer preferences have been resolved and learn from the missteps of early entrants. In these cases, joint venture or internal development may be preferred.

The Question of Comparative Cost The question of which mode of entry is most cost-effective is a critical one, given the need for a diversification strategy to pass the cost-of-entry test. Acquisition can be a high-cost mode of entry due to the need to pay a premium over the share price of the target company. When the premium is high, the price of the deal will exceed the worth of the acquired company as a stand-alone business by a substantial amount. Moreover, the true cost of an acquisition must include the *transaction costs* of identifying and evaluating potential targets, negotiating a price, and completing other aspects of

Transaction costs are the costs of completing a business agreement or deal of some sort, over and above the price of the deal. They can include the costs of searching for an attractive target, the costs of evaluating its worth, bargaining costs, and the costs of completing the transaction.

deal making. In addition, the true cost must take into account the costs of integrating the acquired company into the parent company's portfolio of businesses.

Strategic alliances and other types of partnerships may provide a way to conserve on such entry costs. But even here, there are organizational coordination costs and transaction costs that must be considered, including settling on the terms of the arrangement. If the partnership doesn't proceed smoothly and is not founded on trust, these costs may be significant. In making the choice about how to proceed, the firm should also consider the possibility of even simpler arrangements. If the objective is simply to leverage a brand name and company logo, for example, a strategic alliance centered on licensing may be the lowest-cost alternative. Licensing is particularly attractive if the company lacks other resources and capabilities that are needed for an entry move. Harley-Davidson, for example, has chosen to license its brand name to makers of apparel as an alternative to entering the apparel industry, for which it is ill suited.

CHOOSING THE DIVERSIFICATION PATH: RELATED VERSUS UNRELATED BUSINESSES

Related businesses possess competitively valuable cross-business value chain and resource matchups; **unrelated businesses** have dissimilar value chains and resource requirements, with no competitively important cross-business relationships at the value chain level.

Once a company decides to diversify, it faces the choice of whether to diversify into **related businesses, unrelated businesses,** or some mix of both. Businesses are said to be *related* when their value chains exhibit competitively important cross-business relationships. By this, we mean that there is a close correspondence between the businesses in terms of how they perform *key* value chain activities and the resources and capabilities each needs to perform those activities. The big appeal of related diversification is to build shareholder value by leveraging these cross-business relationships into competitive advantages, thus allowing the company as a whole to perform better than just the sum of its individual businesses. Businesses are said to be *unrelated* when the resource requirements and key value chain activities are so dissimilar that no competitively important cross-business relationships exist.

The next two sections explore the ins and outs of related and unrelated diversification.

STRATEGIC FIT AND DIVERSIFICATION INTO RELATED BUSINESSES

A related diversification strategy involves building the company around businesses where there is *strategic fit with respect to key value chain activities and competitive assets.* **Strategic fit** exists whenever one or more activities constituting the value chains of different businesses are sufficiently similar as to present opportunities for cross-business sharing or transferring of the resources and capabilities that enable these activities.[12] Prime examples of such opportunities include:

LO 2

Gain an understanding of how related diversification strategies can produce cross-business strategic fit capable of delivering competitive advantage.

- *Transferring specialized expertise, technological know-how, or other competitively valuable capabilities from one business's value chain to another's.*
- *Combining the related value chain activities of separate businesses into a single operation to achieve lower costs.* For instance, it is often feasible to manufacture the products of different businesses in a single plant, use the same warehouses for shipping and distribution, or have a single sales force for the products of different businesses (because they are marketed to the same types of customers).
- *Exploiting common use of a well-known brand name that connotes excellence in a certain type of product range.* For example, Yamaha's name in motorcycles gave the company instant credibility and recognition in entering the personal-watercraft business, allowing it to achieve a significant market share without spending large sums on advertising to establish a brand identity for the WaveRunner. Sony's name in consumer electronics made it easier for Sony to enter the market for video games with its PlayStation console and lineup of PlayStation video games. Apple's well-known and highly popular iPods gave the firm instant credibility and name recognition in launching its iPhones and iPads.

CORE CONCEPT

Strategic fit exists when the value chains of different businesses present opportunities for cross-business resource transfer, lower costs through combining the performance of related value chain activities or resource sharing, cross-business use of a potent brand name, and cross-business collaboration to build stronger competitive capabilities.

- *Sharing other resources that support corresponding value chain activities of the businesses, such as relationships with suppliers or a dealer network.* After acquiring Marvel Comics in 2009, the Walt Disney Company saw to it that Marvel's iconic characters, such as Spiderman, Iron Man, and the Black Widow, were shared with many of the other Disney businesses, including its theme parks, retail stores, and video game business. (Disney's characters, starting with Mickey Mouse, have always been among the most valuable of its resources.)
- *Engaging in cross-business collaboration and knowledge sharing to create new competitively valuable resources and capabilities.*

Related diversification is based on value chain matchups with respect to *key* value chain activities—those that play a central role in each business's strategy and that link to its industry's key success factors. Such matchups facilitate the sharing or transfer of the competitively important resources and capabilities that enable the performance of these activities and underlie each business's quest for competitive advantage. By facilitating the sharing or transferring of such important competitive assets, related diversification can boost each business's prospects for competitive success.

The resources and capabilities that are leveraged in related diversification are *specialized resources and capabilities*. By this, we mean that they have very *specific* applications; their use is restricted to a limited range of business contexts in which these applications are competitively relevant. Because they are adapted for particular applications, specialized resources and capabilities must be utilized by certain kinds of businesses operating in specific types of industries to have value; they have limited utility outside this specific range of industry and business applications. This is in contrast to *generalized resources and capabilities* (such as general management capabilities, human resource management capabilities, and general accounting services), which can be applied usefully across a wide range of industry and business types.

L'Oréal is the world's largest beauty products company, with more than $25 billion in revenues and a successful strategy of related diversification built upon leveraging a highly specialized set of resources and capabilities. These include 18 dermatologic and cosmetic research centers, R&D capabilities and scientific knowledge concerning skin and hair care, patents and secret formulas for hair and skin care products, and robotic applications developed specifically for testing the safety of hair and skin care products. These resources and capabilities are highly valuable for businesses focused on products for human skin and hair—they are *specialized* to such applications, and, in consequence, they are of little or no value beyond this restricted range of applications. To leverage these resources in a way that maximizes their potential value, L'Oréal has diversified into cosmetics, hair care products, skin care products, and fragrances (but not food, transportation, industrial services, or any application area far from the narrow domain in which its specialized resources are competitively relevant). L'Oréal's businesses are related to one another on the basis of its value-generating specialized resources and capabilities and the cross-business linkages among the value chain activities that they enable.

Corning's most competitively valuable resources and capabilities are specialized to applications concerning fiber optics and specialty glass and ceramics. Over the course of its 150-year history, it has developed an unmatched understanding of fundamental glass science and related technologies in the field of optics. Its capabilities now span a variety of sophisticated technologies and include expertise in domains such as custom glass composition, specialty glass melting and forming, precision optics, high-end transmissive coatings, and opto-mechanical materials. Corning has leveraged these specialized capabilities into a position of global leadership in five related market segments: display technologies based on glass substrates, environmental technologies using ceramic substrates and filters, optical fibers and cables for telecommunications, optical biosensors for drug discovery, and specialty materials employing advanced optics and specialty glass solutions. The market segments into which Corning has diversified are all related by their reliance on Corning's specialized capability set and by the many value chain activities that they have in common as a result.

General Mills has diversified into a closely related set of food businesses on the basis of its capabilities in the realm of "kitchen chemistry" and food production technologies. Its businesses include General Mills cereals, Pillsbury and Betty Crocker baking products, yogurts, organic foods, dinner mixes, canned goods, and snacks. Earlier it had diversified into restaurant businesses on the mistaken notion that all food businesses were related. As a result of exiting these businesses in the mid-1990s, the company was able to improve its overall profitability and strengthen its position in its remaining businesses. The lesson from its experience—and a takeaway for the managers of any diversified company—is that it is not product relatedness that defines a well-crafted related diversification strategy. Rather, the businesses must be related in terms of their key value chain activities and the specialized resources and capabilities that enable these activities.[13] An example is Citizen Holdings Company, whose products appear to be different (watches, miniature card calculators, handheld televisions) but are related in terms of their common reliance on miniaturization know-how and advanced precision technologies.[14]

While companies pursuing related diversification strategies may also have opportunities to share or transfer their *generalized* resources and capabilities (e.g. information systems; human resource management practices; accounting and tax services; budgeting, planning, and financial reporting systems; expertise in legal and regulatory affairs; and fringe-benefit management systems), the most competitively valuable opportunities for resource sharing or transfer always come from leveraging their specialized resources and capabilities. The reason for this is that specialized resources and capabilities drive the key value-creating activities that both connect the businesses (at points where there is strategic fit) and link to the key success factors in the markets where they are competitively relevant. Figure 8.1 illustrates the range of opportunities to share and/or transfer specialized resources and capabilities among the value chain activities of related businesses. It is important to recognize that even though generalized resources and capabilities may be shared by multiple business units, such resource sharing alone cannot form the backbone of a strategy keyed to related diversification.

> **CORE CONCEPT**
>
> Related diversification involves sharing or transferring *specialized* resources and capabilities. **Specialized resources and capabilities** have very specific applications and their use is limited to a restricted range of industry and business types, in contrast to **generalized resources and capabilities** that can be widely applied and can be deployed across a broad range of industry and business types.

Figure 8.1 Related Businesses Provide Opportunities to Benefit from Competitively Valuable Strategic Fit

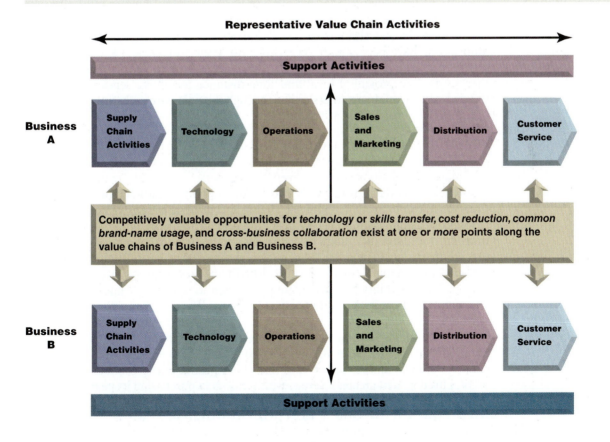

Identifying Cross-Business Strategic Fit along the Value Chain

Cross-business strategic fit can exist anywhere along the value chain—in R&D and technology activities, in supply chain activities and relationships with suppliers, in manufacturing, in sales and marketing, in distribution activities, or in customer service activities.[15]

Strategic Fit in Supply Chain Activities   Businesses that have strategic fit with respect to supply chain activities can perform better together because of the potential for skills transfer in procuring materials, the sharing of capabilities in logistics, the benefits of added collaboration with common supply chain partners, and/or added leverage with shippers in securing volume discounts on incoming parts and components. Dell Computer's strategic partnerships with leading suppliers of microprocessors, circuit boards, disk drives, memory chips, flat-panel displays, wireless capabilities, long-life batteries, and other PC-related components have been an important element of the company's strategy to diversify into servers, data storage devices, networking components, and LCD TVs—products that include many components common to PCs and that can be sourced from the same strategic partners that provide Dell with PC components.

Strategic Fit in R&D and Technology Activities   Businesses with technology-sharing benefits can perform better together than apart because of potential cost savings in R&D, potentially shorter times in getting new products to market, and more innovative products or processes. Moreover, technological advances in one business can lead to increased sales for both. Technological innovations have been the driver behind the efforts of cable TV companies to diversify into high-speed Internet access (via the use of cable modems) and, further, to explore providing local and long-distance telephone service to residential and commercial customers either through a single wire or by means of VoIP (voice over Internet protocol) technology.

Manufacturing-Related Strategic Fit   Cross-business strategic fit in manufacturing-related activities can represent an important source of competitive advantage in situations where a diversifier's expertise in quality manufacture and cost-efficient production methods can be transferred to another business. When Emerson Electric diversified into the chain-saw business, it transferred its expertise in low-cost manufacture to its newly acquired Beaird-Poulan business division; the transfer drove Beaird-Poulan's new strategy—to be the low-cost provider of chain-saw products—and fundamentally changed the way Beaird-Poulan chain saws were designed and manufactured. Another benefit of production-related value chain matchups is the ability to consolidate production into a smaller number of plants and significantly reduce overall production costs. When snowmobile maker Bombardier diversified into motorcycles, it was able to set up motorcycle assembly lines in the same manufacturing facility where it was assembling snowmobiles. When Smucker's acquired Procter & Gamble's Jif peanut butter business, it was able to combine the manufacture of its own Smucker's peanut butter products with those of Jif, plus it gained greater leverage with vendors in purchasing its peanut supplies.

Strategic Fit in Sales and Marketing Activities   Various cost-saving opportunities spring from diversifying into businesses with closely related sales and marketing activities. When the products are sold directly to the same customers, sales costs can often be reduced by using a single sales force and avoiding having two different salespeople call on the same customer. The products of related businesses can be promoted at the same Web site and included in the same media ads and sales brochures. After-sale service and repair organizations for the products of closely related businesses can often be consolidated into a single operation. There may be opportunities to reduce costs by consolidating order processing and billing and using common promotional tie-ins. When global power-tool maker Black & Decker acquired Vector Products, it was able to use its own global sales force and distribution facilities to sell and distribute the newly acquired Vector power inverters, vehicle battery chargers, and rechargeable spotlights because the types of customers that carried its power tools (discounters like Walmart and Target, home centers, and hardware stores) also stocked the types of products produced by Vector.

A second category of benefits arises when different businesses use similar sales and marketing approaches; in such cases, there may be competitively valuable opportunities to transfer selling, merchandising, advertising, and product differentiation skills from one business to another. Procter & Gamble's product lineup includes Folgers coffee, Tide laundry detergent, Crest toothpaste, Ivory soap, Charmin toilet tissue, Gillette razors and blades, Duracell batteries, Oral-B toothbrushes, and Head & Shoulders shampoo. All of these have different competitors and different supply chain and production requirements, but they all move through the same wholesale distribution systems, are sold in common retail settings to the same shoppers, are advertised and promoted in much the same ways, and require the same marketing and merchandising skills.

Distribution-Related Strategic Fit Businesses with closely related distribution activities can perform better together than apart because of potential cost savings in sharing the same distribution facilities or using many of the same wholesale distributors and retail dealers to access customers. When Conair Corporation acquired Allegro Manufacturing's travel bag and travel accessory business in 2007, it was able to consolidate its own distribution centers for hair dryers and curling irons with those of Allegro, thereby generating cost savings for both businesses. Likewise, since Conair products and Allegro's neck rests, ear plugs, luggage tags, and toiletry kits were sold by the same types of retailers (discount stores, supermarket chains, and drugstore chains), Conair was able to convince many of the retailers not carrying Allegro products to take on the line.

Strategic Fit in Customer Service Activities Opportunities for cost savings from sharing resources or for greater differentiation through skills transfer can come from strategic fit with respect to customer service activities, just as they do along other points of the value chain. For example, cost savings may come from consolidating after-sale service and repair organizations for the products of closely related businesses into a single operation. Likewise, different businesses can often use the same customer service infrastructure. For instance, an electric utility that diversifies into natural gas, water, appliance sales and repair services, and home security services can use the same customer data network, the same customer call centers and local offices, the same billing and customer accounting systems, and the same customer service infrastructure to support all of its products and services. Through the transfer of best practices in customer service across a set of related businesses or through sharing resources such as proprietary information about customer preferences, a multibusiness company can create a differentiation advantage through higher-quality customer service.

Strategic Fit, Economies of Scope, and Competitive Advantage

What makes related diversification an attractive strategy is the opportunity to convert cross-business strategic fit into a competitive advantage over business rivals whose operations do not offer comparable strategic-fit benefits. The greater the relatedness among a diversified company's businesses, the bigger a company's window for converting strategic fit into competitive advantage via (1) transferring skills or knowledge, (2) combining related value chain activities to achieve lower costs, (3) leveraging the use of a well-respected brand name or other differentiation-enhancing resources, and (4) using cross-business collaboration and knowledge sharing to create new resources and capabilities and drive innovation.

The Path to Competitive Advantage and Economies of Scope

Sharing or transferring valuable specialized assets among the company's businesses can help each business perform its value chain activities more proficiently. This translates into competitive advantage for the businesses in one or two basic ways: (1) The businesses can contribute to greater efficiency and lower costs relative to their competitors, and/or (2) they can provide a basis for differentiation so that customers are willing to pay relatively more for the businesses' goods and services. In either or both of these ways, a firm with a well-executed related diversification strategy can boost the chances of its businesses attaining a competitive advantage.

Related businesses often present opportunities to eliminate or reduce the costs of performing certain value chain activities; such cost savings are termed **economies of scope**—a concept distinct from *economies of scale.* Economies of *scale* are cost savings that accrue directly from a larger-size operation; for example, unit costs may be lower in a large plant than in a small plant, lower in a large distribution center than in a small one, lower for large-volume purchases of network advertising than for small-volume purchases. Economies of *scope,* however, stem directly from resource sharing, facilitated by strategic fit along the value chains of related businesses. Such economies are open only to a multibusiness enterprise that enables its businesses to share technology, perform R&D together, use common manufacturing or distribution facilities, share a common sales force or distributor-dealer network, use the same established brand name, and/or share other commonly employed resources and capabilities. *The greater the cross-business economies associated with resource sharing and strategic fit, the greater the potential for a related diversification strategy to yield a competitive advantage based on lower costs than those of rivals.*

From Competitive Advantage to Added Profitability and Gains in Shareholder Value

The competitive advantage potential that flows from economies of scope and the capture of other strategic-fit benefits is what enables a company pursuing related diversification to achieve $1 + 1 = 3$ financial performance and the hoped-for gains in shareholder value. The strategic and business logic is compelling: Capturing the benefits of strategic fit along the value chains of its related businesses gives a diversified company a clear path to achieving competitive advantage over undiversified competitors and competitors whose own diversification efforts don't offer equivalent strategic-fit benefits.[16] Such competitive advantage potential provides a company with a dependable basis for earning profits and a return on investment that exceeds what the company's businesses could earn as stand-alone enterprises. Converting the competitive advantage potential into greater profitability is what fuels $1 + 1 = 3$ gains in shareholder value—the necessary outcome for satisfying the better-off test and proving the business merit of a company's diversification effort.

There are four things to bear in mind here:

1. Capturing cross-business strategic-fit benefits via a strategy of related diversification builds shareholder value in ways that shareholders cannot undertake by simply owning a portfolio of stocks of companies in different industries.
2. The capture of cross-business strategic-fit benefits is possible only via a strategy of related diversification.
3. The benefits of cross-business strategic fit come from the transferring or sharing of competitively valuable resources and capabilities among the businesses—resources and capabilities that are *specialized* to certain applications and have value only in specific types of industries and businesses.
4. The benefits of cross-business strategic fit are not automatically realized when a company diversifies into related businesses; *the benefits materialize only after management has successfully pursued internal actions to capture them.*

> Diversifying into related businesses where competitively valuable strategic-fit benefits can be captured puts a company's businesses in position to perform better financially as part of the company than they could have performed as independent enterprises, thus providing a clear avenue for boosting shareholder value.

DIVERSIFICATION INTO UNRELATED BUSINESSES

An unrelated diversification strategy discounts the merits of pursuing cross-business strategic fit and, instead, focuses squarely on entering and operating businesses in industries that allow the company as a whole to increase its earnings. Companies that pursue a strategy of unrelated diversification generally exhibit a willingness to diversify into *any industry* where senior managers see an opportunity to realize consistently good financial results. Such companies are frequently labeled *conglomerates* because their business interests range broadly across diverse industries. Companies that pursue unrelated diversification nearly always enter new businesses by acquiring an established company rather than by forming a start-up subsidiary within their own corporate structures or participating in joint ventures.

With a strategy of unrelated diversification, the emphasis is on satisfying the attractiveness and cost-of-entry tests and each business's prospects for good financial performance. Thus, with an unrelated diversification strategy, company managers spend much time and effort screening acquisition candidates and evaluating the pros and cons of keeping or divesting existing businesses, using such criteria as:

LO 3

Become aware of the merits and risks of corporate strategies keyed to unrelated diversification.

- Whether the business can meet corporate targets for profitability and return on investment.
- Whether the business is in an industry with attractive growth potential.
- Whether the business is big enough to contribute *significantly* to the parent firm's bottom line.

But the key to successful unrelated diversification is to go beyond these considerations and ensure that the strategy passes the better-off test as well. This test requires more than just growth in revenues; it requires *growth in profits*—beyond what could be achieved by a mutual fund or a holding company that owns the businesses without adding any value. Unless the different businesses are more profitable together under the corporate umbrella than they are apart as independent businesses, *the strategy cannot create economic value for shareholders.* And unless it does so, there is *no real justification for unrelated diversification,* since top executives have a fiduciary responsibility to maximize long-term shareholder value.

Building Shareholder Value via Unrelated Diversification

Given the absence of cross-business strategic fit with which to create competitive advantages, building economic shareholder value via unrelated diversification ultimately hinges on the ability of the parent company to improve its businesses via other means. Critical to this endeavor is the role that the parent company plays *as a corporate parent.* To the extent that a company has strong *parenting capabilities*—capabilities that involve nurturing, guiding, grooming, and governing constituent businesses—a corporate parent can propel its businesses forward and help them gain ground over their market rivals. Corporate parents also contribute to the competitiveness of their unrelated businesses by sharing or transferring *generalized resources and capabilities* across the businesses—competitive assets that have utility in any type of industry and that can be leveraged across a wide range of business types as a result. Examples of the kinds of generalized resources that a corporate parent leverages in unrelated diversification include the corporation's reputation, credit rating, and access to financial markets; governance mechanisms; a corporate ethics program; a central data and communications center; shared administrative resources such as public relations and legal services; and common systems for functions such as budgeting, financial reporting, and quality control.

The three principal ways in which a parent company can further the prospects of its unrelated businesses and increase long-term economic shareholder value are discussed below.

Astute Corporate Parenting   An effective way for a diversified company to improve the performance of its otherwise unrelated businesses is through astute corporate parenting. *Corporate parenting* refers to the role that a diversified corporation plays in nurturing its component businesses through the provision of top management expertise, disciplined control, financial resources, and other types of generalized resources and capabilities such as long-term planning systems, business development skills, management development processes, and incentive systems.[17]

One of the most important ways that corporate parents contribute to the success of their businesses is by offering high-level oversight and guidance.[18] The top executives of a large diversified corporation have among them many years of accumulated experience in a variety of business settings and can often contribute expert problem-solving skills, creative strategy suggestions, and first-rate advice and guidance on how to improve competitiveness and financial performance to the heads of the company's various business subsidiaries; this is especially true in the case of newly acquired businesses. Particularly astute high-level guidance from corporate executives can help the subsidiaries perform better than they would otherwise be able to do through the efforts of the business-unit heads alone.[19]

The outstanding leadership of Royal Little, the founder of Textron, was a major reason that the company became an exemplar of the unrelated diversification strategy while he was CEO. Little's bold moves transformed the company from its origins as a small textile manufacturer into a global powerhouse known for its Bell helicopters, Cessna aircraft, and host of other strong brands in a wide array of industries. Norm Wesley, CEO of the conglomerate Fortune Brands from 1999 to 2007, is similarly credited with driving the sharp rise in the company's stock price while he was at the helm. Fortune Brands is now the $7 billion maker of products ranging from spirits (e.g., Jim Beam bourbon and rye, Gilbey's gin and vodka, Courvoisier cognac) to golf products (e.g., Titleist golf balls and clubs, FootJoy golf shoes and apparel, Scotty Cameron putters) to hardware (e.g., Moen faucets, American Lock security devices, Therma-Tru doors).

Corporate parents can also create added value for their businesses by providing them with other types of generalized or parenting resources that lower the operating costs of the individual businesses or that enhance their operating effectiveness. The administrative resources located at a company's corporate headquarters are a prime example. They typically include legal services, accounting expertise and tax services, and other elements of the administrative infrastructure, such as risk management capabilities, information technology resources, and resources concerning public relations and corporate communications. Providing individual business with such types of generalized and support resources and capabilities creates value by lowering companywide overhead costs, since each business would otherwise have to duplicate the centralized activities.

Corporate brands that do not connote any specific type of product are another type of generalized corporate resource that can be shared among unrelated businesses. GE's brand is an example, having been applied to businesses as diverse as financial services (GE Capital), medical imaging (GE medical diagnostics), and lighting (GE lightbulbs). Corporate brands that are applied in this fashion are sometimes called *umbrella brands*. Utilizing a well-known corporate name (GE) in a diversified company's individual businesses has potential not only to lower costs (by spreading the fixed cost of developing and maintaining the brand over many businesses) but also to enhance each business's customer value proposition by linking its products to a name that consumers trust. In similar fashion, a corporation's reputation for well-crafted products, for product reliability, or for trustworthiness can lead to greater customer willingness to purchase the products of a wider range of a diversified company's businesses. Incentive systems, financial control systems, and a company's culture are other types of generalized corporate resources that may prove useful in enhancing the daily operations of a diverse set of businesses.

Judicious Cross-Business Allocation of Financial Resources

Widely diversified firms may also be able to create added value by serving as an internal capital market and allocating surplus cash flows from some businesses to fund the capital requirements of other businesses. This can be particularly important when interest rates are high or credit is unusually tight (such as in the wake of the worldwide banking crisis that began in 2008) or in economies with less well developed capital markets. Under these conditions, an unrelated diversifier with strong financial resources can add value by shifting funds from business units generating excess cash (more than they need to fund their own operating requirements and new capital investment opportunities) to other, cash-short businesses with appealing growth prospects. A parent company's ability to function as its own internal capital market enhances overall corporate performance and boosts shareholder value to the extent that its top managers have better access to information about investment opportunities internal to the firm than do external financiers and can avoid the costs of external borrowing.

Acquiring and Restructuring Undervalued Companies

One way for parent companies to add value to unrelated businesses is by acquiring weakly performing companies at a bargain price and then *restructuring* their operations (and perhaps their strategies) in ways that produce sometimes dramatic increases in profitability. **Restructuring** refers to overhauling and streamlining the operations of a business—combining plants with excess capacity, selling off redundant or underutilized assets, reducing unnecessary expenses, revamping its product offerings, instituting new sales and marketing approaches, consolidating administrative functions to reduce overhead costs, instituting new financial controls and accounting systems, and otherwise improving the operating efficiency and profitability of a company. Restructuring sometimes involves transferring seasoned managers to the newly acquired business, either to replace the top layers of management or to step in temporarily until the business is returned to profitability or is well on its way to becoming a major market contender.

Restructuring is often undertaken when a diversified company acquires a new business that is performing well below levels that the corporate parent believes are achievable. Diversified companies that have capabilities in restructuring (sometimes called *turnaround capabilities*) are often able to significantly boost the performance of weak businesses in a relatively wide range of industries. Newell Rubbermaid (whose diverse product line includes Sharpie pens, Levolor window treatments, Bernzomatic propane torches, Goody hair accessories, Aprica strollers and car seats, Calphalon cookware, and Lenox power and hand tools) developed such a strong set of turnaround capabilities that the company was said to "Newellize" the businesses it acquired.

Successful unrelated diversification strategies based on restructuring require the parent company to have considerable expertise in identifying underperforming target companies and in negotiating attractive acquisition prices so that each acquisition passes the cost-of-entry test. The capabilities in this regard of Lords James Hanson and Gordon White, who headed up the storied British conglomerate Hanson Trust, played a large part in Hanson's impressive record of profitability through the early 1990s.

The Path to Greater Shareholder Value through Unrelated Diversification

For a strategy of unrelated diversification to produce companywide financial results above and beyond what the businesses could generate operating as stand-alone entities, corporate executives must:

- Do a superior job of diversifying into new businesses that can produce consistently good earnings and returns on investment (to satisfy the attractiveness test).
- Do an excellent job of negotiating favorable acquisition prices (to satisfy the cost-of-entry test).
- Do a superior job of corporate parenting via high-level managerial oversight and resource sharing, financial resource allocation and portfolio management, or restructuring underperforming businesses (to satisfy the better-off test).

The best corporate parents understand the nature and value of the kinds of resources at their command and know how to leverage them effectively across their businesses. Those that are able to create more value in their businesses than other diversified companies have what is called a **parenting advantage**.[20] When a corporation has a parenting advantage, its top executives have the best chance of being able to craft and execute an unrelated diversification strategy that can satisfy all three tests and truly enhance long-term economic shareholder value.

The Drawbacks of Unrelated Diversification

Unrelated diversification strategies have two important negatives that undercut the pluses: very demanding managerial requirements and limited competitive advantage potential.

Demanding Managerial Requirements Successfully managing a set of fundamentally different businesses operating in fundamentally different industry and competitive environments is a very challenging and exceptionally difficult proposition.[21] Consider, for example, that corporations like General Electric and Berkshire Hathaway have dozens of business subsidiaries making hundreds and sometimes thousands of products. While headquarters executives can glean information about the industry from third-party sources, ask lots of questions when making occasional visits to the operations of the different businesses, and do their best to learn about the company's different businesses, they still remain heavily dependent on briefings from business-unit heads and on "managing by the numbers"—that is, keeping a close track on the financial and operating results of each subsidiary. Managing by the numbers works well enough when business conditions are normal and the heads of the various business units are capable of consistently meeting their numbers. But the problem comes when things start to go awry in a business due to exceptional circumstances and corporate management has to get deeply involved in the problems of a business it does not know all that much about. Because every business tends to encounter rough sledding at some juncture, unrelated diversification is thus a somewhat risky strategy from a managerial perspective.[22] Just one or two unforeseen problems or big strategic mistakes (like misjudging the importance of certain competitive forces, not recognizing that a newly acquired business has some serious resource deficiencies and/or competitive shortcomings, or being too optimistic about turning around a struggling subsidiary) can cause a precipitous drop in corporate earnings and crash the parent company's stock price.

Hence, competently overseeing a set of widely diverse businesses can turn out to be much harder than it sounds. In practice, comparatively few companies have proved that they have top management capabilities that are up to the task. There are far more companies whose corporate executives have failed at delivering consistently good financial results with an unrelated diversification strategy than there are companies with corporate executives who have been successful.[23] Unless a company truly has a parenting advantage, the odds are that the result of unrelated diversification will be 1 + 1 = 2 or less.

Limited Competitive Advantage Potential The second big negative is that *unrelated diversification offers a limited potential for competitive advantage beyond what each individual business can generate on its own.* Unlike

> **CORE CONCEPT**
>
> A diversified company has a **parenting advantage** when it is more able than other companies to boost the combined performance of its individual businesses through high-level guidance, general oversight, and other corporate-level contributions.

> Relying solely on the expertise of corporate executives to wisely manage a set of unrelated businesses is *a much weaker foundation for enhancing shareholder value* than is a strategy of related diversification.

a related diversification strategy, unrelated diversification provides no cross-business strategic-fit benefits that allow each business to perform its key value chain activities in a more efficient and effective manner. A cash-rich corporate parent pursuing unrelated diversification can provide its subsidiaries with much-needed capital, may achieve economies of scope in activities relying on generalized corporate resources, and may even offer some managerial know-how to help resolve problems in particular business units, but otherwise it has little to offer in the way of enhancing the competitive strength of its individual business units. In comparison to the highly specialized resources that facilitate related diversification, the generalized resources that support unrelated diversification tend to be relatively low value, for the simple reason that they are more common. Unless they are of exceptionally high quality (such as GE's world-renowned general management capabilities), resources and capabilities that are generalized in nature are less likely to provide a source of competitive advantage for diversified companies. *Without the competitive advantage potential of strategic fit in strategically important value chain activities, consolidated performance of an unrelated group of businesses stands to be little more than the sum of what the individual business units could achieve if they were independent, in most circumstances.*

Inadequate Reasons for Pursuing Unrelated Diversification

When firms pursue an unrelated diversification strategy for the wrong reasons, the odds are that the result will be $1 + 1 = 2$ or less. Rationales for unrelated diversification that are not likely to increase shareholder value include the following:

- *Risk reduction.* Managers sometimes pursue unrelated diversification in order to reduce risk by spreading the company's investments over a set of truly diverse industries whose technologies and markets are largely disconnected. But this cannot create long-term shareholder value since the company's shareholders can more flexibly (and more efficiently) reduce their exposure to risk by investing in a diversified portfolio of stocks and bonds.
- *Growth.* While unrelated diversification may enable a company to achieve rapid or continuous growth, firms that pursue growth for growth's sake are unlikely to maximize shareholder value. While growth can bring more attention and prestige to a firm from greater visibility and higher industry rankings, only profitable growth—the kind that comes from creating added value for shareholders—can justify a strategy of unrelated diversification.
- *Stabilization.* In a broadly diversified company, there's a chance that market downtrends in some of the company's businesses will be partially offset by cyclical upswings in its other businesses, thus producing somewhat less earnings volatility. In actual practice, however, there's no convincing evidence that the consolidated profits of firms with unrelated diversification strategies are more stable or less subject to reversal in periods of recession and economic stress than the profits of firms with related diversification strategies.
- *Managerial motives.* Unrelated diversification can provide benefits to managers such as higher compensation (which tends to increase with firm size and degree of diversification) and reduced employment risk. Diversification for these reasons is far more likely to reduce shareholder value than to increase it.

Because unrelated diversification strategies *at their best* have only a limited potential for creating long-term economic value for shareholders, it is essential that managers not compound this problem by taking a misguided approach toward unrelated diversification, in pursuit of objectives that are more likely to destroy shareholder value than create it.

COMBINATION RELATED-UNRELATED DIVERSIFICATION STRATEGIES

There's nothing to preclude a company from diversifying into both related and unrelated businesses. Indeed, in actual practice the business makeup of diversified companies varies considerably. Some diversified companies are really *dominant-business enterprises*—one major "core" business accounts for 50 to 80 percent of total revenues and a collection of small related or unrelated businesses accounts for the remainder. Some diversified companies are *narrowly diversified* around a few (two to five) related or unrelated businesses. Others are *broadly diversified* around a wide-ranging collection of related businesses, unrelated businesses, or a mixture of both. And a number of multibusiness enterprises have diversified into unrelated areas but have a collection of related businesses within each area—thus giving them a business portfolio consisting of *several unrelated groups of related businesses.* There's ample room for companies to customize their diversification strategies to incorporate elements of both related and unrelated diversification, as may suit their own competitive asset profile and strategic vision. *Combination related-unrelated diversification strategies have particular appeal for companies with a mix of valuable competitive assets, covering the spectrum from generalized to specialized resources and capabilities.*

Figure 8.2 shows the range of alternatives for companies pursuing diversification.

EVALUATING THE STRATEGY OF A DIVERSIFIED COMPANY

Strategic analysis of diversified companies builds on the concepts and methods used for single-business companies. But there are some additional aspects to consider and a couple of new analytical tools to master. The procedure for evaluating the pluses and minuses of a diversified company's strategy and deciding what actions to take to improve the company's performance involves six steps:

1. Assessing the attractiveness of the industries the company has diversified into, both individually and as a group.
2. Assessing the competitive strength of the company's business units and determining which are strong contenders in their respective industries.

LO 4

Gain command of the analytical tools for evaluating a company's diversification strategy.

Figure 8.2   **Strategy Alternatives for a Company Pursuing Diversification**

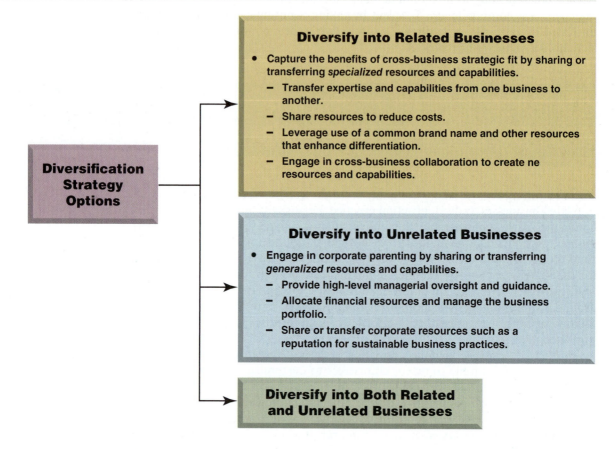

3. Checking the competitive advantage potential of cross-business strategic fit among the company's various business units.

4. Checking whether the firm's resources fit the requirements of its present business lineup.

5. Ranking the performance prospects of the businesses from best to worst and determining what the corporate parent's priority should be in allocating resources to its various businesses.

6. Crafting new strategic moves to improve overall corporate performance.

The core concepts and analytical techniques underlying each of these steps merit further discussion.

Step 1: Evaluating Industry Attractiveness

A principal consideration in evaluating a diversified company's business makeup and the caliber of its strategy is the attractiveness of the industries in which it has business operations. Answers to several questions are required:

1. *Does each industry the company has diversified into represent a good market for the company to be in?* Ideally, each industry in which the firm operates will pass the attractiveness test.

2. *Which of the company's industries are most attractive, and which are least attractive?* Comparing the attractiveness of the industries and ranking them

from most to least attractive is a prerequisite to wise allocation of corporate resources across the various businesses.

3. *How appealing is the whole group of industries in which the company has invested?* The answer to this question points to whether the group of industries holds promise for attractive growth and profitability. A company whose revenues and profits come chiefly from businesses in relatively unattractive industries probably needs to look at divesting businesses in unattractive industries and entering industries that qualify as highly attractive.

The more attractive the industries (both individually and as a group) a diversified company is in, the better its prospects for good long-term performance.

Calculating Industry Attractiveness Scores for Each Industry into Which the Company Has Diversified
A simple and reliable analytical tool involves calculating quantitative industry attractiveness scores, which can then be used to gauge each industry's attractiveness, rank the industries from most to least attractive, and make judgments about the attractiveness of all the industries as a group.

Assessing industry attractiveness involves a consideration of the conditions of each business's macro-environment as well as its competitive environment—the very same factors that are used to evaluate the strategy of a single-business company, as discussed in Chapter 3. Key indicators of industry attractiveness thus include:

- Social, political, regulatory, and environmental factors
- Seasonal and cyclical factors
- Industry uncertainty and business risk
- Market size and projected growth rate
- Industry profitability
- The intensity of competition (five forces)
- Emerging opportunities and threats

In addition, it is critically important to consider those aspects of industry attractiveness that pertain *specifically* to a company's diversification strategy. This involves looking at all the industries in which the company has invested to assess their resource requirements and to consider whether there is good cross-industry strategic fit. The following measures are typically used to gauge industry attractiveness from this multibusiness perspective:

- *The presence of cross-industry strategic fit.* The more an industry's value chain and resource requirements match up well with the value chain activities of other industries in which the company has operations, the more attractive the industry is to a firm pursuing related diversification.
- *Resource requirements.* Industries having resource requirements that match those of the parent company or are otherwise within the company's reach are more attractive than industries in which capital and other resource requirements could strain corporate financial resources and organizational capabilities.

After a set of attractiveness measures that suit a diversified company's circumstances has been identified, each attractiveness measure is assigned a weight reflecting its relative importance in determining an industry's attractiveness—it is weak methodology to assume that the various attractiveness measures are equally important. The intensity of competition in an industry should nearly always carry a high weight (say, 0.20 to 0.30). Strategic-fit considerations should be assigned a high weight in the case of companies with related diversification strategies; but for companies with an unrelated diversification strategy, strategic fit with other industries may be dropped from the list of attractiveness measures altogether. The importance weights must add up to 1.

Next, each industry is rated on each of the chosen industry attractiveness measures, using a rating scale of 1 to 10 (where a *high* rating signifies *high* attractiveness and a *low* rating signifies *low* attractiveness). *Keep in mind here that the more intensely competitive an industry is, the lower the attractiveness rating for that industry.* Likewise, the more the resource requirements associated with being in a particular industry are beyond the parent company's reach, the lower the attractiveness rating. On the other hand, the presence of good cross-industry strategic fit should be given a very high attractiveness rating, since there is good potential for competitive advantage and added shareholder value. Weighted attractiveness scores are then calculated by multiplying the industry's rating on each measure by the corresponding weight. For example, a rating of 8 times a weight of 0.25 gives a weighted attractiveness score of 2.00. The sum of the weighted scores for all the attractiveness measures provides an overall industry attractiveness score. This procedure is illustrated in Table 8.1.

Interpreting the Industry Attractiveness Scores Industries with a score much below 5 probably do not pass the attractiveness test. If a company's industry attractiveness scores are all above 5, it is probably fair to conclude that the group of industries the company operates in is attractive as a whole. But the group of industries takes on a decidedly lower degree of attractiveness as the number of industries with scores below 5 increases, especially if industries with low scores account for a sizable fraction of the company's revenues.

Table 8.1   Calculating Weighted Industry Attractiveness Scores*

Industry Attractiveness Measure	Importance Weight	Industry A Rating/ Score	Industry B Rating/ Score	Industry C Rating/ Score	Industry D Rating/ Score
Market size and projected growth rate	0.10	8/0.80	5/0.50	7/0.70	3/0.30
Intensity of competition	0.25	8/2.00	7/1.75	3/0.75	2/0.50
Emerging opportunities and threats	0.10	2/0.20	9/0.90	4/0.40	5/0.50
Cross-industry strategic fit	0.20	8/1.60	4/0.80	8/1.60	2/0.40
Resource requirements	0.10	9/0.90	7/0.70	10/1.00	5/0.50
Seasonal and cyclical influences	0.05	9/0.45	8/0.40	10/0.50	5/0.25
Societal, political, regulatory, and environmental factors	0.05	10/0.50	7/0.35	7/0.35	3/0.15
Industry profitability	0.10	5/0.50	10/1.00	3/0.30	3/0.30
Industry uncertainty and business risk	0.05	5/0.25	7/0.35	10/0.50	1/0.05
Sum of the assigned weights	1.00				
Overall weighted industry attractiveness scores		**7.20**	**6.75**	**5.10**	**2.95**

*Rating scale: 1 = very unattractive to company; 10 = very attractive to company.

For a diversified company to be a strong performer, a substantial portion of its revenues and profits must come from business units with relatively high attractiveness scores. It is particularly important that a diversified company's principal businesses be in industries with a good outlook for growth and above-average profitability. Having a big fraction of the company's revenues and profits come from industries with slow growth, low profitability, or intense competition tends to drag overall company performance down. Business units in the least attractive industries are potential candidates for divestiture, unless they are positioned strongly enough to overcome the unattractive aspects of their industry environments or they are a strategically important component of the company's business makeup.

The Difficulties of Calculating Industry Attractiveness Scores
There are two hurdles to using this method of evaluating industry attractiveness. One is deciding on appropriate weights for the industry attractiveness measures, since they have a subjective component; different analysts may have different views about which weights are appropriate for the different attractiveness measures. The second hurdle is gaining sufficient command of the industry to assign more accurate and objective ratings. Generally, a company can come up with the statistical data needed to compare its industries on such factors as market size, growth rate, seasonal and cyclical influences, and industry profitability. Cross-industry fit and resource requirements are also fairly easy to judge. But the attractiveness measure on which judgment weighs most heavily is intensity of competition. It is not always easy to conclude whether competition in one industry is stronger or weaker than in another industry because of the different types of competitive influences that prevail and the differences in their relative importance. In the event that the available information is too skimpy to confidently assign a rating value to an industry on a particular attractiveness measure, then it is usually best to use a score of 5, which avoids biasing the overall attractiveness score either up or down.

But despite the hurdles, calculating industry attractiveness scores is a systematic and reasonably reliable method for ranking a diversified company's industries from most to least attractive—numbers like those shown for the four industries in Table 8.1 help pin down the basis for judging which industries are more attractive and to what degree.

Step 2: Evaluating Business-Unit Competitive Strength

The second step in evaluating a diversified company is to appraise how strongly positioned each of its business units is in its respective industry. Doing an appraisal of each business unit's strength and competitive position in its industry not only reveals its chances for industry success but also provides a basis for ranking the units from competitively strongest to competitively weakest and sizing up the competitive strength of all the business units as a group.

Calculating Competitive Strength Scores for Each Business Unit
Quantitative measures of each business unit's competitive strength can be calculated using a procedure similar to that for measuring industry attractiveness.

The following factors are used in quantifying the competitive strengths of a diversified company's business subsidiaries:

- Relative market share. A business unit's *relative market share* is defined as the ratio of its market share to the market share held by the largest rival firm in the industry, with market share measured in unit volume, not dollars. A 10 percent market share, for example, does not signal much competitive strength if the leader's share is 50 percent (a 0.20 relative market share), but a 10 percent share is actually quite strong if the leader's share is only 12 percent (a 0.83 relative market share)—this why a company's relative market share is a better measure of competitive strength than a company's market share based on either dollars or unit volume.
- Costs relative to competitors' costs.
- Ability to match or beat rivals on key product attributes.
- Brand image and reputation.
- Other competitively valuable resources and capabilities.
- Ability to benefit from strategic fit with the company's other businesses.
- Ability to exercise bargaining leverage with key suppliers or customers.
- Caliber of alliances and collaborative partnerships with suppliers and/or buyers.
- Profitability relative to competitors. Above-average profitability is a signal of competitive advantage, while below-average profitability usually denotes competitive disadvantage.

After settling on a set of competitive strength measures that are well matched to the circumstances of the various business units, weights indicating each measure's importance need to be assigned. A *case can be made for using different weights* for different business units whenever the importance of the strength measures differs significantly from business to business, but otherwise it is simpler just to go with a single set of weights and avoid the added complication of multiple weights. As before, the importance weights must add up to 1. Each business unit is then rated on each of the chosen strength measures, using a rating scale of 1 to 10 (where a *high* rating signifies competitive *strength* and a *low* rating signifies competitive *weakness*). In the event that the available information is too skimpy to confidently assign a rating value to a business unit on a particular strength measure, then it is usually best to use a score of 5, which avoids biasing the overall score either up or down. Weighted strength ratings are calculated by multiplying the business unit's rating on each strength measure by the assigned weight. For example, a strength score of 6 times a weight of 0.15 gives a weighted strength rating of 0.90. The sum of the weighted ratings across all the strength measures provides a quantitative measure of a business unit's overall market strength and competitive standing. Table 8.2 provides sample calculations of competitive strength ratings for four businesses.

Interpreting the Competitive Strength Scores
Business units with competitive strength ratings above 6.7 (on a scale of 1 to 10) are strong market contenders in their industries. Businesses with ratings in the 3.3-to-6.7 range have moderate competitive strength vis-à-vis rivals. Businesses with ratings below 3.3 are in competitively weak market positions. If a diversified company's business units all have competitive strength scores above 5, it is fair to conclude that its business units are all fairly strong market contenders in their respective industries.

Table 8.2 Calculating Weighted Competitive Strength Scores for a Diversified Company's Business Units*

Competitive Strength Measure	Importance Weight	Business A in Industry A Rating/ Score	Business B in Industry B Rating/ Score	Business C in Industry C Rating/ Score	Business D in Industry D Rating/ Score
Relative market share	0.15	10/1.50	1/0.15	6/0.90	2/0.30
Costs relative to competitors' costs	0.20	7/1.40	2/0.40	5/1.00	3/0.60
Ability to match or beat rivals on key product attributes	0.05	9/0.45	4/0.20	8/0.40	4/0.20
Ability to benefit from strategic fit with company's other businesses	0.20	8/1.60	4/0.80	8/0.80	2/0.60
Bargaining leverage with suppliers/ buyers; caliber of alliances	0.05	9/0.45	3/0.15	6/0.30	2/0.10
Brand image and reputation	0.10	9/0.90	2/0.20	7/0.70	5/0.50
Competitively valuable capabilities	0.15	7/1.05	2/0.30	5/0.75	3/0.45
Profitability relative to competitors	0.10	5/0.50	1/0.10	4/0.40	4/0.40
Sum of the assigned weights	1.00				
Overall weighted competitive strength scores		**7.85**	**2.30**	**5.25**	**3.15**

*Rating scale: 1 = very weak; 10 = very strong.

But as the number of business units with scores below 5 increases, there's reason to question whether the company can perform well with so many businesses in relatively weak competitive positions. This concern takes on even more importance when business units with low scores account for a sizable fraction of the company's revenues.

Using a Nine-Cell Matrix to Simultaneously Portray Industry Attractiveness and Competitive Strength

The industry attractiveness and business strength scores can be used to portray the strategic positions of each business in a diversified company. Industry attractiveness is plotted on the vertical axis and competitive strength on the horizontal axis. A nine-cell grid emerges from dividing the vertical axis into three regions (high, medium, and low attractiveness) and the horizontal axis into three regions (strong, average, and weak competitive strength). As shown in Figure 8.3, high attractiveness is associated with scores of 6.7 or greater on a rating scale of 1 to 10, medium attractiveness to scores of 3.3 to 6.7, and low attractiveness to scores below 3.3. Likewise, high competitive strength is defined as scores greater than 6.7, average strength as scores of 3.3 to 6.7, and low strength as scores below 3.3. *Each business unit is plotted on the nine-cell matrix according to its overall attractiveness score and strength score, and then it is shown as a "bubble."* The size of each bubble is scaled to the percentage of revenues the business generates relative to total corporate revenues. The bubbles in Figure 8.3 were located on the grid using the four industry attractiveness scores from Table 8.1 and the strength scores for the four business units in Table 8.2.

The locations of the business units on the attractiveness-strength matrix provide valuable guidance in deploying corporate resources to the various business units. In general, *a diversified company's prospects for good overall performance are*

Figure 8.3   **A Nine-Cell Industry Attractiveness–Competitive Strength Matrix**

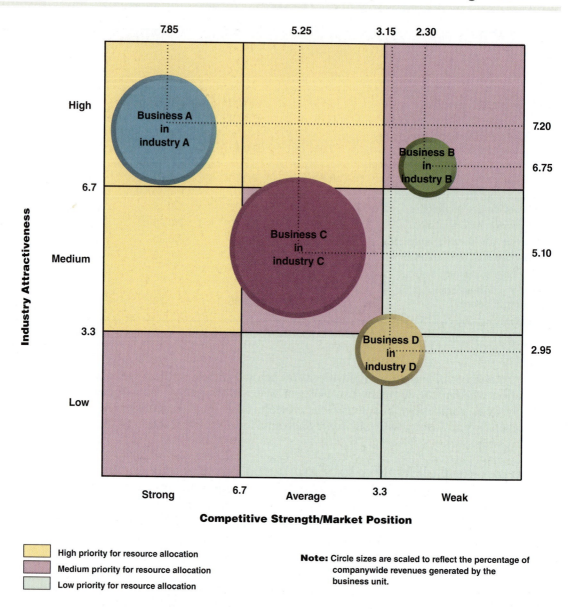

enhanced by concentrating corporate resources and strategic attention on those business units having the greatest competitive strength and positioned in highly attractive industries—specifically, businesses in the three cells in the upper left portion of the attractiveness-strength matrix, where industry attractiveness and competitive strength/market position are both favorable. The general strategic prescription for businesses falling in these three cells (for instance, business A in Figure 8.3) is "grow and build," with businesses in the high-strong cell standing first in line for resource allocations by the corporate parent.

Next in priority come businesses positioned in the three diagonal cells stretching from the lower left to the upper right (businesses B and C in Figure 8.3). Such businesses usually merit medium or intermediate priority in the parent's resource

allocation ranking. However, some businesses in the medium-priority diagonal cells may have brighter or dimmer prospects than others. For example, a small business in the upper right cell of the matrix (like business B), despite being in a highly attractive industry, may occupy too weak a competitive position in its industry to justify the investment and resources needed to turn it into a strong market contender and shift its position leftward in the matrix over time. If, however, a business in the upper right cell has attractive opportunities for rapid growth and a good potential for winning a much stronger market position over time, it may merit a high claim on the corporate parent's resource allocation ranking and be given the capital it needs to pursue a grow-and-build strategy—the strategic objective here would be to move the business leftward in the attractiveness-strength matrix over time.

Businesses in the three cells in the lower right corner of the matrix (like business D in Figure 8.3) typically are weak performers and have the lowest claim on corporate resources. Most such businesses are good candidates for being divested (sold to other companies) or else managed in a manner calculated to squeeze out the maximum cash flows from operations—the cash flows from low-performing/low-potential businesses can then be diverted to financing expansion of business units with greater market opportunities. In exceptional cases where a business located in the three lower right cells is nonetheless fairly profitable (which it might be if it is in the low-average cell) or has the potential for good earnings and return on investment, the business merits retention and the allocation of sufficient resources to achieve better performance.

The nine-cell attractiveness-strength matrix provides clear, strong logic for why a diversified company needs to consider both industry attractiveness and business strength in allocating resources and investment capital to its different businesses. A good case can be made for concentrating resources in those businesses that enjoy higher degrees of attractiveness and competitive strength, being very selective in making investments in businesses with intermediate positions on the grid, and withdrawing resources from businesses that are lower in attractiveness and strength unless they offer exceptional profit or cash flow potential.

Step 3: Checking the Competitive Advantage Potential of Cross-Business Strategic Fit

While this step can be bypassed for diversified companies whose businesses are all unrelated (since, by design, strategic fit is lacking), a high potential for converting strategic fit into competitive advantage is central to concluding just how good a company's related diversification strategy is. Checking the competitive advantage potential of cross-business strategic fit involves searching for and evaluating how much benefit a diversified company can gain from cross-business resource and value chain matchups.

But more than just strategic-fit identification is needed. The real test is what competitive value can be generated from strategic fit. To what extent can cost savings be realized? How much competitive value will come from cross-business transfer of skills, technology, or intellectual capital? Will transferring a potent brand name to the products of other businesses increase sales significantly? Will cross-business collaboration to create or strengthen competitive capabilities lead to significant gains in the marketplace or in financial performance? Without significant strategic fit and

The greater the value of cross-business strategic fit in enhancing a company's performance in the marketplace or on the bottom line, the more competitively powerful is its strategy of related diversification.

Figure 8.4   Identifying the Competitive Advantage Potential of Cross-Business Strategic Fit

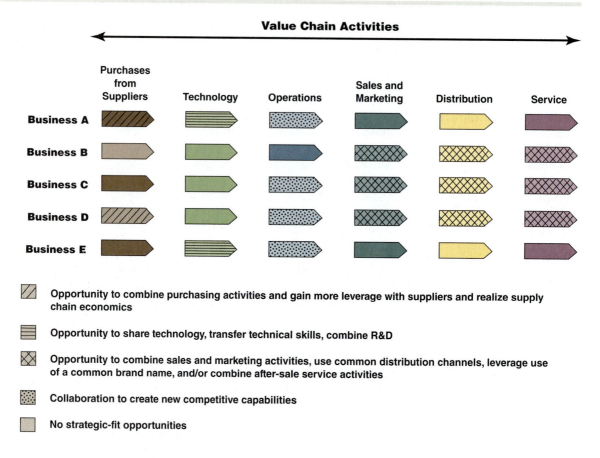

Opportunity to combine purchasing activities and gain more leverage with suppliers and realize supply chain economics

Opportunity to share technology, transfer technical skills, combine R&D

Opportunity to combine sales and marketing activities, use common distribution channels, leverage use of a common brand name, and/or combine after-sale service activities

Collaboration to create new competitive capabilities

No strategic-fit opportunities

dedicated company efforts to capture the benefits, one has to be skeptical about the potential for a diversified company's businesses to perform better together than apart.

Figure 8.4 illustrates the process of comparing the value chains of a company's businesses and identifying opportunities to exploit competitively valuable cross-business strategic fit.

CORE CONCEPT

A diversified company exhibits **resource fit** when its businesses add to a company's overall resource strengths and have matching resource requirements and/or when the parent company has adequate corporate resources to support its businesses' needs and add value.

Step 4: Checking for Resource Fit

The businesses in a diversified company's lineup need to exhibit good **resource fit.** In firms with a related diversification strategy, resource fit exists when the firm's businesses strengthen its overall mix of resources and capabilities and when the businesses have matching resource requirements at points along their value chains that are critical for the businesses' market success. In companies pursuing unrelated diversification, resource fit exists when the parent company has capabilities *as a corporate parent* of unrelated businesses, resources of a general nature that it can share or transfer to its component businesses, and corporate resources sufficient to support its entire group of businesses without being spread too thin. Resource fit in terms of a sufficiency

of corporate resources to manage and support the entire enterprise is also relevant for related diversifiers and companies pursuing a mixed diversification strategy; Firms pursuing related diversification can also benefit from leveraging the resources of the corporate parent.

Financial Resource Fit   One dimension of resource fit concerns whether a diversified company can generate the internal cash flows sufficient to fund the capital requirements of its businesses, pay its dividends, meet its debt obligations, and otherwise remain financially healthy. While additional capital can usually be raised in financial markets, it is important for a diversified firm to have a healthy **internal capital market** that can support the financial requirements of its business lineup. The greater the extent to which a diversified company is able to fund investment in its businesses through internally generated cash flows rather than from equity issues or borrowing, the more powerful its financial resource fit and the less dependent the firm is on external financial resources. This can provide an important competitive advantage over single business rivals when credit market conditions are tight, as they have been in the United States and abroad in recent years.

A *portfolio approach* to ensuring financial fit among a firm's businesses is based on the fact that different businesses have different cash flow and investment characteristics. For example, business units in rapidly growing industries are often **cash hogs**—so labeled because the cash flows they are able to generate from internal operations aren't big enough to fund their expansion. To keep pace with rising buyer demand, rapid-growth businesses frequently need sizable annual capital investments—for new facilities and equipment, for new product development or technology improvements, and for additional working capital to support inventory expansion and a larger base of operations. A business in a fast-growing industry becomes an even bigger cash hog when it has a relatively low market share and is pursuing a strategy to become an industry leader.

In contrast, business units with leading market positions in mature industries may be **cash cows**—businesses that generate substantial cash surpluses over what is needed to adequately fund their operations. Market leaders in slow-growth industries often generate sizable positive cash flows *over and above what is needed for growth and reinvestment* because their industry-leading positions tend to enable them to earn attractive profits and because the slow-growth nature of their industry often entails relatively modest annual investment requirements. Cash cows, although not always attractive from a growth standpoint, are valuable businesses from a financial resource perspective. The surplus cash flows they generate can be used to pay corporate dividends, finance acquisitions, and provide funds for investing in the company's promising cash hogs.

Viewing a diversified group of businesses as a collection of cash flows and cash requirements (present and future) is a major step forward in understanding what the financial ramifications of diversification are and why having businesses with good financial resource fit can be important. For instance, *a diversified company's businesses exhibit good financial resource fit when the excess cash generated by its cash cow businesses is sufficient to fund the investment requirements of*

CORE CONCEPT

A strong **internal capital market** allows a diversified company to add value by shifting capital from business units generating *free cash flow* to those needing additional capital to expand and realize their growth potential.

CORE CONCEPT

A **cash hog** business generates cash flows that are too small to fully fund its operations and growth and requires cash infusions to provide additional working capital and finance new capital investment.

CORE CONCEPT

A **cash cow** business generates cash flows over and above its internal requirements, thus providing a corporate parent with funds for investing in cash hog businesses, financing new acquisitions, or paying dividends.

promising cash hog businesses. Ideally, investing in promising cash hog businesses over time results in growing the hogs into self-supporting *star businesses* that have strong or market-leading competitive positions in attractive, high-growth markets and high levels of profitability. Star businesses are often the cash cows of the future—when the markets of star businesses begin to mature and their growth slows, their competitive strength should produce self-generated cash flows more than sufficient to cover their investment needs. The "success sequence" is thus cash hog to young star (but perhaps still a cash hog) to self-supporting star to cash cow. While the practice of viewing a diversified company in terms of cash cows and cash hogs has declined in popularity, it illustrates one approach to analyzing financial resource fit and allocating financial resources across a portfolio of different businesses.

Aside from cash flow considerations, there are two other factors to consider in assessing whether a diversified company's businesses exhibit good financial fit:

- *Does the company have adequate financial strength to fund its different businesses and maintain a healthy credit rating?* A diversified company's strategy fails the resource-fit test when the company's financial resources are stretched across so many businesses that its credit rating is impaired. Severe financial strain sometimes occurs when a company borrows so heavily to finance new acquisitions that it has to trim way back on capital expenditures for existing businesses and use the big majority of its financial resources to meet interest obligations and to pay down debt. Many of the world's largest banks (e.g., Royal Bank of Scotland, Citigroup, HSBC) recently found themselves so undercapitalized and financially overextended that they were forced to sell off some of their business assets to meet regulatory requirements and restore public confidence in their solvency.

- *Do any of the company's individual businesses not contribute adequately to achieving companywide performance targets?* A business exhibits poor financial fit with the company if it soaks up a disproportionate share of the company's financial resources, makes subpar bottom-line contributions, is too small to make a material earnings contribution, or is unduly risky (such that the financial well-being of the whole company could be jeopardized in the event it falls on hard times).

Nonfinancial Resource Fit   Just as a diversified company must have adequate financial resources to support its various individual businesses, it must also have a big-enough and deep-enough pool of managerial, administrative, and competitive capabilities to support all of its different businesses. The following two questions help reveal whether a diversified company has sufficient nonfinancial resources:

- *Does the company have (or can it develop) the specific resources and capabilities needed to be successful in each of its businesses?*[24] Sometimes a diversified company's resources and capabilities are poorly matched to the resource requirements of one or more businesses it has diversified into. For instance, BTR, a multibusiness company in Great Britain, discovered that the company's resources and managerial skills were quite well suited for parenting its industrial manufacturing businesses but not for parenting its distribution businesses (National Tyre Services and Texas-based Summers Group). As a result, BTR decided to divest its distribution businesses and focus exclusively on diversifying around small industrial manufacturing.[25] For companies pursuing related diversification strategies, a mismatch between the company's competitive assets and the key success factors of an industry can be serious enough to warrant divesting businesses in that industry or not acquiring a new business. In contrast, when a company's resources and capabilities are a good match with the key success factors of industries it is not presently in, it makes sense to take a hard look at acquiring companies in these industries and expanding the company's business lineup.

- *Are the company's resources being stretched too thinly by the resource requirements of one or more of its businesses?* A diversified company must guard against overtaxing its resources and capabilities, a condition that can arise when (1) it goes on an acquisition spree and management is called on to assimilate and oversee many new businesses very quickly or (2) it lacks sufficient resource depth to do a creditable job of transferring skills and competencies from one of its businesses to another. The broader the diversification, the greater the concern about whether the company has sufficient managerial depth to cope with the diverse range of operating problems its wide business lineup presents. Plus, the more a company's diversification strategy is tied to transferring its existing know-how or technologies to new businesses, the more it has to develop a big-enough and deep-enough resource pool to supply these businesses with sufficient capability to create competitive advantage.[26] Otherwise, its competitive assets end up being thinly spread across many businesses, and the opportunity for competitive advantage slips through the cracks.

Step 5: Ranking the Performance Prospects of Business Units and Assigning a Priority for Resource Allocation

Once a diversified company's strategy has been evaluated from the perspective of industry attractiveness, competitive strength, strategic fit, and resource fit, the next step is to rank the performance prospects of the businesses from best to worst and determine which businesses merit top priority for resource support and new capital investments by the corporate parent.

The most important considerations in judging business-unit performance are sales growth, profit growth, contribution to company earnings, and return on capital invested in the business. Sometimes, cash flow is a big consideration. As a rule, the prior analyses, taken together, signal which business units are likely to be strong performers on the road ahead and which are likely to be laggards. And it is a short step from ranking the prospects of business units to drawing conclusions about whether the company as a whole is capable of strong, mediocre, or weak performance in upcoming years.

The rankings of future performance generally determine what priority the corporate parent should give to each business in terms of resource allocation. *Business subsidiaries with the brightest profit and growth prospects and solid strategic and resource fit generally should head the list for corporate resource support.* More specifically, corporate executives must be diligent in steering resources out of low-opportunity areas into high-opportunity areas. Divesting marginal businesses is one of the best ways of freeing unproductive assets for redeployment. Surplus funds from cash cows also can be used to finance the range of chief strategic and financial options shown in Figure 8.5. Ideally, a company will have enough funds to do what is needed, both strategically and financially. If not,

Figure 8.5	**The Chief Strategic and Financial Options for Allocating a Diversified Company's Financial Resources**

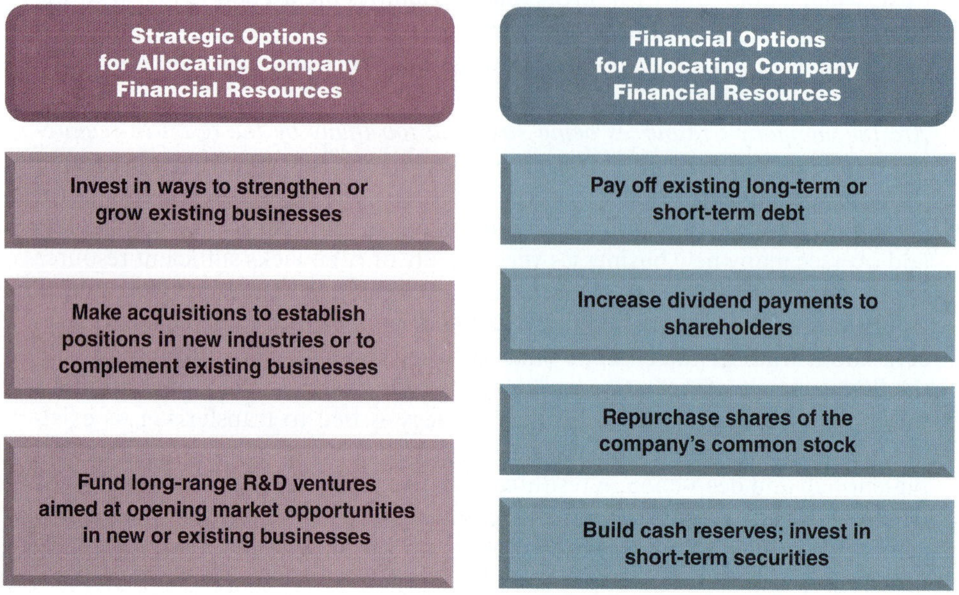

Strategic Options for Allocating Company Financial Resources	Financial Options for Allocating Company Financial Resources
Invest in ways to strengthen or grow existing businesses	Pay off existing long-term or short-term debt
Make acquisitions to establish positions in new industries or to complement existing businesses	Increase dividend payments to shareholders
	Repurchase shares of the company's common stock
Fund long-range R&D ventures aimed at opening market opportunities in new or existing businesses	Build cash reserves; invest in short-term securities

strategic uses of corporate resources should usually take precedence unless there is a compelling reason to strengthen the firm's balance sheet or divert financial resources to pacify shareholders.

Step 6: Crafting New Strategic Moves to Improve Overall Corporate Performance

LO 5

Understand a diversified company's four main corporate strategy options for solidifying its diversification strategy and improving company performance.

The diagnosis and conclusions flowing from the five preceding analytical steps set the agenda for crafting strategic moves to improve a diversified company's overall performance. Corporate strategy options once a company has diversified boil down to four broad categories of actions (see Figure 8.6):

1. Sticking closely with the existing business lineup and pursuing the opportunities these businesses present.
2. Broadening the company's business scope by making new acquisitions in new industries.
3. Divesting some businesses and retrenching to a narrower base of business operations.
4. Restructuring the company's business lineup with a combination of divestitures and new acquisitions to put a whole new face on the company's business makeup.

Sticking Closely with the Existing Business Lineup	The option of sticking with the current business lineup makes sense when the company's present businesses offer attractive growth opportunities and can be counted on to create economic value for shareholders. As long as the company's set of existing businesses puts it in good position for the future and these businesses

Figure 8.6 A Company's Four Main Strategic Alternatives After It Diversifies

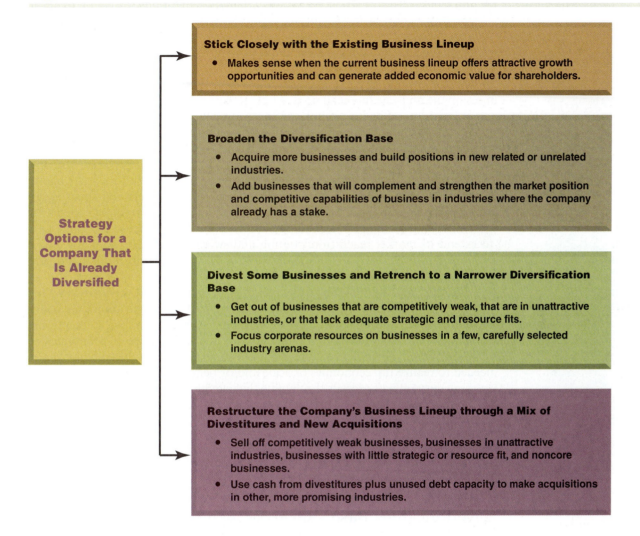

have good strategic and resource fit, then rocking the boat with major changes in the company's business mix is unnecessary. Corporate executives can concentrate their attention on getting the best performance from each of the businesses, steering corporate resources into areas of greatest potential and profitability. The specifics of "what to do" to wring better performance from the present business lineup have to be dictated by each business's circumstances and the preceding analysis of the corporate parent's diversification strategy.

However, in the event that corporate executives are not entirely satisfied with the opportunities they see in the company's present set of businesses and conclude that changes in the company's direction and business makeup are in order, they can opt for any of the three other strategic alternatives that follow.

Broadening a Diversified Company's Business Base Diversified companies sometimes find it desirable to build positions in new industries, whether related or unrelated. There are several motivating factors. One is the potential for transferring resources and capabilities to other related or complementary businesses. A second is rapidly changing conditions in one or more of a company's core businesses brought on by technological, legislative, or new product innovations that alter buyer preferences and resource requirements. For instance, the passage of legislation in the United States allowing banks, insurance companies, and stock brokerages to enter each other's businesses spurred a raft of acquisitions and mergers to create full-service financial enterprises capable of meeting the multiple financial needs of customers.

A third, and often very important, motivating factor for adding new businesses is to complement and strengthen the market position and competitive capabilities of one or more of the company's present businesses. Procter & Gamble's acquisition of Gillette strengthened and extended P&G's reach into personal care and household products—Gillette's businesses included Oral-B toothbrushes, Gillette razors and razor blades, Duracell batteries, and Braun shavers and small appliances. Cisco Systems built itself into a worldwide leader in networking systems for the Internet by making 130 technology-based acquisitions between 1993 and 2008 to extend its market reach from routing and switching into IP telephony, home networking, wireless LAN, storage networking, network security, broadband, and optical and broadband systems.

Another important avenue for expanding the scope of a diversified company is to grow by extending the operations of existing businesses into additional country markets. Expanding a company's geographic scope may offer an exceptional competitive advantage potential by facilitating the full capture of economies of scale and learning/experience curve effects. In some businesses, the volume of sales needed to realize full economies of scale and/or benefit fully from experience and learning curve effects exceeds the volume that can be achieved by operating within the boundaries of just one or several country markets, especially small ones.

Illustration Capsule 8.1 describes how Johnson & Johnson has used acquisitions to diversify far beyond its well-known Band-Aid and baby care businesses and become a major player in pharmaceuticals, medical devices, and medical diagnostics.

Divesting Some Businesses and Retrenching to a Narrower Diversification Base

Retrenching to a narrower diversification base is usually undertaken when top management concludes that its diversification strategy has ranged too far afield and that the company can improve long-term performance by concentrating on building stronger positions in a smaller number of core businesses and industries. Hewlett-Packard spun off its testing and measurement businesses into a stand-alone company called Agilent Technologies so that it could better concentrate on its PC, workstation, server, printer and peripherals, and electronics businesses.

But there are other important reasons for divesting one or more of a company's present businesses. Sometimes divesting a business has to be considered because market conditions in a once-attractive industry have badly deteriorated. A business can become a prime candidate for divestiture because it lacks adequate strategic or resource fit, because it is a cash hog with questionable long-term potential, or because it is weakly positioned in its industry with little prospect the corporate parent can realize a decent return on its investment in the business. Sometimes a company acquires businesses that, down the road, just do not work out as expected even though management has tried all it can think of to make them profitable. Subpar performance by some business units is bound to occur,

ILLUSTRATION CAPSULE 8.1

Managing Diversification at Johnson & Johnson: The Benefits of Cross-Business Strategic Fit

Johnson & Johnson (J&J), once a consumer products company known for its Band-Aid line and its baby care products, has evolved into a $61 billion diversified enterprise consisting of some 250-plus operating companies organized into three divisions: pharmaceuticals, medical devices and diagnostics, and consumer health care products. Over the past decade J&J has made acquisitions totaling more than $50 billion; about 10 to 15 percent of J&J's annual growth in revenues has come from acquisitions. Much of the company's recent growth has been in the pharmaceutical division, which in 2009 accounted for 36 percent of J&J's revenues and 41 percent of its operating profits.

While each of J&J's business units sets its own strategies and operates with its own finance and human resource departments, corporate management strongly encourages cross-business cooperation and collaboration, believing that many of the advances in 21st-century medicine will come from applying advances in one discipline to another. J&J's drug-coated stent grew out of a discussion between a drug researcher and a researcher in the company's stent business. The innovative product helps prevent infection after cardiac procedures. (When stents are inserted to prop open arteries following angioplasty, the drug coating helps prevent infection.) A gene technology database compiled by the company's gene research lab was shared with personnel from the diagnostics division, who developed a test that the drug researchers used to predict which patients would most benefit from an experimental cancer therapy. J&J's liquid Band-Aid product (a liquid coating applied to hard-to-cover places like fingers and knuckles) is based on a material used in a wound-closing product sold by the company's hospital products company. Scientists from three separate business units worked collaboratively toward the development of an absorbable patch that would stop bleeding on contact. The development of the instant clotting patch was expected to save the lives of thousands of accident victims since uncontrolled bleeding was the number-one cause of death due to injury.

J&J's corporate management maintains that close collaboration among people in its diagnostics, medical devices, and pharmaceutical businesses—where numerous examples of cross-business strategic fit exist—gives J&J an edge on competitors, most of whom cannot match the company's breadth and depth of expertise.

Sources: Amy Barrett, "Staying on Top," *BusinessWeek,* May 5, 2003, pp. 60–68; Johnson & Johnson 2007 Annual Report; www.jnj.com (accessed July 29, 2010).

thereby raising questions of whether to divest them or keep them and attempt a turnaround. Other business units, despite adequate financial performance, may not mesh as well with the rest of the firm as was originally thought. For instance, PepsiCo divested its group of fast-food restaurant businesses to focus its resources on its core soft-drink and snack-food businesses, where their resources and capabilities could add more value.

On occasion, a diversification move that seems sensible from a strategic-fit standpoint turns out to be a poor *cultural fit.*[27] Several pharmaceutical companies had just this experience. When they diversified into cosmetics and perfume, they discovered their personnel had little respect for the "frivolous" nature of such products compared to the far nobler task of developing miracle drugs to cure the ill. The absence of shared values and cultural compatibility between the medical research and chemical-compounding expertise of the pharmaceutical companies and the fashion/marketing orientation of the cosmetics business was the undoing of what otherwise was diversification into businesses with technology-sharing potential, product-development fit, and some overlap in distribution channels.

> **Diversified companies need to divest low-performing businesses or businesses that don't fit in order to concentrate on expanding existing businesses and entering new ones where opportunities are more promising.**

There's evidence indicating that pruning businesses and narrowing a firm's diversification base improves corporate performance.[28] A useful guide to determine whether or when to divest a business subsidiary is to ask, "If we were not in this business today, would we want to get into it now?"[29] When the answer is no or probably not, divestiture should be considered. Another signal that a business should become a divestiture candidate is whether it is worth more to another company than to the present parent; in such cases, shareholders would be well served if the company sells the business and collects a premium price from the buyer for whom the business is a valuable fit.[30]

Selling a business outright to another company is far and away the most frequently used option for divesting a business. But sometimes a business selected for divestiture has ample resources and capabilities to compete successfully on its own. In such cases, a corporate parent may elect to spin the unwanted business off as a financially and managerially independent company, either by selling shares to the investing public via an initial public offering or by distributing shares in the new company to existing shareholders of the corporate parent.

Restructuring a Diversified Company's Business Lineup through a Mix of Divestitures and New Acquisitions

> **CORE CONCEPT**
>
> **Companywide restructuring** *(corporate restructuring)* involves divesting some businesses and acquiring others so as to put a whole new face on the company's business lineup.

If there is a serious mismatch between the company's resources and the type of diversification it has pursued, then a **companywide restructuring** effort may be called for. Restructuring a diversified company on a companywide basis *(corporate restructuring)* involves divesting some businesses and acquiring others so as to put a whole new face on the company's business lineup.[31] Performing radical surgery on a company's group of businesses may also be an appealing strategy alternative when its financial performance is being squeezed or eroded by:

- Too many businesses in slow-growth, declining, low-margin, or otherwise unattractive industries (a condition indicated by the number and size of businesses with industry attractiveness ratings below 5 and located on the bottom half of the attractiveness-strength matrix—see Figure 8.3).
- Too many competitively weak businesses (a condition indicated by the number and size of businesses with competitive strength ratings below 5 and located on the right half of the attractiveness-strength matrix).
- Ongoing declines in the market shares of one or more major business units that are falling prey to more market-savvy competitors.
- An excessive debt burden with interest costs that eat deeply into profitability.
- Ill-chosen acquisitions that haven't lived up to expectations.

Companywide restructuring can also be mandated by the emergence of new technologies that threaten the survival of one or more of a diversified company's

ILLUSTRATION CAPSULE 8.2

VF's Corporate Restructuring Strategy That Made It the Star of the Apparel Industry

VF Corporation's corporate restructuring, which includes a mix of divestitures and acquisitions, has provided its shareholders with returns that are more than five times greater than shareholder returns provided by competing apparel manufacturers. Its total return to investors in 2009 (a year in which the economy was down and many manufacturers were struggling) was 38.7 percent. VF's growth in revenue and earnings made it number 310 on *Fortune*'s list of the 500 largest U.S. companies in 2009. In 2010, it earned a spot on *Fortune*'s "World's Most Admired Companies" list.

The company's corporate restructuring began in 2000 when it divested its slow-growing businesses, including its namesake Vanity Fair brand of lingerie and sleepwear. The company's $136 million acquisition of North Face in 2000 was the first in the series of many acquisitions of "lifestyle brands" that connected with the way people lived, worked, and played. Since the acquisition and turnaround of North Face, VF has spent $2.8 billion to acquire 18 additional businesses. New apparel and lifestyle brands acquired by VF Corporation include Vans skateboard shoes, Nautica, Eagle Creek, John Varvatos, 7 For All Mankind sportswear, Reef surf wear, and Lucy athletic wear. The company also acquired a variety of apparel companies specializing in apparel segments such as uniforms for professional baseball and football teams and law enforcement personnel.

VF Corporation's acquisitions came after years of researching each company and developing a relationship with an acquisition candidate's chief managers before closing the deal. The company made a practice of leaving management of acquired companies in place, while bringing in new managers only when necessary talent and skills were lacking. In addition, companies acquired by VF were allowed to keep long-standing traditions that shaped culture and spurred creativity. For example, the Vans headquarters in Cypress, California, retained its half-pipe and concrete floor so that its employees could skateboard to and from meetings.

In 2009, VF Corporation was among the most profitable apparel firms in the industry, with net earnings of $461 million. The company expected new acquisitions that would push VF's revenues to $11 billion by 2012.

Sources: Suzanne Kapner, "How a 100-Year Old Apparel Firm Changed Course," *Fortune,* April 9, 2008, online edition; www.vfc.com (accessed July 29, 2010).

important businesses. On occasion, corporate restructuring can be prompted by special circumstances—such as when a firm has a unique opportunity to make an acquisition so big and important that it has to sell several existing business units to finance the new acquisition or when a company needs to sell off some businesses in order to raise the cash for entering a potentially big industry with wave-of-the-future technologies or products.

Candidates for divestiture in a corporate restructuring effort typically include not only weak performers or those in unattractive industries but also business units that lack strategic fit with the businesses to be retained, businesses that are cash hogs or that lack other types of resource fit, and businesses incompatible with the company's revised diversification strategy (even though they may be profitable or in an attractive industry). As businesses are divested, corporate restructuring generally involves aligning the remaining business units into groups with the best strategic fit and then redeploying the cash flows from the divested business to either pay down debt or make new acquisitions to strengthen the parent company's business position in the industries it has chosen to emphasize.[32]

Over the past decade, corporate restructuring has become a popular strategy at many diversified companies, especially those that had diversified broadly into many different industries and lines of business. In 2008, GE's CEO Jeffrey Immelt announced that GE would spin off its industrial division, which included GE appliances, lighting, and various industrial businesses. Earlier, he had led GE's withdrawal from the insurance business by divesting several companies and spinning off others. He further restructured GE's business lineup with two other major initiatives: (1) spending $10 billion to acquire British-based Amersham and extend GE's Medical Systems business into diagnostic pharmaceuticals and biosciences, thereby creating a $15 billion business designated as GE Healthcare, and (2) acquiring the entertainment assets of debt-ridden French media conglomerate Vivendi Universal Entertainment and integrating its operations into GE's NBC division, thereby creating a broad-based $13 billion media business positioned to compete against Walt Disney, Time Warner, Fox, and Viacom. Illustration Capsule 8.2 discusses how VF Corporation shareholders have benefited through the company's large-scale restructuring program.

KEY POINTS

1. The purpose of diversification is to build shareholder value. Diversification builds shareholder value when a diversified group of businesses can perform better under the auspices of a single corporate parent than they would as independent, stand-alone businesses—the goal is to achieve not just a $1 + 1 = 2$ result but, rather, to realize important $1 + 1 = 3$ performance benefits. Whether getting into a new business has potential to enhance shareholder value hinges on whether a company's entry into that business can pass the attractiveness test, the cost-of-entry test, and the better-off test.

2. Entry into new businesses can take any of three forms: acquisition, internal start-up, or joint venture/strategic partnership. The choice of which is best depends on the firm's resources and capabilities, the industry's entry barriers, the importance of speed, and the relative costs.

3. There are two fundamental approaches to diversification—into related businesses and into unrelated businesses. The rationale for *related* diversification is to benefit from *strategic fit:* Diversify into businesses with matchups along their respective value chains, and then capitalize on the strategic fit by sharing or transferring the resources and capabilities that enable the matching value chain activities in order to gain competitive advantage.

4. *Unrelated* diversification strategies surrender the competitive advantage potential of strategic fit at the value chain level in return for the potential that can be realized from superior corporate parenting. An outstanding corporate parent can benefit its businesses through (1) providing high-level oversight and making available other corporate resources, (2) allocating financial resources across the business portfolio, and (3) restructuring underperforming acquisitions.

5. Related diversification provides a stronger foundation for creating shareholder value than unrelated diversification, since the *specialized resources and*

capabilities that are leveraged in related diversification tend to be more valuable competitive assets than the *generalized resources and capabilities* underlying unrelated diversification, which in most cases are relatively common and easier to imitate.

6. Analyzing how good a company's diversification strategy is consists of a six-step process:

Step 1: *Evaluate the long-term attractiveness of the industries into which the firm has diversified.* Industry attractiveness needs to be evaluated from three angles: the attractiveness of each industry on its own, the attractiveness of each industry relative to the others, and the attractiveness of all the industries as a group.

Step 2: *Evaluate the relative competitive strength of each of the company's business units.* The purpose of rating the competitive strength of each business is to gain a clear understanding of which businesses are strong contenders in their industries, which are weak contenders, and the underlying reasons for their strength or weakness. The conclusions about industry attractiveness can be joined with the conclusions about competitive strength by drawing an industry attractiveness–competitive strength matrix that helps identify the prospects of each business and what priority each business should be given in allocating corporate resources and investment capital.

Step 3: *Check for cross-business strategic fit.* A business is more attractive strategically when it has value chain relationships with the company's other business units that offer potential to (1) realize economies of scope or cost-saving efficiencies, (2) transfer technology, skills, know-how, or other resource capabilities from one business to another, (3) leverage use of a trusted brand name or other resources that enhance differentiation, and (4) build new resources and competitive capabilities via cross-business collaboration. Cross-business strategic fit represents a significant avenue for producing competitive advantage beyond what any one business can achieve on its own.

Step 4: *Check whether the firm's resource mix fits the resource requirements of its present business lineup.* In firms with a related diversification strategy, resource fit exists when the company's businesses add to its overall resource position and when they have matching resource requirements at the value chain level. In companies pursuing unrelated diversification, resource fit exists when the parent company has generalized resources that can add value to its component businesses and when it has corporate resources sufficient to support its entire group of businesses without spreading itself too thin. When there is financial resource fit among the businesses of any type of diversified company, the company can generate internal cash flows sufficient to fund the capital requirements of its businesses, pay its dividends, meet its debt obligations, and otherwise remain financially healthy.

Step 5: *Rank the performance prospects of the businesses from best to worst, and determine what the corporate parent's priority should be in allocating resources to its various businesses.* The most important considerations in judging business-unit performance are sales growth, profit growth, contribution to company earnings, and the return on capital invested in the business. Normally, strong business units in attractive industries have significantly better performance prospects than weak businesses or businesses in unattractive industries. Business subsidiaries with the brightest profit and growth prospects and solid strategic and resource fit generally should head the list for corporate resource support.

Step 6: *Crafting new strategic moves to improve overall corporate performance.* This step entails using the results of the preceding analysis as the basis for devising actions to strengthen existing businesses, make new acquisitions, divest weak-performing and unattractive businesses, restructure the company's business lineup, expand the scope of the company's geographic reach into new markets around the world, and otherwise steer corporate resources into the areas of greatest opportunity.

7. Once a company has diversified, corporate management's task is to manage the collection of businesses for maximum long-term performance. There are four different strategic paths for improving a diversified company's performance: (1) sticking with the existing business lineup, (2) broadening the firm's business base by diversifying into additional businesses or geographic markets, (3) retrenching to a narrower diversification base by divesting some of its present businesses, and (4) restructuring the company's business lineup with a combination of divestitures and new acquisitions to put a whole new face on the company's business makeup.

ASSURANCE OF LEARNING EXERCISES

LO 1, LO 2

1. See if you can identify the value chain relationships that make the businesses of the following companies related in competitively relevant ways. In particular, you should consider whether there are cross-business opportunities for (1) transferring skills/technology, (2) combining related value chain activities to achieve economies of scope, and/or (3) leveraging the use of a well-respected brand name or other resources that enhance differentiation.

OSI Restaurant Partners

- Outback Steakhouse
- Carrabba's Italian Grill
- Roy's Restaurant (Hawaiian fusion cuisine)
- Bonefish Grill (market-fresh fine seafood)
- Fleming's Prime Steakhouse & Wine Bar

L'Oréal

- Maybelline, Lancôme, Helena Rubinstein, Kiehl's, Garner, and Shu Uemura cosmetics
- L'Oréal and Soft Sheen/Carson hair care products
- Redken, Matrix, L'Oréal Professional, and Kerastase Paris professional hair care and skin care products
- Ralph Lauren and Giorgio Armani fragrances
- Biotherm skincare products
- La Roche–Posay and Vichy Laboratories dermocosmetics

Johnson & Johnson

- Baby products (powder, shampoo, oil, lotion)
- Band-Aids and other first-aid products
- Women's health and personal care products (Stayfree, Carefree, Sure & Natural)
- Neutrogena and Aveeno skin care products
- Nonprescription drugs (Tylenol, Motrin, Pepcid AC, Mylanta, Monistat)
- Prescription drugs
- Prosthetic and other medical devices
- Surgical and hospital products
- Acuvue contact lenses

LO 1, LO 3

2. A defining characteristic of unrelated diversification is few cross-business commonalities in terms of key value chain activities. Peruse the business group listings for Lancaster Colony shown below, and see if you can confirm that it has diversified into unrelated business groups.

Lancaster Colony's business lineup

- Specialty food products: Cardini, Marzetti, Girard's, and Pheiffer salad dressings; T. Marzetti and Chatham Village croutons; Jack Daniels mustards; Inn Maid noodles; New York and Mamma Bella garlic breads; Reames egg noodles; Sister Schubert's rolls; and Romanoff caviar
- Candle-lite brand candles marketed to retailers and private-label customers chains
- Glassware, plastic ware, coffee urns, and matting products marketed to the food service and lodging industry

If need be, visit the company's Web site (www.lancastercolony.com) to obtain additional information about its business lineup and strategy.

LO 1, LO 2, LO 3

3. The Walt Disney Company is in the following businesses:

- Theme parks
- Disney Cruise Line
- Resort properties
- Movie, video, and theatrical productions (for both children and adults)
- Television broadcasting (ABC, Disney Channel, Toon Disney, Classic Sports Network, ESPN and ESPN2, E!, Lifetime, and A&E networks)
- Radio broadcasting (Disney Radio)
- Musical recordings and sales of animation art
- Anaheim Mighty Ducks NHL franchise
- Anaheim Angels major-league baseball franchise (25 percent ownership)
- Books and magazine publishing

- Interactive software and Internet sites
- The Disney Store retail shops

Based on the above listing, would you say that Walt Disney's business lineup reflects a strategy of related diversification, unrelated diversification, or a combination of related and unrelated diversification? Be prepared to justify and explain your answer in terms of the nature of Disney's shared or transferred resources and capabilities and the extent to which the value chains of Disney's different businesses seem to have competitively valuable cross-business relationships.

If need be, visit the company's Web site (http://corporate.disney.go.com/index.html?ppLink=pp_wdig) to obtain additional information about its business lineup and strategy.

EXERCISES FOR SIMULATION PARTICIPANTS

LO 1, LO 2, LO 3

1. In the event that your company had the opportunity to diversify into other products or businesses of your choosing, would you opt to pursue related diversification, unrelated diversification, or a combination of both? Explain why.

LO 1, LO 2

2. What specific resources and capabilities does your company possess that would make diversifying into related businesses attractive? Indicate what kinds of strategic-fit benefits could be captured by transferring these resources and competitive capabilities to newly acquired related businesses.

LO 1, LO 2

3. If your company opted to pursue a strategy of related diversification, what industries or product categories could it diversify into that would allow it to achieve economies of scope? Name at least two or three such industries or product categories, and indicate the specific kinds of cost savings that might accrue from entry into each.

LO 1, LO 2

4. If your company opted to pursue a strategy of related diversification, what industries or product categories could it diversify into that would allow it to capitalize on using its present brand name and corporate image to good advantage in the newly entered businesses or product categories? Name at least two or three such industries or product categories, and indicate *the specific benefits* that might be captured by transferring your company's brand name to each.

ENDNOTES

[1] For a more detailed discussion of when diversification makes good strategic sense, see Constantinos C. Markides, "To Diversify or Not to Diversify," *Harvard Business Review* 75, no. 6 (November–December 1997), pp. 93–99.

[2] For a discussion of how hidden opportunities within a corporation's existing asset base may offer growth to corporations with declining core businesses, see Chris Zook, "Finding Your Next Core Business," *Harvard Business Review* 85, no. 4 (April 2007), pp. 66–75.

[3] Michael E. Porter, "From Competitive Advantage to Corporate Strategy," *Harvard Business Review* 45, no. 3 (May–June 1987), pp. 46–49.

[4] Rita Nazareth, "CEOs Paying 56% M&A Premium Shows Stocks May Be Cheap (Update3)," *Bloomberg.com,* December 21, 2009, www.bloomberg.com/apps/news?pid=20603037&sid=ahPolYY.zgQ.

[5] Ibid.

[6] Michael E. Porter, *Competitive Strategy: Techniques for Analyzing Industries and Competitors* (New York: Free Press, 1980), pp. 354–55.

[7] A. Shleifer and R. Vishny, "Takeovers in the 60s and the 80s—Evidence and Implications," *Strategic Management Journal* 12 (Winter 1991), pp. 51–59; T. Brush, "Predicted Change in Operational Synergy and Post-Acquisition Performance of Acquired Businesses," *Strategic Management Journal* 17, no. 1 (1996), pp. 1–24; J. P. Walsh, "Top Management Turnover Following Mergers and Acquisitions," *Strategic Management Journal* 9, no. 2 (1988), pp. 173–83; A. Cannella and D. Hambrick, "Effects of Executive Departures on the Performance of Acquired Firms," *Strategic Management Journal* 14 (Summer 1993), pp. 137–52; R. Roll, "The Hubris Hypothesis of Corporate Takeovers," *Journal of Business* 59, no. 2 (1986), pp. 197–216; P. Haspeslagh and D. Jemison, *Managing Acquisitions* (New York: Free Press, 1991).

[8] M. L. A. Hayward, "When Do Firms Learn from Their Acquisition Experience? Evidence from 1990–1995," *Strategic Management Journal* 23, no. 1 (2002), pp. 21–29; G. Ahuja and R. Katila, "Technological Acquisitions and the Innovation Performance of Acquiring Firms: A Longitudinal Study," *Strategic Management Journal* 22, no. 3 (2001), pp. 197–220; H. Barkema and F. Vermeulen, "International Expansion through Start-Up or Acquisition: A Learning Perspective," *Academy of Management Journal* 41, no. 1 (1998), pp. 7–26.

[9] Haspeslagh and Jemison, *Managing Acquisitions,* pp. 344–45.

[10] Yves L. Doz and Gary Hamel, *Alliance Advantage: The Art of Creating Value through Partnering* (Boston: Harvard Business School Press, 1998), chaps. 1 and 2.

[11] J. Glover, "The Guardian," March 23, 1996, www.mcspotlight.org/media/press/guardpizza_23mar96.html.

[12] Michael E. Porter, *Competitive Advantage* (New York: Free Press, 1985), pp. 318–19 and pp. 337–53; Porter, "From Competitive Advantage to Corporate Strategy," pp. 53–57. For an empirical study supporting the notion that strategic fit enhances performance (provided the resulting combination is competitively valuable and difficult to duplicate by rivals), see Constantinos C. Markides and Peter J. Williamson, "Corporate Diversification and Organization Structure: A Resource-Based View," *Academy of Management Journal* 39, no. 2 (April 1996), pp. 340–67.

[13] David J. Collis and Cynthia A. Montgomery, "Creating Corporate Advantage," *Harvard Business Review* 76, no. 3 (May–June 1998), pp. 72–80; Markides and Williamson, "Corporate Diversification and Organization Structure."

[14] Markides and Williamson, "Corporate Diversification and Organization Structure."

[15] For a discussion of the strategic significance of cross-business coordination of value chain activities and insight into how the process works, see Jeanne M. Liedtka, "Collaboration across Lines of Business for Competitive Advantage," *Academy of Management Executive* 10, no. 2 (May 1996), pp. 20–34.

[16] For a discussion of what is involved in actually capturing strategic-fit benefits, see Kathleen M. Eisenhardt and D. Charles Galunic, "Coevolving: At Last, a Way to Make Synergies Work," *Harvard Business Review* 78, no. 1 (January–February 2000), pp. 91–101; Constantinos C. Markides and Peter J. Williamson, "Related Diversification, Core Competences and Corporate Performance," *Strategic Management Journal* 15 (Summer 1994), pp. 149–65.

[17] A. Campbell, M. Goold, and M. Alexander, "Corporate Strategy: The Quest for Parenting Advantage," *Harvard Business Review* 73, no. 2 (March–April 1995), pp. 120–32.

[18] C. Montgomery and B. Wernerfelt, "Diversification, Ricardian Rents, and Tobin-Q," *RAND Journal of Economics* 19, no. 4 (1988), pp. 623–32.

[19] Ibid.

[20] Ibid.

[21] For a review of the experiences of companies that have pursued unrelated diversification successfully, see Patricia L. Anslinger and Thomas E. Copeland, "Growth through Acquisitions: A Fresh Look," *Harvard Business Review* 74, no. 1 (January–February 1996), pp. 126–35.

[22] Of course, management may be willing to assume the risk that trouble will not strike before it has had time to learn the business well enough to bail it out of almost any difficulty. But there is research that shows this is very risky from a financial perspective; see, for example, M. Lubatkin and S. Chatterjee, "Extending Modern Portfolio Theory," *Academy of Management Journal* 37, no. 1 (February 1994), pp. 109–36.

[23] For research evidence of the failure of broad diversification and trend of companies to focus their diversification efforts more narrowly, see Lawrence G. Franko, "The Death of Diversification? The Focusing of the World's Industrial Firms, 1980–2000," *Business Horizons* 47, no. 4 (July–August 2004), pp. 41–50.

[24] For an excellent discussion of what to look for in assessing this type of strategic fit, see Campbell, Goold, and Alexander, "Corporate Strategy: The Quest for Parenting Advantage."

[25] Ibid., p. 128.

[26] A good discussion of the importance of having adequate resources, as well as upgrading corporate resources and capabilities, can be found in David J. Collis and Cynthia A. Montgomery, "Competing on Resources: Strategy in the 90s," *Harvard Business Review* 73, no. 4 (July–August 1995), pp. 118–28.

[27] Peter F. Drucker, *Management: Tasks, Responsibilities, Practices,* (New York: Harper & Row, 1974), p. 709.

[28] See, for example, Constantinos C. Markides, "Diversification, Restructuring, and Economic Performance," *Strategic Management Journal* 16 (February 1995), pp. 101–18.

[29] Drucker, *Management: Tasks, Responsibilities, Practices,* p. 94.

[30] Collis and Montgomery, "Creating Corporate Advantage."

[31] For a discussion of why divestiture needs to be a standard part of any company's diversification strategy, see Lee Dranikoff, Tim Koller, and Anton Schneider, "Divestiture: Strategy's Missing Link," *Harvard Business Review* 80, no. 5 (May 2002), pp. 74–83.

[32] Evidence that restructuring strategies tend to result in higher levels of performance is contained in Markides, "Diversification, Restructuring, and Economic Performance."

CHAPTER 9

ETHICS, CORPORATE SOCIAL RESPONSIBILITY, ENVIRONMENTAL SUSTAINABILITY, AND STRATEGY

> Business is the most important engine for social change in our society.
>
> **—Lawrence Perlman**
> *Former CEO of Ceridian Corporation*

> It takes many good deeds to build a good reputation and only one bad one to lose it.
>
> **—Benjamin Franklin**
> *American Statesman, Inventor, and Philosopher*

> Corporations are economic entities, to be sure, but they are also social institutions that must justify their existence by their overall contribution to society.
>
> **—Henry Mintzberg, Robert Simons, and Kunal Basu**
> *Professors*

> Companies have to be socially responsible or shareholders pay eventually.
>
> **—Warren Shaw**
> *Former CEO of LGT Asset Management*

LEARNING OBJECTIVES

LO 1. Understand how the standards of ethical behavior in business relate to the ethical standards and norms of the larger society and culture in which a company operates.

LO 2. Recognize conditions that can give rise to unethical business strategies and behavior.

LO 3. Gain an understanding of the costs of business ethics failures.

LO 4. Gain an understanding of the concepts of corporate social responsibility and environmental sustainability and of how companies balance these duties with economic responsibilities to shareholders.

Clearly, a company has a responsibility to make a profit and grow the business—in capitalistic or market economies, management's fiduciary duty to create value for shareholders is not a matter for serious debate. Just as clearly, a company and its personnel also have a duty to obey the law and play by the rules of fair competition. But does a company have a duty to go beyond legal requirements and operate according to the ethical norms of the societies in which it operates—should all company personnel be held to some standard of ethical conduct? And does a company have a duty or obligation to contribute to the betterment of society independent of the needs and preferences of the customers it serves? Should a company display a social conscience and devote a portion of its resources to bettering society? How far should a company go in protecting the environment, conserving natural resources for use by future generations, and ensuring that its operations do not ultimately endanger the planet?

The focus of this chapter is to examine what link, if any, there should be between a company's efforts to craft and execute a winning strategy and its duties to (1) conduct its activities in an ethical manner, (2) demonstrate socially responsible behavior by being a committed corporate citizen and directing corporate resources to the betterment of employees, the communities in which it operates, and society as a whole, and (3) adopt business practices that conserve natural resources, protect the interests of future generations, and preserve the well-being of the planet.

WHAT DO WE MEAN BY *BUSINESS ETHICS*?

Ethics concerns principles of right or wrong conduct. **Business ethics** is the application of ethical principles and standards to the actions and decisions of business organizations and the conduct of their personnel.[1] Ethical principles in business are not materially different from ethical principles in general because business actions have to be judged in the context of society's standards of right and wrong. There is not a special set of ethical standards applicable only to business situations. If dishonesty is considered unethical and immoral, then dishonest behavior in business—whether it relates to customers, suppliers, employees, shareholders, competitors, government, or society—qualifies as equally unethical and immoral. If being ethical entails not deliberately harming others, then recalling a defective or unsafe product is ethically necessary. If society deems bribery unethical, then it is unethical for company personnel to make payoffs to government officials or bestow gifts and other favors on prospective customers to win or retain business. In short, ethical behavior in business situations requires adhering to generally accepted norms about right or wrong conduct. As a consequence, company managers have an obligation—indeed, a duty—to observe ethical norms when crafting and executing strategy.

WHERE DO ETHICAL STANDARDS COME FROM—ARE THEY UNIVERSAL OR DEPENDENT ON LOCAL NORMS?

LO 1

Understand how the standards of ethical behavior in business relate to the ethical standards and norms of the larger society and culture in which a company operates.

Notions of right and wrong, fair and unfair, ethical and unethical are present in all societies and cultures. But there are three distinct schools of thought about the extent to which ethical standards travel across cultures and whether multinational companies can apply the same set of ethical standards in any and all locations where they operate. Illustration Capsule 9.1 describes the difficulties Apple has faced in trying to enforce a common set of ethical standards across its vast global supplier network.

The School of Ethical Universalism

According to the school of **ethical universalism,** the most important concepts of what is right and what is wrong are *universal* and transcend culture, society, and religion.[2] For instance, being truthful (or not being deliberately deceitful) strikes a chord of what's right in the peoples of all nations. Likewise, demonstrating integrity of character, not cheating, and treating people with courtesy and respect are concepts that resonate with people of virtually all cultures and religions. In most societies, people would concur that it is unethical for companies to knowingly expose workers to toxic chemicals and hazardous materials or to sell products known to be unsafe or harmful to the users.

CORE CONCEPT

The school of **ethical universalism** holds that common understandings across multiple cultures and countries about what constitutes right and wrong give rise to universal ethical standards that apply to members of all societies, all companies, and all businesspeople.

Common moral agreement about right and wrong actions and behaviors across multiple cultures and countries gives rise to universal ethical standards that apply to members of all societies, all companies, and all businesspeople. These universal ethical principles set forth the traits and behaviors that are considered virtuous and that a good person is supposed to believe in and to display. Thus, adherents of the school of ethical universalism maintain it is entirely appropriate to expect all businesspeople to conform to these universal ethical standards.[3]

The strength of ethical universalism is that it draws on the collective views of multiple societies and cultures to put some clear boundaries on what constitutes ethical business behavior and what constitutes unethical business behavior regardless of the country or culture in which a company's personnel are conducting activities. This means that in those instances where basic moral standards really do not vary significantly according to local cultural beliefs, traditions, or religious convictions, a multinational company can develop a code

ILLUSTRATION CAPSULE 9.1

Many of Apple's Suppliers Flunk the Ethics Test

Apple requires its suppliers to comply with the company's Supplier Code of Conduct as a condition of being awarded contracts. To ensure compliance, Apple has a supplier monitoring program that includes audits of supplier factories, corrective action plans, and verification measures. In the company's 24-page 2010 Progress Report on Supplier Responsibility, Apple reported that in 2009 it conducted 102 audits of supplier facilities in such countries as China, the Czech Republic, Malaysia, the Philippines, Singapore, South Korea, Taiwan, Thailand, and the United States; 80 of these audits were first-time audits and 22 were repeat audits.

Apple distinguishes among the seriousness of infractions, designating "core violations" as those that go directly against the core principles of its Supplier Code of Conduct and must be remedied immediately. During the 2009 audits, 17 such violations were discovered, including 3 cases of underage labor, 8 cases involving excessive recruitment fees, 3 cases of improper hazardous waste disposal, and 3 cases of deliberately falsified audit records. Apple responded by ensuring that immediate corrective actions were taken, placing violators on probation, and planning to audit them again in a year's time.

While all six of Apple's final assembly manufacturers had high compliance scores—on average, registering well above 90 percent compliance on all issues—other suppliers did not fare so well on the 2009 audits. At 60 of the audited facilities, workers were required to work more than 60 hours per week more than 50 percent of the time—Apple sets a maximum of 60 hours per week (except in unusual or emergency circumstances). In 65 of the audited facilities, workers were found to have been required to work more than six consecutive days a week at least once per month—Apple requires at least one day of rest per seven days of work (except in unusual or emergency circumstances).

At 48 facilities, Apple found that overtime wages had been calculated improperly, resulting in underpayment of overtime compensation. Apple

auditors discovered that at 24 facilities workers were being paid less than the specified minimum wage and that at 45 facilities wage deductions were used to discipline employees. At 57 of the audited facilities, worker benefits (for such things as retirement, sick leave, or maternity leave) were below the legally required amounts.

Apple requires suppliers to provide a safe working environment and to eliminate physical hazards to employees where possible. But the 2009 audits revealed that workers were not wearing appropriate protective personal equipment at 49 facilities. Violations were found at 70 facilities where workers were improperly trained, where unlicensed workers were operating equipment, and where required inspections of equipment were not being conducted. Apple auditors found that 44 facilities had failed to conduct environmental impact assessments, 11 facilities did not have permits for air emissions, and 4 facilities did not meet the conditions specified in their emission permits. Moreover, the audits revealed that 55 supplier facilities did not have any personnel assigned to ensuring compliance with Apple's Supplier Code of Conduct.

For Apple, the audits represent a starting point for bringing its suppliers into compliance, through greater scrutiny, education and training of suppliers' personnel, and incentives. Apple collects quarterly data to hold its suppliers accountable for their actions and makes procurement decisions based, in part, on these numbers. Suppliers that are unable to meet Apple's high standards of conduct ultimately end up losing Apple's business.

Sources: Apple's 2010 Progress Report on Supplier Responsibility; Dan Moren, "Apple Releases 2010 Report on Supplier Responsibility," *Macworld.com,* February 23, 2010, www.macworld.com/article/146653/2010/02/suppliers_2010.htm (accessed July 1, 2010); Andrew Morse and Nick Wingfield, "Apple Audits Labor Practices: Company Says Suppliers Hired Underage Workers, Violated Other Core Policies," *Wall Street Journal Online,* March 1, 2010, http://online.wsj.com/article/SB10001424 05274870423130457509192070410154.html (accessed July 1, 2010); Nicholas Kolakowski, "Apple Finds Violations during 2009 Supplier and Manufacturer Audit," *eWeek.com,* March 1, 2010, www.eweek.com/c/a/Mobile-and-Wireless/Apple-Finds-Violations-During-2009-Supplier-and-Manufacturer-Audit-522622/ (accessed July 1, 2010).

of ethics that it applies more or less evenly across its worldwide operations.[4] It can avoid the slippery slope that comes from having different ethical standards for different company personnel depending on where in the world they are working.

The School of Ethical Relativism

Apart from a select set of universal moral prescriptions—like being truthful and trustworthy—that apply in every society and business circumstance, there are meaningful variations in the ethical standards by which different societies judge the conduct of business activities. Indeed, differing religious beliefs, social customs, traditions, and behavioral norms frequently give rise to different standards about what is fair or unfair, moral or immoral, and ethically right or wrong. The school of **ethical relativism** holds that when there are cross-country or cross-cultural differences in what is deemed ethical or unethical in business situations, it is appropriate for local moral standards to take precedence over what the ethical standards may be in a company's home market. The thesis is that what constitutes ethical or unethical behavior on the part of local businesspeople is properly governed by local ethical standards rather than the standards that prevail in other locations.[5] Consider the following examples.

The Use of Underage Labor

In industrialized nations, the use of underage workers is considered taboo. Social activists are adamant that child labor is unethical and that companies should neither employ children under the age of 18 as full-time employees nor source any products from foreign suppliers that employ underage workers. Many countries have passed legislation forbidding the use of underage labor or, at a minimum, regulating the employment of people under the age of 18. However, in India, Bangladesh, Botswana, Sri Lanka, Ghana, Somalia, and more than 100 other countries, it is customary to view children as potential, even necessary, workers.[6] Many poverty-stricken families cannot subsist without the income earned by young family members; sending their children to school instead of having them work is not a realistic option. In 2006, the International Labor Organization estimated that 191 million children ages 5 to 14 were working around the world.[7] If such children are not permitted to work—due to pressures imposed by activist groups in industrialized nations—they may be forced to go out on the streets begging or to seek work in parts of the "underground" economy such as drug trafficking and prostitution.[8] So if all businesses in countries where employing underage workers is common succumb to the pressures of activist groups and government organizations to stop employing underage labor, then have they served the best interests of the underage workers, their families, and society in general?

The Payment of Bribes and Kickbacks

A particularly thorny area facing multinational companies is the degree of cross-country variability in paying bribes.[9] In many countries in eastern Europe, Africa, Latin America, and Asia, it is customary to pay bribes to government officials in order to win a government contract, obtain a license or permit, or facilitate an administrative ruling.[10] Likewise, in many countries it is normal to make payments to prospective customers in order to win or retain their business. In some developing nations, it is difficult for any company, foreign or domestic, to move goods through customs without paying off low-level officials.[11] A *Wall Street Journal* article reported that

30 to 60 percent of all business transactions in eastern Europe involved paying bribes and the costs of bribe payments averaged 2 to 8 percent of revenues.[12] Some people stretch to justify the payment of bribes and kickbacks on grounds that bribing government officials to get goods through customs or giving kickbacks to customers to retain their business or win new orders is simply a payment for services rendered, in the same way that people tip for service at restaurants.[13] But while this is a clever rationalization, it rests on moral quicksand.

Companies that forbid the payment of bribes and kickbacks in their codes of ethical conduct and that are serious about enforcing this prohibition face a particularly vexing problem in countries where bribery and kickback payments are an entrenched local custom.[14] Refusing to pay bribes or kickbacks in these countries (so as to comply with the company's code of ethical conduct) is very often tantamount to losing business to competitors willing to make such payments—an outcome that penalizes ethical companies and ethical company personnel (who may suffer lost sales commissions or bonuses). On the other hand, the payment of bribes or kickbacks not only undercuts the company's code of ethics but also risks breaking the law. U.S. companies are prohibited by the Foreign Corrupt Practices Act (FCPA) from paying bribes to government officials, political parties, political candidates, or others in all countries where they do business. The Organization for Economic Cooperation and Development (OECD) has antibribery standards that criminalize the bribery of foreign public officials in international business transactions—as of 2009, the 30 OECD members and 8 nonmember countries had adopted these standards.[15] In 2008, Siemens, one of the world's largest corporations and headquartered in Munich, Germany, was fined $1.6 billion by the U.S. and German governments for bribing foreign officials to help it secure huge public works contracts around the world. Investigations revealed that Siemens created secret offshore bank accounts and used middlemen posing as consultants to deliver suitcases filled with cash, paying an estimated $1.4 billion to over 4,000 well-placed government officials in Asia, Africa, Europe, the Middle East, and Latin America between 2001 and 2007. An estimated 300 Siemens sales employees, executives, and board members were being investigated in 2009 for their roles in the scheme. The evidence gathered indicated that such bribes were a core element of Siemens' strategy and business model.

Penalizing companies for overseas bribes is becoming more widespread internationally. The Serious Fraud Office (SFO) in London held a landmark investigation in December 2009 of DePuy International, a subsidiary of Johnson & Johnson, for bribing Greek officials to purchase products. This comes after DePuy was fined over $311 million by the U.S. government for kickbacks to U.S. surgeons in 2007.[16]

Ethical Relativism Equates to Multiple Sets of Ethical Standards   The existence of varying ethical norms such as those cited above explains why the adherents of ethical relativism maintain that there are few absolutes when it comes to business ethics and thus few ethical absolutes for consistently judging a company's conduct in various countries and markets. Indeed, ethical relativists argue that while there are some general moral prescriptions that apply regardless of the business circumstance, there are plenty of situations where ethical norms must be contoured to fit the local customs, traditions, and notions of fairness shared by the parties involved. They argue that a "one-size-fits-all" template for judging the ethical appropriateness of business actions and the behaviors of company personnel simply does not exist—in other

Under ethical relativism, there can be no one-size-fits-all set of authentic ethical norms against which to gauge the conduct of company personnel.

words, ethical problems in business cannot be fully resolved without appealing to the shared convictions of the parties in question.[17] While European and American managers may want to impose standards of business conduct that give heavy weight to such core human rights as personal freedom, individual security, political participation, and the ownership of property, managers in China may have a much weaker commitment to these kinds of human rights. Japanese managers may prefer ethical standards that show respect for the collective good of society. Muslim managers may wish to apply ethical standards compatible with the teachings of Mohammed. Clearly, there is some merit in the school of ethical relativism's view that what is deemed right or wrong, fair or unfair, moral or immoral, ethical or unethical in business situations depends partly on the context of each country's local customs, religious traditions, and societal norms. Hence, there is a kernel of truth in the argument that businesses need some room to tailor their ethical standards to fit local situations. A company has to be very cautious about exporting its home-country values and ethics to foreign countries where it operates—"photocopying" ethics is disrespectful of other cultures and neglects the important role of moral free space (in which there is room to accommodate local ethical standards).

Pushed to the Extreme, Ethical Relativism Breaks Down

While the ethical relativism rule of "When in Rome, do as the Romans do" appears reasonable, it nonetheless presents a big problem—when the envelope starts to be pushed, as will inevitably be the case, *it is tantamount to rudderless ethical standards.* Consider, for instance, the following example: In 1992, the owners of the *SS United States,* an aging luxury ocean liner constructed with asbestos in the 1940s, had the liner towed to Turkey, where a contractor had agreed to remove the asbestos for $2 million (versus a far higher cost in the United States, where asbestos removal safety standards were much more stringent).[18] When Turkish officials blocked the asbestos removal because of the dangers to workers of contracting cancer, the owners had the liner towed to the Black Sea port of Sevastopol, in the Crimean Republic, where the asbestos removal standards were quite lax and where a contractor had agreed to remove more than 500,000 square feet of carcinogenic asbestos for less than $2 million. There are no moral grounds for arguing that exposing workers to carcinogenic asbestos is ethically correct, regardless of what a country's law allows or the value the country places on worker safety.

A company that adopts the principle of ethical relativism and holds company personnel to local ethical standards necessarily assumes that what prevails as local morality is an adequate guide to ethical behavior. This can be ethically dangerous—it leads to the conclusion that if a country's culture is accepting of bribery or environmental degradation or exposing workers to dangerous conditions (toxic chemicals or bodily harm), then so much the worse for honest people and environmental protection and safe working conditions. Such a position is morally unacceptable. Even though bribery of government officials in China is a common practice, when Lucent Technologies found that managers in its Chinese operations had bribed government officials, it fired the entire senior management team.[19]

Moreover, from a global markets perspective, ethical relativism results in a maze of conflicting ethical standards for multinational companies wanting to address the very real issue of which ethical standards to enforce companywide. It is a slippery slope indeed to resolve such ethical diversity without any kind of higher-order moral compass. Imagine, for example, that a multinational company (in the name of ethical relativism) permits company personnel to pay bribes and kickbacks in countries where such payments are customary but forbids them to make such payments in countries where bribes and kickbacks are considered unethical or illegal. Or that the company says it is appropriate to use child labor in its plants in countries where underage labor is acceptable but inappropriate to employ child labor at the remainder of its plants. Having thus adopted conflicting ethical standards for operating in different countries, company managers have little moral basis for enforcing any ethical standards companywide—rather, the clear message to employees would be that the company has no ethical standards or principles of its own. This is scarcely strong moral ground to stand on.

> Codes of conduct based on ethical relativism can be *ethically dangerous* for multinational companies by creating a maze of conflicting ethical standards.

Ethics and Integrative Social Contracts Theory

Social contract theory provides a middle position between the opposing views of universalism (that the same set of ethical standards should apply everywhere) and relativism (that ethical standards vary according to local custom).[20] According to **integrated social contracts theory,** universal ethical principles or norms based on the collective views of multiple cultures and societies combine to form a "social contract" that all individuals, groups, organizations and businesses in all situations have a duty to observe. *Within the boundaries of this social contract,* local cultures or groups can specify what other actions may or may not be ethically permissible. While this system leaves some "moral free space" for the people in a particular country (or local culture or even a company) to make specific interpretations of what other actions may or may not be permissible, universal ethical norms always take precedence. Thus, local ethical standards can be *more* stringent than the universal ethical standards, but never less so.

> ### CORE CONCEPT
>
> According to **integrated social contracts theory,** universal ethical principles based on the collective views of multiple societies form a "social contract" that all individuals and organizations have a duty to observe in all situations. *Within the boundaries of this social contract*, local cultures or groups can specify what additional actions may or may not be ethically permissible.

Hence, while firms, industries, professional associations, and other business-relevant groups are "contractually obligated" to society to observe universal ethical norms, they have the discretion to go beyond these universal norms and specify other behaviors that are out of bounds and place further limitations on what is considered ethical. For example, both the legal and medical professions have standards regarding what kinds of advertising are ethically permissible that extend beyond the universal norm that advertising not be false or misleading. Similarly, food products companies are beginning to establish ethical guidelines for judging what is and is not appropriate advertising for food products that are inherently unhealthy and may cause dietary or obesity problems for people who eat them regularly or consume them in large quantities.

The strength of integrated social contracts theory is that it accommodates the best parts of ethical universalism and ethical relativism. It is indisputable that cultural differences impact how business is conducted in various parts of the world and that these cultural differences sometimes give rise to different ethical norms. But it is just as indisputable that some ethical norms are more authentic or universally applicable than others, meaning that in many instances of cross-country differences one side may be more "ethically correct" than another. In such instances, resolving cross-cultural differences over what is ethically permissible entails applying the rule that *universal or "first-order" ethical norms override the local or "second-order" ethical norms.* A good example is the payment of bribes and kickbacks. Yes, bribes and kickbacks seem to be common in some countries, but does this justify paying them? Just because bribery flourishes in a country does not mean it is an authentic or legitimate ethical norm. Virtually all of the world's major religions (e.g., Buddhism, Christianity, Confucianism, Hinduism, Islam, Judaism, Sikhism, and Taoism) and all moral schools of thought condemn bribery and corruption.[21] Therefore, a multinational company might reasonably conclude that the right ethical standard is one of refusing to condone bribery and kickbacks on the part of company personnel no matter what the local custom is and no matter what the sales consequences are.

Granting an automatic preference to local-country ethical norms presents vexing problems to multinational company managers when the ethical standards followed in a foreign country are lower than those in its home country or are in conflict with the company's code of ethics. Sometimes—as with bribery and kickbacks—there can be no compromise on what is ethically permissible and what is not. *This is precisely what integrated social contracts theory maintains—adherence to universal or "first-order" ethical norms should always take precedence over local or "second-order" norms.* Consequently, integrated social contracts theory offers managers in multinational companies clear guidance in resolving cross-country ethical differences: Those parts of the company's code of ethics that involve universal ethical norms must be enforced worldwide, but *within* these boundaries there is room for ethical diversity and opportunity for host-country cultures to exert *some* influence in setting their own moral and ethical standards. Such an approach avoids the discomforting case of a self-righteous multinational company trying to operate as the standard bearer of moral truth and imposing its interpretation of its code of ethics worldwide no matter what. And it avoids the equally disturbing case for a company's ethical conduct to be no higher than local ethical norms in situations where local ethical norms permit practices that are generally considered immoral or when local norms clearly conflict with a company's code of ethical conduct.

> According to integrated social contracts theory, adherence to universal or "first-order" ethical norms should always take precedence over local or "second-order" norms.

HOW AND WHY ETHICAL STANDARDS IMPACT THE TASKS OF CRAFTING AND EXECUTING STRATEGY

Many companies have acknowledged their ethical obligations in official codes of ethical conduct and statements of company values. In the United States, for example, the Sarbanes-Oxley Act, passed in 2002, requires that companies whose stock is publicly traded have a code of ethics or else explain in writing to the Securities and Exchange Commission (SEC) why they do not. But there's a big difference between having a code of ethics that serves merely as public window dressing and having ethical standards that truly paint the white lines for a company's actual strategy and business conduct.[22] *The litmus test of whether a company's code of ethics is cosmetic is the extent to which it is embraced in crafting strategy and in operating the business day to day.*

It is up to senior executives to walk the talk and make a point of considering three sets of questions whenever a new strategic initiative is under review:

- Is what we are proposing to do fully compliant with our code of ethical conduct? Are there any areas of ambiguity that may be of concern?

- Is it apparent that this proposed action is in harmony with our core values? Are any conflicts or potential problems evident?

- Is there anything in the proposed action that could be considered ethically objectionable? Would our stakeholders, our competitors, the SEC, or the media view this action as ethically objectionable?

Unless questions of this nature are posed—either in open discussion or by force of habit in the minds of strategy makers—there's room for strategic initiatives to become disconnected from the company's code of ethics and stated core values. If a company's executives believe strongly in living up to the company's ethical standards, they will unhesitatingly reject strategic initiatives and operating approaches that don't measure up. However, in companies with a cosmetic approach to ethics, any strategy-ethics-values linkage stems mainly from a desire to avoid the risk of embarrassment and possible disciplinary action should strategy makers be held accountable for approving a strategic initiative that is deemed by society to be unethical and perhaps illegal.

While most company managers are careful to ensure that a company's strategy is within the bounds of what is legal, evidence indicates they are not always so careful to ensure that all elements of their strategies and operating activities are within the bounds of what is considered ethical. In recent years, there have been revelations of ethical misconduct on the part of managers at such companies as Enron, Tyco International, HealthSouth, Adelphia, Royal Dutch/Shell, Parmalat (an Italy-based food products company), Rite Aid, Mexican oil giant Pemex, AIG, Citigroup, several leading brokerage houses, mutual fund companies, investment banking firms, and a host of mortgage lenders. Much of the crisis in residential real estate that emerged in the United States in 2007–2008 stemmed from consciously unethical strategies at certain banks and mortgage companies to boost the fees they earned on processing home mortgage applications by deliberately lowering lending standards and finding ways to secure mortgage approvals for home buyers who lacked sufficient income to make their monthly mortgage payments. Once these lenders earned their fees on the so-called subprime loans (a term used for high-risk mortgage loans to home buyers with dubious qualifications to repay the loans), they secured the assistance of investment banking firms to bundle those and other mortgages into collateralized debt obligations (CDOs), found means of having the CDOs assigned triple-A bond ratings, and auctioned them to unsuspecting investors, who later suffered huge losses when the high-risk borrowers began to default on their loan payments (government authorities later forced some of the firms that auctioned off these CDOs to repurchase them at the auction price and bear the losses themselves).

The consequences of crafting strategies that cannot pass the test of moral scrutiny are manifested in sizable fines, devastating public relations hits, sharp drops in stock prices that cost shareholders billions of dollars, and criminal indictments and convictions of company executives. The fallout from all these scandals has resulted in heightened management attention to legal and ethical considerations in crafting strategy.

WHAT ARE THE DRIVERS OF UNETHICAL STRATEGIES AND BUSINESS BEHAVIOR?

LO 2

Recognize conditions that can give rise to unethical business strategies and behavior.

Confusion over conflicting ethical standards may suggest one reason for the lack of an effective moral compass in business dealings and why certain elements of a company's strategy may be unethical. But apart from this, three main drivers of unethical business behavior stand out:[23]

- Faulty oversight that implicitly allows the overzealous pursuit of personal gain, wealth, and self-interest.

- Heavy pressures on company managers to meet or beat short-term performance targets.

- A company culture that puts profitability and business performance ahead of ethical behavior.

Faulty Oversight and the Overzealous Pursuit of Personal Gain, Wealth, and Self-Interest   People who are obsessed with wealth accumulation, greed, power, status, and their own self-interest often push ethical principles aside in their quest for personal gain. Driven by their ambitions, they exhibit few qualms in skirting the rules or doing whatever is necessary to achieve their goals. A general disregard for business ethics can prompt all kinds of unethical strategic maneuvers and behaviors at companies. According to a civil complaint filed by the Securities and Exchange Commission, the chief executive officer (CEO) of Tyco International, a well-known $35.6 billion manufacturing and services company, conspired with the company's chief financial officer (CFO) to steal more than $170 million, including a company-paid $2 million birthday party for the CEO's wife held on an island off the coast of Italy, a $7 million Park Avenue apartment for his wife, and secret interest-free loans to finance personal investments and purchase lavish artwork, yachts, estate jewelry, and vacation homes. Tyco's CEO and CFO were further charged with conspiring to reap more than $430 million from sales of stock, using questionable accounting to hide their actions, and engaging in deceptive accounting practices to distort the company's financial condition from 1995 to 2002. In 2005, both Tyco executives were convicted on multiple counts of looting the company and sent to jail.

Responsible corporate governance and oversight by the company's corporate board is necessary to guard against self-dealing and the manipulation of information to disguise such actions by a company's managers. **Self-dealing** occurs when managers take advantage of their position to further their own private interests rather than those of the firm. As discussed in Chapter 2, the duty of the corporate board (and its compensation and audit committees in particular) is to guard against such actions. A strong, independent board is necessary to have proper oversight of the company's financial practices and to hold top managers accountable for their actions.

A particularly egregious example of the lack of proper oversight is the case of Enron Corporation, a former diversified energy company that has become a symbol of corporate corruption and fraud. Andrew Fastow, Enron's chief financial officer (CFO), set himself up as the manager of one of Enron's off-the-books partnerships and as the part-owner of another, allegedly earning extra compensation of $30 million for his owner-manager roles in the two partnerships; Enron's board of directors agreed to suspend the company's conflict-of-interest rules designed to protect the company from this very kind of executive self-dealing. Although *Fortune* magazine had named Enron "America's Most Innovative Company" for six years running, in the end it turned out that Enron's real creativity was in its accounting practices. Enron's eventual downfall resulted not only in the company's bankruptcy in 2001 but also in the dissolution of its auditor, Arthur Andersen, which was one of the top-five accounting firms at the time.

> **CORE CONCEPT**
>
> **Self-dealing** occurs when managers take advantage of their position to further their own private interests rather than those of the firm.

Illustration Capsule 9.2 discusses the more recent multibillion-dollar Ponzi schemes perpetrated at Bernard L. Madoff Investment Securities and alleged at Stanford Financial Group.

Heavy Pressures on Company Managers to Meet or Beat Short-Term Earnings Targets Performance expectations of Wall Street analysts and investors create enormous pressure on management to do whatever it takes to deliver good financial results each and every quarter. Executives at high-performing companies know that investors will see the slightest sign of a slowdown in earnings growth as a red flag and drive down the company's stock price. In addition, slowing growth or declining profits could lead to a downgrade of the company's credit rating if it has used lots of debt to finance its growth. The pressure to "never miss a quarter"—so as not to upset the expectations of analysts, investors, and creditors—prompts nearsighted managers to engage in short-term maneuvers to make the numbers, regardless of whether these moves are really in the best long-term interests of the company. Sometimes the pressure induces company personnel to continue to stretch the rules until the limits of ethical conduct are overlooked.[24] Once ethical boundaries are crossed in efforts to "meet or beat their numbers," the threshold for making more extreme ethical compromises becomes lower.

Several top executives at the former telecommunications company WorldCom were convicted of concocting a fraudulent $11 billion accounting scheme to hide costs and inflate revenues and profit over several years; the scheme was said to have helped the company keep its stock price propped up high enough to make additional acquisitions, support its nearly $30 billion debt load, and allow executives to cash in on their lucrative stock options. HealthSouth's chief financial managers were convicted of overstating the company's earnings by $1.4 billion between 1996 and 2002 in an attempt to hide the company's slowing growth from investors. A 2007 internal investigation at Dell Computer found that executives had engaged in a scheme to manipulate the company's accounting data to meet investors' quarterly earnings expectations. The fraudulent accounting practices inflated the company's earnings by $150 million between 2002 and 2006. The executives were terminated by Dell Computer in 2007.

Company executives often feel pressured to hit financial performance targets because their compensation depends heavily on the company's performance. During the late 1990s, it became fashionable for boards of directors to grant lavish bonuses, stock option awards, and other compensation benefits to executives for meeting specified performance targets. So outlandishly large were these rewards that executives had strong personal incentives to bend the rules and engage in behaviors that allowed the targets to be met. Much of the accounting manipulation at the root of recent corporate scandals has entailed situations in which executives benefited enormously from misleading accounting or other shady activities that

ILLUSTRATION CAPSULE 9.2

Investment Fraud at Bernard L. Madoff Investment Securities and Stanford Financial Group

Bernard Madoff engineered the largest investment scam in history to accumulate a net worth of more than $800 million and build a reputation as one of Wall Street's most savvy investors—he was appointed to various Securities and Exchange Commission panels, invited to testify before Congress on investment matters, made chairman of Nasdaq, and befriended by some of the world's most influential people. Madoff deceived Wall Street and investors with a simple Ponzi scheme that promised investors returns that would beat the market by 400 to 500 percent. The hedge funds, banks, and wealthy individuals that sent Bernard L. Madoff Investment Securities billions to invest on their behalf were quite pleased when their statements arrived showing annual returns as high as 45 percent. But, in fact, the portfolio gains shown on these statements were fictitious. Funds placed with Bernard Madoff were seldom, if ever, actually invested in any type of security—the money went to cover losses in his legitimate stock-trading business, fund periodic withdrawals of investors' funds, and support Madoff's lifestyle (including three vacation homes, a $7 million Manhattan condominium, yachts, and luxury cars).

For decades, the Ponzi scheme was never in danger of collapse because most Madoff investors were so impressed with the reported returns that they seldom made withdrawals from their accounts, and when they did withdraw funds Madoff used the monies being deposited by new investors to cover the payments. Madoff's deception came to an end in late 2008 when the dramatic drop in world stock prices caused so many of Madoff's investors to request withdrawals of their balances that there was not nearly enough new money coming in to cover the amounts being withdrawn. As with any Ponzi scheme, the first investors to ask Madoff for their funds were paid, but those asking later were left empty-handed. All told, more than 1,300 account holders lost about $65 billion when Bernard Madoff admitted to the scam in December 2008. As of late October 2009, investigators had located assets of only about $1.4 billion to return to Madoff account holders. Madoff was sentenced to 150 years in prison for his crimes.

Increased oversight at the Securities and Exchange Commission after the December 2008

Madoff confession led to the June 2009 indictment of R. Allen Stanford and five others who were accused of running an investment scheme similar to that perpetrated by Bernard Madoff. Stanford was alleged to have defrauded more than 30,000 Stanford Financial Group account holders out of $7 billion through the sale of spurious certificates of deposit (CDs). The CDs marketed by Stanford Financial Group were issued by the company's Antiguan subsidiary, Stanford International Bank, and carried rates that were as much as three to four times greater than the CD rates offered by other financial institutions. Stanford claimed that the Stanford International Bank was able to provide such exceptional yields because of its investment in a globally diversified portfolio of stocks, bonds, commodities, and alternative investments and because of the tax advantages provided by the bank's location in Antigua. All the investments made by Stanford International Bank were said to be safe and liquid financial instruments monitored by more than 20 analysts and audited by Antiguan regulators. In fact, the deposits were invested in much riskier private equity placements and real estate investments and were subject to severe fluctuations in value. The statements provided to CD holders were alleged by prosecutors to be based on fabricated performance and phony financial statements.

Federal prosecutors also alleged that deposits of at least $1.6 billion were diverted into undisclosed personal loans to Allen Stanford. At the time of Stanford's indictment, he ranked 605th on *Forbes* magazine's list of the world's wealthiest persons, with an estimated net worth of

(Continued)

$2.2 billion. Stanford was a notable sports enthusiast and philanthropist—he supported a cricket league in Antigua and professional golf tournaments in the United States and contributed millions to the St. Jude Children's Research Hospital and museums in Houston and Miami.

Stanford also pledged $100 million to support programs aimed at slowing global warming. In May 2009, Stanford Investment Bank disclosed that it owed $7.2 billion to about 28,000 account holders. Its total assets at the time stood at $1 billion, including $46 million in cash.

Developed with C. David Morgan.

Sources: James Bandler, Nicholas Varchaver, and Doris Burke, "How Bernie Did It," *Fortune Online,* April 30, 2009 (accessed July 7, 2009); Duncan Greenberg, "Billionaire Responds to SEC Probe," *Forbes Online,* February 13, 2009 (accessed July 9, 2009); Katie Benner, "Stanford Scandal Sets Antigua on Edge," *Fortune Online,* February 25, 2009 (accessed July 9, 2009); Alyssa Abkowitz, "The Investment Scam-Artist's Playbook," *Fortune Online,* February 25, 2009 (accessed July 9, 2009); Kathryn Glass, "Stanford Bank Assets Insufficient to Repay Depositors," *Fox Business.com*, May 15, 2009 (accessed July 9, 2009); Bill McQuillen, Justin Blum, and Laurel Brubaker Calkins, "Allen Stanford Indicted by U.S. in $7 Billion Scam," *Bloomberg.com*, June 19, 2009 (accessed July 9, 2009); Jane J. Kim, "The Madoff Fraud: SIPC Sets Payouts in Madoff Scandal," *Wall Street Journal* (Eastern Edition), October 29, 2009, p. C4.

allowed them to hit the numbers and receive incentive awards ranging from $10 million to $100 million.

The fundamental problem with **short-termism**—the tendency for managers to focus excessive attention on short-term performance objectives—is that it doesn't create value for customers or improve the firm's competitiveness in the marketplace; that is, it sacrifices the activities that are the most reliable drivers of higher profits and added shareholder value in the long run. Cutting ethical corners in the name of profits carries exceptionally high risk for shareholders—the steep stock price decline and tarnished brand image that accompany the discovery of scurrilous behavior leave shareholders with a company worth much less than before—and the rebuilding task can be arduous, taking both considerable time and resources.

> ### CORE CONCEPT
>
> **Short-termism** is the tendency for managers to focus excessively on short-term performance objectives at the expense of longer-term strategic objectives. It has negative implications for the likelihood of ethical lapses as well as company performance in the longer run.

A Company Culture That Puts Profitability and Business Performance Ahead of Ethical Behavior

When a company's culture spawns an ethically corrupt or amoral work climate, people have a company-approved license to ignore "what's right" and engage in any behavior or employ any strategy they think they can get away with.[25] At such companies, unethical people are given free reign, and otherwise honorable people may succumb to the many opportunities around them to engage in unethical practices. A perfect example of a company culture gone awry on ethics is Enron.[26]

Enron's leaders encouraged company personnel to focus on the current bottom line and to be innovative and aggressive in figuring out how to grow current earnings—regardless of the methods. Enron's annual "rank and yank" performance evaluation process, in which the lowest-ranking 15 to 20 percent of employees were let go, made it abundantly clear that bottom-line results were what mattered most. The name of the game at Enron became devising clever ways to boost revenues and earnings, even if this sometimes meant operating outside established policies. In fact, outside-the-lines behavior was celebrated if it generated profitable new business.

A high-performance/high-rewards climate came to pervade the Enron culture, as the best workers (determined by who produced the best bottom-line results) received impressively large incentives and bonuses (amounting to as much as

$1 million for traders and even more for senior executives). On Car Day at Enron, an array of luxury sports cars arrived for presentation to the most successful employees. Understandably, employees wanted to be seen as part of Enron's star team and partake in the benefits granted to Enron's best and brightest employees. The high monetary rewards, the ambitious and hard-driving people whom the company hired and promoted, and the competitive, results-oriented culture combined to give Enron a reputation not only for trampling competitors at every opportunity but also for internal ruthlessness. The company's super-aggressiveness and win-at-all-costs mindset nurtured a culture that gradually and then more rapidly fostered the erosion of ethical standards, eventually making a mockery of the company's stated values of integrity and respect. When it became evident in fall 2001 that Enron was a house of cards propped up by deceitful accounting and a myriad of unsavory practices, the company imploded in a matter of weeks—one of the biggest bankruptcies of all time, costing investors $64 billion in losses.

More recently, a team investigating an ethical scandal at oil giant Royal Dutch/Shell Group that resulted in the payment of $150 million in fines found that an ethically flawed culture was a major contributor to why managers made rosy forecasts that they couldn't meet and why top executives engaged in maneuvers to mislead investors by overstating Shell's oil and gas reserves by 25 percent (equal to 4.5 billion barrels of oil). The investigation revealed that top Shell executives knew that a variety of internal practices, together with unrealistic and unsupportable estimates submitted by overzealous, bonus-conscious managers in Shell's exploration and production group, were being used to overstate reserves. An e-mail written by Shell's top executive for exploration and production (who was caught up in the ethical misdeeds and later forced to resign) said, "I am becoming sick and tired of lying about the extent of our reserves issues and the downward revisions that need to be done because of our far too aggressive/optimistic bookings."[27]

In contrast, when high ethical principles are deeply ingrained in the corporate culture of a company, culture can function as a powerful mechanism for communicating ethical behavioral norms and gaining employee buy-in to the company's moral standards, business principles, and corporate values. In such cases, the ethical principles embraced in the company's code of ethics and/or in its statement of corporate values are seen as integral to the company's identity, self-image, and ways of operating. Stories of former and current moral heroes are kept in circulation, and the deeds of company personnel who display ethical values and are dedicated to walking the talk are celebrated at internal company events. The message that ethics matters—and matters a lot—resounds loudly and clearly throughout the organization and in its strategy and decisions. Illustration Capsule 9.3 discusses GE's approach to building a culture that combines demands for high performance with expectations for ethical conduct.

WHY SHOULD COMPANY STRATEGIES BE ETHICAL?

There are two reasons why a company's strategy should be ethical: (1) because a strategy that is unethical is morally wrong and reflects badly on the character of the company personnel and (2) because an ethical strategy can be good business and serve the self-interest of shareholders.

How General Electric's Top Management Built a Culture That Fuses High Performance with High Integrity

GE's CEO, Jeffrey Immelt, has made it a priority to foster a culture built on high ethical standards. The company's heavy reliance on financial controls and performance-based reward systems—which are necessary because of GE's broad multinational diversification—could easily tempt managers at all levels to cut corners, engage in unethical sales tactics, inaccurately record revenues or expenses, or participate in corrupt practices prevalent in the many emerging markets where GE competes. Immelt and GE's other top managers clearly recognize that without a strong ethical culture, there would be little to deter the company's thousands of managers across the globe from pursuing the many types of unethical behavior that would, on the surface, boost performance.

The first step in establishing an ethical culture at GE was for its top management to forcefully communicate the company's principles that should guide decision making. Jeffrey Immelt begins and ends each annual meeting of the company's 220 officers and 600 senior managers with a recitation of the company's fundamental ethical principles. Immelt and GE's other managers are careful to not violate these principles themselves or give implied consent for others to skirt these principles, since human nature makes subordinates at all levels ever vigilant for the signs of hypocrisy in the actions of higher-ups. The importance of walking the talk justifies GE's "one strike and you're out" standard for its top management. For example, a high-level manager in an emerging market was terminated for failing to conduct required diligence on a third-party vendor known for its shady business practices, including the payment of bribes to local officials. Another executive was fired from GE for agreeing to a large and important Asian customer's request to falsify supplier documents that were used by regulatory agencies.

With so many ethical standards prevailing in the more than 100 countries where GE operates, the company has turned to global ethical standards rather than allowing local cultures to shape business behavior. The company's global standards cover such topics as how to best evaluate suppliers' environmental records

and working conditions in its manufacturing businesses and how to avoid money-laundering schemes or aiding and abetting financial services customers engaged in tax evasion or accounting fraud. Operating-level managers are formally responsible for ensuring ethical compliance in their divisions and are required to submit quarterly tracking reports to GE's corporate offices on key indicators such as spills, accident rates, and violation notices. Managers of operating units falling in the bottom quartile on the quarterly assessments are required to submit plans for improving the ethical shortcomings. GE also evaluates the ethical performance of its 4,000 managers who are responsible for profit centers or are key contributors on business teams.

GE's approach to culture building also includes instilling such principles into the behavior of the company's 300,000-plus employees with no managerial responsibility. Employees are provided training to help them understand the company's ethical principles and how those principles can help them make decisions in the ethical gray areas that arise while making everyday decisions. In Immelt's words, "At a time when many people are more cynical than ever about business, GE must seek to earn this high level of trust every day, employee by employee."* GE also allows employees to lodge anonymous complaints about ethics compliance; the complaints are evaluated by more than 500 employees around the world with either full-time or part-time ombudsperson capacity. About 20 percent of the

(Continued)

1,500 concerns lodged annually lead to serious discipline. Hourly employees are also included in annual assessments of ethical performance and are rewarded through bonuses, promotions, or recognition for identifying or resolving ethical issues at the operating level.

* *General Electric*, "The Spirit and the Letter," January 2008, www.ge.com/citizenship/reporting/spirit_and_letter.jsp.

Developed with C. David Morgan.

Source: Based on the discussion of GE's culture-building process by the company's former legal counsel in Ben W. Heineman, Jr., "Avoiding Integrity Land Mines," *Harvard Business Review* 85, no. 4 (April 2007), pp. 100–8.

The Moral Case for an Ethical Strategy

Managers do not dispassionately assess what strategic course to steer. Ethical strategy making generally begins with managers who themselves have strong moral character (i.e., who are trustworthy, have integrity, and truly care about conducting the company's business in an honorable manner). Managers with high ethical principles are usually advocates of a corporate code of ethics and strong ethics compliance, and they are genuinely committed to upholding corporate values and ethical business principles. They demonstrate their commitment by displaying the company's stated values and living up to its business principles and ethical standards. They understand there's a big difference between adopting value statements and codes of ethics and ensuring that they are followed strictly in a company's actual strategy and business conduct. As a consequence, ethically strong managers consciously opt for strategic actions that can pass the strictest moral scrutiny—they display no tolerance for strategies with ethically controversial components.

LO 3

Gain an understanding of the costs of business ethics failures.

The Business Case for Ethical Strategies

In addition to the moral reasons for adopting ethical strategies, there may be solid business reasons. Pursuing unethical strategies and tolerating unethical conduct not only damages a company's reputation but also may result in a wide-ranging set of other costly consequences. Figure 9.1 shows the types of costs a company can incur when unethical behavior on its part is discovered, the wrongdoings of company personnel are headlined in the media, and it is forced to make amends for its behavior. The more egregious are a company's ethical violations, the higher the costs and the bigger the damage to its reputation (and to the reputations of the company personnel involved). In high-profile instances, the costs of ethical misconduct can easily run into the hundreds of millions and even billions of dollars, especially if they provoke widespread public outrage and many people were harmed. The penalties levied on executives caught in wrongdoing can skyrocket as well, as the 150-year prison term sentence of financier Bernie Madoff illustrates.

Conducting business in an ethical fashion is not only morally right—it is in a company's enlightened self-interest.

The fallout of ethical misconduct on the part of a company goes well beyond the costs of making amends for the misdeeds. Rehabilitating a company's shattered reputation is time-consuming and costly. Customers shun companies known for their shady behavior. Companies known to have engaged in unethical conduct have difficulty in recruiting and retaining talented employees; indeed, many people take a company's ethical reputation into account when deciding whether to accept a job

Figure 9.1   **The Costs Companies Incur When Ethical Wrongdoing Is Found Out**

Visible Costs	Internal Administrative Costs	Intangible or Less Visible Costs
• Government fines and penalties • Civil penalties arising from class-action lawsuits and other litigation aimed at punishing the company for its offense and the harm done to others • The costs to shareholders in the form of a lower stock price (and possibly lower dividends)	• Legal and investigative costs incurred by the company • The costs of providing remedial education and ethics training to company personnel • Costs of taking corrective actions • Administrative costs associated with ensuring future compliance	• Customer defections • Loss of reputation • Lost employee morale and higher degrees of employee cynicism • Higher employee turnover • Higher recruiting costs and difficulty in attracting talented employees • Adverse effects on employee productivity • The costs of complying with often harsher government regulations

Source: Adapted from Terry Thomas, John R. Schermerhorn, and John W. Dienhart, "Strategic Leadership of Ethical Behavior," *Academy of Management Executive* 18, no. 2 (May 2004), p. 58.

offer.[28] Most ethically upstanding people are repulsed by a work environment where unethical behavior is condoned; they don't want to get entrapped in a compromising situation, nor do they want their personal reputations tarnished by the actions of an unsavory employer. Creditors are usually unnerved by the unethical actions of a borrower because of the potential business fallout and subsequent risk of default on loans.

All told, a company's unethical behavior risks doing considerable damage to shareholders in the form of lost revenues, higher costs, lower profits, lower stock prices, and a diminished business reputation. To a significant degree, therefore, ethical strategies and ethical conduct are *good business.* Most companies understand the value of operating in a manner that wins the approval of suppliers, employees, investors, and society at large. Most businesspeople recognize the risks and adverse fallout attached to the discovery of unethical behavior. Hence, companies have an incentive to employ strategies that can pass the test of being ethical. Even if a company's managers are not of strong moral character and personally committed to high ethical standards, they have good reason to operate within ethical bounds, if only to (1) avoid the risk of embarrassment, scandal, and possible disciplinary action for unethical conduct on their part and (2) escape being held accountable for unethical behavior by personnel under their supervision and their own lax enforcement of ethical standards.

> Shareholders suffer major damage when a company's unethical behavior is discovered. Making amends for unethical business conduct is costly, and it takes years to rehabilitate a tarnished company reputation.

STRATEGY, CORPORATE SOCIAL RESPONSIBILITY, AND EVIRONMENTAL SUSTAINABILITY

LO 4

Gain an understanding of the concepts of corporate social responsibility and environmental sustainability and of how companies balance these duties with economic responsibilities to shareholders.

The idea that businesses have an obligation to foster social betterment, a much-debated topic in the past 50 years, took root in the 19th century when progressive companies in the aftermath of the industrial revolution began to provide workers with housing and other amenities. The notion that corporate executives should balance the interests of all stakeholders—shareholders, employees, customers, suppliers, the communities in which they operated, and society at large—began to blossom in the 1960s. Some years later, a group of chief executives of America's 200 largest corporations, calling themselves the Business Roundtable, came out in strong support of the concept of **corporate social responsibility:**[29]

> Balancing the shareholder's expectations of maximum return against other priorities is one of the fundamental problems confronting corporate management. The shareholder must receive a good return but the legitimate concerns of other constituencies (customers, employees, communities, suppliers and society at large) also must have the appropriate attention. . . . [Leading managers] believe that by giving enlightened consideration to balancing the legitimate claims of all its constituents, a corporation will best serve the interest of its shareholders.

Today, corporate social responsibility (CSR) is a concept that resonates in western Europe, the United States, Canada, and such developing nations as Brazil and India.

CORE CONCEPT

Corporate social responsibility (CSR) refers to a company's *duty* to operate in an honorable manner, provide good working conditions for employees, encourage workforce diversity, be a good steward of the environment, and actively work to better the quality of life in the local communities where it operates and in society at large.

What Do We Mean by *Corporate Social Responsibility?*

The essence of socially responsible business behavior is that a company should balance strategic actions to benefit shareholders against the *duty* to be a good corporate citizen. The underlying thesis is that company managers should display a *social conscience* in operating the business and specifically take into account how management decisions and company actions affect the well-being of employees, local communities, the environment, and society at large.[30] Acting in a socially responsible manner thus encompasses more than just participating in community service projects and donating monies to charities and other worthy social causes. Demonstrating social responsibility also entails undertaking actions that earn trust and respect from all stakeholders—operating in an honorable and ethical manner, striving to make the company a great place to work, demonstrating genuine respect for the environment, and trying to make a difference in bettering society. As depicted in Figure 9.2, corporate responsibility programs commonly include the following elements:

- *Making efforts to employ an ethical strategy and observe ethical principles in operating the business.* A sincere commitment to observing ethical principles is a necessary component of a CSR strategy simply because unethical conduct is incompatible with the concept of good corporate citizenship and socially responsible business behavior.

Figure 9.2   The Five Components of a Corporate Social Responsibility Strategy

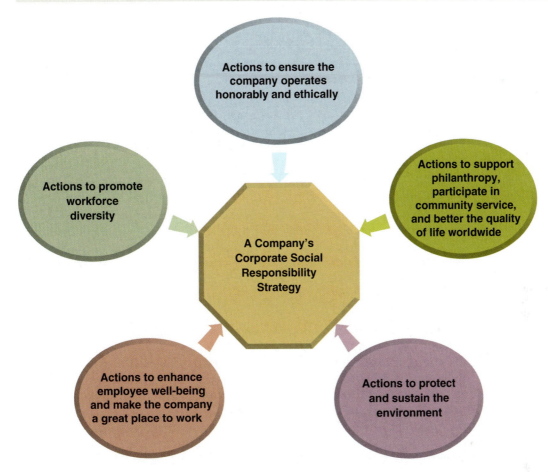

Source: Adapted from material in Ronald Paul Hill, Debra Stephens, and Iain Smith, "Corporate Social Responsibility: An Examination of Individual Firm Behavior," *Business and Society Review* 108, no. 3 (September 2003), p. 348.

- *Making charitable contributions, supporting community service endeavors, engaging in broader philanthropic initiatives, and reaching out to make a difference in the lives of the disadvantaged.* Some companies fulfill their philanthropic obligations by spreading their efforts over a multitude of charitable and community activities—for instance, Microsoft and Johnson & Johnson support a broad variety of community, art, and social welfare programs. Others prefer to focus their energies more narrowly. McDonald's, for example, concentrates on sponsoring the Ronald McDonald House program (which provides a home away from home for the families of seriously ill children receiving treatment at nearby hospitals). British Telecom gives 1 percent of its profits directly to communities, largely for education—teacher training, in-school workshops, and digital technology. Leading prescription drug maker GlaxoSmithKline and other pharmaceutical companies either donate or heavily discount medicines for distribution in the least developed nations. Companies frequently reinforce their philanthropic efforts by encouraging employees to support charitable causes and participate in community affairs, often through programs that match employee contributions.

- *Taking actions to protect the environment and, in particular, to minimize or eliminate any adverse impact on the environment stemming from the company's own business activities.* Social responsibility as it applies to environmental protection entails actively striving to be a good steward of the environment. This means using the best available science and technology to reduce environmentally harmful aspects of the company's operations *below the levels required by prevailing environmental regulations.* It also means putting time and money into improving the environment in ways that extend past a company's own industry boundaries—such as participating in recycling projects, adopting energy conservation practices, and supporting efforts to clean up local water supplies. Retailers like Walmart and Home Depot in the United States and B&Q in the United Kingdom have pressured their suppliers to adopt stronger environmental protection practices in order to lower the carbon footprint of their entire supply chains.[31]

- *Taking actions to create a work environment that enhances the quality of life for employees.* Numerous companies exert extra effort to enhance the quality of life for their employees, both at work and at home. This can include on-site day care, flexible work schedules, workplace exercise facilities, special leaves for employees to care for sick family members, work-at-home opportunities, career development programs and education opportunities, special safety programs, and the like.

- *Taking actions to build a workforce that is diverse with respect to gender, race, national origin, and other aspects that different people bring to the workplace.* Most large companies in the United States have established workforce diversity programs, and some go the extra mile to ensure that their workplaces are attractive to ethnic minorities and inclusive of all groups and perspectives. At some companies, the diversity initiative extends to suppliers—sourcing items from small businesses owned by women or ethnic minorities, for example. The pursuit of workforce diversity can be good business. At Coca-Cola, where strategic success depends on getting people all over the world to become loyal consumers of the company's beverages, efforts to build a public persona of inclusiveness for people of all races, religions, nationalities, interests, and talents have considerable strategic value.

The particular combination of socially responsible endeavors a company elects to pursue defines its **corporate social responsibility (CSR) strategy.** Illustration Capsule 9.4 describes John Deere's approach to corporate social responsibility—an approach that corresponds closely to the description in Figure 9.2. But the specific components emphasized in a CSR strategy vary from company to company and are typically linked to a company's core values. General Mills, for example, builds its CSR strategy around the theme of "nourishing lives" to emphasize its commitment to good nutrition as well as philanthropy, community building, and environmental protection.[32] Starbucks' CSR strategy includes four main elements (ethical sourcing, community service, environmental stewardship, and farmer support), all of which have touch points with the way that the company procures its coffee—a key aspect of its product differentiation strategy.[33] Some companies use other terms, such as *corporate citizenship, corporate responsibility,* or *sustainable responsible business (SRB)* to characterize their CSR initiatives.

CORE CONCEPT

A company's **CSR strategy** is defined by the specific combination of socially beneficial activities the company opts to support with its contributions of time, money, and other resources.

ILLUSTRATION CAPSULE 9.4

John Deere's Approach to Corporate Social Responsibility

Principal Components of John Deere's Corporate Social Responsibility Strategy	Specific Actions to Execute the Strategy
Adhering to the core values of integrity, quality commitment, and innovation *Integrity* means telling the truth, keeping our word, and treating others with fairness and respect. *Quality* means delivering the value customers, employees, shareholders, and other business partners expect every day. *Commitment* means doing our best to meet expectations over the long run. *Innovation* means inventing, designing, and developing breakthrough products and services that customers want to buy from John Deere.	• Committing to ethical behavior and fair dealing in all relationships • Providing Business Conduct Guidelines that show employees how they are expected to carry out company business • Creating an Office of Corporate Compliance to ensure ethical and fair business practices are maintained throughout global operations • Instituting a 24-hour hotline for confidential anonymous reporting of ethical violations • Offering employees professional guidance when they feel they are operating in complicated or ambiguous business and cultural situations
Engaging in philanthropy and community betterment	• Supporting agricultural development in resource-poor countries • Providing increased access to financing for the rural poor in Africa (in partnership with Opportunity International) • Helping start *BackPack* programs in the U.S. to supply supplemental food for school-age children • Supporting a variety of higher educational programs and such programs as Junior Achievement, FFA, and the National 4-H Council • Instituting an employee matching gift program
Conserving resources and sustaining the environment	• Establishing ambitious greenhouse-gas reduction goals to be achieved over the next 5 to 10 years • Mandating the use of recycling and waste reduction practices across all company operations • Implementing a worldwide Environmental Management System geared to ISO14001 standards • Helping to develop long-term comprehensive climate change strategies through EPS's Climate Leaders Program • Designing products to conserve water, encourage biofuel development, and support sustainable agriculture
Supporting and enhancing the workforce	• Maintaining effective workplace safety programs—more than 1,000 awards from the U.S. National Safety Council • Providing programs to promote employee health and wellness and work-life balance • Establishing global occupational health programs keyed to local health issues and infrastructure

(Continued)

313

Principal Components of John Deere's Corporate Social Responsibility Strategy	Specific Actions to Execute the Strategy
	• Helping employees with career development through mentoring, coaching, and a programmatic approach • Creating a continuous learning environment with extensive training opportunities and a tuition reimbursement program
Promoting diversity and inclusiveness	• Creating an inclusive culture in which employees of all backgrounds can develop their leadership potential • Providing training and tools designed to make work teams more diverse, productive, and effective • Sponsoring employee networks that bring together people from around the world with shared interests, gender, ethnicity, or skills • Encouraging diversity within the company's dealer and supplier base • Supporting minority education programs and collegiate diversity initiatives

Source: Information posted at www.deere.com (accessed July 8, 2010).

Although there is wide variation in how companies devise and implement a CSR strategy, communities of companies concerned with corporate social responsibility (such as CSR Europe) have emerged to help companies share best CSR practices. Moreover, a number of reporting standards have been developed, including ISO 26000—a new internationally recognized standard for social responsibility produced by the International Standards Organization (ISO).[34] Companies that exhibit a strong commitment to corporate social responsibility are often recognized by being included on lists such as *Corporate Responsibility* magazine's "100 Best Corporate Citizens" or *Corporate Knights* magazine's "Global 100 Most Sustainable Corporations."

Corporate Social Responsibility and the Triple Bottom Line

CSR initiatives undertaken by companies are frequently directed at improving the company's "triple bottom line"—a reference to three types of performance metrics: *economic, social, environmental.* The goal is for a company to succeed simultaneously in all three dimensions, as illustrated in Figure 9.3.[35] The three dimensions of performance are often referred to in terms of the "three pillars" of "people, planet, and profit." The term *people* refers to the various social initiatives that make up CSR strategies, such as corporate giving, community involvement, and company efforts to improve the lives of its internal and external stakeholders. *Planet* refers to a firm's ecological impact and environmental practices. The term *profit* has a broader meaning with respect to the triple bottom line than it does otherwise. It encompasses not only the profit a firm earns for its shareholders but also the economic impact that the company has on society more generally, in terms of the overall value that it creates and the overall costs that it imposes on society. For example, Procter & Gamble's Swiffer cleaning system, one of the company's best-selling products, not only offers an earth-friendly design but also outperforms less ecologically friendly alternatives in terms of its broader economic impact: It

Figure 9.3 **The Triple Bottom Line: Excelling on Three Measures of Company Performance**

Source: Developed with help from Amy E.Florentino.

reduces demands on municipal water sources, saves electricity that would be needed to heat mop water, and doesn't add to the amount of detergent making its way into waterways and waste treatment facilities. Nike sees itself as bringing people, planet, and profits into balance by producing innovative new products in a more sustainable way, recognizing that sustainability is key to its future profitability.

Many companies now make a point of citing the beneficial outcomes of their CSR strategies in press releases and issue special reports for consumers and investors to review. Staples, the world's largest office products company, makes reporting an important part of its commitment to corporate responsibility; the company posts a "Staples Soul Report" on its Web site that describes its initiatives and accomplishments in the areas of diversity, environment, community, and ethics. Triple-bottom-line (TBL) reporting is emerging as an increasingly important way for companies to make the results of their CSR strategies apparent to stakeholders and for stakeholders to hold companies accountable for their impact on society. The use of standard reporting frameworks and metrics, such as those developed by the Global Reporting Initiative, promotes greater transparency and facilitates benchmarking CSR efforts across firms and industries.

Investment firms have created mutual funds comprising companies that are excelling on the basis of the triple bottom line in order to attract funds from environmentally and socially aware investors. The Dow Jones Sustainability World Index is made up of the top 10 percent of the 2,500 companies listed in the Dow Jones World Index in terms of economic performance, environmental performance, and social performance. Companies are evaluated in these three performance areas, using indicators such as corporate governance, climate change mitigation, and labor practices. Table 9.1 shows a sampling of the companies selected for the Dow Jones Sustainability World Index in 2009 and 2010.

Table 9.1   **A Selection of Companies Recognized for Their Triple Bottom Line Performance in 2009 and 2010**

Name	Market Sector	Country
Johnson & Johnson	Health care and pharmaceuticals	United States
PepsiCo	Food and beverages	United States
adidas	Athletic footwear, apparel, and equipment	Germany
Intel	Technology	United States
Unilever	Food and beverages	Netherlands
Samsung	Electronics	Korea
Nokia	Technology	Finland
Caterpillar	Machinery and equipment	United States
Roche AG	Health care	Switzerland
Air France–KLM	Travel and leisure	France
3M	Adhesives and abrasives	United States
Procter & Gamble	Consumer goods	United States
Sony	Electronics	Japan
BMW	Automobiles and parts	Germany
Novartis	Health care	Switzerland
IBM	Technology	United States
CEMIG	Utilities	Brazil
Cisco Systems	Technology	United States
General Electric	Technology	United States
Coca-Cola	Beverages	United States

Sources: Dow Jones indexes, STOXX Limited, and SAM Group, www.sustainability-indexes.com/07_htmle/indexes/djsiworld_supersectorleaders.html, www.sustainability-indexes.com/07_htmle/publications/factsheets.html (accessed July 5, 2010).

What Do We Mean by *Sustainability* and *Sustainable Business Practices?*

The term *sustainability* is used in a variety of ways. In many firms, it is synonymous with corporate social responsibility; it is seen by some as a term that is gradually replacing CSR in the business lexicon. Indeed, sustainability reporting and TBL reporting are often one and the same, as illustrated by the Dow Jones Sustainability Index, which tracks the same three types of performance measures that constitute the triple bottom line.

More often, however, the term takes on a more focused meaning, concerned with the relationship of a company to its *environment* and its use of *natural resources,* including land, water, air, plants, animals, minerals, fossil fuels, and biodiversity. It is widely recognized that the world's natural resources are finite and are being consumed and degraded at rates that threaten their capacity for renewal. Since corporations are the biggest users of natural resources, managing and maintaining these resources is critical for the long-term economic interests of corporations.

For some companies, this issue has direct and obvious implications for the continued viability of their business model and strategy. Pacific Gas and Electric has begun measuring the full carbon footprint of its supply chain to become not only "greener" but a more efficient energy producer.[36] Beverage companies such as Coca-Cola and PepsiCo are having to rethink their business models because of the prospect of future worldwide water shortages. For other companies, the connection is less direct, but all companies are part of a business ecosystem whose economic health depends on the availability of natural resources. In response, most major companies have begun to change *how* they do business, emphasizing the use of **sustainable business practices,** defined as those capable of meeting the needs of the present without compromising the ability to meet the needs of the future.[37] Many have also begun to incorporate a consideration of environmental sustainability into their strategy-making activities.

Environmental sustainability strategies entail deliberate and concerted actions to operate businesses in a manner that protects natural resources and ecological support systems, guards against outcomes that will ultimately endanger the planet, and is therefore sustainable for centuries.[38] One aspect of environmental sustainability is keeping use of the Earth's natural resources within levels that can be replenished via the use of sustainable business practices. In the case of some resources (like crude oil, fresh water, and the harvesting of edible fish from the oceans), scientists say that use levels either are already unsustainable or will be soon, given the world's growing population and propensity to consume additional resources as incomes and living standards rise. Another aspect of sustainability concerns containing the adverse effects of greenhouse gases and other forms of air pollution so as to reduce global warming and other undesirable climate and atmospheric changes. Other aspects of sustainability include greater reliance on sustainable energy sources, greater use of recyclable materials, the use of sustainable methods of growing foods (so as to reduce topsoil depletion and the use of pesticides, herbicides, fertilizers, and other chemicals that may be harmful to human health or ecological systems), habitat protection, environmentally sound waste management practices, and increased attempts to decouple environmental degradation and economic growth (according to many scientists, economic growth has historically been accompanied by declines in the well-being of the environment).

Unilever, a diversified producer of processed foods, personal care, and home cleaning products, is among the many committed corporations pursuing sustainable business practices. The company tracks 11 sustainable agricultural indicators in its processed-foods business and has launched a variety of programs to improve the environmental performance of its suppliers. Examples of such programs include special low-rate financing for tomato suppliers choosing to switch to water-conserving irrigation systems and training programs in India that have allowed contract cucumber growers to reduce pesticide use by 90 percent while improving yields by 78 percent. Unilever has also reengineered many internal processes to improve the company's overall performance on sustainability measures. For example, the company's factories have reduced water usage by 63 percent and total waste by 67 percent since 1995 through the implementation of sustainability initiatives. Unilever has also redesigned packaging for many of

CORE CONCEPT

Sustainable business practices are those that meet the needs of the present without compromising the ability to meet the needs of the future.

CORE CONCEPT

A company's **environmental sustainability strategy** consists of its deliberate actions to protect the environment, provide for the longevity of natural resources, maintain ecological support systems for future generations, and guard against ultimate endangerment of the planet.

its products to conserve natural resources and reduce the volume of consumer waste. For example, the company's Suave shampoo bottles were reshaped to save almost 150 tons of plastic resin per year, which is the equivalent of 15 million fewer empty bottles making it to landfills annually. As the producer of Lipton Tea, Unilever is the world's largest purchaser of tea leaves; the company has committed to sourcing all of its tea from Rainforest Alliance Certified farms by 2015, due to their comprehensive triple-bottom-line approach toward sustainable farm management.

Crafting Corporate Social Responsibility and Sustainability Strategies

While CSR and environmental sustainability strategies take many forms, those that both provide valuable social benefits *and* fulfill customer needs in a superior fashion may also contribute to a company's competitive advantage.[39] For example, while carbon emissions may be of some concern for financial institutions such as Wells Fargo, Toyota's sustainability strategy for reducing carbon emissions has produced both competitive advantage and environmental benefits. Its Prius hybrid electric- and gasoline-powered automobile is not only among the least polluting automobiles but is also the best-selling hybrid vehicle in the United States; it has earned the company the loyalty of fuel-conscious buyers and given Toyota a green image. Green Mountain Coffee Roasters' commitment to protect the welfare of coffee growers and their families (in particular, making sure they receive a fair price) also meets its customers' wants and needs. In its dealings with suppliers at small farmer cooperatives in Peru, Mexico, and Sumatra, Green Mountain pays "fair-trade" prices for coffee beans (in 2009, the fair-trade prices were a minimum of $1.26 per pound for conventional coffee versus market prices of $0.65 per pound). Green Mountain also purchases about 29 percent of its coffee directly from farmers so as to cut out intermediaries and see that farmers realize a higher price for their efforts—coffee is the world's second most heavily traded commodity after oil, requiring the labor of some 20 million people, most of whom live at the poverty level.[40] Its consumers are aware of these efforts and purchase Green Mountain coffee, in part, to encourage such practices.

CSR strategies and environmental sustainability strategies are more likely to contribute to a company's competitive advantage if they are linked to a company's competitively important resources and capabilities or value chain activities. Thus, it is common for companies engaged in natural resource extraction, electric power production, forestry and paper products, motor vehicles, and chemical production to place more emphasis on addressing environmental concerns than, say, software and electronics firms or apparel manufacturers. Companies whose business success is heavily dependent on high employee morale or attracting and retaining the best and brightest employees are somewhat more prone to stress the well-being of their employees and foster a positive, high-energy workplace environment that elicits the dedication and enthusiastic commitment of employees, thus putting real meaning behind the claim "Our people are our greatest asset." Ernst & Young, one of the four largest global accounting firms, stresses its "People First" workforce diversity strategy that is all about respecting differences, fostering individuality, and promoting inclusiveness so that its more than 144,000 employees in 140 countries

> CSR strategies and environmental sustainability strategies that both provide valuable social benefits *and* fulfill customer needs in a superior fashion can lead to competitive advantage. Corporate social agendas that address only social issues may help boost a company's reputation for corporate citizenship but are unlikely to improve its competitive strength in the marketplace.

can feel valued, engaged, and empowered in developing creative ways to serve the firm's clients. As a service business, Marriot's most competitively important resource is also people. Thus its social agenda includes providing 180 hours of paid classroom and on-the-job training to the chronically unemployed. Ninety percent of the graduates from the job training program take jobs with Marriott, and about two-thirds of those remain with Marriott for more than a year. At Whole Foods Market, an $8 billion supermarket chain specializing in organic and natural foods, its environmental sustainability strategy is evident in almost every segment of its company value chain and is a big part of its differentiation strategy. The company's procurement policies encourage stores to purchase fresh fruits and vegetables from local farmers and screen processed-food items for more than 400 common ingredients that the company considers unhealthy or environmentally unsound. Spoiled food items are sent to regional composting centers rather than landfills, and all cleaning products used in its stores are biodegradable. The company also has created the Animal Compassion Foundation to develop natural and humane ways of raising farm animals and has converted all of its vehicles to run on biofuels.

Not all companies choose to link their corporate environmental or social agendas to their value chain, their business model, or their industry. For example, Chick-Fil-A, an Atlanta-based fast-food chain with over 1,400 outlets in 38 states, has a charitable foundation that funds two scholarship programs and supports 12 foster homes as well as a summer camp for some 1,900 campers.[41] However, unless a company's social responsibility initiatives become part of the way it operates its business every day, the initiatives are unlikely to catch fire and be fully effective. As an executive at Royal Dutch/Shell put it, corporate social responsibility "is not a cosmetic; it must be rooted in our values. It must make a difference to the way we do business."[42] The same is true for environmental sustainability initiatives.

The Moral Case for Corporate Social Responsibility and Environmentally Sustainable Business Practices

The moral case for why businesses should act in a manner that benefits all of the company's stakeholders—not just shareholders—boils down to "It's the right thing to do." Ordinary decency, civic-mindedness, and contributions to the well-being of society should be expected of any business.[43] In today's social and political climate, most business leaders can be expected to acknowledge that socially responsible actions are important and that businesses have a duty to be good corporate citizens. But there is a complementary school of thought that business operates on the basis of an implied social contract with the members of society. According to this contract, society grants a business the right to conduct its business affairs and agrees not to unreasonably restrain its pursuit of a fair profit for the goods or services it sells. In return for this "license to operate," a business is obligated to act as a responsible citizen, do its fair share to promote the general welfare, and avoid doing any harm. Such a view clearly puts a moral burden on a company to take corporate citizenship into consideration and do what's best for shareholders within the confines of discharging its duties to operate honorably, provide good working conditions to employees, be a good environmental steward, and display good corporate citizenship.

> Every action a company takes can be interpreted as a statement of what it stands for.

The Business Case for Corporate Social Responsibility and Environmentally Sustainable Business Practices

Whatever the moral arguments for socially responsible business behavior and environmentally sustainable business practices, it has long been recognized that it is in the enlightened self-interest of companies to be good citizens and devote some of their energies and resources to the betterment of employees, the communities in which they operate, and society in general. In short, there are reasons why the exercise of social and environmental responsibility may be good business:

- *Such actions can lead to increased buyer patronage.* A strong visible social responsibility or environmental sustainability strategy may give a company an edge in differentiating itself from rivals and in appealing to consumers who prefer to do business with companies that are good corporate citizens. Ben & Jerry's, Whole Foods Market, Stonyfield Farm, and the Body Shop have definitely expanded their customer bases because of their visible and well-publicized activities as socially conscious companies. More and more companies are also recognizing the cash register payoff of social responsibility strategies that reach out to people of all cultures and demographics (women, retirees, and ethnic groups).

- *A strong commitment to socially responsible behavior reduces the risk of reputation-damaging incidents.* Companies that place little importance on operating in a socially responsible manner are more prone to scandal and embarrassment. Consumer, environmental, and human rights activist groups are quick to criticize businesses whose behavior they consider to be out of line, and they are adept at getting their message into the media and onto the Internet. Pressure groups can generate widespread adverse publicity, promote boycotts, and influence like-minded or sympathetic buyers to avoid an offender's products. Research has shown that product boycott announcements are associated with a decline in a company's stock price.[44] When a major oil company suffered damage to its reputation on environmental and social grounds, the CEO repeatedly said that the most negative impact the company suffered—and the one that made him fear for the future of the company—was that bright young graduates were no longer attracted to working for the company.[45] For many years, Nike received stinging criticism for not policing sweatshop conditions in the Asian factories that produced Nike footwear, causing Nike cofounder and former CEO Phil Knight to observe that "Nike has become synonymous with slave wages, forced overtime, and arbitrary abuse."[46] In 1997, Nike began an extensive effort to monitor conditions in the 800 factories of the contract manufacturers that produced Nike shoes. As Knight said, "Good shoes come from good factories and good factories have good labor relations." Nonetheless, Nike has continually been plagued by complaints from human rights activists that its monitoring procedures are flawed and that it is not doing enough to correct the plight of factory workers. As this suggests, a damaged reputation is not easily repaired.

- *Socially responsible actions and sustainable business practices can lower costs and enhance employee recruiting and workforce retention.* Companies with

> The higher the public profile of a company or its brand, the greater the scrutiny of its activities and the higher the potential for it to become a target for pressure group action.

deservedly good reputations for social responsibility and sustainable business practices are better able to attract and retain employees, compared to companies with tarnished reputations. Some employees just feel better about working for a company committed to improving society.[47] This can contribute to lower turnover, better worker productivity, and lower costs for staff recruitment and training. For example, Starbucks is said to enjoy much lower rates of employee turnover because of the company's socially responsible practices as well as superior employee benefits and management efforts to make Starbucks a great place to work. Making a company a great place to work pays dividends in recruitment of talented workers, more creativity and energy on the part of workers, higher worker productivity, and greater employee commitment to the company's business mission/vision and success in the marketplace. Sustainable business practices are often concomitant with greater operational efficiencies. For example, when a U.S. manufacturer of recycled paper, taking eco-efficiency to heart, discovered how to increase its fiber recovery rate, it saved the equivalent of 20,000 tons of waste paper—a factor that helped the company become the industry's lowest-cost producer.[48]

- *Opportunities for revenue enhancement may also come from CSR and environmental sustainability strategies.* The drive for sustainability and social responsibility can spur innovative efforts that in turn lead to new products and opportunities for revenue enhancement. Electric cars such as the Chevy Volt and the Tesler Roadster are one example. In many cases, the revenue opportunities are tied to a company's core products. PepsiCo and Coca-Cola, for example, have expanded into the juice business to offer a healthier alternative to their carbonated beverages. GE has created a profitable new business in wind turbines. In other cases, revenue enhancement opportunities come from innovative ways to reduce waste and use the by-products of a company's production. Tyson Foods now produces jet fuel for B52 bombers from the vast amount of animal waste resulting from its meat product business. Staples has become one of the largest nonutility corporate producers of renewable energy in the United States due to its installation of solar power panels in all of its outlets (and sale of what it does not consume in renewable energy credit markets).

- *Well-conceived CSR strategies and sustainable business practices are in the best long-term interest of shareholders.* Social responsibility strategies and strategies to promote environmental sustainability can work to the advantage of shareholders in several ways. They help avoid or preempt legal and regulatory actions that could prove costly and otherwise burdensome. In addition, when CSR and sustainability strategies increase buyer patronage, offer revenue-enhancing opportunities, lower costs, increase productivity, and reduce the risk of reputation-damaging incidents, they contribute to the total value created by a company and improve its profitability. In this manner, well-conceived socially and environmentally responsible strategies can enhance shareholder value even as they address the needs of other company stakeholders. While some question whether addressing social needs is truly in the interest of a company's shareholders, the answer depends on how well such strategies are crafted and whether they contribute to the success of the company's business model. A review of 135 studies indicated there is a positive, but small, correlation between good corporate behavior and good financial

> Socially responsible strategies that create value for customers and lower costs can improve company profits and shareholder value at the same time that they address other stakeholder interests.

how to implement the strategy, and move forward to get all the pieces into place. Company personnel must understand—in their heads and hearts—why a new strategic direction is necessary and where the new strategy is taking them.[3] Instituting change is, of course, easier when the problems with the old strategy have become obvious and/or the company has spiraled into a financial crisis.

But the challenge of successfully implementing new strategic initiatives goes well beyond managerial adeptness in overcoming resistance to change. What really makes executing strategy a tougher, more time-consuming management challenge than crafting strategy are the wide array of managerial activities that must be attended to and the number of bedeviling issues that must be worked out. It takes first-rate "managerial smarts" to zero in on what exactly needs to be done to put new strategic initiatives in place and, further, how best to get these things done in a timely manner that yields good results. Demanding people-management skills and perseverance are required to get a variety of initiatives launched and moving and to integrate the efforts of many different work groups into a smoothly functioning whole. Depending on how much consensus building and organizational change is involved, the process of implementing strategy changes can take several months to several years. To achieve *real proficiency* in executing the strategy can take even longer.

Like crafting strategy, *executing strategy is a job for a company's whole management team, not just a few senior managers.* While the chief executive officer and the heads of major units (business divisions, functional departments, and key operating units) are ultimately responsible for seeing that strategy is executed successfully, the process typically affects every part of the firm—all value chain activities and all work groups. Top-level managers must rely on the active support and cooperation of middle and lower managers to institute whatever new operating practices are needed in the various functional areas and operating units to achieve proficient strategy execution. It is middle and lower-level managers who ultimately must ensure that work groups and frontline employees do a good job of performing strategy-critical value chain activities and produce operating results that allow companywide performance targets to be met. In consequence, strategy execution requires every manager to think through the answer to the question: *"What does my area have to do to implement its part of the strategic plan, and what should I do to get these things accomplished efficiently and effectively?"*

CORE CONCEPT

Good strategy execution requires a *team effort.* All managers have strategy-executing responsibility in their areas of authority, and all employees are active participants in the strategy execution process.

A FRAMEWORK FOR EXECUTING STRATEGY

LO 1

Gain an understanding of what managers must do to execute strategy successfully.

Executing strategy entails figuring out the specific techniques, actions, and behaviors that are needed for a smooth strategy-supportive operation—and then following through to get things done and deliver results. The idea is to make things happen and make them happen right. The first step in implementing strategic change is for management to communicate the case for organizational change so clearly and persuasively to organization members that a determined commitment takes hold throughout the ranks to find ways to put the strategy into place, make

Once managers have decided on a strategy, the emphasis turns to converting it into actions and good results. Putting the strategy into place and getting the organization to execute it well call for different sets of managerial skills. Whereas crafting strategy is largely a market-driven and resource-driven activity, executing strategy is an operations-driven activity revolving around the management of people and business processes. Whereas successful strategy making depends on strategic vision, solid industry and competitive analysis, and shrewd market positioning, successful strategy execution depends on doing a good job of working with and through others; allocating resources; building and strengthening competitive capabilities; creating an appropriate organizational structure; instituting strategy-supportive policies, processes, and systems; motivating and rewarding people; and instilling a discipline of getting things done. Executing strategy is an action-oriented, make-things-happen task that tests a manager's ability to direct organizational change, achieve continuous improvement in operations and business processes, create and nurture a strategy-supportive culture, and consistently meet or beat performance targets.

Experienced managers are emphatic in declaring that it is a whole lot easier to develop a sound strategic plan than it is to execute the plan and achieve the desired outcomes. According to one executive, "It's been rather easy for us to decide where we wanted to go. The hard part is to get the organization to act on the new priorities."[1] In a recent study of 1,000 companies, government agencies, and not-for-profit organizations in over 50 countries, 60 percent of employees rated their organizations poor in terms of strategy implementation.[2] *Just because senior managers announce a new strategy doesn't mean that organization members will embrace it and move forward enthusiastically to implement it.* Senior executives cannot simply direct immediate subordinates to abandon old ways and take up new ways, and they certainly cannot expect the needed actions and changes to occur in rapid-fire fashion and still lead to the desired outcomes. Some managers and employees may be skeptical about the merits of the strategy, seeing it as contrary to the organization's best interests, unlikely to succeed, or threatening to their departments or careers. Moreover, employees may have misconceptions about the new strategy or have different ideas about what internal changes are needed to execute it. Long-standing attitudes, vested interests, inertia, and ingrained organizational practices don't melt away when managers decide on a new strategy and begin efforts to implement it—especially if only a few people have been involved in crafting the strategy or if the rationale for strategic change requires quite a bit of salesmanship. It takes adept managerial leadership to convincingly communicate a new strategy and the reasons for it, overcome pockets of doubt and disagreement, secure the commitment and enthusiasm of key personnel, gain agreement on how to implement the strategy, and move forward to get all the pieces into place. Company personnel must understand—in their heads and hearts—why a new strategic direction is necessary and where the new strategy is taking them.[3] Instituting change is, of course, easier when the problems with the old strategy have become obvious and/or the company has spiraled into a financial crisis.

But the challenge of successfully implementing new strategic initiatives goes well beyond managerial adeptness in overcoming resistance to change. What really makes executing strategy a tougher, more time-consuming management challenge than crafting strategy are the wide array of managerial activities that must be attended to and the number of bedeviling issues that must be worked out. It takes first-rate "managerial smarts" to zero in on what exactly needs to be done to put new strategic initiatives in place and, further, how best to get these things done in a timely manner that yields good results. Demanding people-management skills and perseverance are required to get a variety of initiatives launched and moving and to integrate the efforts of many different work groups into a smoothly functioning whole. Depending on how much

consensus building and organizational change is involved, the process of implementing strategy changes can take several months to several years. To achieve *real proficiency* in executing the strategy can take even longer.

Like crafting strategy, *executing strategy is a job for a company's whole management team, not just a few senior managers.* While the chief executive officer and the heads of major units (business divisions, functional departments, and key operating units) are ultimately responsible for seeing that strategy is executed successfully, the process typically affects every part of the firm—all value chain activities and all work groups. Top-level managers must rely on the active support and cooperation of middle and lower managers to institute whatever new operating practices are needed in the various functional areas and operating units to achieve proficient strategy execution. It is middle and lower-level managers who ultimately must ensure that work groups and frontline employees do a good job of performing strategy-critical value chain activities and produce operating results that allow companywide performance targets to be met. In consequence, strategy execution requires every manager to think through the answer to the question: *"What does my area have to do to implement its part of the strategic plan, and what should I do to get these things accomplished efficiently and effectively?"*

A FRAMEWORK FOR EXECUTING STRATEGY

LO 1

Gain an understanding of what managers must do to execute strategy successfully.

Executing strategy entails figuring out the specific techniques, actions, and behaviors that are needed for a smooth strategy-supportive operation—and then following through to get things done and deliver results. The idea is to make things happen and make them happen right. The first step in implementing strategic change is for management to communicate the case for organizational change so clearly and persuasively to organization members that a determined commitment takes hold throughout the ranks to find ways to put the strategy into place, make

CHAPTER 10

BUILDING AN ORGANIZATION CAPABLE OF GOOD STRATEGY EXECUTION

People, Capabilities, and Structure

> Strategies most often fail because they aren't executed well.
>
> **—Larry Bossidy and Ram Charan**
> *CEO Honeywell International, author and consultant*

> People are not your most important asset. The right people are.
>
> **—Jim Collins**
> *Professor and author*

> Of all the things I've done, the most vital is coordinating the talents of those who work for us and pointing them toward a certain goal.
>
> **—Walt Disney**
> *Founder of the Disney Company*

LEARNING OBJECTIVES

LO 1. Gain an understanding of what managers must do to execute strategy successfully.

LO 2. Learn why hiring, training, and retaining the right people constitute a key component of the strategy execution process.

LO 3. Understand that good strategy execution requires continuously building and upgrading the organization's resources and capabilities.

LO 4. Gain command of what issues to consider in establishing a strategy-supportive organizational structure and organizing the work effort.

LO 5. Become aware of the pros and cons of centralized and decentralized decision making in implementing the chosen strategy.

[21] P. M. Nichols, "Outlawing Transnational Bribery through the World Trade Organization," *Law and Policy in International Business* 28, no. 2 (1997), pp. 321–22.

[22] For an overview of widely endorsed guidelines for creating codes of conduct, see Lynn Paine, Rohit Deshpandé, Joshua D. Margolis, and Kim Eric Bettcher, "Up to Code: Does Your Company's Conduct Meet World-Class Standards?" *Harvard Business Review* 83, no. 12 (December 2005), pp. 122–33.

[23] For survey data on what managers say about why they sometimes behave unethically, see John F. Veiga, Timothy D. Golden, and Kathleen Dechant, "Why Managers Bend Company Rules," *Academy of Management Executive* 18, no. 2 (May 2004), pp. 84–89.

[24] For more details, see Ronald R. Sims and Johannes Brinkmann, "Enron Ethics (Or: Culture Matters More than Codes)," *Journal of Business Ethics* 45, no. 3 (July 2003), pp. 244–46.

[25] Veiga, Golden, and Dechant, "Why Managers Bend Company Rules," p. 36.

[26] The following account is based largely on the discussion and analysis in Sims and Brinkmann, "Enron Ethics," pp. 245–52. Perhaps the definitive book-length account of the corrupt Enron culture is Kurt Eichenwald, *Conspiracy of Fools: A True Story* (New York: Broadway Books, 2005).

[27] Chip Cummins and Almar Latour, "How Shell's Move to Revamp Culture Ended in Scandal," *Wall Street Journal,* November 2, 2004, p. A14.

[28] Archie B. Carroll, "The Four Faces of Corporate Citizenship," *Business and Society Review* 100/101 (September 1998), p. 6.

[29] Business Roundtable, "Statement on Corporate Responsibility," October 1981, p. 9.

[30] For an argument that the concept of corporate social responsibility is not viable because of the inherently conflicted nature of a corporation, see Timothy M. Devinney, "Is the Socially Responsible Corporation a Myth? The Good, the Bad, and the Ugly of Corporate Social Responsibility," *Academy of Management Perspectives* 23, no. 2 (May 2009), pp. 44–56.

[31] Sarah Roberts, Justin Keeble, and David Brown, "The Business Case for Corporate Citizenship" (study conducted by Arthur D. Little for the World Economic Forum), p. 3, www.afic.am (accessed June 9, 2009). A revised and more wide-ranging version of this study can be found at www.bitc.org.uk/document.rm?id = 5253.

[32] "General Mills' 2010 Corporate Social Responsibility Report Highlights New and Longstanding Achievements in the Areas of Health, Community, and Environment" (CSR press release), *CSRwire,* April 15, 2010, www.csrwire.com/press_releases/29347-General-Mills-2010- Corporate-Social-Responsibility-report-now-available.html.

[33] Arthur A. Thompson and Amit J. Shah, "Starbucks' Strategy and Internal Initiatives to Return to Profitable Growth," a case study appearing in the Cases section of this text.

[34] Adrian Henriques, "ISO 26000: A New Standard for Human Rights?" Institute for Human Rights and Business, March 23, 2010, www.institutehrb.org/blogs/guest/iso_26000_a_new_standard_for_human_rights.html?gclid = CJih7NjN2aICFVs65Qo-drVOdyQ (accessed July 7, 2010).

[35] Gerald I. J. M. Zetsloot and Marcel N. A. van Marrewijk, "From Quality to Sustainability," *Journal of Business Ethics* 55 (2004), pp. 79–82.

[36] Tilde Herrera, "PG&E Claims Industry First with Supply Chain Footprint Project," *GreenBiz.com,* June 30, 2010, www.greenbiz.com/news/2010/06/30/pge-claims-industry-first-supply-chain-carbon-footprint-project.

[37] This definition is based on the Brundtland Commission's report, which described sustainable development in a like manner: United Nations General Assembly, "Report of the World Commission on Environment and Development: Our Common Future," 1987, www.un-documents.net/wced-ocf.htm, transmitted to the General Assembly as an annex to document A/42/427—"Development and International Co-operation: Environment" (retrieved February 15, 2009).

[38] See, for example, Robert Goodland, "The Concept of Environmental Sustainability," *Annual Review of Ecology and Systematics* 26 (1995), pp. 1–25; J. G. Speth, *The Bridge at the End of the World: Capitalism, the Environment, and Crossing from Crisis to Sustainability* (New Haven, CT: Yale University Press, 2008).

[39] For an excellent discussion of crafting corporate social responsibility strategies capable of contributing to a company's competitive advantage, see Michael E. Porter and Mark R. Kramer, "Strategy & Society: The Link between Competitive Advantage and Corporate Social Responsibility," *Harvard Business Review* 84, no. 12 (December 2006), pp. 78–92.

[40] World Business Council for Sustainable Development, "Corporate Social Responsibility: Making Good Business Sense," January 2000, p. 7, www.wbscd.ch (accessed October 10, 2003). For a discussion of how companies are connecting social initiatives to their core values, see David Hess, Nikolai Rogovsky, and Thomas W. Dunfee, "The Next Wave of Corporate Community Involvement: Corporate Social Initiatives," *California Management Review* 44, no. 2 (Winter 2002), pp. 110–25. See also Susan Ariel Aaronson, "Corporate Responsibility in the Global Village: The British Role Model and the American Laggard," *Business and Society Review* 108, no. 3 (September 2003), p. 323.

[41] www.chick-fil-a.com (accessed June 1, 2009).

[42] N. Craig Smith, "Corporate Responsibility: Whether and How," *California Management Review* 45, no. 4 (Summer 2003), p. 63.

[43] For an excellent discussion of the social responsibilities that corporations have in emerging countries where many people live in poverty, see Jeb Brugmann and C. K. Pralahad, "Cocreating Business's New Social Compact," *Harvard Business Review* 85, no. 2 (February 2007), pp. 80–90.

[44] Wallace N. Davidson, Abuzar El-Jelly, and Dan L. Worrell, "Influencing Managers to Change Unpopular Corporate Behavior through Boycotts and Divestitures: A Stock Market Test," *Business and Society* 34, no. 2 (1995), pp. 171–96.

[45] Ibid., p. 3.

[46] Tom McCawley, "Racing to Improve Its Reputation: Nike Has Fought to Shed Its Image as an Exploiter of Third-World Labor Yet It Is Still a Target of Activists," *Financial Times,* December 2000, p. 14; Smith, "Corporate Responsibility," p. 61.

[47] Smith, "Corporate Responsibility," p. 63; see also World Economic Forum, "Findings of a Survey on Global Corporate Leadership," www.weforum.org/corporatecitizenship (accessed October 11, 2003).

[48] Roberts, Keeble, and Brown, "The Business Case for Corporate Citizenship," p. 6.

[49] Joshua D. Margolis and Hillary A. Elfenbein, "Doing Well by Doing Good: Don't Count on It," *Harvard Business Review* 86, no. 1 (January 2008), pp. 19–20. Of some 80 studies that examined whether a company's social performance is a good predictor of its financial performance, 42 concluded yes, 4 concluded no, and the remainder reported mixed or inconclusive findings. See Smith, "Corporate Responsibility," p. 65; Lee E. Preston and Douglas P. O'Bannon, "The Corporate Social-Financial Performance Relationship," *Business and Society* 36, no. 4 (December 1997), pp. 419–29; Ronald M. Roman, Sefa Hayibor, and Bradley R. Agle, "The Relationship between Social and Financial Performance: Repainting a Portrait," *Business and Society* 38, no. 1 (March 1999), pp. 109–25; Joshua D. Margolis and James P. Walsh, *People and Profits* (Mahwah, NJ: Lawrence Erlbaum, 2001).

[50] "Performance and Socially Responsible Investments," *The Social Investment Forum,* 2009, www.socialinvest.org/resources/performance.cfm (accessed November 15, 2009).

[51] Glenn Cheney, "Sustainability Looms as a Bigger Issue," *Accounting Today,* May 18, 2009, www.accessmylibrary.com/article-1G1-199972817/sustainability-looms-bigger-issue.html (accessed November 15, 2009).

LO 4

2. In what ways, if any, is your company exercising corporate social responsibility and good corporate citizenship? What are the elements of your company's CSR strategy? Are there any changes to this strategy that you would suggest?

LO 3, LO 4

3. If some shareholders complained that you and your co-managers have been spending too little or too much on corporate social responsibility, what would you tell them?

LO 4

4. Is your company striving to conduct its business in an environmentally sustainable manner? What specific *additional* actions could your company take that would make an even greater contribution to environmental sustainability?

LO4

5. In what ways is your company's environmental sustainability strategy in the best long-term interest of shareholders? Does it contribute to your company's competitive advantage or profitability?

ENDNOTES

[1] James E. Post, Anne T. Lawrence, and James Weber, *Business and Society: Corporate Strategy, Public Policy, Ethics,* 10th ed. (Burr Ridge, IL: McGraw-Hill Irwin, 2002), p. 103.
[2] For research on what are the universal moral values (six are identified—trustworthiness, respect, responsibility, fairness, caring, and citizenship), see Mark S. Schwartz, "Universal Moral Values for Corporate Codes of Ethics," *Journal of Business Ethics* 59, no. 1 (June 2005), pp. 27–44.
[3] See Mark. S. Schwartz, "A Code of Ethics for Corporate Codes of Ethics," *Journal of Business Ethics* 41, nos. 1–2 (November–December 2002), pp. 27–43.
[4] Ibid., pp. 29–30.
[5] T. L. Beauchamp and N. E. Bowie, *Ethical Theory and Business* (Upper Saddle River, NJ: Prentice-Hall, 2001), p. 8.
[6] Based on information in U.S. Department of Labor, "The Department of Labor's 2002 Findings on the Worst Forms of Child Labor," 2003, accessible at www.dol.gov/ILAB/media/reports.
[7] U.S. Department of Labor, "The Department of Labor's 2006 Findings on the Worst Forms of Child Labor," 2006, www.dol.gov/ilab/programs/ocft/PDF/2006OCFTreport.pdf; ibid., p. 17.
[8] W. M. Greenfield, "In the Name of Corporate Social Responsibility," *Business Horizons* 47, no. 1 (January–February 2004), p. 22.
[9] For a study of why such factors as low per-capita income, lower disparities in income

distribution, and various cultural factors are often associated with a higher incidence of bribery, see Rajib Sanyal, "Determinants of Bribery in International Business: The Cultural and Economic Factors," *Journal of Business Ethics* 59, no. 1 (June 2005), pp. 139–45.
[10] For data relating to bribe-paying frequency in 30 countries, see Transparency International, *2007 Global Corruption Report,* p. 332, and *2008 Global Corruption Report,* p. 306, www.globalcorruptionreport.org.
[11] Thomas Donaldson and Thomas W. Dunfee, "When Ethics Travel: The Promise and Peril of Global Business Ethics," *California Management Review* 41, no. 4 (Summer 1999), p. 53.
[12] John Reed and Erik Portanger, "Bribery, Corruption Are Rampant in Eastern Europe, Survey Finds," *Wall Street Journal,* November 9, 1999, p. A21.
[13] For a study of "facilitating" payments to obtain a favor (such as expediting an administrative process, obtaining a permit or license, or avoiding an abuse of authority), which are sometimes condoned as unavoidable or are excused on grounds of low wages and lack of professionalism among public officials, see Antonio Argandoña, "Corruption and Companies: The Use of Facilitating Payments," *Journal of Business Ethics* 60, no. 3 (September 2005), pp. 251–64.
[14] Donaldson and Dundee, "When Ethics Travel," p. 59.
[15] See "OECD Convention on Combating Bribery of Foreign Public Officials in

International Business Transactions," www.oecd.org/document/21/0,3343,en_2649_34859_2017813_1_1_1_1,00.html (accessed May 22, 2009).
[16] Michael Peel, "Landmark Bribery Case Goes to Trial," *Financial Times,* December 2, 2009, p. 4 (retrieved December 27, 2009, from ABI/INFORM Global, document ID:1913325051).
[17] Thomas Donaldson and Thomas W. Dunfee, *Ties That Bind: A Social Contracts Approach to Business Ethics* (Boston: Harvard Business School Press, 1999), pp. 35 and 83.
[18] Based on a report in M. J. Satchell, "Deadly Trade in Toxics," *U.S. News & World Report,* March 7, 1994, p. 64, and cited in Donaldson and Dunfee, "When Ethics Travel," p. 46.
[19] R. Chen and C. Chen, "Chinese Professional Managers and the Issue of Ethical Behavior," *Ivey Business Journal* 69, no. 5 (May/June 2005), pp. 1–5.
[20] Two of the definitive treatments of integrated social contracts theory as applied to ethics are Thomas Donaldson and Thomas W. Dunfee, "Towards a Unified Conception of Business Ethics: Integrative Social Contracts Theory," *Academy of Management Review* 19, no. 2 (April 1994), pp. 252–84, and Donaldson and Dunfee, *Ties That Bind,* especially chaps. 3, 4, and 6. See also Andrew Spicer, Thomas W. Dunfee, and Wendy J. Bailey, "Does National Context Matter in Ethical Decision Making? An Empirical Test of Integrative Social Contracts Theory," *Academy of Management Journal* 47, no. 4 (August 2004), p. 610.

9. The moral case for social responsibility boils down to a simple concept: It's the right thing to do. There are also solid reasons why CSR and environmental sustainability strategies may be good business—they can be conducive to greater buyer patronage, reduce the risk of reputation-damaging incidents, provide opportunities for revenue enhancement, and lower costs. Well-crafted CSR and environmental sustainability strategies are in the best long-term interest of shareholders, for the reasons above and because they can avoid or preempt costly legal or regulatory actions.

ASSURANCE OF LEARNING EXERCISES

LO 1, LO 2, LO 3, LO 4

1. Assume that you are the sales manager at a European company that makes sleepwear products for children. Company personnel discover that the chemicals used to flameproof the company's line of children's pajamas might cause cancer if absorbed through the skin. After this discovery, the pajamas are banned from sale in the European Union and the United States, but senior executives of your company learn that the children's pajamas in inventory and the remaining flameproof material can be sold to sleepwear distributors in certain East European countries where there are no restrictions against the material's use. Your superiors instruct you to make the necessary arrangements to sell the inventories of banned pajamas and flameproof materials to East European distributors. How would you handle this situation?

LO 4

2. Review Microsoft's statements about its corporate citizenship programs at www.microsoft.com/about/corporatecitizenship. How does the company's commitment to global citizenship provide positive benefits for its stakeholders? How does Microsoft plan to improve social and economic empowerment in developing countries through its Unlimited Potential program? Why is this important to Microsoft shareholders?

LO4

3. Go to www.nestle.com, and read the company's latest sustainability report. What are Nestlé's key sustainable environmental policies? How is the company addressing social needs? How do these initiatives relate to the company's principles, values, and culture and its approach to competing in the food industry?

EXERCISES FOR SIMULATION PARTICIPANTS

LO 1

1. Is your company's strategy ethical? Why or why not? Is there anything that your company has done or is now doing that could legitimately be considered "shady" by your competitiors?

wrong behaviors give rise to universal ethical standards that apply to members of all societies, all companies, and all businesspeople.

- According to the *school of ethical relativism,* different societal cultures and customs have divergent values and standards of right and wrong. Thus, what is ethical or unethical must be judged in the light of local customs and social mores and can vary from one culture or nation to another.

- According to the *integrated social contracts theory,* universal ethical principles or norms based on the collective views of multiple cultures and societies combine to form a "social contract" that all individuals in all situations have a duty to observe. Within the boundaries of this social contract, local cultures or groups can specify what additional actions are not ethically permissible. However, when local ethical norms are more permissive than the universal norms, universal norms always take precedence.

3. Confusion over conflicting ethical standards may provide one reason why some company personnel engage in unethical strategic behavior. But three other factors prompt unethical business behavior: (1) faulty oversight that implicitly sanctions the overzealous pursuit of wealth and personal gain, (2) heavy pressures on company managers to meet or beat short-term earnings targets, and (3) a company culture that puts profitability and good business performance ahead of ethical behavior. In contrast, culture can function as a powerful mechanism for promoting ethical business conduct when high ethical principles are deeply ingrained in the corporate culture of a company.

4. Business ethics failures can result in three types of costs: (1) visible costs, such as fines, penalties, and lower stock prices, (2) internal administrative costs, such as legal costs and costs of taking corrective action, and (3) intangible costs, such as customer defections and damage to the company's reputation.

5. The term *corporate social responsibility* concerns a company's *duty* to operate in an honorable manner, provide good working conditions for employees, encourage workforce diversity, be a good steward of the environment, and support philanthropic endeavors in local communities where it operates and in society at large. The particular combination of socially responsible endeavors a company elects to pursue defines its corporate social responsibility (CSR) strategy.

6. The triple bottom line refers to company performance in three realms: economic, social, environmental. Increasingly, companies are reporting their performance with respect to all three performance dimensions.

7. *Sustainability* is a term that is used in various ways, but most often it concerns a firm's relationship to the environment and its use of natural resources. Sustainable business practices are those capable of meeting the needs of the present without compromising the world's ability to meet future needs. A company's environmental sustainability strategy consists of its deliberate actions to protect the environment, provide for the longevity of natural resources, maintain ecological support systems for future generations, and guard against ultimate endangerment of the planet.

8. CSR strategies and environmental sustainability strategies that both provide valuable social benefits *and* fulfill customer needs in a superior fashion can lead to competitive advantage.

deservedly good reputations for social responsibility and sustainable business practices are better able to attract and retain employees, compared to companies with tarnished reputations. Some employees just feel better about working for a company committed to improving society.[47] This can contribute to lower turnover, better worker productivity, and lower costs for staff recruitment and training. For example, Starbucks is said to enjoy much lower rates of employee turnover because of the company's socially responsible practices as well as superior employee benefits and management efforts to make Starbucks a great place to work. Making a company a great place to work pays dividends in recruitment of talented workers, more creativity and energy on the part of workers, higher worker productivity, and greater employee commitment to the company's business mission/vision and success in the marketplace. Sustainable business practices are often concomitant with greater operational efficiencies. For example, when a U.S. manufacturer of recycled paper, taking eco-efficiency to heart, discovered how to increase its fiber recovery rate, it saved the equivalent of 20,000 tons of waste paper—a factor that helped the company become the industry's lowest-cost producer.[48]

- *Opportunities for revenue enhancement may also come from CSR and environmental sustainability strategies.* The drive for sustainability and social responsibility can spur innovative efforts that in turn lead to new products and opportunities for revenue enhancement. Electric cars such as the Chevy Volt and the Tesler Roadster are one example. In many cases, the revenue opportunities are tied to a company's core products. PepsiCo and Coca-Cola, for example, have expanded into the juice business to offer a healthier alternative to their carbonated beverages. GE has created a profitable new business in wind turbines. In other cases, revenue enhancement opportunities come from innovative ways to reduce waste and use the by-products of a company's production. Tyson Foods now produces jet fuel for B52 bombers from the vast amount of animal waste resulting from its meat product business. Staples has become one of the largest nonutility corporate producers of renewable energy in the United States due to its installation of solar power panels in all of its outlets (and sale of what it does not consume in renewable energy credit markets).

- *Well-conceived CSR strategies and sustainable business practices are in the best long-term interest of shareholders.* Social responsibility strategies and strategies to promote environmental sustainability can work to the advantage of shareholders in several ways. They help avoid or preempt legal and regulatory actions that could prove costly and otherwise burdensome. In addition, when CSR and sustainability strategies increase buyer patronage, offer revenue-enhancing opportunities, lower costs, increase productivity, and reduce the risk of reputation-damaging incidents, they contribute to the total value created by a company and improve its profitability. In this manner, well-conceived socially and environmentally responsible strategies can enhance shareholder value even as they address the needs of other company stakeholders. While some question whether addressing social needs is truly in the interest of a company's shareholders, the answer depends on how well such strategies are crafted and whether they contribute to the success of the company's business model. A review of 135 studies indicated there is a positive, but small, correlation between good corporate behavior and good financial

> Socially responsible strategies that create value for customers and lower costs can improve company profits and shareholder value at the same time that they address other stakeholder interests.

performance; only 2 percent of the studies showed that dedicating corporate resources to social responsibility harmed the interests of shareholders.[49] Another indicator is the performance of mutual funds dedicated to socially responsible investments (SRIs) relative to other types of funds. The longest-running SRI index, the Domini 400, has continued to perform competitively, slightly outperforming the S&P 500 (the top-500 firms in the Standard and Poor's Index).[50] Similarly, the Dow Jones Sustainability Index has performed comparably to the Dow Jones Large Cap and Total Market Indexes.[51]

In sum, companies that take social responsibility and environmental sustainability seriously can improve their business reputations and operational efficiency while also reducing their risk exposure and encouraging loyalty and innovation. Overall, companies that take special pains to protect the environment (beyond what is required by law), are active in community affairs, and are generous supporters of charitable causes and projects that benefit society are more likely to be seen as good investments and as good companies to work for or do business with. Shareholders are likely to view the business case for social responsibility as a strong one, particularly when it results in the creation of more customer value, greater productivity, lower operating costs, and lower business risk—all of which should increase firm profitability and enhance shareholder value even as the company's actions address broader stakeholder interests.

> There's little hard evidence indicating shareholders are disadvantaged in any meaningful way by a company's actions to be socially responsible.

Companies are, of course, sometimes rewarded for bad behavior—a company that is able to shift environmental and other social costs associated with its activities onto society as a whole can reap large short-term profits. The major cigarette producers for many years were able to earn greatly inflated profits by shifting the health-related costs of smoking onto others and escaping any responsibility for the harm their products caused to consumers and the general public. Only recently have they been facing the prospect of having to pay high punitive damages for their actions. Unfortunately, the cigarette makers are not alone in trying to evade paying for the social harms of their operations for as long as they can. Calling a halt to such actions usually hinges on (1) the effectiveness of activist social groups in publicizing the adverse consequences of a company's social irresponsibility and marshaling public opinion for something to be done, (2) the enactment of legislation or regulations to correct the inequity, and (3) widespread actions on the part of socially conscious buyers to take their business elsewhere.

KEY POINTS

1. Ethics concerns standards of right and wrong. Business ethics concerns the application of ethical principles and standards to the actions and decisions of business organizations and the conduct of their personnel. Ethical principles in business are not materially different from ethical principles in general.

2. There are three schools of thought about ethical standards for companies with international operations:
   - According to the *school of ethical universalism,* common understandings across multiple cultures and countries about what constitutes right and

it work, and meet performance targets. The ideal condition is for managers to arouse enough enthusiasm for the strategy to turn the implementation process into a companywide crusade. Management's handling of the strategy implementation process can be considered successful if and when the company achieves the targeted strategic and financial performance and shows good progress in making its strategic vision a reality.

The specifics of how to execute a strategy—the exact items that need to be placed on management's action agenda—always need to be customized to fit the particulars of a company's situation. The hot buttons for successfully executing a low-cost provider strategy are different from those for executing a high-end differentiation strategy. Implementing a new strategy for a struggling company in the midst of a financial crisis is a different job from that of making minor improvements to strategy execution in a company that is doing relatively well. Moreover, some managers are more adept than others at using particular approaches to achieving the desired kinds of organizational changes. Hence, there's no definitive managerial recipe for successful strategy execution that cuts across all company situations and all types of strategies or that works for all types of managers. Rather, the specific actions required to implement a strategy—the "to-do list" that constitutes management's action agenda—always represent management's judgment about how best to proceed in light of prevailing circumstances.

The Principal Components of the Strategy Execution Process

Despite the need to tailor a company's strategy-executing approaches to the particulars of its situation, certain managerial bases must be covered no matter what the circumstances. Ten basic managerial tasks crop up repeatedly in company efforts to execute strategy (see Figure 10.1):

1. Staff the organization with managers and employees capable of executing the strategy well.
2. Build the organizational capabilities required for successful strategy execution.
3. Create a strategy-supportive organizational structure.
4. Allocate sufficient budgetary (and other) resources to the strategy execution effort.
5. Institute policies and procedures that facilitate strategy execution.
6. Adopt best practices and business processes that drive continuous improvement in strategy execution activities.
7. Install information and operating systems that enable company personnel to carry out their strategic roles proficiently.
8. Tie rewards and incentives directly to the achievement of strategic and financial targets.
9. Instill a corporate culture that promotes good strategy execution.
10. Exercise the internal leadership needed to propel strategy implementation forward.

How well managers perform these 10 tasks has a decisive impact on whether the outcome of the strategy execution effort is a spectacular success, a colossal failure, or something in between.

Figure 10.1   The 10 Basic Tasks of the Strategy Execution Process

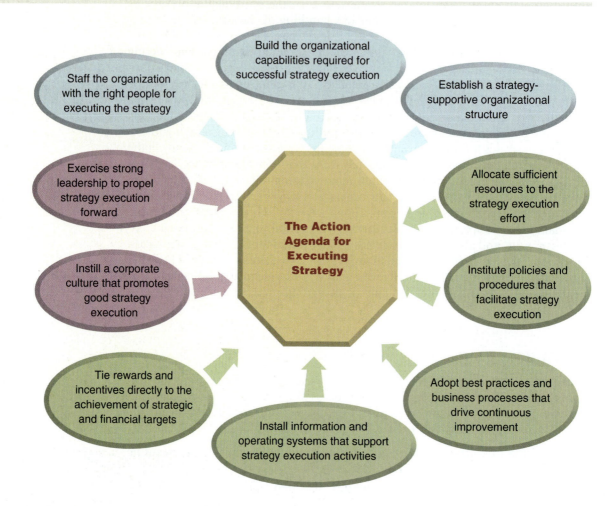

In devising an action agenda for executing strategy, the way for managers to start is with *a probing assessment of what the organization must do differently to carry out the strategy successfully.* They should then consider *precisely how to make the necessary internal changes* as rapidly as possible. Successful strategy implementers have a knack for diagnosing what their organizations need to do to execute the chosen strategy well and figuring out how to get things done cost-efficiently and with all deliberate speed. They are masters in promoting results-oriented behaviors on the part of company personnel and following through on making the right things happen in a timely fashion.[4]

In big organizations with geographically scattered operating units, the action agenda of senior executives mostly involves communicating the case for change, building consensus for how to proceed, installing strong managers to move the process forward in key organizational units, directing resources to the right places, establishing deadlines and measures of progress, rewarding those who achieve implementation milestones, and personally leading the strategic change process. Thus, the bigger the organization, the more that successful strategy execution depends on the cooperation and implementing skills of operating managers who can promote needed changes at the lowest organizational levels and deliver results. In small organizations, top managers can deal directly with frontline managers and employees, personally orchestrating the action steps and implementation sequence, observing firsthand how implementation is progressing, and deciding how hard and how fast to push the process along. Regardless of the organization's size and whether implementation involves sweeping or minor changes, the most important leadership trait is a strong, confident sense of what to do and how to do it. Having a strong grip on these two things comes from understanding the circumstances of the organization and the requirements for effective strategy execution. Then it remains for company personnel in strategy-critical areas to step up to the plate and produce the desired results.

> The two best signs of good strategy execution are whether a company is meeting or beating its performance targets and performing value chain activities in a manner that is conducive to company-wide operating excellence.

What's Covered in Chapters 10, 11, and 12   In the remainder of this chapter and the next two chapters, we will discuss what is involved in performing the 10 key managerial tasks that shape the process of executing strategy. This chapter explores the first three of these tasks (highlighted in blue in Figure 10.1): (1) staffing the organization with people capable of executing the strategy well, (2) building the organizational capabilities needed for successful strategy execution, and (3) creating an organizational structure supportive of the strategy execution process. Chapter 11 concerns the tasks of allocating resources, instituting strategy-facilitating policies and procedures, employing business process management tools and best practices, installing operating and information systems, and tying rewards to the achievement of good results (highlighted in green in Figure 10.1). Chapter 12 deals with the two remaining tasks: creating a strategy-supportive corporate culture and exercising the leadership needed to drive the execution process forward (highlighted in purple in Figure 10.1).

BUILDING AN ORGANIZATION CAPABLE OF GOOD STRATEGY EXECUTION: WHERE TO BEGIN

Building an organization capable of good strategy execution depends foremost on ensuring that the resources and capabilities that are the basis for the strategy are in place, ready to be deployed. Recall from Chapter 4 that these include the skills, talents, experience, and knowledge of the company's human resources (managerial and otherwise). Proficient strategy execution depends heavily on competent personnel of all types, but because of the many managerial tasks involved and the role of leadership in strategy execution, assembling a strong management team is especially important.

If the strategy being implemented is a new strategy, the company may need to add to its resource and capability mix in other respects as well. But renewing, upgrading, and revising the organization's resources and capabilities is a part of the strategy execution process even if the strategy is fundamentally the same, since resources depreciate and conditions are always changing. Thus, augmenting and strengthening the firm's core competencies and seeing that they are suited to the current strategy are also top priorities.

Figure 10.2   **Building an Organization Capable of Proficient Strategy Execution: Three Types of Paramount Actions**

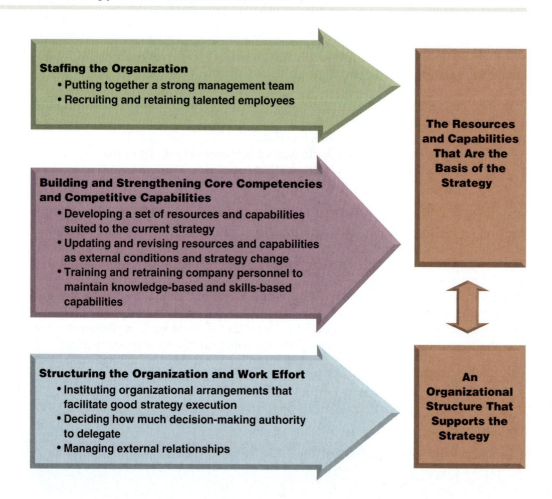

Structuring the organization and work effort is another critical aspect of building an organization capable of good strategy execution. An organization structure that is well matched to the strategy can help facilitate its implementation; one that is not well suited can lead to higher bureaucratic costs and communication or coordination breakdowns. As shown in Figure 10.2, three types of organization-building actions are paramount:

- *Staffing the organization:* putting together a strong management team, and recruiting and retaining employees with the needed experience, technical skills, and intellectual capital.

- *Building and strengthening core competencies and competitive capabilities:* developing proficiencies in performing strategy-critical value chain activities and updating them to match changing market conditions and customer expectations.

- *Structuring the organization and work effort:* organizing value chain activities and business processes, establishing lines of authority and reporting relationships, deciding how much decision-making authority to delegate to lower-level managers and frontline employees, and managing external relationships.

STAFFING THE ORGANIZATION

No company can hope to perform the activities required for successful strategy execution without attracting and retaining talented managers and employees with suitable skills and intellectual capital.

LO 2

Learn why hiring, training, and retaining the right people constitute a key component of the strategy execution process.

Putting Together a Strong Management Team

Assembling a capable management team is a cornerstone of the organization-building task.[5] While different strategies and company circumstances sometimes call for different mixes of backgrounds, experiences, management styles, and know-how, *the most important consideration is to fill key managerial slots with smart people who are clear thinkers, capable of figuring out what needs to be done, good at managing people, and skilled in delivering good results.*[6] The task of implementing challenging strategic initiatives must be assigned to executives who have the skills and talents to turn their decisions into results that meet or beat the established performance targets. Without a smart, capable, results-oriented management team, the implementation process is likely to be hampered by missed deadlines, misdirected or wasteful efforts, and managerial ineptness.[7] Weak executives are serious impediments to getting optimal results because they are unable to differentiate between ideas that have merit and those that are misguided—the caliber of work done under their supervision usually suffers accordingly.[8] In contrast, managers with strong strategy-implementing capabilities have a talent for asking tough, incisive questions; they know enough about the details of the business to be able to ensure the soundness of the decisions of the people around them, and they can discern whether the resources people are asking for to put the strategy in place make sense. They are good at getting things done through others, partly by making sure they have the right people under them and that these people are put in the right jobs.[9] They consistently follow through on issues, monitor progress carefully, make adjustments when needed, and keep important details from slipping through the cracks. In short, they understand how to drive organizational change, and they have the managerial skills and discipline requisite for first-rate strategy execution.

> Putting together a talented management team with the right mix of experiences, skills, and abilities to get things done is one of the first strategy-implementing steps.

Sometimes a company's existing management team is up to the task; at other times it may need to be strengthened or expanded by promoting qualified people from within or by bringing in outsiders whose experiences, talents, and leadership styles better suit the situation. In turnaround and rapid-growth situations, and in instances when a company doesn't have insiders with the requisite know-how, filling key management slots from the outside is a fairly standard organization-building approach. In addition, it is important to ferret out and replace managers who, for whatever reasons, either do not buy into the case for making organizational changes or do not see ways to make things better.[10] For a management team to be truly effective at strategy execution, it must be composed of managers who recognize that organizational changes are needed and who are ready to get on with the process. Weak executives and die-hard resisters have to be replaced or sidelined, perhaps by shifting them to areas where they cannot hamper new strategy execution initiatives.

The overriding aim in building a management team should be to assemble a *critical mass* of talented managers who can function as agents of change and further the cause of first-rate strategy execution. Every manager's success is enhanced (or limited) by the quality of his or her managerial colleagues and the degree to which they freely exchange ideas, debate ways to make operating improvements, and join forces to tackle issues and solve problems.[11] When a first-rate manager enjoys the help and support of other first-rate managers, it's possible to create a managerial whole that is greater than the sum of individual efforts—talented managers who work well together as a team can produce organizational results that are dramatically better than what one or two star managers acting individually can achieve.[12]

Illustration Capsule 10.1 describes General Electric's widely acclaimed approach to developing a top-caliber management team.

Recruiting, Training, and Retaining Capable Employees

Assembling a capable management team is not enough. Staffing the organization with the right kinds of people must go much deeper than managerial jobs in order for strategy-critical value chain activities to be performed competently. *The quality of an organization's people is always an essential ingredient of successful strategy execution—knowledgeable, engaged employees are a company's best source of creative ideas for the nuts-and-bolts operating improvements that lead to operating excellence.* Companies like Google, Microsoft, McKinsey & Company, Southwest Airlines, Cisco Systems, Amazon.com, Procter & Gamble, PepsiCo, Nike, Electronic Data Systems (EDS), Goldman Sachs, and Intel make a concerted effort to recruit the best and brightest people they can find and then retain them with excellent compensation packages, opportunities for rapid advancement and professional growth, and interesting assignments. Having a pool of "A players" with strong skill sets and lots of brainpower is essential to their business.

> In many industries, adding to a company's talent base and building intellectual capital are more important to good strategy execution than additional investments in capital projects.

Microsoft makes a point of hiring the very brightest and most talented programmers it can find and motivating them with both good monetary incentives and the challenge of working on cutting-edge software design projects. McKinsey & Company, one of the world's premier management consulting firms, recruits only cream-of-the-crop MBAs at the nation's top-10 business schools; such talent is essential to McKinsey's strategy of performing high-level consulting for the world's top corporations. The leading global accounting firms screen candidates not only on the basis of their accounting expertise but also on whether they possess the people skills needed to relate well with clients and colleagues. Southwest Airlines goes to considerable lengths to hire people who can have fun and be fun on the job; it uses special interviewing and screening methods to gauge whether applicants for customer-contact jobs have outgoing personality traits that match its strategy of creating a high-spirited, fun-loving, in-flight atmosphere for passengers. Southwest Airlines is so selective that only about 3 percent of the people who apply are offered jobs.

In high-tech companies, the challenge is to staff work groups with gifted, imaginative, and energetic people who can bring life to new ideas quickly and inject into the organization what one Dell executive calls "hum."[13] The saying "People are our most important asset" may seem trite, but it fits high-technology companies precisely. Besides checking closely for functional and technical skills, Dell tests

ILLUSTRATION CAPSULE 10.1

How General Electric Develops a Talented and Deep Management Team

General Electric (GE) is widely considered to be one of the best-managed companies in the world, partly because of its concerted effort to develop outstanding managers. It ranked number one among the best companies for leadership in the most recent global survey conducted by the Hay Group. For starters, GE strives to hire talented people with high potential for executive leadership; it then goes to great lengths to expand the leadership, business, and decision-making capabilities of all its managers. The company spends about $1 billion annually on training and education programs. In 2009, all of its 191 most-senior executives had spent at least 12 months in training and professional development during their first 15 years at GE.

Four key elements undergird GE's efforts to build a talent-rich stable of managers:

1. GE makes a practice of transferring managers across divisional, business, or functional lines for sustained periods of time. Such transfers allow managers to develop relationships with colleagues in other parts of the company, help break down insular thinking in business "silos," promote the sharing of cross-business ideas and best practices, and build a mindset open and adaptive to international markets. There is an enormous emphasis at GE on transferring ideas and best practices from business to business and making GE a "boundaryless" company.

2. In selecting executives for key positions, GE is strongly disposed to candidates who exhibit what are called the four E's—enormous personal *energy,* the ability to *energize* others, *edge* (a GE code word for instinctive competitiveness and the ability to make tough decisions in a timely fashion—saying yes or no, and not maybe), and *execution* (the ability to carry things through to fruition). Considerable attention is also paid to problem-solving ability, experience in multiple functions or businesses, and experience in driving business growth (as indicated by good market instincts, in-depth knowledge of particular markets, customer touch, and technical understanding).

3. All managers are expected to be proficient at what GE calls *workout*—a process in which managers and employees come together to confront issues as soon as they come up, pinpoint the root cause of the issues, and bring about quick resolutions so that the business can move forward. Workout is GE's way of training its managers to diagnose what to do and how to do it.

4. Each year GE sends about 10,000 newly hired and longtime managers to its John F. Welch Leadership Development Center (generally regarded as one of the best corporate training centers in the world) for a three-week course on the company's Six Sigma quality initiative. GE's Leadership Development Center also offers advanced courses for senior managers that may focus on a single management topic for a month. All classes involve managers from different GE businesses and different parts of the world. Some of the most valuable learning comes between formal class sessions when GE managers from different businesses trade ideas about how to improve processes and better serve the customer. This knowledge sharing not only spreads best practices throughout the organization but also improves each GE manager's knowledge.

One of the keys to the success of the management development process at GE is its ability to be adapted to a changing environment: "It's a constant evolution," according to Chief Learning Officer Susan Peters.* Under the leadership of Jack Welch, GE's CEO from 1980 to 2001, training activities were

(Continued)

337

focused around cost cutting, efficiency, and deal making. His successor, Jeffrey Immelt, adapted the focus of development programs to drive toward new goals of risk taking, innovation, and customer focus. Recently, GE has tackled the ascendancy of emerging markets by increased focus on global capability development, including the development of the China Learning Center in Shanghai. This has had a visible impact on the organization: In the last seven years the proportion of non-U.S. executives has doubled, from 15 percent to more than 30.

As a key part of talent development, talent assessment and feedback are approached with characteristic GE energy. Each of GE's 85,000 managers and professionals is graded in an annual process that divides them into five tiers: the top 10 percent, the next 15 percent, the middle 50 percent, the next 15 percent, and the bottom 10 percent. Everyone in the top tier gets stock awards, nobody in the fourth tier gets shares of stock, and most of those in the fifth tier become candidates for being weeded out. Business heads are pressured to wean out "C" players. CEO Jeffrey Immelt personally reviews the performance reviews of the top-600 employees each year, as part of GE's intensive, months-long performance review process.

* D. Brady, "Can GE Still Manage?" *Bloomberg BusinessWeek,* April 25, 2010, pp. 26–32.

Developed with Jeffrey L. Boyink.

Sources: GE Web site (accessed June 2010); Hewitt Associates, "Managing Leadership in Turbulent Times—Why and How the Global Top Companies for Leaders Optimize Leadership Talent in Emerging Markets" (White Paper), www.hewittassociates.com/_MetaBasicCMAssetCache_/Assets/Articles/2009/Managing_Leadership_Turbulent_Times_033009.pdf; D. Brady, "Can GE Still Manage?" *Bloomberg BusinessWeek,* April 25, 2010, pp. 26–32; "Hay Group Study Identifies Best Companies for Leadership," *Bloomberg BusinessWeek.com,* February 18, 2010, www.greatleadershipbydan.com/2010/02/bloomberg-businessweekcomhay-group.html.

> The best companies make a point of recruiting and retaining talented employees—the objective is to make the company's entire workforce (managers and rank-and-file employees) a genuine competitive asset.

applicants for their tolerance of ambiguity and change, their capacity to work in teams, and their ability to learn on the fly. Companies like Amazon.com, Google, and Cisco Systems have broken new ground in recruiting, hiring, cultivating, developing, and retaining talented employees—almost all of whom are in their 20s and 30s. Cisco goes after the top 10 percent, raiding other companies and endeavoring to retain key people at the companies it acquires. Cisco executives believe that a cadre of star engineers, programmers, managers, salespeople, and support personnel is the backbone of the company's efforts to execute its strategy and remain the world's leading provider of Internet infrastructure products and technology.

The practices listed below are common among companies dedicated to recruiting, training, and retaining the most capable people they can find:

1. Spending considerable effort on screening and evaluating job applicants—selecting only those with suitable skill sets, energy, initiative, judgment, aptitude for learning, and personality traits that mesh well with the company's work environment and culture.

2. Putting employees through training programs that continue throughout their careers.

3. Providing promising employees with challenging, interesting, and skill-stretching assignments.

4. Rotating people through jobs that span functional and geographic boundaries. Providing people with opportunities to gain experience in a variety of international settings is increasingly considered an essential part of career development in multinational or global companies.

5. Making the work environment stimulating and engaging so that employees will consider the company a great place to work. Progressive companies work hard at creating an environment in which employees are made to feel that their views and suggestions count.

6. Striving to retain talented, high-performing employees via promotions, salary increases, performance bonuses, stock options and equity ownership, fringe-benefit packages, and other perks.

7. Coaching average performers to improve their skills and capabilities, while weeding out underperformers and benchwarmers.

BUILDING AND STRENGTHENING CORE COMPETENCIES AND COMPETITIVE CAPABILITIES

High among the organization-building priorities in the strategy execution process is the need to build and strengthen competitively valuable core competences and capabilities. As explained in Chapter 4, a company's ability to perform the value-creating activities that express its strategy derives from its resources and capabilities. In the course of crafting strategy, managers identify the resources and capabilities that will enable the firm's strategy. In executing the strategy, managers deploy those resources and capabilities in the form of value-creating activities. But the first step is to ensure that the necessary resources and capabilities are in place and that they are renewed, upgraded, or augmented, as needed.

> **LO 3**
>
> Understand that good strategy execution requires continuously building and upgrading the organization's resources and capabilities.

If the strategy being implemented is new, company managers may have to acquire new resources, significantly broaden or deepen certain capabilities, or even add entirely new competencies in order to put the strategic initiatives in place and execute them proficiently. But even if the strategy has not changed materially, good strategy execution involves refreshing and strengthening the firm's resources and capabilities to keep them in top form. Moreover, it involves augmenting and modifying them to keep pace with evolving market needs and competitive conditions.

Three Approaches to Building and Strengthening Capabilities

Building core competencies and competitive capabilities is a time-consuming, managerially challenging exercise. While some assistance can be gotten from discovering how best-in-industry or best-in-world companies perform a particular activity, trying to replicate and then improve on the competencies and capabilities of others is, however, much easier said than done—for the same reasons that one is unlikely to ever become a good golfer just by studying what Tiger Woods does.

> Building new competencies and capabilities is a multistage process that occurs over a period of months and years. It is not something that is accomplished overnight.

With deliberate effort, well-orchestrated organizational actions, and continued practice, however, it is possible for a firm to become proficient at capability building despite the difficulty. Indeed, by making capability-building activities a routine part of their strategy execution endeavors, some firms are able to develop *dynamic capabilities* that assist them in managing resource and capability change, as discussed in Chapter 4. The most common approaches to capability building include (1) internal development, (2) acquiring capabilities through mergers and acquisitions, and (3) accessing capabilities via collaborative partnerships.[14]

Developing Capabilities Internally   Capabilities develop incrementally along an evolutionary development path as organizations search for solutions to their problems. The process is a complex one, since capabilities are the product of bundles of skills and know-how that are integrated into organizational routines and deployed within activity systems through the combined efforts of teams and work groups that are often cross-functional in nature, spanning a variety of departments and locations. For instance, the capability of speeding new products to market involves the collaborative efforts of personnel in R&D, engineering and design, purchasing, production, marketing, and distribution. Similarly, the capability to provide superior customer service is a team effort among people in customer call centers (where orders are taken and inquiries are answered), shipping and delivery, billing and accounts receivable, and after-sale support. The process of building a capability begins when managers set an objective of developing a particular capability and organize activity around that objective.[15] Managers can ignite the process by having high aspirations and setting "stretch goals" for the organization.[16]

Because the process is incremental, the first step is to develop the *ability* to do something, however imperfectly or inefficiently. This entails selecting people with the requisite skills and experience, upgrading or expanding individual abilities as needed, and then molding the efforts of individuals into a collaborative effort to create an organizational ability. At this stage, progress can be fitful since it depends on experimentation, active search for alternative solutions, and learning through trial and error.[17]

As experience grows and company personnel learn how to perform the activities consistently well and at an acceptable cost, the ability evolves into a tried-and-true competence or capability. Getting to this point requires a continual investment of resources and systematic efforts to improve processes and solve problems creatively as they arise. Improvements in the functioning of a capability come from task repetition and the resulting learning by doing of individuals and teams.[18] But the process can be accelerated by making learning a more deliberate endeavor and providing the incentives that will motivate company personnel to achieve the desired ends.[19] This can be critical to successful strategy execution when market conditions are changing rapidly.

> A company's capabilities must be continually refreshed and renewed to remain aligned with changing customer expectations, altered competitive conditions, and new strategic initiatives.

It is generally much easier and less time-consuming to update and remodel a company's existing capabilities as external conditions and company strategy change than it is to create them from scratch. Maintaining capabilities in top form may simply require exercising them continually and fine-tuning them as necessary. Refreshing and updating capabilities require only a limited set of modifications to a set of routines that is otherwise in place. Phasing out an existing capability takes significantly less effort than adding a brand-new one. Replicating a company capability, while not an easy process, still begins with an established template.[20] Even the process of augmenting a capability may require less effort if it involves the recombination of well-established company capabilities and draws on existing company resources.[21] Companies like Cray in large computers and Honda in gasoline engines, for example, have leveraged the expertise of their talent pool by frequently re-forming high-intensity teams and reusing key people on special projects designed to augment their capabilities. Canon combined miniaturization capabilities that it developed in producing calculators with its existing capabilities in precision optics to revolutionize the 35-mm camera market.[22] Toyota, en route to overtaking General Motors as the global leader in motor vehicles, has aggressively upgraded its capabilities in fuel-efficient hybrid engine technology and constantly fine-tuned its famed Toyota Production System to enhance its already proficient capabilities in manufacturing top-quality vehicles at relatively low costs—see Illustration Capsule 10.2.

Toyota's Legendary Production System: A Capability That Translates into Competitive Advantage

The heart of Toyota's strategy in motor vehicles is to outcompete rivals by manufacturing world-class, quality vehicles at lower costs and selling them at competitive price levels. Executing this strategy requires top-notch manufacturing capability and super-efficient management of people, equipment, and materials. Toyota began conscious efforts to improve its manufacturing competence over 50 years ago. Through tireless trial and error, the company gradually took what started as a loose collection of techniques and practices and integrated them into a full-fledged process that has come to be known as the Toyota Production System (TPS). The TPS drives all plant operations and the company's supply chain management practices. TPS is grounded in the following principles, practices, and techniques:

- *Use just-in-time delivery of parts and components to the point of vehicle assembly.* The idea here is to cut out all the bits and pieces of transferring materials from place to place and to discontinue all activities on the part of workers that don't add value (particularly activities where nothing ends up being made or assembled).

- *Develop people who can come up with unique ideas for production improvements.* Toyota encourages employees at all levels to question existing ways of doing things—even if this means challenging a boss on the soundness of a directive. Former Toyota president Katsuaki Watanabe encouraged the company's employees to "pick a friendly fight." Also, Toyota doesn't fire its employees who, at first, have little judgment for improving work flows; instead, the company gives them extensive training to become better problem solvers.

- *Emphasize continuous improvement.* Workers are expected to use their heads and develop better ways of doing things, rather than mechanically follow instructions. Toyota managers tout messages such as "Never be satisfied" and "There's got to be a better way." Another mantra at Toyota is that the *T* in TPS also stands for "Thinking." The thesis is that a work environment where people have to think generates the wisdom to spot opportunities for making tasks

simpler and easier to perform, increasing the speed and efficiency with which activities are performed, and constantly improving product quality.

- *Empower workers to stop the assembly line when there's a problem or a defect is spotted.* Toyota views worker efforts to purge defects and sort out the problem immediately as critical to the whole concept of building quality into the production process. According to TPS, "If the line doesn't stop, useless defective items will move on to the next stage. If you don't know where the problem occurred, you can't do anything to fix it."

- *Deal with defects only when they occur.* TPS philosophy holds that when things are running smoothly, they should not be subject to control; if attention is directed to fixing problems that are found, quality control along the assembly line can be handled with fewer personnel.

- *Ask yourself "Why?" five times.* While errors need to be fixed whenever they occur, the value of asking "Why?" five times enables identifying the root cause of the error and correcting it so that the error won't recur.

- *Organize all jobs around human motion to create a production/assembly system with no wasted effort.* Work organized in this fashion is called "standardized work" and people are trained to observe standardized work procedures (which include supplying parts to each process on the

(Continued)

assembly line at the proper time, sequencing the work in an optimal manner, and allowing workers to do their jobs continuously in a set sequence of subprocesses).

- *Find where a part is made cheaply, and use that price as a benchmark.*

The TPS utilizes a unique vocabulary of terms (such as *kanban, takt-time, jikoda, kaizen, heijunka, monozukuri, poka yoke,* and *muda*) that facilitates precise discussion of specific TPS elements. In 2003, Toyota established its Global Production Center to efficiently train large numbers of shop-floor experts in the latest TPS methods and better operate an

increasing number of production sites worldwide. Since then, additional upgrades and refinements have been introduced, some in response to the large number of defects in Toyota vehicles that surfaced in 2009–2010.

There's widespread agreement that Toyota's ongoing effort to refine and improve on its renowned TPS gives it important manufacturing capabilities that are the envy of other motor vehicle manufacturers. Not only have such auto manufacturers as Ford, Daimler, Volkswagen, and General Motors attempted to emulate key elements of TPS, but elements of Toyota's production philosophy have been adopted by hospitals and postal services.

Sources: Information posted at www.toyotageorgetown.com; Hirotaka Takeuchi, Emi Osono, and Norihiko Shimizu, "The Contradictions That Drive Toyota's Success," *Harvard Business Review* 86, no. 6 (June 2008), pp. 96–104; Taiichi Ohno, *Toyota Production System: Beyond Large-Scale Production* (New York: Sheridan, 1988).

Managerial actions to develop core competencies and competitive capabilities generally take one of two forms: either strengthening the company's base of skills, knowledge, and intellect or coordinating and integrating the efforts of the various work groups and departments. Actions of the first sort can be undertaken at all managerial levels, but actions of the second sort are best orchestrated by senior managers who not only appreciate the strategy-executing significance of strong capabilities but also have the clout to enforce the necessary cooperation and coordination among individuals, groups, departments, and external allies.[23]

Acquiring Capabilities through Mergers and Acquisitions

Sometimes a company can refresh and strengthen its competencies by acquiring another company with attractive resources and capabilities.[24] An acquisition aimed at building a stronger portfolio of competencies and capabilities can be every bit as valuable as an acquisition aimed at adding new products or services to the company's lineup of offerings. The advantage of this mode of acquiring new capabilities is primarily one of speed, since developing new capabilities internally can take many years of effort. Capabilities-motivated acquisitions are essential (1) when a market opportunity can slip by faster than a needed capability can be created internally and (2) when industry conditions, technology, or competitors are moving at such a rapid clip that time is of the essence.

At the same time, acquiring capabilities in this way is not without difficulty. Capabilities involve tacit knowledge and complex routines that cannot be transferred readily from one organizational unit to another. This may limit the extent to which the new capability can be utilized. For example, the Newell Company acquired Rubbermaid in part for its famed product innovation capabilities. Transferring these capabilities to other parts of the Newell organization proved easier said than done, however, contributing to a slump in the firm's stock prices that lasted for some time. Integrating the capabilities of two firms involved in a merger or acquisition may pose an additional challenge, particularly if there are underlying incompatibilities in their supporting systems or processes. Moreover, since internal fit is important, there is always the risk that under new management the acquired capabilities may not be as productive as they had been. In a worst-case scenario, the acquisition process may end up damaging or destroying the very capabilities that were the object of the acquisition in the first place.

Accessing Capabilities through Collaborative Partnerships

Another method of acquiring capabilities from an external source is to access them via collaborative partnerships with suppliers, competitors, or other companies having the cutting-edge expertise. There are three basic ways to pursue this course of action:

1. *Outsource the function requiring the capabilities to a key supplier or another provider.* Whether this is a wise move depends on what can be safely delegated to outside suppliers or allies versus what internal capabilities are key to the company's long-term success. As discussed in Chapter 6, outsourcing has the advantage of conserving resources so that the firm can focus its energies on those activities most central to its strategy. It may be a good choice for firms that are too small and resource-constrained to execute all the parts of their strategy internally.

2. *Collaborate with a firm that has complementary resources and capabilities in a joint venture, strategic alliance, or other type of partnership established for the purpose of achieving a shared strategic objective.* This requires launching initiatives to identify the most attractive potential partners and to establish collaborative working relationships. Since the success of the venture will depend on how well the partners work together, potential partners should be selected as much for their management style, culture, and goals as for their resources and capabilities.

3. *Engage in a collaborative partnership for the purpose of learning how the partner does things, internalizing its methods and thereby acquiring its capabilities.* Since this method involves an abuse of trust, it not only puts the cooperative venture at risk but also encourages the firm's partner to treat the firm similarly or refuse further dealings with the firm.

Upgrading Employee Skills and Knowledge Resources

Good strategy execution also requires that employees have the skills and knowledge resources they will need to perform their tasks well. Employee training thus plays an important role in the strategy execution process. Training and retraining are important when a company shifts to a strategy requiring different skills, competitive capabilities, and operating methods. Training is also strategically important in organizational efforts to build skills-based competencies. And it is a key activity in businesses where technical know-how is changing so rapidly that a company loses its ability to compete unless its employees have cutting-edge knowledge and expertise. Successful strategy implementers see to it that the training function is both adequately funded and effective. If the chosen strategy calls for new skills, deeper technological capability, or the building and using of new capabilities, training should be placed near the top of the action agenda.

The strategic importance of training has not gone unnoticed. Over 600 companies have established internal "universities" to lead the training effort, facilitate continuous organizational learning, and help upgrade company capabilities. Many companies conduct orientation sessions for new employees, fund an assortment of competence-building training programs, and reimburse employees for tuition and other expenses associated with obtaining additional college education, attending professional development courses, and earning professional certification of one kind or another. A number of companies offer online, just-in-time training courses to employees around the clock. Increasingly, employees at all levels are expected to take an active role in their own professional development and assume responsibility for keeping their skills up to date and in sync with the company's needs.

Strategy Execution Capabilities and Competitive Advantage

As firms get better at executing their strategies, they develop capabilities in the domain of strategy execution much as they build other organizational capabilities. Superior strategy execution capabilities allow companies to get the most from their organizational resources and competitive capabilities. In this way they contribute to the success of a firm's business model. But excellence in strategy execution can also be a more direct source of competitive advantage, since more efficient and effective strategy execution can lower costs and permit firms to deliver more value to customers. Superior strategy execution capabilities may also enable a company to react more quickly to market changes and beat other firms to the market with new products and services. This can allow a company to profit from a period of uncontested market dominance.

Because strategy execution capabilities are socially complex capabilities that develop with experience over long periods of time, they are hard to imitate. And there is no substitute for good strategy execution. (Recall the tests of resource advantage from Chapter 4.) As such, they may be as important a source of sustained competitive advantage as the capabilities that drive a firm's strategies. Indeed, they may be a far more important avenue for securing a competitive edge over rivals in situations where it is relatively easy for rivals to copy promising strategies. In such cases, the only way for firms to achieve lasting competitive advantage is to outexecute their competitors.

Superior strategy execution capabilities are the only source of sustainable competitive advantage when strategies are easy for rivals to copy.

ORGANIZING THE WORK EFFORT WITH A SUPPORTIVE ORGANIZATIONAL STRUCTURE

LO 4

Gain command of what issues to consider in establishing a strategy-supportive organizational structure and organizing the work effort.

There are few hard-and-fast rules for organizing the work effort to support good strategy execution. Every firm's organization chart is partly a product of its particular situation, reflecting prior organizational patterns, varying internal circumstances, executive judgments about reporting relationships, and the politics of who gets which assignments. Moreover, every strategy is grounded in its own set of organizational capabilities and value chain activities. But some considerations in organizing the work effort are common to all companies. These are summarized in Figure 10.3 and discussed in the following sections.

Figure 10.3   Structuring the Work Effort to Promote Successful Strategy Execution

Deciding Which Value Chain Activities to Perform Internally and Which to Outsource

The advantages of a company's having an outsourcing component in its strategy were discussed in Chapter 6, but there is also a need to consider the role of outsourcing in executing the strategy. Aside from the fact that another company (because of its experience, scale of operations, and specialized know-how) may be able to perform certain value chain activities better or cheaper than a company can perform them internally, outsourcing can also sometimes make a positive contribution to better strategy execution. Managers too often spend inordinate amounts of time, mental energy, and resources haggling with functional support groups or other internal bureaucracies over needed services, leaving less time for them to devote to performing strategy-critical activities in the most proficient manner.

> Wisely choosing which activities to perform internally and which to outsource can lead to several strategy-executing advantages—lower costs, heightened strategic focus, less internal bureaucracy, speedier decision making, and a better arsenal of organizational capabilities.

One way to reduce such distractions is to outsource the performance of assorted administrative support functions and perhaps even selected primary value chain activities to outside vendors, thereby enabling the company to concentrate its full energies on performing the value chain activities that are at the core of its strategy, where it can create unique value. For example, E. & J. Gallo Winery outsources 95 percent of its grape production, letting farmers take on weather-related and other grape-growing risks while it concentrates its efforts on wine production and sales.[25] Broadcom, a global leader in chips for broadband communication systems, outsources the manufacture of its chips to Taiwan Semiconductor, thus freeing company personnel to focus their full energies on R&D, new chip design, and marketing. Nike concentrates on design, marketing, and distribution while outsourcing virtually all production of its shoes and sporting apparel.

Such heightened focus on performing strategy-critical activities can yield three important execution-related benefits:

- *The company improves its chances for outclassing rivals in the performance of strategy-critical activities and turning a core competence into a distinctive competence.* At the very least, the heightened focus on performing a select few value chain activities should promote more effective performance of those activities. This could materially enhance competitive capabilities by either lowering costs or improving quality. Whirlpool, ING Insurance, Hugo Boss, Japan Airlines, and Chevron have outsourced their data processing activities to computer service firms, believing that outside specialists can perform the needed services at lower costs and equal or better quality. A relatively large number of companies outsource the operation of their Web sites to Web design and hosting enterprises. Many business that get a lot of inquiries from customers or that have to provide 24/7 technical support to users of their products across the world have found that it is considerably less expensive to outsource these functions to specialists (often located in foreign countries where skilled personnel are readily available and worker compensation costs are much lower) than to operate their own call centers.

- *The streamlining of internal operations that flows from outsourcing often serves to decrease internal bureaucracies, flatten the organizational structure, speed internal decision making, and shorten the time it takes to respond to changing market conditions.*[26] In consumer electronics, where advancing technology drives new product innovation, organizing the work effort in a manner that expedites getting next-generation products to market ahead of rivals is a critical competitive capability. The world's motor vehicle manufacturers have found that they can shorten the cycle time for new models by outsourcing the large majority of their parts and components from independent suppliers and then working closely with their vendors to swiftly incorporate new technology and better integrate individual parts and components to form engine cooling systems, transmission systems, and electrical systems.

- *Partnerships can add to a company's arsenal of capabilities and contribute to better strategy execution.* By building, continually improving, and then leveraging partnerships, a company enhances its overall organizational capabilities and strengthens its competitive assets—assets that deliver more value to customers and consequently pave the way for competitive success. Soft-drink and beer manufacturers cultivate their relationships with their bottlers and distributors to strengthen access to local markets and build loyalty, support, and commitment for corporate marketing programs, without which their own sales and growth are weakened. Similarly, fast-food enterprises like McDonald's and Taco Bell find it essential to work hand in hand with franchisees on outlet cleanliness, consistency of product quality, in-store ambience, courtesy and friendliness of store personnel, and other aspects of store operations. Unless franchisees continuously deliver sufficient customer satisfaction to attract repeat business, a fast-food chain's sales and competitive standing will suffer quickly. Companies like Boeing, Aerospatiale, Verizon Communications, and Dell have learned that their central R&D groups cannot begin to match the innovative capabilities of a well-managed network of supply chain partners.[27]

However, as was emphasized in Chapter 6, a company must guard against going overboard on outsourcing and becoming overly dependent on outside suppliers.

A company cannot be the master of its own destiny unless it maintains expertise and resource depth in performing those value chain activities that underpin its long-term competitive success.[28] As a general rule, therefore, it is the strategically less important activities—like handling customer inquiries and providing technical support, doing the payroll, administering employee benefit programs, providing corporate security, managing stockholder relations, maintaining fleet vehicles, operating the company's Web site, conducting employee training, and managing an assortment of information and data processing functions—for which outsourcing makes the most strategic sense.

Aligning the Firm's Organizational Structure with Its Strategy

The design of the firm's **organizational structure** is a critical aspect of the strategy execution process. The organizational structure comprises the formal and informal arrangement of tasks, responsibilities, and lines of authority and communication by which the firm is administered.[29] It specifies the linkages among parts of the organization, the reporting relationships, the direction of information flows, and the decision-making processes. It is a key factor in strategy implementation since it exerts a strong influence on how well managers can coordinate and control the complex set of activities involved.[30]

> **CORE CONCEPT**
>
> A firm's **organizational structure** comprises the formal and informal arrangement of tasks, responsibilities, lines of authority, and reporting relationships by which the firm is administered.

A well-designed organizational structure is one in which the various parts (e.g., decision-making rights, communication patterns) are aligned with one another and also matched to the requirements of the strategy. With the right structure in place, managers can orchestrate the various aspects of the implementation process with an even hand and a light touch. Without a supportive structure, strategy execution is more likely to become bogged down by administrative confusion, political maneuvering, and bureaucratic waste.

Good organizational design may even contribute to the firm's ability to create value for customers and realize a profit. By enabling lower bureaucratic costs and facilitating operational efficiency, it can lower a firm's operating costs. By facilitating the coordination of activities within the firm, it can improve the capability-building process, leading to greater differentiation and/or lower costs. Moreover, by improving the speed with which information is communicated and activities are coordinated, it can enable the firm to beat rivals to the market and profit from a period of unrivaled advantage.

Making Strategy-Critical Activities the Main Building Blocks of the Organizational Structure   In any business, some activities in the value chain are always more critical to successful strategy execution than others. For instance, a ski apparel manufacturer must be good at styling and design, low-cost manufacturing, distribution (convincing an attractively large number of retailers to stock and promote the company's brand), and marketing and advertising (building a brand image that generates buzz and appeal among ski enthusiasts). In discount stock brokerage, the strategy-critical activities are fast access to information, accurate order execution, efficient record keeping and transactions processing, and good customer service. In specialty chemicals, the critical activities are R&D, product innovation, getting new products onto the market quickly, effective marketing, and expertise in assisting customers.

Where such is the case, it is important for management to build its organizational structure around proficient performance of these activities, making them the centerpieces or main building blocks in the enterprise's organizational structure.

The rationale for making strategy-critical activities the main building blocks in structuring a business is compelling: If activities crucial to strategic success are to have the resources, decision-making influence, and organizational impact they need, they have to be centerpieces in the organizational scheme. Making them the focus of structuring efforts will also facilitate their coordination and promote good internal fit—an essential attribute of a winning strategy, as summarized in Chapter 1. To the extent that implementing a new strategy entails new or altered key activities or capabilities, different organizational arrangements may be required.[31]

Matching Type of Organizational Structure to Strategy Execution Requirements

Organizational structures can be classified into a limited number of standard types. The type that is most suitable for a given firm will depend on the firm's size and complexity as well as its strategy. As firms grow and their needs for structure evolve, their structural form is likely to evolve from one type to another. The four basic types are the *simple structure,* the *functional structure,* the *multidivisional structure,* and the *matrix structure,* as described below.

1. Simple Structure   A **simple structure** is one in which a central executive (often the owner-manager) handles all major decisions and oversees the operations of the organization with the help of a small staff.[32] Simple structures are also known as *line-and-staff structures,* since a central administrative staff supervises line employees who conduct the operations of the firm, or *flat structures,* since there are few levels of hierarchy.[33] It is characterized by limited task specialization; few rules; informal relationships; minimal use of training, planning, and liaison devices; and a lack of sophisticated support systems. It has all the advantages of simplicity, including low administrative costs, ease of coordination, flexibility, quick decision making, adaptability, and responsiveness to change.[34] Its informality and lack of rules may foster creativity and heightened individual responsibility.

Simple organizational structures are typically employed by small firms and entrepreneurial start-ups. The simple structure is the most common type of organizational structure since small firms are the most prevalent type of business. As an organization grows, however, this structural form becomes inadequate to the demands that come with size and complexity. In response, growing firms tend to alter their organizational structure from a simple structure to a functional structure.

2. Functional Structure   A **functional structure** is one that is organized along functional lines, where a function represents a major step in the firm's value chain, such as R&D, engineering and design, manufacturing, sales and marketing, logistics, and customer service. Each functional unit is supervised by functional line managers who report to the chief executive officer and a corporate staff. This arrangement allows functional managers to focus on their area of responsibility, leaving it to the CEO and headquarters to provide direction and ensure that their activities are coordinated and integrated. Functional structures are also known as *departmental structures,* since the functional units are commonly called departments, and *unitary structures* or *U-forms,* since a single unit is responsible for each function.

In large organizations, functional structures lighten the load on top management, relative to simple structures, and make for a more efficient use of managerial resources. Their primary advantage, however, is due to greater task specialization, which promotes learning, enables the realization of scale economies, and offers productivity advantages not otherwise available. Their disadvantage is that the departmental boundaries can inhibit the flow of information and limit the opportunities for cross-functional cooperation and coordination.

It is generally agreed that some type of functional structure is the best organizational arrangement when a company is in just one particular business (regardless of which of the five generic competitive strategies it opts to pursue). For instance, a technical instruments manufacturer may be organized around research and development, engineering, supply chain management, assembly, quality control, marketing, and technical services. A discount retailer, such as Dollar General or Kmart, may organize around such functional units as purchasing, warehousing and distribution, store operations, advertising and sales, merchandising, and customer service. Functional structures can also be appropriate for firms with high-volume production, products that are closely related, and a limited degree of vertical integration. For example, General Motors now manages all of its brands (e.g., Cadillac, Oldsmobile, Chevrolet, Buick) under a common functional structure designed to promote technical transfer and capture economies of scale.[35]

> Functional structures are also called *departmental* structures, *unitary* structures, or *U-forms.*

As firms continue to grow, they often become more diversified and complex, placing a greater burden on top management. At some point, the centralized control that characterizes the functional structure becomes a liability, and the advantages of functional specialization begin to break down. To resolve these problems and address a growing need for coordination across functions, firms generally turn to the multidivisional structure.

3. Multidivisional Structure A **multidivisional structure** is a decentralized structure consisting of a set of operating divisions organized along market, customer, product, or geographic lines, and a central corporate headquarters, which monitors divisional activities, allocates resources, performs assorted support functions, and exercises overall control. Since each division is essentially a business, the divisions typically operate as independent profit centers (i.e., with profit/loss responsibility) and are organized internally along functional lines.[36] Division managers oversee day-to-day operations and the development of business-level strategy, while corporate executives attend to overall performance and corporate strategy, the elements of which were described in Chapter 8. Multidivisional structures are also called *divisional structures* or *M-forms,* in contrast with the U-form (functional) structure.

> **CORE CONCEPT**
>
> A **multidivisional structure** is a decentralized structure consisting of a set of operating divisions organized along business, product, customer group, or geographic lines, and a central corporate headquarters that allocates resources, provides support functions, and monitors divisional activities.

Multidivisional structures are common among companies pursuing some form of diversification strategy or global strategy, with operations in a number of businesses or countries. When the strategy is one of unrelated diversification, as in a conglomerate or holding company, the divisions generally represent separate industries. When the strategy is based on related diversification, the divisions may be organized according to markets, customer groups, product lines, geographic regions, or technologies. In this arrangement, the decision about where to draw the divisional lines depends foremost on the nature of the relatedness and the strategy-critical building blocks, in terms of which businesses have key value chain activities in common. For example, a company selling closely related products to business customers as well as two types of end consumers—online buyers and in-store buyers—may organize its divisions according to customer groups since the value chains involved in serving the three groups differ. Another company may organize by product line due to commonalities in product development and production within each product line. Multidivisional structures are also common among vertically integrated firms. There the major building blocks are often divisional units performing one or more of the major processing steps along the value chain (e.g., raw-material production, components manufacture, assembly, wholesale distribution, retail store operations).

Multidivisional structures offer significant advantages over functional structures in terms of facilitating the management of a complex and diverse set of operations.[37] Putting business-level strategy in the hands of division managers while leaving corporate strategy to top executives reduces the potential for information overload and improves the quality of decision making in each domain. This also minimizes the costs of coordinating divisionwide activities while enhancing top management's ability to control a diverse and complex operation. Moreover, multidivisional structures can help align individual incentives with the goals of the corporation and spur productivity by encouraging competition for resources among the different divisions.

But a divisional business-unit structure can also present some problems to a company pursuing related diversification, because having independent business units—each running its own business in its own way—inhibits cross-business collaboration and the capture of cross-business synergies. To solve this type of problem, firms turn to more complex structures, such as the matrix structure.

4. Matrix Structure   A **matrix structure** is a combination structure in which the organization is organized along two or more dimensions at once (e.g., business, geographic area, value chain function) for the purpose of enhancing cross-unit communication, collaboration, and coordination. In essence, it overlays one type of structure onto another type. Matrix structures are managed through multiple reporting relationships, so a middle manager may report to several bosses. For instance, in a matrix structure based on product line, region, and function, a sales manager for plastic containers in Georgia might report to the manager of the plastics division, the head of the southeast sales region, and the head of marketing.

Matrix organizational structures have evolved from the complex, overformalized structures that were popular in the 60s, 70s and 80s but often produced inefficient, unwieldy bureaucracies. The modern incarnation of the matrix structure is generally a more flexible arrangement, with a single primary reporting relationship that can be overlaid with a temporary secondary reporting relationship as need arises. For example, a software company that is organized into functional departments (software design, quality control, customer relations) may assign employees from those departments to different projects on a temporary basis, so an employee reports to a project manager as well as to his or her primary boss (the functional department head) for the duration of a project.

Matrix structures are also called *composite structures* or *combination structures*. They are often used for project-based, process-based, or team-based management.

Such approaches are common in businesses involving projects of limited duration, such as consulting, architecture, and engineering services. The type of close cross-unit collaboration that a flexible matrix structure supports is also needed to build competitive capabilities in strategically important activities, such as speeding new products to market, that involve employees scattered across several organizational units.[38] Capabilities-based matrix structures that combine process departments (like new product development) with more traditional functional departments provide a solution.

An advantage of matrix structures is that they facilitate the sharing of plant and equipment, specialized knowledge, and other key resources—they lower costs by enabling the realization of economies of scope. They also have the advantage of flexibility in form and may allow for better oversight since supervision is provided from more than one perspective. A disadvantage is that they add an additional layer of management, thereby increasing bureaucratic costs and decreasing response time to new situations.[39] In addition, there is a potential for confusion among employees due to dual reporting relationships and divided loyalties. While there is some controversy over the utility of matrix structures, the modern approach to matrix structures does much to minimize their disadvantages.[40]

> Matrix structures are also called *composite* structures or *combination* structures.

Determining How Much Authority to Delegate

On average, larger companies with more complex organizational structures are more decentralized in their decision making than smaller firms with simple structures—by necessity and by design. Under any organizational structure, however, there is still room for considerable variation in how much authority top managers retain and how much is delegated to down-the-line managers and employees. In executing strategy, then, companies must decide how much authority to delegate to the managers of each organizational unit—especially the heads of divisions, functional departments, and other operating units—and how much decision-making latitude to give individual employees in performing their jobs. The two extremes are to *centralize decision making* at the top (the CEO and a few close lieutenants) or to *decentralize decision making* by giving managers and employees considerable decision-making latitude in their areas of responsibility. As shown in Table 10.1, the two approaches are based on sharply different underlying principles and beliefs, with each having its pros and cons.

LO 5

Become aware of the pros and cons of centralized and decentralized decision making in implementing the chosen strategy.

Centralized Decision Making: Pros and Cons   *In a highly centralized organizational structure, top executives retain authority for most strategic and operating decisions and keep a tight rein on business-unit heads, department heads, and the managers of key operating units; comparatively little discretionary authority is granted to frontline supervisors and rank-and-file employees.* The command-and-control paradigm of centralized structures is based on the underlying assumptions that frontline personnel have neither the time nor the inclination to direct and properly control the work they are performing and that they lack the knowledge and judgment to make wise decisions about how best to do it—hence the need for managerially prescribed policies and procedures, close supervision, and tight control. The thesis underlying authoritarian structures is that strict enforcement of detailed procedures backed by rigorous managerial oversight is the most reliable way to keep the daily execution of strategy on track.

One advantage of an authoritarian structure is tight control by the manager in charge—it is easy to know who is accountable when things do not go well.

Table 10.1   Advantages and Disadvantages of Centralized versus Decentralized Decision Making

Centralized Organizational Structures	Decentralized Organizational Structures
Basic Tenets • Decisions on most matters of importance should be in the hands of top-level managers who have the experience, expertise, and judgment to decide what is the best course of action. • Lower-level personnel have neither the knowledge, the time, nor the inclination to properly manage the tasks they are performing. • Strong control from the top is a more effective means for coordinating company actions.	**Basic Tenets** • Decision-making authority should be put in the hands of the people closest to, and most familiar with, the situation. • Those with decision-making authority should be trained to exercise good judgment. • A company that draws on the combined intellectual capital of all its employees can outperform a command-and-control company.
Chief Advantages • Fixes accountability through tight control from the top. • Eliminates goal conflict among those with differing perspectives or interests. • Allows for quick decision making and strong leadership under crisis situations.	**Chief Advantages** • Encourages company employees to exercise initiative and act responsibly. • Promotes greater motivation and involvement in the business on the part of more company personnel. • Spurs new ideas and creative thinking. • Allows fast response to market change. • May entail fewer layers of management.
Primary Disadvantages • Lengthens response times by those closest to the market conditions because they must seek approval for their actions. • Does not encourage responsibility among lower-level managers and rank-and-file employees. • Discourages lower-level managers and rank-and-file employees from exercising any initiative.	**Primary Disadvantages** • Top management lacks "full control"—higher-level managers may be unaware of actions taken by empowered personnel under their supervision. • Puts the organization at risk if empowered employees happen to make "bad" decisions. • Can impair cross-unit collaboration.

This structure can also reduce goal conflict among managers from different parts of the organization who may have different perspectives, incentives, and objectives. For example, a manager in charge of an engineering department may be more interested in pursuing a new technology than is a marketing manager who doubts that customers will value the technology as highly. Another advantage of a command-and-control structure is that it can enable a more uniform and swift response to a crisis situation that affects the organization as a whole.

But there are some serious disadvantages as well. Hierarchical command-and-control structures make a large organization with a complex structure sluggish in responding to changing market conditions because of the time it takes for the review/approval process to run up all the layers of the management bureaucracy. Furthermore, to work well, centralized decision making requires top-level managers to gather and process whatever information is relevant to the decision. When the relevant knowledge resides at lower organizational levels (or is technical, detailed, or hard to express in words), it is difficult and time-consuming to get all the facts and nuances in front of a high-level executive located far from the scene of the action—full understanding of the situation cannot be readily copied from one mind to another. Hence, centralized decision making is often impractical—the larger the company and the more scattered its operations, the more that decision-making authority must be delegated to managers closer to the scene of the action.

Decentralized Decision Making: Pros and Cons   *In a highly decentralized organization, decision-making authority is pushed down to the lowest organizational level capable of making timely, informed, competent decisions.* The objective is to put adequate decision-making authority in the hands of the people closest to and most familiar with the situation and train them to weigh all the factors and exercise good judgment. Decentralized decision making means, for example, that employees with customer contact are empowered to do what it takes to please customers. At Starbucks, for example, employees are encouraged to exercise initiative in promoting customer satisfaction—there's the oft-repeated story of a store employee who, when the computerized cash register system went offline, enthusiastically offered free coffee to waiting customers.[41]

> The ultimate goal of decentralized decision making is to put authority in the hands of those persons or teams closest to and most knowledgeable about the situation.

The case for empowering down-the-line managers and employees to make decisions regarding daily operations and strategy execution is based on the belief that a company that draws on the combined intellectual capital of all its employees can outperform a command-and-control company.[42] The challenge in a decentralized system is in maintaining adequate control. With decentralized decision making, top management maintains control by determining the limits to authority for each type of position, installing companywide strategic control systems, holding people accountable for their decisions, instituting compensation incentives that reward people for doing their jobs in a manner that contributes to good company performance, and creating a corporate culture where there's strong peer pressure on individuals to act responsibly.[43]

Decentralized organization structures have much to recommend them. Pushing decision-making authority down to subordinate managers, work teams, and individual employees shortens organizational response times and spurs new ideas, creative thinking, innovation, and greater involvement on the part of all company personnel. Moreover, in worker-empowered structures, jobs can be defined more broadly, several tasks can be integrated into a single job, and people can direct their own work. Fewer layers of managers are needed because deciding how to do things becomes part of each person's or team's job. Today's online communication systems and smart phones make it easy and relatively inexpensive for people at all organizational levels to have direct access to data, other employees, managers, suppliers, and customers. They can access information quickly (via the Internet or company network), readily check with superiors or whomever else as needed, and take responsible action. Typically, there are genuine gains in morale and productivity when people are provided with the tools and information they need to operate in a self-directed way.

But decentralization also has some disadvantages. Top managers lose an element of control over what goes on (since empowered subordinates have authority to act on their own) and may thus be unaware of actions being taken by personnel under their supervision. Such lack of control can put a company at risk in the event that empowered employees make unwise decisions. Moreover, because decentralization gives organizational units the authority to act independently, there is risk of too little collaboration and coordination between different organizational units.

Many companies have concluded that the advantages of decentralization outweigh the disadvantages. Over the past 15 to 20 years, there's been a decided shift from authoritarian multilayered hierarchical structures to flatter, more decentralized structures that stress employee empowerment. This shift reflects a strong and growing consensus that authoritarian, hierarchical organizational structures are not well suited to implementing and executing strategies in an era when extensive information and instant communication are the norm and when a big fraction of the organization's most valuable assets consists of intellectual capital and resides in the knowledge and capabilities of its employees.

Capturing Cross-Business Strategic Fit in a Decentralized Structure

Diversified companies striving to capture the benefits of synergy between separate businesses have to beware of giving business-unit heads full rein to operate independently. Cross-business strategic fit typically has to be captured either by enforcing close cross-business collaboration or by centralizing performance of functions requiring close coordination at the corporate level.[44] For example, if businesses with overlapping process and product technologies have their own independent R&D departments—each pursuing its own priorities, projects, and strategic agendas—it's hard for the corporate parent to prevent duplication of effort, capture either economies of scale or economies of scope, or encourage more collaborative R&D efforts. Where the potential for cross-business R&D synergies exist, the best solution is usually to centralize the R&D function and have a coordinated corporate R&D effort that serves the interests of both the individual businesses and the company as a whole. Likewise, centralizing the related activities of separate businesses makes sense when there are opportunities to share a common sales force, use common distribution channels, rely on a common field service organization, use common e-commerce systems, and so on.

> Efforts to decentralize decision making and give company personnel some leeway in conducting operations must be tempered with the need to maintain adequate control and cross-unit coordination.

Facilitating Collaboration with External Partners and Strategic Allies

Organizational mechanisms—whether formal or informal—are also required to ensure effective working relationships with each major outside constituency involved in strategy execution. Strategic alliances, outsourcing arrangements, joint ventures, and cooperative partnerships present immediate opportunities and open the door to future possibilities, but little of value can be realized without active management of the relationship. Unless top management sees that constructive organizational bridge building with strategic partners occurs and that productive working relationships emerge, the value of cooperative relationships is lost and the company's power to execute its strategy is weakened. If close working relationships with suppliers are crucial, then supply chain management must enter into considerations regarding how to create an effective organizational structure. If distributor/dealer/franchisee relationships are important, someone must be assigned the task of nurturing the relationships with forward channel allies. If working in parallel with providers of complementary products and services contributes to enhanced organizational capability, then cooperative organizational arrangements have to be put in place and managed to good effect.

Building organizational bridges with external allies can be accomplished by appointing "relationship managers" with responsibility for making particular strategic partnerships or alliances generate the intended benefits. Relationship managers have many roles and functions: getting the right people together, promoting good rapport, seeing that plans for specific activities are developed and carried out, helping adjust internal organizational procedures and communication systems, ironing out operating dissimilarities, and nurturing interpersonal cooperation. Multiple cross-organization ties have to be established and kept open to ensure proper communication and coordination.[45] There has to be enough information sharing to make the relationship work and periodic frank discussions of conflicts, trouble spots, and changing situations.

Organizing and managing a network structure provides another mechanism for encouraging more effective collaboration and cooperation among external partners. A **network structure** is the arrangement linking a number of independent organizations involved in some common undertaking. A well-managed network structure typically includes one firm in a more central role, with the responsibility of ensuring that the right partners are included and the activities across the network are coordinated. The high-end Italian motorcycle company Ducati operates in this manner, assembling its motorcycles from parts obtained from a hand-picked integrated network of parts suppliers.

Further Perspectives on Structuring the Work Effort

All organization designs have their strategy-related strengths and weaknesses. To do a good job of matching structure to strategy, strategy implementers first have to pick a basic design and modify it as needed to fit the company's particular business lineup. They must then (1) supplement the design with appropriate coordinating mechanisms (cross-functional task forces, special project teams, self-contained work teams, and so on) and (2) institute whatever networking and communications arrangements it takes to support effective execution of the firm's strategy. Some companies may avoid setting up "ideal" organizational arrangements because they do not want to disturb existing reporting relationships or because they need to accommodate other situational idiosyncrasies, yet they must still work toward the goal of building a competitively capable organization.

The ways and means of developing stronger core competencies and organizational capabilities (or creating altogether new ones) have to fit a company's own circumstances. Not only do different companies and executives tackle the capabilities-building challenge in different ways, but the task of building different capabilities requires different organizing techniques. Thus, generalizing about how to build capabilities has to be done cautiously. What can be said unequivocally is that building a capable organization entails a process of consciously knitting together the efforts of individuals and groups. Organizational capabilities emerge from establishing and nurturing cooperative working relationships among people and groups to perform activities in a more efficient, value-creating fashion. While an appropriate organizational structure can facilitate this, organization building is a task in which senior management must be deeply involved. Indeed, effectively managing both internal organization processes and external collaboration to create and develop competitively valuable organizational capabilities remains a top challenge for senior executives in today's companies.

KEY POINTS

1. Executing strategy is an action-oriented, operations-driven activity revolving around the management of people and business processes. The way for managers to start in implementing a new strategy is with *a probing assessment of what the organization must do differently to carry out the strategy successfully.* They should then consider *precisely how to make the necessary internal changes* as rapidly as possible.

2. Good strategy execution requires a *team effort.* All managers have strategy-executing responsibility in their areas of authority, and all employees are active participants in the strategy execution process.

3. Ten managerial tasks crop up repeatedly in company efforts to execute strategy: (1) staffing the organization well, (2) building the necessary organizational capabilities, (3) creating a supportive organizational structure, (4) allocating sufficient resources, (5) instituting supportive policies and procedures, (6) adopting processes for continuous improvement, (7) installing systems that enable proficient company operations, (8) tying incentives to the achievement of desired targets, (9) instilling the right corporate culture, and (10) exercising internal leadership.

4. The two best signs of good strategy execution are whether a company is meeting or beating its performance targets and performing value chain activities in a manner that is conducive to companywide operating excellence. *Shortfalls in performance signal weak strategy, weak execution, or both.*

5. Building an organization capable of good strategy execution entails three types of organization-building actions: (1) *staffing the organization*—assembling a talented management team, and recruiting and retaining employees with the needed experience, technical skills, and intellectual capital; (2) *building and strengthening core competencies and competitive capabilities*—developing proficiencies in performing strategy-critical value chain activities and updating them to match changing market conditions and customer expectations; and (3) *structuring the organization and work effort*—instituting organizational arrangements that facilitate good strategy execution, deciding how much decision-making authority to delegate, and managing external relationships.

6. Building core competencies and competitive capabilities is a time-consuming, managerially challenging exercise that can be approached in three ways: (1) developing capabilities internally, (2) acquiring capabilities through mergers and acquisitions, and (3) accessing capabilities via collaborative partnerships.

7. In building capabilities internally, the first step is to develop the *ability* to do something, through experimentation, active search for alternative solutions, and learning by trial and error. As experience grows and company personnel learn how to perform the activities consistently well and at an acceptable cost, the ability evolves into a tried-and-true capability. The process can be accelerated by making learning a more deliberate endeavor and providing the incentives that will motivate company personnel to achieve the desired ends.

8. As firms get better at executing their strategies, they develop capabilities in the domain of strategy execution. Superior strategy execution capabilities allow companies to get the most from their organizational resources and competitive capabilities. But excellence in strategy execution can also be a more direct source of competitive advantage, since more efficient and effective strategy execution can lower costs and permit firms to deliver more value to customers. Superior

strategy execution capabilities are hard to imitate and have no good substitutes. As such, they can be an important source of *sustainable* competitive advantage. Any time rivals can readily duplicate successful strategies, making it impossible to *outstrategize* rivals, the chief way to achieve lasting competitive advantage is to *outexecute* them.

9. Structuring the organization and organizing the work effort in a strategy-supportive fashion has four aspects: (1) deciding which value chain activities to perform internally and which ones to outsource; (2) aligning the firm's organizational structure with its strategy; (3) deciding how much authority to centralize at the top and how much to delegate to down-the-line managers and employees; and (4) facilitating the necessary collaboration and coordination with external partners and strategic allies.

10. To align the firm's organizational structure with its strategy, it is important to make strategy-critical activities the main building blocks. There are four basic types of organizational structures: the simple structure, the functional structure, the multidivisional structure, and the matrix structure. Which is most appropriate depends on the firm's size, complexity, and strategy.

ASSURANCE OF LEARNING EXERCISES

LO 2, LO 3

1. Review the Careers link on L'Oréal's worldwide corporate Web site (go to www.loreal.com and click on the company's worldwide corporate Web site option). The section provides extensive information about personal development, international learning opportunities, integration of new hires into existing teams, and other areas of management development. How do the programs discussed help L'Oréal to hire good people and build core competencies and competitive capabilities? Please use the chapter's discussions of recruiting, training, and retaining capable employees and building core competencies and competitive capabilities as a guide for preparing your answer.

LO 4

2. Examine the overall corporate organizational structure chart for Exelon Corporation. The chart can be found by going to www.exeloncorp.com and using the Web site search feature to locate "organizational charts." Does it appear that strategy-critical activities are the building blocks of Exelon's organizational arrangement? Is its organizational structure best characterized as a departmental structure tied to functional, process, or geographic departments? Is the company's organizational structure better categorized as a divisional structure? Would you categorize Exelon's organizational structure as a matrix arrangement? Explain your answer.

LO 5

3. Using Google Scholar or your university library's access to EBSCO, InfoTrac, or other online databases, do a search for recent writings on decentralized decision making and employee empowerment. According to the articles you find in the various management journals, what are the conditions under which decision making should be pushed down to lower levels of management?

EXERCISES FOR SIMULATION PARTICIPANTS

LO 5

1. How would you describe the organization of your company's top management team? Is some decision making decentralized and delegated to individual managers? If so, explain how the decentralization works. Or are decisions made more by consensus, with all co-managers having input? What do you see as the advantages and disadvantages of the decision-making approach your company is employing?

LO 3

2. What specific actions have you and your co-managers taken to develop core competencies or competitive capabilities that can contribute to good strategy execution and potential competitive advantage? If no actions have been taken, explain your rationale for doing nothing.

LO 1, LO 4

3. What value chain activities are most crucial to good execution of your company's strategy? Does your company have the ability to outsource any value chain activities? If so, have you and your co-managers opted to engage in outsourcing? Why or why not?

ENDNOTES

[1] As quoted in Steven W. Floyd and Bill Wooldridge, "Managing Strategic Consensus: The Foundation of Effective Implementation," *Academy of Management Executive* 6, no. 4 (November 1992), p. 27.

[2] As cited in Gary L. Neilson, Karla L. Martin, and Elizabeth Powers, "The Secrets of Successful Strategy Execution," *Harvard Business Review* 86, no. 6 (June 2008), pp. 61–62.

[3] Jack Welch with Suzy Welch, *Winning* (New York: HarperBusiness, 2005), p. 135.

[4] For an excellent and very pragmatic discussion of this point, see Larry Bossidy and Ram Charan, *Execution: The Discipline of Getting Things Done* (New York: Crown Business, 2002), chap. 1.

[5] For an insightful discussion of how important staffing an organization with the right people is, see Christopher A. Bartlett and Sumantra Ghoshal, "Building Competitive Advantage through People," *MIT Sloan Management Review* 43, no. 2 (Winter 2002), pp. 34–41.

[6] The importance of assembling an executive team that has an exceptional ability to gauge what needs to be done and an instinctive talent for figuring out how to get it done is discussed in Justin Menkes, "Hiring for Smarts," *Harvard Business Review* 83, no. 11 (November 2005), pp. 100–9, and Justin Menkes, *Executive Intelligence* (New York: HarperCollins, 2005), especially chaps. 1 to 4.

[7] See Bossidy and Charan, *Execution: The Discipline of Getting Things Done*, chap. 1.

[8] Menkes, *Executive Intelligence*, pp. 68, 76.

[9] Bossidy and Charan, *Execution: The Discipline of Getting Things Done*, chap. 5.

[10] Welch with Welch, *Winning*, pp. 141–42.

[11] Menkes, *Executive Intelligence*, pp. 65–71.

[12] Jim Collins, *Good to Great* (New York: HarperBusiness, 2001), p. 44.

[13] John Byrne, "The Search for the Young and Gifted," *BusinessWeek*, October 4, 1999, p. 108.

[14] See chapters 5 and 6 in Helfat et al., *Dynamic Capabilities: Understanding Strategic Change in Organizations* (Malden, MA: Blackwell, 2007); R. Grant, *Contemporary Strategy Analysis*, 6th ed. (Malden, MA: Blackwell, 2008).

[15] C. Helfat and M. Peteraf, "The Dynamic Resource-Based View: Capability Lifecycles," *Strategic Management Journal*, 24, no. 10 (October 2003), pp. 997–1010.

[16] G. Hamel and C. K. Prahalad, "Strategy as Stretch and Leverage," *Harvard Business Review* 71, no. 2 (March/April 1993), pp. 75–84.

[17] G. Dosi, R. Nelson, and S. Winter (eds.), *The Nature and Dynamics of Organizational Capabilities* (Oxford, England: Oxford University Press, 2001).

[18] C. Helfat and M. Peteraf, "The Dynamic Resource-Based View: Capability Lifecycles."

[19] S. Winter, "The Satisficing Principle in Capability Learning," *Strategic Management Journal* 21, nos. 10/11 (October/November 2000), pp. 981–96; M. Zollo and S. Winter, "Deliberate Learning and the Evolution of Dynamic Capa-

bilities," *Organization Science* 13, no. 3 (May/June 2002), pp. 339–51.

[20] G. Szulanski and S. Winter, "Getting It Right the Second Time," *Harvard Business Review* 80 (January 2002), pp. 62–69; S. Winter and G. Szulanski, "Replication as Strategy," *Organization Science* 12, no. 6 (November/December 2001), pp. 730–43.

[21] B. Kogut and U. Zander, "Knowledge of the Firm, Combinative Capabilities, and the Replication of Technology," *Organization Science* 3, no. 3 (August 1992), pp. 383–97.

[22] C. Helfat and R. Raubitschek, "Product Sequencing: Co-Evolution of Knowledge, Capabilities and Products," *Strategic Management Journal* 21, nos. 10/11 (October/November 2000), pp. 961–80.

[23] Robert H. Hayes, Gary P. Pisano, and David M. Upton, *Strategic Operations: Competing through Capabilities* (New York: Free Press, 1996), pp. 503–7. Also see Jonas Ridderstråle, "Cashing In on Corporate Competencies," *Business Strategy Review* 14, no. 1 (Spring 2003), pp. 27–38; Danny Miller, Russell Eisenstat, and Nathaniel Foote, "Strategy from the Inside Out: Building Capability-Creating Organizations," *California Management Review* 44, no. 3 (Spring 2002), pp. 37–55.

[24] S. Karim and W. Mitchell, "Path-Dependent and Path-Breaking Change: Reconfiguring Business Resources Following Business," *Strategic Management Journal* 21, nos. 10/11 (October/November 2000), pp. 1061–82; L. Capron, P. Dussague, and W. Mitchell,

"Resource Redeployment Following Horizontal Acquisitions in Europe and North America, 1988–1992," *Strategic Management Journal* 19, no. 7 (July 1998), pp. 631–62.
[25] J. B. Quinn, *Intelligent Enterprise* (New York: Free Press, 1992), p. 43.
[26] Ibid., pp. 33 and 89; J. B. Quinn and F. Hilmer, "Strategic Outsourcing," *McKinsey Quarterly* 1 (1995), pp. 48–70; Jussi Heikkilä and Carlos Cordon, "Outsourcing: A Core or Non-core Strategic Management Decision," *Strategic Change* 11, no. 3 (June–July 2002), pp. 183–93; and J. B. Quinn, "Strategic Outsourcing: Leveraging Knowledge Capabilities," *Sloan Management Review* 40, no. 4 (Summer 1999), pp. 9–21. A strong case for outsourcing is presented in C. K. Pralahad, "The Art of Outsourcing," *Wall Street Journal,* June 8, 2005, p. A13. For a discussion of why outsourcing initiatives fall short of expectations, see Jérôme Barthélemy, "The Seven Deadly Sins of Outsourcing," *Academy of Management Executive* 17, no. 2 (May 2003), pp. 87–98.
[27] Quinn, "Strategic Outsourcing: Leveraging Knowledge Capabilities," p. 17.
[28] Quinn, *Intelligent Enterprise,* pp. 39–40; also see Gary P. Pisano and Willy C. Shih, "Restoring American Competitiveness," *Harvard Business Review* 87, nos. 7–8 (July–August 2009), pp. 114–25; Barthélemy, "The Seven Deadly Sins of Outsourcing."
[29] A. Chandler, *Strategy and Structure* (Cambridge, MA: MIT Press, 1962).
[30] E. Olsen, S. Slater, and G. Hult, "The Importance of Structure and Process to Strategy Implementation," *Business Horizons* 48, no. 1 (2005), pp. 47–54; H. Barkema, J. Baum, and E. Mannix, "Management Challenges in a New Time", *Academy of Management Journal* 45, no. 5 (October 2002), pp. 916–30.

[31] The importance of matching organization design and structure to the particular requirements for good strategy execution was first brought to the forefront in a landmark study of 70 large corporations conducted by Professor Alfred Chandler of Harvard University. Chandler's research revealed that changes in an organization's strategy bring about new administrative problems that, in turn, require a new or refashioned structure for the new strategy to be successfully implemented and executed. He found that structure tends to follow the growth strategy of the firm—but often not until inefficiency and internal operating problems provoke a structural adjustment. The experiences of these firms followed a consistent sequential pattern: new strategy creation, emergence of new administrative problems, a decline in profitability and performance, a shift to a more appropriate organizational structure, and then recovery to more profitable levels and improved strategy execution. See Chandler, *Strategy and Structure*.
[32] H. Mintzberg, *The Structuring of Organizations* (Englewood Cliffs, NJ: Prentice Hall, 1979); C. Levicki, *The Interactive Strategy Workout,* 2nd ed. (London: Prentice Hall, 1999).
[33] Chandler, *Strategy and Structure*.
[34] Mintzberg, *The Structuring of Organizations*.
[35] Grant, *Contemporary Strategy Analysis*.
[36] Chandler, *Strategy and Structure*.
[37] O. Williamson, *Market and Hierarchies* (New York: Free Press, 1975); R. M. Burton and B. Obel, "A Computer Simulation Test of the M-Form Hypothesis," *Administrative Science Quarterly* 25 (1980), pp. 457–76.
[38] J. Baum and S. Wally, "Strategic Decision Speed and Firm Performance," *Strategic Management Journal* 24 (2003), pp. 1107–29.

[39] C. Bartlett and S. Ghoshal, "Matrix Management: Not a Structure, a Frame of Mind," *Harvard Business Review,* July–August 1990, pp. 138–45.
[40] M. Goold and A. Campbell, "Structured Networks: Towards the Well Designed Matrix," *Long Range Planning* 36, no. 5 (2003), pp. 427–39.
[41] Iain Somerville and John Edward Mroz, "New Competencies for a New World," in Frances Hesselbein, Marshall Goldsmith, and Richard Beckard (eds.), *The Organization of the Future* (San Francisco: Jossey-Bass, 1997), p. 70.
[42] The importance of empowering workers in executing strategy and the value of creating a great working environment are discussed in Stanley E. Fawcett, Gary K. Rhoads, and Phillip Burnah, "People as the Bridge to Competitiveness: Benchmarking the 'ABCs' of an Empowered Workforce," *Benchmarking: An International Journal* 11, no. 4 (2004), pp. 346–60.
[43] A discussion of the problems of maintaining adequate control over empowered employees and possible solutions is presented in Robert Simons, "Control in an Age of Empowerment," *Harvard Business Review* 73 (March–April 1995), pp. 80–88.
[44] For a discussion of the importance of cross-business coordination, see Jeanne M. Liedtka, "Collaboration across Lines of Business for Competitive Advantage," *Academy of Management Executive* 10, no. 2 (May 1996), pp. 20–34.
[45] Rosabeth Moss Kanter, "Collaborative Advantage: The Art of the Alliance," *Harvard Business Review* 72, no. 4 (July–August 1994), pp. 105–6.

CHAPTER 11

MANAGING INTERNAL OPERATIONS

Actions That Promote Good Strategy Execution

> True motivation comes from achievement, personal development, job satisfaction, and recognition.
>
> **—Frederick Herzberg**
> *Expert on motivation*

> Note to salary setters: Pay your people the least possible and you'll get the same from them.
>
> **—Malcolm Forbes**
> *Late publisher of Forbes Magazine*

> Leadership almost always involves cooperative and collaborative activity that can occur only in a conducive context.
>
> **—Lt. General William G. Pagonis**
> *Retired U.S. Army officer and author*

LEARNING OBJECTIVES

LO 1. Learn why resource allocation should always be based on strategic priorities.

LO 2. Understand how well-designed policies and procedures can facilitate good strategy execution.

LO 3. Learn how process management tools that drive continuous improvement in the performance of value chain activities can help an organization achieve superior strategy execution.

LO 4. Recognize the role of information and operating systems in enabling company personnel to carry out their strategic roles proficiently.

LO 5. Appreciate how and why the use of well-designed incentives and rewards can be management's single most powerful tool for promoting adept strategy execution and operating excellence.

I n Chapter 10, we emphasized the importance of building organization capabilities and structuring the work effort so as to perform execution-critical value chain activities in a coordinated and competent manner. In this chapter, we discuss five additional managerial actions that promote good strategy execution:

- Allocating resources to the drive for good strategy execution.
- Instituting policies and procedures that facilitate strategy execution.
- Using process management tools to drive continuous improvement in how value chain activities are performed.
- Installing information and operating systems that enable company personnel to carry out their strategic roles proficiently.
- Using rewards and incentives to promote better strategy execution and the achievement of strategic and financial targets.

ALLOCATING RESOURCES TO THE STRATEGY EXECUTION EFFORT

Early in the process of implementing a new strategy, managers need to determine what resources (in terms of funding, people, etc.) will be required for good strategy execution and how they should be distributed across the various organizational units involved. A company's ability to marshal the resources needed to support new strategic initiatives has a major impact on the strategy execution process. Too little funding slows progress and impedes the efforts of organizational units to execute their pieces of the strategic plan proficiently. Too much funding wastes organizational resources and reduces financial performance. Both outcomes argue for managers to be deeply involved in reviewing budget proposals and directing the proper amounts of resources to strategy-critical organizational units. This includes carefully screening requests for more people and new facilities and equipment, approving those that hold promise for making a contribution to strategy execution and turning down those that don't. Should internal cash flows prove insufficient to fund the planned strategic initiatives, then management must raise additional funds through borrowing or selling additional shares of stock to willing investors.

LO 1

Learn why resource allocation should always be based on strategic priorities.

A change in strategy nearly always calls for budget reallocations and resource shifting. Previously important units having a lesser role in the new strategy may need downsizing. Units that now have a bigger strategic role may need more people, new equipment, additional facilities, and above-average increases in their operating budgets. Implementing a new strategy requires managers to take an active and sometimes forceful role in shifting resources, downsizing some functions and upsizing others, not only to amply fund activities with a critical role in the new strategy but also to avoid inefficiency and achieve profit projections. It requires putting enough resources behind new strategic initiatives to fuel their success and making the tough decisions to kill projects and activities that are no longer justified. Honda's strong support of R&D activities allowed it to develop the first motorcycle airbag, the first low-polluting four-stroke outboard marine engine, a wide range of ultra-low-emission cars, the first hybrid car (Honda Insight) in the U.S. market, and the first hydrogen fuel cell car (Honda Clarity). However, Honda managers had no trouble stopping production of the Honda Insight in 2006 when its sales failed to take off and then shifting resources to the development and manufacture of other promising hybrid models, including a totally redesigned Insight that was launched in the United States in 2009.

Visible actions to reallocate operating funds and move people into new organizational units signal a determined commitment to strategic change and frequently are needed to catalyze the implementation process and give it credibility. Microsoft has made a practice of regularly shifting hundreds of programmers to new high-priority programming initiatives within a matter of weeks or even days. At Harris Corporation, where the strategy was to diffuse research ideas into areas that were commercially viable, top management regularly moved groups of engineers out of low-opportunity activities into its most promising new commercial venture divisions. Fast-moving developments in many markets are prompting companies to abandon traditional annual or semiannual budgeting and resource allocation cycles in favor of resource allocation processes supportive of more rapid adjustments in strategy.

The bigger the change in strategy (or the more obstacles that lie in the path of good strategy execution), the bigger the resource shifts that will likely be required. Merely fine-tuning the execution of a company's existing strategy seldom requires big movements of people and money from one area to another. The desired improvements can usually be accomplished through above-average budget increases to organizational units launching new initiatives and below-average increases (or even small budget cuts) for the remaining organizational units. However, there are times when strategy changes or new execution initiatives need to be made without adding to total company expenses. In such circumstances, managers have to work their way through the existing budget line by line and activity by activity, looking for ways to trim costs and shift resources to higher-priority activities where new execution initiatives are needed. In the event that a company needs to make significant cost cuts during the course of launching new strategic initiatives, then managers have to be especially creative in finding ways to do more with less and execute the strategy more efficiently. Indeed, it is not unusual for strategy changes and the drive for good strategy execution to be conducted in a manner that entails achieving considerably higher levels of operating efficiency and, at the same time, making sure key activities are performed as effectively as possible.

The funding requirements of good strategy execution must drive how capital allocations are made and the size of each unit's operating budget. Under-funding organizational units and activities pivotal to the strategy impedes successful strategy implementation.

A company's operating budget must be both *strategy-driven* (in order to amply fund the performance of key value chain activities) and *lean* (in order to operate as cost-efficiently as possible).

Figure 11.1   **How Policies and Procedures Facilitate Good Strategy Execution**

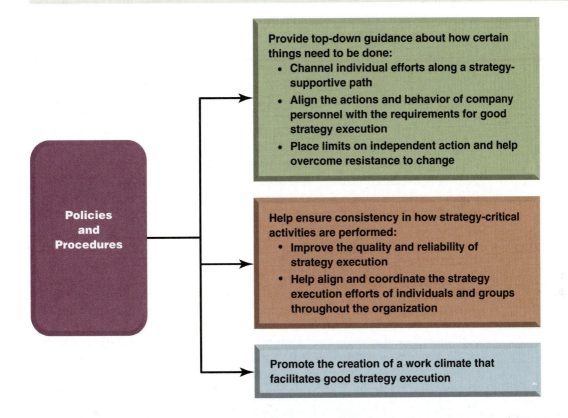

INSTITUTING POLICIES AND PROCEDURES THAT FACILITATE STRATEGY EXECUTION

A company's policies and procedures can either support or obstruct good strategy execution. Any time a company moves to put new strategy elements in place or improve its strategy execution capabilities, some changes in work practices and the behavior of company personnel are usually required. Managers are thus well advised to examine whether existing policies and procedures support such changes and to proactively revise or discard those that are out of sync.

As shown in Figure 11.1, well-conceived policies and operating procedures facilitate strategy execution in three ways:

- *They provide top-down guidance regarding how things need to be done.* Policies and procedures provide company personnel with a set of guidelines for how to perform organizational activities, conduct various aspects of operations, solve problems as they arise, and accomplish particular tasks. In essence, they represent a store of organizational or managerial knowledge about efficient and effective ways of doing things. They clarify uncertainty about how to proceed in executing strategy and align the actions and behavior of company personnel

LO 2

Understand how well-designed policies and procedures can facilitate good strategy execution.

Well-conceived policies and procedures aid strategy execution; out-of-sync ones hinder effective execution.

with the requirements for good strategy execution. Moreover, they place limits on ineffective independent action. When they are well matched with the requirements of the strategy implementation plan, they channel the efforts of individuals along a path that supports the plan and facilitates good strategy execution. When existing ways of doing things are misaligned with strategy execution initiatives, actions and behaviors have to be changed. Under these conditions, the managerial role is to establish and enforce new policies and operating practices that are more conducive to executing the strategy appropriately. Policies are a particularly useful way to counteract tendencies for some people to resist change. People generally refrain from violating company policy or going against recommended practices and procedures without gaining clearance and having strong justification.

- *They help ensure consistency in how execution-critical activities are performed.* Policies and procedures serve to standardize the way that activities are performed and encourage strict conformity to the standardized approach. This is important for ensuring the quality and reliability of the strategy execution process. It helps align and coordinate the strategy execution efforts of individuals and groups throughout the organization—a feature that is particularly beneficial when there are geographically scattered operating units. For example, eliminating significant differences in the operating practices of different plants, sales regions, customer service centers, or the individual outlets in a chain operation helps a company deliver consistent product quality and service to customers. Good strategy execution nearly always entails an ability to replicate product quality and the caliber of customer service at every location where the company does business—anything less blurs the company's image and lowers customer satisfaction.

- *They promote the creation of a work climate that facilitates good strategy execution.* A company's policies and procedures help to set the tone of a company's work climate and contribute to a common understanding of "how we do things around here." Because discarding old policies and procedures in favor of new ones invariably alters the internal work climate, managers can use the policy-changing process as a powerful lever for changing the corporate culture in ways that produce a stronger fit with the new strategy. The trick here, obviously, is to come up with new policies or procedures that catch the immediate attention of company personnel, quickly shift their actions and behavior, and then become embedded in how things are done.

To ensure consistency in product quality and service behavior patterns, McDonald's policy manual spells out detailed procedures that personnel in each McDonald's unit are expected to observe. For example, "Cooks must turn, never flip, hamburgers. If they haven't been purchased, Big Macs must be discarded in 10 minutes after being cooked and French fries in 7 minutes. Cashiers must make eye contact with and smile at every customer." Nordstrom has a company policy of promoting only those people whose personnel records contain evidence of "heroic acts" to please customers—especially customers who may have made "unreasonable requests" that require special efforts. This induces store personnel to dedicate themselves to outstanding customer service, consistent with the requirements of executing a strategy based on exceptionally high service quality. To ensure that its R&D activities are responsive to customer needs and expectations, Hewlett-Packard requires its R&D people to make regular visits to customers to learn about their problems and learn their reactions to HP's latest new products.

One of the big policy-making issues concerns what activities need to be rigidly prescribed and what activities ought to allow room for independent action on the part of empowered personnel. Few companies need thick policy manuals to direct the strategy execution process or prescribe exactly how daily operations are to be conducted. Too much policy can be as much of a hindrance as wrong policy and as confusing as no policy. There is wisdom in a middle approach: *Prescribe enough policies to give organization members clear direction and to place reasonable boundaries on their actions; then empower them to act within these boundaries in whatever way they think makes sense.* Allowing company personnel to act with some degree of freedom is especially appropriate when individual creativity and initiative are more essential to good strategy execution than standardization and strict conformity. Instituting policies that facilitate strategy execution can therefore mean more policies, fewer policies, or different policies. It can mean policies that require things be done according to a strictly defined standard or policies that give employees substantial leeway to do activities the way they think best.

USING PROCESS MANAGEMENT TOOLS TO STRIVE FOR CONTINUOUS IMPROVEMENT

Company managers can significantly advance the cause of superior strategy execution by using various process management tools to drive continuous improvement in how internal operations are conducted. One of the most widely used and effective tools for gauging how well a company is executing pieces of its strategy entails benchmarking the company's performance of particular activities and business processes against "best-in-industry" and "best-in-world" performers.[1] It can also be useful to look at "best-in-company" performers of an activity if a company has a number of different organizational units performing much the same function at different locations. Identifying, analyzing, and understanding how top-performing companies or organizational units conduct particular value chain activities and business processes provides useful yardsticks for judging the effectiveness and efficiency of internal operations and setting performance standards for organizational units to meet or beat.

LO 3

Learn how process management tools that drive continuous improvement in the performance of value chain activities can help an organization achieve superior strategy execution.

How the Process of Identifying and Incorporating Best Practices Works

A **best practice** is a technique for performing an activity or business process that has been shown to consistently deliver superior results compared to other methods.[2] To qualify as a legitimate best practice, the technique must have a proven record in significantly lowering costs, improving quality or performance, shortening time requirements, enhancing safety, or delivering some other highly positive operating outcome. Best practices thus identify a path to operating excellence. For a best practice to be valuable and transferable, it must demonstrate success over time, deliver quantifiable and highly positive results, and be repeatable.

CORE CONCEPT

A **best practice** is a method of performing an activity that has been shown to consistently deliver superior results compared to other methods.

Figure 11.2   **From Benchmarking and Best-Practice Implementation to Operating Excellence**

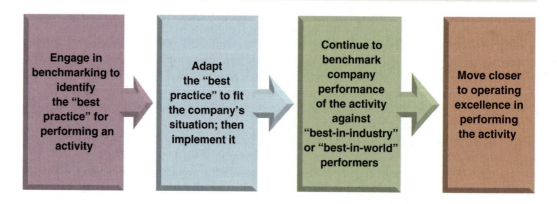

As discussed in Chapter 4, *benchmarking* is the backbone of the process of identifying, studying, and implementing best practices. A company's benchmarking effort looks outward to find best practices and then proceeds to develop the data for measuring how well a company's own performance of an activity stacks up against the best-practice standard. For individual managers, benchmarking involves being humble enough to admit that others have come up with world-class ways to perform particular activities yet wise enough to try to learn how to match, and even surpass, them. But, as shown in Figure 11.2, the payoff of benchmarking comes from adapting the top-notch approaches pioneered by other companies to the company's own operation and thereby boosting, perhaps dramatically, the proficiency with which strategy-critical value chain tasks are performed.

However, benchmarking is more complicated than simply identifying which companies are the best performers of an activity and then trying to imitate their approaches—especially if these companies are in other industries. Normally, the outstanding practices of other organizations have to be *adapted* to fit the specific circumstances of a company's own business, strategy, and operating requirements. Since each organization is unique, the telling part of any best-practice initiative is how well the company puts its own version of the best practice into place and makes it work.

Indeed, a best practice remains little more than another company's interesting success story unless company personnel buy into the task of translating what can be learned from other companies into real action and results. The agents of change must be frontline employees who are convinced of the need to abandon the old ways of doing things and switch to a best-practice mindset. *The more that organizational units use best practices in performing their work, the closer a company moves toward performing its value chain activities as effectively and efficiently as possible.* This is what excellent strategy execution is all about.

Legions of companies across the world now engage in benchmarking to improve their strategy execution efforts. Scores of trade associations and special-interest organizations have undertaken efforts to collect best-practice data relevant to a particular industry or business function and make their databases available online to members. Good examples include The Benchmarking Exchange (**www.benchnet.com**); Best Practices, LLC

> The more that organizational units use best practices in performing their work, the closer a company comes to achieving effective and efficient strategy execution.

(www.best-in-class.com); and the American Productivity and Quality Center (www.apqc.org). Benchmarking and best-practice implementation have clearly emerged as legitimate and valuable managerial tools for promoting operational excellence and enhancing strategy execution.

Business Process Reengineering, Total Quality Management, and Six Sigma Quality Programs: Tools for Promoting Operating Excellence

In striving for operating excellence, many companies have also come to rely on three other potent process management tools: business process reengineering, total quality management (TQM), and Six Sigma quality control techniques. Indeed, these three tools have become globally pervasive techniques for implementing strategies keyed to cost reduction, defect-free manufacture, superior product quality, superior customer service, and total customer satisfaction. The following sections describe how business process reengineering, TQM, and Six Sigma programs can contribute to top-notch strategy execution and operating excellence.

Business Process Reengineering Companies scouring for ways to improve their operations have sometimes discovered that the execution of strategy-critical activities is hindered by an organizational arrangement where pieces of the activity are performed in several different functional departments, with no one manager or group being accountable for optimal performance of the entire activity. This can easily occur in such inherently cross-functional activities as customer service (which can involve personnel in order filling, warehousing and shipping, invoicing, accounts receivable, after-sale repair, and technical support), new product development (which typically involves personnel in R&D, design and engineering, purchasing, manufacturing, and sales and marketing), and supply chain management (which cuts across such areas as purchasing, inventory management, manufacturing and assembly, warehousing, and shipping).

To address the suboptimal performance problems that can arise from this type of situation, many companies have opted to *reengineer the work effort,* pulling the pieces of strategy-critical activities out of different departments and creating a single department or work group to take charge of the whole process and perform it in a better, cheaper, and more strategy-supportive fashion. The use of cross-functional teams has been popularized by the practice of **business process reengineering,** which involves radically redesigning and streamlining the workflow (often enabled by cutting-edge use of online technology and information systems), with the goal of achieving quantum gains in performance of the activity.[3]

> **CORE CONCEPT**
>
> **Business process reengineering** involves radically redesigning and streamlining how an activity is performed, with the intent of achieving dramatic improvements in performance.

When done properly, business process reengineering can produce dramatic operating benefits. Hallmark reengineered its process for developing new greeting cards, creating teams of mixed-occupation personnel (artists, writers, lithographers, merchandisers, and administrators) to work on a single holiday or greeting card theme; the reengineered process speeded development times for new lines of greeting cards by up to 24 months, was more cost-efficient, and increased customer satisfaction.[4] In the order-processing section of General Electric's circuit breaker division, elapsed time from order receipt to delivery was cut from three weeks to three days by consolidating six production units into one, reducing a variety of former inventory and handling steps, automating the design system to replace a human custom-design process, and cutting the organizational layers between managers and workers from three to one. Productivity rose 20 percent in one year, and unit manufacturing costs dropped 30 percent. Northwest Water, a British utility, used process reengineering to eliminate 45 work depots that served as home bases to crews who installed and repaired water and sewage lines and equipment. Under the reengineered arrangement, crews worked directly from their vehicles, receiving assignments and reporting work completion from computer terminals in their trucks. Crew members became contractors to Northwest Water rather than employees, a move that not only eliminated the need for the work depots but also allowed Northwest Water to eliminate a big percentage of the bureaucratic personnel and supervisory organization that managed the crews.[5]

Reengineering of value chain activities has been undertaken at many companies in many industries all over the world, with excellent results at some firms.[6] At companies where it has produced only modest results, this is usually because of ineptness and/or lack of wholehearted commitment from the top. While business process reengineering has been criticized for its use by some companies as an excuse for downsizing, it has nonetheless proved itself as a useful tool for streamlining a company's work effort and moving closer to operational excellence. It has also inspired more technologically based approaches to integrating and streamlining business processes, such as *Enterprise Resource Planning,* a software-based system implemented with the help of consulting companies such as SAP (the leading provider of business software).

Total Quality Management Programs
Total quality management (TQM) is a philosophy of managing a set of business practices that emphasizes continuous improvement in all phases of operations, 100 percent accuracy in performing tasks, involvement and empowerment of employees at all levels, team-based work design, benchmarking, and total customer satisfaction.[7] While TQM concentrates on producing quality goods and fully satisfying customer expectations, it achieves its biggest successes when it is extended to employee efforts in *all departments*—for example, human resources, billing, accounting, and information systems—that may lack pressing, customer-driven incentives to improve. It involves reforming the corporate culture and shifting to a total quality/continuous improvement business philosophy that permeates every facet of the organization.[8] TQM aims at instilling enthusiasm and commitment to doing things right from the top to the bottom of the organization. Management's job is to kindle an organizationwide search for ways to improve, a search that involves all company personnel exercising initiative and using their ingenuity. TQM doctrine preaches that there's no such thing as "good enough" and that everyone has a responsibility to participate in continuous improvement. TQM is thus a race without a finish. Success comes from making little steps forward each day, a process that the Japanese call *kaizen.*

TQM takes a fairly long time to show significant results—very little benefit emerges within the first six months. The long-term payoff of TQM, if it comes, depends heavily on management's success in implanting a culture within which the TQM philosophy and practices can thrive. TQM is a managerial tool that has attracted numerous users and advocates over several decades, and it can deliver good results when used properly.

Six Sigma Quality Programs   Six Sigma programs offer another way to drive continuous improvement in quality and strategy execution. This approach entails the use of advanced statistical methods to identify and remove the causes of defects (errors) and variability in performing an activity or business process. When performance of an activity or process reaches "Six Sigma quality," there are *no more than 3.4 defects per million iterations* (equal to 99.9997 percent accuracy)[9]

There are two important types of Six Sigma programs. DMAIC (define, measure, analyze, improve, and control) is an improvement system for existing processes falling below specification and needing incremental improvement. The DMADV process of define, measure, analyze, design, and verify is used to develop *new* processes or products at Six Sigma quality levels. DMADV is sometimes referred to as a Design for Six Sigma, or DFSS. Both Six Sigma programs are overseen by personnel who have completed Six Sigma "master black belt" training and are executed by personnel who have earned Six Sigma "green belts" and Six Sigma "black belts." According to the Six Sigma Academy, personnel with black belts can save companies approximately $230,000 per project and can complete four to six projects a year.[10]

The statistical thinking underlying Six Sigma is based on the following three principles: All work is a process, all processes have variability, and all processes create data that explain variability.[11] To illustrate how these three principles drive the metrics of DMAIC, consider the case of a hypothetical janitorial company that wants to improve the caliber of work done by its cleaning crews and thereby improve customer satisfaction. The janitorial company's Six Sigma team can pursue quality enhancement and continuous improvement via the DMAIC process as follows:

- *Define.* Because Six Sigma is aimed at reducing defects, the first step is to define what constitutes a defect. Six Sigma team members might decide that leaving streaks on windows is a defect because it is a source of customer dissatisfaction.
- *Measure.* The next step is to collect data to find out why, how, and how often this defect occurs. This might include creating a process flow map of the specific ways that cleaning crews go about the task of cleaning a commercial customer's windows. Other metrics may include recording what tools and cleaning products the crews use to clean windows.
- *Analyze.* After the data are gathered and the statistics analyzed, the company's Six Sigma team may discover that the tools and window-cleaning techniques of certain employees are better than those of other employees because their tools and procedures leave no streaked windows—a "best practice" for avoiding window streaking is thus identified and documented.
- *Improve.* The Six Sigma team implements the documented best practice as a standard way of cleaning windows.
- *Control.* The company teaches new and existing employees the best-practice technique for window cleaning. Over time, there is significant improvement in customer satisfaction and increased business.

Six Sigma's DMAIC process is a particularly good vehicle for improving performance when there are *wide variations* in how well an activity is performed.[12] For instance, airlines striving to improve the on-time performance of their flights have

CORE CONCEPT

Six Sigma programs utilize advanced statistical methods to improve quality by reducing defects and variability in the performance of business processes.

more to gain from actions to curtail the number of flights that are late by more than 30 minutes than from actions to reduce the number of flights that are late by less than 5 minutes. Likewise, FedEx might have a 16-hour average delivery time for its overnight package service operation, but if the actual delivery time varies around the 16-hour average from a low of 12 hours to a high of 26 hours, such that 10 percent of its packages are delivered over 6 hours late, then it has a huge reliability problem of the sort that Six Sigma programs are well suited to address.

Since the mid-1990s, thousands of companies and nonprofit organizations around the world have used Six Sigma programs to promote operating excellence. Such manufacturers as Motorola, Caterpillar, DuPont, Xerox, Alcan Aluminum, BMW, Volkswagen, Nokia, Owens Corning, Boeing, and Emerson Electric have employed Six Sigma techniques to improve their strategy execution and increase production quality. General Electric (GE), one of the most successful companies implementing Six Sigma training and pursuing Six Sigma perfection across the company's entire operations, estimated benefits on the order of $10 billion during the first five years of implementation; its Lighting division, for example, cut invoice defects and disputes by 98 percent, while GE Capital Mortgage improved the chances of a caller reaching a "live" GE person from 76 to 99 percent.[13] Illustration Capsule 11.1 describes Whirlpool's use of Six Sigma in its appliance business.

Six Sigma is, however, not just a quality-enhancing tool for manufacturers. At one company, product sales personnel typically wined and dined customers to close their deals, but the costs of such entertaining were viewed as excessively high.[14] A Six Sigma project that examined sales data found that although face time with customers was important, wining, dining, and other types of entertainment were not. The data showed that regular face time helped close sales, but that time could be spent over a cup of coffee instead of golfing at a resort or taking clients to expensive restaurants. In addition, analysis showed that too much face time with customers was counterproductive. A regularly scheduled customer picnic was found to be detrimental to closing sales because it was held at a busy time of year, when customers preferred not to be away from their offices. Changing the manner in which prospective customers were wooed resulted in a 10 percent increase in sales. Six Sigma has also been used to improve processes in health care. A Milwaukee hospital used Six Sigma to improve the accuracy of administering the proper drug doses to patients. DMAIC analysis of the three-stage process by which prescriptions were written by doctors, filled by the hospital pharmacy, and then administered to patients by nurses revealed that most mistakes came from misreading the doctors' handwriting.[15] The hospital implemented a program requiring doctors to enter the prescription on the hospital's computers, which slashed the number of errors dramatically. Bank of America, Starwood Hotels, Penske Truck Leasing, Jacksonville Electric Authority (JEA), United Heath Group, Amazon.com, and the United States Army, Navy, Air Force, and Marine Corps also have reportedly used Six Sigma techniques successfully in their operations.

While many enterprises have used Six Sigma methods to improve the quality with which activities are performed, there is evidence that Six Sigma techniques can stifle innovation and creativity.[16] The essence of Six Sigma is to reduce variability in processes, but creative processes, by nature, include quite a bit of variability. In many instances, breakthrough innovations occur only after thousands of ideas have been abandoned and promising ideas have gone through multiple iterations and extensive prototyping. Google CEO Eric Schmidt has commented

Whirlpool's Use of Six Sigma to Promote Operating Excellence

Top management at Whirlpool Corporation (with 67 manufacturing and technology centers around the globe and sales in some 170 countries totaling $17 billion in 2009) has a vision of Whirlpool appliances in "Every Home . . . Everywhere with Pride, Passion, and Performance." One of management's chief objectives in pursuing this vision is to build unmatched customer loyalty to the Whirlpool brand. Whirlpool's strategy to win the hearts and minds of appliance buyers the world over has been to produce and market appliances with top-notch quality and innovative features that users will find appealing. In addition, Whirlpool's strategy has been to offer a wide selection of models (recognizing that buyer tastes and needs differ) and to strive for low-cost production efficiency, thereby enabling Whirlpool to price its products very competitively. Executing this strategy at Whirlpool's operations in North America (where it is the market leader), Latin America (where it is also the market leader), Europe (where it ranks third), and Asia (where it is number one in India and has a foothold with huge growth opportunities elsewhere) has involved a strong focus on continuous improvement, lean manufacturing capabilities, and a drive for operating excellence. To marshal the efforts of its 67,000 employees in executing the strategy successfully, management developed a comprehensive Operational Excellence program with Six Sigma as one of the centerpieces.

The Operational Excellence initiative, which began in the 1990s, incorporated Six Sigma techniques to improve the quality of Whirlpool products and, at the same time, lower costs and trim the time it took to get product innovations into the marketplace. The Six Sigma program helped Whirlpool save $175 million in manufacturing costs in its first three years.

To sustain the productivity gains and cost savings, Whirlpool embedded Six Sigma practices within each of its manufacturing facilities worldwide and instilled a culture based on Six Sigma and lean manufacturing skills and capabilities. In 2002, each of Whirlpool's operating units began taking the Six Sigma initiative to a higher level by first placing the needs of the customer at the center of every function—R&D, technology, manufacturing, marketing, and administrative support—and then striving to consistently improve quality levels while eliminating all unnecessary costs. The company systematically went through every aspect of its business with the view that company personnel should perform every activity at every level in a manner that delivers value to the customer and leads to continuous improvement on how things are done.

Whirlpool management believes that the company's Operational Excellence process has been a major contributor in sustaining the company's position as the leading global manufacturer and marketer of home appliances.

Source: www.whirlpool.com, accessed September 25, 2003, November 15, 2005, August 16, 2008, and July 9, 2010; Lexis-Nexis-Edgar Online, exhibit type: exhibit 99 - additional exhibits, filing date: June 21, 2010.

that the innovation process is "anti-Six Sigma" and that applying Six Sigma principles to those performing creative work at Google would choke off innovation at the company.[17]

James McNerney, a GE executive schooled in the constructive use of Six Sigma, became CEO at 3M Corporation and proceeded to institute a series of Six Sigma–based principles. McNerney's dedication to Six Sigma and his elimination of 8 percent of the company's workforce did cause 3M's profits to jump shortly after his arrival, but the application of Six Sigma in 3M's R&D and new product development activities soon proved to stifle innovation and new product introductions, undermining the company's long-standing reputation for innovation. 3M's researchers complained that the innovation process did not lend itself well to the extensive data collection and analysis required under Six Sigma and that too much time was spent completing reports that outlined the market potential and possible manufacturing concerns for projects in all stages of the R&D pipeline. Six Sigma rigidity and a freeze on 3M's R&D budget from McNerney's first year as CEO through 2005 was blamed for the company's drop from first to seventh place on the Boston Consulting Group's Most Innovative Companies list.[18]

A blended approach to Six Sigma implementation that is gaining in popularity pursues incremental improvements in operating efficiency, while R&D and other processes that allow the company to develop new ways of offering value to customers are given freer rein. Managers of these *ambidextrous organizations* are adept at employing continuous improvement in operating processes but allowing R&D to operate under a set of rules that allows for the development of breakthrough innovations. However, the two distinctly different approaches to managing employees must be carried out by tightly integrated senior managers to ensure that the separate and diversely oriented units operate with a common purpose. Ciba Vision, a global leader in contact lenses, has dramatically reduced operating expenses through the use of continuous improvement programs, while simultaneously and harmoniously developing new series of contact lens products that have allowed its revenues to increase by 300 percent over a 10-year period.[19] An enterprise that systematically and wisely applies Six Sigma methods to its value chain, activity by activity, can make major strides in improving the proficiency with which its strategy is executed without sacrificing innovation. As is the case with TQM, obtaining managerial commitment, establishing a quality culture, and fully involving employees are all of critical importance to the successful implementation of Six Sigma quality programs.[20]

The Difference between Business Process Reengineering and Continuous Improvement Programs like Six Sigma and TQM

Business process reengineering and continuous improvement efforts like TQM and Six Sigma both aim at improved productivity and reduced costs, better product quality, and greater customer satisfaction. The essential difference between business process reengineering and continuous improvement programs is that reengineering aims at *quantum gains* on the order of 30 to 50 percent or more, whereas programs like TQM and Six Sigma stress *incremental progress,* striving for inch-by-inch gains again and again in a never-ending stream. The two approaches to improved performance of value chain activities and operating excellence are not mutually exclusive; it makes sense to use them in tandem. Reengineering can be used first to produce a good basic design that yields quick, dramatic improvements in performing a business process. Total quality programs can then be used as a follow-on to reengineering and/or best-practice implementation, delivering gradual improvements over a longer period of time. Such a two-pronged approach to implementing operational excellence is like a marathon race in which you run the first 4 miles as fast as you can and then gradually pick up speed the remainder of the way.

Business process reengineering aims at one-time quantum improvement, while continuous improvement programs like TQM and Six Sigma aim at ongoing incremental improvements.

Capturing the Benefits of Initiatives to Improve Operations

The biggest beneficiaries of benchmarking and best-practice initiatives, reengineering, TQM, and Six Sigma are companies that view such programs not as ends in themselves but as tools for implementing company strategy more effectively. The skimpiest payoffs occur when company managers seize on them as something worth trying—novel ideas that could improve things. In most such instances, they result in strategy-blind efforts to simply manage better.

There's an important lesson here. Business process management tools all need to be linked to a company's strategic priorities to contribute effectively to improving the strategy's execution. Only strategy can point to which value chain activities matter and what performance targets make the most sense. Without a strategic framework, managers lack the context in which to fix things that really matter to business-unit performance and competitive success.

To get the most from initiatives to execute strategy more proficiently, managers must have a clear idea of what specific outcomes really matter. Is it high on-time delivery, lower overall costs, fewer customer complaints, shorter cycle times, a higher percentage of revenues coming from recently introduced products, or what? Benchmarking best-in-industry and best-in-world performance of most or all value chain activities provides a realistic basis for setting internal performance milestones and longer-range targets.

Once initiatives to improve operations are linked to the company's strategic priorities, then comes the managerial task of building a total quality culture that is genuinely committed to achieving the performance outcomes that strategic success requires.[21] Managers can take the following action steps to realize full value from TQM or Six Sigma initiatives and promote a culture of operating excellence:[22]

1. Visible, unequivocal, and unyielding commitment to total quality and continuous improvement, including a vision concerned with quality and specific, measurable objectives for increasing quality and making continuous improvement.
2. Nudging people toward quality-supportive behaviors by:
   a. Screening job applicants rigorously and hiring only those with attitudes and aptitudes right for quality-based performance.
   b. Providing quality training for most employees.
   c. Using teams and team-building exercises to reinforce and nurture individual effort (the creation of a quality culture is facilitated when teams become more cross-functional, multitask-oriented, and increasingly self-managed).
   d. Recognizing and rewarding individual and team efforts to improve quality regularly and systematically.
   e. Stressing prevention (doing it right the first time), not inspection (instituting ways to correct mistakes).
3. Empowering employees so that authority for delivering great service or improving products is in the hands of the doers rather than the overseers—*improving quality has to be seen as part of everyone's job.*
4. Using online systems to provide all relevant parties with the latest best practices, thereby speeding the diffusion and adoption of best practices throughout the organization. Online systems can also allow company personnel to exchange data and opinions about how to upgrade the prevailing best practices.

5.   Emphasizing that performance can, and must, be improved because competitors are not resting on their laurels and customers are always looking for something better.

If the quality initiatives are linked to the strategic objectives and if all organization members buy into a supporting culture of operating excellence, then a company's continuous improvement practices become decidedly more conducive to proficient strategy execution.

> The purpose of using benchmarking, best practices, business process reengineering, TQM, and Six Sigma programs is to improve the performance of strategy-critical activities and thereby enhance strategy execution.

In sum, benchmarking, the adoption of best practices, business process reengineering, TQM, and Six Sigma techniques all need to be seen and used as part of a bigger-picture effort to execute strategy proficiently. Used properly, all of these tools are capable of improving the proficiency with which an organization performs its value chain activities. Not only do improvements from such initiatives add up over time and strengthen organizational capabilities, but they also help build a culture of operating excellence. All this lays the groundwork for gaining a competitive advantage.[23] While it is relatively easy for rivals to also implement process management tools, it is much more difficult and time-consuming for them to instill a deeply ingrained culture of operating excellence (as occurs when such techniques are religiously employed and top management exhibits lasting commitment to operational excellence throughout the organization).

INSTALLING INFORMATION AND OPERATING SYSTEMS

> **LO 4**
>
> Recognize the role of information and operating systems in enabling company personnel to carry out their strategic roles proficiently.

Company strategies can't be executed well without a number of internal systems for business operations. Southwest Airlines, Singapore Airlines, Lufthansa, British Airways, and other successful airlines cannot hope to provide passenger-pleasing service without a user-friendly online reservation system, an accurate and speedy baggage handling system, and a strict aircraft maintenance program that minimizes problems requiring at-the-gate service that delay departures. FedEx has internal communication systems that allow it to coordinate its over 80,000 vehicles in handling an average of 8.0 million packages a day. Its leading-edge flight operations systems allow a single controller to direct as many as 200 of FedEx's 664 aircraft simultaneously, overriding their flight plans should weather problems or other special circumstances arise. In addition, FedEx has created a series of e-business tools for customers that allow them to ship and track packages online, create address books, review shipping history, generate custom reports, simplify customer billing, reduce internal warehousing and inventory management costs, purchase goods and services from suppliers, and respond to quickly changing customer demands. All of FedEx's systems support the company's strategy of providing businesses and individuals with a broad array of package delivery services (from premium next-day to economical five-day deliveries) and enhancing its competitiveness against United Parcel Service, DHL, and the U.S. Postal Service.

Otis Elevator, the world's largest manufacturer of elevators, with some 2.3 million elevators and escalators installed worldwide, has a 24-hour remote electronic monitoring system that can detect when an elevator or escalator installed on a customer's site has any of 325 problems.[24] If the monitoring system detects a problem, it analyzes and diagnoses the cause and location, then makes the service call to an Otis mechanic at the nearest location, and helps the mechanic (who is equipped with a Web-enabled cell phone) identify the component causing the problem. The company's maintenance system helps keep outage times under three hours. All trouble-call data are relayed to design and manufacturing personnel, allowing them to quickly alter design specifications or manufacturing procedures when needed to correct recurring problems. All customers have online access to performance data on each of their Otis elevators and escalators.

Amazon.com ships customer orders of books, CDs, toys, and myriad other items from fully computerized warehouses with a capacity of over 17½ million square feet in 2010. The warehouses are so technologically sophisticated that they require about as many lines of code to run as Amazon's Web site does. Using complex picking algorithms, computers initiate the order-picking process by sending signals to workers' wireless receivers, telling them which items to pick off the shelves in which order. Computers also generate data on misboxed items, chute backup times, line speed, worker productivity, and shipping weights on orders. Systems are upgraded regularly, and productivity improvements are aggressively pursued. In 2003 Amazon turned their inventory over 20 times annually in an industry whose average was 15 turns; by 2009 its industry turnover had decreased to an unprecedented 12. Amazon's warehouse efficiency and cost per order filled was so low that one of the fastest-growing and most profitable parts of Amazon's business was using its warehouses to run the e-commerce operations of large retail chains such as Target.

Most telephone companies, electric utilities, and TV broadcasting systems have online monitoring systems to spot transmission problems within seconds and increase the reliability of their services. At eBay, there are systems for real-time monitoring of new listings, bidding activity, Web site traffic, and page views. Kaiser Permanente spent $3 billion to digitize the medical records of its 8.2 million members so that it could manage patient care more efficiently.[25] IBM makes extensive use of social software applications such as Lotus Connections to support its 1,796 online communities, having discovered that many of its employees depend on these tools to do their work.[26] In businesses such as public accounting and management consulting, where large numbers of professional staff need cutting-edge technical know-how, companies have developed systems that identify when it is time for certain employees to attend training programs to update their skills and know-how. Many companies have cataloged best-practice information on their intranets to promote faster transfer and implementation organizationwide.[27]

Well-conceived state-of-the-art operating systems not only enable better strategy execution but also strengthen organizational capabilities—sometimes enough to provide a competitive edge over rivals. For example, a company with a differentiation strategy based on superior quality has added capability if it has systems for training personnel in quality techniques, tracking product quality at each production step, and ensuring that all goods shipped meet quality standards. If the systems it employs are advanced systems that have not yet been adopted by rivals, the systems may provide the company with a competitive advantage as long as the costs of deploying the systems do not outweigh their benefits. Similarly, a company striving to be a low-cost provider is competitively stronger if it has an unrivaled benchmarking system that identifies opportunities to implement best practices and drive costs out of the business. Fast-growing companies get an important assist from having capabilities in place to recruit and train new employees in large numbers and from investing in infrastructure that gives them the capability to handle rapid growth as it occurs. It is nearly always better to put infrastructure and support systems in place before they are actually needed than to have to scramble to catch up to customer demand.

Instituting Adequate Information Systems, Performance Tracking, and Controls

Accurate and timely information about daily operations is essential if managers are to gauge how well the strategy execution process is proceeding. Information systems need to cover five broad areas: (1) customer data, (2) operations data, (3) employee data, (4) supplier/partner/collaborative ally data, and (5) financial performance data. All key strategic performance indicators must be tracked and reported in real time where possible. Long the norm, monthly profit-and-loss statements and monthly statistical summaries are fast being replaced with daily statistical updates and even up-to-the-minute performance monitoring, made possible by online technology. Most retail companies have automated online systems that generate daily sales reports for each store and maintain up-to-the-minute inventory and sales records on each item. Manufacturing plants typically generate daily production reports and track labor productivity on every shift. Many retailers and manufacturers have online data systems connecting them with their suppliers that monitor the status of inventories, track shipments and deliveries, and measure defect rates.

Real-time information systems permit company managers to stay on top of implementation initiatives and daily operations and to intervene if things seem to be drifting off course. Tracking key performance indicators, gathering information from operating personnel, quickly identifying and diagnosing problems, and taking corrective actions are all integral pieces of the process of managing strategy implementation and exercising adequate control over operations. A number of companies have recently begun creating "electronic scorecards" for senior managers that gather daily or weekly statistics from different databases about inventory, sales, costs, and sales trends; such information enables these managers to easily stay abreast of what's happening and make better on-the-spot decisions.[28] Telephone companies have elaborate information systems to measure signal quality, connection times, interrupts, wrong connections, billing errors, and other measures of reliability that affect customer service and satisfaction. British Petroleum (BP) has outfitted rail cars carrying hazardous materials with sensors and global-positioning systems (GPS) so that it can track the status, location, and other information about these shipments via satellite and relay the data to its corporate intranet. Companies that rely on empowered customer-contact personnel to act promptly and creatively in pleasing customers have installed online information systems that make essential customer data accessible to such personnel through a few keystrokes; this enables them to respond more effectively to customer inquiries and deliver personalized customer service.

Statistical information gives managers a feel for the numbers; briefings and meetings provide a feel for the latest developments and emerging issues; and personal contacts add a feel for the people dimension. All are good barometers.

> Having state-of-the-art operating systems, information systems, and real-time data is integral to superior strategy execution and operating excellence.

Managers must identify problem areas and deviations from plans before they can take action to get the organization back on course, by either improving the approaches to strategy execution or fine-tuning the strategy. Jeff Bezos, Amazon's CEO, is an ardent proponent of managing by the numbers. As he puts it, "Math-based decisions always trump opinion and judgment. The trouble with most corporations is that they make judgment-based decisions when data-based decisions could be made."[29]

Monitoring Employee Performance   Information systems also provide managers with a means for monitoring the performance of empowered workers to see that they are acting within the specified limits.[30] Leaving empowered employees to their own devices in meeting performance standards without appropriate checks and balances can expose an organization to excessive risk.[31] Instances abound of employees' decisions or behavior having gone awry, sometimes costing a company huge sums or producing lawsuits aside from just generating embarrassing publicity.

Scrutinizing daily and weekly operating statistics is one of the important ways in which managers can monitor the results that flow from the actions of empowered subordinates without resorting to constant over-the-shoulder supervision; if the operating results flowing from the actions of empowered employees look good, then it is reasonable to assume that empowerment is working. But close monitoring of operating performance is only one of the control tools at management's disposal. Another valuable lever of control in companies that rely on empowered employees, especially in those that use self-managed work groups or other such teams, is peer-based control. Because peer evaluation is such a powerful control device, companies organized into teams can remove some layers of the management hierarchy and rely on strong peer pressure to keep team members operating between the white lines. This is especially true when a company has the information systems capability to monitor team performance daily or in real time.

TYING REWARDS AND INCENTIVES TO STRATEGY EXECUTION

It is essential that company personnel be enthusiastically committed to executing strategy successfully and achieving performance targets. Company managers typically use an assortment of motivational techniques and rewards to enlist organizationwide commitment to executing the strategic plan. Indeed, a properly designed reward structure is management's most powerful tool for mobilizing organizational commitment to successful strategy execution. But incentives and rewards do more than just strengthen the resolve of company personnel to succeed—they also focus their attention on the accomplishment of specific strategy execution objectives. Not only do they spur the efforts of individuals to achieve those aims, but they also help to coordinate the activities of individuals throughout the organization by aligning their personal motives with the goals of the organization. In this manner, reward systems serve as an indirect type of control mechanism that conserves on the more costly control mechanism of supervisory oversight.

LO 5

Appreciate how and why the use of well-designed incentives and rewards can be management's single most powerful tool for promoting adept strategy execution and operating excellence.

A properly designed reward structure is management's most powerful tool for mobilizing organizational commitment to successful strategy execution and aligning efforts throughout the organization with strategic priorities.

To win employees' sustained, energetic commitment to the strategy execution process, management must be resourceful in designing and using motivational incentives—both monetary and nonmonetary. The more a manager understands what motivates subordinates and the more he or she relies on motivational incentives as a tool for achieving the targeted strategic and financial results, the greater will be employees' commitment to good day-in, day-out strategy execution and achievement of performance targets.[32]

Incentives and Motivational Practices That Facilitate Good Strategy Execution

CORE CONCEPT

Financial rewards provide **high-powered incentives** when rewards are tied to specific outcome objectives.

Financial incentives generally head the list of motivating tools for gaining wholehearted employee commitment to good strategy execution and focusing attention on strategic priorities. They provide *high-powered* motivation for individuals to increase their efforts when rewards are tied to specific outcome objectives. A company's package of monetary rewards typically includes some combination of base-pay increases, performance bonuses, profit-sharing plans, stock awards, company contributions to employee 401(k) or retirement plans, and piecework incentives (in the case of production workers). But most successful companies and managers also make extensive use of nonmonetary incentives. Some of the most important nonmonetary approaches companies can use to enhance motivation are listed below:[33]

- *Provide attractive perks and fringe benefits.* The various options include full coverage of health insurance premiums, college tuition reimbursement, generous paid vacation time, on-site child care, on-site fitness centers, getaway opportunities at company-owned recreational facilities, personal concierge services, subsidized cafeterias and free lunches, casual dress every day, personal travel services, paid sabbaticals, maternity and paternity leaves, paid leaves to care for ill family members, telecommuting, compressed workweeks (four 10-hour days instead of five 8-hour days), flextime (variable work schedules that accommodate individual needs), college scholarships for children, and relocation services.

- *Give awards and other forms of public recognition to high performers, and celebrate the achievement of organizational goals.* Many companies hold award ceremonies to honor top-performing individuals, teams, and organizational units and to showcase company successes. This can help create healthy competition among units and teams within the company, but it can also create a positive esprit de corps among the organization as a whole. Other examples include special recognition at informal company gatherings or in the company newsletter, tangible tokens of appreciation for jobs well done, and frequent words of praise.

- *Rely on promotion from within whenever possible.* The practice of promoting from within helps bind workers to their employer, and employers to their workers, providing strong incentives for good performance. Moreover, promoting from within helps ensure that people in positions of responsibility have knowledge specific to the business, technology, and operations they are managing.

- *Invite and act on ideas and suggestions from employees.* Many companies find that their best ideas for nuts-and-bolts operating improvements come from the suggestions of employees. Moreover, research indicates that the moves of many companies to push decision making down the line and empower employees increases employees' motivation and satisfaction as well as their productivity. The use of self-managed teams has much the same effect.

- *Create a work atmosphere in which there is genuine caring and mutual respect among workers and between management and employees.* A "family" work environment where people are on a first-name basis and there is strong camaraderie promotes teamwork and cross-unit collaboration.

- *State the strategic vision in inspirational terms so that employees feel they are a part of something very worthwhile in a larger social sense.* There's strong motivating power associated with giving people a chance to be part of something exciting and personally satisfying. Jobs with noble purpose tend to inspire employees to give their all. As described in Chapter 9, this not only increases productivity but reduces turnover and lowers costs for staff recruitment and training as well.

- *Share information with employees about financial performance, strategy, operational measures, market conditions, and competitors' actions.* Broad disclosure and prompt communication send the message that managers trust their workers and regard them as valued partners in the enterprise. Keeping employees in the dark denies them information useful to performing their jobs, prevents them from being intellectually engaged, saps their motivation, and detracts from performance.

- *Maintain attractive office space and facilities.* A workplace environment that is attractive and comfortable usually has decidedly positive effects on employee morale and productivity. An appealing work environment is particularly important when workers are expected to spend long hours at work.

For specific examples of the motivational tactics employed by several prominent companies (many of which appear on *Fortune*'s list of the 100 best companies to work for in America), see Illustration Capsule 11.2.

Striking the Right Balance between Rewards and Punishment

Decisions on salary increases, incentive compensation, promotions, key assignments, and the ways and means of awarding praise and recognition are potent attention-getting, commitment-generating devices. Such decisions seldom escape the closest employee scrutiny, thus saying more about what is expected and who is considered to be doing a good job than virtually any other factor. While most approaches to motivation, compensation, and people management accentuate the positive, companies also combine positive rewards with the risk of punishment. At General Electric, McKinsey & Company, several global public accounting firms, and other companies that look for and expect top-notch individual performance, there's an "up-or-out" policy—managers and professionals whose performance is not good enough to warrant promotion are first denied bonuses and stock awards and eventually weeded out. A number of companies deliberately give employees heavy workloads and tight deadlines—personnel are pushed hard to achieve "stretch" objectives and are expected to put in long hours (nights and weekends if need be). At most companies, senior executives and key personnel in underperforming units are pressured to raise performance to acceptable levels and keep it there or risk being replaced.

What Companies Do to Motivate and Reward Employees

Companies have come up with an impressive variety of motivational and reward practices to help create a work environment that energizes employees and promotes better strategy execution. Here's a sampling of what companies are doing:

- Google has a sprawling 20-building headquarters complex known as the Googleplex where its several thousand employees have access to 19 cafes and 60 snack centers, unlimited ice cream, four gyms, heated swimming pools, ping-pong and pool tables, and community bicycles to go from building to building. Management built the Googleplex to be "a dream workplace" and a showcase for environmentally correct building design and construction.

- Lincoln Electric, widely known for its piecework pay scheme and incentive bonus plan, rewards individual productivity by paying workers for each nondefective piece produced. Workers have to correct quality problems on their own time—defects in products used by customers can be traced back to the worker who caused them. Lincoln's piecework plan motivates workers to pay attention to both quality and volume produced. In addition, the company sets aside a substantial portion of its profits above a specified base for worker bonuses. To determine bonus size, Lincoln Electric rates each worker on four equally important performance measures: (1) dependability, (2) quality, (3) output, and (4) ideas and cooperation. The higher a worker's merit rating, the higher the incentive bonus earned; the highest-rated workers in good profit years receive bonuses of as much as 110 percent of their piecework compensation.

- At JM Family Enterprises, a Toyota distributor in Florida, employees get attractive lease options on new Toyotas and enjoy on-site amenities such as a heated lap pool, a fitness center, a free nail salon, free prescriptions delivered by a "pharmacy concierge," and professionally made take-home dinners. Exceptionally high performers are flown to the Bahamas for cruises on the 172-foot company yacht.

- Wegmans, a family-owned grocer with 75 stores on the East Coast of the United States, provides employees with flexible schedules and benefits that include onsite fitness centers. The company's approach to managing people allows it to provide a very high level of customer service not found in other grocery chains. Employees ranging from cashiers to butchers to store managers are all treated equally and viewed as experts in their jobs. Employees receive 50 hours of formal training per year and are allowed to make decisions that they believe are appropriate for their jobs. The company's 2009 annual turnover rate is only 7 percent, which is less than one-half the 19 percent average turnover rate in the U.S. supermarket industry.

- Nordstrom, widely regarded for its superior in-house customer service experience, typically pays its retail salespeople an hourly wage higher than the prevailing rates paid by other department store chains plus a commission on each sale. Spurred by a culture that encourages salespeople to go all out to satisfy customers and to seek out and promote new fashion ideas, Nordstrom salespeople earn nearly 65 percent more than the average sales employee at competing stores. The typical Nordstrom salesperson earns nearly $38,900 per year, but top performers can earn salaries in the six figures.[34] Nordstrom's rules for employees are simple: "Rule #1: Use your good judgment in all situations. There will be no additional rules."

(Continued)

- At W. L. Gore (the maker of GORE-TEX), employees get to choose what project/team they work on, and each team member's compensation is based on other team members' rankings of his or her contribution to the enterprise.
- At Ukrop's Super Markets, a family-owned chain, stores stay closed on Sunday; the company pays out 20 percent of pretax profits to employees in the form of quarterly bonuses; and

the company picks up the membership tab for employees if they visit their health club 30 times a quarter.
- At biotech leader Amgen, employees get 16 paid holidays, generous vacation time, tuition reimbursements up to $10,000, on-site massages, discounted car-wash services, and the convenience of shopping at on-site farmers' markets.

Sources: Fortune's lists of the 100 best companies to work for in America, 2002, 2004, 2005, 2008, 2009, and 2010; Jefferson Graham, "The Search Engine That Could," *USA Today,* August 26, 2003, p. B3; company Web sites (accessed June 2010).

As a general rule, it is unwise to take off the pressure for good individual and group performance or play down the adverse consequences of shortfalls in performance. There is no evidence that a no-pressure/no-adverse-consequences work environment leads to superior strategy execution or operating excellence. As the CEO of a major bank put it, "There's a deliberate policy here to create a level of anxiety. Winners usually play like they're one touchdown behind."[35] High-performing organizations nearly always have a cadre of ambitious people who relish the opportunity to climb the ladder of success, love a challenge, thrive in a performance-oriented environment, and find some competition and pressure useful to satisfy their own drives for personal recognition, accomplishment, and self-satisfaction.

However, if an organization's motivational approaches and reward structure induce too much stress, internal competitiveness, job insecurity, and fear of unpleasant consequences, the impact on workforce morale and strategy execution can be counterproductive. Evidence shows that managerial initiatives to improve strategy execution should incorporate more positive than negative motivational elements because when cooperation is positively enlisted and rewarded, rather than coerced by orders and threats (implicit or explicit), people tend to respond with more enthusiasm, dedication, creativity, and initiative.[36]

Linking Rewards to Strategically Relevant Performance Outcomes

To create a strategy-supportive system of rewards and incentives, a company must reward people for accomplishing results, not for just dutifully performing assigned tasks. To make the work environment results-oriented, managers need to focus jobholders' attention and energy on what to *achieve* as opposed to what to *do*. It is flawed management to tie incentives and rewards to satisfactory performance of duties and activities instead of desired business outcomes and company achievements.[37] In any job, performing assigned tasks is not equivalent to achieving intended outcomes. Diligently showing up for work and attending to one's job assignment does not, by itself, guarantee results. Employee productivity among employees at Best Buy's corporate headquarters rose by 35 percent after the company began to focus on the results of each employee's work rather than on employees' willingness to come to work early and stay late.

> Incentives must be based on accomplishing the right results, not on dutifully performing assigned tasks.

> The key to creating a reward system that promotes good strategy execution is to make measures of good business performance and good strategy execution the *dominating basis* for designing incentives, evaluating individual and group efforts, and handing out rewards.

Ideally, performance targets should be set for every organizational unit, every manager, every team or work group, and perhaps every employee—targets that measure whether strategy execution is progressing satisfactorily. If the company's strategy is to be a low-cost provider, the incentive system must reward actions and achievements that result in lower costs. If the company has a differentiation strategy based on superior quality and service, the incentive system must reward such outcomes as Six Sigma defect rates, infrequent need for product repair, low numbers of customer complaints, speedy order processing and delivery, and high levels of customer satisfaction. If a company's growth is predicated on a strategy of new product innovation, incentives should be tied to factors such as the percentages of revenues and profits coming from newly introduced products.

Incentive compensation for top executives is typically tied to such financial measures as revenue and earnings growth, stock price performance, return on investment, and creditworthiness or to strategic measures such as market share growth. However, incentives for department heads, teams, and individual workers may be tied to performance outcomes more closely related to their strategic area of responsibility. In manufacturing, incentive compensation may be tied to unit manufacturing costs, on-time production and shipping, defect rates, the number and extent of work stoppages due to equipment breakdowns, and so on. In sales and marketing, there may be incentives for achieving dollar sales or unit volume targets, market share, sales penetration of each target customer group, the fate of newly introduced products, the frequency of customer complaints, the number of new accounts acquired, and customer satisfaction. Which performance measures to base incentive compensation on depends on the situation—the priority placed on various financial and strategic objectives, the requirements for strategic and competitive success, and what specific results are needed in different facets of the business to keep strategy execution on track.

Illustration Capsule 11.3 provides a vivid example of how one company has designed incentives linked directly to outcomes reflecting good execution.

Guidelines for Designing Effective Incentive Compensation Systems

As explained above, the first principle in designing an effective incentive compensation system is to tie rewards to performance outcomes directly linked to good strategy execution and targeted strategic and financial objectives. But for a company's reward system to truly motivate organization members, inspire their best efforts, and sustain high levels of productivity, it is equally important to observe the following additional guidelines in designing and administering the reward system:

- *Make the financial incentives a major, not minor, piece of the total compensation package.* Performance payoffs must be at least 10 to 12 percent of base salary to have much impact. Incentives that amount to 20 percent or more of total compensation are big attention-getters, likely to really drive individual or team efforts. Incentives amounting to less than 5 percent of total compensation have a comparatively weak motivational impact. Moreover, the payoff for high-performing individuals and teams must be meaningfully greater than the payoff for average performers, and the payoff for average performers meaningfully bigger than that for below-average performers.

- *Have incentives that extend to all managers and all workers, not just top management.* Lower-level managers and employees are just as likely as senior executives to be motivated by the possibility of lucrative rewards.

ILLUSTRATION CAPSULE 11.3

Nucor Corporation: Tying Incentives Directly to Strategy Execution

The strategy at Nucor Corporation, one of the three largest steel producers in the United States, is to be *the* low-cost producer of steel products. Because labor costs are a significant fraction of total cost in the steel business, successful implementation of Nucor's low-cost leadership strategy entails achieving lower labor costs per ton of steel than competitors' costs. Nucor management uses an incentive system to promote high worker productivity and drive labor costs per ton below rivals'. Each plant's workforce is organized into production teams (each assigned to perform particular functions), and weekly production targets are established for each team. Base-pay scales are set at levels comparable to wages for similar manufacturing jobs in the local areas where Nucor has plants, but workers can earn a 1 percent bonus for each 1 percent that their output exceeds target levels. If a production team exceeds its weekly production target by 10 percent, team members receive a 10 percent bonus in their next paycheck; if a team exceeds its quota by 20 percent, team members earn a 20 percent bonus. Bonuses, paid every two weeks, are based on the prior two weeks' actual production levels measured against the targets.

Nucor's piece-rate incentive plan has produced impressive results. The production teams put forth exceptional effort; it is not uncommon for most teams to beat their weekly production targets anywhere from 20 to 50 percent. When added to their base pay, the bonuses earned by Nucor workers make Nucor's work force among the highest-paid in the U.S. steel industry. From a management perspective, the incentive system has resulted

in Nucor having labor productivity levels 10 to 20 percent above the average of the unionized workforces at several of its largest rivals, which in turn has given Nucor a significant labor cost advantage over most rivals.

After years of record-setting profits, Nucor struggled in the economic downturn of 2008–2010, along with the manufacturers and builders who buy its steel. But while bonuses have dwindled, Nucor showed remarkable loyalty to its production workers, avoiding layoffs by having employees get ahead on maintenance, perform work formerly done by contractors, and search for cost savings. Morale at the company has remained high and Nucor's CEO Daniel DiMicco has received thank-you notes from grateful employees by the basketful. As industry growth resumes, Nucor will have a well-trained workforce still in place, more committed than ever to achieving the kind of productivity for which Nucor is justifiably famous. When the turnaround comes, DiMicco has good reason to expect Nucor to be "first out of the box."

Sources: Company Web site (accessed July 2010); N. Byrnes, "Pain, but No Layoffs at Nucor," *Bloomberg Businessweek,* March 26, 2009.

- *Administer the reward system with scrupulous objectivity and fairness.* If performance standards are set unrealistically high or if individual/group performance evaluations are not accurate and well documented, dissatisfaction with the system will overcome any positive benefits.
- *Ensure that the performance targets each individual or team is expected to achieve involve outcomes that the individual or team can personally affect.* The role of incentives is to enhance individual commitment and channel behavior in

beneficial directions. This role is not well served when the performance measures by which company personnel are judged are outside their arena of influence.

- *Keep the time between achieving the targeted performance outcome and the payment of the reward as short as possible.* Companies like Nucor Steel and Continental Airlines have discovered that weekly or monthly payments for good performance work much better than annual payments. Nucor pays weekly bonuses based on prior-week production levels, while Continental pays employees a bonus whenever actual on-time flight performance meets or beats the monthly on-time target. Annual bonus payouts work best for higher-level managers and for situations where the outcome target relates to overall company profitability or stock price performance.

- *Avoid rewarding effort rather than results.* While it is tempting to reward people who have tried hard yet fallen short of achieving performance targets because of circumstances beyond their control, it is ill advised. The problem with making exceptions for unknowable, uncontrollable, or unforeseeable circumstances is that once "good excuses" start to creep into justifying rewards for subpar results, the door is open for all kinds of reasons why actual performance has failed to match targeted performance. A "no excuses" standard is more even-handed, easier to administer, and more conducive to creating a results-oriented work climate.

> The unwavering standard for judging whether individuals, teams, and organizational units have done a good job must be whether they meet or beat performance targets that reflect good strategy execution.

Once an organization's incentive plan is designed, it must be communicated and explained. Everybody needs to understand how his or her incentive compensation is calculated and how individual/group performance targets contribute to organizational performance targets. The pressure to continuously improve strategy execution and achieve performance objectives should be unrelenting, with no loopholes for rewarding shortfalls in performance. People at all levels must be held accountable for carrying out their assigned parts of the strategic plan, and they must understand that their rewards are based on the caliber of results achieved. But with the pressure to perform should come meaningful rewards. Without an ample payoff, the system breaks down, and managers are left with the less workable options of issuing orders, trying to enforce compliance, and depending on the goodwill of employees.

KEY POINTS

1. Implementing and executing a new or different strategy calls for managers to identify the resource requirements of each new strategic initiative and then consider whether the current pattern of resource allocation and the budgets of the various subunits are suitable.

2. Company policies and procedures facilitate strategy execution when they are designed to fit the strategy and its objectives. Anytime a company alters its strategy, managers should review existing policies and operating procedures and replace those that are out of sync. Well conceived policies and procedures aid the task of strategy execution by (1) providing top-down guidance to company personnel regarding how certain things need to be done and what the boundaries are on independent actions and decisions, (2) enforcing

consistency in the performance of strategy-critical activities, thereby improving the quality of the strategy execution effort and aligning the actions of company personnel, however widely dispersed, and (3) promoting the creation of a work climate conducive to good strategy execution.

3. Competent strategy execution entails visible unyielding managerial commitment to best practices and continuous improvement. Benchmarking, best-practice adoption, business process reengineering, total quality management (TQM), and Six Sigma programs are important process management tools for promoting better strategy execution.

4. Company strategies can't be implemented or executed well without a number of support systems to carry on business operations. Real-time information systems and control systems further aid the cause of good strategy execution.

5. Strategy-supportive motivational practices and reward systems are powerful management tools for gaining employee commitment and focusing their attention on the strategy execution goals. The key to creating a reward system that promotes good strategy execution is to make measures of good business performance and good strategy execution the *dominating basis* for designing incentives, evaluating individual and group efforts, and handing out rewards. Positive motivational practices generally work better than negative ones, but there is a place for both. While financial rewards provide high-powered incentives, there's also place for nonmonetary incentives. For an incentive compensation system to work well, (1) the monetary payoff should be a major percentage of the compensation package, (2) the use of incentives should extend to all managers and workers, (3) the system should be administered with care and fairness, (4) each individual's performance targets should involve outcomes the person can personally affect, (5) rewards should promptly follow the determination of good performance, and (6) rewards should be given for results and not just effort.

ASSURANCE OF LEARNING EXERCISES

LO 3

1. Using your favorite search engine, do a search on the term *best practices*. Browse through the search results to identify at least five organizations that have gathered a set of best practices and are making the best-practice library they have assembled available to members.

LO 3

2. Read some of the recent Six Sigma articles posted at isixsigma.com. Prepare a one-page report to your instructor detailing how Six Sigma is being used in various companies and what benefits these companies are reaping from Six Sigma implementation.

LO 3

3. Review the profiles and applications of the latest Malcolm Baldrige National Quality Award recipients at www.baldrige.nist.gov. What are the standout features of the companies' approaches to managing operations? What do you

find impressive about the companies' policies and procedures, use of best practices, emphasis on continuous improvement, and use of rewards and incentives?

LO 5

4. Consult the issue of *Fortune* containing the latest annual "100 Best Companies to Work For" (usually a late-January or early-February issue), or else go to www.fortune.com to access the list, and identify at least five compensation incentives and work practices that these companies use to enhance employee motivation and reward them for good strategic and financial performance. You should identify compensation methods and work practices that are different from those cited in Illustration Capsule 11.2.

LO 5

5. Using Google Scholar or your university library's access to online business periodicals, search for the term *incentive compensation* and prepare a 1- to 2-page report for your instructor discussing the successful (or unsuccessful) use of incentive compensation plans by various companies. Based on the research you found, what factors seem to determine whether incentive compensation plans succeed or fail?

EXERCISES FOR SIMULATION PARTICIPANTS

LO 1

1. Have you and your co-managers allocated ample resources to strategy-critical areas? If so, explain how these investments have contributed to good strategy execution and improved company performance.

LO 3

2. Is benchmarking data available in the simulation exercise in which you are participating? If so, do you and your co-managers regularly study the benchmarking data to see how well your company is doing? Do you consider the benchmarking information provided to be valuable? Why or why not? Cite three recent instances in which your examination of the benchmarking statistics has caused you and your co-managers to take corrective actions to boost company performance.

LO 2, LO 3, LO 4

3. What actions, if any, is your company taking to pursue continuous improvement in how it performs certain value chain activities?

LO 5

4. Does your company have opportunities to use incentive compensation techniques? If so, explain your company's approach to incentive compensation. Is there any hard evidence you can cite that indicates your company's use of incentive compensation techniques has worked? For example, have your company's compensation incentives actually increased productivity? Can you cite

evidence indicating that the productivity gains have resulted in lower labor costs? If the productivity gains have *not* translated into lower labor costs, is it fair to say that your company's use of incentive compensation is a failure?

LO 2, LO 3, LO 4

5. Are you and your co-managers consciously trying to achieve "operating excellence"? What are the indicators of operating excellence at your company? Based on these indicators, how well does your company measure up?

LO 3

6. What hard evidence can you cite that indicates your company's management team is doing a *better* or *worse* job of achieving operating excellence and executing your strategy than are the management teams at rival companies?

ENDNOTES

[1] For a discussion of the value of benchmarking in implementing and executing strategy, see Christopher E. Bogan and Michael J. English, *Benchmarking for Best Practices: Winning through Innovative Adaptation* (New York: McGraw-Hill, 1994) chaps. 2 and 6; Mustafa Ungan, "Factors Affecting the Adoption of Manufacturing Best Practices," *Benchmarking: An International Journal* 11, no. 5 (2004), pp. 504–20; Paul Hyland and Ron Beckett, "Learning to Compete: The Value of Internal Benchmarking," *Benchmarking: An International Journal* 9, no. 3 (2002), pp. 293–304; Yoshinobu Ohinata, "Benchmarking: The Japanese Experience," *Long-Range Planning* 27, no. 4 (August 1994), pp. 48–53.

[2] www.businessdictionary.com/definition/best-practice.html (accessed December 2, 2009).

[3] M. Hammer and J. Champy, *Reengineering the Corporation: A Manifesto for Business Revolution* (New York: Harper Collins Publishers, 1993), pp. 26–27.

[4] Information on the greeting card industry is posted at www.answers.com (accessed July 8, 2009), and "Reengineering: Beyond the Buzzword," *BusinessWeek*, May 24, 1993, www.businessweek.com (accessed July 8, 2009).

[5] Gene Hall, Jim Rosenthal, and Judy Wade, "How to Make Reengineering Really Work," *Harvard Business Review* 71, no. 6 (November–December 1993), pp. 119–31.

[6] For more information on business process reengineering and how well it has worked in various companies, see James Brian Quinn, *Intelligent Enterprise* (New York: Free Press, 1992), p. 162; Ann Majchrzak and Qianwei Wang, "Breaking the Functional Mind-Set in Process Organizations," *Harvard Business Review* 74, no. 5 (September–October 1996), pp. 93–99; Stephen L. Walston, Lawton. R. Burns, and John R. Kimberly, "Does Reengineering Really Work? An Examination of the Context and Outcomes of Hospital Reengineering Initiatives," *Health Services Research* 34, no. 6 (February 2000), pp. 1363–88; Allessio Ascari, Melinda Rock, and Soumitra Dutta, "Reengineering and Organizational Change: Lessons from a Comparative Analysis of Company Experiences," *European Management Journal* 13, no. 1 (March 1995), pp. 1–13. For a review of why some company personnel embrace process reengineering and some don't, see Ronald J. Burke, "Process Reengineering: Who Embraces It and Why?" *TQM Magazine* 16, no. 2 (2004), pp. 114–19.

[7] For some of the seminal discussions of what TQM is and how it works, written by ardent enthusiasts of the technique, see M. Walton, *The Deming Management Method* (New York: Pedigree, 1986); J. Juran, *Juran on Quality by Design* (New York: Free Press, 1992); Philip Crosby, *Quality Is Free: The Act of Making Quality Certain* (New York: McGraw-Hill, 1979); S. George, *The Baldrige Quality System* (New York: Wiley, 1992). For a critique of TQM, see Mark J. Zbaracki, "The Rhetoric and Reality of Total Quality Management," *Administrative Science Quarterly* 43, no 3 (September 1998), pp. 602–36.

[8] For a discussion of the shift in work environment and culture that TQM entails, see Robert T. Amsden, Thomas W. Ferratt, and Davida M. Amsden, "TQM: Core Paradigm Changes," *Business Horizons* 39, no. 6 (November–December 1996), pp. 6–14.

[9] For easy-to-understand overviews of what Six Sigma is all about, see Peter S. Pande and Larry Holpp, *What Is Six Sigma?* (New York: McGraw-Hill, 2002); Jiju Antony, "Some Pros and Cons of Six Sigma: An Academic Perspective," *TQM Magazine* 16, no. 4 (2004), pp. 303–6; Peter S. Pande, Robert P. Neuman, and Roland R. Cavanagh, *The Six Sigma Way: How GE, Motorola and Other Top Companies Are Honing Their Performance* (New York: McGraw-Hill, 2000); Joseph Gordon and M. Joseph Gordon, Jr., *Six Sigma Quality for Business and Manufacture* (New York: Elsevier, 2002). For how Six Sigma can be used in smaller companies, see Godecke Wessel and Peter Burcher, "Six Sigma for Small and Medium-Sized Enterprises," *TQM Magazine* 16, no. 4 (2004), pp. 264–72.

[10] Based on information posted at www.isixsigma.com (accessed November 4, 2002).

[11] Kennedy Smith, "Six Sigma for the Service Sector," *Quality Digest Magazine*, May 2003, www.qualitydigest.com (accessed September 28, 2003).

[12] Del Jones, "Taking the Six Sigma Approach," *USA Today*, October 31, 2002, p. 5B.

[13] Pande, Neuman, and Cavanagh, *The Six Sigma Way*, pp. 5–6.

[14] Smith, "Six Sigma for the Service Sector."

[15] Jones, "Taking the Six Sigma Approach," p. 5B.

[16] See, for example, "A Dark Art No More," *Economist* 385, no. 8550 (October 13, 2007), p. 10; Brian Hindo, "At 3M, a Struggle between Efficiency and Creativity," *BusinessWeek*, June 11, 2007, pp. 8–16.

[17] As quoted in "A Dark Art No More."

[18] Hindo, "At 3M, a Struggle between Efficiency and Creativity."

[19] For a discussion of approaches to pursuing radical or disruptive innovations while also seeking incremental gains in efficiency, see Charles A. O'Reilly and Michael L. Tushman, "The Ambidextrous Organization," *Harvard Business Review* 82, no. 4 (April 2004), pp. 74–81.

[20] Terry Nels Lee, Stanley E. Fawcett, and Jason Briscoe, "Benchmarking the Challenge to Quality Program Implementation," *Benchmarking: An International Journal* 9, no. 4 (2002), pp. 374–87.

[21] For a recent study documenting the imperatives of establishing a supportive culture, see Milan Ambrož, "Total Quality System as a Product of the Empowered Corporate Culture," *TQM Magazine* 16, no. 2 (2004), pp. 93–104. Research confirming the factors that are important in making TQM programs successful in both Europe and the United States is

presented in Nick A. Dayton, "The Demise of Total Quality Management," *TQM Magazine* 15, no. 6 (2003), pp. 391–96.

[22] Judy D. Olian and Sara L. Rynes, "Making Total Quality Work: Aligning Organizational Processes, Performance Measures, and Stakeholders," *Human Resource Management* 30, no. 3 (Fall 1991), pp. 310–11; Paul S. Goodman and Eric D. Darr, "Exchanging Best Practices Information through Computer-Aided Systems," *Academy of Management Executive* 10, no. 2 (May 1996), p. 7.

[23] Thomas C. Powell, "Total Quality Management as Competitive Advantage," *Strategic Management Journal* 16 (1995), pp. 15–37. See also Richard M. Hodgetts, "Quality Lessons from America's Baldrige Winners," *Business Horizons* 37, no. 4 (July–August 1994), pp. 74–79; Richard Reed, David J. Lemak, and Joseph C. Montgomery, "Beyond Process: TQM Content and Firm Performance," *Academy of Management Review* 21, no. 1 (January 1996), pp. 173–202.

[24] Based on information at www.otiselevator .com (accessed July 9, 2009).

[25] "The Web Smart 50," *BusinessWeek,* November 21, 2005, pp. 87–88.

[26] Aishah Mustapha, "Net Value: Social Software a New Way to Work," *The Edge Malaysia (Weekly),* February 16, 2009.

[27] Such systems speed organizational learning by providing fast, efficient communication,

creating an organizational memory for collecting and retaining best-practice information, and permitting people all across the organization to exchange information and updated solutions. See Goodman and Darr, "Exchanging Best Practices Information through Computer-Aided Systems," pp. 7–17.

[28] "The Web Smart 50," pp. 85–90.

[29] Fred Vogelstein, "Winning the Amazon Way," *Fortune* 147, no. 10 (May 26, 2003), pp. 60–69.

[30] For a discussion of the need for putting appropriate boundaries on the actions of empowered employees and possible control and monitoring systems that can be used, see Robert Simons, "Control in an Age of Empowerment," *Harvard Business Review* 73 (March–April 1995), pp. 80–88.

[31] Ibid. Also see David C. Band and Gerald Scanlan, "Strategic Control through Core Competencies," *Long Range Planning* 28, no. 2 (April 1995), pp. 102–14.

[32] The importance of motivating and empowering workers so as to create a working environment that is highly conducive to good strategy execution is discussed in Stanley E. Fawcett, Gary K. Rhoads, and Phillip Burnah, "People as the Bridge to Competitiveness: Benchmarking the 'ABCs' of an Empowered Workforce," *Benchmarking: An International Journal* 11 no. 4 (2004), pp. 346–60.

[33] Jeffrey Pfeffer and John F. Veiga, "Putting People First for Organizational Success,"

Academy of Management Executive 13, no. 2 (May 1999), pp. 37–45; Linda K. Stroh and Paula M. Caliguiri, "Increasing Global Competitiveness through Effective People Management," *Journal of World Business* 33, no. 1 (Spring 1998), pp. 1–16; articles in *Fortune* on the 100 best companies to work for (various issues).

[34] Jenni Mintz, "Nordstrom Opening in Three Weeks: Company Plans 'Tailgate Party for Women' and Other Events", *Ventura County Star* (California), *McClatchy-Tribune Regional News,* August 12, 2008.

[35] As quoted in John P. Kotter and James L. Heskett, *Corporate Culture and Performance* (New York: Free Press, 1992), p. 91.

[36] Clayton M. Christensen, Matt Marx, and Howard Stevenson, "The Tools of Cooperation and Change," *Harvard Business Review* 84, no. 10 (October 2006), pp. 73–80.

[37] See Steven Kerr, "On the Folly of Rewarding A While Hoping for B," *Academy of Management Executive* 9, no. 1 (February 1995), pp. 7–14; S. Kerr and E. Davies, "Risky Business: The New Pay Game," *Fortune* 134, no. 2 (July 22, 1996) pp. 94–96; and Doran Twer, "Linking Pay to Business Objectives," *Journal of Business Strategy* 15, no. 4 (July–August 1994), pp. 15–18.

CHAPTER 12

CORPORATE CULTURE AND LEADERSHIP

Keys to Good Strategy Execution

> The biggest levers you've got to change a company are strategy, structure, and culture. If I could pick two, I'd pick strategy and culture.
>
> **—Wayne Leonard**
> *Chairman and CEO, Entergy Corporation*

> Success goes to those with a corporate culture that assures the ability to anticipate and meet customer demand.
>
> **—Tadashi Okamura**
> *Former Chairman and CEO of Toshiba Corporation*

> The soft stuff is always harder than the hard stuff.
>
> **—Roger Enrico**
> *Former CEO of PepsiCo*

LEARNING OBJECTIVES

LO 1. Be able to identify the key features of a company's corporate culture and appreciate the role of a company's core values and ethical standards in building corporate culture.

LO 2. Gain an understanding of how and why a company's culture can aid the drive for proficient strategy execution and operating excellence.

LO 3. Learn the kinds of actions management can take to change a problem corporate culture.

LO 4. Understand what constitutes effective managerial leadership in achieving superior strategy execution.

In the previous two chapters, we examined six of the managerial tasks that drive good strategy execution: building a capable organization, marshaling the needed resources and steering them to strategy-critical operating units, establishing appropriate policies and procedures, driving continuous improvement in value chain activities, creating the necessary operating systems, and providing the incentives needed to ensure employee commitment to the strategy execution process. In this chapter, we explore the two remaining managerial tasks that contribute to good strategy execution: creating a strategy-supportive corporate culture and exerting the internal leadership needed to drive the implementation of strategic initiatives forward and achieve higher plateaus of operating excellence.

INSTILLING A CORPORATE CULTURE THAT PROMOTES GOOD STRATEGY EXECUTION

Every company has its own unique culture. The character of a company's culture or work climate is a product of the core values and business principles that executives espouse, the standards of what is ethically acceptable and what is not, the work practices and norms of behavior that define "how we do things around here," the approach to people management and style of operating, the "chemistry" and the "personality" that permeates the work environment, and the stories that get told over and over to illustrate and reinforce the company's values, business practices, and traditions. The meshing together of shared values, beliefs, business principles, and traditions into a style of operating, behavioral norms, ingrained attitudes, and work atmosphere defines a company's **corporate culture.**[1] A company's culture is important because it influences the organization's actions and approaches to conducting business—in a very real sense, the culture is the company's automatic, self-replicating "operating system"—it can be thought of as the organizational DNA.[2] As we learned in Chapter 4, a superior corporate culture can also be a source of sustainable competitive advantage under some circumstances.

Corporate cultures vary widely. For instance, the bedrock of Walmart's culture is dedication to zealous pursuit of low costs and frugal operating practices, a strong work ethic, ritualistic headquarters meetings to exchange ideas and review problems, and company executives' commitment to visiting stores, listening to customers, and soliciting suggestions from employees. General Electric's culture is founded on a hard-driving, results-oriented atmosphere; extensive cross-business sharing of ideas, best practices, and learning; reliance on "workout sessions" to identify, debate, and resolve burning issues; a commitment to Six Sigma quality; and a globalized approach to operations. At Nordstrom, the corporate culture is centered on delivering exceptional service to customers—the company's motto is "Respond to unreasonable customer requests," and each out-of-the-ordinary request is seen as an opportunity for a "heroic" act by an employee that can further the company's reputation for unparalleled customer service. Nordstrom makes a point of promoting employees noted for their heroic acts and dedication to outstanding service; the company motivates its salespeople with a commission-based compensation system that enables Nordstrom's best salespeople to earn more than double what other department stores pay. Illustration Capsule 12.1 relates how Google and Albert-Culver describe their corporate cultures.

CORE CONCEPT

Corporate culture refers to the character of a company's internal work climate—as shaped by a system of *shared* values, beliefs, ethical standards, and traditions that define behavioral norms, ingrained attitudes, accepted work practices, and styles of operating.

Identifying the Key Features of a Company's Corporate Culture

LO 1

Be able to identify the key features of a company's corporate culture and appreciate the role of a company's core values and ethical standards in building corporate culture.

A company's corporate culture is mirrored in the character or "personality" of its work environment—the factors that underlie how the company tries to conduct its business and the behaviors that are held in high esteem. Some of these factors are readily apparent, and others operate quite subtly. The chief things to look for include the following:

- The values, business principles, and ethical standards that management preaches and *practices*—these are the key to a company's culture, but actions speak much louder than words here.
- The company's approach to people management and the official policies, procedures, and operating practices that provide guidelines for the behavior of company personnel.
- The atmosphere and spirit that pervades the work climate. Is the workplace vibrant and fun? Methodical and all business? Tense and harried? Highly competitive and politicized? Are people excited about their work and emotionally connected to the company's business, or are they just there to draw a paycheck? Is there an emphasis on empowered worker creativity, or do people have little discretion in how jobs are done?
- The way managers and employees interact and relate to one another—the reliance on teamwork and open communication, the extent to which there is good camaraderie, whether people are called by their first names, whether co-workers spend little or lots of time together outside the workplace, and what the dress codes are (the accepted styles of attire and whether there are casual days).
- The strength of peer pressure to do things in particular ways and conform to expected norms—what actions and behaviors are encouraged on a peer-to-peer basis?

The Corporate Cultures at Google and Alberto-Culver

Founded in 1998 by Larry Page and Sergey Brin, two Ph.D. students in computer science at Stanford University, Google has become world-renowned for its search engine technology. Google.com was the most frequently visited Internet site in 2009, attracting over 844 million unique visitors monthly from around the world. Google has some unique ways of operating, and its culture is also rather quirky. The company describes its culture as follows:

Though growing rapidly, Google still maintains a small company feel. At lunchtime, almost everyone eats in the office café, sitting at whatever table has an opening and enjoying conversations with Googlers from different teams. Our commitment to innovation depends on everyone being comfortable sharing ideas and opinions. Every employee is a hands-on contributor, and everyone wears several hats. Because we believe that each Googler is an equally important part of our success, no one hesitates to pose questions directly to Larry or Sergey in our weekly all-hands ("TGIF") meetings—or spike a volleyball across the net at a corporate officer.

We are aggressively inclusive in our hiring, and we favor ability over experience. We have offices around the world and dozens of languages are spoken by Google staffers, from Turkish to Telugu. The result is a team that reflects the global audience Google serves. When not at work, Googlers pursue interests from cross-country cycling to wine tasting, from flying to frisbee.

As we continue to grow, we are always looking for those who share a commitment to creating search perfection and having a great time doing it.

Our corporate headquarters, fondly nicknamed the Googleplex, is located in Mountain View, California. Today it's one of our many offices around the globe. While our offices are not identical, they tend to share some essential elements. Here are a few things you might see in a Google workspace:

- *Local expressions of each location, from a mural in Buenos Aires to ski gondolas in Zurich, showcasing each office's region and personality.*
- *Bicycles or scooters for efficient travel between meetings; dogs; lava lamps; massage chairs; large inflatable balls.*

- *Googlers sharing cubes, yurts and huddle rooms—and very few solo offices.*
- *Laptops everywhere—standard issue for mobile coding, email on the go and note-taking.*
- *Foosball, pool tables, volleyball courts, assorted video games, pianos, ping pong tables, and gyms that offer yoga and dance classes.*
- *Grassroots employee groups for all interests, like meditation, film, wine tasting and salsa dancing.*
- *Healthy lunches and dinners for all staff at a variety of cafés.*
- *Break rooms packed with a variety of snacks and drinks to keep Googlers going.*

The Alberto-Culver Company, with fiscal 2009 revenues of more than $1.4 billion, is the producer and marketer of Alberto VO5, TRESemmé, Motions, Soft & Beautiful, Just for Me, and Nexxus hair care products; St. Ives skin care products; and such brands as Molly McButter, Mrs. Dash, Sugar Twin, and Static Guard. Alberto-Culver brands are sold in more than 120 countries.

At the careers section of its Web site, the company described its culture in the following words:

Building careers is as important to us as building brands. We believe that passionate people create powerful growth. We believe in a workplace built on values and believe our best people display those same values in their families and their communities. We believe in recognizing and rewarding accomplishment and celebrating our victories.

We believe the best ideas work their way—quickly—up an organization, not down. We believe that we should take advantage of every ounce of your talent on teams and cross-functional activities, not just assign you to a box.

We believe in open communication. We believe that you can improve what you measure, so we survey and spot check all the time. For that same reason, everyone has specific goals so that their expectations are in line with their managers' and the company's.

We believe that victory is a team accomplishment. We believe in personal development. We believe if you talk with us you will catch our enthusiasm and want to be a part of the Alberto-Culver team.

Sources: Information posted at www.google.com and www.alberto.com (accessed June 30, 2010); S. McClellan, "Alberto Culver Launches Global Search: The Client's Annual U.S. Ad Spending Alone Touches $100 Mil.," *Adweek*, January 29, 2010, www.adweek.com/aw/content_display/news/account-activity/e3i68e64a3cf2727350dd0013083626e8ae.

- The actions and behaviors that are explicitly encouraged and rewarded by management in the form of compensation and promotion.
- The company's revered traditions and oft-repeated stories about "heroic acts" and "how we do things around here."
- The manner in which the company deals with external stakeholders (particularly vendors and local communities where it has operations)—whether it treats suppliers as business partners or prefers hard-nosed, arm's-length business arrangements, and the strength and genuineness of the commitment to corporate citizenship and environmental sustainability.

The values, beliefs, and practices that undergird a company's culture can come from anywhere in the organizational hierarchy, most often representing the business philosophy and managerial style of influential executives but also resulting from exemplary actions on the part of company personnel and consensus agreement about appropriate norms of behavior.[3] Typically, key elements of the culture originate with a founder or certain strong leaders who articulated them as a set of business principles, company policies, operating approaches, and ways of dealing with employees, customers, vendors, shareholders, and local communities where the company has operations. Over time, these cultural underpinnings take root, become embedded in how the company conducts its business, come to be accepted by company managers and employees alike, and then persist as new employees are encouraged to embrace the company values and adopt the implied attitudes, behaviors, and work practices.

The Role of Core Values and Ethics

The foundation of a company's corporate culture nearly always resides in its dedication to certain core values and the bar it sets for ethical behavior. The culture-shaping significance of core values and ethical behaviors accounts for one reason why so many companies have developed a formal values statement and a code of ethics. Many executives want the work climate at their companies to mirror certain values and ethical standards, partly because they are personally committed to these values and ethical standards but also because they are convinced that adherence to such values and ethical principles will promote better strategy execution, make the company a better performer, and improve its image.[4] And, not incidentally, strongly ingrained values and ethical standards reduce the likelihood of lapses in ethical and socially approved behavior that mar a company's reputation and put its financial performance and market standing at risk, as discussed in Chapter 9.

> A company's culture is grounded in and shaped by its core values and ethical standards.

As depicted in Figure 12.1, a company's stated core values and ethical principles have two roles in the culture-building process. First, a company that works hard at putting its stated core values and ethical principles into practice fosters a work climate in which company personnel share strongly held convictions about how the company's business is to be conducted. Second, the stated values and ethical principles provide company personnel with guidance about the manner in which they are to do their jobs—which behaviors and ways of doing things are approved (and expected) and which are out-of-bounds. These values-based and ethics-based cultural norms serve as yardsticks for gauging the appropriateness of particular actions, decisions, and behaviors, thus helping steer company personnel toward both doing things right and doing the right thing.

Figure 12.1   The Two Culture-Building Roles of a Company's Core Values and Ethical Standards

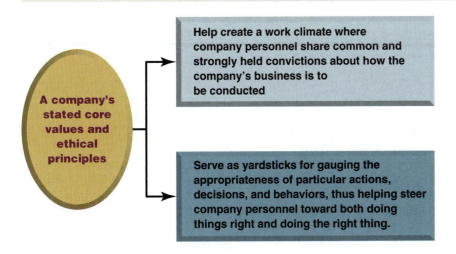

A company's stated core values and ethical principles

Help create a work climate where company personnel share common and strongly held convictions about how the company's business is to be conducted

Serve as yardsticks for gauging the appropriateness of particular actions, decisions, and behaviors, thus helping steer company personnel toward both doing things right and doing the right thing.

Transforming Core Values and Ethical Standards into Cultural Norms   Once values and ethical standards have been formally adopted, they must be institutionalized in the company's policies and practices and embedded in the conduct of company personnel. This can be done in a number of different ways.[5] Tradition-steeped companies with a rich folklore rely heavily on word-of-mouth indoctrination and the power of tradition to instill values and enforce ethical conduct. But most companies employ a variety of techniques, drawing on some or all of the following:

> A company's values statement and code of ethics communicate expectations of how employees should conduct themselves in the workplace.

1.   Giving explicit attention to values and ethics in recruiting and hiring to screen out applicants who do not exhibit compatible character traits.

2.   Incorporating the statement of values and the code of ethics into orientation programs for new employees and training courses for managers and employees.

3.   Having senior executives frequently reiterate the importance and role of company values and ethical principles at company events and in internal communications to employees.

4.   Using values statements and codes of ethical conduct as benchmarks for judging the appropriateness of company policies and operating practices.

5.   Making the display of core values and ethical principles a big factor in evaluating each person's job performance—there's no better way to win the attention and commitment of company personnel than by using the degree to which individuals observe core values and ethical standards as a basis for compensation increases and promotion.

6.   Making sure that managers, from the CEO down to frontline supervisors, are diligent in stressing the importance of ethical conduct and observance of core values. Line managers at all levels must give serious and continuous attention to the task of explaining how the values and ethical code apply in their areas.

7. Encouraging everyone to use his or her influence in helping enforce observance of core values and ethical standards—strong peer pressure to exhibit core values and ethical standards is a deterrent to wayward behavior.

8. Periodically having ceremonial occasions to recognize individuals and groups who display the company values and ethical principles.

9. Instituting ethics enforcement procedures.

To deeply ingrain the stated core values and high ethical standards, companies must turn them into *strictly enforced cultural norms.* They must put a stake in the ground, making it unequivocally clear that living up to the company's values and ethical standards has to be "a way of life" at the company and that there will be little toleration of errant behavior.

The Role of Stories   Frequently, a significant part of a company's culture is captured in the stories that get told over and over again to illustrate to newcomers the importance of certain values and the depth of commitment that various company personnel have displayed. One of the folktales at FedEx, world renowned for the reliability of its next-day package delivery guarantee, is about a deliveryman who had been given the wrong key to a FedEx drop box. Rather than leave the packages in the drop box until the next day when the right key was available, the deliveryman unbolted the drop box from its base, loaded it into the truck, and took it back to the station. There, the box was pried open and the contents removed and sped on their way to their destination the next day. Nordstrom keeps a scrapbook commemorating the heroic acts of its employees and uses it as a regular reminder of the above-and-beyond-the-call-of-duty behaviors that employees are encouraged to display. When a customer was unable to find a shoe she was looking for at Nordstrom, a salesman found the shoe at a competing store and had it shipped to her, at Nordstrom's expense.[6] At Frito-Lay, there are dozens of stories about truck drivers who went to extraordinary lengths in overcoming adverse weather conditions in order to make scheduled deliveries to retail customers and keep store shelves stocked with Frito-Lay products. At Microsoft, there are stories of the long hours programmers put in, the emotional peaks and valleys in encountering and overcoming coding problems, the exhilaration of completing a complex program on schedule, the satisfaction of working on cutting-edge projects, the rewards of being part of a team responsible for a popular new software program, and the tradition of competing aggressively. Such stories serve the valuable purpose of illustrating the kinds of behavior the company reveres and inspiring company personnel to perform similarly. Moreover, each retelling of a legendary story puts a bit more peer pressure on company personnel to display core values and do their part in keeping the company's traditions alive.

Perpetuating the Culture   Once established, company cultures are perpetuated in six important ways: (1) by screening and selecting new employees that will mesh well with the culture, (2) by systematic indoctrination of new members in the culture's fundamentals, (3) by the efforts of senior managers to reiterate core values in daily conversations and pronouncements, (4) by the telling and retelling of company legends, (5) by regular ceremonies honoring employees who display desired cultural behaviors, and (6) by visibly rewarding those who display cultural norms and penalizing those who don't.[7] *The more new employees a company is hiring, the more important it becomes to screen job applicants every bit as much for how well their values, beliefs, and personalities match up with the* *culture as for their technical skills and experience.* For example, a company that stresses operating with integrity and fairness has to hire people who themselves have integrity and place a high value on fair play. A company whose culture revolves around creativity, product innovation, and leading change has to screen new hires for their ability to think outside the box, generate new ideas, and thrive in a climate of rapid change and ambiguity. Southwest Airlines—whose two core values, "LUV" and fun, permeate the work environment and whose objective is to ensure that passengers have a positive and enjoyable flying experience—goes to considerable lengths to hire flight attendants and gate personnel who are witty, cheery, and outgoing and who display "whistle while you work" attitudes. Fast-growing companies risk creating a culture by chance rather than by design if they rush to hire employees mainly for their talents and credentials and neglect to screen out candidates whose values, philosophies, and personalities aren't a good fit with the organizational character, vision, and strategy being articulated by the company's senior executives.

As a rule, companies are careful to hire people who they believe will fit in and embrace the prevailing culture. And, usually, job seekers lean toward accepting jobs at companies where they feel comfortable with the atmosphere and the people they will be working with. Employees who don't fit in well at a company tend to leave quickly, while employees who thrive and are pleased with the work environment stay on, eventually moving up the ranks to positions of greater responsibility. The longer people stay at an organization, the more that they come to embrace and mirror the corporate culture—their values and beliefs tend to be molded by mentors, co-workers, company training programs, and the reward structure. Normally, employees who have worked at a company for a long time play a major role in indoctrinating new employees into the culture.

Forces That Cause a Company's Culture to Evolve   However, cultures aren't static—just like strategy and organization structure, they evolve. New challenges in the marketplace, revolutionary technologies, and shifting internal conditions—especially eroding business prospects, an internal crisis, or top executive turnover—tend to breed new ways of doing things and, in turn, drive cultural evolution. An incoming CEO who decides to shake up the existing business and take it in new directions often triggers a cultural shift, perhaps one of major proportions. Likewise, diversification into new businesses, expansion into foreign countries, rapid growth that brings an influx of new employees, and merger with or acquisition of another company can all precipitate significant cultural change.

Company Cultures Can Be Strongly or Weakly Embedded

Company cultures vary widely in strength and influence. Some are strongly embedded and have a big influence on a company's operating practices and the behavior of company personnel. Others are weakly ingrained and have little effect on behaviors and how company activities are conducted.

Strong-Culture Companies   The hallmark of a **strong-culture company** is the dominating presence of certain deeply rooted values, behavioral norms, and operating approaches that are widely shared and "regulate" the conduct of a company's business and the climate of its workplace.[8] Strong cultures emerge over a period of years (sometimes decades) and are never an overnight phenomenon. In strong-culture companies, senior managers make a point of reiterating the company's principles and values to organization members and explaining how they relate to its business environment. But, more importantly, the managers make a conscious effort to display these principles in their own actions and behavior—they walk the talk and *insist* that *company values and business principles be reflected in the decisions and actions taken by all company personnel.* An unequivocal expectation that company personnel will act and behave in accordance with the adopted values and ways of doing business leads to two important outcomes: (1) Over time, the values come to be widely shared by rank-and-file employees—people who dislike the culture tend to leave—and (2) individuals encounter strong peer pressure from co-workers to observe the culturally approved norms and behaviors. Hence, a strongly implanted corporate culture ends up having a powerful influence on behavior because so many company personnel are accepting of cultural traditions and because this acceptance is reinforced by both management expectations and co-worker peer pressure to conform to cultural norms.

Two factors contribute to the development of strong cultures: (1) a founder or strong leader who established core values, principles, and practices that are viewed as having contributed to the success of the company, and (2) a sincere, long-standing company commitment to operating the business according to these established traditions and values, thereby creating an internal environment that supports decision making based on cultural norms. Continuity of leadership, low workforce turnover, geographic concentration, and considerable organizational success all contribute to the emergence and sustainability of a strong culture.[9]

In strong-culture companies, values and behavioral norms are so ingrained that they can endure leadership changes at the top—although their strength can erode over time if new CEOs cease to nurture them or move aggressively to institute cultural adjustments. The cultural norms in a strong-culture company typically do not change much as strategy evolves, either because the culture constrains the choice of new strategies or because the dominant traits of the culture are somewhat strategy-neutral and compatible with evolving versions of the company's strategy.

Weak-Culture Companies   In direct contrast to strong-culture companies, weak-culture companies lack values and principles that are consistently preached or widely shared (sometimes because the company has had a series of CEOs with differing values and differing views about how the company's business ought to be conducted). As a consequence, few widely revered traditions and few culture-induced norms are evident in employee behavior or operating practices. Because top executives at a weak-culture company don't repeatedly espouse any particular business philosophy or exhibit long-standing commitment to particular values or behavioral norms, individuals encounter little pressure to do things in particular ways. A weak company culture breeds no strong employee allegiance to what the company stands for or to operating the business in well-defined ways. While individual employees may well have some bonds of identification with and loyalty toward their department, their colleagues, their union, or their immediate boss, there's neither passion about the company nor emotional commitment to what it is trying to accomplish—a condition that often results in many employees viewing their company as just a place to work and their job as just a way to make a living.

As a consequence, *weak cultures provide little or no assistance in executing strategy* because there are no traditions, beliefs, values, common bonds, or behavioral norms that management can use as levers to mobilize commitment to executing the chosen strategy. The only plus of a weak culture is that it does not usually pose a strong barrier to strategy execution, but the negative of not providing any support means that culture building has to be high on management's action agenda. Without a work climate that channels organizational energy in the direction of good strategy execution, managers are left with the options of either using compensation incentives and other motivational devices to mobilize employee commitment, supervising and monitoring employee actions more closely, or trying to establish cultural roots that will in time start to nurture the strategy execution process.

Why Corporate Cultures Matter to the Strategy Execution Process

Unlike weak cultures, strong cultures can have a powerful effect on the strategy execution process. This effect may be *positive or negative* since a company's present culture and work climate may or may not be compatible with what is needed for effective implementation and execution of the chosen strategy. When a company's present culture promotes attitudes, behaviors, and ways of doing things that are conducive to first-rate strategy execution, the culture functions as a valuable ally in the strategy execution process.

For example, a corporate culture characterized by frugality and thrift nurtures employee actions to identify cost-saving opportunities—the very behavior needed for successful execution of a low-cost leadership strategy. A culture built around such business principles as outstanding customer satisfaction, operating excellence, and employee empowerment promotes employee behaviors and an esprit de corps that facilitate execution of strategies keyed to high product quality and superior customer service. A culture in which taking initiative, exhibiting creativity, taking risks, and embracing change are the behavioral norms is conducive to successful execution of product innovation and technological leadership strategies.[10]

A culture that is grounded in actions, behaviors, and work practices that are conducive to good strategy implementation assists the strategy execution effort in three ways:[11]

1. *A culture that is well matched to the requirements of the strategy execution effort focuses the attention of employees on what is most important to this effort.* Moreover, it directs their behavior and serves as a guide to their decision making. In this manner, it can align the efforts and decisions of employees throughout the firm and minimize the need for direct supervision.

2. *Culture-induced peer pressure further induces company personnel to do things in a manner that aids the cause of good strategy execution.* The stronger the culture (the more widely shared and deeply held the values), the more effective peer pressure is in shaping and supporting the strategy execution effort. Research has shown that strong group norms can shape employee behavior even more powerfully than can financial incentives.[12]

3. *A company culture that is consistent with the requirements for good strategy execution can energize employees, deepen their commitment to execute the*

strategy flawlessly, and enhance worker productivity in the process. When a company's culture is grounded in many of the needed strategy-executing behaviors, employees feel genuinely better about their jobs, the company they work for, and the merits of what the company is trying to accomplish. As a consequence, greater numbers of company personnel exhibit passion in their work and exert their best efforts to execute the strategy and achieve performance targets.

In sharp contrast, when a culture is in conflict with what is required to execute the company's strategy well, a strong culture becomes a hindrance to the success of the implementation effort.[13] Some of the very behaviors needed to execute the strategy successfully run contrary to the attitudes, behaviors, and operating practices embedded in the prevailing culture. Such a clash poses a real dilemma for company personnel. Should they be loyal to the culture and company traditions (to which they are likely to be emotionally attached) and thus resist or be indifferent to actions that will promote better strategy execution—a choice that will certainly weaken the drive for good strategy execution? Alternatively, should they go along with the strategy execution effort and engage in actions that run counter to the culture—a choice that will likely impair morale and lead to a less-than-wholehearted commitment to management's strategy execution efforts? Neither choice leads to desirable outcomes. Culture-bred resistance to the actions and behaviors needed for good strategy execution, particularly if strong and widespread, poses a formidable hurdle that must be cleared for a strategy's execution to get very far.

This says something important about the task of managing the strategy execution process: *Closely aligning corporate culture with the requirements for proficient strategy execution merits the full attention of senior executives.* The culture-building objective is to create a work climate and style of operating that mobilize the energy and behavior of company personnel squarely behind efforts to execute strategy competently. The more deeply that management can embed execution-supportive ways of doing things, the more that management can rely on the culture to automatically steer company personnel toward behaviors and work practices that aid good strategy execution and veer from doing things that impede it. Moreover, culturally astute managers understand that nourishing the right cultural environment not only adds power to their push for proficient strategy execution but also promotes strong employee identification with and commitment to the company's vision, performance targets, and strategy.

> It is in management's best interest to dedicate considerable effort to establishing a corporate culture that encourages behaviors and work practices conducive to good strategy execution.

Healthy Cultures That Aid Good Strategy Execution

A strong culture, provided it embraces execution-supportive attitudes, behaviors, and work practices, is definitely a healthy culture. Two other types of cultures exist that tend to be healthy and largely supportive of good strategy execution: high-performance cultures and adaptive cultures.

High-Performance Cultures   Some companies have so-called high-performance cultures where the standout traits are a "can-do" spirit, pride in doing things right, no-excuses accountability, and a pervasive results-oriented work climate in which people go all out to meet or beat stretch objectives.[14] In high-performance cultures, there's a strong sense of involvement on the part of company personnel and emphasis on individual initiative and effort. Performance expectations are clearly delineated for the company as a whole, for each organizational unit, and for each individual. Issues and problems are promptly addressed; there's a razor-sharp focus on what needs to be done. The clear and unyielding expectation is that all company personnel, from senior executives to frontline employees, will display high-performance behaviors and a passion for making the company successful. Such a culture—supported by constructive pressure to achieve good results—is a valuable contributor to good strategy execution and operating excellence. Results-oriented cultures are permeated with a spirit of achievement and have a good track record in meeting or beating performance targets.[15]

The challenge in creating a high-performance culture is to inspire high loyalty and dedication on the part of employees, such that they are energized to put forth their very best efforts to do things right and be unusually productive. Managers have to take pains to reinforce constructive behavior, reward top performers, and purge habits and behaviors that stand in the way of high productivity and good results. They must work at knowing the strengths and weaknesses of their subordinates, so as to better match talent with task and enable people to make meaningful contributions by doing what they do best.[16] They have to stress learning from mistakes and building on strengths and must put an unrelenting emphasis on moving forward and making good progress—in effect, there has to be a disciplined, performance-focused approach to managing the organization.

Adaptive Cultures The hallmark of adaptive corporate cultures is willingness on the part of organization members to accept change and take on the challenge of introducing and executing new strategies.[17] Company personnel share a feeling of confidence that the organization can deal with whatever threats and opportunities arise; they are receptive to risk taking, experimentation, innovation, and changing strategies and practices. The work climate is supportive of managers and employees at all ranks who propose or initiate useful change. Internal entrepreneurship on the part of individuals and groups is encouraged and rewarded. Senior executives seek out, support, and promote individuals who exercise initiative, spot opportunities for improvement, and display the skills to implement them. Managers openly evaluate ideas and suggestions, fund initiatives to develop new or better products, and take prudent risks to pursue emerging market opportunities. As in high-performance cultures, the company exhibits a proactive approach to identifying issues, evaluating the implications and options, and moving ahead quickly with workable solutions. Strategies and traditional operating practices are modified as needed to adjust to or take advantage of changes in the business environment.

But why is change so willingly embraced in an adaptive culture? Why are organization members not fearful of how change will affect them? Why does an adaptive culture not break down from the force of ongoing changes in strategy, operating practices, and approaches to strategy execution? The answers lie in two distinctive and dominant traits of an adaptive culture: (1) Any changes in operating practices and behaviors must *not* compromise core values and long-standing business principles (since they are at the root of the culture), and (2) the changes that are instituted must satisfy the legitimate interests of stakeholders—customers, employees, shareowners, suppliers, and the communities where the company operates.[18] In other words, what sustains an adaptive culture is that organization members

As a company's strategy evolves, an adaptive culture is a definite ally in the strategy-implementing, strategy-executing process as compared to cultures that are resistant to change.

perceive the changes that management is trying to institute as *legitimate* and in keeping with the core values and business principles that form the heart and soul of the culture.[19] Not surprisingly, company personnel are usually more receptive to change when their employment security is not threatened and when they view new duties or job assignments as part of the process of adapting to new conditions. Should workforce downsizing be necessary, it is important that layoffs be handled humanely and employee departures be made as painless as possible.

Technology companies, software companies, and Internet-based companies are good illustrations of organizations with adaptive cultures. Such companies thrive on change—driving it, leading it, and capitalizing on it. Companies like Google, Intel, Cisco Systems, eBay, Amazon.com, and Apple cultivate the capability to act and react rapidly. They are avid practitioners of entrepreneurship and innovation, with a demonstrated willingness to take bold risks to create altogether new products, new businesses, and new industries. To create and nurture a culture that can adapt rapidly to shifting business conditions, they make a point of staffing their organizations with people who are flexible, who rise to the challenge of change, and who have an aptitude for adapting well to new circumstances.

In fast-changing business environments, a corporate culture that is receptive to altering organizational practices and behaviors is a virtual necessity. However, adaptive cultures work to the advantage of all companies, not just those in rapid-change environments. Every company operates in a market and business climate that is changing to one degree or another and that, in turn, requires internal operating responses and new behaviors on the part of organization members.

Unhealthy Cultures That Impede Good Strategy Execution

The distinctive characteristic of an unhealthy corporate culture is the presence of counterproductive cultural traits that adversely impact the work climate and company performance.[20] Five particularly unhealthy cultural traits are hostility to change, heavily politicized decision making, insular thinking, behaviors that are driven by greed and a disregard for ethical standards, and the presence of incompatible, clashing subcultures.

Change-Resistant Cultures   In contrast to adaptive cultures, change-resistant cultures—where skepticism about the importance of new developments and a fear of change are the norm—place a premium on not making mistakes, prompting managers to lean toward safe, conservative options intended to maintain the status quo, protect their power base, and guard the interests of their immediate work groups. When such companies encounter business environments with accelerating change, going slow on altering traditional ways of doing things can be a serious liability. Under these conditions, change-resistant cultures encourage a number of undesirable or unhealthy behaviors—viewing circumstances myopically, avoiding risks, not capitalizing on emerging opportunities, taking a lax approach to both product innovation and continuous improvement in performing value chain activities, and responding more slowly than is warranted to market change. In change-resistant cultures, word quickly gets around that proposals to do things differently face an uphill battle and that people who champion them may be seen as something of a nuisance. Executives who don't value managers or employees with initiative and new ideas put a damper on product innovation, experimentation, and efforts to improve. At the same

time, change-resistant companies have little appetite for being first movers or fast followers, believing that being in the forefront of change is too risky and that acting too quickly increases vulnerability to costly mistakes. Hostility to change is most often found in companies with multilayered management bureaucracies that have enjoyed considerable market success in years past and that are wedded to the "We have done it this way for years" syndrome. Before filing bankruptcy in 2009, General Motors was a classic example of a company whose change-resistant bureaucracy was slow to adapt to fundamental changes in its markets, preferring to cling to the traditions, operating practices, and business approaches that had at one time made it the global industry leader.

Politicized Cultures What makes a politicized internal environment so unhealthy is that political infighting consumes a great deal of organizational energy, often with the result that what's best for the company takes a backseat to political maneuvering. In companies where internal politics pervades the work climate, empire-building managers jealously guard their decision-making prerogatives. They have their own agendas and operate the work units under their supervision as autonomous "fiefdoms"; the positions they take on issues are usually aimed at protecting or expanding their own turf. Collaboration with other organizational units is viewed with suspicion, and cross-unit cooperation occurs grudgingly. The support or opposition of politically influential executives and/or coalitions among departments with vested interests in a particular outcome tends to shape what actions the company takes. All this political maneuvering takes away from efforts to execute strategy with real proficiency and frustrates company personnel who are less political and more inclined to do what is in the company's best interests.

Insular, Inwardly Focused Cultures Sometimes a company reigns as an industry leader or enjoys great market success for so long that its personnel start to believe they have all the answers or can develop them on their own. There is a strong tendency to neglect what customers are saying and how their needs and expectations are changing. Such confidence in the correctness of its approach to business and an unflinching belief in the company's competitive superiority breeds arrogance, prompting company personnel to discount the merits of what outsiders are doing and the payoff from studying best-in-class performers. Insular thinking, internally driven solutions, and a must-be-invented-here mindset come to permeate the corporate culture. An inwardly focused corporate culture gives rise to managerial inbreeding and a failure to recruit people who can offer fresh thinking and outside perspectives. The big risk of insular cultural thinking is that the company can underestimate the capabilities and accomplishments of rival companies and overestimate its own progress—until its loss of market position makes the realities obvious.

Unethical and Greed-Driven Cultures Companies that have little regard for ethical standards or that are run by executives driven by greed and ego gratification are scandals waiting to happen, as discussed in Chapter 9. Executives exude the negatives of arrogance, ego, greed, and an "ends-justify-the-means" mentality in pursuing stretch revenue and profitability targets.[21] Senior managers wink at unethical behavior and may cross over the line to unethical (and sometimes criminal) behavior themselves. They are prone to adopt accounting principles that make financial performance look better than it really is. Legions of companies have fallen prey to unethical behavior and greed, most notably WorldCom, Enron, Quest, HealthSouth, Adelphia, Tyco, Parmalat, Rite Aid, Hollinger International, Refco, Marsh & McLennan, Siemens, Countrywide Financial, and Stanford Financial Group, with executives being indicted and/or convicted of criminal behavior.

Incompatible Subcultures   Although it is common to speak about corporate culture in the singular, it is not unusual for companies to have multiple cultures (or subcultures).[22] Values, beliefs, and practices within a company sometimes vary significantly by department, geographic location, division, or business unit. As long as the subcultures are compatible with the overarching corporate culture and are supportive of the strategy execution efforts, this is not problematic. Multiple cultures pose an unhealthy situation when they are composed of incompatible subcultures that embrace conflicting business philosophies, support inconsistent approaches to strategy execution, and encourage incompatible methods of people management. Clashing subcultures can prevent a company from coordinating its efforts to craft and execute strategy and can distract company personnel from the business of business. When incompatible subcultures encourage the emergence of warring factions within the company, they are not just unhealthy—they are downright poisonous.

Incompatible subcultures arise most commonly because of important cultural differences between a company's culture and that of a recently acquired company or because of a merger between companies with cultural differences. Companies with M&A experience are quite alert to the importance of cultural compatibility in making acquisitions and the need to integrate the cultures of newly acquired companies—cultural due diligence is often as important as financial due diligence in deciding whether to go forward on an acquisition or merger. On a number of occasions, companies decided to pass on acquiring particular companies because of culture conflicts they believed would be hard to resolve.

Changing a Problem Culture: The Role of Leadership

LO 3

Learn the kinds of actions management can take to change a problem corporate culture.

When a strong culture is unhealthy or otherwise out of sync with the actions and behaviors needed to execute the strategy successfully, the culture must be changed as rapidly as can be managed. While correcting a strategy-culture conflict can occasionally mean revamping a company's approach to strategy execution to better fit the company's culture, more usually it means altering aspects of the mismatched culture to better enable first-rate strategy execution. The more entrenched the mismatched or unhealthy aspects of a company culture, the more likely the culture will impede strategy execution and the greater the need for change.

Changing a problem culture is among the toughest management tasks because of the heavy anchor of ingrained behaviors and attitudes. It is natural for company personnel to cling to familiar practices and to be wary, if not hostile, to new approaches of how things are to be done. Consequently, it takes concerted management action over a period of time to root out unconstructive behaviors and replace them with new ways of doing things deemed more conducive to executing the strategy.

The single most visible factor that distinguishes successful culture-change efforts from failed attempts is competent leadership at the top. Great power is needed to force major cultural change and overcome the "springback" resistance of entrenched cultures—and great power is possessed only by the most senior executives, especially the CEO. However, while top management must be out front leading the effort, marshaling support for a new culture and instilling the desired cultural behaviors is a job for the whole management team. Middle managers and frontline supervisors play a key role in implementing the new work practices and operating approaches, helping win rank-and-file acceptance of and support for the desired behavioral norms.

As shown in Figure 12.2, the first step in fixing a problem culture is for top management to identify those facets of the present culture that are dysfunctional and pose obstacles to executing new strategic initiatives and meeting company performance targets. Second, managers must clearly define the desired new behaviors and features of the culture they want to create. Third, managers have to convince company personnel of why the present culture poses problems and why and how new behaviors and operating approaches will improve company performance—the case for cultural reform has to be persuasive. Fourth, and most important, all the talk about remodeling the present culture has to be followed swiftly by visible, forceful actions to promote the desired new behaviors and work practices—actions that company personnel will interpret as a determined top management commitment to bringing about a different work climate and new ways of operating.

Making a Compelling Case for Culture Change The way for management to begin a major remodeling of the corporate culture is by selling company personnel on the need for new-style behaviors and work practices. This means making a compelling case for why the culture-remodeling efforts are in the organization's best interests and why company personnel should wholeheartedly join the effort to doing things somewhat differently. Skeptics and opinion leaders have to be convinced that all is not well with the status quo. This can be done by:

- Explaining why and how certain behavioral norms and work practices in the current culture pose obstacles to good execution of strategic initiatives.
- Explaining how new behaviors and work practices will be more advantageous and produce better results. Effective culture-change leaders are good at telling stories to describe the new values and desired behaviors and connect them to everyday practices.
- Citing reasons why the current strategy has to be modified, if the need for cultural change is due to a change in strategy. This includes explaining why the new strategic initiatives will bolster the company's competitiveness and performance and how a change in culture can help in executing the new strategy.

It is essential for the CEO and other top executives to talk personally to company personnel all across the company about the reasons for modifying work practices and culture-related behaviors. Senior officers and department heads have to play a lead role in explaining the need for a change in behavioral norms to those they manage—and the explanations will likely have to be repeated many times. For the culture-change effort to be successful, frontline supervisors and employee opinion leaders must be won over to the cause, which means convincing them of the merits of *practicing* and *enforcing* cultural norms at every level of the organization, from the highest to the lowest. Arguments for new ways of doing things and new work practices tend to be embraced more readily if employees understand how they will benefit company stakeholders (particularly customers, employees, and shareholders).

Figure 12.2   Steps to Take in Changing a Problem Culture

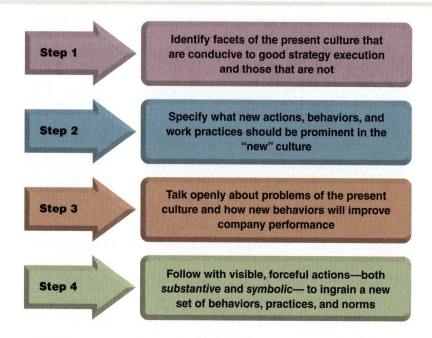

Step 1 — Identify facets of the present culture that are conducive to good strategy execution and those that are not

Step 2 — Specify what new actions, behaviors, and work practices should be prominent in the "new" culture

Step 3 — Talk openly about problems of the present culture and how new behaviors will improve company performance

Step 4 — Follow with visible, forceful actions—both *substantive* and *symbolic*— to ingrain a new set of behaviors, practices, and norms

Until a large majority of employees accept the need for a new culture and agree that different work practices and behaviors are called for, there's more work to be done in selling company personnel on the whys and wherefores of culture change. Building widespread organizational support requires taking every opportunity to repeat the message of why the new work practices, operating approaches, and behaviors are good for company stakeholders.

Management's efforts to make a persuasive case for changing what is deemed to be a problem culture must be *followed quickly* by forceful, high-profile actions across several fronts. The actions to implant the new culture must be both substantive and symbolic.

Substantive Culture-Changing Actions   No culture change effort can get very far with just talk about the need for different actions, behaviors, and work practices. Company executives must give the culture-change effort some teeth by initiating *a series of actions* that company personnel will see as credible and unmistakably indicative of the seriousness of management's commitment to cultural change. The strongest signs that management is truly committed to instilling a new culture include:

• Replacing key executives who are stonewalling needed organizational and cultural changes.

• Promoting individuals who have stepped forward to advocate the shift to a different culture and who can serve as role models for the desired cultural behavior.

• Appointing outsiders with the desired cultural attributes to high-profile positions—bringing in new-breed managers sends an unmistakable message that a new era is dawning.

- Screening all candidates for new positions carefully, hiring only those who appear to fit in with the new culture.

- Mandating that all company personnel attend culture-training programs to learn more about the new work practices and to better understand the culture-related actions and behaviors that are expected.

- Designing compensation incentives that boost the pay of teams and individuals who display the desired cultural behaviors. Company personnel are much more inclined to exhibit the desired kinds of actions and behaviors when it is in their financial best interest to do so.

- Revising policies and procedures in ways that will help drive cultural change.

Executives must take care to launch enough companywide culture-change actions at the outset so as to leave no room for doubt that management is dead serious about changing the present culture and that a cultural transformation is inevitable. The series of actions initiated by top management must create lots of hallway talk across the whole company, get the change process off to a fast start, and be followed by unrelenting efforts to firmly establish the new work practices, desired behaviors, and style of operating as "standard."

Symbolic Culture-Changing Actions There's also an important place for symbolic managerial actions to alter a problem culture and tighten the strategy-culture fit. The most important symbolic actions are those that top executives take to *lead by example.* For instance, if the organization's strategy involves a drive to become the industry's low-cost producer, senior managers must display frugality in their own actions and decisions: inexpensive decorations in the executive suite, conservative expense accounts and entertainment allowances, a lean staff in the corporate office, scrutiny of budget requests, few executive perks, and so on. At Walmart, all the executive offices are simply decorated; executives are habitually frugal in their own actions, and they are zealous in their efforts to control costs and promote greater efficiency. At Nucor, one of the world's low-cost producers of steel products, executives fly coach class and use taxis at airports rather than limousines. If the culture-change imperative is to be more responsive to customers' needs and to pleasing customers, the CEO can instill greater customer awareness by requiring all officers and executives to spend a significant portion of each week talking with customers about their needs. Top executives must be alert to the fact that company personnel will be watching their actions and decisions to see if their actions match their rhetoric. Hence, they need to make sure their current decisions and behaviors will be construed as consistent with the new-culture values and norms.[23]

Another category of symbolic actions includes holding ceremonial events to single out and honor people whose actions and performance exemplify what is called for in the new culture. A point is made of holding events to celebrate each culture-change success (and any other outcome that management would like to see happen again). Executives sensitive to their role in promoting strategy-culture fit make a habit of appearing at ceremonial functions to praise individuals and groups that exemplify the desired behaviors. They show up at employee training programs to stress strategic priorities, values, ethical principles, and cultural norms. Every group gathering is seen as an opportunity to repeat and ingrain values, praise good deeds, expound on the merits of the new culture, and cite instances of how the new work practices and operating approaches have worked to good advantage.

The use of symbols in culture building is widespread. Many universities give outstanding teacher awards each year to symbolize their commitment to good teaching and their esteem for instructors who display exceptional classroom talents. Numerous businesses have employee-of-the-month awards. The military has a long-standing custom of awarding ribbons and medals for exemplary actions. Mary Kay Cosmetics awards an array of prizes ceremoniously to its beauty consultants for reaching various sales plateaus.

How Long Does It Take to Change a Problem Culture?   Planting and growing the seeds of a new culture require a determined effort by the chief executive and other senior managers. A sustained and persistent effort to reinforce the culture at every opportunity through both word and deed is required. Changing a problem culture is never a short-term exercise. It takes time for a new culture to emerge and prevail; overnight transformations simply don't occur. And it takes even longer for a new culture to become deeply embedded. The bigger the organization and the greater the cultural shift needed to produce an execution-supportive fit, the longer it takes. In large companies, fixing a problem culture and instilling a new set of attitudes and behaviors can take two to five years. In fact, it is usually tougher to reform an entrenched problematic culture than it is to instill a strategy-supportive culture from scratch in a brand new organization.

Illustration Capsule 12.2 discusses the approaches used at Chrysler in 2009–2010 to change a culture that was grounded in a 1970s view of the automobile industry.

LEADING THE STRATEGY EXECUTION PROCESS

For an enterprise to execute its strategy in truly proficient fashion and approach operating excellence, top executives have to take the lead in the implementation/execution process and personally drive the pace of progress. The have to be out in the field, seeing for themselves how well operations are going, gathering information firsthand, and gauging the progress being made. Proficient strategy execution requires company managers to be diligent and adept in spotting problems, learning what obstacles lie in the path of good execution, and then clearing the way for progress—the goal must be to produce better results speedily and productively. There has to be constructive, but unrelenting, pressure on organizational units to (1) demonstrate excellence in all dimensions of strategy execution and (2) do so on a consistent basis—ultimately, that's what will enable a well-crafted strategy to achieve the desired performance results.

The strategy execution process must be driven by mandates to get things on the right track and show good results. The specifics of how to implement a strategy and deliver the intended results must start with understanding the requirements for good strategy execution. Afterward comes a diagnosis of the organization's preparedness to execute the strategic initiatives and decisions as to which of several ways to proceed to move forward and achieve the targeted results.[24] In general, leading the drive for good strategy execution and operating excellence calls for three actions on the part of the manager in charge:

• Staying on top of what is happening and closely monitoring progress.

ILLUSTRATION CAPSULE 12.2

Changing the "Old Detroit" Culture at Chrysler

When Chrysler Group LLC emerged from bankruptcy in June 2009, its road to recovery was far from certain. "It was questionable whether they'd survive 2010," said Michelle Krebs, an analyst with auto information provider Edmunds.com. One thing that was holding Chrysler back was its culture—a legacy of "the Old Detroit," which was characterized by finger-pointing and blame shifting whenever problems arose.[a]

Chrysler's management had long been aware of its culture problem. In 2008, Robert Nardelli, Chrysler's autocratic new CEO, placed himself in charge of a wide-ranging culture-change program designed to break the ingrained behaviors that had damaged the company's reputation for quality. Chrysler's slide into bankruptcy was hardly the comeback that the controversial Nardelli envisioned when he was hired for the job by private-equity firm Cerberus Capital Management (which controlled Chrysler from 2007 until 2009).

A strategic partnership ceding management control to Italian automaker Fiat SpA was part of the deal for Chrysler's bankruptcy reorganization, with Fiat's CEO, Sergio Marchionne, becoming Chrysler's CEO as well. In discussing his five-year plan for Chrysler, Marchionne remarked, "What I've learned as a CEO is that culture is not part of the game—it is the game!"[b]

Marchionne put Doug Betts, a veteran of Toyota Motor Corp. and Nissan Motor Co., in charge of a systematic overhaul of Chrysler quality, with cultural change as the fundamental driver. Betts began

by creating new cross-functional teams designed to break down Chrysler's balkanized silos of manufacturing and engineering. Whereas problems were formerly handed off from one department to another, delaying action for an average of 71 days, quality teams are now encouraged to take ownership of solutions.[c] Betts has also taken aim at the climate of fear, replacing concerns over recrimination and retribution with a positive focus on team empowerment and problem solving. By the end of 2009, Betts was saying, "It's different now. People are talking openly about problems now and how to fix [them]."[d] By May 2010, confidence in Chrysler was increasing and sales were up by 33 percent over the same period in the previous year. Analysts were hopeful that Chrysler had finally begun to get it right.

---

[a] Jerry Hirsch, "Chrysler Performance Exceeds Expectations: The Fiat-Managed Company Cut Its Losses to $197 Million and Recorded a $143-Million Operating Profit in the First Quarter of the Year," *Los Angeles Times,* April 22, 2010, http://articles.latimes.com/2010/apr/22/business/la-fi-chrysler-20100422.

[b] Daniel Howes, "Chrysler's Last Chance to Get It Right," *Detroit News,* Business section, 1-dot edition, p. 4B.

[c] Ibid.

[d] Alisa Priddle, "'Different' Chrysler Zeroes In on Quality," *Detroit News,* Business section, 2-dot edition, p. 1A.

Developed with Amy Florentino.

Sources: Robert Snell, "Chrysler Sales Up 33% for May; Ford, GM Rise 23%, 16.6%," *Detroit News:* last updated June 2, 2010, http://detnews.com/article/20100602/AUTO01/6020390/Chrysler-sales-up-33—for-May—Ford—GM-rise-23—16.6-#ixzz0sNQX7iWR; http://topics.nytimes.com/top/reference/timestopics/people/n/robert_l_nardelli/index.html, updated May 1, 2009; Neal E. Boudette, "Nardelli Tries to Shift Chrysler's Culture," *Wall Street Journal,* June 18, 2008, p. B1.

- Putting constructive pressure on the organization to execute the strategy well and achieve operating excellence.
- Initiating corrective actions to improve strategy execution and achieve the targeted performance results.

Staying on Top of How Well Things Are Going

To stay on top of how well the strategy execution process is going, senior executives have to tap into information from a wide range of sources. In addition to talking with key subordinates and reviewing the latest operating results, watching the competitive reactions of rival firms, and visiting with key customers and suppliers to get their perspectives, they usually make regular visits to various company facilities and talk with many different company personnel at many different organization levels—a technique often labeled **managing by walking around (MBWA).** Most managers attach great importance to spending time with people at company facilities, asking questions, listening to their opinions and concerns, and gathering firsthand information about how well aspects of the strategy execution process are going. Facilities tours and face-to-face contacts with operating-level employees give executives a good grasp of what progress is being made, what problems are being encountered, and whether additional resources or different approaches may be needed. Just as important, MBWA provides opportunities to give encouragement, lift spirits, shift attention from the old to the new priorities, and create some excitement—all of which can boost strategy execution efforts.

Jeff Bezos, Amazon.com's CEO, is noted for his practice of MBWA, firing off a battery of questions when he tours facilities and insisting that Amazon managers spend time in the trenches with their people to prevent getting disconnected from the reality of what's happening.[25] Walmart executives have had a long-standing practice of spending two to three days every week visiting Walmart's stores and talking with store managers and employees. Sam Walton, Walmart's founder, insisted, "The key is to get out into the store and listen to what the associates have to say." Jack Welch, the highly effective CEO of General Electric (GE) from 1980 to 2001, not only spent several days each month personally visiting GE operations and talking with major customers but also arranged his schedule so that he could spend time exchanging information and ideas with GE managers from all over the world who were attending classes at the company's leadership development center near GE's headquarters.

Many manufacturing executives make a point of strolling the factory floor to talk with workers and meeting regularly with union officials. Some managers operate out of open cubicles in big spaces populated with open cubicles for other personnel so that they can interact easily and frequently with co-workers. Managers at some companies host weekly get-togethers (often on Friday afternoons) to create a regular opportunity for information to flow freely between down-the-line employees and executives.

Putting Constructive Pressure on Organizational Units to Execute the Strategy Well and Achieve Operating Excellence

Managers have to be out front in mobilizing organizational energy behind the drive for good strategy execution and operating excellence. Part of the leadership task entails nurturing a results-oriented work climate, where performance standards are high and a spirit of achievement is pervasive. Successfully leading the effort to foster a results-oriented, high-performance culture generally entails such leadership actions and managerial practices as:

- *Treating employees as valued partners in the drive for operating excellence and good business performance.* Some companies symbolize the value of individual employees and the importance of their contributions by referring to them as cast members (Disney), crew members (McDonald's), job owners (Graniterock), partners (Starbucks), or associates (Walmart, LensCrafters, W. L. Gore, Edward Jones, Publix Supermarkets, and Marriott International). Very often, there is a strong company commitment to providing thorough training, offering attractive compensation and career opportunities, emphasizing promotion from within, providing a high degree of job security, and otherwise making employees feel well treated and valued.

- *Fostering an esprit de corps that energizes organization members.* The task here is to skillfully use people-management practices calculated to build morale, foster pride in doing things right, promote teamwork, create a strong sense of involvement on the part of company personnel, win their emotional commitment, and inspire them to do their best.[26]

- *Using empowerment to help create a fully engaged workforce.* Top executives must seek to engage the full organization in the strategy execution effort. A fully engaged workforce, one where individuals bring their best to work every day, is necessary to produce great results.[27] So is having a group of dedicated managers committed to making a difference in their organization. The two best things top-level executives can do to create a fully engaged organization are (1) delegate authority to middle and lower-level managers to get the implementation/execution process moving and (2) empower rank-and-file employees to act on their own initiative. Operating excellence requires that everybody contribute ideas, exercise initiative and creativity in performing his or her work, and have a desire to do things in the best possible manner.

- *Making champions out of the people who spearhead new ideas and/or turn in winning performances.* The best champions and change agents are persistent, competitive, tenacious, committed, and fanatical about seeing their ideas through to success. It is particularly important that people who champion an unsuccessful idea not be punished or sidelined but, rather, be encouraged to try again. Encouraging lots of "tries" is important, since many ideas won't pan out.

- *Setting stretch objectives and clearly communicating an expectation that company personnel are to give their best in achieving performance targets.* Stretch objectives—those beyond an organization's current capacities—can sometimes spur organization members to increase their resolve and redouble their efforts to execute the strategy flawlessly and ultimately reach the stretch objectives. When stretch objectives are met, the satisfaction of achievement and boost to employee morale can result in an even higher level of organizational drive.

- *Using the tools of benchmarking best practices, business process reengineering, TQM, and Six Sigma to focus attention on continuous improvement.* These are proven approaches to getting better operating results and facilitating better strategy execution.

- *Using the full range of motivational techniques and compensation incentives to inspire company personnel, nurture a results-oriented work climate, and enforce high-performance standards.* Managers cannot mandate innovative improvements by simply exhorting people to "be creative," nor can they make continuous progress toward operating excellence with directives to "try harder." Rather, they must foster a culture where innovative ideas and experimentation with new ways of doing things can blossom and thrive. Individuals and groups should be strongly encouraged to brainstorm, let their imaginations fly in all directions, and come up with proposals for improving how things are done. This means giving company personnel enough autonomy to stand out, excel, and contribute. And it means that the rewards for successful champions of new ideas and operating improvements should be large and visible.

- *Celebrating individual, group, and company successes.* Top management should miss no opportunity to express respect for individual employees and appreciation of extraordinary individual and group effort.[28] Companies like Mary Kay Cosmetics, Tupperware, and McDonald's actively seek out reasons and opportunities to give pins, ribbons, buttons, badges, and medals for good showings by average performers—the idea being to express appreciation and give a motivational boost to people who stand out in doing ordinary jobs. General Electric and 3M Corporation make a point of ceremoniously honoring individuals who believe so strongly in their ideas that they take it on themselves to hurdle the bureaucracy, maneuver their projects through the system, and turn them into improved services, new products, or even new businesses.

While leadership efforts to instill a results-oriented, high-performance culture usually accentuate the positive, negative reinforcers abound too. Managers whose units consistently perform poorly must be replaced. Low-performing workers and people who reject the results-oriented cultural emphasis must be weeded out or at least employed differently. Average performers should be candidly counseled that they have limited career potential unless they show more progress in the form of additional effort, better skills, and improved ability to execute the strategy well and deliver good results.

Leading the Process of Making Corrective Adjustments

Since strategy execution takes place amid changing environmental and organizational circumstances, there is often a need for corrective adjustments. The process of making corrective adjustments in strategy execution varies according to the situation. In a crisis, taking remedial action fairly quickly is of the essence. But it still takes time to review the situation, examine the available data, identify and evaluate options (crunching whatever numbers may be appropriate to determine which options are likely to generate the best outcomes), and decide what to do. When the situation allows managers to proceed more deliberately in deciding when to make changes and what changes to make, most managers seem to prefer a process of incrementally solidifying commitment to a particular course of action.[29] The process that managers go through in deciding on corrective adjustments is essentially the same for both proactive and reactive changes: They sense needs, gather information, broaden and deepen their understanding of the situation, develop options and explore their pros and cons, put forth action proposals, strive for a consensus, and finally formally adopt an agreed-on course of action.[30] The time frame for deciding what corrective changes to initiate can be a few hours, a few days, a few weeks, or even a few months if the situation is particularly complicated.

Success in making corrective actions hinges on (1) a thorough analysis of the situation, (2) the exercise of good business judgment in deciding what actions to take, and (3) good implementation of the corrective actions that are initiated.

Successful managers are skilled in getting an organization back on track rather quickly. They (and their staffs) are good at discerning what actions to take and in bringing them to a successful conclusion. Managers who struggle to show measurable progress in implementing corrective actions in a timely fashion are often candidates for being replaced.

The challenges of making the right corrective adjustments and leading a successful strategy execution effort are, without question, substantial.[31] Because each instance of executing strategy occurs under different organizational circumstances, the managerial agenda for executing strategy always needs to be situation-specific—there's no generic procedure to follow. But the job is definitely doable. Although there is no prescriptive answer to the question of exactly what to do, any of several courses of action may produce good results. And, as we said at the beginning of Chapter 10, executing strategy is an action-oriented, make-the-right-things-happen task that challenges a manager's ability to lead and direct organizational change, create or reinvent business processes, manage and motivate people, and achieve performance targets.

A FINAL WORD ON LEADING THE PROCESS OF CRAFTING AND EXECUTING STRATEGY

In practice, it is hard to separate leading the process of executing strategy from leading the other pieces of the strategy process. As we emphasized in Chapter 2, the job of crafting, implementing, and executing strategy consists of five interrelated and linked stages, with much looping and recycling to fine-tune and adjust the strategic vision, objectives, strategy, and implementation/execution approaches to fit one another and to fit changing circumstances. The process is continuous, and the conceptually separate acts of crafting and executing strategy blur together in real-world situations. The best tests of good strategic leadership are whether the company has a good strategy and business model, whether the strategy is being competently executed, and whether the enterprise is meeting or beating its performance targets. If these three conditions exist, then there is every reason to conclude that the company has good strategic leadership and is a well managed enterprise.

KEY POINTS

1. Corporate culture is the character of a company's internal work climate—as shaped by a system of *shared* values, beliefs, ethical standards, and traditions that in turn define behavioral norms, ingrained attitudes, accepted work practices, and styles of operating. A company's culture is important because it influences the organization's actions and approaches to conducting business. In a very real sense, the culture is the company's organizational DNA.

2. The key features of a company's culture include the company's values and ethical standards, its approach to people management, its work atmosphere

and company spirit, how its personnel interact, the behaviors awarded through incentives (both financial and symbolic), the traditions and oft-repeated "myths," and its manner of dealing with stakeholders.

3. A company's culture is grounded in and shaped by its core values and ethical standards. Core values and ethical principles serve two roles in the culture-building process: (1) They foster a work climate in which employees share common and strongly held convictions about how company business is to be conducted, and (2) they serve as yardsticks for gauging the appropriateness of particular actions, decisions, and behaviors, thus helping steer company personnel toward both doing things right and doing the right thing.

4. Company cultures vary widely in strength and influence. Some are strongly embedded and have a big impact on a company's practices and behavioral norms. Others are weak and have comparatively little influence on company operations.

5. Strong company cultures can have either positive or negative effects on strategy execution. When they are well matched to the behavioral requirements of the company's strategy implementation plan, they can be a powerful aid to strategy execution. A culture that is grounded in the types of actions and behaviors that are conducive to good strategy execution assists the effort in three ways:

    • By focusing employee attention on the actions that are most important in the strategy execution effort.

    • Through culture-induced peer pressure for employees to contribute to the success of the strategy execution effort.

    • By energizing employees, deepening their commitment to the strategy execution effort, and increasing the productivity of their efforts

6. It is thus in management's best interest to dedicate considerable effort to establishing a strongly implanted corporate culture that encourages behaviors and work practices conducive to good strategy execution.

7. Strong corporate cultures that are conducive to good strategy execution are healthy cultures. So are high-performance cultures and adaptive cultures. The latter are particularly important in dynamic environments. Strong cultures can also be unhealthy. The five types of unhealthy cultures are (1) those that are change-resistant, (2) those that are characterized by heavily politicized decision making, (3) those that are insular and inwardly focused, (4) those that are ethically unprincipled and infused with greed, and (5) those that are composed of incompatible subcultures. All five impede good strategy execution.

8. Changing a company's culture, especially a strong one with traits that don't fit a new strategy's requirements, is a tough and often time-consuming challenge. Changing a culture requires competent leadership at the top. It requires making a compelling case for cultural change and employing both symbolic actions and substantive actions that unmistakably indicate serious commitment on the part of top management. The more that culture-driven actions and behaviors fit what's needed for good strategy execution, the less managers must depend on policies, rules, procedures, and supervision to enforce what people should and should not do.

9. Leading the drive for good strategy execution and operating excellence calls for three actions on the part of the manager in charge:

- Staying on top of what is happening and closely monitoring progress. This is often accomplished through managing by walking around (MBWA).
- Putting constructive pressure on the organization to execute the strategy well and achieve operating excellence.
- Initiating corrective actions to improve strategy execution and achieve the targeted performance results.

ASSURANCE OF LEARNING EXERCISES

LO 1, LO 2

1. Go to www.google.com. Click on the About Google link and then on the Corporate Info link. Under the Culture link, read what Google has to say about its culture. Also, in the "Our Philosophy" section, read "Ten things Google has found to be true." How do the "ten things" and Google's culture aid in management's attempts to execute the company's strategy?

LO 1, LO 2

2. Go to the Jobs section at www.intel.com, and see what Intel has to say about its culture under the links for Careers, Diversity, and The Workplace. Does what's on this Web site appear to be just recruiting propaganda, or does it convey the type of work climate that management is actually trying to create? Explain your answer.

LO 3

3. Using Google Scholar or your university library's access to EBSCO, Lexis-Nexis, or other databases, search for recent articles in business publications on "culture change." Give examples of three companies that have recently undergone culture-change initiatives. What are the key features of each company's culture-change program? What results did management achieve at each company?

LO 1, LO 2

4. Go to www.jnj.com, the Web site of Johnson & Johnson, and read the J&J Credo, which sets forth the company's responsibilities to customers, employees, the community, and shareholders. Then read the "Our Company" section. Why do you think the credo has resulted in numerous awards and accolades that recognize the company as a good corporate citizen?

LO 4

5. In the last couple of years, Liz Claiborne, Inc., has been engaged in efforts to turn around its faltering Mexx chain. Use your favorite browser to search for information on the turnaround plan at Mexx, and read at least two articles or reports on this subject. Describe in 1 to 2 pages the approach being taken to turn around the Mexx chain. In your opinion, have the managers involved been demonstrating the kind of internal leadership needed for superior strategy execution at Mexx? Explain your answer.

EXERCISES FOR SIMULATION PARTICIPANTS

LO 1, LO 2

1. If you were making a speech to company personnel, what would you tell them about the kind of corporate culture you would like to have at your company? What specific cultural traits would you like your company to exhibit? Explain.

LO 1

2. What core values would you want to ingrain in your company's culture? Why?

LO 3, LO 4

3. Following each decision round, do you and your co-managers make corrective adjustments in either your company's strategy or how well the strategy is being executed? List at least three such adjustments you made in the most recent decision round. What hard evidence (in the form of results relating to your company's performance in the most recent year) can you cite that indicates the various corrective adjustments you made either succeeded or failed to improve your company's performance?

LO 4

4. What would happen to your company's performance if you and your co-managers stick with the status quo and fail to make any corrective adjustments after each decision round?

ENDNOTES

[1] Jennifer A. Chatham and Sandra E. Cha, "Leading by Leveraging Culture," *California Management Review* 45, no. 4 (Summer 2003), pp. 20–34.
[2] Joanne Reid and Victoria Hubbell, "Creating a Performance Culture," *Ivey Business Journal* 69, no. 4 (March–April 2005), p. 1.
[3] John P. Kotter and James L. Heskett, *Corporate Culture and Performance* (New York: Free Press, 1992), p. 7. See also Robert Goffee and Gareth Jones, *The Character of a Corporation* (New York: HarperCollins, 1998).
[4] For several perspectives on the role and importance of core values and ethical behavior, see Joseph L. Badaracco, *Defining Moments: When Managers Must Choose between Right and Wrong* (Boston: Harvard Business School Press, 1997); Joe Badaracco and Allen P. Webb. "Business Ethics: A View from the Trenches," *California Management Review* 37, no. 2 (Winter 1995), pp. 8–28; Patrick E. Murphy, "Corporate Ethics Statements: Current Status and Future Prospects," *Journal of Business Ethics* 14 (1995), pp. 727–40; and Lynn Sharp Paine, "Managing for Organizational Integrity," *Harvard Business Review* 72, no. 2 (March–April 1994), pp. 106–17.
[5] For a study of the status of formal codes of ethics in large corporations, see Emily F.

Carasco and Jang B. Singh, "The Content and Focus of the Codes of Ethics of the World's Largest Transnational Corporations," *Business and Society Review* 108, no. 1 (January 2003), pp. 71–94, and Patrick E. Murphy, "Corporate Ethics Statements: Current Status and Future Prospects," *Journal of Business Ethics* 14 (1995), pp. 727–40. For a discussion of the strategic benefits of formal statements of corporate values, see John Humble, David Jackson, and Alan Thomson, "The Strategic Power of Corporate Values," *Long Range Planning* 27, no. 6 (December 1994), pp. 28–42. An excellent discussion of whether one should assume that company codes of ethics are always ethical is presented in Mark S. Schwartz, "A Code of Ethics for Corporate Codes of Ethics," *Journal of Business Ethics* 41, nos. 1–2 (November–December 2002), pp. 27–43.
[6] Chatham and Cha, "Leading by Leveraging Culture."
[7] Kotter and Heskett, *Corporate Culture and Performance,* pp. 7–8.
[8] Terrence E. Deal and Allen A. Kennedy, *Corporate Cultures* (Reading, MA: Addison-Wesley, 1982), p. 22. See also Terrence E. Deal and Allen A. Kennedy, *The New Corporate Cultures: Revitalizing the Workplace after Downsizing, Mergers, and Reengineering*

(Cambridge, MA: Perseus Publishing, 1999); Chatham and Cha, "Leading by Leveraging Culture."
[9] Vijay Sathe, *Culture and Related Corporate Realities* (Homewood, IL: Irwin, 1985).
[10] Avan R. Jassawalla and Hemant C. Sashittal, "Cultures That Support Product-Innovation Processes," *Academy of Management Executive* 16, no. 3 (August 2002), pp. 42–54.
[11] Kotter and Heskett, *Corporate Culture and Performance,* pp. 15–16. Also see Chatham and Cha, "Leading by Leveraging Culture."
[12] Chatham and Cha, "Leading by Leveraging Culture."
[13] Kotter and Heskett, *Corporate Culture and Performance,* p. 5.
[14] For a discussion of how to build a high-performance culture, see Reid and Hubbell, "Creating a Performance Culture," pp. 1–5.
[15] A strategy-supportive, high-performance culture can contribute to competitive advantage; see Jay B. Barney and Delwyn N. Clark, *Resource-Based Theory: Creating and Sustaining Competitive Advantage* (New York: Oxford University Press, 2007), chap. 4.
[16] Reid and Hubbell, "Creating a Performance Culture," pp. 2 and 5.

[17] This section draws heavily on the discussion of Kotter and Heskett, *Corporate Culture and Performance,* chap. 4.

[18] There's no inherent reason why new strategic initiatives should conflict with core values and business principles. While conflict is always possible, most strategy makers lean toward choosing strategic initiatives that are compatible with the company's character and culture and that don't go against ingrained values and beliefs. After all, the company's culture is usually something that strategy makers have had a hand in building and perpetuating, so they are not often anxious to undermine core values and business principles without serious soul-searching and compelling business reasons.

[19] For a more in-depth discussion of using values as legitimate boundaries, see Rosabeth Moss Kanter, "Transforming Giants," *Harvard Business Review* 86, no. 1 (January 2008), pp. 43–52.

[20] Ibid., chap. 6.

[21] See Kurt Eichenwald, *Conspiracy of Fools: A True Story* (New York: Broadway Books, 2005).

[22] Ibid., p. 5.

[23] Judy D. Olian and Sara L. Rynes, "Making Total Quality Work: Aligning Organizational Processes, Performance Measures, and Stakeholders," *Human Resource Management* 30, no. 3 (Fall 1991), p. 324.

[24] For excellent discussions of the problems and pitfalls in leading the transition to a new strategy and to fundamentally new ways of doing business, see Larry Bossidy and Ram Charan, *Confronting Reality: Doing What Matters to Get Things Right* (New York: Crown Business, 2004); Larry Bossidy and Ram Charan, *Execution: The Discipline of Getting Things Done* (New York: Crown Business, 2002), especially chaps. 3 and 5; John P. Kotter, "Leading Change: Why Transformation Efforts Fail," *Harvard Business Review* 73, no. 2 (March–April 1995), pp. 59–67; Thomas M. Hout and John C. Carter, "Getting It Done: New Roles for Senior Executives," *Harvard Business Review* 73, no. 6 (November–December 1995), pp. 133–45; Sumantra Ghoshal and Christopher A. Bartlett, "Changing the Role of Top Management: Beyond Structure to Processes," *Harvard Business Review* 73, no. 1 (January–February 1995), pp. 86–96.

[25] Fred Vogelstein, "Winning the Amazon Way," *Fortune,* May 26, 2003, p. 64.

[26] For a more in-depth discussion of the leader's role in creating a results-oriented culture that nurtures success, see Benjamin Schneider, Sarah K. Gunnarson, and Kathryn Niles-Jolly, "Creating the Climate and Culture of Success," *Organizational Dynamics,* Summer 1994, pp. 17–29.

[27] Michael T. Kanazawa and Robert H. Miles, *Big Ideas to Big Results* (Upper Saddle River, NJ: FT Press, 2008), p. 96.

[28] Jeffrey Pfeffer, "Producing Sustainable Competitive Advantage through the Effective Management of People," *Academy of Management Executive* 9, no.1 (February 1995), pp. 55–69.

[29] James Brian Quinn, *Strategies for Change: Logical Incrementalism* (Homewood, IL: Richard D. Irwin, 1980), pp. 20–22.

[30] Ibid., p. 146.

[31] For a good discussion of the challenges, see Daniel Goleman, "What Makes a Leader," *Harvard Business Review* 76, no. 6 (November–December 1998), pp. 92–102; Ronald A. Heifetz and Donald L. Laurie, "The Work of Leadership," *Harvard Business Review* 75, no. 1 (January–February 1997), pp. 124–34; Charles M. Farkas and Suzy Wetlaufer, "The Ways Chief Executive Officers Lead," *Harvard Business Review* 74, no. 3 (May–June 1996), pp. 110–22. See also Michael E. Porter, Jay W. Lorsch, and Nitin Nohria, "Seven Surprises for New CEOs," *Harvard Business Review* 82, no. 10 (October 2004), pp. 62–72.

PART 2

Readings in Crafting and Executing Strategy

Business Models, Business Strategy, and Innovation

David J. Teece

University of California, Berkeley

Whenever a business enterprise is established, it either explicitly or implicitly employs a particular business model that describes the design or architecture of the value creation, delivery, and capture mechanisms it employs. The essence of a business model is in defining the manner by which the enterprise delivers value to customers, entices customers to pay for value, and converts those payments to profit. It thus reflects management's hypothesis about what customers want, how they want it, and how the enterprise can organize to best meet those needs, get paid for doing so, and make a profit. The purpose of this article is to understand the significance of business models and explore their connections with business strategy, innovation management, and economic theory.

INTRODUCTION

Developments in the global economy have changed the traditional balance between customer and supplier. New communications and computing technology, and the establishment of reasonably open global trading regimes, mean that customers have more choices, variegated customer needs can find expression, and supply alternatives are more transparent. Businesses therefore need to be more customer-centric, especially since technology has evolved to allow the lower-cost provision of information and customer solutions. These developments in turn require businesses to reevaluate the value propositions they present to customers—in many sectors, the supply-side-driven logic of the industrial era has become no longer viable.

This new environment has also amplified the need to consider not only how to address customer needs more astutely but also how to capture value from providing new products and services. Without a well-developed business model, innovators will fail to either deliver or capture value from their innovations. This is particularly true of Internet companies, where the creation of revenue streams is often most perplexing because of customer expectations that basic services should be free.

A business model articulates the logic and provides data and other evidence that demonstrates how a business creates and delivers value to customers. It also outlines the architecture of revenues, costs, and profits associated with the business enterprise delivering that value. The different elements that need to be determined in business model design are listed in Figure 1.

The issues related to good business model design are all interrelated, and lie at the core of the fundamental question asked by business strategists—how does one build a sustainable competitive advantage and turn a supernormal profit? In short, a business model defines how the enterprise creates and delivers value to customers, and then converts payments received to profits.[1] To profit from innovation, business pioneers need to excel not only at product innovation but also at business model design, understanding business design options as well as customer needs and technological trajectories. Developing a successful business model is insufficient to ensure competitive

Reprinted from *Long Range Planning* 43, no. 2/3 (April 2010), pp. 172–194, by David Teece, "Business Models, Business Strategy and Innovation" with permission from Elsevier Science.

Figure 1   Elements of Business Model Design

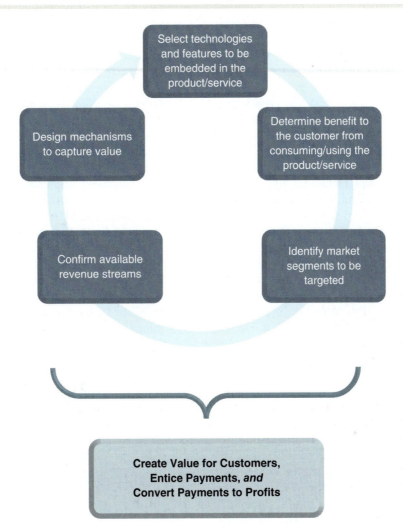

advantage, as imitation is often easy: a differentiated (and hard to imitate)—yet effective and efficient—business model is more likely to yield profits. Business model innovation can itself be a pathway to competitive advantage if the model is sufficiently differentiated and hard to replicate for incumbents and new entrants alike.

In essence, a business model embodies nothing less than the organizational and financial "architecture" of a business.[2] It is not a spreadsheet or computer model, although a business model might well become embedded in a business plan and in income statements and cash flow projections. But, clearly, the notion refers in the first instance to a conceptual, rather than a financial, model of a business. It makes implicit assumptions about customers, the behavior of revenues and costs, the changing nature of user needs, and likely competitor responses. It outlines the business logic required to earn a profit (if one is available to be earned) and, once adopted, defines the way the enterprise "goes to market." But it is not quite the same as a strategy: the distinction and the relationship between the two will be discussed later.

Despite lineage going back to when societies began engaging in barter exchange, business models have only been explicitly catapulted into public consciousness during the last decade or so. Driving factors include the emerging knowledge economy, the growth of the Internet and e-commerce, the outsourcing and offshoring of many business activities, and the restructuring of the financial services industry around the world. In particular, the way in which companies make money nowadays is different from the industrial era, where scale was so important and the capturing value thesis was relatively simple (i.e., the enterprise simply packed its technology and intellectual property into a product which it sold, either as a discrete item or as a bundled package). The existence of electronic computers that allow low-cost financial statement modeling has facilitated the exploration of alternative assumptions about revenues and costs.

Additional impetus has come from the growth of the Internet, which has raised anew, and in a transparent way, fundamental questions about how businesses deliver value to the customer, and how they can capture value from delivering new information services that users often expect to receive without charge. It has allowed individuals and businesses easy access to vast amounts of data and information, and customer power has increased as comparison shopping has been made easier. In some industries, such as the recording industry, Internet-enabled digital downloads compete with established channels (such as physical product sales) and, partly because of the ubiquity of illegal digital downloading, the music recording industry is being challenged to completely rethink its business models. The Internet is not just a source of easy access to digital data; it is also a new channel of distribution and for piracy, which clearly makes capturing value from Internet transactions and flows difficult for recording companies, performers, and songwriters alike. More generally, the Internet is causing many "bricks and mortar" companies to rethink their distribution strategies—if not their whole business models.

Notwithstanding how the Internet has devastated the business models of industries like music recording and news, Internet companies themselves have struggled to create viable business models. Indeed, during the dot-com boom and bust of 1998–2001, many new companies with zero or negative profits (and unprecedentedly low revenues) sought financial capital from the public markets, which—at least for a short while—accommodated them. Promoters managed to

persuade investors that traditional revenue and profitability models no longer applied—and that the dot-com companies would (eventually) figure out (highly) profitable business models. Few have, causing one commentator to remark that "the demise of a popular but unsustainable business model now seems inevitable."[3]

No matter what the sector, there are criteria that enable one to determine whether or not one has designed a good business model. A good business model yields value propositions that are compelling to customers, achieves advantageous cost and risk structures, and enables significant value capture by the business that generates and delivers products and services. "Designing" a business correctly, and figuring out, then implementing—and then refining—commercially viable architectures for revenues and for costs are critical to enterprise success. It is essential when the enterprise is first created; but keeping the model viable is also likely to be a continuing task. Superior technology and products, excellent people, and good governance and leadership are unlikely to produce sustainable profitability if business model configuration is not properly adapted to the competitive environment. Some preliminary criteria for business model design are suggested throughout this article, and summarized in a later section.

BUSINESS MODELS— THE THEORETICAL FOUNDATION

The concept of a business model lacks theoretical grounding in economics or in business studies. Quite simply there is no established place in economic theory for business models; and there is not a single scientific paper in the mainstream economics journals that analyzes or discusses business models in the sense they are defined here. (Possible exceptions are the literature on investment in basic research, which economists recognize as being unsupported by private business models [see below], and the literature on bundling, inasmuch as it deals—indirectly—with different revenue models.) The absence of consideration of business models in economic theory probably stems from the ubiquity of theoretical constructs that have markets solving the problems that—in the real world—business models are created to solve.

Economic theory implicitly assumes that trades take place around tangible products: intangibles are, at best, an afterthought. In standard approaches to competitive markets, the problem of capturing value is quite simply assumed away: inventions are often assumed to create value naturally and, enjoying protection of iron-clad patents, firms can capture value by simply selling output in established markets, which are assumed to exist for all products and inventions. Thus there are no puzzles about how to design a business—it is simply assumed that if value is delivered, customers will always pay for it. Putting so-called "public goods" and "free rider" issues to one side, business models are quite simply redundant because producers/suppliers can create and capture value simply through disposing their output at competitive market prices. Such models clearly assume away the essential business design issues that are the subject of this article.

In short, figuring out business models for a new or existing product or business is an unnecessary step in textbook economics, where it is not uncommon to work with theoretical constructs which assume fully developed spot and forward markets, strong property rights, the costless transfer of information, perfect arbitrage, and no innovation.[4] In mainstream approaches, there is simply no need to worry about the value proposition to the customer, or the architecture of revenues and costs, or about mechanisms to capture value.[5] Customers will buy if the price is less than the utility yielded; producers will supply if price is at or above all costs including a return to capital—the price system resolves everything and business design issues simply don't arise.

But general equilibrium models with (one-sided) markets and perfect competition are a caricature of the real world. Intangible products are in fact ubiquitous, two-sided markets are common, and customers don't just want products; they want solutions to their perceived needs. In some cases, markets may not even exist, so entrepreneurs may have to build organizations in order to perform activities for which markets are not yet ready. Accordingly, in the real world, entrepreneurs and managers must give close consideration to the design of business models and even to

building businesses to execute transactions which cannot yet be performed in the market.

It's also true that business models have no place within the theoretical constructs of planned economies (just as in a perfectly competitive economy). While central planners do need to understand the stages in the production system, in a supply-driven system—where consumers merely get what the system produces—business models simply aren't necessary. There is no problem associated with producers capturing value because value doesn't even have to be captured; the state decides what and how to produce, and how to pay for it all.

While business models have no place in economic theory, they likewise lack an acceptable place in organizational and strategic studies, and in marketing science. However, there has been some limited discussion and research on new organizational forms. Williamson, for instance, recognizes that "the 1840s marked the beginning of a great wave of organizational change that has brought us the modern corporation."[6] As discussed earlier, new organizational forms can be a component of a business model;[7] but organizational forms are not business models. Clearly, the study of business models is an interdisciplinary topic which has been neglected—despite their obvious importance, it lacks an intellectual home in the social sciences or business studies. This article aims to help remedy this deficiency.

EXAMPLES OF BUSINESS MODELS

Business models are necessary features of market economies where there are consumer choice, transaction costs, heterogeneity among consumers and producers, and competition. Profit-seeking firms in competitive environments will endeavor to meet variegated consumer wants through the constant invention and presentation to the consumer of new value propositions. Business models are often necessitated by technological innovation, which creates both the need to bring discoveries to market and the opportunity to satisfy unrequited customer needs. At the same time, as indicated earlier, new business models can themselves represent a form of innovation. There are a plethora of business model possibilities: some will be much better adapted to customer needs and business environments than others. Selecting, adjusting, and/or improving business models is a complex art. Good designs are likely to be highly situational, and the design process is likely to involve iterative processes. New business models can both facilitate and represent innovation—as history demonstrates.

Traditional Industries

A striking early American example of 19th-century business model innovation was Swift and Company's "reengineering" of the meat packing industry. Prior to the 1870s, cattle were shipped live by rail from the midwestern stockyard centers like Omaha, Kansas City, and Chicago to East Coast markets where the animals were slaughtered and the meat sold by local butchers. Gustavus Swift sensed that if the cattle could be slaughtered in the Midwest and shipped already dressed to distant markets in refrigerated freight cars, great economies in "production"/centralization and transportation could be achieved, along with an improvement in the quality of the final product.

Swift's new business model quickly displaced business models involving a network of shippers, East Coast butchers, and the railroads. His biggest challenge was the absence of refrigerated warehouses to store the beef near point of sale, which were not part of the existing distribution system. Swift set about creating a nationwide web of refrigerated facilities, often in partnerships with local jobbers. "Once Swift overcame the initial consumer resistance to meat slaughtered days before in distant places, his products found a booming market because they were as good as freshly butchered meats and were substantially cheaper—Swift's success quickly attracted imitators—by the 1890s, men like Phillip Armour had followed on Swift's heels."[8]

A more recent example is containerization. Malcolm McLean, owner of a large U.S. trucking company, was convinced that conventional shipping was highly inefficient because shipping companies typically broke bulk at dockside, and cargo ships spent most of their time in port being loaded or unloaded. In 1955 he hired an engineer to design a road trailer body that could be detached from its chassis and stacked on ships. McLean acquired a small steamship company,

renamed it Sea-Land Industries (it eventually became absorbed into the Maersk Line). He developed steel frames to hold the containers, first on the top decks of tankers, and then on the world's first specialized cellular containership, the *Gateway City,* launched in 1957. To promote the standardization necessary to develop the industry, McLean made Sea-Land's patents available royalty free to the International Standards Organization (ISO). Sea-Land began service on North Atlantic routes in 1966. When R. J. Reynolds bought Sea-Land for $530 million in 1969, McLean received $160 million for his share and retired.[9]

Another U.S. example of successful business model innovation is Southwest Airlines, where the founder surmised that most customers wanted direct flights, low costs, reliability, and good customer service, but didn't need "frills." To achieve these goals, Southwest eschews the hub-and-spoke model associated with alliances, nor does it allow interlining of passengers and baggage, or sell tickets through travel agencies—all sales are direct. Aircraft are standardized on the Boeing 737, allowing greater efficiency and operating flexibility. Southwest's business model—which was quite distinct from those of the major carriers—followed elements of a discount airline model first pioneered in the United Kingdom by Freddie Laker. Although Laker Airways eventually failed—as did other early followers in the United States such as People's Express—Easy Jet has implemented a similar model in Europe, so far successfully.

The "razor–razor blade model" is another classic (and quite generic) case of a well-known business revenue model (which is just one component of a business model), which involves pricing razors inexpensively, but aggressively marking up the consumables (razor blades). Jet engines for commercial aircraft are priced the same way—manufacturers know that engines are long lived, and maintenance and parts is where Rolls Royce, GE, Pratt & Whitney, and others make their money. So engines are sold relatively inexpensively—but parts (and service) involve considerable markups and represent an income stream that may continue for decades.

In the sports apparel business, sponsorship is a key component of today's business models. Nike, Adidas, Reebok, Canterbury, and others sponsor football and rugby clubs and teams, providing kit and sponsorship dollars as well as royalties streams from the sale of replica products. After building brand on the field, these companies endeavor to leverage their brand into off-field products, often with considerable success. On-field sponsorship is almost a sine qua non for brand authenticity. However, this model is readily imitated, and its viability for any particular apparel company depends on the sponsor's particular abilities to leverage on-field sponsorships into off-field sales. Relationships with clubs, teams, team managers, and club owners become important in the mix.

Performing artists have several business models they can employ. Their revenue sources might include live productions, movies, sales of physical CDs through stores, or online music sales through virtual stores such Apple's iTunes.[10] Stars might decide to use concerts as their main revenue generator, or to spend less time performing and more in the recording studio, using concerts primarily to stimulate sales of recordings. In earlier days when piracy was limited, the Beatles demonstrated that stars could quit live performances and continue to do well on royalties from the sale of recorded music. Then, in the 80s and 90s, the music video became an important source of revenue, and more recently, "soundtracks" to video games have become a significant source of revenue for some artists. In short, multiple revenue streams are available, and the particular revenue model employed can depend on the marketplace, on a star's contextual talents and preferences, and on the quality of copyright protection afforded to recorded music.

Business models must morph over time as changing markets, technologies, and legal structures dictate and/or allow. For instance, the business model that U.S. investment banks had employed for almost 20 years largely disappeared in 2008. From at least the 1950s through the 1990s, the investment banking function usually generated most of the banks' revenues. However, for Goldman Sachs (arguably the industry leader) that figure had fallen to 16 percent by 2007, while revenues from trading and principal investment had grown to 68 percent, leading it and other investment banks to morph their business models into something quite different—and more risky—than traditional investment banking.

Subprime mortgages and other problematic assets became securitized and injected into the system, encouraged by Freddie and Fannie (and by Congress) with results that subsequently hit the headlines. In September 2008, Goldman Sachs and Morgan Stanley (the last two independent investment banks left standing in the United States after the takeover of Bear Stearns by JP Morgan Chase, the bankruptcy of Lehman Brothers, and Merrill Lynch's absorption by Bank of America) converted themselves into federally chartered commercial banks. By accepting government regulation by the Federal Deposit Insurance Corporation (FDIC), Goldman Sachs and Morgan Stanley will need to maintain lower leverage, and accept lower risk and lower returns. In their need for a source of stable funds, both have (albeit reluctantly) made significant business model changes—in short, they have been obliged to abandon their old models entirely.

The Information/Internet Industries

As noted earlier, the information industries have always raised challenging business model issues because information is often difficult to price, and consumers have many ways to obtain certain types without paying. Figuring out how to earn revenues (i.e., capture value) from the provision of information to users/customers is a key (but not the only) element of business model design in the information sector. The rules for strategic engagement promulgated by Shapiro and Varian are core elements of strategy in the information services sector.[11]

As traditional information providers, newspapers have employed a revenue model for decades in which the paper is sold quite inexpensively (usually at a nominal level, insufficient to cover costs), while publishers looked to advertising revenue to cover remaining costs plus provide a profit. In recent years, this business model has been undermined by websites like eBay and Craigslist that have siphoned off advertising revenues from job and real estate listings and classified ads: many newspapers have gone out of business.

The Internet has enabled traditional industries like DVD rentals to adopt a more modern online posture. Netflix (**www.netflix.com**) enables customers to order DVDs online and have expedited delivery by the U.S. Postal Service as a more convenient alternative to going to a rental facility, renting the DVD, and returning it several days later. Monthly fees are what sustain Netflix.

The emergence of the Internet, Napster, and its clones has obliged music recording companies to rethink their business models, which they have been doing along several fronts. On one front, they are moving to greatly increase the royalty rate for Internet "broadcast" of their content, while on another, they are moving to capture advertising revenues associated with that content. For instance, MySpace Music (http://music.myspace.com) enables users to listen to songs from Universal, Sony BMG, and Warner Music, and provides free advertising-supported streaming, with easy access to Amazon.com for music purchases. Another example is the Nokia Comes with Music (CWM) handset, which comes with "free," unlimited music downloads for a year, with Nokia passing on a fee to the recording companies.

A recent example of an Internet business model is Flickr (www.flickr.com), which has been described as "a poster child for Web 2.0 [offering] users a way to share photos easily."[12] Flickr's friendly and easy-to-use Web interface and its free photo management and storage service are noted as great examples of a Web 2.0 "freemium" (free and premium) business model, characterized by Fred Wilson as:

> Give your service away for free, possibly ad supported but maybe not, acquire a lot of customers very efficiently through word of mouth, referral networks, organic search marketing, etc., then offer premium-priced value-added services or an enhanced version of your service to your customer base.

The Flickr business model (which actually evolved from gaming to online photo sharing, harnessing user feedback generated through blogs) essentially gives away the services that amateur photographers want most: photo sharing, online storage, indexing, and tagging. Shuen notes that low-cost online distribution and marketing and investment are associated with "revenue from multiple streams, including value-added premium services and customer acquisition." Flickr's multiple revenue stream business model involves collecting subscription fees, charging advertisers for contextual advertising, and receiving sponsorship

and revenue-sharing fees from partnerships with retail chains and complementary photo service companies. Yahoo bought Flickr in March 2005 for tens of millions of dollars.

A business model pioneered by one company in one space may be adopted by another company in another space. The "freemium" model has been adopted by Adobe (for its PDF reader), Skype and MySpace, while Outshouts Inc. (www.outshouts.com) has applied Flickr's multiple revenue streams model to online Web videos, allowing users to personalize and disseminate videos for business or consumer purposes. While it is common with Internet start-ups, the multiple revenue stream approach is by no means new. Besides theatrical releases and looking to exploit an obvious extra revenue stream—the sequel—movie studios have long sought revenues from "ancillary" licensing (toys, T-shirts, lunchboxes, backpacks), and more recently from video games and soundtracks.

Freemium business models are also deployed by a large number of software companies (such as Linux, Firefox, and Apache) that operate in the open source marketplace. The standard form (or "kernel") of the software is licensed under an open source license and then a premium version with additional features and/or associated services is made available under commercial license terms. One theory is that "vendors" get customers (often, and ideally with the IT organization bypassing Procurement Departments altogether—because, after all, the software is "free") hooked on the free product, and then subsequently convert them into paying customers through the sale of complementary software and/or service. However, conversion rates to paying customers have been poor, and it's not clear the model works.

The discussion so far has focused mainly on the impact of technology on value and its delivery. However, technology can have an equally transformative effect on the cost side of the business model. New "cloud-based" computing models, for example, remove the need for small companies to invest up-front in expensive servers—instead they can buy server capacity in small slices, as needed, according to their monthly needs. The size of such slices continues to shrink—services such as Amazon's EC2, for example, even allow customers to buy virtual server capacity for a single transaction, measured in milliseconds. This kind of innovation transforms previous "fixed plus variable" cost models into entirely variable cost models, greatly improving efficiency and reducing early-stage capital requirements.

BUSINESS MODELS, STRATEGY AND SUSTAINABLE COMPETITIVE ADVANTAGE

A business model articulates the logic, the data, and other evidence that support a value proposition for the customer, and a viable structure of revenues and costs for the enterprise delivering that value. In short, it's about the benefit the enterprise will deliver to customers, how it will organize to do so, and how it will capture a portion of the value that it delivers. A good business model will provide considerable value to the customer and collect (for the developer or implementor of the business model) a viable portion of this in revenues. But developing a successful business model (no matter how novel) is insufficient in and of itself to ensure competitive advantage. Once implemented, the gross elements of business models are often quite transparent and (in principle) easy to imitate—indeed, it is usually just a matter of a few years, if not months, before an evidently successful new business model elicits imitative efforts. In practice, successful business models very often become, to some degree, "shared" by multiple competitors.

As described, a business model is more generic than a business strategy. Coupling strategy analysis with business model analysis is necessary in order to protect whatever competitive advantage results from the design and implementation of new business models. Selecting a business strategy is a more granular exercise than designing a business model. Coupling competitive strategy analysis to business model design requires segmenting the market, creating a value proposition for each segment, setting up the apparatus to deliver that value, and then figuring out various "isolating mechanisms" that can be used to prevent the business model/strategy from being undermined through imitation by competitors or disintermediation by customers.[13]

Strategy analysis is thus an essential step in designing a competitively sustainable business model. Unless the business model survives the filters which strategy analysis imposes, it is unlikely to be viable, as many business model features are easily imitated. For instance, leasing versus owning is an observable characteristic of business models that competitors can replicate. The "newspaper revenue model"—that is, low cost for the newspaper, use of advertising (including classifieds) to help cover the costs of generating content—is easy to replicate, and has been implemented with little variation in thousands of geographically separate "markets" throughout the world.

Having a differentiated (and hard-to-imitate)—but at the same time effective and efficient—architecture for an enterprise's business model is important to the establishment of competitive advantage. The various elements need to be cospecialized to each other, and work together well as a system. Both Dell Inc. and Walmart have demonstrated the value associated with their business models (while Webvan and many other dotcoms demonstrated just the opposite). Dell and Walmart's business models were different, were superior, and required supporting processes that were hard for competitors to replicate (at least in the United States—elsewhere, new entrants could adopt key elements of the model and preempt Walmart, as Steven Tindall has demonstrated so ably in New Zealand with The Warehouse). Both Dell and Walmart have also constantly adjusted and improved their processes over time. Michael Dell, founder of Dell, notes:

> This belief—that by working directly with customers we could get them technology faster, provide a better level of service, and provide better value—was the basis of the business—the fundamental business system was quite powerful and delivered lots of value to our customers—we screwed up lots of things, but the one thing we got right was this core business model, and it masked any other mistakes.[14]

Dell's competitors were incumbents that had difficulty in replicating its strategy, as selling direct to customers would upset their existing channel partners and resellers: as a new entrant, Dell had no such constraints. Another critical element of Dell's success, beyond the way it organized its value chain, was the choice of products it sold through its distribution system. Over time, Dell developed (dynamic) capabilities around deciding which products to build beside desktop and laptop computers, and has since added printers, digital projectors, and computer-related electronics. Of course, the whole strategy depended on the availability of numerous noncaptive suppliers able to produce at very competitive prices.

Magretta points out that the business model of discount (big-box) retailing had been around long before Walmart founder Sam Walton (in his words) "put good sized stores into little one-horse towns which everybody else was ignoring."[15] Once in place, the towns Walmart had selected were too small to support another similar sized store, so a difficult to replicate first mover advantage had been created. Walmart promoted national brands at deep discounts, supported by innovative and lean purchasing logistics and IT systems: these were elements of its strategy that made its business model difficult to imitate.

Search engine development and the Google story is another interesting business model illustration. Early efforts in this field, including Lycos, Excite, Alta Vista, Inktomi, and Yahoo, would find lots of information—perhaps too much—and present it to users in an unhelpful manner, with maybe thousands of results presented in no discernible or useful order. Alta Vista presented links, but without using them as aids to searching. Larry Page, one of the founders of Google, surmised that counting links to a website was a way of ranking its popularity (much like higher citation counts in scientific journals point to more important contributions to the literature), and decided to use the number of links to important sites as a measure of priority. Using this link-based approach, Page and his colleagues at Google devised an Internet site ranking system—the PageRank algorithm—which went on to be their core product/service offering, and one which has proved very valuable to users. The challenge was to tune the product offering and devise a business model to capture value, which was not easy in a world in which consumers expected search to be free.

The business model developed around Google's product/service innovation required heavy investment in computing power as well as in software.

Google writes its own software and (remarkably) builds its own computers. It takes advantage of its considerable computing power to count words and links, and to combine information about words and links. This allows the Google search engine to take more factors into account than others currently in the market. The Google revenue model eschewed funding from advertisers: directed search biased to favor advertisers was perceived by Google's founders as degrading to the integrity of the search process and to its emerging brand. Accordingly, it decided that the essence of its revenue model would be sponsored links—that is, no pop-ups or other graphics interfering with the search. In short, Page and Brin found a way to accommodate advertising (thereby enabling revenue generation) without subtracting from the search experience, and arguably enhancing it.[16] However, they also adopted an integrated approach (by fulfilling their own software and hardware requirements) to keep control of their product/service offering, ensuring its delivery and its quality.

Business model choices define the architecture of the business, and expansion paths develop from there on out. But once established, enterprises often encounter immense difficulty in changing business models—witness the difficulties American Express and Discover Card have experienced in trying to morph to hybrid models where they issue cards themselves while simultaneously looking to persuade banks as partners to act as card issuers for them. This is clearly incongruous—their main competitors (Visa and MasterCard, which provide network services only and don't compete with banks in issuing credit cards) are not hobbled by such relationship conflicts, and are clearly likely to be the bank's preferred partners. Thus American Express and Discover are unlikely to have (and indeed have not had) much success trying to replicate the Visa/MasterCard business model while still maintaining their own internal issuing and acquiring functions.[17]

In short, innovating with business models will not, by itself, build enterprise-level competitive advantage. However, new business models, or refinements to existing ones, like new products themselves, often result in lower cost or increased value to the consumer; if not easily replicated by competitors, they can provide an opportunity to generate higher returns to the pioneer, at least until their novel features are copied. These issues are summarized in Figure 2 and explored in more detail later.

BARRIERS TO IMITATING BUSINESS MODELS

This section attempts to distill those factors that affect the ease or otherwise of imitating business models. At a superficial level all business models might seem easy to imitate—certainly the basic idea and the business logic behind a new model is unlikely itself to enjoy intellectual property protection. In particular, a new business model, being more general than a business method, is very unlikely to qualify for a patent, even if certain business methods underpinning it may be patentable. Descriptions of a business model may enjoy copyright protection, but that is unlikely to be a barrier to copying its basic core "idea." What then is it, if anything, that is likely to impede the copycat behavior that can so quickly erode the business model pioneer's advantage? Three factors would seem to be relevant.

First, implementing a business model may require systems, processes, and assets that are hard to replicate—such was the situation with potential entrants into the towns too small to sustain a Walmart competitor. Similarly, while at some level Dell's direct-to-user (consumers and businesses) business model is obvious (you simply disintermediate wholesalers and retailers), when Gateway Computers tried to implement a similar model, its failure to achieve anywhere near Dell's performance levels has been attributed to the inferior implementation of processes. Capabilities matter. Likewise, when Netflix pioneered delivery of DVDs by mail using a subscription system, Blockbuster video responded with a similar offering. But Netflix held on to its lead, both because it was not handicapped by Blockbuster's cannibalization concerns and because it had patents on the "ordered list" (which it later accused Blockbuster of infringing) by which subscribers indicated online their movie preferences.

Second, there may be a level of opacity (Rumelt has referred to this opacity as "uncertain imitability") that makes it difficult for outsiders to understand in sufficient detail how a business model is implemented, or which of its elements in fact constitute the source of customer acceptability.[18]

Third, even if it is transparently obvious how to replicate a pioneer's business model, incumbents in the industry may be reluctant to do so if it

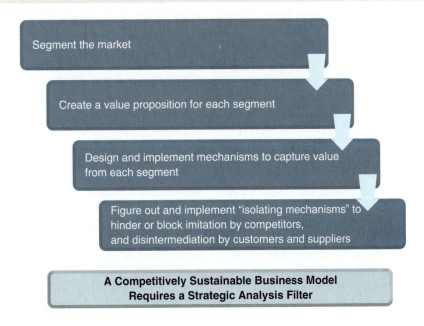

Figure 2   Steps to Achieve Sustainable Business Models

involves cannibalizing existing sales and profits or upsetting other important business relationships. When incumbents are constrained in this way, the pioneer of a new business model may enjoy a considerable period of limited competitive response. Notwithstanding these constraints, competition is likely to be vigorous because other new entrants, similarly unconstrained by incumbency and cannibalization anxieties, will be equally free to enter.

Business Model Learning

The moves made by an incumbent competitor to overcome such barriers to respond to Netflix's entry into DVD rentals provide an interesting illustration of business model learning and adjustment. To respond to Netflix's competitive inroads into its DVD store-rental model, Blockbuster purchased assets from NetLearn in April 2002, including those of **DVDRentalCentral. com**, a subscriber-based online DVD rental service, which it renamed FilmCaddy and operated separately from the rest of the Blockbuster business. In August 2004, Blockbuster shut down FilmCaddy and launched Blockbuster Online, its new online rental service that allowed customers to rent unlimited DVDs (three at a time) for a monthly fee. Its initial plan included no due dates or extended viewing fees, and also gave subscribers two free in-store movie rentals each month. In November 2006, it launched Blockbuster Total Access, coupling its online business with its in-store capabilities to allow online customers the option of returning their DVDs through the mail or exchanging them for free in-store movie rentals at over 5,000 Blockbuster stores.

Clearly, most elements of the Netflix business model were relatively easy to copy, and, although Blockbuster was undoubtedly constrained by the cannibalization of its in-store rentals by its online business, these moves reflected its attempts to respond (defensively) to Netflix. Netflix had figured out an approach and made the investments required to establish the online market. But Blockbuster responded by leveraging its brand equity and its network of physical stores to try to capture value from a modified version of the model Netflix had created: at minimum, it was intent on minimizing damage to its in-store franchise. Its guiding principle in responding appeared to be

to offer customers all the functionality of Netflix plus several distinguishing features—associated with using its retail store footprint—which Netflix couldn't easily match. Blockbuster's stores also complemented its online strategy, by offering customers a choice of how to return their rented DVDs. While Netflix had no retail presence with which to respond to this element of Blockbuster's offering directly, it did have some limited patent protection, with two patents that provided its business model some protection—in particular, to its "ordered list" for movie selection. While these patents did not cover online DVD rental per se, they did cover methods allowing users to pay a flat fee to have a maximum number of movies out at any one time, and to return a fixed number of movies within a fixed time period.

In short, Blockbuster implemented a close facsimile of the Netflix business model (even its website was very similar, featuring stars, recommendations, box shots, and the "dynamic queue") and achieved reasonable success, undoubtedly blunting Netflix's growth. While Blockbuster Online was a good defensive move, Netflix's pioneering status and its capacity to improve its business model, and enforce its patents, helped undergird its competitive advantage.

BUSINESS MODELS TO CAPTURE VALUE FROM TECHNOLOGICAL INNOVATION

The Profiting from Innovation Framework

Figuring out how to capture value from innovation is a key element of business model design. This is a topic on which this author has written extensively, although the treatment hitherto was not couched in the language of business model design. This section is more forthright in that regard.

Every new product development effort should be coupled with the development of a business model which defines its "go-to-market" and "capturing value" strategies. Clearly technological innovation by itself does not automatically guarantee business or economic success—far from it. This was a theme in the author's earlier work, "Profiting from Innovation,"[19] which outlined a contingent approach with respect to how to organize the production system/value chain, taking into account the "appropriability regime" and the innovator's prior asset positioning. Notwithstanding that scholars have recognized that technological innovation without a commercialization strategy is as likely to lead to the (self-) destruction of creative enterprises as it is to profitable (Schumpeterian) creative destruction, technological innovation is often assumed by some to lead inexorably to commercial success. It rarely does. When executives think of innovation, they all too often neglect the proper analysis and development of business models which can translate technical success into commercial success. Good business model design and implementation, coupled with careful strategic analysis, are necessary for technological innovation to succeed commercially: otherwise, even creative companies will flounder. Quintessential examples of firms that succeeded at technological innovation but failed to get the business model and the technology strategy right included EMI (the CAT scanner) and Xerox (the personal computer).[20]

But there are a plethora of other examples too. Eli Whitney's 1793 invention of the cotton gin greatly increasing the ease with which cotton could be separated from the pod—but still he died a poor man. Even Thomas Edison—with his portfolio of 1,000+ patents and personal fame from inventing a durable electric light bulb, electricity as a system, motion pictures, and phonographs—failed commercially on many fronts. For example, he abandoned the recording business after arguably failing to get its business model right by insisting that Edison disks be designed to work only on Edison phonographs (although his early phonograph also suffered from poor sound reproduction, recordings that were too brief, and cylinders that could only survive a few playings). In short, getting the business model *and* the technology strategy right is necessary to achieve commercial viability if sustainable competitive advantage is to be built and innovators are to profit from their innovations.

Figuring out how to deliver value to the customer—and to capture value while doing so—are the key issues in designing a business model: it is not enough to do the first without the second. The imperfections in the market for know-how make capturing value from its production and sale inherently difficult,[21] and may often necessitate a business model where know-how is bundled into products and complementary assets used to realize value to the innovator. This involves some of the trickiest and most frustrating issues that entrepreneurs and managers must address.

The Profiting from Innovation framework is an effort to help entrepreneurs and strategists figure out appropriate business model/designs and technology strategies by delineating important features of business model choice, and predicting the outcomes from those choices. The framework employs contracting theory,[22] and recognizes two extreme modes (models) by which innovators can capture value from innovation:

- At one end of the scale stands the integrated business model, in which an innovating firm bundles innovation and product together, and assumes the responsibility for the entire value chain from A to Z including design, manufacturing, and distribution. Clearly, companies that have the right assets already in place are well equipped to do this; but the framework also indicates when the internal development and commercialization strategy is a necessity.

- The other extreme case is the outsourced (pure licensing) business approach, one that has been embraced by a number of companies, like Rambus (semiconductor memory) and Dolby (high-fidelity noise reduction technology). With respect to licensing versus internal commercialization by the innovator, the framework yields answers calibrated according to the strength of the appropriability/intellectual property regime. Thus one could license—and expect the licensing model to work—only if one had strong intellectual property rights: without them, the licensee might well be the one who captures value, at the expense of the innovator.

- In between there are hybrid approaches involving a mixture of the two approaches (e.g., outsource manufacturing; providing company-owned sales and support). Hybrid approaches are the most common, but they also require strong selection and orchestration skills on the part of management.[23]

The Profiting from Innovation framework can thus be considered as a tool to help design business models, and using it allows one to map business model selection to type of innovation, while simultaneously enabling one to figure out where intellectual property monetization through licensing is likely to be viable, and where it's not, or where some kind of vertical integration is indicated.[24] Although (by construction) it is silent on many issues such as market segmentation and the choice of product features, it nevertheless can provide insights into how a value chain ought to be assembled. And it can predict winners and losers from the competitive process in the context where a customer need is being met.

"Public" Goods and the Bundling and Unbundling of Inventions and Products

Inventors and innovators rarely enjoy strong intellectual property protection. One well-studied (and reasonably well understood) situation where there are serious value-capture problems is investment in basic research and the production of scientific knowledge. Basic research usually ends up in scientific publications, so it is hard—if not impossible—to secure strong intellectual property protection for scientific knowledge. As a result, it is very difficult to charge for discoveries, even if they have the potential to generate high value for society, so very few firms invest in basic research. Spill-overs (externalities) are simply too large; profiting from discovery is simply too difficult. There is no easy for-profit business model for capturing value from scientific discoveries in a world where science wants to be open and rapid dissemination of scientific knowledge through journals, conferences, and professional contacts is almost inevitable: not surprisingly, most basic research is not funded by business firms, but by governments.

Investment in scientific research is an example of what economists call "public goods," a circumstance in which the economic activity in question generates positive externalities, or "spillovers." As there is no good (private) business model that can support value capture, government funding and/or philanthropy is required and provided. Viewed in this way, the concept of the "business model" can be integrated into almost a century of economic thought about the design of institutions and the role of enterprise and government in civil society. Market "failures" occur in the context of innovation when private business models for capturing value draw forth insufficient investment in R&D.

Putting basic science to one side, the most common business model to capture value from inventions is to embed them in a product, rather than simply trying to sell designs or intellectual property. This approach allows those that invest in R&D to ameliorate (to some degree) their lack of intellectual property protection. The latest cell phone, digital camera, or automobile doesn't come with a price for the product and an unbundled price for know-how and/or intellectual property: invention/technology and product are typically bundled together, although (in theory) they don't need to be.

This discussion makes it apparent that market failures (with respect to R&D investment) are partly a function of the ability (or lack thereof) of entrepreneurs to create viable business models using the mechanisms available to them. As noted, one way to try and get around market failures in the "market for inventions" is to bundle invention(s) and complements into products. But too often, firms (and in particular small startups) underemploy the available mechanisms, just offering customers "items" of technology such as devices or discrete technology components. Just by itself, this may not represent a customer solution; a business model based on simply selling an invention—or even an innovative component or item—may not enable the innovator to capture a significant share of the value that might be generated by their innovative technology, unless it has ironclad patent protection and is critical to an important and already recognized application. The proper "marketing" of new technology often requires much more.[25] The bundled provision of complementary products and services is often necessary, not just to help capture value, but to help create it in the first place.

The problem is quite general. When value delivery involves employing intangible (know-how) assets, pricing and value capture are difficult because of the nonexistence of perfect property rights, which means that markets can't work well, as Coase and many others have explained.[26]

As illustrated above, many Internet services are simply provided for "free" as a way to build brand and to indirectly promote a related value-added service, and we have seen how a mixture of revenue approaches is usually required when trying to sell on the Internet.[27] But bundling, while a common and helpful approach, isn't always necessary. When the innovator has a strong patent, it is sometimes possible to capture value either by naked licensing—or even outright sale—of intellectual property. Different models of value capture are available where intellectual property rights exist and can be enforced—so designing business models often requires the skill of the intellectual property lawyer as well as that of the entrepreneur.

To summarize: the traditional revenue model used by innovators to capture value from technology involves the consumer buying (and paying for) products that have intellectual property embedded within them—the method is so common that it is rarely noticed or reflected on.[28] This works well, particularly if an attractive bundled solution can be offered, if there is strong intellectual property, or if imitability is otherwise difficult. Many scientific discoveries and inventions are poorly protected by intellectual property rights, and require business models that feature public funding, or crafty ways to otherwise capture positive spillovers.

Business Models as Innovation

Technological innovation is lionized in most advanced societies; that is a natural and desirable reflection of the values of a technologically progressive society. However, the creation of new organizational forms (like the Skunk Works and the multidivisional organizational structure), organizational methods (like the moving assembly line), and in particular new business models are of equal—if not greater—importance to society, and to the business enterprise. While such innovation may seem less heroic to many citizens—even to many scientists and engineers—without it technological innovation may be bereft of reward for pioneering individuals, as well as for pioneering enterprises and nations.

The capacity of a firm (or nation) to capture value will be deeply compromised unless the capacity exists to create new business models.

As noted, even an inventor as celebrated as Thomas Edison had a questionable track record in terms of business model innovation, abandoning the recording business and also failing to get direct (rather than alternating) current adopted as the industry standard for electricity generation and transmission. History shows that, unless they can offer compelling value propositions to consumers/users *and* set up (profitable) business systems to satisfy them with the requisite quality at acceptable price points, the innovator will fail, even if the innovation itself is remarkable, and goes on to be widely adopted by society. Of course, this makes management, entrepreneurship, and business model design and implementation as important to economic growth as is technological innovation itself. Technological creativity that is not matched by business resourcefulness and creativity (in designing business models) may not yield value to the inventor or even to their society.

As discussed and illustrated in many earlier examples, technological innovation often needs to be matched with business model innovation if the innovator is to capture value. There are of course exceptions—for example, small improvements in the manufacturing process (even if cumulatively large) will usually not require business model innovation, and value can be captured by lowering price and expanding the market and market share. But the more radical the innovation, and the more challenging the revenue architecture, the greater the changes likely to be required to traditional business models. And, as indicated by some of the earlier examples, business model innovation may help to establish a differentiable competitive advantage. Dell didn't bring any improvements to the technology of the personal computer—but it did combine both suppliers' and its own organizational/distribution system innovations to deliver compelling value to end users—as have Southwest Airlines, Virgin, Virgin Blue, and Jet-Blue in the air passenger transport sector.

Sometimes the creation of new business models leads to the creation of new industries. Consider the payment card industry (the core of which is credit and debit cards). The card companies provide network services, associate with banks who issue the cards, and associate with acquirers who sign up merchants to accept credit cards. Early on in the life of the industry, merchants were unwilling to accept a payment card that few

consumers carried, just as card holders didn't want cards that merchants did not accept. As Evans and Schmalensee note, inventing a new business model for credit—the credit card—"required the industry's founders to invest enormous amounts of capital and ingenuity."[29]

Companies should be seeking and considering improvements to business models—particularly difficult to imitate improvements that add value for customers—at all times. Changing the firm's business model literally involves changing the paradigm by which it goes to market, and inertia is likely to be considerable. Nevertheless, it is preferable for the firm to initiate such a change itself, rather than have it dictated by external events, as several investment banks in the United States and elsewhere have experienced recently.

THE ROLE OF DISCOVERY, LEARNING, AND ADAPTATION

Designing a new business model requires creativity, insight, and a good deal of customer, competitor, and supplier information and intelligence. There may be a significant tacit component. An entrepreneur may be able to intuit a new model but not be able to rationalize and articulate it fully; so experimentation and learning are likely to be required. As mentioned earlier, the evolving reality impacting customers, society, and the cost structure of the business must be understood. It is often the case that the right business model may not be apparent up front, and learning and adjustments will be necessary: new business models represent provisional solutions to user/customer needs proposed by entrepreneurs/managers. As Shirky recognizes, a business model is provisional in the sense that it is likely over time to be replaced by an improved model that takes advantage of further technological or organizational innovations. The right business model is rarely apparent early on in emerging industries: entrepreneurs/managers who are well positioned, who have a good but not perfect business model template but who can learn and adjust, are those more likely to succeed.[30]

Technological change often provides the impetus for new and better ways to satisfy customer needs. The horse, then the railroad, the auto, and the airplane have all been technological solutions to society's basic transport needs that successively complemented and displaced each other, and formed the basis of competing business models for carrying people from one place to another. The Internet and the communication and computer revolution have empowered customers, and both allowed and required more differentiation in product/service offerings. Social networking is also trumping the age-old ability of using advertising to get to an audience. As Peter Sealey has noted with respect to new movies releases, "the star-power opening is fading in importance and the marketing and releasing of movies is going into new territory where the masses are molding the opinion of a movie,"[31] and studio executives are having to recognize these new realities and adjust their business models accordingly.

In short, one needs to distill fundamental truths about customer desires, customer assessments, the nature and likely future behavior of costs, and the capabilities of competitors when designing a commercially viable business model. Traditional market research will not often be enough to identify as-yet-unarticulated needs and/or emerging trends. Changes with respect to the relative merits of particular organizational and technological solutions to customer needs must also be considered.

Consider again the question of how society will gather and distribute the news of the day. First it was the town crier; later the newspaper; today the Internet has become increasingly important. Communication costs have dropped dramatically; but now advertising revenues are shrinking too. Generally, when the underlying technology changes, and an established logic for satisfying consumer needs (e.g., newspapers for providing news) is overturned, the business model must change too. But technological change is not always a trigger—or always necessary—to reshaping the business model.

Not surprisingly, the invention of new business models can originate from many potential sources. What business models pioneers often possess—or develop—is an understanding of some "deep truth" about the fundamental needs of consumers and how competitors are or are not satisfying those needs, and of the technological and organizational possibilities (and trajectories) for improvement—some of them, though, just

stumble into such understandings. In almost every case, however, a new business model is successfully pioneered only after considerable trial and error.

Those entrepreneurs who understand "deep truths" and can figure out what customers want and design a better way to satisfy them (and build sustainable organizations to address these customer needs) are business pioneers. They may or may not use new technology, but they must understand customer needs, technological possibilities, and the logic of organization. Put differently, a business model articulates the underlying business, or "industrial logic," of a firm's go-to-market strategy. Once articulated, it is likely that the logic will have to be tested and retested, adjusted, and tuned as the evidence with respect to provisional assumptions becomes clarified.

Netflix (discussed above), the largest online DVD rental service in the United States, offers a flat-fee DVD movie rental service that, by 2007, was serving over 6 million subscribers from its collection of 75,000 titles.[32] Subscribers can use the website's browse function to search for movies by genre, and use an extensive movie recommendation system based on other users' ratings to add to their ordered list for delivery via mail. At its initial launch, the Netflix business model was based on a pay-per-rental service, but this initial pricing model did not succeed, and the company almost failed. It was clear to management Netflix had to rejig its business model and, between September and October 1999, it reinvented itself with a subscription model (the Marque Program). It ended its pay-per-rental model entirely and evolved the monthly fee program to allow subscribers to rent any number of DVDs per month (although only a limited number at any one time). The model was supported by a system of regional distribution centers which ensured next-day delivery to over 90 percent of subscribers. Clearly, it took a while to be able to ascertain the right price points and the manner of pricing that was most acceptable to the customer base for its new service; but as Netflix management figured out viewer convenience, wants, and willingness to pay, it adjusted its business model accordingly. This ability to perceive and adapt saved Netflix and laid the foundation for its growth and development: by 2006 it had reached almost $1 billion in revenues.

Selecting the right "architecture" and pricing model for a business does not just require

understanding the choices available; assembling the evidence needed to validate conjectures and hunches about costs, customers, competitors, complementors, distributors, and suppliers takes detailed fact-specific inquiry and a keen understanding of customer needs and customer willingness to pay as well as of competitor positioning and likely competitive responses. Entrepreneurs and executives must make many informed guesses about the future behavior of customer and competitor, as well as of costs. As the evidence with respect to initial conjectures becomes available, they need to adjust accordingly. Being fast in learning and making the requisite adjustments to the model is important.

A helpful analytic approach for management is likely to involve systematic deconstruction/unpacking of existing business models, and an evaluation of each element with an idea toward refinement or replacement. The elements of a business model must be designed with reference to each other, and to the business/customer environment and the trajectory of technological development in the industry. While the questions are not as crisp as one would like, and the answers are likely to be ambiguous, endeavoring to answer them will impose some discipline and at least help one sort business propositions that are likely to be viable from those that are not. For instance, business propositions that are no more than good ideas fall short; likewise, propositions that involve capturing 1 percent of huge markets show a lack of understanding of differences among (potential) customers, market segments, and competition. And a wonderfully novel (gimmicky) product concept that meets the needs of but a handful of potential customers is unlikely to yield much value. Periodic review can increase the chances of avoiding blind spots: long-lived structural elements—choices made perhaps decades ago in different environments—need to be scrutinized especially thoroughly.

A provisional business model must be evaluated against the current state of the business ecosystem, and also against how it might evolve. Questions to consider (which are summarized in Figure 3) include:

• How does the product or service bring utility to the consumer? How is it likely to be used? Inasmuch as innovation requires the provision of complements, are the necessary complements already available to the consumer with

Figure 3   Questions to Ask About a (Provisional) Business Model

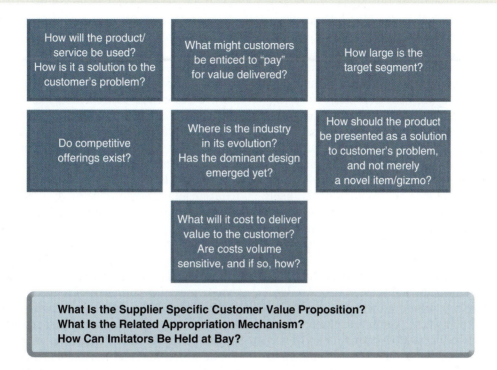

How will the product/service be used? How is it a solution to the customer's problem?

What might customers be enticed to "pay" for value delivered?

How large is the target segment?

Do competitive offerings exist?

Where is the industry in its evolution? Has the dominant design emerged yet?

How should the product be presented as a solution to customer's problem, and not merely a novel item/gizmo?

What will it cost to deliver value to the customer? Are costs volume sensitive, and if so, how?

What Is the Supplier Specific Customer Value Proposition?
What Is the Related Appropriation Mechanism?
How Can Imitators Be Held at Bay?

the convenience and price that are desirable (or possible)?

- What is the "deep truth" about what customers *really* value, and how will the firm's service/product offering satisfy those needs? What might the customer "pay" for receiving this value?
- How large is the market? Is the product/service honed to support a mass market?
- Are there alternative offerings already in the market? How is the offering superior to them?
- Where is the industry in its evolution? Has a "dominant design" emerged? Strategic requirements are likely to be different in the pre- and post-paradigmatic periods.[33]
- What are the (contractual) structures needed to combine the activities that must be performed to deliver value to the consumer? Both lateral and vertical integration and outsourcing issues need to be considered. (Contract theory/transaction cost economics is a useful lens through which to view many of these issues. So is capability theory.)
- What will it cost to provide the product/service? How will those costs behave as volume and other factors change?

- What is the nature of the appropriability regime? How can imitators be held at bay, and how should value be delivered, priced, and appropriated?

As the author has noted in previous work, beyond specifying a realistic revenue architecture, designing a business model also involves determining the set of lateral (complementary) and vertical activities that must be performed and assessing whether and how they can be performed sufficiently cheaply to enable a profit to be earned, and who is to perform them. It involves figuring out the market entry strategy—while entry timing is a strategic, rather than a business model, issue, it may depend in part on the business model employed, particularly the complements already in place.[34]

When establishing a new business there is likely to be uncertainty with respect to all of the above. Disappointments are certain to arise as a new business is built, but success rates can be improved if the architects of the business model learn quickly and are able to adjust within a range that still yields a satisfactory profit.

Of course, once a business model is successfully established, changing technology and

enhanced competition will require more than defenses against imitation. It is also likely that even successful business models will at some point need to be revamped, and possibly even abandoned. For example, as the value proposition associated with the traditional personal computer software licensing model (whereby periodic updates would require the purchase of new software licenses and additional maintenance costs) has weakened for some customers, Microsoft has changed elements of its business model to allow renting so as to compete with cheap or free Web alternatives. According to one source, Microsoft is "overhauling not only what it makes but how to deliver and charge for it."[35] Microsoft has apparently begun to offer its Exchange e-mail server program for a monthly fee, as well as a barebones version of Office for free, supported in part by online advertising. (In fact, it appears now to be offering some products under the freemium philosophy described earlier.) The evidence is not yet in as to whether it will work well for both Microsoft and its customers.

Clearly, designing good business models is in part an art. The chances of good design are greater if entrepreneurs and managers have a deep understanding of user needs, consider multiple alternatives, analyze the value chain thoroughly so as to understand just how to deliver what the customer wants in a cost-effective and timely fashion, adopt a neutrality or relative efficiency perspective to outsourcing decisions, and are good listeners and fast learners. Useful tools include the various types of market research that lead to a deep understanding of the user, along with elements of the Profiting from Innovation framework such as the innovation cycle, appropriability regimes, complementary assets, and intellectual property systems.

The selection/design of business models is a key microfoundation of dynamic capabilities—the sensing, seizing, and reconfiguring skills that the business enterprise needs if it is to stay in sync with changing markets,[36] and which enable it not just to stay alive but to adapt to and itself shape the (changing) business environment. Dynamic capabilities help govern evolutionary fitness, and help shape the business environment itself. Get the business model wrong, and there is almost no chance of business success—get it right, and customize it for a market segment and build in

non-imitable dimensions, and it will contribute to the firm's competitive advantage.

Magretta claims that business models are "variations on the generic value chain underlying all businesses." This view would seem to overlook that a business model is only partly about how to organize the value chain—it is also about figuring out the value proposition to the customer as well as the value capture mechanism. A sustainable business model is as much (as the current author has noted) about where to position within the value chain (i.e., what are the key bottleneck assets to own/control in order to capture value). Clearly, the industry must perform various activities in the value chain—but which one(s) the firm chooses to undertake is very much a business model choice.

Recognized (but not fully developed here) is the notion that a business model cannot be assessed in the abstract; its suitability can only be determined against a particular business environment or context. Neither business strategies, business structures, nor business models can be properly calibrated absent assessment of the business environment; and of course the business environment itself is, in part, a choice variable: that is, firms can both select a business environment and be selected by it, and they can also shape their environment.

Zott and Amit bravely endeavor to hypothesize as to the appropriate mapping of business models to two product market choices: cost leadership and differentiation.[37] However, our state of understanding as to the precise relationship between business model choice and enterprise performance is both highly context-dependent and rather primitive. In certain contexts (e.g., market entry strategies for innovators), testable propositions have been advanced (including by the current author), but strategic studies will have to advance further as a field before mapping can be anything other than suggestive.

Of course, it may very well take time to get a business model right. Pioneers, in particular, are often forced to make only educated guesses as to what customers want, what they will pay for, and the cost structures associated with various ways to organize. As the author's "Profiting from Innovation" paper discusses, especially in the pre-paradigmatic industry evolution phase, it is necessary to stay flexible; experiment with the product and the business model and learn, both from one's own and one's competitors' activities; and to keep sufficient financial resources on hand to remain an industry participant—and hopefully the market leader—by the time the "dominant design" emerges in the market. Indeed, one hopes to be the promoter/owner of this dominant design—and to have the capacity to capitalize on the situation.

CONCLUSION

All businesses, either explicitly or implicitly, employ a particular business model. A business model describes the design or architecture of the value creation, delivery, and capture mechanisms employed. The essence of a business model is that it crystallizes customer needs and ability to pay, defines the manner by which the business enterprise responds to and delivers value to customers, entices customers to pay for value, and converts those payments to profit through the proper design and operation of the various elements of the value chain. Put differently, a business model reflects management's hypothesis about what customers want, how they want it and what they will pay, and how an enterprise can organize to best meet customer needs and get paid well for doing so. The goal of this article has been to advance understanding of the considerable significance of business models and to explore their connections to business strategy, innovation management, and economic theory.

One key conclusion of the analysis is that, to be a source of competitive advantage, a business model must be something more than just a good logical way of doing business. A model must be honed to meet particular customer needs. It must also be non-imitable in certain respects, either by virtue of being hard to replicate or by being unpalatable for competitors to replicate because it would disturb relationships with existing customers, suppliers, or important alliance partners. A business model may be difficult for competitors to replicate for other reasons too. There may be complicated process steps or strong intellectual property protection, or organizational structures and arrangements may exist that will stand in the way of implementing a new business model. Good business model design and implementation involves assessing such internal factors as well as external factors concerned with customers, suppliers, and the broader business environment.

The paucity of literature (both theoretical and practical) on the topic is remarkable, given the importance of business design, particularly in the context of innovation. The economics literature has failed to even flag the importance of the phenomenon, in part because of an implicit assumption that markets are perfect or very nearly so. The strategy and organizations literature has done little better. Like other interdisciplinary topics, business models are frequently mentioned but rarely analyzed; therefore, they are often poorly understood. Not surprisingly, it is common to see great technological achievements fail commercially because little, if any, attention has been given to designing a business model to take them to market properly.

This can and should be remedied. Increased understanding of the essence of business models and their place in the corpus of the social and organizational sciences should help our understanding of a variety of subjects including market behavior, competition, innovation, strategy and competitive advantage. Our understanding of the nature of the firm itself, together with the role of entrepreneurs and managers in the economy and in society, should also benefit from a better appreciation of business models and their role in entrepreneurship, innovation, and business performance.

ENDNOTES

[1] There are other (related) definitions of a business model. See R. Amit and C. Zott, Value creation in e-business, *Strategic Management Journal* 22, 493–520 (2001); and C. Zott and R. Amit, The fit between product market strategy and business model: implications for firm performance, *Strategic Management Journal* 29, 1–26 (2008) define a business model as "the structure, content, and governance of transaction" between the focal firm and its exchange partners (e.g., customers, vendors, complementors). For yet another alternate definition, see Chesbrough and Rosenbloom (see following).

[2] H. Chesbrough and R. S. Rosenbloom, The role of the business model in capturing value from innovation: evidence from xerox corporation's technology, *Industrial and Corporate Change* 11(3), 529–555 (2002).

[3] The end of the free lunch—again, *The Economist* 390(8623) (March 21, 2009).

[4] See K. Arrow, *The Limits of Organization,* Norton, New York (1974). The Arrow–Debreu model of competitive equilibrium has everything priced; but, as Arrow himself notes elsewhere, "in a strictly technical and objective sense, the price system does not work. You simply cannot price certain things" (p. 22) and "trust and similar values, loyalty and truth telling—are not commodities for which trade in the open market is technically possible or even meaningful" (p. 23). "A firm . . . provides another major area within which price relations are held in partial abeyance" (p. 25).

[5] The structure-conduct-performance paradigm in the field of industrial organization is possibly an exception. It stressed that concentrated markets were more profitable. If translated into management/strategy nostrums, as Michael Porter, *Competitive Strategy,* Free Press (1982), did, it suggest the benefits of either scale or differentiation as profit drivers. While scale and differentiation may still assist as profit drivers, the situation in the modern economy is that in many circumstances, these nostrums can be quite misleading.

[6] O. E. Williamson, *Organizational innovation: the transaction-cost approach (1983),* in J. Ronen (ed.), Lexington Books, Lexington, MA (1983).

[7] R. Miles, G. Miles, C. Snow, K. Blomquist, and H. Rocha, Business Models, Organizational Forms, and Managerial Values, working paper, UC Berkeley, Haas School of Business (2009). The authors note how new business models, new organizational forms, new management approaches, and entrepreneurship are the foci of different groups of scholars who rarely meet.

[8] G. Porter, *The Rise of Big Business, 1860–1910,* Harland Davidson, Arlington Heights, Illinois (1973), p. 49.

[9] C. W. Ebeling, Evolution of a box: the invention of the intermodal shipping container revolutionized the international transportation of goods, *Invention and Technology* (2009), 8–9.

[10] Apple's iTunes music store is an example of a business model innovation, and was the first legal pay-as-you-go method for downloading music. *Time* magazine hailed it as "the coolest invention for 2003."

[11] See C. Shapiro and H. Varian, *Information Rules: A Strategic Guide to the Network Economy,* Harvard Business School Press, Boston, MA (1999). The rules for strategic engagement that they promulgate are core elements of strategy in the information

services sector, and here—as elsewhere—the design of business models to support sustainable competitive advantage must be informed by strategy analysis.

[12] A. Shuen, *Web 2.0: A Strategy Guide* O'Reilly, Sebastopol (2008), p. 2.

[13.] See also J. B. Harreld, C. A. O'Reilly and M. L. Tushman, Dynamic capabilities at IBM: driving strategy into action, *California Management Review* 49(4) (2007).

[14] M. Dell, *The Early Entrepreneurial Years in Starting a Business,* Harvard Business School Press (2008). Indeed, a critical element of Dell's success is not just the way it has organized the value chain but also the products that it decides to sell through its distribution system. The initial products were personal computers, but now include printers, digital projectors, and computer-related electronics.

[15.] Quoted in J. Magretta, Why business models matter, *Harvard Business Review* 6 (2002).

[16] For an insightful treatment of the Google story, see D. A. Vise, *The Google Story,* Bantam Dell, New York (2008).

[17] See J. M. de Figueiredo and D. J. Teece, Mitigating procurement hazards in the context of innovation, *Industrial and Corporate Change* 5(2) (1996) for an analysis of some ways to mitigate the hazards of competing with one's suppliers.

[18] S. Lippman and R. Rumelt, Uncertain imitability: an analysis of interfirm differences in efficiency under competition, *Bell Journal of Economics* 13, 413–438 (1982).

[19] D. J. Teece, Profiting from technological innovation: implications for integration, collaboration, licensing and public policy, *Research Policy* 15(6), 285–305 (1986); D. J. Teece, Reflections on profiting from technological innovation, *Research Policy* 35(8), 1131–1146 (2006).

[20] See D. J. Teece (1986) ibid.; and G. Pisano and D. J. Teece, How to capture value from innovation: shaping intellectual property and industry architecture, *California Management Review* 50(1), 278–296 (2007).

[21] D. J. Teece, The multinational enterprise: market failure and market power considerations, *Sloan Management Review* 22(3), 3–17 (1981).

[22] S. Winter, The logic of appropriability: from Schumpeter to Arrow to Teece, *Research Policy* 35, 1100–1106 (2006).

[23] D. J. Teece, Explicating dynamic capabilities: the nature and microfoundations

of (sustainable) enterprise performance, *Strategic Management Journal* 28(13), 1319–1350 (2007).

[24] An application of the framework in the biotech industry context is discussed in G. Pisano, *Science Business: The Promise, the Reality, and the Future of Biotech,* Harvard Business School Press (2006), which includes a careful analysis of the sources of failure in the market for know-how.

[25] For further development of this idea, see W. Davidow, *High Technology Marketing,* Free Press (1986).

[26] R. Coase, The problem of social cost, *Journal of Law and Economics* 3, 1–44 (1960).

[27] The proliferation of illegal digital downloads of recorded music has led recording companies to try to insist on (and sometimes achieve) so-called 360 contracts, so they can participate in all sources of revenue from their artists activities—branded clothing, performances, and other public appearances—as well as just recorded music.

[28] D. J. Teece (1986) op. cit. at Ref 19; D. Somaya and D. J. Teece, Patents, licensing and entrepreneurship: effectuating innovation in multi-invention contexts, in Sheshinki, Baumol, and Strom (eds.), *Entrepreneurship, Innovation, and the Growth of Free-Market Economies,* Princeton University Press (2007).

[29] D. Evans and R. Schmalensee, *Paying with Plastic,* MIT Press, Cambridge, MA (1999), p. 3.

[30] C. Shirky, *Here Comes Everybody: The Power of Organizing Without Organizations,* Penguin, New York (2008).

[31] See Claudia Eller, Little Love this Summer for A-List Movie Actors, *Los Angeles Times,* 29 June, 2009.

[32] http://ir.netflix.com (visited April 2007).

[33] See D. J. Teece (1986) op. cit. at Ref 19.

[34] W. Mitchell and Dual Clocks, Entry order influences on industry incumbents and newcomer market share and survival when specialized assets retain their value; *Strategic Management Journal* 12(2), 85–100 (1991).

[35] Peter Burrows, Microsoft defends its empire, *BusinessWeek,* p. 28 (6 July 2009).

[36] D. J. Teece, G. Pisano, and A. Shuen, Dynamic capabilities and strategic management, *Strategic Management Journal* 18(7), 509–533 (1997); D. J. Teece (2007), op. cit. at Ref 23; D. J. Teece, *Dynamic Capabilities and Strategic Management: Organizing for Innovation and Growth,* Oxford University Press (2009).

[37] C. Zott and R. Amit (2008), op. cit. at Ref 1.

The Power of Vision: Statements That Resonate

Sooksan Kantabutra
Madihol University, Bangkok, Thailand

Gayle C. Avery
Macquarie University, Sydney, Australia

In a fast-changing world, the question for many senior managers is: "What leadership strategy is needed for my organization to stay competitive and to thrive?" To many academics and consultants, visionary leadership or leadership with vision as a core component is the answer. Although scholars, corporate trainers, and management consultants often emphasize the importance of espousing a vision and even suggest characteristics of an effective vision, no one really knows what such a vision looks like (Avery, 2004). In today's corporate world, we can observe that vision statements appear with a wide variety of characteristics, as these examples demonstrate:

> Year after year, Westin and its people will be regarded as the best and most sought after hotel and resort management group in North America. (Westin Hotels & Resorts)

> FirstEnergy will be a leading regional energy provider, recognized for operational excellence, customer service and its commitment to safety; the choice for long-term growth, investment value and financial strength; and a company driven by the leadership, skills, diversity and character of its employees. (FirstEnergy)

> Macy's, Inc., is a premier national retailer with brands that reflect the spirit of America. The timeless values that made our nation strong are the same values that make our company strong:
>
> - A belief in the promise of the future with the energy and determination to get us there.
> - A belief that our heritage mirrors the optimism, inclusion and integrity that provide for both stability and growth.
> - A belief that taking advantage of the right opportunities will continue to lead us to success in all that we do. (Macy's, Inc.)

Adding to the confusion is when practitioners and consultants have great difficulty in differentiating vision from other related terms of mission, values, beliefs, principles, and strategy. This is illustrated in Sage Software's "Corporate Vision and Strategy" as follows:

> As Sage Software has grown, we've been guided by a simple statement of purpose: to help make it easier for our customers to manage their business processes. Standing behind that purpose are our principles for operating the business—with a focus on agility, innovation, trust and integrity, and simplicity—all of which keep us closely connected with our customers. . . .
>
> We are confident in achieving those successes for our customers and have developed a strategy to guide our efforts. With the support of our customers, and through the dedication of our employees and partners, we invite you to share in that vision.

Some organizations already have a vision, but how effective is it? How should senior managers go about developing an effective vision? We know that vision is the starting point of any organizational transformation process and should

Reprinted from "The Power of Vision: Statements that Resonate," by Sooksan Kantabutra and Gayle C. Avery, *Journal of Business Strategy* 31, no. 1 (2010), pp. 37–45. Copyright © Emerald Group Publishing Limited. All rights reserved.

underpin business strategy. But senior managers have often been developing vision statements unaware of what the empirical evidence tells us about constructing an effective vision. According to many leadership scholars, senior managers need to distinguish between "strong" and "weak" visions (Rafferty and Griffin, 2004), as well as "positive" and "negative" (Senge, 1990) visions to ensure their vision is effective. This is particularly important in geographically dispersed organizations where people down the line must share the same vision. Given that senior managers want to develop a "right" vision, knowing about the latest research findings about vision is critical.

We first investigated this issue among retailers in Sydney, the most populous city of Australia (Kantabutra and Avery, 2007), and then their counterparts in Thailand's Bangkok, one of Asia's most populous cities (Kantabutra, 2008a). Our findings reveal that powerful visions that make a significant impact on customer and employee satisfaction—the bottom line of any business—possess certain characteristics: conciseness, clarity, abstractness, challenge, future orientation, stability, and desirability or the ability to inspire. We found similar results by examining the vision statements of *Fortune*'s "Best Companies to Work For," a set of high-performing organizations from a wide range of industries in the USA (Levering and Moskowitz, 2002). Our research has led us to believe that these findings about the characteristics of powerful visions have important implications for leaders working across a wide range of industries, and possibly across different cultures.

Even if one already accepts that vision is critical to organizational performance, our research has identified a few practical guidelines for creating effective visions. In this article, we analyze and describe characteristics of effective visions, and offer practical tips for leaders.

VISIONS THAT WORK

For almost three decades, scholars have argued that vision is important to leadership, strategy implementation, and change. Kenneth Leithwood and colleagues (Leithwood et al., 1996) even point out that vision building is intended to create a fundamental, ambitious sense of purpose, one

to be pursued over many years. Despite its clear importance in the management literature, vision is still not defined in a generally agreed-upon manner (Kantabutra and Avery, 2002). This is a critical issue because how we define *vision* affects how it is espoused by practicing managers and studied by scholars. Indeed, a survey of practicing managers found little agreement as to what they thought *vision* is (Baetz and Bart, 1996), and in the corporate world today there is no commonly agreed definition for a vision.

Avoiding the definitional issue altogether, Robert Baum and his colleagues (Baum et al., 1998) chose not to define vision in advance, but to accept the term as each *individual leader defines it*. They argued that it is the leader's actual vision that guides his or her choices and actions. This approach makes sense to us for three reasons. First, each leader develops a vision in his or her own way, sometimes rationally and objectively, often intuitively and subjectively. Second, visionary leadership often varies from leader to leader on important dimensions. For example, vision has been found to differ based on the leader's style, the content of the vision, and the context in which it takes root. Third, every leader induces his/her followers to act on the vision by using a range of techniques, such as legitimate authority, modeling, intellectual stimulation, goal setting, rewarding and punishing, organizational restructuring, and team building.

Adopting the definition based upon what individual leaders regard as a vision offers a pragmatic way around the definitional confusion in the vision literature. This approach was adopted by Robert Baum and colleagues (Baum et al., 1998) in their study of American start-up firms. They found that vision—based upon the definition espoused by each individual leader—had a statistically significant and positive impact on venture growth. Therefore, we adopted this vision definition for both our Sydney and Bangkok studies.

WHAT DO "POWERFUL" VISIONS LOOK LIKE?

Although business strategy and leadership writers have proposed different characteristics that a vision should have, some commonly shared characteristics can be identified (Kantabutra, 2008b). These include:

1. Conciseness.
2. Clarity.
3. Future orientation.
4. Stability.
5. Challenge.
6. Abstractness.
7. Desirability or ability to inspire.

These seven vision characteristics hold varying degrees of empirical support in the research literature, as well as face validity among managers. Nonetheless, few if any studies have incorporated all of them into a single vision construct for thorough empirical testing. This is the approach that we followed in our research.

Both our retail store studies used the above framework to explore the relationship between vision characteristics and organizational performance, as measured by customer and employee satisfaction. Both these measures are regarded as leading indicators of financial performance.

In the real world, many factors potentially affect organizational performance, and need to be taken into account by researchers. These are known as vision "realization factors." In our research, we included the following factors that previous research indicated were likely to affect realizing a vision:

• Communicating the vision.
• Aligning organizational processes and systems to suit the vision.
• Empowering others to act to achieve the vision.
• Motivating staff.

We hypothesized that rating higher on these factors would demonstrate the existence of a more powerful vision. We further predicted that more powerful visions would be associated with stronger organizational performance.

THE SAMPLES

The samples were drawn from apparel stores in Sydney and in Bangkok that sell brand-new, finished clothing products for individual use, excluding shoes and accessories. Both independent stores and those belonging to a parent company were sampled. All were located in a shopping mall and had their own identity, being in a clearly defined walled area.

A total of 19 of Sydney's major shopping centers were selected and all qualifying stores approached. Of these, 111 stores (70 percent) agreed to participate, with 48 stores (30 percent) declining. From the participating stores, store managers and up to three staff and three customers were interviewed. Store managers refer to those full-time store employees who manage their own stores and are stationed there daily. The latter criterion is important because we were interested in the effects of one manager's vision only. Staff includes full-time, part-time, and casual employees working under the store managers. Customers comprise individuals who were observed buying a product during our visit. If no customer was observed buying during our visit, we returned later until three customers agreed to participate or three visits were made to the store. One hundred and forty-eight staff members and 214 customers participated in our Sydney study.

A total of 12 malls in major Bangkok shopping areas were selected. All qualifying stores in each center were approached. Of these, 126 stores (88.7 percent) agreed to participate, with 16 stores (11.3 percent) declining. From the participating shops, store managers and up to half of each store's total staff members were asked to respond to store manager and staff questionnaires. Based on the number of staff determined for each store, the same number of customers for each respective store was also asked to respond to a customer questionnaire. If no customer was observed buying during our visit, we returned later until the determined number of customers agreed to participate or three visits were made to the store. Store managers, staff, and customers were defined in the same way as those of the Sydney samples. A total of 251 staff members and 258 customers were surveyed in Bangkok.

The store managers were asked to answer questions concerning their vision and organizational alignment, while staff members were asked about vision communication, motivation, and empowerment, as well as their level of job satisfaction. Customers responded to questions concerning their level of customer satisfaction with the store.

DOES VISION MAKE A DIFFERENCE?

From our results, we confirmed prior findings that powerful business visions possess all seven characteristics—conciseness, clarity, abstractness, challenge, future orientation, stability, and desirability or inspiration. Robert Baum and colleagues (Baum et al., 1998) were among the first who found positive relationships between vision characteristics of brevity, challenge, future orientation, aspiring, abstractness, clarity, stability and vision content, and organizational performance in entrepreneurial firms. They surveyed CEOs of architectural woodwork firms, and found that vision characteristics and vision content were directly related to venture growth, as measured by sales, profits, employment, and net worth in these entrepreneurial firms. These vision characteristics were strongly related to venture growth through their effects on vision communication. In our Australian study, we discovered that when one or more of the seven characteristics were missing from a vision, there was no significant effect on either staff or customer satisfaction. Visions with the seven characteristics also impacted the satisfaction of both customers and staff in Bangkok retail stores in significant, positive ways. How each characteristic combines with the other six characteristics to create this effect is explained next.

A vision's conciseness is indicated by whether the vision statement is brief; effective visions contain between 11 and 22 words, rendering them easy to communicate and remember. This was the case in both retail studies where concise visions were indeed frequently communicated.

Clear visions directly point at a prime goal. They can be understood without extended presentation and discussion, often in five minutes. The following is an example of a store manager vision that rates highly on both conciseness and clarity: "to be known as the most interesting store in Sydney."

At the same time, however, powerful visions certainly do not consist of a one-time, specific goal or productivity target (e.g., sales or profit) that can be met and then discarded. They are also abstract, such as the example above. After all, a vision is meant to act as a guide for a wide range of business activities over a long period of time. More critically, abstract visions suggest a longer-term goal that also allows for individual interpretations. This characteristic provides a basis for achieving support from a broader base of stakeholders. This abstractness also allows staff members to apply their own creativity within the framework of their store manager's vision as they carry out daily store operations. An example of a vision rated highly on abstractness is: "to be the market leader in fashionability." This abstract vision allows staff members from all store functions (e.g., designers, front officers, and even support officers) to interpret the vision in their own creative ways as they carry out daily store operations for their store to become "the market leader in fashionability."

In addition, effective visions are challenging—being challenged motivates staff members to try their best to achieve desired outcomes. Challenging visions possess a high but achievable degree of difficulty enabling staff members to enhance their self-esteem as they seek to achieve the store's vision. In our studies, challenging visions usually aim at achieving a national or international status for the store and/or its brand, such as "to be the best retailer in Australia."

Powerful visions clearly indicate the long-term perspective of the business, and the future environment in which it functions. This is because a vision has no power to inspire staff members or attract their commitment unless it offers a view of a clearly better future.

In addition, powerful visions are *stable*. They do not shift in response to short-term trends, technology changes, or market changes, although they must be flexible enough to weather fluctuations. An example of an effective vision with these two characteristics is: "to be the best retailer in New South Wales." This vision statement indicates the long-term perspective of the business (to be the best retailer) and the future environment in which it functions (New South Wales). It is also stable, because no matter how far it is projected into the future, being the best retailer will still be meaningful, despite any change in markets or technology.

Since the hallmark of management is achieving results through others, the ability to motivate staff is central to leadership. As a consequence, powerful visions must be highly desirable and inspiring. They state a goal that directly inspires staff.

An especially strong vision statement in our studies incorporating the seven characteristics is "to be the number one retailer in Australia." This vision statement is brief, pointing directly at a prime goal. Aiming to be the number one retailer in Australia makes this vision statement very challenging and inspiring. Unlikely to be affected by technology or market changes, it also indicates the long-term perspective of the organization and the future environment in which it functions. This vision statement is abstract, inclusive to all organizational interests. Anyone in the organization can use this vision to guide his/her daily operations. Some other powerful visions in our studies include:

> To remain the flagship store of the company by excellent customer service, having the best product and a beautiful store.

> To be the number one choice for youth in surfwear, streetwear and to also do this at the best quality yet the cheapest price.

> To bring the store to its full potential, giving it recognition as one of the best in the company.

HOW DOES VISION MAKE A DIFFERENCE?

Since the literature so consistently emphasizes the importance of vision sharing between leader and followers, we investigated this relationship further in the Sydney retail stores (Kantabutra and Avery, 2005). More specifically, we examined the relationships between vision components shared between store managers and their staff, the way store managers motivate and empower staff to achieve and sustain the shared vision, staff enactment of the vision, and both customer and staff satisfaction.

Instead of investigating the seven vision characteristics alone, these analyses also took into account vision content. It makes more sense to investigate both characteristics and content when it comes to understanding how vision is shared between the leader and followers. Vision content examined in our study focused on images relating to customer and staff satisfaction in the vision statement—because both staff and customer satisfaction are critical to organizational performance.

Our analysis reveals that the shared vision characteristics and content have positive, direct effects on both customer and staff satisfaction. Moreover, staff use of the shared vision to guide their daily operations; and employee motivation and empowerment are critical to staff satisfaction. The most surprising discovery, perhaps a convincing endorsement for the essence of shared vision, is that sharing both vision characteristics and vision content is especially important to customer and staff satisfaction. Simply sharing a vision is even more important than either the leader's efforts at motivation and empowerment, or employees actually using the shared vision to guide their daily activities.

In the Sydney study, in addition to shared vision being important, empowering staff directly improved customer satisfaction, while motivation and empowerment of staff directly predicted improvements in staff satisfaction. Organizational alignment and vision communication predicted improvements in staff satisfaction, but only indirectly.

The vision realization factors appear to operate differently in Bangkok retail stores. Motivation of staff is the only direct predictor of enhanced staff satisfaction, while empowerment of staff, organizational alignment, and vision communication indirectly predicted improvements in staff satisfaction. On the other hand, vision, vision communication, empowerment of staff, motivation of staff, and staff satisfaction indirectly predicted improvements in customer satisfaction.

DO THESE FINDINGS APPLY MORE BROADLY?

Of course, we must be careful about overstating the results of a few studies, even when they are built upon a foundation of earlier research. Thus, it is natural to ask, "Are these findings about vision specific to the retail industry?" In response to this question, we followed up the earlier studies with additional research aimed at determining whether these findings could apply in other industries.

To begin to answer this question, we analyzed 41 available vision statements from the 2002 *Fortune*'s "Best Companies to Work For." This sample comprised high-performing U.S.

companies from a wide range of industries. These organizations claim that their vision statements guide their strategic behaviors, strategies and plans.

Our analysis suggests that the vision statements used by these *Fortune* best companies also reflect the seven characteristics found in the Sydney and Bangkok research. Judged against the seven vision characteristics, the most powerful vision statement from our *Fortune* best companies sample is: "to be recognized as the best professional services firm in the world" (Deloitte Touche Tohmatsu). This vision statement is concise, pointing directly at a prime goal. It is unlikely to be affected by technology or market changes. Very challenging and desirable, this vision statement indicates the long-term perspective of the organization and the future environment in which it functions. No matter how large or dispersed the organization, everyone can use the vision to guide his or her daily operations because it is abstract. Other visions from the *Fortune* sample that strongly conform with the seven attributes are shown as follows:

> To provide the most useful and ethical financial services in the world. (Charles Schwab Corporation)
> To be a world-class provider of food and services. (Ukrop's Food Group)

This research leads us to believe that the seven characteristics of powerful visions found among Sydney and Bangkok apparel retailers, and previously among U.S. start-up firms, could apply across different industries and even cultures.

LINKING VISION AND RESULTS

At first glance, one may question what is so new and original about the samples of effective vision statements from both the Sydney and Bangkok retailers and the *Fortune* best companies. These sample vision statements may not appear to contain innovative ideas. In some cases, they highlight simple, known ideas. However, simplicity and banality do not limit the value of powerful visions.

Kotter (1999) found in his research that successful visions do not have to be brilliantly innovative; in fact, some of the best ones are not. Effective business visions can even have an almost mundane quality, often consisting of fundamental ideas that are already well known. We believe this is because a vision is used to guide organizational members, and therefore needs to encompass all organizational interests. That is, the more inclusive a vision, the more mundane. Although this quality seems obvious, Daft (2005) found in his research of business organizations that many visions fail to adequately involve employees. The more specific, unique, and innovative a vision statement, the less likely it will appeal to a wide range of organizational interests and stakeholders.

In addition, we found that the retail store managers' visions enhanced staff satisfaction in both Sydney and Bangkok. This applies especially to those managers who actively communicate their visions, model their visions through their own actions, and motivate and empower their staff to act on the visions. Furthermore, where store managers align store management systems to match their visions, staff satisfaction is enhanced. In such settings, visions displaying the seven characteristics also positively affected the satisfaction of both customers and staff. This is important because customer and staff satisfaction are frequently correlated with financial and other performance measures.

HOW DIFFERENTLY SHOULD MANAGERS NOW DEVELOP A VISION?

Clearly, more research is still needed into characteristics of powerful visions and vision realization factors. However, our studies, building on prior research, suggest several interesting practical implications. An organizational vision should be shared by organizational members. Vision sharing can be developed when each manager first develops a vision and then communicates it to organizational members or when all organizational members derive a vision. In particular, research suggests that visions that are concise, clear, future-oriented, stable, challenging, abstract, and inspiring are likely to bring about better performance outcomes than visions without these characteristics. Appropriate realization factors should also be put in place. For example, the vision should be aligned with the strategy, and the people empowered.

Some specific guidelines for developing a vision are provided below. A leader should espouse a vision that:

- Is brief (so that it can be remembered and repeated easily).
- Contains a prime goal to be achieved.
- Can encompass all organizational interests.
- Is not a one-time, specific goal that can be met and then discarded.
- Provides a source of motivation for employees to do their best by including a degree of difficulty or stretch (e.g., to achieve a national/international status).
- Offers a long-term perspective for the organization and indicates the future environment in which it will function.

- Is unlikely to be changed by market or technology changes.
- Is viewed as desirable by employees.

Visions containing these characteristics are expected to bring about higher performance outcomes, initially through employee and customer satisfaction, than those without.

Simply having a vision that meets the above criteria is not enough. To maximize performance outcomes, managers should also communicate the vision, motivate and empower employees to act on the vision, and align organizational systems to support the vision. As for employees, the research suggests that they too benefit when managers are able to create and shape a vision meeting the attributes described here. This enables followers to work more effectively, and leads to higher job satisfaction. Therefore, managers who work effectively with a powerful vision could benefit from being aware of these characteristics and realization factors.

REFERENCES

Avery, G. C. (2004), *Understanding Leadership,* Sage Publications, London.

Baetz, M. C. and Bart, C. K. (1996), "Developing mission statements which work," *Long Range Planning,* Vol. 29 No. 4, pp. 524–31.

Baum, J. R., Locke, E. A. and Kirkpatrick, S. A. (1998), "A longitudinal study of the relation of vision and vision communication to venture growth in entrepreneurial firms," *Journal of Applied Psychology,* Vol. 83, pp. 43–54.

Daft, R. L. (2005), *The Leadership Experience,* Thomson South-Western, Mason, OH.

Kantabutra, S. (2008a), "Vision effects in Thai retail stores: practical implications," *International Journal of Retail & Distribution Management,* Vol. 36 No. 4, pp. 323–42.

Kantabutra, S. (2008b), "What do we know about vision?" *Journal of Applied Business Research,* Vol. 24 No. 2, pp. 127–38.

Kantabutra, S. and Avery, G. C. (2002), "Proposed model for investigating relationships between vision components and business unit performance," *Journal of Management and Organization,* Vol. 8 No. 2, pp. 22–39.

Kantabutra, S. and Avery, G. C. (2005), "Essence of shared vision: empirical investigation," *New Zealand Journal of Human Resources Management,* Vol. 5, pp. 1–28.

Kantabutra, S. and Avery, G. C. (2007), "Vision effects in customer and staff satisfaction: an empirical investigation," *Leadership & Organization Development Journal,* Vol. 28 No. 3, pp. 209–29.

Kotter, J. P. (1999), *What Do Leaders Really Do?* Harvard Business School Press, Boston, MA.

Leithwood, K., Tomlinson, D. and Genge, M. (1996), "Transformational school leadership," in Leithwood, K., Chapman, J., Corson, D., Hallinger, Ph. and Hart, A. (Eds.), *International Handbook of Educational Leadership and Administration,* Kluwer, Dordrecht.

Levering, R. and Moskowitz, M. (2002), "Best companies to work for: the best in the worst of times," *Fortune,* Vol. 145 No. 3, pp. 148–68.

Rafferty, A. E. and Griffin, M. A. (2004), "Dimensions of transformational leadership: conceptual and empirical extensions," *The Leadership Quarterly,* Vol. 15 No. 3, pp. 329–54.

Senge, P. M. (1990), *The Fifth Discipline: The Art and Practice of the Learning Organization,* Currency Doubleday, New York, NY.

Finding Your Strategy in the New Landscape

Pankaj Ghemawat

IESE Business School,
University of Navarra, Spain

The 2008 crash hit cross-border business hard. The value of international trade was projected to decline by as much as 9% in 2009. Foreign direct investment has plunged even more: After dropping 15% in 2008, it fell by more than 40% in 2009. Though we may have reached the bottom, the prospects for the medium term don't look promising. For much of the next decade, we can reasonably expect to see weak global growth, pressures from overcapacity, persistently high unemployment, volatility in the financial markets, costlier capital, a greatly expanded role for governments, a much larger burden of regulation and taxation for all, and maybe even increased protectionism. If we experience a second crash, as some experts worry, these conditions could all worsen.

It goes without saying that global firms must factor these developments into their strategies in the new decade. For some, the response will be to retrench and focus on home markets. This already seems to be happening: If you look at the annual reports of the world's 100 largest companies, you'll find that the percentage of firms in developed economies that emphasized international or global business in their letters to shareholders declined from 51% in 2006 to 31% in 2008. (In contrast, the percentage increased among the few companies from emerging economies in the group.) And use of the words "global" and "globalization," while up significantly, was mostly in references to the economic slowdown and its impact on company performance.

Becoming homebodies, however, may be a bad idea for firms based in the developed world. Early data for 2009 indicate that China accounted for 66% of global growth in GDP (excluding countries with negative growth) and India for 11%. Indonesia accounted for the third-largest portion, 4%. Though 2009 was an abnormal year—developed economies will snap back—the economic clout of big emerging markets, particularly China and India, is likely to increase over the next few decades, not just the next few years. According to recent World Bank projections, by 2050 China and India will together account for nearly 50% of global GDP—about the same as the G7's current share, which is expected to decline to 25%. (These GDP figures are all nominal and not adjusted for purchasing power parity.) And since per capita incomes in China and India are projected to be only one-half to one-third the size of those in advanced economies, there's room for even higher growth rates in these markets after 2050. The same holds true in many other emerging markets as well.

That said, managers cannot afford to ignore the risks of pursuing a global strategy in the uncertain years ahead. To successfully negotiate the rockier path before them, they must change their strategic approach in several dimensions. My purpose in these pages is to suggest what direction they might take across this new, more rugged terrain. I'll look first at how the crisis affects a company's basic strategic environment and then explore how that translates into changes in product and market focus, organizational and supply chain structures, talent management choices, and, of increasing importance, the management of corporate reputation and identity. In other words, I'll take you through the hub and spokes of a typical strategy wheel, outlining the steps that firms should consider taking with each. (See the exhibit "New Strategy Directions.")

STRATEGY AND COMPETITION

Most companies' global strategies have been based on a vision of a world that's steadily, even rapidly, becoming more integrated, where the key challenge is keeping up with that integration. But given what we've witnessed in the past two years, it makes more sense to adopt a vision in which national differences remain pronounced (and may become even more so), and managing those differences is the primary challenge. Companies whose strategies currently emphasize smoothing differences and achieving economies of scale across national boundaries may need to shift toward adapting to local conditions. Companies whose strategies emphasize arbitrage—taking advantage of differences—may need to make the same shift; now is not the time to be perceived as an exploitative foreigner.

Resource allocation processes will have to change, too. During the years of rising asset prices, many companies came to think of global strategy as one long asset-accumulation play that involved relatively little risk. The idea was to invest abroad and, if that didn't work out, resell at a capital gain. That may be why, according to a survey of *HBR* readers, 88% of managers in precrisis days thought of global strategy as an imperative, almost an article of faith, rather than as a set of options to be carefully evaluated.

New Strategy Directions

Companies need to rethink their strategies in response to the changed economic landscape. This wheel describes the adjustments they should consider for each component of strategy.

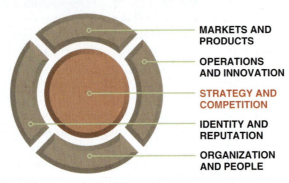

- MARKETS AND PRODUCTS
- OPERATIONS AND INNOVATION
- STRATEGY AND COMPETITION
- IDENTITY AND REPUTATION
- ORGANIZATION AND PEOPLE

STRATEGY AND COMPETITION

Adapt to local differences

Invest more selectively

Watch for emerging-market competition

MARKETS AND PRODUCTS

Focus on underserved segments everywhere

Recognize price pressures

Cultivate requisite variety

OPERATIONS AND INNOVATION

Rethink the scope of offshoring

Simplify supply chains

Import process innovations from emerging economies

Move R&D to where the researchers and the market growth are

ORGANIZATION AND PEOPLE

Re-create country manager functions

Relocate key functions

Develop a globally representative talent pool

Exploit communication technologies

IDENTITY AND REPUTATION

Build a strong corporate identity

Emphasize corporate citizenship

Restore the reputation of business in general

Idea in Brief

In the aftermath of the 2008 crash **demand will remain weak for several years,** with governments taking a more active, possibly protectionist role. Many companies will need to try harder to adapt to local norms. Firms also must be more discriminating about investments and pay more attention to emerging-market competitors and to rebuilding their own reputations.

The large developing economies still represent the best market opportunities, but companies will need to expand into underserved segments in richer countries. This will mean offering more-customized products at lower prices. Emerging economies will also play a bigger role in both process and product innovation.

The organizational power of the local country unit will grow, and firms will transfer more key functions away from the home base. At the same time they will have to cultivate a more diverse talent pool to reflect the new organizational reality. Managing a more diverse workforce will require a strong corporate identity and investments in communication technologies.

Now that the bubble has burst, many firms are being reminded that a significant portion of their global operations subtract, rather than add, economic value. This isn't just a result of the crisis; it was true in the years leading up to the downturn. Of course, some global investments will pay off in the long run. Nevertheless, in a postbubble world, where the cost and even the availability of capital are issues, firms will need to be more ruthless about terminating long-standing loss makers—and more selective in pursuing new opportunities. Some of this selectivity can be imposed by raising hurdle rates and tightening assumptions around terminal values. Some firms are also trying out other approaches, such as allocating resources according to their articulated strategic priorities. A number of large companies have turned on the investment spigots in China and, to a lesser extent, India—and for other platforms for growth—while tightening the financial taps elsewhere. Other companies have responded to resource constraints by offshoring, outsourcing, and forging strategic alliances (which seem to be on an upsurge).

Many companies from the developed world also need to widen their competitive focus. Last year, in the space of two weeks, I spoke with the two market leaders in a particular product category about globalization. It was clear that the two companies were mostly focused on each other. I tried to point out that if they considered China to be their major area for growth, it behooved them to pay at least as much attention to local Chinese competitors as they did to each other, especially since their sector was not R&D- or advertising-intensive (the two clear markers of multinational advantage). As the economies of China and other developing nations surge, they will produce formidable homegrown rivals, of ever larger size and reach—an issue that Thomas Hout and I reviewed in "Tomorrow's Global Giants? Not the Usual Suspects" (*HBR* November 2008).

Let's turn now to how these strategic shifts play out in the functional components of a multinational's strategy.

MARKETS AND PRODUCTS

When it comes to customers and product choices, three main changes are likely.

First, multinationals from advanced economies will have to rethink their customer targeting. In large emerging markets they have traditionally focused on the urban elite, who can buy premium products in upscale retail outlets. Going forward, companies will need to penetrate more geographies, channels, and income levels. Within China, many successful multinationals have already developed strategies at the provincial level and are now working at the level of clusters of cities and rolling inland from the coast. India is seeing a similar pattern.

At home, multinationals should also look for ways to target underserved segments. Walmart, for example, has begun a major push into U.S. urban markets. The top 15 metropolitan areas represent more than a third of the total U.S. market, but Walmart's share in them is only 4%, compared with 10% in the United States overall. The company's new urban strategy involves smaller store formats and more attention to mobilizing local political support.

Second, most markets will experience pressures on pricing. Economic weakness and extra capacity, and possibly a shift in the zeitgeist from excess to frugality, have already pushed prices downward. Expansion into poorer markets at home and abroad will intensify this trend. This will require companies to do some repositioning—even in the luxury products sector in booming markets such as China. According to *Forbes,* Tiffany has faltered in China because its stores are small and offer only a limited range of high-end products. Louis Vuitton and Gucci, in contrast, have prospered with larger stores that offer many items at price points of several hundred dollars, which appeal to the luxury "entrants" and to gift buyers, who account for a large portion of luxury purchases in China.

Finally, multinationals will have to develop products and services that are fundamentally different from what they're used to selling, as well as regional varieties of offerings, as local differences in, for instance, taste, price sensitivity, and infrastructures for service and delivery become more important. This is obviously a challenge: If it's hard for a company to recognize that what worked in New York isn't working in Mumbai, it will be even harder for it to recognize that what worked in Mumbai may not work in Nagpur. But the savvier players are already trying this approach. Nokia's 1,000-plus-employee R&D force in India has engaged in extensive product adaptation, some of it focused on rural and other lower-income markets. The results include a basic mobile phone that doubles as a flashlight for use during power outages and a phone designed to be shared by multiple people.

OPERATIONS AND INNOVATION

On the supply side, several interrelated shifts are taking place. The pressing need to reduce global trade imbalances from record and clearly

unsustainable levels, the rise of protectionism, and concerns about the environment are undermining the traditional "Chimerica" model, in which the United States imports large volumes of goods from China. Before the crisis, companies became accustomed to offshoring, but they should at least take a second look at the practice now. It's noteworthy that the U.S. global giants that were financially healthy and confident enough to make major operations investments recently have stressed that they made those investments at home. Intel, for example, has talked up its new U.S. semiconductor plants, and GE its new U.S. wind turbine facilities. Of course, these are just two particularly vivid examples; both companies continue to invest substantially if quietly overseas. But that holds its own lesson: When offshoring does make sense, managing the discourse around it is more important than ever.

Unless protectionism spikes, significant offshoring will most likely continue. But supply chains will need to become shorter, simpler, and more robust, which means they'll require major reconfiguration. In the recent past the division of tasks across countries became ever finer and more complex; the manufacture of some garments, for instance, might have involved as many as 40 processing steps in a dozen countries. Now increased concerns about the environment and sensitivity to energy prices, not to mention the possibility of protectionism, appear to be reversing that trend. A 2009 survey of logistics providers revealed that nearly one-quarter of North American and European clients had taken steps to shorten their supply chains during the previous year. In the airline industry, international carriers continue to debate the sustainability of flying empty aircraft to developing countries in Asia and Central America, where costs are lower, for routine maintenance.

Perspectives on skills and process innovations are also changing. Traditionally, companies tended to transfer older, less-automated technology to plants in less-developed countries. Those plants didn't contribute to technological advances. But recent reports on manufacturing firms—for instance, the global components survey sponsored by the Alfred P. Sloan Foundation—reveal that many Western multinationals have actually started to import some of their less-automated processes back into plants in high-wage regions. Their experience in low-wage countries has shown them that labor-intensive plants can be more flexible than, yet just as reliable as, more-automated plants. It also turns out that the gain in flexibility can more than compensate for the higher wage bill. The flow of knowledge and innovation in operations has begun to reverse, with plants in places like Mexico becoming models for plants in the United States.

A reversal is happening in product innovation, too. It's clear from labor projections that technical manpower is growing rapidly in emerging markets and that multinationals will have to shift the locus of R&D there. The projections forecast a shortfall in the global supply of many categories of engineers and other technical personnel, in a field already dominated by graduates of universities and technical schools in India and China. Consequently, large high-tech firms with interests in emerging markets are starting to think hard about basing their R&D efforts in those countries. Intel, in fact, has already designed one chip almost entirely in India: the Xeon 7400 processor, which it rolled out in 2008.

ORGANIZATION AND PEOPLE

As operational norms and patterns in learning and innovation begin to reflect the new opportunities and constraints, so too will norms around organizational structure and talent.

Before the crash, many companies were moving toward globally integrated structures. But the notion that we live in a world where the constituent parts of enterprises can and should be bound ever more tightly together has been challenged by contagion, economic volatility, and changing political sentiments. We may therefore see some organizational power flow back to country managers as companies tone down their attempts to eliminate or exploit cross-border differences and instead look to adapt to local conditions.

But in view of the other new priorities on the agenda—bringing lower-end products to market sooner; dealing with local rivals more aggressively; taking out costs in design and manufacturing; and expanding faster into new segments and territories—more changes are called for. Because local knowledge has become critical and the need to shorten learning and action cycles more

urgent, companies must go beyond simply setting up local operations and start building deep local connections. A number of companies have begun moving some key functions out of headquarters. IBM's global procurement office, for instance, is now located in Shenzhen, China. Cisco set up Cisco East as a second headquarters in Bangalore. Perhaps the most dramatic example is provided by the GM reorganization. The company's Mexican and Canadian operations will continue reporting to the person overseeing the United States, but operations pretty much everywhere else apart from Europe will now report to the head of China, which last year overtook the United States as the automaker's largest market in terms of number of vehicles supplied. This is a basic realignment of the power structure within a hitherto U.S.-centric GM: The China operation is now regarded by many as the more interesting part of the company. Looking forward, people are talking of more multinationals with dual headquarters, one in the West and one in Asia (most likely China).

Such organizational power shifts will demand fundamental changes in the diversity of management ranks. The profile of most large U.S. corporations still reflects past patterns of operations, rather than intended future patterns. Their management is still dominated by Americans, and few have really come to terms with diversity. A Boston Consulting Group study of large multinationals and their aspirations in 16 rapidly developing economies conducted before the crisis found a gross mismatch between the amount of growth targeted in these geographies (about 33% then, and probably more now) and the percentage of top personnel from or located in them (less than 10% then and probably now as well). Clearly, this is not sustainable.

Finally, we have to become much smarter about the way we manage interactions among diverse, far-flung employees. Although companies have globalized their footprints, their managers still communicate across geographies mostly by traveling to and fro, holding conference calls, and, to a lesser extent, e-mail. Companies rarely exploit the new collaborative tools of the Web, such as chat rooms and online bulletin boards, to build a stronger sense of community.

The challenges of cross-border communication can be quite subtle. Language barriers, for example, are less of a problem for those providing information than for those receiving it; it's easy for a Chinese manager to make a comprehensible presentation in English but harder to get people listening to it to invest in comprehension. Research shows, for example, that people very quickly tune out when they have trouble understanding an accent. Companies could do far more to take advantage of modern communications to close not only geographic but also cultural and demographic distances.

IDENTITY AND REPUTATION

Establishing a strong one-firm identity will be key to managing long-distance interactions in the days ahead. Firms that have clear and well-understood values and communication norms but also respect diversity are likely to deal better with cultural and national differences in developing, communicating, and executing strategies. Strong global leadership-development programs can also help—although in the present environment these seem to be subject to the same kinds of cuts as, say, golf tournament sponsorships. The general point is that firms will need to invest in organizational glue if they are to remain more than the sum of their parts.

The identity challenge posed in the new environment is not only internal. With government taking on an expanded role as investor, customer, regulator, and tax collector, corporate diplomacy is becoming a more important component of strategy in the postcrisis world. In such an environment, the insistence that the marketplace should completely dictate outcomes is unlikely to win friends and influence people. CEOs and other executives will need to spend more time managing government relationships.

Beyond simply dealing with the government, however, companies need to come to grips with the fact that the general reputation of business is at an all-time low. In a recent survey conducted in the United States, the Pew Research Center asked the public how much people in 10 occupations contributed to the well-being of society. Business executives were ranked at the very bottom of the group. Only 21% of respondents thought they contributed a lot, while 23% thought lawyers, the second-least-favored occupation, did. (The military and teaching professions ranked the highest; with scores of 84% and 77%, respectively.)

Though attitudes look a little bit more positive in emerging markets, the standing of capitalism and private business enterprise is being challenged in fundamental ways. Any company that wants to thrive in this environment has to reassess its efforts to bolster its reputation in particular and the reputation of business in general. Because it's not going to be business as usual!

Rebuilding the reputation of business may also help with the broader challenge of protectionism. Since studies show that protectionism flourishes when trust in economic institutions is low, the restoration of trust in business may help contain it.

That concludes our whirl around the strategy wheel. If there is one overarching message to take away from the trip, it's that for the typical multinational the postcrisis world requires a somewhat looser approach to strategy and organization than was popular just a few years ago. A second important message is that multinationals must increase diversity in their ranks but, at the same time, build cohesive corporate cultures and tighten their talent management practices. That creates a tension, of course. Nevertheless, developed-world companies have to become more cosmopolitan in their worldview and more discriminating in their investment choices. They still have time—but not much—to make that adjustment and to exploit what remain strong advantages in many sectors.

Getting into Your Competitor's Head

Hugh Courtney
University of Maryland

John T. Horn
McKinsey & Company

Jayanti Kar
McKinsey & Company

The global financial crisis that erupted in 2008 shows, with painful clarity, that we live in an interdependent business world. In bleak times and fair, the success of a company's strategy often depends greatly on the strategies of its competitors. In periods of financial turmoil, for instance, the prospects—and even survival—of a bank often depend on the near-term M&A of its rivals. Similarly, the ultimate success of Boeing's new commercial jet, the 787 Dreamliner, will depend on the way Airbus positions, markets, and sells its new and competing A380 and A350. Pfizer's ability to sustain market share and profitability in the market for cholesterol-lowering treatments will depend on the moves of the company's branded and generic pharmaceutical competitors, to say nothing of biotech and medical-product companies developing alternative treatments.

This strategic interdependence implies that the ability to anticipate your competitors' strategies is essential. Yet a recent survey of business executives found that the actions and reactions of potential rivals almost never play a role in, for example, decisions to introduce and price new products.[1] An important reason for this neglect, we believe, is that strategic-planning tools, such as game theory and scenario planning, are of limited use unless a company can correctly define the key elements of the strategic game, especially the strategic options and objectives of competitors. This is no easy task. Rare is the company that truly understands what its competitors and their decision makers care about most, how they perceive their assets and capabilities, and what all this means for their strategies. A company with such insights could reverse-engineer the moves of competitors and predict what they were likely to do. In a credit crunch, for instance, such a company would be well positioned to buy financial and nonfinancial assets at attractive prices if it knew that poorly capitalized competitors would avoid new risk and therefore not bid for these assets.

Getting inside your competitor's head is difficult because companies (and their decision makers) usually are not alike. At any time, a company has assets, resources, market positions, and capabilities it must protect, leverage, and build upon. Different endowments imply different strategies even in the same general market environment. What's more, even a competitor with similar endowments may pursue different strategies if its owners, stakeholders, and decision makers have a different objective.

So if you want to anticipate rather than react to strategic moves, you must analyze a competitor at two levels: organizational and individual. At the organizational level, you have to think like a strategist of your competitor by searching for the perfect strategic fit between its endowments and its changing market environment. At the

Reprinted from *McKinsey Quarterly* Issue 1 (2009), pp. 128–37. This article was originally published in McKinsey Quarterly, www.mckinseyquarterly.com. Copyright © 2009 McKinsey & Company. All rights reserved. Reprinted by permission.

individual level, you have to think like the decision makers of the competitor, identifying who among them makes which decisions and the influences and incentives guiding their choices. This approach moves you beyond the data-gathering efforts of most competitive-intelligence functions, toward a thought process that helps turn competitive intelligence into competitive insights. While our approach won't eliminate surprises, it will help you better understand your competitors and their likely moves and eliminate some of the guesswork that undermines the development of strategies in an increasingly interdependent business world.

THINK LIKE YOUR COMPETITOR'S STRATEGIST

When your competitor resembles you, chances are it will pursue similar strategies—what we call symmetric competition. When companies have different assets, resources, capabilities, and market positions, they will probably react to the same market opportunities and threats in different ways—what we call asymmetric competition. One of the keys to predicting a competitor's future strategies is to understand how much or little it resembles your company.

In the fast-food industry, for example, two leading players, McDonald's and Burger King, face the same market trends but have responded in markedly different ways to the obesity backlash. McDonald's has rolled out a variety of foods it promotes as healthy. Burger King has introduced high-fat, high-calorie sandwiches supported by in-your-face, politically incorrect ads. As the dominant player, McDonald's is the lightning rod for the consumer and government backlash on obesity. It can't afford to thumb its nose at these concerns. Smaller players like Burger King, realizing this, see an opportunity to cherry-pick share in the less health-conscious fast-food segment. Burger King competes asymmetrically.

Companies can determine whether they face symmetric or asymmetric competition by using the resource-based view of strategy: the idea that they should protect, leverage, extend, build, or acquire resources and capabilities that are valuable, rare, and

inimitable and that can be successfully exploited. Resources come in three categories: tangible assets (for example, physical, technological, financial, and human resources), intangible assets (brands, reputation, and knowledge), and current market positions (access to customers, economies of scale and scope, and experience). Capabilities come in two categories: the ability both to identify and to exploit opportunities better than others do.

In the video-game-console business, the strategies of Microsoft and Sony, which are attempting to dominate next-generation systems, are largely predictable—based on each company's tangible and intangible assets and current market position. Although the core businesses of the two competitors will be affected by video game consoles differently, both sides see them as potential digital hubs replacing some current stand-alone consumer electronic devices, such as DVD players, and interconnecting with high-definition televisions, personal computers, MP3 players, digital cameras, and so forth.

For Sony, which has valuable businesses in consumer electronics and in audio and video content, it is important to establish the PlayStation as the living-room hub, so that any cannibalization of the company's consumer electronics businesses comes from within. After the recent victory of Sony's Blu-ray standard over Toshiba's HD-DVD, Sony stands to realize a huge payoff in future licensing revenues. The PlayStation, which plays only Blu-ray disks, is thus one of the company's most important vehicles in driving demand for Blu-ray gaming, video, and audio content.

Microsoft has limited hardware and content businesses but dominates personal computers and network software. Establishing the Xbox as the living-room hub would therefore help to protect and extend its software businesses. For Microsoft, it is crucial that the "digital living room" of the future should run on Microsoft software. If an Apple product became the hub of future "iHome" living rooms, Microsoft's software business might suffer.

Sony and Microsoft therefore have different motives for fighting this console battle. Yet the current market positions (existing businesses and economies of scope), tangible assets (patents, cash), and intangible assets (knowledge, brands) of both companies suggest that they will compete aggressively to win. It was predictable that they would produce consoles which, so far, have been far superior technologically to previous systems and interconnect seamlessly with the Internet, computers, and a wide variety of consumer electronics devices. It was also predictable that both companies would price their consoles below cost to establish an installed base in the world's living rooms quickly. The competition to win exclusive access to the best third-party developers' games, as well as consumer mind-share, will also probably continue to be waged more aggressively than it was in previous console generations. For Microsoft and Sony, the resource-based view of strategy helps us to understand that this battle is about far more than dominance in the video game industry and thus to identify the aggressive strategies both are likely to follow.

Nintendo, in contrast, is largely a pure-play video game company and thus an asymmetric competitor to Microsoft and Sony. The resource-based view of strategy explains why Nintendo's latest console, the Wii, focuses primarily on the game-playing experience and isn't positioned as a digital hub for living rooms. The Wii's most innovative feature is therefore a new, easy-to-use controller appealing to new and hardcore gamers alike. The Wii has few of the expensive digital-hub features built into the rival consoles and thus made its debut with a lower retail price.

Applying the resource-based view of strategy to competitors in a rigorous, systematic, and fact-based way can help you identify the options they will probably consider for any strategic issue. But if you want to gain better insight into which of those options your competitors are likeliest to choose, you have to move beyond a general analysis of their communications, behavior, assets, and capabilities and also think about the personal perceptions and incentives of their decision makers.

THINK LIKE YOUR COMPETITOR'S DECISION MAKERS

Since the objectives of corporate decision makers rarely align completely with corporate objectives, companies often act in ways that seem inconsistent with their stated strategic intentions or with the unbiased assessments of outsiders about the best paths for them to follow. So if you want to predict the next moves of a competitor, you must often consider the preferences and incentives of its decision makers.

The key to getting inside the head of a competitor making any decision is first identifying who is most likely to make it and then figuring out how the objectives and incentives of that person or group may influence the competitor's actions. In most companies, owners and top managers make divestment decisions, for example. Strategic pricing and service decisions are often made, within broad corporate guidelines, by frontline sales personnel and managers.

Owners and Other Important Stakeholders

The objectives of the person or group with a controlling interest in your competitor probably have a major influence on its strategy. Sometimes, personal preferences are particularly relevant: it's likely that Virgin's pioneering foray into the commercial space travel industry partially reflects the adventurous tastes of its charismatic founder, Sir Richard Branson. For family-owned or -controlled businesses—public or private—family values, history, and relationships may drive strategy. A competitor owned by a private-equity firm is likely to focus on near-term performance improvements to generate cash and make the company more attractive to buyers. While every private-equity firm is different, you can often forecast the tactics any given one will take by studying its history, since many such firms often repeat their successful strategies.

Other stakeholders may also profoundly influence a company's strategy, so it often pays to get inside their heads as well. You can't evaluate any large strategic moves GM or Ford might make without considering the interests of the United Auto Workers and how those interests might check or facilitate such moves. The importance of nonowner stakeholders in driving a company's strategy varies by country of origin too. If you compete with a Chinese company, the Chinese government is often a critical stakeholder. In Europe, environmental organizations and other nongovernmental stakeholders exert more power over corporate decision making than they do in the United States.

Top-Level Management

Since the owners of companies hire top-level management to pursue the owners' strategic objectives, a Martian might think that management's decisions reflect those interests. Earthlings know that this may or may not be true. That's why you must study your competitor's top team.

First, that analysis provides another source of insight into the objectives of the company's owners. When James McNerney arrived at 3M in 2001, for instance, he brought along his belief in GE's "operating system," a centralized change-management methodology that inspired GE's successful approach to Six Sigma, globalization, and e-Business. If you were a 3M competitor, McNerney's history suggested that he would try to turn 3M, which had traditionally favored a fairly loose style of experimentation, into a more operationally accountable company. His hiring signaled the 3M board's intention to focus more aggressively than before on costs and quality. It surely came as no surprise to 3M's board or to the company's competitors that one of McNerney's first strategic moves was to launch a corporate Six Sigma program.

And of course, senior executives aren't always perfect "agents" for a company's owners, whose personal interests and incentives may differ from theirs. Such agency problems quite commonly bedevil even companies with the best governance practices, so it often pays to focus on the objectives of senior leaders as well.

General Managers and Frontline Employees

Competitors of a decentralized company must focus not only on the objectives of its owner and corporate leaders but also on those of business unit leaders, middle management, and even frontline staff. Until recently, for example, Ford was decentralized, with each geographic region run almost independently. Automotive competitors that wished to predict Ford's behavior would have needed to focus on the statements and actions of each regional and brand manager, because the company's objectives could vary from location

to location and across divisions. But since Alan Mullaly took over as CEO in 2006, he has moved to coordinate some decisions and platforms across divisions and regions. Competitors must now understand what is still decided by regional managers and what by Detroit.

For certain decisions, frontline employees and managers are also important, especially if they make pricing, marketing, service, and operational decisions that significantly influence a company's competitive advantage. Even if decision making is more centralized, the incentives of frontline employees may be misaligned with the objectives of a company's owners or senior leaders. Agency problems may inspire the front line to undercut these objectives.

Suppose, for example, that the head of a division at one of your competitors wants its commissioned sales force to promote a new product. If the sales force is enjoying strong sales from established products, reps may hesitate to risk their compensation to promote the new one. A knowledge of such agency problems—which can often be detected through the chatter between your frontline sales force and the customers you share with competitors—can have great strategic importance for your company. In this case, agency problems will probably delay the point when the new product wins significant sales. You could exploit that time lag to fortify your own presence in the market and possibly to preempt the competitor's new offering.

REACH A POINT OF VIEW

What happens once you have a better sense of the options your competitors may consider and the way they may evaluate those options?

Let's say that your company's market environment is relatively stable and that you have much useful information about your main competitors and their decision makers. You can then apply game theory to determine, with considerable confidence, the strategies your competitors will probably follow to maximize their objectives, as well as the way your own choices may influence those strategies. Suppose, however, that even your best efforts don't give you a clear picture of the resources of your competitors or their decision makers' objectives. Then it is often best to avoid trying to predict the competition's exact behavior and instead to use scenario planning to test your company's strategic possibilities.

In a financial crisis, for example, even the best competitive-intelligence efforts may provide incomplete, excessively complex, or inconsistent information on the competition's strategies and thus fail to support game theory or scenario planning. We have found that one way of generating a point of view in such situations is to conduct "war games." In these exercises, each team, representing a specific competitor, receives a fact pack about that company and its decision makers. The teams then make key strategic decisions for the companies they represent. Through several rounds of competition, every team can act on its own strategies and react to the moves of other teams. The war game forces the players to combine incomplete, and perhaps inconsistent, information on competitors to develop a point of view about which moves make the most and least sense for them and are therefore the most and least likely moves for them to make.

No matter how thorough and insightful your analysis may be, two things are almost sure to happen: your competitor will make some moves you considered unlikely, and some of your data will quickly become obsolete. When a competitor acts

in unexpected ways, your company has a crucial learning opportunity. Why were you wrong? Did you, say, miss an important agency problem that undermined the execution of the strategy you thought the competitor would follow? Did the market environment change, creating new threats and opportunities for the competitor? Did it bring in a new chairman or CEO? You must diagnose your mistakes, learn from them, and ensure that you use the latest data to develop your point of view.

Learning from your mistakes means managing these competitive-insight activities as an ongoing process for real-time strategic planning and decision making, not as an annual or biannual event in a bureaucratic planning process. Particularly in dynamic markets, where companies have to make decisions constantly, information about competitors must be updated as soon as possible (see Exhibit 1).

One key to making this ongoing process more insightful is tapping into the latest competitive intelligence dispersed throughout the frontline workforce. An e-mail address, a blog, or a shared database could let sales reps report on the latest pricing, promotion, negotiation, and sales tactics that competitors use with key customers or customer segments. Engineers might

Exhibit 1   The Competitor-Insight Loop

The competitor-insight loop

4 Synthesize, learn, and repeat
- Synthesize information to a point of view about which moves make the most and least sense for your competitor
- Learn from ongoing indicators and monitoring
- Repeat

1 Listen to your competitor
- Gather basic competitive intelligence—what are your competitors saying?
- Use pattern recognition— do recent moves and counter-moves reveal strategy?

3 Think like the decision makers for your competitor
- Who is the likely decision maker?
- Are the decision makers' interests aligned with those of the company's owners?

2 Think like a strategist for your competitor
- What are its assets, capabilities, market positions?
- How might it protect, extend, and leverage them?

use such facilities to report the latest product pipeline rumors from professional conferences. When possible, companies should also establish appropriate information-sharing arrangements with key partners; suppliers, for example, may provide the latest intelligence on future input prices. As Ken McGee argues in *Heads Up,* most of the information needed for sound business strategy decisions is already available. You just have to create a process to capture and synthesize it meaningfully.

Particularly today, no company is an island. Those that most accurately perceive the competitive landscape as it is and is likely to be in the future have a distinct competitive advantage. Our process—focusing on changes in the resources, decision-making structures, and compensation systems of competitors—moves beyond the usual updates on key market trends and uncertainties. Its rewards are huge: fewer surprises from competitors and more opportunities to shape markets to your own advantage.

ENDNOTE

[1] David Montgomery, Marian Chapman Moore, and Joel Urbany, "Reasoning about competitive reactions: Evidence from executives," *Marketing Science,* 2005, Volume 24, Number 1, pp. 138–49.

Operational Capabilities: Hidden in Plain View

Barbara B. Flynn
Indiana University

Steven Melnyk
Michigan State University

Sarah Jinhui Wu
Fordham University

OPERATIONAL CAPABILITIES 101

Operational capabilities are a lot like love: we know them when we see them, but it can be difficult to articulate precisely what they are. There has been much discussion about the importance of operational capabilities to the competitive success of U.S. businesses. However, it is difficult to develop and nurture operational capabilities when we do not have a good handle on how to recognize them.

Furthermore, there is a tendency to throw around terms like "capabilities," "resources," and "best practices" as though they are interchangeable; they are, in fact, very different. Each is important in its own way, but effective operations strategy requires understanding the differences between them and deploying each in the most effective way.

In this article, we focus primarily on operational capabilities, developing the concept in a way that is easy to understand and visualize. We then briefly differentiate between operational capabilities and other closely related concepts, focusing on implications for managers.

Reprinted from *Business Horizons*, Vol. 53, No. 3 (May 2010), pp. 247–256, by Barbara B. Flynn, Sarah Jinhui Wu, and Steven Melnyk, "Operational capabilities: Hidden in Plain View," with permission from Elsevier.

WADING IN

What are capabilities? In attempting to answer this question, it is helpful to look to the strategic management literature, which has studied the concept of capability—in general—for many years. By understanding the broader concept of capabilities, we can isolate their key features and apply them in an operations context. Although strategic management researchers use various terms to define capabilities, there seems to be consensus that a capability is not the same as a resource, but rather that it represents a distinctive and superior way of allocating, coordinating, and deploying resources (Amit & Schoemaker, 1993; Schreyogg & Kliesch-Eberl, 2007).

Examining how capabilities are developed better illustrates their essential attributes. Strategic management scholars argue that capabilities can be purposely built by focusing on the complex interactions between a firm's resources (Amit & Schoemaker, 1993; Dierickx & Cool, 1989), deeply rooted within its idiosyncratic social structure (Schreyogg & Kliesch-Eberl, 2007) and spanning functions and hierarchical levels (Grant, 1996; Zeitz, Mittal, & McCauly, 1999). As such, capabilities become embedded into the fabric of a firm through managers' deliberate decisions over time (Grewal & Slotegraaf, 2007). Specifically, capabilities are embedded in organizational processes that are focused on coordination, learning, and transformation (Harreld, O'Reilly, & Tushman, 2007). They are distinct behavioral patterns that are unique to a firm, because each firm's organizational units are unique and different from those of every other firm (Teece, Pisano, & Shuen, 1997). Capabilities are tacit social processes, which means that they emerge gradually over time—so gradually that participants may not even be aware of their existence and may ultimately take them for granted (Leonard-Barton, 1992).

As social processes, capabilities are path dependent, influenced by factors such as firm history (Teece et al., 1997); the actions of decision makers at the individual, group, and firm levels (Rothaermel & Hess, 2007); and the firm's learning process (Schreyogg & Kliesch-Eberl, 2007). They provide a way for the firm to make sense of its environment (Schreyogg & Kliesch-Eberl, 2007), giving it a means of configuring its resources at various levels (Lee & Kelley, 2008). Capabilities facilitate problem-solving decision making under conditions of uncertainty (Dosi, Hobday, & Marengo, 2003), allowing managers to deal with ambiguous and ill-structured tasks (Schreyogg & Kliesch-Eberl, 2007). Thus, they are validated through experience, by a process of identifying problems, applying the embedded skill sets, and verifying that the desired results have been attained. To summarize, according to the strategic management literature:

- Capabilities are *firm-specific.*
- Capabilities *emerge gradually* over time.
- Capabilities are *tacit*; participants may be unaware of their existence.
- Capabilities are *path dependent*, influenced by a firm's history and the actions of its decision makers.
- Capabilities are *empirically validated*, through their application to problems faced by a firm.

WHAT ARE OPERATIONAL CAPABILITIES?

How does this apply in an operations context? Synthesizing the research on capabilities and applying it in the operations context, we offer the following definition of operational capabilities:

Operational capabilities are firm-specific sets of skills, processes, and routines, developed within the operations management system, that are regularly used in solving the problems faced by a unit and which provide that unit—and, ultimately, the firm—with the means of configuring the resources of the operations management system to meet the firm's distinctive needs and challenges.

In order to better clarify the boundaries of operational capabilities, it is crucial to differentiate them from interrelated constructs; particularly, resources and operational practices. Resources form a firm's foundation, consisting of the firm's capacity and all of its stocks (Wang & Ahmed, 2007). In contrast, operational practices are fairly standardized activities, programs, or procedures that have been developed to address the attainment of certain specific operational goals or objectives (Flynn, Sakakibara, & Schroeder, 1995). For instance, while just-in-time (JIT) strives to reduce and eliminate all forms of waste, the goal of total productive maintenance (TPM) is to maximize equipment effectiveness (Cua, McKone, & Schroeder, 2001). Operational capabilities, then, provide unity, integration, and direction to resources and operational practices. Operational capabilities encapsulate both explicit elements—for example, resources and operational practices—and tacit elements that are less visible—such as know-how, skill sets, and leadership—for handling a variety of problems or dealing with uncertainty. That is, operational capabilities draw on resources and operational practices to generate outcomes consistent with desired results. Operational capabilities help the firm generate solutions that "make sense."

AN EXAMPLE FROM THE KITCHEN

While what we've discussed may seem to make sense in the abstract, it is vital to develop a working picture of operational capabilities and how they are different from resources and operational practices. To this end, consider the illustrative metaphor of a restaurant kitchen. A kitchen's resources include assets, such as stoves (number, size, type); the size of the kitchen; the pantry (size, types of ingredients); its layout; and the kitchen staff (size, skill level, knowledge, experience). These resources determine how much food can be prepared and the bounds of what can and cannot be done in the kitchen, just as an organization's resources determine the boundaries of what the firm can do. However, resources—in and of themselves—only define potential, because they are passive and reactive. They are like a stick of dynamite: nothing happens to the dynamite until it is lit, when it reacts to the flame and explodes. Similarly, a stove can't prepare a meal. Like all resources, a stove is passive and has potential, but it can't do anything on its own.

What about operational practices? Operational practices are essentially recipes. They provide generic instructions on how the various resources (e.g., ingredients, stoves) can be combined to make a meal. Once the ingredients and process have been documented as a recipe, the recipe becomes a standard solution that can be applied every time we want to make the same meal, much like the way that best practices are followed in a factory. However, although many kitchens may use the same chocolate mousse recipe, there is no guarantee that the resulting mousses will all look and taste the same. In fact, it wouldn't be surprising to find that the sweetness or creaminess of the ensuing mousses are different, because the recipe provides only basic guidance about how to combine resources; it does not capture the impact of less tangible and explicit factors, such as the freshness and quality of the ingredients, the chef's skill in setting the stove's flame at the proper height, or precise measurements of ingredients.

So, how does this relate to operational capabilities? A restaurant kitchen's capability is more than a stove, a chef, and/or a recipe; it is the capacity to leverage the chef's skill sets to deploy the kitchen's resources and recipes to create dishes that reflect the restaurant's history, style of cooking, and the preferences of its customers.

The traits of operational capabilities that we listed are evident in many ways in a restaurant kitchen. First, although the chef is a critical resource, she needs to extend her standard training from cooking school and customize it to her kitchen's specific context; for example, its menu, affordability, acceptable ingredients, cuisine history, and customers' needs. The restaurant itself has a history that has shaped its character, including the type of chef that was hired and whether she was hired through internal promotion, from a similar restaurant, or from a restaurant that this establishment wanted to emulate. This history makes the restaurant unique. Therefore, a kitchen's operational capabilities are *firm specific*, and a chef would be unable to take them with her if she moved to the kitchen of a different restaurant.

Second, restaurants often use apprenticeships, whereby a chef learns how to cook and prepare meals, as well as mastering the rules that govern how the various ingredients can and cannot be combined. Although the chef already learned how to cook during her formal culinary training, it probably took years for the chef to complete her apprenticeship. Graduating from a well-known cooking school may get a new chef in the door, but she still needs to master the subtleties which make her kitchen unique, observing interactions between kitchen staff and picking up clues from the context of the kitchen. It is in this way that the kitchen's operational capabilities are passed on to future generations of chefs, illustrating *path dependence*.

Third, a kitchen's operational capabilities are formed in a system whereby various resources—such as the chef's skill, supplier relationships, kitchen equipment, and chef/staff relationships—interact in a harmonious way, which takes time to develop. Thus, operational capabilities *emerge gradually over time*.

Fourth, if one wants to learn about a specific main course—say, roast duck—the chef could easily write down the recipe and perhaps emphasize a few key points. However, the chef cannot articulate all the subtleties of making roast duck, since she has taken many things (e.g., relationships with staff and suppliers) for granted over the years and they seem like second nature to her. However, these are the necessary, but intangible, elements associated with the kitchen's operational capabilities. Thus, the operational capabilities of the kitchen are *tacit* and deeply embedded, and are not easily observed, even by those who work in the kitchen.

Lastly, the existence of operational capabilities is reflected in the kitchen's ability to solve its primary strategic problem. The famous Quan-JuDe (全聚德) in Beijing has long been regarded as the most authentic Peking Duck restaurant in the world. The uniqueness of its roast duck comes from an overall cooking process that integrates explicit resources, practices, and tacit elements (e.g., know-how, skill sets, leadership) which have become institutionalized over time. Over the 100-year history of QuanJuDe, neither the ingredients nor the recipe for roast duck have changed much. Yet, today's customers live in a fast-paced world, where they cannot afford to spend hours waiting for a meal to be prepared. Therefore, QuanJuDe had to update its process to more quickly prepare its roast duck, while retaining the original flavor. Thus, the restaurant's operational capabilities were *empirically validated* through diners' reactions to traditional roast duck prepared using updated methods.

It is the chef—more properly known as the "chef de cuisine"—and staff (the executive chef, sous chef, expediter, pastry chef, chef de garde, and various line cooks) that determine how the kitchen's resources are used in addressing the various problems it faces; for example, whether the kitchen's resources are used to prepare Italian meals or Chinese meals, and whether the kitchen prepares unique meals for a small clientele or standard meals for a large volume of diners. The specific problem to be solved is critical, since it determines which types of "solutions" are acceptable and which are not. It also affects how the chef interacts with the staff and the nature of their relationship (whether they work collaboratively or are tightly controlled). In solving these problems, the chef and her staff are themselves the product of a process, ultimately shaping the types of meals prepared, the types of customers targeted, and the restaurant's ability to innovate by creating new and unique dishes that reflect the inimitable characteristics of the restaurant, its style of cooking, or the region in which the restaurant is located. They may not be able to articulate the subtleties of making roast duck or chocolate mousse, because it seems like second nature to them. Thus, the operational capabilities of a restaurant are tacit and deeply embedded.

To summarize, while resources are passive and reactive—like dynamite or a stove—both operational practices and operational capabilities are active and proactive. While resources are readily observable and operational practices combine resources in a relatively explicit and observable way, operational capabilities are tacit and difficult to articulate. Because they are intertwined with resources, operational practices, and even organizational culture, operational capabilities are very difficult to see or identify.

Resources like stoves can be directly purchased from factory markets. That means they can be easily transferred across firms. Similarly, operational practices can be learned from competitors through benchmarking, making them relatively easy to transfer across firms. However, it is the elusive nature of operational capabilities that makes them key to competitive advantage. Because they evolve within a firm and are time and path dependent, it is very difficult to transfer operational capabilities between firms. They are institutionalized within a particular firm, making operational capabilities a powerful competitive weapon.

EMERGENT OPERATIONAL CAPABILITIES

Based on our definition of operational capabilities, we searched through the literature for potentially critical operational capabilities. Our starting point was research conducted by Swink and Hegarty (1998), which proposed seven capabilities relevant in an operations context: improvement, innovation, integration, acuity, control, agility, and responsiveness. Although this work provides a solid foundation, several of these capabilities require further refinement in terms of their dimensionality and uniqueness. Thus, we introduced perspectives drawn from other literature on operational capabilities.

Schroeder, Bates, and Junttila (2002) empirically demonstrated that the operational capabilities inherent in firm-specific, path-dependent learning resulted in the development of proprietary production processes that confer competitive advantage. Although there are many different firm-specific practices associated with the development of proprietary production processes, each reflects an underlying ability to customize a process to meet the unique needs of a firm's products and target markets. It is this commonality that reflects an operational capability. Consequently, we included operational customization as an additional operational capability.

Teece et al. (1997) argued that the ability to sense the need to reconfigure a firm's asset structure, and accomplish the necessary internal and external transformation, is valuable when a firm is faced with a rapidly changing external environment. This construct overlaps somewhat with the operational capability that Swink and Hegarty (1998) termed agility. In many studies (e.g., Christopher, 2000; Fliedner & Vokurka, 1997; Swink & Hegarty, 1998), agility is operationalized by flexibility's two dimensions: volume and variety. However, agility is a higher level construct than flexibility (Aitken, Christopher, & Towill, 2002; Sharifi & Zhang, 2001; Zhang & Sharifi, 2007), because it includes the ability to sense unexpected demand, maintain flexible responses, and implement synchronized operations. This draws on two other operational capabilities: process responsiveness and the ability to reconfigure resources. Thus, we define operational reconfiguration as the ability of a firm in a dynamic environment to reconfigure its asset structure and accomplish the necessary internal and external transformations.

Swink and Hegarty (1998) defined integration in a relatively narrow way, only considering the integration between the operations function and the product/process design function. Considering the need for integration/coordination with other internal functions and external supply chain partners (Escrig-Tena & Bou-Llusar, 2005; Teece et al., 1997), we expanded Swink and Hegarty's definition to emphasize the cooperation skills needed to achieve this broad integration. We renamed this *operational cooperation,* in order to suggest an operational capability that is manifested both internally and externally. Furthermore, acuity—which Swink and Hegarty defined as the ability to understand customers' needs, and convey valuable information and insights regarding products and processes—largely relies on effective cooperation between marketing and operations. We view this as subsumed by the broader operational capability of operational cooperation.

FOCUS GROUP

To verify our proposed set of operational capabilities, we utilized a focus group of eight middle-level managers who worked primarily in the operations area of a single firm that produced household appliances. Asked to compare our suggested operational capabilities with those they experienced on the job, these participants had worked in operations and supply chain management for 14.75 years, with a minimum of 8 years and a maximum of 25 years. Five worked at the plant level, while three were employed at the division level. The number of plants/divisions they had worked for varied from 1 to 6, with a mean of 2.25. Thus, each participant was knowledgeable about his or her firm and its operational capabilities.

The participants were first introduced to the concept of operational capabilities, and then were asked to develop a list of what they believed to be key operational capabilities, listing a total of 15 items (see Table 1). Of this number, 11 of the 15 items listed mapped well to the operational capabilities that we had identified based on the literature. Thus, there was substantial agreement between the focus group and our list of operational capabilities. The four items that did not correspond to items on our list of operational capabilities were carefully assessed, in order to determine whether they should be added to our list.

Our analysis revealed that one item actually represented an outcome, while the other three reflected organizational—rather than operational—capabilities; thus, the original set of operational capabilities was retained. "Dependability and reliability" is a process outcome rather than an operational capability, because it focuses on process performance, not on the way in which process performance is achieved. "Control of the supply chain" goes beyond the domain of operational capabilities, since having control of the supply chain can be related to factors such as brand name, unique technology, and order size. While this may reflect a capability of an organization, it is not an operational capability because it cuts across functions. Similarly, "value creation for core customers" focuses on creating value for customers, which is an organizational—rather than an operational—capability. Finally, "new product testing facility" is also an organizational capability because it reflects the ability to quickly change both the design of new products and reduce new product introduction lead time.

Table 1   **Operational Capabilities Identified from the Literature and by the Focus Group**

Focus Group	Literature
• Collaboration and trust with partners	Operational cooperation
• Intellectual property and know-how (specialized tooling, technology, equipment)	Operational customization
• Specialization (service experts)	
• Process customization	
• Responsiveness	Operational responsiveness
• Sense of urgency to meet short lead time	
• Fulfillment of customers' orders	
• Process improvement to make price competitive	Operational improvement
• Process standardization	
• Radical process innovation	Operational innovation
• Change management	Operational reconfiguration
• New product testing facility	Others
• Control of the supply chain	
• Value creation for core customers	
• Dependability and reliability	

KEY OPERATIONAL CAPABILITIES

Through our review of the literature and discussion with focus group participants, we developed a list of six key operational capabilities. Each is described next.

Operational Improvement

Operational improvement is based on the concept that Swink and Hegarty (1998) called "improvement." It consists of differentiated skills, processes, and routines for incrementally refining and reinforcing existing operations processes. By "differentiated," we mean that these skills, processes, and routines were developed in a way that was unique to the organization. For example, over time, a restaurant kitchen may develop efficient approaches for preparing its specialties. This might include assigning tasks to those with the most appropriate skills, developing shortcuts that do not affect the taste of a dish, learning which dishes can go into the oven at the same time, learning which parts of the dish can be prepared ahead of time, and so forth. Similarly, an organization may develop the ability to complete its routine work in the most

efficient way possible, through assigning various tasks to those who are most qualified to complete them; developing shortcuts that do not affect the end product; developing approaches for multiprocessing; learning which parts of a job can be done in advance and held in inventory, and which must be completed at the last minute; and so forth. This ability develops over time and is empirically validated as the organization experiments with different approaches for completing the task, and learns about the skills and abilities of the employees who are involved. An organization with an operational improvement capability will have the ability to continuously adapt the process as new employees are added and as particular features of the job at hand change over time. Furthermore, the ability to improve processes will be transferred to the organization's other processes. Thus, operational improvement capability is embedded in the organization, not in particular people. Similarly, even if a chef leaves a restaurant for other employment, the process and the ability to incrementally refine it remain.

Operational Innovation

While operational improvement is based on incremental change, operational innovation focuses on radical change. Operational innovation is centered on what Swink and Hegarty (1998) term "improvement" capability. It represents the differentiated skills, processes, and routines for radically improving existing operations processes or for creating and implementing new and unique manufacturing processes. A chef borrows from different recipes and uses her experiences and knowledge to create a few specialties for her restaurant. For example, Brennan's in New Orleans is widely acknowledged as having the best bananas Foster. Brennan's has been around since 1946, and the original chef who created this recipe is long gone. The restaurant's recipe for bananas Foster is publically available via the Brennan's website, so it is clearly something beyond the recipe that causes Brennan's to have the best bananas Foster. The unique process for making bananas Foster—which at Brennan's involves a tableside cart cooking arrangement, complete with flaming liqueur—was an operational innovation when it was developed, and it remains difficult to precisely imitate. Similarly, a restaurant may develop recipes that capitalize on the unique skills of its staff and the specific assets in the kitchen. For example, a restaurant with a skilled pastry chef and confectionery oven may develop innovative pastry-based entrees like Beef Wellington, to present a course in a manner unique from other establishments.

Operational Customization

While operational improvement focuses on incremental change and operational innovation focuses on radical change, operational customization has at its core the creation of something unique. Operational customization is based on the notion put forth by Schroeder et al. (2002) regarding "proprietary process and equipment." It consists of differentiated skills, processes, and routines for the creation of knowledge through extending and customizing operations processes and systems. A kitchen skilled in operational customization has the ability to create something completely unique. Consider a mother whose college-aged child returns home after a long absence. Mom will prepare whatever the child wants for dinner; this could entail shopping for unusual ingredients, scanning the Internet for special recipe ideas, and perhaps even purchasing additional resources such as a donut fryer or ice cream freezer.

Similar operational innovations can be seen on the television program *Iron Chef,* which features competitions between chefs that focus on the novel use of a particular ingredient during each episode—for example, artichokes one week and sea bass the next—to create uniquely specialized dishes. Likewise, a manufacturer that is strong in operational customization will have the ability to produce exactly what a customer desires. This requires having flexible equipment, access to a wide variety of materials, and employees who are skilled and experienced at interpreting vaguely articulated client desires, using general purpose equipment to translate them into products that meet the customers' needs.

Operational Cooperation

Operational cooperation builds upon the concepts of "skills for cooperation" (Escrig-Tena & Bou-Llusar, 2005) and Swink and Hegarty's (1998) "integration" and "acuity." It is defined as differentiated skills, processes, and routines for creating healthy and stable relationships with people from various internal functional areas, as well as external supply chain partners. In a restaurant setting, the purchasing staff works closely with the chef, in order to buy the best-quality ingredients in a timely manner. For example, in a Thai restaurant, papaya is commonly used in both hot and cold dishes. Because the freshness of the papaya greatly influences the flavor of the dishes, the effectiveness of the purchasing staff to work with both the chef and suppliers is crucial for obtaining the best papayas. Although individual members of the purchasing staff may form relationships with particular suppliers, operational cooperation moves beyond personal relationships to institutional relationships that transcend the particular individuals.

Operational Responsiveness

Operational responsiveness is based on the "responsiveness" construct put forth by Swink and Hegarty (1998). At its core is the ability to quickly modify a standard product to meet the unique needs of an individual customer. Operational responsiveness is defined as differentiated skills, processes, and routines for reacting quickly and easily to changes in inputs or output requirements.

For example, a restaurant may be known for its ability to customize its dishes for vegetarians, patrons with gluten or peanut allergies, or patrons with religious dietary restrictions. Because this customization involves removing ingredients that may contribute significantly to the taste of a particular dish, operational responsiveness capability is important in responding to customer needs by developing dishes that have the same taste without a particular ingredient.

Operational Reconfiguration

Operational reconfiguration is based on "reconfiguration" as articulated by Teece et al. (1997), and "agility" as offered by Swink and Hegarty (1998). Because a strategic mismatch between an organization's operations strategy and its market environment can be devastating, the ability to sense subtle points about the market environment and react appropriately can be a potent competitive weapon. Operational reconfiguration is the differentiated skills, processes, and routines for accomplishing any transformations needed to reestablish the fit between operations strategy and the market environment, if their equilibrium has been disturbed. For example, a chef may replace ingredients in a standard recipe in order to cater to the tastes of customers in a particular environment. Many Chinese restaurants in the United States replace traditional Chinese green vegetables, which are unfamiliar to U.S. customers, with the more familiar broccoli. The taste of the dishes remains the same, but U.S. customers view them as less exotic than dishes which include unfamiliar Chinese green vegetables. Similarly, there are many anecdotes about mistakes made by U.S. businesses as they marketed their products in a different culture without being savvy to the nuances of that culture.

HIDDEN IN PLAIN VIEW

This study provided a rationale for viewing operational capabilities as critical to success at both the operations and corporate levels. We suggest operational capabilities are much like a "secret ingredient" because, as with the purloined letter of Edgar Allan Poe (1845), operational capabilities are essentially hidden in plain view. That is, operational capabilities are present but overlooked

both by the managers who work with them and by researchers. They are taken for granted. They fail to generate attention because they do not seem unusual. This is due to the very nature of operational capabilities: they are tightly embedded in the organizational fabric of the operations management system. This embeddedness is the result of three factors: (1) the interconnectedness of operational capabilities with resources and operational practices, (2) linkages between operations capabilities and the social network, and (3) the fit with the primary problems that the firm and its operations management address. This embeddedness makes operational capabilities tacit in nature and path dependent. These traits, in turn, create a barrier to imitation (Grewal & Slotegraaf, 2007). As a result, operational capabilities are crucial in understanding and explaining performance variability. Thus, while resources and operational practices are critical, they are not sufficient.

Operational capabilities are the secret ingredient that is hidden in plain view for several reasons. First, operational capabilities are not as obvious and tangible as operational practices and resources. When trying to explain success, managers tend to focus on factors that are readily perceived and relatively easy to duplicate and implement. This is what Spear and Bowen (1999) and Spear (2004) observed when describing how others viewed the success of Toyota. While observers saw Toyota using general purpose equipment, statistical process control, and cross-functional employees, what they did not as readily observe was how Toyota had extended and customized all of these elements to address its specific problems. In sum, they did not see Toyota's "DNA" (Spear & Bowen, 1999). A critical element of this DNA is Toyota's operational capabilities. Employing this perspective, it is evident why even the most detailed and precise duplication efforts by mimicking companies could not achieve the same level of performance. The resources and practices that work so well at Toyota might not fit the implementing organization's culture or history, or may not even be consistent with the problem that the firm is interested in solving; these elements are central attributes of operational capabilities. This observation is also supported by research conducted by Westphal, Gulati, and Shortell (1997). When studying corporate experiences with total quality management (TQM), they found that the factors which explained high performers could not adequately explain low performers. The high performers understood, expanded, and tailored TQM and its specific practices to their unique needs, resource profiles, and interfirm relationships. In contrast, the lower performers blindly imitated techniques and tools without any modification or adjustment. While the former group developed operational capabilities and subsequently improved performance, the latter group did not. A similar explanation is provided by the four stages of Hayes and Wheelwright (1984). Stage II firms (externally neutral) strive to improve through extensive and indiscriminant imitation of competitors. In contrast, Stage III firms are more successful in their improvement efforts by screening potential new resources and practices for consistency with operations strategy.

Second, operational capabilities are closely linked to resources and operational practices. This interconnectedness makes operational capabilities difficult to identify separately; consequently, their existence may be overlooked. There is a tendency for both managers and researchers to confuse resource and operational practices with operational capabilities. For example, Eisenhardt and Martin (2000) and Lee and Kelley (2008) have noted that "best practices" can be viewed as a type of capability. Yet, Teece (2007) disagreed with this position, stating that, under certain conditions, best practices are not capabilities, nor does their use lead to a sustainable competitive advantage. This position was repeated by Hayes, Pisano, Upton, and Wheelwright (2005). Such confusion is not surprising given the close linkages that exist between operational capabilities, resources, and operational practices.

Third, the development of operational capabilities is associated with the culture and history of a particular firm and the specific problems that it is striving to solve. There are two types of fit related to operational capabilities: fit with organizational culture and history, and fit with the specific problem being addressed (e.g., cost reduction vs. radical product innovation). Both types of fit tend to be overlooked in cross-sectional/benchmarking analysis. For example, Toyota's operational capabilities were built to solve the company's primary problem: given its production lines, how could it be flexible enough to change the product mix to accommodate changing demand (Womack, Jones, & Roos, 1990)? While General Motors (GM) spent a great deal of time and money studying Toyota's success, its management did not appreciate that GM and Toyota were solving fundamentally different problems. To GM, the central issue was that of reducing cost, producing the most with a given level of resources. In contrast, Toyota was more interested in improving flexibility, minimizing the level of resources needed to satisfy a given level of demand.

This may be one of the reasons why the best practices construct cannot be applied universally: they must be developed to fit the specific problem being solved and the specific environment in which they will be deployed, and they must be extended—that is, improved upon in unique ways—so that they help the system offer customers better solutions (Westphal et al., 1997). Managers from one firm, when studying another, tend to view activities through a lens built on the assumption that the firm being studied is solving the same type of problem, or problems, that the observers are. This myopia prevents them from seeing and assessing operational capabilities.

CLOSING COMMENTS

The goal of operations strategy is to help managers develop, position, and align managerial policies and resources in a way that is consistent with the organization's overall business strategy. This level of planning and decision making focuses on developing operations into a source of sustainable competitive advantage. In addressing this objective, managers must speak to the dynamic tension that exists between the two critical elements of strategy: efficiency and effectiveness. Efficiency is concerned with issues related to reducing cost for a given level of demand or increasing output for a given level of resources. In contrast, effectiveness deals with how well the operations process internally supports the overall corporate strategy and externally supports the organization in meeting or exceeding the needs of critical customers, relative to its competitors.

The tension between efficiency and effectiveness is evidenced in the historical competition between Kmart and Walmart. During the late 1970s, Kmart enjoyed an enormous size advantage, which translated into substantial efficiencies in purchasing, distribution, and marketing. At the time, Walmart was only a small niche player. Within a decade, however, Walmart transformed itself into a giant in the discount retail industry and has continued growing. The secret of Walmart's success lies in its effectiveness in satisfying customer needs; Walmart uses cross-docking in replenishing its inventory, which makes goods available when and where customers want them, without the need to hold a lot of costly inventory.

One strategy for improving operations efficiency is to study other organizations and apply those practices and tools that have been successfully used by them. By focusing on operations practices such as JIT and TQM, managers deal with activities that are highly observable, easy to articulate, and well defined. In applying best practices from other firms and benchmarking leading firms, though, it must be recognized that we are introducing a force for homogenization and standardization of practices. When everyone implements best practices, they become the norm. While the adoption of such practices can improve operations and corporate performance to a certain extent, it cannot help a firm develop and maintain a sustainable competitive advantage. This approach also runs counter to the central concept of strategic management: that is, the need to differentiate a firm and its capabilities from those offered by its competitors.

In the context of operations strategy, we can argue that while efficiency comes from operational practices, effectiveness is based on operational capabilities. Yet, for many managers, operations practices and operational capabilities remain a source of major confusion. In part, this confusion reflects the fact that these two concepts have not been clearly articulated and delineated with sufficient precision. Operational capabilities need to be clearly defined and systematically identified, because operations performance is the result of operational capabilities. How a manufacturer can change or shape its operations performance depends on how it invests in operations capabilities.

We have proposed a conceptual definition of operational capabilities and a metaphor which captures their essential traits. These traits help us differentiate operational capabilities from operational practices and resources, and understand the process by which competitive advantage is developed. In addition, we provided a comprehensive framework of operational capabilities that covers six salient dimensions. This concept of operational capabilities forms a foundation for improved understanding of dynamic capabilities and their development process, which is imperative in today's turbulent environment.

REFERENCES

Aitken, J., Christopher, M., & Towill, D. (2002). Understanding, implementing, and exploiting agility and leanness. *International Journal of Logistics: Research and Applications, 5*(1), 59–74.

Amit, R., & Schoemaker, P. J. H. (1993). Strategic assets and organizational rent. *Strategic Management Journal, 14*(1), 33–46.

Christopher, M. (2000). The agile supply chain, competing in volatile markets. *Industrial Marketing Management, 29*(1), 37–44.

Cua, K. O., McKone, K. E., & Schroeder, R. G. (2001). Relationship between implementation of TQM, JIT, and TPM, and manufacturing performance. *Journal of Operations Management, 19*(6), 675–694.

Dierickx, I., & Cool, K. (1989). Asset stock accumulation and sustainability of competitive advantage. *Management Science, 35*(12), 1504–1511.

Dosi, G., Hobday, M., & Marengo, L. (2003). Problem-solving behavior, organizational forms and the complexity of tasks. In C. E. Helfat (Ed.), *The SMS Blackwell handbook of organizational capabilities* (pp. 167–192). Malden, MA: Blackwell.

Eisenhardt, K. M., & Martin, J. A. (2000). Dynamic capabilities: What are they? *Strategic Management Journal, 21*(10–11), 1105–1121.

Escrig-Tena, A. B., & Bou-Llusar, J. C. (2005). A model for evaluating organizational competencies: An application in the context of a quality management initiative. *Decision Sciences, 36*(2), 221–257.

Fliedner, D., & Vokurka, R. J. (1997). Agility: Competitive weapon of the 1990s and beyond? *Production and Inventory Management Journal, 38*(3), 19–24.

Flynn, B. B., Sakakibara, S., & Schroeder, R. G. (1995). Relationship between JIT and TQM: Practices and performance. *Academy of Management Journal, 38*(5), 1325–1360.

Grant, R. (1996). Toward a knowledge-based theory of the firm. *Strategic Management Journal, 17*(SI Winter), 109–122.

Grewal, R., & Slotegraaf, R. J. (2007). Embeddedness of organizational capabilities. *Decision Sciences, 38*(3), 451–488.

Harreld, J. B., O'Reilly, C. A., & Tushman, M. L. (2007). Dynamic capabilities at IBM: Driving strategy into action. *California Management Review, 49*(4), 21–43.

Hayes, R. H., Pisano, G. P., Upton, D. M., & Wheelwright, S. C. (2005). *Operations, strategy, and technology: Pursuing the competitive edge.* Hoboken, NJ: Wiley Higher Education.

Hayes, R. H., & Wheelwright, S. C. (1984). *Restoring our competitive edge: Competing through manufacturing.* New York: John Wiley.

Lee, H., & Kelley, D. (2008). Building dynamic capabilities for innovation: An exploratory study of key management practices. *R&D Management, 38*(2), 155–168.

Leonard-Barton, D. (1992). Core capabilities and core rigidities: A paradox in managing new product development. *Strategic Management Journal, 13*(2), 111–125.

Poe, E. A. (1845). *The purloined letter.* Retrieved from http://xroads.virginia.edu/HYPER/POE/purloine.html.

Rothaermel, F. T., & Hess, A. M. (2007). Building dynamic capabilities: Innovation driven by individual-, firm-, and network-level effects. *Organizational Science, 18*(6), 898–921.

Schreyogg, G., & Kliesch-Eberl, M. (2007). How dynamic can organizational capabilities be? Towards a dual-process model of capability dynamization. *Strategic Management Journal, 28*(9), 913–933.

Schroeder, R. G., Bates, K. A., & Junttila, M. A. (2002). A resource-based view of manufacturing strategy and the relationship to manufacturing performance. *Strategic Management Journal, 23*(2), 105–117.

Sharifi, H., & Zhang, Z. (2001). Agile manufacturing in practice: Application of a methodology. *International Journal of Operations and Production Management, 21*(5/6), 772–794.

Spear, S. J. (2004). Learning to lead at Toyota. *Harvard Business Review, 82*(5), 78–86.

Spear, S. J., & Bowen, H. K. (1999). Decoding the DNA of the Toyota production system. *Harvard Business Review, 77*(5), 96–106.

Swink, M., & Hegarty, W. H. (1998). Core manufacturing capabilities and their links to product differentiation. *International Journal of Operations and Production Management, 18*(4), 374–396.

Teece, D. (2007). Explicating dynamic capabilities: The nature and microfoundations of (sustainable) enterprise performance. *Strategic Management Journal, 28*(13), 1319–1350.

Teece, D. J., Pisano, G., & Shuen, A. (1997). Dynamic capabilities and strategic management. *Strategic Management Journal, 18*(7), 509–533.

Wang, C. L., & Ahmed, P. K. (2007). Dynamic capabilities: A review and research agenda. *International Journal of Management Reviews, 9*(1), 31–51.

Westphal, J. D., Gulati, R., & Shortell, S. M. (1997). Customization or conformity? An institutional and network perspective on the content and consequences of TQM adoption. *Administrative Science Quarterly, 42*(2), 366–394.

Womack, J. P., Jones, D. T., & Roos, D. (1990). *The machine that changed the world.* New York: Rowson Associates.

Zeitz, G., Mittal, V., & McCauly, B. (1999). Distinguishing adoption and entrenchment of management practices: A framework for analysis. *Organization Studies, 20*(5), 741–776.

Zhang, Z., & Sharifi, H. (2007). Towards theory building in agile manufacturing strategy: A taxonomical approach. *IEEE Transactions on Engineering Management, 54*(2), 351–370.

Orchestrating the New Dynamic Capabilities

Amy Shuen
CEIBS (China Europe International
Business School)

Sandra Sieber
IESE Business School
University of Navarra, Spain

EXECUTIVE SUMMARY

Over a decade ago, "dynamic capabilities" were introduced to the business world as a way for companies to get ahead in times of rapid technological change through orchestration, recombination and transformative collaboration. Now, with the advent of Web 2.0 and the opportunities that presents, dynamic capabilities achieve a new relevance. The emerging technological landscape enables firms to put dynamic capabilities into practice easier than ever before, since it allows for ongoing collaboration and interaction between companies and users, hence fostering new types of innovation. In this article, the authors outline the principles behind Web 2.0-empowered business models, giving managers numerous ideas they can try out immediately, at low cost, and with potentially much higher ROI than could ever be achieved with a non-Web-enabled business. Why not put your own dynamic capabilities to the test? You're only a click away.

When Skype first burst onto the scene, everyone predicted the familiar story of disruptive innovation in the telecom industry, where the new destroys the old way of doing business in a spiraling zero-sum game. Fast-forward to the present: Apple's iPhone has shown a new win–win path to success using collaborative innovation on the Web. The iPhone brought together thousands of handset makers, operators, and software developers, giving them a considerable share of a market already worth $2 billion a year, and reinvented several industries in the process.

In a similar fashion, diverse companies—from Google and Amazon, to IBM, Cisco, and Intuit—are continuing to innovate their business models and grow, despite the economic crisis, with revenue and success widely shared. Many industry leaders are wondering if the core principles of strate-

Reprinted from "Orchestrating the New Dynamic Capabilities," by Amy Shuen and Sandra Sieber, *IESE Insight*, Issue 3 (2009), pp. 58–65. Reprinted with permission.

Sophie Mancuso contributed to this article.

gic management and competitive advantage have changed. The answer, we argue, is a resounding yes.

Here's why: The Web has changed the economics of business and collaboration. Companies can no longer conceive of their capabilities in isolation, but must learn to co-create them within a broader, dynamic and non-zero-sum ecosystem of external partners. The new "managed" but open ecosystems range from "orchestrated" standards-based networks of developers, to communities and "crowds" of lead users and bloggers, to e-commerce affiliates, to complementary businesses that cross industry divides.

A highly cited *Strategic Management Journal* article from 1997 once defined "dynamic capabilities" as a company's strategic ability to combine inside and outside competences to address volatile environments and periods of rapid change. *Orchestration* was lauded over positioning, *management innovation* and *combinations* over structure, and *transformative collaboration* over traditional strategizing as the means of gaining competitive advantage.

Few could have predicted when that article was written the widespread social transformation that the Web, broadband, and mobile technologies would trigger, nor the exponential growth of Google, Facebook, Twitter, Amazon, and Apple—businesses that rely on the economics of network effects, social influence, viral distribution, and Web-enabled business models. Now, thanks to Web 2.0 business models and platforms, collective user value, along with ways to more productively monetize and enhance the "wisdom of the crowd," has become commonplace. It's the modern version of the old fable "Stone Soup," in which hungry villagers each contribute whatever they can spare—a carrot here, a potato there, some leftover scraps of meat. In the end, everyone enjoys a hearty, collectively co-created soup. The Web is today's soup pot, taking individual contributions, remixing them, and redistributing them as something new across many networks with almost zero costs.

This year, Berkeley's Oliver Williamson won the Nobel Memorial Prize in Economic Sciences for his research on the transaction costs underlying industrial structure and organizational boundaries. These are the very same transaction and coordination costs that Web-enabled business models are transforming substantially. Little wonder that "collaborative innovation" and the new "dynamic capabilities" of orchestrating knowledge, ecosystems, partnerships, and collective user value across multiple industrial and geographic boundaries have become top strategic priorities for the Fortune 500 agenda.

THE NEW COLLABORATIVE MATRIX

Web 2.0 has changed the rules of business. But it isn't simply about building Web-based businesses to put the old-style ones out of the picture. It's about using a company's own "dynamic capabilities" to orchestrate and recombine the best of what the online world has to offer while multiplying the value of existing networks of users and partners. New-style click-and-mortar, online-offline network partnerships focus on bridging and building new networks so that everyone gains, and potential competitors become potential partners. Figure 1 shows at least three ways to combine users with company capabilities profitably and speedily. The New Collaborative Matrix has its roots in traditional innovation theory, but wouldn't be as profitable or as successful without the help of digital-plus-network economics.

Democratized Innovation

The lower left-hand corner of the innovation matrix reminds us that many peer-to-peer, or user-to-user, innovations produce positive network effects, but the benefits become public goods or consumer surplus. Wikipedia is an example of positive network externalities in which many benefit from the widespread sharing and distribution of digital knowledge or music. However, the founders did not capture or internalize the pecuniary value of these network effects. In contrast, the other three boxes show that collective network effects can be successfully monetized and create new business value.

Crowdsourcing

How many users of Google, YouTube, Flickr, Amazon, or Trip Advisor realize that their usage, clicks, tags, photos, videos, reviews, comments, and participation in online contests and polls are being turned into positive network effects by *crowdsourcing,* which makes the site better for everyone? The main difference between user-to-company and user-to-user innovation is that a company is able to capture tangible, monetary benefits of the user in exchange for continued innovation and improvement. There are numerous well-known examples: IBM, which identified and developed several fast-growing, high-potential new businesses via its global Innovation Jams; and Google's PageRank and AdWords algorithms, which both improve the relevance of search results for users while pricing advertising according to relevant clicks. But it doesn't stop there: Threadless.com harnesses the power of the online community to design funky T-shirts; and the mining company Goldcorp mobilizes prospectors to find gold for them.

Figure 1   The New Collaborative Matrix

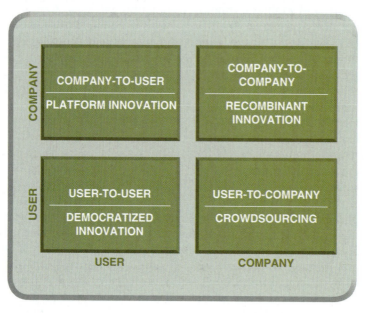

Source: Based on concepts originally published in *Web 2.0: A Strategy Guide* by Amy Shuen (O'Reilly Media, 2008).

Platform Innovation

Company-to-user innovation is when a company provides the platform for users and developers to distribute their software, applications, or digital goods, such as music or games, to their social or professional networks, or simply to the market-place at large. IBM, Apple, and Facebook spring to mind, but Neopets and South Korea's Cyworld also stand out in this regard.

Recombinant Innovation

Perhaps the best-known example of company-to-company innovation is Apple. Before the iTunes store, it had already teamed up with Gracenote to give the names of the tracks to consumers rip-ping CDs. But rather than working against the record companies by encouraging consumers to download music illegally, Apple wanted to legitimize the sale of music online, so it worked with record companies, convincing them to collaborate and sell music digitally. The result was a win–win situation, with all parties dependent on each other for success.

As we can see from these examples, you don't have to invent the wheel to have a successful project. By simply working with other companies, you can make something highly valuable for a specific group of consumers and users. The big-gest challenge for companies innovating in these areas is to convert from an ingrained culture of competition to collaboration. It's not easy to turn around and preach "give to get" and "let's revenue-share," but the payoffs are worth it.

HOW TO MULTIPLY YOUR DYNAMIC CAPABILITIES

Build on Collective User Value

The first and critical step is to start thinking exponentially rather than incrementally. The Web makes it 10 times faster for any company with an existing network of relationships to orchestrate 10 times the users and 10 times the partners to connect and combine for new value creation. And you don't have to be a Fortune 500 company, or an online store, to benefit. Governments, public agencies, and nonprofits are relatively lacking in capital, assets, and resources, but they have managed to achieve great things simply by lever-aging their rich social capital. Barack Obama's use of Web 2.0 during his bid for the White House serves as an excellent example (see Figure 2).

This same comparison of the ROI and cash flow curves of Web 2.0, Web 1.0, and traditional approaches characterizes many other cases.

Reading 6 Orchestrating the New Dynamic Capabilities　　　　　**R-55**

A great example of a company that built itself on collective user value is the photo-sharing site Flickr. It initially offered users free online space to store and organize photos with features to comment and tag. Of course, word soon spread, and as people contributed to Flickr, they made it better and better. When the site had a critical mass of users, popularity, and information, it offered a premium service to those willing to pay for more benefits. With virtually zero marketing costs and low-cost online distribution and capital investment, Flickr managed to create a number of positive revenue streams quickly to cover the cost of the free services it offered.

Nevertheless, coming up with a viable business model based on collective user value is not without its challenges. First, you need to start from a blank slate and honestly look at your business from the customers' point of view: What are their real needs? How do you propose to address them? This is crucial, as in order for your effort to be effective, the collaboration and cooperation must be conceived in ways that users consider helpful and valuable to them.

Once people get engaged, you need to clarify the different types of value that are created by their contributions, and then decide on the revenue model. This normally implies a cost structure that allows the top contributors to be rewarded in some way, for collective user value to be incentivized, and then monetizing this value.

An interesting example in this vein is that of professional online networks, of which there are currently several vying for dominance in Europe. The initial leader—the German company Xing—has managed to develop a business model that relies heavily on its community, which numbered some 8 million in August 2009. Apart from the usual staying-in-touch with colleagues and job contacts, Xing facilitates over 30,000 specialized groups and 90,000 live networking events a year, organized by members for members. So far,

Figure 2　The Multiplied Advantages of Web 2.0

A traditional brick-and-mortar business spends a lot at the outset before seeing any profit. Think of the traditional pavement-pounding, knocking-on-doors approach to drumming up sales, or getting out the vote.

A typical Web 1.0 method is "robocalling" – automated dialing of phone lists using a prerecorded message. This requires an expensive initial outlay, which will only see returns over time. it also risks alienating potential supporters who don't like being interrupted at meal times. Besides, would you rather receive a call from an old friend or an impersonal machine?

In the 2008 U.S. presidential election, Barack Obama used Web 2.0 innovation: The initial cost of his iPhone downloads was much lower, and the payback was enormous almost immediately. There were about 5,000 downloads the first day, and within minutes people had a powerful tool that enabled them to call their "first degree of separation" friends and associates in key battleground states using their iPhone contact lists. What's

more, they received up-to-the-minute coverage and position statements on key campaign talking points. This generated half a million phone calls in the run-up to the election. One simple application turned supporters nationwide into a powerful, targeted, evangelistic telesales force. The rest is history.

Now, imagine getting that kind of multiplied response from marketing your own product or service. Every business could use a similar customized sales and customer relationship management tool on their company cell phones.

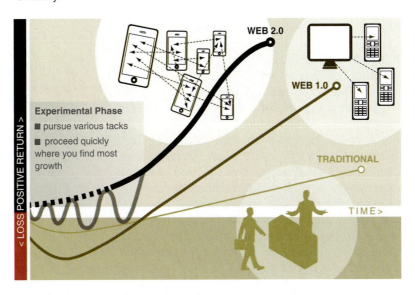

Source: Based on concepts originally published in *Web 2.0: A Strategy Guide* by Amy Shuen (O'Reilly Media, 2008).

users have acknowledged the value of these services, and the site currently counts around 700,000 paying Premium Members. In the midst of the crisis, Xing announced a 35 percent increase in total revenues to 21.54 million euros for the first six months of 2009, largely driven by Premium Membership revenues, which were up by 41 percent in 2009 over 2008. The international leader, LinkedIn, which is aggressively entering the European market, has adopted a different approach by building a large user base that only gets limited services, while some lead users—headhunters and recruiters—pay a significant sum for the possibility of browsing the huge database that LinkedIn has, and afterward contacting individual profiles.

Tactical Questions to Consider:
* Do you allow users to participate on your site with their own ideas?
* How do you support your most active community members?

Activate Network Effects

For most of us, traffic has negative connotations. But in the digital world, it's good news for business. Why? Because under certain conditions online traffic may be made up of network effects, which, put simply, are the effect each user has on the value of a product or service. They are very often at the heart of the new Web business models. If strong network effects exist, this may have a potentially huge effect on the overall profitability of a company.

Activating network effects, however, is tricky, since one has to understand that there are different kinds of effects, and that a misunderstanding of the effect has vast implications on the overall viability of the envisioned strategy. The five different kinds of network effects are direct, indirect, demand-side, cross-network and social.

A classic example of a *direct network effect* is the telephone. An individual telephone was useless but as people bought them, their value increased. *Indirect network effects* are when the popularity of a product or service spawns the production of increasingly valuable complementary goods—for example, the iPod and its accessories. *Demand-side effects* are, as we saw with Flickr, when willingness to pay for a service increases as more and more people use it. *Cross-network effects* are when a rise in usage by one group of users increases the value of a complementary product or service to

another distinct group of users, such as reader-writer software pairs. Lastly, *social or local network effects,* such as instant messaging, are when a user is influenced directly by the decisions of other consumers.

Network effects are the results of users jumping on the bandwagon. For this reason, they can mean the difference between your company having the lion's share or the leftovers of a competitive market. If two companies are locked in battle and one is slightly ahead of the other, network effects can tip the scales in favor of one of the competitors. Positive feedback can amplify the stronger company so that it gets stronger while the reverse is true of the weaker. In such tippy markets, network effects are so powerful that they can ultimately determine the rise or fall of entire companies.

In order to make network effects work, you need to figure out what yours are and how you can measure their value. Find out which groups could generate positive network effects for you and how you can get them to do so. Free or highly subsidized services, such as Google's search engine, are usually the answer. In addition, figure out a way to monetize the business model by finding a group of users that has a positive willingness to pay. Google gets almost all of its revenue from advertising, by placing ads (that then need to be clicked on) on either its own or third-party pages. Don't forget that network effects accumulate exponentially, and once you have activated them, the sky's the limit, because one network effect gives birth to more, which in turn give birth to even more and so on.

Tactical Questions to Consider:
* As users visit your site, do you learn from their activities, or just present information to them?
* If you are in a competitive race, how do your users see your offerings versus your competitor's?

Work Through Social Networks

While people might think of social networking as a particular kind of Web 2.0 application, it can enrich projects even when it isn't the central focus. The communities built by social networks can serve to strengthen the appeal of an endeavor. Members of a community naturally influence each other, so positive network effects can be triggered left, right, and center. As in the physical world, once key influencers are talking about a product or service, everybody will be, but the pace of this picks up online.

Again, the extreme power law of the Web means that once a network has a critical mass, more and more want to join, and the number of members grows exponentially. As we see with websites such as Facebook, Flickr, and MySpace, social networks acquire customers fast. They can attract tens of millions of new, active, and frequently engaged customers in a short amount of time, bringing with them valuable storehouses of openly uploaded, digital, personal and social content. This content can be turned into cash through charging certain users. But the value of this base can also be immediately monetized through target revenue advertising. Just think, while Google can offer advertisers the relevance of a keyword, Facebook gives them a personalized view of the consumers they want to reach.

Facebook isn't just a great audience for advertisers, though; developers are able to distribute their applications on the site. Consider possibilities within your own organization. Very often, IT projects have to be pushed back because of a lack of programming resources available internally. Outsourcing may be a solution. But traditional outsourcing only partially overcomes the resourcing problem, since the solution will be restricted to available capacity. What if we try to organize the idle capacity of IT programmers from virtually any country on earth, and go for crowdsourcing?

"What could you accomplish with a team of 225,534?" poses TopCoder.com, citing the number of developers in 200 countries that it counts among its software development community—and that number is constantly rising. TopCoder proposes a novel method of building and delivering software. TopCoder receives a project from a corporate client, and breaks it down into manageable pieces, which are then put out for competition online. Programmers in the community write the pieces that are put together according to the client's requirements and time frame. The client only pays the prize money for the chosen result, not for the hours of time the developers may have spent coming up with various solutions. Since several teams are competing for the same project, the quality of the winning solution is usually quite high. With this business model, TopCoder

has turned an age-old labor problem into a business proposition.

Tactical Questions to Consider:
- Do you provide mechanisms for your users to communicate among themselves?
- Could user information, like profiles, create advertising value for you?

Multiply Your Partners Through Syndication

In the online world, almost anything can be syndicated, because everything is in digital bits that can be copied at no extra cost. But the online syndication of competences takes it to a whole new level. When a company has the dynamic capabilities to change its initial business model and embrace syndication, it can find itself in a different league.

Originally an online bookseller, Amazon soon wised up to the fact that a lead in the market would be difficult to maintain when competitors were a click away. So, in 2001, it decided to sell shelf space, or zShops, to rivals. Sales increased by 34 percent in 2003 and at the end of that year Amazon posted its first profit after operating at a loss for a decade. Today, zShops have morphed into Amazon Marketplace, and Amazon has become the online platform for a broad range of online retailers, providing them back-office services, such as its shopping cart or payment system, which they never would have had the resources to build on their own. Paradoxically, Amazon gained competitive advantage by openly selling company secrets to potential rivals, and then turning them into a new set of partners and affiliates. Again, like Apple, IBM, and other network-savvy corporations, Amazon preferred to take advantage of a small segment of businesses in the long tail, and then expanding that market sliver exponentially, while sharing revenue with others.

The online phenomenon of mashups also sees companies working with each other. Mash-ups are digital open remixing of information from different sources. For example, HousingMaps.com combined the rentals on Craigslist with Google maps so that viewers could instantly see where addresses were. Two formerly unrelated sites were remixed to produce something that was more useful than its parts to a certain group of users. Web

2.0 competence syndication can turn competitors, ecosystem partners, and a broad range of small and medium enterprises into loyal, revenue-generating, revenue-sharing users, while increasing economies of scale and scope. This is a long way from the game theory of business strategy in the 80s, which saw keeping rivals on their toes as the key to success.

Tactical Questions to Consider:

- Are there aspects of your business that you could sell or syndicate as services?
- Could you work with businesses that might feel threatened by your projects?
- Do you have a product or service that could complement an existing Web service?

NO EXCUSES

Though many examples of the new high-tech business models are Web-based, traditional businesses have no excuse for failing to take full advantage of these opportunities as well. Let's look at some who have done just that.

Webkinz

This stuffed-toy company used dynamic capabilities and Web 2.0 to meet the demands of the Noughties child who likes teddy bears and computer games. The plush toys are no different from any others in the physical sense, but each comes with a secret code that enables its owner to enter the online Webkinz World, a virtual play area with its own economy. Every time you buy a pet, play a game, answer questions, or do activities, you get KinzCash to be spent in the online store. In addition, you interact with other pet owners through Webkinz chat. However, accounts expire within a year, unless another Webkinz animal is purchased, so kids have to keep buying if they want to remain part of the world.

The Webkinz business model has a big element of recombinant innovation, where a company took a classic product and mixed it with new technology to make something more valuable than the sum of its parts. The Webkinz World exploits a range of network effects including: direct—the experience of being part of the world gets better as more people join; indirect—the stuffed toys encourage complementary products in the shop;

and social—the online chat room connects fellow pet owners who influence each other.

Zopa

In the current economy, access to credit is increasingly difficult for consumers and enterprises alike. But money hasn't vanished. Part of the difficulty arises from a lack of trust in the system. This is precisely where social financiers such as Zopa.com come in. These platforms want to cut out the traditional middleman—the bank—and connect lenders and borrowers directly. So, if someone has some spare money to lend, he or she can check out the lending options, and then proceed directly to the description of a potential borrower and the motives of his or her financial need. The lender sets the lending rate that suits him or her, and the loan enters an online auction. Thus, social lending is putting risk assessment, rates, and returns back in the hands of individual lenders and borrowers themselves, and eschewing the overheads and money-making schemes employed by banks, which many regard with cynicism in the wake of the crisis.

GE/Google Smart Grid

GE provides consumers with wireless "smart meters" and Google makes the detailed energy data available to users via their laptops. In a pilot project involving Oklahoma G&E, even teenagers got in on the act, unplugging the toaster after breakfast when they knew down to the cent the value of doing so, as their minute-by-minute energy use was being calculated and fed to them via the Web. GE has recombined an old product (metering) with information technologies, and used aspects of Web 2.0 in its business model. Vitally, this innovation has an energy-saving motive at its core, which these days gives any project an added edge.

Lego

The Danish company Lego allows customers to design their own Lego sets through its "Design byME" initiative. This program, launched in October 2009 as a continuation of its Lego Factory customization program, allows users to create their own Lego product, from beginning to end, providing all the necessary information and tools to get the job done. Customers download digital design software provided by Lego at no charge. They custom-design their own dream Lego models on computer, right down to the box and building guide. Then the product can be ordered online and shipped to their door.

Maybe some of these ideas inspire you. Try them out. The low cost and high connectivity of the Web means you can experiment easily—indeed, experimentation is key to finding out what works and what doesn't. Once you've seen the difference it makes, you can build in the directions that you find the most growth.

WEB 3.0 AND BEYOND

Like backseat passengers on a road trip, we tend to ignore the amazing scenery whizzing past us as we impatiently ask the driver, "Are we at Web 3.0 yet?" If we date the start of the first generation of the Web to Netscape going public in 1995, then it took us a full decade to reach the "cross-over point" in 2005—the year when more bits, bytes, and digital goods were being uploaded and shared on the Web than were being downloaded. So, if it took 10 years to go from Web 1.0 to Web 2.0—from static to dynamic, from passive users to active contributors—and we are nearly halfway through the second decade of the Web, what's next on the horizon?

Part of our impatience is due to the instant gratification we have come to expect from the Web, and we're disappointed that the Web at work doesn't look that much different from the Web at home. This, in itself, says a lot about how we've changed.

John Chambers, CEO of Cisco, speaking at an O'Reilly Media Web 2.0 Summit, pointed out that the new Web paradigm has reversed the usual sequence of technology and business innovation. In the past, disruptive high-tech innovations, such as semiconductor chips, began life in big industry labs, and then trickled down to the mass market in simplified versions, after proving their commercial worth in the professional world. Customers had to be educated by companies on how to use these new products and services, with a small group of early adopters and lead users acting as pioneers before opening up the path to mainstream acceptance.

Those days are fast disappearing. We're witnessing a quantum social shift that has business implications for both digital and traditional industries. All around us, we see industry transformations and network convergence—in media, entertainment, music, telecom, financial services, energy, life sciences, health care, consumer electronics, precious metals. Even everyday branded products like Heinz Ketchup and Doritos are bringing new collaborative innovation and dynamic capabilities to the forefront. In the United States, Europe, and Asia, whole new ecosystems and networks of small businesses are forming around these leaders.

The next Web crossover point will be when the world puts the Web to work in jumping the digital divide and bringing local entrepreneurs and users at the bottom of the pyramid into the networked, digital knowledge economy. A few promising and influential innovators in this area include Kiva, the world's first online microlending platform connecting lenders to entrepreneurs across the globe.

Another example is the pharmaceutical distributor McKesson, which has been an IT innovator in providing preventive and emergency services to homeless people in partnership with state health and hospital agencies. In return for a free cell phone and monthly minutes, previously hard-to-reach but at-risk groups such as homeless people can be monitored and receive health care and medical advice to reduce the likelihood of high-cost emergency room and acute-care cases down the road.

Such initiatives are pursuing collaborative innovation on a large scale, connecting digital, financial, and knowledge-based capabilities and resources with external networks of local partners and government agencies. The Web of the future, we believe, will see more "feet on the street," featuring even greater transparency, visibility, localization, and distribution to global participants at the bottom of the pyramid.

Low-Cost Strategy through Product Architecture: Lessons from China

Hua Wang
Euromed Management Ecole
de Marseille, France

Chris Kimble
Euromed Management Ecole
de Marseille, France

INTRODUCTION

The global financial downturn that began in 2008 has pushed much of the world's car industry into crisis; carmakers serving the U.S. market, including strong performers like Toyota and Honda, have experienced double-digit declines in their sales. The Chinese car industry, on the other hand, is booming. It overtook the U.S. industry in 2008 to become the second largest in the world, producing 9.4 million vehicles.

Foreign carmakers located in China have played their part, but local players such as Geely, Chery, and BYD have also had a role in the expansion. This article will argue that the rapid growth of indigenous Chinese carmakers is driven not by low labor costs, but by innovations in product architecture that have enabled Chinese carmakers to follow a low-cost strategy while still producing products that are broadly equivalent to their foreign counterparts. By changing the product design, local carmakers with less than 15 years' experience have managed to produce cars in the same product category as their Western competitors but at a significantly lower price.

We begin by briefly highlighting the link between breakthrough strategies and product design. We follow this with a discussion of product architecture and identify a form of transitional product architecture created by Chinese carmakers known as a quasi-open modular architecture. We then present a case study of a Chinese carmaker, Geely, which illustrates the nature of the car industry in China and shows the impact that this transitional architecture can have. Finally, we address the possible implications of this approach for car production by the mainstream U.S. and European car industry.

BREAKTHROUGH STRATEGIES AND PRODUCT DESIGN

Breakthrough Strategies

The notion of breakthrough strategy has its own literature and is dealt with elsewhere (e.g., Markides, 2000). Our aim here is not to enter into a discussion of these ideas but to outline the key concepts. Although there is disagreement on points of detail, there is broad agreement on the key features:

- A breakthrough strategy involves a radical or fundamental shift in the way in which things are done.
- A breakthrough strategy is not about playing the existing game better but about changing the rules of the game.
- A breakthrough strategy involves a complete reconceptualization or reconfiguration of an existing business model.

For the purposes of this paper, we will simply define a breakthrough strategy as the successful

Reprinted from "Low-Cost Strategy Through Product Architecture: Lessons From China," by Hua Wang and Chris Kimble, *Journal of Business Strategy*, Vol. 31, No. 3 (2010), pp. 12–20. Copyright © Emerald Group Publishing Limited. All rights reserved.

introduction of a radical change in the way a business operates that creates an entirely new way of doing business. Success, in this context, is defined in terms of the company's ability to outperform its competitors significantly.

Examples of companies that achieve this sort of breakthrough are often drawn from the high-tech sector. For example, eBay based its business operations on the same principles as long-established auction houses such as Christie's and Sotheby's, but achieved a breakthrough by the dematerialization of the auction process, coupled with the creation of PayPal, which both makes payment easier and generates additional revenue for eBay. Although most of the recent literature on breakthrough strategies tends to focus on the alignment of IT and business strategy, other approaches can be followed.

Product Design

Fraser (2007) describes how companies can achieve strategic breakthroughs by applying the principles of design to business strategy. She describes this as consisting of three interacting gears. The first gear is user understanding; being able to reframe the business through the eyes of the customer. She describes this as "more than marketing 101" (Fraser, 2007, p. 68), as it involves a deep and profound understanding of the customer's needs.

The second gear is concept visualization, where an abstract understanding of users' needs becomes a concrete expression of what the product should be and how it will serve the customer's needs. Finally, the third gear, what Fraser calls strategic business design, involves applying abductive reasoning—making the conceptual leap to think, "If feature X were possible, all of our ideas about what we want to do with the product would follow naturally" (Figure 1).

The following section will present an approach that makes such a link between strategy and design. To do this, we will need to narrow the field of design to a subcategory known as product architecture.

PRODUCT ARCHITECTURE: THE MISSING LINK IN BREAKTHROUGH STRATEGY?

Product architecture is a conceptual representation of the physical components that go to make up a product, together with any interactions between them that affect the functioning of that product. Takahiro Fujimoto argues that a fit between

Figure 1   The Three Gears of Design

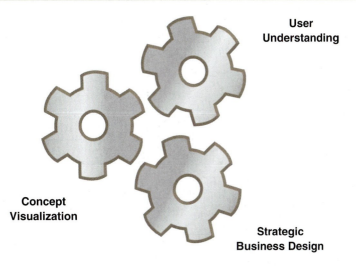

User Understanding

Concept Visualization

Strategic Business Design

Source: Adapted from Fraser (2007).

capabilities in manufacturing and product architecture can create an advantage for a particular industry in a particular country or region and identifies product architecture as one of the most important sources of a country's comparative advantage (Fujimoto, 2007).

Fujimoto defines product architecture in terms of an approach that links the functional and structural design of a product. He divides product architecture along two dimensions: modular-integral and open-closed. The modular-integral dimension refers to the level of integration of the components in a product. Products with a high degree of component integration have many-to-many links between their components, meaning that the product has to be produced as a single integrated unit. A low level of component integration means that components have a simple one-to-one correspondence and can be treated as discrete modules. The open-closed dimension refers to the level of standardization. An open architecture implies the existence of industry-level standards for components; a closed architecture means that standardization exists only within the boundaries of a single firm.

By combining these two dimensions, Fujimoto identifies three possible forms of product architecture: open-modular, closed-modular, and closed-integral. According to Fujimoto, the fourth

category, open-integral, is a logical contradiction and a practical impossibility (Figure 2).

Fujimoto's classification of product architecture provides us with a useful way to think about the links between the design of products and the strategic positioning of a company. For example, the often-repeated story of IBM (Baldwin and Clark, 1997) can be recast in terms architectural evolution.

Viewed in this way, IBM's story is as follows. In the 1950s, computers were specialized, custom-built machines created to perform specific tasks, clearly corresponding to the closed-integral cell in Fujimoto's model. At that time, IBM was the market leader in the manufacture of custom-built data-processing machines such as the IBM 704. However, in response to growing demand in the 1960s, IBM began to introduce new products such as the IBM System 360 range that shared the same hardware and software. This moved IBM into the closed-modular cell in the model. In the late 1970s and early 1980s, a new market for desktop computing began to emerge in which Apple was the market leader. IBM launched its own desktop PC in 1981 and, in order to cut costs and speed up development time, outsourced heavily (Figure 3). This effectively moved the desktop into the third open-modular cell of Fujimoto's model, which in turn created the conditions for companies such

Figure 2   Fujimoto's Taxonomy of Product Architecture

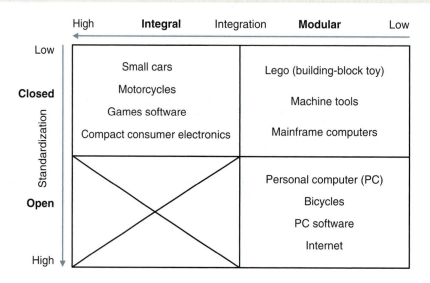

Figure 3   The IBM Story in Terms of an Evolution in Product Architecture

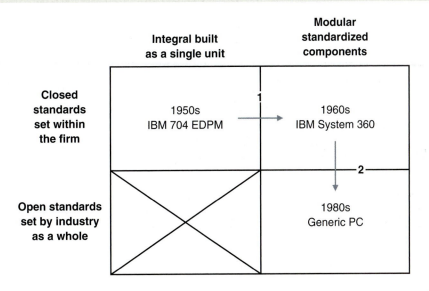

as Intel and Microsoft to make a strategic breakthrough and become the new market leaders.

Although there is no single pattern to architectural evolution, according to Baldwin and Clark (1997), the general trend is a movement from closed-integral to open-modular architectures, a trajectory that can also be seen in the production of complex mechanical products such as cars.

For example, according to Langlois (2002), the 1930s marked the transition from craftsman-built, open-modular car production to a mass-production closed-integral model. This model remained dominant until the 1990s, when, driven by competitive pressures, a number of leading European carmakers began to move to a closed-modular type production, for example, platform sharing between Citroën and Peugeot cars in the PSA group, or Volkswagen, Audi, Skoda, and Seat in the Volkswagen group. However, this modularity has remained at the company, rather than the industrial, level; consequently, the change from closed to open product architectures that we can see in the PC industry is not present in the U.S. or European car industry.

In China, however, carmakers and their suppliers have begun to move toward a more open, modular form of production based on what is termed a quasi-open modular product architecture. Fujimoto describes this development in the following way:

> Imitation-turned-versatile parts are being gathered and assembled by numerous companies and this is different from a full-fledged open architecture based on a carefully worked-out plan as seen in various digital products made by American companies. (Fujimoto, 2002, p. 35)

In China, best-selling foreign cars are routinely imitated through reverse engineering. Major components from those foreign cars, such as engines and chassis, have, through repetitive remodeling, become defacto generic components that can be used by indigenous manufacturers. By mixing and matching remodeled components from existing cars, Chinese manufacturers are able to produce completely new cars more quickly and at a much lower price than their foreign counterparts are able to achieve (Figure 4). Although this approach is a radical departure from Western practices, it remains only a quasi-open modular architecture, as the modularity of the remodeled components has not yet reached the industry level.

The analysis of the case study that follows provides a concrete illustration of how this quasi-open

Figure 4   The Emerging Chinese Automobile Industry

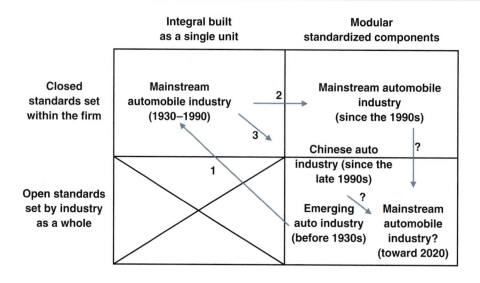

modular architecture works in practice and additionally illustrates some of the unique features of the Chinese car industry that contributed to its emergence.

CASE STUDY—CHINA GEELY AUTOMOBILE CO. LTD

Method

The methodology used to produce this case study was an in-depth, longitudinal case history (Yin, 2003). The study was undertaken over a period of five years and was divided into three stages. The first stage was a preliminary field study that took place over a period of a year in 2002; the second stage was an in-depth investigation conducted between January and April 2006; the final stage involved onsite interviews and was carried out between March and May 2007. The majority of interviewees for this final stage were middle- or senior-level managers who had at least 15 years' experience as carmakers. This approach afforded a broader understanding of the Chinese market and moved beyond the experiences of a single firm. The full details of the case study have been published elsewhere (Wang, 2008).

Findings and Analysis

In 1998, a successful private manufacturer of refrigerators and motorcycles in China named Geely made what might have appeared to be a surprising decision and expanded into the production to motorcars. At the time, there were already around 120 carmakers in China and the central government was actively promoting a car industry based around a small number of state-owned companies. The approval process for any new projects was extremely severe. Geely had little credibility as a car manufacturer and was compelled to resort to some rather creative and unorthodox practices, such as listing their first cars in the less-regulated bus category.

Despite such an inauspicious start, in December 2001, Geely was registered officially as a carmaker and became the first privately owned car manufacturer in China. In less than 10 years, it has become the ninth-largest carmaker in China. It sold 230,000 units in 2008, a year-on-year increase of 11.6 percent, and succeeded in increasing its exports by 79.8 percent. In addition, it has expanded its production capacity to 500,000 units and has set up five new manufacturing sites. The company's success in crafting a breakthrough strategy from such unpromising beginnings is based in part on its founder's deep understanding of Chinese markets, and in part on the innovations it has made in its product architecture.

Refrigerators, motorcycles, and cars were the three products most affected by the rise in living standards and purchasing power that followed the economic reforms of the 1980s (Wang, 2008). The Chinese middle class, who buy these goods, are highly price sensitive but also very concerned about the appearance of the product, which is an outward expression of their social status. Geely was able to identify precisely what the consumer wanted but, in addition, was able to develop a new product architecture that allowed it to produce a low-price/low-cost product that was designed to meet specific local needs.

As elsewhere, components from best-selling foreign cars were reverse-engineered and copied, but the approach pioneered by Geely differed from traditional copying in one important respect: the architecture of the copied product was progressively altered in such a way that the high-level mixing and matching of components from different sources became possible.

Geely experienced at least two stages in the development of their product architecture. In the first stage, architectural changes were based on simple imitation. The first model produced in 1998, the Haoqing, was based on the Charade, which was itself the result of technology transfer from Toyota's affiliate, Daihatsu. The Charade was produced by the state-owned FAW Xiali. Initially, around 60 percent of components (including the engine and transmission) were purchased directly from FAW Xiali, with copied components accounting for another 10 percent. Thus, around 70 percent of the components of the Haoqing were interchangable with that of the Charade.

Later, in the second stage, the capability of mixing and matching components was increased. The Maple, which entered production in 2002, was based on the combination of two foreign models already produced in China: the French Citroën ZX and the Charade (originally from Japan). The body and chassis of the Maple were based on the imitation and remodeling of Citroën ZX, while the engine was based on the remodeling of a Toyota engine. From this point of view, the Maple was more of an open-modular design than the Haoqing.

Combining components from cars designed with an integral or closed modular architecture

(the Citroën ZX and Charade) to build a car with a quasi-open modular architecture (the Maple) was a major technical challenge for Geely. Architectural change requires a significantly higher level of technological and engineering capability than copying. The more recent cars produced by Geely have reached a high level of modularity, going well beyond the closed modular model typical of leading Western carmakers. For example, the engine produced by Geely can fit into bodies derived from several different foreign models, each produced by different manufacturers. Additionally, cars produced by Geely can also accommodate a number of other engines that can be bought in the open market. A senior manager at Geely explains:

> During the design period, enough space has been reserved for an engine. We've tried to assemble different engines on the same car, and all of them work without the need to change the rest of the car's architecture.

In short, the interface between the engine and the rest of the car has been designed to allow the manufacturer to mix and match major components in a flexible and efficient way. This architectural innovation, both at the level of the engine and that of the whole car, has helped Geely to significantly reduce its costs (Wang, 2008). For example, Geely's MR4790Q engine can be produced at one-third of the price of a Toyota engine because the components of Toyota's engine have become "imitation-turned-versatile" parts that can be produced at low costs and in large volumes. In terms of total cost, Geely's plant manager observed:

> If our competitors are selling their vehicles (of the same category) at prices as low as ours, they are losing money, whereas we still make profit.

The final element in Geely's breakthrough is that it has enabled the creation of innovative interfirm relationships that support its overall strategy. A high percentage (around 70 percent) of components, including parts of the engine, are outsourced; consequently, Geely and its suppliers need to work very closely together. Geely strives to lower the price but must also maintain an acceptable level of quality to meet the local market's needs. To achieve this goal, it has built on its links with its suppliers from its motorcycle business who are experienced in high-volume production at low costs. This category accounts for 50 percent of its total number of suppliers. To ensure quality is maintained, the suppliers of big companies such as Volkswagen, Toyota, PSA, Nissan, and General Motors are also integrated into the sourcing system. Having Geely, as the customer helps those suppliers realize economies of scale because of the higher production volume. Thus, the architectural innovation that has taken place at Geely, is now contributing to a wider change at the industrial level (Figure 5).

CONCLUSION: IMPLICATIONS FOR THE AUTOMOBILE GIANTS

Attaining low-cost production is a perennial challenge for most manufacturers. The current incremental approach toward cost reduction using existing product architectures, which predominates in the Western car industry, seems to be reaching its limits; only a radical architectural change in product design will allow a company to lower its costs so significantly that its competitors will find the move hard to follow. In just a single decade, through its innovative use of product architecture, Geely has moved from having no experience of carmaking to a position where it is the ninth-largest carmaker in China and is

able to produce and sell cars that are significantly cheaper than its foreign counterparts. In 2009, Geely announced a sales growth of 25 percent and no job cuts despite the financial crisis and a global economic downturn.

Although Geely's progress has been dramatic, it is by no means an exceptional case in China's car industry. Other local carmakers, including Chery, BYD, and Great Wall are making similar progress using similar methods. We estimate that cars featuring quasi-open architectures now represent around 30 percent of total production in China. In addition to the carmakers, developments among component suppliers are reinforcing the move toward quasi-open architectures. For example, Mitsubishi is selling its engines to at least 21 different carmakers in China and Delphi's engine management system has become modular so that it can be used with any Mitsubishi engine in order to increase its sales. In short, the Chinese market has become the crucible from which a new product architecture for automobiles has begun to emerge: local consumers, carmakers, and leading component suppliers are all contributing to expansion of the quasi-open architectural paradigm.

Leading carmakers in other parts of the world are confronting multiple challenges to their position; so far, the response seems to have been to continue to adhere to closed product architectures. However, technological advances such as greater fuel efficiency or the development of

Figure 5   **Three Gears Model in the Chinese Automobile Industry**

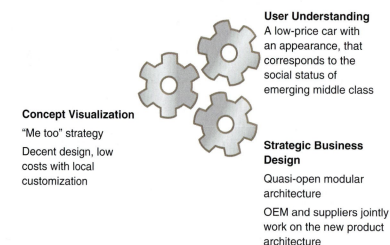

User Understanding
A low-price car with an appearance, that corresponds to the social status of emerging middle class

Concept Visualization
"Me too" strategy
Decent design, low costs with local customization

Strategic Business Design
Quasi-open modular architecture
OEM and suppliers jointly work on the new product architecture

technically complex hybrid or other forms of so-called green cars have failed to stimulate sales in mature markets due to their high price. Abandoning the low-cost bottom of the pyramid, as the market in developing countries is sometimes referred to, to local manufacturers could be a strategic mistake, as these are exactly the markets where the innovations that seem set to produce low-cost strategic breakthroughs appear to be happening.

Developments such as the quasi-open architecture found in Chinese car manufacturing seem to have the potential to produce cars of comparable quality to those of the established carmakers, but at a significantly lower cost. Mainstream Western carmakers may have the edge on new technology, but this alone seems unlikely to give them the strategic breakthrough they need. The current carmaking giants and others need to be fully aware of the strategic potential of innovations in product architecture, both as a potential driver of breakthrough strategy and as a threat to the current position. Manufacturers based in the mature markets of the United States and Europe ignore the lessons of low-cost production through innovations in product architecture that are beginning to emerge from China at their peril.

REFERENCES

Baldwin, C. Y. and Clark, K. B. (1997), "Managing in an age of modularity," *Harvard Business Review,* Vol. 75 No. 5, pp. 84–93.

Fraser, H. M. A. (2007), "The practice of breakthrough strategies by design," *Journal of Business Strategy,* Vol. 28 No. 4, pp. 66–74.

Fujimoto, T. (2002), "Thinking about the China's manufacturing industry from the perspective of product architecture," *Keizai Sangyo Janaru,* pp. 34–7.

Fujimoto, T. (2007), "Architecture-based comparative advantage: a design information view of manufacturing", *Evolutionary and Institutional Economics Review,* Vol. 4 No. 1, pp. 55–112.

Langlois, R. N. (2002), "Modularity in technology and organization," *Journal of Economic Behavior and Organization,* Vol. 49 No. 1, pp. 19–37.

Markides, C. C. (2000), *All the Right Moves: A Guide to Crafting Breakthrough Strategy,* Harvard Business School Press, Boston, MA.

Wang, H. (2008), "The innovation in the product architecture: a study of Chinese automobile industry," *Asia Pacific Journal of Management,* Vol. 25 No. 3, pp. 509–35.

Yin, R. K. (2003), *Case Study Research: Design and Methods,* Sage, Thousand Oaks, CA.

Innovation Strategies Combined

Frank T. Rothaermel
Georgia Institute of Technology

Andrew M. Hess
University of Virginia

Continuous innovation is the engine that drives highly successful companies such as Apple, General Electric, Google, Honda, Hewlett-Packard, Microsoft, Procter & Gamble, Sony, Tata group, and many others. Innovation is an especially potent competitive weapon in tough economic times because it allows companies to redefine the marketplace in their favor and achieve much-needed growth. However, achieving continuous innovation is very hard, and most attempts fail.

One increasingly popular way to think about innovation is to conceive of it as an open rather than a closed system—a concept Henry Chesbrough and others have written about. To continue to be innovative in a world of widely distributed knowledge, many companies are recognizing that they must open their innovation process to combine internal with external R&D. That can be done by bringing in new human capital, engaging in strategic alliances, or acquiring technology ventures. By the same token, internal inventions that a company decides not to pursue should be not simply shelved, but rather considered for commercialization through licenses, spin-offs, or joint ventures.

If an open innovation system does in fact help drive growth and performance, managers need to answer two critical questions:

1. Which innovation strategies should the company pursue?
2. Which innovation strategies go well together?

To answer these important questions, we spent five years studying how global pharmaceutical companies have built innovative capabilities in biotechnology. We documented, in great detail, the annual R&D expenses of 81 global pharmaceutical companies over a 22-year period, along with every biotech and non-biotech patent the companies filed, every scientist who worked for one of the companies, all alliances entered into and all acquisitions consummated during that period. In particular, we tracked approximately 900 acquisitions, 4,000 alliances, 13,200 biotechnology patents, 110,000 non-biotechnology patents, and 135,000 scientists; we used U.S. biotechnology patents granted as a proxy for innovation in this industry. Although the global pharmaceutical industry is unique to some extent, we believe that our findings also hold for many other industries, because new knowledge, human capital, strategic alliances, and acquisitions increasingly determine the success or failure of individual businesses across a large number of industries today.

DECIDING WHICH INNOVATION STRATEGY TO PURSUE

The question of which innovation strategies to pursue is critical, because corporate executives have multiple strategies for achieving innovation at their disposal. They can decide to spend more on internal R&D, hire and retain the best human capital, ally with innovative companies, or buy innovation through acquisitions. Each strategy has its distinct pros and cons, as captured in Figure 1.

In addition to examining those four fundamental innovation strategies, we also examined two different components of recruiting and retaining superior human capital; our study distinguished between exceptional "star" scientists and more typical "non-star" scientists. When considering the importance of human capital, most CEOs think about how to recruit and retain exceptional star performers. Non-star performers, however, often get overlooked. And yet these rank-and-file knowledge workers are critical to innovative success. While star scientists can cue a company to shifts in the knowledge environment and direct the organization toward promising new areas, non-star scientists are the ones who integrate new knowledge into processes and routines—and thereby execute the organizational changes necessary to be innovative.

WHICH INNOVATION STRATEGIES GO WELL TOGETHER?

Although researchers have a fairly good understanding of innovation strategies *individually,* the effects of pursuing various innovation strategies simultaneously have not been known. That is a significant problem, because clearly, executives can decide to pursue multiple innovation levers

Figure 1   Four Approaches to Innovation

Companies have a variety of innovation levers at their disposal, but each strategy has its pros and cons and each requires different competencies.

Innovation Strategy	Upsides	Downsides	Some Exemplar Companies		Requirements
Recruiting and Retaining Superior Human Capital	• Better control of IP • Long-term growth focus • Difficult for competitors to imitate	• Organic growth is slower • Challenge of identifying and valuing superior human capital	• Goldman Sachs • Google • Merck	• Research In Motion • Southwest Airlines • W.L. Gore	• Astute strategic human resource management • Organizational flexibility
Internal R&D Spending	• Internalization of skills and capabilities • Full capture of returns	• Full risk exposure • Long time horizon • Uncertain returns	• Apple • BMW • Hewlett-Packard		• Culture of risk tolerance • Organizational flexibility • Long-term commitment
Strategic Alliances	• Shared risk • Multiple, small-scale investments provide strategic options • Faster than internal development	• Potential loss of IP control • Challenge of alignment of goals • Shared returns	• IBM • Eli Lilly • Oracle • Procter & Gamble		• Dedicated function for the management of partnerships
Acquisitions	• Faster than growing organically • Acquire innovative technologies before start-ups become competitors	• Risk of overpaying • Cultural integration concerns • Involves relying on others for innovation	• Cisco • General Electric • Pfizer • Microsoft		• Capability to identify and assimilate acquisition targets

simultaneously. They can, for example, combine internal R&D spending with acquisitions, or the recruitment of superior human capital with alliances. Many other permutations are possible, thereby significantly increasing the complexity that companies face when attempting to innovate. Moreover, the business world is complex and messy—and does not conform to the convenience found in most academic studies of keeping everything else equal while studying the effects of one single innovation strategy at a time.

What happens when different innovation strategies are pursued simultaneously? Which innovation strategies go well together, and which do not? In Figure 2, we present a simplified version of some of the results from our study, which were reported in detail in an article in *Organization Science*. Green arrows denote strategies that go well together, while red arrows show combinations that reduced the effectiveness of a company's investment in innovation strategies. (Blue boxes indicate that there was neither a synergistic effect nor one that decreased expected innovative performance.)

As the matrix indicates, the combination of star and non-star performers enhances innovative performance: Our research highlights the complementary roles that star and non-star performers play. Moreover, our findings also show synergies between internal R&D expenditures and alliances—and suggest that a strong internal R&D capability allows a company to select and pursue the most promising strategic alliances. Finally, alliances and acquisitions frequently reinforce each other.

On the other hand, in some cases, pursuing multiple innovation strategies simultaneously can actually reduce the effectiveness of a company's investments in innovation strategies. For example, our findings suggest that the type of knowledge obtained through alliances and through rank-and-file knowledge workers is often redundant. Similarly, investments in star performers and R&D spending can also apparently lead to redundant outcomes when both strategies are pursued simultaneously.

UNDERSTANDING THESE FINDINGS

To foster successful innovation, managers must be able not only to weigh the strengths and weaknesses of each innovation mechanism but also to understand and predict how these mechanisms are likely to interact when used in tandem. The resources and capabilities required to pull any one innovation lever are not independent of those needed to pull a different lever. Due to mounting performance pressures, managers often choose a grab-bag approach to innovating, by employing a variety of available mechanisms simultaneously—without knowing the possible deleterious interaction effects.

In contrast, our research points to important yet frequently overlooked interdependencies across different innovation strategies. When pursued in tandem, some innovation levers positively reinforce one another, while others compensate

Figure 2   The Effects of Simultaneous Innovation Strategies

Our detailed study of large pharmaceutical companies' innovation strategies in biotechnology found that combining some strategies tended to result in synergies that improved innovation performance, but other strategy

	NON-STARS	STARS	R&D	ALLIANCES	ACQUISITIONS
NON-STARS	—	↑	■	↓	■
STARS	↑	—	↓	■	■
R&D	■	↓	—	↑	■
ALLIANCES	↓	■	↑	—	↑
ACQUISITIONS	■	■	■	↑	—

combinations interacted negatively. Green arrows denote strategies that go well together, while red arrows show combinations that can reduce the effectiveness of a company's investments in innovation. Blue boxes indicate that there was neither a synergistic effect nor one that decreased expected innovative performance.

for one another. Our study empirically validates the conclusion that just because executives *can* pull a certain innovation lever, does not mean they *should*. Using more innovation strategies at once is not always better!

Although the results from our study are intriguing and valuable to managers, an important caution is in order. Our research is focused on understanding the innovation efforts of established, and, for the most part, large companies (e.g., average, inflation-adjusted annual R&D expenditures of more than $850 million). Given their size, many of the companies studied have already developed competencies in specific innovation levers. For example, one pharmaceutical company may have traditionally focused on internally developing its research capabilities, while several others may have more often chosen to build their innovation capabilities through acquisitions and alliances. What's more, there is no clear overlap between the capabilities needed for developing a company's human capital and those needed for successfully managing alliances. Consequently, for the companies we studied, the negative effects on innovation associated with combining certain innovation strategies may reflect the opportunity costs of not focusing more on an innovation approach that hones the company's existing, underlying competencies and harnesses its prior experience. The results could be different for biotechnology start-up companies. For example, given the endemic resource constraints of technology start-ups, we speculate that the negative consequences of combining noncompatible innovation strategies may be even more pronounced. On the other hand, biotech start-ups tend to be more nimble than large companies and are less burdened with red tape. Our findings

suggest that start-ups that have a keen understanding of the effectiveness of their different innovation levers and how to combine them can execute a winning innovation strategy.

Overall, our study found that the strategy that appears to have the greatest impact on innovative performance is developing and fostering human capital. One potential reason for the importance of this innovation strategy is related to the notion of time horizons. For established companies, alliances and acquisitions are often executed for the purposes of filling a specific need or anticipated gap in the innovation pipeline. Indeed, some acquisitions are consummated out of panic, rather than from any long-term vision for a future stream of innovations. In contrast, sustainable innovation is a long-term strategy that requires an equally long-term strategic commitment by the business—such as a strategy of developing superior human capital.

Our goal is not to offer managers a one-size-fits-all recipe for successful innovation. Such a fool's errand would miss one of the points of our study, which is that the utilization of an innovation lever is itself a significant investment that carries the burden of all path-dependent activities. Rather than pulling every lever possible, managers should carefully weigh the unforeseen costs—often opportunity costs—associated with interdependencies between different innovative mechanisms. Maximizing scale of inputs does not equal maximizing innovative outputs. Recognizing this, managers should resist the siren song of the innovation grab bag in favor of a more deliberate approach to innovation that weighs not only where the organization is today but also where it was yesterday and where it hopes to be tomorrow.

RELATED RESEARCH

Rothaermel, F. T., and Hess, A. M. (2007), "Building dynamic capabilities: innovation driven by individual-, firm-, and network-level effects," *Organization Science*, Vol. 18 No. 6, pp. 898–921.

Managing Strategic Alliances: What Do We Know Now, and Where Do We Go from Here?

Prashant Kale
Rice University

Harbir Singh
University of Pennsylvania

EXECUTIVE OVERVIEW

Alliances present a paradox for firms. On the one hand, firms engage in a large number of alliances to secure and extend their competitive advantage and growth; on the other hand, their alliances exhibit surprisingly low success rates. In this paper, we discuss how firms can address these failures by identifying some of the primary drivers of alliance success. First, we discuss how firms can achieve success with any individual alliance by considering critical factors at each phase of the alliance life cycle. Second, we show how firms can increase their overall alliance success by developing and institutionalizing firm-level capabilities to manage alliances. Third, we highlight emerging issues in the alliance context, including the need to recognize a new class of alliances between firms and not-for-profit organizations or individuals, the benefits of taking a "portfolio approach" to alliance strategy and management, and the opportunity to transfer one's alliance capabilities to the effective management of other interfirm relationships, including acquisitions.

THE ALLIANCE PARADOX

In the last two decades, alliances have become a central part of most companies' competitive and growth strategies. Alliances help firms strengthen their competitive position by enhancing market power (Kogut, 1991), increasing efficiencies (Ahuja, 2000), accessing new or critical resources or capabilities (Rothaermel & Boeker, 2008), and entering new markets (Garcia-Canal, Duarte, Criado, & Llaneza, 2002). By the turn of this century many of the world's largest companies had over 20 percent of their assets, and over 30 percent of their annual research expenditures, tied up in such relationships (Ernst, 2004). A study by Partner Alliances reported that over 80 percent of Fortune 1,000 CEOs believed that alliances would account for almost 26 percent of their companies' revenues in 2007–08 (Kale, Singh, & Bell, 2009). Nevertheless, alliances also tend to exhibit high failure rates (Dyer, Kale, & Singh, 2001). Studies have shown that between 30 percent and 70 percent of alliances fail; in

other words, they neither meet the goals of their parent companies nor deliver on the operational or strategic benefits they purport to provide (Bamford, Gomes-Casseres, & Robinson, 2004). Alliance termination rates are reportedly over 50 percent (Lunnan & Haugland, 2008), and in many cases forming such relationships has resulted in shareholder value destruction for the companies that engage in them (Kale, Dyer, & Singh, 2002).

This creates a paradox for firms. On the one hand, companies face significant obstacles in ensuring sufficient success with alliances. On the other hand, they need to form a greater number of alliances than before, and must increasingly rely on them as a means of enhancing their competitiveness and growth. If this is indeed the case,

Reprinted from "Managing Strategic Alliances: What Do We Know Now, and Where Do We Go From Here?" by Prashant Kale and Harbir Singh, *Academy of Management Perspectives*, Vol. 23, No. 3 (August 2009), pp. 45–62. Copyright © 2009 by Academy of Management. Reproduced with permission of Academy of Management via Copyright Clearance Center.

managers need a better understanding of what really underlies alliance success and how firms can manage alliances better. This paper takes a step in addressing these questions by drawing on insights gained from prior and current research on this subject. We examine these issues at two different levels of analysis.

First, we focus at the level of a single alliance between two or more firms, investigating the major factors that explain the success of a given alliance; this has been the primary focus of most alliance research until recently. Second, we focus on a firm as a whole that is engaged in not just one but multiple alliances over time, and we explain how it can get better at managing them. In other words, how can it develop a firm-level "alliance capability" so as to enjoy greater and repeatable success across all its alliances? Scholars have begun studying the latter issue only recently, but it is particularly important as, in a world where firms rely more than ever on alliances, having a superior capability to manage them is in itself a source of competitive advantage.[1]

We conclude the paper by discussing both emerging opportunities and challenges at both levels of analysis. First, at the alliance level firms need to recognize the growing importance of a new class of alliances in addition to the traditional firm-to-firm alliance: alliances between firms and not-for-profit entities, including nongovernmental organizations (NGOs), and alliances between firms and individuals (such as Procter & Gamble's Connect + Develop relationships established to foster and accelerate innovations). Second, at the firm level, companies need to develop another kind of capability in the alliance context apart from the capability to enable greater and repeatable success across their set of alliances—firms also need to learn how to manage their alliance portfolio as a whole. We term this "alliance portfolio capability," and later in this paper we describe some of its constituents. Third, we suggest that if firms have a capability to manage alliances successfully they have an opportunity to leverage this proficiency to effectively manage acquisitions, which are traditionally considered to be a different mode of inorganic growth from alliances. In doing so, we highlight some opportunities for fruitful synthesis between alliances research and acquisitions research, which otherwise have been pursued as distinct and separate streams of research.

WHAT DETERMINES THE SUCCESS OF A SINGLE ALLIANCE?

A strategic alliance is a purposive relationship between two or more independent firms that involves the exchange, sharing, or codevelopment of resources or capabilities to achieve mutually relevant benefits (Gulati, 1995). A strategic alliance can span one or more parts of the value chain and have a variety of organizational configurations typically based on the absence or presence of equity in the relationship (for example, joint ventures represent one type of an equity-based alliance). Figure 1 provides an overview of the range of interfirm relationships that can be categorized as strategic alliances. The success of any single alliance depends on some key factors that are relevant at each stage of alliance evolution (Gulati, 1998). These include (a) the formation phase, wherein a firm deciding to initiate an alliance selects an appropriate partner, (b) the design phase, wherein a firm (and its partner) set up appropriate governance to oversee the alliance, and (c) the postformation phase, wherein a firm manages the alliance on an ongoing basis to realize value (Schreiner, Kale, & Corsten, 2009). Given the hundreds of articles that have studied these issues over two decades, it is not feasible to examine every aspect in detail. Therefore, we briefly review only those factors that prior research considers most important. Figure 2 provides an overview of the main phases of the alliance life cycle and factors in each phase that are critical to alliance success. In the process, we also extend prior work by highlighting conditions under which some of these factors have a stronger impact on alliance success, and/or the relationships between them.[2]

Alliance Formation Phase: Partner Selection and Fit

Previous research has focused extensively on partner selection during alliance formation and its

Figure 1   **Scope of Interfirm Relationships**

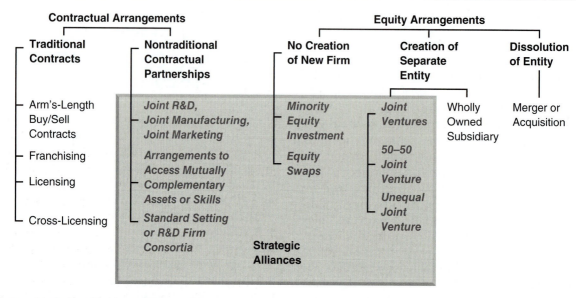

Source: Adapted from Yoshino and Rangan, 1995.

Figure 2   **A Single Alliance: Key Success Factors**

implications for alliance success. A review of more than 40 studies (Shah & Swaminathan, 2008) showed that the following partner traits have a positive influence on alliance performance: partner complementarity, partner commitment, and partner compatibility or fit. Partner complementarity is the extent to which a partner contributes non-overlapping resources to the relationship, such that one partner brings those value-chain resources or capabilities the other lacks and vice versa (Dyer & Singh, 1998; Harrigan, 1988; Mowery, Oxley, & Silverman, 1996). Resource-based theories suggest that the greater the complementarity between partners, the greater the likelihood of alliance success, and many studies have found support for this.

However, partner complementarity alone is insufficient for alliance formation and success. A partner firm must be compatible with the focal firm (Beamish, 1987) and committed to the relationship. Partner compatibility refers to the fit between partners' working styles and cultures, whereas commitment includes the willingness of a partner not only to make resource contributions required by the alliance but also to make short-term sacrifices to realize the desired longer-term benefits (Gundlach, Achrol, & Mentzer, 1995).

While all three partner attributes—complementarity, commitment, and compatibility—are vital to the success of an individual alliance, emerging research shows that managers need to appreciate under which conditions some of these attributes are more critical to alliance success than others. To illustrate, partner complementarity seems to have greater impact on alliance success when one partner is relatively younger than the other (Rothaermel & Boeker, 2008), or when the alliance is such that it is difficult for partners to fully specify the exact outcomes expected from that alliance. In the latter case partner complementarity is important, as it provides assurance that due to extant complementarity of resources or products outcome benefits are likely to be positive even if it is difficult to fully assess them (Shah & Swaminathan, 2008). Often, complementarity implies greater interdependence between alliance partners. In that case, complementarity positively affects alliance success only when partners establish the processes necessary to manage those interdependences (Dyer & Singh, 1998).

On the other hand, commitment seems particularly critical in alliances where partners have identified the specific benefits they expect to gain by coming together, but remain relatively unclear about the exact processes necessary to achieve them. In these alliance relationships, partner commitment is more important than usual, as partners must be willing to dedicate costly resources to the relationship and pledge to work with each other even when they realize that some adaptation might be required in the future in light of the uncertainty that exists. Overall, managers need to pay attention to such contingencies while

selecting partners that are generally complementary, compatible, and committed.

Alliance Design Phase: Choice and Implementation of Alliance Governance

An alliance exposes a firm to several transaction or coordination hazards that can adversely affect the firm itself or its partner. Thus, how a firm constructs alliance governance during the design phase of the alliance life cycle is crucial to alliance success. Literature has highlighted three primary mechanisms to address governance issues in an alliance.

First, transaction costs theory has proposed that equity ownership is an effective mechanism to govern alliances (Williamson, 1985). In an alliance, a firm can expose itself to opportunistic behavior by its alliance partner if it has invested in relationship-specific assets in order to derive expected benefits, or if there is uncertainty regarding market conditions facing the relationship. In such situations, creating an equity-based alliance (wherein one partner takes an equity stake in the other, or both partners create a new, independent venture wherein both take a stake) is critical to success, as equity has three governance properties to address the hazards involved. First is the property of "mutual hostages," in which shared equity aligns the mutual interests of the partners (Hennart, 1988); by owning equity, partners are required to make ex ante commitments toward the alliance, and their concern for their investment reduces the possibility of future opportunistic behavior. Second, equity facilitates hierarchical supervision to monitor day-to-day functioning of the alliance and address contingencies as they arise (Kogut, 1988). And third, equity ownership creates a basis for each partner to receive a share of the returns from the alliance in proportion to its level of ownership. This in turn creates an incentive for partners to cooperate with one another. Numerous studies have provided evidence for the effectiveness of equity in governing alliances (David & Han, 2004).

Contractual provisions in the alliance agreement represent the second mechanism of effective governance (Mayer & Argyres, 2004; Poppo & Zenger, 2002; Reuer & Arino, 2007), but this aspect has received attention in research only recently. Contracts help manage exchange hazards in a variety of ways. A contract clearly sets forth mutual rights and obligations of partners by specifying each firm's inputs to the alliance, processes by which exchanges will occur and disputes will be resolved, and expected outputs from the relationship. Contracts also limit information disclosures by partners during the operation of the alliance, specify how each partner will interact with third parties, and outline ways in which the alliance will end. Two more aspects that increase contractual effectiveness in governing alliances are enforcement provisions that relate to IP protection and the specification of breaches that might necessitate termination or adjudication, and informational provisions that facilitate required coordination between alliance partners (Reuer & Arino, 2007).

Self-enforcing governance, relying on goodwill, trust, and reputation (Granovetter, 1985; Gulati, 1995; Uzzi, 1997), is the third mechanism of effective alliance governance. At times, it is referred to as "relational governance." Relational governance enhances the likelihood of alliance success by reducing transaction costs in several ways: (a) Contracting costs are minimized because firms trust their partners to behave fairly; (b) monitoring costs are lower because external, third-party monitoring is not required; and (c) costs of complex adaptation are lowered because partners are willing to be flexible in response to unforeseen circumstances. In addition, relational governance enables partners to work together in implementing value-creation initiatives that need sharing of tacit knowledge between partners, exchanging resources that are difficult to price, and offering responses that are not explicitly called for in the contract (Zajac & Olsen, 1993). Finally, if relational governance is based on some resource dependence between partners, it acts as an effective means to monitor and control partner behavior (Filatotchev, Stephan, & Jindra, 2008).

However, in making choices about alliance governance, it is important to understand some of the subtle relationships between the various governance mechanisms. First, as recent work (Reuer & Arino, 2007) has shown, contractual complexity does not vary across equity and nonequity alliances. This finding implies that

equity alone is insufficient to guarantee successful alliance governance and that these mechanisms might actually complement each other in driving alliance success. Second, there are different views of the relationships between formal governance (based on equity ownership or contracts) and informal governance (based on trust). One school of thought suggests that one type of mechanism substitutes or crowds out the other such that informal relational governance reduces the need for formal governance (Bradach & Eccles, 1989; Gulati, 1995), or that inclusion of formal governance mechanisms actually hinders the development of relational governance in alliances (Ghoshal & Moran, 1996). A second school of thought sees these mechanisms as being complementary in enhancing alliance success such that relational governance amplifies the positive effects of formal governance further (Poppo & Zenger, 2002) and enables partners to more easily accept formal contractual governance despite the incomplete and ambiguous nature of contractual clauses (Gulati & Nickerson, 2008). Recent work by Puranam and Vanneste (2009) takes a further step in outlining conditions affecting the nature of the relationships (negative or positive) among these different mechanisms. They show how the nature of these relationships actually varies based on whether a manager makes governance choices in alliances by selecting a particular level of governance complexity to *match* the need for safeguards based on expected hazards, or whether she tries to maximize alliance performance given the attributes of the transactions involved.

Postformation Alliance Management: The Roles of Coordination and Trust

Appropriate decisions linked to partner selection and alliance governance positively affect the likelihood of success of every alliance. However, to realize the expected benefits, firms must also proactively manage an evolving entity such as an alliance *after* it is up and running. Two factors are especially important during the postformation phase of the alliance life cycle: managing coordination between partners and developing trust between them.

Alliance partners must coordinate their actions to manage their interdependence and realize the benefits of their relationship. But severe coordination problems can result from the lack of sufficient knowledge about how one's actions are interdependent with the other's, what decision rules a partner is likely to use, how to allocate resources, or how information should be handled (Gulati, Lawrence, & Puranam, 2005; Gulati & Singh, 1998; Schreiner et al., 2009). Coordination problems refer to the difficulties of aligning actions between partners. These problems can arise even when partners' interests are fully aligned with each other. To manage coordination successfully, alliance partners can use any or all of three classic mechanisms: programming, hierarchy, and feedback (Galbraith, 1977).

Programming is the least complex of the three mechanisms. It involves developing clear guidelines on what specific tasks need to be carried out by each partner, who exactly is accountable for each task, and a timetable for implementing them. This mechanism facilitates coordination by improving the clarity and predictability of partner actions, reducing frustration, and increasing decision-making speed. Use of interfirm knowledge-sharing routines (Dyer & Singh, 1998) to share critical task-related information is another dimension of this aspect.

The use of hierarchy, the second coordination mechanism, includes the creation of a formal role or structure with authority and decision-making ability to oversee ongoing interactions between partners and to facilitate information and resource sharing. As an example, a firm can appoint a separate dedicated alliance manager to manage this, or both partners can create an alliance review committee to play this role. Finally, in cases where partners need to regularly inform each other of their respective actions or decisions, or they must periodically evaluate the evolving nature of their interdependence and adapt to it, feedback mechanisms such as joint teams and collocation are helpful in order to quickly process pertinent information and mobilize resources accordingly. Of course, the exact nature of various coordination mechanisms and the extent to which they are required depends on the nature of interdependence between partners. Alliances with reciprocal interdependence generally need the greater and more complex coordination mechanisms of the

ones listed above as compared with those with either sequential or pooled interdependence (Gulati et al., 2005; Gulati & Singh, 1998).

Many studies find that trust between partners is critical to alliance success, not only because it facilitates alliance governance, as described earlier, but also because it helps partners work more cooperatively. Trust comprises two parts: a structural component, which refers to a type of expectation that one's partner will not act opportunistically due to a mutual hostage situation (Bradach & Eccles, 1989), and a behavioral component, which refers to the degree of confidence a firm has in its partner's reliability and integrity (Madhok, 1995). The former type of trust is akin to deterrence-based trust, which arises from the use of governance mechanisms such as shared equity or contractual agreements (Gulati, 1995), and the latter to knowledge-based trust, which gradually emerges as two partners interact and develop norms of reciprocity (Zaheer, McEvily, & Perrone, 1998) and fairness. The behavioral component of trust is particularly critical to effective functioning of the alliance during the postformation phase.

However, if it is so important, *how can firms create trust in their relationships, and how exactly does it help?* Trust develops through a cyclical process of bargaining, interaction, commitment, and execution between the concerned firms (Ring & Van de Ven, 1994). Based on this idea, scholars have identified several trust-building mechanisms. A firm can build trust by demonstrating that it trusts its partner firm by making large, unilateral commitments. By voluntarily placing itself in a position of vulnerability, a firm invites the alliance partner to reciprocate in kind, and interfirm trust gradually develops between the two (Mayer, Davis, & Schoorman, 1995). A second way is to demonstrate one's own trustworthiness (instead of being just trusting) by scrupulously honoring all commitments, and making sure to commit to only those actions that are within a firm's power and ability to execute. By making commitments and living up to the expectations, a firm can earn its partner's trust (Zaheer & Harris, 2006). A third driver of interfirm trust is interpersonal trust, sometimes referred to as "relational capital" (Kale, Singh, & Perlmutter, 2000). Such interpersonal trust most often develops between the individuals from the two firms that interact with each other at the alliance interface. It is linked to the social bonds that develop between these individuals as they work regularly with each other, understand each other's working style, and are stable in their respective roles (Schreiner et al., 2009). Finally, interfirm trust also depends on institutional factors including the location or national culture of the concerned firms (Dyer & Chu, 2003), or the existence of industry-level arrangements to facilitate interactions between them (McEvily, Perrone, & Zaheer, 2003).

Developing trust during the postformation phase of an alliance is critical to its success in many ways. It facilitates greater information sharing between partners (Dyer & Chu, 2003), lowers perceptions of relational risk, and promotes the willingness of partners to adapt the alliance to evolving contingencies (Doz, 1996). Trust between partners also enables them to simultaneously achieve two objectives generally considered mutually exclusive: Trust not only enables them to share valuable know-how with their alliance partner but also protects against the opportunistic acquisition of proprietary knowledge by the partner (Kale et al., 2000). Apart from these positive outcomes, studies show that trust also leads to increased partner satisfaction with the alliance and the achievement of joint action and goal fulfillment (Schreiner et al., 2009). Consequently, the scope and longevity of the alliance increase (Jap & Anderson, 2003).

HOW TO BUILD A FIRM-LEVEL CAPABILITY FOR ALLIANCE SUCCESS?

Turning our attention to the level of the firm gives rise to another important question in light of the alliance paradox highlighted earlier: If most firms engage in multiple alliances over time, and their overall alliance success rates are generally low, how does a firm develop its capability to manage alliances to achieve greater, repeatable alliance success than others? In an environment where alliances are an important part of a firm's strategy, having a firm-level alliance capability to manage alliances would indeed be a source of competitive advantage (Gulati, 1998). Only recently has this subject received attention. We review this research and highlight three main building blocks underlying the development of alliance capability in firms: prior alliance experience, creation of a dedicated alliance function, and implementation of firm-level processes to accumulate and leverage alliance management know-how and skills. Figure 3 provides an overview of these factors and their relationship to one another.

Building Alliance Capability through Experience

Quite simply, a firm can develop its alliance capability by having greater experience in doing alliances.

Figure 3   **Drivers of Firm-Level Alliance Capability**

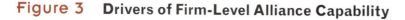

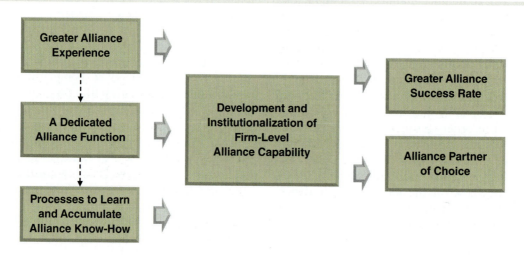

Implicit feedback from alliance experience helps build alliance management skills through tacit "learning by doing." Researchers have recently found empirical support for the role of experience in explaining a firm's alliance capability and success. Anand and Khanna (2000) conducted one of the first studies in this domain and found that firms with greater alliance experience received a more positive response from stock markets when they formed or announced a new alliance. According to them, favorable market reaction suggests that firms with greater alliance experience presumably have greater alliance capability and hence are more likely to succeed with the new alliance they have formed. Others have found that prior experience leads to greater alliance success not only in terms of creating shareholder value but also in the focal firm's ability to achieve its stated objectives in future alliances (Kale et al., 2002).

Creating an Alliance Function to Build Alliance Capability

Although experience is a useful mechanism for building a firm's alliance capability, Anand and Khanna (2000) found that this does not fully explain why some firms enjoy greater success with alliances than others do. Emerging research addresses this gap by highlighting the role of a second mechanism in building firm-level alliance capability. The adoption of higher-order organizing principles, such as creating a separate structure or entity that is responsible for coordinating and managing a firm's overall alliance activity, is critical in this regard (Kale et al., 2002). A separate organizational unit to manage alliances, commonly referred to as a "dedicated alliance function," is vital in building an organization's alliance capability. Companies such as Hewlett-Packard (Alliance Analyst, 1996), Eli Lilly (Dyer et al., 2001; Gueth, 2005), and Philips Electronics (Kale et al., 2009) have demonstrated the successful use of this mechanism.

The dedicated alliance function provides several benefits to firms (Dyer et al., 2001; Kale et al., 2002). First, it is a focal point for capturing and storing alliance management lessons and best practices from the firm's own prior and current alliance experiences as well as leveraging that knowledge throughout the organization as

time and occasion warrant. The managers in this function become repositories of alliance management know-how by virtue of their repeated involvement in the various alliances of the firm. Second, the dedicated alliance function enhances the visibility and awareness of a firm's alliances among external stakeholders (investors, customers, government), thus enlisting their buy-in and support. Third, a dedicated alliance function provides legitimacy and support for a firm's alliances and helps garner internal resources necessary for alliance success. Fourth, it acts as a mechanism to monitor the performance of the firm's alliances in order to identify potential trouble spots before they become an issue. The dedicated alliance function can then take necessary action in a timely manner to escalate or resolve those conflicts. Empirical studies (Hoang & Rothaermel, 2005; Kale et al., 2002) have shown a positive link between the existence of a dedicated alliance management function and a firm's alliance capability and overall alliance success. Firms that have a dedicated alliance function to coordinate their alliance activities enjoy a much greater alliance success rate (around 70 percent) than firms without one (around 40 percent). Moreover, these studies have found that the alliance function is relatively more important than prior experience in building a firm's alliance capability. Firms can establish this function in many different ways—they can organize it around key partners, businesses, functions, geography, or some combination of the same based on which of these dimensions is most important.

Establishing Learning Processes to Build Alliance Capability

New research provides insight into a third mechanism used to develop alliance capability in firms (Kale & Singh, 2007). Building on the knowledge-based view of the firm (Grant, 1996), which suggests that organizations improve their skills to manage a given task by accumulating and applying knowledge relevant to that task, this work emphasizes the role of certain learning processes in building alliance capability. Firms can implement four deliberate processes to learn, accumulate, and leverage alliance management knowledge either from their own alliance experience or from that of others. Usually, individual managers in a firm are the primary repository of useful alliance management experience and knowledge gained from prior or current alliance experience. As such, a firm can undertake efforts to help individual alliance managers articulate their personally held know-how of alliance management. By doing so, the firm can capture and externalize that knowledge so other managers in the firm can learn from those experiences.

A firm can go a step further and codify its accumulated alliance management know-how in the form of usable knowledge objects, such as alliance management guidelines, checklists, and manuals, that incorporate best practices to manage the different phases and decisions in the alliance life cycle. Hewlett-Packard and Eli Lilly were some of the early adopters of this practice—they developed such codified tools and templates to help managers assess the fit of potential alliance partners, draw up alliance agreements, assess alliance performance, and so on. The codification process facilitates the replication and transfer of alliance best practices within a firm, creating what is essentially a toolkit for managers. Figure 4 provides examples of various codified resources that some alliance-capable firms have developed for personal use.

It is important to note, however, that it is not possible to articulate or codify *all* know-how,

especially knowledge that is tacit or personal in nature (Winter, 1987). However, a firm can leverage such alliance know-how by having knowledge-sharing processes to exchange tacit and individually held alliance management know-how across the organization. Creating communities of personal interaction (Seely Brown & Duguid, 1991), such as cross-company alliance committees, task forces, or other forums, to exchange alliance experience and best practices among alliance managers is one of the means companies have used to achieve this goal (Draulans, deMan, & Volberda, 2003; Kale & Singh, 2007).

Finally, some companies use a fourth process to help individual managers internalize and absorb relevant alliance management know-how that exists in different parts of the firm, through formal and informal means. This internalization process stresses "learning how," wherein the recipient focuses on acquiring a recipe of how to undertake a specific alliance-related task or decision rather than just conceptually understanding why it works. In practical terms, when some firms have adopted this process they have created an "alliance apprenticeship" in which newer managers work with experienced alliance managers and soak up useful knowledge from them. Other firms send their managers to formal alliance training programs that are conducted either internally by the firm or by outsiders.

Figure 4   Examples of Codified Tools to Manage Alliances

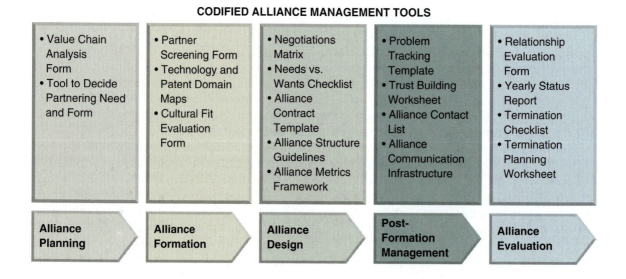

CODIFIED ALLIANCE MANAGEMENT TOOLS

- Value Chain Analysis Form
- Tool to Decide Partnering Need and Form

- Partner Screening Form
- Technology and Patent Domain Maps
- Cultural Fit Evaluation Form

- Negotiations Matrix
- Needs vs. Wants Checklist
- Alliance Contract Template
- Alliance Structure Guidelines
- Alliance Metrics Framework

- Problem Tracking Template
- Trust Building Worksheet
- Alliance Contact List
- Alliance Communication Infrastructure

- Relationship Evaluation Form
- Yearly Status Report
- Termination Checklist
- Termination Planning Worksheet

Alliance Planning → Alliance Formation → Alliance Design → Post-Formation Management → Alliance Evaluation

Collectively, the four learning processes we have described are directed toward building and institutionalizing a firm's alliance capability through articulating, codifying, sharing, and internalizing alliance management know-how and skills to help the firm manage its future alliances more effectively. Kale and Singh (2007) equated these learning processes to a higher-order dynamic capability (Eisenhardt & Martin, 2000; Zollo & Winter, 2002) that helps firms extend, modify, and improve their organizational capability to manage alliances. The empirical evidence shows that these processes have a strong influence on a firm's alliance capability and overall alliance success.

When Do These Mechanisms Really Matter and How Do They Relate to One Another?

Alliance experience, a dedicated alliance function, and organizational processes to learn and leverage alliance management know-how are three important mechanisms to develop and institutionalize an organizationwide capability in alliance management. However, it would be useful for managers to know the specific conditions under which some of these mechanisms are more effective in developing alliance capability, and the relationships among them. Emerging research has begun to shed light on some of these issues, but others remain unresolved.

Concerning alliance experience, it seems that prior experience is more useful in developing capabilities to manage certain kinds of alliances than others. In their work, Anand and Khanna (2000) found that prior experience with joint ventures is useful in developing skills to manage future joint ventures, but this does not hold true for contractual nonequity alliances. This may be because, as an alliance form, joint ventures show greater similarity in terms of structure, design, and governance issues across different situations (which makes it possible to transfer learning) as compared to contractual nonequity alliances. Sampson (2005) observed that prior experience helps develop alliance skills when that experience is more recent, as the benefits derived from experience depreciate over time. The usefulness of experience also varies by the degree of its specificity; experience in alliances with a particular

partner help a firm build its capability to manage future alliances successfully with that same partner, whereas general alliance experience is less useful in this regard. This research seems to suggest that, even though experience is a critical mechanism for building alliance capability, its relevance varies by its type, specificity, and timing.

The relevance of the dedicated alliance function also seems to vary across different business or firm conditions. We find that a dedicated alliance function helps develop alliance skills more effectively in larger firms than in smaller ones (Rothaermel & Boeker, 2008). This is plausible as the use of organizing principles to collect and disseminate relevant knowledge is perhaps more necessary in larger firms, where the knowledge has to be collated from and shared with diverse sources/individuals. This may not be the case in smaller firms where key individuals interact directly and frequently with each other. The use of this function also depends on the extent of functional relatedness across different alliances of a firm and the know-how required for managing them (Kale et al., 2002). But many other questions related to the creation and usefulness of the alliance function remain unanswered: If a firm were to create such a function, where exactly should it be located in the organizational setup, who should head it, who should it report to, what should be the composition of the individuals who comprise it, and how does its role evolve and change over time? Given the cost and effort involved in setting up a dedicated alliance function, future research must study these questions in detail. Similar questions arise about the alliance learning processes described earlier. While the literature has observed the efficacy of these processes, the following issues are worth examining: Will continual use of these processes turn them into "rituals" that are routinely followed, without the deliberate effort necessary to learn from them? Will implementation of these processes create a bureaucracy whose costs outweigh the resultant benefits?

The investigation of relationships among the three primary mechanisms used to develop alliance capability (alliance experience, a dedicated alliance function, and alliance learning processes) is necessary as well. Some scholars have suggested that the use of explicit mechanisms, such the dedicated alliance function or specific processes to articulate or codify alliance know-how, enhances the direct effect of implicit mechanisms such as alliance experience (Zollo & Winter, 2002) in building a firm's alliance capability. In other words, these mechanisms interact with and moderate each other in explaining a firm's alliance capability and success. However, more recent research has shown (Kale & Singh, 2007) that these mechanisms are actually mediating in nature—that is, the dedicated alliance function mediates the impact of alliance experience on a firm's alliance capability and overall alliance success. In turn, alliance-learning processes of articulation and codification further mediate the effect of the dedicated alliance function in building a firm's alliance capability.

Creating Capabilities: Time Frames and Challenges

In recent applied work we explored the actual time required to implement alliance capability development in an organization. In a multiyear collaboration with Dr. John Bell (he was the previous vice president of corporate alliances for Philips, and is a management scholar who studies alliances), we tracked the development of alliance capability within Philips, a large multinational with operations in more than 150 countries and a range of businesses in electronics (music systems, televisions, etc.), lifestyle products (shavers, coffee makers, lighting fixtures), and health care (large-scale medical imaging products, patient monitoring systems). Observing that Philips had myriad interfirm relationships without organized coordination, Bell conceived of and implemented an alliance capability development process that started in 2001. He set up the Corporate Alliance Office at Philips and over the next seven years his team, armed with a strong mandate from the CEO and board, implemented a set of decisions and management processes to improve Philips's alliance capability. Bell implemented many of the practices and processes discussed in the previous section of this paper. Several key observations worth discussion emerged from that experience.

First, the process of building alliance capability in a large corporation is a slow and multiyear process. It took Bell more than seven years to gradually and informally introduce some of the alliance management processes we have described. It was only in the latter portion of the

seven years that he created a well-defined process and codified the firm's accumulated alliance know-how into usable tools and templates. Second, as in most organizations, creating capabilities that rest on knowledge-based processes requires consistent sponsorship and support from senior management. This is a factor worth noting particularly because it is one that often remains unmeasured in large sample studies, as the nature of top management commitment does not lend itself to easy empirical representation. Third, the impact of the alliance function is easier to observe with rich, multifaceted data in a single firm than in a more reduced form or larger sample study. By studying a single organization like Philips over an extended period, we were able to observe how the organization was able to derive increased revenues or greater new product introductions through its alliances. We were also able to see how line managers increasingly embraced alliance relationships as a vehicle to pursue growth opportunities after they became more proficient in managing alliances. As such, it was possible to identify the effectiveness of the dedicated alliance function. Through it all, it became clear that alliance capability building is time-consuming and draws on intangible assets such as knowledge and decision/management processes. On the positive side, and in justification of the time, effort, and resources required, building alliance capability provides enduring benefits to a firm.

EMERGING ISSUES IN ALLIANCES: WHERE DO WE GO FROM HERE?

Extant literature provides valuable insights into successful alliance management. But scholars also need to address new issues that emerge on the alliance frontier. In the next section, we outline some of these issues and offer preliminary suggestions on how to think about them.

From Firm-to-Firm Alliances to a New Class of Alliances

Extant alliance literature has focused mainly on alliances between two or more commercial or for-profit firms. Today, many firms are engaging in two new types of alliances: those with not-for-profit entities and/or nongovernmental organizations, and formal collaborations with individuals. Partnerships with the former type of entity are becoming important in several situations. In today's evolving business environment, society views firms as entities that are responsible for serving not only the interests of their shareholders but also the interests of other stakeholders within the community. Often, commercial firms are unable to meet this obligation on their own, and hence they collaborate with not-for-profit entities or NGOs that might be better positioned to understand the needs of these other stakeholders. Further, to accelerate their growth many firms are expanding in emerging economies by serving poor consumers at the so-called bottom of the pyramid. These efforts require unconventional means and business models to address this new class of customer (Prahalad, 2006), and NGOs and grassroots organizations that interact directly with these customers might understand them better than commercial firms do. Thus, commercial firms often partner with such organizations to address this large untapped market. Finally, in their quest to tap new and innovative ideas from outside their own organizations, firms are collaborating not only with other organizations (of any kind) but also directly with single persons or individuals. Initiatives including P&G's Connect ≦ Develop (Houston & Sakkab, 2006) and "open innovation" (Chesbrough, 2005) are prominent examples of this kind.[3]

Both types of collaboration, those with non-profits or NGOs and those with individuals, represent a new class of alliances quite different from the traditional interfirm alliances studied in academic literature. We consider them alliances because in both cases, the entities involved in the relationship bring distinct but valuable resources to meet mutually beneficial objectives, and they are often required to make investments that are specific to the concerned relationship. Nevertheless, these alliances are different, not only because the objective function of a firm's alliance partner is different (as compared to a traditional for-profit organization) but also because the concerned partner has a different set of skills and organizational culture. Thus, the challenges of managing such alliances and the factors and best practices that lead to success may also be different from

what we know from our study of traditional interfirm alliances. Current academic research has very little to say about how to successfully manage this emerging class of alliances. Hence, future research must investigate this issue in greater depth.

From Individual Alliances to Alliance Portfolios

It is beneficial to know the best practices of managing a single alliance between two or more firms. However, firms could also benefit significantly by assuming a portfolio approach to alliances in the future. As discussed earlier, most firms today engage in more than one alliance. For example, a pharmaceutical firm might have one alliance with partner A to source a new technology, a second alliance with partner B to facilitate its entry into a new geographical market, a third alliance with partner C to jointly manufacture a core compound, and so on. Even when it comes to sourcing a new technology, a firm may have alliances with more than one partner to achieve the same objective. Each individual alliance is important, and a firm certainly needs to have a sound strategic logic for its alliance and adopt appropriate best practices in each stage of its life cycle. Nevertheless, a firm can gain additional advantages by considering its entire set of individual alliances as one portfolio, and managing it as such.

In shifting the level of analysis to the entire alliance portfolio and away from each individual alliance within that portfolio, though, new issues arise. A firm needs to know how to configure its alliance portfolio (Hoffmann, 2007) along several dimensions. It must first assess the extent to which its portfolio is complete such that collectively all its alliances meet its strategic needs. Second, in building the alliance portfolio, firms must guard against competition that might arise between individual alliances in that portfolio. If a firm undertakes more than one alliance for the same purpose, greater overlap in the benefits offered by each individual alliance may increase to the extent that one alliance rivals another alliance in the portfolio. This in turn can lead to significant adversities that might ultimately outweigh the benefits. Third, some alliances in a firm's portfolio may actually complement, rather than compete with, each other such that the benefits they offer are extra-additive in nature. For example, a pharmaceutical firm may have one alliance with a firm to in-source a new molecule for a drug that targets a particular disease, and at the same time have a second alliance with another firm to get a specific technology to test the efficacy of that molecule in a speedy and cost-effective way. In this scenario, the benefits derived from the first alliance are accentuated because of the second alliance in the firm's portfolio, and vice versa. The greater the existence of such complementarity between individual alliances in a firm's portfolio, the greater will be the firm's opportunity to generate extra-additive benefits from those alliances.

For the reasons outlined above, conceptually it is useful to take a portfolio approach to alliances. Thus far, however, very few academics (Hoffmann, 2007; Lavie, 2006) have paid attention to it. In practice too, the portfolio approach to alliance strategy and management is still in its infancy. In a survey of 76 companies, we found that only 30 percent of them consider or manage their alliances as a portfolio in building their alliance strategy; even among those firms that do, most look only at the degree of competition that exists between different alliances in the portfolio. Only a small proportion of firms consider completeness of the alliance portfolio, and an even smaller number assess the extent of complementarity across individual alliances in the portfolio. This implies that most firms still focus mainly on each individual alliance, and they do not fully exploit synergy benefits that might exist across their individual alliances by considering them as part of one portfolio.

The capabilities necessary to manage alliances as a portfolio are different from the alliance capability discussed earlier. So far, in conceptualizing alliance capability scholarly literature has focused primarily on the constituent skills required to successfully manage a single alliance through the different stages of its life cycle (e.g., partner selection skills, alliance governance skills, skills to create trust between partners in a given alliance), and recent literature has now also shown how a firm can develop an organizationwide alliance capability for repeatable and greater alliance success. Nevertheless, looking ahead we think it is important to distinguish between a firm's alliance capability, which refers to the firm's ability to manage each single alliance successfully, and a firm's alliance *portfolio* capability, which refers to its ability

to manage its set of alliances as a portfolio. In our view, alliance portfolio capability comprises multiple dimensions, including the skills to configure an alliance portfolio (to create a set of complete, noncompetitive, and complementary alliances), to foster and maintain trust across different alliance partners in the portfolio, to resolve conflicts between alliances in the portfolio, to coordinate strategies and operations across alliances in the portfolio, to create routines to share operational know-how across individual alliances in the portfolio, to monitor the extra-additive benefits (and costs) that arise due to interaction between different individual alliances in the portfolio, and so on. So far, little academic research has been done on this subject (Sarkar et al., forthcoming), and more work in this direction would be beneficial.

A Relational Organization: From Managing Alliances to Managing Acquisitions

In a strategic alliance two or more firms come together to access or exchange resources and capabilities to enhance their competitive advantage or growth while retaining their respective independence and identity (Gulati, 1995). However, instead of doing an alliance, a firm can also use a very different mode to access resources of another firm: It can acquire that firm. In an acquisition, the focal company (i.e., the acquirer firm) purchases control rights over the assets and operations of another firm (i.e., the acquired firm), and in the process the two companies usually become one organization to realize the desired benefits of coming together. Quite rightly, most scholars generally consider alliances to be a very different organizational mode than acquisitions, given differences in terms of the control, ownership, and independence of the firms involved in each case. Consequently, two separate research streams have evolved to study issues associated with these two very distinct organizational modes. But looking ahead we believe there is an opportunity to share insights from the world of alliances, in terms of both research and practice, with respect to managing certain kinds of acquisitions. Here's why. The success of an acquisition relies on how an acquirer manages the acquired firm after completing the transaction (Haspeslagh & Jemison, 1991).

During the postacquisition management phase, the acquirer has to make decisions on two critical aspects: the extent to which it integrates the acquired firm with itself, and the extent to which it replaces managerial resources of the acquired firm (Zollo & Singh, 2004). Research shows that in most cases, an acquirer fully integrates the acquired organization within itself, combining the boundaries of the two firms. Consequently, the acquired company loses its separate identity and independence in the market; this approach to integration is referred to as absorption or structural integration. The acquirer typically also replaces most of the acquired firms' senior executives with its own, and even in cases where it chooses to retain them it limits their decision-making freedom.

However, recent studies show that some acquirers take a very different approach to managing their acquisitions in certain settings: when large companies acquire small entrepreneurial firms for their technological or knowledge-based skills (Puranam & Srikanth, 2007), or when firms from emerging economies acquire larger firms in developed economies to enhance their global presence or competitiveness (Kale & Singh, 2008). In both of these cases, most acquirers leave the acquired firm structurally separate so that the latter maintains its identity in the market. The acquirer also retains most senior employees in the acquired firm and gives them operating freedom in running the acquired company. There are several reasons for taking this approach to acquisitions. By not integrating the acquired company into itself, an acquirer minimizes the complexities that arise during the postacquisition period and avoids the disruption of resources and routines that results when two companies attempt to combine their operations. Maintaining a separate organization is also beneficial if the acquired firm has a unique identity in the minds of its key stakeholders (customers, regulators, shareholders) and maintenance of that identity generates business value for the firm. Retaining senior executives of the acquired firm and giving them independence and autonomy creates a positive climate within the acquired firm and sends a positive, symbolic signal to its stakeholders. It also allows the acquirer firm to retain the industry- or context-specific expertise of the acquired firm's management/employees and leverage their human and social

capital for mutual gains. This is relevant when an acquirer buys a target for its intellectual capital and expertise. At the same time, the two companies still need to coordinate some of their activities and operations to realize potential synergies that exist between them.

The aforementioned description suggests that, although the concerned transactions are an acquisition from an ownership standpoint, the manner in which an acquirer manages them makes them more like an alliance between two firms. The Renault-Nissan relationship, Cisco's acquisitions of some small technology companies, and the Tata Group's acquisition of Corus Steel in the United Kingdom are examples of such transactions. This is because, unlike in a traditional acquisition, in this approach both the acquirer and acquired firms remain independent and relatively autonomous—and yet, how do they then interact with each other to achieve some of the desired benefits of coming together? To manage such acquisitions the acquirer needs to recognize the issues and best practices discussed earlier as important in the postformation phase of an alliance. First, the acquirer needs to choose appropriate coordination mechanisms to leverage the interdependence between the two separate firms. Second, it needs to build trust between the two firms such that employees in each firm work in the interests of both firms and are willing to share relevant know-how with each other for mutual benefit. Third, it needs to establish appropriate mechanisms to resolve or escalate any conflicts that might arise.

We term this approach a "partnering approach to acquisitions." What it implies is that if a firm is skilled in managing alliances and has a collaborative capability or mindset, that firm could be equally effective in managing acquisitions that call for such an approach to handling postacquisition integration. Therefore, firms can extend their alliance capability into a broader relational capability that can sometimes be leveraged to manage certain other interfirm relationships, such as acquisitions, too. Thus far, very few academics or practitioners have recognized this opportunity, let alone studied or addressed it, but we hope that will change in the future. From a practical standpoint, taking this approach may call for some changes in how firms are organized internally. As we mentioned before, in our fieldwork we have studied many companies that have created a dedicated alliance team or function to oversee their overall alliance activity. Some of the firms we have observed have an additional team to oversee and coordinate their acquisition activity. In the majority of cases, these two teams are structurally separate and operate in their own silos. However, if alliance management capabilities are useful in managing some kinds of acquisitions, there exists a need for learning or capability transfer between these teams, and it would be helpful if they worked in close concert with one another and had relevant mechanisms to enable that. Cisco is one of the few companies that seem to have taken this step.

CONCLUSION

Alliances are widespread in today's business landscape. In the face of growing competition, the high rate of technological change, and discontinuities within most industries, firms pursue a large number of alliances to access new resources, enter new markets or arenas, or minimize their risk. Yet there is a paradox: They frequently fail to reap the anticipated benefits of most of their alliances. In this paper we have discussed how firms can address this paradox to improve their likelihood of alliance success by focusing on two different levels of analysis: (a) the level of an individual alliance a firm engages in, and (b) the level of the firm as a whole that is engaged in more than one alliance over time. At the level of a single alliance of a firm, we highlighted how certain factors at each stage of the alliance life cycle are critical to alliance success. If a firm selects a complementary, compatible, and committed partner at the time of alliance formation, and makes relevant choices with respect to alliance design in terms of equity or contractual or relational governance, the alliance is more likely to succeed. During the postformation stage,

alliance success depends on the effective use of relevant coordination mechanisms to manage the interdependence between the two firms and the successful development of trust between partners as the alliance evolves. We also highlight specific conditions when the above-mentioned aspects are more pivotal to alliance success.

In settings where alliances are a central element of strategy and firms engage in more than one alliance over time, they stand to benefit by building their alliance capability. The idea, supported by empirical evidence, is that firms improve their overall alliance success if they take systematic action to develop processes and talent in support of alliance management. Alliance capability requires attention to both a dedicated alliance function within a firm and a set of institutionalized processes to accumulate and leverage alliance management know-how across the firm. These soft factors underlying a firm's overall alliance success perform better when championed by a firm's leaders; frequent restructuring and inconsistent support are recipes for the loss of accumulated learning. Yet the path to development of alliance capabilities remains both uncertain and time-consuming. As we saw in the example of a large corporation, despite strong championing by the CEO and a sustained effort to incorporate alliance management processes within the firm, building effective alliance capability can take between 5 and 10 years. This may well be a window into the development of capabilities in general.

Looking into the future, managers face new challenges and issues with respect to alliances. Firms need to learn how to manage certain new types of alliances, generate incremental value by taking a portfolio approach to managing their alliances, and realize gains by extending their alliance capabilities to become relational organizations that are adept at successfully managing other interfirm relationships too, including acquisitions.

ENDNOTES

[1] A vast literature examines a firm's network of interorganizational relationships, including alliances. We acknowledge the importance of the network perspective in providing useful insights regarding alliances. However, given its broad scope a detailed incorporation of the network perspective is beyond the scope of this paper.

[2] Joint ventures are also a form of alliance. Hence, many of the alliance success factors we discuss are relevant to success in joint ventures as well. However, because joint

ventures also entail the creation of a separate entity by the partners concerned, which is not the case in other types of alliances, they have certain unique issues and challenges worth addressing. For a more complete review of the issues that are unique to joint venture management, please refer to a recent article by Beamish and Lupton (2009).

[3] Most companies have traditionally relied on internal innovation, where new products and services are developed by the companies' in-house R&D teams. But in these two approaches to innovation, which are a radical alternative to the internal innovation model, companies connect with external sources for new ideas: university and government

labs, Web-based talent markets, suppliers, and even individual inventors. Companies then develop these new ideas, sourced from external partners, into new and refined profitable products—swiftly and cheaply—by using their firm's own R&D and other resources.

REFERENCES

Ahuja, G. (2000). Collaboration networks, structural holes and innovation: A longitudinal study. *Administrative Science Quarterly, 45*(3), 425–456.

Alliance Analyst. (1996). *Managing alliances: Skills for the modern era.* Philadelphia: PA.

Anand, B., & Khanna, T. (2000). Do firms learn to create value? The case of alliances. *Strategic Management Journal, 21*(3), 295–315.

Bamford, J., Gomes-Casseres, B., & Robinson, M. (2004). *Envisioning collaboration: Mastering alliance strategies.* San Francisco: Jossey-Bass.

Beamish, P. (1987). Joint ventures in LDCs: Partner selection and performance. *Management International Review, 27*(1), 23–27.

Beamish, P., & Lupton, N. (2009). Managing joint ventures. *Academy of Management Perspectives, 23*(2), 75–94.

Bradach, J., & Eccles, R. (1989). Price, authority and trust: From ideal types to plural forms. *Annual Review of Sociology, 15*(1), 97–112.

Chesbrough, H. (2005). *Open innovation: The new imperative for creating and profiting from technology.* Cambridge, MA: Harvard Business School Press.

David, R. J., & Han, S. K. (2004). A systematic assessment of the empirical support for transaction cost economics. *Strategic Management Journal, 25*(1), 39–58.

Doz, Y. (1996). The evolution of cooperation in strategic alliances: Initial conditions or learning processes? *Strategic Management Journal, 17*(7), 55–83.

Draulans, J., deMan, A., & Volberda, H. (2003). Building alliance capability: Management techniques for superior alliance performance. *Long Range Planning, 36*(2), 151–166.

Dyer, J., & Chu, W. (2003). The role of trustworthiness in reducing transaction costs and improving performance. *Organization Science, 14,* 57–68.

Dyer, J., Kale, P., & Singh, H. (2001). How to make strategic alliances work. *Sloan Management Review, 42*(4), 37–43.

Dyer, J., & Singh, H. (1998). The relational view: Cooperative strategy and sources of interorganizational competitive advantage. *Academy of Management Review, 23*(4), 660–679.

Eisenhardt, K., & Martin, J. (2000). Dynamic capabilities: What are they? *Strategic Management Journal, 21*(10–11), 1105–1121.

Ernst, D. (2004). Envisioning collaboration. In J. Bamford, B. Gomes-Casseres, & M. Robinson (Eds.), *Mastering alliance strategies.* San Francisco: Jossey-Bass.

Filatotchev, I., Stephan, J., & Jindra, B. (2008). Ownership structure, strategic controls and export intensity of foreign invested firms in emerging economies. *Journal of International Business Studies, 39*(7), 1133–1148.

Galbraith, J. (1977). *Organization design.* Reading, MA: Addison-Wesley.

Garcia-Canal, E., Duarte, C., Criado, J., & Llaneza, A. (2002). Accelerating international expansion through global alliances. *Journal of World Business, 37*(2), 91–107.

Ghoshal, S., & Moran, P. (1996). Bad for practice: A critique of the transaction cost theory. *Academy of Management Review, 21*(1), 13–34.

Granovetter, M. (1985). Economic actions and social structure: A theory of embeddedness. *American Journal of Sociology, 91*(3), 481–510.

Grant, R. (1996). Toward a knowledge-based theory of the firm. *Strategic Management Journal, 17,* Winter Special Issue, 109–122.

Gueth, A. (2005). Entering into an alliance with big pharma: Benchmarks for drug delivery contract service providers. *Pharmaceutical Technology, 25*(10), 132–135.

Gulati, R. (1995). Does familiarity breed trust? The implications of repeated ties for contractual choice in alliances. *Academy of Management Journal, 38*(1), 85–112.

Gulati, R. (1998). Alliances and networks. *Strategic Management Journal, 19*(4), 293–317.

How Emerging Giants Are Rewriting the Rules of M&A

Nirmalya Kumar

London Business School

Mergers and acquisitions, the stuff of newspaper headlines, quite often fail. Around 50% of mergers don't achieve their business objectives, and takeovers cause the shareholders of most acquirers to lose money, according to several studies conducted over the past four decades. Yet, in an ironic twist, companies from developing countries such as China, India, Malaysia, Russia, and South Africa are using M&A as their main globalization strategy today.

Even after the economic crisis engulfed the world in the last quarter of 2008, the Indian technology major Tata Consultancy Services picked up Citigroup Global Services (the North American bank's India-based outsourcing division) for $505 million in October 2008; another Indian technology company, HCL, bought Britain's Axon Group for $672 million in December 2008; and China's Minmetals made a $1.7 billion bid for the Australian company OZ Minerals in February 2009. In fact, emerging giants clinched 26% of the previous year's takeover deals between developed countries and developing ones, a recent A.T. Kearney study shows.

Fueling the trend is the fact that many emerging giants are cash rich. Economies like China and India grew at near double-digit rates over the past 15 years, and that, along with corporations' restructuring, resulted in profit margins of 10%, twice those in the developed world. Reflecting those companies' bloated balance sheets, a survey conducted by HBR and the World Economic Forum in 2008 found that 50% of CEOs from developing economies plan to finance their bids with internal resources and 46% by issuing fresh equity. They aren't worried about diluting shareholdings: Business families or founder-promoters hold large stakes in companies in developing nations. Those majority shareholdings also ensure that CEOs won't lose control if stock prices fall, so smart ones can focus on generating long-term value. Moreover, suitors from developing countries are finding the valuations of companies more attractive after the recent stock market crashes in the United States and Europe.

Cash isn't the only factor behind the M&A wave. My research indicates that emerging giants can also create value from takeovers more easily than corporations from developed countries. U.S. and European companies, inhibited by slow-growing home markets, acquire rivals primarily to become bigger and thus create economies of scale. After every merger, executives try to identify synergies, fashion efficient processes, and reduce head count so that costs will fall. In a slow-growing market, lowering costs to enhance margins is the only way to boost profits. This storyline is easy to sell to investors; a CEO can describe a merger's benefits beforehand and demonstrate some of them soon afterward.

By contrast, when emerging giants pursue cross-border acquisitions in particular, they don't search for traditional synergies or try to lower their costs. They buy Western companies to gain complementary competencies—that is, to learn to deploy assets such as technologies and brands, and capabilities such as new business models and

Ring, P., & Van de Ven, A. (1994). Developmental processes of cooperative interorganizational relationships. *Academy of Management Review, 19*(1), 90–118.

Rothaermel, F., & Boeker, W. (2008). Old technology meets new technology: Complementarities, similarities and alliance formation. *Strategic Management Journal, 29*(1), 47–77.

Sampson, R. (2005). Experience effects and collaborative returns in R&D alliances. *Strategic Management Journal, 26*(8), 1009–1031.

Sarkar, M., Aulakh, P., & Madhok, A. (2009). Process capabilities and value generation in alliance portfolios. *Organization Science, 20*(3), 583–600.

Schreiner, M., Kale, P., & Corsten, D. (2009). What really is alliance management capability and how does it impact alliance outcomes and success? *Strategic Management Journal, 30*(13), 1395–1419.

Seely Brown, J., & Duguid, P. (1991). Organizational learning and communities-of-practice: Toward a unified view of working, learning, and innovation. *Organization Science, 2*(1), 40–56.

Shah, R., & Swaminathan, V. (2008). Factors influencing partner selection in strategic alliances: The moderating role of alliance context. *Strategic Management Journal, 29*(5), 471–494.

Uzzi, B. (1997). Social structure and competition in interfirm networks: The paradox of embeddedness. *Administrative Science Quarterly, 42*(1), 35–67.

Williamson, O. (1985). *The economic institutions of capitalism: Firms, markets, relational contracting.* New York: Free Press.

Winter, S. G. (1987). Knowledge and competence as strategic assets. In D. J. Teece (Ed.), *The competitive challenge: Strategies for industrial innovation and renewal.* New York: Harper Collins.

Yoshino, M., & Rangan., S. (1995). *Strategic alliances: An entrepreneurial approach to globalization.* Boston: Harvard Business School Press.

Zaheer, A., & Harris, S. (2006). Inter-organizational trust. In O. Shenkar & J. J. Reuer (Eds.), *Handbook of strategic alliances.* Thousand Oaks, CA: Sage Publications.

Zaheer, A., McEvily, B., & Perrone, V. (1998). Does trust matter? Exploring the effects of interorganizational and interpersonal trust on performance. *Organization Science, 8*(1), 141–159.

Zajac, E., & Olsen, C. (1993). From transaction cost to transactional value analysis: Implications for the study of inter-organizational strategies. *Journal of Management Studies, 30*(1), 131–147.

Zollo, M., & Singh, H. (2004). Deliberate learning in corporate acquisitions: Post-acquisition strategies and integration capabilities in US bank mergers. *Strategic Management Journal, 25*(13), 1233–1256.

Zollo, M., & Winter, S. (2002). Deliberate learning and the evolution of dynamic capabilities. *Organization Science, 13*(3), 339–351.

How Emerging Giants Are Rewriting the Rules of M&A

Nirmalya Kumar
London Business School

Mergers and acquisitions, the stuff of newspaper headlines, quite often fail. Around 50% of mergers don't achieve their business objectives, and takeovers cause the shareholders of most acquirers to lose money, according to several studies conducted over the past four decades. Yet, in an ironic twist, companies from developing countries such as China, India, Malaysia, Russia, and South Africa are using M&A as their main globalization strategy today.

Even after the economic crisis engulfed the world in the last quarter of 2008, the Indian technology major Tata Consultancy Services picked up Citigroup Global Services (the North American bank's India-based outsourcing division) for $505 million in October 2008; another Indian technology company, HCL, bought Britain's Axon Group for $672 million in December 2008; and China's Minmetals made a $1.7 billion bid for the Australian company OZ Minerals in February 2009. In fact, emerging giants clinched 26% of the previous year's takeover deals between developed countries and developing ones, a recent A.T. Kearney study shows.

Fueling the trend is the fact that many emerging giants are cash rich. Economies like China and India grew at near double-digit rates over the past 15 years, and that, along with corporations' restructuring, resulted in profit margins of 10%, twice those in the developed world. Reflecting those companies' bloated balance sheets, a survey

conducted by HBR and the World Economic Forum in 2008 found that 50% of CEOs from developing economies plan to finance their bids with internal resources and 46% by issuing fresh equity. They aren't worried about diluting shareholdings: Business families or founder-promoters hold large stakes in companies in developing nations. Those majority shareholdings also ensure that CEOs won't lose control if stock prices fall, so smart ones can focus on generating long-term value. Moreover, suitors from developing countries are finding the valuations of companies more attractive after the recent stock market crashes in the United States and Europe.

Cash isn't the only factor behind the M&A wave. My research indicates that emerging giants can also create value from takeovers more easily than corporations from developed countries. U.S. and European companies, inhibited by slow-growing home markets, acquire rivals primarily to become bigger and thus create economies of scale. After every merger, executives try to identify synergies, fashion efficient processes, and reduce head count so that costs will fall. In a slow-growing market, lowering costs to enhance margins is the only way to boost profits. This storyline is easy to sell to investors; a CEO can describe a merger's benefits beforehand and demonstrate some of them soon afterward.

By contrast, when emerging giants pursue cross-border acquisitions in particular, they don't search for traditional synergies or try to lower their costs. They buy Western companies to gain complementary competencies—that is, to learn to deploy assets such as technologies and brands, and capabilities such as new business models and ventures also entail the creation of a separate entity by the partners concerned, which is not the case in other types of alliances, they have certain unique issues and challenges worth addressing. For a more complete review of the issues that are unique to joint venture management, please refer to a recent article by Beamish and Lupton (2009).

[3] Most companies have traditionally relied on internal innovation, where new products and services are developed by the companies' in-house R&D teams. But in these two approaches to innovation, which are a radical alternative to the internal innovation model, companies connect with external sources for new ideas: university and government labs, Web-based talent markets, suppliers, and even individual inventors. Companies then develop these new ideas, sourced from external partners, into new and refined profitable products—swiftly and cheaply—by using their firm's own R&D and other resources.

REFERENCES

Ahuja, G. (2000). Collaboration networks, structural holes and innovation: A longitudinal study. *Administrative Science Quarterly, 45*(3), 425–456.

Alliance Analyst. (1996). *Managing alliances: Skills for the modern era.* Philadelphia: PA.

Anand, B., & Khanna, T. (2000). Do firms learn to create value? The case of alliances. *Strategic Management Journal, 21*(3), 295–315.

Bamford, J., Gomes-Casseres, B., & Robinson, M. (2004). *Envisioning collaboration: Mastering alliance strategies.* San Francisco: Jossey-Bass.

Beamish, P. (1987). Joint ventures in LDCs: Partner selection and performance. *Management International Review, 27*(1), 23–27.

Beamish, P., & Lupton, N. (2009). Managing joint ventures. *Academy of Management Perspectives, 23*(2), 75–94.

Bradach, J., & Eccles, R. (1989). Price, authority and trust: From ideal types to plural forms. *Annual Review of Sociology, 15*(1), 97–112.

Chesbrough, H. (2005). *Open innovation: The new imperative for creating and profiting from technology.* Cambridge, MA: Harvard Business School Press.

David, R. J., & Han, S. K. (2004). A systematic assessment of the empirical support for transaction cost economics. *Strategic Management Journal, 25*(1), 39–58.

Doz, Y. (1996). The evolution of cooperation in strategic alliances: Initial conditions or learning processes? *Strategic Management Journal, 17*(7), 55–83.

Draulans, J., deMan, A., & Volberda, H. (2003). Building alliance capability: Management techniques for superior alliance performance. *Long Range Planning, 36*(2), 151–166.

Dyer, J., & Chu, W. (2003). The role of trustworthiness in reducing transaction costs and improving performance. *Organization Science, 14*, 57–68.

Dyer, J., Kale, P., & Singh, H. (2001). How to make strategic alliances work. *Sloan Management Review, 42*(4), 37–43.

Dyer, J., & Singh, H. (1998). The relational view: Cooperative strategy and sources of interorganizational competitive advantage. *Academy of Management Review, 23*(4), 660–679.

Eisenhardt, K., & Martin, J. (2000). Dynamic capabilities: What are they? *Strategic Management Journal, 21*(10–11), 1105–1121.

Ernst, D. (2004). Envisioning collaboration. In J. Bamford, B. Gomes-Casseres, & M. Robinson (Eds.), *Mastering alliance strategies.* San Francisco: Jossey-Bass.

Filatotchev, I., Stephan, J., & Jindra, B. (2008). Ownership structure, strategic controls and export intensity of foreign invested firms in emerging economies. *Journal of International Business Studies, 39*(7), 1133–1148.

Galbraith, J. (1977). *Organization design.* Reading, MA: Addison-Wesley.

Garcia-Canal, E., Duarte, C., Criado, J., & Llaneza, A. (2002). Accelerating international expansion through global alliances. *Journal of World Business, 37*(2), 91–107.

Ghoshal, S., & Moran, P. (1996). Bad for practice: A critique of the transaction cost theory. *Academy of Management Review, 21*(1), 13–34.

Granovetter, M. (1985). Economic actions and social structure: A theory of embeddedness. *American Journal of Sociology, 91*(3), 481–510.

Grant, R. (1996). Toward a knowledge-based theory of the firm. *Strategic Management Journal, 17,* Winter Special Issue, 109–122.

Gueth, A. (2005). Entering into an alliance with big pharma: Benchmarks for drug delivery contract service providers. *Pharmaceutical Technology, 25*(10), 132–135.

Gulati, R. (1995). Does familiarity breed trust? The implications of repeated ties for contractual choice in alliances. *Academy of Management Journal, 38*(1), 85–112.

Gulati, R. (1998). Alliances and networks. *Strategic Management Journal, 19*(4), 293–317.

Gulati, R., Lawrence, P., & Puranam, P. (2005). Adaptation in vertical relationships: Beyond incentive conflict. *Strategic Management Journal, 26*(5), 415–440.

Gulati, R., & Nickerson, J. (2008). Interorganizational trust, governance form and exchange performance. *Organization Science, 19*(5), 688–710.

Gulati, R., & Singh, H. (1998). The architecture of cooperation: Managing coordination costs and appropriation concerns in strategic alliances. *Administrative Science Quarterly, 43*(4), 781–814.

Gundlach, G., Achrol, R., & Mentzer, J. (1995). The structure of commitment in exchange. *Journal of Marketing, 59*(1), 78–92.

Harrigan, K. (1988). Joint ventures and competitive strategy. *Strategic Management Journal, 9*(2), 141–158.

Haspeslagh, P., & Jemison, D. (1991). *Managing acquisitions.* New York: Free Press.

Hennart, J. (1988). A transaction cost theory of equity joint ventures. *Strategic Management Journal, 9*(1), 36–74.

Hoang, H., & Rothaermel, F. (2005). The effects of general and partner-specific experience on joint R&D project performance. *Academy of Management Journal, 48*(2), 332–345.

Hoffmann, W. (2007). Strategies for managing a portfolio of alliances. *Strategic Management Journal, 28*(8), 827–856.

Houston, L., & Sakkab, N. (2006). Connect and develop: Inside Procter and Gamble's new model for innovation. *Harvard Business Review,* March, 1–8.

Jap, S., and Anderson, E. (2003). Safeguarding interorganizational performance and continuity under ex post opportunism. *Management Science, 49,* 1684–1701.

Kale, P., Dyer, J., & Singh, H. (2002). Alliance capability, stock market response and long-term alliance success: The role of the alliance function. *Strategic Management Journal, 23*(8), 747–767.

Kale, P., & Singh, H. (2007). Building firm capabilities through learning: The role of the alliance learning process in alliance capability and success. *Strategic Management Journal, 28*(10), 981–1000.

Kale, P., & Singh, H. (2008). Emerging multinationals: A partnering approach to acquisitions. *Strategic Management Society India Conference.* Hyderabad: India.

Kale, P., Singh, H., & Bell, J. (2009). Relating well: Building capabilities for sustaining alliance networks. In P. Kleindorfer & Y. Wind (Eds.), *The network challenge: Strategies for managing the new interlinked enterprise.* London: Pearson Press.

Kale, P., Singh, H., & Perlmutter, H. (2000). Learning and protection of proprietary assets in strategic alliances: Building relational capital. *Strategic Management Journal, 21*(3), 217–237.

Kogut, B. (1988). A study of the life cycle of joint ventures. *Management International Review, 28,* 39–52.

Kogut, B. (1991). Joint ventures and the option to expand and acquire. *Management Science, 37*(1), 19–34.

Lavie, D. (2006). The competitive advantage of interconnected firms: An extension of the resource-based view. *Academy of Management Review, 31*(3), 638–658.

Lunnan, R., & Haugland, S. (2008). Predicting and measuring alliance performance: A multidimensional analysis. *Strategic Management Journal, 29*(5), 545–556.

Madhok, A. (1995). Revisiting multinational firms' tolerance for joint ventures: A trust-based approach. *Journal of International Business Studies, 26*(1), 117–137.

Mayer, K., & Argyres, C. (2004). Learning to contract: Evidence from the personal computer industry. *Organization Science, 15*(4), 394–410.

Mayer, R., Davis, J., & Schoorman, F. (1995). An integration model of organizational trust. *Academy of Management Review, 20,* 709–734.

McEvily, B., Perrone, V., & Zaheer, A. (2003). Trust as an organizing principle. *Organization Science, 14*(1), 91–104.

Mowery, D., Oxley, J., & Silverman, B. (1996). Strategic alliances and interfirm knowledge transfer. *Strategic Management Journal, 17*(Winter Special Issue), 77–91.

Poppo, L., & Zenger, T. (2002). Do formal contracts and relational governance function as substitutes or complements? *Strategic Management Journal, 23*(8), 707–725.

Prahalad, C. K. (2006). *The fortune at the bottom of the pyramid.* Upper Saddle River, NJ: Wharton School Publishing.

Puranam, P., & Srikanth, K. (2007). What they do vs. what they know: How acquirers leverage technology acquisitions. *Strategic Management Journal, 28*(8), 805–825.

Puranam, P., & Vanneste, B. (2009). Trust and governance: Untangling a tangled web. *Academy of Management Review, 34*(1), 11–28.

Reuer, J., & Arino, A. (2007). Strategic alliance contracts: Dimensions and determinants of contractual complexity. *Strategic Management Journal, 28*(3), 313–330.

Idea in Brief

- Half of mergers don't deliver their hoped-for business value. Yet companies from developing countries are defying that statistic, using **M&A** as their main globalization strategy and generating more value from takeovers than their counterparts from developed nations.
- Unlike Western companies, which use **M&A** primarily to increase size and efficiency, emerging giants acquire firms to obtain competencies, technology, and knowledge essen-

tial to their strategy. They avoid overturning acquisitions' management structures and people, ensuring smoother integration. And they have a clear long-term vision guiding their actions; they are willing to wait for a takeover to pay off.
- By applying these **M&A** principles, Indian aluminum producer Hindalco became one of the world's largest aluminum manufacturers.

innovation skills—that will help them become global leaders. Operating costs aren't an issue; the emerging giant knows it can transform an acquisition's economics simply by switching to the low-cost resources and business processes in its home country. In addition, developing countries will increasingly absorb Western companies' output of technologically superior products. Many slow-growing companies with low margins can be turned into fast-growing, high-margin enterprises by their acquirers in developing countries, the logic of "reverse" M&A suggests.

To realize their objectives, companies from developing countries are using new techniques to identify targets and integrate them. They acquire only to meet strategic goals; they don't completely assimilate acquisitions; and CEOs focus on the long term while planning take-overs and evaluating results. One company showing the way is India's Hindalco, which has used M&A to become one of the world's largest manufacturers of aluminum. In the process, the Indian commodities player turned into an integrated global major and boosted revenues by 30 times, from $500 million to $15 billion, in just seven years. Although the current recession is hurting Hindalco, its strategies are a harbinger of how emerging giants will increasingly approach M&A in the global market and gain an advantage over companies that use more traditional acquisition strategies (see Exhibit 1).

HINDALCO'S GLOBAL AMBITIONS

Unknown outside India until recently, Hindalco is the flagship company of the $28 billion Aditya Birla Group, one of the country's oldest and most diversified family business houses. Set up in 1857, the group went overseas in the 1970s when the founder's great-great-grandson, Aditya Birla, established 19 joint ventures in Egypt, Indonesia, Malaysia, the Philippines, and Thailand. It was unusual for Indian entrepreneurs to operate abroad in those days, and the experience laid the foundations of the group's global ambitions. After Aditya's death, in 1995, son Kumar Birla continued to focus on growth; by 1999, the group was one of the world's biggest manufacturers of cement, carbon black, and viscose staple fiber.

By then, Hindalco had grown into India's largest aluminum producer, with a nearly 40% share of the market. It had built a dozen processing plants and also captive power plants and coal mines, and the organization concentrated on upstream operations such as bauxite mining, alumina refining, and aluminum smelting. It was a commodity manufacturer predominantly focused on the Indian market, although it exported a fifth of its output. Senior executives in the group, like Debu Bhattacharya, who became Hindalco's CEO in July 2003, were dissatisfied with that.

Exhibit 1   Two Approaches to M&A

Emerging giants have different reasons from Western corporations for acquiring companies abroad. They also use novel integration techniques and measure performance in light of long-term goals. It's too early to tell if their approach will work—but if it does, it will take cross-border M&A to new heights.

	Traditional Approach to M&A	Emerging Giants' Approach to M&A
Rationale	The aim of a takeover is usually to lower costs, though some companies use acquisitions to obtain technologies, enter niches, or break into new countries.	The aim is to obtain new technologies, brands, and consumers in foreign countries.
Synergy Levels	The acquirer and the acquisition usually have the same business model. Even when a company takes over a start-up, the approach to market is the same.	The acquirer is often a low-cost commodity player, while the acquisition is a value-added branded-products company.
Integration Speed	The buyer makes several changes in the acquisition soon after the takeover. It slows the quest for synergies thereafter.	Integration is slow-moving at first. After a while, the buyer starts pulling the acquisition closer.
Organizational Fallout	High executive turnover and head-count reduction are likely at first. Culture clashes occur and productivity declines, but things settle down over time.	Little interference, executive turnover, or head-count reduction occurs right after the acquisition. Although it's too soon to tell as of now, tensions could simmer over the long run and blow up.
Goals	The buyer has clear short-term aims but may not have thought through long-term goals.	The acquirer's short-term objectives may be fuzzy, but its long-term vision for the acquisition is clear.

Hindalco could do better, they believed, because India had large reserves of bauxite and the company boasted low processing costs.

A turn-of-the-century strategy review convinced top management that Hindalco could become a global leader by expanding the aluminum business, manufacturing more value-added products, and selling both aluminum and aluminum products all over the world. However, success factors in upstream and downstream businesses differ, so Hindalco decided to pursue a two-pronged strategy: It would generate economies of scale in the aluminum manufacturing business by setting up projects in India, and it would use cross-border acquisitions to break into the product market. The latter would be risky; Hindalco had never before acquired a company. It would therefore have to learn to integrate acquisitions and, at the same time, absorb new capabilities.

CLIMBING THE M&A COMPETENCY STAIRWAY

Hindalco didn't immediately cast about for targets overseas. Instead, it patiently executed small takeovers, first in India and later abroad, before making a big global play. Each of the initial acquisitions, my research suggests, taught the company something new and served as a stepping-stone toward another acquisition (see Exhibit 2). Combined, those moves created an M&A competency stairway, as I call it, which the company steadily climbed over a period of eight years.

The process started in 2000. Canada's Alcan, one of the aluminum industry's global leaders, wanted to merge with France's Pechiney and Switzerland's Alusuisse to focus on the upstream business. It decided to pull out of India, where it had only a downstream operation, and put its

Exhibit 2   Lessons Learned from Each Acquisition

Indian aluminum producer Hindalco acquired several companies before it picked up Atlanta-headquartered giant Novelis in 2007. From each takeover, the Indian enterprise learned new industry-related skills and M&A techniques. It needed to cultivate both kinds of capabilities to acquire a North American company more than twice its size.

ACQUISITIONS

							Novelis North America 2007
					St. Anne Nackawic Pulp Mill Canada 2005	Minacs Worldwide Canada 2006	
			Nifty; Mount Gordon Australia 2003				
Indal; Annapurna Foils India 2000	2001	2002		2004			

- How to bid for, negotiate with, and integrate companies in India
- How to manage a large customer-focused, value-added products business
- How to turn around a small Indian company in receivership

- How to take over, turn around, and operate companies in a developed market
- How to list companies on a stock exchange abroad and manage investor relations

- How to manage a global supply chain as a buyer and a seller
- How to manage price fluctuations and foreign exchange risks across countries

- How to acquire, assimilate, and delist a company in North America
- How to manage a large, HR-intensive multinational operation

55% equity stake in Indal—the longtime leader in the Indian market—on the block. A bidding war ensued, and in July 2000, Hindalco, which had long coveted Indal, managed to land the prize catch for a total of $230 million .

This takeover enabled Hindalco to straddle the length of the industry's value chain. Over the past nine years, the company has become adept at developing aluminum products such as sheets, foils, and extrusions, and manufacturing them cost-effectively. It has developed the ability to brand products, distribute them to retailers and other business customers, and cultivate customer relationships. From Indal, Hindalco inherited a small company, Annapurna Foils, which had gone into receivership. Hindalco's executives, who had never had to nurse a company back to health, joined the team dealing with the situation. By installing cutting-edge equipment, reengineering processes, and fostering demand for packaging foils, such as lid foil and confectionery wrap, they helped turn around Annapurna.

Hindalco also learned to cope with touchy postmerger integration issues. For example, Alcan had operated in India since 1938, and its Indian managers prided themselves on their values and processes. Indal's managers worried that after the merger, Hindalco's "family business" ways

would drive out their "professional management" culture. To reassure them, Hindalco decided to retain all of Indal's senior managers. Kumar Birla made it a point to send out the message, internally and externally, that the group "acquires talent, not just assets" and that it would always deploy the best person for the job. Hindalco has tried to live up to that claim. For instance, Indal's CFO, S. Talukdar, continued in that role until 2005, when the two companies formally merged, and then stepped in as Hindalco's CFO—a rare postmerger occurrence. Hindalco's approach helped turn Indal into a growth machine: Its profits were five times as big in 2006 as they were in 1999.

Three years after picking up the majority stake in Indal, Hindalco felt it could tackle cross-border acquisitions. A nascent copper division took over the Nifty and Mount Gordon mines, two Australian companies, one of which was in receivership and the other was heading there. The companies were small, but the takeovers forced Hindalco to cut its teeth in a developed country, where, among other challenges, labor costs were high and regulations were strict. It used the opportunity to create an overseas company. After merging the two acquisitions, Hindalco made a public offering and listed Aditya Birla

Minerals—the first Indian company to trade publicly in Australia—on the Australian Securities Exchange.

Hindalco's growing confidence in its ability to take over and turn around companies spread throughout the Aditya Birla Group. In 2005 the group picked up a pulp mill in Canada to feed its fiber plants in China, India, Indonesia, and Thailand. The deal allowed the group's managers to cope with the dynamics of a global supply chain from the perspectives of both sellers and buyers, and to understand the intricacies of hedging foreign exchange and price risks in different countries. The next year, the group's outsourcing services unit, TransWorks Information, bought a Canadian company, Minacs Worldwide, to create a global player in that field.

The experience the Aditya Birla Group gained through all these takeovers convinced Hindalco that it was time to go after the big one. In December 2006, after the group had scooped up six companies in six years, Hindalco made a bid for Novelis, one of the world's largest producers of flat-rolled aluminum and aluminum products. The Atlanta-headquartered company's facilities were new; it had earned a reputation for technological innovation; and its customers included Anheuser-Busch, Coca-Cola, Ford, Tetra Pak, and ThyssenKrupp. Novelis had reported a 2005 profit of $90 million, but for fiscal 2006 it was projecting a loss of between $240 million and $285 million. That's because it had been born with a large amount of debt on its books. In addition, the company had entered into fixed-price long-term contracts with four major customers, and when raw materials prices rose sharply in 2005, Novelis started losing money on those deals.

Hindalco's unsolicited offer took Novelis's board by surprise. The board later warmed to the idea of a sale and initiated a competitive bidding process. In May 2007, Hindalco succeeded in picking up Novelis for $6 billion—the second-largest takeover by an Indian company in the United States. If Hindalco hadn't gained a wealth of M&A experience, it probably wouldn't have overcome the diffidence of many emerging-market companies and made a bid for a North American corporation more than twice its size.

STICKING TO STRATEGIC ACQUISITIONS

It may appear as though Hindalco acquired firms willy-nilly, as most Western enterprises do. However, it pursued companies such as Indal and Novelis only after it had carefully figured out what it would achieve by buying them. Hindalco identified its weaknesses and targeted only those corporations whose purchase would offset them, as I shall demonstrate next. So far, it hasn't shown much interest in using M&A to grow quickly or to deal with overcapacity.

Three years before the Novelis bid, Hindalco identified four types of companies in the aluminum industry: Miners like Rio Tinto and BHP Billiton mainly extract bauxite and convert it into aluminum. Aluminum producers such as Dubal and Rusal make aluminum because they have inexpensive access to energy, which accounts for 40% of production costs. Downstream producers such as Novelis and Sapa buy aluminum on the London Metal Exchange and convert it into aluminum products. And integrated giants like Alcoa and Alcan combine upstream and downstream operations.

There are good companies of all four kinds, so no single business model is preferable. Enterprises that focus on upstream rather than downstream operations are more profitable, but their profits fluctuate more. That's because speculators on commodity exchanges influence aluminum prices, whereas consumer demand mostly determines product prices.

Hindalco was then an upstream player, so its profits varied every year. It decided to add downstream operations for a few reasons: First, the company wanted to steady the profit stream. Second, it realized it had to be globally competitive at home since India wasn't a protected market anymore. And third, to move away from the commodity business, Hindalco had to manufacture value-added products. Making aluminum at competitive prices requires economies of scale, process skills, and cheap raw materials. Selling value-added aluminum products demands attention to quality, service, and brands; product development skills; and a knack for forging customer relationships—capabilities that Hindalco didn't possess. To learn them, it decided to acquire the leading downstream companies: Indal in India and Novelis overseas. The objective was to gain new competencies—not to get big fast or to reduce costs.

Once it has identified a target, Hindalco doesn't worry much about the stock market's reaction. The day after it announced the Novelis deal, for instance, Hindalco's scrip price fell (on February 11, 2007) by 13% and its market capitalization declined by $600 million. In the 2006–2007 annual report, Birla acknowledged the adverse impact of the takeover on Hindalco's bottom line. He asked shareholders to be patient: "I do realize that in the short-term [the acquisition] does cause a strain on your Company's Balance Sheet. However, if you look at the bigger picture, this is one of the most striking acquisitions and over the long-term will undeniably create enormous shareholder value."

This philosophy, which will stand Birla in good stead as Hindalco battles the current recession, is one of the distinguishing features of takeovers by emerging giants. Unlike the many Western companies that merely pay lip service to the idea of generating value in the long run, smart emerging giants are content to reap the benefits from takeovers over time. In an interview for this article, Birla told me: "I'm not worried. Investors may have a short-term perspective, but my vision is to build a world-class company that is still the leader four decades from now." One downside of this approach is that if the logic driving an acquisition is flawed, it will be too late before the company realizes its mistake. Companies like Hindalco can conceal a multitude of sins by telling investors, "We know best; trust us."

ALLOWING INTEGRATION TO EVOLVE

Hindalco's management doesn't believe in the 30-day or 100-day integration plan; it allows the postmerger process to evolve naturally and rarely intervenes. By the time the company bid for Novelis, it had developed a simple, four-step process to help meet its initial postmerger objectives. The steps are standard ones, relating to finance, organizational issues, business processes, and markets, but the Indian company prioritizes them in a

unique way. Most Western and Asian companies spend a lot of time after a merger tackling knotty organizational issues—that is, who's going to get what job—as well as financial ones. Hindalco resolves those issues quickly and then focuses on integrating business processes to score immediate wins and combining markets to create long-term value.

Financial Integration

Instead of centralizing the financial operations after taking over a company, Hindalco tackles only the reporting systems at first. Senior executives want the acquirer and the acquired to speak the same financial language, see the same reports, and set similar benchmarks—as soon as possible. Managers from Novelis and Hindalco worked side by side to get their reporting periods aligned. Prior to June 2007, Hindalco's financial year ended on March 31 whereas Novelis's ended on December 31, so standardization was essential. Other teams took up the consolidation of quarterly results and ensured that both entities met the guidelines of regulators such as the Securities and Exchange Board of India and the U.S. Securities and Exchange Commission. Taxation too required an integration team; Hindalco and Novelis had to meet the tax laws in all the countries in which they operated, but they wanted to optimize the tax bill as well. In none of these cases did Hindalco insist on doing things its way; it shared best practices with Novelis, and vice versa, so that they could find common ground.

Organizational Integration

Hindalco doesn't disturb an acquisition's management structure, systems, or people unless necessary. For example, it kept Novelis people in all the top management jobs there—including COO Martha Finn Brooks, who has held her position since 2005. Moreover, in the first six months after the takeover, Hindalco deputed just two of its own executives to Novelis: It sent an expert from its copper division to institutionalize a risk-management process and installed a senior executive in Novelis's logistics department to help improve its global supply chain. This dampened the fears at Novelis that "the Indians were coming." By sending two of its best people, Hindalco was able to impress Novelis's executives, who now routinely check with the Indian company before going outside the group for ideas or people.

Business Process Integration

Hindalco looks for easy and painless business wins in the short term. For instance, it has set up a company in India to manage Novelis's information technology systems because of the availability of inexpensive engineers there. Hindalco didn't lay off Novelis employees, but it stopped the hiring of consultants. By 2010 the IT project will reduce the merged entity's costs by $40 million a year. Similarly, Hindalco noticed that Novelis's stock turns—the number of times inventory sells—were six a year, compared with its own 20. If stock turns at Novelis were to increase by just one, the company reckons, that would free $50 million to $70 million in working capital. Hindalco has set Novelis a target of seven to 12 stock turns a year by 2010, which could free about $300 million in working capital. Novelis has started overhauling its supply chain management and inventory control practices, but it's too early to say what the results will be. Besides, the company's sales are falling in the current slowdown, so its stock turns are unlikely to rise.

Wherever Hindalco has felt that Novelis had superior processes, the acquirer has learned from the acquired. For instance, the U.S. company relies on value-based management systems, so Hindalco has enlisted Novelis's managers to develop similar processes in all its units in India. On the basis of analyses of competitors, markets, plants, financials, and customer data, they are developing planning models that will enable Hindalco to craft better strategies for the future.

Market Integration

Despite the competition in the Indian market, Hindalco can easily stoke demand in India for the products of companies it acquires. This type of integration is peculiar to emerging giants, which have fast-growing home markets. For example, India's demand for aluminum products is projected to almost double from 1 million tons in 2007 to 1.9 million tons in 2012, and half of that increase in demand will be for the kind of flat-rolled

products Novelis produces. Thus, India could absorb a third of the North American company's output in three years' time. Even then, India's per capita consumption of aluminum will be one kilogram compared with China's 9 kilograms and the United States' 25. If Hindalco can grow India's consumption to 2.25 kilograms—a quarter of China's current consumption—India will consume everything that Novelis produces today. The first signs of change are visible. Two years before the Novelis deal, Hindalco sounded out the world's majors about setting up can-making operations in India. None were interested, but after the Novelis takeover, five entered India. Hindalco is supplying all of them with flat-rolled aluminum from a Novelis plant in South Korea. When the volumes become bigger, the company will set up a plant in India to manufacture flat-rolled aluminum.

The future of these investment plans will of course depend on how well Hindalco weathers the global recession, which has shrunk the demand for aluminum and aluminum products. Although the price of aluminum fell by about one-third in the last three months of 2008, the Indian company's revenues grew by 1.8% and it reported a profit of $395 million for the period from April to December 2008. By contrast, Novelis's performance suffered: Sales fell by 1.7% in the nine months leading up to December 31, 2008; in the last quarter of the calendar year, they tumbled by 20%. The company realized a huge net loss of $1.9 billion from April to December. This included a one-time financial charge of $1.5 billion, which Novelis, like several other North American companies, incurred because its value fell by that amount in 2008, and the SEC required that the sum be written off. Excluding all the financial charges, Novelis recorded a pretax loss of $32 million for the quarter, compared with a loss of $22 million for the same period in 2007.

Hindalco believed that Novelis's steady earnings would help offset the fluctuations in its profits from year to year. It did not anticipate a meltdown of the market, with demand all along the value chain falling so dramatically. Hindalco has faced other problems at Novelis as well. For instance, Hindalco has not been able to commercialize Novelis's technologies quickly. It has several products in its innovation funnel, but their development is moving at a very slow pace.

As with most acquisitions, Hindalco took over Novelis when the stock market was at its peak. When booms become busts, acquirers often run into problems as interest costs rise and debt repayments come due. Not only will it take Hindalco longer than it expected to realize the benefits of the Novelis acquisition, but the Indian company will have to invest a lot of money to ride out this storm. What will help, though, is the fact that Hindalco developed a clear long-term strategy and adhered to it while making acquisitions.

Traditionally, the desire to consolidate has driven acquisitions. However, emerging giants are taking over companies abroad to connect sophisticated technologies and brands with low costs and relatively high growth rates at home. Western multinational companies can fight back by giving global mandates to their overseas subsidiaries. But that will happen only when the locus of M&A shifts from the corporate headquarters in the developed world to regional headquarters in emerging markets.

The American Model of the Multinational Firm and the "New" Multinationals from Emerging Economies

Mauro F. Guillén
University of Pennsylvania

Esteban García-Canal
Universidad de Oviedo, Spain

EXECUTIVE OVERVIEW

The traditional American model of multinational enterprise (MNE), characterized by foreign direct investment (FDI) aimed at exploiting firm-specific capabilities developed at home and a gradual country-by-country approach of internationalization, dominated the global economy during much of the post–World War II period. In the last two decades, however, new MNEs from emerging, upper-middle-income, or oil-rich countries have followed completely different patterns of international expansion. In this paper we analyze the processes through which these firms became MNEs and to what extent we need a new theory to explain their international growth.

The modern multinational enterprise (MNE) as we know it today has its origins in the second industrial revolution of the late 19th century. British, North American, and continental European firms expanded around the world on the basis of intangible assets such as technology, brands, and managerial expertise. The climax of their worldwide expansion was reached during the 1950s and 60s, as trade and investment barriers gradually fell around the world (Chandler, 1990; Kindleberger, 1969; Vernon, 1979; Wilkins, 1974).

While significant variations in the strategy and structure of North American and European multinationals were documented at the time (e.g., Stopford & Wells, 1972) and the rise of Japanese multinationals during the 1970s and 80s added yet more diversity to the global population of multinational corporations, firms expanding from relatively rich and technologically advanced countries tended to share a core set of features. Chief among them were their technological, marketing, and managerial strengths, which enabled them to overcome the so-called liability of foreignness in a variety of markets, investing for the most part in wholly or majority-owned subsidiaries, transferring technology, products,

and knowledge from headquarters to far-flung operations around the globe, and relying on elaborate bureaucratic and financial controls.

This relatively straightforward state of affairs is changing rapidly. Since the 1990s, the global competitive landscape has become increasingly populated by MNEs originating in countries that are not among the most advanced in the world. These "new" MNEs come from (a) upper-middle-income economies such as Spain, Portugal, South Korea, and Taiwan; (b) emerging economies such as Brazil, Chile, Mexico, China, India, and Turkey; (c) developing countries such as Egypt, Indonesia, and Thailand; and (d) oil-rich countries such as the United Arab Emirates, Nigeria, and Venezuela. The new MNEs operate internationally using multiple entry modes, ranging from alliances and joint ventures to wholly owned subsidiaries. Some of them are small and product focused, while others are large and diversified across many industries. The literature has referred to

"The American Model of the Multinational Firm and the 'New' Multinationals From Emerging Economies," by Mauro F. Guillen and Esteban Garcia-Canal, *Academy of Management Perspectives*, Vol. 23, No. 2 (May 2009), pp. 23–35. Copyright © 2009 by Academy of Management. Reproduced with permission of Academy of Management via Copyright Clearance Center.

them in a variety of ways, including "third-world multinationals" (Wells, 1983), "latecomer firms" (Mathews, 2002), "unconventional multinationals" (Li, 2003), "challengers" (BCG, 2008), and "emerging multinationals" (Accenture, 2008; *Economist,* 2008; Goldstein, 2007). While they may not possess the most sophisticated technological or marketing skills in their respective industries, they have expanded around the world in innovative ways. They have become key actors in foreign direct investment and cross-border acquisitions (UNCTAD, 2006).

The new multinationals from the BRIC[1] countries have made great inroads into the global economy. Among Brazilian firms, Companhia Vale do Rio Doce and Metalúrgica Gerdau are among the largest firms in mining and steel, Embraer holds with Bombardier of Canada a duopoly in the global regional jet market, and Natura Cosméticos has a presence in both Latin America and Europe. Lukoil, Gazprom, and Severstal are among the Russian multinationals, while India boasts an army of firms not only in IT and outsourcing services, in which companies such as Infosys, TCS, and Wipro are among the largest in the world, but also in steel, automobiles, and pharmaceuticals. Chinese firms have irrupted with force in global markets not only as exporters but also as foreign investors, and in every industry from mining and oil to chemicals and steel. In electrical appliances and electronics, China boasts three increasingly well-known firms: Haier, Lenovo, and Huawei.

Multinationals from the so-called Asian tiger economies—those that industrialized during the 1960s—are among the earliest new multinationals from countries other than the most advanced. Taiwan, a country that excels both at technological and process innovation, has proved to be the most fertile ground for outward foreign investors, including such powerhouses as Formosa Plastics, Taiwan Semiconductor, and Acer. Following a path to development much more oriented toward large-scale industry, South Korea is home to some of the best-known names in the electronics and appliances industries (Samsung and LG) and automobiles (Hyundai and Kia). The city-state of Singapore has bred multinationals in food and beverages (Fraser and Neave, Want Want), electronics (Olam), telecommunications (Singtel), real estate (Capitaland), transportation (Neptune Orient Lines), and hotels (City Developments).

For its part, Hong Kong is home to a large number of multinationals in a similar set of industries, led by Hutchinson Whampoa, the world's largest port operator.

In addition to South Korea and Taiwan, Spain has produced the largest number of truly global multinationals among the countries that back in the 1960s were still attempting to develop a solid industrial base. In food processing, Spanish companies have made important acquisitions in Europe, Asia, and the Americas, turning themselves into the world's largest producers of rice and olive oil and the second-largest of pasta. In the textiles and clothing sector, Spain has also produced companies of international stature, such as global denim leader Tavex (now merged with Brazil's Santista); Inditex, which owns the world's second-most-valuable brand (Zara); and Pronovias, the largest bridal-wear designer and manufacturer. Spanish firms in telecommunications (Telefónica), electricity (Endesa, Iberdrola), and banking (Santander, BBVA) are among the largest MNEs in their respective industries.

In Spanish-speaking Latin America some firms from Mexico and Argentina stand out as formidable global competitors. In food processing, Bimbo and Gruma are among the largest in their respective market niches, namely, packaged bread and tortillas. In cement, Cemex is the second- or third-largest, depending on the specific product. Grupo Modelo is the third-largest brewery in the world. These companies have made acquisitions or greenfield investments in North America, Asia, and Europe. Argentina's Tenaris is the global leader in seamless steel tubes, and Industrias Metalúrgicas Pescarmona is a major firm in the crane business.

The Middle East is also becoming the home base of major multinational corporations, including DP World of Dubai (the world's second-largest port operator), Orascom (the Egyptian construction and telecommunications group with major operations throughout Africa and the Middle East), Mobile Telecommunications Company (the Kuwaiti giant), and Enka Insaat ve Saayi (the Turkish infrastructure group).

The proliferation of the new MNEs has taken observers, policymakers, and scholars by surprise. Many of these firms were marginal competitors just a decade ago; today they are challenging some of the world's most accomplished and established multinationals in a wide variety of industries and markets. The unexpected rise to prominence of firms such as Cemex of Mexico, Embraer of Brazil, Haier of China, Tata Consultancy Services of India, and Banco Santander of Spain raises three fundamental questions: First, do these firms share some common features that distinguish them from the traditional American model of the MNE? Second, what advantages have made it possible for them to operate and compete not only in host countries at the same or lower level of economic development but also in the richest economies? Third, why have they been able to expand abroad at dizzying speed, in defiance of the conventional wisdom about the virtues of a staged, incremental approach to international expansion? Before being in a position to answer these questions, one must begin by outlining the established theory of the MNE.

THE THEORY OF THE MULTINATIONAL FIRM

Although MNEs have existed for a very long time, scholars first attempted to understand the nature and drivers of their cross-border activities during the 1950s. The credit for providing the first comprehensive analysis of the MNE and of foreign direct investment goes to economist Stephen Hymer, who in his doctoral dissertation observed that the "control of the foreign enterprise is desired in order to remove competition between that foreign enterprise and enterprises in other countries . . . or the control is desired in order to appropriate fully the returns on certain skills and abilities" (Hymer, 1960, p. 25). His key insight was that the multinational firm possesses certain kinds of proprietary advantages that set it apart from purely domestic firms, thus helping it overcome the "liability of foreignness."

Multinational firms exist because certain economic conditions and proprietary advantages make it advisable and possible for them to profitably undertake production of a good or service in a foreign location. It is important to distinguish between vertical and horizontal foreign expansion in order to fully understand the basic economic principles that underlie the activities of MNEs in general and the novelty of the "new" MNEs in particular.

Vertical Expansion

Vertical expansion occurs when the firm locates assets or employees in a foreign country with the purpose of securing the production of a raw material, component, or input (backward vertical expansion) or the distribution and sale of a good or service (forward vertical expansion). The necessary condition for a firm to engage in vertical expansion is the presence of a comparative advantage in the foreign location. The advantage typically has to do with the prices or productivities of production factors such as capital, labor, or land. For instance, a clothing firm may consider production in a foreign location due to lower labor costs.

It is important, though, to realize that the mere existence of a comparative advantage in a foreign location does not mean that the firm ought to vertically expand. The necessary condition of lower factor costs or higher factor productivity, or both, is not sufficient. After all, the firm could benefit from the comparative advantage in the foreign location simply by asking a local producer to become its supplier. The sufficient condition justifying a vertical foreign investment refers to the possible reasons encouraging the firm to undertake foreign production by itself rather than relying on others to do the job. The two main reasons are uncertainty about the supply and asset specificity. If uncertainty is high, the firm would prefer to integrate backward into the foreign location to make sure that the supply chain functions smoothly, and that delivery timetables are met. Asset specificity is high when the firm and the foreign supplier need to develop joint assets in order for the supply operation to take place. In that situation the firm would prefer to expand backward in order to avoid the "hold-up" problem, that is, opportunistic behavior on the part of the foreign supplier trying to extract rents from the firm. These necessary and sufficient conditions also apply in the case of forward vertical expansion into a foreign location. Uncertainty and asset specificity with, say, a foreign distributor would compel the firm to take things into its own hands and invest in the foreign location in order to make sure that the goods or services reach the buyer in the appropriate way and at a reasonable cost.

Horizontal Expansion

Horizontal expansion occurs when the firm sets up a plant or service delivery facility in a foreign location with the goal of selling in that market, and without abandoning production of the good or service in the home country. The decision to engage in horizontal expansion is driven by forces different than those for vertical expansion. Production of a good or service in a foreign market is desirable in the presence of protectionist barriers, high transportation costs, unfavorable currency exchange rate shifts, or requirements for local adaptation to the peculiarities of local demand that make exporting from the home country unfeasible or unprofitable. As in the case of vertical expansion, these obstacles are a necessary condition for horizontal expansion, but not a sufficient one. The firm should ponder the relative merits of licensing a local producer in the foreign market or establishing an alliance against those of committing to a foreign investment. The sufficient condition for setting up a proprietary plant or service facility has to do with the possession of intangible assets—brands, technology, know-how, and other firm-specific skills—that make licensing a risky option because the licensee might appropriate, damage, or otherwise misuse the firm's assets.[2]

Scholars in the field of international management have also acknowledged that firms in possession of the requisite competitive advantages do not become MNEs overnight, but in a gradual way, following different stages. According to the framework originally proposed by researchers at the University of Uppsala in Sweden (Johanson & Vahlne, 1977; Johanson & Wiedersheim-Paul, 1975), firms expand abroad on a country-by-country basis, starting with those more similar in terms of sociocultural distance. They also argued that in each foreign country firms typically followed a sequence of steps: on-and-off exports, exporting through local agents, sales subsidiary, and production and marketing subsidiary. A similar set of explanations and predictions were proposed by Vernon (1966, 1979) in his application of the product life cycle to the location of production. According to these perspectives, the firm commits resources to foreign markets as it accumulates knowledge and experience, managing the risks of expansion and coping with the liability of foreignness. An important corollary is that the firm expands abroad only as fast as its experience and knowledge allow.

ENTER THE "NEW" MULTINATIONALS

The early students of the phenomenon of MNEs from developing, newly industrialized, emerging, or upper-middle-income countries focused their attention on both the vertical and the horizontal investments undertaken by these firms, but they were especially struck by the latter. Vertical investments, after all, are easily understood in terms of the desire to reduce uncertainty and minimize opportunism when assets are dedicated or specific to the supply or the downstream activity, whether the MNE comes from a developed country or not (Caves, 1996, pp. 238–241; Lall, 1983; Lecraw, 1977; Wells, 1983). The horizontal investments of the new MNEs, however, are harder to explain because they are supposed to be driven by the possession of intangible assets, and firms from developing countries were simply assumed not to possess them, or at least not to possess the same kinds of intangible assets as the classic MNEs from the rich countries (Lall, 1983, p. 4). This paradox becomes more evident with the second wave of FDI from the developing world, the one starting in the late 1980s. In contrast with the first wave of FDI from emerging countries that took place in the 1960s and 70s, the new MNEs of the 1980s and 90s aimed at becoming world leaders in their respective industries, not just marginal players (Mathews, 2006). In addition, the new MNEs do not come only from emerging countries. Some firms, labeled as born-globals or born-again born-globals (Bell, McNaughton, & Young, 2001), have emerged from developed countries following accelerated paths of internationalization that challenge the conventional view of international expansion.

The main features of the new MNEs, as compared to the traditional ones, appear in Table 1. The dimensions in the table highlight the key differences between new and conventional MNEs. Perhaps the most startling one has to do with the accelerated pace of internationalization of the

Table 1   The New Multinational Enterprises Compared to Traditional Multinationals

Dimension	New MNEs	Traditional MNEs
Speed of internationalization	Accelerated	Gradual
Competitive advantages	Weak: Upgrading of resources required	Strong: Required resources available in-house
Political capabilities	Strong: Firms used to unstable political environments	Weak: Firms used to stable political environments
Expansion path	Dual path: Simultaneous entry into developed and developing countries	Simple path: From less to more distant countries
Default entry modes	External growth: Alliances and acquisitions	Internal growth: Wholly owned subsidiaries
Organizational adaptability	High, because of their meager international presence	Low, because of their ingrained structure and culture

new MNEs, as firms from emerging economies have attempted to close the gap between their market reach and the global presence of the MNEs from developed countries (Mathews, 2006).

A second feature of the new MNEs is that all of them, no matter the home country, have been forced to deal not only with the liability of foreignness but also with the liability and competitive disadvantage that stem from being late-comers lacking the resources and capabilities of established MNEs from the most advanced countries. For this reason, the international expansion of the new MNEs runs in parallel with a capability upgrading process through which newcomers seek to gain access to external resources and capabilities in order to catch up with their more advanced competitors, that is, to reduce their competitiveness gap with established MNEs (Aulakh, 2007; Li, 2007; Mathews, 2006). However, despite lacking the resource endowment of MNEs from developed countries, the new MNEs usually have an advantage over them, as they tend to possess better political capabilities. As the new MNEs are more used to dealing with discretionary and/or unstable governments in their home country, they are better prepared than the traditional MNEs to succeed in foreign countries characterized by a weak institutional environment (Cuervo-Cazurra & Genc, 2008). Taking into account the high growth rates of emerging countries and their peculiar institutional environments, political capabilities have been especially valuable for the new MNEs.

The first two features taken together point to another key characteristic of the new MNEs: They face a significant dilemma when it comes to international expansion because they need to balance the desire for global reach with the need to upgrade their capabilities. They can readily use their home-grown competitive advantages in other emerging or developing countries, but they must also enter more advanced countries in order to expose themselves to sophisticated, cutting-edge demand and develop their capabilities. This tension is reflected in Figure 1. Firms may evolve in a way that helps them upgrade their capabilities or gain geographic reach, or both. Along the diagonal, the firm pursues a balanced growth path. Above the diagonal it enters the region of capability building, in which the firm sacrifices the number of countries entered (its geographic reach) so as to close the gap with other competitors, especially in the advanced economies. Below the diagonal the firm enters the unsustainable region because prioritizing global reach without improving firm competencies jeopardizes the capability upgrading process. The tension between capability upgrading and gaining global reach forces the new MNEs to enter developed and developing countries simultaneously from the beginning of their international expansion. Entering developing countries helps them gain size and operational experience and generate profits, while venturing into developed ones contributes primarily to the capability upgrading process. The new MNEs

Figure 1 Expansion Paths of New MNEs in Developed and Developing Countries

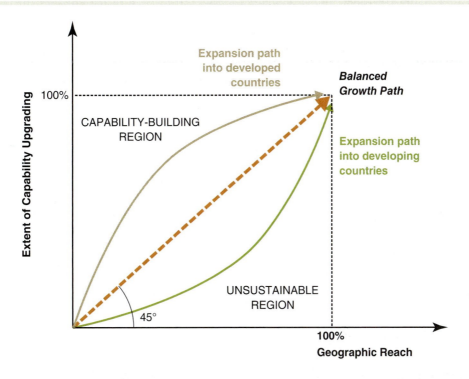

have certainly tended to expand into developing countries at the beginning of their international expansion and limit their presence in developed countries to only a few locations where they can build capabilities, either because they have a partner there or because they have acquired a local firm. As they catch up to established MNEs, they begin to invest more in developed countries.

A fourth feature of the new MNEs is their preference for entry modes based on external growth. Global alliances (García-Canal et al., 2002) and acquisitions (Rui & Yip, 2008) are used by these firms to simultaneously overcome the liability of foreignness in the country of the partner/target and to gain access to their competitive advantages with the aim of upgrading their own resources and capabilities. When entering into global alliances, the new MNEs have used their home market position to facilitate the entry of their partners in exchange for reciprocal access to the partners' home markets and/or technology. Besides the size of the domestic market, the stronger the position of new MNEs in it the greater their bargaining power to enter into these alliances. This fact

is illustrated by the case of some new MNEs competing in the domestic appliances industry, such as China's Haier, Mexico's Mabe, and Turkey's Arcelik, whose international expansion was boosted by alliances with world leaders that allowed them to upgrade their technological competencies (Bonaglia et al., 2007). Capability upgrading processes based on acquisitions have been possible in some cases due to the new MNEs' privileged access to financial resources, because of government subsidies or capital market imperfections, as illustrated by the Chinese MNEs (Buckley et al., 2007).

A final feature of the new MNEs is that they enjoy more freedom to implement organizational innovations to adapt to the requirements of globalization because they do not face the constraints typical of established MNEs. As major global players with long histories, many MNEs from the developed economies suffer from inertia and path dependence due to their deeply ingrained values, culture, and organizational structure. Mathews (2006) showed how the new MNEs from Asia have adopted a number of innovative organizational forms that suited their needs, including networked and decentralized structures.

When analyzing the foreign investments of the new MNEs of the 1960s and 1970s, scholars focused their attention on two important questions: their motivations and their proprietary, firm-specific advantages, if any. The following sections deal with these two issues.

Motivations of New MNEs

Table 2 summarizes the main motivations identified in the literature. As noted above, scholars documented and readily explained the desire of some of the new MNEs to create backward linkages into sources of raw materials or forward linkages into foreign markets in order to reduce uncertainty and opportunism in the relationship between the firm and the supplier of the raw material, or between the firm and the distributor or agent in the foreign market. Research documented, especially in the cases of South Korean and Taiwanese firms, their drive to internalize backward and forward linkages through the creation of trading companies, in some cases with government encouragement and financial support (Fields, 1995, pp. 183–237). For example, while during the 1960s a tiny proportion of South Korea's exports reached foreign markets through the distribution and sale channels established by South Korean firms, by the 1980s roughly 50 percent of them were fully internalized, that is, handled by the exporters themselves (Cho, 1987). As would be expected, the new MNEs felt the pressures of uncertainty and asset specificity more strongly if they had developed intangible assets. For instance, using evidence from a representative cross-sectional sample of 837 Spanish exporting firms as of 1992, Campa and Guillén (1999) found that those with greater expenditures on R&D were more likely to internalize export operations. A recent survey of the empirical evidence

Table 2   Motivations for Foreign Direct Investment by the New Multinational Enterprises

Motivation	Description	References
Backward linkage into raw materials	Firm seeks to secure supplies of crucial inputs in the face of uncertainty or asset specificity	Fields, 1995; Lall, 1983; UNCTAD, 2006; Wells, 1983
Forward linkage into foreign markets	Firm seeks to secure access to the market in the presence of asset specificity	Fields, 1995; UNCTAD, 2006; Wells,1983
Home-country government curbs	Firm attempts to overcome growth restrictions imposed by the government in its home market	Lall, 1983; UNCTAD, 2006; Wells, 1983
Spreading of risk	Firm locates assets in different countries to manage risk	Lecraw, 1977
Movement of personal capital abroad	Firm invests abroad so that owners diversify their exposure to any one country	Wells, 1983
Following a home-country customer to foreign markets	Firm follows home-country customers as they expand horizontally to other countries	UNCTAD, 2006; Wells, 1983
Investment in new markets in response to economic reforms in the home country	Firm enjoying monopolistic or oligopolistic position in the home market is threatened by liberalization, deregulation, and/or privatization policies	Goldstein, 2007; Guillén, 2005
Acquisition of firm-specific intangible assets	Firm invests or acquires assets in more developed countries	Lall, 1983; UNCTAD, 2006
Exploitation of firm-specific intangible assets	See Table 3	

concluded that many of the new MNEs, especially in the extractive and manufacturing sectors, became multinationals when they internalized backward or forward linkages (UNCTAD, 2006).

Scholars also documented that developing-country MNEs wished to expand abroad in order to overcome limitations imposed by the home-country government in the domestic market. In many developing and newly industrialized countries, limitations such as licensing systems, quota allocations, and export restrictions kept firms from having enough growth opportunities at their disposal, hence the desire to expand abroad (Lall, 1983; Wells, 1983). In part related to the previous motive, firms felt the need to spread risks by locating assets in different countries (Lecraw, 1977). This motivation was driven by the macroeconomic and political volatility characteristic of so many developing and newly industrialized countries. A variation on this effect has to do with the case of family-owned MNEs from developing countries under the threat of government scrutiny or confiscation (Wells, 1983).

The early literature on the new MNEs also identified buyer-supplier relationships as motives for a supplier establishing production facilities in a foreign country in which the buyer already had a presence (UNCTAD, 2006; Wells 1983). In some cases, both the buyer and the supplier are home-country firms that followed each other abroad, while in others the buyer is a multinational from a developed country that asks its supplier in a developing or newly industrialized country to co-locate either in its home country or in other countries (Guillén, 2005).

Firm-Specific Assets

Scholars also devoted attention to the proprietary, firm-specific intangible assets of the new MNEs, noting that they engaged in foreign direct investment with the purpose of not only acquiring such assets but also exploiting existing ones. Foreign expansion with a view to acquiring intangible assets, especially technology and brands, was not very important during the 1970s and 1980s, but has become widespread in the last two decades (UNCTAD, 2006). With the advent of current account and currency exchange liberalization in many developing and newly industrialized countries, the new MNEs have enjoyed more of a free

hand in terms of making acquisitions, including multibillion-dollar deals. Many of these have targeted troubled companies or divisions located in the United States and Europe that possess some brands and product technology that the new MNE is in a better position to exploit because of its superior or more efficient manufacturing abilities.

Acquisitions have not been the only way to gain access to intangible assets. The evidence suggests that the acceleration in the international expansion of the new MNEs has been backed by a number of international alliances aimed at gaining access to critical resources and skills that allow these firms to catch up to MNEs from developed countries. As argued above, these alliances and acquisitions have been critical for these firms to match the competitiveness of MNEs from developed countries. For this reason the international expansion of new MNEs runs in parallel with the process of upgrading their capabilities. Sometimes, however, capability upgrading precedes international expansion. This is the case, for instance, for some state-owned enterprises that undergo a restructuring process before their internationalization and privatization (Cuervo & Villalonga, 2000).

In other cases the capability upgrading process can follow international expansion. This can happen in regulated industries, where firms face strong incentives to commit large amounts of resources and to establish operations quickly, whenever and wherever opportunities arise, and frequently via acquisition as opposed to greenfield investment (García-Canal & Guillén, 2008; Sarkar et al., 1999). As opportunities for international expansion in these industries depend on privatization and deregulation, some firms lacking competitive advantages expand abroad on the basis of free cash flows as opportunities arise.

As noted above, horizontal investments seemed to pose a challenge to established theories of the MNE. The literature had emphasized since the late 1950s that MNEs in general undertake horizontal investments on the basis of intangible assets such as proprietary technology, brands, or knowhow. The early literature on the new multinationals simply assumed that firms from developing or newly industrialized countries lacked the kind of intangible assets characteristic of American, Japanese, and European multinationals

(Lall, 1983, p. 4). In fact, study after study found that the new multinationals scored lower on technology, marketing skill, organizational overhead, scale, capital intensity, and control over foreign subsidiaries than their rich-country counterparts (e.g., Lall, 1983; Lecraw, 1977; Wells, 1983).

Still, horizontal investments cannot be explained without the presence of intangible assets of some sort. Table 3 summarizes the main types of intangible assets possessed by the new MNEs, as reflected in the existing literature. During the 1970s and 1980s, the scholarly attention focused on capabilities such as the adaptation of technology to the typically smaller scale markets of developing and newly industrialized countries, their cheaper labor, or imperfect input markets (Ferrantino, 1992; Heenan & Keegan, 1979, Lall, 1983; Lecraw, 1977; Tolentino, 1993). Consumer-good MNEs from these countries were also found

to possess a different kind of intangible asset, namely, "ethnic brands" that appealed not only to customers in the home market but also to the ethnic diaspora in foreign countries, especially in Europe and the United States (Ferrantino, 1992; Goldstein, 2007, pp. 117–122; Lecraw, 1977; Wells, 1983). Other scholars noted that the new MNEs possessed an uncanny ability to incrementally improve available products and to develop specialized variations for certain market niches (Lall, 1983; UNCTAD, 2006).

During the 1980s, students of the so-called East Asian miracle highlighted yet another intangible asset, one having to do with the ability to organize production and to execute large-scale projects efficiently with the help of technology borrowed from abroad in industries as diverse as steel, electronics, automobiles, shipbuilding, infrastructure development, and turnkey plant

Table 3   Intangible Assets of the New Multinational Enterprises

Intangible Asset	Description	References
Technology adaptation	Adaptation of available technology to small-scale product markets, cheap labor, and/or imperfect input markets	Ferrantino, 1992; Heenan & Keegan, 1979; Lall, 1983; Lecraw, 1977; Tolentino, 1993
Early adoption of new technology	Implementation of new technology developed by someone else, especially in infrastructure industries such as construction, electricity, or telecommunications	Guillén, 2005; UNCTAD, 2006
Ethnic branding	Consumer brands with appeal to immigrant home-country communities abroad	Ferrantino, 1992; Heenan & Keegan, 1979; Lall, 1983; Lecraw, 1977; Wells, 1983
Efficient production and project execution	Ability to absorb technology, combine resources, and innovate from an organizational point of view in ways that reduce costs and enhance learning	Amsden & Hikino, 1994; Goldstein, 2007; Guillén, 2000; Kock & Guillén, 2001; Mathews, 2006; UNCTAD, 2006
Product innovation	Incremental product improvements; specialized products for market niches	Lall, 1983; UNCTAD, 2006
Institutional entrepreneurial ability	Skills or know-how needed to operate in the peculiar institutional conditions of less developed countries	Caves, 1996; Lall, 1983; Lecraw, 1993
Expertise in the management of acquisitions	Experience gained in the home country in the management of M&As and corporate restructuring that help to extract value from cross-border acquisitions	Guillén, 2005
Networking skills	Ability to develop networks of cooperative relationships	Buckley et al., 2007; Dunning, 2002; Mathews, 2006
Political know-how	Advantage in dealing with host governments and with political risk in less developed countries	García-Canal & Guillén, 2008; Lall, 1983; Lecraw, 1977

construction (Amsden & Hikino, 1994). Scholars also proposed that these capabilities facilitated the growth of diversified business groups (Guillén, 2000; Kock & Guillén, 2001), which in turn made it easier for firms within the same group to expand and invest abroad by drawing on shared financial, managerial, and organizational resources (Goldstein, 2007, pp. 87–93; Guillén, 2002; Lall, 1983, p. 6; Mathews, 2006; UNCTAD, 2006). A specific type of managerial skill that becomes critical in accelerated internationalization is the ability to effectively manage mergers and acquisitions or strategic alliances. These abilities become critical when extracting value from such organizational combinations, which are necessary to learn and gain access to critical external knowledge and resources (Kale et al., 2000; Zollo & Singh, 2004). Guillén (2005) has shown that the accrued skills in the management of M&A and corporate restructuring by large Spanish firms competing in regulated industries have been critical for their international expansion in Latin America. Buckley et al. (2007), analyzing the success of Chinese firms capitalizing on the Chinese diaspora, argued that some firms have the ability to engage in beneficial relationships with other firms that have valuable resources needed to succeed in global markets. The adoption of network-based structures has also helped the development of the new MNEs by making easier the coordination of the international activities (Mathews, 2006). However, home-country networks in several cases have also allowed these firms to take advantage of the experience of the firms from the network (Elango & Pattnaik, 2007; Yiu et al., 2007).

In more recent years, students of the new MNEs have drawn attention to other types of intangible assets. On the technology side, research has documented that firms in developing, newly industrialized and upper-middle-income countries face lower hurdles when it comes to adopting new technology than do their more established counterparts in rich countries. This is especially the case in industries such as construction, electricity, port operations, and telecommunications, in which companies from Brazil, Chile, Mexico, South Korea, Spain, and Dubai, among other countries, have demonstrated a superior ability to borrow technology and organize efficient operations across many markets (Guillén, 2006; UNCTAD, 2006).

Another area of recent theoretical and empirical research has to do with the political know-how that the new MNEs seem to possess by virtue of having been forced to operate in heavily regulated environments at first, and then rapidly deregulating ones, as illustrated by the expansion of Spanish banking, electricity, water, and telecommunications firms throughout Latin America and, more recently, Europe (García-Canal & Guillén, 2008). This "political" capability was not lost on the early students of the new MNEs; they duly pointed out that these firms possessed an "institutional entrepreneurial ability" that enabled them to operate effectively in the peculiar political, regulatory, and cultural conditions characteristic of developing countries (Caves, 1996; Goldstein, 2007, pp. 99–102; Lall, 1983; Lecraw, 1993). Political and regulatory risk management was identified in some early studies as a key competitive capability (Lall, 1983; Lecraw, 1977). In the last 20 years, a new twist has been added to this theoretical insight after the observation that the new MNEs are making acquisitions and increasing their presence in the infrastructure industries of the rich countries of Europe and North America, including electricity generation and distribution; telecommunications; water; and airport, port, and toll-highway operation, among others (Guillén, 2005). The recent corporate expansion into Latin America of Spanish firms from regulated industries illustrates how firms tend to invest in those countries where their political capabilities are more valuable, that is, those with high political instability, as shown by García-Canal and Guillén (2008). An interesting result of this study is that Spanish firms from regulated industries reduced over time their propensity to invest in politically unstable countries, showing that it is easier to move from politically unstable countries to stable ones than the other way around.

Patterns of Expansion

An important point that early students of the new MNEs underplayed was that, depending on the home country, these foreign-investing firms tended to emerge from certain industries and not others (UNCTAD, 2006). Thus, the South Korean MNEs have excelled in automobiles and electronics, the Taiwanese in component manufacturing, the Brazilian in automotive and aerospace products, the Mexican in ethnic brands and in producer goods such as cement, the Spanish in regulated and infrastructure industries, the Indian in information services, the Chinese (so far) in simple assembled goods, and so on. In so doing, firms originating from developing, newly industrialized, and upper-middle-income countries have accumulated proprietary intangible assets that have enabled them to successfully compete through internalized exports and horizontal investments even in the most advanced countries in the world.

This process of "reverse" foreign direct investment from home countries at a lower level of development than the host countries to which it is directed is anomalous only in a superficial way. The overall level of development of a country, as measured by such aggregate indicators as GDP per capita, more likely than not conceals a heterogeneous mix of backward and world-class industries and firms. Many countries around the world include pockets or enclaves of excellence surrounded by relatively mediocre or even inefficient producers. The literature on geographical clusters and agglomeration economies has shown that firms build capabilities as they interact with others located in close proximity (Cortright, 2006; Porter, 1998). This literature emphasizes that the country level of analysis is not the appropriate one for understanding the impact of location and geography. Ironically, one of the facilitating factors in the development of these clusters and enclaves of excellence could be incoming FDI and outsourcing agreements from firms located in developed countries that contributed to the formation of industrial clusters in less developed ones (McKendrick et al., 2001; Meyer, 2004).

The new MNEs have tended to follow some of the patterns of expansion consistent with product life cycle and staged theories of internationalization, as they have tended to expand first into countries located within the same region (Goldstein, 2007; Lall, 1983; Wells, 1983). In addition, when stepping outside their home region, they have tended to emphasize areas culturally, politically, or economically similar, as in the case of the Spanish firms' expansion into Latin America (Guillén, 2005). However, notable exceptions to this pattern have to do with investments in search of strategic assets (Goldstein, 2007, pp. 85–87) and the rapid pace

at which they have expanded their global reach (Mathews, 2006).

CONCLUSION

The new MNEs are the result of both imitation of established MNEs from the rich countries—which they have tried to emulate both strategically and organizationally—and innovation in response to the peculiar characteristics of emerging and developing countries. The context in which their international expansion has taken place is also relevant. The new MNEs have emerged from countries with weak institutional environments, property rights regimes, legal systems, and so on. Experience in the home country was especially valuable for the new MNEs because many countries with weak institutions are growing fast, and these MNEs developed the capabilities to compete in such challenging environments.

In addition, the new MNEs have flourished at a time of market globalization in which, despite local differences that still remain, global reach and global scale are crucial. The new MNEs have responded to this challenge by embarking on an accelerated international strategy based on external growth aimed at upgrading their capabilities and increasing their global market reach. When implementing this strategy, the new MNEs took advantage of their market position in the home country, and, ironically, their meager international presence allowed them to adopt a strategy and organizational structure that happens to be most appropriate to the current international environment in which emerging economies are growing very fast.

It is also important to note that the established MNEs from the rich countries have adopted some of the behaviors of the new multinationals. Increased competitive pressure from the latter in industries such as cement, steel, electrical appliances, construction, banking, and infrastructure has prompted many American and European firms to become much less reliant on traditional product-differentiation strategies and vertically integrated structures. To a certain extent, the rise of networked organizations (e.g., Bartlett & Ghoshal, 1989) and the extensive shift toward outsourcing represent competitive responses to the challenges faced by established

MNEs. Finally, a special type of new MNE is the so-called born-global firm, which resembles the new MNE in many ways but has emerged from developed countries.

Taking all these developments into account, it is clear that the American model of MNE is fading. In effect, globalization, technical change, and the coming of age of the emerging countries have facilitated the rise of a new type of MNE in which foreign direct investment is driven not only by the exploitation of firm-specific competencies but also by the exploration of new patterns of innovation and ways of accessing markets. In addition, the new MNEs have expanded rapidly, without following the gradual staged model of internationalization.

It is important to note, however, that the decline of the American model of the MNE does not necessarily imply the demise of existing theories of the MNE. In fact, the core explanation for the existence of MNEs remains: In order to pursue international expansion the firm needs to possess capabilities allowing it to overcome the liability of foreignness; no firm-specific capabilities, no multinationals. Our analysis of the new MNEs has shown that their international expansion was possible due to some valuable capabilities developed in the home country, including project-execution and political and networking skills, among other nonconventional ones. Thus, the lack of the classic technological or marketing capabilities does not imply the absence of other valuable capabilities that may provide the foundations for international expansion. It is precisely for this reason that the new MNEs are here to stay.

ENDNOTES

[1] Brazil, Russia, India, and China.
[2] For a summary of the basic economic model of the multinational firm, see Caves (1996).

Stephen Hymer (1960) was the first to observe that firms expand horizontally to protect (and monopolize) their intangible assets.

REFERENCES

Accenture. (2008). *The rise of the emerging-market multinational.* Retrieved April 8, 2009, from http://www.accenture.com/NR/rdonlyres/2835C9BA-2077-4C68-B1CD-8B87DC9F009B/0/MPW2Jan08.pdf.

Amsden, A. H., & Hikino, T. (1994). Project execution capability, organizational know-how and conglomerate corporate growth in late industrialization. *Industrial and Corporate Change, 3*(1), 111–147.

Aulakh, P. S. (2007). Emerging multinationals from developing economies: Motivations, paths and performance. *Journal of International Management, 13*(3), 235–240.

Bartlett, C. A., & Ghoshal, S. (1989). *Managing across borders: The transnational solution.* Boston: Harvard Business School Press.

BCG. (2008). *The 2008 BCG 100 new global challengers: How top companies from rapidly developing economies are changing the world.* Retrieved April 8, 2009, from http://www.bcg.com/impact_expertise/publications/publication_list.jsp?pubID=2495.

Bell, J., McNaughton, R., & Young, S. (2001). Born-again global firms: An extension to the born global phenomenon. *Journal of International Management, 7*(3), 173–190.

Bonaglia, F., Goldstein, A., & Mathews, J. A. (2007). Accelerated internationalization by emerging markets multinationals: The case of the white goods sector. *Journal of World Business, 42,* 369–383.

Buckley, P. J., Clegg, L. J., Cross, A. R., Liu, X., Voss, H., & Zheng, P. (2007). The determinants of Chinese outward foreign direct investment. *Journal of International Business Studies, 38,* 499–518.

Campa, J. M., & Guillén, M. F. (1999). The internalization of exports: Firm and location-specific factors in a middle-income country. *Management Science, 45*(11), 1463–1478.

Caves, R. E. (1996). *Multinational enterprise and economic analysis.* New York: Cambridge University Press.

Chandler, A. D. (1990). *Scale and scope: The dynamics of industrial capitalism.* Cambridge, MA: Harvard University Press.

Cho, D.-S. (1987). *The general trading company: Concept and strategy.* Lexington, MA: Lexington Books.

Cortright, J. (2006). *Making sense of clusters: Regional competitiveness and economic development.* (Discussion Paper). Washington, DC: The Brookings Institution Metropolitan Policy Program.

Cuervo, Á., & Villalonga, B. (2000). Explaining the variance in the performance effects of privatization. *Academy of Management Review, 25,* 581–590.

Cuervo-Cazurra, Á., & Genc, M. (2008). Transforming disadvantages into advantages: Developing-country MNEs in the least developed countries. *Journal of International Business Studies, 39,* 957–979.

Economist. (2008, January 10). The challengers. *The Economist.*

Elango, B., & Pattnaik, C. (2007). Building capabilities for international operations through networks: A study of Indian firms. *Journal of International Business Studies, 38,* 541–555.

Ferrantino, M. J. (1992). Technology expenditures, factor intensity, and efficiency in Indian manufacturing. *Review of Economics and Statistics, 74*(4), 689–700.

Fields, K. J. (1995). *Enterprise and the State in Korea and Taiwan.* Ithaca, NY: Cornell University Press.

García-Canal, E., & Guillén, M. F. (2008). Risk and the strategy of foreign location choice in regulated industries. *Strategic Management Journal, 29,* 1097–1115.

García-Canal, E., López Duarte, C., Rialp Criado, J., & Valdés Llaneza, A. (2002). Accelerating international expansion through global alliances: A typology of cooperative strategies. *Journal of World Business, 37*(2), 91–107.

Goldstein, A. (2007). *Multinational companies from emerging economies.* New York: Palgrave Macmillan.

Guillén, M. F. (2000). Business groups in emerging economies: A resource-based view. *Academy of Management Journal, 43*(3), 362–380.

Guillén, M. F. (2002). Structural inertia, imitation, and foreign expansion: South Korean firms and business groups in China, 1987–1995. *Academy of Management Journal, 45*(3), 509–525.

Guillén, M. F. (2005). *The rise of Spanish multinationals: European business in the global economy.* Cambridge, England: Cambridge University Press.

Heenan, D. A., & Keegan, W. J. (1979). The rise of third world multinationals. *Harvard Business Review, 57*(January–February), 101–109.

Henisz, W. J. (2003). The power of the Buckley and Casson thesis: The ability to manage institutional idiosyncrasies. *Journal of International Business Studies, 34,* 173–184.

Hoffmann, W. H. (2007). Strategies for managing a portfolio of alliances. *Strategic Management Journal, 28*(8), 827–856.

Hymer, S. (1960/1976). *The international operations of national firms: A study of direct foreign investment.* Cambridge, MA: The MIT Press.

Johanson, J., & Vahlne, J. E. (1977). The internationalization process of the firms: A model of knowledge development and increasing foreign market commitments. *Journal of International Business Studies, 8*(1), 23–32.

Johanson, J., & Wiedersheim-Paul, F. (1975). The internationalization of the firm: Four Swedish cases. *Journal of Management Studies,* October, 305–322.

Kale, P., Singh, H., & Perlmutter, H. V. (2000). Learning and protection of proprietary assets in strategic alliances: Building relational capital. *Strategic Management Journal, 21,* 217–237.

Kindleberger, C. P. (1969). *American business abroad.* New Haven, CT: Yale University Press.

Kock, C., & Guillén, M. F. (2001). Strategy and structure in developing countries: Business groups as an evolutionary response to opportunities for unrelated diversification. *Industrial & Corporate Change, 10*(1), 1–37.

Lall, S. (1983). *The new multinationals.* New York: Wiley.

Lecraw, D. (1977). Direct investment by firms from less developed countries. *Oxford Economic Papers, 29*(November), 445–457.

Li, P. P. (2003). Toward a geocentric theory of multinational evolution: The implications from the Asian MNEs as latecomers. *Asia Pacific Journal of Management, 22*(2), 217–242.

Li, P. P. (2007). Toward an integrated theory of multinational evolution: The evidence of Chinese multinational enterprises as latecomers. *Journal of International Management, 13*(3), 296–318.

Mathews, J. A. (2002). *Dragon multinationals: A new model of global growth.* New York: Oxford University Press.

Mathews, J. A. (2006). Dragon multinationals. *Asia Pacific Journal of Management, 23,* 5–27.

McKendrick, D. G., Doner, R. F., & Haggard, S. (2001). *From Silicon Valley to Singapore: Location and competitive advantage in the hard disk drive industry.* Palo Alto, CA: Stanford University Press.

Meyer, K. E. (2004). Perspectives on multinational enterprises in emerging economies. *Journal of International Business Studies, 35,* 259–276.

Porter, M. E. (1988). Clusters and the new economics of competition. *Harvard Business Review, 76*(6), 77–90.

Rui, H., & Yip, G. S. (2008). Foreign acquisitions by Chinese firms: A strategic intent perspective. *Journal of World Business, 43,* 213–226.

Sarkar, M. B., Cavusgil, S. T., & Aulakh, P. S. (1999). International expansion of telecommunications carriers: The influence of market structure, network characteristics and entry imperfections. *Journal of International Business Studies, 30,* 361–382.

Stopford, J. M., & Wells, L. T. (1972). *Managing the multinational enterprise.* New York: Basic Books.

Tolentino, P. E. E. (1993). *Technological innovation and third world multinationals.* London: Routledge.

UNCTAD (United Nations Conference on Trade and Development). (2006). *World Investment Report 2006.* New York: United Nations.

Vernon, R. (1966). International investment and international trade in the product cycle. *Quarterly Journal of Economics, 80,* 190–207.

Vernon, R. (1979). The product cycle hypothesis in a new international environment. *Oxford Bulletin of Economics and Statistics, 41*(4), 255–267.

Wells, L. T. (1983). *Third world multinationals: The rise of foreign investment from developing countries.* Cambridge, MA: The MIT Press.

Wilkins, M. (1974). *The maturing of multinational enterprise: American business abroad from 1914 to 1970.* Cambridge, MA: Harvard University Press.

Yiu, D. W., Lau, C. M., & Bruton, G. D. (2007). International venturing by emerging economy firms: The effects of firm capabilities, home country networks, and corporate entrepreneurship. *Journal of International Business Studies, 38,* 519–540.

Zollo, M., & Singh, H. (2004). Deliberate learning in corporate acquisitions: Post-acquisition strategies and integration capability in U.S. bank mergers. *Strategic Management Journal, 25,* 1233–1256.

Core Competencies for Diversifying: Case Study of a Small Business

Paul Trott
University of Portsmouth, UK

Colin Wheeler
University of Portsmouth, UK

Tom Maddocks
Barcroft Ltd, Dorset, UK

- This paper addresses a significant gap within the present body of work on the resource-based view of the firm: the lack of empirical research on the resource-based perspective within the SME sector (Newbert, 2007).

- This study applies the resource-based view and core competencies analysis in a very practical situation: a small manufacturing firm in the UK. The study is the result of a two-year "action research" project where the researcher was embedded within the firm. The manufacturing firm supplies hydraulic tube assemblies to the yellow construction industry and has experienced rapid growth over the past 10 years. Using a causal mapping methodology the findings reveal distinctive capabilities that the firm is able to use as a basis for diversification into the leisure marine industry.

- The findings contribute to the body of literature on the resource-based view of the firm by providing a methodological approach which helps to uncover core competencies in practice.

INTRODUCTION: GROWING A SUCCESSFUL MANUFACTURING FIRM

Diversifying away from your main business and revenue stream that has provided a stable and profitable business for over 30 years is full of risks and uncertainty. This paper illustrates how a manufacturing company in the United Kingdom (UK), supplying one of the UK's fastest-growing private businesses, AED,[1] set about this difficult task using core competencies analysis as a basis for diversification.

Founded in 1972 and now located in Dorset, Steel-Tubes Limited[2] has extensive experience in the tube manipulation industry and in particular the fabrication of rigid hydraulic tube assemblies for the construction machinery market. Steel-Tubes is a leading supplier to the yellow goods industry, with an established customer base which includes JCB, Caterpillar, and Hitachi. With a turnover of £15 million, the company is one of the largest tube manipulators in the UK. While Steel-Tubes has been successful, with constant growth in turnover and employees, it has grown into a position where 80 percent of the business is from one customer. This is, however, a strategy that Steel-Tubes purposely undertook seven years ago. Having seen the potential growth of AED, over the past five years, it focused on growing the business from 50 percent to 80 percent from AED. Having captured this growth, the longer-term strategy is now on reducing the dependency on the single customer and the yellow goods industry.

Reprinted from "Core Competencies for Diversifying: Case Study of a Small Business," by Paul Trott, Tom Maddocks, and Colin Wheeler, *Strategic Change*, Vol. 18, No. 1/2 (January 2009), pp. 27–43. Copyright © John Wiley & Sons, Inc. All rights reserved.

It is sometimes easy to overlook the success the company has achieved in growing the business from £9 million to £15 million over the past five years. While this has largely been supplying a single customer, this customer has been very demanding and continues to be so. For example, orders are placed with lead times of several months, but changes are made to these orders a few weeks prior to delivery. Further, a JIT manufacturing system does not allow for suppliers to operate late deliveries. Operating within such a manufacturing environment demands a range of special skills not just in manufacturing but also in quality management, logistics, and customer service. The quality standards set for the products being produced are equivalent to the highest in the industry and the products produced perform in harsh and demanding environments. Steel-Tubes has so far managed to fight off competitors who have entered the market by offering a better quality product delivered on time. Indeed, competitors have found it difficult to meet the demanding requirements of the customer—AED. By any measure this small company in Dorset is an example of a successful manufacturing company producing high-quality steel products on time every week for an industry-leading company.

All these successes have been achieved within a firm of 250 employees, 230 of whom work on the factory floor. The firm can be characterized by its craft-based approach to manufacturing and quality. Emphasis is placed on quality and service rather than on efficiency and cost minimization. The very small management team is headed by an accountant with many years of experience in this and related manufacturing industries. The small group of managers within the firm have few formal qualifications (the managing director is one of only two with a university education), but many years of industry experience. It is this in-depth knowledge of the industry and the customer that seems to play a significant role in the firm's success. The managing director, however, is aware of the limited formal business expertise within the firm to analyze and develop a strategy for diversification.

The yellow goods industry continues to grow, with JCB competing with Caterpillar and CNH of the USA, Komatsu of Japan, and Volvo of Sweden. Competition is fierce, and AED continues to put further pressure on its suppliers to lower costs and demand more for less. The dependency on one customer, however, is also growing and will continue to grow as long as sales from AED outweigh total sales from other customers. This causes problems for Steel-Tubes, as AED is able to dictate terms that are disadvantageous, such as demanding short lead times and instant response to new or adjusted orders, causing disruption in production. Dependency on one customer in a focused industry means that Steel-Tubes is vulnerable to changes in AED's strategy, as well as changes in the construction machinery industry. AED is also realizing the potential threat that being dependent on a sole supplier poses to their business and is currently looking at secondary suppliers for hydraulic tube assemblies. Having recently expanded into China and India, it is reasonable to conclude that AED may also be planning to outsource parts from these countries in the future.

The key challenge for Steel-Tubes was how to identify a strategy to diversify and enable it to build a business to generate a revenue stream beyond the yellow goods industry. This raises many questions, not least of which is whether the firm is able to undertake the work necessary to devise such a strategy. Over the past few years the senior management team has discussed the diversification issue many times. Opportunities for diversification almost always resulted in the usual suspects: products that contained steel tubes—golf trolleys, tubular furniture, lamp posts, etc. The senior management team recognized that if it was to carry out a rigorous diversification analysis it did not have the resources or necessary skills internally to undertake such an exercise. In 2006, Steel-Tubes secured a two-year Department of Trade & Enterprise Knowledge Transfer Partnership Associate to help it develop opportunities for diversification. This was the preferred method of choice for the managing director of Steel-Tubes, partly because he wanted to work closely with the project and recognized that there were many idiosyncrasies with the business that would take a long time to appreciate and understand. Given the available resource, a two-year project leveraging expertise from a business school seemed to offer the opportunity for a research project that would involve learning over a longer-term period (these are also the conditions most suitable for "action research").

This was in preference to external consultancy firms whose approach and methodology would almost certainly have been on a much shorter time scale, especially given the available resources. The next section explores the strategic management literature in general and the resource-based view (RBV) of the firm with respect to diversification.

THE CONCEPTS OF THE RBV AND CORE COMPETENCIES ANALYSIS

For the academic discipline of strategic management, the landscape has changed considerably in little more than 10 years. The RBV emerged as the contemporary and dominant approach to strategy development. Virtually all the strategy journals and most of the business and management journals featured articles written from a resource-based perspective. Moreover, the language of the RBV—such as resources, capabilities, and competencies—now fills the mainstream business press. So what are the key concepts of the RBV?

If the RBV is dependent on the two key principles that firms are different and these differences are relatively stable, then a key question arises: How does one identify these differences that determine the success of a firm? It is the detail that is significant here, and by differences we mean strengths. It is around this concept of strengths that so much of the debate has taken place.

Strengths have been interpreted as resources, capabilities, and competencies (Wernerfelt, 1984; Barney, 1991). Hamel and Prahalad (1994) developed the idea of core competencies for a very specific type of resource. Indeed, they developed three tests that they argue can be used to identify core competencies, namely "customer value," "competitor differentiation," and "extendibility." Yet, despite the widespread acknowledgment of the salience of core competencies for acquiring and sustaining a competitive position, the notion of core competencies has remained largely amorphous (Onyeiwu, 2003). Indeed, there is a tendency in the literature to characterize core competencies as any asset that enhances firm performance. According to Hamel and Prahalad (1994), a firm's ability to generate profits from its technology assets depends on the level of protection it has over these assets and the extent to which firms are able to imitate these competencies. For example, are competencies at the periphery or the center of a firm's long-term success? If they are at the center and difficult for firms to imitate, then long-term profits are assured; for example, over the past 50 years few firms have been able to imitate Honda's success in developing performance engines.

Increasingly, economists are using the notion that firms possess discrete sets of capabilities or competencies as a way of explaining why firms are different and how firms change over time. To summarize: competitive advantage resides not in a firm's products but in its competencies. These are defined as knowledge, skills, management processes, and routines acquired over time that are difficult to replicate—this is most likely because they are constantly changing or being updated. However, knowledge or technology in itself does not mean success; firms must be able to convert intellect, knowledge, and technology into offerings that customers want. This ability is referred to as a firm's competencies: *the ability to use its assets to perform value-creating activities.* This frequently means integrating several assets such as product technology and distribution, product technology and marketing effort, distribution and marketing. Indeed, it is the investment in intangible assets that seems to be a determinant of core competencies (Onyeiwu, 2003).

RBV and Dynamic Capabilities

It is Jay Barney (1991) who is considered by many to have made a significant contribution to the debate on the RBV when he argued that there can be heterogeneity of firm-level differences among firms that allow some of them to sustain competitive advantage. He therefore emphasized strategic choice, where responsibility lies with the firm's management to identify, develop, and deploy resources to maximize returns. He further proposed that above-industry-average rents can be earned from resources when they are valuable, rare, imperfectly imitable, and non-substitutable (so-called VRIN attributes).

A key issue for debate within the literature has been over what form resources take. It is now widely accepted that resources include tangible ones such as patents, properties, proprietary technologies and intangible resources such as relationships and trust built up over time (Galbreath and Galvin, 2004). It is this wider interpretation of the concept of resources—and in particular the recognition that resources include information, knowledge, and skills—that has further developed the concept of RBV.

Significantly, the idea that firms develop firm-specific routines as they conduct their business differentiated the concept of RBV from the more static SWOT framework. Teece et al. (1997) put forward the idea that firms develop dynamic capabilities that are difficult to replicate and it is this that makes firms different. This seems to chime well with Edith Penrose's (1959) idea that it is resources that enable firms to create services or flows. But the technology capability of the firm frequently dictates what is possible and what can or cannot be achieved in a given time frame; hence a firm's opportunities are constrained by its current position and current knowledge base (i.e., it is path-dependent). This introduces the notion of technological trajectories (Dosi, 1982; Nelson and Winter, 1982). Acquiring knowledge about technology takes time, involves people and experiments, and requires learning. To exploit technological opportunities a firm needs to be on the "technology escalator," that is, firms cannot move easily from one path of knowledge and learning to another. According to Teece et al. (1997), the choices available to the firm in terms of future direction are dependent on its own capabilities; that is, the firm's level of technology, skills developed, intellectual property, managerial processes, and routines. Furthermore, they argue that the choices made by any firm must take place in an environment characterized by changing levels of technology, changing market conditions, and changing societal demands. Teece et al. (1997) refer to this concept as the dynamic capabilities of firms. This is significant within the debate on the RBV as it implies a shift in focus from protecting rare, inimitable, and non-substitutable resources (the so-called VRIN framework) to continuously creating resources and capabilities in order to compete (Kogut and Zander, 1982; Teece et al., 1997; Winter, 2003).

In a review of the empirical research on the RBV of the firm, Newbert (2007: 137) examines the issue of distinguishing among resources, capabilities, and core competencies and finds:

> It is perhaps no surprise that capabilities and core competencies have been found to be far more significant in explaining competitive advantage and performance than resources.

Newbert further argues that resources have received a great deal of empirical attention because, relative to capabilities and core competencies, they are easy to measure. For example, the construct human capital is the most widely studied resource as it can be operationalized along dimensions such as demographics in certain roles/positions, whereas capabilities and core competencies are difficult to access and identify. Indeed, he presents the identification of capabilities and core competencies as a major methodological challenge which necessitates a greater need for primary data collection techniques and will, by its nature, introduce a greater potential for respondent bias.

Core Competencies as a Basis for Diversification

The RBV emphasizes the theme of sustained success within the research; diversification can be viewed as the other side of the same coin. It is growing the firm through utilizing the firm's resources, capabilities, and competencies, which is at the heart of this approach to strategy development (Clark, 2000). The commonly accepted theory of diversification is the resource-based perspective.

The previous discussions illustrate that there has been a considerable debate amongst academics on the pages of many of the highly regarded strategic management journals. Indeed, despite the confusion that exists regarding terminology, much of the debate has focused on the validity or not of the RBV as a theory (Gibbert, 2006a,b; Levitas and Ndofor, 2006; Connor, 1991), and all the practical applications have been within multinational firms and from a corporate-level perspective. Empirical research in this field is almost entirely focused upon large and multibusiness organizations, with the result that the vast SME sector has been largely ignored. Indeed, Petts

(1997) and Mills and Platts (2001) argue that there has been little application of the concepts to SMEs, manufacturing or otherwise. While this may be a function of the "growing pains" of the school of thought, this represents a significant gap within the present body of RBV/competencies literature. It is not our intention here to test the validity of the RBV framework. Rather, we aim to show how the theoretical framework and an empirical method could be used by managers of firms. This study attempts to apply the resource-based perspective and core competencies analysis in a very practical situation: a small manufacturing firm in the UK. The research questions therefore are:

1. What are the core competencies of Steel-Tubes Limited?
2. How can core competencies be identified within a small manufacturing firm?
3. How can core competencies be used as a basis for diversification?

METHODOLOGY

Given that the associate was to be embedded within the company working alongside the senior management team, the research lends itself to an in-depth study of the firm's resources and core competencies. The research methodology adopted for this project is most accurately described as action research. Action research is problem-centered, user-centered, and action-oriented. It involves the firm and its members in active learning, problem-finding, and a problem-solving process. It adopts a "scientific" method in the form of data-gathering, forming hypotheses, testing hypotheses, and measuring results; this is an integral part of the process (Johnson, 1976). Data are not simply returned to the firm in the form of a written report, but instead are fed back in meetings, and the firm and the researcher collaborate in identifying and ranking specific problems and in devising methods for finding their real causes. In this study an iterative inquiry process was developed within Steel-Tubes, which led to data-driven collaborative research in the form of three phases of enquiry to understand underlying causes. These findings have been used to try to develop organizational change (Reason and Bradbury, 2001).

Identifying resources and competencies within firms presents a considerable challenge to researchers (Rouse and Daellenbach, 2002). This is particularly so when there are strong relations of complimentarity and co-specialization among individual resources, so that it is not necessarily the individual resources but rather the way resources are clustered and how they interact with one another that are important to a firm's competitive advantage. Causal maps provide a method of analysis for researchers and managers within firms to uncover complex systems in the areas of quality, strategy, and information systems (Fiol and Huff, 1992). These causal maps are known by many names, including Ishikawa (fishbone) diagrams, cause-and-effect diagrams, impact wheels, issue trees, strategy maps, and risk-assessment mapping tools. Causal maps can be used by managers to focus attention on the root causes of a problem, find critical control points, guide risk management and risk mitigation efforts, formulate and communicate strategy, and teach the fundamental causal relationships in a complex system (Scavarda et al., 2006). In the social sciences, a causal map is generally considered to be a type of cognitive map, which is an individual's mental model of the relationships (causal or otherwise) among the elements of a system. Typically, causal maps are drawn with nodes representing concepts, ideas, or areas. The nodes are linked with unidirectional arcs that represent beliefs about the causal relationships among these nodes. Synthesizing causal maps from a number of respondents results in a "collective causal map."

Eden and Ackerman's modeling of competencies using a causal mapping methodology is ideally suited to identifying relationships among assets, distinctive competencies, and outcomes. The mapping process using diagrams helps managers within the firm identify and recognize relationships between capabilities where previously they were unrecognized. The relationship between patterns of competencies and the goals of an organization are used as the basis for establishing core distinctive competencies and for developing and exploring the business model which informs strategic direction (Eden and Ackerman, 2000).

The analysis in this paper relies on content analysis and cognitive maps. Cognitive maps have been defined as:

Graphic representations that locate people in relation to their information environment. Maps provide a frame of reference for what is known and believed. (Fiol and Huff, 1992: 267)

There are many different types of cognitive maps. For example, causal maps (e.g. Bougon et al., 1977) have been extensively discussed and used in the management literature (see the special issue of the *Journal of Management Studies*, 1992, **29**(3) for a review). In the study presented here, the cognitive maps are derived using Eden and Ackerman's framework (Eden and Ackerman, 2000). The cognitive maps produced in the study can be interpreted by drawing on the insights offered by personal constructs (Homer and Oliva, 2001; Pavlov and Saeed, 2004; Howick et al., 2006).

Cognitive mapping is a soft systems approach that enables the researcher to establish people's views and why they hold these views. The technique is fairly simple to use and hence does not require extensive training; typically, the interviews last about an hour (Eden, 1983). Further, it is a modeling technique that elicits a person's understanding of a process in his own words. The constructed cognitive map (model) uses the participant's own language and thus facilitates ease of understanding of the model. This is important for receiving feedback on the developed model. Immediate problems are presented if the model cannot be easily understood by the participant.

A number of studies have suggested that an in-depth interview, in the style required for cognitive mapping, cannot be started without detailed knowledge and preparation (Marshall and Rossman, 1989). Burgess says it is essential to get to know the people before detailed conversations can occur. In this case, this criterion has been met following the immersion within the organization by the associate for two years. Table 1 illustrates the additional information and data to which such a process provides access. The direct interactive modeling technique of cognitive mapping using elite semistructured interviews was thus selected as an appropriate method for revealing the core competencies of the organization.

The research was designed in three phases. Phase 1 was an exploratory approach using focus groups to uncover competencies and capabilities within the firm. Phase 2 examined and evaluated

Table 1 Information Available Due to KTP Project Structure

Immersion within the organization provides access to:

1. Internal documentation.
2. Attendance at and information from internal meetings.
3. Information from informal discussions with colleagues.
4. Confidential information.
5. Historical and present data.

the identified variables in more detail. Phase 3 explored links and relationships between the variables using a mapping technique.

Phase 1: Focus Groups

In order to gain a perspective from the different management perspectives, the focus groups were divided into two groups: senior managers (five) and middle managers (seven). By dividing the sessions into these groups the fear of any repercussions from senior colleagues is limited and more honest and complete findings were more likely. The sessions were tape-recorded and anonymity was assured. The questions were designed to be explorative and to create discussion within the groups (see Table 2). The questions selected were split into groups, with each group aiming to cover a different objective. One group of questions aimed to identify resources and capabilities and the other to discover informal systems within Steel-Tubes.

In order to triangulate the findings from Phase 1 and avoid in-built bias, interviews were held with two of the firm's major customers and two potential customers to identify requirements seen as necessary in order to compete and be successful in the yellow construction goods industry. These findings were compared to those identified internally in Phase 1.

Phase 2: Focus Groups

In the second session the senior and middle management groups were combined. The objective this time was to establish which of the issues raised during the previous sessions are core to enabling

Table 2   Phase 1 Focus Group Questions

1. Steel-Tubes does lots of things, but what does it do well?
2. Which activities does Steel-Tubes struggle to do well, and which ones do they do very well?
3. What formal and informal systems exist within Steel-Tubes to allow them to deliver benefit to their customers?
4. How do the formal and informal systems complement Steel-Tubes' activities and how do they inhibit them?
5. What activities deliver the most customer benefit in terms of adding value?
6. What does Steel-Tubes do that competitors can't do? For instance, high quality, flexibility, cutting and plating its own products.
7. What resources does it have that help it to succeed?
8. Are these unique in any way?
9. In terms of unique capabilities are there areas in which Steel-Tubes has adapted and changed over the years which have enabled it to continue to be successful?
10. How is Steel-Tubes able to be so flexible?
11. How could Steel-Tubes offer the same level of service to other customers as they do to their major customer?

Steel-Tubes to compete and which ones are key to Steel-Tubes' success. This was done in the form of an attribute scoring exercise, where each of the participants scored the success factors identified in the previous sessions in terms of importance (see Appendix 1). Discussions of why people scored the attributes the way they did then took place, with the emphasis on the difference between senior and middle management views. Hafeez et al. (2002) designed a scoring exercise as part of the methodology outlined in their paper, and this was used as a template. By scoring the attributes of a company it is easier to identify the importance of each one in relation to the others. This is important as it is the relationships among the attributes which are considered to underpin a company's competitive advantage and which are likely to lead to core competencies (Wernerfelt, 1984; Hamel and Prahalad, 1994; Barney, 2002; Eden, 2006).

Phase 3: Focus Groups

For the third sessions, the participants were split into the two groups in Phase 1. This session was designed to build on the findings from the previous sessions and determine the relationships among the identified attributes. Causal mapping was used in the third phase of focus groups as it offers a visible method of showing linkages between the capabilities and resources that were identified in the earlier sessions. The key objective was to establish assets, capabilities, and outcomes and explore linkages among them through the development of a collective causal map.

Opportunities for Related Diversification

The final part of the research was to identify opportunities for diversification using the core competencies. The biggest challenge for this part of the research was addressing the scope and size of analysis required. In order to help narrow the search, an initial screening was undertaken to try to identify those industries that were large consumers/users of steel tube. This was based on the initial guiding principle for the research that any market opportunity had to be related in some form to the firm's heritage and skills (that is, 25 years of bending steel tube)—especially given the size of the firm and limited resources. This provides structure to the search and ensures that any opportunity will be realistic and less likely to be naive and impracticable. Hence, the diversification opportunities examined are related to existing technological capabilities. Having established the core competencies of Steel-Tubes, these were to be used as drivers to identify possible opportunities and assess them for suitability in terms of diversification. The heavy users of small bore tubular steel were the starting point for the search and investigation. Clearly, the final business decision regarding choice of diversification would necessarily be based on traditional business information, such as:

- Size of market.
- Potential customers.

- Volume of steel tube used.
- Potential competitors.
- Barriers to entry/exit.
- Resources needed for diversification.
- Investment costs.

FINDINGS AND ANALYSIS

All the sessions were approached by all the participants with a willing and positive attitude, reflected in the quantity and quality of the data gathered. The focus groups uncovered many resources and capabilities. Many of these were raised in both sessions, suggesting that these may be fundamental to Steel-Tubes' sustained competitiveness. It was clear after analyzing the results from the focus groups in Phase 1 that the services Steel-Tubes offers, coupled with the high-quality products produced, were key factors behind Steel-Tubes' success. The attributes that enable Steel-Tubes to offer an exceptional service were identified as follows:

1. *Accommodating production operation.* An issue which was raised in both groups was the constant "disruption" to production. Having investigated this further, it seems disruption is caused to the order of the queues for processes. It was explained that although disruption to the order of the queues happens quite regularly, this has little effect on productivity or the actual production processes. Further evidence of this ability is that approximately 33 percent of all parts produced are less than one year old, which suggests new products are introduced to the production line on a regular basis.

2. *Experience in small batch production.* This year, the average order has been approximately 300, with a range of 20 to 1,500 but a mean average of 52 per batch. Further research is required into batch sizes as this will be part of the criterion to investigate market opportunities and therefore it is important to understand what is meant by a small batch size and whether or not this differs among industries.

3. *Extent and skills of the prototyping service.* The benefits and negative effects of prototypes being developed on production machines needs to be explored, particularly the way in which Steel-Tubes is able to cope with this disruption on the production line caused by the prototyping service. This is further evidence of the ability to deal with disruption; the way in which Steel-Tubes is able to control an environment where prototyping and the production line work harmoniously, as opposed to working as separate entities in a traditional setup and as the literature would suggest, is most effective.

4. *A comprehensive in-house production service.* Although this has been identified as a key success factor for Steel-Tubes, it is not yet clear if this is a unique resource within the industry. Further investigation will need to be done to establish the full capabilities of the two plants in order to provide a basis for benchmarking against other companies.

5. *In-built capacity.* More investigation is needed to discover what happens to orders that are at the back of the queues. It is not yet clear if the nightshift production schedule consists of orders which have been postponed during the day or if nightshift production schedules are postponed to accommodate incomplete orders from the day shift. If this is the case, are orders constantly postponed until they are considered urgent or is there an in-built capacity in production which accommodates these postponed orders?

6. *Planning and logistics.* The planning and logistics department is responsible for ensuring the right parts are being pushed through the production line and that they get shipped on time. It is important to understand the way in which this is managed in order to benchmark this against other companies.

Good teamwork at the operational level and the knowledge of bending being tacit in individuals are two areas which also enable Steel-Tubes to offer an exceptional customer service. However, they are currently two issues which are relevant to the project but at present will not be investigated. This is because they will be more important when researching market opportunities and will offer bias as to whether or not opportunities are realistic.

Factors and Outcomes Identified from Customers

The interviews were held at the customer's place of business and lasted approximately one hour. Not surprisingly, there was considerable similarity with those from within the firm. The key factors necessary for success in this industry were:

1. On-time deliveries.
2. Quality.
3. Rapid response.
4. Competitive price.
5. Experience of working within the industry.
6. Production planning & scheduling.

Given the findings from Phase 1, variables 1 to 4 were identified as necessary outcomes rather than capabilities or assets. These feed into the causal mapping exercise in Phase 3.

Analysis from Phase 2

Further analysis of each of the capabilities identified was undertaken using a scoring method based on the work of Hafeez et al. (2002). By scoring the attributes of a company it is easier to identify the importance of each one in relevance to the others. It is the relationships among the attributes which are considered to underpin a company's competitive advantage and are likely to lead to core competencies. Barney (2002), Eden (2006), and Hamel and Prahalad (1994) recognize that some attributes are more important than others and that they have to be ranked in some way in order to be able to distinguish between ones which are crucial to core competencies (this is shown in Table 3).

Analysis from Phase 3

The findings from Phase 2 feed directly into Phase 3. Figure 1 shows a causal map with three layers. The outcomes at the top of the map can be distinguished from distinct competencies as they tend to be factors that are demanded by customers. These were identified by correlating findings from Phase 1 and findings from interviews with customers. Whereas distinct competencies are the effect of processes within the firm (here a process is defined as a series of activities, which are linked together and managed),

Table 3 Findings from Focus Group 2 Scoring

	Commercial Manager	Prototype Manager	Quality Manager	Logistics Manager	Dispatch Manager	Poole General Manager	Production Coordinator	Commercial Estimator	Production Manager	Production Director	Quality Controller	Total
Knowledge and experience of bending	1	4	3	4	5	5	4	5	5	4	5	4
Good teamwork at the operational level	2	2	4	5	4	3	5	5	4	5	4	43
Comprehensive in-house production capability	4	2	1	5	2	3	5	3	5	5	5	40
High perceived quality in the industry	2	5	3	2	5	4	4	4	4	3	4	40
Flexible accommodating production system	3	3	5	3	1	4	3	4	5	4	4	39
Extent and skills of the prototyping service	4	4	2	2	2	4	4	5	3	4	4	38
Planning and logistics systems	3	2	2	4	3	4	3	3	4	4	4	36
In-built production capacity	3	3	4	3	4	2	2	4	3	4	3	35
Experience in small batch production	2	2	4	1	3	4	4	2	3	3	3	31
Total	24	27	28	29	29	33	34	35	36	36	36	

Figure 1   **Identification of Core Competencies within Steel-Tubes Limited: Collective Cognitive Mapping**

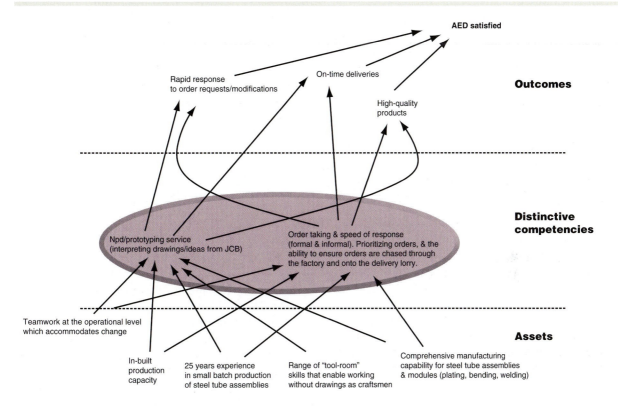

it is the ability to manage distinct competencies that separates them from assets, which cannot be managed. The map illustrates many links and relationships that have been identified between the resources and capabilities. This illustrates how Steel-Tubes' flexible manufacturing system contributes to its success in terms of provision of service and how it is integral to Steel-Tubes. The two distinctive competencies that were identified through an analysis of Steel-Tubes' business model were:

1. A flexible production system allowing rapid response to orders.
2. A personal service to customers utilizing specialist prototyping expertise.

As a final test for the validity of these core competencies, they have been compared to three questions devised by Hamel and Prahalad (1994):

1. Does it add customer value?

2. Does it differentiate your company from your competitors?

3. Does it offer a base of expansion for your company?

There is clear evidence from Steel-Tubes' main customer that it values the firm's ability to respond rapidly to its orders. Sometimes Steel-Tubes is able to turn round a request in 24 hours, something that competitors are either unwilling (high cost implications) or unable to do.

Using Barney's (2002) VRIO framework, it is possible to analyze the capabilities identified and explore whether there is congruence. Table 4 shows the attributes within the VRIO framework. This offers three attributes that have the characteristics of core competencies as identified by Barney. The distinctive competencies identified seem to satisfy all of Hamel and Prahalad's (1994) tests and Barney's (2002) VRIO framework, so it is fair to conclude that the above are realistic core competencies for Steel-Tubes Limited.

Table 4   Steel-Tubes' Competencies Using Barney's (2002) VRIO Framework

Attribute	Valuable	Rare	Costly to Imitate	Exploitable
Experience in small batch production	No			
In-built production capacity	No			
Good teamwork at the operational level	No			
Planning and logistics systems	Yes	No		
Comprehensive in-house production	Yes	Yes	No	
Knowledge and experience of bending	Yes	Yes	No	
Flexible accommodating production system	Yes	Yes	Yes	Yes
Extent and skills of the prototyping service	Yes	Yes	Yes	Yes
High perceived quality in the industry	Yes	Yes	Yes	Yes

Opportunities for Related Diversification

Table 5 shows the list of potential industry and market opportunities generated by discussions with steel tube suppliers into tube-related sectors. Column 1 contains the long list of industry sectors identified by both steel tube suppliers as heavy users of small bore steel tube and tube bending machine suppliers as users of their machines. Columns 2 and 3 are the two core competencies for Steel-Tubes identified by the earlier analysis. Each of these industries was examined with respect to these competencies to see if the competencies could be exploited. The emphasis of the analysis was on the industry structure, supply chains, and nature of supplier relationships. There were two industries that provided a positive match with both of the core competencies: the leisure marine industry and specialist automotive.

The predominant material used for tubular products in the marine industry is stainless steel. Similarly, low-volume automotive markets also use stainless steel tubular products. These two sectors have characteristics that match the core competencies of Steel-Tubes. In addition, stainless steel in these markets carries a premium price due to the aesthetic value of the products. Another positive factor of producing small bore stainless steel tubular assemblies is the supplier gap within the marine industry, which should make for an easier market entry strategy.

CONCLUSIONS

This paper has illustrated how a small manufacturing firm supplying the yellow construction machine industry was able to use core competencies analysis to identify distinctive capabilities as a basis for diversification. Following this study, Steel-Tubes Limited decided to enter the leisure marine market. It has since secured its first order and supplied its first product: a stainless-steel mast for radar to the UK's second largest producer of leisure marine vessels.

These findings provide some much-needed empirical research from the SME sector, which has thus far been overlooked within the area of the resource-based perspective. Virtually all studies using the RBV have focused on large multinational firms as a basis of analysis (Petts, 1997; Mills and Platts, 2001).

This study has shown how the core competencies of an SME can be identified using a causal mapping methodology. The methodology to identify the core competencies used here had three phases based on focus groups, a scoring process for competencies, and the development of causal maps (Hafeez et al., 2002). The core competencies were further evaluated using the tests suggested by Hamel and Prahalad (1994) and Barney (2002), and cross-checked with customers, suppliers, and competitors. The analysis of core competencies of the firm guided the diversification analysis. It is the relationship between assets and capabilities which is so crucial for small firms. This is especially so for

Table 5   Analysis of Opportunities for Diversification

Industry Sectors That Are Heavy Users of Small Bore Steel Tube	Flexible Production System Allowing Rapid Response to Orders	Personal Service to Customers, Utilizing Prototyping Expertise
Aerospace	X	
Agricultural equipment		
Agricultural process plants		
Air conditioners and heaters		
Boilers		
Composite substitutes for metal tubes		
Defense	X	
Health care		
Leisure equipment		
Locomotive		
Lorries/buses		
Leisure marine	X	X
Material handling		
Mining		
Offshore oil and gas		
Recycling and waste management		
Renewable energy		
Shop fittings		
Specialist automotive	X	X

small firms where the assets are likely to be on a smaller scale than those of large firms. For Steel Tubes it is not only the ability of the firm to have flexibility in its manufacturing operations, but also the ability to respond quickly to customer orders that is central to the success of the firm's business model. Hence, it is agility in manufacturing rather than simply flexibility which enables the firm to configure operations to order and gives Steel-Tubes its distinctive capability and core competencies. Steel-Tubes has since invested further in this part of its activities and employed more people within its newly recognized capability-product prototyping.

The casual mapping methodology cited in this paper can be used by other SMEs, but it should be noted that the resources and skills required are significant. The mapping process requires extensive discussions between the lead researcher and individuals, both inside and outside the firm (Marshall and Rossman, 1989), and the organization of the interviews and focus groups and the analysis of the data all take time. In addition,

Steel-Tubes went through the KTP approval process with the DTI, recruited a graduate, and then introduced that person to all aspects of the firm's operations. It was crucial during this period that the graduate was able to develop the trust and confidence of Steel-Tubes' management. The project also required the company's management to engage fully with the process.

Although technically employed by the Knowledge Transfer Partnership, the graduate spent virtually all of his time at Steel-Tubes Limited and in this respect was "embedded" in the firm. He developed a highly detailed understanding of the firm, not only because he has been there for more than a year at the time of writing but also because the mapping process demands extensive interaction with the company, suppliers, customers, and to an extent, competitors. So the experience of carrying out the analysis of Steel-Tubes suggests that it is essential for firms to ensure that a full and detailed understanding of the firm is developed during the process.

The findings offer support for Newbert's (2007) arguments relating to distinguishing among resources, capabilities, and core competencies. The methodology presented here offers clear evidence of the challenges in attempting to identify a firm's core competencies. Indeed, the paper illustrates the high level of support and company involvement required in order to identify core competencies. It is therefore no surprise that resources have received far greater attention because, as this paper has shown, relative to capabilities and core competencies they are easy to measure.

APPENDIX 1: ATTRIBUTE SCORING EXERCISE

Below is the list of attributes that have been identified as key to Steel-Tubes' success. Using numbers 1–5, please score each of the attributes depending on how important you perceive them to be: 1 being of low importance, 5 being of high importance. However, you are only able to use the number 3 twice.

Key attribute	Score
Comprehensive in-house production capability	
Experience in small batch production	
Planning and logistics systems	
Flexible accommodating production system	
In-built production capacity	
Extent and skills of the prototyping service	
Good teamwork at the operational level	
Knowledge and experience of bending	
High perceived quality in the industry	

ENDNOTES

[1] The name of the firm has been changed to ensure anonymity.

[2] The name of the firm has been changed to ensure anonymity.

REFERENCES

Barney J. 1991. Firm resources and sustained competitive advantage. *Journal of Management* **17**: 99–120.

Barney JB. 2002. *Gaining and Sustaining Competitive Advantage,* 2nd ed. Prentice-Hall: Upper Saddle River, NJ.

Bougon M, Weick K et al. 1977. Cognition in organizations: an analysis of the Utrecht Jazz Orchestra. *Administrative Science Quarterly* **22**: 606–639.

Clark D. 2000. Implementation issues in core competence strategy making. *Strategic Change* **9**(2): 115–127.

Conner K. 1991. A historical comparison of resource-based theory and five schools of thought within industrial organization economics: do we have a new theory of the firm? *Journal of Management* **17**: 121–154.

Dosi G. 1982. Technical paradigms and technological trajectories: a suggested interpretation of the determinants and directions of technical change. *Research Policy* **11**(3): 147–162.

Eden C, Jones S, Sims D. 1983. *Messing about in Problems.* Pergamon: Oxford.

Eden C. 2006. Core competence analysis. Seminar held at Open University Business School, 18 October.

Eden C, Ackerman F. 2000. Mapping distinctive competencies: a systemic approach. *Journal of the Operational Research Society* **51**(1): 12–20.

Fiol C, Huff A. 1992. Maps for managers: where are we? Where do we go from here? *Journal of Management Studies* **29**(3): 267–285.

Galbreath J, Galvin P. 2004. Which resources matter? A fine grained test of the resource-based view of the firm. Academy of Management Best Paper Proceedings, New Orleans, LA, August.

Gibbert M. 2006a. Generalizing about uniqueness: an essay on an apparent paradox in the resource-based view. *Journal of Management Inquiry* **15**(2): 124–134.

Gibbert M. 2006b. Munchausen, Black Swans, and the RBV: response to Levitas and Ndofor. *Journal of Management Inquiry* **15**(2): 145–151.

Hafeez K, Zhang Y, Malak N. 2002. Core competence for sustainable competitive advantage: a structured methodology for identifying core competence. *IEEE Transactions on Engineering Management* **49**(1): 28–35.

Hamel G, Prahalad CK. 1994. Competing for the future. *Harvard Business Review* **72**(4): 122–128.

Homer J, Oliva R. 2001. Maps and models in system dynamics: a response to Coyle. *System Dynamics Review* **17**(4): 357–363.

Howick S, Ackermann F, Andersen D. 2006. Linking event thinking with structural thinking: methods to improve client value in projects. *System Dynamics Review* **22**(2): 113–140.

Johnson RA. 1976. *Management, Systems, and Society: An Introduction*. Goodyear Publishing Co.: Pacific Palisades, CA: 222–224.

Kogut B, Zander U. 1982. Knowledge of the firm, combinative capabilities, and the replication of technology. *Organization Science* **3**(3): 383–397.

Levitas E, Ndofor HA. 2006. What to do with the resource-based view? A few suggestions for what ails the RBV that supporters and opponents might accept. *Journal of Management Inquiry* **15**(2): 135–144.

Marshall C, Rossman GB. 1989. *Designing Qualitative Research*. Sage: London.

Mills J, Platts K. 2001. Applying resource-based theory: methods, outcomes and utility for managers. Proceedings of the 8th International Conference of the European Operations Management Association, Bath, pp. 177–190.

Nelson RR, Winter SG. 1982. *An Evolutionary Theory of Economic Change*. The Belknap Press of Harvard University: Cambridge, MA.

Newbert SL. 2007. Empirical research on the resource-based view of the firm: an assessment and suggestions for future research. *Strategic Management Journal* **28**: 121–146.

Onyeiwu S. 2003. Some determinants of core competencies: evidence from a binary-logit analysis. *Technology Analysis and Strategic Management* **15**(1): 43–63.

Pavlov OV, Saeed K. 2004. A resource-based analysis of peer-to-peer technology. *System Dynamics Review* **20**(3): 237–262.

Penrose ET. 1959. *The Theory of the Firm*. John Wiley: New York, NY.

Petts N. 1997. Building growth on core competences—a practice approach. *Long Range Planning* **30**(4): 551–561.

Reason P, Bradbury H. 2001. *Handbook of Action Research*. Sage: London.

Rouse MJ, Daellenbach US. 2002. More thinking on research methods for the resource-based perspective. *Strategic Management Journal* **23**(10): 949–963.

Scavarda AJ, Bouzdine-Chameeva T, Goldstein SM, Hays JM, Hill AV. 2006. A methodology for constructing collective causal maps. *Decision Sciences* **37**(2): 263–283.

Teece DJ, Pisano G, Shuen A. 1997. Dynamic capabilities and strategic management. *Strategic Management Journal* **18**(7): 509–533.

Wernerfelt B. 1984. A resource based view of the firm. *Strategic Management Journal* **5**(2): 171–180.

Globalfocusing: Corporate Strategies under Pressure

Klaus E. Meyer
University of Bath, UK

- On the global stage, competitive advantages are gained by creating, transferring, and exploiting competences across operations and locations internationally.
- In consequence, conglomerates are redesigning their strategies to focus on core businesses, yet with a global scope. De-diversification and internationalization thus complement each other in a process of "globalfocusing."
- This paper outlines the shifts in the relative barriers to entry to countries and industries that have been driving these processes of change in corporate strategies on the global stage.
- On this basis, implications of the change in global strategy are derived for decision-makers in both business and politics who are operating in the volatile global economy.

INTRODUCTION

Businesses across Europe face a continuously shifting and increasingly open competitive environment. In the 1980s, many companies focused on their national markets, but served a variety of different industry segments. In the new millennium, such domestic focus has become rare as European integration and globalization have changed the nature of competition. On the global stage, competitive advantages are gained by creating, transferring, and exploiting competences across operations and locations internationally. Businesses thus face enhanced opportunities for international growth, while the benefits of expanding into other industries domestically have diminished.

In consequence, conglomerates are redesigning their strategies to focus on narrowly defined core industries with a global scope. Thus, they simultaneously accelerate their internationalization while reducing their product diversification. De-diversification and internationalization thus complement each other in a process of "globalfocusing" (Meyer, 2006). This process is driven by shifts in the relative transferability of resources and capabilities across industries and countries due to the globalization of markets, resources, supply chains, and business models.

These changes in corporate strategies create new challenges for business leaders and policy-makers. Business leaders not only have to manage international competition, but have to pursue strategies that create and exploit complementarities and linkages in the global net of their operations. This requires changes of corporate strategies that involve new capabilities and may be risky to implement. Policy-makers face businesses that are operating at supranational levels, and thus less likely to react to national policies. Yet national resource endowments, especially human capital, continue to attract business operations and thus national competitiveness.

Reprinted from "Globalfocusing: Corporate Strategies Under Pressure," by Klaus E. Meyer, *Strategic Change*, Vol. 18, No. 5/6 (August 2009), pp. 195–207. Copyright © John Wiley & Sons, Inc. All rights reserved.

CASE EXAMPLES

The process of globalfocusing often evolves over many years, even decades. Nokia is renowned as a leading brand for mobile headsets, yet as recently as two decades ago the mobile phone business generated merely 10 percent of the revenues of what was then an industrial conglomerate in Finland (Figure 1a, Table 1). Nokia quite literally hit gold with its mobile handset design and marketing, and then focused its resources on exploiting this gold mine, selling its other business units along the way. The main restructuring occurred in one major wave in the early 1990s, and since then Nokia has grown its competences in mobile telephony and is exploiting these competences increasingly by developing and marketing other communications devices. While focusing its product scope, Nokia has established its brand globally, backed up by global operations.

The phenomenon is equally common among medium-size companies, especially in business-to-business markets. For example, Danisco A/S was established in 1989 by a merger creating a Danish conglomerate integrating businesses loosely related to the food industry. Over the next two decades, it has gone through several phases of restructuring in which peripheral business units were sold, while businesses were acquired to strengthen the core business (Figure 1b, Table 1). Waves of rapid restructuring were followed by periods of organic growth, until such growth necessitated reconsideration of what is core, and what is periphery. In consequence, in March 2009 Danisco completed the sale of its erstwhile largest business unit, Danisco Sugar.

Change in a similar direction can be observed in major European conglomerates, though rarely as radical as in these two case examples. While strengthening the international operations of its core business, for example, BASF divested its pharmaceuticals business, Siemens divested many of its IT-related businesses, while Philips divested 25 businesses in 1998 alone. In Spain, banks BBVA and Santander have divested their investment portfolios in industrial firms while growing their core banking business internationally. Other conglomerates, such as British Cadbury-Schweppes, have split themselves into two independent companies.

These companies engaged in long-term restructuring from a conglomerate to a focused but highly international strategy over the past two decades. This process has created global players in single industries that have left those industries where they could not achieve market leadership. However, implementing such a strategic change is subject to substantial risks, as illustrated by the failure of the Daimler-Chrysler merger.

COMPETITIVE ADVANTAGES OF THE GLOBAL SPECIALIST

Operating on the global stage provides companies with opportunities to create competences that may provide a competitive edge over domestic firms. These opportunities arise from the exposure to a diversity of markets, resources, and regulatory regimes. By linking operations across the different locations, multinational firms can develop unique competitive advantages (Ghoshal, 1987; Ghemawat, 2007; Dunning and Lundan, 2008):

1. *Global scale.* Greater economies of scale can be attained by supplying multiple national markets from one site, thus reducing costs of, for instance, product development, production, and distribution networks. Global scale moreover enhances bargaining power vis-à-vis business partners and governments.

2. *Global supply chains.* Firms can exploit comparative cost advantages across locations by disaggregating production and sourcing operations across different locations. This allows them to arbitrage even small differences in costs, especially for labor and raw materials.

3. *Global R&D.* Integration of research and development (R&D) sites around the world allows access to a diversity of talent and knowledge clusters, and interaction with the most innovative customers, suppliers, and researchers. Recently, the annual *Global Innovation 1000* report by Booz & Company (Jaruzelski and Dehoff, 2008) highlighted these contributions of global R&D. Notably, the report suggests that international linkages, rather than increased R&D spending per se, contribute to improved corporate performance.

Figure 1a   Nokia OY 1990–2008

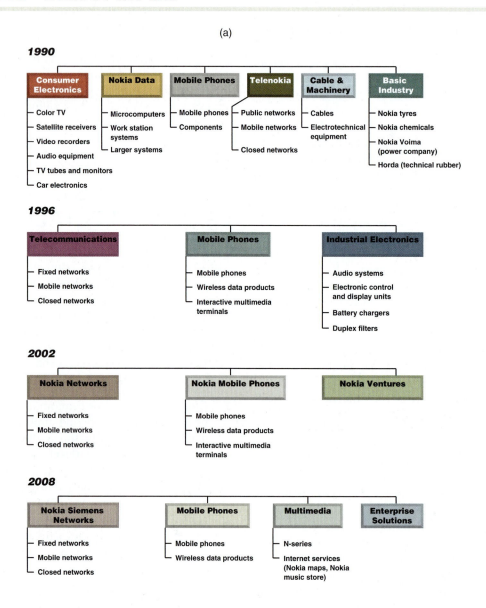

(a)

4. *Global knowledge management.* The exchange of operational knowledge, experience, and competence linkages across operations and locations is a potential source for innovations and new competencies. By creating and sharing databases and human capital across operations, firms thus create a global knowledge pool that can support each individual operation.

5. *Global customers.* Businesses serving other businesses often work with customers that themselves have a global scope of operation, and expect delivery of the same product or service at multiple sites. Firms with global distribution networks and production sites in many business hubs are often better positioned to supply these key account customers, for example in the automotive sector.

Any of these international linkages provide multinational enterprises with opportunities to create and exploit resources. Compared to domestic competitors, they thus have potentially

Figure 1b   **Danisco A/S 1990–2008**

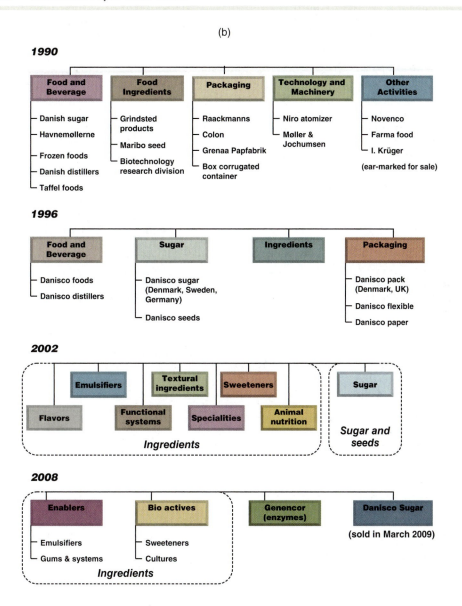

(b)

stronger operational capabilities, and more markets in which to apply them. Single-country operations cannot realistically replicate the cost and dynamic advantages of an operation integrating multiple locations. Thus, even medium-size firms, such as the infamous German Hidden Champions, develop strategies aimed to dominate global niche markets (Simon, 1996; Venohr and Meyer, 2009).

RESOURCES SHAPE THE GROWTH ARC

Half a century ago, Edith Penrose (1959) argued that the growth of firms is driven by their resource endowments, particularly their managerial resources. Firms continuously develop new resources and seek applications for them,

Table 1   Shifts in Corporate Strategies, 1990 to 2009

	1990	2009
Nokia (Finland)	"Nokia is a European technology company, the turnover of which in 1990 was 22.1 mrd Finnish marks. 84% of turnover comes from EFTA and EC countries. The group is divided into six divisions . . . Main products are colour TVs and monitors, micro computers and terminals, mobile phones, digital telephone exchanges and telecommunication networks, cables and cable machinery as well as tires and chemicals for forest industry." (1990) (a)	"We make a wide range of mobile devices with services and software that enable people to experience music, navigation, video, television, imaging, games, business mobility and more. Developing and growing our offering of consumer Internet services, as well as our enterprise solutions and software, is a key area of focus. We also provide equipment, solutions and services for communications networks through Nokia Siemens Networks." (2009) (b)
Danisco (Denmark)	"The company wishes to be a first-class supplier to the international food and beverage industry on the global market and be a supplier of high-quality foods and branded goods on selected European markets. Danisco's activities have been divided into four sectors for the food-oriented area . . . a sector has been established for activities outside this area." (1990) (c)	"Danisco develops and produces functional ingredients primarily for the food and beverage industries but also for some non-food sectors." "Produced mainly from natural raw materials such as plant oil and vegetables, the broad product range is backed by top technical services, creating innovative, high-quality solutions used in many packaged consumer goods around the globe." "The main functionality of Danisco ingredients is to create or improve taste, texture, nutritional profile and/or food protection in the final consumer products." (2009) (d)

Sources:

(a) Nokia annual report 1990, translated by Päivi Karhunen, Helsinki School of Economics.
(b) Nokia website, accessed June 2009.
(c) Danisco annual report 1989/1990.
(d) Danisco website, accessed June 2009.

thus accumulating resources in a dynamic process. However, resources are typically bundled and thus indivisible and difficult to sell separately, which results in "slack" resources that are not required for current operations, but can be a source of internal growth. The growth of a firm is thus a process of resource accumulation and redeployment. Firms expand when they have resources that they can share with new operations to strengthen existing market positions, to expand into new industries (i.e., product diversification), or to go international.

However, the nature of a firm's resources shapes the path of its growth (Figure 2). In particular, resources shape the relative merits of growth by domestic diversification, or by internationalization of the core business. Some capabilities may be specific to a country, but may be profitably transferred to other industries within this country. For example, the in-depth knowledge of consumers and marketing practices may enable strategies of "brand extension" to loosely related products. Other resources are more specific to an industry but may be exploited in this industry in other countries. For example, technological expertise for product development can be a foundation for international growth.

Resources drive growth, yet lack of resources can be a key constraint to corporate growth. Resources, especially managerial resources, can only be built at a limited pace, known in the literature as the "Penrose constraint" (Tan and Mahoney, 2005). Rapid growth of any particular business may thus require firms to free resources elsewhere, for instance by divestment of peripheral activities and the acquisition of

Figure 2   Country and Industry-Specificity of Resources

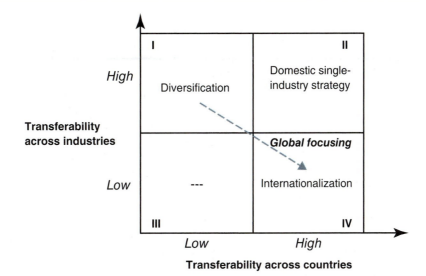

Note: The arrow indicates change induced by liberalization and globalization of industries.

Source: Revised from Meyer (2006).

complementary resources external to the firm. The implementation of an acquisition, however, requires scarce managerial resources in the acquiring firm, while acquired management teams often cannot be readily integrated with the existing top management. Divestments would free managerial resources and thus enable new growth.

These processes of corporate growth are normally continuous over long periods of time, yet they are disruptive at times of strategic shift. Periods of organic growth may be followed by waves of acquisitions and divestments. Once a firm exceeds its optimal size, after a period of growth, it may spin off or sell a division to free managerial and financial resources for reinvestment into more profitable activities. Even when it has been profitable to use resources to develop a new operation, this operation may in the long run generate more revenues outside the governance of the founding firm. Resource-sharing that was important during the establishment phase may become less important relative to, say, linkages of distribution channels. Thus, when synergies with another firm outweigh the costs of the transaction, a divestment is appropriate. Such divestments are a natural part of corporate growth that has become more common in the twenty-first century as markets for corporate assets have become considerably more efficient.

Divestments allow the reallocation of resources to new activities. Thus, when opportunities for profitable international growth of one unit exceed the potential of another existing business unit, the latter may be divested. The divestment then generates human and financial resources that allow overcoming the Penrose constraint, and thus enable faster internationalization.

The relative merits of alternative corporate growth paths, and hence the optimal scope in terms of product diversification and internationalization, are grounded in the transferability of the firm's resources across industries and countries. With the globalization of markets and supply chains, global operations may offer higher resource rents. At the same time, conglomerates lose their relative competitiveness. These shifts in the competitive landscape are likely to induce firms to globalfocus, as indicated by the diagonal arrow in Figure 2.

In the language of economics, this process may be described with the concept of barriers to entry (BTE). Traditionally, high BTE into countries constrained international growth. In recent decades, such technological and administrative barriers have been reduced, while BTE to industries gained in relative importance as a result of increasing complexity of technologies and supply chains. The relative height of BTE respectively to industries and countries thus determines the relative merits of diversification and internationalization strategies. Shifts in the *relative* BTE can trigger shifts in the international and product scope of firms.

DRIVERS OF CHANGE

The shifts in the competitive landscape that change the transferability of resources across industries and countries arise from complementary external and internal forces: market liberalization, financial markets, dynamics of global competition, and managerial leadership.

Market Liberalization

The institutional framework of a country encompasses the formal and informal rules according to which firms act; it thus moderates how firms compete, grow, survive, or fail. When these rules fall short of securing efficient functioning of markets, firms may organize transactions within a conglomerate. For example, human capital may be developed internally rather than externally, with career paths within a conglomerate rather than individuals switching jobs frequently. Thus, reputable conglomerates benefit from access to the best university graduates, who are then allocated across the businesses according to need. Other resources that can be shared across businesses include network relationships and bargaining positions vis-à-vis state bureaucracies or national retail chains. Domestic growth based on sharing such resources may thus be a suitable growth strategy in weakly transparent and network-intensive contexts.

The institutional context changes with legal changes aimed to make markets more efficient, for example by reducing tariffs or non-tariff barriers to international trade. Such liberalization reduces BTE and thus makes it easier for importers or foreign investors to compete. Moreover, information on potential partners and employees becomes more readily available, which reduces incumbents' advantage from their country-specific knowledge and networks. Liberalization thus lowers the costs of moving goods and people across borders, and thereby creates

opportunities to create capabilities grounded in global operations. In a liberalized environment, it is easier to attain competitive advantages with business models that coordinate and integrate geographically dispersed operations.

If product diversification is motivated by the need to overcome inefficiencies in the domestic business environment, then changes in the institutional framework would be expected to trigger changes in the scope of companies (Kock and Guillén, 2000; Peng et al., 2003). Foreign entrants are likely to create competitive pressures on local firms to adapt organizational structures suitable for the new environment. In the EU, continuous union-wide liberalization created such pressures in many industries, notably the Internal Market 1992 program. Consequently, corporate growth, which in the 1970s may have occurred by entry into related or even unrelated industries within a domestic market, may now focus on internationalization. The liberalization thus encourages focused strategies in global—or at least Europe-wide—niche markets. For instance, Danisco's aforementioned sale of its sugar division has in part been triggered by changes in the EU sugar market regime.

Liberalization initially often led to national mergers and acquisitions as some governments aimed to promote domestic mergers that create "national champions" operating across multiple sectors and thus, supposedly, big enough to withstand tougher competition. Yet this policy misunderstands how international competition works. In the long run, in open markets industry specialists are likely to gain competitive advantages over national conglomerates, and thus diversified national champions created by political motives are likely to eventually face restructuring. Market liberalization is thus likely to trigger global-focusing, albeit possibly with considerable time lags.

Industry Dynamics

On the global stage, technological and organizational capabilities are benchmarked against competitors worldwide, rather than nationally, and their business models designed to exploit global linkages and integration. Globally operating firms create pressures on their competitors to invest in order to stay ahead in core businesses, where they can achieve market leadership, and thus to globalfocus.

These competitive pressures move up and down the value chain, especially when customers move toward global sourcing or global marketing. International operations become essential when markets transcend national borders, competitors operate globally, and customers seek delivery at multiple sites around the world. Globalfocusing can thus become a self-reinforcing process within an industry.

These industry dynamics create different pressures for competitors and for customers. If competitors lower their costs through global integration, this creates pressures to strengthen operational capabilities or to exit. If customers adopt global sourcing, suppliers may have to expand their international scope to retain their internationally operating customers. Many firms in business-to-business markets may thus be induced to invest overseas by the internationalization of their customers. Global-focusing is particularly astute in business-to-business industries. Consumer goods manufacturers face different consumers in each country and may find it easier to extend their brand to related products and thus to prosper with diversification strategies.

Financial Markets

Financial markets are an important mediator between competitive pressures and corporate change. A widespread belief in the financial investment community suggests that conglomerates trade at a discount. Corporate communications thus often point to financial market pressures when explaining changes of strategy. Recent research sheds doubt on the prevalence of such a discount control, for antecedents of diversification appear to eliminate any statistically significant discount (Campa and Kedia, 2002); in fact, some studies outside Anglo-American countries find group-affiliated firms to benefit from a "diversification premium" (Kogut et al., 2002; Khanna and Yafeh, 2007). Such scientific evidence may have eased pressures to focus in recent years—the belief is still widespread and can influence managerial decisions, especially in contexts of highly imperfect information.

The liberalization of financial markets in recent decades has made it easier for financial investors to cross national boundaries, while many once privately held businesses have raised capital on the stock market. Financial investors, especially international financial investors, thus play an increasing role in shaping managerial objectives. This impacts on strategies because, firstly, investors with a large portfolio of financial assets are less interested in the risk diversification that conglomerates may offer (because they can diversify risk by diversifying their own financial portfolio). Secondly, international investors are more aware of development outside the company's home market, and may thus prefer investing in companies that exploit such opportunities. The recent financial crisis may, however, have raised the awareness of the benefits of at least moderate diversification, thus softening the pressures for narrow focusing.

Financial markets thus reinforce the effects of competition on the design of corporate strategy. They are likely to be particularly vigilant when the stock market performance is weak. Thus, divestment of peripheral activities is more likely to be initiated when a company has been underperforming on the stock market.

Corporate Leadership

Corporate change is initiated and implemented by leaders at the helm of an organization. The competences, experiences, and mental models of these decision makers thus play a crucial role in shaping corporate strategies. In particular, the educational and experiential knowledge base of business leaders influences their assessment of existing resources and the potential value that these resources may create in alternative business strategies (Hambrick and Mason, 1984; Lyles and Schwenk, 1992).

Globalization has changed this experience and knowledge base of top managers. The new generation of business leaders have often been trained in business schools outside their own country, and thus have wider experience horizons and better understanding of international business opportunities while facing lower cognitive barriers. They are thus better equipped to recognize business opportunities for efficiency improvements and growth through integrated global operations, or by entering markets in other locations.

Changes in strategy are thus often associated with changes in top management, especially with generational change. The cognitive barriers and lack of experience that have inhibited internationalization in the past no longer apply in the 21st century. New leaders may thus initiate or facilitate major shifts in the global strategy of a firm, and its associated strategic and organizational changes. In this way, globalization thus influences the competences of top managers, and thus indirectly their assessment of alternative opportunities to leverage their resources.

MANAGEMENT CHALLENGES

The globalfocusing trend challenges how managers have to conceptualize their business. In the 1980s, companies may have had a choice between being a big fish in a small pond and being a small fish in a big pond. They do not have that choice any longer, at least not in Europe. Globalization has created one big ocean, where (almost) every firm competes with any other firm that happens to offer similar products or services. Thus, the competitive challenge is to observe the industry worldwide and to recognize threats and opportunities on that level.

New business opportunities often arise with new business models that integrate operations at different locations worldwide (Kenney and Florida, 2004; Ghemawat, 2007). To recognize and implement such opportunities, firms need new organizational structures and capabilities throughout the organization that make interaction across borders a way of life for individuals in many functional departments, not only in top management. Often, such a global organization will be built through mergers and acquisitions, which presents leadership challenges of integration management in cross-border, cross-cultural contexts. Thus, the leadership challenge is to create corporate capabilities, especially human capital and communications infrastructure, that can create and exploit global linkages. This requires managers with a global mindset, and with the linguistic and cross-cultural competences to operate across large distances.

The implementation of a globalfocusing strategy is, however, subject to substantial risks:

- Businesses competing globally need a solid understanding of the global industry, its competitive dynamics, and potential entrants originating from other countries. The complexity is likely much higher than in a purely domestic industry, which makes it more challenging for business leaders to be well informed and to take appropriate action.

- On the global stage, firms face coordination challenges (and thus costs) between businesses based in different countries. This is likely to be of concern, especially when it involves cross-cultural management challenges for companies that hitherto have not operated internationally.

- Globalfocusing often involves acquisitions of other businesses abroad. Yet, many corporate acquisitions are set to fail to reach their strategic objectives; in particular, the operational integration of the acquired unit often fails to realize the synergies envisaged at the time of the acquisition deal. Yet, these synergies are the essence of acquisitions motivated by globalfocusing strategies.

Thus, the risk management challenge is to recognize and assess new forms of risk, not only in the external environment, but in the implementation of complex tasks within a global organization.

POLICY CHALLENGES

Corporate strategies integrating operations and leveraging resources on the global stage diminish the scope for national industrial policy. Societies may feel attached to high-profile companies domiciled in their midst, yet this is only partly economically justified. Most companies keep most of their high-value-added activities close to home, and it is in the interest of home government to keep it that way. Yet these operations will only be able to realize their full potential if they can interact with operations elsewhere with a minimum of friction. Since business models depend on the effective integration of operations, any government policy that directly or indirectly causes friction to cross-border activities, such as the movement of goods and people, may negatively affect the competitiveness of such firms.

Thus, policies aiming to induce companies to pursue a particular strategy are likely to have counterproductive side-effects. In particular, a national champion policy aiming to create big domestic firms expected to withstand the challenges from foreign competition may be misplaced.

Rather, firms that are best able to utilize the variations across the world are most likely to survive and prosper; thus, policies that support the international competitiveness of the home-based firm may yield stronger long-term impact.

Host governments aiming to attract and retain activities may rather focus on creating an attractive environment for selected types of high-value-added activities and specializations. The location of different operational units of a global specialist is determined by the comparative advantages of different host countries. Hence, host country policies designed to improve dynamic comparative advantages can act as a magnet for multinational firms to locate economic activity. On the other hand, policies aiming to attract all the stages of a value chain are bound to fail (Buckley, 2009).

GLOBALFOCUSING DURING THE GLOBAL FINANCIAL CRISIS

How is the global financial crisis likely to affect the trends outlined in this paper? In 2008, the reduced efficiency of financial markets and higher borrowing costs may have impeded firms' ability to engage in acquisitions, yet by 2009 opportunities have arisen for cash-rich firms to acquire businesses that are struggling financially due to the slump in demand, or due to reduced availability of capital. However, in the short term, we may see less of the systematic and long-term restructuring of organizations aimed at building a globally integrated organization according to a strategic design, as in the cases of Danisco and Nokia. This type of visionary, radical change requires efficient financial markets.

In the long term, two scenarios are conceivable. At the time of writing (June 2009), the financial crisis had triggered the deepest recession since the 1930s, yet several indicators suggest that the bottom of the recession may have been reached in April 2009. Importantly, many of the driving forces of globalization remain intact, including comparative advantages, information and communication technology, and global business competences of both decision-makers and their organizations. Thence, firms with a global organization—able to benefit from global supply chains, global market access, or global product development—are likely to continue to enjoy competitive advantages over those competing only in their domestic market (Meyer, 2009). Thus, international growth will continue to be the preferred option, rather than domestic diversification.

However, another scenario is possible. If the financial crisis was to induce substantive protectionist policies, then the costs of international operations may well outweigh their benefits. Traditional trade protectionism is constrained by, for example, the rules of the WTO. Yet government policies such as stimulus programs with implicit buy-local conditions, and major bail-outs of national champions (such as car makers), may inhibit international linkages. This could conceivably lead to a reversal of the trends outlined in this paper. Those with a wider horizon than local politicians may suffer, including both consumers that appreciate broad choice and low prices and forward-thinking businesses that have developed integrative business models.

REFERENCES

Buckley PJ. 2009. The impact of the global factory on economic development. *Journal of World Business.* Online advance: DOI 10.1016/j. jwb.2008.05.003.

Campa JM, Kedia S. 2002. Explaining the diversification discount. *Journal of Finance* 57: 1731–1762.

Dunning JH, Lundan S. 2008. *Multinational Enterprises and the Global Economy,* 2nd ed. Edward Elgar: Cheltenham, UK.

Ghemawat P. 2007. *Redefining Global Strategy.* Harvard Business School Press: Boston.

Ghoshal S. 1987. Global strategy: an organizing framework. *Strategic Management Journal* 8: 425–440.

Hambrick DC, Mason P. 1984. Upper echelons: the organization as a reflection of its top managers. *Academy of Management Review* 9: 193–206.

Jaruzelski B, Dehoff K. 2008. Beyond borders: the Global Innovation 1000. *Business + Strategy* 53: 53–68 [http://www.strategy-business.com/media/file/sb53_08405.pdf].

Kenney M, Florida R (eds). 2004. *Locating Global Advantage: Industry Dynamics in the International Economy.* Stanford University Press: Stanford, CA: 1–22.

Khanna T, Yafeh Y. 2007. Business groups in emerging markets: paragon or parasites? *Journal of Economic Literature* 65: 331–372.

Kock CJ, Guillén MF. 2000. Strategy and structure in developing countries: business groups as an evolutionary response to opportunities for unrelated diversification. *Industrial and Corporate Change* 10: 77–113.

Kogut B, Walker D, Anand J. 2002. Agency and institutions: national divergence in diversification behavior. *Organization Science* 13: 162–178.

Lyles MA, Schwenk CR. 1992. Top management, strategy and organizational knowledge structures. *Journal of Management Studies* 29: 155–174.

Meyer KE. 2006. Globalfocusing: from domestic conglomerates to global specialists. *Journal of Management Studies* 43(5): 1109–1144.

Meyer KE. 2009. Corporate strategies during the global downturn: initiating a forward-looking debate. SSRN working paper, http://papers.ssrn.com/sol3/papers.cfm?abstract_id = 1373024.

Peng MW, Lee S-H, Wang DYL. 2003. What determines the scope of the firm over time. *Academy of Management Review* 30: 622–633.

Penrose ET. 1959. *The Theory of the Growth of the Firm.* Basil Blackwell: Oxford.

Simon H. 1996. *Hidden Champions, Lessons from 500 of the World's Best Unknown Companies.* Harvard Business School Press: Boston.

Tan D, Mahoney JT. 2005. Examining the Penrose effect in an international business context: the dynamics of Japanese firm growth in US industries. *Managerial and Decision Economics* 25: 113–127.

Venohr B, Meyer KE. 2009. Uncommon common sense management. *Business Strategy Review* 20(1): 38–43.

Making the Most of Corporate Social Responsibility

Tracey Keys
IMD Business School (International Institute for Management Development), Switzerland

Kees van der Graaf
IMD Business School (International Institute for Management Development), Switzerland

Thomas W. Malnight
IMD Business School (International Institute for Management Development), Switzerland

Too often, executives have viewed corporate social responsibility (CSR) as just another source of pressure or passing fad. But as customers, employees, and suppliers—and, indeed, society more broadly—place increasing importance on CSR, some leaders have started to look at it as a creative opportunity to fundamentally strengthen their businesses while contributing to society at the same time. They view CSR as central to their overall strategies, helping them to creatively address key business issues.

The big challenge for executives is how to develop an approach that can truly deliver on these lofty ambitions—and, as of yet, few have found the way. However, some innovative companies have managed to overcome this hurdle, with smart partnering emerging as one way to create value for both the business and society simultaneously. Smart partnering focuses on key areas of impact between business and society and develops creative solutions that draw on the complementary capabilities of both to address major challenges that affect each partner. In this article, we build on lessons from smart partnering to provide a practical way forward for leaders to assess the true opportunities of CSR.

MAPPING THE CSR SPACE

There is no single accepted definition of CSR, which leads to plenty of confusion about what constitutes a CSR activity. We can begin to develop a working definition of CSR by thinking about its dual objectives—benefiting business and society—and the range of potential benefits in each case (Exhibit 1).

Many businesses pursue CSR activities that can best be termed pet projects, as they reflect the personal interests of individual senior executives. While these activities may be presented with much noise and fanfare, they usually offer minimal benefits to either business or society. In the middle are efforts that can make both sides feel good but that generate limited and often one-sided benefits. With philanthropy, for example, corporate donations confer the majority of benefits on society (with potential but often questionable reputational benefits to the

Exhibit 1   **Corporate Social Responsibility: The Landscape**

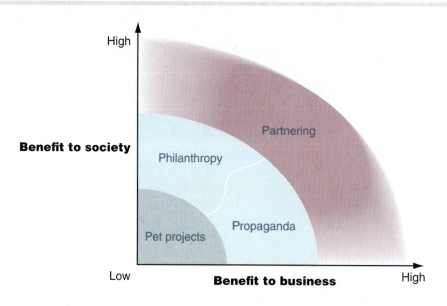

business). Similarly, in what's best referred to as propaganda, CSR activities are focused primarily on building a company's reputation with little real benefit to society. Some cynics suggest that this form of CSR is at best a form of advertising—and potentially dangerous if it exposes a gap between the company's words and actions.

None of these approaches realize the opportunities for significant shared value creation that have been achieved through smart partnering. In such ventures, the focus of the business moves beyond avoiding risks or enhancing reputation and toward improving its core value creation ability by addressing major strategic issues or challenges. For society, the focus shifts from maintaining minimum standards or seeking funding to improving employment, the overall quality of life, and living standards. The key is for each party to tap into the resources and expertise of the other, finding creative solutions to critical social and businesses challenges.

So how does this work? The examples in the two accompanying boxes (see "Addressing Rural Distribution Challenges in India" and "Ensuring Sustainable Supplies of Critical Raw Materials") illustrate smart partnering initiatives at Unilever. Both address long-term strategic challenges facing the company and help to build creative partnerships that accrue significant benefits to both sides.

Initial questions for any leader should be, "Where have you focused CSR activities in the past?" and, more important, "Where should you focus them for the future?" All organizations have to balance limited resources and effort, so the challenge is how best to deploy yours to maximize the benefits to your business (and your shareholders and stakeholders), as well as to society. Start by mapping your current portfolio of CSR initiatives on the framework shown in Exhibit 1 and ask: What are the objectives of our current initiatives? What benefits are being created, and who realizes these? Which of these initiatives helps us to address our key strategic challenges and opportunities?

FOCUSING CSR CHOICES: GUIDING PRINCIPLES

Companies are likely to have activities scattered across the map, but that's not where they have to stay—nor is it how the benefits of CSR are maximized. Many companies start with pet projects, philanthropy, or propaganda because these activities are quick and easy to decide on and implement. The question is how to

Addressing Rural Distribution Challenges in India

More than 70 percent of India's population resides in rural villages scattered over large geographic areas with very low per capita consumption rates. For multinationals, the cost of reaching and serving these rural markets is significant, as typical urban distribution approaches do not work. Hindustan Unilever Limited's Project Shakti overcame these challenges by actively understanding critical societal and organizational needs. HUL partnered with three self-help groups, whose members were appointed as Shakti entrepreneurs in chosen villages. These entrepreneurs were women, since a key aim for the partnership was to help the rural female population develop independence and self-esteem. The entrepreneurs received extensive training and borrowed money from their self-help groups to purchase HUL products, which they then sold in their villages. By 2008, Shakti provided employment for 42,000 women entrepreneurs covering nearly 130,000 villages and 3 million households every month. In the same year, HUL sales through the project approached $100 million. Dalip Sehgal, then executive director of New Ventures at HUL, noted: "Shakti is a quintessential win–win initiative and overcame challenges on a number of fronts. It is a sales and distribution initiative that delivers growth, a communication initiative that builds brands, a micro-enterprise initiative that creates livelihoods, a social initiative that improves the standard of life, and catalyzes affluence in rural India. What makes Shakti uniquely scalable and sustainable is the fact that it contributes not only to HUL but also to the community it is a part of."[1]

[1] V. Kasturi Rangan and Rohithari Rajan, "Unilever in India: Hindustan Lever's Project Shakti," Harvard Business School case 9-505-056, June 27, 2007.

move toward CSR strategies that focus on truly cocreating value for the business and society. The accompanying examples suggest three principles for moving toward this goal.

1. *Concentrate your CSR efforts.* Management time and resources are limited, so the greatest opportunities will come from areas where the business significantly interacts with—and thus can have the greatest impact on—society. These are areas where the business not only can gain a deeper understanding of the mutual dependencies but also in which the highest potential for mutual benefit exists.

2. *Build a deep understanding of the benefits.* Even after selecting your chosen areas of opportunity, finding the potential for mutual value creation is not always straightforward. The key is finding symmetry between the two sides and being open enough to understand issues both from a business and a societal perspective.

3. *Find the right partners.* These will be those that benefit from your core business activities and capabilities—and that you can benefit from in turn. Partnering is difficult, but when both sides see win–win potential there is greater motivation to realize the substantial benefits. Relationships—particularly long-term ones that are built on a realistic understanding of the true strengths on both sides—have a greater opportunity of being successful and sustainable.

Applying these principles to choosing the appropriate CSR opportunities prompts additional questions—namely: What are the one or two critical areas in our business where we interface with and have an impact on society and where significant opportunities exist for both sides if we can creatively adjust the relationship? What are the core long-term needs for us and for society that can be addressed as a result? What resources or capabilities do we need, and what do we have to offer in realizing the opportunities?

Ensuring Sustainable Supplies of Critical Raw Materials

Unilever's Lipton unit is the world's largest buyer of tea. In 1999, Unilever Tea Kenya started a pilot program in Kericho, in southwestern Kenya, to apply company sustainability principles to the production of tea. The initiative focused on improving productivity, sustainability, and environmental management, as well as energy and habitat conservation. For Unilever, growing pressure on natural resources means that securing high-quality supplies of critical raw materials in the long term is of paramount strategic importance.

The Kericho initiative had a direct impact on the company's ability to control the supply of tea not just today but also into the future, while simultaneously enhancing Unilever's corporate reputation with both consumers and employees. Company leadership felt that higher short-term costs were far outweighed by the long-term strategic edge Unilever gained for its raw-materials supplies and brands. In 2008, as a signal of its commitment, Unilever expanded the scope of its sustainable-agriculture program, pursuing certification from the Rainforest Alliance for all Lipton tea farms by 2015.

For society, the initiative increased farmer revenue through a 10 to 15 percent premium paid above market prices. Additionally, it focused on topics of significant concern for governments and farmers alike, including improving farmer skills, environmental protection, and sustainable production methods (such as developing a self-sufficient ecosystem), as well as enhancing local associated jobs. All these factors contributed to strengthened rural income, skills, and living standards.

BUILDING THE BUSINESS CASE

In smart partnering, mutual benefit not only is a reasonable objective, it is also required to ensure long-term success. But this commitment must be grounded in value-creation potential, just like any other strategic initiative. Each is an investment that should be evaluated with the same rigor in prioritization, planning, resourcing, and monitoring.

Now you need to define the array of potential benefits for both the business and for society. This will not always be easy, but a clear business case and story is important if you are to get the company, its shareholders, and its stakeholders on board.

You can assess the benefits across the following three dimensions:

1. *Time frame.* Be clear on both the short-term immediate objectives and the long-term benefits. In smart partnering, the time frame is important, as initiatives can be complex and take time to realize their full potential.

2. *Nature of benefits.* Some benefits will be tangible, such as revenue from gaining access to a new market. Others will be equally significant, but intangible, such as developing a new capability or enhancing employee morale.

3. *Benefit split.* Be clear about how benefits are to be shared between the business and society. If they are one-sided, be careful you are not moving into the philanthropy or propaganda arena. Remember that if the aim is to create more value from partnering than you could do apart, then benefits must be shared appropriately.

Exhibit 2 outlines two contrasting benefit arrays for the Unilever examples discussed in the accompanying sidebars. With Project Shakti, the short-term tangible benefits are extremely clear and powerful, while in the case of Kericho the long-term intangible benefits are strategically critical for both the business and the communities in which it operates. Remember that it is not essential to have benefits in every section of the matrix. However, if you are struggling with any of the dimensions—for example, there are no long-term or tangible benefits or if most of the benefits are one-sided—go back and ask if this is a real partnering opportunity where significant mutual value creation is possible.

Exhibit 2   Plotting the Benefits

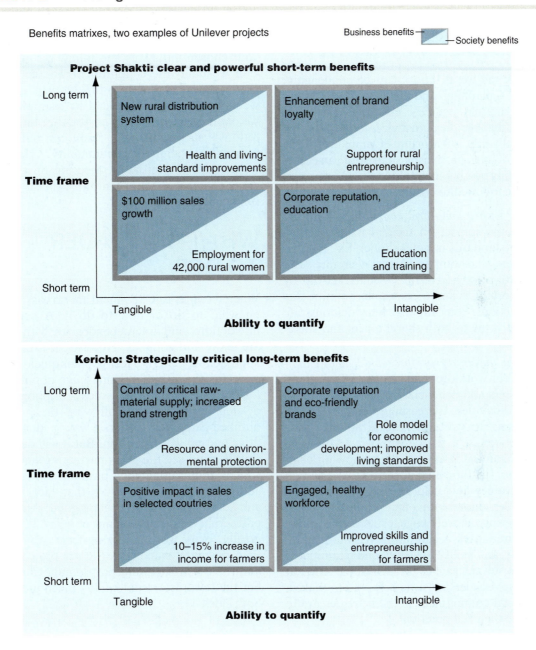

Benefits matrixes, two examples of Unilever projects   Business benefits ─────── Society benefits

Project Shakti: clear and powerful short-term benefits

Time frame

Long term
- New rural distribution system
- Health and living-standard improvements
- Enhancement of brand loyalty
- Support for rural entrepreneurship

- $100 million sales growth
- Employment for 42,000 rural women
- Corporate reputation, education
- Education and training

Short term

Ability to quantify: Tangible → Intangible

Kericho: Strategically critical long-term benefits

Time frame

Long term
- Control of critical raw-material supply; increased brand strength
- Resource and environmental protection
- Corporate reputation and eco-friendly brands
- Role model for economic development; improved living standards

- Positive impact in sales in selected coutries
- 10–15% increase in income for farmers
- Engaged, healthy workforce
- Improved skills and entrepreneurship for farmers

Short term

Ability to quantify: Tangible → Intangible

As you develop a clear array of benefits, a business case, and a story to communicate to all stakeholders, ask: Do we have a clear understanding of the entire array of benefits and the associated business case, on which we can focus, assess, and manage the potential CSR activity? Does the activity focus on fundamental value creation opportunities where we can really partner with society to realize simultaneous benefits? Are the opportunities significant, scalable, and supportive of our overall strategic priorities?

IMPLEMENTING CSR WITH CONSISTENCY AND DETERMINATION

Partnering, as we all know, can be challenging. It requires planning and hard work to assess potential mutual benefits, establish trust, and build and manage the activities, internally as well as externally. But is it worth it? Companies at the forefront of such partnering suggest the answer is a resounding yes, but an additional two principles need to be followed to ensure success:

- *Go in with a long-term commitment.* Having a positive impact on societal issues such as living standards is not a "quick fix" project. Leaders who want to partner therefore need to have a long-term mind-set backed up by solid promises and measurable commitments and actions. Your initiative must demonstrate added value to both shareholders and stakeholders over time.

- *Engage the entire workforce and lead by example.* Your workforce can be one of your greatest assets and beneficiaries when it comes to CSR activities. Increasingly, employees are choosing to work for organizations whose values resonate with their own. Attracting and retaining talent will be a growing challenge in the future, so activities that build on core values and inspire employees are key. Unilever, along with other leaders in smart partnering, actively engages its employees in such initiatives, seeing improved motivation, loyalty, and ability to attract and retain talent as a result. Engaging the workforce starts at the top. Leaders must be prepared to make a personal commitment if the activities are to realize their full potential.

This is the tough bit of the process: taking action, rather than speaking about it, and keeping up the momentum even when targets are far in the future. As you plan the implementation of your chosen initiatives and follow through, ask: Can we build the commitment we need across the organization to make this happen—and are we as leaders willing to lead by example? Have we planned effectively to ensure that implementation is successful, with resources, milestones, measurement, and accountability? How can we manage the initiative, focusing on the total array of benefits sought, not just the short-term financials?

WHAT'S A LEADER TO DO?

When it comes to CSR, there are no easy answers on what to do or how to do it. A company's interactions and interdependencies with society are many and complex. However, it is clear that approaching CSR as a feel-good or quick-fix exercise runs the risk of missing huge opportunities for both the business and society. Taking a step-by-step approach and following the principles outlined here offers leaders a way to identify and drive mutual value creation. But it will demand a shift in mind-set: the smart partnering view is that CSR is about doing good business and creatively addressing significant issues that face business and society, not simply feeling good. And smart partnering is not for the faint of heart. It requires greater focus, work, and long-term commitment than do many standard CSR pet projects, philanthropic activities, and propaganda campaigns, but the rewards are potentially much greater for both sides.

Business as Environmental Steward: The Growth of Greening

Eric G. Olson
Ernst & Young

Attitudes are changing toward the environment to encourage innovation for conservation, and the benefits from this source of innovation are certain to outlive our current generation. Initiatives at enterprises of all sorts and sizes that improve environmental impact are increasing in number and the trend continues to accelerate as more attitudes change.

Many corporate initiatives that benefited the environment in the past were the result of new legislation, community pressure, or customer safety concerns. They have also come from reactive calls to action for specific environmental threats such as acid rain, ozone layer depletion, and excessive pollution and smog. However, with the evidence that science shows us about the acceleration of global warming and associated climate change, there is a growing consensus that transformations to protect the environment should be more pervasive and much larger steps than those already being taken are needed.

In many respects, the driving forces behind the current wave of business transformation for improved environmental stewardship have never been as strongly aligned as they are today, and the potential for some forces to become even stronger in the future is poignantly real.

DRIVING FORCES FOR ENVIRONMENTAL STEWARDSHIP ARE ALIGNED AS NEVER BEFORE

Among the difficult challenges that business leaders and practitioners face today is to understand the driving forces that encourage environmental stewardship in the context of their own operations. Historically, the driving forces behind profitable business decisions and efficient practices have been perceived to conflict with environmentally conscientious behavior. Until only a few years ago, the most visible environmental stewards were often found chained to trees, lying in front of bulldozers protesting deforestation, or organizing and leading boycotts against the activities of "big business." Today, the past perception of negativity and confrontation between environmental stewardship and

Reprinted from "Business as Environmental Steward: The Growth of Greening," by Eric G. Olson, *Journal of Business Strategy*, Vol. 30, No. 5 (2009), pp. 4–13. Copyright © Emerald Group Publishing Limited. All rights reserved.

profitable business activity is oftentimes being replaced with a positive spirit of collaboration and partnership. Indeed, many businesses are learning to focus on improving efficiency to lower their environmental impact, which also improves business performance.

This transformation of perception, and in many respects the reality behind the perception, has begun because multiple forces pushing enterprises to become better environmental stewards have aligned in the right direction. Moreover, the stage is set for those forces to remain aligned far into the future. Figure 1 illustrates the topography of forces that drive enterprises to improve their environmental stewardship, presented in the context of the foundational drivers, their impacts that influence all of the global community, and risks that need to be mitigated. These forces do not exist in isolation, but are interdependent and often reinforcing. For example, if market risk from rapidly changing consumer preferences toward "green" products is high, the reputational risk for businesses that do not take steps to be more efficient and "green" will also be higher. As business leaders already know, where risk can be mitigated or managed in a topography like this, there is also opportunity to realize benefits and create

value. Each of these drivers is discussed next, with illustrative ties to issues that are important in business management.

FOUNDATIONAL DRIVERS ARE ONES THE WORLD MUST LEARN TO MANAGE

Foundational drivers are ones that the world must learn to manage in order to avoid adverse impacts on the environment and earth's natural resources. Global climate and weather change receive much attention, but population growth and industrialization are also important forces behind the need to improve environmental sustainability.

Climate and Weather Change from Global Warming

Global warming and associated climate and weather change have received worldwide attention not only because of the accepted changes already caused to planet earth but also because of

Figure 1   Topography of Forces That Encourage and Drive Business Action

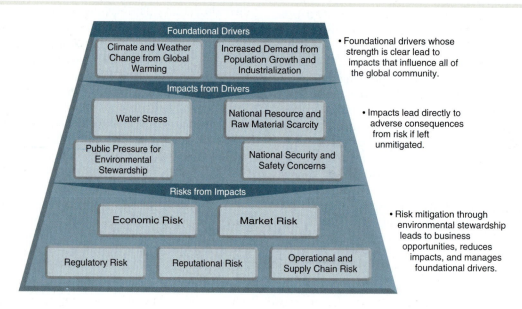

extreme predictions for the future that are being made based on increasingly sound scientific facts. Some changes that have already occurred are clearly documented, although complete agreement on specific details is still a matter of discussion and critics remain.

There is a growing consensus and supporting scientific evidence that increasing concentrations of greenhouse gases are likely to accelerate the rate of climate and weather change. Scientists predict that the average global surface temperature could rise by as much as 4.5 degrees Fahrenheit over the next 50 years, and up to 10 degrees in the next century. Evaporation will increase as the climate warms, which will increase average global precipitation. Soil moisture is likely to decline in many regions, and intense rainstorms could become more frequent. Sea level may eventually rise two feet (Global Warming Trends, 2009) or more along most of the U.S. coast. Obviously, the effects of global warming and associated climate change are shared by the entire planet, and if they are to be slowed down or even reversed, all the stakeholders that contribute to greenhouse gas emissions can and should contribute to a solution.

For the anthropogenic greenhouse gas emissions, which are those that can be attributed to human activity and our combustion of fossil fuels, nearly every economic sector contributes significantly. Therefore, every sector can play a role in reducing emissions from human activity. Power stations make the highest contribution at 21.3 percent; industrial processes follow at 16.8 percent; then transportation fuels at 14.0 percent, agricultural byproducts at 12.5 percent, fossil fuel retrieval, processing, and distribution at 11.3 percent, residential, commercial, and other sources at 10.3 percent, and finally waste disposal and treatment at 3.4 percent (U.S. Environmental Protection Agency, 2008).

By understanding global warming and associated climate and weather change as driving forces for improving their positions as environmental stewards, businesses can gain valuable insight into what actions can be taken in several ways.

First, by identifying and measuring key performance indicators that characterize the carbon footprint of an organization or significant operational area, an enterprise provides a solid foundation for managing and reducing greenhouse gas emissions. The often-heard saying "If you can measure it, you can manage it" certainly applies here. Appropriate accountability can be established if sufficient information granularity and reporting are achieved to show where greenhouse gases might be attributed to business activity in departments, plants, or products.

Second, by understanding where the most significant sources of greenhouse gas emissions come from, businesses can evaluate all their options to prioritize and target the highest contributors to their carbon footprints for optimization and improvement. Whether the appropriate action is to replace inefficient machinery with devices that consume less energy or installing renewable energy producing equipment, enterprises are now able to build business cases for different alternatives that support environment stewardship, reduce costs, and increase profitability.

Third, by measuring and understanding how the operations of an enterprise contribute to greenhouse gas emissions, business leaders can evaluate their extended value chain to make better decisions as environmental stewards and influence activity outside the walls of their own company. Some companies are already considering environmental stewardship performance in evaluating suppliers and business partners as part of a balanced scorecard approach, and other companies are building stronger relationships with customers through recycling programs and incentives that build loyalty and encourage repeat business, as well as cross-selling and up-selling. Companies are also sharing the "carbon footprint burden" with specially designed programs. For example, some companies are purchasing "clean" electricity off of the grid that is generated from renewable sources such as wind farms and solar panels, and trading carbon credits in other programs. In 2008, Dell was one company that announced it had become a "carbon neutral" company, in part, by increasing its purchase of green electricity.

Finally, a more sophisticated understanding of greenhouse gas emissions can open up opportunities for companies to develop new products, create relationships with new business partners, and even grow entirely new business segments that create higher value for new and existing customers, improve environmental impact on a very broad scale, and create a competitive advantage through sustained differentiation. Indeed, companies that are learning to master a more sophisticated view of greenhouse gas emissions, global warming, and associated climate and weather change already have the advantage of being first movers in many instances, and in some cases the followers are not far behind.

INCREASED DEMAND FROM POPULATION GROWTH AND INDUSTRIALIZATION

Even after the threat of global warming and associated climate change are adequately addressed and sustainability of the planet's health demonstrated, the world's population will continue to grow, more than 30 percent from 2010 to 2050 (United Nations Population Division, 1999), and draw from increasingly scarce natural resources such as oil and other fossil fuels, water, minerals, agricultural land, and clean air. As different countries and geographic regions work to raise the living standards for their societies, industrialization will lead to additional demand. Developing regions of the world now have an enormous opportunity to industrialize with the complementary objective of environmental sustainability, without some of the burdensome legacy infrastructure in other regions whose economies went through their industrial revolution more than a century ago.

Environmental risk, which is often described as the threat of adverse effects arising from human activity, includes a host of hazards that organizations have consistently worked to avoid in the past. Even though management of environmental risk has been a driving force behind environmental stewardship for many decades now, new pressures from sources such as resource exploitation, unmitigated waste, residential and commercial

real estate development, population growth, industrialization, and even climate change are giving cause for renewed attention. Avoiding such outcomes as oil and chemical spills, toxic waste contamination, health hazards, and unsafe environmental conditions continues to be a top priority for most businesses.

IMPACTS FROM DRIVERS LEAD TO ADVERSE CONSEQUENCES WITHOUT ENVIRONMENTAL STEWARDSHIP

Without widespread improvements in environmental stewardship, impacts from the foundational drivers will lead to adverse consequences around the world. Among these consequences are water stress, natural resource and raw material scarcity, public pressure, and national security and safety concerns.

Water Stress

Water is a natural resource that is sometimes overlooked as one that is increasingly scarce or under stress because its availability is highly dependent on regional conditions. Some regions will continue to enjoy plentiful water even with global warming, while others will inevitably find themselves surprisingly short supplied as global climate change affects weather patterns and the distribution of fresh water.

According to the Intergovernmental Panel on Climate Change (IPCC), increasing temperatures and extreme weather patterns are already taking their toll on crop yields, which are declining in many parts of Asia. The panel reported in 2007 that future climate change attributable to global warming is expected to put close to 50 million extra people at risk of hunger by 2020, and rising to 132 million and 266 million by 2050 and 2080, respectively. It also suggests that rising air temperatures could decrease rain-fed rice yields by 5 to 12 percent in China, and net cereal production in South Asian countries could decline by 4 to 10 percent by the end of this century (United Nations Environment Programme, 2007). After those scenarios were evaluated and with newer information available in 2009, C. Field of the Carnegie Institute for Science said greenhouse gas emissions are "now outside the entire envelope of possibilities" considered in the 2007 report of the IPCC. Carbon emissions have been growing at 3.5 percent per year since 2000, which is up sharply from the 0.9 percent per year in the 1990s (Schmidt, 2009). Clearly the imperatives to better manage natural resources, such as fresh water, and reduce greenhouse gas emissions globally are here to stay. Expanding industrialization and population growth also require increasing amounts of usable water and can lead to shortages even without drought or climate change.

Natural Resource and Raw Material Scarcity

The outlook appears equally risky for some raw materials when long-term predictions are considered. By some estimates, the minerals due to run out within 50 years are copper, lead, mercury, nickel, gallium, tin, zinc, and phosphorous. Although most businesses and even government enterprises have difficulty formulating strategy around deadlines as far out as 50 years, it is still important for today's businesses to recognize that the supply of some common raw materials is not infinite and as global industrialization continues, there is likelihood that price instability may represent a rising business risk. Even if predictions like these are only partly true, businesses that take action to conserve today and explore different alternatives to stay "ahead of the curve" will be well positioned to reap enormous rewards as others strive to catch up in the future.

Oil and other fossil fuels are also natural resources whose capacity to meet growing demand may be limited, and their eventual scarcity routinely receives "front-page" attention. What is even scarcer than the fossil fuels, though, with many decades of supply still remaining, is our ability to burn them without causing adverse global climate and weather change.

Public Pressure for Environmental Stewardship

Climate change and adverse weather patterns, broader spreading of infectious disease, increased glacial ice flow and melting, and redistribution of plant and animal life are only a few phenomena being linked to global warming, which serve to strengthen public pressure for improved environmental stewardship. The public is also sympathetic to endangered species that may perish because of global warming and associated climate change, especially "charismatic megafauna," as may be the case for polar bears as their ice-rich habitat melts without being replenished each year.

Public pressure as a driving force for the green movement is currently positive in most regions of the world, and serving to push environmental improvement steadily forward. However, the possibility of public pressure shifting from being a positive driving force to a more negative, inflamed one is an impact to be watchful for. Public pressure in the form of unrest is certainly more likely when food production declines while population rises, basic natural resources become scarce, water supplies become more stressed, and other adverse changes occur in the environment such as more frequent and more severe natural disasters.

National Security and Safety Concerns

Resource scarcity, by itself, is enough cause to spark national and even international security concerns. In extreme scenarios, countries and regions where natural resources are found might raise protectionist economic barriers, forge new alliances with unexpected partners, and shift where global economic strength exists. Combining this impact with public unrest as supplies of all sorts become scarce, the national security concern is even clearer. When global conditions become dire enough, riots, corruption, sanctions, and military action to protect sovereign borders are all potential adverse impacts.

Of course, the safety of all living organisms and their habitats is another obvious concern from increased severe weather patterns, floods, fires, and other events of nature. For example, increases in fires, floods and hurricanes all pose a safety risk to people and property that are a great cause for concern.

RISKS THAT REQUIRE MITIGATION TO MANAGE DRIVERS AND CAPTURE BUSINESS VALUE

Appropriately mitigating risk can lead to significant business value as environmental stewardship improvements also result in differentiated products, more efficient operations, and a more sustainable world.

Economic Risk from Energy, Water, and Other Natural Resource Prices

The economics driving energy and raw material prices is one force that many businesses are working to understand better, and then leveraging that understanding toward improving their environmental stewardship. How high energy and commodity prices can go in a given economic cycle, or how long a retreat in prices can be sustained with the headwind of global industrialization is a matter of great debate, and economists and industry analysts continue to have differing points of view. Despite the ongoing debate, one fact has become clear in recent years. That is, as long as energy and commodity prices for scarce raw materials remain unpredictable and long-term global demand sustains heightened levels, initiatives that reduce energy consumption and raw materials waste have stronger value propositions, and therefore make more business sense to implement. One notable exception might be for water management, where the price for water in many areas of the world is still much lower than its actual economic value.

With wide fluctuations in petroleum prices and cheap energy being harder to rely upon, businesses across all industry segments are now taking a close look at their energy usage, and formulating what can be done to reduce consumption or shift to a less risky source with a more stable long term cost. For some enterprises, the first step has been simply to install straightforward technology devices, such as motion-sensitive light switches, and train employees on energy-saving practices they can use in their everyday work. Other companies have taken larger steps to instrument their inventory of energy consuming equipment, implement new technology to monitor and optimize energy consumption, or appoint new roles in the organization with ownership and accountability for achieving business and environmental impact benefits. Still others have reconfigured their operations to utilize alternative and renewable energy sources in order to reduce dependence on fossil fuels that have more volatile and unpredictable price fluctuations.

It is an obvious conclusion and fortunate outcome that efforts to reduce energy consumption and natural resource waste also reduce overall greenhouse gas emissions and improve environmental stewardship. Economic risk associated with increasingly scarce raw materials has spurred conservation activities across all industries, which include innovative efforts to reduce waste, recycle existing material, and search for lower-cost and more sustainable substitutes.

Economics, price volatility, and the associated risks, by themselves, are insufficient driving forces to sustain the current green movement. It is easy to justify business decisions that reduce energy consumption and natural resource waste when commodity prices are high and global economies are growing rapidly. However, the consequence of reducing demand from conservation efforts even in an active and vibrant economy is an inevitable drop in price. Economic recession and slower growth also contribute to lower consumption as economic cycles play out. So, if improved environmental stewardship were to rely on price pressure alone as a driving force, the world would be destined to experience an endless ebb and flow of cyclical activity in the absence of new taxation or "cap-and-trade" mechanisms.

Market Risk from Poor Response to Changing Consumer Preferences

The heightened awareness and changing preferences of consumers is also a driving force that is necessitating the transformation for businesses to become better environmental stewards. Consumers are looking not only for new products and services that simultaneously address global warming and volatile energy prices but also for environmentally conscious companies from which to make their purchases. New product and service strategies, business models, and entirely new businesses have been made possible by simple consumer demand for environmentally friendly products. For companies of all sizes, product portfolios and marketing focus is shifting from an environmentally cavalier atmosphere to an eco-friendly one. Although individuals and organizations that support actions such as living in trees to disrupt logging activities are still far from mainstream, it is becoming increasingly difficult for a business to be too eco-friendly from a consumer's point of view.

In some cases the change in business strategy to capture the attention of customers can be simple, such as increasing recycled content and accentuating that fact in product labeling, as Starbucks has done for some time with its beverage cups and heat protectors. Other subtle product changes can also be effective, such as redesigning a water bottle to reduce plastic content and explaining the reason for the new eco-friendly design to customers through low-cost label changes. For other companies, where larger research and development investments are being made to support more sophisticated eco-friendly products, risks are higher, as are potential rewards in the marketplace. Eco-friendly automobiles have been in development for years, and are just now growing in popularity.

New business success stories are also springing up in areas that have struggled to be profitable in the past. Companies that assess real estate properties for renewable energy opportunities and others that install new equipment are benefiting because of a new emphasis from consumers to reduce their own carbon footprint. Other businesses that extend the scope of recycling programs are also more successful now that consumers increasingly view recycling as an obligation rather than a nuisance.

To heighten consumer awareness, labeling standards are emerging such as "Carbon Labeling," first introduced in the United kingdom in 2007. Carbon labeling articulates the total carbon emissions from bringing a product to the store shelf. As claims to having eco-friendly products increase from companies around the world, standards, oversight, and regulation are certain to follow in order to identify false claims and clarify the meaning and importance of others.

Regulatory Risk from Government Action and Legislation

The combination of regulatory risk from new legislation and global agreements is a driving force that is expected to accelerate the trend toward environmental sustainability.

In 1997 the United Nations held a conference on climate change in Kyoto, Japan, that resulted in an international agreement to fight global warming and associated climate change. The Kyoto Protocol was then adopted; it became effective in 2005 and calls for reductions in emissions of greenhouse gases by industrialized nations. In 2008 at another meeting in Japan, the Group of Eight (G-8) leading industrial nations endorsed halving world emissions of greenhouse gases by 2050, but set no near-term targets.

Other, more binding proposals are also being developed and turned into law. The United Kingdom Climate Change Act, proposed in 2007 and becoming law in 2008, aims to move the UK to a low carbon economy and society with an 80 percent cut in emissions by 2050 from a 1990 baseline. Even though aviation and shipping are excluded, the impact to businesses of all sorts will be substantial.

Regulatory proposals are being actively developed not only at the global and country level but also at the industry, state, and local levels.

In real estate markets, there is a growing recognition that state energy efficiency standards are getting more strict. In 2007 it was predicted that future legislation would require commercial buildings to be zero-net-energy consumers by 2050 (Freedman, 2007). For this to be even partly true, a paradigm shift is needed in the construction industry. In fact, Lockwood (2006) points out, "A substantial body of experience and a set of tested standards have made 'green' a realistic choice for most building projects."

Even water as a valuable and scarce resource receives attention from governments around the world, and associated regulatory risks can be significant. For example, in 2002 the Coca-Cola Company had an operating license that allowed use of ground water in Kerala, India, canceled because of water management and supply concerns.

Other industries are also facing a more restrictive legislative environment that is pressing businesses to become better environmental stewards. As early as 2003 the European Union enacted the Waste from Electrical and Electronic Equipment (WEEE) and the Restriction of Hazardous Substances (RoHS) directives, which were both pieces of legislation focused primarily on the reduction of damage to the environment arising from the use of certain hazardous substances in electrical and electronic equipment. More recently, Germany integrated the intent of both directives into its own laws with the Act Governing the Sale, Return and Environmentally Sound Disposal of Electrical and Electronic Equipment, also known as the ElektroG. This law establishes new responsibilities for companies that sell their products in the German market. Among other responsibilities, firms must take back, recycle, and dispose of the products they sell.

Some electronics companies, such as Lenovo and Dell, have voluntarily initiated their own take-back, recycling, and disposal programs. Hewlett-Packard, Sony, Apple, Asus, and Toshiba, among others also have take-back programs.

As some companies voluntarily adopt practices in one country that are being enforced through legislation in another, the broader trend toward increased corporate social responsibility plays an important role.

Reputational Risk from Failure to Strengthen Corporate Social Responsibility

The increased reputational risk as corporate social responsibility strengthens is another driving force that is making it easier for companies to improve their position as environmental stewards.

Corporate social responsibility (CSR) is no longer viewed as simply a regulatory or discretionary cost of doing business. Instead, it is increasingly viewed as an investment that brings financial returns. Environmental stewardship is a significant part of corporate social responsibility, but also included are societal and market responsibilities as well. In 2008, a survey of 250 business leaders on corporate social responsibility found that 68 percent of them are now utilizing CSR as an opportunity and a platform for growth (Pohle and Hittner, 2008). Today, more than ever before with the onset of the information age, the actions of an enterprise, its leaders, and its employees are highly visible and more readily judged by society. Not surprisingly, when this visibility uncovers actions that are perceived to be originating from low ethical standards, often regardless of their actual legality, business value and customer loyalty can easily be lost and difficult to regain. Stakeholders in the investment community will perceive the enterprise with higher risk, customers will choose competing products when other factors in their decision are equal, and community support might be lost as well.

While many actions focus on improving responsibility toward society and social values, a growing number of them target environmental stewardship. Tesco provides one example, which is the fourth-largest retail chain in the world that operates in the grocery and other industry segments. The company runs 75 percent of its delivery fleet on biodiesel fuel, had labeled 70,000 of its products with carbon counts for consumer awareness by 2008, and will meet the electricity and heating needs of a distribution center in Goole, UK, with a straw-powered combined heat and power plant that will generate enough electricity to run eight Tesco stores. The electricity is almost carbon neutral because the amount of greenhouse gas emissions is around the same that the straw absorbs while growing. To extend the benefits even further, the ashes from the process will be made available for other industries or local farmers to use, and all excess electricity will be sold back to the grid (*Environmental Leader,* 2008).

Businesses adopting ethical standards for environmental stewardship that are higher than current legislative requirements are in many cases also gaining competitive advantage, winning customer loyalty and market share, and lowering their business risk. Reducing environmental impact often leads directly to higher profitability through increased sales or decreased costs, but also can lower the risk from adverse environmental impact events. When adverse environmental events occur, companies that are known for high levels of environmental responsibility can potentially have an easier time maintaining customer trust, loyalty, and support.

Operational and Supply Chain Risk from Inefficiencies and Environmental Changes

Operational and supply chain risk from inefficiencies, environmental hazards, and extreme adverse weather patterns is another driving force that is pushing businesses to invest in the necessary initiatives to become better environmental stewards. For example, as some enterprises improve their efficiency and lower their resulting cost structure, other businesses that do not are increasingly at risk of being unable to compete effectively with higher operating costs. Polluted water supplies and increased hurricane activity are examples of other kinds of risk to business operations.

One emerging practice that some businesses are now adopting is to favor suppliers and other business partners that run environmentally conscious businesses, thus directing more business to them. A complete transition to such practices requires fundamental changes to well-established procurement processes and supplier performance measurement systems, so it will take some time. However, the risk is growing for suppliers that do not improve their environmental stewardship, and in the future they will have more difficulty competing for business with low environmental stewardship status.

Luckily, there is a growing number of mature, proven solutions as well as innovative, high-impact new ones that businesses can apply across all industries to improve their operations and become better environmental stewards. Without these existing solutions for companies to evaluate and utilize, the task of improving environmental stewardship would certainly be much more difficult.

BUSINESS LEADERS ARE ALREADY RESPONDING TO THE DRIVING FORCES

Not only is it becoming clear that virtually any stakeholder can do more to improve environmental stewardship; it is also increasingly less acceptable for some stakeholders to do nothing. Emerging business models are being designed to accomplish a range of objectives, from recognizing and rewarding knowledge and experience of sustainability practices in employees, to enabling improvements in the extended value chain that include the activities of suppliers and business partners.

Across industries and for enterprises of all sizes, the ability to assess the driving forces that are pushing organizations to improve their environmental stewardship is also helping them to better identify and prioritize new opportunities. Businesses are identifying and taking action with initiatives that are simultaneously improving environmental impact and improving their own business performance.

Opportunities have been available to improve environmental stewardship across most enterprises for many years, but only recently have all the driving forces aligned in the right direction to prompt the worldwide call to action that is being witnessed today.

REFERENCES

Environmental Leader (2008), "Tesco powers distribution center on straw," July 22, available at: www. environmentalleader.com/2008/07/22/tescopowers-distribution-center-on-straw.

Freedman, R. (2007), "Climate-change crossfire," *Realtor® Magazine,* p. 15, The National Association of Realtors®, August, available at: www.realtor.org/archives/frontlinesledeaug07.

Global Warming Trends (2009), "Global warming—climate," available at: www.globalwarmingtrends.com (accessed March 20, 2009).

Lockwood, C. (2006), "Building the green way," *Harvard Business Review,* June, pp. 129–37.

Pohle, G. and Hittner, J. (2008), "Attaining sustainable growth through corporate social responsibility," IBM Institute for Business Value, IBM

Global Business Services, available at: www.935.ibm.com/services/us/gbs/bus/pdf/gbe03019-usen-02.pdf.

Schmidt, R.E. (2009), "Climate warming gases rising faster than expected," *USAToday.com,* February 16, available at: www.usatoday.com/tech/science/2009-02-14-climate-report_N.htm.

United Nations Environment Programme (2007), "Millions at risk of hunger and water stress in Asia unless global greenhouse emissions cut," April 10, available at: www.unep.org/Documents.

Multilingual/Default.asp? Article ID = 5551 &Document ID = 504&l = en.

United Nations Population Division (1999), "The world at six billion, part 1," p. 5, October 12, available at: www.un.org/esa/population/publications/sixbillion/sixbilpart1.pdf.

U.S. Environmental Protection Agency (2008), "Inventory of US greenhouse gas emissions and sinks: 1990–2006," U.S. Greenhouse Gas Inventory Reports, April 15, available at: http://epa.gov/climatechange/emissions/downloads/08_CR.pdf.

Recurring Failures in Corporate Governance: A Global Disease?

Nandini Rajagopalan
University of Southern California

Yan Zhang
Rice University

INDIA'S ENRON? SATYAM COMPUTER'S BILLION-DOLLAR CORPORATE FRAUD

On January 7, 2009, B. Ramalinga Raju—founder and chairman of Satyam Computer Services, one of India's largest and most respected software and IT services companies—admitted that he had committed India's biggest corporate fraud, having manipulated the company's income statements, cash flows, and balance sheet for more than seven years. The $1.47 billion fraud on the Satyam (meaning *truth,* in Sanskrit) balance sheet included overstated revenues and profits, acts that were perpetrated by the founder and his brother, the company's CEO, to attract more business and avoid any possible hostile takeover. "It was like riding a tiger, not knowing how to get off without being eaten," Raju wrote in his confession statement ("India's Enron," 2009). Prior to this turn of events—which resulted in the arrests of the chairman, the CEO, and the CFO of the company, and pending criminal indictments as well—Satyam had been widely recognized for exemplary corporate governance, and Raju hailed as a role model for successful business and entrepreneurship. The founder and his co-conspirators reported fictitious cash deposits, misstated accounts receivables and accounts payables, understated liabilities, and overstated assets; these falsities only came to the fore when Raju tried to buy two other firms owned by his family. Shareholders revolted against the acquisition proposal because they viewed the planned purchases as attempts to prop up other failing family businesses by siphoning cash out of the profitable software firm.

Even before the Satyam scandal erupted, Indian shareholders had already lost more than $2 billion from corporate frauds and bad governance since 2003 ("Corporate India's Governance Crisis," 2009). In a January 7, 2009, report issued by an analyst at one of India's leading investment houses, only 4 out of 68 Indian companies were found to adhere to "highly desirable" disclosure standards; more than half the companies on the list that did not make the grade were well-known firms with significant global presence ("Corporate India's Governance Crisis," 2009).

CHINA'S TOXIC MILK SCANDAL: NEGLIGENCE OR CRIMINAL INTENT?

In September 2008, the Sanlu Group—maker of one of the oldest and most popular brands of infant formula in China—was charged with a heinous act: the company was alleged to have added the toxic chemical melamine to its baby milk powder in effort to boost the mixture's protein content. By the time of the discovery, Sanlu's contaminated baby milk powder had affected nearly

Reprinted from *Business Horizons*, Vol. 52, No. 5 (November 2009), pp. 545–552, by Nandini Rajagopalan and Yan Zhang, "Recurring Failures in Corporate Governance: A Global Disease?," with permission from Elsevier.

294,000 Chinese infants, and killed 6. Sanlu, which is 43 percent owned by New Zealand's Fonterra, received a bankruptcy order from a Shijiazhuang Court in December 2008, and four of its top executives were given long prison sentences in January 2009. Under the Chinese Civil Servants Law, which took effect in 2005, and the State Council Regulations on the Punishment of Civil Servants of Administrative Organs, enacted in 2007, heads of administrative bodies who fail to fulfill their duties and cause serious problems that could have been avoided face removal from their jobs and other, more severe, punishment. Indeed, several senior government officials in China have been brought down by the scandal, including the head of the General Administration of Quality Supervision, Inspection, and Quarantine (AQSIQ).

Milk powder from 22 other Chinese companies tested positive for melamine, too, with Sanlu's product at the top of the ranking. Apparently, adding melamine to increase the protein content of dairy products had been an industry-wide practice. Some of the affected companies issued recalls of their dairy products, and other countries began testing Chinese dairy products or removing them from stores. The scandal decimated Chinese dairy exports, and re-exposed long-standing concerns about food security, corruption, and lack of political checks and balances (Wikipedia, 2009).

U.S. FINANCIAL GIANTS' QUESTIONABLE CONDUCT: EXECUTIVE PAYOUTS

Since mid-2008, the U.S. banking industry has been in the deepest recession since the Great Depression of the 1930s. While investors have borne the bulk of the losses and taxpayers have shelled out trillions of dollars to keep financial giants afloat, executives and employees of these banks appropriated disproportionate shares of the profits when the market was booming ("Bank Incentives," 2009). In the three years prior to its collapse, Bear Stearns paid $11.3 billion in employee compensation and benefits, while its shareholders received only around $1.4 billion of JPMorgan Chase stock—currently worth

only half of that amount—after its fall. Lehman Brothers distributed $21.6 billion in the three years before 2007, while its shareholders got nothing because the company went bankrupt. Merrill Lynch paid staff over $45 billion during the three years prior to 2007, but its shareholders got shares in Bank of America that are now worth just $9.6 billion, less than one-fifth of the original offer value. Citigroup paid $34.4 billion to its employees in 2007, but is now valued at just $18.1 billion. The most outrageous case is probably AIG, the insurance and financial services giant: it lost $61.7 billion in the fourth quarter of 2008 and received more than $170 billion in federal bailouts. However, AIG paid over $165 million in bonuses to executives by March 21, 2009, as part of a total payout of $450 million. These highly visible and notorious examples have reinforced the public perception that banking is simply a gravy train for employees ("Attacking," 2009).

While the specific form of corporate governance failure, the magnitude of the fraud, and the final effects on employees, customers, or shareholders may be different across these three national contexts, what is common is the frequency of occurrence of large-scale breakdowns in corporate governance in both developed and developing economies. Understanding why these failures recur, and the intended and actual effects of proposed governance solutions in each of these contexts, is a worthwhile exercise—even if it only serves to illuminate the complexity and magnitude of challenges confronting regulators and governments keen to restore confidence in their country's corporate sector and financial markets.

WHY DO GOVERNANCE FAILURES OCCUR?

Governance Failures in the United States

Roe (2005) traces the recurring breakdowns in American corporate governance to two core and enduring instabilities in the American governance context: (1) the separation of ownership and control, with ownership resting with distant and diffuse shareholders while control is exercised by hired managers; and (2) a decentralized and porous regulatory system, in which multiple regulators with partial authority contribute to a flexible, specialized, and comprehensive regulatory framework while there is no single, unified regulatory agency that oversees the disparate regulatory efforts and resolves potential conflicts and inconsistencies across regulatory agencies. These two core attributes of the U.S. governance framework have obvious strengths, but they are also beset by weaknesses that come to the fore each time U.S. corporations and stakeholders experience a governance crisis.

For instance, the separation of ownership and control is acknowledged as facilitating significant economies of scale in the operation of large firms, the hiring and retention of highly qualified managerial talent, the ease of entry into and exit from markets, and the availability of capital to meet the financing needs of entrepreneurs and start-up firms, and so on. However, on the down side, this separation exacerbates the problems posed by incentive misalignment, self-serving behaviors pursued by managers, entrenchment of powerful managers who may lack the skills and knowledge to manage in changing environments, and so forth. Indeed, Roe argues that the separation of ownership and control explains the recurrent breakdowns the United States corporate sector and financial markets have witnessed over several decades, including the problems associated with hostile takeovers and failure of competitive forces in the 1970s and 1980s, insider trading in the 1980s, excessive executive pay in the 1990s, and the collapse of Enron and other corporate giants in the 21st century.

The porous and decentralized regulatory structure, on the other hand, poses challenges that serve to restrain the power of regulators and the effectiveness of governance reforms intended to check egregious corporate conduct. Managers of large firms and their auditors and accountants can influence both the formulation as well as the implementation of regulations and laws through lobbying the SEC, preemptively litigating, influencing Congress through elected representatives, and so on. In sum, these fundamental characteristics of the governance system result in instabilities that can never be solved once and for all; instead, each crisis leads to a specific set of solutions that are intended to fix the immediate problems, even though the next breakdown is inevitable given the inherent instabilities of the underlying system. While Roe's conclusions are quite alarming, and some may disagree that governance breakdowns are inevitable, it cannot be disputed that for all practical purposes it is impossible to design a fail-proof governance system that conserves the benefits of separation of ownership and control and decentralized regulation while preventing the abuses of power and privilege that inevitably accompany these institutions. Interestingly, the governance failures in developing world contexts, including the examples discussed earlier from India and China, cannot be attributed to either separation of ownership and control or decentralized regulation, because neither of these factors exists in these countries to a degree that they can be blamed for recent acts of corporate fraud.

GOVERNANCE FAILURES IN INDIA AND CHINA

In contrast to the problems that underlie the governance context in the United States, the governance failures witnessed in developing nations like India and China stem not from the separation of ownership and control, but from the concentration of ownership and control within state-owned, public-sector units, or family-owned businesses, and from the pyramidal ownership structures that dominant shareholders use to achieve greater control of the firm (Rajagopalan & Zhang, 2008). For instance, in India a majority of the largest companies are family owned, and their founders—for example, as in the Satyam case discussed earlier—often exercise control to such an extent that they can misstate financial reports and create shadow companies through complex cross-holdings that deal with one another in financially dubious and even potentially illegal ways ("Corporate India's Governance Crisis," 2009; Rajawat, 2009). In China, the government controls about 70 percent of the stakes of publicly listed companies in the Shenzhen and Shanghai Stock Exchanges, and most businesspeople believe that corruption, especially bribery of government officials, is a necessary condition and a norm for conducting business (Rajagopalan & Zhang, 2008).

In both countries, the fundamental problem of concentration of ownership and control in the same hands is further exacerbated by: (1) the lack of incentives for firms and their managers to implement governance reforms, (2) underdeveloped external monitoring systems and weak regulatory agencies, and (3) a shortage of qualified independent directors. While India's formal financial reporting standards essentially meet international standards for accountability and transparency, and its principal regulator—the Securities and Exchange Board of India—is set up to be independent of the government ("Bank Incentives," 2009), enforcement of governance laws is often weak and characterized by significant loopholes. Political connections also often undermine the independence and will of enforcement agencies ("Did SEBI," 2009). In other words, while the United States governance context needs to deal with the challenges posed by a decentralized and porous regulatory system, developing countries lack a regulatory structure with the political will and judicial support to enforce reforms that are enacted.

GOVERNANCE REFORMS: WHY DON'T THEY WORK?

Recent Reforms in the United States: Mixed Evidence on Their Effectiveness

In the wake of Enron and other major scandals in the financial sector that contributed to the recent financial meltdown and ensuing global economic crisis, the United States government and regulatory agencies have focused on enacting new laws, such as the Sarbanes-Oxley Act of 2002, and developing a broader range of stricter monitoring and enforcement mechanisms. These mechanisms are intended not only to generally align managerial interests with those of shareholders but also to ensure greater and more complete transparency in financial accounting, to increase the accountability of executives and directors for reckless and irresponsible risk-taking that results in significant losses to shareholders, to deter potential frauds, and to allow more effective apprehension and prosecution of the perpetrators of these frauds.

A quick review of the most common safeguards in place, however, reveals significant disconnects between the intended benefits and realized effects, and many of these gaps can be attributed to the two fundamental instabilities of the United States governance system discussed earlier in this article (Roe, 2005). On the one hand, managers who control a corporation are inevitably in a better position to manipulate governance mechanisms to promote their own economic well-being, often exploiting legal loopholes, and the dispersed shareholder base can do little to prevent such abuse. On the other hand, decentralized and "siloed" regulatory agencies are unable to coordinate monitoring and enforcement efforts at a level needed to prevent the commission of frauds that cut across regulatory boundaries. The information gaps and significant lapses in regulatory vigilance that preceded the Enron fiasco were repeated with even more dire consequences in the more recent subprime mortgage crisis and ensuing financial meltdowns that decimated once-venerated and iconic Wall Street firms.

One widely used government practice that has failed to achieve the desired objective is equity-based executive compensation. Agency theory suggests that "the most direct solution to [the] agency problem is to align the incentives of executives with the interests of shareholders by granting (or selling) stock and stock options to the CEO" (Hall & Liebman, 1998, p. 656). At their peak in 2001, stock options accounted for over 50 percent of the pay of CEOs of major United States firms (Sanders & Hambrick, 2007). However, stock options give executives a strong incentive to take excessive risk because the downside risk is zero, because the lowest value of stock options is zero, while the upside gain is unlimited. Research has shown that options-loaded CEOs deliver more big losses than big gains (Sanders & Hambrick, 2007). Moreover, the use of options in executive compensation also gives executives an incentive to manipulate the options grant dates, leading to the corporate fraud of stock option backdating. In a recent stock option backdating case, a firm picked a past date when its stock price was particularly low to be the stock option grant date, and thereby increased the value of the stock options (Heron & Lie, 2009; Lie, 2005). Heron and Lie (2009) estimated that 13.6 percent of all option grants to top executives during the period 1996–2005 were backdated or otherwise manipulated.

Indeed, some have argued that equity-based compensation is partly responsible for the recent meltdown of the financial sector. The base packages, including pay and bonuses, for executives in the financial sector were sufficiently large to make them feel financially secure. That gave bankers a license to gamble their equity-based pay in hopes of earning the huge payouts that would take them into the ranks of the über-wealthy ("Bank Incentives," 2009; "Attacking," 2009).

Governance Reforms in India and China: Failures in Implementation

As noted in the previous section, the contexts in India and China pose different challenges compared with the United States and other advanced economies when it comes to governance failures. This is primarily because the broader institutional, economic, and legal-regulatory environments in these nations are in the initial stages of evolution as compared with economies in which the governance context has evolved over many decades of experience with capitalism.

In both India and China, regulatory bodies have advocated comprehensive and rigorous reforms intended to bolster the credibility and integrity of listed companies, to facilitate access to capital for new businesses and expansion of existing businesses, to achieve more transparency and accountability of corporate managers, and to enforce adherence to international standards of accounting and financial reporting. For instance, China's Company Law, enacted in December 1993, was an important starting point in the evolution of governance reforms; it was followed by the China Securities Law in December 1998 and, more recently, the Code of Corporate Governance for Listed Companies in China, enacted in January 2002. The latter, in particular, was designed to further strengthen the requirements related to accounting procedures and information disclosure, selection of independent directors, and shareholder rights and protection.

In India, the most significant milestone in the evolution of corporate governance was the estab-

lishment of the Securities and Exchange Board of India (SEBI) in 1992, an event followed by a series of overarching and comprehensive governance reforms implemented by the Indian government based on the recommendations of four independent governance committees: the Bajaj Committee in 1996, the Birla Committee in 2000, the Chandra Committee in 2002, and the Murthy Committee in 2003. For more details on the recommendations from these committees and the ensuing governance reforms, see Rajagopalan and Zhang (2008).

Notwithstanding the scope and urgency of the reforms enacted in both countries, however, there is widespread agreement that both countries are very weak when it comes to enforcing these reforms. Indeed, in a 2004 report on the implementation of corporate governance codes in India, the World Bank noted serious gaps and lapses, particularly in relation to the role of nominee directors from financial institutions, stock-listing laws and regulations, insider trading, and dividend and share-transfer transactions (World Bank, 2004).

While appropriate in many ways, the response of the Indian government following the Satyam crisis was still criticized as being too slow. For instance, while the disclosure of fraud was made on a Wednesday morning, the first resulting crucial decision—which was to dismiss the entire board of directors—was only made on Friday night. In a scathing critique of the government's response timing, published in India's leading business journal, Dubey (2009) sarcastically notes:

> So what if crucial time was lost in the intervening 70-odd hours when the company, its finances, its accounts, and IT infrastructure remained in the hands of people who were part of the management that committed the fraud. So what if the Centre and the State debated for three days about who would initiate legal action against the Rajus. So what if incriminating evidence may have been destroyed as Satyam investigators have discovered . . . they are unable to locate the company's bank statements. (p. 64)

Dubey (2009) goes on to note:

> India must also build a consensus on separating economic fraud investigators and offices such as the SIFO from political clutches such as the Ministry of Corporate Affairs. Business and politics are so well intertwined in the country that political control can potentially influence investigators. . . . All of this could be avoided if business fraud or

bankruptcy investigators were given the statutory authority and the independence to swing into action without waiting for a political nod. (p. 65)

As a direct result of the Sanlu milk powder scandal, China passed its first food safety law—effective June 1, 2009—in an effort to restore consumer confidence. Under the new law, consumers can get financial compensation of up to 10 times the price of the product, in addition to compensation for any harm caused by tainted food. The law also bans food safety supervision agencies from advertising food products and states that individuals, including celebrities, who advertise for a substandard product may also be held liable for damages. While this new law represents an important step in the monitoring and strengthening of food safety standards, some are skeptical about its chance of success. The new law did not create a single, powerful body—akin to the U.S. Food and Drug Administration (FDA)—to handle food safety. China's Departments of Health, Agriculture, Quality Supervision, Industry, and Commerce Administration will all share the responsibilities of monitoring the country's food supply. In addition, China has 450,000 registered food production and processing enterprises, with the vast majority employing just 10 people or less. A United Nations report last year noted that the challenge of overseeing these small businesses is one of China's biggest hurdles in ensuring food safety.

DETERRING GOVERNANCE FRAUDS: A COST-BENEFIT APPROACH

Because financial frauds, product tampering, and many other violations of governance laws can be viewed as corporate crimes, we draw on the broader, well-established economics of crime literature (e.g., Eide, Rubin, & Shepherd, 2006) to argue that the likelihood of such violations is contingent upon two factors: (1) the costs associated with committing a fraud, and (2) the benefits derived from committing that fraud. The higher the costs imposed on the perpetrator and the lower the benefits associated with the fraud, the lower the likelihood that the fraud will be committed.

Deterring Fraud by Increasing the Costs

The costs associated with committing a governance fraud generally depend upon three factors. The first is the probability that the deviant behavior will be discovered, which substantially depends upon the monitoring mechanisms in place. The greater the probability that the fraud will be discovered, the less likely it is that a company or its management will commit a fraud.

The second factor is the size or extent of the punishment (e.g., financial fines, loss of liberty) if a fraud is detected and, relatedly, who will be affected, monetarily or otherwise, by the punishment. Severe punishment—for example, being banned from an industry/functional area if certain violations are uncovered—will discourage a company and the management. In many cases, however, because the company pays for the punishment, the threat of punishment may have limited effect in disciplining management behavior. For instance, in May 2002, Merrill Lynch paid a $100 million fine to settle with the State of New York after its analysts were caught denigrating the companies they touted to investors during the technology bubble era. Indeed, the major purpose of the SEC's recent requirement for CEOs and CFOs to personally certify their companies' financial statements is to narrow the legal loophole between a company's financial statements and its senior executives' individual responsibilities, thereby enhancing the quality of a company's financial disclosures (Zhang & Wiersema, 2009). Once they have certified their companies' financial statements, subsequent revisions of the statements could potentially expose executives to criminal charges.

The third factor is the likelihood that the punishment will be enforced, which depends upon the effectiveness and speed of the legal system in place. Especially in emerging markets such as China and India, the major problem regarding corporate governance is not the absence of laws but the lack of timely and consistent enforcement of the laws that already exist (Rajagopalan & Zhang, 2008).

Because of the relative maturity and sophistication of governance laws, and the legal and regulatory frameworks in developed economies like the United States, the costs associated with corporate frauds are quite significant; white-collar criminals can access the best legal representation, though, which can sometimes reduce the probability and size of the punishment. In comparison, as noted earlier, monitoring and enforcement of governance laws is particularly lax in both India and China, albeit for somewhat different reasons, and the breakdowns in implementation serve to reduce the costs associated with committing these crimes, especially because the most powerful business people and corporate families are also very well connected with leading politicians, who can in turn often influence regulatory agencies. Therefore, the potential cost of committing a fraud is relatively lower in developing countries than in developed countries.

Deterring Fraud by Reducing the Benefits

The benefits associated with a fraud depend upon the utility function of the individual or group committing the fraud. Of course, this utility function can also be generated at more aggregate levels for a top management team or an entire corporation, depending upon growth and profitability targets, schemes for division of profits, and so on. The utility derived from fraudulent acts reflects both financial and nonfinancial benefits (e.g., political power, prestige, social standing). In both developed and developing economies, the benefits associated with corporate frauds can be substantial although, again, the magnitude and nature of these benefits can vary across these environments. In developed nations, the winner-take-all syndrome, the increasing disparity between pay and performance, and the excessive risk-taking witnessed in the recent collapse of large financial institutions have resulted at least partly from the disproportionate benefits bestowed on a few at the uppermost echelons of the corporate sector. Whether CEOs and senior managers are paid for their performance or not is a topic of continued debate in both academic and business circles. However, the prevalence of huge financial payouts for top executives and the low personal risk associated with performance failures have clearly increased the pecuniary benefits associated with deviant corporate behaviors.

In developing nations, the benefits appear to stem from the spurt of economic opportunities created by the opening of once-closed economies and the encouragement of private enterprise in industries once dominated by the public sector. While the overall opportunities for wealth creation have increased, the distribution of such wealth continues to be lopsided. Business press articles in recent years have documented the increasing number of millionaires and billionaires in both China and India, the rapid growth and profitability experienced by the largest business houses and families, and the rapidly increasing salaries and benefits at the top executive levels. The winner-take-all syndrome that may have driven individual and corporate excesses in developed nations is now permeating emerging economies as well, where the asymmetry in the distribution of rewards is further exacerbated by lax governance regimes and poor enforcement mechanisms.

In summary, the recurrence of corporate frauds depends upon both the potential costs and benefits of committing the frauds. Developed nations have been able to deal with the cost side of governance failures relatively effectively, although recent corporate excesses have renewed concerns about these aspects. Developed nations, though, are faced equally with the twin challenges of increasing the costs and decreasing the benefits associated with corporate frauds and excesses. These differences have implications for the direction in which reforms need to be directed, especially because—as we argue later—attempts in developing nations to curb the benefits may have the costly effect of curbing individual and corporate ambition and entrepreneurship, with serious debilitating effects on overall growth and prosperity.

Governance Challenge in the United States: Costs versus Benefits

While there is certainly room for bolstering the monitoring and enforcement sides of the governance situation in the United States, especially in relation to coordinating and sharing information across different regulators, we believe that influencing the payoffs associated with corporate and individual misconduct should be more of a priority than tweaking the regulatory code further. It is indeed gratifying to note that the new Obama administration is beginning to focus on this issue, especially in the context of executive compensation, given that compensation and equity ownership are after all the most significant benefits. Reforms being considered include, among other things, the following: (1) banks receiving federal rescue money must agree to executive pay restrictions and to a ban on big paychecks for departing executives, known as *golden parachutes;* (2) advisory voting on executive compensation; (3) restrictions on deferred compensation; (4) a clearer definition of performance-based pay; (5) limits on severance payments for senior executives; (6) broader "claw back" provisions to recoup bonuses; (7) higher levels of engagement of the SEC in different aspects of corporate governance, especially in the compensation of senior executives; and (8) greater transparency in company disclosures, and enhanced personal accountability of senior executives ("Attacking," 2009; Solomon & Paletta, 2009).

At the same time, changes to executive compensation systems have to be made very cautiously because past attempts—such as the 1984 decision in the United States to cap severance payments at three times base pay by imposing a special tax on payments above that level and the $1 million cap imposed on the tax deductibility of executive salaries—have often had unintended negative consequences leading to even higher financial benefits for top executives ("Attacking," 2009). Instead, strengthening the ability of shareholders to monitor pay deals ex ante and making "say on pay" votes by shareholders mandatory at public firms may curb compensation abuses more effectively than one-size-fits-all reforms that unintentionally incentivize the exploitation of loopholes or, even more troubling, thwart innovation and entrepreneurship.

Curbing Corporate Frauds in China and India: Costs versus Benefits

In developing nations like China and India the governance regime is characterized by relatively low costs of committing corporate frauds, due to lax monitoring and weak enforcement, as well as high benefits, due to rapid growth opportunities and windfall economic gains for the winners. For practical and policy reasons, however, it is difficult

for these economies to simultaneously and aggressively tackle both challenges. Attempting to tackle the benefits side too aggressively—by controlling/regulating salary levels, hiring and promotion decisions, investment decisions, and so forth—can have the unintended and potentially disastrous effect of curbing much-needed entrepreneurship, talent retention, and ambitious growth and profitability targets. Given the nascent stage of economic development in countries like India and China, we believe that it may be more prudent to concentrate on the cost side, and focus on stricter implementation and enforcement of monitoring and punishment mechanisms, at least in the short to mid term.

For instance, the Reports on the Observance of Standards and Codes (ROSC) noted that many of the sanctions and enforcement rules currently in place in India were inadequate, and that monetary sanctions were particularly in need of adjustment (World Bank, 2008). While the sanctions imposed by the stock exchange included warnings, suspension of trading, and delisting, it did not include monetary fines that were high enough to deter noncompliance. The ROSC also recommended better coordination of the roles and responsibilities of the three regulatory agencies charged with enforcing governance norms over listed companies in order to minimize regulatory lapses and oversights.

Any benefits-side reforms that are considered should be carefully assessed for their potential adverse effects on the managerial talent market, and on the corporate growth and wealth-creation strategies. Given that even developed nations have only recently begun to worry about the benefits side of the equation, a "wait and learn" attitude may be advisable for developing nations. We hasten to add that we are not arguing in favor of completely eschewing benefits-side reforms in developing nation contexts. Indeed, governance reforms should aim to increase the costs and reduce the benefits associated with corporate frauds for maximum deterrence. For example, China's new food safety law has increased consumers' financial compensation for tainted food, from the price of the product up to 10 times the price of the product. While this change certainly increases the costs for a firm to commit the sort of fraud that Sanlu did, it may not be a sufficient deterrent if the economic gains to be reaped from fraudulent acts are potentially huge in relation to the costs. Indeed, to minimize the likelihood of corporate frauds and related crimes, it is imperative not only to increase the costs associated with the crime (ex post punishment), but also to reduce the benefits derived by the person or group considering such acts (ex ante utility).

CONCLUDING REMARKS

The recurrence of corporate governance crises in highly developed, as well as developing, economies reminds us that the price of economic growth and opportunity is indeed eternal vigilance. Understanding the differences in the institutional contexts helps us to realize that what works to curb governance failures in one context may be less effective in another, and that the timing and focus of reforms should reflect the realities of the economic and institutional conditions that different nations face. Ultimately, the most effective and sustainable governance reforms will be those that simultaneously increase the costs of corporate frauds and decrease the benefits that individuals and corporations can derive from ignoring governance norms and laws.

REFERENCES

Attacking the corporate gravy train. (2009, May 30). *The Economist,* 71–73.

Bank incentives are all wrong. (2009, January 29). *The Economist.* Retrieved from http://www.economist.com/displaystory.cfm?story_id=13036810&CFID=59669704&CFTOKEN=26151850.

Corporate India's governance crisis. (2009, February 2). *BusinessWeek,* 78–79.

Did SEBI ignore Satyam under political pressure? (2009). *The Economic Times.* Retrieved from http://economictimes.indiatimes.com/articleshow/3969014.cms.

Dubey, R. (2009, January 26). Create a special force. *Business World,* 64–65.

Eide, E., Rubin, P. H., & Shepherd, J. M. (2006). Economics of crime. *Foundations and trends in microeconomics.* Boston: World Scientific Publishing Co.

Hall, B. J., & Liebman, J. B. (1998). Are CEOs really paid like bureaucrats? *Quarterly Journal of Economics, 113*(3), 653–691.

Heron, R. A., & Lie, E. (2009). What fraction of stock option grants to top executives have been backdated or manipulated? *Management Science, 55*(4), 513–525.

India's Enron. (2009, January 8). *The Economist.* Retrieved from http://www.economist.com/business/displaystory.cfm?story_id=12903424.

Lie, E. (2005). On the timing of CEO stock option awards. *Management Science, 51*(5), 802–812.

Rajagopalan, N., & Zhang, Y. (2008). Corporate governance reforms in China and India: Challenges and opportunities. *Business Horizons, 51*(1), 55–64.

Rajawat, Y. K. (2009, January 26). Anatomy of a fraud. *Business World,* 66–68.

Roe, M. J. (2005). The inevitable instability of American corporate governance. *Corporate Governance Law Review, 1*(1), 1–19.

Sanders, G., & Hambrick, D. C. (2007). Swinging for the fences: The effects of CEO stock options on company risk taking and performance. *Academy of Management Journal, 50*(5), 1055–1078.

Solomon, D., & Paletta, D. (2009, May 13). U.S. eyes bank pay overhaul. *The New York Times.* Retrieved from http://online.wsj.com/article/SB124215896684211987.html.

Wikipedia. (2009). *Timeline of the 2008 Chinese milk scandal.* Retrieved from http://en.wikipedia.org/wiki/Timeline_of_the_2008_Chinese_milk_scandal.

World Bank. (2004). *Report on the observance of standards and codes (ROSC), corporate governance country assessment: India.* Washington, DC: World Bank–IMF.

World Bank. (2008). *Reports on the observance of standards and codes (ROSC) for corporate governance.* Retrieved from www.worldbank.org/ifa/rosc_cg.html.

Zhang, Y., & Wiersema, M. (2009). Stock market reaction to CEO certification: The signaling role of CEO backgrounds. *Strategic Management Journal, 30*(7), 693–710.

Creative Execution

Eric Beaudan
Odgers Berndtson, Canada

Eric Beaudan is the leadership Assessment Practice Director at Odgers Berndtson, one of Canada's largest executive search firms. This article is extracted from his forthcoming book, Creative Execution.

Call it unconventional or unorthodox, but Creative Execution—which can be all of these things—is designed to differentiate the company sharply and take it to previously unattainable heights. Leaders will understand why and how after they've read this article.

Fire your imagination and travel back to another time, more than 200 years ago. The year is 1805 and almost all of Europe lies within Napoleon Bonaparte's grasp. Only one nation stands in his way of achieving total European domination: England. With 200,000 crack troops assembled in northern France, the Emperor is counting on Admiral Villeneuve to join forces with the Spanish and secure the Straits of Dover for the force that will invade England. Surveying the scene, the Emperor says, "Let us be masters of the Straits for six hours and we shall be masters of the world."

Standing in the way of Napoleon's grandiose scheme is the Royal Navy's most capable admiral, Horatio Nelson, who had already decimated the French fleet that escorted Napoleon's army to Egypt in 1798, and pursued the French fleet from North Africa to the West Indies and back. Admiral Villeneuve is well aware of Nelson's prowess. Although his fleet bristles with 33 ships of the line, including the first-rate Spanish ship *Santissima Trinidad,* the world's largest warship with 130 guns, Villeneuve knows that Nelson's 27 men-of-war are in peak fighting condition.

When Nelson finally catches Villeneuve off Cape Trafalgar the morning of October 21, 1805, he achieves a monumental victory. The English sink or capture 18 French ships, with over 14,000 French and Spanish killed in action, 10 times more than the English. Taken prisoner aboard his flagship, Villeneuve commits suicide a few days after the battle. Napoleon's dreams of European hegemony are shattered in one fell swoop.

NELSON'S TOUCH

How did Nelson achieve such an overwhelming victory? The answer is that Nelson mastered what I call Creative Execution—the ability to execute a strategy so well conceived, understood, and embraced by all that it almost guarantees a successful outcome, even against the odds. Nelson's captains knew that they were going to win before the battle even started. They called their approach, quite simply, the Nelson Touch.

The Nelson Touch was anything but gentle. Nelson sought to not just defeat the Combined Fleet but to crush it. Instead of the traditional "line of battle," in which two parallel lines of warships pounded each other from a safe distance—which led to long, inconclusive battles—Nelson decided to break through the enemy line at a 90-degree angle and attack individual ships from close quarters. His plan would ensure that the English, who could load and fire their guns almost twice as fast as the French and Spanish, could sink or disable enemy ships on a much larger scale than a long-range shoot out would allow. At Trafalgar, Nelson divided his fleet into two lines, one led by himself on the *Victory,* and the other led by Admiral Collingwood aboard the *Royal Sovereign.* Both lines cut through the center of the French and Spanish combined fleet and engaged in close-quarter action against the enemy (see Figure 1).

I've mapped Nelson's Touch against the five key ingredients of the Creative Execution formula I developed to break down the winning strategies of great leaders in history and business. By mastering these five ingredients, leaders will learn how to construct a Creative Execution formula that differentiates their organization and

Figure 1   Nelson's Battle Plan at Trafalgar

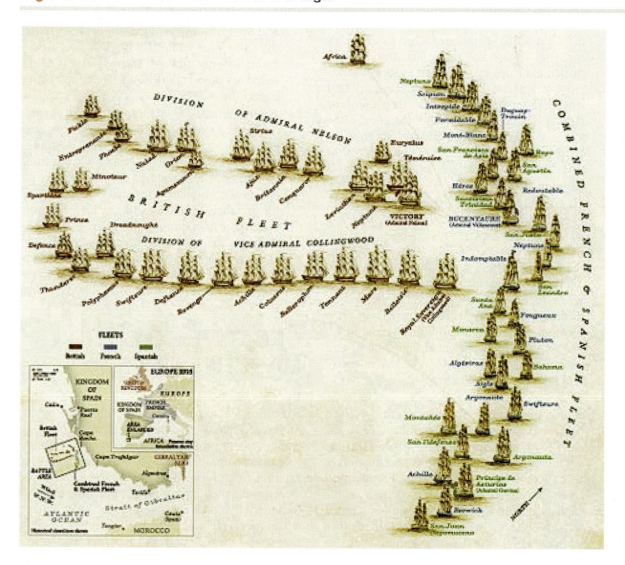

vastly increases their ability to achieve extraordinary results against the odds.

FIVE INGREDIENTS OF CREATIVE EXECUTION

1. *A unique strategy understood and accepted by everyone.* The first ingredient of Creative Execution—indeed of all execution—is a unique, compelling strategy. Nelson's choice of strategy and tactics—to force a decisive battle with the Combined Fleet, approach the enemy line at a right angle, and use superior firepower to overwhelm each ship in close-quarter combat—was both visionary and compelling. Nelson invited different ships' captains to his cabin every night to discuss and refine his strategy, and drilled his ships every day to ensure that his crews maintained the gunnery accuracy that was the key to success. The fleet's unique strategy of breaking through the enemy line and its competitive advantage in gunnery accuracy provided the double hammer blow that splintered the French and Spanish Combined Fleet.

2. *Candid dialogue.* The openness with which Nelson dealt with his peers and superiors was a hallmark of his personality. He fervently promoted his strategy within the Admiralty, shared it openly with his crew, and encouraged his captains to debate his ideas. Nelson understood that if he was to achieve the tactical breakthrough he was seeking, he would need to lay down the Royal Navy's tradition of silent disagreement, and encourage his captains to take the initiative and break established norms.

3. *Clear roles and accountabilities.* Once he shared his strategy with his captains, Nelson had the document published for all, so it was clear who was responsible for what. The fleet would be divided into two attacking forces that would slice through the French and Spanish center—with clear instructions for each attacking line. Nelson even sent out a terse reminder: "In case signals can neither be seen nor understood, a captain can do no wrong by placing his ship alongside an enemy." First lieutenants were told how to press the attack should their captain be killed in action.

4. *Bold action.* Nelson had demonstrated his willingness to take bold action before Trafalgar. At the Battle of the Nile in 1798, he annihilated a French fleet in a night action when no other fleet had previously fought at night. His reputation for decisive action was so great after the Battle of the Nile that Admiral Villeneuve "sensed he was fighting not just an enormously gifted and bold opponent but an entire institution built on excellence and precision, overloading the odds from the start."[1] Upon seeing Nelson's attack formation, the Spanish Admiral exclaimed "We are doomed!" Even though the French and Spanish ships had the opportunity to fire the first shots while the English fleet slowly made its way toward them, Nelson boldly sailed his ships right through the center of the enemy line.

5. *Visible leadership.* Only by being visible during the skirmishes that occur throughout execution can leaders unleash people's creative powers. At Trafalgar, Nelson refused to remove his decorations or cover his Admiral's uniform. He was convinced that his presence on the deck of the *Victory* would encourage his sailors to fight harder. Halfway through the battle, a French sharpshooter spotted Nelson in his uniform and shot him. Nelson died after being taken belowdecks—and became an instant hero.

CREATIVE EXECUTION MARCHES EAST

By the middle of the 20th century, Creative Execution ceased to be used exclusively by the military. Thanks to revolutions in technology, capital, talent, and global development, Creative Execution migrated from its Western founders to Japan, China, India, and the Middle East. If you were among the 1 billion people watching the 2008 Summer Olympics opening ceremonies in Beijing, where over 10,000 performers put on a show that took seven years to put together, you're well aware of that fact. As well, large-scale innovation,

Compelling strategy. The first ingredient of successful execution is a unique and compelling strategy that clearly outlines what you will do—or won't do—in order to achieve outstanding results	• Nelson's strategy for breaking through the enemy fleet's line at Trafalgar • Google's decision to focus on Internet search, instead of content • Four Seasons' approach to building mid-size hotels • Toyota's efforts to meet customer needs in every market
Candid dialogue. Openness to other people's ideas, honest debate, disagreements, and resolution are critical to effective teamwork and execution. Creating a culture of candor improves employee engagement and drives innovation.	• Nelson's encouragement of "creative disobedience" • Larry Page and Sergey Brin's annual letter to Google shareholders • Toyota employees make on average 600,000 suggestions for improving the company or manufacturing processes each year
Clear roles & accountabilities. Managers and employees need to understand how their individual roles and accountabilities connect to the strategy. Clear roles drive expectations and cement people's commitment to specific actions.	• Thomes Cook's CEO made each of his direct reports the CEO of a strategic initiative • Each Toyota employee is empowered to pull an andon cord that stops the entire production line • Each captain in Nelson's fleet knew what to do in case the flagship couldn't send proper signals
Bold action. Bold action generates incredible momentum. It firmly propels the organization toward its new direction, and provides the first tangible taste of how the strategy will be deployed.	• General Schwarzkopf's famous "left hook" in Desert Strom • Google is in the process of digitizing the content of all the libraries in the world • Toyota's early investment in hybrid technology
Visible leadership. Visible leadership of the organization's senior leaders is necessary to maintain a common focus, keep track of execution milestones, and create a postive culture of learning, courage, and perseverance.	• Nelson's insistence that he should wear his Admiral's uniform at Trafalgar • Akio Toyoda describes himself as the "owner-chef" at Toyota • COO Katie Taylor visits up to 30 Four Seasons hotels every year

which the United States demonstrated through unique feats such as the Berlin Airlift of 1948 and the race to the moon in the 1960s, is just as vibrant in South Korea and BRIC countries as it is in New York and Silicon Valley.

Consider these two examples:

• Over 70 percent of Boeing's highly touted 787 Dreamliner, a carbon-composite aircraft that took its maiden flight in December 2009, is designed and manufactured in China, Russia, and India. Not only are Chinese workers bending sheet metal for the Dreamliner, but Chinese and Indian designers are putting together the specs for the aircraft.

Likewise, in 2008, European aircraft maker Airbus opened its first plant outside Europe in China—where it now employs 600 workers to assemble the popular A320 airplane. And so China is no longer just buying Boeing and Airbus's planes—which is what it did in the 1980s and 1990s—it is actually learning how to design, manufacture, and assemble the planes. This significant shift will likely see China form its own aircraft industry in the near future.

• In the United Arab Emirate of Abu Dhabi, a T-shaped island with barely 1 million inhabitants, engineers are building a new, high-tech, zero-carbon-emission city called Masdar, or "the source" in Arabic. Masdar will rely exclusively on solar and renewable energy sources to power 50,000 houses and 1,500 businesses. To keep the city cool and minimize energy requirements, Masdar will be walled, and its streets will be narrow and shaded. The city will be completed in 2016, at a cost of roughly $22 billion.

With $1 trillion at its disposal from oil revenues managed through the Abu Dhabi Sovereign Wealth Fund (which recently bought a 15 percent stake in London's Gatwick Airport, and a 10 percent stake in Hyatt Hotels), Abu Dhabi's grandiose plans aren't restricted to Masdar. In 2009, the Emirate signed a $1.6 billion agreement with the French national museums to build a branch of the Louvre on the island of Saadiyat, as part of a $27 billion development project. Renowned architect Frank Gehry is building a modern art museum there, while Japanese architect Tadao Ando is erecting a maritime museum and arch. In the next five years, the Creative Execution burst under way in Abu Dhabi will present us with another version of Dubai that, seemingly, grew out of nothing to become a world-class megalopolis.

GOOGLE THIS

While Creative Execution is thriving in BRIC countries and the Middle East, it has not entirely vanished from the United States or Europe. Take Google, which since its inception has experienced 10 years of double (and sometimes triple) digit growth. Back in October 2007, Google's share price of $700 made it more valuable than mighty Microsoft, with a market cap of $220 billion. Google continues to push the boundaries of creative development, whether it's through the stunning scenery of Google Mars or clever customization of advertising for its Gmail users. In 2009, while other tech companies were struggling, Google increased it revenues by 17 percent in the last quarter alone—adding another cool $1 billion to its topline.

Using the Creative Execution formula, we can map out Google's rise from start-up to global leader in Internet search:

Unique strategy. From the get-go, the unique appeal of cofounders Larry Page and Sergey Brin's algorithm is what set Google apart from other Internet search engines. While attending Stanford University, Page and Brin designed a formula—called PageRank—that analyzes links to and from all the websites on the Internet, and determines how important each website is, based on the number of links that refer back to it. While early Internet providers like AOL and Netscape focused on e-mail services and measured their success by keeping users inside a "walled garden," Google kept its main page simple and let the logic of PageRank take users out of its site as quickly as possible.

What appeared at first blush to be a proposition for losing money on the Internet turned into a scalable gold mine. By sticking to their unique strategy and focusing on Internet search, rather than content, Page and Brin built a company that owns 60 percent of the global Internet search market, and has emerged as "the most formidable challenger that Microsoft has ever faced."[2]

Candid dialogue. Google's culture of candid dialogue is rooted in the friendship between Page and Brin, who met on Stanford's campus in the summer of 1995. As Google's own philosophy states, "Ideas are traded, tested and put into practice with an alacrity that can be dizzying. Meetings that would take hours elsewhere are frequently little more than a conversation in line for lunch and few walls separate those who write the code from those who write the checks."

Since Google's 2004 IPO, Brin and Page have upheld their pledge to take turns writing a direct, open letter to shareholders at the beginning of every year, where they explain the company's direction. Their original IPO letter, inspired by Warren Buffet's essays, made it clear to all potential shareholders that the company would not attempt to "smooth out" its quarterly results, a common practice among publicly traded companies. This candor and straight talk from Page and Brin, as well as their commitment to keeping PageRank safe from the influence of advertisers, remains fundamental to Google's success.

Clear roles and accountabilities. When Eric Schmidt joined Google as CEO in 2001, he brought the business experience that Google needed to balance the creative energy and technical genius that Page and Brin brought to the table. The three have been collaborating for so long that, as Brin and Page acknowledge, "decisions are often made by one of us, with the others being briefed later. . . . We can often predict differences of opinion among the three of us."[3] In the early days of Google, Page and Brin were so close that they actually shared a rectangular workstation at the Googleplex, Google's head office in Mountain View, California.

Within the company itself, Google employees feel an unusual sense of shared direction and accountability. Part of this operating philosophy is reflected in Google's structure, which consists of teams without the usual layers of middle management. Schmidt, Page, and Brin realize that to attract and keep the world's best computer scientists and innovators, they need to keep the structure flat and provide their engineers with space to think creatively. The enduring rule that engineers must spend 20 percent of their time pursuing their own independent projects is a unique example of Google's commitment to Creative Execution.

Bold action. From the get-go, Google's founders never shied away from taking bold, decisive action to move the company forward. Page and Brin's first big decision was to download the entire Internet on Google's computers, and use its web crawler to unleash the PageRank algorithm on each page. Google takes a bold approach to new product development, often releasing beta versions of its technology to let users provide critical feedback.

The idea of digitizing every single book in the world, whether it's written in English, French, or Urdu, seems outrageous. Yet that's exactly what Google set out to do in 2002, boldly ignoring the possibility of a legal quagmire which publishers threw up as soon as the University of Michigan announced its intention to be the pilot site. Google took a similar bold step with its decision to ignore the public backlash about its Gmail product, correctly foreseeing that it could maintain user confidentiality and trust even if it allowed its algorithm to "read" people's mail and display corresponding ads next to their text.

Visible leadership. From their humble beginnings in a Palo Alto garage to ringing the bell at the New York Exchange in 2004, the day of Google's IPO, Page and Brin have displayed the kind of visible leadership of which Admiral Nelson would approve. The pair successfully stood up to the SEC and Wall Street investment firms when they set the rules for their IPO, insisting that the initial share price be set at a fairly high $85.00, and cutting investment firms' traditional fees by 50 percent. Google's decision to lift the censorship of its Chinese website, or leave China altogether, is another example of the founders' commitment to living up to their unique motto, Do No Evil.

Page and Brin aren't the only visible Google executives. Take Marissa Mayer, who joined the company as employee number 20. Mayer remains an icon for Google, not only because she was the company's first female engineer, but because of her huge impact on the look and feel of Google's products, which she edits for style, color and nonsense-free content. The *New York Times* described Mayer as "the rare executive who has become—at least in the sometimes cloistered world of computer geeks—a celebrity."[4] By hiring talented executives like Mayer and Eric Schmidt, Page and Brin have created a diversified, highly capable leadership team at Google.

MAKING CREATIVE EXECUTION WORK FOR YOU

You may think that Creative Execution worked for Nelson and for Google, but that it may not work for you because you're not an Admiral, a CEO, or a Middle East oil tycoon. But Creative Execution can help anyone achieve great results against the odds, in any organization. To unleash Creative Execution in your organization, you need to do the following.

Evaluate Your Strategy

Is your existing strategy so unique and compelling that it gets you and other people excited, just like the Nelson Touch? Does it identify an opportunity just as striking as the one Page and Brin discovered when they decided to focus on Internet search, when all their competitors were focused on serving up proprietary content?

As a consultant, I worked with the senior leaders of companies like Thomas Cook in North America and Bank of Montreal to evaluate whether executives understood, accepted, and fully embraced their organization's direction. We found that, in typical organizations, there were serious disconnects between executives' interpretation of the strategy and the levels of acceptance across the organization. This was usually the result of several tendencies:

- Relying excessively on external advisers, consultants, and industry experts to design strategy. Thomas Cook hired a strategy consulting firm to create a clever new direction, but had to work much harder than it had anticipated to get its people and leadership team on board. Lesson learned? Invest your team's time in thinking through and shaping your strategy. Don't present them with a fait accompli.

- Staying "within the boundaries" of what others are doing. Page, Brin, and Nelson created their own strategic vision, which contradicted the established principles of naval warfare and the Internet business. Don't be afraid to seek out contrarian views and defy the logic that's prevalent in your industry.

- Assuming that everyone is on board. That's rarely the case at the beginning of any significant change initiative. The leader's role is to continually promote, explain, and hear the voices of people charged with execution.

- Not being clear about who's in charge. At Thomas Cook Financial Services, the CEO insisted that each of his direct reports be the owner of a strategic initiative. This created clear roles and accountabilities for making change happen.

Encourage Bold Thinking

The second key to making Creative Execution work is to ensure that your compelling strategy doesn't become a straightjacket but rather an empowering tool. As a Creative Execution leader, you must walk a fine line between creating a bold direction and getting people energized so that they take ownership of the strategy, and apply their creative thinking to its successful execution.

The biggest mistake leaders make is to assume that once they have conceived a strategy, execution is a mundane task which barely deserves their attention. Creative Execution leaders use strategy as a stepping stone to unleash the bold thinking and creativity of everyone on their team. They make execution—not strategy—the focus of their work. They don't insist that everyone blindly follow the strategy, but encourage what Admiral Nelson called "creative disobedience," namely, using critical thinking skills to make decisions and solve problems as they emerge. Nelson took that thinking one step further when he directly disobeyed an order from his boss early in his career and charged into an enemy fleet instead of withdrawing. Nelson later claimed that he never saw the signal to withdraw, even though his flag officer had clearly drawn his attention to it.

By giving your people carte blanche to think and act boldly, you will:

1. Send the message that you care deeply about execution.
2. Build up trust and collaboration.
3. Unleash people's creative skills and energy.
4. Learn to push your organization's boundaries.

Lead from the Front

Leading from the front, in warfare or business, is what keeps people focused on their tasks, and is the centerpiece of Creative Execution. Even in the age of Twitter and GPS, there's no substitute for a leader, whether a CEO or product manager, who spends time in the trenches with the people who deal directly with customers and feel first-hand the impact of his or her decisions.

Kathleen Taylor, COO of Toronto-based Four Seasons Hotels and Resorts, visits up to 30 hotels each year from Doha to Shanghai. At that rate, she manages to see every Four Seasons property at least once every three years. Not only does Katie meet with employees and all department heads (a total of 30 to 40 people in each hotel), but she also spends private time with each general manager and their family to show her appreciation for their commitment to the company. She's leading from the front, even in places like the Middle East where you might not expect a woman to be front and center. Just like Katie, your job as a Creative Execution leader is to be visible in order to personally infuse your strategy and direction with meaning.

THE CREATIVE EXECUTION CHALLENGE

I've delved into the lives and achievements of extraordinary leaders and companies in the process of writing about Creative Execution. Each situation led to the execution of an uncommon strategy, with remarkable results. The common thread in each case was a clearly articulated formula that provided a watertight link between strategy and execution. Shaping, applying, and evolving that unique formula is the fundamental function of leadership (see Figure 2).

Marcel Proust wrote that "the voyage of discovery consists not in seeing new landscapes but in having new eyes." Having new eyes will help you design a Creative Execution formula that's unique to you, and lets you to tap into the creative potential of your organization. That's the challenge which Nelson and Google so brilliantly embraced, and which can be your key to achieving great results against the odds (see Figure 3).

Figure 2   The Creative Execution Loop

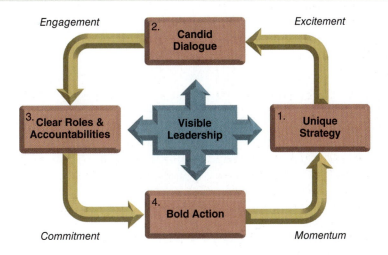

Figure 3   Are you a Creative Execution Leader?

Leaders Who Undermine Creative Execution . . .	Leaders Who Foster Creative Execution . . .
• Treat strategy development as an exclusive exercise for people at the top of the organization. • Believe that execution will take place because they will insist on it, or because the strategy itself is too brilliant to fail. • Want everyone to follow the plan, regardless of circumstances. • View even small failures as unbearable. • Rely on formal hierarchy and communications to engage people and make things happen.	• Treat strategy development as an opportunity to engage their people in rethinking the future. • Believe that execution will take place because they fervently encourage candid dialogue about the strategy and what it means. • Are comfortable with "creative disobedience." • Personally lead and model the behaviors needed to make change happen. • View mistakes and failures as part of the growth process. • Stay visible and approachable, especially in times of doubt or crisis.

ENDNOTES

[1] Arthur Herman, *To Rule the Waves,* HarperCollins, 2004, p. 384.
[2] Randall Stross, *Planet Google,* p. 8.
[3] Sergey Brin and Larry Page, "An Owner's Manual for Google Shareholders," 2004.
[4] *New York Times,* Sunday, March 11, 2009, B1.

Only the Right People Are Strategic Assets of the Firm

David W. Crain
Pepperdine University

Sometime shortly before the current Great Recession ends, companies seeking to jump-start growth will start hiring. Because of record layoffs in the past few years, these growth seekers will be looking at the biggest and best-trained talent pool in history. Finding good people will be easy. But unless firms learn how to select new workers to match their core strategy they will miss a rare opportunity to recruit the right people.

For example, Starbucks is known for its cordial and knowledgeable coffee brewers known as "baristas." Starbucks is an outstanding example of a company whose frontline people have become strategic assets of the firm. Starbucks' customers come in for the coffee, but they often come back because baristas greet them by name, remember their favorite beverage, and educate them about new beverage choices. As evidence the baristas are strategic assets, Starbucks reports that customers often follow their favorite ones when the servers move to a new location. Starbucks competes with other coffee outlets by offering a special retreat for its customers, a place where servers remember customers' likes and have a comfy chair waiting for them. It provides a comfort zone away from home and office. Clearly, the baristas are essential to Starbucks, business model.[1]

The rise in importance of such crucial cadres of employees follows the transformation of the economy from one of manufacturing to service delivery. In manufacturing, workers assembled and moved components to create products—tangible goods and merchandise. People engaged in such activities, productive as they might be, are rarely encountered by customers. In contrast, in service-based industries such as health care, retailing, transportation, professional services, financial services, and food services, employees are in direct contact with customers, either personally or electronically, completing transactions that are part tangible and part experiential. In such industries, people have become integral to the value proposition.

Now, innovative service providers no longer just shave pennies from call center costs, but instead are learning to reconsider their service delivery employees as critical contributors to the value of the firm's offering.[2] In the traditional manufacturing firm, where people assemble products, it is natural to view customer service units as overhead, groups whose economic costs must be controlled and minimized. But when people are in direct contact with customers, often influencing the amount of sale and customer loyalty, they become strategic assets of the firm. This is not new. Professional-services firms—lawyers, engineers, and physicians—long have understood their skilled professionals to be strategic assets. To be sure, physicians might be described as delivering medical services, but patients come back for the doctor's interpersonal skills and the relationship that develops, often described as "bedside manner." In such situations, customers grow more attached to the service professional than to the firm.

Service companies, then, provide the most conspicuous opportunity to study how employees

Reprinted from "Only the Right People Are Strategic Assets of the Firm," by David W. Crain, *Strategy and Leadership*, Vol. 37, No. 6 (2009), pp. 33–38. Copyright © Emerald Group Publishing Limited. All rights reserved.

can become more valuable strategic assets. Two questions emerge:

- Is there a way to tell how people in a service firm are viewed and managed as strategic assets?
- How can they become strategic assets if they currently aren't?

Examining highly successful companies in two industries—retail services and transportation services—provides an opportunity to look at practices that management uses to transform its people into strategic assets. Inexorably, these practices boil down to:

- Recruiting and retaining the right people.
- Training and developing them.

RETAIL SERVICES—WALMART

Walmart's strategies are tightly focused on achieving low-cost leadership in its industry and implementation requires tough-minded management. For example, Walmart pays its line management employees significantly less than Costco, one of its main rivals. To understand the role played by people in Walmart's operations, its various internal functions are broken down into activities performed by its people and reassembled into an activity map.[3] Exhibit 1 shows Walmart's strategic goals supported by the tactical activities of its people.[4]

Walmart has made implementation of its low-cost leadership strategy part of every employee's job. This is a remarkable achievement given that, in many of America's corporations, most employees have only a vague understanding of their firm's strategy or its goals.

It is well understood how Walmart achieves low prices through vast scale economies and hard bargaining with suppliers. But that is just part of the low-cost retail story. What isn't so well known is how Walmart, after achieving the lowest possible cost of goods sold, assures low-cost leadership by reducing its cost of operations through activities like aggressive deployment of technology and inventory control. Early on, Walmart also learned the power of shrinkage reduction, an ongoing activity that permeates every facet of the organization.

Shrinkage in a retail environment can be described as product losses that occur between the receiving dock and the cash register due to breakage, damage, spoilage, diversion, and theft. In a typical retail operation, shrinkage is an expense against revenues, averaging about 2 percent. In much of the industry, shrinkage has long been dismissed as insignificant and inevitable. But a 2 percent expense is significantly magnified in an operation whose gross margins are 23 percent and whose operating margins are but 6 percent.[5] Shrinkage reduction is a strategic goal that all employees in a retail operation can contribute to, from company leadership (by setting strategic goals) down to the lowest stocking clerk or point-of-sale cashier (by making it a job-performance objective).

Implementing corporate strategy in most companies is profoundly different. Through strategic initiatives, strategy implementation is usually handed off to interdepartmental task forces—terms like "Change Team" come to mind—staffed by executives and mid-level managers. The adopted strategy rarely penetrates deeper into the organization with the result that lower-level managers and stocking clerks usually have no idea of their company's strategy or strategic goals.

Methodology for strategy implementation and measurement can make strategy part of every employee's performance. The Balanced Scorecard approach pioneered by Harvard professor Robert Kaplan and his co-author David Norton is a management-by-objectives method that translates corporate strategic goals into employee-performance goals that can be measured at all levels of employee activity.[6] For an operation like Walmart, achieving a strategic goal of even 1 percent company-wide shrinkage becomes a measurable performance objective for store managers and store employees alike. Tied to a system of performance bonuses, such performance planning becomes powerfully linked to implementation of company strategy.

Inherent in Balanced Scorecard methods is the concept that achieving corporate strategic objectives requires establishing "learning and growth objectives" for the organization as well as its people. This suggests two powerful people-management concepts:

- Employee education ("learning and growth") is a valid component of employee performance that can't be met without setting education performance objectives.

Exhibit 1   Walmart's Activity Map Linking Activities to Strategic Objectives

- Successful strategy implementation requires employee education, training and development.[7]

Thus, for a retailer seeking reduction of shrinkage, employees need to be taught the meaning of shrinkage and how it impacts company operations. They need to be taught effective tactics and also how to use high-tech tools (such as radio-frequency identification tags) employed in shrinkage reduction.

In retail operations, other critical success targets[8] can be achieved through employee performance measures like sales per square foot, inventory turnover and same-store sales. Walmart, through employee activities like inventory management, aggressive deployment of technology, and financial efficiency, can link employee-performance plans

directly to the strategy. For people in such a work environment, strategy isn't some abstract concept discussed by executives at off-site planning retreats; these people touch the strategy every day. As a result, they become increasingly valuable strategic assets of the firm.

TRANSPORTATION SERVICES—JETBLUE

JetBlue came to market offering amenities air travelers want: satellite TV, snacks, extra legroom, and wide leather seats. It achieved this through listening to customers' needs and through aggressive deployment of technology in its aircrafts' cabins and on the ground. These activities that comprise JetBlue's business model have been analyzed in various writings[9] and are depicted in the activity map of Exhibit 2.

In addition to its modern fleet of aircraft, JetBlue seeks new ways to recruit and retain world-class employees. JetBlue offers flexible job contracts and full benefits, even for its work-at-home employees.[10] As a result, the company is overwhelmed with job applicants—and achieves a significant competitive advantage by being able to pick the best possible people. These superior employees, especially those who come in contact with the customer, are without question strategic assets, whether they work in the air or on the ground.

Unlike Walmart, which manages and recruits with a steely-eyed focus on low-cost leadership, JetBlue picks its people to fit its vibrant, fun-loving, safety-conscious service culture, a core strategic asset:

Strength of Our People. We believe that we have developed a strong and vibrant service-oriented company culture built around our five key values: safety, caring, integrity, fun and passion. Our success depends on our ability to continue hiring and retaining people who are friendly, helpful, team-oriented and committed to delivering the JetBlue Experience to our customers. Our culture is reinforced through an extensive orientation program for our new employees, which emphasizes the importance of customer service, productivity and cost control. We also provide extensive training for our employees, including a leadership program and other training that emphasizes the importance of safety.[11]

Job applicants are asked to recount incidents that show fit between their past behavior and JetBlue's values. After such a recruiting dialogue involving the value of safety, JetBlue hired a rival's flight mechanic who, despite being under

Exhibit 2   JetBlue's Activity Map Linking Activities to Strategic Objectives

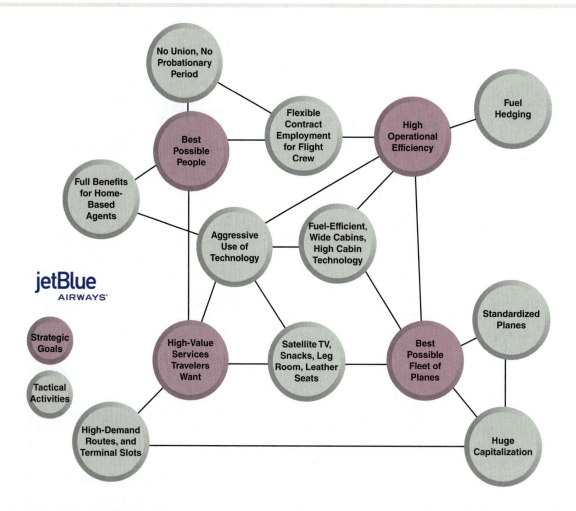

pressure from the rival's management, refused to "sign off" an international flight whose plane wasn't in complete safety compliance.

Selection and retention of people is guided by finding the best fit between a candidate and the corporation's culture and values. Management consultant and best-selling author Jim Collins warns that the old adage "People are your most important asset" is misleading. In fact, it's only the "right" people who are a company's most important asset.[12]

PEOPLE AS STRATEGIC ASSETS IN THE 21ST CENTURY

If you want your people to be strategic assets, you need to recruit people who can implement strategy. Both Walmart and JetBlue make certain they have the people they need—Walmart through arduous training and development and weeding out those who don't fit the culture[13] and JetBlue in its selection of top candidates and then careful training and development. To make people strategic assets of the firm:

- Criteria for selection and retention of people must be consistent with company values.
- Performance management must be linked through measurement to the firm's strategic goals.

In today's service-based companies, employees are "the center of organizational performance."[14] For the service-based firm, where people deliver the service (Walmart) or where they become inseparable from the service (JetBlue and Starbucks), employees feel they are valued because they possess an acute awareness of the impact they have on their company's strategy. In short, in these best-in-class firms, Walmart and JetBlue, people have become strategic assets of the firm.

ENDNOTES

[1] Author's interviews with Starbucks workers.
[2] Peter F. Drucker was the first to note that one segment of the employee population, "knowledge workers," were no longer cost centers. See his *Post-Capitalist Society,* Harper Business, 1993, and *The Essential Drucker,* Harper Collins, 2001.
[3] Michael Porter introduced the concept of activity maps in *Competitive Advantage: Creating and Sustaining Superior Performance,* Free Press, 1985. The visual presentation of activity maps can be found in Porter's later article, "What is strategy," *Harvard Business Review,* November–December 1996. There are no arrows on activity maps because cause-and-effect relationships are fluid and often reversed.
[4] Harvard Business School Case #9-794-024, "Walmart Stores, Inc.," August 6, 1996, provides a thorough review of Walmart's business practices up to its international (horizontal) expansion, while Harvard Business School Case 9 -799-118, "Walmart in 1999," August 30, 1999, describes international expansion fueled by aggressive use of technology. The reader is also referred to the PBS program, "Is Walmart good for America?" WGBH Edu-

cational Foundation (2004), for insights into Walmart's supply-chain activities.
[5] Margins are Walmart five-year averages. Put another way, 2 percent of Walmart's 2008 revenue would be a not "insignificant" $8 billion in losses due to breakage and theft. The 2 percent shrink is a long-standing figure for retail. In 2007, the national retail average had fallen to 1.6 percent, likely due to Walmart's vigilance. See the National Retail Federation report dated June 11, 2007.
[6] Robert S. Kaplan and David P. Norton, *The Strategy-focused Organization,* Harvard Business School Press, 2001.
[7] At Fluor Corporation (1999) a strategic goal involving weighted average cost of capital became embedded in management-training classes throughout the corporation: How is WACC calculated? Why is it important to company performance? And what can employees do to meet WACC goals?
[8] For a discussion linking critical success factors to strategic goals, see Stanley C. Abraham, *Strategic Planning: A Practical Guide for Competitive Success,* Thomson South-Western, 2006.

[9] See, for example, Harvard Business School Case #9-801-354, "JetBlue Airways: Starting from Scratch," October 29, 2001, which describes the foundation and beginnings of JetBlue.
[10] JetBlue, op. cit., and "Some companies rethink the telecommuting trend," *The Wall Street Journal,* February 28, 2008.
[11] JetBlue's stated values have been unswerving in its annual filings from the beginning. This statement is from JetBlue's 2008 Annual Report, February 13, 2009.
[12] James C. Collins, *Good to Great,* Harper Business, 2001. Collins's dictum often has been mistaken for selection and retention policy. But the emphasis is not on people's experience or even their skills and knowledge. Rather, employees' innate capabilities matter most—in short, do they share the firm's values and can they be trained?
[13] Walmart's view is a reflection of the old adage, "Strategy is 90 percent implementation," attributable to a 1989 interview with Scandinavian Airlines' CEO Jan Carlzo.
[14] Peter F. Drucker, *Post-Capitalist Society,* Harper Business, 1993.

Six Sigma at Your Service

Peter Guarraia
Bain and Company

Gib Carey
Bain and Company

Alistair Corbett
Bain and Company

Klaus Neuhaus
Bain and Company

Lean Six Sigma is justly famous for making a better car or widget. Since 1986 at least (the roots of the movement go back to the early 1900s), the Six Sigma process—made popular by companies such as Motorola, Toyota, and General Electric—has become a time-tested methodology for repeatedly producing products while using the most exacting tolerances for quality control. But now service companies are pushing this defect-reduction methodology to a new level. Banks are trying to use it to jump-start growth, telecommunications giants are aiming it at costs, and even retailers are trying it out to serve their customers better.

There's only one trouble: diffused too far and wide, even the best quality control initiative can become a scattershot technique without a focus on major results. All too often, companies train and deploy cadres of Lean Six Sigma experts, known as "black belts," only to see few major improvements from their work. Proof of this comes in a recent Bain & Company management survey of 184 companies. A full 80 percent of executives say their Lean Six Sigma efforts are failing to drive the anticipated value. Moreover, 74 percent say they are not gaining the expected competitive edge because they haven't achieved their savings targets.

Worse yet, unfocused Six Sigma efforts actually *slow* improvement efforts. When managers are unsure how best to deploy the Lean Six Sigma, black belts treat all problems, big and small, with the same approach. Attacking problems piecemeal is virtually guaranteed to yield less than optimal solutions.

And because of this ground-up perspective, it is also almost certain to miss those critical, company-wide improvements that will make the biggest difference.

Such a lack of focus becomes even more critical today, when a sharp fall-off in business needs to be addressed with bold, extremely targeted measures—measures that can substantially increase cost savings, trim the most waste, and boost revenues. In other words, it is management's job to know exactly where to put black belts to work, not let them wander off on their own quests.

A BUSINESS X-RAY?

Some services companies have discovered the solution to this lack of focus. They've added a step at the beginning of the Lean Six Sigma process—something we call a diagnostic X-ray—that allows them to identify the biggest opportunities for gains. Performed by a small advance team of black belts, the diagnostic X-ray consists of three steps.

First, the X-Ray team starts with a procedure called "value-stream mapping." This reveals the largest sources of wasted time and materials in current processes, which also yields the best places for reducing costs.

Next, the team checks the efficiency of company processes (such as bill collecting) by

Reprinted from "Six Sigma at Your Service, by Peter Guarraia, Gib Carey, Alistair Corbett, and Klaus Neuhaus, *Business Strategy Review*, Vol. 20, No. 2 (Summer 2009), pp. 56–61. Copyright © John Wiley & Sons, Inc. All rights reserved.

measuring actual performance against internal and external benchmarks, including competitors. The test allows the team to gauge shortcomings and establish improvement targets.

Finally, they set priorities, focusing on process improvements that will have the biggest impact.

Once let loose on the thorniest problems, black belts can then do what they do best: improving inefficient or poorly designed processes through Lean Six Sigma's famed DMAIC sequence—define, measure, analyze, improve, and control. Simply put, these steps are now sighted on the targets of highest opportunity.

Some may find it surprising that a quality-improvement technique can "translate" from a factory floor to, say, a claims office. And it's equally surprising that service firms are helping perfect this methodology. But when you consider that the goal of pleasing valuable customers—whether it's the buyer of a Lexus or a holder of a large annuity—is the same for all businesses, it's understandable how Lean Six Sigma can fit the bill. Indeed, as Lean Six Sigma spreads, it is helping a growing range of companies meet a vast range of new objectives—everything from spending less on equipment to redesigning stores for efficiency to performing a better job of stocking and replenishing inventory. In fact, perhaps the best way to see how Six Sigma is reshaping the services industry is to take a quick tour of an array of companies who have made quality the hallmark of providing a service instead of building a product.

NEW CLAIMS TO FAME: AN INSURANCE COMPANY FINDS PROFITS IN ITS CLAIMS PROCESSES

A laser-guided approach to Six Sigma, for example, recently paid off for a major UK insurance company that found itself at a crossroads. Fast-changing market conditions were jeopardizing the insurer's ambitious plans to grow its market share by 150 percent. And that wasn't the worst of it. The insurer also estimated that if it did nothing, half its profits were at risk. Management knew in its bones that the root problem was inefficient internal processes, but various random efforts to streamline them had failed. So the company decided to try a different approach: perform a diagnostic X-ray of its business to know where to focus its efforts.

Instead of spreading out all over the company, the X-ray team's first move was to develop a map of the insurer's claims processes. That exercise revealed the largest problem in high definition: costs were out of control. The reason? Too many activities. There were, in fact, 189 separate ones, by actual count. The team's creation of a business-process fact base that involved looking at every step in the claims process, from account setup to claims handling, revealed this jumble.

Analysis showed that the claims process could be broken down into seven major steps. Each step was then broken out so that the team could look at time spent and staffing levels. This breakdown helped the company zero in on major inefficiencies. It also resulted in a significant discovery; the insurer was spending the same amount of time and money on each and every claim—be it for a highly valued customer such as a global corporation or a single individual.

But while the team could now clearly see where to improve costs, it still needed to know by how much. In other words, what was the ultimate goal of the Six Sigma process? For that, they turned to benchmarking. Looking internally, they found both the best-in-process efficiency—and the worst. For example, in one unit, the claims-handling process represented 11 percent of total costs, while at another business unit it was only 6 percent.

The X-ray team also found that the placement process—gathering customer information, placing insurance, issuing certificates, handing over processing to the back office, and chasing client payments—took twice as long in one business unit as it did in another. Armed with this knowledge, the firm began to develop standardized processing times.

Benchmarking also helped the team track its costs by activity—an insight that allowed the insurer to better understand client risk. The company was able to see where it made money, exposing the most- to least-profitable business units. This cost curve starkly showed how the company could tailor service to better align its costs to what clients actually value. It also allowed the insurer to break its customers into three value segments based on overall profitability.

But a management question remained: Were all the possible changes literally worth the effort? Or were some more lucrative than others? Data to determine that would be developed in the final phase of the X-ray team's work, in which the group came up with solid numbers for adopting each of the various solutions. Out of this investigation came a list of the top three opportunities for boosting revenues and cost savings, while simultaneously better meeting customer needs.

This critical winnowing process—skipped in the past in the rush to deal with myriad problems—set the stage for unleashing the entire horde of trained black belts. Not only did they now have their marching orders, the black belts also had a set of priorities. What were they?

First, they set out to re-price some policies—charging more to clients who were expensive to serve and raising prices for smaller clients who demanded tailored service. Within the first year, re-pricing alone earned the insurer an additional 10 percent of the company's profits.

Second, the black belts worked on a series of organizational changes, such as standardizing the processing times across business units—boosting profits by an additional 10 percent.

Third, over a span of 30 months, the insurer invested in technology upgrades that included sophisticated cost-modelling tools. This investment allowed business units to calculate such details as how many hours employees need to spend on gold-standard clients versus other customer segments. The cost analysis also challenged staffing assumptions, such as how large a sales team it needed. Ultimately, the IT investments helped deliver an additional 30 percent profit increase.

CREDIT WHERE CREDIT IS DUE: A BANK SPEEDS ITS CREDIT PROCESSES

In a case that sounds like a foreshadowing of today's financial turmoil, a major Australian commercial bank not long ago found itself in need of just such a Lean Six Sigma diagnostic X-ray when its local residential-property market suddenly cratered in an economic downturn. Moving quickly, it shifted its focus to its robust commercial banking division—and grew handily.

To make the transition, the bank knew that it needed to overhaul credit processes at every level—from loan handling to credit policies to the sales force and credit approval teams. Unfortunately, its existing loan-approval procedure did not set speed records; in fact, it plodded. The unfortunate result: new investments from valued customers who needed—and expected—quick action were going elsewhere. In a nutshell, the bank had to become more agile, increasing the speed, accuracy, and efficiency of credit processes and decision making.

Beyond identifying the problem, the diagnostic X-ray team pinpointed major trouble spots. Among these was a lack of uniformity in loan application approvals. This institutional randomness resulted in delays and errors requiring costly rework. Compounding the problem, credit officers too often made lending decisions based on personal judgement. Long-standing institutional lending policies were observed in the breach. On top of that, all loans—large and small—had to move through the same initial layers of approval, causing even more delays.

This glacial pace was not true throughout the bank; the diagnostic team discovered this fact after benchmarking different bank branches. For example, the team found that one branch expedited loan application decisions by simply assigning a credit officer to work alongside loan managers on the bank floor. With mapping and benchmarking results in hand, the X-ray team then prioritized a small list of big opportunities. One of the most effective was to develop a fast track for processing lower-risk loans. Today, nearly half of all loan applications get expedited treatment, and errors requiring rework have dropped by 25 percent. As a result, even as its real estate loan operations continue to languish, new commercial business is fuelling growth at 2.5 times the market.

HOLDING THE PHONE: A MOBILE PHONE COMPANY MAKES MORE OF ITS CALL CENTER

Lean Six Sigma can help companies not only on the ground in real estate but over the airways. A leading European mobile phone company was bleeding customers. It knew exactly why it had the problem, if not exactly how to fix it: the company's customer service center was abysmal. Swamped with calls, the center's operators had racked up a poor track record for resolving customer problems. And, with its limited budget, the center wasn't likely to provide its own solution.

The company thus had to devise a two-pronged solution: a new call-center strategy that would transform the facility from a cost center into a revenue generator, and the ability to zero in on the most critical initiatives to improve customer service. The diagnostic X-ray laid the groundwork for the Lean Six Sigma work that led to the twin solutions. The X-ray showed that the biggest cost saver (and customer boon) would be to redesign systems so operators could resolve problems on the first call. This not only allowed the company to eliminate hand-offs but also made it possible to reduce staff count.

To turn the call center into a revenue generator, the X-ray process conducted customer and competitor surveys to create three distinct customer groups, based on their customer value. That ultimately led to devising service plans for each customer segment. And who better to sell that than someone who has just created a satisfied customer? Indeed, by knowing exactly where to focus its efforts, the mobile phone company's new call-center strategy has improved customer service and started generating revenue. Thanks to its newly empowered operators, the company is on track to save 25 percent of its operating costs in less than three years.

A BEAUTIFUL MARRIAGE: A BANK INTEGRATES MERGED OPERATIONS

Six Sigma can also be applied to a company's culture. Indeed, a company's personality not only affects how it treats, or mistreats, customers, it can threaten the success of mergers. So discovered a major U.S. financial institution faced with a culture clash after an acquisition.

The story is common enough in the world of mergers and acquisitions. In this case, when a U.S. merchant bank acquired its major competitor, management was divided on how to run the merged business. The vastly different business practices generated friction that drove a number of top performers from the acquired company out the door. Hardly a defect-reduction problem, one might think. Yet management deployed the diagnostic X-ray to build a consensus around how best to integrate operating practices and quickly identify top areas for improvement. In effect, the tool moved the discussion from personalities to processes.

In the value-stream mapping phase, the diagnostic team compared loan-approval processes. What became immediately apparent was that while the merchant bank was better at assessing larger, riskier deals, its approvals took much longer. On the other hand, the acquired bank was faster and delivered better customer service—but its deals typically were smaller. The team's follow-up benchmarking of competitor practices showed that the merchant bank had many unnecessary approval steps, which frustrated its best customers—new and old.

To quickly plug the brain drain, the team prioritized dramatic improvements that all could buy into. At the top of the list was a loan approval system with a fork in the path: lower-risk deals would take a simpler route, while harder deals would go through a more rigorous, but standardized, process. The solution incorporated the best of both cultures: the acquired bank's speed and predictability with the acquiring bank's sophistication for handling larger deals.

Ultimately, the merger stayed intact. And the solution allowed the merged entity to accelerate approvals and increase its average deal size by 35 percent.

SWEATING THE DETAILS: A RETAILER BECOMES MORE CUSTOMER-FRIENDLY

While attacking big problems with Lean Six Sigma produces the most dramatic results, sometimes that overall picture is composed of a welter of details. In the United States, one big-box retail market leader figured it needed to wade into the minutiae of store activities to stave off inroads from general merchandise discounters and to keep its strong growth on track.

The cost of its initial solution—making stores more customer friendly—was skyrocketing faster than it was delivering results. The retailer needed a customer-focused strategy that it could afford over the long haul. Like its namesake, the preliminary X-ray had to reveal what was below the surface.

The X-ray team laboriously mapped more than 100 operations in store after store to determine how many hours were spent each week on routine tasks—everything from opening and closing stores to pricing, taking inventory, restocking shelves, and filling orders placed through the retailer's website. Mundane tasks that consumed lots of time went to the top of list for streamlining. The members also compared the workings of individual outlets and their efficiency.

No process was too small for review. One time waster that emerged was the requirement that employees fill out a lengthy form each time a customer requested price matching. What for? Employees reported that the form was never looked at again. Also on the list: the haphazard system for filling online orders. While the retailer was encouraging customers to place online orders for pickup at a nearby store, nobody at the store necessarily knew where the merchandise was. The team found out why: unless an employee was stationed at a computer, the store had no way of knowing when an order arrived. Also, items were stacked virtually anywhere, causing delays as employees searched for the right product.

The X-ray team unearthed another important failing: the stocking system was supposed to keep high-profit items on store shelves. Indeed, it was more important to have a $100 high-margin core item in stock than a $5 accessory. But by watching employees and checking merchandise holes on shelves, the team realized that workers weren't following the high-margin inventory plan. Why not? Employees said the plan was too detailed to follow.

Back at corporate headquarters, the team prioritized these minuscule findings that added up to huge savings. Once the black belts were dispatched, they eventually generated an incredible $50 million in annual cost reductions from a variety of small process tweaks and from simply revamping systems for inventory restocking and online order pickups.

BLACK BELTS REQUIRED?

A "black belt" is an employee trained in Six Sigma approaches and technology with deep experience using the techniques to deliver change to the business. Sometimes the diagnostic X-ray is enough in itself; you don't always need to send in black belts to fix a problem. Black belts are often most valuable when attacking well-defined opportunities, but may not be ideal for leading the X-ray process. Also, small efforts requiring less analytical or process rigor might not require a blackbelt's experience. That's exactly what a UK energy company found when it sought ways to curb operating costs that had ballooned to some $1 billion annually.

When the X-ray team mapped and benchmarked costs related to all aspects of customer service—from pursuing new customers, and setting up accounts, to measuring energy use and collecting payments—it unearthed several cost-saving opportunities. But the biggest one was a total surprise. The company discovered that nearly 50 percent of its meter-reading expenses were avoidable, largely by reducing the number of times it reads a meter. No team of black belts was needed to simply change the schedules.

But that didn't mean they were totally unnecessary. As the energy provider ranked other cost-saving opportunities, it found additional quick wins. In the end, the detailed X-ray of the energy provider's major processes showed how it could reduce 30 percent of its total costs while at the same time more effectively competing for new customers and improving customer service. When the black belts were set to work on these initiatives, challenges worthy of allocating their valuable time and skills, the energy leader was back on track to achieve stronger cost performance.

AT YOUR SERVICE

Looking to the future, service companies' increasing adoption of quality-improvement techniques that have already been in use for at least five decades (in the case of Toyota) may have other surprising outcomes. This is especially likely as new sources of energy are developed in the face of wildly fluctuating petroleum costs and global warming. After all, Chevrolet, which plans to introduce its all-electric Volt vehicle in 2010, has already begun negotiations with electric utilities to ensure enough inexpensive electricity is available to power them. That tremendous demand for electricity will certainly test current procedures in the utility industry (in both senses of "current") and probably employ a lot of black belts. But in the broader perspective, the convergence of Lean Six Sigma across industries may be arriving just as many industries converge into a new and better model for operating in the 21st century.

RESOURCES

Sandra L. Furterer (editor), *Lean Six Sigma in Service,* CRC Press, 2009.

The Story Is the Message: Shaping Corporate Culture

John Marshall
Lighthouse Academies Inc.

Matthew Adamic
Consultant

INTRODUCTION

A few decades ago, "corporate culture" might have referred to a company's dress code or its working hours. Today, however, most business leaders recognize that organizational culture is both more sophisticated and more powerful than anything contained in an employee manual. One of the key elements in developing and defining corporate culture is the narrative: a story told by a leader that becomes not only part of a company's folklore but eventually the unconscious fabric of employees' behavior patterns.

While nearly all leaders attempt to align the goals of their employees with organizational goals and communicate a sense of vision and purpose, it is clear that some individuals and companies are distinctly more effective than others. What made Ronald Reagan the "Great Communicator"? Why does Southwest Airlines have a more clearly defined corporate culture than most of its competitors? How was MCI able to take on AT&T and succeed when few people outside of the company believed it would be possible?

In a series of interviews with leaders in organizations noted for effective corporate storytelling, four distinct characteristics emerged: purpose, allusion, people, and appeal. Narratives told with a particular purpose in mind, which allude to a company's history and role in the market, told by the right person to the proper audience, and that contain an inspiring emotional appeal are far more likely to impact corporate culture and employee behavior than those which fall short on any one of these categories (see Figure 1).

PURPOSE

The first basic principle of an effective corporate narrative is achieving a particular purpose: to applaud and foster a certain type of behavior or ingrain a tenet of corporate culture. Like other forms of management communication, it "must be a planned process—there must be a strategy" (Smith, 1991). Effective stories, even those told in a folksy, informal style, are related for a specific reason. Phil Condit, former president and CEO of Boeing, describes the importance of storytelling and specifically mentions Herb Kelleher, his counterpart at Southwest Airlines:

> If you go back to tribal behavior . . . one of the most critical people in any tribe was the shaman, the fundamental storyteller. Keep in mind, [his] job was not one of historical accuracy. Instead, [it] was to tell stories that influenced and guided behavior. Stories were modified in order to achieve the appropriate kind of culture. I've watched Herb tell stories: he watches the reaction of people and his story then takes on new and different nuances depending upon his audience and the reaction he is hoping for. . . . Stories are powerful because we remember them. I think Herb is Southwest's shaman; he is the storyteller, and those stories get repeated and retold and they form the fabric of the Southwest culture. (Freiberg and Freiberg, 1996)

John Marshall is an Education Pioneers Fellow based at Lighthouse Academies Inc., Boston, MA, USA. Matthew Adamic is an independent consultant, specializing in ethnographic research.

Reprinted from "The Story is the Message: Shaping Corporate Culture," by Jon Marshall and Matthew Adamic, *Journal of Business Strategy*, Vol. 31, No. 2 (2010), pp. 18–23. Copyright © Emerald Group Publishing Limited. All rights reserved.

Figure 1   The Four Components of Effective Corporate Storytelling

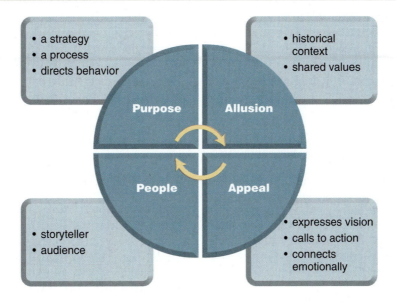

Many of Kelleher's stories are designed to illustrate Southwest's dedication to customer service, including a nearly legendary tale of a gate agent who took the extraordinary step of accompanying an elderly passenger on a flight to ensure he reached his destination without incident. Frank Wright, a retired Southwest Airlines pilot, confirmed the impact of Kelleher's stories on the culture of the organization and that Kelleher's purpose was understood. "It's the good to great theory: while a good employee would have a cordial, procedurally correct customer encounter, a great employee would [act like the agent in the story]" (F. Wright, pers. comm., 17 April 2009). Ideally, the story not only reaches its immediate audience but spreads through word of mouth and managers at all levels until it becomes part of corporate heritage and culture.

In the interview, Wright also noted several important caveats for storytellers in organizations. "Does the story have to be true? Absolutely! Will it be embellished? Probably. Will it morph? Without a doubt. [Should] it have a humorous slant? Yes, because that laughter will enable listeners to remember the story and will encourage others to re-tell the incident." Like epic poems passed down and adapted by each generation, corporate narratives become part of a culture over which the original storyteller has little control. Consequently, an effective story must have a purpose that is unambiguous and that will survive any subsequent edits.

ALLUSION

Jim Parker, who served as Southwest Airlines' General Counsel for 15 years before succeeding Herb Kelleher as CEO, emphasizes the importance of a cultural and historical context for a narrative:

> People remember stories a lot better than they remember lectures, so I try to make my point through stories. It's important to give people a connection to the past so they feel like they have more than just a job, and instead feel like they are part of a mission. (J. Parker, pers. comm., 4 May 2009)

This observation echoes a research study which found that "leaders [can] inspire extraordinary commitment and devotion by including many references to a collective's history and tradition . . . [and] shared values" (Shamir et al., 1994). A successful narrative should, therefore, be told in the proper context; it must allude to a common history and culture.

Another company noted for its use of corporate narrative was MCI, which began as an upstart challenger in the telecommunications industry and eventually shattered the monopoly of AT&T (Bell Telephone). Larry Bouman, who left AT&T and was hired as a manager by MCI in 1975, explained that certain stories were essential to the culture, including

> the "David versus Goliath" story that evolved from the very first press reporting about MCI and the eventual FCC decision . . . [which] authorized MCI to construct its first interstate microwave radio network. How a small company from Joliet, Illinois . . . led to the eventual breakup of the Bell System became the story of success for generations of MCI employees. The story provided continued motivation and a constant reminder that anything . . . could be accomplished. (L. Bouman, pers. comm., 23 April 2009)

Bouman further explained how his

> co-workers [at AT&T] didn't think anyone could [compete] with AT&T because [it] had a monopoly. [At MCI], there was energy, vision, and a can-do attitude. When I started meeting people, everyone was energized—they really wanted to [accomplish Founder and Chairman William McGowan's goal], which by all accounts was impossible.

Jerry Adamic, who was hired by Bouman and joined MCI in 1984, explained that "the environment in which those things happened made it a passion; it wasn't just a job, it was a holy war against . . . AT&T" (J. Adamic, pers. comm., 24 April 2009). Even after the breakup of the Bell System, MCI drew energy from its cultural origins as an upstart and its narratives alluded to and celebrated a history of innovation and overcoming seemingly insurmountable challenges.

PEOPLE

Narratives require two parties: the storyteller and the audience. For a story to have the maximum impact on corporate culture, both the leader and the audience must be committed to the medium of the story as a means of communicating a vision. Unsurprisingly, the better the story is, the greater the impact it is likely to have. This does not suggest, however, that only those with special talent should use narratives. According to Allan et al. (2002), "nearly everyone can be, and should be, a story-teller." Nonetheless, certain leaders possess a special charisma and a knack for weaving image-laden stories that set them apart as visionaries and champions of corporate culture.

The more difficult part of the equation is typically the audience. Particularly for companies that lack a culture of strong visionary leadership, even powerful and compelling stories may fall on deaf ears. A Carnegie Mellon study suggests that this phenomenon is widespread: two-thirds of the 400 managers and professionals surveyed responded that their company's leaders did not engender "a clear understanding of a corporate vision, mission and goals" and an even smaller fraction believed their top managers could "motivate employees and implement a vision successfully" (Kelley, 1989). For leaders trying to change a cynical culture, therefore, the need for powerful and persuasive communication is even more acute.

One way a leader can improve the likelihood that his stories will become part of corporate culture is to select managers and hire employees who share a common set of goals and who will receive and repeat a story. Frank Wright of Southwest explains that

> hiring is the key to get employees to do legendary acts. Interview questions like "tell me a specific time you felt it was best to break the rules in your last job" or "tell me about a time you went over and above the call of duty" are very effective. (F. Wright, pers. comm., 24 April 2009)

Jerry Adamic noted that at MCI, "storytelling was part of the culture because of the passion [for] the company; current employees wanted to tell the stories and new employees wanted to hear the stories" (J. Adamic, pers. comm., 24 April 2009). In these companies, both the hiring and enculturation processes select individuals who will embrace the leader's vision and enhance the corporate culture.

MIT social psychologist Edgar Schein (1997) notes that "leaders create cultures, but cultures, in turn, create the next generation of leaders." This transmission of culture is evident at Southwest Airlines where Herb Kelleher's ideas are still embraced years after his retirement. "[Southwest] has developed a generation of future leaders who daily live the core values and business principles that have contributed to creating and preserving the Southwest culture." With energetic employees determined to preserve both the stories and the values Kelleher promoted, Southwest has "created a tribe of shamans who have woven . . . a tight culture that would take years to unravel" (Freiberg and Freiberg, 1996).

APPEAL

The defining element of an effective story is an appeal or call to action that expresses a leader's vision for his company. A narrative is little more than an entertaining anecdote unless it conveys a particular appeal. Southwest's Jim Parker explains that "storytelling is a better way to make people understand your point . . . It's better than just saying 'customer service is important' " (J. Parker, pers. comm., 4 May 2009). At MCI, the appeal was based on the mission of proving to AT&T that they could in fact compete: "A lot of it was built up as an 'us versus them' mentality" (J. Adamic, pers. comm., 24 April 2009).

A story becomes an appeal when it connects emotionally with the audience. According to Allan et al. (2002), "most Northern European and North American organizations have cultures that severely limit any reference to the emotions of the people involved . . . [yet] people do have feelings all the same." The most effective storytellers consciously make emotional appeals to their audiences: "The more skilled the teller, the more likely the listener is to absorb the emotional content of a story in a constructive way." Like a military commander rallying his troops before a battle or a coach firing up a sports team before a big game, a business leader can, in certain situations, use an emotional appeal to a common goal or shared values to inspire his employees.

A story that emphasizes an appeal to certain values, however, also implies responsibility. "[As a leader], it's important to remember that everything you do touches people's lives, and it's going to become a part of the culture, so you don't do things lightly" (Allan et al., 2002). Appropriately, Parker illustrated this with a story:

> After 9/11, Southwest was the only airline that didn't furlough; we didn't ask people to take job cuts or pay cuts. . . . I still run into people . . . who

thank me for not cutting jobs or pay after 9/11, and they'll tell a story about how they were about to buy a house or get married or send a child off to college and how important it was for them to have the job and money. I feel they'll be telling that story for years to come. Things like that get passed down from one generation to the next; it's part of the company culture. The driving force of the decisions we made after 9/11 was the fact that we'd spent 30 years building up our culture, and I think doing otherwise would have destroyed it. (J. Parker, pers. comm., 4 May 2009)

In this way, the company leaders embraced their own long-standing appeal to treat others with fairness and kindness, and in doing so, cemented the place of these values in corporate culture.

LEADERSHIP AND STORIES

A quality that distinguishes transformational leaders is the ability to communicate a vision and inspire others to action. According to Phil Harkins (1999), while each leader must develop a unique voice,

> great leaders often use stories to translate their messages. Stories connect and become part of the lore of the organization. A story can translate a leader's voice, especially when that story is repeated . . . throughout the organization. It can reflect values and principles without overburdening the listener with theory.

President Ronald Reagan offers a perfect illustration of this ability. In the 1984 campaign, Reagan repeated stories of Americans hit hard by taxes and advocated a plan of "fundamental tax reform." His strategy worked: voters embraced his stories, his allusions to America's history of rebellion against taxation, and his plan of action. Reagan won the election in a landslide and his reforms were adopted despite the fact that the opposition party controlled Congress.

Although the formula for communication success seems straightforward, many leaders struggle to express their ideas and particularly find the story an unfamiliar and even uncomfortable medium. According to Robert McKee (2003), "too often, they get lost in the accoutrements of companyspeak: PowerPoint slides, dry memos, and hyperbolic missives from the corporate communications department." While storytelling is a skill that everyone practices in family and social settings, many find it difficult to employ this skill in the workplace. While "many people in organizations receive training in the preparation of reports and in making presentations . . . [few companies employ] a similar approach to . . . storytelling skills" (Allan et al., 2002). Even with training and practice, few leaders will achieve the charisma and innate ability of Reagan, Kelleher, or McGowan, but all can employ the same strategies and techniques of persuasion and influence.

CONCLUSION

In an increasingly complex and fast-paced world, leaders must penetrate the mire of facts and institutionalized reports if they are to inspire and emotionally appeal to their employees. Stories have a unique ability to, as Allan et al. (2002) put it, "grab people's attention quickly and economically. Narratives work better than other ways of stimulating learning because they are a central part of human [cognition]." Just as humans contextualize other parts of life in stories, people want to feel that their work lives are part of larger story in which they play an important role. For this to happen, they must understand the company's history, its values, its present challenges, and where it—and they—will be in the future. A story that contains allusion to the past, a purpose in the present, and an appeal to a shared vision achieves these goals. Truly great stories will bolster morale in times of crisis and motivate employees to accomplish more than they believed possible, and that is the essence of great leadership.

REFERENCES

Allan, J., Fairtlough, G. and Heinzen, B. (2002), *The Power of the Tale: Using Narratives for Organisational Success*, John Wiley & Sons, Aldershot.

Freiberg, K. and Freiberg, J. (1996), *NUTS! Southwest Airlines' Crazy Recipe for Business and Personal Success*, Bard Press, Austin, TX.

Harkins, P. (1999), *Powerful Conversations: How High-Impact Leaders Communicate*, McGraw-Hill, New York, NY.

Kelley, R. (1989), *Gold Collar Worker Survey*, Carnegie Mellon University, Pittsburgh, PA, quoted in Smith, A. (1991), *Innovative Employee Communication: New Approaches to Improving Trust, Teamwork, and Performance*, Prentice-Hall, Englewood Cliffs, NJ, p. 69.

McKee, R. (2003), "Storytelling that moves people," *Harvard Business Review*, June, p. 53.

Schein, E. (1997), *Organizational Culture and Leadership*, available at: www.tnellen.com/ted/tc/schein.html (accessed 6 May 2009).

Shamir, B., Arthur, M. and House, R. (1994), "The rhetoric of charismatic leadership: a theoretical extension, a case study, and implications for research," *Leadership Quarterly*, Vol. 5, pp. 25–42, quoted in Emerich, C., Brower, H., Feldman, J. and Garland, H. (2001), "Images in words," *Administrative Science Quarterly*, No. 46, pp. 527–57.

Smith, A. (1991), *Innovative Employee Communication: New Approaches to Improving Trust, Teamwork, and Performance*, Prentice-Hall, Englewood Cliffs, NJ.

PHOTO CREDITS

ORGANIZATION INDEX

NAME INDEX

A

Aaronson, Susan Ariel, 326
Abkowitz, Alysa, 305
Abraham, Stanley C., R-175
Achrol, R., R-75, R-88
Ackerman, F., R-116, R-117, R-124, R-125
Adamic, Jerry, R-184, R-185
Adamy, Janet, 8
Agle, Bradley R., 326
Ahlstrand, Bruce, 47
Ahmed, P. K., R-42, R-51
Ahuja, G., 291, R-87
Aitken, J., R-45, R-50
Alexander, Marcus, 246, 291
Allan, J., R-185, R-186
Ambroz, Milan, 387
Amit, R., 131, R-19, R-20, R-21, R-41, R-50
Amsden, A. H., R-106, R-107, R-109
Amsden, Davida M., 387
Amsden, Robert T., 387
Anand, B., R-79, R-81, R-87
Anand, J., 244, R-136
Anderson, D., R-125
Anderson, E., R-78, R-88
Ando, Tadao, R-166
Anslinger, Patricia L., 291
Antony, Jiju, 387
Argandoña, Antonio, 325
Argyres, C., R-75, R-88
Arino, A., R-75, R-76, R-88
Armour, Philip, R-6
Arnold, David J., 245
Arrow, Kenneth, R-21
Arthur, M., R-186
Ascari, Alessio, 387
Ash, Mary Kay, 20
Aulakh, P. S., 245, R-89, R-102, R-109, R-111
Avery, Gayle C., R-22, R-23, R-26, R-28

B

Badaracco, Joseph L., 416
Baetz, M. C., R-23, R-28
Bailey, Wendy J., 325
Bain, J. S., 88
Baldwin, C. Y., R-62, R-63, R-67
Bamford, James, 201, R-72, R-87
Band, David C., 388
Bandler, James, 305
Bareilles, Sara, 191
Barkema, H., 291, R-359
Barnevik, Percy, 204
Barney, Jay B., 131, 416, R-114, R-118, R-120, R-121, R-122, R-124
Barrett, Amy, 283
Barringer, Bruce, 47
Bart, C. K., R-23, R-28

Barthélemy, Jérôme, 201, 359
Bartlett, Christopher A., 131, 201, 245, 358, 359, 417, R-108, R-109
Basu, Kumal, 292
Bates, K. A., R-44, R-51
Baum, J. Robert, 359, R-23, R-25, R-28
Baumol, William, R-21
Beamish, P., R-75, R-87
Beatles, R-7
Beauchamp, T. L., 325
Beaudan, Eric, R-162
Beckett, Ron, 387
Beckhard, Richard, 359
Bell, H., R-72
Bell, J., R-101, R-109
Bell, John, R-82, R-88
Benner, Katie, 305
Bergen, Mark E., 131, 201
Bettcher, Kim Eric, 326
Betts, Doug, 409
Bezos, Jeff, 176, 377, 410
Bhattacharya, Arindam K., 239, 245
Bhattacharya, Debu, R-91
Birchall, Dav W., 131
Birinyi, Laszlo, 49
Birla, Aditya, R-91
Birla, Kumar, R-91, R-93, R-95
Blank, Arthur, 169
Bleeke, Joel, 201, 245
Bloomquist, K., R-21
Bluedorn, Allen C., 47
Blum, Justin, 305
Boeker, W., R-72, R-75, R-81, R-89
Bogan, Christopher E., 387
Bonaglia, F., R-103, R-109
Bonaparte, Napoleon, R-162
Bontis, Nick, 131
Bossidy, Larry, 328, 358, 417
Bou-Llusar, J. C., R-45, R-47, R-50
Boudette, Neal E., 409
Bougon, M., R-117, R-124
Bouman, Larry, R-184
Bouzdine-Chameeva, T., R-125
Bowen, H. K., R-48, R-51
Bower, Joseph L., 201
Bowie, N. E., 325
Boyink, Jeffrey L., 338
Bradach, J., R-76, R-77, R-87
Bradbury, H., R-116, R-125
Brady, D., 338
Branson, Richard, R-37
Brin, Sergey, 393, R-10, R-165, R-166–R-167, R-168, R-170
Brinkman, Johannes, 326
Briscoe, Jason, 387
Brohan, Mark, 176
Bromley, Philip, 47
Brooks, Martha Finn, R-95
Brower, H., R-186

Brown, David, 326
Brown, Robert, 47
Brown, Shona L., 18
Brugmann, Jeb, 326
Brush, T., 291
Bruton, G. D., R-111
Bryce, David J., 200
Buckley, P. J., 244, R-103, R-107, R-109, R-135
Buckley, R., R-106
Buffett, Warren, R-167
Burcher, Peter, 387
Burke, Doris, 305
Burke, Ronald J., 387
Burnah, Philip, 359, 388
Burns, Lawton R., 387
Burrows, Peter, R-21
Burton, R. M., 359
Byrne, John, 358
Byrnes, N., 383

C

Caliguiri, Paula M., 388
Calkins, Laurel Brubaker, 305
Camp, Robert C., 132
Campa, J. M., R-104, R-109, R-133, R-135
Campbell, Andrew, 246, 291, 359
Cannella, A., 291
Capron, L., 244, 358
Carasco, Emily F., 416
Carey, Gib, R-176
Carlzo, Jan, R-175
Carroll, Archie B., 326
Carroll, Lewis, 20
Carter, John C., 417
Carver, John, 47
Cavanagh, Roland H., 387
Caves, R. E., R-101, R-106, R-107, R-109
Cavusgil, S. T., R-111
Cha, Sandra E., 416
Chadha, A., 245
Chambers, John, R-59
Champy, James, 164, 387
Chandler, Alfred D., Jr., 359, R-98, R-109
Chapman, J., R-28
Charan, Ram, 328, 358, 417
Charney, Dov, 188
Chatain, O., 201
Chatham, Jennifer A., 416
Chatterjee, S., 291
Chen, C., 325
Chen, Ming-Jer, 201
Chen, R., 325
Cheney, Glenn, 326
Chesbrough, Henry, R-20, R-68, R-83, R-87
Chittoor, R., 245
Cho, D.-S., R-104, R-110
Christensen, Clayton M., 18, 388

SUBJECT INDEX

Resource-based view of the firm
  approach to strategy development, R-114
  competitive advantage, R-114
  conclusions on, R-122–R-124
  creating resource capabilities, R-115
  and diversification, R-115–R-116
  and dynamic capabilities, R-114–R-115
  firm-specific routines, R-115
  identifying core competencies, R-114
  key principles, R-114
  key success factors, R-119–R-120
  research findings and analysis, R-119–R-123
  research methodology
    action research, R-116
    causal maps, R-116
    cognitive maps, R-116–R-117
    focus groups, R-117–R-118
    identifying diversification opportunities, R-118–R-119
  small and medium-sized businesses, R-116
  and SWOT analysis, R-115
  technology capability, R-115
  VRIN attributes, R-114, R-115
Resource bundles, 99, 120
Resource fit
  definition, 276
  in diversified companies, 276–279
  financial, 277–278
  nonfinancial, 278–279
  related diversification, 276–277
  unrelated diversification, 276–277
Resources
  adequate for diversification, 278–279
  aggressive spending on, 143–144
  avoiding overtaxing, 279
  and barriers to entry, R-131–R-132
  basis of competitive attack, 168
  in best-cost provider strategy, 157–158
  better in some locations, 228
  bundling of, R-130
  categories of, R-36
  causal ambiguity, 101
  competitive assets, 93–102
  competitively superior, 101
  contrasted with capabilities, R-42
  country-specific, R-131
  cross-border sharing, 229–231
  cutting-edge, 102
  definition, 100–101
  in diversification decisions, 252–253
  divestment for reallocation of, R-131
  durable value, 102
  easily perceived and duplicated, R-48
  easily transferred, R-44
  forms of, R-115
  for growth of global companies, R-129–R-132
  industry-specific, R-131
  intangible, 97–98
  linked to operational capabilities, R-49
  of local companies to compete, 240–241
  overcoming lack of, R-130–R-131
  as passive and reactive, R-43
  Penrose constraint, R-130–R-131
  reason for mergers and acquisitions, 181
  relation to value chain, 119–120
  requirements for diversification, 269
  social complexity, 100–101
  specialized vs. generalized, 255–257
  for successful differentiation, 150
  tangible, 97–98
  tests of competitive power

  available substitutes, 101
  competitively valuable, 100
  hard to copy, 100–101
  rarity, 100
  transferability across industries/countries, R-131
  used in foreign markets, 206–207
  VRIN attributes, R-114, R-115
Resource-sharing, R-131
Restriction on Hazardous Substances directive (EU), R-150
Restructuring, 281
  companywide, 284
  corporate, 284
  examples, 286
  following divestiture, 285
  necessitated by large acquisition, 285
  through divesting and new acquisition, 284–286
  undervalued companies, 264
  at VF Corporation, 285
Results-oriented work climate, 411–412
Retailers
  bargaining power, 67–68
  coordinating with, 148
  franchising strategies, 217–218
  vision studies of, R-24–R-27
Retailing
  lean Six Sigma for, R-179–R-180
  reaching strategic objectives, R-172–R-173
Retail space as barrier to entry, 60
Retaliation
  for below-market pricing, 233–234
  signaling, 173
Retraining, 343–344
Retrenching, 281
  after financial crisis, R-29
  to narrow diversification base, 282–284
Return on invested capital, 94
Return on investment, R-53, R-55
Return on sales, 94
Return on total assets, 94
Revenue enhancement, 320–321
Reverse engineering, in China's auto industry, R-63
Reverse foreign direct investment, R-108
Rewards
  balanced with punishment, 379–381
  company examples, 380–381
  in corporate culture, 396
  linked to performance, 381–384
  scrupulous administration of, 383
  strategy execution objectives, 377
  for success, 412
Risk reduction, wrong reason for diversification, 266
Risks
  of exchange rate shifts, 211–213
  political, 211
Rivalry
  and buyer demand
    cost of brand switching, 56
    in fast-growing markets, 56
  cutthroat, 59
  and diversity of competitors, 58
  factors affecting strength of, 57
  fierce or strong, 59
  in foreign markets, 209
  in globally competitive markets, 58
  and high exit barriers, 57–58
  identical vs. differentiated products, 56–58
  moderate or normal, 59

  as number of competitors increases, 58
  and unused production capacity, 58
  varying by industry, 55
  weak, 59
Rivals; see also Industry rivals
  accessing costs of, 115
  adopting or improving ideas of, 169
  chosen for attack, 170–171
  competitive battles among, 54–56
  competitive weapons, 56
  cost advantage over, 140–141
  costs and prices competitive with, 108–120
  deterred by profit sanctuaries, 234
  following differentiation, 151
  low-cost advantage over, 137
  signaling retaliation, 173
  strategy for competitive edge over, 54
  ways of competing, 54–55
Robotic production, 140
ROI; see Return on investment
Royal Navy, R-162–R-165
Runner-up firms, attack on, 171
Russia
  McDonald's experience in, 237
  new MNEs, R-99

S

S. S. United States, 298
Safety concerns, R-147–R-148
Sales
  in differentiation strategy, 148
  incentive compensation, 283
  Six Sigma program for, 370
  strategic fit, 258–259
  value chain activity, 111
Santissima Trinidad, R-162
Sarbanes-Oxley Act, 43, 300, R-156
Scenario planning, R-35, R-39
Schumpeterian creative destruction, R-13
Scientific research, bundled into products, R-14–R-15
Scientists, star and nonstar, R-69
Scope of the firm
  decisions, 177–178
  horizontal, 178
  outsourcing decisions, 178
  vertical, 178
Screening new employees, 396
Sea level changes, R-145
Search engine development, R-10
"Second-order" ethical norms, 300
Securities and Exchange Commission, 42, 300, R-95, R-155
  on certifying financial statements, R-158
  and executive compensation, R-160
  failure in Madoff fraud, 303
  lobbying by large firms, R-155
  and Tyco International, 302
Securities and Exchange Commission Board of India, R-95, R-156, R-157
Securities Law, China, R-157
Self-dealing, 302
Self-enforcing governance, R-76
Self-managed work groups, 377
Self-manufacturing, 67
Sellers, number of, in relation to buyers, 68
Separation of ownership and control; see Ownership and control
Serious Fraud Office, United Kingdom, 297